THE OXFORD HANDBOOK OF

JOHN

The Oxford Handbook of John Donne presents [...] Donne studies and provides tools to orient scholarship in [...] the twenty-first century and beyond. Though profoundly historical in its orientation, the *Handbook* is not a summary of existing knowledge but a resource that reveals patterns of literary and historical attention and the new directions that these patterns enable or obstruct. Part I—Research resources in Donne Studies and why they matter—emphasizes the heuristic and practical orientation of the *Handbook*, examining prevailing assumptions and reviewing the specialized scholarly tools available. This section provides a brief evaluation and description of the scholarly strengths, shortcomings, and significance of each resource, focusing on a balanced evaluation of the opportunities and the hazards each offers. Part II—Donne's genres—begins with an introduction that explores the significance and differentiation of the numerous genres in which Donne wrote, including discussion of the problems posed by his overlapping and bending of genres. Essays trace the conventions and histories of the genres concerned and study the ways in which Donne's works confirm how and why his 'fresh invention' illustrates his responses to the literary and non-literary contexts of their composition. Part III—Biographical and historical contexts—creates perspective on what is known about Donne's life; shows how his life and writings epitomized and affected important controversial issues of his day; and brings to bear on Donne studies some of the most stimulating and creative ideas developed in recent decades by historians of early modern England. Part IV—Problems of literary interpretation that have been traditionally and generally important in Donne Studies—introduces students and researchers to major critical debates affecting the reception of Donne from the 17th through to the 21st centuries.

Jeanne Shami is Professor of English at the University of Regina, Saskatchewan, where she has taught since 1977. She is past president of the John Donne Society (2002–03) and has won its award for distinguished publication three times (1996, 2000, 2003).

Dennis Flynn is Professor of English at Bentley University and a past president of the John Donne Society. He has published numerous reviews and articles in Donne studies; authored *John Donne and the Ancient Catholic Nobility*; and co-edited three volumes in the ongoing Donne Variorum project as well as *John Donne's Marriage Letters at The Folger Shakespeare Library*.

M. Thomas Hester is Alumni Distinguished Professor of English at North Carolina State University and the author/editor of numerous books and articles on Renaissance literature. At present he is an editor of *The Oxford Edition of the Prose Letters of Donne*, with Dennis Flynn and Ernest W. Sullivan, II. He is also Editor of *The John Donne Journal*.

THE OXFORD HANDBOOK OF

JOHN DONNE

Edited by
JEANNE SHAMI,
DENNIS FLYNN,
and
M. THOMAS HESTER

OXFORD
UNIVERSITY PRESS

OXFORD
UNIVERSITY PRESS

Great Clarendon Street, Oxford OX2 6DP
United Kingdom

Oxford University Press is a department of the University of Oxford.
It furthers the University's objective of excellence in research, scholarship,
and education by publishing worldwide. Oxford is a registered trade mark of
Oxford University Press in the UK and in certain other countries

© Oxford University Press 2011

The moral rights of the author have been asserted

First published 2011
First published in paperback 2016

All rights reserved. No part of this publication may be reproduced, stored in
a retrieval system, or transmitted, in any form or by any means, without the
prior permission in writing of Oxford University Press, or as expressly permitted
by law, by licence or under terms agreed with the appropriate reprographics
rights organization. Enquiries concerning reproduction outside the scope of the
above should be sent to the Rights Department, Oxford University Press, at the
address above

You must not circulate this work in any other form
and you must impose this same condition on any acquirer

Published in the United States of America by Oxford University Press
198 Madison Avenue, New York, NY 10016, United States of America

British Library Cataloguing in Publication Data

Data available

Library of Congress Cataloging in Publication Data

Data available

ISBN 978–0–19–921860–8 (Hbk.)
ISBN 978–0–19–871557–3 (Pbk.)

Links to third party websites are provided by Oxford in good faith and
for information only. Oxford disclaims any responsibility for the materials
contained in any third party website referenced in this work.

In Memoriam
Grace Hester
Albert C. Labriola
Michael W. Price
Camille Wells Slights

Acknowledgements

The editors accord thanks to a number of persons who have assisted in varying capacities. First, thanks to the Handbook's board of advisors, Peter Beal, Heather Dubrow, Michael Questier, and Annabel Patterson, with special thanks to Heather and Annabel for stepping in to help at some crucial moments.

At many critical points during this process, the editors have been able to draw on the advice and expertise of colleagues in the John Donne Society, here thanking Dayton Haskin, Gary A. Stringer, and Heather Dubrow in particular for their commitment to Donne studies, for their collaborative spirit, and for their generosity.

Individual thanks also to the following institutions and persons who have helped in the preparation of this book:

Jeanne Shami thanks her co-editors, M. Thomas Hester and Dennis Flynn, and her assistant, Anne James, for their efforts to bring this project to completion. They have contributed immeasurably to the quality of the volume, and have rescued her from many errors and infelicities. She would also like to thank the University of Regina for continuing to support her research, and in particular for a grant from the President's Fund in the project's last stages. To the Social Sciences and Humanities Research Council of Canada also, for funding her research including this project, she is grateful for ongoing assistance. Thanks also to Annabel Patterson, who at an important moment offered sharp, intelligent, and practical advice with candour, generosity, and patience; and to Katrin Ettenhuber, for allowing access to her forthcoming research on Donne and Augustine. Finally, she would like to thank her husband Ken Mitchell for his love and patient support, and her children Andrew and Julia for their good humour and encouragement.

M. Thomas Hester thanks his co-editors Jeanne Shami and Dennis Flynn for their patience and help in a difficult time. Thanks also to Heather Dubrow for stepping in to make her valuable contribution; to Annabel Patterson for her reflections and advice; and to Gene Melton for his expertise and helpfulness. Finally, he thanks his daughter Claire for her companionship and love.

Dennis Flynn thanks his co-editors Jeanne Shami and M. Thomas Hester for their patience and inspiration at various crucial moments throughout the project from its inception, especially Jeanne for her outstanding leadership. To Bentley University, especially former Dean of Arts and Sciences Catherine Davy; former English Department Chairperson Maureen Goldman; and English Department Chairperson Wiley C. Davi, thanks for their confidence, constancy, and sustentation. And to Judith Kamber, Mara Flynn (with Mae Belle, Max, John, and Lina), Anna Flynn (with Aurora), and Molly Flynn: thanks for their forbearance and their deeply reciprocated love.

Finally, all three editors would like to accord special thanks to Anne James, a graduate student at the University of Alberta, for her contributions to this project. They cannot be summarized under 'research assistance' because they have involved a level of commitment, expertise, judgement, and good sense incommensurate with that designation. Based in Regina, SK, Anne was an invaluable resource to Jeanne Shami, both personally and professionally, offering encouraging and sensible advice; accomplishing assigned tasks cheerfully, competently, and expeditiously; and taking on increasing responsibilities as the project approached its conclusion. We are grateful for her collaborative spirit.

Contents

List of illustrations	xv
List of maps	xviii
List of contributors	xix
Note to readers	xxviii
List of short forms	xxix

General introduction   1
JEANNE SHAMI, M. THOMAS HESTER, AND DENNIS FLYNN

PART I: RESEARCH RESOURCES IN DONNE STUDIES AND WHY THEY MATTER

Introduction   9
JEANNE SHAMI

1. The composition and dissemination of Donne's writings   12
GARY A. STRINGER

2. John Donne's seventeenth-century readers   26
ERNEST W. SULLIVAN, II

3. Archival research   34
LARA M. CROWLEY

4.I. Editing Donne's poetry:
from John Marriot to the Donne *Variorum*   43
GARY A. STRINGER

4.II. Editing Donne's poetry: the Donne *Variorum* and beyond   56
RICHARD TODD

5.	Modern scholarly editions of the prose of John Donne Ernest W. Sullivan, II	65
6.	Research tools and their pitfalls for Donne studies Donald R. Dickson	81
7.	Collaboration and the international scholarly community Hugh Adlington	89

PART II: DONNE'S GENRES

	Introduction Heather Dubrow and M. Thomas Hester	99
8.	The epigram M. Thomas Hester	105
9.	The formal verse satire Gregory Kneidel	122
10.	The elegy R. V. Young	134
11.I.	The paradox Michael W. Price	149
11.II.	The paradox: *Biathanatos* Ernest W. Sullivan, II	153
12.	Menippean Donne Anne Lake Prescott	158
13.	The love lyric Dayton Haskin	180
14.	The verse letter Margaret Maurer	206

15.	The religious sonnet R. V. Young	218
16.	Liturgical poetry Kirsten Stirling	233
17.	The problem Michael W. Price	242
18.	The controversial treatise Graham Roebuck	249
19.	The essay Jeffrey Johnson	264
20.	The anniversary poem Graham Roebuck	273
21.	The epicede and obsequy Claude J. Summers	286
22.	The epithalamion Camille Wells Slights	298
23.	The devotion Kate Narveson	308
24.	The sermon Jeanne Shami	318
25.	The prose letter Margaret Maurer	348

PART III: BIOGRAPHICAL AND HISTORICAL CONTEXTS

Introduction   365
Dennis Flynn and Jeanne Shami

26.I.	The English Reformation in the mid-Elizabethan period PATRICK COLLINSON	371
26.II.	Donne's family background, birth, and early years DENNIS FLYNN	383
27.I.	Education as a courtier ALEXANDRA GAJDA	395
27.II.	Donne's education DENNIS FLYNN	408
28.I.	Donne's military career ALBERT C. LABRIOLA	424
28.II.	The Earl of Essex and English expeditionary forces PAUL E. J. HAMMER	435
29.I.	Donne and Egerton: the court and courtship STEVEN W. MAY	447
29.II.	Donne and late Elizabethan court politics ANDREW GORDON	460
30.I.	Donne's wedding and the Pyrford years DENNIS FLYNN	471
30.II.	New horizons in the early Jacobean period ANTHONY MILTON	483
31.I.	The death of Robert Cecil: end of an era JOHANN SOMMERVILLE	495
31.II.	Donne's travels and earliest publications DENNIS FLYNN	506
32.I.	Donne's decision to take orders JEANNE SHAMI	523

32.II.	The rise of the Howards at court ALASTAIR BELLANY	537
33.I.	Donne and court chaplaincy PETER MCCULLOUGH	554
33.II.	The hazards of the Jacobean court KENNETH FINCHAM	566
34.I.	Donne's readership at Lincoln's Inn and the Doncaster embassy EMMA RHATIGAN	576
34.II.	International politics and Jacobean statecraft MALCOLM SMUTS	589
35.I.	Donne: the final period CLAYTON D. LEIN	600
35.II.	Donne, the patriot cause, and war, 1620–1629 SIMON HEALY	616
36.I.	The English nation in 1631 ARNOLD HUNT	632
36.II.	The death of Donne ALISON SHELL	646

PART IV: PROBLEMS OF LITERARY INTERPRETATION THAT HAVE BEEN TRADITIONALLY AND GENERALLY IMPORTANT IN DONNE STUDIES

	Introduction DENNIS FLYNN	661
37.	Donne and apostasy ACHSAH GUIBBORY	664

38.	Donne, women, and the spectre of misogyny THERESA M. DIPASQUALE	678
39.	Donne's absolutism DEBORA SHUGER	690
40.	Style, wit, prosody in the poetry of John Donne ALBERT C. LABRIOLA	704
41.	Do Donne's writings express his desperate ambition? HUGH ADLINGTON	718
42.	'By parting have joyn'd here': the story of the two (or more) Donnes JUDITH SCHERER HERZ	732
43.	Danger and discourse LYNNE MAGNUSSON	743

Bibliography 756
Index 813

List of Illustrations

Ill. 1.1. *HSShe* **in the Westmoreland ms. (NY3), fo. 37**, the sole seventeenth-century manuscript including this poem, *HSShow*, and *HSVex*, none of which appeared in any early edition and all of which remained undiscovered until the 1890s. (Henry W. and Albert A. Berg Collection of English and American Literature, The New York Public Library, Astor, Lenox and Tilden Foundations. Reproduced with permission.)

Ill. 4.II.1. Holograph verse letter (*Carey*) to Lady Lettice Carey and Mrs Essex Rich, the sisters of Lord Robert Rich, who visited Donne at Amiens in early 1612, when this letter was likely written. (University of Oxford, Bodleian Library, MS. Eng. Poet d. 197, recto. Reproduced with the kind permission of the Bodleian Library, University of Oxford.)

Ill. 4.II.2. Page from Sermon with holograph corrections: This scribal manuscript, corrected in Donne's hand, was identified in the British Library in 1992 by Jeanne Shami. (© The British Library Board. MS. Royal 17.B.XX.)

Ill. 4.II.3. Sequences of Holy Sonnets in the seventeenth-century artefacts (*Donne Variorum* 7.1.LXII). This table lists (left to right) the successive arrangements of Holy Sonnets in extant seventeenth-century manuscripts and editions, thus describing the early transmissional history of the poems. (Reproduced with the permission of Indiana University Press.)

Ill. 7.1. The Friendship Oak, a 500-year-old live oak tree that overlooks the Gulf of Mexico on the Gulf Park Campus of the University of Southern Mississippi (Long Beach, MS), birthplace of the John Donne Society. (Photo, Gary A. Stringer.)

Ill. 10.1. Gary A. Stringer's stemma for the revised text of *ElBrac* (*Donne Variorum* 2.46). (Reproduced with the permission of Indiana University Press.)

Ill. 13.1. Summer House, Pyrford, Surrey. (Photo, Suzanne Knights, http://commons.wikimedia.org/wiki/File:John_Donne_house_Pyrford.jpg.)

Ill. 15.1. Gary A. Stringer's stemma of seventeenth-century artefacts containing the Holy Sonnets (*Donne Variorum* 7.1.LXIV). (Reproduced with the permission of Indiana University Press.)

Ill. 20.1. Elizabeth Drury's tomb, All Saints Church, Hawstead, Suffolk. (Photo, Paul Parrish.)

Ill. 24.1. John Donne as Dean of St Paul's, said to have been painted by Cornelius Johnson (oils, 1620, St Paul's Cathedral, London, hanging in the deanery). (Reproduced by permission of the Dean and Chapter of St Paul's Cathedral, London.)

Ill. 26.I.1. Donne's sheaf of snakes seal (Folger Shakespeare Library, L.b.534). This red wax seal was used by Donne for letters sent throughout his life. The sheaf of seven snakes was a charge in the arms Donne claimed, indicating his paternal descent from Welsh gentry. (Reproduced by permission of the Folger Shakespeare Library.)

Ill. 26.II.1. Loseley, Guildford, Surrey. Built by Anne More Donne's grandfather Sir William More in 1569, this was the house in which he (not her father) raised and educated her. It is still the residence of direct descendants, the More–Molyneux family. (Photo, Loseley Park Estate Office.)

Ill. 29.I.1. Elizabeth Wolley, damaged funeral monument, now standing (with the even more severely damaged sculpture of her second husband, Sir John Wolley) in the crypt of St Paul's Cathedral, London. (Reproduced by permission of the Dean and Chapter of St Paul's Cathedral.)

Ill. 30.II.1. Samuel Ward's 'Double Deliverance' ('Deo Trin-vni Britanniae bis ultori…') Interest in the Gunpowder Plot revived at times of political crisis throughout the seventeenth century. This print, 'invented' by Samuel Ward and printed at Amsterdam in 1621, was one of the first pictorial representations circulated in England. (© The Trustees of the British Museum.)

Ill. 32.I.1. John Donne as a royal chaplain in 1616 (portrait miniature by Isaac Oliver in the Royal Collection at Buckingham Palace). (The Royal Collection © 2009, Her Majesty Queen Elizabeth II.)

Ill. 33.II.1. Old St Paul's, engraving by Wenceslaus Hollar. BL Maps 3545 (4). This is the cathedral remodelled by Inigo Jones in the 1630s. (© The British Library Board, BL Maps 3545 (4).)

Ill. 34.I.1. Interior, Trinity Chapel, Lincoln's Inn, London. The altar, pulpit, and altar rails all date from after Donne's time. (Image © John N. Wall. Reproduced by permission.)

Ill. 34.I.2. Reconstruction of interior floorplan of Trinity Chapel, Lincoln's Inn, 1623, showing disposition of pulpit, communion table, and seating arrangements. (Drawing by Eugene W. Brown, AIA, reproduced with his permission [cf. Wall 2007].)

Ill. 35.I.1. Gold Medal of the Synod of Dort by Jan van Bylaer, awarded to Donne by the Staaten-Generaal at the conclusion of the Doncaster embassy to the Netherlands. (Reproduced by permission of the Syndics of The Fitzwilliam Museum, Cambridge.)

Ill. 35.I.2. Signatures and seals of Bishop Mountain, John Donne, and Sir Anthony Browne, 1622. Detail from Essex County PRO MS D/DBg 1/27. (Reproduced by courtesy of Essex Public Record Office.)

Ill. 36.I.1. Frontispiece for *Deaths Duell* (1632), line engraving by Martin Droeshout. (© National Portrait Gallery, London. Reproduced by permission.)

Ill. 36.II.1. Donne's funeral monument, sculpted by Nicholas Stone and stored for over 200 years after the 1666 fire of London in the crypt of St Paul's Cathedral, London. (Reproduced by permission of the Dean and Chapter of St Paul's Cathedral.)

Ill. 38.1. Portrait of Donne, by an unknown artist (oil on panel, c.1595, National Portrait Gallery 6795), known as the 'Lothian portrait' since its discovery in 1959 at Newbattle Abbey. (© National Portrait Gallery, London; reproduced by permission.)

Ill. 43.1. Frontispiece of *Poems, by J. D.* (1635), engraved by William Marshall. (Reproduced by permission of the Huntington Library, San Marino, California.)

List of Maps

Map 25.1. Detail from Map of Surrey taken from *Surrey described and divided into hundreds* by John Norden/John Speed (1610). British Library Maps C.7.c.5 (44). This detail shows important Donne locations including Pyrford, Mitcham, Twickenham, Loseley, and Croydon. (© The British Library Board, BL Maps C.7.c.5 (44).)

Map 27.II.1. Map of the 1585 siege of Antwerp, showing Parma's camp on high ground at Calloo, the surrounding flooded plain, and the canal dug between Calloo and Steeken, all described in the translations of Donne's Latin Epigrams. (Back endpaper of Jervis Wegg, *The Decline of Antwerp under Philip of Spain* [London: Methuen, 1924].)

Map 28.I.1. Map of England, Cadiz, and the Azores, showing Donne's destinations in 1596 and 1597. (James Winny, *A Preface to John Donne*, [Pearson Education Limited, © Longman Group Limited 1970, 1981, 19].)

Map. 28.II.1. Map of the '1596 raid on Cadiz, showing the line of the English attack in the harbour.' From Sir Walter Raleigh by Raleigh Trevelyan (Penguin Books, 2002). Text © Raleigh Trevelyan, 2002. Map © Penguin Books Ltd, 2002.

Map 29.I.1. Map of London entitled 'Londen over Lunden die Hauperstatt in Engellande' on pages lviii–lix of *Cosmographey: das ist, Beschreibung aller Lander* (1598) by Sebastian Münster. (© The British Library Board, Shelfmark 569.h.1.)

Map 29.I.2. Map of Donne's London, a schematic drawing reprinted from *A Preface to Donne*, James Winny, Pearson Education Limited, © Longman Group Limited 1970, 1981, 182, corresponding to those on the Münster map (above), but including landmarks relevant to Donne.

Map 30.I.1. Map of Pyrford, detail (CUL Maps MS Plans 759a). Map of Pyrford showing the estate of Sir Francis Wolley after his death in 1614. (Reproduced by kind permission of the Syndics of Cambridge University Library, Maps.Ms. Plans.758–9a.)

Contributors

Hugh Adlington is Lecturer in English at the University of Birmingham. He is the author of numerous essays on early modern writers, including John Donne, John Milton, and Thomas Browne. He is the co-editor of the *Oxford Handbook to the Early Modern Sermon*, and editor of *The Oxford Edition of the Sermons of John Donne*, Volume 2.

Alastair Bellany is Associate Professor of History at Rutgers University. He is the author of *The Politics of Court Scandal in Early Modern England: News Culture and the Overbury Affair, 1603–1660* (Cambridge, 2002), and co-editor (with Andrew McRae) of *Early Stuart Libels: An Edition of Poetry from Manuscript Sources* (2005: www.earlystuartlibels.net). He is currently working on a series of projects on the representation and reputation of George Villiers, Duke of Buckingham, including a book (with Thomas Cogswell) on Buckingham's 1628 assassination.

Patrick Collinson is Emeritus Regius Professor of Modern History at the University of Cambridge, and a Fellow of Trinity College, an acclaimed historian of post-Reformation English religious history. His *The Elizabethan Puritan Movement* (1967) was based on a doctoral thesis supervised by Sir John Neale and led to the series of his seminal books and essays, including *Archbishop Grindal: The Struggle for a Reformed Church* (1979), *The Religion of Protestants: The Church in English Society, 1559–1625* (1982), and 'The Monarchical Republic of Queen Elizabeth I' (1987).

Lara M. Crowley is Assistant Professor of English at Texas Tech University. Her articles on Renaissance literature and manuscript studies have appeared in *Modern Philology*, *English Manuscript Studies, 1100–1700*, *John Donne Journal*, and *English Literary Renaissance*, and her studies have been supported by such groups as the Andrew W. Mellon Foundation and the National Endowment for the Humanities. She is also an assistant editor for the John Donne Letters Project and for *The Variorum Edition of the Poetry of John Donne: Songs and Sonets*. Her current book project is entitled 'Interpreting Manuscripts: John Donne's Poetry and Prose in Early Modern England'.

Donald R. Dickson, Professor of English at Texas A&M University, is the author of *The Tessera of Antilia: Utopian Brotherhoods and Secret Societies in the Early*

Seventeenth Century (1998) and *The Fountain of Living Waters: The Typology of the Waters of Life in Herbert, Vaughan, and Traherne* (1987). He has edited (and translated) Thomas and Rebecca Vaughan's *Aqua Vitæ: Non Vitis: Or, The radical Humiditie of Nature: Mechanically, and Magically dissected By the Conduct of Fire, and Ferment* (2001) and *The Poetry of John Donne* (Norton Critical Editions, 2007). He has published articles in such journals as *Huntington Library Quarterly*, *Renaissance Quarterly*, *The Seventeenth Century*, *Notes and Records of the Royal Society*, *Renaissance and Reformation*, *John Donne Journal*, and *George Herbert Journal*, among others. He is associate general editor of *The Variorum Edition of the Poetry of John Donne*.

Theresa M. DiPasquale is Associate Professor of English at Whitman College in Walla Walla, WA. She has won the John Donne Society's Award for Distinguished Publication three times: for *Literature and Sacrament: The Sacred and the Secular in John Donne* (1999); for 'Donne's *Epigrams*: A Sequential Reading', *Modern Philology*, 104/3 (2007); and for *Refiguring the Sacred Feminine: The Poems of John Donne, Aemilia Lanyer, and John Milton* (2008). She is also the author of articles on Renaissance poetry in journals including *Philological Quarterly*, *Journal of English and Germanic Philology*, and *John Donne Journal*. Her current research includes work on Donne's conception of time. She is married to Lee Keene and they have one son, Dominic.

Heather Dubrow, the John D. Boyd, SJ, Chair in the Poetic Imagination at Fordham University, has published six single-authored books, most recently *The Challenges of Orpheus: Lyric Poetry and Early Modern England* (2008). Her other publications include a co-edited collection of essays, the overview of twentieth-century Shakespeare criticism in The Riverside Shakespeare, and numerous essays on early modern literature and on pedagogy. Also a poet, she is the author of two chapbooks and of poems in many journals.

Kenneth Fincham is Professor of History at the University of Kent. He specializes in the politics and religion of early modern England, and has published *Prelate as Pastor: The Episcopate of James I* (1990), edited *The Early Stuart Church 1603–1642* (1993) and *Visitation Articles and Injunctions of the Early Stuart Church* (2 vols., 1994–8), and co-authored, with Nicholas Tyacke, *Altars Restored: The Changing Face of English Religious Worship 1547–c.1700* (2007). Currently he is working on the Church of England in the period 1640–65. He is also one of the Directors of the Database of the Church of England 1540–1835 (www.theclergydatabase.org.uk).

Dennis Flynn is Professor of English at Bentley University. He is author of *John Donne and the Ancient Catholic Nobility* (1995), as well as numerous essays; co-editor (with M. Thomas Hester and Robert P. Sorlien) of *John Donne's Marriage Letters at The Folger Shakespeare Library* (2005); and an Assistant Textual Editor of *The Variorum*

Edition of the Poetry of John Donne. At present he is an editor of *The Oxford Edition of the Prose Letters of Donne*, with M. Thomas Hester and Ernest W. Sullivan, II.

Alexandra Gajda is Lecturer in Early Modern History at the University of Birmingham. She is writing a monograph on Robert Devereux, second Earl of Essex, and late Elizabethan political culture.

Andrew Gordon coordinates the English programme at the University of Aberdeen, where he is also Co-Director of the Centre for Early Modern Studies. He is the author of articles on diverse aspects of Renaissance culture, from early modern correspondence and manuscript circulation to libels and civic space. He has co-edited collections on literature and mapping and on urban citizenship, and a monograph entitled *Writing the City* is forthcoming.

Achsah Guibbory is Ann Whitney Olin Professor of English at Barnard College, Columbia University. She has published numerous articles and essays on seventeenth-century literature and culture, as well as several books, the most recent of which are *Ceremony and Community from Herbert to Milton* (1998) and *The Cambridge Companion to John Donne* (2006). Her book *Christian Identity, Jews, and Israel in Seventeenth-Century England* is forthcoming from Oxford University Press.

Paul E. J. Hammer is Professor of History at the University of Colorado at Boulder. His publications include *The Polarisation of Elizabethan Politics: The Political Career of Robert Devereux, 2nd Earl of Essex, 1585–1597* (1999), *Elizabeth's Wars: War, Government and Society in Tudor England, 1544–1604* (2003), *Warfare in Early Modern Europe* (edited, Ashgate, 2007), and many articles on Elizabethan politics and political culture. He is currently completing a book on the Essex Rising and the end of Elizabethan politics.

Dayton Haskin teaches English and comparative literature at Boston College. He is the author of *Milton's Burden of Interpretation* and of *John Donne in the Nineteenth Century* and is also a contributing editor to *The Variorum Edition of the Poetry of John Donne*. He has written on a range of topics related to Donne, including the Sermons, the erotic and the religious poems, the first American editions of the poetry, the biography, and the history of the writer's reputation. At present he is studying the early fabrication of a literature curriculum in American colleges at the end of the nineteenth century and writing a book on what happened to Shakespeare and Milton when they were turned into academic subjects.

Simon Healy is Senior Researcher at the History of Parliament Trust, London, and author of 244 articles in *The House of Commons 1604–29*, ed. J. P. Ferris and A. D. Thrush (forthcoming, 2010). Research interests include state formation, English

Crown finances 1540–1640, the confessional state, political culture, the north of England, Wales, and the Marches during the early modern period.

Judith Scherer Herz is Professor of English at Concordia University, Montreal. Her publications include numerous articles on Donne, Milton, and seventeenth-century writing. Her current research focuses on the presence of Donne in modern and contemporary poetry. She has also published two books on E. M. Forster as well as articles on Forster and Leonard Woolf. She is a former President of ACCUTE (the Association of Canadian College and University Teachers of English) and of the John Donne Society.

M. Thomas Hester, Alumni Distinguished Professor of English at North Carolina State University, is author/editor of numerous books and articles on Renaissance literature—most recently, *Donne's Marriage Letters in the Folger Shakespeare Library* (with Dennis Flynn and Robert P. Sorlien) and *Talking Renaissance Texts: Essays on the Humanist Tradition* (with Jeffrey Kahan). At present he is an editor of *The Oxford Edition of the Prose Letters of Donne*, with Dennis Flynn and Ernest W. Sullivan, II. He is also editor of the *John Donne Journal*.

Arnold Hunt is a curator of manuscripts at the British Library. His publications include *The Art of Hearing: English Preachers and their Audiences 1590–1640* (2010). He is currently editing Donne's Sermons at St Dunstan's for the forthcoming *Oxford Edition of the Sermons of John Donne*.

Jeffrey Johnson is Department Chair and Professor of English at East Carolina University. He is the author of *The Theology of John Donne*, a past president of the John Donne Society, and associate chief editor of the Commentary for *The Variorum Edition of the Poetry of John Donne*.

Gregory Kneidel is Associate Professor of English at the University of Connecticut. He is author of *Rethinking the Turn to Religion in Early Modern English Literature* (2008) and is working on a book on Donne and law.

Albert C. Labriola died on 11 March 2009, but not before completing with grace and dispatch two essays for this Handbook. At Duquesne University he had been acting dean of the McAnulty College and Graduate School of Liberal Arts, distinguished university professor, Professor of English, and was celebrated internationally as a Renaissance scholar. A member of the Donne *Variorum* Advisory Board, he was volume commentary editor for the *Songs and Sonets*, a past president of the John Donne Society, and a founding member of the organization.

Clayton D. Lein is Professor of English at Purdue University. He is editor of *British Prose Writers of the Early Seventeenth Century* (1995) and has published widely in such journals as *English Literary Renaissance*, *John Donne Journal*, *Eighteenth-Century Studies*, *Studies in English Literature*, *Comparative Literature*, and *University of Toronto Quarterly*. He has won many teaching awards, including the 'Teacher of the Year' award from the Indiana Humanities Council (1993), and has been inducted into Purdue's Book of Great Teachers. His most recent article, 'At the Porch to the Temple: Herbert's Progress to Bemerton', will appear in *George Herbert's Pastoral: New Essays on the Poet and Priest of Bemerton* (2010).

Lynne Magnusson is Professor of English at the University of Toronto. She has published extensively on Shakespeare's language, early modern women's writing, the genre of the letter, and discourse analysis, and is the author of *Shakespeare and Social Dialogue*, a co-author of *Reading Shakespeare's Dramatic Language*, and co-editor of *The Elizabethan Theatre*, vols. *XI–XV*. The recent recipient of a Canada Council Killam Research Fellowship, she is working to complete *The Transformation of the English Letter, 1520–1620*, the Norton Critical Edition of *Shakespeare's Sonnets*, and a study offering historicist approaches to the language of Shakespeare's early plays.

Margaret Maurer, the William Henry Crawshaw Professor of Literature at Colgate University, has published essays on Donne's verse and prose letters. She also writes on Shakespeare and is an editor, with Barry Gaines, of *Three Shrew Plays* (2010).

Steven W. May is adjunct Professor of English at Emory University, Atlanta, and Senior Research Fellow at Sheffield University. His books include *The Elizabethan Courtier Poets* (1991), an edition of *Queen Elizabeth I: Selected Works* (2004), and *Elizabethan Poetry: A Bibliography and First-Line Index of English Verse, 1559–1603* (2004). His research interests centre on English Renaissance manuscript culture, the Tudor court, and editing early modern documents.

Peter McCullough is Fellow and Tutor in English at Lincoln College, Oxford. He is author of *Sermons at Court: Religion and Politics in Elizabethan and Jacobean Preaching* (Cambridge, 1998), numerous articles on early modern religious writing and publishing, and editor of *Lancelot Andrewes: Selected Sermons and Lectures* (Oxford, 2006). He is the general editor of *The Oxford Edition of the Sermons of John Donne* (Oxford, forthcoming).

Anthony Milton is Professor of Early Modern History at the University of Sheffield and author of *Catholic and Reformed: The Roman and Protestant Churches in English Protestant Thought 1600–1640* (1995) and *Laudian and Royalist Polemic in Seventeenth-Century England: The Career and Writings of Peter Heylyn* (2007). He is the editor of *The British Delegation and the Synod of Dort 1619–19* (2005) and has also written articles on censorship, the public sphere, Anglo-Palatine relations, and other aspects of religious politics in seventeenth-century England. He is currently working on a monograph provisionally entitled 'England's Second Reformation: The Battle for the Church of England 1636–66'.

Kate Narveson is an Associate Professor of English at Luther College, where she teaches medieval and Renaissance literature. She has published on John Donne, George Herbert, and other early modern devotional writers, on methodological issues in studying religion and literature, and on the trope of poetic immortality. She is currently working on a book-length study of the ways in which lay Scripture literacy led to the rise of a culture of devotional writing among ordinary men and women in early modern England.

Anne Lake Prescott teaches at Barnard College and Columbia University. The author of *French Poets and the English Renaissance* and *Imagining Rabelais in Renaissance England*, as well as co-editor of *Female and Male Voices in Early Modern England: A Renaissance Anthology* and *Renaissance Historicisms*, she has published essays on Thomas More, Clément Marot, Marguerite de Navarre, Louise Labé, Philip Sidney, Michael Drayton, Renaissance jokes, England's rejection of the Gregorian Calendar, and early modern psalmody. Co-editor of *Spenser Studies* and of an Ashgate series of texts by or concerning early modern women, she is a former president of the Sixteenth Century Society and member of the board of the Renaissance Society of America. She is on the editorial board of *SEL*, the *Sidney Journal*, and the *John Donne Journal*.

Michael W. Price died on 11 May 2006, leaving among his papers the drafts of two essays for this volume. He was 41, had earned his doctoral degree from Purdue University, and was Professor of English at Grove City College in western Pennsylvania. He wrote, presented, and published a number of essays on Donne and was a member of the John Donne Society.

Emma Rhatigan is Lecturer in Early Modern Literature in the School of Literature, Language, and Linguistics at the University of Sheffield. She is currently writing a book on preaching at Lincoln's Inn and editing a volume of Donne's Lincoln's Inn Sermons for *The Oxford Edition of the Sermons of John Donne* (forthcoming). She is also co-editing, with Hugh Adlington and Peter McCullough, the forthcoming *Oxford Handbook of the Sermon in Early Modern Britain*.

Graham Roebuck is Professor Emeritus at McMaster University, where, for more than forty years, he taught Humanities and English Literature. He continues to pursue his interests in early modern studies. Early works include *Clarendon and Cultural Continuity*—'definitive' and 'indispensable' for the study of Clarendon's works and the literature of the English Civil Wars. Recent works include *The Mysterious and* *the Foreign in Early Modern England* (2008), co-edited with M. Silcox and H. Ostovich. Since 1986 he has been Director of the McMaster Stratford Seminars on Shakespeare and the Theatre. He is past president of the Toronto Renaissance and Reformation Colloquium and past president (2004–5) of the John Donne Society.

Jeanne Shami is Professor of English at the University of Regina, where she has taught since 1977, and author of *John Donne and Conformity in Crisis in the Late Jacobean Pulpit* (2003). In 1992 she discovered a manuscript sermon by John Donne (corrected in his own hand), and published her findings in 1996 as *John Donne's 1622 Gunpowder Plot Sermon: A Parallel-Text Edition*. She is past president of the John Donne Society and has won three of its awards for distinguished publication (1996, 2000, 2003). Currently, she is serving as a consulting editor to *The Oxford Edition of the Sermons of John Donne* and as an assistant editor of *The Oxford Edition of the Letters of John Donne*. She is also commentary editor for the Verse Letters volume of the Donne *Variorum* project, and a member of its Advisory Board.

Alison Shell teaches in the English Department at University College London. She was formerly Professor in the Department of English Studies at Durham University. She has written *Catholicism, Controversy and the English Literary Imagination, 1558–1660* (1999) and *Oral Culture and Catholicism in Early Modern England* (2007), as well as several articles and book chapters on early modern literature and religion.

Debora Shuger is a UCLA Distinguished Professor of English and author of *Censorship and Cultural Sensibility* (2006), *Political Theologies in Shakespeare's England* (2001), *The Renaissance Bible* (1994), *Habits of Thought in the English Renaissance* (1990), and *Sacred Rhetoric* (1988), as well as numerous articles on early modern culture, religion, and literature.

Camille Wells Slights, Professor Emerita, University of Saskatchewan, is the author of articles on early modern literature published in such journals as *PMLA*, *English Literary History*, and *Shakespeare Quarterly* and two books, *The Casuistical Tradition in Shakespeare, Donne, Herbert, and Milton* (1981) and *Shakespeare's Comic Commonwealths* (1993). She received the Donne Society Award for Distinguished Publication in the *John Donne Journal* for 1993. After retiring from teaching in 2004 she moved to Wolfville, Nova Scotia, where she continued to work on a study of the conscience and of constructions of subjectivity in seventeenth-century British literature. She died in July 2009, a few days after submitting the present article to the editors.

Malcolm Smuts is Professor of History at the University of Massachusetts Boston and author of numerous publications on the politics and political culture of early Stuart England, including *Court Culture and the Origins of a Royalist Tradition in England* (1987) and *Culture and Power in England 1585–1685* (1998).

Johann Sommerville is Professor of History at the University of Wisconsin, Madison. His publications include *Royalists and Patriots: Politics and Ideology in England 1603–1640* (1999), and editions of the political writings of King James VI and I and Sir Robert Filmer in the series Cambridge Texts in the History of Political Thought.

Kirsten Stirling is *maître d'enseignement et de recherche* in English literature at the University of Lausanne, Switzerland, and has an MA and PhD from the University of Glasgow. Her research interests include John Donne's Holy Sonnets, word/image approaches to literary texts, and Scottish literature. She is the author of *Bella Caledonia: Woman, Nation, Text* (2008).

Gary A. Stringer is Emeritus Professor of English at the University of Southern Mississippi, Research Professor of English at Texas A&M University, and the general editor of *The Variorum Edition of the Poetry of John Donne*.

Ernest W. Sullivan, II is the Edward S. Diggs Endowed Chair in English at Virginia Tech. He has authored *The Influence of John Donne: His Uncollected Seventeenth-Century Printed Verse*; edited *Biathanatos by John Donne*, *The First and Second Dalhousie Manuscripts: Poems and Prose by John Donne and Others*, *The Harmony of the Muses*; and co-edited *Puzzles in Paper: Concepts in Historical Watermarks*; vols. 2, 6, 7, and 8 of *The Variorum Edition of the Poetry of John Donne*; and vols. 1 and 2 of *The Complete Works of Abraham Cowley*. He is co-proprietor of *The Thomas L. Gravell Watermark Archive: An Online Database of Watermarks from the 15th–19th Centuries*. He is a senior textual editor for *The Variorum Edition of the Poetry of John Donne*, general textual editor for *The Complete Works of Abraham Cowley*, and a past president of the John Donne Society.

Claude J. Summers is William E. Stirton Professor Emeritus in the Humanities at the University of Michigan–Dearborn. He has published widely on Renaissance and modern literature. A past president of the John Donne Society of America, he is general editor of glbtq.com—an online encyclopedia of gay, lesbian, bisexual, transgender, and queer culture.

Richard Todd is Professor of British Literature after 1500 at the University of Leiden, the Netherlands. He is the author of *The Opacity of Signs: Acts of Interpretation in George Herbert's 'The Temple'* (1986). He has also published widely on non-dramatic aspects of early modern British literature, including several case studies on Constantijn Huygens's draft manuscript translations of scribal originals of poems by John Donne (now in the possession of the Koninklijke Bibliotheek [Royal Library] in The Hague), in *English Manuscript Studies* (2002) and elsewhere. He is currently serving on the editorial team of the *Songs and Sonnets* volume 4 of *The Variorum Edition of the Poetry of John Donne* (1995–) http://donnevariorum.tamu.edu.

R. V. Young is Professor of English at North Carolina State University and a former editor of the *John Donne Journal.* He is currently the editor of *Modern Age: A Quarterly Review.* His book *Doctrine and Devotion in Seventeenth-Century Poetry* (2000) won the annual award for the best contribution to Donne studies in 2002. His bilingual edition of Justus Lipsius' *Concerning Constancy* is forthcoming.

Note to readers

In this *Handbook*, for Donne's poems we have used the *Variorum* texts so far published (Anniversaries, Epicedes and Obsequies, Epigrams, Epithalamions, miscellaneous poems, Elegies, and Holy Sonnets); Satires, including *Metem*, and Verse Letters are cited from Milgate's edition (1967) and remaining poems from the edition of C. A. Patrides (1985).

Short forms for citations of these and other standard editions of Donne's writings are:

1622 Sermon	Donne, J. (1996b). *John Donne's 1622 Gunpowder Plot Sermon: A Parallel-Text Edition*, transcribed and edited by J. Shami. Pittsburgh: Duquesne University Press.
Biathanatos	Donne, J. (1984a). *Biathanatos*, ed. E. W. Sullivan, II. Newark: University of Delaware Press.
Courtier's Library	Donne, J. (1930). *The Courtier's Library*, ed. E. M. Simpson. London: The Nonesuch Press.
Devotions	Donne, J. (1975). *Devotions Upon Emergent Occasions*, ed. A. Raspa. Montreal: McGill-Queen's University Press.
Essayes	Donne, J. (2001). *Essayes in Divinity*, ed. A. Raspa. Montreal: McGill-Queen's University Press.
Letters	Donne, J. (1977). *Letters to Severall Persons of Honour*, ed. M. T. Hester. Delmar, NY: Scholars' Facsimiles and Reprints.
Marriage Letters	Donne, J. (2005). *The Marriage Letters of John Donne at The Folger Shakespeare Library*, ed. M. T. Hester, R. P. Sorlien, and D. Flynn. Washington, DC: The Folger Shakespeare Library.
Milgate	Donne, J. (1967b). *John Donne: The Satires, Epigrams and Verse Letters*, ed. W. Milgate. Oxford: Clarendon Press.
Paradoxes	Donne, J. (1980). *John Donne Paradoxes and Problems*, ed. H. Peters. Oxford: Clarendon Press.
Patrides	Donne, J. (1985). *The Complete English Poems of John Donne*, ed. C. A. Patrides. London: J. M. Dent & Sons.
Problems	Donne, J. (1980). *John Donne Paradoxes and Problems*, ed. H. Peters. Oxford: Clarendon Press.

Pseudo-Martyr	Donne, J. (1993). *Pseudo-Martyr*, ed. A. Raspa. Montreal: McGill-Queen's University Press.
Sermons	Donne, J. (1953–62). *The Sermons of John Donne*, ed. G. R. Potter and E. M. Simpson. 10 vols. Berkeley and Los Angeles: University of California Press.
TMC	Matthew, T. and Donne, J., jr. (1660). *A Collection of Letters, made by Sr Tobie Mathews Kt.* London.
Variorum	Donne, J. (1995–). *The Variorum Edition of the Poetry of John Donne*, vols. 2, 6, 7.1, and 8, ed. G. A. Stringer *et al.* Bloomington and Indianapolis: Indiana University Press.

In the interests of convenience and economy, short forms are used for references to Donne's poems quoted or cited in the essays. We have adopted as standard the short forms used by the Donne *Variorum*, whose editors state: 'These forms are based on traditional headings or numberings except in cases where traditional designations are confusing, imprecise, or nonexistent.' Donne's own headings for his poems, given the absence of holographs, are unknown.

List of Short Forms

Air	Air and Angels ['Twice or thrice had I loved']
AltVic	A Letter Written by Sir H. G. and J. D. Alternis Vicibus ['Since every tree begins']
Amic	Amicissimo et Meritissimo Ben Jonson ['Quod arte ausus es hic tua']
Anniv	The Anniversary ['All kings and all their favorites']
Annun	Upon the Annunciation and Passion ['Tamely frail body']
Antiq	Antiquary ['If in his study']
Apoth	Apotheosis Ignatij Loyolae ['Qui sacer antefuit']
Appar	The Apparition ['When by thy scorn']
AutHook	Ad Autorem ['Non eget Hookerus']
AutJos	Ad Autorem ['Emendare cupis Joseph']
Bait	The Bait ['Come live with me']
BB	To Mr. B. B. ['Is not thy sacred hunger']
BedfCab	Epitaph on Himself: To the Countess of Bedford ['That I might make your cabinet']

BedfDead	To the Countess of Bedford: Begun in France ['Though I be dead and buried']
BedfHon	To the Countess of Bedford ['Honor is so sublime']
BedfReas	To the Countess of Bedford ['Reason is our soul's left hand']
BedfRef	To the Countess of Bedford ['You have refined me']
BedfShe	Elegy to the Lady Bedford ['You that are she']
BedfTwi	To the Countess of Bedford: On New-Year's Day ['This twilight of two years']
BedfWrit	To the Countess of Bedford ['To have written then']
Beggar	A Lame Beggar ['I am unable, yonder beggar cries']
Blos	The Blossom ['Little thinkest thou']
BoulNar	Elegy upon the Death of Mrs. Boulstrode ['Language thou art too narrow']
BoulRec	Elegy on Mrs. Boulstrode ['Death, I recant']
Break	Break of Day ['Tis true, 'tis day']
Broken	The Broken Heart ['He is stark mad']
Cales	Cales and Guiana ['If you from spoil']
Calm	The Calm ['Our storm is past']
Canon	The Canonization ['For God's sake hold your tongue']
Carey	A Letter to the Lady Carey and Mrs. Essex Rich ['Here where by all']
CB	To Mr. C. B. ['Thy friend whom thy deserts']
Christ	A Hymn to Christ at the Author's Last Going into Germany ['In what torn ship soever']
Citizen	A Tale of a Citizen and his Wife (noncanonical) ['I sing no harme, goodsooth']
Commun	Community ['Good we must love']
Compu	The Computation ['For the first twenty years']
ConfL	Confined Love ['Some man unworthy']
Corona	La Corona
Cor1	'Deign at my hands'
Cor2	Annunciation ['Salvation to all that will is nigh']
Cor3	Nativity ['Immensity cloistered in thy dear womb']
Cor4	Temple ['With his kind mother who partakes thy woe']
Cor5	Crucifying ['By miracles exceeding power of man']
Cor6	Resurrection ['Moist with one drop of thy blood']
Cor7	Ascension ['Salute the last and everlasting day']
Coryat	Upon Mr. Thomas Coryat's Crudities ['Oh to what height']
Cross	The Cross ['Since Christ embraced']
Curse	The Curse ['Whoever guesses, thinks, or dreams']
Damp	The Damp ['When I am dead']

Disinher	Disinherited ['Thy father all from thee']
Dissol	The Dissolution ['She is dead']
Dream	The Dream ['Dear love, for nothing less']
Eclog	Eclogue at the Marriage of the Earl of Somerset ['Unseasonable man, statue of ice']
Ecst	The Ecstasy ['Where, like a pillow on a bed']
ED	To E. of D. with Six Holy Sonnets ['See, Sir, how as the sun's']
EdHerb	To Sir Edward Herbert ['Man is a lump']
EG	To Mr. E. G. ['Even as lame things']
EgDD	Epigraph from Death's Duel ['Corporis haec animae']
Elegies:	
ElAnag	The Anagram ['Marry and love thy Flavia']
ElAut	The Autumnal ['No spring nor summer beauty']
ElBed	Going to Bed ['Come, Madam, come']
ElBrac	The Bracelet ['Not that in color it was like thy hair']
ElChange	Change ['Although thy hand and faith']
ElComp	The Comparison ['As the sweet sweat of roses in a still']
ElExpost	The Expostulation ['To make the doubt clear']
ElFatal	On His Mistress ['By our first strange and fatal interview']
ElJeal	Jealousy ['Fond woman which would'st have thy husband die']
ElNat	'Nature's lay idiot'
ElPart	His Parting From Her ['Since she must go']
ElPerf	The Perfume ['Once and but once found in thy company']
ElPict	His Picture ['Here take my picture']
ElProg	Love's Progress ['Whoever loves, if he do not propose']
ElServe	'Oh, let not me serve so'
ElVar	Variety ['The heavens rejoice in motion']
ElWar	Love's War ['Till I have peace with thee']
EpEliz	Epithalamion upon…the Lady Elizabeth ['Hail, Bishop Valentine']
EpLin	Epithalamion Made at Lincoln's Inn ['The sunbeams in the east']
EtAD	Epitaph for Ann Donne ['Annae/Georgii More de filiae']
EtED	Epitaph for Elizabeth Drury ['Quo pergas, viator']
EtRD	Epitaph for Robert and Anne Drury ['Roberti Druri/quo vix alter']
EtSP	John Donne's Epitaph…in St. Paul's Cathedral ['Iohannes Donne/Sac: Theol: Profess:']
Expir	The Expiration ['So, so, break off']
Fare	Farewell to Love ['Whilst yet to prove']
Father	A Hymn to God the Father ['Wilt thou forgive']
Faust	Faustinus ['Faustinus keeps his sister']

Fever	A Fever ['Oh do not die']
FirAn	The First Anniversary. An Anatomy of the World ['When that rich']
Flea	The Flea ['Mark but this flea']
Fun	The Funeral ['Whoever comes to shroud me']
FunEl	A Funeral Elegy [''Tis lost to trust a tomb']
Gaz	Translated out of Gazaeus ['God grant thee thine own wish']
GHerb	To Mr. George Herbert with One of My Seals ['Qui prius assuetus serpentum']
Goodf	Goodfriday, 1613. Riding Westward ['Let man's soul be a sphere']
GoodM	The Good Morrow ['I wonder by my troth']
Ham	An Hymn to the Saints and to the Marquis Hamilton ['Whether that soul which now comes']
Har	Obsequies upon the Lord Harrington ['Fair soul, which wast not only']
Harb	The Harbinger to the Progress (by Joseph Hall) ['Two souls move here']
Heart	'When my heart was mine own'
Henry	Elegy on the Untimely Death of…Prince Henry ['Look to me, Faith']
Hero	Hero and Leander ['Both robbed of air']
HG	To Sr. Henry Goodyere ['Who makes the past a pattern']

Holy Sonnets:

HSBatter	'Batter my heart'
HSBlack	'O my black soul'
HSDeath	'Death be not proud'
HSDue	'As due by many titles'
HSLittle	'I am a little world'
HSMade	'Thou hast made me'
HSMin	'If poisonous minerals'
HSPart	'Father part of his double interest'
HSRound	'At the round earth's imagined corners'
HSScene	'This is my play's last scene'
HSShe	'Since she whom I loved'
HSShow	'Show me dear Christ'
HSSighs	'O might those sighs'
HSSouls	'If faithful souls'
HSSpit	'Spit in my face'
HSVex	'O to vex me'
HSWhat	'What if this present'
HSWhy	'Why are we by all creatures'
HSWilt	'Wilt thou love God'

	LIST OF SHORT FORMS xxxiii

HuntMan   To the Countess of Huntingdon ['Man to God's image']
HuntUn   To the Countess of Huntingdon ['That unripe side of earth']
HWHiber   H. W. in Hibernia Belligeranti ['Went you to conquer?']
HWKiss   To Sir Henry Wotton ['Sir, more than kisses']
HWNews   To Sir Henry Wotton ['Here's no more news']
HWVenice   To Sir H. W. at His Going Ambassador to Venice ['After those reverend papers']

Ignatius, verse from:
   IgAver   'Aversa facie Janum referre'
   IgFeath   'Feathers or straws swim on the water's face'
   IgFlow   'As a flower wet with last night's dew'
   IgLark   'The lark by busy and laborious ways'
   IgNoise   'With so great noise and horror'
   IgOper   'Operoso tramite scandent'
   IgPiece   'That the least piece which thence doth fall'
   IgPlum   'Aut plumam, aut paleam'
   IgQual   'Qualis hesterno madefacta rore'
   IgResemb   'Resemble Janus with a diverse face'
   IgSport   'My little wandering sportful soul'
   IgTanto   'Tanto fragore boatuque'
ILBlest   To Mr. I. L. ['Blest are your north parts']
ILRoll   To Mr. I. L. ['Of that short roll']
Image   'Image of her whom I love'
InAA   Inscription in the Album Amicorum of Michael Corvinus ['In propria venit']
Ind   The Indifferent ['I can love both fair and brown']
InLI   Inscription in a Bible Presented to Lincoln's Inn ['In Bibliotheca Hospitii']
Jet   A Jet Ring Sent ['Thou art not so black']
Jug   The Juggler ['Thou callest me effeminate']
Julia   Julia (non-canonical) ['Hearke newes, ô Enuy']
Klock   Klockius ['Klockius so deeply hath sworn']
Lam   The Lamentations of Jeremy ['How sits this city']
Lect   A Lecture upon the Shadow ['Stand still and I will read']
Leg   The Legacy ['When I died last']
Liar   The Liar ['Thou in the fields walkest']
Libro   De Libro Cum Mutuaretur ['Doctissimo Amicissimoque v. D. D. Andrews']
Licent   A Licentious Person ['Thy sins and hairs']
Lit   A Litany ['Father of heaven and him']

LovAlch	Love's Alchemy ['Some that have deeper digged']
LovDeity	Love's Deity ['I long to talk with some old']
LovDiet	Love's Diet ['To what a cumbersome unwieldiness']
LovExch	Love's Exchange ['Love, any devil else but you']
LovGrow	Love's Growth ['I scarce believe my love to be so pure']
LovInf	Lovers' Infiniteness ['If yet I have not all thy love']
LovUsury	Love's Usury ['For every hour that thou wilt spare me']
Macaron	In Eundem Macaronicon ['Quot, dos haec, linguists']
Mark	Elegy on the Lady Markham ['Man is the world']
Martial	Raderus ['Why this man gelded Martial']
Merc	Mercurius Gallo-Belgicus ['Like Aesop's fellow slaves']
Mess	The Message ['Send home my long strayed eyes']
Metem	Metempsychosis ['I sing the progress of a deathless soul']
MHMary	To the Lady Magdalen Herbert, of St. Mary Magdalen ['Her of your name']
MHPaper	To Mrs. M. H. ['Mad paper stay']
NegLov	Negative Love ['I never stooped so low']
Niobe	Niobe ['By children's birth and death']
Noct	A Nocturnal upon St. Lucy's Day [''Tis the year's midnight']
Para	The Paradox ['No lover saith, I love']
Philo	An Obscure Writer ['Philo with twelve years' study']
Phrine	Phrine ['Thy flattering picture, Phrine']
Praise	To the Praise of the Dead and the Anatomy (by Joseph Hall) ['Well died the world']
Prim	The Primrose ['Upon this primrose hill']
Prohib	The Prohibition ['Take heed of loving me']
Pyr	Pyramus and Thisbe ['Two by themselves each other']
Ralph	Ralphius ['Compassion in the world again is bred']
Relic	The Relic ['When my grave is broke up again']
Res	Resurrection Imperfect ['Sleep, sleep, old sun']
RWEnvy	To Mr. R. W. ['Kindly I envy thy song's']
RWMind	To Mr. R. W. ['Muse not that by thy mind']
RWSlumb	To Mr. R. W. ['If as mine is thy life a slumber be']
RWThird	To Mr. R. W. ['Like one who in her third widowhood']
RWZeal	To Mr. R. W. ['Zealously my muse']
Sal	To the Countess of Salisbury ['Fair, great, and good']
Sappho	Sappho to Philaenis ['Where is that holy fire']

Satires:
Sat1	'Away thou fondling motley humorist'
Sat2	'Sir, though (I thank God for it) I do hate'

Sat3	'Kind pity chokes my spleen'
Sat4	'Well, I may now receive and die'
Sat5	'Thou shalt not laugh in this leaf, Muse'
SB	To Mr. S. B. ['O thou which to search']
SecAn	The Second Anniversary. Of the Progress of the Soul ['Nothing could make me sooner']
SelfAc	A Self Accuser ['Your mistress, that you follow whores']
SelfL	Self Love ['He that cannot choose but love']
SGo	Song ['Go, and catch a falling star']
Sheaf	A Sheaf of Miscellany Epigrams
Sheaf 1–61:	individual poems within Sheaf
Ship	A Burnt Ship ['Out of a fired ship']
Sickness	A Hymn to God My God, in My Sickness ['Since I am coming']
Sidney	Upon the Translation of the Psalms by Sir Philip Sidney ['Eternal God, (for whom who ever dare …)']
Sorrow	Elegia ['Sorrow, who to this house']
SSweet	Song ['Sweetest love, I do not go']
Stat	Stationes from Devotions ['Insultus morbi primus']
Storm	The Storm ['Thou which art I']
SunRis	The Sun Rising ['Busy old fool, unruly sun']
Tilman	To Mr. Tilman after He Had Taken Orders ['Thou whose diviner soul']
Token	Sonnet. The Token ['Send me some token']
Triple	The Triple Fool ['I am two fools, I know']
TWHail	To Mr. T. W. ['All hail sweet poet']
TWHarsh	To Mr. T. W. ['Haste thee harsh verse']
TWHence	To Mr. T. W. ['At once from hence']
TWPreg	To Mr. T. W. ['Pregnant again']
Twick	Twickenham Garden ['Blasted with sighs and surrounded with tears']
Under	The Undertaking ['I have done one braver thing']
ValBook	A Valediction of the Book ['I'll tell thee now']
ValMourn	A Valediction Forbidding Mourning ['As virtuous men pass mildly away']
ValName	A Valediction of My Name in the Window ['My name engraved herein']
ValWeep	A Valediction of Weeping ['Let me pour forth']
Wall	Fall of a Wall ['Under an undermined and shot-bruised wall']
Will	The Will ['Before I sigh my last gasp']
Wing	Sir John Wingfield ['Beyond th'old pillars']
Witch	Witchcraft by a Picture ['I fix mine eye on thine']
WomCon	Woman's Constancy ['Now thou has loved me one whole day']

GENERAL INTRODUCTION

JEANNE SHAMI, M. THOMAS HESTER, AND DENNIS FLYNN

INTENDED as a source of directions, a guard against misdirections, and an indicator of new directions, this Handbook is *not* intended as a mere summary of existing knowledge but rather reveals critical patterns of literary and historical work on John Donne's writings and the new directions that these patterns have enabled or obstructed. In several respects it breaks new ground even while it introduces scholars to the history of Donne studies, providing conceptual tools to orient and unfold Donne scholarship.

In the first of the fifty-six essays contributed, Gary A. Stringer estimates that Donne made public, in print or in the pulpit, 'close to 75 per cent' of his extant writings, despite the facts (paraphrasing the words of Annabel Patterson) that 'the state in which Donne lived not only practised official government censorship, but also routinely intercepted citizens' personal mail and spied on their private conversations', and that 'the possibility of running afoul of the authorities was an inescapable condition of nearly every verbal utterance'. In the last of these essays, Lynne Magnusson adds that 'Elizabethan practices of print censorship can by no means account adequately for the acute apprehension, to be found in so many of Donne's writings, that linguistic interaction and practical communication are fraught with risks deriving from state or religious authority'. In these two statements we recognize a main concern of Donne studies to date, and a pointer towards work to be carried forward by Donne scholars.

Donne began to publish his writings early in the reign of James I. This departure was not prompted by any easing of censorship, nor by any whim of Donne's own.

Donne's publications seem to express instead his daring and his resolution to extend, to carry forward, some of the impulses that had prompted and continued to prompt those of his writings issued in manuscript, but to do so as well in a public and officially sanctioned format that was not only more widely accessible but also more dangerous. In all four Parts of this volume, Donne's daring and resolution are prominent features of various discussions.

Donne's writings are seen here first in relation to textual bibliography, archival research, and other academic scholarship, actively and often collaboratively exploring the history and culture of early modern England. Study of Donne's writings at the forefront of disciplines is today assuming the indicative function for English literary scholarship that a century earlier was taken on by study of Shakespeare's writings. A congeries of traditionally insoluble scholarly problems about Donne and his writings has gradually come, during the past few generations, into more distinct focus and discernible order through application of new expertise and technology. As a result, the tools set forth and explained in Part 1 of the Handbook have shown and still promise clear progress and intensity for the field, especially through recent organization of collaborations by teams of scholars, such as the Indiana Donne *Variorum*, the Oxford *Sermons* and *Letters* editions (and this Handbook), grounded in the annual conferences of the John Donne Society and the *John Donne Journal*. These undertakings have been called forth especially by the continuing success of the *Variorum*, growing our comprehension of the shape of Donne's career as a writer, including the ways and circumstances in which his writings were disseminated in manuscript and in print.

The daring of Donne's Epigrams, Satires, Elegies, and Verse Letters of the 1590s tended to rule out their publication before his death. As the chosen genres for his earliest poetry, these illustrate his interest not only in the history of poetic genres but in the cunning way classical poets had penetrated them with the often dangerous history of their own times. Donne outdid them, according to a connoisseur of daring, Ben Jonson, who (referring to one of the Verse Letters) told William Drummond that Donne was 'the first poet in the World in some things'. From this beginning in what Thomas Carew called 'fresh invention' grew the full array of Donne's genres, unequalled in excellence and variety by the work of any other English writer and discussed in succession by the Part 2 essays of this Handbook. His initial, richly satirical efforts issued next, at the start of the seventeenth century, in the mock-epic *Metem*, treated first among Donne's 'Menippean' writings by Anne Lake Prescott, who lists also various examples of this generic capacity, all of which Donne at various points invested with his energies: 'dream visions, trips to the underworld or the moon, degrading metamorphoses, lists (with their curious tendency, even when seriously meant, to edge into risibility), formal paradoxes, mock encomia, parodic speeches, collections of grotesqueries, imaginary societies, Lucianic dialogues, and in the Renaissance imaginary libraries'. These are all component parts of Donne's authorship, not to be dismissed or neglected synecdochically (J. R. Roberts 1982b: 62–3).

Donne's foison in subgenres such as these, not only in his early years, as Prescott observes, can suggest an 'all-male atmosphere' that is 'quite unlike many of the lyrics for which Donne is now better loved', although in some ways these love lyrics or 'Songs and Sonets', many of them addressed to or uttered by various fictional or actual women, also stretch and confuse generic classification, as do the Menippean writings. Dayton Haskin's Part 2 essay notes about the 'Songs and Sonets' that, although Donne must have begun writing them at about the same time as his other poems of the 1590s, 'It is not clear that Donne himself thought of these poems as a group'. Haskin bases this thinking on the evidence compiled by the *Variorum* editors, that 'these poems entered manuscript circulation one by one at different times, perhaps over a period of more than two decades'. Whether they were designed as a group or not, these poems differ from other poetic kinds that Donne circulated by genre, sometimes arranged in sequences. Moreover, they do not have the clear classical precedent so characteristic of Donne's other early genres, although they do seem at least partly to derive thematically from classical Latin love poetry and formally from medieval and later rhyming verse about love relationships.

Another genre Donne adopted from late medieval and Renaissance practice was the sonnet, used both for Verse Letters and, in both individual poems and sequences of poems, for his Holy Sonnets. R. V. Young's essay on the religious sonnet sequences is exemplary work on these poems, informed by the *Variorum*. As Young remarks:

The lucubrations of the textual editors, while providing a satisfying explanation of the textual problems associated with the Holy Sonnets, challenge the ingenuity of interpreters by complicating the hermeneutic problem. They endorse [Helen] Gardner's sense that the poems are sequential, and that Donne conceived of them as an interrelated set; but, instead of one sequence of twelve and another of four, the *Variorum* offers two sets of twelve with four different poems in each and with different arrangements. If the poems are designed to be read and comprehended in sequence—in the manner of Sir Philip Sidney's *Astrophil & Stella* or Samuel Daniel's *Delia*—as the textual evidence suggests, then it is incumbent upon critics to explain what is *meant* by Donne's substantial revision.

Young's essay is the first fruit of such scholarly commitment and stands as a model for the student of Donne inclined to use such conceptual tools as the *Variorum* makes available.

Even more complex generic problems are posed by Donne's first major publications in prose and poetry, *Pseudo-Martyr* and the Anniversary poems. As Graham Roebuck points out, these are both works of mixed genre. *Pseudo-Martyr* is a controversial treatise, but it incorporates in its historical and journalistic enterprise such 'ambiguous' literary forms as the anatomy and the disputed question. Likewise, the *Anniversaries* are an 'elaborate confection', a 'rich assembly and mixture of genres, and echoes of genres'. As such, these works illustrate the truth that genres are human attempts to codify, civilize, and resolve difficult and complex social situations as well as lenses through which we understand writing.

This truth is nowhere more applicable than in the study of Donne's Sermons, of which he deliberately made public more examples, in print or from the pulpit, than of any other genre. As Jeanne Shami states, Donne's Sermons were 'the culmination of his intellectual life, the repository of his moral and political thought, and, at their best, his finest literary creations'. In them Donne found a way to deal proportionately with the dangers that had led him to feel fear and shame about his earliest writings. The Sermons show Donne engaging fully in the public sphere all the impulses characteristic of his earlier work disseminated to friends in manuscript.

Applicable generally to work on Donne's genres, Dayton Haskin's essay on the love lyrics dwells also on the extent to which these poems have been or should be read in relation to Donne's biography. To help solve this problem he lays out tentatively a 'hermeneutic' that may 'release' readers of the Handbook from the sense 'that we are ultimately reading under the sort of biographical imperative that is built into devoting a handbook to a single author'; and in particular Haskin cautions that in reading Part 2 essays on genres we should not 'ultimately give way to questions that are shot through with implications for understanding "Donne" himself'. Haskin's hermeneutic encompasses interpreting the formal variety of the love lyrics, including (1) their 'peculiar' stanza forms (of which he counts more than forty different varieties); (2) their use of conceits and striking effects of closure; (3) their possibly having been addressed to known or implied readers, as if serving one function of Verse Letters; (4) a related consideration, their evidently having been designed to provoke some response from an undisclosed addressee, their presenting what Margaret Maurer (discussing the Verse Letters and using Donne's own phrase) identifies as 'emergent occasions'; and (5) the question Haskin broached earlier in his essay, the collection and arrangement of the love lyrics, the question 'whether Donne regarded these poems as constituting a group'. Readers of the Handbook may find parts of this hermeneutic also of use for the study of particular genres other than Donne's love lyrics.

As Haskin here and elsewhere implies, the use of biographical and historical evidence in Donne studies is a contested site, a consideration reflected in the editors' design of Part 3 of the Handbook: eleven pairs of chronologically but otherwise loosely linked essays, matching segments of Donne's biography with brief, serial characterizations of the history of his time. This pairing of biographical essays with essays by historians is intended to augment recognition by Donne scholars of the important work carried on by early modern English historians since the 1970s, work that has put all studies of the period on a new footing. For example, Part 3 begins with Patrick Collinson's guide to new conceptual tools for Donne's biographers, reviewing the work of such historians as Eamon Duffy and Michael C. Questier, both enriching and complicating our sense of the background in religion and politics of Donne's family history and earliest years. Later, Paul E. J. Hammer presents new perspectives on Donne's participation in the Cadiz raid and Azores voyage, conventionally conceived (by Walton and later biographers) as an expression of Donne's allegiance to Robert Devereux, Earl of Essex. Johann Sommerville reviews issues surrounding the

Gunpowder Plot and the Oath of Allegiance, suggesting some of the complexity of Donne's attitude and response. Alastair Bellany deals with the volatile politics that followed the death of Robert Cecil, Earl of Salisbury, when the royal court was badly split by rival factions, the Spanish-leaning Howards and the Protestant 'patriots' who had clustered around Prince Henry until his death six months after Salisbury's; in this unstable context, Bellany conjectures, Donne may have approached King James's favourite, Robert Carr, Viscount Rochester, as 'the best available point of access to the King'. Malcolm Smuts focuses on the aftermath of Donne's participation in the embassy of James Hay, Viscount Doncaster, arguing that, despite distress at the seemingly Spanish direction of King James's policies in 1620, Donne's diplomatic experience led him to see that 'growing division among British Protestants and shrill attacks on the King's behaviour would only play into the hands of Spain' as well as of 'British Catholics, church papists, and anti-Calvinists who hoped to exploit the foreign-policy debacle to dilute the evangelical character of the English church'. Arnold Hunt discerns brief and heavily coded political statements in Donne's preaching during the final years of his life, concluding that 'Donne seems to have been slow to adapt' to the new, Laudian, and anti-Calvinist religious agenda, remaining aligned until the end with a moderate Calvinism 'acceptable to Laud while still remaining within the bounds of Reformed orthodoxy', a middle ground that was difficult to find by the early 1630s, as contrast with other preachers demonstrates.

In the study of Donne's biography, it has been clear at least since Augustus Jessopp that Donne's formative period coincided with the most dramatic and dangerous period for English Catholics, when their persecution was most virulent. Donne himself wrote about how deeply he and his family were involved in the persecution. Yet our sense of this important formative influence, despite what we know (and can learn) about the lasting psychological effects of such experience, remains sketchy and still haunted by questions like fixing the date of Donne's 'conversion' to the Church of England, or deciding about 'apostasy' in his writings. Such terms have derived from, and been captives of, a historical tradition that defined religious history along lines of confessional controversy. Moreover, students of Donne still tend to deal with these questions as traditional students of literature, parsing the theology, philology, and decorum of Donne's poetry and prose. To some extent we may feel that what actually happened to Donne either cannot be learned or is already known, through Walton or others, adequately enough for literary analysis—our prime interest in Donne—to carry on without further irritable searching after fact. As long as this attitude prevails, we are not able to give a truly coherent account of Donne's formative years and their effects on his later life and writings.

The sequence of biographical essays, although in general they describe the outline of Donne's life, are not intended to supply a biography but instead to highlight important biographical issues calling for further work. Many of these issues have been problems unrecognized or misconceived at various times since Izaak Walton published his *Life of Donne* in the seventeenth century. Many deficiencies of Walton's work were exposed by David Novarr's *The Making of Walton's Lives* (1958); consequently, with a few exceptions, Walton is generally used in Part 3 essays advisedly, with discretion and some hazard, unless his testimony can be supported by independent evidence. For example, Dennis Flynn departs markedly from the presentation by Walton and subsequent biographers of Donne's problematic education and university years, discussing evidence until now mainly ignored by students of Donne. Steven W. May details much new evidence about Donne's years in the employ of Master of the Rolls and Lord Keeper Thomas Egerton, another traditionally obscure biographical topic. Flynn again devotes attention to biographical cruxes in his essays on Donne's wedding and on Donne's response to the Gunpowder Plot and Oath of Allegiance. Jeanne Shami focuses on Donne's decision to take orders and primarily on the ambivalent quality of the main evidence for understanding it, Walton's *Life* and Donne's extant correspondence; exploring widely divergent accounts of Donne's situation, as well as of his inner life and motivations at the time of this decision, Shami traces 'a more nuanced path' through the various considerations that complicated his resolution to pursue 'divinity' by highlighting his central dilemma to realize both '*ambition* (to serve, to be recognized publicly and remembered for one's talents, to advance in the world) and *honour* (to serve with integrity, to be held accountable for one's principles, to contribute to the public good)'. Clayton D. Lein studies Donne's career at the transition between the reigns of James I and Charles I, describing Donne as public spokesperson for the English Church, as defined by its king and head; as the Church's most imaginative architect from the pulpit; and as a practising pastoral administrator in legal, educational, and charitable work in his parish assignments as well as at St Paul's. Emphasizing the significance of the parish for Donne throughout his life, Alison Shell concludes Part 3 with a biographical essay that reviews Donne's death through his many anticipative writings and actions expressing 'the era's basic moral obligation to keep death constantly in mind'; recalling Donne's 'most famous' piece of prose, 'No Man is an *Iland*...', Shell remarks that church bells 'defined a parish unit'; she notes the 'startlingly paradoxical' effect of Donne's proverbial injunction, 'never send to know for whom the bell tolls', in which 'one's interests are so closely identified with one's neighbour's' that 'not to try to find out who is dying' becomes 'the acme of neighbourliness'.

Part 4 of the Handbook deals in reception history, focusing on seven key problems—literary, biographical, and cultural—that have traditionally vexed studies of Donne's writings and life: Achsah Guibbory on Donne's so-called apostasy; Theresa M. DiPasquale on his misogyny; Debora Shuger on his political absolutism; Albert C. Labriola on the qualities of his versification; Hugh Adlington on his ambition; Judith Scherer Herz on Donne's own critical trope—Jack Donne and the Dean of St Paul's—as well as on many of its critical metamorphoses; and Lynne Magnusson on Donne and danger. Each chapter sums up the controversy and offers new ways to disentangle old habits of thought.

PART I

RESEARCH RESOURCES IN DONNE STUDIES AND WHY THEY MATTER

INTRODUCTION

JEANNE SHAMI

PART 1 of the *Oxford Handbook of John Donne* emphasizes the heuristic and practical orientation of the Handbook by examining prevailing assumptions and reviewing or introducing students and researchers to some of the specialized scholarly tools available for Donne studies. Chapters in this section provide a brief evaluation and description of the scholarly strengths, shortcomings, and significance of each resource, focusing on a balanced evaluation of the opportunities and the hazards each offers.

Part 1 begins with two essays situating Donne's writings in terms of his status as primarily a 'manuscript author', read by particular, identifiable individuals during his life and a variety of readers in his early print afterlife. Gary A. Stringer's essay on 'The Composition and Dissemination of Donne's Writings' introduces the controversial subject of the production, circulation, and transmission of Donne's writings in the sixteenth and seventeenth centuries among various coteries, dedicatees, and named recipients, concluding that 'Donne at various times availed himself of each of the modes of communication available to him, choosing print, oral delivery, or manuscript circulation in accordance with the various meanings he intended for—and felt comfortable in conveying to—particular audiences at particular times'. The essay pays particular attention to 'the vulnerability of manuscript texts not just to errors of inadvertency or misjudgement, but to deliberate scribal tampering', in addition to considering questions regarding the intended recipients of the poems, precise dating of many of Donne's writings, Donne's practices of revision, and the authoritative canon of Donne's writings.

Ernest W. Sullivan II's essay on Donne's early (seventeenth-century) readership establishes the range of readers and the variety of uses to which Donne's works were put in the first generations after their dissemination and publication. The essay thus challenges the perception of Donne's seventeenth-century readers as comprising primarily the 'intellectual elite' with access to his manuscripts, by demonstrating that a great many more people were 'reading/writing Donne (particularly his works in print) much more frequently and over a much greater time-span than has been thought', and that these writings had 'commercial, social, and personal value for a great diversity of readers'. Sullivan's focus on the practices of reading and interpretation of Donne's writings over the course of the seventeenth century redraws our picture of Donne's seventeenth-century influence on his society's language and culture across the social spectrum.

Following these two introductory essays, Lara M. Crowley's essay introduces readers to the importance of archival work in advancing Donne studies. Here we mean archives, first and foremost, as the archive of Donne's own writings, including the many contemporary copies—both manuscript and print—of his writings. However, archival research is also introduced as important for adding new information to the biographical, historical, and contextual fields in which these writings are situated. Thus, 'opportunities in archival research extend beyond the important goals of establishing informed texts, their likely periods of composition, and (in some cases) the sequences in which they circulated, to such issues as Donne's attitudes towards print and patronage'. Archival research also promises to yield knowledge of the literary tastes of Donne's readers, as we increase our awareness of and familiarity with early modern practices of manuscript compilation and circulation. The essay also offers practical advice for navigating archival collections even as it expresses the exciting possibilities opening up for Donne scholars in this kind of research.

Essays by Stringer, Richard Todd, and Sullivan explore the important issues of what we read when we read John Donne's writings, how close these writings are to Donne's originals, the history of establishing texts for Donne studies and their impact on criticism of his works, and debates over which writings are canonical. Together these essays demonstrate the importance of establishing the texts of Donne's writings as foundational to all other scholarly activity. Every edition represents the best efforts of an expert to provide an accurate and reliable representation of the work, and provides the necessary biographical, historical, critical, and factual information to begin a thorough and intellectually satisfying study of the work. 'Any reader who wants to understand any literary work has to start with its scholarly edition.' So, Stringer and Todd describe and analyse the complex textual tradition of editing Donne's poetic texts, culminating in the work of the Donne *Variorum* project, which has provided the most comprehensive, accurate, and scholarly edition of Donne's poetry available to his readers based on the most thorough investigation of all bibliographical evidence (including all known manuscripts) collated using state-of-the-art technological programs, and interpreted according to sound principles of textual editing that eschew the 'eclectic' texts of all former editions.

Sullivan tackles the state of the text for all of Donne's prose works, providing for all readers of Donne an overview of the work of the textual bibliographer and a scholarly review of available editions of Donne's prose.

Donald R. Dickson's essay introduces scholars to essential scholarly tools outside the archives and the established texts in an essay dealing with short-cuts to research—both the opportunities afforded by these tools as well as the pitfalls associated with them. Electronic databases (e.g. the online sermons available through Brigham Young University) and concordances (both print and now electronic—i.e. DigitalDonne) that allow readers to search and manipulate text, as well as printed volumes (such as John R. Roberts's annotated bibliographies) that gather together and annotate critical resources are described and evaluated. This chapter is intended to facilitate research, but cautions users to remain aware of the hazards of short-cuts of any kind to the scholarly enterprise.

Finally, Hugh Adlington's essay demonstrates that perhaps the most important and underused research tool in the kit is the international scholarly community. This essay indicates the international scope of interest in Donne and the principal organizations that facilitate exchange of ideas, but it is also intended to inspire greater engagement with Donne scholars around the world, and to seek opportunities and occasions for working together—in teams—on large projects such as the Donne *Variorum*, the Oxford *Letters* project, and the Oxford *Sermons* project, as well as on smaller projects where both established and emerging scholars can converse.

Together, these essays set the tone, prepare the textual and contextual ground, and highlight the tools available for advancing Donne studies into the twenty-first century. No readers hoping to approach the subjects of subsequent chapters should do so without first making themselves familiar with the scholarly landscape sketched here in Part 1.

CHAPTER 1

THE COMPOSITION AND DISSEMINATION OF DONNE'S WRITINGS

GARY A. STRINGER

1

When John Donne died on 31 March 1631, at the age of 59, he left behind a body of written work remarkable for both its volume and its variety. These writings—or those that have survived and are itemized in Geoffrey Keynes's bibliography—include (*a*) three treatises on controversial religio-moral questions (*Biathanatos*, a casuistical justification of suicide; *Pseudo-Martyr*, an argument that Roman Catholics ought to take the Oath of Allegiance; and *Conclave Ignati/Ignatius his Conclaue*, an attack, in separate Latin and English versions, on the Jesuits); (*b*) 160 Sermons (dating variously from 1615 to 1631); (*c*) *Deuotions Vpon Emergent Occasions* (a set of twenty-three meditations prompted by a life-threatening illness that Donne endured in 1623); (*d*) thirty-five brief prose pieces, which include twelve Paradoxes (e.g. 'That it is possible to find some vertue in some women'), nineteen Problems (e.g. 'Why haue Bastards best Fortunes?'), two characters ('…of a Scot at the first sight' and '…of a Dunce'), 'An Essay of Valour', and 'Newes from the very Countrey' (on this latter work, see Chs. 3 and 5); (*e*) *Essayes in Divinity* (a series of learned 'Disquisitions', 'Meditations', and 'Prayers' on the opening verses of

Genesis and Exodus); and (*f*) about 230 Prose Letters, written to a variety of friends, acquaintances, and actual or potential patrons. They also include (*g*) approximately 200 poems, totalling slightly over 9,100 lines, that fall broadly across the spectrum of generic types.

An emphasis in recent years on Donne's involvement in the manuscript culture of his time has tended to make us forget just how much of his work he actually published. Dedicated to King James and prefaced with an introductory epistle signed 'Iohn Donne', *Pseudo-Martyr* (392 quarto pages) was printed in 1610, and—though they remained technically anonymous until 1634—the two versions of *Ignatius* (Latin, 35 quarto pages; English, 143 duodecimo pages) both appeared in print the following year. Between 1622 and 1627, moreover, after rising to the deanship of St Paul's and achieving international prominence as a preacher, he published six individual Sermons (totalling 437 pages) that had been delivered on 'special' occasions (two to a royal audience), and shortly thereafter Donne acceded to the importunity of 'Friends' (*Letters* 249) and published the record of his 1623 sickness as *Devotions*, dedicating the work to Prince Charles. A crude tabulation shows that, even if we define 'publication' strictly as 'disseminated in print', during his lifetime Donne published about 42 per cent of the 3,849 pages of prose he had written; and if we broaden the definition to include the normal mode of 'publishing' sermons—proclaiming them orally in a public forum—this figure is close to 75 per cent. What remained unpublished at his death, disseminated only in manuscript, were *Biathanatos*, the short proses, *Essayes in Divinity*, the Letters, and most of the poems.

As Annabel Patterson and others have reminded us, the state in which Donne lived not only practised official government censorship, but also routinely intercepted citizens' personal mail and spied on their private conversations, and the possibility of running afoul of the authorities was an inescapable condition of nearly every verbal utterance. Against the background of this 'repressive culture' (A. Patterson 1984: 92), as the brief survey above suggests, Donne at various times availed himself of each of the modes of communication available to him, choosing print, oral delivery, or manuscript circulation in accordance with the various meanings he intended for—and felt comfortable in conveying to—particular audiences at particular times. And his appreciation of the relative advantages and limitations of each of these media would seem to have been very much like our own. When he determined to reach the broadest possible audience in the most enduring form, he chose print: *Pseudo-Martyr*, for instance, treats a politically charged topic of pressing national (and even international) concern, and printing it enables Donne—as one who had needed to 'blot out, certaine impressions of the Romane religion' before 'binding... [his] conscience' to any 'locall' one (13)—to exhort the English Catholic community (as well, of course, as to position himself among the loyal supporters of state policy) in the most public way possible. Similarly, when re-entering the arena of theologico-political controversy with *Conclave Ignati/Ignatius His Conclaue*, Donne published the work in both English and Latin in an attempt to appeal to both a local English and an international European audience. In publishing the *Devotions* in 1624, moreover, Donne seems to have embraced something like an official obligation to minister the record of his ordeal as 'holy delight' (*Letters* 249) to the general Christian community. And even if the original promptings may have come from the king or other sponsors, the desire to ensure wider dissemination and greater permanence must largely account for Donne's printing of the six Sermons of 1622–7, as well as for the fact that, if what Izaak Walton says is true, among his remains at his death were 'sixscore of his Sermons all written [out for posthumous publication] with his own hand' (1658: 88).

The writings that did *not* see print during Donne's life (or that had not been publicly declaimed from the pulpit) are ones that—for a variety of reasons—Donne deemed inappropriate for general scrutiny. By definition, of course, personal letters are of concern only to the sender and the receiver (and perhaps a circle of select friends). And the *Essayes in Divinity*—either because, as Donne's son averred when publishing the work in 1651, they represent the 'many debates betwixt God and himself, whether he were worthy, and competently learned to enter into Holy Orders' ('To the Reader', 5) or because, in the more cynical reading of Edmund Gosse, they are mere 'scholastic exercises' written to demonstrate 'the soundness of Donne's orthodoxy and the breadth of his learning' to the Archbishop (2.63)—serve a private agenda that apparently contemplates an audience of, at most, one (see also Ch. 19). With respect to the brief prose pieces, by contrast, Donne intended an audience, but deliberately sought to restrict circulation to a few trusted recipients for fear of the embarrassment—or worse—that public exposure of his authorship might entail. In a Letter enclosing some Paradoxes, sent to an unnamed friend in about 1600, Donne promises 'to acquaint' the recipient with 'all' his writings, but worries that 'to...[his] satyrs there belongs some feare and to some elegies and these [Paradoxes] perhaps shame' and threatens not to share his writings further unless he receives by return letter 'an assurance vpon the religion of your frendship that no coppy shalbee taken for any respect of these or any other my compositions sent to you' (LRO, Finch DG. 7. Lit. 2, fo. 308^v). And with *Biathanatos* he was even more circumspect. In a Letter accompanying a manuscript of the work sent to Sir Robert Ker (Earl of Ancrum) in 1619, Donne characterizes the treatise as the 'misinterpretable' work of a younger '*Jack Donne*, and not...D[r]. *Donne*', averring that 'no hand hath passed upon it to copy it' and that it had been communicated 'onely to some particular friends in both Universities, then when I writ it' (*Letters* 21–2).

Most of Donne's poetry also was unprinted during his lifetime, the principal exceptions being the individually published *Anniversaries* triptych—*FirAn* (1611), *FunEl* (1611), and *SecAn* (1612)—and *Henry*, which was included in the third edition of Josuah Sylvester's commemorative volume *Lachrymae Lachrymarum* (1613). Written over a period of about forty years, in several languages, the approximately 200 poems that make up this extraordinary body of work range in length from one to just over 500 lines and include a remarkable variety of poetic kinds: Satires, love

Elegies, Epigrams, Songs and Sonets, Epithalamions, Letters, poems commendatory of other literary works, philosophical meditations, Epicedes and Obsequies, Holy Sonnets and Hymns, versifications of books of the Bible and other occasional religious poems, assorted lapidary verse, and a further few items that defy generic classification. The intended audiences for these poems were correspondingly diverse, including, in Arthur Marotti's summation, various 'coterie[s]' of readers—'friends, acquaintances, patrons, patronesses, and the woman he married' (1986: x). The generic kinds, of course, are not always neatly aimed at a single category of readers: some of the Songs and Sonets, for instance, are probably or certainly written for Anne More (*LovGrow*) or (later) Anne Donne (*ValWeep*), while others apparently address his patroness Lucy Russell, Countess of Bedford (*Twick*), fellow poets (*Bait*), and the general gaggle of young wits with whom he associated as a young man about London in the 1590s (*SGo*, *Ind*). The recipients or subjects of some of the poems—especially of the Verse Letters, the Epicedes, the *Anniversaries*, (two of) the Epithalamions, and the funerary inscriptions—can be specifically identified, while the intended recipients of others remain conjectural. Precise dates are likewise impossible to assign to most of the poems.

Various reasons for Donne's refusal to publish his poems may be (and have been) advanced. One—although the above-noted quantity, generic variety, and length of Donne's labour in the vineyard that distinguish this body of work show the writing of poetry to have been a defining element of his being—is that Donne harboured a gentlemanly disdain for the role of the poet and, in particular, sought to avoid the 'stigma' (J. W. Saunders 1951: 139) of printing his verse. Indeed, some support for this view may be picked out of his own words. Responding in a Letter of about 1610 to Henry Goodere's suggestion that he compose commendatory verses to the Countess of Huntingdon, for instance, Donne declines partly on grounds that 'that knowledge which she hath of me, was in the beginning of a graver course, then of a Poet, into which (that I may also keep my dignity) I would not seem to relapse' (*Letters* 103). A few years later, in a Letter to George Garrard of 14 April 1612, he reinvokes the spectre of the poet's lack of dignity and links it specifically with print publication: 'Of my Anniversaries, the fault that I acknowledge in my self, is to have descended to print any thing in verse, which though it have excuse even in our times, by men who professe, and practise much gravitie; yet I confesse I wonder how I declined to it, and do not pardon my self' (*Letters* 238). The apparent disparagement of poetry and printing in these passages cannot be totally discounted, of course, but each must be appreciated in the full context within which it occurs. The position Donne had held when the young Elizabeth Stanley (later Countess of Huntingdon) had previously known him at York House was that of Chancellor Egerton's trusted secretary, a man apparently chosen for the fast track to a significant public career. Donne—or anyone—might well have regarded that as a 'graver course, then of a poet', especially one who might seem to be seeking favours from a noble lady whose respect he had once been able to take for granted.

And Donne's 'acknowledge[ment]' of the 'fault' of 'descend[ing] to print' must be viewed in light of the condemnation, noted further on in the Letter, of the *content* of the *Anniversaries*: certain unnamed 'Ladies'—no doubt ones who had already been or wished to become the subjects of Donne's praise themselves—had apparently complained that what Donne had said of 'Mistris *Drewry* was not so', that he had 'said too much' (*Letters* 239), a criticism echoed in Ben Jonson's rebuke that 'if … [the *Anniversaries*] had been written of ye Virgin Marie it had been something' (1–2.133).

Another possible factor in Donne's eschewal of print for these works is the venerable status that manuscripts, especially of belletristic writings, continued to occupy long after the invention of printing. Michael Drayton's address 'To the Generall Reader' that prefaces *Poly-Olbion*, for instance, complains of the 'great disaduantage' that accompanies publication of his poem: 'it commeth out at this time, when Verses are wholly deduc't to Chambers, and nothing esteem'd in this lunatique Age, but what is kept in Cabinets, and must only passe by Transcription…' (A1). And scholars like Peter Beal (1998) and Harold Love (1993) have demonstrated the widespread reliance on 'scribal publication' that thrived in the 1620s and 1630s and persisted late into the century. Donne himself seems to acknowledge this tradition in a Latin Verse Letter to one Dr Andrews (*Libro*), who—before returning to Donne a borrowed book that his children had mutilated—repaired the damaged artefact with manuscript replacement pages: '*Parturiunt madido quae nixu praela, recepta, / Sed quae scripta manu, sunt veneranda magis*' ('Things brought forth by the wet labours of the press are acceptable, / But those written by hand are more to be venerated'; *Milgate* 112, ll. 1–2). Whether this is to be understood as a categorical endorsement of manuscript over print rather than as a tactful gesture calculated to reduce his friend's embarrassment is not clear, but we do know that none of the over 200 books from Donne's library that has yet come to light is a manuscript; and we know—from the reference in the Letter below to an 'old [manuscript] book' that Donne had sought to borrow when gathering material for a planned edition of his poems—that his alleged veneration of manuscripts did not extend to the maintenance of a comprehensive holograph collection of his own poems. A Letter written to Goodere in 1614 provides perhaps the most reliable perspective on this matter. Having already determined to enter the church, Donne informs Goodere of a project he is forced to undertake as 'a valediction to the world before I take Orders':

…I am brought to a necessity of printing my Poems, and addressing them to my L[ord]. Chamberlain [Robert Carr, Earl of Somerset]. This I mean to do forthwith; not for much publique view, but at mine own cost, a few Copies. I apprehend some incongruities in the resolution; and I know what I shall suffer from many interpretations: but I am at an end, of much considering that; and, if I were as startling in that kinde, as ever I was, yet in this particular, I am under an unescapable necessity… By this occasion I am made a Rhapsoder of mine own rags, and that cost me more diligence, to seek them, then it did to make them.

This made me aske to borrow that old book of you, which it will be too late to see, for that use, when I see you: for I must do this, as a valediction to the world, before I take Orders. (*Letters* 196–7)

Donne then turns to a specific concern about the contents of the intended edition, asking whether Goodere had

ever made any such use of the letter in verse, *A nostre Countesse* [of Huntingdon] *chez vous*, as that I may not put it in, amongst the rest to persons of that rank; for I desire very very much, that something should bear her name in the book, and I would be just to my written words to my L. *Harrington*, to write nothing after that. I pray tell me as soon as you can, if I be at liberty to insert that: for if you have by any occasion applied any pieces of it, I see not, that it will be discerned, when it appears in the whole piece. (*Letters* 197–8)

These excerpts point to the more fundamental motives behind Donne's systematic attempt to restrict most of his poetry to manuscript circulation, motives partly similar to those that inhibited publication of some of the prose. While the 'interpretations' he dreads having to 'suffer' may include a general disapprobation of the act of publication itself (the 'fault' of having 'descended to print'), the admission that he has 'ever'—if not now so much as formerly—been 'startling in that kinde' (i.e. 'afraid of print') suggests that his deeper concern is with the specific imputations of moral and/or political impropriety that he knows 'publique view' of the poems will draw upon him—the same issues of 'feare' and 'shame' that had animated his negotiations with the friend fifteen years previously. The second excerpt underscores his awareness that, even if perfectly decent purposes may be accomplished by tailoring poems to specific audiences and circumstances, doing so may implicate one in a web of (potentially treacherous) expectations and obligations. In the 1610 Letter to Goodere quoted above, he cites as the principal reason for declining to address the Countess of Huntingdon directly his exclusive devotion to the Countess of Bedford—he has, he says, 'reserved [for her] not only all the verses, which I should make, but all the thoughts of womens worthinesse' (*Letters* 104). Here, he finds in the promise made to Lord Harington in the end of *Har*—'in thy Graue I do interre my Muse' (l. 256)—a binding prohibition against composing a new poem on Lady Huntingdon for the proposed edition, incidentally noting the possible further complication—which he treats as unexceptionable—that Goodere may have appropriated the original Verse Letter for his own uses. In sum, the 'interpretations' to which Donne fears the proposed edition will open him include not only moral and political indiscretions, but also breaches of ethics and etiquette. As his experience with the *Anniversaries* shows, print publication at any time, not just in 1614, would have rendered him similarly vulnerable. Although, for whatever reasons, the 'Somerset edition' never appeared, that he was willing to contemplate it at this time is a measure of the extreme pressure Carr must have been placing upon him.

2

The strictness of Donne's efforts to control the manuscript circulation of individual poems and even of whole genres undoubtedly varied according to differences in subject matter, purpose, and intended audience, and his attitude towards such dissemination must also have fluctuated over time, as the course of life inexorably transformed 'Jack Donne' into 'D[r]. Donne'. Even his most diligent efforts, however, were doomed to fail, and his poems eventually became widely known among his contemporaries, as the original recipients shared copies with others, who in turn shared them with still others in ever-expanding circles of manuscript dissemination. Indeed, the section on Donne in Peter Beal's *Index of English Literary Manuscripts* lists 3,997 whole or partial copies of individual Donne poems in the manuscript record (and others have come to light since the *Index* appeared), and those that survive constitute only a fraction of what must have originally existed. Unfortunately, among these thousands of manuscript copies only four brief inscriptions, a Latin Epitaph on his wife, and a single Verse Letter—the sixty-three-line *Carey*—are written in Donne's own hand. And the remaining scribal transcriptions, produced by scores of individuals often working from copies many stages removed from Donne's originals, are full of textual errors. Most of these, of course, are the result of simple ineptitude or carelessness, but some of them reflect the deliberate efforts of various copyists to improve Donne's poems aesthetically or to purge them of objectionable material. An additional factor complicating the interpretation of the manuscript evidence is that Donne revised many of his poems over the course of time, some of them more than once, and sent these revised versions into circulation alongside the originals, begetting strains of authentic variation within the surrounding sea of error.

Depending on a number of factors—how long a given poem drifted around in the manuscript pool, which social networks it circulated within, its level of popularity with readers, the diligence (and success) of Donne's efforts to limit its circulation, and, surely, chance—the number of surviving copies of particular poems varies widely: of the (early) Elegy *ElBrac*, for instance, sixty-three manuscript copies remain, while only four full transcriptions of the lyric *Fare* are extant, and the Holy Sonnet *HSShe*, written after the death of Anne Donne in 1617, survives in only a single manuscript copy. Donne originally handed the poems around individually or in small sequences, and during the 1590s and the first two decades of the seventeenth century collections of varying size and composition found their way into dozens of contemporary diaries, commonplace books, and handwritten anthologies of poetry. In the 1620s, after Donne had written most of the poems and redirected his creative energies to the composition of Sermons, it became possible to pull together more or less comprehensive collections of his poems; and scribally assembled collections from this period provided almost all the texts printed in the

Ill. 1.1. *HSShe* in the Westmoreland ms. (NY3), fo. 37, the sole seventeenth-century manuscript including this poem, *HSShow*, and *HSVex*, none of which appeared in any early edition and all of which remained undiscovered until the 1890s. The Westmoreland ms., inscribed in the hand of Donne's friend Rowland Woodward, has very high authority among the seventeenth-century manuscripts of Donne's poems. (Henry W. and Albert A. Berg Collection of English and American Literature, The New York Public Library, Astor, Lenox and Tilden Foundations. Reproduced with permission.)

seventeenth-century editions of Donne's collected *Poems*, the first of which was published two years after his death (Donne 1633b; see Ch. 4.I). The unregulated proliferation of Donne's poems within manuscript circles inevitably resulted in problems of attribution, and the resulting indeterminacy of canon is one of the persisting consequences of Donne's failure either to leave behind an authoritative holograph collection or to fix his poems in print. In some cases Donne's poems were ascribed to others; even more frequently the poems of others were ascribed to him, as copyists sought to fill up their collections with works putatively by the age's greatest writer of 'conceited Verses' (Baker 156). And the 'private friends' (1633b: ^{2}A2) who sponsored—and presumably supplied John Marriot with the primary manuscripts for—the editions from 1633 onward were unable to assemble a complete and uncontaminated canon. The 1633 *Poems* contains two spurious poems—William Basse's 'An Epitaph upon Shakespeare' and a versification of 'Psalm 137', persuasively ascribed to Francis Davison by Donne's late nineteenth-century editors A. B. Grosart (Donne 1872–3: 2.xxvi) and E. K. Chambers (Donne 1896: 2.303)—and lacks about forty poems that have subsequently been accepted into the canon, five of which are Elegies that Marriot had in hand, but was refused permission to print. The expanded edition of 1635 drops the Basse epitaph, retains the psalm (which remains in the canon until the dismissal by Grosart in 1873), and adds an additional twenty-eight poems from various manuscripts, including three of the disallowed Elegies and a dozen items—including a sixth satire—that are now regarded as spurious. The Restoration edition of 1669 presents a further ten canonical poems, leaving nearly twenty still to be unearthed, and adds one further spurious poem—a seventh satire that begins 'Sleep, next Society and true friendship'. With slight variations, the canon thus established passed on into the eighteenth- and early nineteenth-century editions; but in his edition of 1872–3 A. B. Grosart expanded the canon by some forty-one poems, incorporating items previously printed as Donne's by F. G. Waldron (1802) and John Simeon (1856) and adding others from manuscripts of which he had become aware. All of these forty-one additions except the Elegy *ElWar* and the Epigram *Liar* are now regarded as illegitimate, and doubts about their authenticity were raised almost immediately by Grosart's successor E. K. Chambers, whose 1896 edition labelled thirty-four of them 'Doubtful' and rejected seven outright, along with four others that had been regarded as authentic since at least 1669. At the same time Chambers appended eleven previously 'Uncollected' poems, including the authentic *AltVic* and *Macaron*.

Chambers's sporadic attempts to apply critical and bibliographical standards in the separation of the (canonical) sheep from the (spurious) goats were decisively eclipsed by Herbert Grierson in 1912. Correctly assigning authorship in many cases, Grierson relegated to appendices all the poems proposed by Grosart and Chambers except *Liar* and *ElWar*, expunged from the canon all the spurious items from *1669* except the ode 'Vengeance will sit above our faults', and printed a further inventory of twenty-two poems that 'frequently accompany' Donne's in the manuscripts that

Grierson knew. Owing to the reappearance of the Westmoreland manuscript in the 1890s, moreover, Grierson was able to expand the roster of authentic poems by two Epigrams, four Verse Letters, and three Holy Sonnets, and except for a further handful of Epigrams, these are the last additions accepted into the canon, although Helen Gardner, Grierson's successor in the Oxford University Press series, classified as 'Dubia' eight poems that had been embraced as Donne's since the seventeenth century, including *Sappho, ElExpost, ElPart, Julia, Citizen, ElVar, Token*, and *SelfL*. Excepting *Token*, and *SelfL*, which have not yet been considered, the ongoing *Variorum*, on the other hand, has accepted as authentic all these poems except *Julia* and *Citizen*, which are printed as 'Dubia' and provided with a somewhat reduced textual apparatus. The Elegy *ElVar* has recently been persuasively attributed to Nicholas Hare by Mark Bland (2008).

Indeterminacy of text is a second consequence of the way Donne handled his poems. As these works passed along the channels of manuscript circulation, copyists inevitably misread their predecessor's handwriting, made slips of the pen, lost track of their place in the copy-text, decided to 'improve' the poem as they transcribed it, or found themselves baffled by the sheer difficulty that Donne's poetry sometimes presents, and the cumulative result of these actions—as is suggested above—can be a welter of confusion. In their struggles to penetrate the obscurity of 'Loues naturall lation' in line 47 of *ElAut*, for example, transcribers proposed a wide variety of solutions, including 'naturall=lation', 'naturall station', 'natur-alation', 'naturall latean', 'naturall motion', 'Naturallatyon', and 'Nature a'lation'. One baffled copyist, admitting defeat, even penned only 'natural', leaving a following blank space to be filled in later. Neither did the entry of the poem into print clear up the mystery: in the initial printing in the 1633 *Poems*, John Marriot conjectured the unique 'motion natural'; in the second edition two years later he adopted from manuscript the more regular, but still incorrect, 'natural station'; and—except for Robert Chamberlain's 'natural action' in the 1654 *Harmony of the Muses*—one or the other of these readings appeared in every subsequent edition until Herbert Grierson restored the authorial 'naturall lation' in 1912.

The manuscripts of the forty-eight-line love Elegy *ElBed*, which survives in some sixty-seven artefacts, form a virtual casebook of the bewildering variety of changes that typically crept into manuscript texts as they circulated promiscuously through the culture. The headings on the poem range from mere generic labels ('*A Sonnett*', '*Elegie*') to numberings ('*Elegie*. 2ᵈ', '*Elegy. 7*', '*Elegia Decima Octava.*') to subject labels ('An inuitation of his mʳˢ to bedd', 'To his Mʳⁱˢ as shee was going to bed') to combinations that identify both content and author ('Dr. Donne. Going to bedd', 'Dr Donne to his m.ʳˢ going to bed', 'I: D: to his wife going to bedd'). The addressee of the poem is variously referred to as 'Madame', 'Ladie', or 'Mistresse' (l. 1); her 'girdle' is either 'glistering' or 'glittering' like 'heauens zones [or *loue* or *zone*]' (l. 5); and she is invited to 'Vnlase', 'Vntie', or 'Vnpinne' herself (l. 9) so that she can 'safely [or *softly* or *so softly*] tredd' (l. 17) in 'this Loues halowed [or *Love-hallowed*] temple;

this soft [or *same*] bedd' (ll. 17–18). According to one manuscript lineage the purpose of the 'spangled breastplate' which the mistress 'weare[s]' is 'That the eyes of busy fooles may be stopt there' (ll. 7–8); in another group the syntax is changed, and the lover urges her to remove the breastplate 'That I may see my shrine that shines soe faire'. And the stunning line composed exclusively of prepositions (l. 26), which expresses the lover's anticipatory exploration of the mistress's body, exhibits almost every imaginable permutation. He demands that she 'Licence... [his] roving hands' to go 'Before, behind, between, above, below', 'Before, behind, aboue, betweene, belowe', 'Behind, before, betweene, aboue, belowe', 'Behinde, before, above, betweene, belowe', 'Betweene, before, beneath, aboue, belowe', and 'Aboue, behinde, before, beneath, belowe'—among other possible routes.

The single most jarring variant in the poem appears in line 46, and it illustrates the vulnerability of manuscript texts not just to errors of inadvertency or misjudgement, but to deliberate scribal tampering. As the lover beseeches his mistress to 'Cast all, yea this whight linnen hence' and reveal herself in full nakedness, he avers—in the authorial version—that 'Ther [or *Here*] is no penance, much lesse innocence'. A second line of transmission, however, begun by someone distraught at the stark libertinism of this avowal (or at the linkage of such a licentious sentiment with Donne) reads 'due to innocence', and subsequent scribes in the chain of transmission further sanitize the phrase to 'for pure [or *true*] innocence'. Indeed, a major group of manuscripts in the line of transmission reposition lines 31–2—'To enter in these bonds, is to be free / Then where my hand is sett, my seale shalbee'— to follow the expurgated line 46, apparently intending to transmute the original Ovidian seduction into a decent request from a groom to his bride that she yield up his marital rights. A marginal note beside line 31 in the Bridgewater ms. (HH1) shows that other seventeenth-century readers wanted to construe the poem in this same way: 'why may not a man write his owne Epithalamion if he can doe it so modestly' (fo. 106^v).

Responsibility for some of the textual variation found in the manuscripts of Donne's poems must be laid at the poet's own feet. Donne may have been no more prone to revise a completed poem than the next writer, but the comparative ease of 'publishing' in manuscript meant that he could (and frequently did) hand out early drafts of works that he subsequently found reason to change before distributing further. Motivated by either aesthetic or ideological considerations (or both), these revisions can range from minor tinkering to extensive recasting. In lines 11–12 of *ElBrac*, for instance, Donne originally refers to 'Angels' that might have 'stray'd or gone / From the first State of their Creation' because of a 'taint', but the recognition that this seemed to blame God for the angels' fall led him subsequently to revise 'taint' to 'fault' (see *Variorum* 2.8). The subject matter of *Sat3*, on the other hand, proved so 'startling' that Donne revised the poem extensively to fine-tune images or concepts. The original version, for instance, asserts that God made the religious seeker to stand 'Soldier' in 'this world's garrison'; in revision the seeker becomes a 'sentinell' (l. 31). Donne originally declares that 'On a high hill / Ragged and steepe Truthe dwells'; his revision labels the hill 'huge' and 'cragged' and asserts that on it truth 'stands'. The original enjoins the seeker to 'strive so that before age, death's twilight, / Thy Mind rest'; the revised version prescribes rest for the 'soule'. And a dozen further changes scattered throughout bespeak Donne's revisionary return to the poem to nuance his meaning (see Stringer 2007: 300–4).

Even seemingly innocuous love lyrics were subject to such adjustment. *Relic*, for instance, exists in two authorial versions that differ substantively in nine of the poem's thirty-three lines. In the first version, the lover-poet imagines that the future gravedigger who finds the 'Bracelet of bright haire about the bone' might interpret it as 'a loving couple' '**Who hop'd** that this device might be **a** way' (l. 9) to unite their souls at judgement day; the revised version strengthens this to '**Which thought** that this device might be **some** way'. The first version refers to 'a time, or land / **Where** misdeuotion doth Command' (ll. 12–13); the second version stresses time over place: '**When** misdeuotion…' The mistress is originally promised '**You shalbee** a Mary Magdalen' (l. 17); in the revision, she is addressed more tenderly—'**Thou shalt bee**'. The earlier version declares that 'at such **Tyme**, Myracles are sought' (l. 20); the revision pluralizes 'Tyme' to '**tymes**'. In the first rendition the poet declares 'I would **haue that age** by this paper taught' (l. 21); in the second he strikes a less assertive note—'I would **that age were** by this paper taught'. And in lines 25–6, Donne originally declares 'Difference of sex we neuer knew / More then our guardian Angells doe', but in revision tightens this syntax to 'Difference of sexe **no more wee** knew / **Then** our Guardian Angells doe'. Then, two final alterations—'betwixt those meales' to 'betweene those meales' (l. 28) and 'Our hands ne're touch't the seales' to '…those seales' (l. 29)—complete the rewriting of the poem. Whether Donne effected these changes for purely aesthetic reasons is not clear, but something in the talk of graves, relics, mis-devotion, bishops, and kings clearly made the editor of the 1633 *Poems* sufficiently nervous that he carefully picked through both these versions as he went about concocting a text that he deemed fit to print.

Variations of the sort described above obviously pose enormous challenges for anyone wishing to separate what Donne wrote from the scribal changes imposed upon it, but examination of the manuscripts can also provide insights into Donne's mind and art—and into the changing conditions under which he wrote—that might well not exist had he forestalled circulation of his poems by putting printed versions before the public. Any authorial revision—whether it be of 'taint' to 'fault' in *ElBrac* or of 'Truthe dwells' to 'truth stands' in *Sat3* or of 'You shalbee' to 'Thou shalt bee' a 'Mary Magdalen' in *Relic* or of 'Or presently, I know not, see that face' to 'But my euer wakeing part shall see that face' in line 7 of the Holy Sonnet *HSScene*—inevitably raises questions of motive that may lead to a better understanding of the poem. The same can be true of scribal changes: not only does awareness that various squeamish copyists sought to convert *ElBed* from a seduction poem into a hymeneal hymn open a window on the early reception of the poem, but examination of the devices used in the attempt can enhance our appreciation of both the structure and the theme of Donne's version. Further examples abound. Manuscript copyists, for instance, saw puns on Donne's name everywhere, and constantly call attention to this possibility by spelling 'done' as 'donne' ('When thou hast donne thou hast not donne' in *Father* is almost inevitable). At the end of *Bait*, the scribe of the Crewe manuscript (TM1)—relying on the lingering use of 'i' for both 'i' and 'j' in manuscript orthography—even detects a pun on Donne's first name, integrating an attribution into the last line of the poem to point out the wordplay—'that fish that is not caught therby / Alas, is wiser farr then I: D'. Even scribal trivializations can be instructive—a collation of the early texts of *Canon*, for instance, shows that in about half of the three-dozen manuscripts of the poem, the lovers are invoked in the last stanza as 'yo^u whom reverend loue / made one anothers Hermitage', while the remaining copies give the corrupt scribal '…one anothers Pilgrimage'. Nothing can help us appreciate what a striking conceit Donne has here created so much as seeing it destroyed by an uncomprehending copyist. All such evidence of scribal—or authorial—manipulation of the text was erased when regularized spelling and various printing conventions were imposed in Marriot's print shop and each poem rendered in an edited, monolithic version, however, and until manuscripts of Donne's writings become available on the Web, modern readers who wish to engage with this material must pick it out of the textual apparatus provided in the *Variorum* and other scholarly editions.

A final consequence of Donne's having limited his poems to manuscript circulation—or rather, the element in his conception of the functions of poems that made manuscript the inevitable medium of dissemination—is that for a great many of these works the social contexts into which they were originally introduced and apart from which they can be only partially understood remain indeterminate. Is the Elegy commonly called 'The Autumnall' (*ElAut*) a 'late Elizabethan eleg[y]' in which Donne's speaker sets out to explain the paradox that 'far from alienating people, age may actually refine intimacies', but gets shanghaied by his own conceit into voicing a 'gerontophobic rant' (C. Martin 36 n. 4, 36, 50) that undercuts his original encomiastic impulse? Or did Donne write it about 1610 and give it, along with copies of his religious verses, to his friend Magdalen Herbert, who received it as a gracious compliment to the 'Beauties of her body, and minde' (Walton 1670: *Life of…Herbert* 15)? There is no evidence in the nearly fifty manuscripts of the poem to settle the dating question, and the headings—none of which may be Donne's—range from none at all to simply 'Elegie' to 'Eligy Autumnal' to 'Elegie. Autumnal on the Ladie Shandoys' to 'A Paradox of an ould Woman', to 'In commendation of declining Beawtie', to 'The widow', to 'Elegye 12: On the Lady Herbert afterwards Danuers'. Does *Flea* embody an annoying sexist fantasy of superior male cleverness that Donne wrote to entertain the sports at the Mermaid Tavern? Or was it part of his courtship of Anne More, who he knew would enjoy the joke and give him a kiss for his pains? The original recipients of *Martial* could no doubt identify the 'Katherin', who 'for the courts sake put downe stues', even though modern editors cannot; and there was no need for Donne to identify by name the subject of his early Epicede *Sorrow*—the audience for whom the poem was originally composed knew well enough who had died. Of course, knowing the date or the addressee of a poem does not necessarily tell us how to read it correctly. The Verse Letter to the Countess of Bedford beginning 'Reason is our Soules left hand' (*BedfReas*), for instance, opens with a conceit so extravagant that it seems to verge on blasphemy: 'Reason is our Soules left hand, Faith her right, / By these wee reach divinity, that's you...' (ll. 1–2), and continues to elaborate the notion for another thirty-six lines. What relationship between Donne and Lady Bedford is embedded in these lines? Does Donne here debase himself in a sycophantic bid for patronage? Or does he rather employ a playful language of compliment that delights and ennobles both parties?

Donne himself was aware that questions such as these attached to some of his writings, and repeatedly throughout his career—from the early 'feare &...shame' letter that accompanied the Paradoxes to his 1614 Letter to Goodere lamenting the 'interpretations' entailed in the projected edition of his poems to the 1619 Letter to Robert Ker that accompanied the 'misinterpretable' *Biathanatos*—expressed concern about how his works would be received. And this was not simply a question of whether readers would like what he said; it was also a question of whether they would understand what he meant. In the Letter accompanying the Paradoxes he is at pains to teach the recipient how to read them. Calling them 'swaggerers' that will be 'quiet enough if you resist them', he asserts that 'if they make you to find better reasons against them they do there office:... for they are rather alarums to truth to arme her then enemies' (LRO, MS Finch DG. 7, Lit. 2, fo. 308^v). Such instructions, for whatever guidance they might have provided, did not accompany these 'swaggerers' when they were eventually published after Donne's death, and the result has been 'substantial confusion and ambiguity regarding Donne's intended messages' (Sullivan 2007: 423). Whatever similar 'metacommentary' may have surrounded the original distribution of his poems—whether in the form of written remarks, oral comments, or merely understandings implicit in the relationships Donne had with his various recipients—is also now lost. Part of the ongoing challenge for modern readers is to reconstruct these contexts in so far as possible.

CHAPTER 2

JOHN DONNE'S SEVENTEENTH-CENTURY READERS

ERNEST W. SULLIVAN, II

IDENTIFYING John Donne's seventeenth-century readers (A. J. Smith and Dayton Haskin have chronicled Donne's eighteenth- and nineteenth-century readers) provides important information about the nature of Donne's poetry as well as its role in early modern culture. Our conception of Donne's readers as persons of great intellectual and aesthetic sophistication has been shaped largely by England's greatest literary critics: Ben Jonson's line in 'To John Donne' ('Longer a knowing, then most wits doe liue'; 8.34, l. 5) and his observation 'that Donne himself for not being understood would perish' (1–2.138); John Dryden's comment in *A Discourse Concerning the Original and Progress of Satire* that Donne 'affects the Metaphysicks...and perplexes the Minds of the Fair Sex with nice Speculations of Philosophy' (1956– : 4.7); Samuel Taylor Coleridge's comment on Donne's 'intenseness and peculiarity of thought' (1836–9: 1.149); and T. S. Eliot's description of Donne's poetry as characterized by 'rapid association of thought which requires considerable agility on the part of the reader' (242). Arthur Marotti has described Donne's intended audience as a coterie of fellow intellectuals and cultural superheroes like Sir Walter Ralegh (1986: 3). Moreover, Ilona Bell (2000) has argued that Anne More read some of her future husband's verse and prose.

Donne himself, in his verse and prose, recognized the intellectual complexity of his work, the difficulty of reading it, and the kind of reader he hoped for. In *Sat2*, he writes that 'Pöetry...Ridlingly it catch men' (ll. 5–8), and in *BedfRef* that 'darke texts need notes' (l. 11). In a Letter of 1600, Donne alerts his anonymous addressee to the ambiguous nature of his Paradoxes: 'they were made rather to deceaue tyme then her daught^r truth...if they make y^o to find better reasons against them they do there office...they are rather alarums to truth to arme her then enemies' (LRO, MS Finch DG. 7, Lit. 2, fo. 308^v; E. M. Simpson 1948: 316), and in a 1607 Letter, he describes his Problems as 'light flashes' and 'hawkings' (*Letters* 88). In a Letter to Robert Ker accompanying a manuscript of *Biathanatos*, Donne identifies his select intended audience, the complex nature of the work, and the ambiguity of his readers' response: 'it is upon a misinterpretable subject...onely to some particular friends in both Universities, then when I writ it, did communicate it...there was a false thread in it, but not easily found' (*Letters* 21–2). Certainly, Donne expected his readers to read with discretion—'If therefore of Readers, which Gorionides obserues to be of foure sortes, (Spunges, which attract all without distinguishing; Howerglasses, which receiue, and power out as fast; Baggs, which retayne onely the dregs of the Spices and let the Wine escape, And Siues which retayne the best onely) I find some of the last sort, I doubt not but they may be hereby enlight'ned' (*Biathanatos* 32)—but not to obsess over every detail at the expense of his message— 'Iust as a perfect Reader doth not dwell / On every sillable, nor stay to spell / Yet without doubt hee doth distinctly see / And lay together every A and B' (*Har* ll. 93–6).

Some of Donne's seventeenth-century readers fell within his parameters and those of the literary critics, some did not; the ones who did not have the most interesting implications for our understanding of the role of Donne's verse in early modern culture. Smith's *John Donne: The Critical Heritage* was the first focused effort to identify specifically Donne's readers: on page 4, Smith identifies thirteen 'known readers' (whom he categorizes as 'associates or correspondents' of Donne's) and an additional forty-one less certain readers listed in his table of contents (vii–viii)— generally persons who referred to Donne or who appeared to have been influenced by Donne. Presently, using the criterion that anyone who wrote a complete line of Donne verse into his or her own writing must have read Donne, we can identify sixty certain readers even though we cannot assume that the listed compiler or author of a work is the Donne reader: there are cases of ambiguous authorship and cases where someone other than the listed author or compiler was responsible for the Donne material. For example, 'S. N.', compiler of *The Loyal Garland*, counts as one of sixty-one compilers but not as one of the sixty identifiable readers. Amusingly, Donne had only contempt for such readers/writers:

> But hee is worst, who (beggarly) doth chaw
> Others wits fruits, and in his ravenous maw
> Rankly digested, doth those things out-spue,
> As his owne things;' and they are his owne, 'tis true,
> For if one eate my meate, though it be knowne
> The meate was mine, th'excrement is his owne.
>   (*Sat2* ll. 25–30)

There are sixty-one of these poets (including Ben Jonson, Henry Vaughan, Abraham Cowley, Thomas Carew, Francis Beaumont, Andrew Marvell, and John Dryden), dramatists (including John Webster, Margaret Cavendish, George Etherege, Thomas Killigrew, and Nathaniel Lee), essayists (including Thomas Barlow, Thomas Blount, Thomas Dekker, William Drummond of Hawthornden, Katherine Thimelby, and Mary de la Rivière Manley), biographers/historians (including Henry Holland, Izaak Walton, William Dugdale, and Payne Fisher), composers (including Alfonso Ferrabosco, Pelham Humphryes, John Playford, and William Corkine), translators (including Georg Rodolf Weckherlin, Johann Grindal, Constantijn Huygens, and Henrik Rintjus), and compilers of verse miscellanies (including Donne's son John, William Basse, John Mennes, John Gough, Robert Chamberlain, Samuel Sheppard, Abraham Wright, Joshua Poole, Henry Stubbs, and William Winstanley). During the seventeenth century, these authors (not including the younger Donne) produced 251 volumes containing over 653 complete or fragmentary Donne verses, giving Donne quite a large writership/readership (Sullivan 1993: 2). As the work of the *Variorum Edition of the Poetry of John Donne* proceeds, it should be possible to add to the list of known Donne readers by identifying the copyists and owners of the more than 250 manuscripts containing Donne's verse and prose. Presently, we can only list with certainty Rowland Woodward, Nathaniel Rich, Francis Russell (fourth Earl of Bedford), Giles Oldisworth, and William Drummond of Hawthornden (mentioned above) as having transcribed Donne's poems in the seventeenth century. Peter Beal (1980) has identified many seventeenth-century owners of manuscripts containing Donne's poems, but proving that the owners read the manuscripts is problematic.

In addition, there are several other groups of specific and virtually certain readers. It seems reasonable to infer that the eighteen (not including Rowland Woodward and Edward Herbert, counted elsewhere) known recipients of Donne's Verse Letters read the poems written to them, including Elizabeth Stanley, Countess of Huntingdon; Magdalen Herbert; Lucy Russell, Countess of Bedford; Lady Lettice Carey and Essex Rich, daughters of Robert Rich, third Baron Rich; Catherine Howard, Countess of Salisbury; Sir Henry Wotton; Sir Robert and Anne Drury (for whom Donne wrote *FirAn* and *SecAn*); Robert Carr, Earl of Somerset, and his wife Lady Frances Howard; as well as Lady Elizabeth, Queen of Bohemia and Friedrich V, Count Palatine (couples for whom Donne wrote the Epithalamions *Eclog* and *EpEliz*); Christopher Brooke; Samuel Brooke; George Herbert; Edward Tilman; and Dr Richard Andrews. We could add six more names to this list if we could identify with certainty other Verse Letter recipients 'T. W.', 'E. G.', 'B. B.', 'I. L.', 'I. W.', and 'L. of D.' (or 'E. of D.').

Known recipients of Donne Prose Letters (and therefore almost certain readers) not included above are Anne Donne; Sir George More; Robert More; George Garrard; Sir Henry Goodere; Lady Bridget Kingsmill; Sir Edward Herbert; Thomas Roe; George Villiers, Marquess of Buckingham; Sir Thomas Egerton; Sir Robert Cotton; Henry, Prince of Wales; Sir Robert Harley; William Trumbull; Sir Dudley

Carleton; Sir Henry Marten; Sir Nicholas Carew; Sir Edward Conway; John Williams; Lionel Cranfield, Earl of Middlesex; and James Hay, Earl of Carlisle.

We can also reasonably add the following recipients (not included above) of presentation copies of Donne published works: William Feilding, first Earl of Denbigh; the Earl of Kingsmill; a 'Mr Lee at the Cockpitt'; an 'Edward Carter Esq'; William Cavendish, Marquess of Newcastle; Aubrey de Vere, twentieth Earl of Oxford; an 'I. Marckham'; and a 'William Hodges' were presented with copies of the first edition of *Biathanatos* by the younger Donne. Donne himself, of course, presented King James I with the manuscript of *Pseudo-Martyr*.

If we assume that the author of 'The printer to the Understanders' (Miles Flesher); the author of the 'Hexastichon Bibliopolae'; the publisher, John Marriot; and the authors of the 'Elegies Upon the Author' published in the 1635 second edition of Donne's poems also read verse by the subject of their elegies, we can add another fifteen names (including those of Lucius Cary, Viscount Falkland; Henry King; and Richard Corbett, Bishop of Norwich).

The specifically identifiable individuals in the above groups of Donne readers do not much affect our present perception of Donne's seventeenth-century audience as the intellectual elite; however, the reality that a great many more people (most of whom cannot be specifically identified) were reading/writing Donne (particularly his works in print) much more frequently and over a much greater time span than has been thought does imply two important new facts about Donne's seventeenth-century readers: (1) Donne's readers during his lifetime were not limited to those with access to manuscripts (Donne's friends and the elite); and (2) Donne's audience had not disappeared by the time of the Restoration, suggesting a wider and more enduring appeal of his poetry.

Smith (1975) most clearly states the received view that during Donne's lifetime his readership was limited to those with access to his manuscripts: the 'peculiar circumstances in which he wrote and was read specifically exclude that possibility [that Donne's 'poetry had a revolutionary impact while he was still writing'], for his poems were not, and could not have been, widely known in his own day. No more than five of them and some bits of another three were printed in his lifetime and no collected edition appeared until two years after his death, so that his contemporaries could have read most of his work only in manuscript' (2). In fact, twenty-five rather than five of Donne's poems were published in their entirety (and another six in part) during his lifetime by identifiable readers of Donne (Sullivan 1993: 5–6). The sixty volumes containing 154 printings and reprintings of these poems published by Donne's identifiable readers prior to his death in 1631 prove that his poetry had a larger readership during his lifetime than the traditional view allows (ibid. 6).

Smith also states the received view that Donne's readership disappeared after the Restoration: 'It is plain that by the last three decades of the century Donne's poetry had become a mere curiosity which the amateur might indifferently patronise or discount' (1975: 12). Some of these so-called amateurs who wrote Donne's verse into the first published versions of their own post-1670 works include Andrew Marvell, Nathaniel Lee, Jane Barker, John Dryden, and Mary de la Rivière Manley. Certainly the existence of sixty-nine volumes by identifiable readers of Donne, printing 266 complete or partial Donne poems after 1670, proves that Donne maintained a substantial readership through the Restoration (Sullivan 1993: 7).

The identification of specific seventeenth-century readers of Donne's work has important implications for our understanding of how Donne was read and used by his contemporaries, readings and uses that we would not expect from reading many of Donne's literary critics. After complaints by Ben Jonson ('that Done for not keeping of accent deserved hanging'; 1–2.133), John Dryden ('Wou'd not *Donn's* Satires, which abound with so much Wit, appear more Charming, if he had taken care of his Words, and of his Numbers?'; 1956– : 4.78), and Samuel Johnson ('for the modulation was so imperfect, that they were only found to be verses by counting the syllables'; 2006: 1.200), one would not expect many musical settings of Donne's verse. Even so, Alfonso Ferrabosco's 1609 *AYRES* contains the earliest printing of, and a musical score for, Donne's *Expir* (C2^v); and William Corkine's *THE SECOND BOOK OF AYRES* (1612) contains the earliest printing of, and a musical score for, Donne's *Break* (B1^v). In 1659 John Playford published musical settings for Francis Beaumont's adaptation of Donne's *SGo* (11) and Thomas Carew's adaptation of Donne's *Damp* (102). Finally, in 1688 Pelham Humphryes contributed a musical setting of Donne's *Father* to Henry Playford's *Harmonia Sacra* (51–2). Given the frequently asserted complexity and abstract subject matter of Donne's verse, one might not expect much translation into foreign languages either; however, Georg Rodolf Weckherlin translated six of Donne's poems into German, Constantijn Huygens translated nineteen into Dutch, and Henry Stubbs published translations of three more into Greek.

Aware of Dryden's observation (1956– : 4.7) that Donne 'perplexes the Minds of the Fair Sex with nice Speculations of Philosophy', we would not expect many women amongst Donne's readers, yet these include possibly Anne Donne and certainly Lucy Russell; Elizabeth Stanley; Magdalen Herbert; Katherine Thimelby; Lettice Carey; Essex Rich; Catherine Howard; Anne Drury; Frances Howard; Mary de la Rivière Manley; and Margaret Cavendish, Duchess of Newcastle (who uses her character Lady Ward's ability to quote lines 35–6 of Donne's *Storm* in her play *The Second Part of the Lady Contemplation* [219] as proof of her heroine's wit and intellectual independence).

The most common use of Donne's verse by his fellow poets would today be judged plagiarism. Despite his complaints about Donne, Dryden (1692) stole lines 5–6 of Donne's *Har* (22) and lines 61–2 of *BoulNar* (23) for insertion into his poem 'Eleonora'; and works by poets as diverse as Daniel Baker, Francis Beaumont, Aston Cokayne, Thomas Carew, Henry Fitzjeffery, William Habington, Francis Quarles, Henry Vaughan, and John Webster contain unacknowledged lines from Donne.

Probably the most interesting result of identifying Donne's seventeenth-century readers is the completely unexpected audience for Donne that may be inferred from the works produced by Donne's readers/authors and the unexpected ways in which that audience read Donne. The title pages of books by some of the authors identifiable as Donne readers by the presence of Donne's verse in their writings frequently act as advertisements for these books, carefully establishing their intended use and target audience; and the commercial success of these works, as measured by the number of their editions, certainly implies the existence of the target audience and its satisfaction with the usefulness of Donne's verse. These title pages and the contents of the works make it clear that Thomas Carew got it right in his elegy when he crowned Donne as presiding over '*The universall Monarchy of wit*' (Donne 1633b: 388, l. 96). Donne's verse had a huge readership among the barely literate, who appreciated its wit and who adapted Donne's witty lines into their own voice. One such example of Donne's witty appeal to the lower class would be Samuel Sheppard's parody of seventeenth-century almanacs, *Merlinus Anonymus. An Almanack and no Almanack. A Kalendar, and no Kalendar. An Ephemeris (between jest, and earnest), for the year 1653*. Explaining 'The Parts of the Kalendar', Sheppard describes his fourth column (where he locates overall 224 lines from twenty-two Donne poems) as 'a pure Chronicle…of some…remarkable passages, during the war, laugh, and be laxative' (A4). For January, this column contains the following entries: 'The fall of a Chimney neer Saint *Peter Pauls Wharfe*, 1643', 'Mistresse *E: G.* carted 1644', 'Mr: *Newton* delivered his Dogg over into the hands of Squire *Low*, 1645', 'A cart of Hay over thrown in Smithfeild, 1645', '*Nan Sharpe* (Rectresse of *Sodome*, and *Gubernatrix* of *Gomorah*) married to a Beadle, lash her Sirrah', and lines 15–16 of Donne's *Calm* ('The fighting place now seamens rages supply; / And all the tackling is a frippery'; A5ᵛ). Evidently a seventeenth-century reader would find Donne's description of a ruined warship transformed into an overdressed strumpet as witty as a 'Rectresse of *Sodome*' married to a 'Beadle'.

More often, Donne's barely literate readers adapted his wit to improving their own verbal facility, as encouraged by '*W: B. Esquire*'s' preface to his translated and enlarged version of Michael Scott's *The Philosopher's Banquet*: 'wee haue here certaine Epigrams and Iestes…interlaced, with excellent positions, witty questions and answers vpon diuers and sundry arguments, the perfect vse and insight whereof doth accomplish a man for discourse, behauiour and argument at the Table of our superiours' (A4ᵛ). While the title pages and prefaces of such self-help books clearly indicate that their compilers are aware of the semi-literate nature of their audience, their implication that this audience would first read and then speak/write Donne's verse provides insight into the social and economic power of verse at the lower levels of seventeenth-century society; and the changes in these title pages and contents of the volumes through their often several editions illustrate an important evolution in Donne's seventeenth-century reading audience.

Consider the level of literacy and use of Donne's verse anticipated by 'The Authors Preface to the Reader' of John Gough's 1645 *The Academy of Complements*:

thou hast choise and select Complements set thee down in a form, which upon an occasion offered, thou mayest imitate, or with a little alteration make use of: thou hast in the next place variety of Subjects, with expression to the height of eloquence penn'd to quicken thy minde upon the like objects presented to thy view or fancy, thou has witty disputes, amorous discourses... Thou hast exquisite Letters... then thou hast Dedications, Superscriptions fitted to thy own desires for thy use, upon any sudden occasion... in summe, both Eloquence and Love, with their secrets and mysteries, are made naked, and manifestly revealed to the weakest judgement. (A5^v–A6)

The 1645 edition contains lines 1–2, 4–3, and 5–6 of *Break* (166). The edition of 1646 adds a section titled 'a new Schoole of Love' (110–27) and lines 15–18 of *Break* (136). The editions of 1650, 1654, 1658, 1663, and 1670 add *Ind* on pages 231–2.

By 1684 the anticipated audience of *The Academy of Complements* had changed from predominantly male to predominantly female, as suggested by the new title page:

THE Academy OF COMPLEMENTS WITH Many New Additions OF Songs and Catches *A-la-mode*, STORED With Variety of Complemental and Elegant Expressions, of LOVE and COURTSHIP. Also Witty and Ingenious Dialogues and Discourses, *Amorous and Jovial*. With Significant LETTERS upon Several Occasions. Composed for the use of *Ladies* and *Gentlewomen. By the most refined* Wits *of this Age*.

In this edition, the sexually suggestive first stanza of *Break* and the risqué *Ind* disappear. On the other hand, the admonition of the female speaker of lines 15–18 of *Break* remains:

> The fair, the false love can
> Admit all but the busie man:
> He that hath business, and makes love, does do
> Such wrong as if a married man should woo.
>
> (94)

Voiced by a female speaker, these lines could easily be adapted into a female reader's letter; Donne had become the literal voice of a generation of real-life Lady Wards. Another work by Samuel Sheppard, *The Marrow of Complements*, creates a sample prose letter (41–2), presumably to be used by a rejected suitor, out of Donne's *ElExpost*.

In the hands of educator Joshua Poole, this extension of Donne's readership for the purpose of improving the discourse of readers goes all the way to very young schoolchildren. His *The English Parnassus* ('A COLLECTION Of all Rhyming Monosyllables, The choicest Epithets, and Phrases: With some General Forms upon all Occasions, Subjects, and Theams, Alphabetically digested') provides anonymous verse (including twenty-three fragments from Donne) which 'his Schollers in that private School, at *Hadley*, Kept in the house of Mr. *Francis Atkinson*' (A5) could read and then assemble into poems for their classes, much as John Webster, Henry Vaughan, and John Dryden read and used Donne's verse.

So what do we learn about Donne's poetry and how it was read by specifically identifying his seventeenth-century readers? We learn that Donne's writings had commercial, social, and personal value for a great diversity of readers during the entire century. Perhaps surprisingly, given the large role of religion in seventeenth-century English culture and Donne's fame among his own contemporaries as Dean of St Paul's, Donne's seventeenth-century readers, unlike his readers in our own century, had very little interest in his Divine Poems: in fact only eight of the thirty-six Divine Poems appear outside of his collected editions, with twenty-four of their twenty-nine appearances occurring in the various printings of Walton's *Life of Donne*. Much of the value of Donne's work for his seventeenth-century readers attaches to its wittiness: seventeen of the works by our identified authors have some form of the word 'wit' on their title pages. Ascertaining whether Donne's work helped to create a love of verbal wit that permeated language at every level of Renaissance society or simply satisfied an already present demand may be impossible; however, identifying these readers and their uses of Donne's writing shows the scale of Donne's influence on early modern English language, literature, society, and culture. And as more of Donne's readers are identified, it will be possible to sharpen our perception of how his work (and literature generally) circulated through and influenced early modern culture as well as how it was read and interpreted by contemporaries. Donne very nearly placed his individual talent within the tradition when he wrote 'I ame / The Trumpet, at whose voice the people came' (*SecAn* ll. 527–8); identifying his readers and their uses of his work shows that he was the literal voice of the people as well.

CHAPTER 3

ARCHIVAL RESEARCH

LARA M. CROWLEY

Donne and manuscripts

'What Printing-presses yield we think good store, / But what is writ by hand we reverence more'. Edmund Blunden's translation of Donne's Latin encomium of manuscripts reminds us that Donne composed poetry primarily for a manuscript medium. Traditionally, scholars prized his few extant holographs, but non-holographic copies of Donne's poetry and prose in numerous Renaissance verse miscellanies, commonplace books, and other manuscripts were relatively neglected by scholars prior to the nineteenth century, when pioneers such as Alexander B. Grosart and E. K. Chambers began to consult them (Haskin 2007). Herbert J. C. Grierson's seminal 1912 edition drew significant attention to archival materials by analysing and cataloguing multiple manuscripts containing Donne's verse (see Ch. 4.I). Grierson, however, still based texts on the earliest printed collection of Donne's poems (Donne 1633*b*). Although manuscript verse collections were often compiled during authors' lifetimes, frequently by members of their literary circles, printed verse collections were usually published posthumously and based on whichever literary manuscript(s) editors or printing houses could obtain. The 1633 *Poems By J. D.*, for example, was based primarily on Cambridge University Library Additional MS 5778c, known as the Cambridge-Balam manuscript; thus, this first printed collection proves a 'second-hand manuscript' (Sullivan 1994: 298). Yet, twentieth-century editors of Donne and his fellow poets generally followed Grierson's example in consulting manuscript copies for textual variants rather than for copy-texts. Then, in 1980, Peter Beal published the first volume of the *Index of English Literary Manuscripts*. This expansive catalogue of extant copies of works by writers such as Donne—the most popular English manuscript poet of his time—initiated a dramatic shift in scholarly attention to 'what is writ by hand'.

Beal's continued archival research has been supplemented by the textual editors of *The Variorum Edition of the Poetry of John Donne*, whose monumental contributions include providing manuscript versions as copy-texts. We now know of over 4,000 separate transcriptions of poems by Donne in at least 245 extant manuscripts in the United Kingdom, Ireland, the United States, South Africa, and Japan—a small fraction of the Donne manuscripts that must have been compiled in the sixteenth and seventeenth centuries (*Variorum*, 'General Introduction', vol. 3: forthcoming). We also recognize that, in contrast to previous assumptions, most manuscript collections reflect multiple textual traditions.

Further study of early modern English manuscripts by scholars such as Margaret J. M. Ezell, Mary Hobbs, Grace Ioppolo, Harold Love, Arthur F. Marotti, Steven W. May, and H. R. Woudhuysen has broadened our understanding of matters such as scribal publication, manuscript compilation, circulation of texts, and scribal variants. For example, while scribal variants can indicate errors (such as a hasty copyist's slip of the pen or eye-skip) or efforts by copyists to 'improve' texts, they can also represent such circumstances as an author's revision or a verse collector's appropriation of a text for present circumstances—the latter affording invaluable information regarding cultural politics and literary reception. Evidence suggests that there was an outpouring of small groups and collections of Donne's manuscript poems in the 1620s and 1630s, some travelling beyond Britain, as Constantijn Huygens's 1630 translation of four Donne poems attests. Copies of individual poems circulated even earlier, such as the version of *Metem* found in Folger Shakespeare Library MS V.a.241, owned by a Roger Bradon c.1620. Donne's verse Satires might have circulated with *Storm* and *Calm* as early as the 1590s, long before they first appeared in print, although dating manuscripts with certainty rarely proves possible. Yet, analyses of seventeenth-century papers and individual (and particularly identifiable) scribes could throw light on the dating of archival materials, validating or challenging modern assumptions.

Archival materials include not only manuscript copies of poetry, prose fiction, and even plays, but also items such as letters, book lists, family ledgers, warrants, and numerous other handwritten documents that can illuminate texts, as well as the world in which they were composed, disseminated, and received. Thus, opportunities in archival research extend beyond the important goals of establishing informed texts, their likely periods of composition, and (in some cases) the sequences in which they circulated, to such issues as Donne's attitudes towards print and patronage. As Beal observes (1998: 31–2), the multitude of manuscript copies of Donne's works could reflect a more complex perspective on publication than appears if we take his single remark regarding his theologically sensitive *Biathanatos*—that he forbid it 'the Presse, and the Fire' (*Letters* 22)—to encapsulate his stance on print. For example, Donne's reluctance to publish his poems at

Somerset's urging could reflect concern about being subsumed further into Somerset's faction, thus inadvertently offending patrons like the Countess of Bedford (Eckhardt 2006). Study of manuscripts as gifts can illuminate patronage systems: writers ranging from the professional scribe Ralph Crane (Bodleian, MS Rawlinson poetry 61) to the courtier poet Sir John Harington (IT, MS 538, vol. 43) offered influential friends and patrons manuscripts containing their works. Such study enhances our understanding of literary networks and even intellectual affinities, a potential impetus for Donne's giving a copy of *Biathanatos* with autograph corrections to Sir Edward Herbert (Bodleian, MS e Musaeo 131). Manuscript versions were sometimes requested. For example, King James I requested that Donne provide him with a copy of his 1622 Gunpowder Plot Sermon; in 1992 Jeanne Shami discovered the manuscript that Donne supplied—a scribal copy with his own autograph corrections (*1622 Sermon*).

Shami's exciting find illustrates that manuscript archives are rife with potential insights, even discoveries. Often manuscript study encourages alteration of prevailing paradigms for early modern literary culture. Contrary to modern assumptions, for example, seventeenth-century manuscript compilers continued to copy Donne's verse long after publication of the 1633 *Poems*. Some even collated printed and manuscript texts, suggesting keen contemporary interest in variants. This habit extended to copying printed texts: Sir Samuel Tuke copied from the 1635 *Poems* extracts from twenty-four poems, two Prose Letters, the epistle to *Metem*, and two elegies for Donne (BL, Add MS. 78423, fos. 43^v–44^r), providing a glimpse into the preferences and practices of a seventeenth-century reader. Similarly, extracts from the second edition of Donne's *Juvenilia* appear in Bodleian MS English poetry e 112 (fos. 103^r–108^v). Study of this manuscript, mislabelled 'unimportant' in the only recent scholarly edition of Donne's Paradoxes and Problems (Donne 1980: lii n.1), seems to offer a contemporary literary interpretation: beneath the title of 'That a wise man is known by much laughing', someone added 'wch I see nothing here to proue I.N.' (fo. 105^v). Most likely 'I.N.' represents John Newdigate, of Arbury Hall, Nuneaton, Warwickshire—an early reader of Donne's heavily encoded and playful prose. This enigmatic remark could indicate that Newdigate considered Donne's line of argument unconvincing or rather that Newdigate, believing himself a wise man, found nothing funny in the Paradox.

Significant knowledge regarding the literary tastes of seventeenth-century readers and writers is lost when we limit attention to printed volumes alone. Archival evidence suggests that most compilers of manuscript miscellanies gathered such items as political satires, religious materials, and letters by famous courtiers, particularly those involved in scandals like the Earl of Essex's 1601 uprising and the 1613 Overbury affair. As Joshua Eckhardt shows, they also collected verse libels and erotic poems, intermingled in manuscripts with items of various literary forms and genres (2009; see also Bellany 2002). Collectors frequently jumbled together a wide variety of poems in miscellanies, lewd lyrics alongside pious and devotional texts. Many of these manuscript works, particularly sexually explicit verses, remain unprinted. Unpublished manuscript poems that describe female body parts, techniques of seduction, and sexual intercourse accompany such poems as *ElBed*—one of the most frequently copied Donne poems in Renaissance manuscripts. The poem's popularity in manuscripts might reflect its print censorship, for it was one of five Elegies denied publication in 1633, remaining solely in manuscript until 1654 when printed in *The Harmony of the Muses*. But study of the poem in Rosenbach ms. 239/22 (fos. 52^v–53^r) reveals that verse censorship of a kind was not limited to print, for an owner of the manuscript miscellany nearly obliterated Donne's risqué Elegy (McLeod). Generally, such verses reveal the preferences as well as the wide-ranging preoccupations of manuscript compilers, predominantly educated young men of the universities or the Inns of Court who probably represented the principal contemporary audiences for Donne's sophisticated (and often bawdy) verse.

Dealing with Manuscripts and Their Repositories

Manuscript studies continue to illuminate works by Donne and his contemporaries within their historical and cultural contexts, yet many scholars remain wary of the archives. For some, reservations stem from practical concerns, such as distance from collections or lack of travel funding, although numerous scholars are awarded travel fellowships and grants each year from home institutions, libraries, and (for the fortunate few) national foundations. For others, reservations result from lack of training in archival research methods. For years literary scholarship and textual scholarship were generally regarded as separate fields of inquiry (bibliographers provided texts, and critics analysed them), but a growing emphasis on book history has encouraged the merging of fields in the academy. Training in bibliography, however, has been somewhat slow to catch up with scholarly interest. At a recent meeting of the Renaissance Society of America, I heard an eminent literary critic respond to a suggestion that she might benefit from attending to a particular collection of papers by saying, 'but I would have to learn palaeography'. Even senior scholars can be limited by archival shyness, but manuscript studies can be integrated into a research portfolio at any point in one's career.

Manuscript collections are generally housed in university and college libraries, large libraries and repositories, and local record offices. Each archive maintains some form of finding aid for its collections. Although some archives publish their guides (usually in limited print runs), such tools are frequently available only on-site, but one can find more and more information about collections online. In fact, in this increasingly digital age, proximity to manuscript collections proves less essential for embarking on archival research, especially if one contacts a venue's archivist(s). In my experience, patient and generous archivists and library staff members have frequently answered critical questions and proffered valuable advice. Consulting an archivist with expertise in one's collections of interest prior to and during a visit can result in a more productive research trip.

Naturally, each research experience is shaped by the expectations and practices of the venue. While examining the famous Burley manuscript (LRO, MS Finch DG. 7, Lit. 2) in the Leicestershire Record Office in 2007, I realized that nearly all of my fellow researchers were local citizens exploring their family histories. In accordance with their readers' needs and their own resources, archives' policies and procedures vary and should be consulted in advance: some libraries, for example, allow visitors only on certain days during limited hours, and most archives require letters of introduction. On the day of Shami's previously mentioned discovery she was initially unable to enter the British Museum's Manuscript Reading Room because she lacked such a letter from 'a person of repute'. Thirst and luck took Shami to the Museum Tavern across the street, where she happened upon friends, including Stella Revard, who by chance had a few sheets of Southern Illinois University letterhead on which to pen the necessary authorization (*1622 Sermon*: ix).

Many groups of manuscripts and early printed volumes were gathered by families or by enterprising collectors like Sir Robert Cotton in the sixteenth and seventeenth centuries, Sir William Petty in the eighteenth century, and Sir Thomas Phillipps in the nineteenth century. Eventually, most collections made their way to centralized locations, but they maintain titles that reflect previous ownership, such as the Lansdowne manuscripts at the British Library, collected by Petty, first Marquess of Lansdowne (1737–1805). The Loseley manuscripts, papers related to the More family whose descendants still reside at Loseley Park, constitute an important collection for Donne scholars. While some papers remain at Loseley, others were deposited at the Surrey History Centre in Woking, and still others were sold by the family to the Folger Shakespeare Library. The latter group includes an autograph Letter to George More announcing Donne's marriage to More's daughter Anne, which can be viewed in printed facsimile (*Marriage Letters* 2005).

Study of Donne manuscripts begins by familiarizing oneself with these and other archives containing his works. *Variorum* volumes list extant manuscripts with copies of Donne's poems, and critical editions of his prose works identify various manuscripts, although additional artefacts surface regularly. While examining papers in Cheshire archives in 1996 Dennis Flynn unearthed manuscript copies of Donne's letter to the Countess of Montgomery in the Cheshire Record Office; *Father*, in the Chester City Record Office; and *ElBrac* among the papers of Sir Richard Grosvenor in the archives of Eaton Hall, Eccleston. Discovery of these items 'illustrates the fact that even in well-trodden Record Offices such manuscripts may still be found to lodge among seemingly unrelated papers' (Flynn 2000a: 291). In 2006 Beal discovered copies of Donne's Paradoxes, and the supposedly spurious characters and essay on valour, among the Gell family papers in the Derbyshire Record Office in Matlock (MS D258/7/13/6 [vi]). Like most collections, these papers were catalogued, but even the most knowledgeable archivists cannot recognize every untitled and/or unattributed item.

One should not assume that a previously explored archive has been exhausted, for discoveries continue to be made in literary manuscripts pored over by other scholars who sought other things. For example, while studying Donne's prose Paradoxes and Problems in British Library MS Stowe 962, an early seventeenth-century miscellany examined frequently for its works by Donne, Thomas Carew, Ben Jonson, Sir Walter Ralegh, and others, I encountered a seventy-four-line poem entitled 'The Earle of Southampton prisoner, and condemned. to Queen Elizabeth'. The poem appeared to be a copy of a verse epistle composed by Henry Wriothesley, third Earl of Southampton and dedicatee of Shakespeare's *Venus and Adonis* and *Lucrece*, as well as a possible intended audience for Shakespeare's *Sonnets*. Although the Earl was convicted of treason and sentenced to death in February 1601 for his leadership in Essex's uprising, the Queen, for reasons never explained fully, commuted Southampton's sentence to life in the Tower (King James I released him in 1603). Although I hesitated to defer my work on Donne's prose, I recalled that Southampton is not acknowledged as a poet. Thus, I sought previous scholarship on the poem, but to my surprise I found no mention of it. In addition, my analysis of available evidence, such as the Earl's four known contemporary Tower writings, suggested that Southampton probably did compose this verse petition (Crowley forthcoming). One hopes that scholars will identify additional manuscript copies that shed further light upon the poem and its authorship. Our extensive and increasing knowledge regarding manuscript culture impels us not only to analyse long-overlooked collections like the Gell papers, but also to re-examine familiar volumes like British Library MS Stowe 962.

Advances in digital humanities are enhancing our study of all collections, although we must not forget foundational printed research tools, such as Steven W. May and William A. Ringler's first-line index of Tudor poetry. Future studies of Donne and his fellow poets would benefit greatly from expansion of this work to include Jacobean and Caroline poetry. Printed indices for individual archives, such as the *First-line index of English poetry, 1500–1800, in manuscripts of the Bodleian Library, Oxford*, also prove valuable, although online first-line search engines are under development. Yet, online research tools, such as the Union First Line Index of English Verse, accessible through the Folger Shakespeare Library website, are becoming increasingly available. Some libraries, such as the University of Leeds, have launched excellent manuscript search engines, making libraries' holdings accessible far from their reading rooms and providing impetus to update catalogues. The National Archives has taken the lead in centralizing manuscript scholarship via its online 'Access to Archives', a search engine of manuscript catalogues throughout England. A single search for 'Henry Goodere' provides references and descriptions from multiple manuscripts in fifteen collections housed in such locations as the Warwickshire County Record Office. Yet, searching for items requires ingenuity and patience: the same search for 'Henry Goodere' lists manuscripts pertaining to other men by that name housed in archives including the Shakespeare Birthplace Trust Records Office (in part because searchable date-spans refer to entire collections, not individual manuscripts), and a search for 'Henry Goodyer' affords five different results. Thus, in searching archives one needs to try every conceivable variation on titles, locations, and author names (e.g. 'Henry'/'Henrie' and 'Goodere'/'Goodyer'/'Goodyear'). In addition, not all British archival collections are covered in 'Access to Archives'. While we must recognize such limitations, these online research tools will continue to grow more user-friendly and more precise.

In 2011 Beal, Woudhuysen, and John Lavagnino will make accessible to the public an online tool that will become crucial for study of Donne's manuscript texts: the *Catalogue of English Literary Manuscripts*, an expanded version of Beal's original printed *Index* that will list all extant copies of works by Donne and approximately 200 contemporary authors. In addition, Donne scholars will soon have access to images of multiple manuscript poems, for *Variorum* editors are digitizing significant collections—an effort that will enable 'archival' research far from archives. While there is no substitute for working with material artefacts, these and other resources will encourage undergraduate and graduate students throughout the world to explore Donne manuscripts.

Numerous online and printed guides are available to assist one in learning how to read and analyse manuscripts. Italic scripts in seventeenth-century manuscripts prove easy for modern readers to decipher, but secretary scripts can present initial challenges. Yet, training in common letter forms and conventions can be accomplished via a printed palaeographical guide, such as *Elizabethan Handwriting, 1500–1650: A Manual*, or an online program, although many scholars simply develop such skills through practice. For learning how to investigate, describe, and categorize manuscripts, handbooks like D. C. Greetham's *Textual Scholarship: An Introduction* prove useful starting-points, and Beal's recent *A Dictionary of English Manuscript Terminology:1450–2000* has already become an indispensable resource. One also benefits from reading the foundational scholarship previously mentioned and additional scholarly essays on Donne manuscripts in journals like the *John Donne Journal* and *English Manuscript Studies, 1100–1700*, in order to become more likely to contribute mature observations and genuine discoveries.

In pursuit of such contributions, pitfalls in archival research frequently (and perhaps ironically) result from enthusiasm, from rushing to conclusions about a seemingly exciting 'find'. When Flynn, for example, discovered that a 'Mr John Donnes' accompanied the Earl of Derby to France as a gentleman waiter in 1585, he hoped in *John Donne and the Ancient Catholic Nobility* to offer a logical answer to a long-standing question: where was Donne during his teenage years? It had been assumed previously, despite a lack of evidence, that Donne spent several years studying at Cambridge. Flynn astutely suggested that, since Donne would have been required to take the same Oath of Supremacy at Cambridge that would have been demanded had he returned to Oxford after Michaelmas 1584, his uncle Jasper Heywood arranged these travels abroad so that Donne might avoid the persecution of Catholics in England. Yet, in a review of Flynn's book, Steven W. May pointed out that to Elizabethans 'Mr' (meaning master) was a title of respect unlikely to refer to a boy in his early teens; thus, 'Mr John Donnes' probably refers to a person older than the poet (May 1998). Flynn's use of archival evidence in constructing this argument, combined with May's corrective, reminds us that manuscript scholars should foster the courage to challenge prior assumptions but also remain cautious in determining what new evidence might reveal. Manuscript research affords the thrills of literary detective work but requires scepticism, precision, and a willingness to spend numerous hours studying documents without immediate rewards. But rewards frequently come, sometimes in the form of discovering significant manuscript copies of texts, such as *Biathanatos* (Beal 1998).

Study of Donne's poetry and prose in manuscripts will continue to enrich our understanding of the production, dissemination, and reception of his works in early modern England. In Beal's 2004 forum on 'The Future of Renaissance Manuscript Studies', May attests: 'Overall, no area of study in English literature offers more promise of ongoing, genuine discoveries than manuscript research. The manuscripts, so long neglected, contain a wealth of new and unstudied information not only about Renaissance poetry but about the broader Renaissance culture in which it was produced' (2004: 61). For example, ongoing archival research related to Donne's preaching venues by scholars such as Jeffrey Johnson, Emma Rhatigan, and John Wall throws light on Donne's clerical career and on seventeenth-century Church of England worship practices more generally. I am particularly interested in Donne's contemporary audiences and how, through study of his poetry and prose within manuscript contexts, we uncover clues to early interpretations, thereby enhancing modern exegesis. I argued recently, for instance, that study of the previously mentioned copy of Donne's perplexing *Metem* among its surrounding manuscript contents in Folger MS V. a. 241 suggests that at least one contemporary reader interpreted the poem as a political satire on court favourites, probably Robert Cecil (Crowley 2007a). Donne's apocrypha also merit attention, for more poems in seventeenth-century manuscripts seem to be misattributed to Donne than to any other poet. Canons of Renaissance poets are not permanently fixed. Analysis of manuscript attributions could clarify cases of disputed authorship, as well as Renaissance readers' attitudes towards the concepts of authors and authorship. Even spurious ascriptions cast light on contemporary perspectives on Donne and 'the company [his] poems were accustomed to keep' (Love 1993: 6)—poems by John Roe and others that tend to accompany groups of Donne's poems in manuscript miscellanies.

Archival research can alter modern conceptions of early modern writers, canons, texts, and contexts. We still have much to learn about the psychology of manuscript compilation and circulation in the period, and the wealth of surviving manuscript copies of Donne's works presents exceptional opportunities to study the nature of textual transmission (Beal 2002). As we strive to illuminate Donne's poetry and prose, we must obey his own command in *ValBook*: 'Study our manuscripts' (l. 10).

For significant contributions to this chapter, I am obliged to Peter Beal, whose vast knowledge of literary manuscripts is matched by his generosity. 'What Printing-presses yield we think good store, / But what is writ by hand we reverence more' is Edmund Blunden's translation of the first two lines of Donne's Latin poem *Libro*: '*Parturiunt madido quae nixu praela, recepta, / Sed quae scripta manu, sunt veneranda magis*' [*Milgate* 112, ll. 1–2]). Beal offered the second line of Donne's Latin poem as the motto for his Index (1980: v), and the poem was subsequently adopted in translation by the Manuscript Department of the British Library.

CHAPTER 4.1

EDITING DONNE'S POETRY: FROM JOHN MARRIOT TO THE DONNE *VARIORUM*

GARY A. STRINGER

THE tradition of editing Donne's poems contains three phases: an early one covering the period 1633–69, in which the publisher John Marriot and his immediate successors, using such manuscripts as they were able to lay hands on, took on the initial challenge of publishing a comprehensive collection of Donne's poems; a middle one, in which editors from Jacob Tonson in 1719 to J. R. Lowell in 1855 produced a series of editions based on the seventeenth-century editions (and on each other); and a final one, beginning with Alexander Grosart in 1872 and continuing to the present time, in which editors—while still largely dependent on the efforts of their predecessors—have sporadically reverted to manuscript material in their attempts to improve the received text and establish the canon of Donne's verse.

Seven editions/issues of Donne's collected poems were published in the seventeenth century: in 1633, 1635, 1639, 1649, 1650, 1654, and 1669 (*Variorum* sigla A–G). We do not know exactly who sponsored the first edition—the introductory 'The Printer to the Understanders' cites the support merely of 'private friends' (^{2}A2)—nor do we know whether the numerous verbal emendations and (especially) regularizations of metre evident throughout the volume reflect the work of some editor other than Marriot (Donne's literary executor Henry King has been suggested), but we do know that on 13 September 1632 Marriot entered a manuscript of Donne's 'verses and Poems' into the Stationers' Register and a few months later brought forth the 406-page *Poems, by J. D. with Elegies on the Authors Death*. As Herbert J. C. Grierson was the first to recognize, this edition derived its texts mainly from a Group-I and (to a lesser extent) a Group-II manuscript, supplemented with material drawn from 'previously printed editions' (the *Anniversaries* and *Henry*) and other 'miscellaneous' sources (Donne 1912: 2.xcvii). Further, Grierson plausibly attributed A's somewhat chaotic organization to the fact that Marriot had only catch-as-catch-can access to manuscript sources of the poems while assembling the volume. Grierson's editorial successors—especially Helen Gardner, C. Wesley Milgate, and the *Variorum* editors—have refined his conclusions, identifying Cambridge University Library MS Add. 5778(c) (Group I; *DV* siglum C2), Trinity College Dublin MS 877 (Group II; *DV* siglum DT1), and the National Library of Wales Dolau Cothi MS 6748 (Group II; *DV* siglum WN1) as the specific sources of particular poems. The *Variorum* Elegies volume further identifies a handful of readings (e.g. 'lawlesse law' in *ElComp* l. 9) that A's editor can have obtained only from the O'Flahertie ms. (Group III; *DV* siglum H6), an artefact upon which the 1635 edition drew heavily for additional poems, a more rational organizational scheme, and many 'corrections' to the text. Barely a month after Marriot registered his manuscript with the Stationers, the O'Flahertie scribe wrote 'finishd this 12 of October 1632' on that artefact's title page. Stringer (*Variorum* 2.lxxviii–lxxix) speculates that shortly thereafter H6's owner attempted to register his own manuscript with the Stationers, learned of the Marriot edition already in press, and subsequently struck a deal that allowed Marriot access to H6, with the results above noted: arriving late onto the scene, H6 could supply only a few targeted readings for A, but was used extensively in the revised and expanded second edition of 1635 (B).

Drawing material from not only H6, but also two other manuscripts to a lesser degree (see *Variorum* 2.lxxix–lxxx), B adds nearly thirty poems (a dozen of them spurious—see Ch. 1) and organizes its contents generically under section headings also adapted from H6. Imposing an organizational scheme that would establish the general shape of all subsequent seventeenth-century editions, B begins with four items of front matter—'The Printer to the Understanders', two brief hexastiches (from and to the bookseller), and the (misplaced) Prose Letter meant to introduce *Metem*—and proceeds as follows: 'Songs and Sonets', 'Epigrams', 'Elegies', 'Epithalamions', 'Satyres', 'Letters to Severall Personages' (Verse Letters), 'Funerall Elegies' (beginning with the *Anniversaries* and continuing with 'Epicedes and Obsequies Upon the deaths of sundry Personages'), Prose Letters, 'The Progress of the Soule' (*Metem*), 'Divine Poems' (beginning with *Corona* and the 'Holy Sonnets'), 'Elegies Upon the Author'. The 1639 edition (C) is a page-for-page resetting of B, and there are only minor additions in the three issues of the fourth edition (D–F), most notably of the Elegy *ElVar*, the lyric *SelfL*, and some prose pieces in the 1650 issue (E), edited by Donne's son. More extensive changes, however, appear in the carelessly edited Restoration edition of 1669 (G), which is based on the text of the fourth edition, but supplemented by the addition of whole poems and individual readings derived from perhaps as many as seven additional manuscripts (see *Variorum* 2.lxxxi). In addition to a spurious first stanza for *Break* and the spurious seventh satire mentioned in Chapter 1, G substitutes a full version of *ElPart* for the truncated version introduced in B and—in the morally looser climate of the Restoration—ventures to print from manuscript *ElProg* and *ElBed*, which had fallen to the censor's axe in 1633. (For a precise register of the enlargement of the corpus of poems in the collected editions from 1633 through 1669 and the organization of the volumes' contents, see the first-line indexes on the *Variorum*'s website: http://donnevariorum.tamu.edu. Images of A, B, and G are online at http://DigitalDonne.tamu.edu.)

After the Restoration edition of 1669, the manuscript tradition of Donne's poetry dropped out of sight for nearly 200 years, and—with some few adversions to prior seventeenth-century editions—G's was ultimately the primary source text for all editions until that of Grosart in 1872–3. The bookseller Jacob Tonson set his 1719 edition of Donne's *Poems on Several Occasions* (*Variorum* siglum H) into type from G, basically following its organizational scheme; and—mediated through Tonson—G's text was perpetuated in John Bell's *The Poetical Works of Dr. John Donne* (1779; *Variorum* siglum I), which reordered the contents but based the text directly on H; Robert Anderson's *The Poetical Works of Dr. John Donne* (1793; siglum J), which was based on I and followed its organizational scheme; Alexander Chalmers's *The Poems of John Donne, D. D.* (1810; siglum K), which reverted to H for its setting text and plan of organization; and James Russell Lowell's *The Poetical Works of Dr. John Donne* (1855; siglum M), which also reverted to H for the text, but re-sequenced the contents. Into the stream leading to the succeeding four editions, Tonson introduced a few careless errors (e.g. 'these sighs' [for the authorial 'those sighs'] in *HSSighs* 1); but he also made the occasional independent correction (changing e.g. G's ungrammatical 'hurt reach' to 'hurts reach' in *ElPict* 14) and, on even rarer occasions, adopted emendations from either B or C, his alteration of G's 'place' to the correct 'pass' in *ElBrac* 63, for example. I–K manifest no consultation of either manuscripts or earlier editions (see *Variorum* 2.lxxxiii for specifics on how this process of transmission plays out in the Elegies). In the summation of Dayton Haskin, each editor from Tonson through Chalmers 'tended to anchor his work in that of his recent predecessors, emending eclectically, and often impressionistically' (2002b: 206). The lone exception was Henry Alford, who, editing the poems in volume 6 of his *The Works of John Donne* (1839; *Variorum* siglum L), prints a selection of the poems from A, supplementing them with a handful of 'Poems Not in the Edition of 1633' and—according to notes scattered throughout the volume—occasionally comparing J.

Although their editors were obviously concerned to present a readable text, by modern standards the editions from Tonson through Alford were essentially popular rather than scholarly, and I, J, and K were all presented as volumes in ongoing series of 'complete' editions of the 'Poets of Great Britain' (I, J) or of 'the English Poets' (K). The rudiments of a critical approach, however, can be seen in Lowell's *Poetical Works* (1855; siglum M), itself included in 'the series of "British Poets" then in course of publication by Little, Brown, & Company, in Boston' (Donne 1895: vii). Lowell based his edition on Tonson, but—despite having only limited access to the earlier seventeenth-century editions—cited 'more textual variants than any reader of Donne's poetry had ever seen before' (Haskin 2002b: 176), drawing most of these from B, but (by way of Alford's edition) also recording a few from A. After publication, until his death in 1891, Lowell continued to record variants from the earlier editions, showing a growing scepticism towards the received G-based text, and this awakening critical attitude eventually bore fruit in the Grolier Club edition of 1895 (O), in which Charles Eliot Norton and Mabel Burnett, Lowell's daughter, more fully realized Lowell's dream of a genuine scholarly edition.

For his *Complete Poems of John Donne* (2 vols., 1872–3; *Variorum* siglum N), published as part of the 'Fuller Worthies Library', Alexander B. Grosart asserts that he collated all the early editions 'with prolonged carefulness' (1.xii), and he set poems into type variously from A, B, C, and G, sequencing the genres in a Satires-to-Divine Poems order. Except for F. G. Waldron's publication of *ElWar* in 1802 and John Simeon's publication of *Liar* in 1856, moreover, Grosart was the first editor since 1669 to print a Donne poem from manuscript, using four artefacts from the British Library (Add. 18,647 [B7], Harley 4955 [B32], Harley 5110 [B33], and Lansdowne 740 [B40]), Haselwood-Kingsborough I (HH4), and the Stephens manuscript (H7), then in private hands in London. Unfortunately, none of these manuscripts is particularly reliable, and H7—to which Grosart ascribed 'very great weight' (Donne 1872–3: 1.3)—is especially corrupt, as Norton and other editors shortly pointed out. Nevertheless, Grosart specifies his copy-text for each poem, records a great many textual variants, and provides brief (though, in many respects, inaccurate) bibliographical descriptions of the seventeenth-century editions. Thus, although it was, in Haskin's words, 'the most careless edition of Donne ever printed' (2002b: 181), Grosart's may fairly be characterized as the first scholarly edition of Donne's poetry, and his work stimulated later critiques that led to more extensive consideration of manuscript evidence in the editing of Donne. (For Grosart's efforts to augment the canon, see Ch. 1.)

Prompted by their regard for Lowell's long-standing interest in Donne's poems and a desire to preserve the 'many hundreds' (Donne 1895: viii) of marginal emendations that Lowell had recorded in his personal copy of M, in the 'Grolier Club edition' of 1895 (siglum O) Norton and Burnett aspired to present a text 'more nearly correct and more intelligible than any hitherto printed' (ix). Their approach was to publish a carefully corrected text of A (though they modernized the spelling and introduced their own organizational scheme), supplementing it with other poems that had first appeared in the subsequent seventeenth-century editions and recording all verbal variants to the copy-text in footnotes. Although this edition made no use of manuscripts in preparing the text, Norton published in 1896 an essay on 'The Text of Donne's Poems' in which he not only reviewed Grosart's work in detail and harshly dismissed it (2–3), but also provided the first scholarly treatment of Donne's manuscripts, describing H7 (by this time in the Harvard library) more accurately than Grosart had and also describing two other manuscripts—the 'Carnaby' (H3) and the 'Norton' (H4)—that he had acquired (7–13). Norton listed from all three manuscripts exceptional variants he thought worth attention as possible improvements of the text of A. Throughout, however, he remained of the view that manuscript readings generally establish the comparative trustworthiness of A.

Norton's essay also took notice of, and reviewed favourably, Edmund K. Chambers's two-volume *Poems of John Donne* (Donne 1896; *Variorum* siglum P), published as part of the 'Muse's Library' series. Unlike the Grolier Club edition, P was based not on A alone, but drew eclectically on B through G as well as on occasional manuscript evidence for specific readings. Chambers, like Norton, believed that A presented the most reliable text of the poems, requiring of course to be supplemented with some poems first printed in later seventeenth-century editions; Chambers also made sporadic use of evidence from about twenty manuscripts (including the ones previously consulted by Grosart) held mainly at Oxford or the British Library, an accessible fraction of what he called the 'innumerable' manuscripts (1896: 1.v). Like Grosart before him, Chambers provided a description of the seventeenth-century editions and their contents, and his research led him early to the conclusion later substantiated by the *Variorum* editors that some of Donne's poems exist 'in several more or less revised forms' (1.xliv). Apparently following B, Chambers opened his edition with 'Songs and Sonets', but thereafter diverged into an organizational scheme of his own devising. His augmentation of the canon is described in Chapter 1.

With the publication of P the stage was set for Grierson's landmark Oxford edition of 1912, the two-volume *Poems of John Donne* (*Variorum* siglum Q), which—as Grierson recalls in his preface—began in frustration at the unavailability of an adequate text from which to teach his students (Donne 1912: 1.iii) and developed in explicit reaction to the unsatisfactory efforts of his three immediate predecessors. He deplored N for its many inaccuracies and the whimsicality of its editorial method, especially criticizing its reliance on H7, which he thought of all manuscripts the 'worst, the fullest of obvious and absurd blunders' (2.cv). And he deprecated Chambers's eclecticism, his abandonment of A in favour of the 'often erroneous emendations of the later editions', and his modernizing of the punctuation while at the same time failing to preserve any 'record of the changes made' (1.iv). Grierson found the plan of the Grolier editors—accurately to reproduce the text of A and to add poems not contained in A from their first printings in subsequent editions—'the soundest' of the approaches used by these forerunners, but complained that in O, as in P, 'the punctuation has been freely altered throughout' and that 'no record of these changes is preserved in the textual notes', even when these changes altered the meaning of the text as originally printed (2.cxiv).

To this problem Grierson originally proposed a solution almost identical to that of the Grolier editors—to present a text based on the printed editions, using A as copy-text wherever possible and supplementing it with later first printings of poems not included in A. But his initial collations revealed that A was 'certainly not faultless' and that the later editions, particularly G, were 'very carelessly edited and corrupt' (1.iv). Encouraged by Norton's suggestion in his 1896 essay that 'corrections' might be 'obtained' from manuscripts—which for Grierson at some point came to hold 'at least the same interest and importance as the Quartos have for the editor of Shakespeare' (2.lxxviii)—he thus undertook an initial collation of certain manuscripts available in the British Library, concluding from this study that the deficiencies of A could not be overcome by 'bas[ing] a text on any single extant manuscript' or even by 'mak[ing] an eclectic use of a few of them' (1.v). This conclusion, in turn, led to a radical expansion of Grierson's plans, and he eventually undertook to locate, describe, and take account of all the seventeenth-century artefacts containing Donne's poems, prints and manuscripts alike. Accordingly, he first discusses the publication history of Donne's poems, mentioning the *Anniversaries* and *Henry* before proceeding to the various editions of the collected *Poems*. For all editions from A through Tonson (H) he gives formal bibliographical descriptions (including typographical facsimiles of their title pages) that with various degrees of specificity detail their formats, contents, organizational patterns, and relationships to each other. He then similarly describes the manuscripts of which he was aware, itemizing thirty-seven in his sigla list and discussing about thirty in considerable detail. Among these artefacts Grierson distinguishes three (he announces 'four', but never specifies the last) classes: (*a*) 'collections of portions of Donne's poems, e.g. the *Satyres*' (2.lxxix); (*b*) manuscripts that 'are, or aim at being, complete collections of Donne's poems' (2.lxxxii–lxxxiii); and (*c*) miscellaneous collections that include some Donne poems along with other contents (2.cvi). Further, within the second class he identifies 'three main groups' the first two of which, with some variation, each descends 'from a single stream' or 'head' and embodies a common textual tradition, while members of the third are less closely associated, but still 'tend to follow a common tradition' (2.cxi). (Expanded and partly realigned by the discoveries and analyses of later editors, these groups remain central to all discussions of the texts of Donne's poems.) As noted above in this chapter, Grierson's comparative analysis of the texts and contents of the prints and manuscripts led him to posit that a manuscript closely resembling the Leconfield (C8), a member of his Group I, 'was used for a large, and textually the best, part of the edition of 1633' (2.lxxxiv), that a 'manuscript resembling' *A18* (B7), *N* (H4), and *TC* (CT1 and DT1)—Grierson's Group II—was another of the 'sources of the edition' (2.xciv–xcv), and that the remaining poems derived either from previous printings or from 'more miscellaneous and less trustworthy sources' (2.xcvii). He also recognized that the O'Flahertie manuscript

(H6) and another 'resembling closely' the Carnaby (H3) and the Phillipps (O21) had contributed to the text and contents of B in 1635 (2.xcviii).

Having amassed and analysed a huge corpus of manuscript data, Grierson then outlined a method for using this material 'to get back as close as may be to what the poet wrote himself' (2.cxii). The method entailed collating them 'and establishing what one might call the agreement of the manuscripts whether universal or partial, noting in the latter case the comparative value of the different groups' (2.cxvii). The 'first result of a collation of the manuscripts', Grierson averred, was 'to vindicate' the edition of 1633 (A) (2.cxviii), and the frequency-of-appearance approach was validated by the fact that 'in about nine cases out of ten' readings in A that had such manuscript support also met the criterion of 'intrinsic probability'; for readings in the 'later editions' that had similar manuscript support, he further observed, there was 'a good deal to be said' (2.cxvii–cxviii). To avoid being trapped in an inflexible method, however, Grierson also asserted his belief that '[i]n some cases the manuscripts *alone* give us what is obviously the correct reading' (2.cxix) and that 'occasionally the correct reading has been preserved in only one or two manuscripts' (2.cxx). And his willingness to credit minority—or even unique—manuscript testimony in given instances is sometimes difficult to distinguish from the eclecticism he so deplored in Chambers. For instance, because the Westmoreland ms. (*Variorum* siglum NY3) resolves what Grierson reads as a logical contradiction in lines 57–8 of *EpLin* (2.98), he accepts its unique 'nill' (for 'will') in line 57: 'His steeds nill be restrained'. Similarly, in *Sat4* line 38, for no specified reason, he prefers the 'He speaks no language' found in the Oxford Queen's College ms. (*Variorum* siglum OQ1) and the Dyce ms. (*Variorum* siglum VA1) for the '...one language' that appears in all the prints and other manuscripts known to him. On occasion Grierson even adopted readings that had *no* manuscript support, printing as the last line of *Father* the editions' 'I feare no more'; and—on no artefactual authority whatsoever—he rewrites *ElComp* l. 5 as 'on her brow her skin such luster sets' (for 'on her necke...') in an attempt to create an appropriate context for the 'coronets' found in the prints and 'so many MSS' (2.74) at the end of line 6. The reading 'carcanetts' (which *is* consistent with 'neck') was known to Grierson from the highly authoritative NY3, from which he had adopted 'nill' in the epithalamion discussed above, but when his 'agreement' criterion came head-to-head with his 'comparative-value' criterion, he could only fall back on the 'individual preference' for which he disparaged others.

Grierson thought it 'impossible...to construct a complete genealogy' (2.cxi) of the manuscripts he knew, and it never occurred to him to choose copy-texts from various sources on a poem-by-poem basis. Having concluded that A was 'far and away superior to any other single edition and...to any *single* manuscript' (2.cxvi), he thus based each poem on its first printing (A most often), emending it towards manuscript readings when he saw need and adding from manuscript (especially NY3) and a few scattered printings poems that had not previously been published in an edition. For poems identified as existing in multiple authorial versions (he names several lyrics and 'the *Satyres*'), Grierson generally sought to 'retain one tradition pure', recording the variants in his notes (2.cxxi)—though he did print in full two versions of *Father*. With some slight adjustment, he adopts the overall organizational scheme of B. For each poem he identifies the copy-text and sources collated in a set of footnotes that also lists—usually fully and accurately—all substantive and semi-substantive variants in the sources collated and records his editorial emendations, including those of spelling and punctuation. Finally, combining his 'agreement of the manuscripts' principle with historical research, he addresses the problem of canonicity, persuasively rejecting as spurious all but two of the poems that Grosart and Chambers had added (see Ch. 1). Upon the bibliographical, conceptual, and methodological bases thus established by Grierson much of the succeeding Donne editorial enterprise has been built.

In either direct or mediated form, Grierson's text held the stage alone for the next forty years. Sporting a much-reduced apparatus and 'corrected in some places', a more portable, one-volume incarnation of Q was issued by Oxford University Press in 1929 as *The Poems of John Donne* (Donne 1929*b*: xlix; repr. 1933), this edition later providing the text used for Combs and Sullens's *Concordance* (Chicago, 1940). Also in 1929, in what was essentially a reprint of Grierson, the Nonesuch Press published John Hayward's *John Donne, Dean of St. Paul's: Complete Poetry and Selected Prose* (Donne 1929*a*; *Variorum* siglum S), which alters Q's text in the odd instance (e.g. replacing Q's 'glittering' with 'glistering' in *ElBed* line 5), but generally repeats even Q's anomalies and mistranscriptions—'brow' (for 'neck') in *ElComp* line 5 and 'on heavenly things' (for the correct 'in heauenly things') in *HSShe* line 4, for example. S, in turn, subsequently provided the text for Fausset's (modernized) *Poems of John Donne* (Everyman's Library, 1931), Robert Hillyer's *Complete Poetry and Selected Prose...* (Random House, 1941), and Coffin's *Complete Poetry and Selected Prose* (Modern Library, 1946), thus perpetuating Grierson's text in popular editions for the next two decades. Grierson's also became the source-text for many schoolroom anthologies in the twentieth century.

Forty years after Q's first appearance, apparently having determined that the time was ripe for a scholarly successor to Grierson, Oxford University Press published the first of four volumes that over the course of the next twenty-six years would present a complete, re-edited text of Donne's poems: Helen Gardner's *The Divine Poems* (Donne 1952*a* [rev. edn. 1978]; *Variorum* siglum U), Gardner's *The Elegies and the Songs and Sonnets* (1965; *Variorum* Siglum X), Wesley Milgate's *The Satires, Epigrams, and Verse Letters* (1967*b*; *Variorum* siglum Y), and Milgate's *The Epithalamions, Anniversaries, and Epicedes* (Donne 1978*b*; *Variorum* siglum BB). Both Gardner and Milgate explicitly position their editions as successors to Grierson's, accepting his premise that—in Gardner's words—'the only possible basis' for a critical edition is the seventeenth-century prints (1978*a*: xci), and—though variously offering some refinements of his procedures, including the use of manuscripts that had come to light since the publication of Q—affirming 'the general soundness of his methods' (Donne 1967b: v).

According to her preface, two of the main goals Gardner set out to achieve in the 1952 *Divine Poems* were textual in nature: (1) to print the Holy Sonnets in their 'right order' (v), and (2) to 'find a solution' (v) to the problem posed by the facts that Donne's poems first saw print in a non-authoritative, posthumous edition (A) and that, while no holographs exist, the poems exist in a 'great many manuscript copies which antedate the first edition' (v). Gardner's printing of the Holy Sonnets in the 'right' (v) order entails abandoning the sixteen-poem arrangement of 1635 and printing—for the first time since Alford in 1839—the twelve-poem arrangement of A, which is that of its Group-I source. The four poems left over from this rearrangement (Sonnets 'added in 1635'; xii) she rearranges and prints as a numbered four-item set bound together, she thinks, by a 'penitential' (xli) theme; and she concludes by adding the three Sonnets unique to NY3 in a separately numbered group. As the *Variorum* volume on the Holy Sonnets has shown, Gardner is right in recognizing the Group-I and -II order followed in A as authorial, but she understands the reformation of A's Sonnet sequence by the compiler of B as merely an instance of editorial corruption, failing to see that the arrangement of the poems in the Group-III manuscript from which the editor of B derived the four Sonnets 'added in 1635' is also authorial and deserving of recognition (see *Variorum* 7.1.lx–cii *passim*). Thus, while she noteworthily restores the authorial Group-I sequence of A, making it available for critical scrutiny for essentially the first time in over 300 years, Gardner also fabricates a spurious set of 'penitential' Sonnets whose authenticity remained unquestioned until the appearance of the *Variorum* volume half-a-century later (see Ch. 17).

The ultimate aim of Gardner's re-examination of the relationship between the manuscripts and the printed editions is to perfect the text of A (or other first printing of a given poem) by 'eradicating error' (*Variorum* 7.1.lxxxiv), and pursuit of this goal requires her to refine Grierson's proto-genealogical method for assessing the authority of variants. Accordingly, she elaborates a general theory of manuscript transmission, sketching in stemmas for Groups I and II (an implicit rebuttal of Grierson's declaration that such was impossible) and setting forth a set of precise rules for applying Grierson's 'comparative value' criterion in emending the copy-text (see Donne 1952a: xcii–xciii). While applying these rules enables her to correct some errors that Grierson had accepted—she rejects A's emendation of the source-manuscript's 'minutes last point' to '…latest point' in *HScene* line 4, for instance, and refuses the editorially invented 'feare no more' in *Father* line 18—this procedure provides no guidance in instances in which the choice is between two equally valid alternatives. Hence, for example, Gardner follows Grierson in substituting NY3's 'true griefe, for he put it in my brest' for B's Group-III reading 'griefe, for he put it into my brest' in *HSSouls* line 14, implausibly speculating that the Group-III archetype had erroneously omitted 'true' and that 'this was patched by the alteration of "in" to "into"' (1952a: 77; see *Variorum* 7.1.79), but rejects without comment such other NY3 readings as 'burne me, O God' in *HSLittle* line 13, retaining B's 'burne me o Lord'. And even though she directly acknowledges that 'a few readings in W [NY3]...may represent an earlier stage of the text' (70) and finds some of these appealing, she accepts none of them into her reading text. They are thus consigned to the oblivion of the textual apparatus, awaiting the *Variorum*'s development of a 'full genealogy for the poems' and an editorial theory capable of 'dealing with authorial revision' (*Variorum* 7.1.lxxxiv).

In her following edition in 1965, possibly as a result of conversations with Milgate about the Satires volume then in progress, Gardner looks back at her work in *The Divine Poems* and declares her belief that Donne did in fact revise *Corona*, the Holy Sonnets, and *Annun*, even as she avers that—except for three lines of *Curse* and possibly parts of *Will* and *GoodM*—the Elegies and the Songs and Sonets contain no 'variants of a kind to compel the hypothesis of authorial revision' (Donne 1965: lxxxii–lxxxiii). Accordingly, although she now concludes that A requires even 'more thorough and consistent correction from the manuscripts than Grierson undertook' (viii), her textual work in *The Elegies and the Songs and Sonets* is of a methodological piece with that in her previous edition. Gardner's major innovations in this volume are matters of canon and arrangement. She relegates *ElPart, Julia, Citizen, ElExpost, ElVar, Sappho, Token, SelfL,* and the spurious stanza of G's version of *Break* to a section of 'Dubia', and transfers *Image* from the Elegies to the Songs and Sonets. Further, although she uses A as copy-text for the ten Elegies it contains, she abandons A's order in favour of that in NY3 (except that she interpolates *ElProg* into the group), setting the poems 'excepted' from A (see Ch. 1) into type from C2. In a radical departure from tradition and bibliographical precedent, moreover, Gardner attempts to arrange the Songs and Sonets chronologically—she presents a group of poems supposedly composed 'before 1600' and another 'after 1602' (v)—and, within those groups, thematically, her justification being that the order of A is 'wholly irrational' and 'cannot be memorized' (vi).

In his *Satires, Epigrams, and Verse Letters* (Donne 1967b), prepared in close consultation with Gardner, Milgate adheres faithfully to the textual theory developed by his Oxford University Press predecessors, using the first seventeenth-century printing of each poem as copy-text and emending from manuscript in essential accordance with the guidelines previously codified by Gardner, with whom he shares the view that A was 'carefully edited' (lxviii) and therefore must be scrutinized closely for instances of editorial intervention. Accordingly, for the Satires, *Metem*, and the 'Epigrams and verse letters which it contains' (lxx), A serves as copy-text, while the poems not present in A derive variously from B, D, E, Jonson's *Volpone* (1607), Coryate's *Crudities* (1611), NY3, and the flyleaves of two books from Donne's library. Milgate abandons Grierson's arrangement of the poems for a 'more logical and convenient order' (v) based on genre and chronology, but his most significant contribution is the proposal—an expansion of a notion first mentioned by Grierson—that the (first four) Satires exist in an original and two authorially revised forms. Milgate sets the proposition forth in an extended discussion of the manuscript evidence (xlii–lxi), illustrates his conclusions by a comprehensive stemma, and dates the two revisions tentatively to about 1598 (when Donne took up employment with Egerton) and 1607–8 (when he was courting the favour of the Countess of Bedford). Unfortunately, limitations of space (and also, perhaps, editorial theory) prevent Milgate from publishing more than one version of any of the Satires, and the variants that distinguish the earlier versions from the later Group-II text found in A remain buried in the textual notes. Also regrettable is that, since he follows NY3's order and uses it as copy-text for four Epigrams not in A, Milgate does not abandon A altogether and set the entire sequence of Epigrams into type from NY3. Milgate's subsequent edition of the *Epithalamions, Anniversaries, and Epicedes* (Donne 1978b) follows the same editorial principles as his Satires volume, and in addition to the works mentioned in the title, it also includes the 'Elegies upon the Author' that had followed Donne's own poems in the seventeenth-century editions of the collected *Poems*. For the first time ever, moreover, Milgate brings together the six Latin epitaphs and inscriptions—compositions 'mid-way between prose and verse' (v)—that Donne wrote over the years.

Milgate also praises Frank Manley's edition of the *Anniversaries* (1963; *Variorum* siglum W), which—along with Theodore Redpath's '*Editio minor*' of the love lyrics (1956; *Variorum* siglum V)—is one of two mid-century editions that focus on single poetic genres. Except for Bennett, Manley is the first editor since the early seventeenth-century to use their first printings—in 1611 and 1612, respectively—as copy-texts for *FirAn* and *SecAn*, and he collates at least two copies of every printing of the *Anniversaries* from 1611 through 1669 in the search for press variants. Further, he is the first editor ever to make use of the unique errata slip found in Geoffrey Keynes's copy of *SecAn* and described in 1946. In an effort to appeal to both a 'university' and a 'general' readership (vii), Redpath modernizes both spelling and punctuation in his *Songs and Sonets*. He follows Grierson 'completely' with respect to canon, and his text—while 'taking account of' manuscript evidence unearthed after the publication of Q—essentially reproduces Grierson's, including such idiosyncratic interventions as 'Eagers desire' in *Fare* line 30, where all the source texts give 'Eager, desires'. Dropping the extenuating '*Editio minor*' from its title, Redpath's second *Songs and Sonets* (1983; siglum CC) is not a mere revision, but a completely new edition, which, though it continues to modernize spelling and punctuation, contains a 'fairly full' critical apparatus to support a text newly constructed on Q's principles. Having now concluded that 'good sense can be made of the old reading' (151), Redpath reverts to 'Eager, desires' in *Fare* line 30, and he reorganizes the volume's contents according to 'the moods of the poems', perhaps encouraged in this by Gardner's similar previous decision.

Each straddling the line between the scholarly and the popular, four other influential editions of the complete poems appeared between 1942 and 1985—Roger E. Bennett's *The Complete Poems of John Donne* (1942; *Variorum* siglum T); John T. Shawcross's *The Complete Poetry of John Donne* (1967a; siglum Z); A. J. Smith's *John*

Donne: the Complete English Poems (1971a; siglum AA); and C. A. Patrides's *The Complete English Poems of John Donne* (1985; siglum DD). Modernizing spelling and aiming his edition at 'those who wish to read Donne's poetry for pleasure' (xi), Bennett diverges radically from the Griersonian editorial approach, declaring that 'since there is no single authoritative text of any kind available to us', it is 'advisable to base each poem on whatever accessible text has the fewest obvious errors' (xxv). Accordingly, Bennett sets poems into type variously from eight prints (including the 1611 and 1612 first printings of the *Anniversaries*) and six manuscripts to which he had access in American repositories during World War II (H4, H6, HH1, NY3, PM1, and H10), recording a few variant readings in a severely curtailed apparatus. As the diversity of these copy-text choices implies, Bennett's editorial method is thoroughly eclectic, and he readily merges readings from various sources in order to confect the text he prefers, an example being his replacement of the copy-text's (NY3's) 'Now off with those shoes and then safely tread' with H6's 'Off with those shoes you wear, and safely tread' in *ElBed* line 17. Beginning with Songs and Sonets and ending with Divine Poems, Bennett organizes his volume according to a combination of chronological and thematic concerns.

Calling the text of his edition 'eclectic and somewhat subjectively based', Shawcross (1967a) essentially reverts to the Grierson–Gardner approach, basing copy-texts on their earliest printings and emending when 'a later version or the reading of a consensus of manuscripts seems to be closer to Donne's "original"' (xxi). That personal taste is frequently at the base of Shawcross's eclecticism is evident, to take one of many examples, in his handling of *HSSighs* line 8, where—on grounds of metrical smoothness (497)—Shawcross retains the ''Cause I did suffer' that B derived from H6 rather than emending to the 'Because I did suffer' dictated by the consensus of manuscripts. And he is the only editor ever to divide *ElAut* into stanzas and print it among the Songs and Sonets. Shawcross contributes significantly, however, in providing an extensive listing of variants (including many that had not previously been cited) and the fullest catalogue of manuscripts containing Donne poems that had as yet been assembled—159 in all. Grouping the poems by genre and attempting to arrange the genres in chronological order of composition, Shawcross institutes a similarly useful feature in assigning each poem a separate numerical siglum.

One of Keynes's two brief notes on A. J. Smith's 1971 Penguin edition mentions that '[t]he cover has a reproduction of the Lothian portrait with lipstick and other colouring added' (1971a: 216), and, indeed, with its modernized spelling and punctuation, AA veers more towards the popular than the scholarly. The volume's brief preface bespeaks Smith's basic awareness of the complications surrounding Donne's text, though four years after the publication of Shawcross Smith still avers that there are only 'forty-five manuscripts' (13) containing Donne poems; and while averring the primacy of A among the seventeenth-century editions, he declares himself an eclecticist primarily interested in offering 'the richest and most pointed readings of Donne's poems that have good authority in the early versions' (14). Smith's notes merge the explicatory and the textual, and the few manuscript variants he lists—cited unspecifically as '*MS*' or '*MSS*'—seem to be derived from the apparatus of previous scholarly editions. Perhaps (like Redpath) also emboldened by the precedent of Gardner, Smith arranges the Songs and Sonets alphabetically according to their popular titles, placing them at the beginning of a volume organized according to a scheme of his own devising.

Of all the editors in the line of Grierson, Patrides—in his 1985 update of the original 1931 Everyman—is the most persistently determined to base the copy-text on the seventeenth-century editions, especially A; and Patrides defends this devotion on grounds that, 'save for Donne's lifetime, his reputation to our own century is based on the printed versions, not the manuscripts' (Donne 1985: 2). This dogmatic reverence for the prints extends to the preservation of A's 'necke'–'coronets' contradiction, which Grierson had rewritten, and to retention of the compositorial 'assumes a pitious minde' in *HSWhat* line 14, where all manuscripts, including the one upon which A was based, read 'assures a pitious minde'. What few manuscript variants Patrides does cite in his footnotes are cited, as in AA before him, merely as 'a MS' or 'the MSS', and his heavy reliance on Grierson for this information is evident, for example, in his replication of Grierson's mistranscribed 'on heavenly things' in *HSShe* line 4 and 'their head' in *HSShe* line 6, where NY3, the sole source of these poems, reads 'in heauenly things' and 'the head', respectively. Also like Grierson, Patrides arranges the volume's contents in the order of B.

Finally, four recent editions in which readers have had access to Donne deserve brief mention—John Carey's 'Oxford Authors' *Donne* (1990), his subsequent 'World's Classics' *Selected Poetry* (1996a), Ilona Bell's 'Penguin Classics' *Selected Poems* (2006), and Donald R. Dickson's 'Norton Critical Edition' of *John Donne's Poetry* (2007), which includes a substantial selection of the poems. Textually, Carey's modernized editions declare their reliance on only Gardner and Milgate, and while the 1996 *Selected Poetry* arranges the poems by genre, the earlier 'Oxford Authors' volume intermingles poems with various prose works in a chronological scheme intended to provide 'a clear sense of Donne's development, as writer and thinker' (Donne 1990: xxxviii), breaking up such generic groups as the Satires, Elegies, and even the Holy Sonnets in order to distribute poems throughout the volume in accordance with this plan. Bell's edition makes mention of the many manuscript copies of Donne poems cited in Beal's *Index* and the *Variorum*, but bases copy-texts on the 'first published seventeenth-century edition of each poem', emending from the later editions or from manuscript 'when there is a compelling reason to do so' (xlii–xliii). Updating A. L. Clements's prior volume in the same series (1966), Dickson's is the only one of these editions to reflect the scholarly climate generated by the *Variorum* project, using NY3 as the copy-text for all the poems it contains and drawing others from the Trinity College, Dublin manuscript (DT1), the most reliable of the Group IIs, and H6, supporting these choices by a collation of all the seventeenth-century prints.

CHAPTER 4.II

EDITING DONNE'S POETRY: THE DONNE *VARIORUM* AND BEYOND

RICHARD TODD

ORGANIZED in the early 1980s and now having published *The Anniversaries and the Epicedes and Obsequies* (vol. 6); *The Epigrams, Epithalamions, Epitaphs, Inscriptions, and Miscellaneous Poems* (vol. 8); *The Elegies* (vol. 2); and *The Holy Sonnets* (vol. 7.1)—four of a projected eleven physical volumes—the collaborative international project to produce *The Variorum Edition of the Poetry of John Donne* has placed the editing of Donne's poems on a new foundation. (The *Variorum* Commentary's summary of criticism will be treated in Ch. 6.)

As Gary A. Stringer explains in Chapter 1, holographs of the poems have almost entirely vanished, and very little of Donne's verse was published before his death. The remaining texts, though numerous, are all either scribal manuscript transcriptions or posthumous printings based on these transcriptions. Despite the general lack of authorial manuscripts or of printings over which the author might be assumed to have exerted some control, however, until the *Variorum* edition was launched, the reigning wisdom among modern editors was that, in Helen Gardner's words, the early prints formed 'the only possible basis' (1978*a*: xci) for a critical edition. And even such editors as A. B. Grosart (1872–3) and R. E. Bennett (1942), who set some poems into type from manuscript, relied heavily on the received print tradition. With the partial exceptions of Grosart and Bennett, in practice this deference to the efforts of their predecessors has meant that editors have generally regarded the manuscripts primarily as a source from which to 'correct' their print copy-texts and have, consequently, recorded only such manuscript variants as were needed to support their editorial choices. Coupled with the failure to develop a reliable genealogical method and—to varying degrees—with a dearth of information about the manuscripts and their contents, this view of the manuscripts as merely an occasional source of lost authorial readings has had the further effect of causing editors to produce eclectic texts, as they have picked and chosen manuscript readings to satisfy their own sense of what was aesthetically or logically required in given instances.

With the avowed aim of 'recover[ing] and present[ing] exactly what Donne wrote' insofar as the 'available materials' make such a goal feasible (*Variorum* 6.XLIII), the *Variorum* has adopted a different approach, choosing manuscript copy-texts for most of the poems 'simply because they seem in fact and in theory more likely to represent the lost originals accurately than do the early printings' (*Variorum* 6.XLV). And the range of possible choices has been enhanced enormously by the work of Peter Beal, whose coverage of Donne in the *Index of English Literary Manuscripts* (1980) expanded the number of manuscript copies of Donne poems far beyond that known to previous editors (see Ch. 1). For the *Variorum* editors, choice of the copy-text is the product of a painstaking analysis of both the print and manuscript evidence based on collation of every early exemplar of a given poem. Like H. J. C. Grierson before them, the *Variorum* editors recognize that an all-inclusive genealogy of whole manuscripts is not possible, partly because most of them cannot be accurately dated, partly because many once-extant manuscripts that formed links in the evolutionary chain are now missing, but principally because the comprehensive manuscript collections are genealogically mixed, containing copies of individual poems whose proximity to Donne's originals varies widely. Thus—in keeping with the material circumstances under which these works were distributed to their original recipients (see Ch. 1)—they proceed on a poem-by-poem basis, recognizing that 'the possibility of missing copies and the intractability of the surviving evidence also make it impossible to construct a complete genealogy for many of the [individual] poems', but also believing that by collating all copies and analysing the results, 'it is possible to identify patterns of variation that lead back to the least corrupted surviving version[s] of a poem' for use as copy-text (*Variorum* 6. XLVI).

A signal example of the success of this method appears in the *Variorum*'s edition of *Ham* (6.220–1), written to commemorate the death of James Hamilton on 2 March 1625. Lines 19–28 chronicle the utter devastation that befalls the body when the soul flees, but discern in this devastation a lesson in Christian hope, which Donne develops in Platonic terms:

> Never made Body such hast to confesse
> What a Soule was. All former comelynesse
> Fledd in a minute when the Soule was gon
> And hauing lost that beauty would haue none
> So fell our Monasteryes in an instant growne
> Not to lesse houses, but to heapes of stone;
> So sent his body that fayre forme it wore
> Vnto the Spheare of formes, and doth (before
> His body fill vp his Sepulchrall stone)
> Anticipate a Resurrection.
> For as, in his fame, now, his Soule is heere:
> So in the forme thereof his bodye's there.

Though typically intricate, the argument developed in lines 25–30 is not incomprehensible: at death the 'forme' (the soul) of the Marquess's body instantaneously ascended to the 'Spheare of formes' (heaven), thereby prefiguring the body's eventual 'Resurrection' and assuming a role as the body's representative in heaven, just as the Marquesse's 'fame' remains with the body on earth as a representative of the departed 'Soule'. After carefully examining all the data, the *Variorum* editors selected the O'Flahertie ms. (H6) as the copy-text for this poem; every prior printing of the poem, however, from its first appearance in print in 1633 onward, had ultimately been based on a manuscript that read line 27 as 'His **soule shall** fill up his Sepulchrall stone'. Analysis of the poem's entire transmissional history and the consequent selection of H6 as copy-text thus enabled the *Variorum* to give Donne's readers their first ever access to the stunning conceit in these lines.

Once the copy-text has been selected—whether a manuscript or (occasionally) a print—it is treated very conservatively: the copy-text's (frequently idiosyncratic) spelling is retained and its particular punctuation emended only as necessary to obviate misreading (leaving poems printed from manuscript punctuated quite differently from those based on an early edition); manifest errors in the chosen copy-text are corrected (e.g. the copy-text's 'make you numberles' in line 88 of *ElBrac* is emended to the required 'make your number les'); and certain print conventions—such as the expansion of brevigraphs and the capitalization of the first word in each line—are applied to manuscript sources, but the practice of eclectically 'conflat[ing] readings from multiple sources' (6.XLVIII) is eschewed. In volumes 6 and 8, the first to be published, the results of the analysis that led to the selection of each copy-text were presented graphically in a 'Schema of Textual Relationships' that merely grouped texts into families on the basis of shared readings; but as the editors have become increasingly adept at genealogical analysis over the years, they have sometimes been able to develop a full stemma that precisely positions the copy-text in relation to the lost holograph, and in such cases they have been more willing to emend up the line of descent towards that lost original. An example is the treatment of *ElPart*, for which the *Variorum* presents a comprehensive stemma (see 2.365, reproduced in Ch. 17) and justifies the 'more aggressive' emendation of its text as follows: 'While the results may seem to resemble the eclectic texts...deplored above, they in fact do not arise from whim or personal taste, but from the systematic application of the genealogical method' (2.XCIII).

Each volume of the *Variorum* is designed as a stand-alone entity that contains all the methodological and bibliographical information necessary to make its contents intelligible (many complementary tools, including first-line indexes of the seventeenth-century editions and major manuscripts, are available on the project's website: http://donnevariorum.tamu.edu). Accordingly, the front matter includes a list of 'Short Forms of Reference for Donne's Works', mnemonically designed to avoid the confusing system of numbers by which previous editions have variously designated such poems as the Elegies and the Holy Sonnets, for instance; a list of 'Sigla for Textual Sources', which employs a rationalized alphanumeric scheme to organize the several hundred manuscripts and printed editions consulted for the edition; a list of 'Manuscripts Listed by Traditional Classification', which organizes the artefacts by Grierson groups and identifies each by *Variorum* siglum, traditional siglum, and Beal delta number; a brief list of 'Symbols and Abbreviations Used in the Textual Apparatus'; and the 'General Introduction' to the *Variorum* project, which discusses the materials, theory, principles, and procedures used in the edition as a whole. These sections are followed by introductory matter specific to the volume in question, which addresses textual issues pertinent to the volume's particular contents. Depending on whether a given volume includes poems of only one generic type or of several, the organization and placement of this introductory matter may vary, but in every case it addresses a common set of concerns: the date of composition of the poem (or genre) and the historical circumstances surrounding its composition; the place of the poem in Donne's life and evolution as a writer; and the transmissional history of the text, from (in almost all cases) its circulation in manuscript through its appearance in editions from the seventeenth through the twentieth centuries.

These biographical, historical, and bibliographical matters are initially treated expositorily in either a 'General Textual Introduction', a poem-specific textual introduction, or both. As occasional poems assignable to specific dates, for instance, the three Epithalamions in volume 8 can each be individually introduced as an independent bibliographical entity; the Epigrams in that volume, however, as well as the Elegies in volume 2 and the Holy Sonnets in volume 7.1, form organized sequences of items that must be discussed at the group level in a 'General Textual Introduction' as well as individually. Whatever its level, each textual introduction translates the raw data collected in the textual apparatus into a coherent narrative of the work's transmissional history, presents a defence and description of the copy-text, and explains any emendations deemed necessary. The textual introduction is then supported by an extensive textual apparatus that provides far more information than has been recorded in any previous edition. Classes of artefacts whose details are reported here include manuscripts, seventeenth-century editions of the collected *Poems*, seventeenth-century printings in volumes other than the collected editions, modern first printings, and selected modern editions.

Beginning with seventeenth-century sources, the apparatus identifies the copy-text and sources collated, locating the poem by page or folio numbers within each artefact; lists all emendations of the copy-text; and provides a full historical collation. Organized in the 'Historical Collation' section are details pertinent to the format of the various artefacts and their embodiments of the text (imperfections, indentations of the text, and various kinds of 'Miscellaneous' information); a list of all headings/titles affixed to the poem; a line-by-line collation of the source texts; and a list of subscriptions to the poem. The following section of 'Verbal Variants in Selected Modern Editions' replicates the apparatus supplied for seventeenth-century sources, though limiting the detail of the line-by-line collation; and this is followed in turn by a stemma or schema of textual relationships, which is supported by a brief listing of textual variants that justify the stemma or schema. Finally, an 'Analysis of Early Printed Copies' cites press variants and physical peculiarities in the various seventeenth-century printings. Reportage of variants and other detail is designed to serve the interests of a variety of users, and the objective is to provide the data necessary to reconstruct in all essential respects any copy of the text of any poem.

Two distinctive, almost unique, features of the *Variorum*, made possible by the exhaustive accumulation of textual data and the employment of enhanced analytical methods, are the identification of authorial sequences of poems and—in cases where the differences are sufficient to justify such a procedure—the presentation of multiple authorial or bibliographically significant versions of poems and sequences. The volumes published to date have identified authorial sequences of the Elegies, the Epigrams, and the Holy Sonnets, and in the case of the latter two genres the edition has printed multiple authentic sequences that differ not only in the number and order of poems they contain, but also in the texts of individual poems. Volume 8, for instance, presents three different authorial sequences of Epigrams; and Volume 7.1 presents four sequences of the Holy Sonnets: an early twelve-poem, never-before-printed authorial sequence embodied in the Group-III manuscripts; an intermediate sequence uniquely preserved in the Westmoreland ms. (*Variorum* siglum NY3), which repeats—with some authorial revision of the texts of individual sonnets—the twelve-poem Group-III arrangement, but adds not only four 'replacement sonnets' that Donne later substituted for four of the originals in his final arrangement, but also (uniquely) *HSShe*, *HSShow*, and *HSVex*; and a final sequence, found in the Group-I and -II manuscripts, that contains Donne's final revisions to the text and a reordered and reconstituted twelve-poem set of Sonnets. Finally, because it represents the form in which readers have historically encountered the Holy Sonnets and has formed the basis of so much critical and scholarly comment, the *Variorum* prints a typographical facsimile of the editorially constructed sequence introduced in the collected *Poems* of 1635 (B), which recovered from H6 the four Group-III sonnets that had been displaced in Donne's final revision and integrated them into the twelve-poem set that it had received from A. Illustrating the transmissional history of these poems by actually printing the various sequences enables readers to appreciate the extraordinary evolution of this set of poems in a way that no mere description of the process can.

In addition to the bibliographical advances made possible by the appearance of Beal's *Index*, the *Variorum* has also benefited from the recent emergence of computer technology, from the modern availability of more convenient and affordable means of travel, and from access to financial support for scholarly projects through the (American) National Endowment for the Humanities. Important tools used by the *Variorum* editors in the preparation and analysis of the textual evidence, for instance, are *The Donne Variorum Frame File Generator (F-GEN.exe)* and *The Donne Variorum Textual Collation Program (DV-COLL.exe)*, Windows-based computer programs written especially for the project and available free of charge at the *Donne Variorum* website: http://donnevariorum.tamu.edu. *F-GEN* simplifies the rendering of manuscript- or print-derived texts into collatable, electronic files; and *DV-COLL*, which is capable of comparing on a character-by-character basis up to 250 electronic copies of a given poem at once, facilitates analysis of the textual relationships among those copies. Among the most impressive products of these tools are the stemmas mentioned above—of the original and revised versions of *ElBrac* and *ElPart* (2.45–6 and 2.365, respectively) and of the sequences of Holy Sonnets in volume 7.1 (LXIV). Discovery of the kind of precise genealogical relationships illustrated in these stemmas still requires rigorous human analysis, but that process is greatly facilitated by the computer's ability to manipulate large quantities of data; and as a result the *Variorum* is able to establish more accurate and authoritative texts and sequences of Donne's poems than has hitherto been possible.

The *Variorum* project has so far taken about three decades, and less than half of the corpus of Donne's poems has yet been published: projected volumes on the Satires, the Songs and Sonets, the Verse Letters, and the Hymns and occasional religious poems lie in the future, as does a concluding volume—essentially the continually updated DigitalDonne website—that will add formal bibliographical descriptions of the textual artefacts to the first-line indexes and other bibliographical aids already available on the project's website. A great deal of the initial work has involved the immensely time-consuming and expensive business of collecting microfilms or photographs of every known manuscript or print source, transcribing each copy of every poem into a specially designed computer file formatted with *F-GEN*, and then proofreading these files against the originals *on site*, a verification not always possible for earlier editors who lived when travel was more difficult. After nearly thirty years a complete database of verified files has finally been compiled, and the transcriptions used in the editing of the four volumes that have appeared in print are available for download on the *Variorum* website, with others to follow as the edition proceeds. Providing free public access to the tools and materials developed within a project heavily underwritten by public funds is one of the ways in which the *Variorum* editors seek to keep faith with the animating

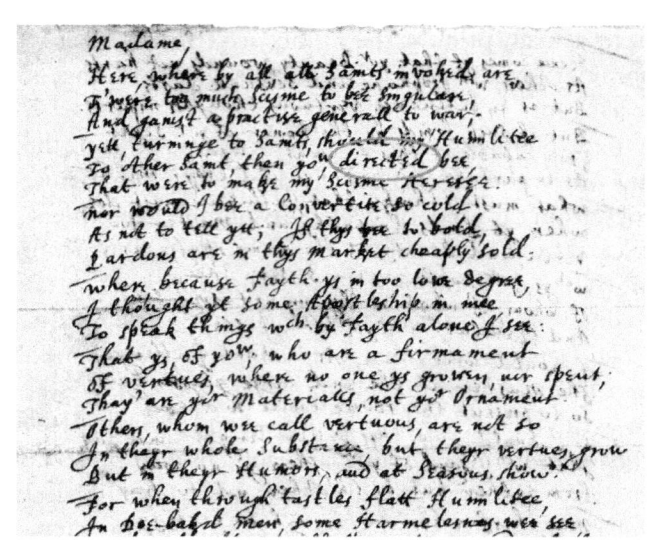

Ill. 4.II.1. Holograph Verse Letter (*Carey*) to Lady Lettice Carey and Essex Rich, the sisters of Lord Robert Rich, who visited Donne at Amiens in early 1612, when this letter was likely written. Apart from book inscriptions this is Donne's only poem extant in holograph, discovered in 1970 among papers of the Duke of Manchester. (University of Oxford, Bodleian Library, MS. Eng. Poet. D. 197, recto. Reproduced with the kind permission of the Bodleian Library, University of Oxford.)

principles of the National Endowment for the Humanities, which has supported the project for over thirty years.

The *Variorum*'s aims and achievements have generally, but not invariably, been met with approbation. In reviewing volume 8, for instance, Brian Vickers opines that in printing three sequences of Epigrams the edition gives 'too much space' to 'some rather mediocre material' (1999: 108) and further laments that the 'pointing' in the edition is at times 'too light' (ibid. 109), citing a passage in *Eclog* as an example. And writing in *The Year's Work in English Studies*, Holly Nelson cites the (unattributed) theoretical objection that the *Variorum* effort is 'imprudent because it is guided by a nostalgic impulse to reach an irretrievably lost original holograph and to exhume authorial intentions' (H. F. Nelson 517). Despite such demurrals, however, it is indisputable that the *Variorum* has reinvented the editing of Donne's poetry. As both beneficiaries of and contributors to the recent growing interest in the material culture of the seventeenth century, the *Variorum* editors have placed themselves in something of the same position that John Marriot faced as he set about gathering manuscript copies of the poems for the first edition of 1633—except that they have accumulated vastly more data than Marriot knew (or would likely have been able to cope with), and they have had the benefit of three-and-a-quarter centuries of editorial hindsight. Remembering that the edition makes available a great deal of material to which readers have not previously had access, including material that can be used to critique its own goals and procedures, we are perhaps best served, as Haskin has suggested, by viewing the textual work of the *Variorum* 'less as an iconic monument than as a critical tool...a ground from which to raise and explore many questions that could not have been productively defined' without the evidence now brought to hand (2002*b*: 207).

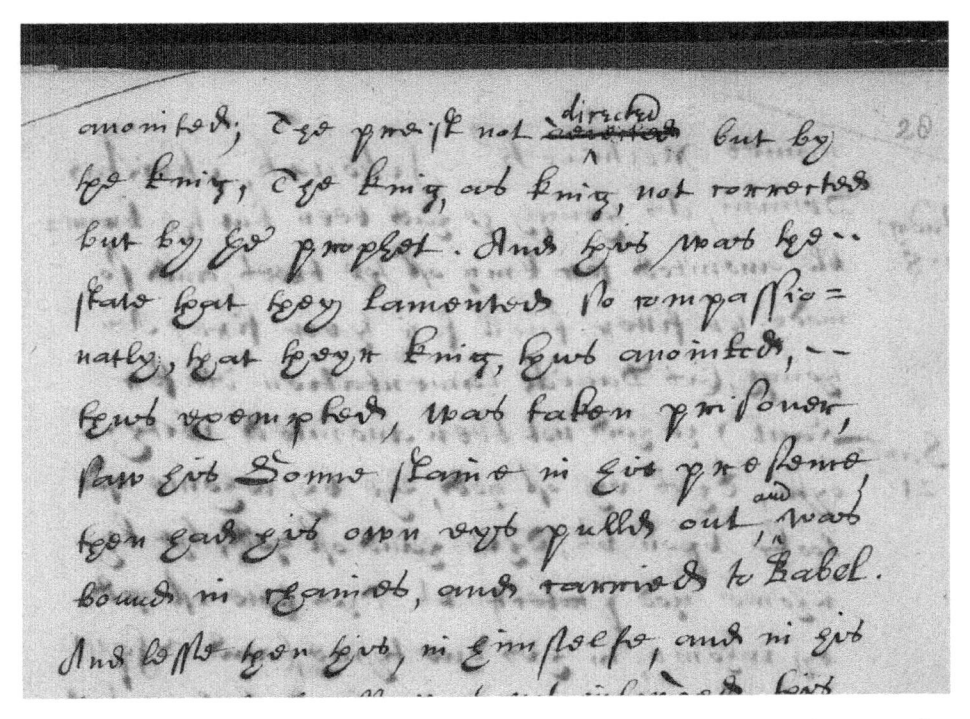

Ill. 4.II.2. Page from Sermon with holograph corrections: This scribal manuscript, corrected in Donne's hand, was identified in the British Library in 1992 by Jeanne Shami. The handwriting of the word 'directed' (BL, MS. Royal.B.XX, fo. 28ʳ, line 1) is virtually identical to that of the same word on line 5 of the holograph Verse Letter. Both have the same long upright ascender on *d*, the same break after the *i* before the *r* begins, the same *r* with high ligature to epsilon *e*. The epsilon *e* leading to a curled-back *d* in the Sermon is identical to the epsilon *e* leading to straight ascender *d* of the poem, but the *d* of the Sermon is one of the most characteristic of Donne's letters. (© The British Library Board. Ms. Royal 17.B.XX.)

Group III		Group IV	Group I	Group II	1633 ed.	1635–69 eds.
B46 H5 HH1	C9–H6	NY3	B32 C2 O20 SP1	B7 CT1 DT1 H4 WN1[1]	A	B-G
Diuine Meditations	Diuine Meditations	Holy Sonnets	Holy Sonnets	none	Holy Sonnets	Holy Sonnets
1. (HSMade)	1. (HSMade)	1. (HSMade)	om	om	om	I. (HSMade)
2. (HSDue)	2. (HSDue)	2. (HSDue)	1. (HSDue)	1. (HSDue)	I. (HSDue)	II. (HSDue)
3. (HSSighs)	3. (HSSighs)	3. (HSSighs)	om	om	om	III. (HSSighs)
4. (HSPart)	4. (HSPart)	4. (HSPart)				
5. (HSBlack)	5. (HSBlack)	5. (HSBlack)	2. (HSBlack)	2. (HSBlack)	II. (HSBlack)	IV. (HSBlack)
						V. (HSLittle)
6. (HSScene)	6. (HSScene)	6. (HSScene)	3. (HSScene)	3. (HSScene)	III. (HSScene)	VI. (HSScene)
7. (HSLittle)	7. (HSLittle)	7. (HSLittle)	om	om	om	
8. (HSRound)	8. (HSRound)	8. (HSRound)	4. (HSRound)	4. (HSRound)	IV. (HSRound)	VII. (HSRound)
						VIII. (HSSouls)
9. (HSMin)	9. (HSMin)	9. (HSMin)	5. (HSMin)	5. (HSMin)	V. (HSMin)	IX. (HSMin)
10. (HSSouls)	10. (HSSouls)	10. (HSSouls)	om	om	om	
11. (HSDeath)	11. (HSDeath)	11. (HSDeath)	6. (HSDeath)	6. (HSDeath)	VI. (HSDeath)	X. (HSDeath)
12. (HSWilt)	12. (HSWilt)	12. (HSWilt)				
	Other Meditations					
	[13] (HSSpit)	13. (HSSpit)	7. (HSSpit)	7. (HSSpit)	VII. (HSSpit)	XI. (HSSpit)
	[14] (HSWhy)	14. (HSWhy)	8. (HSWhy)	8. (HSWhy)	VIII. (HSWhy)	XII. (HSWhy)
	[15] (HSWhat)	15. (HSWhat)	9. (HSWhat)	9. (HSWhat)	IX. (HSWhat)	XIII. (HSWhat)
	[16] (HSBatter)	16. (HSBatter)	10. (HSBatter)	10. (HSBatter)	X. (HSBatter)	XIV. (HSBatter)
			11. (HSWilt)	11. (HSWilt)	XI. (HSWilt)	XV. (HSWilt)
			12. (HSPart)	12. (HSPart)	XII. (HSPart)	XVI. (HSPart)
		17. (HSShe)				
		18. (HSShow)				
		19. (HSVex)				

[1] Lacks poems 9–12

Ill. 4.II.3. Sequences of Holy Sonnets in the seventeenth-century artefacts (*Donne Variorum* 7.1.LXII). This table lists (left to right) the successive arrangements of Holy Sonnets in extant seventeenth-century manuscripts and editions, thus describing the early transmissional history of the poems. For identification of sigla and discussion of bibliographical details, see *Variorum* 7.1.XXXII–XXXVIII and LX–LXIV. (Reproduced with the permission of Indiana University Press.)

CHAPTER 5

MODERN SCHOLARLY EDITIONS OF THE PROSE OF JOHN DONNE

ERNEST W. SULLIVAN, II

1

TEXTUAL bibliographers attempt to provide scholarly editions of works that accurately represent what authors wrote as well as factual and insightful commentary to aid scholars, students, and general readers in understanding texts. Most textual scholarship on Donne's works has concentrated on his poetry (see Chs. 4.I and 4.II); however, in the twentieth century scholarly editions of Donne's prose began to appear.

A brief discussion of how scholarly editions are created will illustrate their value to different readers. Textual bibliographers attempt to identify every manuscript and print version of a text that could have been influenced by the author. The original artefacts containing these texts (paper or vellum manuscripts, books, stones, paintings, etc.) are then examined for their physical details (ink, watermarks, evidence of ownership, etc.) for clues that would establish authenticity, date, provenance, and relationships among the artefacts in order to determine how and when the text was created and evolved. Once this physical evidence has been established, textual bibliographers compare all aspects of every form of the text with those of every other text in order to fill out what can be known about its creation and genesis.

Once all the relationships among all known versions of a text have been worked out, the textual bibliographer can produce a text for a scholarly edition based on which version of the text best represents what the author wrote and which incorporates any revisions for which the author is likely responsible. Finally, the textual introduction outlines the main features of the textual situation and the theoretical approaches used to solve any textual problems, and a textual apparatus reports all the differences among the various states of the text.

Without the scholarly edition, even professional scholars gaining (with much work and expense) access to all of the manuscripts and rare books necessary would still need to sort out much information in order to have confidence in what they were reading. Students could access microfilm or digital images of many printed artefacts (themselves imperfect copies of original manuscripts) and a few manuscripts but would have no way to assess the accuracy of these texts. General readers could access few of these materials on the Internet.

In addition to reliable and accurate texts, scholarly editions provide scholarly commentary on the contents of the text, generally in the form of introductory essays and notes, setting the work in its literary and historical/cultural traditions, dating and placing it in the context of the author's life, and reviewing its critical reception and history, thus providing basic context and information needed to interpret the text intelligently. Recent scholarship has shown the complexity of the problems facing those who would construct scholarly editions of Donne's various prose works. The present and past state of work on these editions shows that different theoretical and practical approaches have been, and will be, required to produce reliable and accurate texts. I will consider the scholarly success or failure of notable editions of Donne's prose works in the order of their original appearance in print.

2

Donne published *Pseudo-Martyr* in 1610. The book does not pose a formidable textual challenge since the only manuscript versions are a few extracts derived from the first printing (Beal 1980: 563), and the work was printed in only one edition. Even so, there are important textual issues: the work was printed with enough proofreading care that many stop-press corrections (corrections made during the printing process that result in different readings in different copies of the work) appear. Donne shows his care for the accuracy of the printing with an errata sheet listing corrections he desired in the text and marginal notes; however, his statements about these corrections are ambiguous ('Those literall and punctuall Errors, which doe not much endanger the sense, I haue left to the discretion and fauour of the Reader, as he shall meete with them. The rest he may be pleased to mend thus' [¶2ᵛ]), leaving the reader to correct what Donne considered errors not affecting meaning.

The commentary for an edition of *Pseudo-Martyr* poses a formidable challenge: the work does not fit easily into any genre; the issues under debate in the Oath of Allegiance and the sources for Donne's arguments are unfamiliar to modern readers; the work has little critical history (requiring the editor to provide the reader with the contexts for interpreting it); and, judging from a table of contents listing fourteen chapters for a work containing only twelve, the book appears incomplete. The only modern edition of *Pseudo-Martyr* is that by Anthony Raspa (1993), an edition marred by a problematical textual theory, text, and commentary.

Even though Raspa examined eighty-two copies of *Pseudo-Martyr* (listed on lvi–lviii, some of them previously unrecorded) and provided a useful discussion of the book's printing, he failed to provide a text that meets modern standards of textual theory and accuracy. The most important textual decision for any editor is the choice of copy-text, the text the editor believes best represents what the author wrote and serves as the basis for the text of the scholarly edition. With only one edition and no separate issues extant (the derivative and fragmentary manuscript material, unmentioned by Raspa, is probably irrelevant to establishing the text of *Pseudo-Martyr*), choice of copy-text would seem an easy task—just pick a copy. In the case of *Pseudo-Martyr*, however, so many corrections were made during the printing process that virtually every copy has a different text. Seventeenth-century printers corrected their texts in units called 'formes' that held all the pages of type used for a single impression rather than by 'leaves' or pages. Ordinarily, an editor would compile a table of these press variants, indicating whether they were printed on an inner or outer forme and whether they represent a corrected or uncorrected state of the text. The editor would then select that copy requiring the least emendation to reveal the corrected state. Raspa does not analyse the variants by inner and outer forme or corrected and uncorrected state, and, finding 'no avowedly superior or inferior copies' (lxxviii), selects two copies as his copy-text based on their having 'survived equally well the intemperies of almost four hundred years' (lxxviii). And even though the two copies selected by Raspa differ in their texts, he does not establish when he is using both copies as copy-text, or one, or the other, or why he might choose one over the other at a particular point. Thus the reader has no idea why any particular reading in the text best represents what Donne wrote. Since Raspa does not tabulate the variants by forme, he has no convenient way to report them all in his textual apparatus, so he abandons textual practice and reports only variants in 'a selected number of other copies' (lxxxviii) without mentioning how those copies were selected. And even when he does report press variants, he does so in modern typography (regularizing the use of i/j, i/y, and u/v), leaving the reader without access to the original reading. Raspa does follow standard practice in reporting emendations he makes to the copy-texts, except that he does not report his changes to spelling, capitalization, and, in the marginal notes, punctuation.

These failures to follow standard textual practice might be less worrisome if there were not so many errors in the text Raspa does provide. These errors begin on his title page for Donne's text, where a hyphen between 'PSEUDO' and 'MARTYR' is omitted; a comma appears after 'MARTYR' where the original has a period; and Raspa prints *'fate'* instead of *'fat'* in the quotation from Deut. 32.15 (1). Overall, Raspa's text will not suffice for scholars performing close readings or requiring lengthy quotations; they might turn instead to the 1974 Scholar's Facsimiles & Reprints reproduction of the British Library first-edition copy (which Raspa uses as one of his two copy-texts) or to the Early English Books Online photographic reproduction of the Huntington Library's first edition copy.

However, Raspa's critical introduction offers a learned and detailed historical, biographical, and theological context for Donne's complex argument to convince English Catholics not to incur a false martyrdom by refusing to take the Oath of Allegiance to King James I. Further, Raspa's commentary elucidates Donne's hundreds of marginal references as well as the persons, places, and things (including theological and legal technicalities) mentioned throughout the volume.

3

In 1611 Donne published *Ignatius His Conclave* in two Latin editions (one in England and one on the continent) and in one English edition. Three subsequent editions in English appeared: in 1626, in 1634/35, and in the *Paradoxes, Problemes, Essayes, Characters*, a collection of Donne's miscellaneous writings published by his son in 1653 (not 1652, the date on the book's title page; see Raspa 2001: lvii). A third Latin edition appeared in 1680. Donne's name did not appear on the title page until the English third edition of 1634. The only surviving manuscript material related to *Ignatius* is an undated and anonymous translation into English titled 'Conclave Ignati: Ignatius his Closet' in the British Library (MS Harl. 1019). The Latin and English versions both contain less-than-thorough errata lists provided by Donne (E5^v and G8, respectively).

The chief textual issues revolve around the primacy of the Latin and English versions of the text and their interrelationship, the relationship of the manuscript to the printed texts, and the extent of Donne's involvement in the printing process. The standard modern edition of both the Latin and English texts of *Ignatius* is that by T. S. Healy (1969). On the basis of substantial external and internal evidence, Healy establishes the priority of the Latin printing. Then, carefully reading the texts themselves, he establishes that Donne wrote the Latin first. Using further evidence in the texts plus echoes in *Biathanatos* (unpublished in 1610), Healy establishes that

Donne himself did the English translation. Healy also establishes that the Latin text printed in England served as the copy-text for the continental Latin edition and appropriately selects the earlier text for his Latin copy-text. Finally, Healy establishes that the 1680 Latin edition derives from the continental Latin edition of 1611.

For his English text, Healy examined the seven known copies of the 1611 first edition, finding no press variants but many errors in the printing. Healy proves that the 1626 edition derives from the 1611, that the editions dated 1634 and 1635 are actually only separate issues of the same typesetting with different title pages, and that (contrary to its title page) the text of *Ignatius* in the 1653 miscellany derives solely from the edition of 1634. He identifies all copies collated and his specific copy-texts: the British Library copy of 1611 printed in England for his Latin and one of two 1611 copies at Harvard for his English text (li). Healy uses the later editions to correct manifest errors in his copy-texts, adopts the readings in the errata lists, and even uses the Latin edition to correct errors in the English. In a footnote (lii), Healy shows his acquaintance with R. C. Bald's discovery (1970) of the manuscript translation, 'Conclave Ignati: Ignatius his Closet', noting that Bald felt the manuscript was simultaneous with Donne's own translation of *Ignatius* and that the translation was not by Donne. Healy's textual work lacks complete bibliographical descriptions of the volumes and reproductions of the title pages (though these are readily available in Keynes 1973: 16–24). The facing-page Latin and English texts make it easy to check differences between the two and have the added advantage that Healy can key his commentary to just the English text.

The critical introduction and commentary are the larger and more complex task facing the editor. Healy provides a learned and useful introduction, examining Donne's Latin and English styles, the historical setting including similar works, connections to Donne's other works, and the nature and targets of Donne's satire. In addition to the commentary noted above, Healy provides appendices of differences between the Latin and English texts, Donne's sources, and Donne's collaboration with Thomas Morton in theological controversy.

4

Donne's Sermons, both in their texts and commentary, present by far the largest challenge of any of his prose works to an editor. The first textual problem is the great mass of text and number of textual artefacts. Only six of Donne's Sermons were printed during his lifetime, the first in 1622 (see Ch. 24). The three great posthumous folio collections of 1640 (*LXXX Sermons*), 1649 (*Fifty Sermons*), and 1660 (*XXVI Sermons*, which actually contains twenty-three Sermons) contain another

153 sermons. One further Sermon, not printed until the twentieth century, exists in two manuscript copies, bringing the total of printed Sermons to 160. In addition to the potentially authoritative printed texts of the Sermons, nineteen Sermons survive in manuscripts; variant readings in these also have potential textual authority.

Henry Alford's 1839 edition of the Sermons was the first post-seventeenth-century edition, but neither its text nor its commentary meets modern standards (but see Haskin 2007: 58–66 for a discussion of the significance of this edition). The only scholarly edition of Donne's Sermons has been that of George Potter and Evelyn Simpson (1953–62). Potter and Simpson revolutionized both textual work and critical commentary on the Sermons with an edition based on collation of all the then known manuscripts and seventeenth-century printed editions.

In spite of the efforts that went into the monumental achievement of Potter and Simpson, their theoretical and methodological approaches no longer meet the standards of a modern scholarly edition. Potter and Simpson chose the three posthumous folio editions as their copy-texts, even though they realized that the earlier quartos and manuscripts often contain 'the text substantially as Donne preached it' (*Sermons* 1.57). Additionally, their collational work on the folios was limited to an unacceptably small number of copies (ten, often inadequately identified); and their account of the stop-press variants these collations were intended to discover shows their failure to understand the process of correction by forme, leaving them unaware of the order in which the corrections were made. And, inevitably, Potter and Simpson could not have known of the manuscript texts of the Sermons discovered after 1962, some of which have reconfigured the relationships among the texts of several of the Sermons and, hence, their relative claims to representing what Donne wrote (*1622 Sermon*; Shami 2008a).

The Potter and Simpson commentary also suffers from theoretical and methodological deficiencies. These editors chose to arrange the Sermons chronologically; however, since sixty-six of the 160 Sermons are undated, Potter and Simpson were forced to guess at dates, yielding a sequence and groupings of limited use to readers. In the commentary itself, Potter and Simpson demurred that 'many passages in the sermons that deserve explanatory or critical consideration we leave to future scholars' (2.v). Lacking modern scholarship on the genre and subgenres of the sermon, Potter and Simpson frequently misunderstood the structural and stylistic features of the Sermons.

A new scholarly edition of Donne's Sermons, sponsored by Oxford University Press, hopes to solve some of the problems of the Potter and Simpson edition by collating many more copies of printed texts and by incorporating the newly discovered manuscripts (at least one of which has corrections in Donne's handwriting: *1622 Sermon* 13–19) and what has been discovered about them. The editors of the new edition will then select their copy-texts by determining which copy is closest in form and date to the Sermon as originally preached by Donne. Instead of grouping the Sermons chronologically, the new editors will organize them by place of preaching. Hence, Donne's carefully constructed links among Sermons composed as a series for the same audience over large periods of time—to the benchers of Lincoln's Inn over an academic term or terms, or at court during Donne's annual month of service there, or the extended series on his prebendal Psalms at St Paul's—will become apparent to readers. The commentary in this new edition will place Donne in the intellectual context of his time and make his Sermons more accessible to students and scholars by annotating his biblical, patristic, scholastic, and contemporary theological sources; identifying his uses of classical and biblical languages; demonstrating his engagement with other disciplines and contemporary political and religious debate; and identifying *loces communes* in his other works (including poetry).

5

Donne's popular essay on his grave illness during November and December of 1623, *Devotions upon Emergent Occasions*, first appeared in print in 1624 (with a second issue in the same year); a second edition was published also in 1624, a third in 1626 (with its second issue in 1627), a fourth in 1634, and a fifth in 1638. John Sparrow (1923a: xxvii) gives evidence that a translation into Dutch was printed in Amsterdam in 1655. This version of the text has been identified by Paul Sellin (1983: 39–42) as Johann Grindal's *Aendachtige Bedenckingen*.

The first edition of the *Devotions* contains an errata list (A6^v), though there is no evidence that Donne proofread the volume during printing. No manuscript text is known to have survived, though Keynes (1973: 82) records a copy of the 1627 edition formerly belonging to Sparrow that contains an English verse rendering of Donne's Latin 'Stationes' preceding each section of the text. However, questions of genre and literary tradition as well as biographical, historical, and cultural context present real problems for the commentary.

The two modern editions are those of Sparrow (1923) and Raspa (1975). Sparrow rightly considers the two 1624 and 1626 editions as alone having authority for his text; he uses the first edition of 1624 as his copy-text, with the second of 1624 and the 1626 edition as the basis for his emendations. Sparrow does not investigate whether Donne was involved in any changes made in the second 1624 and 1626 editions. Aside from regularizing i/j and u/v, Sparrow retains Donne's spelling and punctuation. Sparrow's introduction and commentary are minimal and, given the complexity of the *Devotions*, are not satisfactory for most readers.

In his edition Raspa gives a detailed description of the printing history of the *Devotions*, arguing that flagrant errors in the 1634 and 1638 editions, derived from the earlier editions, discredit their textual authority (xliv–xlv). Incidentally, Raspa muddies the textual waters by arguing that there was only one issue of the first 1624 edition, because the only difference between the two 1624 texts occurs on the title page (xlvi). But this minor change in typesetting without a complete resetting of the type that would constitute a new edition is precisely the hallmark of an 'issue'. Thus, there are actually two issues of the first 1624 edition. Raspa's account of the genesis of the text has the first edition serving as copy-text for the second, the second for the third, the second and possibly the third for the fourth, and the third and fourth for the fifth (xlviii–li). The *Variorum Edition of the Poetry of John Donne*, working with just the preliminary verse 'Stationes', has the first, second, and third editions all influencing the fourth (*Variorum* 8.242–3). Since all editions ultimately derive from the first, Raspa correctly chooses it as his copy-text; however, without explanation or justification he uses three separate copies as his 'master text' (lii). As with Raspa's edition of *Pseudo-Martyr*, there is no analysis of press variants and no explanation of why these copies were selected. Since there is no mention of press variants, all copies must read identically, obviating any need for three separate copy-texts.

Raspa offers a more thorough introduction than does Sparrow: he covers the efforts to identify Donne's disease and, at length, the tradition of Ignatian meditation and its relation to Donne's theology. Raspa's commentary notes are less full than those in his *Pseudo-Martyr*, but still provide extremely valuable aid in sorting through the persons, places, ideas, and cultural connections in the volume.

6

A group of short satirical works (eleven Paradoxes and ten Problems) first appeared in print in Donne's *Juvenilia* (1633), with a second edition in the same year. In *Paradoxes, Problemes, Essayes, Characters* (1653), Donne's son published a third edition (in two issues) of these short prose pieces while adding a twelfth Paradox, seven Problems, two Characters, and an Essay. R. C. Bald (1964: 198–203) found thirteen of the Problems translated into Latin by Louis Rouzee in his *Problematum Miscellaneorum* (1616).

Donne's Paradoxes and Problems present unusual problems for an editor, not only in that they survive in several versions in print and manuscript (Beal 1980: mss. DnJ 4060, DnJ 4061, DnJ 4062, DnJ 4063, DnJ 4068–89, and DnJ 4091–5), and not only because questions have arisen about the authorship of two

Paradoxes, but also (and more fundamentally, as is argued in Chs. 11.I and 17) because most bibliographers and critics have heedlessly accepted their first publisher's grouping them as 'Juvenilia', although they are neither generically nor chronologically proximate.

The standard modern edition is *Paradoxes and Problems* by Helen Peters (1980). Although Peters works very hard to sort out the extensive manuscript materials, her work is compromised by a variety of factors, some beyond her control. Lacking access to the ten Paradoxes in the Burley ms. (LRO, MS Finch, DG. 7, Lit. 2) recovered only in 1980, Peters had to rely on Evelyn Simpson's transcription of Herbert J. C. Grierson's collations of the Burley ms. against their texts in the *Juvenilia* (liv). Peters does not mention Beal (1980) manuscripts DnJ 4084, DnJ 4085–7, and DnJ 4089. Peters's assessment of the manuscripts she did work with is compromised by her reliance on dated and discredited information: for example, that the Burley ms. was Henry Wotton's commonplace book and that Donne's 'Group II' manuscripts result from a collection by Sir Robert Ker (liv and lxii). Peters does not do much better with the simpler textual problems in the printed texts. She argues that the 1633 first edition has a very poor text derived from a manuscript like the Stephens ms. at Harvard (li) and that the second 1633 edition was printed from the first, though she does not explain from where the missing lines of 'Why have Bastards best Fortune' are added (lxxxv). She also argues that the 1653 third edition is printed from the second 1633 edition, though she cannot identify the source of its one additional Paradox and seven additional Problems (lxxxiii). Peters doubts that Donne wrote 'A Defence of Women's Inconstancy' and 'That Virginity is a Vertue', solely because of their infrequent manuscript appearances, even though the first appears in all three seventeenth-century editions, and the second was included by Donne's son in the third edition (lxxxvi–lxxxvii). There seems no sufficient basis for her decision. Even so, her choice of the Westmoreland ms. as copy-text for the Paradoxes (lxxxix) and the O'Flahertie ms. for the Problems (xc) is fortuitous, though not well argued. Faced with multiple authoritative versions of the texts, Peters prints the text she considers final without explaining the basis for her ordering. Her textual notes report only readings from 'representative' artefacts (1 and 23).

Peters's introduction treats the Paradoxes and Problems alike as 'early works of "Jack Donne" written at different periods of his younger life' (xv), of interest mainly because of their similarities to much of Donne's poetry; but although she dates the Paradoxes to the early 1590s she can cite no evidence of them earlier than a Letter Keynes speculatively dates to 1600, when Donne was nearly 30. She uses internal references to date the Problems between 1603 and 1610 (xv), when Donne was no juvenile. She does not explain why the Problems should be referred to as 'early works'. She then usefully examines the history of the genre of the Paradox (xvi–xxii) and the Problem (xxvii–xxxviii) and speculates on Donne's possible revision of some Problems that exist in longer and shorter versions. Her commentary includes useful notes on textual matters and connections to other Donne works but not much glossing or critical analysis.

7

Biathanatos, first published by Donne's son in 1647, is a text that gives a bibliographer nightmares, but for this reason it is also a case study in the importance of textual editing, illustrating the effects of new discoveries on substantive textual issues. It survives in two issues of the 1647 quarto edition, an edition in 1700, a ten-page 'extract' dated 1652–3 by Beal (1980: 560) in Durham Cathedral's MS 132, and two complete manuscripts: one long known at the Bodleian Library, Oxford (MS e Musaeo 131); and another at Canterbury Cathedral (U210/2/2), discovered and described by Beal (1998), a discovery that has complicated the task of editing the book, as Beal points out. Before Beal's discovery of the Canterbury Cathedral ms. two modern editions had been published: one in 1982, edited by Michael Rudick and M. Pabst Battin; and one in 1984, edited by Sullivan. Both editions provide readers with background material for understanding *Biathanatos* in essays on its bibliographical features, connection to Donne's biography, critical reception, and sources, as well as commentaries on the material reflected in Donne's hundreds of marginal citations. Rudick and Battin's edition (Donne 1982: xcvii–xcix) supplies incomplete descriptions of the Bodleian manuscript (M) and the 1647 edition (Q) and non-diplomatic (non-literal) transcriptions of their title pages. Sullivan's supplies complete bibliographical descriptions of M, Q, and the edition of 1700, as well as diplomatic transcriptions of their title pages (xxxvi–lv). Both editions state that the 1700 text derives from Q and has no independent authority (Rudick and Battin xcix), with Sullivan's providing proof (*Biathanatos* lv). The principal differences between the two editions are that, while Rudick and Battin base their 'modern-spelling edition' (not usually a preference of scholarly editors) on Q (ci–ciii), Sullivan preserves seventeenth-century accidentals (spelling, punctuation, capitalization, font, and paragraphing), using M as the basis for his edition (lviii).

Beal's discovery of a second, independently authoritative, manuscript of *Biathanatos* at Canterbury Cathedral, however, has made clear the need for a new edition based on analysis and collation of the Canterbury ms. (as well as the Durham 'extract') to determine its relation to M and Q. Establishing the relationships among Canterbury, M, and Q is essential to selecting the optimum copy-text for a new edition of *Biathanatos*. In addition to the need for clarity about these relationships, further controverted issues will have to be addressed anew, including the dating of M (cf. Donne 1982: xcviii; *Biathanatos* xxxviii; Beal 1998: 36–7) and the significance of the notes duplicating the table of contents that are absent from the margins of M but that do appear in the margins of Q and Canterbury (cf. Donne 1982: cv; *Biathanatos* xxxvi–xxxvii and xxxix–xli; Beal 1998: 51–2).

8

Catalogus Librorum, a Latin introduction to and list of thirty-four imagined books and their often real authors, first appeared in the 1650 edition of *Poems, by J. D.*, edited by John Donne the younger, and was reprinted in the collected poems of 1654, 1669, and 1719. This work also survives in a scribal copy at Trinity College, Cambridge, as '*Catalogus librorum aulicorum incomparabilium et not vendibilium*' ('The Courtier's Library of Rare Books Not for Sale').

The manuscript and printed text differ significantly, and Evelyn M. Simpson in her edition (81) argues that the differences derive from Donne; the text and significance of any supposed authorial revisions pose substantial challenges to an editor, as do arcane contents and unusual genre. The two modern editions are those of Simpson (1930) and Piers Brown (2008), which reproduces Simpson's text. Simpson tries to establish that the manuscript, in omitting two consecutive book titles, reflects an authorial revision of the 1650 printed version (83–5). But she presents no evidence that this skip in the manuscript was not simply an error of the scribe, having no direct connection to Donne. This alternative explanation is ironically supported by Simpson's having settled on 1650 as the text on which to base her edition, arguing that Donne's revision of the *Catalogus* in the Cambridge manuscript was 'hasty and perfunctory' (88). Since both texts contain numerous errors and mistakes, Simpson's preference rests largely (and sensibly) on the more logical ordering and inclusion of items in the 1650 catalogue part of the work, though she does use the manuscript for much of the format (including inserting 'CATALOGUS LIBRORUM' as the heading of the work and adding 'AULICORUM *incomparabilium et* NON VENDIBILIUM' to the heading). Simpson reports the differences between the 1650 and manuscript versions and includes many useful notes on anomalies in the transcription of the manuscript. The textual work, however, is not to modern standards because she does not identify the specific copy of 1650 used as the copy-text, gives no indication of collating its text against multiple copies for press variants, and does not collate its text against the other seventeenth-century printings (the failure to collate the 1669 edition is particularly problematic because some of its texts derive from manuscripts different from those used for the earlier editions). Simpson also provides an English translation by her husband Percy, a brief history of criticism on the *Catalogus*, contexts for its satiric genre, and a discussion of its historical, cultural, and biographical significance. She also provides explanatory notes on all the items in the *Catalogus*. Despite Simpson's good work, the *Catalogus* needs editing to modern textual standards, using post-1930 scholarship on Donne's biography as well as his other satirical and paradoxical works.

The need has not entirely been filled by Brown (2008), whose edition does not utilize textual bibliography, simply reprinting the text of Simpson's Latin edition while providing a new translation and a new introduction. Brown's introduction briefly updates Simpson's history of criticism on the *Catalogus* and places the work more fully in the contexts of humanist reading and secretarial counsel at the late Elizabethan court. As for biographical context, Brown varies little from Simpson, for example accepting (833) her dating of 1611 for an undated Latin Letter Donne wrote to his friend Sir Henry Goodere, mentioning the *Catalogus*. (For a different dating of this letter, see Ch. 30.I.)

9

The text of Donne's *Essayes in Divinity* poses relatively few problems for an editor, though its date, the unusual nature of the work, and its complex ideas and multiple sources present a substantial task. Nothing of the *Essayes in Divinity* survives in manuscript, and it exists in only one authoritative version: the first edition printed in 1651 by Thomas Maxey for Richard Marriot, with its sheets later bound up and published following the text of *Ignatius His Conclave* in both issues of the 1653 *Paradoxes, Problemes, Essayes, Characters*. Sorting out the printing of the text, then, is the major task for the editor of the *Essayes in Divinity*. Of particular interest is a nine-page dedicatory letter that appeared in some but not all copies.

The two modern scholarly editions are by Simpson (1952) and Raspa (2001). In sorting out the different printings, Simpson conjectures (xxviii) that Donne's son, the editor of both printings, for political reasons 'canceled' the original 1651 dedication to 'Sir H. Vane' to dedicate the *Paradoxes, Problemes, Essayes, Characters* to Francis Lord Newport, omitting from that issue signatures A3–7ᵛ of the 1651 text. Keynes, although he accepts Simpson's theory about the suppression of the address to Vane, questions her account of these leaves, first because not all copies of the 1651 issue contain them, and second because in the binding of the 1653 edition 'the cancellation was often very carelessly done', leaving one or more leaves intact (1973: 128). Copies of the 1651 and 1653 dedicatory material come bound in several versions of page order and content, proving the need to examine every possible copy. Simpson does not identify the individual copy of the 1651 text that she uses as her copy-text, though she mentions four she has seen—at the Bodleian Library; Christ Church

College Library, Oxford; Worcester College Library, Oxford; and her own (xxix). On the basis of her own judgement and notes from an 1855 edition of the *Essayes* by Augustus Jessopp, Simpson emends various errors in the text (xxix).

Simpson speculatively dates the *Essayes*, on the basis of their interest in theology, after *Ignatius His Conclave* (ix–x). She then takes up what little critical attention the *Essayes* had received and adds considerable material of her own on the connections between the *Essayes* and Donne's other works. Further, Simpson provides a useful identification of Donne's many sources and an extensive set of notes using her experience in editing Donne's Sermons.

For his edition of 2001 Raspa inspected forty-six copies of the *Essayes in Divinity*, nineteen of them bound alone and presumably issued in 1651, and twenty-seven copies bound into the *Paradoxes, Problemes, Essayes, Characters* (liv–lvi). The examination of so many copies allowed Raspa to prove that the copies lacking the dedicatory address to Vane were equally distributed between the 1651 edition and the *Paradoxes, Problemes, Essayes, Characters*, establishing that there was only one issue of the *Essayes in Divinity* (lxi). Raspa disputes Simpson's conjecture of a political motive for the cancellation of the dedicatory address to Vane and instead attributes the cancellation to the 'strains and stresses of manual mid-seventeenth-century printing' (lxi). On the evidence of the *Stationers' Register* and publishers' records and advertisements, Raspa concludes that after an initial offering of the individual *Essayes* volume in 1651, sales resumed a year-and-a-half later, with two issues of *Paradoxes, Problemes, Essayes, Characters* in the spring of 1653, not 1652 as editors and critics had asserted, accepting the date on the title page, which reflects the old reckoning of 25 March as the turn of the new year (lvii–lxi).

As in his editing of *Pseudo-Martyr* and the *Devotions*, Raspa does not choose just one copy-text. Averring that 'no copy that has survived can be considered as inherently superior to another', he eschews analysis of press variants, arguing that, since leaves imprinted at various stages of the printing process were commonly and promiscuously bound together, there can be no meaningful pattern of variants apart from indications 'of good and bad luck' (lxxiv). Raspa arrives at this conclusion after having collated four additional copies against his chosen copy-texts and having 'checked for further variant frequency' against thirteen additional copies (lxxiv–lxxv). Raspa does list a number of press variants (lxxv); however, in the absence of any systematic analysis of the press variants by formes, the reader is left with no way to tell which variants represent the corrected states and no rationale for why Raspa's three copy-texts were selected, except that they are in 'prime condition' (lxxiv).

Raspa's introduction explains the reliance of the *Essayes* on the ancient tradition of biblical exegesis using the hexapla, hexaemeron, and heptaplus as adapted by Renaissance humanists in England and on the continent; and he explores Donne's use of typology in the *Essayes*. Raspa's commentary goes far beyond the standard explanatory notes to constitute a true commentary: in addition to the standard glosses and identifications, he provides lengthy analyses (some as long as four pages) of Donne's ideas and their historical and theological contexts.

10

Aside from the Sermons, Donne's Prose Letters pose the greatest challenge to an editor: the Letters are numerous, scattered, not easily accessible; new ones continue to appear; the surviving versions of them do not always provide reliable texts; a considerable critical tradition has to be dealt with; and the commentary is made more difficult by the sheer mass of details and the deliberately cryptic nature of their politically, personally, and theologically sensitive texts. Although individual and small groups of Letters had appeared in print earlier, the first major collection of Donne's Letters (129) appeared in 1651 as *Letters to Severall Persons of Honour*, again edited by John Donne the younger. Approximately 228 letters written by Donne survive: thirty-eight in Donne's own handwriting, twenty-seven in scribal copies (some in several copies), and the rest in several print artefacts (some of these printed Letters also exist in manuscript, and some exist in multiple print artefacts). Fortunately the number of Letters surviving in multiple versions in either manuscript or print or both is relatively small (about a quarter of the total), so the individual Letters do not pose the usual problems in determining the genesis of the text. Instead, the chief textual problems posed by the Letters lie in attribution, interference or error by the persons producing the surviving artefacts of the Letters, and the inevitable discovery of new Donne Letters.

Presently, would-be readers of Donne's Letters have only three, obviously unsatisfactory, modern editions: Gosse (1899), Hester (1977), and Oliver (2002). As with the Sermons, a new scholarly edition sponsored by Oxford University Press is under way using a team of editors with access to the materials compiled by Robert P. Sorlien and I. A. Shapiro for their uncompleted editions. Edmund Gosse's 'edition' of Donne's Letters is compromised by his intention to write a biography using the Letters as his main source of biographical material: 'the determination to force Donne's correspondence to illustrate his biography had become a necessary one' (1.xiv). He prints many Letters piecemeal or so rewritten into dialogues and conversations that they are virtually unrecognizable; and, moreover, they are silently modernized in spelling, punctuation, and paragraphing. Even though Gosse recognized the extraordinary deficiencies of the texts, dates, and addresses of the Donne Letters in his main sources (Donne's 1651 *Letters to Severall Persons of Honour* and Toby Matthew's *Collection of Letters* (1660), he readily admits that he has 'not attempted to annotate the Letters' (1.xvi) to solve these problems for readers. Gosse does print nineteen

Donne Letters for the first time, but a comparison of his text of Donne's 1623 Letter to the Duke of Buckingham, printed from a manuscript in Donne's own hand, proves his text no better than the seventeenth-century texts he justifiably derides (Sullivan 1981: 122–3). And, of course, Gosse did not have access to the possibly thirty-five Donne Letters (of which about twenty are likely Donne's) in the Burley ms. (first printed by Simpson 1924: 284–320; 1948: 303–36) or the eight transcribed or holograph Letters discovered since 1924.

M. Thomas Hester's 1977 facsimile edition of the 1651 edition of *Donne's Letters to Severall Persons of Honour* goes far beyond facsimile status: his introduction not only contains a substantial essay, it also utilizes a large body of textual and biographical scholarship to date the Letters and identify their proper recipients. But his edition only provides 129 Donne Letters (one of the Letters is by Donne, but written for a friend) and no commentary. Distinctly less serviceable, Oliver (2002) provides only ninety-five Letters, each with only a brief contextual note and almost no annotation. The texts are also problematical: the spelling, punctuation, and paragraphing have been silently modernized; and corrections of the text have also been made silently. The reader, then, has no way of recovering the readings in the copy-texts. There is no evidence of collation of any texts, and the copy-texts are not identified by specific copy. Oliver's introduction does provide a brief biography of Donne and some analysis of Donne's style, though this analysis in large part tendentiously chastises Donne for his 'questionable qualities' (xiii) and 'the eccentricity of the mentality' (xvi) that gave rise to the Letters.

The forthcoming Oxford University Press edition will attempt to remedy the need for a scholarly edition of Donne's Letters by establishing and printing the entire canon of Donne's Letters (about 230 at present); providing reliable texts by collating multiple original copies (for appropriate Letters) of all possibly authoritative texts; giving a full textual apparatus with a bibliographical description of all the relevant artefacts and a complete reporting of all verbal variants and emendations of the copy-text; printing the Letters in chronological order by establishing their dates (most of these can now be determined); identifying the recipients of nearly all of the Letters; using the dates and recipients to provide a full context for each Letter; and providing commentary that guides readers through the persons, places, ideas, events, and connections to Donne's life and other works. This edition will also include introductory critical and textual essays that will cover Donne's use of the letter genre; the cultural, personal, and theological considerations that affect his markedly cryptic style in many of the Letters; the cultural context for the writing and exchange of letters; and the problems in ascertaining the reliability of the texts in the surviving artefacts.

Clearly, in conclusion, scholarly editions suffer from the vagaries of any human intellectual endeavour. There will always be disagreements over what textual theory or methodology will produce the most reliable text. The incredible complexity and detail of the texts and artefacts on which they are inscribed will inevitably result in human error. Sometimes the surviving artefacts have suffered alteration or damage sufficient to prevent recovery of a perfect text. And then there is every editor's darkest nightmare: the discovery of a new and authoritative version of the text. Even so, scholars and students should seek out and treasure scholarly editions. Every edition represents the best efforts of an expert to provide an accurate and reliable representation of the work, along with as many details as are known of when and how (and even by whom) the work came into being. Additionally, such editions provide the necessary biographical, historical, critical, and factual information to begin a thorough and intellectually satisfying study of the work. Any reader who wants to understand any literary work has to start with its scholarly edition.

CHAPTER 6

RESEARCH TOOLS AND THEIR PITFALLS FOR DONNE STUDIES

DONALD R. DICKSON

This chapter discusses the strengths, shortcomings, and significance of some fundamental research tools for Donne studies both in print and online. Included are assessments of the commentary in the Donne *Variorum*, some online tools and electronic repositories, various concordances for studying linguistic patterns, and specialized bibliographies and research guides. A cautionary word: while these short-cuts can streamline the process of gathering materials, reading an index to the Sermons cannot replace careful study of Donne's writings, just as reading an annotated bibliography (with its second-hand summaries of books and essays) cannot substitute for engaging with the critical tradition that has interpreted Donne's writings.

THE DONNE *VARIORUM*

Without question, the most useful tool in Donne studies to appear in the past twenty-five years has been the *Variorum Edition of the Poetry of John Donne*, edited by Gary A. Stringer *et al*. This edition not only provides a text that is as close to what Donne actually wrote as known evidence will permit (see Ch. 4.II), but also a reliable digest of all the critical commentary on the poems. This commentary provides essential information about the critical and scholarly discussion of both Donne's poems and their intellectual contexts. Two fundamental principles guiding the commentary are completeness and objectivity. The editors summarize all known literary criticism from Donne's time until the present, in English as well as in Czech, Dutch, French, German, Italian, Korean, Japanese, Polish, Portuguese, Russian, and Spanish. No other variorum edition has cast its nets so widely. This vast body of material is summarized without editorial opinion as to its validity, with the main criterion for inclusion being precedence. Thus, the first person to record a critical insight is credited for it (although others who make similar points are often noted by cross-referencing). This principle has the drawback of granting, in practice, the same status to any and all opinions, regardless of merit, obliging readers to evaluate for themselves. But such was the intent of the editors, who did not wish to establish their own 'normative' view of what the poems mean—as other variorum editors have done—but rather to present a summary that would enable scholars to sift the wheat from the chaff for themselves. Like all second-hand summaries, however, these commentaries are to be used with caution. They are intended to direct readers to available scholarly traditions and to encourage hands-on engagement with the works that comprise these traditions, not to render such engagement unnecessary.

Readers will find the critical commentary presented chronologically in narrative form and organized in levels that move from the most general to the most specific. For example, in the Holy Sonnets volume (7.1), at the highest level of organization can be found 'General Commentary on the Holy Sonnets', followed by discussions of 'Dating and Order', 'The Poet/Persona', 'Genre and Traditions', 'Language and Style', 'Prosody', 'Sacred and Profane', 'Themes', and 'The Holy Sonnets and Other Works'. After these presentations of topics common to all the Holy Sonnets, each individual poem is treated with general commentary, then notes and glosses of lines and words. While readers will find such ready access to the entire critical heritage for each poem or generic group of poems a great boon, they will need to reconcile the sometimes conflicting interpretations for themselves.

DigitalDonne

This research tool (http://digitaldonne.tamu.edu), initiated by Stringer at Texas A&M University, offers a sophisticated electronic version of some early print editions of Donne's poetry as well as access to several key manuscript texts upon which the Donne *Variorum* is based, together with tools for textual analysis and manipulation. Already, digital images and transcriptions of three early print editions owned by the Cushing Memorial Library at Texas A&M University have been mounted—*Poems, by J. D. with Elegies on the Authors Death* (1633b), the 1635 second edition, and the 1669 seventh issue—as have images with transcriptions of the St Paul's Cathedral Library ms., the O'Flahertie ms., and the Westmoreland ms. of Donne's poems, along with the O'Flahertie copy of Donne's *Letters to Severall Persons of Honour* (1654). This unique copy contains marginalia and bound-in notes by the mid-nineteenth-century bibliophile and Donne scholar, the Revd T. R. O'Flahertie. DigitalDonne includes the following features:

- images of each volume's spine, covers, and front and back matter;
- side-by-side presentation of 600-dpi colour images of each page of text and the *Donne Variorum* transcription;
- a tilepic capability, permitting zooming-in on images for minute examination;
- tables of contents sortable by order of appearance or poem title with hyperlinks to specific pages in the volume;
- page-by-page and jump-to-next-poem browsing capabilities;
- an on-screen concordance facility that allows users to isolate every occurrence of every word in the volume and to display each item in the context of both the image and the transcription;
- in-context flagging and exhibition of press variants, based on collation of additional copies of the edition against the primary copy;
- a composite list of formes detailing the press variants within each forme;
- a formal bibliographical description of each edition.

Several features make DigitalDonne a powerful research tool, especially its unique concordance capabilities (described below). But equally unprecedented is its comprehensive inventory of stop-press corrections, the first ever assembled for any of the seventeenth-century editions of Donne's *Poems*. (Because type was corrected during printing and uncorrected sheets were routinely bound up with the sheets containing stop-press corrections, each copy of an early book is potentially unique, and many copies of an early printing will be found to differ.) The primary imaged text of *Poems, by J. D.* (1633b) is the White copy (at the Cushing Memorial Library), which has been collated against copies at the Beinecke Library, the Folger Library, the British Library, the John Rylands Library, and St John's College, Oxford. Variants are marked by an asterisk in the text, and a pop-up box indicates whether it is in a corrected or uncorrected state. Elsewhere, a composite list of formes shows where press variants occur within each forme, thus demonstrating the degree to which each sheet was proofed.

DigitalDonne also presents manuscripts of Donne's poetry, making them available for analysis. Users can view these original artefacts under optimal conditions: through capacities built into all standard Web browsers, 600 dpi colour images can easily be magnified to present material details invisible to the naked eye. The transcriptions of these manuscripts in modern typeface (and in a format that makes them easy to manipulate) facilitates an analysis of the texts they contain. DigitalDonne will eventually make available the 5,000 or more transcriptions of the manuscript and early print copies of Donne's poems that the Donne *Variorum* editors have prepared over the years. In addition, a Donne *Variorum* companion website (http://donnevariorum.tamu.edu) presents useful tools for work on the manuscripts and editions that are raw materials for the *Variorum* texts. Some forty first-line indexes of seventeenth-century editions and manuscripts are already available online, along with the Donne *Variorum* Textual Collation software (DV-COLL) to study the various transcriptions. DV-COLL makes it possible to compare multiple versions of the same text. Since only the differences between a lead text and other versions are recorded by DV-COLL, users can easily see textual variations. For example, in line 345 of *Metem*, it is readily apparent that all but two witnesses, B29 and H6 (the Gosse ms. at the Folger and the O'Flahertie ms. at Harvard), read some version of 'outstreat'. Where there is agreement, for example, with 'nor', 'those', or 'thence', nothing is recorded.

158.B29.345	his flesh,	nor suck	those oyles	W^{ch}	thence out	sweat
158.F10.345			Oyles,			streat
158.H06.345	His flesh			w^{ch}		out-sweate
158.C02.345	His	sucke	oyles,			outstreate,
158.CT1.345	His		Oyles,			one streat
158.B07.345	His fflesh,		oyles,	w^{ch}		one streate
158.DT1.345	His fleash,		oyles,			streat
158.H04.345	His		oyles,			streat
158.00A.345	His		oyles,	which		outstreat,
158.00B.345	His		oyles,	which		outstreat,
158.00G.345	His		oyles	which		outstreat,

Thus, scholars can easily visualize differences and study the texts for themselves to verify (or challenge) the *Variorum* results.

Bibliographies

Geoffrey Keynes's *A Bibliography of Dr. John Donne*, first published in 1914, then expanded in 1932, 1958, and 1973, provides an analytical bibliography of Donne's published works that includes a full description of the format and make-up of each book and a facsimile of its title page as well as a list of the volume's contents.

Keynes covers all of Donne's prose works, the Letters, and all the editions of the poetry, including translations and musical settings of his poems. He reconstructs the list of works in Donne's personal library for which there is some evidence of ownership (213 titles), lists surviving images of the poet, and offers a checklist of older critical works, particularly useful for the nineteenth century and earlier. Another essential bibliographical research tool is Ernest W. Sullivan's *The Influence of John Donne: His Uncollected Seventeenth-Century Printed Verse* (1993), which records where Donne's verse was printed, translated, or adapted. While Keynes and Sullivan are indispensable for the bibliographical history of Donne, the three volumes of John R. Roberts's *John Donne: An Annotated Bibliography of Modern Criticism* (1973, 1982, 2004) should be the starting point for serious students of the critical tradition in Donne studies. Covering the years 1912–95, these three volumes provide a comprehensive guide to Donne scholarship. Roberts has provided essentially descriptive (rather than evaluative) annotations for all books, editions, monographs, chapters, essays, and notes written specifically on Donne. These often include substantial quotations or paraphrases that help readers evaluate whether an item is relevant to their research topics and so should be read. The items are arranged chronologically by date of publication (then alphabetically by author within each year) and assigned an item number; since the indexes are keyed to the item numbers, they are very easy to use. Included are an Index of Authors, Editors, Translators, Reviewers, and Illustrators; a Subject Index; and an Index of Donne's Works that is further divided by genre. A simple comparison of the number of items in each of the volumes reveals that enthusiasm for Donne's poetry has only increased since his 'discovery' by T. S. Eliot and other early twentieth-century poets. In the period from 1912 to 1967, 1,280 items were devoted to Donne (with a significant rise in the rate as the advocates of the New Criticism discovered Donne's utility in the post-war era); from 1968 to 1978, 1,044 items; and from 1979 to 1995, 1,572 items *in toto*. Roberts's bibliographies also show that critics continue to privilege Donne's love poems and Holy Sonnets over other genres—such as the Elegies, Verse Letters, Epigrams, and Epithalamions—and pay only scant attention to the Sermons and other prose. Another guide to the dizzying number of books and articles on Donne is the *MLA International Bibliography*, but comparison shows how comprehensive Roberts's work is. Searching the online *MLA International Bibliography* using 'Donne, John' in a subject search yields 630 entries for the years 1968–78 and 905 for 1979–95, whereas Roberts lists 1,044 and 1,572 items respectively for those same periods. One caution in using Roberts's volumes is that their topical indexes differ with each volume. In part, these differences chart the changing critical emphases in Donne studies from 1912 to 1995; in part, however, they reflect the editor's growing awareness of the importance of certain topics to Donne studies. Ideally, an index to all three volumes could be compiled to assist readers in identifying materials from all three volumes related to the 'new' topics.

Concordances

Combs and Sullens's *A Concordance to the English Poems of John Donne* has provided yeoman service since 1940. Combs and Sullens list guide-words in bold type followed by the full line in which the word appears along with an abbreviated reference (poem title, line number, and page reference to Herbert Grierson's one-volume *Poetical Works*). One strength is that guide-words appear in modern spelling while 'Donne's spelling' is used in the quoted lines of the text. Thus all three instances of *firmness* are listed together, even though spelled differently ('firmnesse' in *ValName* line 2, 'firmnes' in *ValMourn* line 35, and 'Firmness' in *ElProg* line 80). But this strength can also be a limitation, since modern spelling flattens out certain ambiguities: for example, the pun on *travel* and *travail* that Donne was fond of. Other limitations include its use of Grierson's edition, which has been replaced by other texts; its omission of nearly 200 common words (such as all pronouns and prepositions and many adverbs); and its omission of the Latin poems. Unlike Combs and Sullens's concordance, Celia Florén's more recent concordance, based on John Carey's modern-spelling edition of the poetry, includes all occurrences of every word in the poems. Useful features include an index of word frequency and a rhyme index. Both of these traditional concordances have now been superseded in terms of flexibility and comprehensiveness by the online concordance feature of DigitalDonne. This online tool can be used with any of the three earliest editions of Donne's poems (i.e. the 1633, 1635, or 1669 editions) and can display words and typographical features such as hyphenated constructs, parentheses, ampersands, and digraphs. Thus a student can find all instances in the 1635 text in which æ-ligatures—or *travel* and *travail*—were used. One weakness of the DigitalDonne concordance is that a search is limited to a single edition. Since the canon grew with each successive edition—*Poems, by J. D.* (1633*b*) contains about thirty fewer poems than a modern text of Donne's poetry—students will need to supplement their searches by consulting other editions. Furthermore, the DigitalDonne concordance is based on old-spelling texts that oblige searchers to be familiar with variant spellings of words. Had the vocabulary lists been lemmatized so that variant spellings of the same word were noted, the search capabilities would have been much enhanced. The ability to concord ampersands, or elision marks, however, makes the DigitalDonne concordance uniquely valuable.

John Donne Sermons

Another online resource for Donne studies is the electronic archive of John Donne Sermons in the Digital Collections at Brigham Young University Library (http://www.lib.byu.edu/dlib/donne). The text for this electronic archive is the ten-volume *Sermons of John Donne*, edited by George Potter and Evelyn Simpson (1953–62), which was scanned digitally and then subjected to optical character recognition (OCR) software to produce a machine-readable and hence searchable text. Files are displayed and printed as individual pages in portable document format (pdf). Although readers can search for any word or string of words in the electronic text or in any of six metadata fields—date (i.e. year), occasion (feast day or liturgical season), audience, location (i.e where a Sermon was preached), Old Testament or New Testament source-text—the results of these searches are not reliable because the text behind the scanned images is not reliable. Metadata fields can be used for basic searches, for example, to find how often Donne preached at Whitehall (28), but such a search does not indicate how often he preached before the king or the nobility 'at court' without specifying Whitehall as the location or those Sermons where the king was likely present but not identified in the title of the Sermon. One other significant limitation of John Donne Sermons is that it does not include the marginal scriptural citations that have been part of the presentation of Donne's Sermons since they were first printed. (Since only one autograph manuscript for a Sermon now exists, we simply do not know if the marginalia usually published as part of the Sermons are Donne's or an early scribe's.) Readers of the online Sermons, thus, do not have access to Potter and Simpson's textual apparatus that corrects and clarifies these marginalia. Troy D. Reeves has prepared *An Index to the Sermons of John Donne* in three volumes (*Index to the Scriptures*, *Index to Proper Names*, and *Index to Topics*). This index provides a fairly accurate listing of Donne's scriptural references and use of proper names, but the first two volumes should be used cautiously because of factual inaccuracies. Volume 3 presents its own difficulties because of its idiosyncratic and partial classification of Sermon topics (see Shami 1984*b*). Both the Index and online keyword-searching tools require considerable judgement from the user: they can direct readers to particular Sermons, but readers must resist the lure of easy access to these complex texts. There is no substitute—once the keywords are located—for reading the entire sermon in which they are located.

Handbooks

A. J. Smith's *John Donne: The Critical Heritage* is a useful compendium of critical observations on Donne from the seventeenth through the nineteenth centuries (and also provides some editorial commentary). The first volume gathers criticism from the seventeenth century until the late nineteenth century and offers an introductory survey of the ebb and flow of Donne's reputation as a poet, though Smith's survey ought to be supplemented by Raoul Granqvist's work and Dayton Haskin's *John Donne in the Nineteenth Century* for a more scholarly account of the history of the developing interest in his life and his Sermons. The second volume, completed by Catherine Phillips, contains writings from 1873 to 1923, when Donne's stature was being substantially enhanced as he became part of the literary canon (but see Haskin 2007: 104–5 on an extremely important omission from this volume). Robert Ray's *A John Donne Companion* (1990) offers a survey of the life and works, as well as an extensive 'dictionary' of ideas, concepts, words, and summaries of poems. Achsah Guibbory's *The Cambridge Companion to John Donne* (2006) also provides a valuable introduction to the poet. Articles by leading scholars offer overviews of his life, the texts, literary contexts, religion, politics, gender, and various aspects of his art. All of these resources, however, are effective only to the extent that they direct the reader to the full texts of both the author and his critics.

CHAPTER 7

COLLABORATION AND THE INTERNATIONAL SCHOLARLY COMMUNITY

HUGH ADLINGTON

According to John R. Roberts's *Annotated Bibliography of Modern Criticism, 1979–1995*, over one hundred books, articles, and notes on Donne's life and work have been published yearly since 1978, providing ample testimony of burgeoning critical interest in Donne studies. Items of interest have appeared in a wide variety of languages and publications, from mainstream university and commercial presses to highly specialized journals, bulletins, and newsletters. This brief chapter aims to indicate the international scope of this surge of interest, the nature of scholarly exchange and collaboration in Donne studies, the principal organizations that facilitate this exchange, and the value of the international scholarly community as a research tool. To that end, the chapter begins by considering two closely linked institutions that have provided a central focus for, and promotion of, Donne studies in the past thirty years: that is, the John Donne Society and the *John Donne Journal: Studies in the Age of Donne*.

Co-founded in 1982 by M. Thomas Hester and Robert V. Young, the *John Donne Journal* (*JDJ*) (http://social.chass.ncsu.edu/jdj) publishes studies of sixteenth- and seventeenth-century poetry and prose, as well as short notes, announcements, and descriptions of manuscripts, texts, and documents. The journal's subtitle, *Studies in the Age of Donne*, reflects its wider historical and literary focus, with each issue containing several articles on authors and texts contemporary with Donne. From 1982 to 1995 the journal was coedited by Hester and Young, sponsored by the John Donne Society, and published twice a year by the English Department at North Carolina State University. In 1995 (vol. 14) the journal became a single-issue annual. Since 2007 the journal has been edited by M. Thomas Hester alone. The journal's print run started at 300 and has subsequently risen to its present 500. Tables of contents for all back issues can be viewed at the *JDJ* website; at the time of writing (2008) there had been eight special issues over the twenty-six years of the journal's run. These were: vol. 4.2 (1985): *The Metaphysical Poets in the Nineteenth Century* (ed. Antony H. Harrison); vol. 5.1–2 (1986): *Essays in Literature and the Visual Arts* (ed. Richard S. Peterson); vol. 9.1 (1990): *Interpreting 'Aire and Angels'* (ed. Achsah Guibbory); vol. 11.1–2 (1992): *The Sermons* (ed. Jeanne Shami); vol. 14 (1995): *New Uses of Biographical and Historical Evidence in Donne Studies* (ed. Dennis Flynn); vol. 21 (2002): *In Memoriam Louis Lohr Martz 1913–2001* (ed. Jonathan F. S. Post and R. V. Young); vol. 24 (2005): *Richard Crashaw* (ed. John R. Roberts and R. V. Young); and vol. 25 (2006): *Literature and Music* (ed. Richard S. Peterson). *JDJ*'s influence in publishing the latest in research, while also providing a forum both for highly specialized and more general pieces, has been considerable, as witnessed by the fact that the journal in 2008 had 200 institutional subscribers and between fifty and seventy-five annual individual subscribers, in twenty-one countries. The journal's usefulness as a research tool might be further enhanced were it available in electronic format, or listed by one or more of the leading online archives of scholarly journals, such as JSTOR, SwetsWise, ProQuest, Literature Online (LION), or Ingenta Connect.

The journal's sponsor, the John Donne Society (JDS), was formally organized in 1986, inspired in part by scholarly meetings of the editors of *The Variorum Edition of the Poetry of John Donne*, the multi-volume edition now in process of publication by Indiana University Press. After meeting annually for nineteen years at the Gulf Park Conference Centre of the University of Southern Mississippi, the society held its twentieth-anniversary meeting in February of 2005 at the Lod and Carole Cook Conference Centre on the campus of Louisiana State University. Each year approximately sixty scholars and students of Donne gather from throughout North America and Western Europe, and from as far away as Australia, Israel, and Hong Kong, to explore and discuss Donne's life and writing. Participants range from promising students to distinguished scholars, some presenting twenty-minute papers in panel/discussion format, some giving lengthier invited talks, and all united by their interest in discussing Donne's writings and their multiple contexts. The proceedings of the JDS Conference also include an annual colloquium on a single work by Donne, usually with three contributors presenting papers on the challenges of teaching that text, followed by a group discussion among presenters and the audience. The aim of the session is to focus attention on teaching Donne's work, with selected papers subsequently being published in the *John Donne Journal*. In 2010 the JDS celebrated its twenty-fifth anniversary.

One of a number of literary societies with interests focused on an early modern English author (others include the Edmund Spenser Society, Christopher Marlowe Society, Ben Jonson Society, and John Milton Society), the JDS is distinguished by its combination of intellectual seriousness and conviviality, both of which are evidenced by the long continuity of its membership. In addition to the annual conference, the John Donne Society, an Allied Member of the Modern Language Association of America (MLA), sponsors two sessions at the annual MLA meeting, held in late December. Typically, one session has a specific topic while the other is an open session. JDS also sponsors an open session at the International Congress

Ill. 7.1. The Friendship Oak, a 500-year-old live oak tree that overlooks the Gulf of Mexico on the Gulf Park Campus of the University of Southern Mississippi (Long Beach, MS), birthplace of the John Donne Society. With lateral roots extending 150 feet in all directions, the Friendship Oak has withstood Katrina and a series of earlier hurricanes. A plaque at the foot of the tree proclaims that those who stand in the shade of its branches will remain friends all their lives. (Photo, Gary A. Stringer.)

on Medieval Studies, Kalamazoo, Michigan, held annually in May. Each year the JDS issues two editions of the *John Donne Society Newsletter*, and, when appropriate, the JDS presents an Award for Distinguished Publication. The JDS website (http://johndonnesociety.tamu.edu) also serves as a forum for discussion, as a bulletin board for notices of upcoming events, and as a source of links to other Donne-related sites. The most significant of these sites as scholarly resources are DigitalDonne, the Donne *Variorum*, and John Donne Sermons Online. The DigitalDonne website (http://digitaldonne.tamu.edu) is a presentation of high-quality digital images of early editions and manuscripts of Donne's poems, accurate transcriptions of the texts of the poems, and tools for the analysis of both artefacts and texts. At time of writing, the website contained fully digitized images of single copies of the 1633, 1635, and 1669 printed editions of Donne's poems, of Donne's 1654 *Letters to Severall Persons of Honour*, and of the St Paul's Cathedral Library and Westmoreland manuscripts of Donne's poems (*Variorum* sigla SP1 and NY3). Further digitization of different editions is planned. The site provides a formal bibliographical description and a composite list of all press variants for each printed edition (see Ch. 6). The Donne *Variorum* website (http://donnevariorum.tamu.edu) provides information about the project's materials, editorial procedures, and personnel, as well as keeping interested students, scholars, and members of the public abreast of progress on the edition.

Aside from the *John Donne Journal*, a large number of other academic periodicals regularly publish scholarly articles on Donne's life and work. Between 1979 and 1995 at least 260 different journals published items on Donne studies (J. R. Roberts 2004: xiii–xxi). Among the most prominent English-language publications are the *Review of English Studies, Studies in English Literature, 1500–1900, The Seventeenth Century, English Literary Renaissance, Essays in Criticism, English Manuscript Studies 1100–1700, Huntington Library Quarterly, Journal of English and Germanic Philology, Prose Studies, Renaissance and Reformation (Renaissance et Réforme)*, and *Renaissance Studies*. Important online journals for Donne studies include *Early Modern Literary Studies* (http://extra.shu.ac.uk/emls/emlshome.html), *Literature Compass* (http://www.blackwell-compass.com/subject/literature), *Early Modern Culture* (http://emc.eserver.org/default.html), *Renaissance Forum* (http://www.hull.ac.uk/renforum), and *Seventeenth-Century News* (http://repositories.tdl.org/tdl/handle/2249.1/5065). Not surprisingly, English-speaking countries comprise the traditional centres of Donne scholarship, chiefly the United States, United Kingdom, Canada, Australia, and Ireland. However, an increasing number of items are written in languages other than English, by scholars from across Western and Eastern Europe, Asia, Africa and the Middle East, and Latin America. Between 1912 and 1968 scholarly articles in Donne studies were published in French, Spanish, Italian, and German, among other languages (J. R. Roberts 1973). Between 1969 and 1978 the range of languages used in publications on Donne had expanded to include French, German, Italian, Spanish, Japanese,

Dutch, Polish, Hungarian, and Russian (J. R. Roberts 1982*a*). Between 1979 and 1995 all of these languages were represented once again, with the addition of Czech, South Korean, Greek, Portuguese, Catalan, Swedish, Chinese, and Danish (J. R. Roberts 2004). Publications on Donne in yet more languages almost certainly exist but are difficult to locate; the linguistic range referred to above, therefore, represents only a part of the whole picture (Olivares; Dean).

The largest concentrations of activity in Donne studies outside of North America, the United Kingdom, Ireland, and Australia are to be found in Western Europe and Japan. The most salient factors underpinning such activity include adequate translations of Donne's works, the inclusion of his writings in school and university textbooks, the organization of dedicated scholarly societies to provide a forum for information exchange and publication, sufficient availability of research funding for graduate projects and beyond, and more intangible factors such as ebbs and flows in cultural opinion. In Iberia, for example, the Spanish and Portuguese Society for English Renaissance Studies (SEDERI—Sociedad Hispano-Portuguesa de Estudios Renacentistas Ingleses) provides a focus in the region for research into early modern English literature and history. Since 1990 SEDERI has published a yearbook of papers presented at its annual conference, with numerous essays (written in English) concerned in particular with the relationship between Donne's work and that of his Spanish and Portuguese contemporaries (Canteli 1994, 1999; Alonso 1996, 1999; Ribes 1996, 1999; Ballesteros; Heffernan; Pablos; Machado; K. Whitlock). In France and other francophone countries, most notably Belgium, Canada, and Switzerland, various translations of Donne's work, not least the parallel-text edition by Robert Ellrodt in 1993, *John Donne: Poésie* (Paris: Imprimerie Nationale), have stimulated further critical studies, including work by scholarly societies such as Groupe d'Études et de Recherche Britanniques (GERB), and Société d'Études Anglo-Américaines XVIIe et XVIIIe Siècles (Donne 1984*b*; Ellrodt). Other active centres of Donne studies in Western Europe, with scholars writing both in English and other languages, include the Netherlands, Germany, Italy, Denmark, and Finland (Daley 1990; Sellin 1982; Barfoot and Todd; Auberlen; Hamburger; Kullmann; Milani; Propris; Bøgh; Salenius). In Eastern European countries such as Russia, Georgia, Poland, the Czech Republic, and Hungary translation of Donne's writing has been widespread, leading to further critical studies of both his poems and prose (Berezkiva; Kruzhkova; Karumidze; Mroczkowski; Sito; Hron; Ferenc 1987, 1989). Assessments of Donne's knowledge and use of specific languages have also been a feature of international research efforts (Goodblatt; Sellin 1988: 109–12; Gabrieli).

In Asia, Japan has traditionally been a leading centre of Donne studies, with institutions such as the English Literary Society of Japan (established in 1917) and the Japan Society of Seventeenth-Century English Literature providing opportunities for scholarly exchange and publication. (ELSJ publishes Japanese and English numbers of its journal, *Studies in English Literature*, twice yearly.) Important scholarly resources produced by Japanese Donne scholars include the online *Hyper-Concordance to the Works of John Donne* (http://victorian.lang.nagoya-u.ac.jp/concordance/donne/), constructed by Mitsuharu Matsuoka in 2003, and Yoshihisa Aizawa's *Bibliography of Writings about Metaphysical Poetry in Japan*, first published in 1982 (covering the period April 1975–March 1979), and updated in 1989 (covering the period April 1979–March 1984). The abundance of Japanese criticism of Donne's work is such that Yoshihisa Aizawa has been appointed Contributing Editor for Japanese Commentary on *The Variorum Edition of the Poetry of John Donne*, the only such appointment for commentary in a language other than English. Scholars in South Korea and India have also produced studies on Donne in recent years (Yu; Choi; Dasgupta; Rajnath). Nevertheless, within Asia it is China that has seen the most significant recent growth in Donne scholarship. According to Kui Yan in a recent article in the *John Donne Journal*: 'Since 1982, Chinese scholars have published about 100 papers and 3 books devoted solely to the study of his works' (2007: 314). In 1999 Chinese scholarly interest in Donne was boosted by Fu Hao's translation of the complete Songs and Sonets, complete Elegies, and most of the Divine Poems—the first time a substantial number of Donne's poems had been published in Chinese translation in a single volume. Other factors contributing to this recent growth in Chinese interest include Donne's elevation to the top five of the Chinese canon of English writers (the other four are Chaucer, Shakespeare, Keats, and Hardy), a consequent increase in financial support for research available from government organizations, and a rise in the number of academic awards and prizes for which Donne studies are eligible (ibid. 329–30). As a result of such support, Donne studies have flourished in China since 2000, with research projects consisting 'primarily of comparative studies, textual analyses, thematic inquiries, and theoretical considerations' (321). Obstacles to further research, however, include 'lack of a translation of Donne's complete works into Chinese, the absence of conversation among China's many Donne scholars, and the difficulties of getting access to recent publications from outside China' (331). With regard to the second of these difficulties, the formation of literary societies dedicated to study of the literature and history of the early modern period at a national level in China may well foster communications between isolated scholars.

Internationally, connections between researchers are promoted by well-established annual conferences, visiting fellowship and scholarship schemes, and international publishing projects. Since its inception in 1986, the John Donne Society, through its annual conference, website, and sponsorship of the *John Donne Journal*, has been instrumental in fostering links between researchers in different countries. Nevertheless, language barriers persist, and increasing environmental concerns over international air travel threaten future freedom of mobility. In the potential absence of face-to-face communication, therefore, IT applications, including email, the Internet, and blogging, may offer the best hope for maintaining international scholarly exchange. Electronic conferencing is one example of the innovative use of such technology. In February 2008 the online journal *Appositions: Studies in Renaissance/ Early Modern Literature and Culture* hosted what was billed as the first ever fully electronic conference in the field of early modern literary and cultural studies. Papers from seventeen scholars from six countries (Australia, Canada, Cyprus, the United Kingdom, Ireland, and the United States) were posted to the conference site (http://appositions.blogspot.com/), and visitors were invited to offer questions and comments via a 'post a comment' link at the foot of each document page. Whether such enterprises will have a significant future impact on Donne studies remains to be seen, but they, like more traditional arenas of scholarly exchange, can only advance what in Donne studies has always been coterminous with the pursuit of knowledge, that is, 'my second religion, friendship' (*Letters* 85).

In short, the international scholarly community constitutes an immensely valuable, but often disregarded, tool for any scholar wanting to make original contributions to Donne studies. Findings from translation studies, and from scholars working in archives of sixteenth- and seventeenth-century materials in countries around the world, have advanced our understanding of the linguistic, historical, and material contexts for Donne's work. Studies of Donne's travels, his reading, and his dealings with international statesmen, scholars, diplomats, and divines, have shed light on broader questions concerning the international exchange of knowledge in the early modern period. Studies that trace the reception of Donne's work, from the seventeenth century to the present day, spill inevitably across national boundaries. As a consequence, such research contributes to our understanding of the respective roles played by educational and commercial institutions, publishing, and individual writers, teachers, and scholars in the process of international canon-formation and the shaping of the public and private evaluation of literature in different regions and different times. The myriad articles, books, and dissertations that issue from researchers around the world also testify to the vast array of interpretive strategies and approaches available to the international scholarly community in Donne studies. To overlook the opportunities offered by international collaboration, or simply to remain unaware of the research activities of scholars in places other than the traditional centres of Donne studies, is to risk both duplication of effort and the cultivation of an inward- rather than outward-looking scholarly community. Scholarly isolationism or parochialism promises little dividend for the growth of knowledge; international pooling of resources and findings, by contrast, offers the researcher more fruitful returns. As Donne himself proposes in *ValBook*: 'Thus vent thy thoughts; abroad I'll studie thee' (l. 28).

PART II

DONNE'S GENRES

INTRODUCTION

HEATHER DUBROW AND
M. THOMAS HESTER

1

STUDYING Donne generically casts new light on issues central to his major writings and to Donne studies in general. At the same time, it is a key for unlocking the complexities of the poems and prose works per se, in so doing also drawing our attention anew to texts such as the Epigrams or Problems, whose genre has tempted us dismissively to relegate them to 'minor' status and hence to neglect them. In addition to points about specific poems, the essays in Part 2, through their attention to genre, reveal many larger, overarching issues about Donne's work, his engagement with both the history of the genres in which he participates and the connections of his genres to historical circumstances, usefully drawing attention to the frequency with which Donne's texts focus on patterns of historical change in other arenas—though this interest in history is as various in its forms and as volatile in its moods as two of the many texts that exemplify it, *Metem* and the *Anniversaries*. M. Thomas Hester suggests that the Epigrams are their author's 'earliest poems, instructive examples *in parvo* of his poetic achievement'; similarly, in many of the poems, even or especially in so-called minor genres, we find kernels of potentialities and pressures that recur elsewhere.

Other significant questions that generic study of Donne encourages us to ask include how his responses to political authority, considered in many essays in this volume, relate to his responses to the authority of established literary conventions. Important also, of course, is how Donne responded to his Catholic heritage and to its religious and cultural challenges in his time. Approaching his work generically again offers useful perspectives. Gregory Kneidel points to *Sat3* as a poem suggesting 'someone who believes that Truth does exist and can be found'; but he finds also in the same lines 'someone who embraced Renaissance scepticism, questioned doctrinaire religion, and deplored the violence it fostered'. R. V. Young's essay on the Elegies notes that 'Donne's Catholic background inevitably created an estrangement between him and an England increasingly dependent on a unique version of Protestantism for its emerging national identity. Yet no one is more English than Donne, no one more of an ingrained Londoner'. Graham Roebuck remarks that in *Pseudo-Martyr* two masters of the Controversial Treatise 'occur in interesting guises': Desiderius Erasmus appears as the subject of unjustified attacks by the Jesuit controversialist Roberto Bellarmino; and Thomas More is invoked not as one who was 'martyred for refusing an oath that denied papal supremacy', but rather as one who translated Lucian and, 'although firm in his Catholic faith, sought to "*deliver the world from superstition, which was crept in under Religion*"'. Kate Narveson finds in Donne's interpretation of the literary form of the Devotion an irenic drive to avoid controversies. And Jeanne Shami demonstrates a cognate drive towards reconciliation in the way sources and readings drawn from different confessions are united in the Sermons.

If our generic organization of Donne's writings can thus revisit, though not always resolve, some of the most pressing issues about his life and work as a whole, that approach is also crucial for understanding texts within particular genres. Kneidel, mapping the ways Donne's formal verse Satires differ from and relate to other texts in that kind, both ancient and modern, explores the nature of Donne's attraction to the form. Michael W. Price and Ernest W. Sullivan II illuminate both Donne's work in the prose Paradox and the place of *Biathanatos* within 'the inherent ambiguity of the genre', expanding 'the reach of the witty paradox into a controversial, intellectually serious, and extended analysis of the ethical, legal, and theological implications of suicide'. Young addresses problems central to *Corona* by tracing its author's adaptations of the sonnet, while Kirsten Stirling shows that Donne's 'invocation of and yet distancing from the liturgical genre is typical' of his other religious verse. Camille Wells Slights's essay shows that Donne's preoccupation with the privacy of lovers is both clarified and explicated when he approaches the wedding poem, a form in which he 'examines this pull between the privacy of love and the collectivity of community from the other side, assuming the voice of outsider rather than lover'. And Claude J. Summers shows how Donne in his funeral poems manifests and manipulates the 'rhetoric of grief' in these 'public poems'.

But the organization of Part 2 also allows—indeed encourages—its authors and readers to adopt new perspectives on questions that extend far beyond John Donne's own canon. A generic approach can illuminate broader debates about early modern literature and about the critical methodologies through which we study Donne's and other eras. This mode of organization also tightens the cohesion of Part 2 to the rest of the

Handbook by offering new perspectives on the issues in other sections: problems of textual bibliography, cultural and biographical contexts, and many challenges in interpretation are crystallized when one addresses Donne's approaches to literary forms.

Building thus on the work of the Donne *Variorum* editors, some of whose contributions have been described in Part 1, Young traces the controversies surrounding whether and how the Holy Sonnets should be read as sequences of poems; in so doing he demonstrates that Donne's canon provides valuable test cases for debates about the material and other conditions of publication, about how these conditions, especially the often vexed interactions among authors, publishers, and printers, create meaning. In particular, Young uses the bibliographical evidence provided by the *Variorum*, evidence of the practices of both scribal and print cultures resulting in the transmission of texts in groups, to explain Donne's purposes and achievements in revising his sequences of Sonnets.

Another question that engages not only Donne scholars but also many other students of early modern culture is periodization. The old contrast of the exuberant Elizabethan age, reaching its apex in the glorious achievements of the 1590s, and the darker Jacobean era exemplified by Donne and Webster has long been discredited, but critics continue to debate alternative methods of organizing and subdividing the period. Because Donne writes both in genres mainly popular in the sixteenth century, such as sonnets and formal verse satires, and in those more characteristic of the succeeding century, notably epithalamions and religious verse, his body of work encourages us to trace the interactions and intersections among decades and styles. In this connection, Dayton Haskin observes that the seventeenth-century editorial heading 'Songs and Sonets', applied to Donne's love lyrics, echoed the title of 'Tottel's Miscellany', and that like that popular sixteenth-century anthology Donne's poems in this genre do not accord with the contrasting tradition of sixteenth-century sonnet cycles, which 'represent an author's lyric self-expression'; belonging rather to the even older tradition of commonplace book and miscellany, Donne's discrete love poems, his first editors realized, 'did not offer a narrative sequence but left poems as aesthetic performances to be read through here and there and in any order that a reader wished'.

2

Donne's approach to genre is typically self-conscious and reflexive: he draws attention to his forms, writes about them as well as writing in them. Or, to put it another way, he often distances himself from the very literary types in which he is participating, as it were introducing them with the 'if' constructions so characteristic of his work, as Hester has shown (1996b: 130). Thus, for example, his Satires and Epithalamions explicitly comment on the problems created by these literary types. *Sat3* famously complains,

> Kinde pitty chokes my spleene; brave scorn forbids
> Those teares to issue which swell my eye-lids;
> I must not laugh, nor weepe sinnes, and be wise,
> Can railing then cure these worne maladies?
>
> (ll. 1–4)

Anne Lake Prescott's essay on Donne's Menippean texts squarely faces the centuries-long issue of 'which texts should count as "Menippean"' and 'how to define the genre, if it is a genre and not a mode or tradition'. Donne and the tradition of humanist scholarship he knew defined it broadly, 'and would also have agreed that this often very erudite genre is particularly given to laughter at pretentious erudition'. Haskin comments about Donne's performance in the Songs and Sonets that these poems 'allow such a large admixture of cynicism about love that they continue to defeat the expectations generally associated with "love poetry"'. And Jeffrey Johnson shows how in the *Essayes* Donne is 'working within [the genre of the essay] even as he redefines the parameters of the genre' through 'the idiosyncratic scepticism of his exegesis', literally offering a 'new genre'.

Donne's predilection for writing in meta-genres (that is, genres about genres) demonstrates patterns manifest in other ways throughout the canon. We clearly see in these reflexive gestures the argumentative strain in Donne: he writes Epithalamions and writes about and against the act of writing them. As we have already implied, the habit in question also participates in its author's curious and very typical blend of immediacy and distance, his tendency to be insider and outsider at once, or to move rapidly between those two positions, often recalling his predilection for including observer figures in texts such as *Ecst* and *Eclog*.

Another characteristic of Donne's genres is his extraordinarily eclectic approach to his literary sources. Witness, for example, the range of literary and theological traditions whose influence on the Sermons is traced in Jeanne Shami's essay. That eclecticism often encompasses extensive interaction with classical models of the genre. Donne approaches such sources aware that, as Claudio Guillén observes, 'a genre is ... an invitation to the actual writing of a work' (72), and Donne of course responds to such invitations with his characteristic delight in innovation. It is tempting but ultimately dangerous to contrast Donne's innovative approach to genres with the putative conventionality of other poets of his time. Poets ranging from the major figures in whom one might anticipate innovation, such as Sidney, to lesser-known writers such as Barnabe Barnes regularly approach genres innovatively. But, bearing that caveat in mind, we can still identify the shapes Donne's innovations assumed, precisely because they are so numerous, as witnessed by the nineteen essays of Part 2, describing Donne's unparalleled range of kind.

Arguably the most intriguing characteristic, even the signature characteristic, of Donne's prosody is his heterometrical couplets, and they can help us encapsulate his generic innovations as well. Such couplets consist of two lines linked by a rhyme and often linked syntactically as well; but they are distinguished by their rhythm, often because one is considerably longer than the other ('Why dost thou thus / Through windowes and through curtaines call on us?' (*SunRis* ll. 2–3). Similarly, Donne's generic innovations link together what is alike in some ways and very different in others—his approach to a generic convention and other approaches; or his work and that of one of his predecessors in the genre; or, more significantly, his sympathetic approach at one point in the text and his more critical approach at another—and the effect in both cases is to startle and unsettle the observer.

Equally telling is how frequently Donne plays genres or their fragments against each other within the same text. Margaret Maurer's essay on the Verse Letters demonstrates that these texts mediate between lyric poetry and occasional writings like sermons and reminds us that the Letters often assume the form of sonnets; Slights's essay explores how and why Donne includes a pastoral prologue in *Eclog*; and similarly, Hester shows that Donne mixes various modes of epigrammatic writing. In combining literary types in these ways Donne often creates a kind of dialogue, which sometimes, but by no means invariably, becomes argumentative, between and among genres. And this is, indeed, only one of many senses in which his involvement with genre is dialogic. That involvement typically sets up implicit conversations with earlier writers, with alternative possibilities for the genre, with opposing genres.

The dog that did not bark in the night, as Sherlock Holmes observes, can tell us more than her noisier kennel-mates. It is revealing that a figure who clearly did not suffer fools gladly writes relatively few poems that parody their genre, and that even in those cases the extent of the parody is debatable because it often seems juxtaposed with some sympathy for the literary type in question. For example, the key to evaluating the degree of mockery in *Metem* or in *Storm* and *Calm*; or deciding whether *Bait* is more attracted to its model than it appears at some points to be; or discerning whether *EpLin* is wholly or even largely parodic—the key is the stance of the poet as an insider on the verge of becoming an outsider or as an outsider with one foot inside the door. Quite simply, these stances are more congenial to Donne and more intriguing to his readers than bald parody. Indeed, dialogue—even or especially a conversation where one speaker is superior—is more attractive to him than simply dismissing the alternative voice through parody.

In fact, given the range of genres in which Donne writes, his decision not to engage in others is revealing. Many long-standing assumptions about this singularly urban and urbane poet are confirmed by the apparent absence of pastoral, one of the most popular genres in his era. At the same time, elements of pastoral do surface occasionally, notably in *Eclog* and especially in *Bait*. These poems remind us yet again that Donne is intrigued with, even preoccupied with, segments of his literary heritage that on some levels are not appealing to him. Witness above all the role of the sonnet in his oeuvre (a topic germane to essays by Haskin, Maurer, and Young), and the related though separable question of his involvement with Petrarchism, of whose discursive practice the sonnet is often the outward and visible sign.

Critics have long debated whether Petrarchism is a mode with which Donne briefly flirted early in his career, before turning determinedly to anti-Petrarchism; or whether significant Petrarchan elements survive throughout. However one resolves that argument in terms of the readings of individual poems, two generalizations do emerge. On the one hand, the lack of conventional love sonnets clearly demonstrates the iconoclasm with which Donne is often and not inappropriately associated; on the other hand, the recuperation of the sonnet form in his Verse Letters, noted in Maurer's essay, and the presence of Petrarchan elements in many other texts demonstrate the openness to a range of generic forms stressed throughout this introduction. The dialogic propensities identified above may further help us to address these conundra about Petrarchism and its favourite genre, the sonnet. As Young remarks, Donne's use of the sonnet to express and explore spiritual turmoil 'could only take poetic form in the matrix of Donne's wide reading and immersion in the literary culture of the late Renaissance. He was conversant with the conventions of Petrarchan love poetry and the sacred parody of these conventions in both native English and continental forms, in the work of such figures as Clément Marot, St John of the Cross, William Alabaster, and Robert Southwell'. Donne, that is, establishes continuing and multivocal dialogues between and among Petrarchan possibilities and rebuttals of them.

In that, as in so many other respects, John Donne talks through, about, and with generic possibilities. As John Frow observes, genre is 'a form of symbolic action' that 'makes things happen by actively shaping the way we understand the world' (2). Indeed, one reason genre interests Donne so much is his intent to shape the world through the symbolic action of language. Studying how and why he writes generically can help shape the way we ourselves see John Donne's worlds.

CHAPTER 8

THE EPIGRAM

M. THOMAS HESTER

1

EPIGRAMS, in a small space, transmit the grammar of death, having originated (their etymology suggests: *epigraphein* [Gk.] → *epigramma* [Lat.] → *epigramme* [Old Fr.]: 'upon' + 'to write') as inscriptions on tombs or buildings, encomia, or memorial markings, an origin that even in the ancient world tended towards satire and, by Donne's time, had expanded to include not only engraved lapidarian testaments but brief, saucy, and racy riddles that a resident at the Inns of Court might well find scratched on the surface of his door or wall. These were a brief, pointed, poetic version of the *graffito* or Pasquil, as Puttenham intimated in his description of the genre as written 'vpon a table, or in a windowe, or vpon the wall or mantel of a chimney in some place of common resort, where it was allowed euery man might come' (Puttenham 142).

Donne's Epigrams were his earliest poems, instructive microcosms of his poetic achievement. In fact, Joseph Spence spoke more truly than he thought or intended when he sought to dismiss most of Donne's poetry as nothing but 'un Tissu d'Epigrammes' (247), for the character of the epigram is mixed into all Donne's genres, often comprising the pointed jests and final turns in his poems, which (in a phrase from one of his Paradoxes) 'cozen your Expectatyonn' (*Paradoxes* 52). In fact, the importance of Donne's poetry to his age might reside less in the rather uneven quality of his Latin and English Epigrams themselves than in their contribution to what has been called 'the epigrammatic transformation' of English poetry in the late sixteenth century (Fowler 1982: 176), for which Donne, along with Jonson, was largely responsible. Indeed, Donne was recognized by Jonson as the best English epigrammatist: 'Who shall doubt, Donne, where I a *Poet* bee, / When I dare send my *Epigrammes* to thee? / That so alone canst judge, so'alone do'st make' (Jonson 8.62), an opinion shared by William Drummond, who thought Donne 'might easily be the best Epigrammatist we have found in English' (Drummond 226). Jonson undoubtedly included Donne's Epigrams when (as Drummond recorded) he 'affirmeth Done to have written all his best pieces err he was 25 years old' (Jonson 1–2.135). Indeed, Donne is the master of the short, pointed poem; his better-known Songs and Sonets 'have something of the epigram' in them, 'as often as not... pointed, or witty, rather than simply passionate' (Fowler 1982: 102). The same is true of many of his Elegies, Verse Letters, and funeral poems; even his mock epic, *Metem*, and his two grandly intellectual *Anniversaries* are transmitted to the reader through a version of the epigrammatic compression he initially borrowed from the traditions of the ancient genre. In his Epigrams (as frequently in his lyrics) the movement is towards the compression of the speaker's utterance into as small a space as possible, almost to reduce the poem to a phrase or even a word. This, of course, is a given of the genre. In most cases, the Donne Epigram (or lyric) does just the opposite of 'elaborating' on a motif or metaphor.

This practice is equally evident in some of the epigrammatic lyrics, in *Flea*, for instance, where the bold sophister's entire argument is compressed into that single word, conspicuous by its absence, 'die'; and in the generic amphiboly (or ambiguous discourse) of *Appar*, where the final word 'innocent' (l. 17) is framed by two opposed and opposing sets of generic frames: the idealistic, Petrarchist 'solicitation'; and the realistic, Ovidian 'my love is spent'. In these senses, Donne seems always to be testing the power or potentiality of words to signify, for the compression of signs into a single phrase or word both satisfies and at the same time destroys the dialectical movement towards clarity and closure. The final turn, twist, or adage, with its expected terminal closure, only opens up the impossibility of signs to resolve the human dilemma presented or signalled in the poem: the 'sullen Writ', as Donne wittily terms *Metem* in its last stanza, 'just so much courts thee, as thou dost it' (l. 512).

In general, and in the Epigrams in particular, Donne is always a revisionist poet, an innovative artist who modifies whatever he borrows, whose imitations are so original that it is difficult to discern their subtext or model, when there is one. Moreover, as is demonstrated in the *Variorum* edition, he revised, rearranged, and modified his Epigrams, creating 'three distinct sequences of poems, each of which differs significantly from the others at both the macro and micro levels' (*Variorum* 8.LVII). He worked on these sequences during a period estimated at perhaps as many as twenty-five years, circulating in the 1590s a group of eight to ten poems; subsequently (no later than 1602) reorganizing and augmenting them in a sequence of twenty; and finally at some later point reducing them to the third sequence of sixteen poems that was published in 1633 and in succeeding seventeenth-century editions (Stringer 1999: 93). Each of these sequences was conceived, unlike many classical and Renaissance epigram collections, to allow a reader 'to observe and absorb the thematic, verbal, and stylistic connections among individual epigrams and to read each poem in relation to others' (DiPasquale 2007: 333—a pioneering essay opening the way for critical discussion of Donne's sequences of Epigrams). In this departure, as in others, Donne gave evidence of what Thomas Carew called 'fresh invention' (Donne 1633*b*: 386, l. 28).

Like other *fin de siècle* Elizabethan epigrammatists, Donne was aware of the two main traditions of classical epigram—Greek and Latin—widely imitated by English poets in the sixteenth century. Probably at an early age Donne became familiar with both traditions, learning of them as part of his education by tutors at home, perhaps from the early 1580s with the advice or influence of his uncle, Jasper Heywood, SJ, an exile returned to perform underground missionary work. Heywood had for nearly two decades in Germany taught the Jesuit *ratio studiorum*, a curriculum in use all over Europe and featuring an emphasis on the *Greek Anthology* and on writing Latin epigrams (Flynn 1995*c*: 183–4). In any case, Donne's awareness of generic tradition can be seen in his earliest purported work as a poet, his sequence of Latin Epigrams, probably written in the mid-1580s, although available only in English translations made after Donne's death by Jasper Mayne (*Variorum* 8.255–69). Apparently, Donne had preserved the Latin originals at least until he lent his only copy to his friend Sir Henry Goodere at some point after the start of their friendship in 1599. In a Latin Letter, Donne requested their return from Goodere, but no copy of the originals is extant despite the fact that translations were published by Mayne in 1652 (Flynn 1984: 126–8; Ch. 27.II below).

Critical assessment of Donne's Latin Epigrams is limited by their unavailability in original Latin texts; their translations cannot be accepted as definitely representing Donne's poems, although they certainly bear some relation to Latin originals. Even from the translations we can discern some generic hallmarks of Donne's style in English Epigrams—compression of utterance into as small a space as possible, thus testing the power or potentiality of words to signify; and manipulation of epigrammatic strategies and conventions to bring into question and open up the adequacy and the creativity of human forms and signs. Nevertheless, as known only in translation, Donne's Latin Epigrams cannot effectively be much discussed or compared to his English Epigrams of the 1590s.

Apart from the evidence of this apprentice work, two sources for Donne's awareness of classical generic tradition are the *Epigrammata* (1518) of his great-grand-uncle Sir Thomas More and the 600 English epigrams of his grandfather John Heywood, published by the hundreds beginning in 1550 and collected in his *Woorkes* (1562). More's *Epigrammata*, a 'bridge between the classical and the native English traditions' of the epigram (Coiro 61), included the earliest Latin translations from the *Greek Anthology* published in England and probably served as a textbook for the young Donne. In More's poems, Donne found not only the Latin tradition of Martial and Catullus, but also the older tradition of the poems Maximus Planudes had anthologized at Constantinople around the turn of the fourteenth century, mainly sententious and proverbial, often in the form of lapidary inscriptions, including also witty and satirical epigrams. One poem Donne almost certainly held in mind is More's Latin translation of a Greek epigram that could well have served as a model for Donne's *Ship*:

> Out of a fyred Ship, which by no way
> But drowning could be rescued from the flame,
> Some men leap'd forthe, and ever as they came
> Nere the foes Ships, did by ther Shott decay.
> So all were lost, which in the Ship were found:
> They in the Sea being burnt, they in the burnt ship drownd.
>
> (*Variorum* 8.7)

This may be compared to More's '*In navim exvstam*':

> *Iam ratis aequoreas oneraria fugerat undas.*
> *Matris at in terrae deperijt sinibus.*
> *Corripitur flammis, atque ardens auxiliares*
> *Quas maris hostiles fugerat, optat aqua…*

A cargo ship had escaped the waves of the sea, but perished on the bosom of her mother, the land. She caught fire, and, as she burned, she wished for help from that which she had escaped—the hostile waters of the sea. (More 1984: no. 36; 120–3)

Striking is the appearance, in both Donne's and More's poems, of images of sinking ships conjoined with paradoxes involving both seawater and fire.

Coiro points out that More's epigrams 'on the brevity of life' seem his most characteristic work in the epigram, 'peculiarly Renaissance meditations' (63)—not surprising in a collection that traces its origins to the tombstone inscription. Although Donne's is not the austere style of More or the proverbial, anecdotal style of Heywood, he does share their dangerous attitudes towards authority. More injected a political dimension into his epigrams that is never apparent in the *Greek Anthology*. The largest number of epigrams on a similar subject in More's *Epigrammata*—twenty-six— are his often derisive poems on kingship (Coiro 67). A common theme for both More and Donne is a daring, caustic, and cautionary treatment of the dangers inherent in positions of power. Among More's poems on figures of authority, perhaps closest to Donne's are epigrams such as '*Quid inter tyrannvm et principem*':

> *Legitimus immanissimis*
> *Rex hoc tyrannis interest.*
> *Seruos tyrannus quos regit,*
> *Rex liberos putat suos.*

A king who respects the law differs from cruel tyrants thus: a tyrant rules his subjects as slaves; a king thinks of his as his own children. (More 1984: no. 109; 162–3)

Or this daring taunt ('*De principe bono et malo*'):

> *Quid bonus est princeps? Canis est custos gregis inde*
> *Qui fugat ore lupos. Quid malus? Ipse lupus.*

What is a good king? He is a watchdog, guardian of the flock, who by barking keeps the wolves from the sheep. What is the bad king? He is the wolf. (no. 115; 164–5)

Not surprisingly, More's many poems on figures of authority were the least imitated and least reprinted of his epigrams in Renaissance anthologies (Coiro 75). Indeed, a similar caution and reluctance may well account for Donne's never having published his Epigrams, including several about figures of authority. If his jibe at the painting of Phrine, for example, is a subtle comment about the cosmetics and (flattering) portraits of the aged Queen Elizabeth (*Variorum* 8.9); if the Queen is also figured in the powerful Katherine (a name derived from the Greek word for 'pure'), who 'for the Coarts sake put downe Stews' (8.9); if *Antiq* by naming 'Hammon' (8.8) dares to critique John Hammond, who devised the 'Bloody Question' put to Catholics suspected of treason, asking whether they supported the papal power to excommunicate the English monarch; and if the 'Earle of Nothing=am' (8.276) is Lord Charles Howard, second Baron of Effingham, then we may hear a note struck by More's daring poems in those of his great-grand-nephew half a century later—and recognize grounds for his guarding their circulation carefully.

Absence of surviving manuscript or print artefacts suggests that Donne's Latin Epigrams did not enjoy a wide circulation, whether because he did not show them to anyone interested in transcribing manuscript copies, or because for most English readers they lacked appeal, or simply because fewer readers troubled to transcribe his Latin than his English poems (or few purchased editions of the Latin that evidently were published in the 1650s). His English Epigrams fared better, most of them circulating in manuscript over a period of years beginning in the late 1590s in Donne's three successively revised authorial sequences (*Variorum* 8.14–16), as did the Elegies, Satires, and Holy Sonnets. The *Variorum* editors remark as 'most noteworthy' two exceptions that appear in only the intermediate sequence, *Cales* and *Wing*, both of which, evidence suggests, may have been withheld from circulation but for a single instance of dissemination. 'Whether Donne regarded these epigrams as politically incendiary or in some other way indecorous, it is clear that he carefully restricted their circulation' (8.18). The same may be said of 'E. of Nottingham', attributed to Donne by Stringer (1991: 71–4); subsequently published in *Variorum* 8.276, it is described in a headnote (270) as a 'recently discovered candidate for addition to the canon' of Donne Epigrams. If, indeed, 'E. of Nottingham' is Donne's, these three guarded poems can be taken together as fruit of Donne's experience during the Cadiz raid of 1596, and all three may express politically critical attitudes both towards the leadership of the expedition by Robert Devereux, second Earl of Essex, and towards factional opposition to Essex (Flynn 1995c: 207–10; but see also Stringer 1991: 72).

2

More did not limit his *Epigrammata* to translations of or poems modelled on Greek epigrams; 'over one hundred (but less than half)' of his poems are based on originals from Greek sources such as Plato, Aristotle, Plutarch, Lucian, and Diogenes Laertius, supplemented by material derived from other classical writers (e.g. Plautus, Cicero, Seneca, and Martial) as well as biblical texts, traditional jests, Aesopic fables, and English love lyrics (McCutcheon 2005: 77). In particular, More's book also seems likely to have directed Donne (possibly through the tutorial skills of Jasper Heywood) towards that second type of epigram, framed in Latin by Catullus and Martial, which came to dominate the short reign of the epigram in the English Renaissance.

This second strain in the classical tradition, to which Donne and most of his fellow poets would eventually more fully incline, was characterized mainly by language compressed to the point of being 'hyperdetermined' (B. H. Smith 205–7), poems often concluding with a satirical reversal or 'sting'. An instructive example of this feature of Donne's art is his *Disinher*: 'Thy father all from thee by his last will / Gaue to the poore; thou hast good title still' (*Variorum* 8.8). As *Milgate* (200) points out, this poem resembles two of Martial's epigrams, III.10 and V.32. Indeed, the disinherited son is a frequent subject in both Roman and English satire; and Martial's IV.70 could be added to the list of classical analogues that deride this comic type. Each of the Latin poems, however, scoffs at a son whose disaster is the result either of his own or of his father's profligacy. The father of Martial's Philomusus, for example, has been such a spendthrift that there is no inheritance left:

> *idem te moriens heredem ex asse reliquit.*
> *exheredavit te, Philomuse, pater.*

At his death he has left you his sole heir. Philomusus, your father has disinherited you. (Martial 1.206–7; III.10, ll. 5–6)

The ungrateful son, Ammianus, has been disinherited because his disrespect has been discovered by his father:

> *Nihil Ammiano praeter aridam restem*
> *moriens reliquit ultimis pater ceris.*
> *fieri putaret posse quis, Marulline,*
> *ut Ammianus mortuum patrem nollet?*

Ammianus' father on his deathbed left him nothing in his last will but a dry rope. Who would have thought, Marcellinus, that Ammianus could be sorry his father died? (1.336–7; IV.70)

And Crispus has been left poor because of his father's dissipation:

> *Quadrantem Crispus tabulis, Faustine, supremis*
> *non dedit uxori. 'cui dedit ergo?' sibi.*

Crispus did not give a farthing to his wife in his last testament, Faustinus. 'To whom did he give then?' To himself. (1.384–5; V.32)

In each case, the Roman heir is 'disinherited' because of some vice in which either he or his father has indulged, and Martial (who like Donne's grandfather Heywood, the professional jester, almost always assumes more the role of jester than of satirist) laughs at the ironic justice of the pathetic victim's predicament.

Donne's poem, however, inverts the usual treatment of this ancient comic type. The focus of the comic irony in *Disinher* is not the conduct of the son or the father before publication of the 'last will', but instead the surprising significance of a philanthropic father's final gesture. Anticipation of a conventional jest about the requiting of a disappointed heir *is* evoked by 'from thee' in the opening clause; and the reader is further encouraged to expect an explanation that the heir has received his just deserts for questionable conduct by the disclosure that the father has given his wealth 'to the poore'. But the surprise of the final part of the compound sentence, 'Thou has good title still', puns on at least two meanings of 'title' and submits the unexpected observation that, as the survivor of a noble and charitable father, the disinherited son has gained the father's 'title' but has been given 'title' only metaphorically or spiritually to the father's wealth. The title of rank, which the father could not donate to the poor, is 'still' 'good' both legally and morally: poor consolation if the poem were to be read as a formal *consolatio*. On the other hand, small comfort is available from the word 'title' if it means the one remaining ground or justification for a claim to the father's goods: the fact that the disinherited son, now that he is 'poore', qualifies for his father's beneficence.

This wry jest is typical of Donne's refusal in his Epigrams to give the reader the conclusion one expects, or has been led to expect, by the initial premises of the poem or by the conventional features of the type being presented. Here the expectation that the son has been rendered poor is overturned by the moral interpretation of the worth that should be 'all' to a loving son—the goodness of his father. In this sense, then, that most important final word of the Epigram surprises and satisfies simultaneously: the son does have a title that is 'still' in the sense of being dead or worthless materially, as the first sentence of the poem anticipates; but finally he has 'good title' *yet*—his 'still' father has bequeathed him a heritage of honour and charity. Rather than an imitation of Martial that ridicules the conventional disinherited or profligate son, Donne's Epigram surprises the reader with its consoling compliment, its ironic advice to a son who must adjust to his father's 'profligate' charity.

The originality of Donne's treatment of this satirical type in *Disinher* is also evinced in his surprising amplification of the proverbial adage that lies behind the final, pointed turn of the poem. If there is a Latin model or analogue for the poem, it is probably a distich from that popular medieval and Renaissance textbook of proverbial wisdom, the *Dicta Catonis*. This widely used collection of homely advice, which appeared in at least six major editions during the sixteenth century, experienced a great educational vogue during the Renaissance for its practical ethics and elementary clarity. (It offers a summa for the advice Polonius gives Laertes, for example.) One of its adages offers advice to a new heir about the wisdom of guarding his heritage carefully:

> *Quod tibi sors dederit tabulis suprema notato,*
> *augendo serva, ne sis quem fama loquatur.*
>
> A heritage bequeathed to you will
> Keep and increase: so save your good name still.
> (Anon. 1935: 610–11)

In his Epigram, Donne wryly applies this advice to the disinherited son, suggesting that the ancient admonition is 'good [advice] still'. Thus, by accommodating this popular and rather commonplace adage to the context of a *disinherited* son, Donne increases the surprise of his poem. Not only does he reverse the usual, expected treatment of the unfortunate-heir type of the satirical epigram; he also illustrates an unforeseen applicability of the pseudo-Cato's advice in the *Dicta Catonis*. The final effect of Donne's wit in *Disinher*, then, is to illustrate once again *in parvo* that union of matter and manner central to his art. The syntagmatic surprise of Donne's distich—its sharp and surprising reversal of expectations created by the first line-and-a-half of the poem—is mirrored by the surprising amplification of the conventional satiric type and the commonplace analogue in the Epigram. Our expectations have been cozened again, like those of the responsive auditor in *Flea*, who is directly but subtly invited to draw certain conclusions about the speaker's conceits and verbal gymnastics; so the readers of *Disinher* are invited to draw certain conclusions, only to have those interpretations corrected, rescinded, or frustrated by the final turn of Donne's witty dialectic and 'fresh invention' (Donne 1633b: 386, l. 28).

3

Perhaps the best introduction to the complex (and complicating) generic manipulation and surprise on which Donne's reputation was founded and reached its fullest achievement is provided by his lapidary Epigram *Wing*:

> Beyond th'old Pillers many'haue trauailed
> Towards the Suns cradle, and his throne, and bed.
> A fitter Piller our Earle did bestow
> In that late Iland; for he well did know
> Farther then Wingefield no man dares to go.
> (*Variorum* 8.8)

In the one sequence where it appears, this Epigram looks back at 'earlier poems on death and entombment' while at the same time completing a group of poems on war (DiPasquale 2007: 350). Suitable as an inscription on the colonel's tomb, resonating with the verbal tension and encapsulated proverbial wisdom demanded of the genre, this poem displays Donne's expertise in the Planudean form of the sepulchral epigram, fulfilling admirably the epigram's function as an abbreviated transfer of cultural codes and values. (On genres as codes see Colie 1973: ch. 2.) As a proverbial epigram it memorializes the intrepid hero of the 1596 Cadiz expedition who was slain near the Pillars of Hercules, those promontories that mythologically marked the boundaries of the known world (and that Emperor Charles V and King Felipe II designated as the *terminus a quo* of the supposedly endless Spanish empire). Donne presents Wingfield as an embodiment of the Hercules emblem: his heroic labours and sacrifice provide a model and a boundary beyond which human heroism dare not on its own aspire.

This same kind of commemorative typology figures in two of Donne's epigrammatic riddles. In *Hero*, just as Wingfield's mythic stature arises from the English colonel's monumental 'travail' as if across the span of the known world (from 'cradle' to 'throne' to 'bed'), so the universality of the lovers' amatory conduct is figured forth in the Empedoclean circularity of their immersion in the four elements: 'Both robd of ayre, we both ly in one ground, / Both whom one fyer had burn'd, one water dround' (*Variorum* 8.7). The just circle of their love has transformed the fragmented, elemental flux into a harmony. Here, however, there is a note of irony in the image of the two lovers as an emblem of the elemental unity of love. For they have achieved an elemental perfection only through their deaths; the circle of their love seems just only through their destruction. Rather than an image of eternity, then, we are left with a sad completeness, for the poem suggests only a literary immortality. The circle of the lovers' actions lies, as the pun on 'lye' suggests. They are 'robd of ayre', victims as much as conquerors; their completeness is achieved only through their final immersion in death. The situation is similar in *Pyr*: 'Two, by themselues, each other, Love and Feare / Slayne, cruell frinds, by parting haue ioynd here' (*Variorum* 8.7). The oxymoronic exigencies of the lovers' situation—'by themselues'/by 'each other', by 'Feare'/by 'Love', 'cruell'/'frinds', 'parting'/'ioynd'—are presented as having been overcome, or 'unmetaphored' (Colie 1974: 11, who discusses various forms of mythic and metaphoric play with genres in the Renaissance) by the essential love of this two-in-one. In the Wingfield encomium, the 'late Iland', itself rendered dead by the victory of the English and the death of the colonel, becomes literally the scene of a sententious proverb that recalls the enduring (and prevailing) nature of his example and provides a reminder of the eternal standards and spiritual cause that Wingfield, Essex, and the English claim to represent.

Wing, then, displays Donne's ability in the Planudean mode of the epigram. Nevertheless, to see the Wingfield poem as an example of this mode only is to miss much of its fun and complexity, for it manifests also generic mixing and witty inversions such as occur in his Epigrams in the Latin epigrammatic style, for example the explicit assaults of *Licent* and *Antiq*. *Licent* presents an ironic literalization of the psalmist's admission that his sins are 'more than the hairs of mine head' (Ps. 40:12) through an amusing amplification of the joke about a syphilitic's 'French crown' (Caricato 155–6): 'Thy Sins and haires may no man equall call / For as thy Sins increase, thy haires do fall' (*Variorum* 8.8). These satirical thrusts are extended by the pun on 'haires'/heirs (prepared for by the synecdochic 'thy sinnes increase'). This pun not only intimates the extent of the satiric victim's contagion, but also transforms the witty Roman epigram into a verification of both the psalmist's adage and the biblical proverb about the visitation of the sins of the father on the son. *Antiq* also transforms biblical figure into topical insult: 'If in his study Hammon hath such care / To'hang all old strange things, let his wife beware' (8). The victim here appears to be the same Haman derided at the conclusion of *Sat5*, who lost all 'when he sold his Antiquities' (l. 87), and who is identified there with the traitorous chief minister of Esther: 5–7 who, selling his treasures in order to pay off assassins, ended up by being hanged on the gallows that his wife advised him to erect for the faithful Mordecai. By selling his 'Antiquities', that is, God's people and the wisdom of their religion (*OED:* 5 and 6), Haman lost his life. In *Antiq*, it is Hammon's *wife*, not his life, that is threatened. In this poem the caustic variation on the traditional image of woman as vessel ('ware') combines with a bitter dash of topical satire to create in fallacious ambiguity that surprise-through-equivocation so frequent in Donne's Epigrams.

In fact, *Antiq* may present an oblique attack on a specific person; as Grierson suggests (Donne 1912: 2.59), the most likely candidate seems to have been John Hammond, the civil lawyer, interrogator of Edmund Campion, cohort of the notorious Richard Topcliffe (who was infamous for the torture of Catholic recusants in his home), and reputed originator of 'the Bloody Question'. In support of Grierson's suggestion of a topical attack on Hammond, it is worth noting that 'old', 'strange', and 'thing' are epithets for Catholics among Establishment controversialists; in *Sat2*, for instance, Donne ironically applies these terms to a court provocateur in order to indict the Establishment's hypocritical administration of the 'huge statute lawes' (l. 112). With or without this topical level of meaning, *Antiq* retains a stinging and satirical typology in its unfolding syntactical disclosure that Hammon's 'care' for his wife should make her wary. As DiPasquale points out, the 'religiopolitical innuendo that hangs about' this poem is particularly important for its appearance in Donne's earliest sequence, of the 1590s, where it is positioned first (2007: 355).

Returning to the Wingfield encomium, if we recall that the imperial motto Felipe of Spain inherited from his father was *plus oultra* ('Farther than')—a motto inscribed across depictions of the Herculean Pillars and above an ever-rising sun in Spanish heraldic emblems—then Donne's epigrammatic 'pillering' of the Spanish is apparent. The emblematic sun of Felipe, which was supposed never to set on the empire, the pillars that marked not the boundary but the start of the nation's empire, and the motto that expressed their expansionist achievements are all here rendered applicable to the daring colonel who died pillaging a Spanish port—'Farther then [*plus oultra*] Wingefield no man dares to go'. The Spanish having been stripped of goods and pride by the daring raid on Cadiz, Donne the assaulting epigrammatist now defiantly waves their own banners in their faces. The lapidary Epigram is in effect not only a riddle and a joke but also a witty assault, fully in the spirit of Martial's comic deflations of his Roman enemies. The encomium ends with 'a sting in its tail'.

Cleverly retorting to the implicit boast of the empire's impresa, Donne exposes at the same time the dangers of epigrammatic enclosures; by turning Felipe's epigrammatic, heraldic emblem against him, he shows the impossibility of (pre)determining the significations of public speech-acts. Literally and generically anglicized by Donne (*plus oultra* = 'Farther then'), the elements of the Spaniard's emblem are compressed into the final line's epitaph for Wingefield and re-create the emblem/epigram, leading into vistas of signification beyond the boundaries of Felipe's hyperdetermined intentions. Here, as in the other Epigrams (and as in the radical re-formations/reconstructions of Petrarchan motifs in his lyrics), Donne shows that no metaphor can be subjected to the imperialism of any single hermeneutic, or interpretive system. The empire of metaphor is finally heuristic; its boundaries are not pillars of interpretive restrictions but imaginative traces of human 'travail'. Even in his most 'Greek' Epigram, then, Donne's tendency is to open up the genre in which he works, here by mixing modes of epigram in order both to fulfil and to surprise generic expectations.

4

If More is the most likely transmitter of the riches of the *Greek Anthology* to Donne, then John Heywood—mercilessly prolific, consciously rough-hewn (and too often dull), and anti-establishmentarian—may be the conduit that oddly embodied for Donne an English style of the Latin epigram as framed by Martial—the style, that is, that came to dominate the short reign of the epigram in the English Renaissance. More, as we have seen, embeds a moral satire in his translations and borrowings, thereby helping to establish the genre as the 'vehicle for a kind of authoritative advice that would have seemed the antithesis of the witty trifles of Martial' (Crane 1986: 169). Heywood, although his work seems unaware not only of the *Greek Anthology* and Martial, but also of the sixteenth-century vogue of humanist, neo-Latin, continental epigrams, succeeded nonetheless in producing a prodigious number of home-grown, trifling poems. The 'mad merry wit' Heywood (whose *An hundred Epigrammes* (1550) was the first book published in England with the term 'epigrams' in its title) offered to Donne—again perhaps through the tutelage of Jasper Heywood—what has been termed by many the 'medieval' epigram, because of an overwhelming focus on anecdote, fabliau, and proverb.

As Caricato observes: 'One seeks in vain here for translations or imitations of the Anthology or Martial' (93). Instead, Heywood's major contributions to the genre are the proverb and the anecdote. For random examples, consider, from among his 'Three hundred Epigrammes, vpon three hundred prouerbes':

Of fortune to fooles. 124.

God sendth fortune to fooles, not to euery chone:
Thou art a foole, and yet fortune thou hast none...;

and:

Of late and neuer. 300.

Better late then neuer. Ye mate,
But as good neuer as to late...

And from 'The fifth hundred of Epygrams':

Of deliuerance from yll. 58.

Wyfe, from all euyll, when shalt thou deliuered bee?
Sir, when I (said she) shalbe deliuered from thee.

(Heywood 1992: fos. T, Yii, and Aaii^v)

These epigrams may seem uneven in quality and wit, rather tame examples of a reliance on the traditional figures and situations of the fabliau, especially in the sexual and marital humour they exude. Yet many of them would seem to have pinched particular nerves at court, apparently serving as satirical exposés of marital disputes, exercising a sharply insulting proclivity carried over perhaps from Heywood's position as an unofficial court jester. And his many epigrams supporting the Catholic faith frequently seem to have tested the bounds of subversion, a lifelong tendency earlier expressed by his stances at court (especially his involvement in a failed plot to topple Archbishop Cranmer), that eventually forced him into exile for the last fourteen years of his life.

Like the 'flippant disrespect' and 'radical viewpoint' concerning kings in More's Latin epigrams (Coiro 70 and 75), Heywood's 'medieval' approach to the epigram may well have influenced some of the central tenets of Donne's own approach to the genre. Court jester during four Tudor reigns, Heywood was finally not flippant at all—as was recognized in the age by authorities and by compatriots such as Camden, Davies, Kendall, and Bastard. For 'under the rough humor of his epigrams, Heywood insisted upon the old loyalties to the Catholic church, to Mary Tudor, and to old-fashioned morals' (Coiro 79). Such, after all, as *King Lear* most eminently illustrates, is the function of the 'fool' at court. From this perspective, Heywood's forty-five-line epigram, 'A keper of the commaundments', may seem his best poem, matched perhaps only by the first epigram of his final collection, 'Of Rebellion', where he announces again his devotion above all else 'to god, queene, countre, and crowne' (quoted by Coiro 79). Coiro evokes Heywood's example to his grandson as the author of provocative and, often, daring epigrams—when she points out that: 'Ironically, while Heywood brought to the epigram a conservative moral standard, a loyalty to the way things used to be, when his epigrams applied the old proverbs against the present times his very conservatism was subversive' (79). To have mixed this subversive generic conservatism with a sexual playfulness derived from the medieval fabliau resulted in a paradoxical play that heralded some of Donne's own English Epigrams, and also some of his translated Latin ones.

As More interspersed radically anti-authoritarian epigrams among humanist translations of the *Greek Anthology*, so Heywood interposed politically incorrect defences of the old religion in his centuries. In this and other ways, he brought a medieval 'fresh invention' to the genre and sought paradoxically (in Crane's words) 'to subvert aphoristic wisdom and return the genre to a stance of amateur frivolity' (1986: 176) by publishing hundreds of poems departing from Tudor Protestant work, such as Robert Crowley's epigrams expressing mainly an anti-Catholic didacticism. In his 'deliberate counterstatement' to such work, Heywood's epigrams counterpose a less serious idiom for a serious purpose, they 'do not directly contradict the voice of authority', but amount to 'anti-authoritarian "trifles" in a deliberately rough, vernacular verse form' that sought to return the epigram to its former, more entertaining style, 'thus undermining its effectiveness as a vehicle of moral and religious authority' (ibid. 178–9). Donne's sequences of Epigrams are mixtures of the aims, styles, motives, and sources of his two forefathers, composers of witty, anti-authoritarian poems that dare to ridicule the powerful and the proud as well as the foolish and the unfortunate. Donne's 'mixed' style inclines towards the authoritative voice of the lapidarian epigram of the *Greek Anthology* before it reverses course in its witty, surprising denouement. The epigrams of both More and Heywood thus tread in their witty thrusts the precarious border of subversion later found in Donne's Epigrams, proposing the same paradoxical mixing and vexing of generic expectations on which Donne's approaches to the epigram, Latin and English, are founded.

If a genre is an invitation to match form to matter, or a set of metaphoric problems to be solved (Guillén 109 ff.), then Donne's Epigrams seem to explore or test the poetics of the epigram itself. We get the pun we expect (usually), the hyperdetermined closure required of the epigram whether it is assaulting, dedicatory, sepulchral, ecphrastic, or amatory. But we also get what Colie describes: something 'more than conventionally "ought" to fit into such a small space, expanding the one sign' (whether the pun or the form as a paradigm) into all 'kinds' of relevant, interrelated, and contradictory meanings (1970: 152). A genre is a metaphor and, as such, in Foucault's words, 'a network of marks in which each of them may play, and does in fact play, in relation to all the others, that of secret or of indicator...a play of resemblances' (34, 41). What we get in Donne's Epigrams is a dramatic illustration of the affective experience of the limitations of this genre—and perhaps, by implication, the innate limitations of any sign or series of signs to enclose the vagaries and interrelated possibilities of human action and expression.

As McCutcheon summarizes More's epigrammatic strategy, More 'characteristically subverts, questions, or reopens an initial claim, inverts an old proverb, or otherwise renders an epigram open-ended, by juxtaposition, by ambiguity of language and allusion, by exploiting different points of view and incongruities of situation, and by innumerable other rhetorical strategies' (2005: 86). The point reinforces our sense of the influence of Heywood and especially of More on Donne's epigrammatic strategies. Two final examples of Donne's subversive Epigrams are *Martial* and *Ralph*, which conclude two of his manuscript sequences, one of them the sequence printed after his death. The first of these two Epigrams is an attack on Matthew Raderus, the Jesuit priest whose 'gelded' 1602 edition of Martial's epigrams expunged all obscene poems:

> Why this Man gelded Martial I muse;
> Except himselfe alone his tricks would vse
> As Katherine, for the Coarts sake put downe Stews.
> (*Variorum* 8.9)

The jest is conveyed by the puns on 'vse' (as sexual intercourse) and 'tricks' (as sexual stratagems), intensified by the description of the *priest* as 'this Man'. The final simile reinforces and amplifies the ridicule established within the initial two lines.

As a former law student and employee of Lord Keeper Egerton, Donne would have been aware of the legal derivations of 'sake', meaning guilt, sin, or crime. He plays on that sense in the simile of the third line: the comparison of the editor to 'Katherin' (whether one of Henry VIII's wives or Catherine de' Medici—or someone else, such as Queen Elizabeth, or even James I—is not clear) elaborates the jest through its suggestion that she prohibited the brothels in order to satisfy the courtiers' libidinous indulgences *within* the court. In fact, identification of the specific queen is not essential to the satire here, for the Latin meaning of 'Katherin' ('pure') conveys the satirical thrust of the ironic simile—it accentuates the wry comparison between a 'pure' queen whose prohibitions may have been intended to serve her own sexual desires and a 'chaste' priest whose excisions may have been intended to further his own sexual knowledge. And the choice of prohibition by a 'queen' (Elizabethan slang meaning both prostitute and homosexual) of prostitutes serving their customers may be intended to insult the editor/priest by facetiously accusing him of sodomy also (Martial's several poems on sodomites were among those cut from Raderus's expurgated edition). However, the final simile only intensifies the sarcasm of the first two lines; the joke is already complete within this distich. One possible reason the simile may have been added is that the allusion to prostitution affects the reader of the next and final poem of the sequence.

Before turning to *Ralph*, it is important to recall that Martial anticipated and himself warned against treating his poems as Raderus did. In one of Martial's several defences of the propriety of *lascivia* to his *iocosa carmina* (droll poems), the Roman poet compares poems to husbands and readers to wives. Despite their many charms, he explains, husbands cannot please their wives '*sine mentula* (without a penis)' and, by the same token, epigrams cannot please their readers unless they are wanton (*ne possint, nisi pruriant, iuvare*; 'they can't unless (sexually) aroused, please'). Recalling the similar defence of Catullus XVI (22), he pleads, therefore,

> *quare deposita severitate*
> *parcas lusibus et iocis rogamus,*
> *nec castrare velis meos libellos.*

So please put prudery aside and spare my jests and jollities; and don't try to emasculate my little books. (1.64–5; I.35, ll. 12–14)

Martial then concludes his apologia with a pert comparison of Priapus (the fertility god of procreation, who had become an emblem of the phallus) to Galli (the raving priests of Cybele who castrated themselves at the conclusion of their rites): '*gallo turpius est nihil Priapo* (nothing is more disgusting than Priapus as Cybele's Eunuch)'. Raderus omitted this epigram from his edition, of course; but it does lie behind Donne's own attack on the editor, as is suggested by the heading given his poem in the Westmoreland ms.: 'Martial: castratus' (*Variorum* 8.9).

A key part of the jest in Donne's poem is conveyed by the reference to the priest as 'this *man*', intimating that he has been less rigid about his priestly vows than even the disgusting *Galli*; indeed, 'himselfe alone his tricks would use' suggests that Raderus is more of a Priapus than a Gallus. If Donne intends the reader to recall Martial's apologia and its central analogies between the pleasures of the reader and the wife and between castrating priests and phallic figures, then the reader, fresh from the simile about Katherine and the prostitutes, is invited to read the following Epigram in the spirit of Martial's *iocosa carmina*.

At first glance, however, *Ralph* seems to disappoint this expectation: 'Compassion in the world againe is bred, / Ralphius is sicke, the Broker keeps his bed' (*Variorum* 8.9). The poem initially impresses us as another of Donne's novel assimilations of a familiar Renaissance proverb: 'A crafty knave needs no broker' (Tilley 359). Ralphius, as the lower-class associations of his name intimate, is certainly a social 'knave'; but Donne inverts the saucy adage so that his knave is not 'crafty' but has a knavish broker who is. The satire of this ironic inversion of the proverb derives from the double meaning of 'keeps': the broker is sickened by the sickness of his client, whose death could bring about a loss of the money Ralphius owes him. But the bed ridden broker is not so 'compassionate', of course, as to return to Ralphius his pawned bed.

The placement of this poem, concluding a sequence immediately after an attack on the editor who 'gelded' Martial's sexually illicit epigrams, raises the possibility that there is more to *Ralph* than a sarcastic quip about an indifferent broker and his pathetic client. The suggestive language of the poem, as well as its sequential context, invites another interpretation of the situation—a reading deriving from the provocative possibilities of 'Compassion...bred...sicke...the broker keeps his bed'. Perhaps the prostitution simile of the previous poem and the oblique reminders of Martial's own warnings about husbands' inability to please their wives '*sine mentula*' are intended to invite a bawdy reading of *Ralph*. Such a possibility is strengthened by the fact that the word 'broker' meant not only a pawnbroker or middleman but was also slang for a bawd, pimp, or pander. If this implication about the situation is followed, then it is also possible that 'keeps his bed' means not only that the broker is bed ridden or refuses to return the bed of Ralphius, but that he sexually possesses his client's wife or regulates those who enjoy their marriage 'bed'. Ralphius could be 'sick' for several reasons: he could be suffering from a venereal disease transmitted as a result of his wife's prostitution, or he could be sick at heart over the broker's business arrangement with her. In this sense, 'Compassion' is 'bred' 'in the world' for several reasons (as suggested by the rhyme of *bed/bred*). Compassion, in the sense of 'suffering together', could result from the spread of venereal disease 'in the world', or from the world's pity for Ralphius the cuckold, or (if ridicule of the wife is intended) from the broker's suffering the same disease that Ralphius has contracted. Even the wife could be an object of pity as a victim of the broker, thus increasing the causes of Ralphius' suffering and thereby including her as another object of the world's 'Compassion'.

Thus, if the suggestive rhyme and the provocative hints about the situation are followed, the overall effect of the anecdote in *Ralph* is broad—but indefinite at the same time, its bases not clarified by the sexual innuendoes of the Epigram. The range of pun and sexual suggestion in the poem does *open up* several possible readings, but the point of the poem may be less to present a clear explanation of the precise causes of Ralphius' plight than to frustrate the expectations 'bred' by the first line-and-a-half of the poem. Ralphius makes a perfect dupe for the epigrammatist's wit, but the reader is left wondering about his own status in the witty world of the poet; it is a bit discomfiting, after all, to know that a joke has been told and not to be sure about the precise point of its ridicule. It might be safest, therefore, to recall again Donne's warnings about our responses to his poems—for example, his wry monition in *Metem* that his satire 'just so much courts thee, as thou dost it, / Let me arrest thy thoughts; wonder with me...' (ll. 511–12). The possibility should not be discounted, that is, that Donne presents a 'gelded' Epigram in *Ralph*, and that the bawdy connotations encouraged by *Martial* and seemingly supported by the sexual hints of this poem are a barometer of the reader's habits of mind and interpretive proclivities. Is Ralphius 'cozened' by the broker? Is that the interpretation of his sickness that we prefer? Under what conditions can compassion be 'bred' 'in the world'? Or in the reader? Or is the truth of the matter simply that the reader 'againe' has been cozened by Donne?

It is with this interpretive dilemma that *Ralph* (and Donne's collection of Epigrams) concludes—not with the maximal closure that is supposed to characterize the epigram but with the creation of questions about Ralphius and the broker, the poet and the reader. For even if we have ignored the potential warning of *Martial* and avoided the traps of a salacious reading of *Ralph* we are still left wondering whose bed the broker 'keeps', and therein made aware that once again we were misled by the initial premises of the poem, by the misdirections laid out in the first line-and-a-half. And even if we have heeded the warning of the 'mus[ing]' English '*Martiall*' in that penultimate poem, we are still left wondering about our own motives, 'Compassion', and wit at the close of the sequence of Donne's Epigrams. According to DiPasquale, in the Epigrams 'Donne gives his readers no respite' (2007: 372), so that, at the conclusion of *Ralph*, regardless of which understanding of Ralphius' situation we choose, we are left wondering at the multiplicity of language, at Donne's exploitation of the diversity of signification. Such 'wonder' is, of course, the ultimate effect 'bred' by the 'fresh invention' of the Epigrams.

CHAPTER 9

THE FORMAL VERSE SATIRE

GREGORY KNEIDEL

IN 1620 a young clergyman named John Cave wrote a poem in which he confessed that his own 'quick brain'd Age' could scarcely 'reach' or even 'find' the 'more pure minde' in the 'well plac'd words' of Donne's formal verse Satires (A. J. Smith 76; thanks to Gary A. Stringer for this reference). Four centuries later Cave's search continues. Donne's Satires remain difficult poems to understand and appreciate. In fact, in our own age, Donne's words hardly seem 'well plac'd', and there is no strong consensus about what was in his mind when he wrote them, much less how it might be considered 'pure'. Our search for the Donne of the Satires is aided to a point by our understanding of the generic conventions of classical formal verse satire. The first section of this chapter outlines some of these conventions. The second section demonstrates the freshness of Donne's reception of his classical models by contrasting his Satires with those of other classicizing Elizabethan formal verse satirists whose words and minds are considerably easier to reach but ultimately less interesting to find.

Juvenal (fl. 100–30 CE), the Roman poet most commonly associated with the outburst of formal verse satire in late Elizabethan England, described the subject of his satires in this way: 'all human activity—prayers, fears, anger, pleasure, joys, hustle and bustle—this is the mishmash of my little book' (*quidquid agunt homines, votum, timor, ira, voluptas, / gaudia, discursus, nostri farrago libelli est* [138–9; 1.85–6]). Though somewhat misleading (there are, for example, few joys in Juvenal), this description provides a convenient template for presenting some of the generic conventions of formal verse satire as it was practised by Juvenal and his two Roman predecessors, Horace (65–8 BCE) and Persius (34–62 CE). Given Juvenal's professed interest in 'all human activity' (literally, 'whatever humans do'), it would be unwise to generalize about the subject matter of the forty poems that comprise the canon of Roman formal verse satire. To be sure, a handful of topics do recur: for example, problems between patrons and their literary and political clients; law and crime; sex and seduction; food and eating; religion and pedagogy; travel within, from, and beyond the city of Rome; literature and satire itself. Such topics converge on what Persius calls, with a whiff of contempt, 'the subtleties of social duty' (*tenuia rerum / officia* [104–5; 5.93–4]) and they often expose the disparity between: (1) what humans should do or think they do; and (2) what they really do (for 'humans' understand, for the most part, 'privileged Roman males'). The satirists promote virtues such as liberty, friendship, self-knowledge, constancy, manliness, and moderation. They attack the corresponding vices of slavery, sycophancy, hypocrisy, ambition, effeminacy, and excess. In the best satires, as frequently in Donne's, these assorted vices are shown to be virtually indistinguishable in practice. Thus Juvenal's 'grim-looking perverts' (148–9; 2.9) are mocked not merely for their prurience, which might in itself be forgiven, but because this prurience manifests or is manifested by other vices (e.g. greed, vanity, passivity, hypocrisy) that together signal the breakdown of Rome's venerable social institutions (e.g. friendship, marriage, patronage, nobility). In a genre stuffed with funny, arresting, and salacious examples of what humans do, it goes without saying that instances of bad behaviour outnumber those of good. Juvenal's inclusive-sounding 'whatever' comes to mean almost exclusively whatever is laughable or offensive or just plain wrong.

Satire in its broadest sense is more typically characterized not so much by its subject matter as by the poet's stance or attitude towards that subject matter. This stance is largely determined by the poet's purpose, which can usually be triangulated somewhere between attack, entertainment, and preaching (Rudd 1). Thus, satire combines elements of invective, comedy, and sermon rhetoric, and the satirist balances, or notably fails to balance, impassioned outrage, wry humour, and ethical guidance. If Horace, Persius, and Juvenal constitute the holy trinity of formal verse satire (with the epigrammatist Martial providing a significantly lesser but recognized generic model), their characteristic stances help to distinguish at least the outlines of their individual practices. Horace laughs at folly and teaches an eclectic ethics with a smile (more entertainment and preaching, less attack). Persius, a young and rather bookish proponent of strict Stoic doctrine, rails against vice (more attack and preaching, less entertainment). Juvenal is slightly more difficult to pin down. He was renowned in Donne's age for the savage indignation of his early satires, for the immoderate passion with which he inveighed against the excesses and irrationality of his age. But Juvenal's career as a satirist was a long one, and he eventually moved beyond indignation towards a posture of amused, or at least ironic, detachment. A measure of coherence was given to Juvenal's divergent stances in the 1950s when his example was used to introduce into the modern critical tradition the theory of the satiric persona. According to this theory, Juvenal himself was not convulsed by the riot of emotions ('prayers, fears, anger, pleasure, joys') that he so frequently flaunts. Instead, he created personae or fictional speaking masks for each poem, almost as if writing what we now call dramatic monologues. Consequently, the stance of each persona must be distinguished, notionally at least, from the beliefs and experiences of the poet himself (see Highet; Anderson; and Kernan 64–80).

Whatever its limitations, persona theory helps to sift out some of the basic ingredients in the 'mishmash' (*farrago*, literally 'cattle-feed'; a coarse play on the likeliest source of the term 'satire', *satura* = a platter of mixed foods) that the Roman verse satirists serve up for their readers. Ancient readers would have associated the satirists' personae with those crafted in theatre, mime, and oratory, and the satirists freely imitated and parodied the formal elements of these genres (e.g. brisk narration and dialogue, exaggerated gestures, stock comparisons). They also borrowed elements from the kindred genres of epigram, verse epistle, familiar letter, academic lecture, philosophical dialogue, Aesopian fable, and Theophrastic character, many of which Donne also produced. Poetic form is also an implicit subject of the programmatic satires that Horace, Persius, and Juvenal wrote to defend their choice of genre, primarily by way of explaining why they did not write epic or elegy (cf. Horace 1.4, 1.10, and 2.1; Persius 1; Juvenal 1). Epic is idealistic. Elegy is effete. Both are dull, derivative, un-Roman, and self-consciously oblivious to the 'hustle and bustle' of lived life. While epic and elegy had fairly clearly defined generic rules, formal verse satire was less well theorized. Instead of following rules, the satirists played off the precedents set by earlier satirists, starting with the genre's putative inventor, Lucilius. Consequently, formal verse satire retained an unpredictability, an openness, that has led some critics to charge that it lacks formal unity, coherence, or design. C. S. Lewis, for example, mused that 'the Roman model [of verse satire], though it has produced great couplets and great paragraphs, has produced no great poem, no poem in which the parts really gain by belonging to the whole' (1954: 468). It is true that one rarely feels that there isn't a line to spare when reading a poem by Persius or Juvenal especially. But the best Roman satires are carefully composed, and most of them seem like formless 'mishmash' only when served alongside an exquisitely prepared dish of Virgilian epic or Horatian ode. No doubt we would appreciate their formal coherence more if we were to sample the poems the satirists themselves scorned, the fourth-rate, puling elegies and droning epics that were published with great fanfare but soon found wrapped around the daily catch at the fishmonger's stall. The *libelli* or 'little books' into which Horace and Juvenal gathered their poems for publication (Horace's eighteen verse satires comprise two books; Juvenal's sixteen comprise five; Persius' six were published posthumously in one) also betray signs of formal and thematic arrangement, an important point to remember when considering Donne's five verse Satires as a coherent sequence.

Style is probably the most important and contentious generic feature of formal verse satire. Lewis once wrote that Donne laboured 'under the influence of the old blunder which connected *satira* with *satyros* and concluded that the one should be as shaggy and "salvage" as the other' (1954: 469). But the blunder was Lewis's. As Alvin Kernan soon pointed out, Donne, almost alone among his peers, says nothing to associate his Satires with rowdy woodland creatures (117). Contrast the merry and hornless satyr that prances across the title page of John Donne the Younger's pathetic compilation of jests, epigrams, and satires, unimaginatively entitled *Donne's Satyr* (London, 1662). Of course, the style of Donne's Satires can be shaggy and savage—or, in less sylvan terms, loose and difficult. But that is because he was following his Roman models. Their satiric style, built on a dactylic hexameter line hijacked from epic, features abrupt transitions; disjointed, even hallucinogenic, dialogue; compressed and distorted syntax; and frequently exotic, obscure, or vulgar word choice. As with their stances, the styles of the three Roman satirists were differentiated in broadly useful terms. Horace titled his satires 'conversations' (*sermones*), deemed his verse pedestrian, and charted a stylistic middle course well below the high flight of epic but above the low vulgarity of comedy. Taking the opposite tack, Juvenal fashioned an expansive, allusive, declamatory, richly figured style designed to arrogate the grandeur of epic. Persius' cramped style caused the most consternation. When Barten Holyday published the first English translation of Persius, he advertised it not merely as Persius Englished but also as something more unthinkable: '*Persius* Vnderstood' (Holyday 1616: A2ʳ). Numerous explanations for Persius' affected obscurity have been proposed: he was young, he was angry, he was driven to incomprehensibility because, in the shared language of stoicism and republicanism endemic to Roman satire, he lacked poetic and personal liberty. In what remains one of the best introductions to the Renaissance theories of satire that Donne would have encountered, John Dryden in 1693 opined that Donne's satiric style most resembled Horace's. But when Dryden wrote of Persius that 'his diction is hard; his Figures are generally too bold and daring; and his Tropes, particularly his Metaphors, insufferably strain'd', he intimated that Persius was something like a metaphysical poet of the Donne school (see G. Williamson 1930: 43; Dryden 1956– : 4.51 and 78).

The Roman satirists remained popular after—and in some ways because—Rome declined and fell. The Church Fathers appreciated their fiery condemnations of the moral depravity that plagued Rome during the very period in which Christianity grew into an organized religion. Augustine, for example, quoted Persius to prove that the old pagan gods, who hadn't managed to prevent the sack of Rome in 410 CE, had in fact never instilled in their followers virtues of any sort (57; quoting Persius 3.66–72). Later Christian moralists and poets found other damning or edifying bits of wisdom in Roman satires, especially Juvenal's long Satire 6, a storehouse of ancient anti-feminism. In a way, the Roman satirists came to resemble the Hebrew prophets: they inveighed against the waywardness of their benighted people but needed the light of Christian doctrine to illuminate the true but hitherto shadowy path to salvation discernible in their poems (see Hester 1982: 3–11). Holyday, rejecting the proposition that Christians should not read poetry as obscene as Juvenal's, extolled his moral uprightness and lamented, 'O that we could Argue him into a Christian!' (1673: A^v). To read the satirists in this essentially medieval way, as Christian moralists *avant la lettre* (or, rather, *avant l'esprit*), one had to ignore their evident delight in depicting and so participating in the vice they saw around them. It helped that their poems circulated primarily in pieces. As with most classical authors, the Roman satirists were received into the Christian West largely as excerpted lines in schoolbooks and collections of sententiae. So, for example, in a 1597 treatise in which he aims to demonstrate the existence of God, the glories of Elizabeth's reign, and the sundry social vices plaguing England, Donne's soon-to-be father-in-law George More quotes a line from Juvenal (cf. G. More 112).

It was not until the Renaissance, when pagan Rome's glories once again began to outshine its failings, that vernacular poets began to imitate rather than merely quote the Roman satirists. Sir Thomas Wyatt (1503–42) became the first to write Roman-style formal verse satires in English. No prophetic voice crying in the wilderness, Wyatt wrote instead as a disgruntled courtier bristling at the abuse of royal power by Henry VIII. Wyatt took as his primary model Horace, who was more dependent upon his emperor, Augustus, than Persius upon Nero or Juvenal upon Domitian (see Burrow). Wyatt's more immediate models were Lodovico Ariosto and Luigi Alamanni, whose satires were later gathered together with those of other early sixteenth-century Italian satirists by Francesco Sansovino in his *Sette libri di Satire* (Venice, 1560). In the latter half of the century a similar tradition of 'satire régulière' would emerge in France (see Magnion and, for developments in Spain, Lerner). It is hard to imagine that Donne did not know the works of these continental vernacular satirists, but his specific debt to them, if any, has not yet been estimated.

Moreover, these antecedent and parallel developments in the genre do not explain why a strain of formal verse satire animated by the spirit of Persius, and especially Juvenal, flashed onto the London literary scene in the mid-to-late 1590s. Certainly the specific contributions of Persius and Juvenal to the Roman tradition of formal verse satire had been expounded much earlier in sixteenth-century poetic treatises (see Baumlin 1986). And certainly satire had flourished in England throughout the century in numerous other modes, many of which were formal and many of which were in verse. A number of socio-political and literary influences have been or might plausibly be proposed: (1) the anxieties of a generation of young, ambitious, over-educated men chasing too few career opportunities; (2) the emergence of modern science and the re-emergence of classical scepticism that together called into question the lofty educational and civic claims of Renaissance humanism; (3) the rise of London as a Rome-like metropolis and the spectre of England as a Rome-like empire; (4) a weariness with the four-decade rule of Elizabeth and countervailing uncertainties about its end; (5) a hyper-competitive literary scene dominated by simpering Petrarchism and indulgent Ovidianism, both ripe for stern satiric castigation; and (6) the fragmentation of English religious culture exacerbated by radical Puritanism and militant Catholicism (for the analogous case of sixteenth-century French formal verse satire, see Salmon 2003: 94). These possible influences are by no means mutually exclusive, and however they are valued, it is, as Anne Lake Prescott has recently argued, wrong to treat the 1590s as a kind of last, brilliant flowering of the Tudor satiric tradition, since it is possible to find earlier satires that were more artistically sophisticated, more socially engaged, and even more adroitly, if less pretentiously, classical (2000: 238).

With the partial exception of literary fashions (which come up in the first half of *Sat2*), all of these themes recur in Donne's Satires: *Sats 2, 4,* and *5* express concerns about entering, and not being able to enter, professional service; *Sats 1, 3,* and *4* critique the intellectual agenda of Renaissance humanism in various ways; *Sats 1* and *4* explore the contradictory impulses of London's cosmopolitanism and England's xenophobia; and *Sats 3, 4,* and *5* especially criticize Elizabeth and her government. The overlapping between these admittedly rough-and-ready groupings reveals something distinctive about Donne's satiric mode, namely its power of synthesis, which is especially evident in his handling of the last topic listed above, religion and religious controversy. The Roman satirists lampoon ancient religious customs and their abuses (cf. Persius 2 and Juvenal 15). And, among Donne's contemporaries, John Marston casts some rather conventional barbs at superstitious Catholics and hypocritical Puritans and denounces a certain Crispus for repeatedly changing religions in pursuit of worldly success:

> Now Iew, then Turke, then seeming Christian,
> Then Atheist, Papist, and straight Puritan,
> Now nothing, any thing, euen what you list,
> So that some guilt may grease his greedy fist.
> (Marston 116, ll.153–6)

But one cannot find in the Roman or other late Elizabethan satirists anything approximating the extended argumentation and searching scepticism of Donne's *Sat3*, in which the papist, Puritan, conformist, the lover of all churches and the lover of none are each first given a name and a brief biography and then dismissed as inadequate. Nor is there in Marston anything like Donne's bracing critique of Elizabethan politics for interfering inappropriately in the pursuit of religious truths. As here, Donne's Satires typically conjoin topics in a way that challenges readers to identify a shared, hidden source of ostensibly dissimilar social injustices. So, for example, while Joseph Hall wrote satires about various poetic genres and about the law, Donne's *Sat2* joins the two themes by attacking first bad poets and then a bad lawyer. What poetry has to do with law is not explicitly stated. Hall treats systematically and rather tediously what Donne treats synthetically but also more enigmatically. Because of their compression and thematic complexity, Donne's Satires are as a group, in Annabel Patterson's frank estimation, 'simply better, more interesting' (2006: 121) than the repetitive productions of Marston or Hall or the shorter but also more narrowly conceived efforts of Everard Guilpin, Thomas Middleton, or William Rankins. One of Donne's signal achievements in the genre was to do much more with much less. In 1614 Thomas Freeman complained: 'Thy [i.e. Donne's] *Satyres* short, too soone we them o'relooke, / I pre thee *Persius* write a bigger booke' (Freeman 'Epigram 84' K2^r).

Donne's Satires were also scarce because he did not have them printed during his lifetime. Instead, he permitted them to circulate in manuscript copies within a coterie of readers—in Ben Jonson's phrase, 'Rare poemes aske rare friends' ('To Lvcy, Covntesse of Bedford, with M^r. Donnes Satyres', Jonson 8.60, l. 6)—who may have consisted initially of other smart, ambitious young men but later came to include other kinds of readers, such as the aristocratic and religious Lucy Russell, Countess of Bedford. By contrast, Marston, Hall, and the others printed their books of satires in close succession, and each compulsively advertised his book's unprecedented audacity and wit so that the satiric persona each presents to his prospective buyers is qualitatively different from the one Donne presents to his more restricted readership. The other late Elizabethan satirists strut and preen like competing shock-radio personalities, promising new heights of wit and grotesquery, parroting each other's gags, and picking fights whose stakes now seem quite trivial (if they ever really mattered at all). Their chief aim was to be known as the nastiest satirist in print—though at times it is difficult to distinguish between nastiness and silliness. Only Marston could pose the premise of much Juvenalian satire (i.e. that it is difficult *not* to write satire) in a question like this: 'O what dry braine melts not sharp mustard rime / To purge the snottery of our slimie time?' (Marston 108, ll.70–1). For his part, Hall wrote three books of milder, Horatian, 'tooth-less' satires but, just as 'lightning' is followed by a 'thunder-clap' (J. Hall 1949: 51, l. 91), he followed them up with three books of harsher, Juvenalian, 'biting' verse (never mind that lightning is more destructive than thunder). The personae crafted by Marston, Hall, and, to a lesser degree, the other late Elizabethan verse satirists are above all designed to seem secure, integral, punishing but not punishable, reproachful but beyond reproach.

When one turns to Donne, the contrast is stark and indicative both of his fresh treatment of his classical models and of his departure from contemporary practice. His *ars satirica* is not articulated in lurid, programmatic detail and must be inferred from his poems themselves. With the partial exception of *Sat2*, he does not snipe at other writers and offers only brief glimpses of the contemporary literary scene. Donne does not grandstand; he never claims to whip, bite, bark, or the like, and, more tellingly, he almost always speaks of corporeal punishment and physical compulsion in negative or at least deeply ambiguous terms. So, to take the best-known example, there is no scholarly consensus about how exactly to describe the stance towards religion and liberty that Donne adopts in *Sat3*. Numerous philosophical and religious traditions have been proposed as sources for its iconic images (e.g. 'On a huge hill, / Cragged, and steep, Truth stands' [ll. 79–80]), for its memorable exhortations (e.g. 'Seeke true religion' [l. 43] and 'doubt wisely' [l. 77]), and for its overall argumentative structure. There are lines that please critics who want Donne to be a traditionalist with a medieval, Catholic mind, that is, someone who believes that Truth does exist and can be found through the cooperation of human effort, divine inspiration, and pious respect for the wisdom of tradition. For example, Donne advises anyone seeking true religion to 'aske thy father which is shee, / Let him aske his; though truth and falsehood bee / Neare twins, yet truth a little elder is' (ll. 71–3). Truth *can* be distinguished from falsehood, and fathers, prominent authority figures in the poem (cf. l. 11 and l. 59), can help to do it. But the same lines also comfort those who want a more radical Donne with a liberal, anti-authoritarian agenda, someone who embraced Renaissance scepticism, questioned doctrinaire religion, and deplored the violence it fostered. For example, if asked, would Donne's father and grandfather really have given the same answer? If so, one of them probably ran afoul of secular and religious authorities, since England's official religion had changed at least three times in the previous sixty years. And yet, wherever we locate the satire in the history of the English Reformation (to say nothing of Donne's own religious biography), few critics can deny William Empson's basic claim that Donne was 'against burning people alive for their religious convictions' (127). The spectre of interrogation, torture, incarceration, and capital punishment haunts several of Donne's other Satires; he is not glib or self-congratulatory about the conventional association of satire and violence.

To state this point differently, Donne frequently introduces into his Satires philosophical or religious principles that mitigate the satiric disdain he voices. Early in several of the Satires he introduces pity, charity, and kindness, concepts that are quite alien to Marston's poems but that coexist closely with hatred and scorn in Donne's (cf. *Sat2* ll. 1–4; 3 ll. 1–2; 4 ll. 1–2). More ominously, Donne also talks a good deal about fear, and it is not the fear that his victims feel when confronted with his satiric wrath. He spends the first half of *Sat4*, a long, graphic, Dantesque tour of Elizabeth's court, conversing with a certain 'thing' who appears to be part courtly parasite, part Jesuit priest, and part agent provocateur. This 'thing' remains determinately unnamed, but it freely dispenses slanderous court gossip: 'Who wasts in meat, in clothes, in horse, he notes; / Who loves Whores, who boyes, and who goats' (ll. 127–8). Donne does not seem to want to know exactly who loves goats. In fact, he senses danger in merely acquiring this knowledge: 'I more amas'd then Circes prisoners, when / They felt themselves turne beasts, felt my selfe then / Becomming Traytor' (ll. 129–31). This remarkable moment suggests that, in Elizabeth's police state, the passive, unwanted acquisition of information could be construed as the commission of treason. A little later Donne reconsiders this experience and insists,

> Low feare
> Becomes the guiltie, not th'accuser; Then,
> Shall I, nones slave, of high borne, or rais'd men
> Fear frownes?
>
> (ll. 160–3)

This is about as close as Donne ever gets to Marston's and Hall's sense of authorial impunity, but it is a perspective Donne can maintain only in the safe, 'wholesome solitarinesse' of his home (l. 155). He goes on to recount the subsequent, equally horrifying, conclusion of his trip to Elizabeth's presence chamber from which he escapes, shaking 'like a spyed Spie', as 'Tyr'd' and 'pleas'd' 'As men which from gaoles to'execution goe' (ll. 237, 229–30). Marston and Hall rarely convey this sense of vulnerability.

It is up to the biographers to explain why Donne felt vulnerable, why he dwelt so often on danger and fear while his contemporaries did not (see Ch. 43). From a generic point of view, however, it is possible to explain how, if not why, Donne created his uniquely vulnerable satiric persona by synthesizing classical models. Donne's *Sat1*, probably the Satire least polluted by an atmosphere of peril, is a good example of Donne's eclectic classicizing. Its basic plot is taken from Horace's delightful Satire 1.9, in which, while taking a chance stroll down Rome's *Via Sacra*, Horace becomes attached to a talkative bore who tactlessly pumps him for personal favours. In his reworking of this satire, Donne becomes a dutiful student induced by a companion, whom he calls a 'fondling motley humorist' (l. 1), to leave his cramped study (ll. 1–52) for a diverting trip through the streets of London (ll. 53–112) to visit the companion's 'Love' (l. 106), who proves to be either unfaithful or just a prostitute (or both). The walk through town, the snippets of sarcastic dialogue between two mismatched personalities, and the comic catastrophe give away the primary Horatian model (the catastrophe, it should be noted, also echoes the conclusion of Horace 1.2). But Donne mixes in elements more commonly identified with Persius and Juvenal as well. Persius often presents himself as a young but serious student, not terribly experienced in the outside world, and so he, rather than the savvy Horace, seems like a more natural model for the reluctant, bookish Donne. Likewise, because Donne's interlocutor does not actually speak (l. 83) until well after he has persuaded Donne to hit the street (l. 52), much of the poem feels less like Horace and more like Prufrockean interior monologue ('"Come, lets goe"' [l. 52]). Critics have argued that such a dialogue between representatives of the spirit and the flesh harks back to a long tradition of Christian devotional writing. But it was Persius who first parodied Horace's trademark sociability and chattiness by admitting that he created a fictional interlocutor purely to have someone to argue with (1.44). Still other elements seem more Juvenalian. In the poem's second half Donne vividly depicts a cityscape awash with agglomerated vice (itchy lust, naked ambition, ostentatious vanity, and, worst of all, constant inconstancy). His language is direct, colourful, and sometimes obscene, and his style frequently veers toward declamation. Other traits borrowed from each of the three Roman satirists could be listed. But already in 1598 Marston, while boasting of his Persian obscurity and Juvenalian indignation, mocked pedantic critics for attaching '*Epethite*[s]' to his satires ('*that's* Persius *vaine*, *That's* Iuvenals, *heere's* Horace' [Marston 138, ll. 94–6]). And it seems best to conclude with Arnold Stein that 'Donne does not make or give himself an easily identifiable character as do earlier and later professional satirists' (1984: 75).

Or, as Juvenal famously put it in a question that betrays the genre's simultaneous obsession with and disregard for genealogies of all sorts, 'What's the use of pedigrees?' (*Stemmata quid faciunt*; 322–3, 8.1).

A similar point about Donne's elusive satiric persona can be made by examining Guilpin's debt to Donne's *Sat1* (see Hester 1984). In the middle of that poem, Donne enters the vice-ridden streets and begins to screw himself up into an indignant moral outrage signalled by repetition of 'sooner' (ll. 53, 57, and 59). But, before he can lash out with savage indignation, Donne suddenly unwinds and wonders, 'But how shall I be pardon'd my offence / That thus have sinn'd against my conscience?' (ll. 65–6). Whether we take the question as ironic or sincere, Donne's posture here contrasts sharply with the posture that Guilpin takes at a similar moment in his *Satire 5*, a poem that seems to be modelled on Donne's. As he enters the street, Guilpin asks, 'Oh what a pageant's this? what foole was I / To leaue my studie to see vanitie?' (D6ʳ). Although he says he *was* a fool, Guilpin now confidently assesses his own previous judgements. The two poems' endings similarly underscore the different kinds of satiric personae that Donne and Guilpin create. Here is the catastrophe of Donne's poem:

> At last his [i.e. the 'humorist's'] Love he in a windowe spies,
> And like light dew exhal'd, he flings from mee
> Violently ravish'd to his lechery.
> Many were there, he could command no more;
> He quarrell'd, fought, bled; and turn'd out of dore
>   Directly came to mee hanging the head,
>   And constantly a while must keepe his bed.
>
> (ll. 106–12)

The joke and the violence here are directed towards Donne's flighty companion; Donne himself emerges comparatively unscathed, though as the proverbial fool following a fool he cannot be said to have gained much standing from his companion's demise. In Guilpin's poem, by contrast, after the poet parts ways with his companion (who has at last found his 'mistress minkes'), he encounters a group of rowdies heading to the tavern after seeing a play. A brawl ensues and Guilpin suddenly steps out of the narrative to impose his moral judgement:

> Enough of these then, and enough of all,
> I may thanke you for this time spent; but call,
> Henceforth I'le keepe my studie, and eschew,
> The scandall of my thoughts, my follies view.
>
> (D7ᵛ)

The closure of Guilpin's poem is more contrived, more edifying, more definitive. He asserts a kind of authorial self-control that is conspicuously absent in Donne.

Critics who see the young Donne as frustrated in his professional ambitions and anxious about his religious beliefs take a rather dim view of the vulnerability of his satiric persona and the openness of his Satires themselves. But a more affirmative view is also possible, and again it can be described in terms of Donne's generic innovations. Romance is conventionally the generic antithesis of satire. But each of Donne's Satires features the pursuit of something, a something usually embodied in or personified by a woman. This is most obviously true in *Sat3*, a remarkable and much-studied poem in which Donne foregoes the pursuit of philosophical 'vertue' and 'earths honour' (ll. 7 and 9) that the classical satirists had undertaken in order to pursue 'faire Religion' and 'heavens joyes' (ll. 5 and 8), aims that are first figured as a 'Mistresse' (l. 5) and then, in the guise of 'Truth' (l. 80), at the summit of a 'huge hill' (l. 79) to be ascended.

But other, less exalted mistresses can be found in the other Satires as well: the prostitute lover in the brisk narrative of *Sat1*; Coscus' Lady in the epistolary *Sat2*; the Queen in the courtly nightmare recounted in *Sat4*; and both the Queen and 'Faire lawes' (l. 69) in *Sat5*, an almost occasional and frankly anticlimactic disquisition on the role of wealth in the administration of law. In the context of these pursuits, it is easier to see Donne's fear as a positive attribute so that, to expand one of Donne's core and transvaluing assertions in *Sat3*, 'feare great courage, and high valour is' (l. 16). In fact, the ordering of the Satires—which, as the forthcoming *Variorum* edition will demonstrate, almost always circulated in groups and in their current order—invites readers to imagine Donne's search or pursuit continuing between poems. *Sat2*'s 'I do hate / Perfectly all this towne' (ll. 1–2) seems to pick up not far from where *Sat1* ends. And the high-minded injunction to seek out 'our Mistresse faire Religion' (l. 5) in *Sat3* leads, as Alexander Pope attempted to conceal and as M. Thomas Hester has more recently revealed, to the rather grim survey of the numerous vestiges of banned Catholic religiosity that one might find in, of all places, Elizabeth's presence chamber (1982: 73–97). (When Pope versified Donne's second and fourth Satires, publishing them together in his 1735 *Works*, he not only embalmed Donne's satiric wit in smarmy cleverness but also removed much of Donne's religious imagery.)

In short, in each of his Satires and throughout his Satires, Donne is looking for something. Perhaps it is an unattainable ideal (truth, liberty, justice); perhaps it is something more personal and circumstantial (employment, admiration, safety). One prevalent view over the past several decades has been that Donne's Satires constitute a 'drama of self-discovery' in, as it were, five acts (see Lauritsen). Whether or not this is true, and regardless of what kind of self we say Donne discovers, it is clear that neither Donne's classical models nor his contemporaries conceived of the same kind of drama. Thus Marston ostentatiously dedicates *The Scourge of Villanie* (1598) to 'his most esteemed, and best beloued Selfe' (94), a self that he clearly thinks he has already discovered.

This point returns us to Cave's 1620 poem, which acknowledged how difficult it was for seventeenth-century readers to discover the Donne of the Satires. In describing this difficulty, Cave invokes 'That Man / who first found out the Perspective which can / make starrs at midday plainly seen' (A. J. Smith 76). This man is the Danish astronomer Tycho Brahe (1546–1601), who sought to popularize 'Crypteria' or observatories built in 'deep concaves in Gardens, where the Stars might be observed even at noon'; these crypteria worked, it was said, by shutting out 'that lustre, which by *reflection*, doth spread about us from the face of the Earth' (Wotton 1650: 298). One might have liked Cave to compare Brahe to Donne at this point, thus implying that Donne had found a satiric 'Perspective', strategically hidden within the garden of late Elizabethan culture, that allowed him to see and critique his social universe plainly and truthfully. But Cave's point is that Donne's *readers* need a special interpretive perspective, a sort of crypterion or 'frame' through which we can 'finde' Donne's 'sense' in the same way we would find stars at midday (A. J. Smith 76). The generic tradition of Roman formal verse satire provides one such interpretive frame, one that requires us to diminish the reflected 'luster' created by other late Elizabethan formal verse satirists without blocking out the dominant light of the classical models that Donne shared with them.

CHAPTER 10

THE ELEGY

R. V. YOUNG

The title Elegies is problematic for many modern readers considering the poems by John Donne gathered under that title. The term 'elegy' is generally associated with poems of mourning, either for the death of an individual (e.g. Milton's *Lycidas*) or for the melancholy fact of human mortality as such (e.g. Gray's *Elegy Written in a Country Churchyard*). There is virtually nothing else in English with the same title comparable to Donne's Elegies, and their erotic themes and ironic tone, often sliding into satire, are comprehensible only if his models among classical poets and their neo-Latin imitators during the Renaissance are taken into account. Once this literary context is established, then Donne's particular contribution to the genre, which he imagines anew in terms of his own peculiar situation in England at the threshold of the seventeenth century, emerges as a remarkable instance of the 'fresh invention planted' with which he is credited by Thomas Carew (Donne 1633*b*: 386, l. 28).

In the Greek and Roman poetry of antiquity, *elegy* means first of all a poem written in the elegiac metre; that is, couplets consisting of a dactylic hexameter line followed by a quasi-pentameter, which is produced by the omission of the last half of the third and sixth feet. Greek poets used elegiacs for a wide variety of poetic purposes, although the term from which it comes, ἔλεγος, most commonly refers to a lament or a song of mourning. In Latin the measure was first used by Ennius and likewise applied to a wide variety of themes and styles over the centuries. Many epigrams are written in elegiacs—most notably those of Martial—and it can be difficult to ascertain at what point a poem ceases to be an epigram and becomes an elegy.

Donne, however, is undoubtedly thinking of the Roman love elegy, which first emerges with Catullus in the middle of the first century before Christ, and which develops into books of elegies with Tibullus, Propertius, and Ovid in the latter half of the century. We have other names of Roman elegists whose work has not survived—Gallus, for example—and there are a handful of poems in the Tibullan collection now attributed to Lygdamus and the woman poet Sulpicia; but Tibullus himself, Propertius, and Ovid are the objects of imitation by Donne and other Renaissance authors. As for these Romans, their chief model was the Alexandrian poet Callimachus, although they mention a certain Philetas, whose work has not survived (Luck 35–6; Veyne 17–18).

The Latin love elegy, like so much else in the literature of classical antiquity, was revived by the neo-Latin poets of the Renaissance. To be sure, the elegiac measure also recovered its versatility. Giovanni Pontano (1429–1503), for example, perhaps the dominant humanist poet of fifteenth-century Italy, deploys the elegy to celebrate, console, and lament the loss of his wife and small children—an application of the genre that would never have occurred to his pagan predecessors. The Latin elegies of Joachim Du Bellay (1522–60) are, likewise, not concerned with love affairs, but with describing his sojourn in Rome (II), establishing peace among Christian princes (IV), praising Ronsard (VI), expressing his longing for France (VII), and various other themes. He comes closer to Donne's English Elegies in some of the poems of his *Amores*, but not all of these are written in the elegiac metre. Moreover, the continuity of the story of his loss and recovery of 'Faustina' is unlike anything in Donne or in classical antiquity.

The neo-Latin elegist who most nearly suggests a possible model for Donne's English Elegies is the Flemish poet Joannes Secundus (1511–36), whose production of popular and highly influential Latin poetry was remarkable in a life of Keatsian brevity. No other neo-Latin poet of the Renaissance imitates so faithfully the Roman erotic elegy in constructing a sequence of poems that display the ebb and flow of amorous passion, involving one or more named women. Indeed, Secundus' obsessive desire for one Julia in the first book of his elegies suggested such kinship to the ardent lover of Cynthia that he was known among Renaissance readers as 'the "Belgian Propertius"' (Endres 41–2). His work was available in England, since we know that Ben Jonson owned a copy of the 1582 edition (ibid. 32). Nevertheless, like Du Bellay's *Amores*, Secundus' elegies seem to intimate a narrative continuity and to represent an intense, personal passion unlike what we find either in the Romans or in Donne. To be sure, the question of sincerity and the relationship between the poems and the reality of the poet's life are vexed issues not only among students of Donne's poetry, but also among scholars of the Roman erotic elegy, which provides a model (cf. Veyne 44 and, for an opposing perspective, the essays collected in Lively and Salzman-Mitchell).

Thomas Campion (1567–1620), better known now for his English songs and for his scheme for introducing classical metres into English poetry, claims to be the first Englishman to compose Latin elegies with his *Elegiarum liber*, included in his *Thomae Campiani Poemata* (1595, rev. edn. 1619). It is of course possible that Donne saw these poems in manuscript before their publication, but there is no evidence of this. He was certainly writing his English Elegies before Campion's Latin poems saw print, and there is little in either set of poems to suggest direct influence in either direction.

The most obvious candidate for Donne's model is Christopher Marlowe's (1564–93) translation of Ovid's *Amores* under the title *Ovid's Elegies*, but here again the dating creates questions. While Marlowe's rendering was (obviously) completed by 1593, the first partial edition was not published before 1598. Some scholars, assuming that Donne knew Marlowe's work in manuscript, have suggested that his version of the *Amores* was at least an inspiration (Wanning 182; LaBranche 359–60; Gill 70; Armstrong 421); but only one asserts a specific verbal similarity between a phrase in Donne's Elegies and a passage in Marlowe's translation (Bedford 222–3). In any case, Donne himself seems to have regarded these poems, like his Satires, as a generic collection or 'book' of Elegies, as a notorious remark in a Letter written around 1600 may suggest: 'to my satyrs there belongs some feare and to some elegies and these perhaps shame' (E. M. Simpson 1948: 316).

Despite the interpretive necessity of placing them in the literary context of the Roman erotic elegy and its Renaissance humanist imitators, a reader who comes to Donne's Elegies after perusing Tibullus, Propertius, and Ovid or Secundus, Du Bellay, and Campion will be struck by their originality. (The *Variorum* editors enhance this originality by including *Sorrow* among the Epicedes and Obsequies [*Variorum* 6.103] rather than among the Elegies, as Gardner does under the title 'A Funeral Elegy'; Ovid, Propertius, and Tibullus all include funerary poems among their elegies, as do their Renaissance imitators, Secundus and Campion.) While there are certainly precedents and models for most features of Donne's Elegies, taken as a whole they are unique. They are distinctive, first, in what Donne leaves out. He makes little use of myth: 'Cupid' turns up only once in the Elegies (*ElProg* l. 28) and again as 'Love' (*ElAut* l. 15), and possibly once more, (*ElProg* ll. 4–5), and 'Venus' also turns up only once, and then as a planet rather than a goddess (*ElPart* l. 7). In Donne's Elegies we encounter no *recusatio*, that is, no self-conscious defence of writing love poetry rather than celebrating military heroism (as, for example, in Propertius 3.3, Tibullus 1.1, Ovid *Amores* 1.1, and Secundus *Elegiarum* 1.1.), and no proclamation of literary immortality either for himself or for his mistress. Indeed, there is no mistress—at least no name attributed to a particular woman in whose love the poetic persona exults, of whose absence or scorn he complains. Traditionally, elegiac love poets have given fictional names to the objects of their passion. Tibullus is charmed by Delia and, in Book II, by Nemesis; Propertius by Cynthia, Ovid by Corinna. Their Renaissance successors imitate this device: Joannes Secundus is tormented by unsatisfied desire for Julia and plots his erotic conquest of Neaera and Venerilla in a second book; Joachim Du Bellay eventually finds more success with Faustina. Campion mentions a certain Sybilla as well as Caspia and Mellea. In declining to provide a name for a particular woman, Donne also forgoes the pretence—inconsistent and shadowy as it usually is—of narrative continuity.

This omission, however, provides Donne with the opportunity to offer an enhanced diversity of personae and hence of tone. If no particular mistress is named, then there is no need to maintain a consistent outlook in the speaker. Donne is thus able to explore a variety of attitudes towards love, as well as a diverse array of erotic situations and problems. Finally, although Donne's speakers are often disillusioned or disappointed, sometimes even a bit absurd, they never assume the posture of comically abject servitude that is a standard feature of the erotic elegy from Catullus into the sixteenth century. The *Variorum* editors have presented a good deal of textual evidence suggesting that the Elegies always constituted a specific set of poems, although the items admitted to the group and their order, as well as the content of individual poems, seem to have been subject to successive revisions. Further, the editors surmise that the sequence of twelve Elegies collected in the Westmoreland ms. (*Variorum* siglum NY3) by Rowland Woodward represents the final set of texts in the definitive arrangement of the book intended by Donne (*Variorum* 2.LXVII–LXX; see Ch. 15 below for a discussion of how the twelve Holy Sonnets of the 1633 edition represent Donne's final intentions for that sequence). The motive and method of revision are exemplified by the relation between *ElBrac* and *ElProg*. The *Variorum* editors conjecture that the former, contrary to the usual assumption, is a later addition to the collection of twelve written to replace *ElProg*. Although the poet may have 'withheld [*ElProg*] from circulation—either because he remained generally uncomfortable with his handling of the material or because the poem resisted technical completion', the poem 'actually opens on an annunciatory note that might well serve to introduce the entire sequence, admonishing "Who euer loues" to begin by properly considering "The right true end of loue"' (2.LXXII). Considering the first twelve Elegies from this perspective makes it fairly easy to construct a rationale for the omission of the remaining six, regarded as authentic by the *Variorum* editors, from the 'Book'.

ElChange closes with a complex conceit of flowing water in order to illustrate a nuanced resolution to the problematic desire for sexual variety: 'To love not any one, nor euery one' (l. 28). The apparently rejected elegy, *ElProg*, closes with a verbally convoluted but conventional proposal to settle down and abandon 'variety' once the perfect woman possessed of all feminine virtues appears: 'Which being found assembled in some one / Wee'le leaue her euer, and loue her alone' (ll. 81–2). It is not difficult to conceive why a poet would prefer a more sophisticated idea in simpler syntax.

ElPart and *ElExpost* are both poems of leave-taking as are *ElFatal* and *ElPict* in the twelve-elegy sequence, and it is, again, not hard to see why the latter two would be favoured. *ElPart* exists in several seventeenth-century versions of widely varying length, and as the *Variorum* editors observe, 'There is thus no easy answer to the problem of selecting a copy-text' and 'to construct a readable text has required a substantial amount of emendation' (2.339). Further, Donne seems to have cannibalized *ElPart* for other Elegies in the final sequence. Both *ElJeal* (esp. ll. 31–2) and

ElFatal (l. 12: 'Thou shallt not Love by meanes so dangerous') seem to echo, for instance, the following lines:

> Wast not enough, that thou didst hazard vs
> To pathes in loue soe darke soe dangerous
> And those so ambusht round with houshould spies
> And over all the towred husbands eyes
> That flam'd with oylie sweat of Ielousie?
>
> (ll. 39–43)

Similarly, *ElExpost* presents a difficult text that suggests incompletion and a plethora of somewhat incoherent narrative details generally uncharacteristic of the first twelve Elegies.

ElAut and *Sappho* are unlike anything else among the Elegies and may never have been part of the proposed book, although the preponderance of textual evidence suggests that both poems are compatible with Donne's work in the genre and properly attributed to him. *ElAut* has been traditionally associated with Lady Magdalen Herbert (for whom, Walton asserts [1675: 267], Donne wrote the poem), a connection that, if true, would make it later than the other Elegies are thought to be. Praising an older woman for the attractiveness of her aged features is cleverly original, and there is nothing surprising in a poet like Donne hazarding such an unconventional kind of compliment and treating it as an innovation in the elegiac tradition. Similarly, *Sappho* stands out as 'the first female homosexual poem in English' (Carey 1981a: 270). Technically, it is a 'heroical epistle' modelled on Ovid's elegiac *Heroides*—hypothetical letters by famous women of Graeco-Roman myth and history to their (usually faithless) lovers. Surprisingly, unlike *ElProg* and *ElBed*, it seems not to have roused the ire of the licencers and appears in every seventeenth-century edition, despite its somewhat graphic depiction of homoerotic love-making. Perhaps it was regarded as such an exotic literary exercise as not to be a threat to morals.

In any case, neither *ElAut* nor *Sappho*, for all their virtues of originality and wit, fits the thematic scheme that emerges from the final sequence of the twelve-elegy book: the uncertainties of love for an alienated young man among the particular perils of London in the 1590s. The uniquely hard edge of Donne's Elegies is a result of their intimate association with a setting of dangerous political and religious repression. Indeed, the innuendo of his language is sometimes so insistent that the erotic concerns of the Elegies seem fused with their political and religious anxieties. As Achsah Guibbory observes, 'These poems reveal a deep sense of the connectedness of private and political human relations' (1990: 829). This 'connectedness' is one of the deeply original elements of the Elegies, and the ultimate import of these relations is one of their most controversial aspects.

ElBrac exemplifies many of the distinctive features of Donne's contribution to the classical love elegy. While it lacks the element of graphic lubriciousness that evidently kept *ElProg* out of the printed editions of Donne's poems until 1669, it was, nonetheless, among the poems 'officially excepted' from the 1633 edition, 'presumably for political or religious reasons'; and 'government authorization had not yet been obtained' when it was included in the second edition of 1635 (*Variorum* 2.8). The 'political or religious' features that might well have been troubling to censors fairly leap off the page, and these are aggravated by a seething tone of disillusioned resentment.

To be sure, gestures of political dissidence make an appearance in Roman erotic elegy, but they never even hint at the fear and hostility that pervade Donne's work. While Ovid was genuinely shocked at his exile by the emperor Augustus, it is generally believed that naughty poems were not the only cause of the emperor's ire. Many of Donne's Elegies are fraught with political and religious implications that are at times barely contained by the erotic fiction. The familiar pun on 'angel'—a coin bearing an image of the Archangel Michael on one face—offers numerous opportunities for irreverence. The mistress's demand in *ElBrac* that the poetic persona melts down 'twelve righteous Angels' in order to replace her lost bracelet is lamented with lugubrious cynicism. This crude secular expropriation of the spiritual mission of biblical angels is matched by an equally reductive mock theologizing of the 'damnation' suffered by 'innocent' coins:

> Shall these twelue innocents, by thy seuere
> Sentence, dradd Iudge, my sins great burden beare?
> Shall they be damn'd and in the furnace throwne
> And punisht for offenses, not their owne.
>
> (ll. 17–20)

The mistress is characterized by the 'divinity' of the conventional Petrarchan beloved, but she manifests not the numinous attributes of love and beauty, but wrathful judgement instead. What is more, her attitude towards her poetic lover is as calculating as his: 'if thou Loue let them alone / For thou wilt loue me lesse, when they are gone' (ll. 53–4).

The contrast between the fated 'angels' and the debased coins of France and Spain would probably not alarm the government (ll. 23–36). Such ridicule of foreigners is a familiar feature of the Elizabethan stage—compare Portia's descriptions of her various suitors in *The Merchant of Venice* (I. ii.), for example. Much of what follows, however, might well give pause to the licenser. The divine implacability of the ruthless mistress could be taken for a comment on the harshness of Queen Elizabeth's reign, especially in view of her appropriation of Petrarchan motifs in dealing with her courtiers (S. Frye 108, 135). It might also suggest the wrath of the Calvinist God removing all hope of escape from the ironclad decree of predestination for those who are not elect, and at least one commentator (Gill 69) has found a derisory image of the burial of Christ in the distraught persona reluctantly surrendering his coins to the fire 'as her only Sonne / The Mother in the hungry graue doth lay' (ll. 80–1). Such flippant allusions to fiery martyrdom and the Our Father

(l. 79: 'thy will be donne') are sufficiently provocative to offend a respectable Elizabethan reader.

It only gets worse when the persona curses the hypothetical 'wretched finder' in terms that evoke the fear posed by agents of the Crown in their vigilance against sedition and assassination:

> May the next thing thou stoopst to reach, containe
> Poyson, whose nimble fume rott thy moist braine:
> Or Libells, or some interdicted thing
> Which negligently kept, thy ruyne bring.
> (ll. 99–102)

In 1593, frequently regarded as the *terminus a quo* for *ElBrac*, Thomas Kyd was arrested by officers of the Lord Mayor searching for the authors of 'libels against strangers' and hauled off to Bridewell Prison. Among his papers were fragments of a disputation denying the divinity of Christ, which Kyd claimed had been left in his lodgings by Christopher Marlowe, who would be killed within three weeks (Harrison 253, 257–8; see R. V. Young 2000c: 253–7 for further reflections on the topical elements in *ElBrac*).

Allusions of this kind to topical issues in Elizabethan London, as well as mockery of moral principle and religious mystery, are common throughout the Elegies. In *ElComp* the skin of the ugly woman resembles 'sun-parch'd quarters on the City gate' (l. 31), a recollection of the grisly destiny of the body parts of those executed for treason. *ElPerf* is a virtual gallery of pictures from the persecution of Catholic recusants in the 1580s and 1590s. The furtive trysts of the lovers are carried out in the manner of secret Masses in great houses, and the mistress's mother has all the marks of a pursuivant, accosting suspects, searching for the appurtenances of Catholic worship, and asking leading questions:

> And when She takes thy hand, and would seeme kind
> Doth search what rings and armelets she can find [...],
> And politiquely will to thee confes
> The Sins of her owne Youths ranke Lustines.
> (ll. 17–19, 23–4)

If the suspicious mother seems to be an agent provocateur attempting to lead her victim into an indiscreet admission, her husband reacts to the persona's 'loud perfume'—which is compared to the incense used in the Catholic liturgy—with a despot's fear: 'so we weare spyed / When like a tyrant king that in his bed / Smelt Gunpowder, the pale wretch shivered' (ll. 41–4; see R. V. Young 1987b for further discussion of the Elegies and the persecution of Catholic recusants). Jacobean readers may have been struck by an ironic, if fortuitous, prophecy of the Gunpowder Plot of 1605 aimed at King James and his Parliament.

The adulterous persona of *ElJeal* concludes by recommending to his mistress that they elude her husband's suspicions by going into a domestic 'exile' from his 'house',

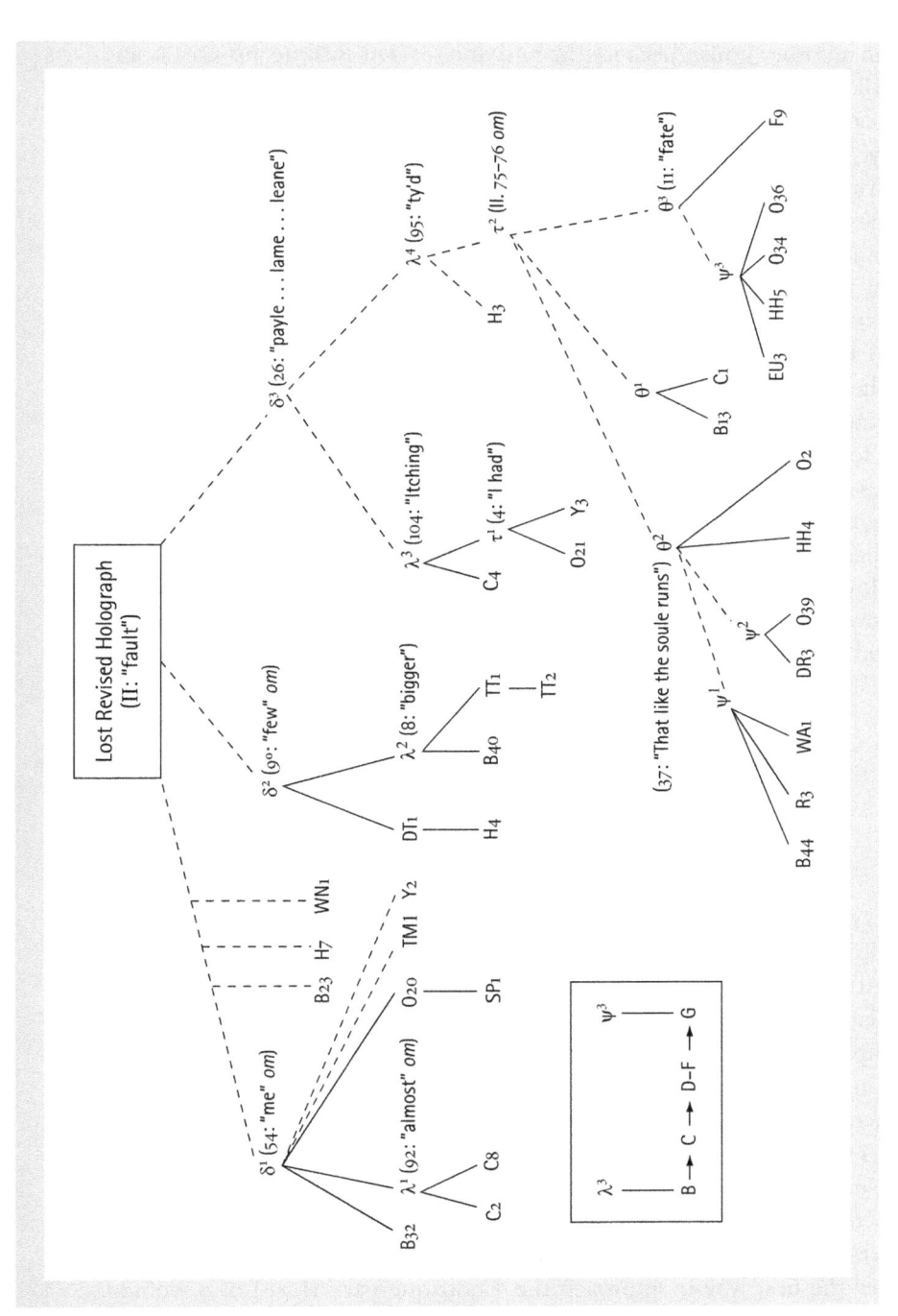

Ill. 10.1. Gary A. Stringer's stemma for the revised text of *ElBrac* (*Donne Variorum* 2.46). This graceful stemma illustrates three major lines of transmission of early copies of the poem deriving from a lost revised holograph not extant. Each of these lines descends through subbranches comprising the traditional manuscript groups I, II, and III. For identification of sigla and discussion of bibliographical details, see *Variorum* 2.XXXII–XXXVII and 11–17. (Reproduced with the permission of Indiana University Press.)

analogous to the actual practice of numerous Catholic recusants (including members of Donne's family), as well as various kinds of Protestant dissidents. The lovers must 'play' in an other house' because the husband's is 'His Realme, his Castle, and his Diocis' (ll. 30, 26). It is difficult to imagine how the poet could have found a more provocative set of comparisons and allusions, but, as in *Sat3*, where 'a Philip, or a Gregory, / A Harry, or a Martin' (ll. 96–7) are equally unsatisfactory sureties for personal salvation, so here 'skorne' for authority is aimed both at 'Londons Maior' and 'the Popes pride' (ll. 31, 34).

Political and religious discontent is prominent in the poet's appropriation of images from the voyages of discovery and schemes for colonization of the New World. *ElWar* seems to imagine an essentially maritime conflict, in Donne's time arising from England's struggle with Spain for control of access to the riches of America—the Cadiz and Islands expeditions, for example, in which the poet himself participated. 'And Midas ioyes our Spanish iourneys giue, / We touch all gold, but find no food to liue' (ll. 17–18), complains the speaker. 'Long Voyages are long consumptions', he adds, '/ And ships are carts for executions' (ll. 25–6).

Of course, this poem owes a good deal to Ovid's risqué comparison between the Roman soldier and the illicit lover, especially in *Amores* 1.9, where the poet depicts the 'armèd' lover, taking advantage of a sleeping husband in order to use his 'weapons' on a drowsy 'foe' (1977: 1.355–9, ll. 21–6). It is not difficult to see the resemblance between Ovid's ridicule of militarism and Donne's equally sardonic take on English forays:

> Here let me warr; in these armes let me ly
> Here let me parle, batter, bleede, and dy.
> Thy armes imprison me, and myne armes thee,
> Thy hart thy ransome is, take myne for mee.
>
> (ll. 29–32)

Donne's Elegy seems more immediate and personal than Ovid's, however, perhaps because his lover addresses a particular woman rather than the Roman poet's shadowy friend Atticus and 'whoever called love idleness' (l. 31).

In thus adapting classical conventions to the issues and concerns of his own time, Donne exemplifies the essence of humanist imitation, which is always an aspiration to emulate and even surpass, rather than merely to copy. While an Ovid or a Propertius wrote in the context of a triumphant Roman empire, extolled by Virgil and Horace, Donne's background was an age of discovery and competitive exploitation of the New World by the emergent European powers. As *ElWar* takes a sardonic view of the conflict between Spain and England in the Atlantic, so *ElProg* reduces the controversies among explorers over the best route to the riches of the 'Indies' to a debate over the best way to approach the 'Centrique part' (l. 36) of a woman. Starting at her face and working downwards—a mock blason—is compared to a lengthy and difficult and ultimately futile sea voyage (ll. 40–72).

Of course, the culmination of this figurative device comes in the notorious *ElBed*, which, like *ElProg*, did not see print until the 1669 edition of Donne's *Poems*:

> Oh my America, my newfound land,
> My kingdome, safelyest when with one man man'd.
> My Myne of pretious stones; my empiree;
> How blest ame I in this discouering thee!
>
> (ll. 27–30)

Lying behind this trope is a good deal of English imperialistic propaganda, much of it motivated by jealousy of Spain's head start in the exploitation of the riches of the New World. What is more, Donne closes out the Elegy with an elaborate tissue of religious metaphors that daringly make light of contemporaneous doctrinal disputes:

> Like pictures, or like bookes gay coverings, made
> For lay men, are all women thus arrayd,
> Themselues are mistique bookes, which only wee
> Whom their imputed grace will dignify
> Must see reuealed.
>
> (ll. 39–43)

Both Catholic clericalism and the Protestant notion of the imputation of Christ's righteousness to the elect are simultaneously reduced to the fashionable whims of a woman of dubious virtue (see R. V. Young 1987b; Hester 1987a, who finds in the lady in the Elegy a mocking image of Queen Elizabeth's expropriation of the iconography of the Blessed Virgin Mary; and Hackett).

The treatment of love within this context of political and religious allusion is often quite ingeniously witty, but also cynical and not infrequently even crude. The tone of the Elegies has occasioned a good deal of critical dismay. Achsah Guibbory speaks for many in accusing the Elegies of 'a persistent misogyny, indeed a revulsion at the female body' (1990: 812; see also Sanders, esp. 39, 40, 41–2; Gill, esp. 55–6; and Carey 1981a: 105–6). Guibbory, 'arguing not that love is a metaphor for politics but that love itself is political—involves power transactions between men and women' (1990: 811), offers an implicit rebuttal to R. V. Young (1987b) and Hester (1987a), who maintain that *ElBed* and some of the other risqué Elegies are focused on political as much as erotic concerns. (The view that Donne the poet, as opposed to the poetic persona, was a misogynist has since been sharply challenged by M. L. Stapleton; see also Ch. 38 below.) Evidence of impatience with and disdain for women as well as a coarse, exploitative view of sexual relationships abounds in the Elegies. The speaker of *ElBrac* regrets the loss of this object not for its tender associations, but on account of 'the bitter cost' (l. 8), and both *ElComp* and *ElAnag* furnish grotesque and repugnant images of women's bodies. In *ElPerf* the furtive lover suggests that his mistress's real attraction, her 'bewtyes bewty, and food of our love', has been correctly identified by her father as 'Hope of his goods' (ll. 10–11); and in

ElProg the essence of a woman becomes merely her vaginal orifice, and the poem ends with a foul analogy for a man who thinks a woman's face an object of love: 'his Error is as great / As whoe by Clister gaue the stomack meate' (ll. 95–6).

An assessment of the Elegies demands, however, a careful consideration of the nature of their discourse and the relationship between a poet and his poems. The speakers of Donne's Elegies—in contrast to the personae of Ovid's *Amores* and the poems of Tibullus and Propertius—do not coalesce into a single, consistent figure. The blasé adulterer who briskly dismisses his mistress's fears of her husband's suspicions in *ElJeal* can hardly be identified with the feckless youth whose elaborate precautions and furtive secrecy are overturned when his mistress's father is alerted by a 'loud perfume' to the presence of an interloper in his house. Apprehended on account of his fashionable scent, the furtive lover of *ElPerf* berates himself for 'the greatest Staine to mans estate / [. . .] to be calld effeminate' (ll. 61–2).

His tone is likewise different both from the seething resentment of the man who must replace his lady's lost bracelet and the arrogant presumption of the speaker of *ElComp*, who in equally extravagant terms extols his own beloved and belittles another woman, imperiously disparaging his listener's taste in feminine charm with a witty turn on a familiar proverb: 'Leaue her, and I will leaue comparing thus / She, and comparisons are odious' (ll. 53–4). *ElAnag* likewise offers the speech of one man ridiculing the erotic propensities of another, but the tropes in this poem are so outlandish and inconsistent that it seems more an exercise in absurdity than a hostile attack. Once the central conceit is in place, the poem becomes a device for generating ingenious insults: 'Though all her parts be not in th'vsuall place / She hath yet an Anagram of a good face' (ll. 15–16). Sheer exuberance of wit makes it impossible to see this as a real attempt to injure a particular woman, even a fictitious character. 'Giue her thyne; and She hath a Maydenhead', the persona chortles early in the poem (l. 8), but towards the close he is recommending 'Flauia' as bride because her husband would never have to fear infidelity on her part, 'Who though seauen yeares She in the Stews had layd / A Nunnery durst receive, and thinke a Mayd' (ll. 47–8). Misogyny should be made of sterner stuff.

The speaker of *ElNat* presents yet another face: the urbane seducer whose ingénue mistress has eventually proven more subtle and less faithful than he. While there is an obvious echo of Ovid's *Amores* 1.4 and Tibullus 1.6 in detailing an erotic code of symbolic objects—for instance, 'the Alphabett / Of flowers [. . .] devisefully beeing sett' (2.127, ll. 9–10)—and in the evident frustration of watching another man enjoy the woman to whom he has served as Ovidian *praeceptor amoris*, Donne's persona is a far more irately jealous victim of ironic comeuppance:

> Must I alas
> Frame and enamell plate, and drinke in glas?
> Chafe waxe for others Seales; breake a Colts force
> And leaue him then, beeing made a redy horse?
>
> (ll. 27–30)

Tibullus, Propertius, and Ovid all create a familiar, consistent character who elicits the reader's amused sympathy; the diversity of Donne's personae evokes a less sympathetic response. Hence Gill's unfavourable contrast between Donne's 'adolescent crudeness' and Ovid's 'suave sophistication' (55) misses the former's originality in *not* asking the reader to identify with the Elegies' dramatized voices.

Now it is true that in the 1590s the historical John Donne had a reputation as a ladies' man: he had to defend himself against the charge 'of having deceivd some gentlewomen before' to his very reluctant father-in-law, Sir George More (*Marriage Letters* 40), and years later he was famously recalled by Sir Richard Baker as, among other things, 'a great visiter of Ladies' (Baker 156). It would, moreover, be exceedingly naive to assume that such a man had never entertained the various disdainful and angry sentiments towards women uttered by the speakers of his Elegies—or that he had never himself expressed them among his coterie at the Inns of Court. What a man is capable of imagining or saying, however, is not the same as a settled opinion. It is one of the functions of literature—especially the short dramatic poem—to explore the shadowed byways and dark corners of human experience and confront whatever is found. Surely we can grant Donne a measure of Shakespeare's negative capability?

The core of his originality is precisely the convergence of classical elegiac convention with a vividly concrete realization of the political and religious circumstances of late Elizabethan England as apprehended by a sensibility rendered exceptionally acute both by nature and heritage. The Elegies are an exemplary embodiment of humanist imitation at its best: the forms and devices of classical poetry are re-imagined in the poet's own historical time and subjected to the power of his wit and passionate awareness. In addition to his sheer poetic talent, Donne also possessed a perspective uniquely suited for the undertaking because he was both an insider and an outsider with respect to the society and cultural milieu that his poems represent. Donne's Catholic recusant background inevitably created an estrangement between him and an England increasingly dependent on a unique version of Protestantism for its emerging national identity. Yet no one is more English than Donne, no one more of an ingrained Londoner. This quality emerges powerfully in a mastery of the English language surpassed in his day only by Shakespeare. Thomas Carew is particularly perceptive in remarking how

> to the awe of thy imperious wit
> Our stubborne language bends, made only fit
> With her tough-thick-ribb'd hoopes to gird about
> Thy Giant phansie.
> (Donne 1633*b*: 386–7, ll. 49–52)

Similarly, Donne is very much an insider among the restless, ambitious young denizens of the Inns of Court, eager for fame and preferment—what nowadays we call *success*—as well as pleasure. There is no reason to suppose that the young Donne was deficient in desire and aspiration. Nevertheless, his keen intelligence and uncommon verbal gift, along with 'the worst voluptuousnes, which is an Hydroptique immoderate desire of humane learning' (*Letters* 51), would have made him an outsider in any time and place.

The mingling of mordant political and religious observations with the predominantly erotic focus of the Elegies intensifies the element of sly cynicism that alternates with an infectious excitement—even at times exuberance—about the possibilities of sexual experience. The restless personae of the Elegies, with their unedifying opinions about women and blasphemous treatment of religion, are extreme dramatic embodiments of the inner conflicts of Elizabethan society itself. The speaker of *ElBrac* cares more about money, his 'twelve righteous Angels' (l. 9), than about the lady whose bracelet he has lost amidst a world in which marriage is more a matter of social and financial prudence than love. His sardonic regard of 'angels' as coins rather than divine messengers reflects a very religious society in which the worship of Mammon still threatens to displace the worship of God. The belligerence of the arrogant lover of *ElComp* likewise reflects an increasingly competitive society in which every aspect of a man's self-presentation—including the woman in his company—is a mark of his stature.

It must be acknowledged as well that the Elegies' brusque, tough-minded rejection of every wisp of sentimentality is in part a literary rebellion against Petrarchan and Neoplatonic idealizations of feminine beauty and sexual attraction. This rebellion is not, however, merely literary: it equally bespeaks an enthusiasm for the physical pleasures of the flesh. Hence the women in Donne's love poems are never on the pedestals of their Petrarchan sisters and are not infrequently found in bed. Sometimes his determined effort to forge an image of sexual experience that is both graphic and novel brings him to the verge of the grotesque. The persona of *ElComp* likens the love-making of his rival and his despicable mistress to a 'Plough' rending 'stony ground' (l. 48), but the embraces the speaker shares with his beloved are like 'Priests [...] handling reuerent Sacrifice' or 'the Surgeon' 'searching wounds' (ll. 50, 51). That the intimacy of physical love should suggest religious violence and wounds is unsurprising in a man of Donne's generation who had witnessed the violence of battle during the Cadiz expedition and bloody public executions at Tyburn. Although Donne imitates the standard elegiac theme of love displacing valour in *ElWar*, he is unique among love elegists in offering a persona who has himself been in combat.

ElWar introduces another note that is unimaginable in Roman elegy with the suggestion that there is 'More glorious service staying to make men' (l. 46) than by actual fighting. Ovid's Corinna is the only woman in Roman elegy to undergo pregnancy (*Amores* 2.13–14), and the poet only finds out because she ends it by abortion and nearly dies herself. In Donne's poem the possibility of pregnancy is treated as a matter of course, indeed a justification, and hardly seems to deter the lover's enthusiasm. The same high spirits may be found in *ElBed*. John Carey is typical in his disapproval, seeing a 'despotic lover [...] ordering his submissive girl-victim to strip' (1981a: 105), but it is quite as easy to imagine a mature, self-possessed woman who is only having difficulty getting out of her 'spangled brestplate' (l. 7) because she is laughing so hard at her lover's extravagant discourse. To suggest that sexual love with a woman is as thrilling as conquering the New World is hyperbole, and the woman who didn't see it would certainly be a fool; but she would be dull indeed if she failed at least to smile at the ingenuity of the compliment.

ElChange closes by saying, 'Change is the Nurcery / Of Musick, Ioye, Life, and Eternity' (ll. 35–6). Whether the man John Donne ever actually regarded love in this light is problematic, but change or variety is certainly an attribute of the Elegies themselves. By the end of the sequence of twelve, constituting Donne's book of Elegies, the gnawing vexation of *ElBrac* and the scornful contempt of *ElComp* have given way to the ruefully humorous tenderness of leave-taking in *ElFatal* and *ElPict*. The latter invokes the familiar notion that lovers exchange souls in its opening couplet, but the poem closes with an idea of love that purports to be more realistic and hence mature than the standard fare of Petrarchism or the erotic elegy. When he returns from his sea voyage, presumably a naval expedition, the discrepancy between the suave young man in the portrait he has left behind and the tanned, aged, and perhaps injured returning veteran will be no cause of diminished love:

> That which in him was fayre or delicate
> Was but the Milke which in Loves childish State
> Did nourse it: Who now is growne strong inough
> To feede on that which to disvsd tasts seems tough.
>
> (ll. 17–20)

Another original feature of Donne's Elegies that is especially prominent in these two final Elegies of the book is a blending of the same sardonic comedy characteristic of the harsher Elegies with passages of solicitous affection. In *ElPict* the speaker's image of himself returning with his 'body a sack of bones, broken within / And powders blew staines scatterd on my skin' (ll. 9–10) seems a droll parody of the exaggerations of returned soldiers, familiar in Elizabethan drama and satire. Similarly, the expostulation by the persona of *ElFatal* that she refrain from disguising herself as his page in order to follow him on his journey compliments the young woman's 'womanly discovering grace', but then brings in an analogy that would never appear in a Petrarchan poem: 'Richly clothd Apes are calld Apes' (ll. 30, 31). Moreover, the speaker does not forbear to evoke the same kind of national satire that emerges in *ElBrac*: 'Men of France, changeable Cameleons', will immediately recognize her sex; and 'Th'indifferent Italian', 'well content to thinke thee Page' (ll. 33, 38, 39), will seek to commit an outrage.

The nature of Donne's style, his 'words masculine persuasive force' (*ElFatal* l. 4), is consistent throughout the Elegies. It is the character and outlook of the personae and the nature of the problems confronted that change and give the sequence of twelve its shape and significance. In the first six Elegies love is marred or at least threatened by a defect in the relationship itself. The arrogant adulterer of *ElJeal* and the somewhat feckless lover of *ElPerf* are faced with discovery of their illicit affairs by a husband and father respectively. In *ElBrac* and *ElServe* the lovers utter their discontent with the overbearing demands of their mistresses—the latter with unmistakable political overtones, threatening to be 'Recusant' (l. 45). *ElNat* presents a lover who, having taught a woman to cheat and deceive, is dismayed when she turns her wiles on him. The poem's title ironically fits the speaker better than the woman to whom he applies it. Even the surly, assertive persona of *ElComp* seems to protest too much in proclaiming in such outlandish fashion the superiority of his mistress.

The tone shifts subtly in the latter half of the set. *ElWar* and *ElBed* are among the most erotically explicit, but avoid the coarse brutality of some of the others. It is instructive to contrast them with *ElProg*, which deploys a similar conceit of a sea voyage of discovery, but closes with a simile of exceptionally grotesque ugliness. *ElChange* seeks to reconcile a love of amorous variety with some kind of faithfulness, and *ElAnag* takes up the same theme as *ElComp*, but in a jocular and considerably less aggressive fashion. The final two poems in the sequence, *ElFatal* and *ElPict*, invoke constancy and the permanence of love despite anticipated separation. The challenges to the lovers in these poems are external to the relationships themselves.

In sum, the erotic Elegies of John Donne, consisting of a set of twelve poems and what might be called an appendix of additional compositions excluded from the set for one reason or another, portray various kinds of love affairs in a context of severe religious and political anxiety. They are unique in the elegiac tradition in the variety of characters and attitudes they portray, and in the immediacy and realism of situations they evoke. While they draw on some of the conventions of the erotic elegy of ancient Rome and its neo-Latin imitators during the Renaissance, in de-emphasizing the mythological machinery of Venus and Cupid and locating themselves firmly in Elizabethan London, Donne's Elegies are exemplary of his 'fresh invention' (Donne 1633*b*: 386, l. 28).

CHAPTER 11.1

THE PARADOX

MICHAEL W. PRICE

THOUGH today considered obscure, a minor genre, the paradox has flourished from time to time since the classical period, enjoying significant popularity in England at the turn of the seventeenth century (T. Burgess 157–6; Colie 1966: 3-40; *Paradoxes* xvi–xxvii). An important problem for criticism is why the paradox emerged and flourished in England at this particular time. It had developed in two related traditions: the mock encomium and the argument against received opinion. In the former, the paradox was like a 'roast'—ironic praise, replete with burlesqued conventions of formal encomium, for someone or something unworthy of praise. In the sixteenth century the outstanding example of the mock encomium was Desiderius Erasmus' famous *Moriae Encomium* (written in 1509), a declamation in praise of folly (and of Thomas More) that raised this tradition of the genre to unparalleled force and complexity. The paradox as argument against received opinion, however, disputed common sense concerning ethical and other doctrines. In the sixteenth century the outstanding examples of paradoxical argument against received opinion were the *Paradossi* of Ortensio Landi (1543). Asserting in the *Paradossi*, among other things, that it is better to be poor than rich, ugly than beautiful, ignorant than wise, or drunk than sober, Landi cleverly turned every schoolboy's mundane rhetorical exercise upon its head.

His book was enormously popular throughout Western Europe and, from a 1553 French version by Charles Estienne, was translated into English by Anthony Munday in 1593 as *The Defence of Contraries: Paradoxes against common opinion, debated in forme of declamations in place of publike censure: only to exercise yong wittes in difficult matters*, with an extension of Estienne's lengthy subtitle: *Wherein is no offence to Gods honour, the estate of Princes, or priuate mens honest actions: but pleasant recreation to beguile the iniquity of time*. Munday's added disclaimers in effect called attention to subversive potential dissimulated under the performative, declamatory style of the paradoxes. In this generic tradition of Erasmian humanism, rhetorically dissimulating in arguments against received opinion, Donne wrote twelve Paradoxes, all but two by the mid-1590s.

Not long after writing his ten early Paradoxes, Donne enclosed copies of them with a Letter to a friend, a Letter that tells us much about why Donne wrote them and what he was doing with this genre. Sending them 'Only in obedience' (published by E. M. Simpson 1948: 316–17) to his friend's importunate request, and providing metacommentary on how to read them, 'for they carry wth them a confession of there lightnes & y^r trouble & my shame', he stressed that he was 'desirous to hyde them wthout any ouer reconing of them or there maker'. Further, Donne's Letter bound his friend, by the 'religion' of their friendship, to refrain from allowing anyone to transcribe copies (316). The facts that one had to apply to Donne for copies and that Donne warned against transcribing them both suggest not only that manuscript circulation of Donne's Paradoxes was rare, but also that his friend may not previously have seen copies and may instead have heard or heard about the Paradoxes only as comic, oral performances for an Inns of Court coterie.

In the same Letter Donne revealed a deliberate rhetorical strategy of his Paradoxes, 'rather to deceave tyme then her daughth^r truth'. That is, although they may seem false they seem so only because their circumstances of composition call for dissimulation: 'they are but swaggerers: quiet enough if y^o resist them. if perchaunce they be pretyly guilt, y^t is there best for they are not hatcht: they are rather alarums to truth to arme her then enemies: & they haue only this advantadg to scape from being caled ill things y^t they are nothings' (316). Three times in this passage Donne stressed that his enclosures had a surface appearance concealing their fundamental nature: they appeared to be swaggerers, but they were really cowards; they appeared to be prettily gilt, but they were really unhatched; and they appeared to be enemies to truth, but they were really only alarms to truth. The heart of the matter of the Paradoxes, Donne stressed, was rhetorical dissimulation.

Both dissimulation and performance were discussed in one notable example of the Paradoxes Donne sent to his friend, 'That a wise man is knowne by much laughing' (*Paradoxes* 14–16), which established these keynotes by alluding to the opening of Erasmus' *Moriae Encomium*, where Folly found a signal of her own merit in her audience's laughter at her mere appearance. Donne's Paradox went on to argue that at comedies or other witty performances (such as oral performance of a paradox), 'I have noted some wch not vnderstanding the iests haue yett chosen this as ye best meanes to seeme wise & vnderstanding to laugh when there companions laughed' (15). He then pointed to the performative quality of English courtly manners, where 'almost every man affects an humor of iesting, & is content to deiect & deforme him self yea to become foole to no other end wch I can spy but to giue his wise companions occasion to laugh' (16). Having sketched these scenes, Donne likened himself to the performers in them, his Paradox to their jests, and his coterie audience to the performers' audiences, inviting wise men, 'if wise men do reade this paradox', to 'laugh both att it and mee' (16). Readers or hearers of these words therefore must either laugh or be thought unwise.

With some uncertainty, however, critics of Donne's Paradoxes have typically scanted their dissimulative features while acknowledging Donne's imitative manipulation of generic conventions: evoking Landi's manner (see Peters's Introduction in *Paradoxes* xxii); recycling stock topics and themes (Pease 38–42); deploying conventional argumentative strategies (Malloch 1956: 194–203); and registering intellectual traditions, such as scepticism, stoicism, and humanism, all generally informing sixteenth-century paradoxes (E. N. S. Thompson 1927: 94–5). Meanwhile, biographical critics, assigning Donne's Paradoxes to the 1590s, have pursued relations between his life and art (Marotti 1986: 45–7; E. M. Simpson 1931: 32–45), though rarely noting the way his Paradoxes expressed Inns of Court performative style. Both kinds of critics have used the Paradoxes to segue into discussion of the Elegies, Satires, and other writings, comparing and contrasting Donne's wit or the positions he articulates on certain topics with his wit or positions on the same topics in earlier or subsequent works (Sanders 27–43; Leishman 77–84).

In fact, despite some genuine insights, on the whole critics have handled Donne's Paradoxes with censure or neglect, often characterizing them as trivial, coarse, or enigmatic (E. M. Simpson 1931: 42) before dismissing them and moving on to other writings (Webber 1963: 4–5). More common than such estimates is a prevalent critical silence about the Paradoxes, which are mentioned if at all as mere *jeux d'esprit* or 'juvenilia', schoolboy exercises or trifles of a misspent youth. This superficial prejudice was encouraged by Donne's first editors, including his son, whose prefatory epistle to the 1653 edition of the *Paradoxes, Problemes, Essayes, Characters* packaged them with the *Essayes in Divinity* as Donne's writings '*of the* least *and* greatest *weight*' (A2^r) respectively, the 'Primroses *and* violets *of the Spring*' (A2^v) as opposed to the 'Fruits *of the Autumn*' (A2^v). Donne's son may truly have thought the Paradoxes trivial; more likely he feigned thinking so in order to distract attention from their subversive subtexts.

In 1633 Henry Seyle printed the first edition of Paradoxes and Problems with the title *Ivvenilia*, even though it contained little if anything that can have been composed before Donne was 20 and much that he seems to have written in his thirties and forties. Earlier, on 14 November 1632, Sir Henry Herbert had been called to appear before Star Chamber to explain 'why hee warranted the booke of D. Duns paradoxes to bee printed' (qtd. in Keynes 1973: 93). While modern critics dismiss these writings as trifles, clearly the Star Chamber did not, despite the title under which the Paradoxes were published.

Critical censure and neglect of Donne's Paradoxes has proceeded from a failure to situate these writings in the coterie context for which they were originally designed and performed, or written and circulated. Like many of the poems, the Paradoxes were written for a hand-picked audience that was both exclusive and known to the author. In this sense, whether presented orally or not, such writings are performances in which an author capitalizes on his nearness to his audience and his audience's nearness to him. To recover the particular social setting chosen for such performance necessitates a heightened critical sensitivity to occasionality, oral qualities, topical references, self-referentiality, and appropriation of culturally encoded, historically specific language. However, such specific properties of Donne's art should not be deployed as reductive heuristics, mischaracterizing Donne's texts as disposable, ephemeral, and deliberately unstable.

Conditions of coterie culture actually facilitated rhetorical dissimulation, both through an esotericism enabling the encoding of subtexts for initiated audiences and through resort to various strategies that could conceal dangerous content in the event a manuscript might miscarry. Such strategies included restricting circulation and misrepresenting writings by trivializing them. For example, when Donne in his Letter to his friend describes his Paradoxes as 'nothings', noting their 'lightnes' and 'shame', although critics have almost unanimously interpreted the characterization literally—as dismissal of, apology for, and embarrassment about the Paradoxes—it is more reasonable to interpret 'nothings' and Donne's other deprecatory remarks about his Paradoxes as irony, merely ostensible admissions. Like Erasmus, Landi, and Munday, he appears to trivialize the Paradoxes in order to facilitate safe transmission of the subversive ideas buried in their subtexts, thereby circumventing the danger posed by conditions of censorship and persecution in sixteenth-century European society. Darkly calling his Paradoxes 'nothings' is part of Donne's careful strategy to manage circulation of and to avoid punishment for his writings by presenting them in an obscure, concealing manner.

Dangerous social conditions certainly motivated obscurity and concealment. Donne's early correspondence alluded several times to fears that writings might miscarry or in some way wind up in the wrong hands, where unintended readers might then use them adversely. And as the ninth satirical book title of his *Courtier's Library* Donne listed '*Quidlibet ex quolibet*; Or, the art of decyphering and finding some treason in any intercepted letter, by Philips' (*Courtier's Library*: 32), referring to Thomas Phelippes, an infamous agent who had been employed for such purposes by Francis Walsingham and Robert Cecil. Donne mentioned the topic again in *Pseudo-Martyr*, where he complained about 'the curious malice of those men, who in this sickly decay, and declining of their cause, can spy out falsifyings in every citation: as in a jealous, and obnoxious state, a Decipherer can pick out Plots, and Treason, in any familiar letter which is intercepted' (*Pseudo-Martyr* 10). Donne was not merely describing a misfortune from which he himself felt immune. Quite the contrary: the fear that his manuscripts might wind up in the wrong hands troubled him, and when he evinced this fear in his Letters, he almost always associated with it a desire to conceal his writings or the sentiments expressed in them.

CHAPTER 11.II

THE PARADOX: *BIATHANATOS*

ERNEST W. SULLIVAN, II

By the Renaissance (see Ch. 11.I), the paradox had a tradition and reputation as a witty but trivial genre, more suited to intellectual jugglery than to serious analysis or commentary. Even so, Donne ultimately employed the inherent ambiguity of the genre, the restriction of his audience to a coterie, and manuscript metacommentary to create a rhetorical strategy that gave him enough plausible deniability to expand the reach of the witty paradox into a controversial, intellectually serious, and extended analysis of the ethical, legal, and theological implications of suicide in his *Biathanatos*, published posthumously in late September or early October of 1647: *A Declaration of that Paradoxe or Thesis, that Selfe-homicide is not so naturally Sinne, that it may neuer be otherwise. Wherein The Nature, and the extent of all those Lawes, which seeme to be violated by this Act, are diligently Surueyd*. Critics who take Donne's shorter Paradoxes and *Biathanatos* seriously as well as those who see the works as elaborate jokes often begin by discussing another paradoxical work by Donne's famous great-grand-uncle: Sir Thomas More's *Utopia*. Critics use More's rhetorical strategy in *Utopia* to show how an author can create disbelief or ambiguity. If the critics take Donne seriously, they argue that Donne lived in an oppressive society, as did More, and, like More, could not risk expressing his opinions explicitly on controversial matters. If the critics think that the Paradoxes as well as *Biathanatos* are not serious, they discuss Donne's genetic predisposition to wit, ambiguity, and intellectual jugglery.

But Donne used a different strategy for creating disbelief than did Thomas More, and Donne's strategy has exponentially increased the level of ambiguity about his creation of disbelief for readers of *Biathanatos* in print form after his death. More intended *Utopia* for publication; thus, he created its disbelief and ambiguity internally, in the work itself. *Utopia* ostensibly outlines an antidote for the collapse of the English economy in the early 1500s and the subsequent weakening of the social order, marked particularly by the rise of thievery. Such a work inevitably criticized the government; thus, More had to create plausible deniability for himself to avoid the collapse of his own economy, and he did so by weaving disbelief into the very fabric of his work. The title itself, *Utopia*, means 'nowhere', leaving government censors to wonder how seriously to take a proposal for an economy that operated without money. Further, More places the proposals in the mouth of a character named Raphael Hythloday whose last name derives from the Greek 'hutlos' (nonsense) and 'daien' (distributor), identifying Hythloday as a pedlar of nonsense. Finally, More has a character named after himself conclude *Utopia* with a disclaimer to the effect that he does not agree with Hythloday and does not think that his ideas would be of much use in England. At this point, various kinds of evidence internal to the work have alerted the reader to suspect Hythloday's credibility, though the reader does not know specifically what to disbelieve.

The difference between the rhetorical strategies of More and Donne and the problem for all of Donne's readers since his death in 1631, then, is that More intended to publish *Utopia* and expected that anyone with access to the printed book could read it; thus, More had to incorporate the elements of his rhetorical strategy for creating disbelief into the work itself. Donne, on the other hand, attempted to guide reader response by restricting circulation of *Biathanatos* in manuscript to personal friends; thus, he had less need to incorporate any strategies for creating disbelief into the work itself because (as long as he was alive) he could personally provide the necessary clues to create disbelief in the form of 'metacommentary': that is, personal Letters or other communications that commented on how the work should be read.

Biathanatos does contain some internal elements that could arguably undercut its veracity and thereby create disbelief; however, these elements are not as pervasive as in *Utopia*, and their effect is a matter of opinion. The first internal clues that might create disbelief appear on the title page. The word 'Paradox' suggests possible ambiguity as does the epigraph '*Non omnia vera esse profiteor. Sed Legentium vsibus inservire*' ('It is openly acknowledged that not all things [spoken of] are true, except they serve the uses of the readers'; *Biathanatos* 181). Occasionally an example or statement in the text seems facetious: for example, in quoting a definition of true repentance from Clement ('*To do no more, and to speake no more, those things, whereof you repent*', 37), Donne comments: 'Of such a repentance as this, our Case is capable enoughe' (37–8). In 1699 John Adams responded, 'Can this be in earnest?' (315), though Adams never doubted the sincerity of

Donne's overall argument. Further, *Biathanatos* contains over one thousand quotations and paraphrases from over one hundred sources, and roughly 10 per cent of Donne's holograph marginal citations for these sources contain some degree of error. This fact might undercut Donne's credibility had he not warned his readers in a note at the end of his Works Cited pages that, 'In citing these *Authors*... I haue trusted mine owne old notes. Which though I haue no reason to suspect, yet I confesse here my lazinesse; and that I did not refresh them with going to the Originall' (5). Everyone knows about old notes. Finally, on at least one occasion Donne significantly misremembers the Bible, alleging that the account that '*Lots* wife was turn'd to a pillar of Salt... grew currant, not from an Euidence in the text' (140). Obviously, Donne forgot Genesis 19:26: 'Now his wife behinde him loked backe, and was turned in to a piller of salt' (Berry fo. 8^v). As we shall see, however, these internal intimations of disbelief, unlike those in *Utopia*, had no effect on early readers with access only to the printed text of *Biathanatos*.

The two Letters Donne wrote about *Biathanatos* show his strategy of restricting its manuscript circulation and of providing metacommentary to prepare his selected readers for disbelief. The first, written to accompany a manuscript of *Biathanatos* entrusted to 'Sr Robert Carre [Ker] *now Earle of* Ankerum' when Donne travelled to Germany, establishes that *Biathanatos* is ambiguous and written for a select audience: 'I have always gone so near suppressing it, as that it is onely not burnt: no hand hath passed upon it to copy it, nor many eyes to read it: onely to some particular friends in both Universities, then when I writ it, I did communicate it' (*Letters* 21). Donne asks Ker to minimize access to the manuscript ('Keep it, I pray, with the same jealousie', 22) and expressly forbids any publication: 'I only forbid it the Presse, and the Fire: publish it not, but yet burn it not' (22). By way of metacommentary, Donne told Ker to let any readers know that it was 'a Book written by *Jack Donne*, and not by D. *Donne*' (22) and 'upon a misinterpretable subject' (21). Donne also described the ambiguous response of some other early readers of the manuscript: 'certainly, there was a false thread in it, but not easily found' (22).

Secondly, Donne's autograph presentation Letter '*To the Noblest knight Sr Edward Herbert*' prefacing the Bodleian Library manuscript of *Biathanatos* reiterates the special nature of his selected audience (Lord Herbert) and prepares Lord Herbert for disbelief: 'ytt [*Biathanatos*] cannot chuse a wholsomer ayre then yor Library, where Autors of all complexions are preserud. If any of them grudge thys Booke a roome, and suspect ytt of new, or dangerous Doctrine, yo^w, who know us all, can best Moderate' (*Biathanatos* 249). Whether *Biathanatos* actually taught 'new, or dangerous Doctrine' was left to the reader.

When John Donne, Jr. published his father's *Biathanatos* in 1647 he provided his own metacommentary, this time in an 'Epistle Dedicatory' and in two letters accompanying special copies presented to potential patrons. Alas, the younger Donne's metacommentary in the 'Epistle Dedicatory' obviates all his father's strategy of suggesting disbelief: 'For, although this Booke appear under the notion of a Paradox, yet, I desire your Lordship [Lord Herbert of Cherbury], to looke upon this Doctrine, as a firme and established truth, *Da vida osar morir* ['to dare death is to live']' (*Biathanatos* 250). Whether the true 'Doctrine' is the Spanish proverb, or that suicide is not a sin, the reader anticipates nothing but 'truth'. In a presentation letter to a Mr. Lee inscribed in a copy of *Biathanatos* at Cambridge University Library, Donne's son describes *Biathanatos* as an 'absolute Originall' (xlv); and in another, also at Cambridge University Library, to Edward Carter, he remarks the 'noueltie of the subiect' (xlv): neither assessment would be true unless *Biathanatos* is indeed the first defence of suicide in English; thus, the younger Donne's metacommentary prepares the reader for originality, not disbelief.

Once *Biathanatos* found its way into print, Donne's strategies of restricting its audience and using his metacommentary to prepare readers for disbelief failed utterly, as we can see in contemporary interpretations from readers who, like most of us, had only the printed book and not Donne's metacommentary: the few clues contained in the work itself were not enough to produce disbelief. Sir William Denny, in *Pelecanicidium: or the Christian Adviser against Self-Murder* (1653), alludes to *Biathanatos* as a sincere defence of suicide: 'the Frequency of such Actions [suicides] might in time arrogate a Kind of Legitimation by Custom, or plead Authority from some late-publisht Paradoxes, That Self-Homicide was Lawfull' ($A5^{r-v}$). Charles Blount, in *The Two First Books of Philostratus* (1680), regarded *Biathanatos* as a defence of suicide: 'I refer you to that excellent Treatise entituled, BIATHANATOS, and written by that eminent Poet and Divine, Dr. *Donn*, the Dean of *Pauls*; wherein, with no weak Arguments, he endeavours to justifie out of Scripture, the Legality of self-Homicide' (154). In 1699 *Biathanatos* elicited a specific and lengthy response from John Adams, who clearly believed *Biathanatos* a defence of suicide and feared that others did, too:

> This [proving suicide lawful] has been pretended to more particularly by a Gentleman of our own Country, with much shew of Learning and Reason, in a Treatise intitled, *Biathanatos*. Which, by the great Character of the Author, rais'd afterwards upon *better* Grounds, by the Agreeableness of the Argument to the present Age, and by its having passed some Years unanswer'd... has been highly esteem'd by *some People*. (J. Adams 41)

More recently, scholars, even with access to Donne's metacommentary for *Biathanatos*, have struggled with disbelief in its arguments. Some, like A. E. Malloch (1958), Rosalie Colie (1966), and Richard E. Hughes, read *Biathanatos* as a joke on itself, while Edmund Gosse, Donald R. Roberts, Evelyn M. Simpson (1948), and I treat it as a serious, though limited, defence of suicide.

So, does one believe what Donne wrote in his Paradoxes and Problems and *Biathanatos*, or does one believe what he wrote about these works in his metacommentary? Or can one reconcile the belief and the disbelief? Again, the comparison with Sir Thomas More is instructive. Though More and Donne differed in their strategies for creating disbelief, they both created disbelief not to undercut the seriousness and legitimacy of their arguments but to create personal, plausible deniability for what even today would qualify as subversive ideas, ideas that most readers then and now would prefer to disbelieve. Even though More and Donne went to great lengths to achieve such deniability through elaborate strategies of disbelief, they both sincerely wanted to initiate intellectual debate over their paradoxical propositions, as Donne makes clear in the pool of Bethesda image from John 5:2–9 that dominates *Biathanatos*: 'as in the Poole of *Bethsaida*, there was no health till the Water was troubled, so the best way to finde the truth in this matter was to debate and vexe it' (30). Thus it is in Donne's early prose as it is in his search for 'true religion' (l. 43) in his *Sat3*: the surest path to the truth is signposted 'doubt wisely' (l. 77).

CHAPTER 12

MENIPPEAN DONNE

ANNE LAKE PRESCOTT

THIS chapter explores some satirical texts by John Donne that seem to have little in common: *Metem*, *The Courtier's Library*, *Ignatius his Conclave*, Verse Letters mocking Thomas Coryate, and a number of 'characters' or essays, some of them of disputed authorship but that are probably or possibly by Donne. Each text has its own character, agenda, and context, but each also relates to that debated genre, Menippean satire, named for the ancient writer Menippos, of whose writings nothing remains but who figures in dialogues by the second-century satirist Lucian. It came to the Renaissance through what remained of works by the Roman Varro, the somewhat better-preserved *Satyricon* of Petronius, Apuleius' *Golden Ass*, Seneca's *Apocolocyntosis* ('Gourdification of Claudius', model for the anonymous *Julius Exclusus* long if uncertainly attributed to Erasmus), and Lucian himself. Modern authorities are in no better agreement as to which texts should count as 'Menippean' than they are on how to define the genre, if it is a genre and not a mode or tradition. We can define it narrowly so as to exclude the ancient satirists Apuleius and Lucian (Relihan 16, 21, 186; Weinbrot 7–8) or more broadly so as to include them (Kirk; Smet).

Renaissance opinion, however, was tolerably clear and broad; the humanist scholars whom Donne knew would have agreed with the laxer definitions, and would also have agreed that this often very erudite genre is particularly given to laughter at pretentious erudition (Blanchard). These Renaissance humanists, including L. B. Alberti, Caelio Secundo Curione, Daniel Heinsius, Justus Lipsius, and John Barclay, imitated the Menippea in Latin, although arguably the greatest of all Menippean satires is François Rabelais's *Gargantua et Pantagruel*. Donne's early English readers might have added William Baldwin's *Beware the Cat*[holic], pamphlets by Thomas Nashe such as *Lenten Stuffe*, Sir John Harington's scatological *Metamorphosis of Ajax*, and John Healey's translation of Joseph Hall's dystopic *Mundus alter et idem*; and not a few would have thought More's *Utopia* Menippean. One French satire sometimes associated with Donne includes a valuable definition: in the 1595 translation of the *Satyre Ménippée* (1594), an attack by several moderate French 'politique' Catholics on the recalcitrant enemies of Henri IV, a 'Discovrse' ascribed to the French printer explains the title:

> As concerning the adiective *Menippized*, it is not new or vnusuall, for it is more then sixteene hundred years agoe, that Varro...made Satyres of this name also, which Macrobius sayth were called Cyniquized, and Menippized: to which he gaue that name because of Menippus the Cynicall Philosopher, who also had made the like before him, al ful of salted iestings, & poudred merie conceits of good words, to make men to laugh, and to discouer the vicious men of his time. And Varro imitating him, did the like in prose, as since his time there hath done the like, Petronius Arbiter, & Lucian in the Greek tongue, & since his time Apuleius, and in our age that good fellow Rabelaiz, who hath passed all other men in contradicting others, and pleasant conceits, if hee would cut off from them some quodlibetarie speeches in tauernes, and his salt and biting words in alehouses. (Le Roy *et al.* 203–4)

Menippean satire is salty, jumbled, cynical, and proud of it. Traditionally, but not always, including both prose and verse, it loves to collect, attract, heap up, include, stuff, toss in. Thanks to the invention of printing, which allowed new forms of visual play, Tom Nashe could use traditional black letter to make an astrologer enemy look old-fashioned and print a woodcut that he feigned to believe shows someone about to relieve himself on 'Ajax' (thus punning on 'a jakes', or privy). Pictures, shaped poems, giants, staves of music, dream visions, macaronics, send-ups, sesquipedalian neologisms, puns, embedded tales, dinner parties, reversals of inside and outside, shifts of gender, jokes, debates, animal combinations, snarky marginal commentary, or silly footnotes—throw it all in and let it bulge. Menippean satire is fat food, carnival, Falstaff. Save elegance and shape for Lenten rationality and self-regulation. Menippean satire can be indecent, affirming the body but often ambivalently. It is literally degrading, but usually so as to trip up the haughty who deserve it, and its send-ups of a constricting and exclusive erudition paradoxically require a learned reader to savour them fully. In the hands of a Lucian the genre may be amoral (it is hard to know if Lucian took anything seriously), but more committed writers can deploy it on behalf of a belief. It is arguably gendered male, even as what some think is its enemy twin, romance, is often thought feminine, for few women could read the many Menippean satires in the Latin where many such texts stayed—and stay. Several works discussed in this essay, although translated, may retain some of this all-male atmosphere and in this regard are quite unlike many of the lyrics for which Donne is now better loved.

If Menippean satire is cannibalistic—like Lucian's whale in *A True Story* swallowing everything it can—it also readily fragments, offering topoi and subgenres exploitable by those not wishing to stage an entire Menippean performance. Hence the dream visions, trips to the underworld or the moon, humiliating metamorphoses, lists (with their curious tendency, even when seriously meant, to edge into risibility), formal paradoxes, mock encomia, parodic speeches, collections of grotesqueries, imaginary societies, Lucianic dialogues, and, in the Renaissance, imaginary libraries. It helps make sense of Donne's satires to remember such sometimes now obscure texts, obscure because minor or because still in Latin. Even minimal ones might at least have made students at the Inns of Court or wits at the Mermaid laugh. Take, for example, a brief vernacular work, the pseudonymous *Maroccus Extaticus. Or, Bankes Bay Horse in a Trance...Anatomizing some abuses and bad trickes of this age* (Dando 1595). Dedicated to a tavern host, the book sports a title that parodies Curione's *Pasquillus Ecstaticus* (1545; published in English in 1566 and 1584), a woodcut, snatches of Skeltonic verse, a talking horse who says (B3^v) he learned Latin 'when I gambolde at Oxforde' (although whether he gamboled/gambled with hooves or dice he does not say), and mistranslations. When the master says philosophically that '*Omnis homo mendax*, Everie man may amend' (a mendacious reading, for the Latin means 'Every man is a liar'), the horse replies, '*Et ut hora sic vita*, A loves a whoore as his lyfe' (C2). And then, anticipating the title of Donne's *FirAn*, he suggests that this dialogue 'be our first lecture of the Anatomie of the world' (D). The 'anatomy' was itself a Menippean mode, as Robert Burton knew. If Donne never wrote a fully Menippean satire, the genre commanded his attention and his imagination. Even some texts by Donne not included in this chapter (*Pseudo-Martyr*, *Biathanatos*, some Letters) show traces of its style (see Chs. 11.II, 18, 20, and 25).

METEMPSYCHOSIS

By 1601, when Donne dated his satirical mock-epic *Metempsychosis* or *The Progresse of the Soule* (in the posthumous 1633 *Poems* edited by John Donne Jr. it has two titles), Robert Cecil had triumphed over the now beheaded Earl of Essex, Elizabeth was ageing fast, times in the late 1590s had been bad, and political irritation was in the air. For the last few years, moreover, and perhaps in response to the purported idealism and self-consciously rich style of *The Faerie Queene* and Petrarchan love sonnets, there had also been a fashion for swaggering negativity, for snarls, barks, bites, bitter pills, lashes, candlelit but vain searches for honesty that might make Diogenes—the doggish *cyn*ic philosopher—leave his barrel for London (Prescott 2000: 226–30). Even a future bishop, Joseph Hall, wrote in 1597 that '*Satyre* should be like the *Porcupine*, / That shoots sharp quilles out in each angry line' (F3^v), and Spenser himself ends the last complete book of his epic with the cynical advice to 'seeke to please, that now is counted wisemens threasure' (*Faerie Queene* 6.12.41). Indeed, so violent and so politically volatile did verse satirists in the later 1590s become that the authorities, with Robert Cecil's involvement, forbade further printing of such texts (McCabe). In its real or assumed cynicism, the brilliant ugliness of many of its images, its moments of hyperbolic misogyny, its contempt for political striving, and its sense of a universe ablaze with corrupt sexuality, *Metem* thus suits the world of still-youngish educated men about town who enjoyed seeming unimpressed by worldly power (or, on the other hand, by Puritan sedition) but who were happy to whip it into shape with their pens. The cynicism could be genuine, if experimental, but surely fashion's productive temptation plays its part.

Granted this taste for showy aggression, for metaphoric punishment and even murder, then, it seems appropriate that the little tribute by J. M[arriot] prefacing the 1633 *Poems* (^{2}A2^v) puns cleverly on winding sheets for the grave's decay and book sheets that give eternity. And, also granted Lucian's Renaissance reputation as a problematic Menippean sceptic and satirist, it seems likewise fitting that a copy of *Metem* is found in a Folger Library manuscript that also contains six Lucianic dialogues (Crowley 2007a: 48 and 54–5). It is true that modern scholars continue to have varied ways of describing the poem. Ronald Corthell (1981) calls it a paradox, although, like the little mock encomia that he notes, paradoxes also recall the Menippea. For Siobhán Collins it is a generically mixed 'riddle', while Kenneth Gross finds 'Rabelaisian wit' (372) and Anthony Parr connects it to Donne's interest in travel (72–4). It has even been vigorously and learnedly argued that *Metem* is more of an epic elaboration on certain patristic or heretical theories of the soul than it is a satire (Mueller 1972: 114 ff.).

Yet the label that accompanies the title, 'Poêma Satyricon', inevitably carries a generic implication and to the educated would recall Petronius, just as would John Barclay's *Euphormionis Satyricon*, first printed in 1603. That the Roman satirist (assuming that tradition has the right Petronius) wrote under the tyrant Nero, who would soon force his friend, accused of joining a treasonous conspiracy, to kill himself, may well add another overtone. Further complicating this already generically mixed work, moreover, the poem's first words, 'I sing', recall Virgil's 'Arma virumque cano' even as the topic and title recall Ovid—whose *Metamorphoses* may stand in the same quasi-satirical relationship to the completed *Aeneid* as some think Donne's apparently uncompleted pseudo-epic stands in relationship to Spenser's likewise unfinished epic, *The Faerie Queene*.

Dedicated to 'Infinity' ('Sacrum Infinitati'), with a brief prefatory epistle or 'porch', as Donne calls it in a not uncommon metaphor imagining a text as a temple or house, *Metem* opens the 1633 *Poems*. Unusually for Donne, it has a date: 16 August 1601, the poet claiming a few lines later that he had lived nearly six 'lustres'—almost thirty years. (I thank Donald R. Dickson for a preview of his introduction to the *Variorum* edition of the poem, which argues that Donne had begun it some time earlier.) Why 16 August? In the Catholic calendar that is St Roch's day, retaining that designation in many English almanacs even after the Reformation. St Roch, often pictured with a dog, was said to help cure the plague and skin diseases (later including the pox), perhaps because tradition reported that he was born at Montpellier with a red cross on his breast. In William Caxton's version of *The Golden Legend* the cross is colourless and on the shoulder, but modern sources on Catholic saints uniformly claim it was red and on the breast (Daniel Royot, professor emeritus at the Sorbonne, graciously sent me extensive material on St Roch, much of it now on trustworthy websites). Is St Roch here because he is a mischievous parallel to Spenser's Redcrosse Knight—a Redcrosse Saint? Or did his dog suggest to Donne the traditionally doggish or *cyn*ical nature of much satire?

In the poem that follows, the soul's 'progress', or journey, takes it from the death-bearing apple in the Garden of Eden to—in order of appearance, but with some temporary visits to additional beings and anticipations of yet others that may complicate a total still reasonably estimated at twelve bodies—a mandrake (that man-shaped root that Donne tells the reader of *SGo* to 'get with child'), a sparrow, a fish, a swan, a sea-pie (or 'oyster-catcher'), a whale, a mouse, a wolf, a dog, an ape, and the biblical woman Themech. The poem evidently imagines an eroticized, even a violently eroticized, universe, for each of the creatures Donne describes was once associated with the *eros*, from the aphrodisiac-eating sea-pie to the mandrake (said by some to grow under a gibbet from the semen left by a hanged man) to the notoriously oversexed ape (Wentersdorf 71–2). Next would have come incarnation in some great person that Donne's preface coyly tells us we will meet at the end of his poem. We meet no such figure in the text as we have it, either because the poem truly is unfinished or because we are meant to deduce the name of someone whom Donne thought it wiser not to mention even in manuscript. Needless to say, there has been speculation. Salisbury, who died in 1612, has for some time been the favourite, and there is little doubt that, like a number of others, Donne viewed that statesman with fear and anger, not least because of sympathy for Essex as one of Cecil's victims, but also because he so despised the government's suspicious eagerness to sniff out sedition (M. van Wyk Smith; Flynn 1987: 164–6; McRae 59–62, 69–71, 188–91; Crowley 2007*a*: 47, 61–2, 69; see also Ch. 31.I).

Partly because of the subtitle, 'First Song', and partly because we never meet the unnamed great person, the poem is regularly called unfinished. The preface, furthermore, seems to promise an Ovidian and Pythagorean adventure, an epic 'progress' or journey (upward along the great chain of being from vegetable to animal to human but downward through worse and worse corruptions) longer and more conclusive than what we have. On the other hand, the poem's structure—fifty-two quasi-Spenserian stanzas of nine pentameter lines and one alexandrine that describe what seem like twelve incarnations—is so neat, so patterned, that it can feel complete, even if there is no full consensus on how to count the twelve (Wentersdorf omits the promised final incarnation, whereas Blackley plausibly includes it while still finding a dozen in what he thinks is a finished poem [ch. 1]).

The allusion to weeks and months, then, assumes a circular time even as the passage from Eden to England and from apple to some modern figure assumes a linear one. There may even be yet another circle implied by the first and last stanzas' references to the biblical Seth's pillars, although we hear that the poem will outlast them temporally.

One reason to find a deliberate temporal patterning in Donne's poem is the frequency with which his contemporaries gestured at time, as line and as circle. Giles Fletcher's 1593 *Licia*, for example, has fifty-two sonnets and, at two lines each, 366 'days' for the leap year 1592; Spenser's *Epithalamion* (1595) has twenty-four stanzas and 365 long lines; and in William Rankins's *Seauen Satyres Applyed to the weeke* (1598) satire circles though a week's worth of planetary influences before reaching a poem on 'the wandering Satyre'. If Donne's tone suits the fashion for satire, his structure thus recalls the period's numerological interests; indeed, early readers might have noted that twelve introductory stanzas are followed by the forty that describe the metamorphoses themselves—and could, to those so inclined, recall the forty years of that earlier wandering towards the Promised Land. Such ironies are reinforced in the 1633 edition by the contrast (whether or not Donne's doing) between the poem's disillusioned conclusion that 'The onely measure is, and judge, opinion' and the catchword 'Holy' at the bottom of the page (27), which when we turn brings us to the Holy Sonnets, the next poem being the circular *Corona*. That *Metem* is dedicated to infinity, moreover, adds another temporal gesture, perhaps an ironic one, suggesting what...? An infinity of psychic migrations? An infinity of corruptions and religious or political innovators?

In recent years critical interest has sometimes focused on how *Metem* relates the 'soul' to the body as it makes its brutal and rapacious way from apple onward and, argues John Carey when defending the poem against those who find it incoherent or ugly, powerfully evoking the physical process of invading a body (1981a: 148–59). The issues involved are complex, as are the implications for the poem. In his seduction poem *Ecst*, Donne refers to the body–soul connection as the 'subtile knot, which makes us man' (l. 64), the 'knot' presumably being the 'reti' or 'net' that some anatomists were beginning to doubt existed and thus, claims Richard Sugg (2000: 15–16), edging into a more materialist and anti-humanist or even irreligious view of the human person. Elizabeth Harvey (2007a: 259 ff.) says something similar when arguing that Donne aims at Spenser. I doubt, though, that the forms in *The Faerie Queene*'s Garden of Adonis (3.6.355 ff.) are 'souls' in a religious sense, or that to imagine a rational soul coexisting with, rather than subsuming, the animal might upset religious orthodoxy. Plato's image of the 'soul' as a charioteer/rider and recalcitrant horse, after all, was a commonplace. For Harvey, Donne's near-Spenserian stanza points to the 'Castle of Alma' in *Faerie Queene* 2 (but is Alma the God-given religious soul?) and a sonnet from the 'Visions of the Worldes Vanitie' (*Complaints*

1591) in which, as in Donne, a tiny creature fells an elephant. Perhaps—and I would add Erasmus' 'Scarabeus aquilam quaerit' in his *Adages* (2005: 178–214), with its great animals brought low by humble ones. It is a sign of how subjective such allusions can be, though, that for Susan Snyder (396–407) Donne parodies the French biblical epics by the Huguenot poet Guillaume Du Bartas as translated by Josuah Sylvester, something for which I find no evidence. And, taking an entirely different view, Wyman Herendeen (9.11) calls the poem Donne's 'palinode' before his turn to religious verse. His argument would at least make sense of stanza 44's seldom-remarked blasphemy: 'This wolfe begot himselfe' upon a dog and thanks to the transmigration of souls was 'Sonne to himselfe, and father too', for 'which Schoolemen would misse / A proper name' (ll. 434–8). One (im)proper name would be 'Trinity'. In later editions *Metem* was moved, but in 1650 it is still followed by the devout *Corona*.

One difficulty, too often ignored in such discussion, is the ambiguity surrounding the word 'soul' in Renaissance discourse. Those who considered such matters could distinguish between the rational soul that might or might not subsume the vegetable and animal souls that human beings in*corp*orate and the probably immortal and certainly unique God-given spirit that Christians believe will be reunited with the body at the Resurrection. The problem for us is that Renaissance writers could be inconsistent, confused, and confusing in their vocabulary, failing to use 'spirit' and 'soul' consistently and adding to the confusion with references to the binary body/soul (or body/spirit) without further specification or explaining how this binary relates to the triple 'vegetable, animal, rational' soul(s) or to, for example, the 'spirits' in the blood (D. P. Walker 146–50), a confusion that supports the claim that the soul's 'characteristics are clearly not those of the Aristotelian or Christian soul' (Tepper 265). In theory, *metempsychosis* of the divine unique soul (or spirit) is heresy, which is why talk about the soul of some great person being infused into the patron or poet one is trying to flatter (a standard compliment) is not to be taken literally in a religious sense. But is it heretical to suppose that an ordinary 'natural' soul of whatever category might migrate? These are deep theological waters that Donne on occasion navigates in his Sermons and Letters. After all, there is no Christian consensus on the soul, as Donne would explain in a Letter to Sir Thomas Lucy (or more probably to Sir Henry Goodere) dated only 9 October at Mitcham. If the soul is infused at birth, how can it acquire the taint of original sin? But if it comes by inheritance then how is it individual or for that matter different from that of an animal? There is as yet, concludes Donne, no full understanding of such matters (*Letters* 11–19; see also Targoff 2008: 11). Most people seem, of course, to have been content with vaguely imagined dichotomies (flesh/spirit, body/mind, reason/passion) and triplicities (animal, vegetable, and rational souls or spirits), so it is hard to blame Donne for being imprecise in this poem, and since he does not make its operative vocabulary or theory clear, probably its readers should hesitate to pin him down.

THE COURTIER'S LIBRARY

Put together between 1601 and 1611, Donne's *Catalogus librorum aulicorum incomparabilium et non vendibilium* ('A Catalogue of Courtiers' Rare Books Not for Sale') is a bibliography in Latin of non-existent texts, translated by Percy Simpson for Evelyn M. Simpson's edition (1930) and more recently by Piers Brown (2008); (see Ch. 11.II). Now commonly called *The Courtier's Library* because of the manuscript's Latin title, it was first printed in the 1650 *Poems*, where it closely follows 'Newes from the very Countrey' and that essay's opening image of 'a Frippery of Courtiers'. Its obvious model is the mock library in Rabelais's *Pantagruel* (ch. 7, 1.250 ff.), sufficiently well known in the fashionable circles to which Donne was peripherally connected for James I to write Salisbury in October of 1605 that the French ambassador was so greedy that he could add an 'art of begging' to the 'bibliothèque of his countryman Rabelais' (Prescott 1998b: 169; on non-books see 167–79 and Spargo). Rabelais's was the first fantasy library but there had been many fantasy books, for example those in the famous *Letters of Obscure Men*, ignorant epistles by non-existent monks and theologians composed by Ulrich von Hutten and others to mock conservative academics; Donne might have read it, granted his ambivalence towards scholastic subtleties and his awareness of the Continent. Rabelais's collection, though, was by far the most famous. His titles can be scatological, as witness the *Ars honeste petandi in societate* ('The art of farting politely in society'; a pun on 'Ars/arse' would not work in French), but many scoff at the ultra-conservative theologians he scorned and who in turn suspected humanists like himself as semi-heretics at best. *De optimatate triparum* ('On good tripe'), for example, is credited to the overweight Noël Béda, who had tried to get the evangelical Marguerite de Navarre censored. Others have more philosophical resonance: *Quaestio subtilissima, utrum Chimera in vacuo bombinans, possit comedere secundas intentiones, et fuit debatua per decem hebdomadas in concilio Constantiensi* ('A most subtle problem, whether the Chimera, buzzing in a vacuum, can eat second intentions, as it was batted around for ten weeks at the Council of Constance') parodies medieval scholasticism, but the question is not uninteresting for those thinking about paradox and nonentity.

There are, to be sure, interesting differences between Donne and Rabelais: the latter's chief targets are what he saw, if sometimes unfairly, as comfortable monastic ignorance, retrograde bigotry like that gripping the Sorbonne, and scholars who resisted humanist learning. Donne's aim is to satirize lazy courtiers, political corruption, and arrogance. But he also satirizes, and like Rabelais with an anger that shows through the comedy although from an opposite perspective, the authorities' suspicious and persecutory anti-Catholicism. He may laugh at the 'vacuousness of courtly accomplishment', observes Claire Preston, but he more dangerously implies an anxious contempt for governmental snooping and misreading (98). Piers Brown (2008: 836 ff.) argues that the list also suggests the tensions felt by those with a more humanist conception of *otium*/leisure who worked as under-appreciated secretaries to their social betters, to which I would add that it is a sign of a cultural shift in attitudes that Donne names more authors than does Rabelais, whose focus is on titles.

By the time Donne finished his *Catalogus*, moreover, others had ventured into the world of titled nothings (in itself a gesture towards airheaded courtiers or dim professors). In Germany Johann Fischart, author of anti-Jesuit poetry, had borrowed Rabelais's books for his own 'Pantagruelischen Bibliothec' (*Catalogus Catalogorum Perpetuo Durabilis* [1590], printed in 'Nowhere'—sceptics would say Strasbourg). In France, during the stormy late 1580s, there had circulated a list of fantasy books said by its compositor(s) to belong to Mme de Montpensier, sister of the Guise brothers and like them a leader of the pro-papist and Spain-friendly League that warred against the Catholic Henri III and the still-Huguenot Henri de Navarre. If Donne read it, and it was popular enough for the chronicler and collector Pierre de l'Estoile (l'Estoile 5.349–57) to acquire a copy in 1587, he probably enjoyed it. This is equal-opportunity satire. Catherine de' Medici figures as translator from the Italian of a *Pot Pourri* of French affairs; the Guise family, from Lorraine, is credited with a book translated from their dialect into 'good French'; and a book on cuckolds is dedicated to Henri de Navarre. There is some indecency, with a 'Lexicon de Fouterie' (a 'dictionary of screwing'), and Donne would have noted Number 62 in particular: 'Treatise in the form of a paradox: that one may be received as a counselor at court without knowing anything' (354). The interest in dialects and words is intriguing, as is the number of women mentioned. This is less the world of beleaguered humanism or overworked secretaries than of a court and a militant opposition with a large role for women (Polachek 433 ff.; the difference between France and Britain in this regard, both in politics and satire, is striking). Closer to home, Donne would have been amused by marginal allusions to non-existent books in the translation of Joseph Hall's Menippean *Mundus alter et idem* (*Discovery of a New World*, 1609). And Sir John Harington's scatological *Metamorphosis of Ajax* (1595) is said by its author to recuperate an episode in Gargantua's career that Rabelais somehow forgot (1962: 68–71).

Donne's ironic preface explains that courtiers lack leisure to read but need the appearance of having done so. This list will thus help those who must sleep until ten and still have time to dress, get the face just right in the mirror, and decide whether to greet so-and-so with a hearty laugh or a raised eyebrow. And then there are meals and entertainment to attend to. There is no mention of anything so vulgar as strenuous service to the state. Leave the classics to schoolteachers and academics, quote no well-known books but rather these, and you will impress those who thought they had heard everything.

There follow thirty-four titles. The Trinity ms. adds three, two by Agrippa and one by the monk Huebald of St-Amand. To be sure these are real paradoxes, perhaps the start of a list of such texts (R. E. Bennett 1933), although we might forgive anyone who thinks '*Baldus in laudem Calvitii*'—Baldus in praise of Baldness—a joke. The books are on such useful topics as determining the sex of, or hermaphroditism in, atoms (a parody, probably, of the alchemical impulse to gender the physical world, but conceivably a glance at James I's complex sexuality). The same item mentions Hugh Plat, famous for inventions and what the age called 'projects' or plats/plots of the sort Jonson likewise satirized and that Donne would have associated with the 'innovation' that drew his satirical eye in other areas of life. Other titles lampoon the torturer Richard Topcliffe or government decipherers who can find treason anywhere. One evokes Rabelais's similarly anti-scholastic parodic *quaestio* concerning a famed monstrous nonentity: '*That the Chimera is a prophecy of Antichrist*, by an anonymous Sorbonist'. The extremes of number mysticism receive a sceptical knock too: *The Judæo-Christian Pythagoras* by the Italian Neoplatonist Pico reports, and not implausibly, that 66 is 99 if you hold the page upside down. To the poet John Davies are ascribed poor anagrams, and if Catholic scholastics are scorned so is Luther. The astrologer John Dee has been gazing ridiculously above the heavens and Donne mentions Dr Tom Thorney, who appears also in 'The Character of a Scot' (see below; and compare the allusion there to a 'knight-wright' to the fantasy title *Apocryphal Knights*). A title or two may sneer at Salisbury.

Some texts are credited to writers such as Erasmus whom Donne admired—the joke is less on them than in the juxtaposition of name and title. There is a little on Hell, a little on venereal disease, and a little scatology. The cleverest example of the last is 'John Harington's *Hercules*, or the Method of Purging Noah's Ark of Excrement'. *Hercules* (title of a 1608 Menippean satire by Heinsius) is a good choice for a book on such a dirty job as sanitizing the Ark, granted the hero's famous use of a diverted river to cleanse the Augean stables, and Harington's *Ajax* had already drafted another Greek hero, whose name was pronounced 'a jakes' (i.e. a privy), in the service of inventing the *water*-closet. Harington seems to hint that England could use a good flush toilet for its sins, and Donne may similarly imply that England could use a Herculean purge. The wit is typical of Donne, being both compressed and wide-ranging. Just as typical is the occasional play with nothingness, the glimpse into the void behind the titles: 'Cardan *On the nullibiety of breaking wind*' is a fine fart joke, but it also recalls not only the emptiness of such lower breath but also the old scholastic question of whether 'nothing'—*nihil*—is not in fact something because it makes a sound when you say it. In late scholastic argument one answer to the dismaying liar paradox was 'nil dicis' (you say nothing), to which one retort was 'But "nothing" is sound, air' (Spade; and for humanist nothing jokes Prescott 1987). The issue was important: for those comfortable with Aristotelian tradition there is no such thing as nothing, but God had created the world from nothing, and by a century or so before Donne's day the zero, with all its attendant jests and worries, had finally won grudging acceptance even in northern Europe.

As the century wore on there would be more imaginary books, and indeed the genre flourishes yet, as witness modern ads for a web-based bookseller featuring such titles as *Making Marriage Work* by Henry VIII or, more magisterially, Jorge Luis Borges's 'Library of Babel' (the science-fiction writer Stanislas Lem's *A Perfect Vacuum* takes the next logical step, offering imaginary book reviews; Donne would relish the title). Especially in a print culture, fantasy books raise disturbing questions about the relation of words to things: under what circumstances do we have words but no referents, signifiers but no signifieds? The implications for the nature of signs and sacraments can be troubling. That may be why Donne alludes elsewhere to the frozen words that Pantagruel and his companions find (see below), and why his friend Ben Jonson was so haunted by the Oracle of the Bottle at the end of Rabelais's fifth book (Prescott 1998*b*: 69–70, 119–22; F. Nichols 1988: 12–13). The bottle, associated with if not actually containing the wine that makes Panurge resolve to marry despite his fears of cuckoldry, says 'Drink!' in German. The accompanying woodcut, though, shows the flask full of words, the same words that Panurge recites in an ecstasy but that, as placed in the image, and in a complexity worthy of Lewis Carroll, praise the bottle itself. Panurge, a prince's companion whom the vexatious would-be companion in Donne's *Sat4* calls a 'pretty linguist', albeit a 'poore gentleman' (ll. 59–60), understands 'Trinch!'; yet the bottle, with its praise said by Panurge in the text but by the bottle itself in the picture, seems to have more words than wine. Donne's courtiers would be dismayed and their secretaries, when not in a tavern, amused.

Donne collected fantasy books both because they make good satire and because they connect with matters that he found compelling: made of nothing, they can in principle be infinite; adding up to zero, they can stretch, in a big enough fantasy library, to infinity. Zero, the 'cipher' that we cannot fully decipher, is in shape and concept uncomfortably but intriguingly close to All.

Ignatius His Conclave

Internal evidence shows that Donne finished *Ignatius* in late 1610. It was printed in Latin in early 1611 and, later that year, appeared in what is probably his translation. No author is identified until 1634, when Donne was dead, a coyness that, whatever its motives, is in keeping with this genre's taste for quasi-anonymity (true, Thomas Coryate seems to have learned the writer's name by 1615; see below). At least the 1611 title page helpfully defines the work as describing a 'late election in hell: wherein many things are mingled by way of satyr'. Donne knew about elections and speeches, after all, having by now been a Member of Parliament. Copies were soon circulating abroad, for l'Estoile bought one that February (see Healy's edition [*Ignatius* xiii–xiv] for such bibliographical information and for reasons to think the translation Donne's own).

A few months earlier François Ravaillac had assassinated France's Henri IV, promulgator of the Edict of Nantes extending to Protestants a limited toleration that many English Catholics would have wished for themselves and that Ravaillac's action, only five years after the 1605 Gunpowder Plot, made even less thinkable in England. *Conclave* is also a contribution (by a man still in need of pleasing the great) to the war of words over the English government's demand that Catholics take the Oath of Allegiance, something that Pope Paul V forbade them to do. The famous Cardinal Bellarmino had written to the Archpriest Blackwell, who had sworn the oath, agreeing with the Pope. The dispute came to engage the energies of the King himself (and James was no mean rhetorician) when in 1609 he exchanged pamphlets with Bellarmino. Donne's *Ignatius*, then, can be read as mocking Bellarmino's writings against James and using, more comically, some of the King's own arguments (*Ignatius* xxi, xxvi). In fact, suggests Eugene Kirk (formerly 'Korkowski') in a 1975 article that makes a definitive case for *Conclave* as a Menippean satire, Donne's timing was good, for his friend Sir Henry Wotton, ambassador to Venice, had sent word to James that a leading pro-Jesuit writer, Caspar Schoppe, was finishing a satire of the King himself (437). *Ignatius* may be a pre-emptive strike that could do Donne no harm with the Crown, and in any case he wrote in a time and place much given to such anti-Catholic satire (Boyce lists many). In Barnabe Rich's 1593 *Greenes Newes both from Heauen and Hell*, for example, a Jesuit impregnates his hostess; in Thomas Dekker's 1606 *Newes From Hell* the infernal regions house bad poets (B4^v), Catholic conspirators (F4), and '*Elizian* Courtiers' (H4) dressed like Frenchmen; and, written c.1610 although printed in 1627, Phineas Fletcher's *Locustae* offers a demon named 'Equivocus', the Moon as 'the Florentines [Galileo's] new world' (G4^v), and the Lucianic world as stage (H2^v). The 'new philosophy', moreover, probably accelerated a fashion for cosmic voyages, and it is possible that Donne had access to Johannes Kepler's *Somnium* (Nicolson 1940*a*: 96 and 1940*b*: 268–75), although Piers Brown argues persuasively for the greater relevance of Kepler's *De Stella Nova* (P. Brown 2009). A 'new star' is a disturbing innovation of the highest order.

Donne opens with a preface by the 'printer' (probably himself) calling this work less scurrilous than some Catholic satires that use Pasquil, the famous libel-covered Roman statue also called Pasquin, to 'butcher and mangle' their own popes and cardinals by reviving Lucian (*Ignatius* 5). Readers now have a hint of the generic context for what is to come; Healy (*Ignatius* 158–61) doubts we can identify anything specific, but Estienne Pasquier's *Iesuites Catechism* (on which see below) makes a good referent. The narrator then explains, after a de-rigueur allusion to the Sorbonne and then to Kepler, Tycho Brahe, and Galileo, that he was swept up in an 'Exstasie', a rush upward that recalls Curione's Pasquin. Rising like a lark and, thanks to the new optics, furnished with special 'spectacles', he cannot quite discern Limbo or Purgatory, but he sees Hell well enough. What follows is dense with allusion, marginal citation of modern works in Latin that include some by the Jesuits' defenders, wordplay, and complex conceits worthy of metaphysical poetry. Thus Ignatius would like to possess the Devil (15; vice versa is the usual arrangement), and when admiring the Pope we should remember Satan lest we focus on the mere image and forget the '*prototype*' (47). We must distinguish Lucifer the Devil from Lucifer the evening star, Venus, and since the new cosmology shows that Venus circles the sun and can show us only her rear, modern astronomers can use her but 'preposterously', or backwards (17). And there is the usual false accusation that Jesuits inspired the murders of Henri III and Henri IV (77) and the usual references to papal cross-dressing and sodomy (43).

What the narrator observes is a power struggle to sit next to a soon-nervous Lucifer, a struggle that entails some formal speeches, the most passionate and impressive given by Ignatius. (Coffin [210] thought Donne somewhat credulous when hearing the astronomers, but for Hassel [331] the credulity belongs to the narrator and the irony to the author.) Each aspirant or celebrity is given to innovation, itself a topic with religious significance, for Catholics and Reformers regularly accused each other of having invented a new Christianity—one reason why Donne makes Ignatius unimpressed by Calvin and Beza as revolutionaries (77; confusingly, though, Satan seems to see Luther as an innovator, albeit one now in Heaven: 87). Those introduced include Mohammed (9), who introduced a new religion; Copernicus, who proposed a new heliocentric cosmos (13); the Jesuit astronomer Christopher Clavius, chief designer of the 1582 Gregorian calendar (17); Paracelsus, who advocated a new chemistry-based pharmacotherapy (19); Machiavelli, codifier of modern statecraft's amoral principles (25); and Columbus, who discovered a new world (69). Even Cecil, at whom Donne may aim some of the satire, is an innovator, bringing new men to politics and sidelining members of the old nobility such as the ninth Earl of Northumberland, whom Donne knew and may also have admired (Flynn 1987: 169–78).

Ignatius Loyola, however, is the worst and most devious innovator of all, creator of the Society of Jesus, an organization that was neither the ancient priesthood nor a traditional monastic order but a phalanx formed along military lines yet able to live amongst civilians and pursue papal interests. Soon famous for clever word-twisting 'equivocation', persuasive argument, plotting (which then had a lexical overlap with innovative 'plats', and 'platforms'), and supposedly encouraging regicide, the Jesuits impressed even those many who hated them. When Ignatius founded the Society he did to the religious scene something like what Copernicus did to the cosmos when he made it harder to know *where* we are, or like what Clavius did to the calendar when he made it harder to know *when* we are—for England had retained the older 'count', thus lagging ten (later eleven) days behind most of the Continent. No wonder, master innovator that he is, that Ignatius wins the debate, although conceding Machiavelli's value to his order. Lucifer, afraid for his throne, arranges to have the Jesuits, now that Galileo has brought the moon closer, emigrate there so as to form a 'Lunatique Church' on that mutable feminine body that will soon grow to be itself a Hell (*Ignatius* 81 ff.). But no. News of efforts to canonize Ignatius leads, after some struggle, to his installation at Lucifer's right hand.

Once more, it helps to give *Conclave* generic company. Well before 1611 there had been satirical reports on some other world—Heaven, Hell, Hades, the moon. Lucian's *True History* was a major model, as was his *Menippos*, and the telescope had made the inner solar system if not easier to visit then easier to see. Donne could have read many such satires, including a scene from *Pantagruel* in which the giant's servant Epistemon reports on the carnival reversals that he saw in Hades while he was (briefly) dead (Rabelais 1.367 ff.). Inevitably, such satirical voyages could purport to have discovered Catholic folly or wickedness. Some are astonishingly sadistic. It was probably the learned Matthias Flacius Illyricus whose *Wonderfull Newes of the Death of Paul the III* (1552?), translated by William Baldwin, relays a report by 'Esquillus' (Pasquil) to 'Mark Forius' (Pasquil's fellow statue Marforius) on Paul III's posthumous transformation into a hag who bleeds menstrual blood into a chalice that is then used in a parodic Mass (Flacius C1). Donne never approached such obscenity, and indeed, despite the eroticized world of *Metem* and hints here and there, he was less given than many to sexualizing the enemy.

Anti-Catholic satire not only launched into space but descended into Hell: in Curione's *Pasquine in a Traunce* (translated 1566?) Pasquin/Pasquil tells Marforius about a dream visit up to what he first thinks is Heaven but turns out to be the Pope's Hell; there, for example, one famous saint is reduced to making rosary beads (fo. 18), and the non-committal Erasmus is tied between a hart's horns to swing with the wind (fo. 75). The allusion in Donne's *Sat4* to one who in 'a trance' 'dreamt he saw hell' (ll. 157–8) is regularly taken as meaning Dante, but the wording much better suits Curione's Pasquine. Curione wrote before the Jesuits had become important enough to be feared, but the years immediately preceding *Ignatius* had seen a number of satires attacking or defending them, some in Latin by such humanist scholars as Heinsius.

The war of snarls and scoffs, however, was complicated by the religious conversions and re-conversions (that of the internationally known Isaac Casaubon, for example, to say nothing of those of Henri IV and Jonson), and indeed, it is important to remember that many people could be both Catholic and anti-Jesuit. On these grounds alone, Donne would have been interested in *The Jesuites Catechism* (1602; see Zuber) by the much-published Estienne Pasquier, translated by William Watson that same year, and reprinted in the late 1670s and 1685, doubtless thanks to fears of the Popish Plot and James II's Catholicism. In this dialogue, which the translator addresses 'To All English Catholicks, that are faithfull subjects to Queene Elizabeth', Donne would have found Pasquil and Marforius, attacks on Jesuits for various regicides, some poetry, wordplay (e.g. on Agnus Dei and a papal bull), connecting (fos. 56–7ᵛ) 'Pape' (Pope) with 'papelards' (hypocrites), and—dear to any Renaissance writer's heart—anagrams: one speaker notes that 'SECTA JESUITARUM' ('the Jesuit sect') is also TUTE MARES VICIAS ('Thou debauchest males') so that, explains a little poem, 'With women you lie not, but with males rather, / Speake Jesuit, how canst thou be a Father?' (fos. 114–15). Jesuits have two souls, one Spanish and the other—when in France—French (1.1.2). But there is worse, for some 'Lucianists' once pictured Satan dressed as a monk to tempt Christ, showing that monks are 'Diabolicall' (fo. 210ᵛ), but in fact the Devil, wanting to look more pious than a monk, transforms himself into Ignatius. The very spirit of division, Ignatius 'represents the person of *Lucifer*', who 'would equall himselfe to his Creator' and exercise power 'over the Universall Church' (fo. 223ᵛ). He is good at disguise, but whatever his habit, he remains the same: 'Cloath an Ape in Tissue, the beast may happily be more proud, but never the lesse deformed' (fo. 225). If Donne did not read this, he should have.

Similarly, the *Satyre Menippée*, which is sometimes mentioned in connection with Donne, was by Catholics anxious to defend Henri IV against those who still opposed him despite his conversion. Much of this work is itself a conclave, a meeting of the Estates, with satirical descriptions, scoffs at Jesuits and Spain, and parodic orations interrupted by poetry. A 1595 supplement, not included in the English translation but highly relevant to Donne, involves a plan, an ironically termed 'saincte entrerprise', to send the Spanish army to the moon so as to extend Spain's empire and, in the words of one modern scholar, 'to give the poor Jesuits, now banished from most European countries, somewhere to go and something to do!' (Ridgely 174; Anon. 1752: 247). As Donne's Ignatius settled into his throne near Lucifer the décor and company must have felt familiar.

Poems for Thomas Coryate's *Crudities*

One subgenre of Menippean satire is the paradoxical praise of something or someone valueless that the writer pretends to like: baldness, for example, or debt, or folly, or in this case a man who willingly plays the fool better than he intended. Thomas Coryate of Odcombe, a man of respectable origin clinging to the fringes of Prince Henry's court, seems to have taken on the role of quasi-jester. His *Coryats Crudities* describes the author's travels abroad in a cheerful but not particularly comic style, and is important for anyone studying early modern travel literature and European response to Eastern cultures.

With a title suggesting not vulgarity but rawness resistant to both physical and mental digestion (K. A. Craik 2004: 1–2), *Crudities* was printed in 1611 with a huge prefatory collection of pseudo-praise, some friendly enough but some disdainful beyond the requirements of joshing friendship. Either Coryate or his printer, William Stansby, added sometimes deliberately uncomprehending notes increasing the carnival. Later that year these 'panegyrics' were printed separately by Thomas Thorpe as *The Odcombian Banquet: Dished Foorth by Thomas the Coriat, and Served in by a Number of noble Wits*... The poems' atmosphere is convivial, erudite, witty, and urbane, evocative of supposed meetings at London's Mitre or Mermaid Taverns of some 'Sireniac' gentlemen—'Sireniac' because a 'mermaid' could then be a 'siren'—but also of the world shared by gentleman wits with ties to the universities, law, and court (O'Callaghan 2007: ch. 5; for more on print-and-drink friendships, Roebuck 1996b: 145–6. Shapiro 1950 gives dates and lists friends; on social subgroups see Ord). The tonality is also Menippean, with a Rabelaisian taste for multiplicity, macaronic wordplay, anagrams, an erudition that mocks itself, images of eating and swilling, words and books as edible and drinkable, allusions to giants and to fantasy voyages. If satire is a *lanx satura*, this platter is heaped high. Like a fraternity initiation, it offers riotous male bonding but it can be harsh; carnival itself, after all, is cruel to those who do not fit in. Coryate's smile as he read these (non-)tributes may have shown some gritted teeth.

To this volume, published after he had begun to appear in print, Donne contributed certainly two poems, *Coryat* (d3–d4) and *Macaron* (d4), and is probably also the 'Dones' who wrote a third (f5ᵛ; the final 'e' and flourish in Donne's signature can resemble an 's', and allusions to Rabelais further suggest that Dones is Donne; see Prescott 1998a and 1998b: 71–2). The 1649 edition omits both the macaronics and the poem by Dones, and mystifyingly puts *Coryat* among the 'Funerall Elegies' (262–4). Whether or not the poems wounded Coryate no one knows, but in 1615 he addressed Donne as the author of the 'two most elegant Latine Bookes, *Pseudomartyr, and Ignatij Conclaue*', in a compliment printed in the 1616 *Greetings from the Court of the Great Mogul* (45; see Roebuck 1996b: 141–3 on its relevance to Donne's 'descent' into print in 1610/11; on Coryate's life see Strachan). In any case, the poems suit this 'celebrity roast', as one scholar has called the prefatory material in *Crudities* (Centerwall 79). They also suit interests and images that appear elsewhere in Donne's work.

The first and longest, in 1611 entitled simply 'Incipit Joannes Donne', calls Coryate's book an 'Infinit worke' with no 'end', presumably no back cover visible from here. It is larger than the world, exotic, monstrous, bulging, a 'Universall Booke', and filled with famous political names, for Coryate is 'As deepe a States-man, as a Gazettier'. It is scattered, multiple, incoherent, its pages like the hacked limbs of heroes dying in foreign battles—or like the bodies of criminals 'cut in Anatomies' (*Milgate* 47–8; Roebuck 1996b: 147 remarks on the poem's images of dismemberment). The pages will have their uses, wrapping pills or helping bind other books. Nor, says Donne with the same sophistical logic that energizes his love poetry, is the author of this book whole: men both reason and laugh, so Coryate is only half a man, which is lucky, since otherwise he would be too huge. His leaves are 'mysticall' because each is, like those of the Sybil, a whole book, but Donne will pass up the chance to peruse them and, overthrown by the author's 'Gyant-wit', rather than 'reade all', would 'reade none'. Here, burlesqued, are matters that Donne elsewhere takes more seriously: the scattered body, an all that is also a nothing, a multiplicity that is also a universality, the nervous comedy of slithering logic, and a touch of anger at the 'deepe States-man' who watches everyone (*Milgate* 47–8). One scholar, astutely calling Donne's poem a 'meditation on print publication', thinks it leaves books soulless and inanimate, this 'progress of the book' being 'unremittingly materialistic and anatomising' (O'Callaghan 2007: 124–6). Given that Coryate's pages are 'mysticall' and paradoxical, however, being all and nothing, endless and trivial, we could as plausibly call them uncanny.

The second poem, *Macaron* (*Milgate* 49), comprises two elegiac couplets mixing Latin, French, Italian, and English. Since these almost unintelligible verses are so seldom discussed I give a transcription with accents added for the metre and a translation by Professor Roger Kuin:

> Quôt, dos hâec, Linguîsts perfêtti, Dîsticha fâiront,
>   Tôt cuerdôs States-mên hîc livre fara tuûs.
> Ês sat à my l'honnêur estre hîc intêso; Car Î leave
>   L'hônra, dê persônne nêstre credûto, tibî
>   Explicit Ioannes Donne.

> As many perfect linguists as this gift, these distichs, will make,
>   So many prudent statesmen will this book of yours have as harvest.
> It is enough for my honour here to be understood; for I leave
>   The honour of being believed by no one to you.

Some pages later in the 1611 edition of *Crudities*, on fo. f5ᵛ, comes the poem by 'Joannes Dones', again entitled 'Incipit Joannes Donne' (reprinted in Centerwall 80–1). Coryate is again (un)praised in terms of endless space and endless size. Had he followed Drake or Magellan to the '*unturn'd cheeke*' of Mother Earth, for example, and then gone yet further, he might have found 'wonders' beyond those Rabelais describes, ones even more likely to vex the Pope. Donne cites Rabelais's land of frozen words in *The Fourth Book* (ch. 55–6), that punning if poignant scene in which the words melt into the cries of an ancient battle (cf. Donne's other allusion to these frozen words in his Letter transcribed in the Burley ms. at fo. 296ᵛ, printed in E. M. Simpson 1948: 310). Here are linguistic paradoxes: words that release their original meaning with time, perhaps like the Gospel after its confinement in the Vulgate (one way to read Rabelais's scene), or perhaps like going into print and so both releasing and re-freezing discourse. The poet also cites not only Pantagruel's fairly genial war with sausages in Book IV but the more certainly anti-Catholic and perhaps less authentic Book V's 'Popehawks' (although the original's 'Papegault' is singular). Donne's convivial participation in the crowd of politically connected and elegantly erudite men jests with matters of acute personal significance.

'Characters'

Satire often includes snatches of vivid characterization meant to entertain, offer social commentary, reinforce a larger argument, or demolish enemies. The most often cited model for characterizing—in the ancient sense of sketching or inscribing—a social type or tendency is Theophrastus (born c.370 BCE), a student of Aristotle who was himself so compelling a teacher, it was said, that he once attracted 2,000 pupils to hear him (Theophrastus 23; see also Smeed). His 'Characters' survived the Middle Ages in a number of manuscripts, with some spurious additions, and began to see print in the early sixteenth century. Casaubon's edition appeared in 1592, and Donne might have known of one, also in Greek, published at Oxford in 1604, and the 1616 translations by John Healey, too late for Donne to have read before writing his own 'characters', are evidence of the genre's popularity.

Once in England, the 'character' mutated so as to include images of vice and virtue, although wit never vanished, if sometimes lingering only as compression. Ralph Johnson's 1665 *Scholars Guide* defines the genre as a 'witty and facetious description of the nature and qualities of some person, or sort of people'. Choose 'a sort of men as will admit of variety of observation, such be, drunkards, usurers, lyars, taylors, excise-men, travellers, pedlars, merchants, tapsters, lawyers, an upstart gentleman, a young Justice, a Constable, an alderman, and the like'. Then 'Express their natures, qualities, conditions, practices, tools, desires, aims, or ends, by witty Allegories, or Allusions, to things or terms in nature, or art...still striving for wit and pleasantness' with 'tart nipping jerks about their vices' and conclude with a 'witty and neat passage, leaving them to the effect of their follies or studies' (15).

The most famous writer of such 'characters' was Sir Thomas Overbury, although whether Sir Thomas himself, murdered while in the Tower during a notorious scandal, wrote any of the sketches credited to him is uncertain. 'Newes from the very Country', ascribed to one 'I. D.', first appears in the 1614 edition of Overbury's characters (G2^v; beginning with the 1615 edition there follows an 'Answere' by 'A. S.'). 'I. D.' could be a number of people, not least John Davies, who wrote *A Second Husband for Sir Thomas Overburies's Wife* (1616), but the 1650 edition of Donne's *Poems* included 'Newes', and extracts are found in the Burley ms. (LRO, MS Finch DG.7, Lit. 2 as discussed in *Problems* 67, 137; I quote Peters's edition even though she classifies the 'Newes' as 'Dubia'). Is it a 'Character'? The 1616 edition of Overbury's *Wife, With New Elegies* ends with a brief definition that gives the Greek name, 'which signifieth to ingrave, or make a deepe Impression'. It is also an Egyptian hieroglyph, we read, 'in little comprehending much', a picture 'quaintlie drawne', and 'wits descant on any plaine song'. Some would call a Donne Sermon wit's descant on a plain text, but is 'Newes' a Theophrastian 'descant'? The definition's appearance at the end of this collection (S2^v–S3) might suggest that the writer considered it some sort of 'character', but as editions added yet more of what the 1622 title page calls 'Wittie Conceits' whoever arranged the contents worked them into more coherent categories, so that 'Newes' now finds itself not with or near 'characters' but firmly linked to other satirical reports from the country, the ocean, and so forth.

In that same 1622 edition we find the more certainly Theophrastian 'Character of a Dunce' (G3–G5) and, separated by a poem but still under the running title 'Characters', an 'Essay of Valour' (Q6–R1), a complex argument that in its terse declarative style resembles something by Bacon even as its personal opening ('I am of opynion') recalls Montaigne. (See *Problems* 62; I quote Peters's edition even though she classifies both 'Dunce' and 'Valour' as 'Dubia'.) In its initial cynicism, though, it is like neither. This 'essay' fits the 'Character' tradition, moreover, for the latter's titles as they came down to the Renaissance allude to such habitual activities or qualities as 'Slander' and 'Arrogance'. 'Dunce' is not credited to Donne or even to an 'I. D.', but was published in Donne's 1652[3] *Paradoxes and Problemes* (fos. D10–D12), as was 'Valour' (fos. D12v–E4). The latter is found also in *Cottoni Posthuma* (321–7), a 1651 collection, put together by James Howell, of texts by or possessed by the late Sir Robert Cotton, a bibliophile who had known Donne; there it is identified as a 'Fancie' and perhaps ironically ascribed to the truly valorous if also poetically lovesick Sir Philip Sidney. In the 1652[3] *Paradoxes and Problemes* we also find the aggressively contemptuous and previously unpublished 'Character of a Scot at the first sight' (fos. D9–D9v), but not 'Newes'. All three pieces are listed under 'Characters' in the 1652 Table of Contents (fo. A8), with 'Dunce' and 'Scot' paired together; here too 'Valour' is generically ambiguous.

Did Donne write all these prose works? Some (e.g. Helen Peters in *Problems* lxxxvii–lxxxviii) have doubted it; others, including myself, are more confident that he did. The question of authorship in Overbury's collection, moreover, is complicated, for as time went on and the anonymous 'wittie conceits' accumulated, the volume's impression of conviviality took on the tone of a group effort. Even the preference for anonymity or initials may be in part designed to suggest the sort of networked friendship or *convivium* found in the poems prefacing *Coryats Crudities*. There remains a major difference, for the Overburian literary party, perhaps because some of its participants had ties to the Court, had a few female wits: 'M^{ris} B. (sometimes, if doubtfully, identified as Cecilia Bulstrode, who had died in 1609) sends 'Newes of my Morning Work' as early as 1614 (fos. H2v–H3) and, in 1618, 'the Lady Southwell' reports on edicts promulgated by the Parliament of 'Eutopia' (O3v–O5v). The question of authorship may remain unsettled, in part because, in the absence of definitive evidence, those who think that the pieces are Donne's may be inclined to see wit and subtlety and those who do not find them interesting may be less apt to think them his. Whether they are juvenilia, as Donne Jr. claimed (1652[3] A5v), is another question, for we lack dates for their composition and 'Scot' was almost certainly written after 1603, when, even according to the traditional definition of 'juvenile' as someone under 30, Donne was now fully adult.

Whatever one thinks of their authenticity or generic identity, they undoubtedly aim at certain types, social scenes, or even individuals. 'Dunce' laughs at clownish stupidity in terms that fit Donne's preoccupations: a dunce is 'a Soule drownd in a lump of flesh' (*Problems* 59), although a soul should of course animate the body. Animating souls should not, though, be like the atheist's sometimes sleepy but sometimes too 'restive' horses. Donne recalls here the traditional Platonic image of the soul as a charioteer or rider trying to control a temperamental steed. He is a 'meere nothing of him selfe' but although tedious almost past endurance is at least 'a foyle for better witts' (60). He lacks a centre and coherence, vomiting mere morsels of meaning that stick in his teeth, and is—repeats Donne—'just Nothing but the subject of Nothing, the Object of contempt'. Take him as he is, concludes the sketch (with charity? resignation? contempt?), for 'there is no hope hee should ever become better' (62). If the concern with soul and body, nothingness, and heaped-up incoherence is familiar in Donne, the focus on the dunce's usefulness to others' wit recalls the crueler pseudo-panegyrics to Coryate and may indeed (Flynn 1973/4: 66–7) point to him.

Donne's brief 'Scot' is clearly aimed at James I (Flynn 1973/4: 67) and just as clearly unprintable while the king or his son lived—when it first saw the light in 1652 England was a regicidal republic. The rustic Scot dresses badly, with stockings pretentiously dyed 'Gules', the heraldic term for 'red'. With a plain face, big nose, and followers who call him 'Laird', he has become a 'knight-wright', an allusion to the King's supposed willingness to sell knighthoods. Now he is off to see a bear-baiting with his 'whore', followed by 'Tom Thorney' (*Problems* 58–9; again I quote Peters's edition even though she classifies 'Scot' as 'Dubia'), identified by a scribe in an early manuscript as a surgeon, which could then mean barber—but since barber-surgeons served as doctors, this Scot or his companion may require treatment for something Donne need not spell out.

'Valour', like so much of Donne's work, ponders a word that relates only problematically to a referent, the essay's scepticism recalling Falstaff's dismissal of 'honour' as a mere 'scutcheon' (*1 Henry IV*, V. i. 143), a shield's painted arms with emptiness behind it. Like a telescope, says Donne, a reputation for valour can make a small man seem large, but when we put on good clothes, good faces, and good wit we become too effeminate to attract women. Scars are more inviting, as is armour. Nicely cynical, but other touches, even the remark that women 'seduced by *Apparrell*' (*Problems* 58–9) must remember that men go naked to bed, recall deeper matters. Should only women remember that clothes do not make the man? *Is* valour mere appearance? After the essay claims that valour is grounded in reason and the effort to do no wrong, the speaker says that since he admires valour he should be a man of few words...and the essay ends promptly on that self-referential note. 'Newes' reports the non-news that the rich are more powerful than the poor; that Jesuits, once rare as apricots, are now everywhere; that Vice is a pike with an appetite for the mere fry of virtues and smaller vices; that afflicted atheists want a God they cannot find; and that, in an image recalling Donne's concern with the authorities' suspicious misinterpretations, an author's sentences are 'like haires in an horse taile, concurre in one roote of beauty and strength, but being pluckt out one by one, serve onely for springes and snares'. Pure Donne, and chilling.

It is possible that three more brief essays are by Donne. Almost certainly not intended for print, they appear first in *Cottoni Posthuma* (1651), gathered under the heading 'Sir Francis Walsinghams Anatomizing Of Honesty, Ambition, and Fortitude' and follow the 'Essay of Valour', separated only by a poem to a faint-hearted lover urging him to keep trying; the poem is likewise ascribed to Sidney but might seem to many ears more in the Cavalier style than in that of Sidney—or of Donne. The essays by 'Walsingham', which the title page says (with what truth nobody can definitively know) were 'written in the year 1590' (Cotton 329), the same year in which their supposed author died. They are concerned, as are most of Theophrastus' own 'characters' (one of which is on 'petty ambition'), more with specific traits or impulses that can belong to a person than with general types of people, and treat those attributes with stylistic compression and often subtle discriminations. These 'anatomies' use a sharp scalpel. They are almost certainly not by Walsingham, any more than 'Valour' is by that statesman's son-in-law Philip Sidney, and Dennis Flynn (1969: 430–8) has made a case for Donne's authorship, noting some lexical overlaps with Donne's eleventh Paradox ('That the Gifts of the Body are better than those of the Mind'). As Flynn observes, these essays contain at least two matters dear to Donne: the relation of body to soul and the utility of gold and coins to clever analogies and witty conceits.

The essay on honesty, in the older sense of lifelong integrity, not of mere truth-telling, distinguishes it from the doing of good deeds and from fame-giving valour, finding in it a certain pleasant malleability, like that of gold, that allows the honest man to receive the impress of friendship, especially in the country—where, we may suppose, honesty is more easily sustained. Ambition, a quality that 'is in Men, as beauty is in women'(Cotton 336), is not, in this essay, confused with the desire to rise at all costs but is rather, to the eye of reason, valuable for spurring those who possess it to do 'brave and worthy acts' (338) worthy of the 'Love, Honour, and Praise' that are 'the greatest Blessings of this world' (but not, presumably, of the next) and that please the mind more than the body (335). 'Fortitude' moves beyond 'this world' when remarking that 'the Perfection of Happinesse consists in the Love of God', which alone can fill 'all the Corners of the Soule' (339). In the little list of secular virtues with which the author concludes the essay, for his focus is on the classical ones that Theophrastus himself knew and not on the Pauline trio of Faith, Hope, and Charity more dear to the Dean of St Paul's, we read that Fortitude is also able to steel us against adversity and can give us a 'Confidence not to be Circumvented by any danger' (340). These virtues attract the praise of others, but temperance is from within, making the body able to prevent disease inside us and mitigating the discomfort of a life with cold, hunger, and need.

It is possible to read these three essays as ironic, and indeed Flynn (1969: 430–8) does so. Certainly the first one flickers with dry wit (to be soft gold ready for coining into friendship sounds more shiny than stable), but it is possible, especially granted the partial subjectivity of all readings, to see the others less as satire than as straightforward meditations on the things of this world, ironic only in so far as the things of this world are not the things of the next and must look inadequate by comparison. If the pieces are by Donne—and Flynn makes a good case—then this is Donne as reflective Bacon, not Donne as laughing Pasquil and certainly not Donne as Hall's disgusted porcupine.

The works this chapter has described are individually interesting; together, and in their political or cultural context—a context extending not only back in time but across the Channel—most of them show that when Donne was thinking beyond traditional verse satire, keeping one eye on the Menippea and another on the censors, he could be clever but serious. What are words? How do they mean? Is there nothing? Can we name it? Can names go on forever? Can souls do so—and how, as they 'progress' to infinity if only in a witty conceit? And can there be a linear infinity if at the end of time, when the square of our maps becomes the circle of eternity, endlessness ends in God? What is a soul, for that matter, and how does it relate to nothing? It had long been said by Augustine and others, who had read Plato, that evil is the absence of good, a *privatio boni*, and yet the sins of the Jesuits must be something, too infernally weighty for the moon. And do they too, like Copernicus and Clavius, call all in doubt by confusing us with equivocations' false logic? If so, let us at least 'doubt wisely'—and laugh.

CHAPTER 13

THE LOVE LYRIC [SONGS AND SONETS]

DAYTON HASKIN

Love lyrics are commonly thought to be short non-narrative poems that, in contexts representing experiences of love and sex, articulate the subjective thoughts and emotions of a single speaker. This definition, like the term itself, emerged relatively recently in the history of thinking about literary kinds. In a handbook committed to interpreting Donne's writings primarily on the basis of distinct genres, it will be instructive to consider what this and other generic designations have to offer to our understanding of the fifty-odd poems that have traditionally been known as Songs and Sonets. The challenge is all the greater because Donne, as illustrated in other chapters of this Handbook, was impatient with generic conventions, and he often worked against the expectations that attended particular literary kinds.

It is not clear that Donne himself thought of these poems as a group. Nor can we assume that all through his life he valued each of them similarly and consistently. The editors of the *Variorum* have compiled evidence that these poems entered manuscript circulation one by one at different times, perhaps over a period of more than two decades, and have observed that the poet seems not to have kept an archive of them. Donne's earliest readers necessarily encountered them piecemeal; and these poems would seem to have as good a claim as any of his verses to qualify as the random 'pieces' that, according to his first biographer, Izaak Walton, 'had been loosely ... scattered in his youth' and that their author later 'wisht ... had been abortive, or so short liv'd that his own eyes had witnessed their funeralls' (Walton 1675: 53). Gradually, they were gathered by others; and posthumously, notably not in the first (1633) but in the second (1635) edition of *Poems by J.D.*, they were presented as belonging to a generic group. It was designated 'Songs and Sonets' and made to lead off the volume.

The prominence given these poems in the mid-1630s may have had something to do with a newly robust reputation that Donne's 'amatory verses' were acquiring. From the fact that references to the lyrics are rare until the 1620s, it can be inferred that Donne probably kept most of them largely out of circulation, perhaps in accord with a principle facetiously stated in the Preface to *Metem* that he liked to write for people who didn't need his poems to be explained. In a Verse Letter to Roland Woodward he had remarked that his Muse had 'showne' to 'few, yet too many' his satires and 'love-song weeds' (*RWThird* ll. 4–5). But in the 1620s discrete poems that must have been discreetly circulating only among a few trusted friends escaped the poet's control. A rapidly accumulating number of manuscripts (many of them still extant) show that the poems were as unruly as they were popular: there are more copies of the Songs and Sonets than of any of Donne's poems in other genres, and the copies carry a greater density of variant readings. Their contemporary cachet suggests that the makers of the 1635 volume, like those who had been responsible in 1623 for placing *The Tempest* at the head of Shakespeare's First Folio, gave pride of place to material that would catch the eye and quicken the desire of someone picking up the volume for the first time. A few moments of browsing through the 1635 *Poems* might reveal that there were plenty of pieces that, while they included bookish and learned references, tapped into the vitality of colloquial speech with an unparalleled mixture of playful and earnest tones.

After 1635 the traditional designation and placement of the Songs and Sonets remained stable through many subsequent editions of the *Poems*, even when love poetry became less prestigious in English literary culture and increasingly, with the rest of Donne's works, most of his love poems garnered less, and less appreciative, attention. Curiously, the history of writing on Donne shows that for more than two centuries his love lyrics were rarely referred to as if they constituted a distinct genre. Between the seventeenth century and the Victorian *fin de siècle* people sometimes spoke of Donne's 'amatory' poems or his 'love' verses, by which they meant the Elegies and other poems as well as the love lyrics; various observers, in remarking on Donne's practice as a 'satirical' poet, had some of his Elegies, Verse Letters, and short love poems as much in mind as his formal Satires. In the nineteenth century, when Walton's *Life of Dr Donne* came widely to be regarded as 'the masterpiece of English biography' (cf. Stephen 1898–1902: 3.38), and as love poetry took on renewed prestige among the Victorians, a growing concern for a less misleading generic classification led editors to propose new headings for the group: 'Lyrical' in A. B. Grosart's edition (1872–3), 'Miscellaneous' in the Grolier Club edition (1895), and 'The Love Poems' in the title of the volume in which the group was for the first time published as a book in its own right (1905), not without the omission of about a dozen poems that Charles Eliot Norton considered unworthy of the poet.

The last decade of the nineteenth century witnessed an extraordinary quickening of interest in the Songs and Sonets, and the late Victorian period has been the only time in history when there was much controversy about membership in the group. To fifty-two poems that in the 1633 first edition appeared mostly in two large batches and were randomly arranged, the 1635 edition had added four more when it brought them all together. In 1873 Grosart, intent on creating an autobiographically revealing edition that would show Donne as a promiscuous rake who had been saved by the love of a good woman, printed 'for the first time' as Donne's more than twenty 'lyrical' poems on love and sex, only to have subsequent editors expose the spuriousness of his claims. The general stability in the canon seems to be owing not so much to an inherent generic criterion as it does to the fact that none of the poems has a better claim to belong with those of any other genre. It is a credit to the intelligence of the Grolier Club editors that, without having bibliographical precedent for the designation 'Miscellaneous', they called attention to a significant way in which these poems constitute a different sort of group than ones gathered according to more strictly generic classifications. As lyric poems, the so-called Songs and Sonets do not answer to a classical precedent in the way that Donne's Epigrams, Elegies, Satires, Verse Letters, Epicedes, Obsequies, and Epithalamions do. Moreover, they differ from the kinds of poems—Elegies, Epigrams, Satires, and Holy Sonnets—that Donne himself sometimes arranged in sequences.

The difficulty about knowing what to call this posthumous collection is telling. None of the poems is a sonnet as that term is commonly understood today. Cumulatively, the poems depict a range of amorous experience that is so fluid and contradictory in its implications as to inhibit generalization. As Neil Keeble has observed, in the best study we have of the generic qualities of these poems, we would suppose that in the Renaissance, amidst the critical revival of interest in classical kinds, considerations of genre would provide a key to understanding Donne's poetic achievement. For this group of poems, however, it turns out that this is the case indirectly at best (Keeble 77). At least three interrelated reasons that it is difficult to assign a generic name may be productively explored in detail: (1) the elasticity of the term 'lyric'; (2) the seeming inappropriateness of the traditional designation 'Songs and Sonets'; and (3) the poet's manifest design of working against (as well as with) the generic conventions he inherited.

Historically, 'lyric' has been defined broadly and variously, and often as a mode rather than a genre. What English speakers have understood by the word has changed considerably over time. In the Romantic period 'lyric' came to refer almost to poetry in general. Its dominant sense today allows for poems on virtually any topic. This development owes something to the proliferation of 'lyric' forms in the Renaissance, when the term served more as a broad general category than as a designation for a specific genre. (Among his '*Lyrick* Pieces' Michael Drayton enumerated odes, hymns, ballads, and several other forms.) Nor was there any theoretical distinction between the melodic 'lyrics' written by, say, Campion or by Shakespeare when he included songs in his plays and the verbal 'lyrics' written, for example, by Donne and Waller. In fact, the word 'lyric' was slow to make its way into currency. Until the eighteenth century it was used chiefly as an adjective, as illustrated in the heading Ben Jonson conferred upon his 'Celebration of Charis in Ten Lyric Pieces' or in John Dryden's reference to the 'sweetness of Mr. Waller's lyric poesy'. Yet there is also evidence that it was on its way to serving as a noun. In the 1580s Sir Philip Sidney praised 'the Earle of Surries Lyricks' (see *OED*, 'lyric'). Three decades later William Drummond of Hawthornden, compiling a list of books that he had read, referred to a manuscript of 'Jhone Dones lyriques' (A. J. Smith 73, quoting National Library of Scotland, MS 2059, Hawthornden MSS. Vol. vii, fo. 336^r). Still, such usage was by no means routine. The traditional name, Songs and Sonets, is hardly more precise. Upon inspection, however, it is somewhat more revealing. In seventeenth-century manuscripts the heading 'Song' often shows up above individual poems by Donne, and scribal references to 'Dunne's sonets' sometimes appear as well. As a heading, 'Songs and Sonets' echoed the title of the sixteenth-century anthology popularly known as 'Tottel's Miscellany'. This volume had launched what we recognize in retrospect as the most lyrical of all periods in English literary history. Through its substantial representation of poems by Wyatt and Surrey it suggested that 'lyrical' verse was courtly and sweet. This association with 'lyrical' performance continued in many of the sonnet cycles. By the 1630s, since poets had ceased writing such cycles, the heading implemented in the 1635 *Poems by J. D.* may have suggested to readers that Donne had written an old-fashioned sort of love poetry. Keeble proposes that calling poems that are not courtly and rarely sweet 'Songs and Sonets' was 'either unwittingly inappropriate or knowingly ironic' and possibly 'parodic' (Keeble 72, 73).

Given that the heading 'Songs and Sonets' suggests a distance between Donne's poems and those of the sonneteers, we may credit the compilers with recognizing that the poems do not represent an author's lyric self-expression; they belong rather to the older tradition of the commonplace book and the miscellany. Tottel had established the miscellany as an aesthetically accomplished type of book, and collections modelled on his *Songs and Sonets* antedated sonnet sequences in English. The miscellany did not offer a narrative sequence but left poems as aesthetic performances to be read through here and there and in any order that a reader wished. George Turberville was working with the miscellany model, for instance, when he brought out his *Epitaphes, Epigrams, Songs and Sonets* (1567). This collection drew the focus away from the poet, as Mary Crane has astutely observed, by presenting the various poems as experiments 'in different kinds of verse', and by showing 'little concern for whether or not they represent incompatible attitudes and ideologies' (Crane 1993: 174). In fact, Turberville made it explicit that the work done by the maker of a miscellany remained preliminary to the gathering and framing activities expected of readers themselves. In his preface, as he introduced a selection of his poems, he indicated that at least some of them were fictional. He suggested that this increased the likelihood that readers would be able to turn them to their own morally useful purposes. Other miscellaneous collections, for instance ones published by George Gascoigne, George Whetstone, and Thomas Watson, also showed poets self-consciously imitating the work of editors. Their volumes gathered up their poems and presented them with a certain irony (especially poems that they dismissed as mere trifles) as material that their readers might be able to use for their own profit. In *Hekatompathia* (1581) Watson presented himself both as an author, who in his youth had written trifling pieces, and as an editor, who in his maturity had isolated them as juvenilia, the better to illustrate his mature repentance. His arrangement of groups of poems created a book more like the sonnet sequences: it adumbrated a larger narrative pattern. While such sequencing was decidedly not Donne's practice, the fact that narrative had come to operate as a principle of organization in miscellaneous collections seems to have influenced the overall arrangement of the genres in the printed editions of Donne's *Poems*. Whatever may have been the conscious design of the anonymous makers of the 1635 edition (see Ch. 1 above), their placing of the 'Songs and Sonets' at the start, their adding a number of biographically revealing Prose Letters in the middle, and their displacing 'Divine Poems' to the end work in concert to suggest a rudimentary biographical narrative. Significantly, however, the arrangement of various poems within the section called 'Songs and Sonets' accords with the fact that very little is known about the order in which they were composed. It respects the likelihood that they were not conceived as a coherent body of verse. And it yields no sign that anyone was trying to make them tell an unfolding story. These poems are better read in the tradition of *silva* illustrated in 'The Forest' section of Ben Jonson's *Works* (1616) and in Milton's late collection of *Poems, &c. upon Several Occasions* (1673). Gathered according to this convention, poems are freed from a literary system dominated by specific occasions and a quest for patronage, and the range of the poet's diverse aesthetic achievements comes more clearly into focus.

The model of the miscellany shows then that, taken together, Donne's love lyrics need not be read serially nor in their entirety. As arrayed in 1635 they display a witty toying with the usual expectations that the words 'songs' and 'sonets' set in motion. They also demonstrate the poet's refusal to go along with the idea that various love poems need to express a single lyric subjectivity. In fact, the compilers' implementation of 'Songs and Sonets' for the heading seems to be respectfully indebted to the Contents page of the O'Flahertie ms. (dated 1632), the main source for the poems that they added in 1635. The scribe who created this manuscript displayed unusual care to classify and arrange Donne's poems generically. The practical basis for separating the short love poems from ones in other genres had something to do with their occasional and miscellaneous qualities. They shared subject matter with the Elegies, but differed formally from them by virtue of their not being in rhyming couplets. They did not fit with poems among the Verse Letters that express affection with a display of erotic imagery because they do not name a particular historical person as their addressee; nor do they presuppose the writer's signature at the close.

(*ValName*, working an intriguing variation on the conventions of the verse letter, stands as the exception that proves this rule.) They were separated from the numbered Holy Sonnets both because they are referable to mortal loves and also on the basis of their conspicuous avoidance of the conventional fourteen-line formats.

When the makers of the 1635 volume implemented the terms 'Songs and Sonets' that had been used by the O'Flahertie scribe, they must have deployed them with an awareness of still current early modern usage, which is to say, a good deal more loosely than we are accustomed to allowing: the one could refer to a poem that had a *potential* to be set to music, and the other to 'A short poem or piece of verse' that was likely 'of a lyrical and amatory character' (*OED*, sense 2). Whether Donne himself had the aversion to musical settings voiced by the speaker of *Triple*, some of his lyrics were set to music; and in *Canon* the speaker is made to refer to secular lyrics as 'hymnes'. In *Ind* Donne has his speaker use the designation 'song', curiously, to distance the first two stanzas of his utterance, which had seemed intensely immediate, and to call attention to their status as a performance (Dubrow 2008: 106–9). Moreover, the fact that the sonnet was not part of the classical repertoire meant that it could readily be infused with the sort of epigrammatic verse in which Donne's contemporaries recognized him as pre-eminent; and the terms 'sonnet' and 'epigram' were both employed for brief poems of varying numbers of lines and rhyme schemes (Keeble 76–7; cf. Colie 1973: 69–75). Thus, elsewhere in *Canon* Donne himself uses 'sonnets' in the sense of short love poems. The choice, then, in 1635 of the designation 'Songs and Sonets' signalled sophisticated readers to notice the unstable relation between the poet and his speakers and the innovations that Donne had wrought within a tradition. Not for nothing did Donne's poetry seem to T. S. Eliot the decisive precedent for the theory that he put forward in 'Tradition and the Individual Talent'.

Admittedly, it is inevitable that any writer will work in some relation to existing genres. In this matter the Songs and Sonets are striking for the considerable resistance that they mount against some frameworks within which contemporary love poems were characteristically lodged. Donne avoids making one woman the fixed subject of every love poem. Like some other love poets, he keeps the identities of the several women in the poems shadowy. Beyond this, he often refrains from marking the sex of the lover or the beloved. He provides no sequence that generates a larger narrative frame for individual poems; and he does not identify the speakers with the poet who writes the verse. For all these reasons and others, the poems prove difficult to place in relation to the dates of known events and circumstances in his own life. At the same time, many of them have so distinctive a ring to them that experienced readers feel something like what Coleridge remarked of *ValMourn*, that 'none but D. could have written' them (1984: 223). This dynamic—a powerful consistency of style and voice coupled with an absence of information about concrete circumstances outside the poems—suggests that the poems benefit from being read within a more ample set of generic considerations than has been considered so far.

Of the three general categories of poetic literature known as epic, dramatic, and lyric, the ancient world developed far more theory about the first two than the third. Even in the Renaissance, the higher genres and narrative forms (especially epic and tragedy) garnered far more critical attention than shorter ones. That relatively few ancient dicta about lyric could be turned into rules helps to account for some radical discontinuities in the history of what is now, retrospectively, commonly called lyric poetry, an amorphous category that, as acknowledged above, has generally included a variety of subgenres. In antiquity lyric poetry was often distinguished from choric verse by virtue of the fact that it was composed to be performed by a single singer and that, as a designation connecting it with a musical instrument suggests, the musical element was considered even more intrinsic to it than to epic and drama. Among the Alexandrian poets, however, and especially among the Romans, who imitated them, lyric poetry was increasingly disconnected from musical performance, and there is extant a large body of lyric poetry written simply to be read rather than performed. By Donne's time it was increasingly taken for granted in the emerging vernacular literatures that short poetic compositions need not be connected with music. Since the Renaissance, the musical dimension of many lyric poems seems at best vestigial. Modern handbooks to literature tend to emphasize the subjective elements that come through in the language of a short poem, more than the aural components, as the constitutive feature of lyric.

Still, there is no gainsaying that Donne's short love poems belong to a broad poetic tradition that we are likely to call lyric. Poems of the sort that we are considering here arose by starts and stops in the long process of the human discovery that love is something to sing about and that various pleasures may be derived from felicitous combinations of words into a coherent sequence of rhythmical and tonal sound patterns. Early manifestations of ancient compositional practice among the Egyptians, the Hebrews, and the Greeks suggest that lyric poetry had its origins in religious activities, including celebratory occasions on the one hand and ritual mourning on the other, and that it was typically performed for an audience. All three cultures eventually produced dozens of types of poems that are 'lyric' in modern senses of the word and that treat an extraordinary number of subjects, including human love. For their part, the Greeks early on distinguished between, on the one hand, 'melic' poems intended to be sung to musical accompaniment and, on the other, iambic and elegiac poems that were chanted. (Melic poetry included wedding songs, but also many other types.) Metre was essential to melic poetry, with lines of equal length generally serving for spoken verse, whereas poems to be sung were more often arranged in phrases of varying lengths combined into stanzas. Eventually, at Alexandria, the works of several *lyrici vates*, including Sappho, Pindar, and Anacreon, were collected and became canonical.

While the Romans largely followed Greek formal precedents, Latin poetry created a number of possibilities that Donne would later exploit. In Latin literature an emerging preponderance of short poems meant to be read (rather than sung) reduced the importance of the aural dimensions, tipping poetic practice in a more cognitive direction. These poems tapped the allusive and enigmatic potential in verbal art, rendering the verse more subjective. They opened greater possibilities for uttering personal desire. They thus made more room for autobiographical expression—and for the interpretation of poems as autobiographical utterances. The representation of particularized experience is found, for instance, in writings by Catullus and Tibullus, whose love poems often suggest concrete occasions of a private nature (as opposed to public celebration or mourning). Much as the Romans' writing of formal satires, epigrams, and epistolary verse provided a decisive precedent for Donne's practice, then, Latin love poetry inspired some of his erotic poems, though less with respect to their metrical than to their thematic features. Still, early modern poets were very conscious of the aural dimensions of verse. Donne made his Elegies specially reminiscent of Ovid's practice by deploying a standard metrical pattern: he implemented the English heroic couplets that Christopher Marlowe had substituted for Latin elegiacs in his translations of the *Amores*. In the poems that came to be called Songs and Sonets, Donne also drew inspiration from Ovidian thematic precedents; but he experimented with a wide variety of metrical and stanzaic patterns that, considered collectively, point up the range of distinctive occasions, experiences, and moods that these poems envisage and convey. This metrical variety was the legacy not of the classical Roman poets, who imitated the Greeks in their deployment of quantitative metres, but of medieval Latin poets and their successors in several European vernaculars, who gradually abandoned strictly quantitative verse and developed the wholly new principle of rhyming. Donne exploited this development to complement and enhance the variety of subjects, situations, and experiences that, according to Puttenham's *Art of English Poesie* (34), are required for love poetry: 'a forme of Poesie variable, inconstant, affected, curious and most witty of any others.'

The late medieval and early modern developments in Western European love poetry that generated the expectation formulated by Puttenham are too numerous and complex to summarize here. In view of Donne's practice, however, it is worth recognizing that its traditions often involved borrowing religious language to express and explore human love. While these traditions were different from, say, the art of South India—where readers also found devotional lyrics permeated by erotic images and discourse, but in poetry as well as sculpture the gods were frequently depicted as enraptured in human sexual pleasure and beseeched to share their sexual ecstasy with their devotees—they sometimes, as in poetry inspired by the biblical Song of Songs, included robust openness to human sexuality as a locus for the intersection of human and divine creativity. Yet during the 300 or so years before Donne began writing a curious bifurcation had taken place, illustrated in the very different sorts of love poems written by Dante and by Petrarch, respectively. The potentially adulterous and generally unrequited love that had been represented in courtly love poetry was adapted by Petrarch; and the poems of pain and sorrow that he wrote for Laura, in life and after her death, proved far more influential for poetic practice than those by Dante celebrating an exalted and purely spiritual love for Beatrice. In England, after the appearance of Sidney's *Astrophil and Stella*, with its lightly veiled fiction of a poet writing sonnets in an attempt to woo an inaccessible mistress, other sonnet sequences provided an entertaining storyline that made the volumes in which they appeared quite different from the miscellanies to which we have already referred. Although Edmund Spenser entered the lists with other poets, his *Amoretti* revised the usual narrative outcome by concluding with a celebration of fulfilled sexual love and authorized marital bliss, punctuated ultimately by an epithalamion. Donne's practice as a love poet was to reject the dominant post-classical framework without ignoring some lingering potentials in the Petrarchan tradition.

Considered as a group, Donne's Songs and Sonets are sufficiently different from preceding English love poetry that, along with the harsh numbers of his Satires and some other poems, they occasioned Ben Jonson's remark that 'for not keeping of accent [Donne] deserved hanging'. They also had much to do with Jonson's prediction 'that Done himself for not being understood would perish' (Jonson 1–2.138). Donne's love poems evince a resolve not to write in strict sonnet form, whether Italian or English, or in fact in any recurring or fixed form. (When it came to metre and rhyme and matters of form generally, 'Variety' proved for Donne as much 'Loves sweetest Part' as a fresh succession of sexual partners is said by the speaker of *Ind* to be his fundamental criterion of pleasure: l. 20.) Collectively but not individually, they avoid any implication that there is but one Stella or Delia to be loved. Each asks readers to envisage a separate occasion and set of circumstances, perhaps even a different cast of characters. (That cast includes a subset of men who are unapologetic about their eager pursuit of sexual love and of women who are fairly sophisticated in the ways of love.) The poems do not generate by any sequential arrangement a larger narrative than is suggested within any individual poem. In fact, although the speakers of the various poems seem to have a recognizable style and a common orientation, unlike Sidney's Astrophil and Spenser's poet-lover, they are not identified with the poet; and they do not promise immortality to the beloved. Perhaps above all, while Donne writes some poems in which the speaker knows the pains of unrequited love and some that powerfully express cynicism about love, the Songs and Sonets avoid giving an overall impression of frustration and failure. There are many poems that represent joyful, mutually fulfilling amatory experiences, unbounded by the social authorization celebrated in Spenser's *Epithalamion*.

These and other aspects of Donne's 'invincible repugnance to the commonplace' are on display in his love poems. As William Minto (862) recognized when he implemented this phrase in the era of Queen Victoria, Donne's own resistance to what had been overworked provides a principal explanation for the corresponding resistance that these poems met, for instance, when Palgrave deliberately excluded every one of them from *The Golden Treasury*. While their freshness of invention had made them attractive to Donne's contemporaries and immediate successors, among the definers of literary taste in the neoclassical period and well into Victorian times their seeming eccentricity was a ground for dismissing them. Dryden was willing to praise the great variety in Donne's poems, even as he complained that Donne 'affects the Metaphysicks, not only in his Satires, but in his Amorous Verses, where Nature only shou'd reign; and perplexes the Minds of the Fair Sex with nice Speculations of Philosophy, when he shou'd ingage their hearts, and entertain them with the softnesses of Love' (Dryden 1956– : 4.7). This observation provided the original of a critique that Dr Johnson deepened and disseminated still more widely. Johnson also accepted Alexander Pope's designation of Donne as the head of a school of 'metaphysical poets'. He observed that its members were 'men of learning', only to propose that 'to shew their learning was their whole endeavour' and to pronounce that in view of their 'desire of exciting admiration', 'they were not successful in representing or moving the affections' (S. Johnson 2006: 1.200, 214). To illustrate how 'far-fetched' metaphysical conceits might be, he cited the conceit of the stiff twin compasses from *ValMourn*, ridiculing its 'absurdity' even as he acknowledged its 'ingenuity'. Yet he also remarked on the usefulness of such conceits 'to those who know their value' (ibid. 1.213).

To overcome the arbitrary limitations within which Donne has often been read, it helps to consider the historic breakthrough recorded by Coleridge in 1811 while he was reading the Songs and Sonets. 'As late as ten years ago,' he wrote in Charles Lamb's copy of the *Poems*, 'I used to seek and find out grand lines and fine stanzas; but my delight has been far greater, since it has consisted more in tracing the leading Thought thro'out the whole. The former is too much like coveting your neighbour's Goods: in the latter you merge yourself in the Author—you *become He*' (1984: 220). The comparison of two lovers to the feet of a compass seems gratuitously extravagant if it is taken in isolation from the poem as a whole. There is nothing in what Johnson observed about *ValMourn* that encourages readers to see the relevance of precisely thirty-six lines to making a verbal circle that will 'end, where [its speaker] begunne' (l. 36), nor anything that suggests that even so astute a reader as he glimpsed the gestalt within which the compass imagery contributes to the drawing of that circle. Nor are the parting, moving, and rejoining of the two feet seen in relation to the series of metaphors that refer to other sorts of separation with which that of the lovers is ultimately, and in so sexually charged a manner, contrasted: 'growes erect' (l. 32) ends the poem on a note of anticipation and adds an additional referent for the word 'where', one that in another poem by Donne is called 'the Centrique part' (*ElProg* l. 36).

The extraordinary frankness with which Donne sometimes depicts sexual intimacy reminds us that he often preferred to write for particular persons known to him (and not necessarily to us) whom he imagined deriving pleasure as they discovered the inner workings of this or that poem. Elsewhere in this Handbook

Margaret Maurer calls attention to the way in which Donne writes this preference into the opening lines of a poem that carries a different sort of charge, *Storm*, where he praises Christopher Brooke as a person who has the intelligence and imagination to understand the daring vision of experience carried by the acute descriptive power that informs the poem (see Ch. 14). To this example we might add that in another Verse Letter, *MHPaper*, Donne goes even further in imagining an ideal reader when he compares his self-possessed and generous addressee to 'majesty [that] doth never feare / Ill or bold speech' and to 'a mother which delights to heare / Her early child mis-speake halfe utter'd words' (*MHPaper* ll. 21–4). This is to say that what remains important for reading Donne's poems today is to take up their inherent challenge, and invitation, to become one of those true friends for whom the poet displayed an ultimate respect when he wrote them as prompts for a mutual construction and experience of knowledge.

Consider the impudence of *SunRis*:

> Busie old foole, unruly Sunne,
> Why dost thou thus,
> Through windowes, and through curtaines call on us?
> Must to thy motions lovers seasons run?
>
> (ll. 1–4)

Dull sublunary readers, remaining outside the intimate workings of the poem, gaze on it with disapproval, missing out on the fun. Inside the poem what 'elements' (to borrow the word as Donne uses it in *ValMourn*) the 'rising' is an unspoken analogy with the couple's lovemaking. This is hinted at in the three sets of five paired lines of varying lengths that make up each stanza: the poem thus intimates the possibility that the speaker's partner contributes to his keeping up this potent discourse in the face of a carnal necessity that is universally encountered though individually experienced. *SunRis* casts the reader into a position analogous to that of the lover's partner, asking participation in the attempt to maintain through three intricately wrought stanzas an otherwise inappropriate and superfluous attitude; this activity is a prelude to a climactic moment that the poem does not deliver all by itself. This is to say that, precisely by leaving the analogy only implicit, Donne transforms a human into a poetic problem and then risks, rather as a stand-up comic might, getting his audience to go along with him. Perhaps only a reader willing to share the task of not letting down is likely to appreciate the tonal shift in the last lines, where the speaker's condescension not only varies but also sustains his impudence, as the lines continue to deny the impotence that a reasonable account of the 'real' state of affairs would induce:

> She'is all States, and all Princes, I,
> Nothing else is.
> Princes doe but play us, compar'd to this,
> All honor's mimique; All wealth alchimie;

>   Thou sunne art halfe as happy'as wee,
>   In that the world's contracted thus.
>   Thine age askes ease, and since thy duties bee
>   To warme the world, that's done in warming us.
>   Shine here to us, and thou art every where;
>   This bed thy center is, these walls, thy spheare.

(ll. 21–30)

Merging with the author thus entails something like a Copernican revolution for merely casual readers: keeping up what he started, rather than expecting him to deliver on his own the earth-shattering climax that would occur if, instead of making our sun to run, we actually got it to stand still. Sincerity here is measured in the lengths to which Donne goes to entertain. Playfulness and earnestness, far from being opposed, act as partners. It is on grounds such as this that we might actually credit Walton's speculation that *ValMourn* was written for someone who, knowing Donne in the biblical sense, would know how to read his poem.

Dr Johnson, in his remarks on the 'metaphysical' poets in his *Life of Cowley*, like Dryden (whose comments on Donne were addressed to the Earl of Dorset), quite overlooks the degree to which Donne credits women in particular with the indulgent sympathy and the wit to merge themselves with the poet's vision: through his speakers Donne puts on displays of wit as performances for readers intelligent and imaginative enough to appreciate how the poet makes a cleverly trotted out piece of learning integral to a textual erotics (I. Bell 2006b). It is for this reason that *Flea*, although even so great a devotee of the poet as Sir Herbert Grierson regretted the fact that it appeared as the first poem in the 1635 edition, actually makes an apt introduction to the poetry. For whatever the woman in that poem ultimately thinks of the speaker's attempts at seduction, her actions between the stanzas show that she enjoys playing the game. Donne's poems are 'metaphysical' as much because they frequently make witty use of terms from scholastic philosophy and from religious discourse as because some of them seem to entail an exalted philosophy of love.

This is specially the case with *Canon*, the piece that prompted Coleridge's observation about the importance of 'trac[ing] the leading Thought thro'out the whole' (1984: 220). While the speaker addresses an unsympathetic observer in this poem, the poet writes, as he did in many Verse Letters, for appreciative women and men. Dryden's complaint about his love poems shows that by the later seventeenth century it was no longer imagined that the likes of Magdalen Herbert and Lucy, Countess of Bedford, had been among Donne's most appreciative readers. Yet, as with the Songs and Sonets generally, *Canon* is a better poem if we allow that the woman, for whom the speaker regards the world as well lost, gestures to the women among the poet's envisaged audience. That audience cannot have been made up solely of a male coterie who regarded Donne, having lost his position in Egerton's household, as writing clever verses to gain patronage and to regain the sort of 'place' of which the speaker of this poem speaks derogatorily. The assumption that Donne wrote only or chiefly for men has underwritten a self-congratulatory 'orthodoxy' in late twentieth-century readings of his poetry. It has proved an important component of readings proposing that late Elizabethan and early Jacobean love poetry is 'really' about place-seeking and court politics. It also promotes taking sexist perspectives in the poems straight, without considering in relation to the workings of a poem as a whole moments when misogynistic discourse is deployed for satiric purposes against sexist dispositions. It wilfully deflects the satire directed in *ValBook* against divines and Petrarchan mistresses and their lovers, lawyers, and statesmen; and it misses the joke upon 'mis-devoted' lovers shared by the speaker and his beloved in *Relic*, which playfully posits a future in which, by a rather benign misunderstanding, 'All women shall adore us, and some men' (Ferry 108). We can imagine that even 'barely literate' readers felt included rather than excluded by the genial playfulness of this prediction. (Elsewhere in this volume Ernest W. Sullivan II's highly informative essay emphasizes the importance of our recognizing that such readers were numerous and that the pleasures they took in reading Donne are not to be discounted; see Ch. 2.)

Donne's true friends, those who read and passed round and copied out his poems with appreciation (if not always with full understanding), participated with him in repeated pleasurable activities of the sort disapproved of by the silenced tongue-wagger chided in the opening of *Canon*. That figure is as reminiscent of the adversaries of Ovid's love-making as he is predictive of unappreciative readers for whom Donne's love poetry remains written 'in cypher'. Donald Guss (157–65) has observed how richly in the middle stanza of this poem Donne has drawn on the resources of Neoplatonism to effect a dramatic realization of a Petrarchan conceit whereby the two lovers are compared to the phoenix. As well as engaging other early modern love poetry, the poem is reminiscent of classical and Troubadour love poems. It also draws learnedly and with precision upon modern revisions in the church's procedures for the beatification of saints. Moreover, by way of the phoenix image, it entails a 'mysterious' comparison of the lovers to the incarnate Son of God who combines two natures in one person, and whose dying and rising provided the very model of the lives of the saints, not all of them martyrs by literal death. (That the lovers understand themselves to be martyrs for sexual pleasure is the *ground* for the central comparison in that third stanza and the justification, such as it is, for the invocation quoted as it were in the final stanza.) Importantly, Donne casts his engagement with the Petrarchan tradition within a larger framework, involving a poetics of desire and fulfilment, as his best readers have intuited (see e.g. Dubrow 1995: 203–48) and as Coleridge recognized when he praised the exuberant creativity with which Donne displayed a 'Lordliness of opulence' and 'pride of doing what he likes with his own' (1984: 219, 220). Such readers just might gather from the poem that Donne invites so serious, if playful, a contemplation of the Incarnation as to prod his readers to think through the dimensions and implications of the efficacy of the sacred 'mystery' whereby the Lord of Creation took on a human body. Where

Spenser's Easter sonnet invoking the 'glorious Lord of lyfe' and encouraging his beloved to act upon the love that was 'the lesson which the Lord us taught' is beautiful, *Canon* is witty and provocative—and ultimately leaves a more suggestive lesson to its readers' powers of devout inference. Like *Relic*, which also envisages a relatively benign misreading of the nature of the lovers' love, it develops an intimacy between the loving couple and the actual readers of the poem, whose understanding is graciously assumed to be superior to that of dull sublunary lovers (Ferry 116–25).

Singling out *Canon* is helpful because at three critical moments this particular poem has either powerfully inhibited or greatly facilitated reading Donne's love lyrics more generally. In the mid-seventeenth century *Canon* epitomized the poetry that Izaak Walton in his *Life and Death of Dr Donne* sought to render nugatory when he proposed that most of the poems had been written before Donne's twentieth year and that Donne himself had wished them out of existence. Walton wrote the *Life* as hagiography, precisely to be included in the first collected edition of the Sermons, where it pre-empted the possibility of seeing in *Canon* the degree to which Donne had been implicated in Catholicism or of reading the poem as the poet's appropriation of the theme of the world well lost. Published in 1640, the *LXXX Sermons* offered an alternative picture of the essential identity of the writer whose *Poems* had recently gone through three editions. It canonized instead a body of writing that clinched Walton's assertion that, when Donne took holy orders, the English Church gained a 'second St. *Austine*' (1675: 38). (The comparison to Augustine left unspoken the implication that any irregular sexual adventures depicted in Donne's poetry, if they referred to the poet's personal experiences, were to be regarded as part of a larger providential pattern in this great saint's life.) Without mentioning *Canon* as such, Walton presented a radically different interpretation of the relations between Donne's public and private identities, famously presenting his marriage as 'the remarkable error of his life' (1675: 52). At the same time, however, Walton managed to give basic information about how the wedding came about and unwittingly created what turned out, once his narrative was detached from the Sermons and took on an independent life, to be the canonical version of a memorable love story.

Along with his account of Donne's 'conversion' from popery to the Church of England, the story of Donne's marriage made Walton's *Life of Donne* intensely interesting to readers in the Romantic and Victorian periods. It prompted many of them to look into Dr Donne's long-neglected love poetry to fill out details of his fascinating life story. Curiously, all through the nineteenth century, as readers increasingly read other poems as referable to Donne's courtship of Anne More and to their marriage, virtually everyone resisted reading *Canon* as an autobiographical utterance. Only at the end of the century was it pointed out that Walton had actually provided precisely the information with which *Canon* could be read as an autobiographical defence of the marriage; and only in the mid-twentieth century was a full-scale biographical reading worked out, offering renewed life to the romantic assumption that Donne often wrote love poems as virtual transcripts of his first-hand experiences.

A second ground on which *Canon* might exert a thoroughgoing influence upon the reading of the Songs and Sonets also bore long-delayed fruit. Coleridge's proposal that Donne's poems are to be read as whole performances, with the reader imaginatively recapitulating the exhilarating process through which the poem was first created, was cited by Cleanth Brooks in his highly influential reading of the poem as a self-referential 'well-wrought urn'. Brooks offered that reading as an introduction to a whole 'theory of poetry', and only thereafter did the poem begin to attract extensive attention. Read precisely as a dramatic monologue, *Canon* became the paradigmatic poem for the practice of the New Criticism.

Ill. 13.1. Summer House, Pyrford, Surrey. Traditionally known as 'Queen Elizabeth's summer house', this banqueting house, formerly attached to the orchard wall near the banks of the River Wey, is all that remains of early architecture on the estate of Anne Donne's cousin, Sir Francis Wolley, where Donne and his family lived in one of two houses belonging to Wolley, both now displaced by a block of 'executive flats'. (Photo, Suzanne Knights, http://commons.wikimedia.org/wiki/File: John_Donne_house_Pyrford.jpg.)

A third ground on which *Canon* has proven generally influential has especially to do with its title, and with popular confusion about the concept of 'canonical' literature. Having become so significant a poem for mid-twentieth-century readers and teachers of poetry, *Canon* later became, in the last quarter of the century, a target of denigration. It was demonstrated to be ripe for deconstruction. It was criticized for silencing the voice of the woman for whom the male speaker presumes to speak. It was adduced as evidence of an ambitious place-seeker's having written, desperately, for a male coterie. Moreover, Donne himself was held up as the epitome of the canonical dead male writer, whose work would have to give way to new voices with an opening of 'the canon'. More recently, in a continuing reaction against the pedagogy connected with Practical Criticism and the New Criticism, Donne, whose love poems have often proven an apt focus for discussion in the classroom, lingers prominently in the background of complaints about the degree to which the dramatic monologue has come to be regarded as the quintessential form of the lyric (Culler 201–6).

Canon also makes an apt window onto the Songs and Sonets because it seems an exception to the general observation that for the love lyrics we do not have information that enables us confidently to locate the date and circumstances of their original composition. Taken together with the fact that for nearly every Donne poem that is to be printed in the *Variorum* the textual editors need to posit the existence of a 'Lost Original Holograph', this state of affairs need not be assumed to be grounds for frustration, however. As a result of the ways in which Donne wrote and distributed his poems, it is a feature of those poems and an object for interpretive exercise. Even *Canon* is written in ways that encourage us to imagine a more general situation than Donne's own loss of a place. It makes no mention of marriage, for instance, and offers no description of the woman or of her status except as the speaker's loving partner. The absence of references to marriage and the married state is also a general characteristic of Donne's love lyrics. To be sure, not all the poems envisage a stable, committed relationship. Those that celebrate longevity, or involve a challenge to achieve it, do so without counting on the social support that might be lent by public institutions (Low 31–64). The intense privacy ascribed to the love relationship is nonetheless presented in ways that tease readers to want to know more, while preserving the speaker and his beloved in the position of greater knowledge and power (as in *SunRis*) than the readers. If, as has been well said, Donne preferred known readers, he must also have preferred for those readers to respond to his poems with a knowing discretion. Since the later nineteenth century, however, once it became increasingly common to believe that a person's secret life, especially secret sexual life, provides a key to understanding a subject's 'nature' and peculiar 'genius', attempts to bracket out biographical considerations when reading the Songs and Sonets have been repeatedly squelched: it is an abiding effect of these poems that readers want to know more about the man who wrote them, and in this frame of mind it is easy to overlook the considerable variety of fictional momentary selves that the poet impersonates for the sake of exploring his themes (see Cruttwell 46).

Given the inevitability of interest in Donne's biography, the best that might be said about the generic characteristics of the Songs and Sonets is that they encourage and frustrate a desire that they beget. Because it is a constitutive feature of these poems that neither singly nor as a group do they enable readers to settle into a consensus about their significance for understanding Donne's personal love-life, it makes sense here to lay out, however tentatively, a modest hermeneutics that arises out of what we have noticed about their generic qualities and about the history of how they have been read. Such practical considerations as are enumerated here, if they seem productive enough in their own right, may release us from a sense that we are ultimately reading under the sort of biographical imperative that is built into devoting a handbook to a single author and organizing it so that these chapters on the genres in which Donne wrote ultimately give way to questions that are shot through with implications for understanding 'Donne' himself. At the same time, these considerations may prove biographically revealing on a different count. As M. Thomas Hester has shown in providing a 'preface' for readers of Donne's lyrics, because the Songs and Sonets evince the poet's thoroughgoing familiarity with a great many learned ideas and practices of his era, they give access to his extraordinarily rich engagement with controverted divinity and theological hermeneutics. Donne wittily adapted these materials to say about amatory and sexual experience in his poetry what no one else had said (Hester 1990a).

Formal variety

When encountering a Donne love lyric on the page, in order to 'trace the leading Thought thro'out the whole' (Coleridge 1984: 220), it makes sense seriously to attend to matters of form. As readers at a great temporal remove from the moments when the poems were composed and entrusted to particular persons, we can nonetheless find pleasures in noting how carefully each poem has been constructed. The formal integrity of the poems is generally to be perceived in retrospect; and the poet's 'foreconceit' (to invoke Sidney's term) requires to be appreciated through riveting our attention upon details and by allowing ourselves to discover what through its form the poem is meant to do. Perhaps not too much should be made of the fact that many of the love lyrics are divided into either two or three stanzas. Still, the frequency with which Donne employs numerical and geometrical imagery in the poems can open us to contemplating the possibility that numerical structure operates significantly in any given poem. The number of lines allotted to a poem is not always as readily correlated with the theme as the thirty-six in *ValMourn* to the

360 degrees of a circle. There are certainly times, however, when the number is suggestive. For instance, if we consider the thirty-three-line *Relic* with the twenty-two-line *Res* (both have eleven-line stanzas), we may remember that thirty-three is the age traditionally ascribed to Christ at his death—and resurrection.

Peculiar stanza forms, so many of which (with their varying line lengths and rhyme schemes) seem to be of Donne's own devising, may be regarded as suggestive of whatever authorial design we are willing to consider relevant to the interpretive task. (Think, for instance, of the inversion of the sonnet form in the two stanzas of *WomCon* and of the heterometric couplet with which this inconstant poem ends; of the way in which the poet unobtrusively implements the word 'love' at the ends of the first and last line in each stanza of *Canon*—and rhymes it with words in the fourth and eighth lines of each stanza to boot.) Given that there are more than forty different stanza forms among the Songs and Sonets, observations about numerical and metrical structure can be productively multiplied (see Dubrow 2008: 172–3). The general upshot of what we have noticed is that great formal variety helps to keep the subject from seeming routine and stale: avoiding standard forms and devising a different form for each particular performance are aspects of making love seem continually new. Variety takes on added importance if we think of some verses as having been written rather like verse letters to be read by the women to whom many speakers address themselves—or by any one woman who had the opportunity to read several of the poems together. This is especially the case for the valedictory poems, among which *ValBook* explicitly and *ValMourn* implicitly involve ways of speaking to a beloved that seem to presuppose long experience in one another's company. Even and especially in reading poems such as these, which suggest a mutual attachment that defies time and change, it is helpful to recall Donne's provocative claim that he worked 'best when [he] had least truth for [his] subiect' (Letter to Sir Robert Carr prefacing *Ham*: *Variorum* 6.219). In so far as he created poems that celebrate 'true love', he performed that love through a demonstration of wit that demands a corresponding exercise of imagination on the part of his reader.

Conceits and 'the shutting up'

Besides attending to the ways in which aspects of form contribute to unifying a given poem, tracing the leading thought through the poem may also enhance our pleasure in seeing how the component parts work together. Many of the Songs and Sonets are organized by a single, sustained comparison of this or that feature of experience to something (e.g. a funeral, a noxious vapour, a sunrise) named in the heading, whether by the author or by an early copyist or compiler. While there were scores of poems written to take up the challenge to write about a flea, Donne's has proven memorable because of the ways in which it provokes sustained attention to one particular flea as an improvised prop in a brief drama of attempted seduction. Similarly, the heading *GoodM* announces a new relationship, one claimed by the speaker to have involved a discontinuity with all preceding ones as powerful as the difference between sleeping and waking; and at the same time, as Grierson understood when he made the poem to lead off not only his edition of Donne's poems but also his great anthology, *Metaphysical Lyrics and Poems of the Seventeenth Century* (1921), between previous love poetry and Donne's. Modernist poets found vital inspiration in Donne's having made so productive a break with his predecessors. Even today, to come upon Donne's voice after hearing Spenser's can seem a difference as great as between night and day.

Besides relying upon poetic form and metaphysical conceits to foster an overall effect, a love lyric by Donne often draws upon a powerful and memorable close to create an impact for which the various preceding lines are understood, retroactively, to have been but a preparation. In a penitential Sermon on Psalm 6:8–10 Donne explained that in 'Metricall compositions … the force of the whole piece, is for the most part left to the shutting up' and 'the whole frame of the Poem is a beating out of a piece of gold, but the last clause is as the impression of the stamp, and that is it that makes it currant' (*Sermons* 6.41). The language here is reminiscent of a line within *ValMourn*; and the 'shutting up' calls attention, in case we have missed it, to the ground on which the seemingly outrageous comparison of the lovers to the feet of a compass has been implemented. In *Break*, in terms more epigrammatic but less 'poetic' than those used by the Juliet who insists to her Romeo that they have heard the nightingale and not the lark, a culminating aphorism epitomizes the system of prosaic values that the speaker criticizes: 'He which hath businesse, and makes love, doth doe / Such wrong, as when a maryed man doth wooe' (ll. 17–18). Elsewhere Donne has written memorably formulated final clauses that, when taken out of context, sound even deadlier. Heard without reference to the poetic argument of the whole poem, *Air*, the lines 'Just such disparitie / As is twixt Aire and Angells puritie, / T'wixt womens love, and mens will ever bee' (ll. 26–8) sound more like a bitter general principle than the rounding out of a challenge to the woman to love the speaker as much as or more than he claims to love her.

It may be that of all Donne's conclusions the 'shutting up' of *Noct* seems the most discontinuous with 'the leading Thought' of the poem. After a sustained attempt to get his audience to imagine utter nothingness, beyond all the nothingness that can be contrasted with something, the speaker of this poem quite unexpectedly grants being and activity to his deceased beloved: 'shee enjoyes her long nights festival' (l. 42). Against everything we have been led to expect, he resolves upon action himself: 'Let mee prepare towards her' (l. 43). Moreover, he wills a radical reinterpretation of the lost future into which he has been claiming that a bereavement beyond all renewal has consigned him: 'and let mee call / This houre her Vigill, and her eve' (ll. 43–4). The most startling claim here, apparently prompted to the speaker's great surprise by his contemplation of what he thought was the difference between his situation and that of young lovers, is 'made currant' by way of an extraordinary syntactic dexterity: while the phrase 'her eve' seems at first a repetition and trivial variation on the phrase 'her Vigill', the words make quite different sense if we read the 'her' preceding 'eve' not as another pronominal adjective but as a half of a double accusative and read 'eve' as a reference to the primordial woman and 'mother of all the living' (Hebrew: *Chavvah*, 'life-giver'; I owe this interpretation to Michael Cowan). Ultimately, the poem, propelled by the memory of a powerful and productive love between two persons made male and female 'in the image of God', credits the biblical promise of a new creation beyond the utter annihilation that the poem has expended great pains to get us to picture. This is one of those places that requires a reader who would merge with the author to dissociate the compelling voice that Donne creates for his speaker from the design of the poem itself.

Known readers and implied readers

In the fourth edition of his *Life of Donne* (1675), more than sixty years after the alleged event in question, Izaak Walton incorporated a version of *ValMourn* and reported that Donne had given a copy of the poem to his wife. This was to transform it into a virtual verse letter by assigning it a known reader. (Walton does not go so far as to claim that Donne necessarily composed the poem for the occasion.) It is possible that a number of Donne's love lyrics were written for and given to particular persons. Yet every one of the Songs and Sonets differs from the Verse Letters in that readers who encounter them in manuscript or print do not find there a specified addressee. This fundamental characteristic of the poems suggests that, even if Donne used one or more as a letter, as is ostensibly the case with his Verse Letters and dramatically the case in *ValBook*, he had in mind other readers beyond the addressee. (His envisaging such a possibility is conspicuously inscribed into *Carey*.) The importance of Donne's having left the identities of lovers in his lyrics unspecified is pointed up by contrast when we consider the Verse Letter *MHPaper*. This poem seems to have been written in the period shortly before the widowed Magdalen Herbert married young Sir John Danvers, at a time when Donne himself was very much a married man. A playful Letter, it presupposes a considerable degree of intimacy and mutual understanding between the writer and the recipient. Its final claim—that his interest in her love-life is for the sake of his being able to love the man she chooses to love—sounds as if it's a discreet acknowledgement of love between two people who are not about to ruin any lives by acting upon their mutual attraction and, moreover, a genuine resolve to take pleasure in a dear friend's happiness. What can be known about these two people outside the poem would seem to enhance our pleasure in reading it, and the inscription that identifies the recipient justifies our bringing knowledge extraneous to the poem to bear. Nonetheless, we will want also to consider the possibility that Donne may not have actually sent his friend the Letter: conceivably, there was a gap between the addressee as a fictional implied reader and the known persons to whom Donne actually showed the poem. The implied reader for whom Donne wrote might trump the actual readers to whom he gave them to read. Or rather, we might say, borrowing Sullivan's phrase, 'the kind of reader he hoped for' (see Ch. 2), that even and especially in poems that Donne composed for known readers he sought to set them the sort of challenge that would stretch their intelligence and imagination and test their interpretive generosity.

Relic offers a different sort of case in point. Another poem about an attraction between two persons, at least one of whom is committed elsewhere, *Relic* is not directly addressed to the woman to whom the speaker pays a powerful tribute in the 'shutting up': 'All measure, and all language, I should passe, / Should I tell what a miracle shee was' (ll. 32–3). (One can imagine, however, a situation in which Donne showed it to an actual woman.) It is doubtful whether the playfulness that prompts us to project a hasty tryst between these two lovers when they get their bodies back on Judgement Day extends to a suggestion that the speaker is himself so attractive that it was miraculous that the woman never gave herself to him. Still, the poem works a witty and powerful variation on the paradigmatic Petrarchan situation. It posits, on the other side of life, after death has parted all who have been married and occurring simultaneously with the consummation of the world, the possibility of an explosive consummation of a passion that has smouldered all through human history. This poem is richer for the woman's identity remaining hidden. A biographical reference would radically alter the whole centre of gravity, making the two historical persons the focus of interest, whereas this is a great poem about the power of a potentially adulterous attraction in human life—and one that wittily suggests an astonishing intimacy between two persons who entitle one another to enjoy this fantasy as a way of enhancing that power by holding it in abeyance.

The case of *Twick* is different still, partly because its title works quite differently from the titles of Donne's other love lyrics. Its reference to the estate of Lucy, Countess of Bedford, seems to place the composition of the poem at least seven years after Donne's marriage, and squarely within the poet's relationship with a known patroness. Yet the title was not necessarily created by Donne. If we exercise a certain scepticism about a connection between the poem and the Countess, it looks in any event like a distinctively Donnean hyperbolic contribution to the Petrarchan poetry of unrequited love. If, on the other hand, we allow the connection suggested by the title, then the poem may be thought to have the sort of interest that late twentieth-century historicist criticism has often taken in it. Critics of this bent have observed that Petrarchism provided men with a way to think about and structure desire, namely, as a lack, an absence that meant they must live constantly in pursuit of something unobtainable. They have, moreover, emphasized the degree to which, from late in the reign of Elizabeth, traditionally erotic discourse came to serve poets as a language with which to seek patronage. From this perspective, *Twick* seems just one more piece of evidence that Donne, ambitious for a place, projected into his writing a fragmented, unstable self. Among those who regard this perspective on the conditions of the writer in early modern England as an orthodoxy, considerations of genre seem rather trivial and effete. Yet if Donne wrote this poem for the Countess herself, its audacious declaration of passion exceeds anything appropriate for a client to say to a patron. It makes sense, therefore, at least to entertain the possibility that the poem is premised upon and contributes to an enhancement of an extraordinary intimacy between the speaker, who is sufficiently distanced from the poet for deniability, and the Countess as the implied reader, who is trusted to read its over-the-top excesses generously, with amusement.

Emergent occasions

Comparing Donne's love lyrics to his Verse Letters can prove useful in another way. In both kinds of poem the discourse is likely designed to provoke a response. There are important differences in the circumstances that each kind entails, however. As Margaret Maurer points out, Donne's designation for particular circumstances was 'emergent occasions' (see Ch. 14), and much of the artistry of his Verse Letters consists in his transformation of these into inspiration for a poetical invention. In a majority of cases the mission of the poem is to overcome the physical distance that separates the writer and the addressee. In the love lyrics, where the identities of the speakers and of the addressees are not disclosed, fictional situations are implied and readers need to exert still greater powers of inference and discrimination to 'merge with the author'. Many of the Songs and Sonets are best read as dramatic monologues that begin at a point reminiscent of situations familiar from other poets' love poems. We rarely appreciate this fully until we've read the whole poem, however, because with Donne's love lyrics the 'emergent occasion' does not so much give rise to the poem as it arises out of the speaker's improvising within the fictive situation. That is, the imagined circumstances in these poems sometimes generate and almost always entail a fictional exigency.

In early modern usage the word 'emergent' generally meant 'rising out of a surrounding medium', such as water (*OED*, A., adj. 1a). As a noun, it referred to an 'outcome, incidental result', or 'unforeseen occurrence, a contingency not specially provided for' (*OED*, B., n., 1 and 2). Both noun and adjective were derived from the Latin *emergens*, meaning 'rising up', 'coming forth', even 'extricating oneself'. Increasingly, the English adjective came to be used in contexts that carried an implication of unexpectedness; and the noun form gave way to the more modern word 'emergency', which includes a sense of urgency and often generates a moment of crisis. (The earliest citation for what the *OED* considers the 'improper' sense 'urgency, pressing need', comes from the eighteenth century. The earliest citation for the sense 'urgently demanding immediate action', however, is quoted from Donne's Second Prebend Sermon, on Ps. 63:7.) In other words, by representing situations in which both the speaker and the addressee find themselves under increasing pressure, Donne anticipated—and likely contributed to—the most significant historical shifts in the sense of the English word, which have to do with defining what we now call an 'emergency'.

Even the more cynical poems where the speakers cavalierly put forward broad generalizations often entail such a dynamic. Take *ConfL*, for instance, read as a poem in which a woman generalizes about how men have, quite unnaturally, imposed constancy upon women. Here, it is her identification of the injustice and her protest against it that emerge like a shark's fin at the surface of the water. Or consider the 'shutting up' of *Commun*, where—as if to acknowledge the validity of the woman's plea and turn it against her—the male speaker advocates callous promiscuity precisely at the expense of women held by men in common: 'And when he hath the kernell eate, / Who doth not fling away the shell?' (ll. 23–4). Here, the shark's teeth emerge, and only the dullest of readers will fail to see that it is the poet who has exposed them. Among lyrics in this vein, *Ind* offers at once a more lighthearted case and a clearer demonstration of the grounds that Donne's prestige as a 'satirical' writer rested upon a much wider base of poems than the formal Satires alone. Like *ConfL* and *Commun*, this poem offers the broadest of generalizations; and like them, it bears the unmistakable traces of oral culture that make even Donne's bookish manuscript poems seem lively and lifelike. Here again the poet directs irony against a speaker, this one performing like a stand-up comic ostensibly for a group of women. It emerges in the self-satisfied third stanza, where the speaker trots out not a learned conceit but an external authority from the realm of classical mythology (this is highly uncharacteristic among the Songs and Sonets) to clinch his case. Here, we might say, the shark metamorphoses into a man, and as a result of his own preferential option he is rendered generic ('indifferent'): he has made himself incapable of significant choice. 'Der Mensch ist, was er isst' (One is what one eats).

At the other end of the spectrum, in poems that seem to project a particularly exalted kind of enduring love, one in which the bodily and the spiritual are said (even if we hear this as a strategy of seduction) to be inextricably intermingled, Donne's speakers encourage the mutual acceptance of a challenge to keep love alive. Even so apparently cynical a poem as *WomCon* may be read as a prod to deepening love—and benefits from being read this way, as Coleridge implicitly understood when he remarked that it should be titled 'Mutual Inconstancy' (1984: 18). For, while its catalogue of not quite fifty ways to leave a lover involves a show of wit, its deconstruction of the standard game-playing promotes kinds of intimacy and mutual recognition between casual lovers that invite the addressee to join in turning a tentative suggestion into a mutual agreement to risk pursuing the relationship further. The sense of crisis is not so sharp here, and the invitation is sufficiently indirect as to leave the addressee a fairly easy way out. This is not the case, however, in poems where the 'shutting up' invites mutual commitment to a relationship that entails high stakes and promises to involve continuing challenges. Consider *GoodM*, a poem that many would read as involving virtually the same initial situation as *WomCon*:

> What ever dyes, was not mixt equally;
> If our two loves be one, or, thou and I
> Love so alike, that none doe slacken, none can die.
> (ll. 19–21)

Or *Lect*, where the invitation is couched in more threatening language: 'Love is a growing, or full constant light; / And his first minute, after noone, is night' (ll. 25–6). Or a more joyous poem, *Anniv*, where instead of declaring, as Shakespeare and others did, that the writing of the poem ensures the immortality of the beloved, the embrace of temporal process offers an experience that the speaker boldly calls 'everlasting day':

> Let us love nobly, and live, and adde againe
> Yeares and yeares unto yeares, till we attaine
> To write threescore, this is the second of our raigne.
> (ll. 28–30)

The power of such poems to convey a sense of exigency is enhanced by their being interspersed in random proximity with other lyrics in which the vagaries of love are prominently on display.

Collection and arrangement

At the outset, we noted some reasons for uncertainty whether Donne regarded these poems as constituting a group. If there is no reason to believe that the poems in the collection traditionally known as Songs and Sonets were all written with a sense that they ultimately belong together, then, say, *Sappho*, and *Metem*, and any number of other poems might just as well be included in an edition with them under the heading 'Miscellaneous'. For two—even three—reasons, however, such an unprecedented gathering would be unhelpful. First, the Songs and Sonets were thought by copyists and compilers to be sufficiently of a piece that, while they were not all brought together until 1635, they were gathered into batches in manuscripts and the number of batches reduced to two in the 1633 edition (1633 printed *Para* apart from the two batches). Second, and more tellingly, the fact that among these poems each is formally different from all the others indicates a measure of conscious deliberation on the part of a maker who did not repeat a given form. In short, there is some reason to think that Donne thought of these poems as a group that might eventually be gathered up by others.

The possibility that the love lyrics would survive and be brought together is in fact inscribed in some of the poems themselves. It is intimated in *Canon* in the claim that the lovers will 'build in sonnets pretty roomes' (l. 32). It hovers over *ValBook* when, referring to 'our manuscripts, those Myriades / Of letters, which have past betwixt thee and me' (ll. 10–11), the speaker counsels the woman from whom he is parting to 'writ[e]' in 'cypher' (l. 21) a book that will distil the essence of their love. (This lack of verbal identification of the couple helps, in fact, to make the poems seem even more intimate, as the emphasis on 'brave' secrecy in *Under* would make explicit.) The idea with which Donne and his lover are playing here is that each individual written piece points to but does not fully embody a perfect ideal that will stand in judgement on all other human loves, and ideas of love, through posterity. As the woman is encouraged to compose 'Annals' (l. 12) that will preserve 'Rule and example' (l. 14) beyond the destruction of all things material, one might suppose that frivolous or cynical bits of writing might require to be excluded. Still, their inclusion sets off more clearly the normative ideal that is to be glimpsed by understanding readers but can never be reduced to ordinary language.

This way of reading *ValBook* has often been anticipated. Many readers have recognized in the poem a potential for glimpsing not so much the normative ideal for loving to which the fourth stanza explicitly refers but a transformative gathering up of Donne's love poetry for readers in future times, readers in whom the poet puts a surprising degree of trust and from whom he posits a good deal of sympathetic understanding (Guibbory 1983). *ValBook*, read from this perspective, also suggests a certain ambivalence on Donne's part that helps account for the poems remaining for some years closely kept and for their having eventually made their way to a larger audience. A related ambivalence is expressed in the Letter of 1619 in which Donne entrusted the manuscript of *Biathanatos* to Robert Ker with the explanation that, 'because it is upon a misinterpretable subject, I have always gone so near suppressing it'; to which he added the instruction to 'Reserve it for me' and 'if I die...forbid it the Presse and the Fire' (*Letters* 21–2). If what Walton reported in 1640 about Donne's desire to see the 'funeralls' (1640: B4ʳ) of his youthful poems accurately reflects conversations that he had had with Donne or had heard about from others, the fact remains that Donne did not, and probably could not, destroy all his love poetry. In the last decade of his life, when it was being more and more widely circulated in manuscript and eventual publication in print must have seemed inevitable, Donne may have felt seriously 'misinterpreted'. Still, the faith that he had once had that, eventually, there would be readers who would understand his love poems sympathetically was not altogether cancelled out. Like children who grow up and act with increasing independence from their parents, Donne's love poems were already in his own lifetime quite beyond his control. He had, as the *Variorum* editors are prepared to illustrate, sent them into the world singly, one by one. Although they bore a distinct family resemblance to one another and this was sometimes recognized by compilers, such as those who kept *Fun*, *Blos*, *Prim*, and *Relic* together in manuscripts, Donne himself seems not to have tried to gather them up, to sort them through, to disown that one and make this one his principal heir; nor did he insist that any cease their unruly behaviour. In short, he wrote these poems in a manner that leaves a great deal of work to posterity.

A third reason that the poems can benefit from their having been gathered into a group, even so miscellaneous a group as does not require us to read them either sequentially or in their entirety, is that they hold one another at arm's length. While knowledge of one poem can help us to understand another, knowledge of all these poems prompts us to take each one as a discrete performance and to experience it in all the intensity that comes from the poet's successful avoidance of having generated a larger narrative.

Whatever may have been the circumstances in which Donne composed them, his love poems clearly include some of the most remarkable pieces that he ever wrote. Many still convey those 'fresh' qualities (in senses of 'fresh' that include 'novel', 'newly made', 'invigorating', 'not stale', 'charged with energy', 'frisky', etc.) that proved compelling to his contemporaries, and also (by anticipation, in the even more modern senses of 'forward', 'impudent', and 'free in behaviour') to readers today. By the time Donne was in his fifties, when the number of manuscript copies of his love lyrics was growing rapidly, his reputation as a poet increasingly rested on them. In the decades that followed their publication in printed books, the Songs and Sonets were frequently, and often badly, imitated; and in the eighteenth century they were routinely denigrated, not least by people who did not trouble themselves to read them. During the nineteenth century, however, as Donne's life became a subject of widespread interest and the Victorians promoted love poetry to renewed prominence, more than any others of his poems the Songs and Sonets garnered a new breadth and quality of attention. This contributed substantially to Donne's belated emergence, in twentieth-century accounts of the history of writing in English, as a figure of major importance. In our time the intensity and quality of pleasures that many readers continue to find in, say, *Flea*, *GoodM*, and *ValMourn* make them favourite points of entry into Donne's oeuvre. And yet other, quite wonderful, poems among the group (e.g. *Appar*) have provoked a good deal of resistance, especially among readers unprepared to countenance an allegedly major love poet writing on several occasions in a cynical or apparently misogynistic vein about love. The poet himself, though he recognized the likelihood that his poems would suffer misinterpretation, seems not to have wanted it any other way: the 'fresh invention' that in 1633 Thomas Carew named as the overriding impression created by Donne's writing suggests that he might have been pleased to foresee that worthy readers would enjoy negotiating the difficulties inherent in trying to fit his love poems into conventional categories.

CHAPTER 14

THE VERSE LETTER

MARGARET MAURER

An influential study of Donne's poetry makes fundamental to an appreciation of his work that he 'preferred known readers for his writing'; he is a coterie poet (Marotti 2006: 35; 1986). Some forty of his poems, addressed to particular persons and printed, many of them, approximately together in early editions of his work, seem obvious instances of this preference. These poems, Verse Letters, vary widely in length (from twelve to 130 lines), somewhat less widely in form (ten-syllable lines and simple rhyme patterns—couplets, triplets, quatrains—predominate). They frequently take as their subject the communicative act itself, often in the context of the writer's concern that he or his correspondent live virtuously. Never so admired as his lyrics, Donne's Verse Letters have always attracted some attention for their consideration of the meaning of virtue and the importance of friendship (L. Stapleton; *Milgate*; Lewalski 1973; Cameron; Scodel 1993; Kneidel 2005). As coterie productions, however, they have generated more interest, seeming to offer or confirm insights into episodes in Donne's life and career (Thomson; Storhoff; Aers and Kress 1978; Maurer 1980; Pebworth and Summers 1984; Klawitter 1992; Flynn 1995*b*; B. Saunders 2000; Cunnington).

Placing Donne's Verse Letters within the genre of poetry they exemplify, however, moves appreciation of them in a somewhat different direction, towards evaluating them as poems and considering how Donne's practice of Verse Letters might be related to the writing he chose to print. Generic considerations render more prominent Donne's art in making particular circumstances, what he called 'emergent occasions', the inspiration of poetical invention. Considered this way, Donne's Verse Letters stand between the lyric poetry, on which his reputation still largely rests and none of which he published, and the great occasional writings that he did publish, notably the *Anniversaries*, *Devotions upon Emergent Occasions*, and his publicly delivered Sermons.

Donne's practice of the Verse Letter is arguably peculiar to him. He seems to have resorted to it more often than other early modern English writers; at least, an unusually large number of his productions in this genre have survived. By the crude measure of counting pages in early editions of his poetry, Verse Letters constitute some 17 per cent of his poetical output. The extent and coherence that his writings in this genre have in *Poems, By J. D. with Elegies on the Authors Death* are reflected by three other, unrelated circumstances. One seems a deliberate act of homage: Ben Jonson paraphrased lines from a Verse Letter (*Calm*) when he told William Drummond that Donne was 'the first poet jn the World jn some things' and noted that Donne had 'written all his best pieces err he was 25 years old' (Jonson 1.135). Another is probably accidental: Donne's only surviving holograph poem is a Verse Letter. To take note of the third, involving his least-known poem, may be merely sentimental: a Latin Verse Letter, unrecorded in any known manuscript and first printed with the Prose Letters of the 1635 *Poems*, has long been assumed to have been written much earlier than it was. Correcting that misconception (Kelliher 1993: 137) leads to the realization that this Verse Letter is certainly among the last and may be the last poem he wrote.

A generic consideration of Donne's Verse Letters is difficult, however, because the form is unusually amorphous. Appreciating his achievement in it requires some theorizing, about the genre itself and about Donne's engagement with it. Practitioners and poetical treatises contemporary to Donne are useful in the former undertaking; and, besides his own practice, Prose Letters in which Donne mentions Verse Letters are helpful for the latter.

There are classical precedents in the genre of the verse letter in Horace and Ovid and numerous exemplars from late antiquity and the Middle Ages. In all, verse letters can seem indistinguishable from other kinds of poetry—from satire, in the case of Horace; elegy, in the case of Ovid; and epigrams, begging poems, dedications, fictional addresses (heroical epistles), and other occasional verses that seem to have been the stock-in-trade of court poets for centuries before the humanist movement drew attention to a letter's capacity to serve, not as an exhibition of rhetorical skill, but, in Justus Lipsius' formulation, as a 'message of the mind' (Lipsius 9). Moreover, as the verse letter can be difficult to distinguish from other kinds of poems, it can also seem not clearly distinct from letters not in verse. Medieval treatises of the *ars dictaminis* (the art of dictated, i.e. written, compositions) included verse models (Curtius 148–54); and Petrarch, who first stimulated interest in letter-writing as a literary form, included two metrical letters with his Latin prose letters to illustrious ancients (Petrarch xxi).

Notwithstanding this amorphousness, early modern theorists recognize the verse letter as a genre of poetry; and what they have to say about it illuminates not only Donne's practice but also subsequent attitudes to poems in this kind. Thomas

Sébillet (*Art poétique françois*, 1548) has little more to say than that Ovid and Clément Marot are masters of *l'épître*, '*une lettre missive mise en vers*' (124), but this brief description says much. Ovid's *Heroides* are imaginary letters in elegiac metre addressed by women in myth to the men who betrayed them; and his late books of elegies, *Tristia* and *Epistulae ex Ponto*, comprise many poems addressed to particular persons. Clément Marot, the prolific occasional poet of the court of Francis I, addressed many of his poems on everyday events to living contemporaries. Sébillet's pairing of Ovid and Marot, then, embraces both classical and indigenous models for verse epistles and both of the contrary expectations that such poems will either reflect on a limited set of topics established by the practice of classical poets or take as their subject some purely incidental matter.

In a treatise published a year later, *La Deffence et Illustration de la Langue Françoyse*, a young Joachim Du Bellay chooses one side over the other, observing that the epistle 'is not a kind of poem that can greatly enrich our vulgar tongue, since they are normally about familiar and domestic matters, unless you wanted to write them in imitation of elegies, like Ovid, or make them sentencious and grave, like Horace' (2006: 374). In the next year a reply to Du Bellay's treatise, Barthélemy Aneau's *Le Quintil horacien* (1550), disputes this, defending Marot's practice (199–200). Thereafter, however, at least in published theory, neoclassicism wins out. Jacques Peletier du Mans (1555) proposes Horace as the best model and rhymed couplets as the most suitable form, noting that the epistle is closely related to elegy (Ovidian) and to satire (Horatian) (275). To Julius Caesar Scaliger (1561), the epistle is a species of elegiac poetry (169). To Antonio Minturno (1564), it is a kind of satire (273), as it is also to Giovanni Viperano (1579), who distinguishes between Horace's satires and his epistles by saying that Horace addressed satires to persons at hand and epistles to persons absent (138). To Pierre Laudun d'Aigaliers (1597), elegy and epistle are closely related (75–8).

In contrast to these notices of the genre and its practitioners in French and Italian is the silence of English theorists. *The Art of English Poesy* (1589) mentions Marot, though not his verse epistles, and also the poetry of Ludovico Ariosto, but not that his satires, as imitated by Luigi Alamanni and subsequently by Thomas Wyatt, were epistolary (Puttenham 107, 148; Wyatt 186–94, 438–52). Silent as well about this kind of poetry is Philip Sidney in his *Defence of Poesie* (1595). Puttenham's failure to mention epistolary poetry is puzzling; Sidney's, however, is no mystery.

The *Defence*'s silence seems inevitably to follow from the way Sidney defines such poetry as he deems worthy of defence. If, as Sidney argues, what makes writing poetical is the idea or foreconceit that informs it, not the rhyming and verse into which its expression might be cast (101), a verse letter is not inherently poetry. That is, 'verse letter' might designate any letter, however loosely conceived, written in verse; and to Sidney 'verse [is] but an ornament and no cause to Poetry' (103). In fact, however, Thomas Moffett says that Sidney himself wrote verse letters and describes them in terms that coincide with what continental theorists with neoclassical predilections say about the genre. The section of his life of Sidney describing Sidney's poetry concludes, 'I pass over letters of most elegant style, in metrical and prose form, which he addressed to the Queen, to friends, but particularly to [the Countess of Pembroke] your honored mother (inheritor of his wit and genius)...'. Moffett closes the sentence by referring to epistolary models: 'if it shall be deemed well to let [Sidney's] epistles go into the everlasting memory of his race and of the republic of letters, may I die if, compared to them, Horace will not seem stupid, Cicero mediocre, and Ovid simply nothing at all, or weak' (74). No verse letters by Sidney have gone into the 'everlasting memory of his race and the republic of letters'; if he wrote any, Donne may or may not have known them.

In the same year that Sidney's *Defence* was published, Thomas Lodge's *A Fig for Momus* appeared. The Wilton circle would have disdained the seven poems Lodge called epistles in his *Fig*. He claims, not entirely accurately, that they 'are in that kind, wherein no Englishman of our time hath publiquely written' (3: 6-7). (George Turberville had included in his 1576 *Epitaphes and Sonnettes* verse epistles about his embassy to Russia in 1568–9.) Nearly all of the fifteen poems in *A Fig* are addressed to or dedicated to some living person. The seven epistles are distinguished from the four satires and four eclogues in being about miscellaneous topics. They are versified essays dedicated, in some cases, to recipients who are not named ('*Ad Momum*') or identified only by initials and, in others, to people with proper names, a Master W. Bolton and Michael Drayton.

Since Lodge is about as various as can be in the kinds of addressees he names for his verse letters, the poems' subjects—a lecture on dogs or dreams or alchemy, a discourse on obesity, a review of the present state of poetry—seem less inspired by the person to whom they are addressed than written as discursive poems and then assigned to recipients. This is also the case with six epistles by Samuel Daniel described, on a second title page of some copies of the 1603 edition of them (Collier 1866: 1.216), as 'after the manner of Horace'. These, too, are verse essays, all on moral topics; and each is addressed to someone in the newly constituted Jacobean court. Manuscript evidence suggests that Daniel may at one point have considered reassigning at least one of them to another person (A. Freeman).

Donne might well have been aware of most if not all of these statements of theory and examples of practice in his days at the Inns of Court when he seems to have been writing his earliest Verse Letters, short poems addressed to recipients identified by initials. Since most are not sonnets, the point of several that are in fourteen lines seems to be to advertise that fact, that is, to declare that they are not such sonnets as Surrey or Spenser might write or to define the form of the sonnet in a new way. They rhyme in couplets and triplets, and if their arguments take a turn, it is as likely to occur in the tenth as in the ninth line. Most are preoccupied with their own creation. They seem to be the productions of a young poet declaring his independence from other poets and enlisting the approval, if not the help, of friends in doing so. An especially full collection of them are in the Westmoreland ms. (*Variorum* siglum

NY3), in the hand of Rowland Woodward, to whom five Verse Letters are addressed, including one in which Donne refers to other kinds of poems he has been writing, 'love-song weeds, and Satyrique thornes' (*RWThird* l. 5).

As Verse Letters, these short works invite comparison to the opening poems in a set of sonnets by the same Du Bellay who had once so conspicuously devalued the example of Marot compared to Horace and Ovid. The sonnets in Du Bellay's *Les Regrets* abjure traditional literary subjects and rhetorical ostentation, professing to attend 'only to what happens here,...I write at random' (2006: 52; 1, ll. 7–8). This protestation that he is writing a kind of anti-poetry, however, actually serves a subtly sophisticated act of imitation. His 'here' is Rome. Writing from Rome to correspondents in France, Du Bellay, as Richard Helgerson observes, reverses the situation of Ovid in the *Tristia*, the title of which is recalled by *Les Regrets* (2006: 9–18).

Like Du Bellay's *Les Regrets*, though less elaborately, Donne's early Verse Letters reflect on what it means to him to be writing the kind of poems he is writing, and a similarly ostentatious perversity of mood seems to characterize them, using some version of the sonnet form but disclaiming any interest in the subtle effects that can be achieved with it, and preoccupied, though usually cynically, with love and poetry, the sonnet's traditional concerns. Du Bellay writes to Pierre Paschal: 'What I want, Paschal, is that whatever I write should be prose in rhyme or rhyme in prose' (2006: 52); Donne tells Mr. T. W., 'if this song be too'harsh for rime.../ 'Twill be good prose, although the verse be evill, / If thou forget the rime as thou dost passe' (*TWHail* ll. 25–8). For Du Bellay, the distance between Italy and France underlies the conceit of many of his poems; and recurringly, too, Donne calls attention to his geographical separation from his correspondent: 'Thy friend, whom thy deserts to thee enchaine, / Urg'd by this inexcusable occasion, / Thee and the Saint of his affection / Leaving behinde' (*CB* ll. 1–4); '[My] slimy rimes bred in our vale below, /...Fly unto that Parnassus, wher thou art. / There thou oreseest London: Here I'have beene, / By staying in London, too much overseene' (*EG* ll. 2–6); 'Your Trent is Lethe; that past, us you forget' (*ILRoll* l. 6). New bibliographical insights emerging from the Donne *Variorum* project suggest that Donne may even have ordered some of these 'sonnets' into a short sequence he sent 'To E. of D.' or 'L. of D.' (*Variorum* 7.1.XCV–XCVII).

Donne's early Verse Letters seem different from any models he might have had, however, in the degree to which they emphasize his dependence on correspondence as a source of inspiration. One describes the poet 'Pregnant' with 'th'old twins Hope, and Feare', as he asks how and where T. W. is and what hopes the poet has for T. W.'s reply, furtively second-guessing every gesture that might deliver it. Finally receiving the reply as 'Almes', he is 'bountifully fed' by reading it and says 'grace' after the 'banquet', 'zealously' embracing the love T. W.'s response has protested,

> though I thinke thy love in this case
> To be as gluttons, which say 'midst their meat,
> They love that best of which they most do eat.
> (*TWPreg* ll. 1, 7, 9, 10, 11, 12–14)

This self-deprecation is the witty point of the poet's representation of his need to indulge in letter-writing. The poem gives the impression that correspondence in verse was an ordinary kind of letter-writing for Donne.

Four Verse Letters addressed to Henry Wotton might seem to support this surmise. Several manuscripts and the early editions include a seventy-line poem, *HWKiss*, that incorporates both a salutation, 'Sir', and a signature, 'Donne', into the metre, and in the case of the signature, the rhyme, of the closing couplet. The poem's argument is introduced by an assertion that Donne relies on letter-writing as a stimulus for thought:

> Sir, more then kisses, letters mingle Soules;
> For, thus friends absent speake. This ease controules
> The tediousnesse of my life: But for these
> I could ideate nothing...
>
> (*HWKiss* ll. 1–4)

Another begins with a triplet similarly ostentatious about being a versified letter:

> Here's no more newes, then vertue:'I may as well
> Tell you *Cales*, or St *Michaels* tale for newes, as tell
> That vice doth here habitually dwell.

This poem ends with a line that incorporates mention of the place from which he sends it: '*At Court*; though *From Court*, were the better stile' (*HWNews* ll. 1–3, 27). Such touches make the poems seem part of a regular correspondence between Donne and Wotton; but two others to Wotton in the Burley ms. (*Variorum* siglum LR1) include elements that suggest otherwise. The Verse Letter titled in most manuscripts and in the early editions 'To Sir *H. W.* at his going Ambassador to *Venice*' is preserved in LR1 with a postscript, not reproduced in the early editions, in which Donne, having concluded the Verse Letter with a valedictory promise to pray for Wotton in his absence, endorses it with a prose note that he compares to a 'pygmey upon a Giant', expressing the hope that he might see Wotton again to 'yett kisse *your* hand' (*Milgate* 233). Another poem, *HWHiber*, existing only in that same manuscript, resembles a Prose Letter, likely to another correspondent entirely (E. M. Simpson 1948: 306), that expresses, with similar images and wording but to very different effect, some of the same ideas. Consequently, these two Verse Letters in the context of this manuscript seem marked by a notable intensity of expression that distinguishes them from Prose Letters.

Donne seems to say just this about Verse Letters in relation to those in prose in a letter to Henry Goodere (*Letters* 85–8) in which he refers to 'a Letter in verse' as a kind of poetry he practised. This Letter begins by describing what Donne calls the superfetative effect of receiving several letters from Goodere at once, saying he can muster only a reply which is 'nothing else but a confession that I should and would write'. Among the letters from Goodere awaiting Donne on his return to London that Tuesday had been one in verse: 'I owed you a Letter in verse before by mine own promise, and now that you think that you have hedged in that debt by a greater by your Letter in verse, I think it now most seasonable and fashionable for me to break.' Donne does not answer Goodere's verse letter in kind; he sends instead two prose Problems and a long-since-written poem.

If, to Donne, a Verse Letter is not simply a letter, it is also not simply a poem detached from particular circumstances; and the single extant Verse Letter to Goodere is an opportunity to observe Donne in the act of turning verses into a Verse Letter, that is, into a poem written to a particular person on a particular occasion. *HG* begins in a detached Horatian mode, as a seemingly disinterested Donne prepares to offer Goodere such moral advice as might be tendered to any one at any time. The first five of the poem's twelve four-line stanzas are elegantly expressed commonplace figures for the effect of the counsels the poem seems to be planning to dispense: turning a 'new leafe' (l. 2) as of a book, not '[Leaving] growing' (l. 6) as a building, providing 'manlyer diet' for the soul (l. 17). With the sixth stanza, however, something more particular enters the poem as Donne introduces a figure that (though this is yet to be admitted) is inspired by the poem's occasion: Donne's taking leave of Goodere, who has broken a promise to return the visit. Pointedly, Donne proposes, as the means whereby spiritual growth can be achieved, that Goodere 'your selfe transplant / A while from hence' (ll. 21–2), that is, leave his customary places and habits. Four stanzas are devoted to this idea—to the virtue of seeking 'outlandish ground' (l. 22), being 'a stranger' (l. 25), 'travaile' (l. 31), and being ashamed to '[lessen] in the aire' (l. 35) like a trained hawk—before the poem returns to its didactic project, listing precepts: love and fear God (l. 38), abjure 'falshood' (l. 41). But the poem persists in this for little more than a stanza before it begs pardon for its sententiousness ('But why doe I touch / Things, of which none is in your practise new, / And Fables, or fruit-trenchers teach as much': ll. 42–4). Then follows the confession of the disappointment that led Donne to write a poem on Goodere's shortcomings:

> But thus I make you keepe your promise Sir,
> Riding I had you, though you still staid there,
> And in these thoughts, although you never stirre,
> You came with mee to Micham, and are here.
>
> (*HG* ll. 45–8)

Donne's pretence is that he has realized in the course of the journey during which he says he composed the poem that Goodere, as the object of his reflections, has in effect travelled though he has never stirred and will take Donne's advice by reading the poem. 'Fetter[ed] in verse' (*Triple* l. 11), Donne's annoyance is tamed by writing the poem and experiencing the paradoxical condition of recommending change to a friend, someone dearly loved for who he is.

While the Prose Letter to Goodere referring to 'a Letter in verse' and 'your Letter in verse' suggests that there were other Verse Letters in the regular, apparently for some years weekly, correspondence Donne sustained with Goodere, this is the only surviving one. Some, if not most, of Donne's longer Verse Letters were likely written in circumstances that did not involve an actual exchange. How to understand this aspect of his practice of the genre is suggested by the opening of what may be his finest Verse Letter (the lines of *Calm* Jonson quoted to Drummond are a continuation of it), *Storm*. Donne begins by asserting that what has stimulated him to write is his anticipation of his Letter's being read by someone who is, by of virtue of their friendship and regardless of whether the friend will reply, a corresponding intelligence:

> Thou which art I, ('tis nothing to be soe)
> Thou which art still thy selfe, by these shalt know
> Part of our passage; And, a hand, or eye
> By *Hilliard* drawne, is worth an history,
> By a worse painter made; and (without pride)
> When by thy judgment they are dignifi'd,
> My lines are such: 'Tis the preheminence
> Of friendship onely to'impute excellence.
>
> (ll. 1–8)

The patently false modesty of this passage does not qualify the compliment to Brooke, to whom Donne is saying that it is the prospect of his friend's appreciation that has stimulated what Clayton D. Lein describes as Donne's 'brilliance in manipulating [classical and Biblical] traditions' (1974: 150) to describe the storm that delayed the Earl of Essex's expedition against Spain in the summer of 1597.

The other of the two Prose Letters establishing that Donne considered the Verse Letter as a kind of poetry he practised is interesting to consider in relation to this point. Its content (*Letters* 194–8) is suffused with references to emergent occasions, circumstances that seem to require of Donne and his correspondent—again Goodere—considerable finesse. It was written in the days before Donne took orders in the church, as he was 'going about to pay debts' (196). After warning Goodere 'that my L. Chancellor hath been moved, and incensed against you' and that there is a 'great danger, obliquely likely to fall' because of how Goodere stands 'towards M. Mathew' (195), Donne tells Goodere that the Earl of Somerset is pressing him to publish his poems, so he is looking to retrieve a Verse Letter:

One thing more I must tell you; but so softly, that I am loath to hear my self: and so softly, that if that good Lady were in the room, with you and this Letter, she might not hear. It is, that I am brought to a necessity of printing my Poems, and addressing them to my L. Chamberlain.... But this is it, I am to ask you; whether you ever made any such use of the letter in verse, *A nostre Countesse chez vous*, as that I may not put it in, amongst the rest to persons of that rank; for I desire very very much, that something should bear her name in the book, and I would be just to my written words to my L. *Harrington*, to write nothing after that. I pray tell me as soon as you can, if I be at liberty to insert that: for if you have by any occasion applied any pieces of it, I see not, that it will be discerned, when it appears in the whole piece. (196–8)

Donne had apparently written a poem to a lady and sent it to Goodere, potentially for Goodere to use, in whole or in part, as his own.

Donne appears not to be concerned that Goodere may have used pieces of the poem in his own act of courtship. What matters as Donne projects including it in his published collection is the effect that a Verse Letter addressed to a particular lady will convey of his respect for and capacity to engage with persons 'of that rank'. He sees her identity, conveyed by her titled name, as an aspect of his poem's expression for readers beyond the coterie they inhabit together. This consideration has important implications for a hermeneutic of Verse Letters. In some cases it is possible to know more about an addressee of a verse letter than the poem itself conveys; and in some cases such information can support interpretive efforts by validating for readers what they perceive of the logic or tone of the poem's argument. Finally, however, since details about an addressee can do no more than that, occasional poetry, the best of it, functions without them. That is, good occasional poetry holds its own with whatever can be known from other sources about the poem's addressee, whether nothing at all or in flat contradiction of what the poem itself suggests. The association of a particular poem on a particular subject with a named addressee who must be presumed to have imputed excellence to it is a significant element of what a verse letter conveys to other readers.

Donne's Verse Letters to noble ladies pose the greatest challenge to readers in this regard. The source of the interpretive difficulties they present is that it can be difficult to believe that the named lady appreciated all of the subtleties of argument and tone that characterize the best and most elaborate of them. In effect, readers can be distracted by the question of how the lady might have responded from focusing on the response the poem anticipates. While it is possible, and even likely, that these poems were sent to and read by their named addressees, there is little evidence to warrant certainty on that point. Consequently, it follows that for most of these poems questions about how a correspondent did in fact respond are not, strictly speaking, relevant. Though they may be relevant for biographers, of Donne or of the lady, they need not interfere with a reader's efforts to appreciate the poem for what it is. What is relevant is in the poem's title, the assertion that a particular person occasioned the poem.

As it happens, the one Donne poem that survives in holograph is a Verse Letter to a noble lady. One commentator has called it 'a close contender for the silliest poem [Donne] ever wrote' (Herz 1994: 141); but even an acceptance of that judgement cannot forestall an appreciation of it if one takes seriously, as one must (and L. E. Semler does), that Donne wrote it anticipating that the lady addressed was equal to its wit (48). *Carey*, written after the publication of the two Anniversary poems that appeared in print while Donne was in France in 1612, is a letter of compliment curiously fashioned to, at once, expose its own extravagance and withstand the charge of extravagance, by posing at first as an intimate address to a single lady ('Madame'), then anticipating that its hyperbolical praises will be seen by the eyes of another lady (the artefact of the Letter in Donne's hand assists imagining its lying open on a table), and then dodging the consequences of that exposure by translating itself into a mirror to extend the Letter's praise to include the peeping other lady, 'your noble worthie sister' (l. 52).

Even more brilliantly, *MHPaper* (addressed to Magdalen Herbert) also uses its epistolary condition to acknowledge its writer's defensiveness, this time his hesitation about what he might properly write to an engaged woman. Donne's solution to this delicate problem adapts, among other classical precedents, the much-imitated conceit of Horace's address to his book (*Epistulae* 1.20). Donne addresses the paper he is inscribing, begging it not to be a Letter, 'Mad paper stay,...lye hid with mee' (ll. 1, 3). Having failed, the poet then imagines at length his Letter's inarticulateness in the lady's presence, manages to devise for it a single stanza of elegant praise, and at last commissions it to be the writer's agent in the lady's letter cabinet to discover the identity of her favourite correspondent so that he might 'love him that shall be lov'd of her' (l. 52).

Early editions of Donne's poetry register that he wrote two poems 'To the Countesse of Huntingdon', one 'To the Countesse of Salisbury', and six to 'The Countesse of Bedford'. All are exercises in formulating extravagant praise of the addressees' beauty, dignity, and goodness in terms that are wittily justified by the argument of the Verse Letter. In the case of the Verse Letter *Sal*, Donne frankly admits (rather than indirectly acknowledging it with something like the mirror conceit of the Verse Letter to the Lady Carey) that 'things like these, have been said by mee / Of others' (ll. 37–8). In a Prose Letter to a friend, who had apparently encouraged him to court the lady, Donne rehearses the main argument he uses in this poem:

I would I could be beleeved, when I say that all that is written of them [by me of others], is but prophecy of her. I must use your favour in getting her pardon, for having brought her into so narrow, and low-rooft a room as my consideration, or for adventuring to give any estimation of her, and when I see how much she can pardon, I shall the better discern how far farther I may dare to offend in that kinde. (*Letters* 260–1)

The issue for Donne, as this Prose Letter makes clear, is whether the addressee's corresponding intelligence will appreciate his efforts to contextualize the hyperbole that the conventions of this kind of poetry impose on him.

In another Letter to Goodere, Donne again expresses hesitation about acceding to Goodere's suggestion that he write a Verse Letter in praise of a countess, partly, he says, 'that I may also keep my dignity' of pursuing 'a graver course, then of a Poet', but also because he has promised another countess that he would reserve 'not only all the verses, which I should make, but all the thoughts of womens worthinesse' for her. Despite these hesitations, he justifies his decision to write the poem:

because I hope she [the other countess] will not disdain, that I should write well of her Picture ['picture' in the sense of another person who has the same qualities as the lady to whom Donne has made the promise, that is, the countess Goodere had suggested Donne court], I have obeyed you thus far, as to write:... If those reasons which moved you to bid me write be not constant in you still, or if you meant not that I should write verses; or if these verses be too bad, or too good, over or under her understanding, and not fit; I pray receive them, as a companion and supplement of this Letter to you.... (*Letters* 103–5)

If the poem referred to here is, as R. C. Bald assumes (1970: 179–80), a Verse Letter to the Countess of Huntingdon, it is likely *HuntMan*. What 'use' Goodere made of it, whether he sent it to the Countess or took advantage of its expressions in some other way, cannot be ascertained; but the readers of *Poems* were presumed to consider the verses not too bad nor too good nor 'over or under her understanding, and not fit'. Regardless of a recipient's actual capacity to appreciate the poem for what it is, early readers of Donne's poetry made it their study to do so.

There are more Verse Letters 'To the Countesse of Bedford' than to any other addressee, and when the other poems Donne wrote about persons or events associated with her are considered with them, Lucy Russell emerges as one of his most important correspondents. The recurring subject of his Verse Letters to her is virtue, morally upstanding but also effective behaviour, a topic that Lucy Russell seems particularly to have inspired Donne to consider. Prose Letters support the further assumption that she received at least some of these Verse Letters as well as other poems Donne wrote (Epicedes and Obsequies on the deaths of her friends and brother); and she may even have responded in kind to his poetry (*Letters* 67). The issue of these poems is the difficulty of acting virtuously in the milieu of the court. This makes the Verse Letters to the Countess, variously contextualizing and qualifying the extravagant praise that is the given of their arguments, illustrative of the dilemma both Donne and the lady faced: he in relation to her, she in relation to those with whom she interacted to gain favours for others, including Donne.

BedfDead seems, in its broken-off condition, to record the inevitable frustration of Donne's attempt to maintain a relationship with the Countess when circumstances required him to court others. The biographical truth of the matter belies what the poem suggests: that is, Donne did not give over his efforts to maintain the association. Their interaction continued after he returned from France, surviving his decisions both to publish the *Anniversaries* and to enter the church. The incomplete poem suggests the poignant fiction that, after all, their relationship could not be sustained. It was printed as such, and it deserves attention as such; but it is not prima facie evidence of what transpired.

One of the most important achievements of twentieth-century scholarship on Donne was to register the distorting effect of Izaak Walton's insinuation that Donne's poetical output evolved from 'facetiously Composed and carelesly scattered' poems ('most of them being written before the twentieth year of his age') to heavenly poetry written 'in his declining age; witnessed then by many Divine Sonnets, and other high, holy, and harmonious Composures' (Walton 1670: 53–4). Actually, Donne wrote very few poems after he took orders in 1615 (Novarr 1980). Most of them are connected to specific events, three are Verse Letters, two are in Latin. That is, when he entered the priesthood Donne became almost entirely an occasional poet; and it is in this capacity that he produced *Libro* (*Milgate* 112–13).

It is an intricately conceited, playful poem written to thank Richard Andrews, who had attended Donne in some of his illnesses, for his extraordinary efforts to return a book Donne had lent him. Andrews's children had damaged the book, and Andrews had restored it by copying it over. Donne's poem takes its conceit from this: a printed text has reverted to manuscript, gone backwards, as it were, into an earlier technology of the written word. Donne makes that circumstance the occasion to reflect on the impossibility of the doctor's doing for him what the doctor had done for the book; Andrews cannot rejuvenate an old man. The poem becomes movingly paradoxical as Donne's words, inscribed by his ageing hand, become involved at last, as in a sermon, with the canonized text of the printed word of God: '*Hei miseris senibus! nos vertit dura senectus / Omnes in pueros, neminem at in Iuvenem. / Hos tibi servasti praestandum, Antique Dierum, / Quo viso, et vivit, et juvenescit Adam*' ('Alas, for poor old men, harsh old age turns us all into children, but it turns no one into a youth. You have reserved that distinction to Yourself, O Ancient of Days, in whose sight, Adam both lives and grows young': ll. 15–18).

In the 1635 *Poems*, where this poem first appeared, it was placed before the first of the Prose Letters, also in Latin, near the end of the volume, as if to stress its epistolary character over its poetical condition. Appreciating it requires reading against that insinuation. A graceful letter of gratitude might be accomplished in prose. Donne has written, instead, a Verse Letter that qualifies its message with the manoeuvres of poetry. The reversion he celebrates in the book's condition inspires his hope in the rejuvenating power of God, who enters the poem, by no means coincidentally, under the name given him by the prophet (Daniel 7:9, 13, 22). There is no better instance of how both the characteristically poetical habits of Donne's mind and his ability to discharge the obligations of a pastoral office were alike stimulated by specific circumstances.

CHAPTER 15

THE RELIGIOUS SONNET

R. V. YOUNG

For Izaak Walton, John Donne was a 'second St. *Austine*' (1675: 38), a young man of somewhat disorderly life who, like the great Church Father, eventually found his true vocation as a Christian clergyman and altered his life decisively and permanently. While modern scholarship has found numerous flaws in Walton's account of Donne's life, the strict dichotomy of sacred and profane can be questioned simply by considering the poetry. Like his secular verse, Donne's religious poems begin with the deployment of conventional genres, which the poet then develops in novel and often surprising ways in accord with his personal vision and the considerable resources of his wit. The same kinds of images and conceits that shape the imaginative world of the love poems form the fabric and texture of Donne's dramatization of religious experience. *ValWeep*, for example, broods upon erotic despair by invoking the image of a globe, while *Sickness* meditates on the mysteries of death by remarking the shortcomings of 'all flatt Maps' (l. 14). The Elegy *ElWar* likewise compares sexual intercourse to combat: 'Here let me parle, batter, bleede, and dy' (l. 30); while the Holy Sonnet *HSBatter* directs the same conceit to a man's fearful strife with God. Donne the man may have made various critical changes in the mode of his life, but the terms in which Donne the poet saw and depicted the world and the texture of his poetry remain remarkably consistent from first to last. In view of the pre-eminence of the sonnet in English love poetry during Donne's early manhood, it is in his religious Sonnets that this ironic convergence of sacred and profane is most acute.

Since the sonnet from Petrarch through Sir Philip Sidney and his imitators had generally served as a vehicle for dramatizing the inward strife of a man struggling with a conscience divided by the competing demands of desire and a kind of erotic idealization, the genre is an inspired choice for manifesting the tensions of an age of religious controversy and conflict. Because of his Catholic recusant upbringing, Donne endured an acute awareness not only of the sometimes violent confrontations between Catholics and Protestants, but also of the dissidence within the various confessional communities, including the Church of England in which he eventually took holy orders. Further, Donne provides an especially marked example of the strain between sacred and profane love that emerges during an era of heightened Christian consciousness. His religious Sonnets may be best apprehended, then, as a series of responses to the spiritual turbulence generated not only by the clash of competing Protestant and Catholic Reformations, but also by the inner turmoil of erotic passion.

Indeed, his spiritual response could only take poetic form in the matrix of Donne's wide reading and immersion in the literary culture of the late Renaissance. He was conversant with the conventions of Petrarchan love poetry and the sacred parody of these conventions in both native English and continental forms, in the work of such figures as Clément Marot, St John of the Cross, William Alabaster, and Robert Southwell. In addition, like all of his religious poetry, the religious Sonnets were influenced by Augustinian and scholastic theology as reshaped by the polemics of the Reformation. All of these sources of Donne's moral and spiritual imagination must be considered along with the poet's peculiar personal situation in the England of Elizabeth and James. Yet the religious Sonnets remain above all poems: the genre deployed for the dramatization of a particular devotional experience reveals more of the meaning than any assessment of theological background or historical context. The poet's deft manipulation of the expectations associated with generic conventions may indeed be regarded as a chief constituent of these poems' unique and enduring significance.

While the Holy Sonnets are the pulsing heart of all Donne's religious poetry, closely associated with them is *Corona*, a finely wrought formal meditation on some of the mysteries traditionally associated with the rosary, but subtly altered, perhaps with the purpose of rendering them inoffensive to moderate Protestant sensibilities in Donne's treatment. The Sonnets of this work prepare the way for the sixteen Holy Sonnets that appear in different combinations in the editions of 1633 and 1635 as well as in numerous manuscripts (in some of which they are called 'Divine Meditations') and for the three late Sonnets unique to the Westmoreland ms. (*Variorum* siglum NY3), first published by Edmund Gosse in the 1890s. These nineteen poems are justly famous and hold a place among the most powerful expressions of religious longing and anxiety in the English language; but their interpretation, difficult enough in view of their innate ambiguities of discourse and tone, is complicated by an elusive textual history. Critics have long debated the proper order of the Sonnets, or whether there is such an order, and hence to what extent the relationship among the Sonnets as a group determines the meanings of the individual poems. The question of sequence is, in turn, folded into debates about the 'Protestant' or 'Catholic' doctrinal orientation of the Holy Sonnets. Moreover, for many years what now appears to be a spurious addition to the title of the Verse Letter, 'To E. of D.', namely, 'with six holy sonnets', has led to a great deal of fruitless conjecture about the dating of the Holy Sonnets or of *Corona* (*Variorum* 7.1.XCV–XCVI). The textual evidence accumulated by the *Variorum* editors now makes it clear that the resolution of these significant questions is best pursued by regarding the generic features of the Holy Sonnets as a sonnet sequence (see Ill. 4.II.3).

A sequence of twelve Holy Sonnets was published in the first edition of Donne's poems in 1633 immediately after *Corona*. Four more Holy Sonnets were interspersed among these and the order rearranged in the edition of 1635, and this remained the arrangement in all subsequent editions until the middle of the twentieth century, although the three religious Sonnets first published by Gosse were added to the end of the sequence in twentieth-century editions. In 1952, in her edition of Donne's *Divine Poems*, Helen Gardner reinstituted the order of 1633 as a distinct sequence, printed the four additional Sonnets of 1635 as a separate group, and treated the three Sonnets unique to the Westmoreland ms. as individual poems standing alone. Gardner's argument is both textual and interpretive: she maintains that the most authoritative manuscripts (of Groups I and II) all affirm the 1633 sequence, and that in this sequence the Holy Sonnets can be interpreted as two sets of linked meditations based on Jesuit practice inspired by St Ignatius Loyola's *Spiritual Exercises*. 'The first', Gardner maintains, 'are quite clearly a short sequence on one of the most familiar themes for a meditation: death and judgement, or the Last Things' (Donne 1978a: xl). 'The last six sonnets do not form a sequence,' she continues; 'but they are on two aspects of a single theme, love', with 7–9 dealing with the Atonement and God's love for man, and 10–12 reflecting on the love man owes to God and neighbour (xli). The four Sonnets added in 1635 Gardner arranged into a group suggesting another set of Ignatian meditations on the theme of penitence (liii).

Gardner's interpretation of the Holy Sonnets in the light of Jesuit meditation received support from Louis Martz (1947), who applied the same interpretive concept to Donne's *Anniversaries* and subsequently discussed a wide range of seventeenth-century poems in terms of Ignatian meditative practice (1954; 2nd edn. 1962). Among subsequent editors, however, only John Shawcross adopted Gardner's arrangement of the Holy Sonnets. By the late 1970s there was a reaction, led by Barbara Lewalski (1973, 1979) against the notion that Donne's poems were significantly influenced, even structurally, by the Jesuits or any other Catholic sources. Lewalski, and her numerous supporters, adhered to the 1635 order of the Holy Sonnets as a convenient, standard way of referring to the poems, among which they allowed no particular order or thematic relationship (Lewalski 1979: 265). The textual argument over the order of the Holy Sonnets thus became an important part of a literary and historical dispute over the meaning of the poems and their relationship to Reformation polemics.

The exhaustive labours of the textual editors of the *Variorum* edition of the Holy Sonnets have in a limited way vindicated Gardner's acceptance of the 1633 sequence without endorsing her interpretation or her explanation of the four additional Sonnets of 1635. This definitive treatment of the text of the Holy Sonnets affirms that 1633 is indeed a sequence, but a revised sequence. The four poems interpolated in the 1635 edition were part of an earlier version that Donne evidently discarded in the process of revision. The *Variorum* editors maintain that the 1633 sequence of twelve favoured by Gardner and found in the Group I and Group II manuscripts is a revision of an earlier sequence of twelve found in the Group III manuscripts. The 1635 ordering is an editorial effort to put the two sequences together and apparently corresponds to no intention of the poet, but retains a historical interest because of the wide influence of that printing on all subsequent editions over the next three centuries. The three poems inscribed in the Westmoreland ms. in the hand of Donne's friend Rowland Woodward seem to have been written ten or more years later than the Sonnets in sequences. They are highly personal poems that Donne or Woodward evidently did not wish to circulate, and they disappeared from view until Gosse published them.

The lucubrations of the textual editors, while providing a satisfying explanation of the textual problems associated with the Holy Sonnets, challenge the ingenuity of interpreters by complicating the hermeneutic problem. They endorse Gardner's sense that the poems are sequential, and that Donne conceived of them as an interrelated set; but, instead of one sequence of twelve and another of four, the *Variorum* offers two sets of twelve with four different poems in each and with different arrangements. If the poems are designed to be read and comprehended in sequence—in the manner of Sir Philip Sidney's *Astrophil & Stella* or Samuel Daniel's *Delia*—as the textual evidence suggests, then it is incumbent upon critics to explain what is *meant* by Donne's substantial revision. Perhaps we should begin by asking whether Gardner's explanation of the thematic unfolding of the 1633 series—six Sonnets on death and judgement preceding six on Christian love—is strengthened or weakened by considering how it revises the earlier version. At the same time, the *Variorum*'s affirmation that all sixteen of the Holy Sonnets published in 1635 were written as elements of a sequence is, in any case, a crucial part of their meaning.

A good place to begin considering the interpretive problem is with *Corona*, which is unequivocally a single poetic structure, a form with secular as well as sacred precedents that the poet has adapted to devotional purposes. As a 'crown' or garland of seven sonnets, linked by having the last line of one Sonnet repeated as the first line of the next until the last line of the last Sonnet repeats the first line of the first, it recalls a tradition of linking sonnets or stanzas of love poetry in praise of a woman, practised in Italian by Annibal Caro and in English by George Gascoigne and George Chapman, as well as the rosary and other devotional schemes (Martz 1954: 107). Gascoigne, in fact, uses a set of linked sonnets for satirical pieces in a sequence of seven sonnets beginning 'In haste post haste, when fyrste my wandring mynde' (Gascoigne 278). The Sonnets of *Corona* are thus mutually interdependent for the manifestation of their full significance, and in this comply with the dominant tradition of the sonnet down to Donne's day. As Patrick F. O'Connell shows, individual

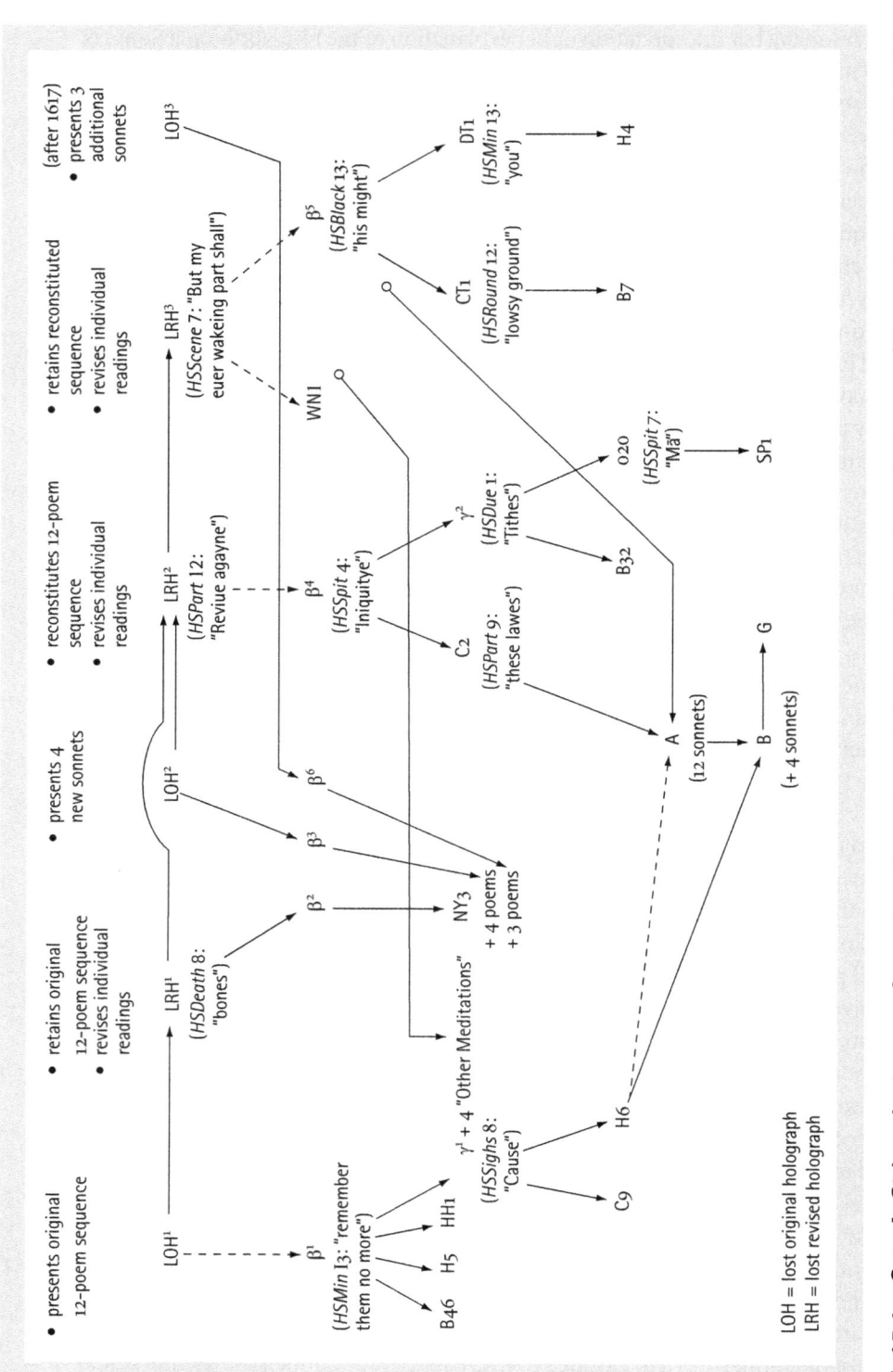

Ill. 15.1. Gary A. Stringer's stemma of seventeenth-century artefacts containing the Holy Sonnets (*Donne Variorum* 7.1.LXIV). This intense stemma portrays the relationships among the artefacts by outlining the genealogy of the poems in two stages, first in artefacts traditionally belonging to Group III, and second in the stage embodied by the Westmoreland ms. (NY3). For identification of sigla and discussion of bibliographical details, see *Variorum* 7.1. XXXII–XXXVIII and LXI–LXVII. (Reproduced with the permission of Indiana University Press.)

pieces of the sequence are incomplete in themselves: 'Indeed the process itself, including the failures, the premature resolutions, and all, is an integral part of the overall pattern that makes up the gift-crown' (130).

Intuition suggests that *Corona* is earlier than the other Holy Sonnets, an initial foray into sacred parody of the secular sonnet sequence, most usually associated with idealized—and thus potentially idolatrous—profane love. Since Donne's Songs and Sonets include no sonnets properly speaking, his use of the sonnet form in a religious context heightens the contrast between the sacred and profane. The idolatry of obsessive carnal desire is, of course, an important motif in the Holy Sonnets, and the poet of exultant lovers '*Canoniz'd* for Love' in *Canon* (l. 36) may well have been conscious of a good deal that required repudiation. It would not be surprising for a man of Donne's background to have recourse to a highly structured devotion like the rosary, familiar to him from his boyhood; and it is equally unsurprising that he would revise this devotion in a way that would make it more compatible with his newly Reformed sensibility. In *Corona*, Donne is devising a Protestant liturgical poem by modifying Catholic materials. Still, its highly visible formal structure necessarily makes *Corona* seem Catholic from the perspective of the Puritan preference for extemporaneous prayer over the liturgical forms retained by the Book of Common Prayer from Catholic worship (H. Davies 1.259, 264). And there are motifs in Donne's sequence that seem distinctively Catholic. The second Sonnet, *Cor2*, for example, declares that in the Virgin's womb the Son 'Can take no sinne, nor thou give' (l. 7), a line that hints at the doctrine of the Immaculate Conception—that the Blessed Virgin was conceived without Original Sin—unless the second clause is mere filler. At the least, it focuses more devotional attention upon the Virgin Mary than was typical among Protestants of this era.

The formality of *Corona* doubtless makes it seem less original and personal than the other Holy Sonnets. Nevertheless, Donne deploys the intricate structure of the poetic crown as a framework for characteristically witty conceits and tough-minded observations. In *Cor3*, 'Starres, and wisemen will travell to prevent / Th'effect of *Herods* jealous generall doome', leading the poetic persona to wonder: 'Was not his pity towards thee wondrous high, / That would have need to be pittied by thee?' (ll. 7–8, 11–12). In *Cor4* Donne invokes a paradox that goes back, by way of St Bernard, to St Augustine: 'The Word but lately could not speake, and loe / It sodenly speakes wonders' (ll. 5–6; cf. R. V. Young 2000a: 91–2). But *Cor5* develops out of a disillusioned vision of fallen human nature:

> Hee faith in some, envie in some begat,
> For, what weake spirits admire, ambitious, hate;
> In both affections many to him ran,
> But Oh! the worst are most, they will and can...
> (ll. 2–5)

In a sense, the 'weake spirits' are hardly more admirable than the 'ambitious'. We are reminded that in the very first Sonnet of *Corona* Donne invokes a theme that will preoccupy him in many of the Holy Sonnets, the authenticity of the persona's love for Christ, in the prayer that he 'Reward my muses white sincerity' (l. 6). The six Sonnets that follow in the sequence may be regarded as a dramatization of the penitent's effort to affirm the 'white sincerity' of his devotion.

Without the prosodic linkage of *Corona*, the order of the Holy Sonnets is not obvious. The evidence provided by the *Variorum* edition, however, compels us to consider them likewise as parts of a sequence and to attempt to interpret them accordingly:

> A signal feature of the manuscript transmission of the Holy Sonnets is that none of the poems has a history of individual circulation. However ordered, these sonnets invariably traveled in groups, a fact suggesting that the concept of sequence was integral to Donne's understanding of the genre from the very beginning. Fortunately...the validity of this implication does not rest on mere inference, for the details of Donne's handling of individual texts as they move forward in the stream of transmission confirm that the ordering of the sonnets was a matter of continuing authorial attention. (*Variorum* 7.1.LX–LXI)

The *Variorum* editors, however, dismiss Gardner's conception of the sequence of 1633 as well as her notion that the four extra Sonnets of 1635 were intended as a short independent set. The first half of the 1633 sequence cannot have been intended as a set of six Sonnets on the Last Things, they maintain, because the poems originally appeared scattered through the original sequence of twelve found in the Group III manuscripts (as poems 2, 5, 6, 8, 9, and 11) along with the additional four Sonnets (poems 1, 3, 7, and 10 of Group III) of 1635 (XCIII). Gardner's efforts to date and organize the Holy Sonnets according to interpretive considerations, such as Donne's evolving ideas about the fate of the soul after death and his poems' relation to an elegy by Lady Bedford, are likewise rejected (XCVII–XCIX).

The *Variorum* thus leaves us not only 'with little upon which to base a theory about when the majority of the Holy Sonnets were written' (C), but also with no theory of the significance of the order of either the original or the revised sequence. Nevertheless, the meaning of a sequence as such depends neither on the time nor the original order in which the individual poems were composed. Gardner's interpretation cannot be simply refuted by demonstrating that the first six Sonnets of the 1633 set were not *originally* intended as a six-part reflection on the Last Things: Donne may very well have perceived in retrospect that six of the original twelve Sonnets could be extracted from a set that evidently failed to satisfy him completely and grouped together as a meditation on the Last Things. The meaning of a passage of poetry is not logically exhausted by the author's intention when he began writing.

Criticism of Gardner's explanation of the 1633 sequence ought to examine how well it accounts for the organization of the poetic argument that she has posited. One might thus observe that the ninth poem in the revised sequence, *HSWhat*, seems to touch on the theme of the Last Things as surely as any of the first six Sonnets, and more than some—*HSDue*, for example. A further difficulty with Gardner's interpretation is that it seems to allow the sequence to fall into two halves with very little that unites it into a single poetic discourse.

A consideration of the way Donne changed the order of the sequence and discarded and added poems suggests that he was indeed striving for a more coherent poetic argument without necessarily devising so rigorous a structure as obtains in *Corona*. The first Sonnet of the original sequence is eliminated from the revised sequence, its place taken by what had been the second Sonnet. A comparison of these two poems suggests reasons for the change. Both deal with the paradox that a human being, a creature made by God in his own image, is liable to utter destruction despite his divine origin: 'Thou hast made me, and shall thy work decay?' (l. 1) begins the original first poem; the second similarly acknowledges, 'first was I made / By thee, and for thee' (ll. 2–3), and wonders: 'Why doth the Deuill thus vsurpe in me?' (l. 9). In the original version, then, the first two Sonnets are a pair on the same theme, but the first immediately veers off into the rhetoric of spiritual terror without really expounding the paradox. The persona expresses his grief and terror over the fear of death and damnation without yet having confronted his situation fully.

If the set is intended to be a meditation, however, the second of the original poems is far more suitable for the first place that it occupies in the revised sequence. It is a less impassioned poem than the first Sonnet of the original set and establishes the theme of the meditation in a more measured fashion:

> As due by many titles I resigne
>   My self to thee ô God; first I was made
> By thee, and for thee, and when I was decay'de
>   Thy bloud bought that the which before was thine.
> I am thy Sun, made with thy self to shine,
>   Thy seruant, whose paines thou hast still repaid
> Thy sheepe, thine Image, And till I betray'd
>   My self a Temple of thy spiritt Divine.
>
>   (ll. 1–8)

By acknowledging the persona's creation, redemption, and continuous spiritual comfort, the octave invokes all three persons of the Trinity, thereby placing the set of Sonnets firmly within the reflective tradition of Christian meditation. Having established in somewhat legalistic terms his dependent relationship with God, the speaking persona, with an abrupt turn in the discourse, devotes the sestet to his spiritual crisis:

> Why doth the Deuill then vsurpe in mee?
>   Why doth hee steale, nay ravish that's thy right?
> Except thou rise, and for thine owne worke fight
>   Oh I shall soone despaire, when I doe see
> That thou lou'st Mankind well, yet wilt not chuse mee
>   And Satan hates mee, yet is loath to loose mee.
>
>   (ll. 9–14)

God has sent his Son to save the world he created and his Holy Spirit to fill the faithful with grace, but the redemption of humanity seems not to be working for this particular sinner, who fears lest he may not be found among the elect. The remaining eleven Sonnets in the revised sequence work out this dilemma, which sets the basic problem and anticipates what follows. The 'Deuill' who seeks to 'vsurpe' and 'rauish' looks forward to the famous *HSBatter*, which first appears as the tenth Sonnet in the revised sequence—a good indication that Donne found new possibilities in the original poems upon reconsidering them. Most important, perhaps, is the new relation that he perceived between *HSDue* and what had been Sonnet 4 in the original sequence, *HSPart*, which becomes the final Sonnet in the revision, providing the final answer to the questions raised in the first poem. The sinner who sees himself in legal and financial terms as *due by many titles* to a lord who has no interest in his creature's *resigning* of what is already owed, finally realizes that the Son, his Saviour, has bestowed upon the sinner 'part of his double interest' (l. 1). The legal jargon of ownership is transfigured in what has become the culmination of the meditation on election by the only *law* that matters for sinful man: 'Thy Lawes Abridgment, and thy last command / Is all but Loue, Oh lett that last will stand. / Finis' (ll. 13–14). *Finis*—'the End'—is included only in the revised sequence, embodying 'Donne's final adjustment of the text of the Holy Sonnets' (*Variorum* 7.1.LXXI), suggesting that Donne thought that he had found a fitting framework for the apparently disparate spiritual cries of the Holy Sonnets by making the second and fourth poems the first and last.

Of the ten poems in between, Gardner was certainly correct to note that they deal with the Last Things and with the love between God and man. Her mistake was perhaps in attempting to reduce the sequence to an excessively schematic arrangement. Still, the revision seems designed to enhance continuity and eliminate some repetition. The first Sonnet of the original sequence (*HSMade*) is probably discarded because it begins with the same equivocal treatment of election as the next (*HSDue*—which becomes first), but then turns abruptly after one line to the terror of death and damnation, a theme covered sufficiently by several poems in the revised version, especially 2–4 (*HSBlack*, *HSScene*, *HSRound*). The third Sonnet of the original version (*HSSighs*) may well have been discarded because Donne takes up the same theme in a more subtle fashion in the new Sonnet 9 of the revision. Both poems recall their speakers' sinful profane passion with the same phrase, 'In my Idolatry' (orig. 3: l. 5, rev. 9: l. 9), while the later version expressly evokes the Last Things in its opening line, 'What if this present were the worlds last night?'

The seventh and tenth Sonnets of the original sequence (*HSLittle*, *HSSouls*) also treat the fire of lust and 'Idolatrous Lovers' (*HSSouls* l. 9 respectively), and Donne may, again, have felt these themes were over-represented in the original sequence. Gardner thought that the four excluded Sonnets were a brief penitential set, but the notions of penitence and the Last Things are not so easily distinguished. Donne evidently wished to add more Sonnets that raised the theme of God's love, which, already present in the final couplet of *HSDue*, calls for further expression as the sequence unfolds. All the new Sonnets, as Gardner perceived, invoke the notion of God's love: both 7 (*HSSpit*) and 8 (*HSWhy*) dwell with wonder on the humility of the suffering Christ, the first of these suggesting that the ungrateful Christians are worse than the Jews who executed the Saviour, the second that human beings, because of sin, are worse than the comparatively innocent beasts over whom men have been given dominion. This eighth Sonnet is in part an answer to the fifth (*HSMin*—9 in the original sequence), which complains that only men and not 'poysonous mineralls', 'Leacherous Goates', 'Serpents Envious' (l. 3), and the like are subject to damnation. Similarly, *HSRound* seems to have been moved from the eighth position in the original sequence to fourth in the revision so that it might be mirrored and answered by the new ninth Sonnet, *HSWhat* (the fourth poem from the end of the sequence). The contrast between the lust for 'Prophane Mistresses' (l. 10) and the self-sacrificing love of Christ in the latter then gives way to Donne's famous call for God to 'ravish' (*HSBatter* l. 14) him away from his betrothal to the Devil.

The culminating Sonnet in the original sequence was also an invocation of human and divine love: 'Wilt thou loue God, as he thee? then digest / My soule, this wholesome meditation' (*HSWilt* ll. 1–2). This is not an inappropriate conclusion to a meditative sequence focusing on Christian love, but Donne may have felt that the sequence should not end with a metapoetic reference to meditation. These Sonnets, after all, strive for structural development without the explicit literariness of *Corona*. Moreover, once he had moved *HSDue* to the opening position, the logic of concluding with *HSPart* may have seemed inexorable. The *law* of love is a paradoxical transcendence of legality, even as it maintains the theme of quasi-legal obligation that opens the sequence, if only by undermining it. Above all, the poem that Donne finally made the culmination of the sequence in its revised form subsumes all the worries that surface in the intervening Sonnets—the striving for grace, which can only be given (*HSBlack*), the *imputation* of righteousness (*HSScene*), the nature of repentance (*HSRound*), and so on—in the comfortable doctrine that God's nature and essence are defined by love. It is a fitting wish for a man of irenic views in an age of religious controversy and conflict. Most important, it is an ideal conclusion for a set of Sonnets that transforms the erotic preoccupations of the conventional love-sonnet sequence—with a supreme act of Donne's witty inventiveness—into a contemplation of the divine lover's sovereign possession of the feminine soul of the Petrarchan lover.

The three final Holy Sonnets, which have been numbered 17–19 since Herbert Grierson's early twentieth-century edition, seem not to be connected with either of the two sequences of twelve and, in all probability, were written much later. Indeed, if *HSShe* refers to the death of Donne's wife on 15 August 1617—as it almost certainly does—then it provides a definite internal *terminus a quo*. Similarly, if *HSShow* refers to the Protestant defeat at the Battle of White Mountain on 29 October 1620—at least a perfectly plausible conjecture—then another *terminus a quo* is provided by internal evidence. It is not much of a leap, then, to infer that the third of these Sonnets, unique to the Westmoreland ms. (*Variorum* siglum NY3) and out of circulation before the twentieth century, was also written about the same time. The key interpretive question about these poems is why, in contrast to *Corona* and the rest of the Holy Sonnets, of which manuscript copies are plentiful, they were evidently kept out of circulation. Gosse, who first printed them, thought that 'they were suppressed by the editors of 1633 and 1635 because of the leaning they betrayed to certain Romish doctrines' (2.109), and Grierson believed that *HSShow*, in particular, seemed to question the validity of the Church of England in which, by 1620, Donne had already been ordained for five years (Donne 1978a: 121). Gardner counters that: 'The sonnet is not merely "compatible with loyalty to the Church of England"; it could hardly have been written by anyone but an Anglican' (ibid. 122). She points out that the irenic conception of the church implied by the poem is made explicitly in *Essayes in Divinity*, and offers only this explanation for the obscurity of *HSShow* before the twentieth century: 'If Donne deliberately withheld it from publication, it might well be because he thought it was too witty a poem for a man of his profession to write' (123).

This explanation overlooks the fact that *Essayes in Divinity* (1651) was itself not published by his son until long after Donne's death, probably because it would have been regarded as scandalously indulgent to Catholicism (see R. V. Young 2000a: 9). Moreover, Gardner invokes what has come to be a controversial and somewhat equivocal definition of 'Anglican', and neglects to ask whether—and if so, why—the other two Sonnets were deliberately withheld from circulation. While it is improbable that the disappearance of these Sonnets for nearly three centuries was merely fortuitous, an actual demonstration that they were intentionally suppressed is difficult. The best we can do is to surmise what Donne—or someone—may have feared the Sonnets could reveal about his thoughts and feelings, and how that might have affected contemporary responses to a man in his position; and the best way to do this is to consider how the Sonnets work as poetry.

As in the final revised sequence of Holy Sonnets, in these individual poems Donne again manages an ironic reinvention of the Petrarchan love sonnet through which sexual desire is subsumed by the formidable love of God, whose possessive demands would overwhelm their hapless human object had the Lord not fulfilled them himself. Although a number of the Songs and Sonets and Elegies as well as some of the religious poems provide tantalizing hints about Donne's relationship with Anne More, *HSShe* is the only poem—apart from the Latin inscription he wrote for her tomb (Hester 1996a: 17–34)—that makes explicit reference to his wife. If, as Louis Martz conjectures, *Noct* is a cry of outraged anguish over Anne's death (1954: 214–15), then the Sonnet may be read as its counterpart: an earnest acceptance of the will of God and vow of unswerving devotion:

> Since She whome I lovd, hath payd her last debt
> > To Nature, and to hers, and my good is dead
> > And her Soule early into heauen rauished,
> Wholy in heauenly things my Mind is sett.
>
> > > > (ll. 1–4)

The poet who had dramatized the quasi-divine 'mystery' of erotic love in *Canon* and exalted the lovers to sexual 'sainthood' here regards human love as ancillary to the love of God:

> Here the admyring her my Mind did whett
> > To seeke thee God; so streames do shew the head,
> > But though I haue found thee,'and thou my thirst hast fed,
> A holy thirsty dropsy melts mee yett.
>
> > > > (ll. 5–8)

In *Sat3* (ll. 103–4) the source of a stream is a trope for God as the source of all earthly political power (in *Sat5* [ll. 29–30] Queen Elizabeth is like the calm headwaters of the Thames); in the Sonnet he is the fountainhead of all earthly love, which, like earthly power, is unsatisfactory in itself. The poet, having discovered the source of true love, remains insatiable nonetheless. Only when every earthly alternative is stripped away will his soul be fully open to divine love:

> But why should I begg more Love, when as thou
> Dost woe my Soule, for hers offring all thine:
> And dost not only feare least I allow
> > My Love to Saints and Angels, things diuine,
> But in thy tender iealosy dost doubt
> Least the World, fleshe, yea Deuill putt thee out.
>
> > > > (ll. 9–14)

Now it is not difficult to see why Donne or anyone close to him might have been reluctant to see this poem read by any but his most intimate friends. First, it is extremely personal, almost undeniably a glimpse of his most tender feelings for his deceased wife and his struggle to sacrifice them to his devotion to the heavenly Master who had 'rauished' her away from the poet. Even more telling, perhaps, is the equivocal treatment of a disputed point between Catholics and Protestants: the reverence paid to saints and angels. To be sure, Donne affirms the Reformation principle that God will brook not even a hint of worship to any created being that would distract the faithful from unwavering attention to the Godhead; nevertheless, the closing couplet suggests that the traditional enemies of the soul—the world, the flesh, and the devil—pose a far more dangerous threat that requires all our vigilance. The implication is that Christians suffer enough temptations without wasting their energy on mutual polemics. Thus the sacred parody of a Petrarchan love sonnet, the literary embodiment of individual erotic obsession, daringly serves as an analogue for a critique of the fruitless preoccupation of the competing confessional communities with imposing their particular worship everywhere, while blind to the greater love of the Father for all his children.

It would have been similarly indiscreet to reveal *HSShow* to any but Donne's most sympathetic associates, who shared his irenic views of Christianity. Gardner is undoubtedly correct in asserting that this Sonnet does not question the validity of the Church of England, but her notion of Anglican tolerance is premature: 'The Anglican, at this period, differed from the Roman Catholic and the Calvinist in not holding a doctrine of the church which compelled him to "unchurch" other Christians' (Donne 1978a: 122). The trouble with this statement is that, if the poem were written about 1620, many if not most of the bishops in the Church of England were themselves Calvinists. What is now considered Anglicanism—a position self-consciously mediating between the extremes of Rome and Geneva and warily conceding to both the designation of true churches or, better, legitimate local branches of the eternal church founded by Christ but subsisting in no earthly institution—had no official standing in the Church of England. It was only beginning to take shape in the minds of men like Richard Hooker, Lancelot Andrewes, and—of course—John Donne.

And this Holy Sonnet is a composition that documents the beginnings of this novel 'ecumenical' vision of the church. In *Sat3* Donne had already questioned the competing claims of religious authority: 'Is not this excuse for mere contraries, / Equally strong? cannot both sides say so?' (ll. 98–9). As religious conflict broke out again in the early stages of the Thirty Years War, human claims to possess the keys to the one true church evidently drew the poet's scorn once again:

> Sleepes She a thousand, then peepes vp one yeare?
> Is She selfe truth and errs? now new, now'outwore?
> Doth She,'and did She, and shall She evermore
> On one, on Seauen, or on no hill appeare?
>
> (ll. 5–8)

Gardner rightly remarks that 'Donne's sarcastic wit' in these lines 'is turned against those, either Calvinist or Roman, who would confine the meaning of the word Church' (Donne 1978a: 122), but it was not a perspective that was widely accepted in his own church. Many Englishmen might also have taken umbrage at the joke he has at the expense of Edmund Spenser's identification of Una, the one truth, with the Church of England in Book I of the *Faerie Queene*: 'Dwells She with vs, or like adventuring knights / First trauaile we to seeke and then make Love?' (ll. 9–10; see Summers 1987). For the small circle of readers who knew all of Donne's poems, the sarcasm would have doubtless been sharpened by the recollection of *Sat3*'s comparison of the typical Englishman's choice of a church to his choice of a mistress. The parody of a Petrarchan sonnet form yet once more conveys an element of the poet's ironic wit by its very form.

Donne's idea of the true church emerges in the shocking conceit of the closing couplet:

> Betray kind husband thy Spouse to our Sights,
>   And let myne amorous Soule court thy mild Dove,
> Who is most trew, and pleasing to thee, then
> When She'is embrac'd and open to most Men.
>
> (ll. 11–14)

The true church is she who best exemplifies the 'last will' (l. 14) of the concluding Sonnet of the revised sequence of twelve; that is, the church that most freely and abundantly manifests the saving love of her 'kind husband'. The blatantly sexual figure—the church is a 'trew' bride by being promiscuous—is indeed startling. But the erotic metaphor is justified both by its frequent appearance in Scripture and by the logic of sacred parody. In the Old Testament, Jerusalem all too often 'plaied the harlot' (Ezek. 16:15) in spite of God who espoused her, whereas in the New Testament Christ is the husband of 'a glorious Church, not hauing spot, or wrincle, or anie suche thing' (Eph. 5:27). But in Donne's conceit, the measure of the church's fidelity is to be 'open to most men', in sharp contrast to the proud, disdainful beauty of the Petrarchan sonnet sequence—Sidney's Stella, for example, or Samuel Daniel's Delia. The meaning of the conceit is thus embodied in the generic form of the Sonnet: the wit and decorum of what at first seems scandalous are achieved by the implied allusion to the idolatrous worship of the pining lover for a merely mortal woman, whose chastity can only be cold and forbidding. The church, however, is true to her divine spouse by embodying his sacrificial love for fallen humanity. As in the Sonnet on his dead wife, this poem deploys an ironic view of the internal *strife* of the frustrated 'idolatrous' Petrarchan lover as a trope for the sectarian strife occasioned by churchmen who make 'idols' of their churches' doctrine and liturgy. It is worth recalling, at this point, the 'courage of straw', in *Sat3*, which demands that 'every hee / Which cryes not, "Goddesse," to thy Mistresse, draw, / Or eate thy poysonous words' (ll. 26–8).

Although it is also a very personal Sonnet, *HSVex* does not manifest the obvious reasons for being withheld from circulation that are apparent in *HSShe* and *HSShow*. Indeed, it could easily have fit into the first version of the sequence of twelve and, in tone and style, is reminiscent of the four Sonnets excluded from the revision. It treats a common penitential theme, backsliding, but with Donne's characteristic paradoxical wit: 'Oh, to vex me, contraryes meete in one: / Inconstancy vnnaturally hath begott / A constant habit...' (ll. 1–3). The sestet opens with an admission that suggests a persona who is more aware of, or perhaps more candid about, the wheedling approach to God that appears in *HSWhat*: 'I durst not view heauen yesterday; and to day / In prayers, and flattering Speaches I court God' (ll. 9–10). This is not a bad description of the procedure of a man who tries to convince the crucified Saviour that he should have the 'piteous minde' of 'Prophane Mistresses' (see *HSWhat* ll. 14, 10). This last of Donne's Holy Sonnets closes with a cry of remorse that shows why the poetic persona of *HSShe* feels that he must worry more about 'the World, fleshe, yea Deuill' than about popish devotions 'to Saints and Angels': 'So my deuout fitts come and go away / Like a fantastique Ague: Save that here / Those are my best dayes, when I shake with feare' (ll. 12–14). This is a very moving poem in its exasperated acknowledgement of spiritual weakness; the poetic persona in his inability to come to terms with the demands of divine love depicts himself in terms reminiscent of Astrophil, sleepless over his frustrated longing for an unattainable Stella. Here, of course, it is the Petrarchan poet who has, through his own pride, become 'unattainable' to an altogether worthy and desirable suitor. Possibly someone who valued Donne's reputation was reluctant to reveal to very many readers that a man of such stature in the Church of England still felt compelled to examine himself so scrupulously. Most reflective Christians, however, can only find such humility in a clergyman salutary and comforting.

The Holy Sonnets are certainly among the treasures of devotional poetry in the English language, and *Corona* likewise manifests an undeniable poetic power. In addition, they provide a fascinating window upon the religious life of the Jacobean era. Above all, what must be acknowledged about Donne's religious Sonnets is their capacity to engage the mind and imagination and to surprise, even startle, the sensibilities after repeated readings as surely as his secular poetry. Donne's skill in deploying the genre of the love sonnet for sacred purposes is thus a measure of the degree to which his poetry embodies a unity that persists beneath—or perhaps above—sectarian strife, the unified vision of a Christian culture that still could see human love pour itself out into the love of God. *Corona* and the Holy Sonnets may perhaps be taken as a late monument to an era before T. S. Eliot's 'dissociation of sensibility' (247).

CHAPTER 16

LITURGICAL POETRY

KIRSTEN STIRLING

HELEN Wilcox describes the religious lyric as 'a genre not so much by birth... but by *baptism*; the lyric was converted and born again' (1994: 24). Similarly, M. Thomas Hester considers Donne's *HSDue* as 'an exploration of the kindness of the religious lyric... a poem in search of its own genre' (1987*b*: 60, 71). The generic classification of Donne's poems on religious subject matter poses even more problems than questions of genre usually do. If 'liturgical poetry' is interpreted strictly, none of Donne's poems qualify for the category since none of them were actually part of the church liturgy; and to interpret the term liturgical 'metaphorically', as P. G. Stanwood does, 'assign[ing] to it an aesthetic function which expresses the ordered movement of time in space' (1979: 91), is to lose sight of the specificities of what liturgical means. Lily Campbell proposes the term 'divine poetry', commonly used in the sixteenth and seventeenth centuries, and objects to the use of near-synonyms such as *devotional*, *religious*, and *theological*, but her study is restricted to poetry 'based directly on the Bible' (4–5). Metrical translations of the Psalms and other poetic parts of the Bible flourished in the sixteenth century, and Donne participated in this movement, though not to a very large extent. To describe his poems as 'liturgical' suggests a somewhat different focus from Louis Martz's description of them as private, interior 'poetry of meditation' (1954; rev. edn. 1962). 'Liturgical' implies some connection to structured, communal practices of worship, and although Donne's 'divine poems' range well beyond the strictly scriptural or liturgical, they contain indirect reference to scriptural passages and many features that could be identified as liturgical—primarily, a concern with commemorative action and with the collective, congregational voice. In the ongoing debate about Donne's personal religious sympathies (see Ch. 37), many critics have demonstrated that his religious poetry draws on both the Catholic liturgy and the liturgy of the Church of England, so the poems might best be called 'para-liturgical', related to church liturgy but going beyond it.

Donne's religious poetry of the early seventeenth century is a continuation of the tremendous outpouring of religious verse that developed in the sixteenth century. Following the example of Luther in Germany, who enthusiastically supported the project of setting spiritual songs to popular secular tunes alongside the translation of the Psalms into the vernacular, Miles Coverdale, who also produced the first complete Bible in English (1535), printed his *Goostly Psalms and Spirituall Songs*, which contained not only translations of the Psalms but also 'original' songs, mostly translated from Luther's German. After Coverdale many more volumes of spiritual songs were produced. Many of these songbooks were intended to counter the rise of secular poetry in England, and, as Coverdale's preface stated, aimed to replace the 'foule and corrupte' ballads dear to the youth of England with more edifying subject matter (qtd. in Campbell 31). However, the rise in English religious poetry cannot entirely be seen as a counter-movement to secular verse, since amongst the proponents of biblical translation and the writing of spiritual verse were Edmund Spenser, Thomas Wyatt, Philip Sidney, and Donne himself (see Zim 1987: 1–4).

The language of the liturgy, and particularly the Book of Common Prayer, had a great influence on the Protestant lyrics of the sixteenth century, as Ramie Targoff demonstrates in *Common Prayer: The Language of Public Devotion in Early Modern England* (2001). A. B. Chambers makes the same point, though less explicitly, in titling his book *Transfigured Rites in Seventeenth-Century English Poetry* (1992). The Book of Common Prayer itself did not contain any verse, a result of both 'practical exigencies' and 'abstract prejudices against rhyme' as Targoff puts it (2001: 57). Yet Sidney, in his *Apology for Poetry*, insists on the status of the Psalms as poetry, describing them as 'a divine poem...heavenly poesy', and concluding that that poetry 'deserveth not to be scourged out of the Church of God' (99). As well as using the Psalms to illustrate the divine origins of poetry, Sidney goes on to identify three 'kinds' of poetry, finding that 'the chiefe both in antiquity and excellency were they that did imitate the inconceivable excellencies of God', and takes David's Psalms as his first example (101–2). The translation of the Psalms into a metrical vernacular had a great influence on the development of religious poetry. More than seventy separate Psalters in English were published between 1530 and 1600 (many in prose) (Zim 1987: 2), not to mention translations of selections from the Psalms. One of the first people to translate Psalms into English was Wyatt, who produced a metrical paraphrase of the seven Penitential Psalms. Spenser is known to have translated them, though unfortunately no copy survives, and Sidney himself embarked upon the translation of the whole Psalter, which was completed by his sister, Mary Herbert, Countess of Pembroke, after his death.

The Psalms are the paradigmatic example of liturgical poetry, not only because they are probably the oldest example of the genre, but also because they manage to be both individual and collective, both voicing the experiences of a first-person speaker and endlessly applicable to the experience of the congregation. Although Donne's contribution to the culture of biblical translation is fairly minimal compared with many of his near-contemporaries—limited, as far as we know, to his *Lam*—his poem *Sidney* (Patrides 467–9), in praise of the Sidneys' translation of the Psalms, lays out his beliefs regarding ideal liturgical poetry and practice. He describes the Psalms themselves as 'the highest matter in the noblest forme' (l. 11), thus, like Sidney in his *Defence*, insisting on the form, the aesthetic quality of divine poetry. Hence his praise of the Sidneys' translation develops into a criticism of the vernacular metrical translation of the Psalms then in use in the Church of England, by Thomas Sternhold, John Hopkins, and others (1562). Donne bemoans 'that these Psalmes are become / So well attyr'd abroad, so ill at home', and asks, 'shall our Church, unto our Spouse and King / More hoarse, more harsh than any other, sing?' (ll. 37–8, 43–4). Donne was not alone in criticizing the Sternhold–Hopkins translation of the Psalms in comparison with versions circulating on the continent, particularly Théodore Beza and Clément Marot's French translation (1543). In contrast to this 'harshness' he outlines an ideal of liturgical song: the united choir of the church on earth singing these 'sweet learned labours' (l. 54) together. Donne describes 'three Quires, heaven, earth and sphears' in order to praise the communal song of the earthly choir above the others: 'our third Quire, to which the first gives eare, / (For, Angels learne by what the Church does here) / This Quire hath all' (ll. 27–9). *Sidney* was written in 1621 at the earliest, since it alludes to the death of Mary Herbert, the Countess of Pembroke (l. 53). Yet a very similar comparison of the three choirs is to be found in the much earlier poem *Lit* (Patrides 456–67), one of the most explicitly liturgical poems under consideration here. The twenty-third stanza states that 'to [God] / A sinner is more musique, when he prayes, / Then spheares, or Angels praises bee, / In Panegyrique Allelujaes' (ll. 199–202). Both poems emphasize the beauty and musicality of man's communication with God which surpass the choirs of spheres and of angels. An important progression between the two poems is that in *Lit* Donne speaks of 'a sinner', whereas in *Sidney* he speaks of 'the Church', implying communal, liturgical prayer rather than individual devotion.

Targoff claims that although *Sidney* describes Donne's vision of ideal liturgical poetry, he never succeeds in 'writing devotional verse that reflects a simultaneously individual and collective voice' (2001: 92). She argues that 'even an ostensibly liturgical work' like *Lit* 'does not ultimately offer prayers that one might plausibly imagine to be either read aloud by a congregation or read privately by anonymous worshippers' (93). But, as Dayton Haskin has pointed out, there is no reason to suppose that *Lit* was intended to be a set prayer (2002a: 64) and therefore no reason to consider it a failure. In attempts to determine the model for Donne's poem critics have identified it with both the structure of the Catholic Latin Litany of the Saints (A. Patterson 2002: 40) and the language of the Litany composed by Cranmer found in the Book of Common Prayer (Wellington). Donne's own mention of his litany in a Letter to Henry Goodere provides no definitive statement regarding his model, but it does make clear that his poem deliberately steers between the litanies of the 'Roman' and 'Reformed' Churches: 'neither the Roman Church need call it defective, because it abhors not the particular mention of the blessed Triumphers in heaven; nor the Reformed can discreetly accuse it, of attributing more than a rectified devotion ought to doe' (*Letters* 34).

Just as *Corona*'s associations with the rosary are 'rendered inoffensive to Protestant sensibilities' (Ch. 15 above), so Donne manages to transform his litany into a prayer that is neither Roman nor Reformed. Anticipating criticism regarding the propriety of 'tak[ing] such divine and publique names, to his own little thoughts', Donne specifies that his litany 'is for lesser Chappels, which are my friends' (*Letters* 33). This invocation of and yet distancing from the liturgical genre is typical of much of Donne's religious verse. Even when he emphasizes the private nature of *Lit*, he metaphorically invokes 'Chappels'. This is the recurrent question in the consideration of Donne's poetry as 'liturgical': at what point do his 'own little thoughts' become 'publique'?

Donne's individual and idiosyncratic wit, which has been endlessly discussed by critics, may seem difficult to reconcile with the liturgical genre, in part because of preconceptions about the turgidity of liturgy, and partly because wit is generally considered to be personal and not communal, not part of the act of communal worship. Wit may also seem too irreverent, not suited to the great purpose of communication with God. The reconciliation of wit with religious subject matter is something that also apparently worried Donne, or at least caused him to insert apologies in both *Lit* and *Sidney*. One of the supplications in *Lit* asks: 'When wee are mov'd to seeme religious / Only to vent wit, Lord deliver us' (ll. 188–9), suggesting that wit may displace the ostensible devotional purpose of the text. *Sidney* opens with the apostrophe:

> Eternall God, (for whom who ever dare
> Seeke new expressions, doe the Circle square,
> And thrust into strait corners of poore wit
> Thee, who art cornerlesse and infinite)
> I would but blesse thy Name, not name thee now.
>
> (ll. 1–5)

Paradoxically, spontaneous apostrophe of God may end up limiting the divine rather than opening up new channels of communication. The prescribed patterns and forms (*Sermons* 7.61) of the liturgy avoid the potential blasphemy of any attempt spontaneously to define God. One of Donne's most extended conceits, *Cross* (*Patrides* 448–50), is a tour de force of wordplay—and image-play—based on the symbol of the cross. The poem lists crosses found in the wings of birds, in the shape of man, in the mast of a ship, in the lines of the globe, and plays on the different meanings of the word: 'make the sign of the cross' but also 'cross out' or 'restrain' ('therefore Crosse / Your joy in crosses': ll. 41–2). The poem itself warns the reader to 'Crosse and correct concupiscence of wit' (l. 58), and it may seem like an outpouring of typically Donnean juxtaposition, except that almost all of these witty resemblances appear in Justius Lipsius' *De Cruce* (Lewalski 1979: 255), so that Donne's wit is traditional, and not original to him. In a similar vein, Walter Ong has demonstrated the importance of wit in Latin hymnody, in the work of Adam of St Victor and Thomas Aquinas among others. Wit and wordplay, in fact, prove to be appropriate to describe the paradoxes of the Christian mysteries of the Incarnation and the Resurrection, and Ong draws a direct parallel between the pun on Donne's name in his *Father* and some of the Latin hymns of Adam of St Victor (315). Thus Donne's wit need not be an impediment to considering his poems liturgically; on the contrary, it connects him to a long tradition of medieval hymnody with its roots in Augustine.

Donne's speaker, in fact, seems to approve the church's use of a similar kind of wit in *Annun* (Patrides 452–4), where he comments on the church's role in creating the liturgical calendar that allows the coincidence of the feasts of the Annunciation and Good Friday in the year 1608: 'This Church, by letting these daies joyne' (l. 33) has permitted the existence of 'this doubtfull day / Of feast or fast' (ll. 5–6). Donne uses this liturgical coincidence to develop one of his favourite themes, one to which he returns in later poetry and in his Sermons: that the beginning and the end of man's life, as on the circumference of a circle, are one and the same point. While the calendrical coincidence of Annunciation and Passion provokes reflection on the life of Christ, Donne's speaker insists that the model of Christ's life is relevant for all mankind: 'Death and conception in mankinde is one' (l. 34). And the last line of the poem, 'And in my life retaile it every day' (l. 46), proposes a related model for liturgical practice: while the joint liturgical celebration prompts meditation upon the events it commemorates, its message should be carried beyond that single day.

A similar reflection can be found in Donne's other poem named after a date in the liturgical calendar, *Goodf* (Patrides 454–6). (Interestingly, the precise temporal location of these two poems in the liturgical calendar means they are among the few of Donne's poems that can be dated with any certainty.) The naming of the feast day (which happens only in the title) gives the structure of the whole poem, because it soon becomes clear that Donne's speaker is riding in the wrong direction, away from the observance of this central event in the Christian calendar. And yet paradoxically, while Donne's speaker claims that this is the wrong direction, he performs the act of commemoration proper to liturgical worship. The crucifixion is made present to the memory rather than the eye of the poem's speaker. The poem enacts the tension between individual desires or obligations and the opposing obligation to contemplate Christ's crucifixion, particularly on the day liturgically set aside for it. The idea of going the wrong way is worked out on different levels, first cosmologically, in the opening conceit that describes man's soul as a 'Spheare...growne / Subject to forraigne motion' (ll. 1, 3–4) and thus 'whirld' out of its correct course, and then geographically, as the speaker is riding west instead of east. Both conceits come together in the developed pun on sun/son: just as the 'intelligence' of the sphere should be governed by the sun (Donne 1967a: 367 n. 11), so on earth the rider should be riding eastwards in the direction of the rising sun, both the liturgically correct direction for the altar of a church and the direction of Jerusalem. Donne began, but did not complete, a longer comparison based on sun/son in the poem *Res*, but the concision of the parallel of Christ with the rising sun in *Goodf* allows him once more to engage wit and paradox to evoke the central mystery of Christianity in two lines. In the east he 'should see a Sunne, by rising set', that is, Christ being killed by being raised on the cross, and he will therefore 'by that setting endlesse day beget' (ll. 11–12).

This 'spectacle' of Christ crucified is hypothetical, since the point of the poem is that Donne's speaker does not see it: because he is facing in the wrong direction, because he is not at church, because he cannot, literally, witness the events of the Passion in this time and place. And yet the speaker describes the spectacle that he 'do[es] not see' in great detail. Part of what he cannot or dare not see is the paradox of the Incarnation, which also preoccupies Donne in *Corona*, and, as in *Corona*, he presents the paradox in spatial terms. 'Could I behold those hands which span the Poles, / . . . peirc'd with those holes?' he asks (ll. 21–2). The question 'could I' is not a question simply of volition but of ability: is it possible for me to contemplate these things now? And the answer seems to be, 'not in this lifetime', as Donne, paraphrasing Exodus 33:20, makes quite clear: 'Who sees Gods face, that is selfe life, must dye' (l. 17). And so, in the deferral of the final confrontation between man and God that is typical of Donne's religious poetry, Donne's speaker postpones his 'turn' towards God's face and at the same time performs a neat twist on the poem's central conceit. He 'turne[s] his back' only to 'receive / Corrections' (ll. 37–8), and only once God has 'burn[t] off [his] rusts' and restored the divine Image, will he be able to 'turne [his] face' (ll. 40–2). The 'turning', therefore, will be in the future. *Goodf* incorporates past, present, and future in its meditation: the past event that is to be commemorated; the present act of memory; and the future justification.

For Targoff, *Goodf* is not a collective and liturgical poem: 'despite the shared occasion that it commemorates, [it] does not strive to speak on behalf of Christian worshippers' (2001: 92). For A. B. Chambers, too, the poem is 'an ego trip as well as a westward ride' (194). Yet this collision of the liturgy with the ego is precisely what gives shape to Donne's religious poetry, and while *Goodf* may be the most developed example of the different trajectories the ego and the liturgy may take, it is a theme that is revisited in the three Hymns Donne wrote after his ordination. A hymn is, by implication, a public genre, and Donne's Hymns are not without problems of generic classification. St Augustine defined a hymn as: 'a singing to the praise of God. If you praise God, and do not sing, you utter no hymn. If you sing, and praise no God, you utter no hymn. If you praise anything which does not pertain to the praise of God, though in singing you praise, you utter no hymn' (note to Psalm 148, qtd. in J. R. Watson 2). While this excludes classical hymns in praise of heroes or pagan gods, it is a reasonable definition of the Christian hymn, and it immediately causes problems for the reading of Donne's. John Shawcross suggests that the earliest of Donne's three Hymns, *Christ* (probably 1619), is mistitled and misclassified. Although the form of the poem, in three regular stanzas (*Patrides* 472-3), resembles a hymn, and resembles the other Hymns in Donne's canon, it is not a song of praise. Rather, Shawcross suggests, it is a prayer, though a communal prayer, since despite the 'I' of the poem, its metaphors and paradoxes can be uttered by all men (1991: 71). The poem was probably written in 1619 when Donne was attached to Lord Doncaster's embassy to Germany (see Emma Rhatigan's analysis of the Doncaster embassy in Ch. 34.I), but despite the autobiographical title the sea journey described in the poem explicitly becomes, from the second line onwards, 'emblematic'. The first two stanzas describe this journey where the ship is the 'embleme of thy Arke' (l. 2), the sea 'an embleme of thy bloode' (l. 4), and the clouds the 'clouds of anger' masking the face of Christ (l. 5). The island is not just the island that Donne's speaker leaves behind him, but it is the island of man that he abjures in the second stanza. The last two stanzas, however, become more difficult; to take up Targoff's argument, harder for a congregation to identify with, and harder to imagine a congregation reading aloud. In the last stanza the speaker's self begins to creep in: the reference to the 'false mistresses' of 'Fame, Wit, Hopes' (l. 28), with its echoes of the 'prophane mistresses' of *HSWhat* (*Variorum* 7.1.25; l. 10), may also refer more to Donne's youth than to that of many of his parishioners. Yet the very stanza where the ego seems to reassert itself in the communal genre ends with the eclipsing of the self: 'Churches are best for Prayer, that have least light: / To see God only, I goe out of sight' (ll. 29-30). This metaphor could function as another definition of Donne's ideal liturgical (or indeed individual) prayer. The self must be subordinated to God and to the prayer itself and must not assert itself through the false mistress of wit. The paradox is that in 'go[ing] out of sight' the praying voice falls silent. Donne returns to the poem's original conceit in the last line: 'to scape stormy dayes, I chuse / An Everlasting night' (l. 31-2). But as this everlasting night ends the Hymn, it seems to be a silent everlasting night.

In contrast to this silence, *Sickness* (1623 or 1631) opens with a similar musical metaphor to the harmony that closes *Sidney*. In *Sidney* Donne ends by hoping that the singing of the 'Sydnean Psalmes' may be 'as our tuning'—a preparation for singing 'th'Extemporall song' after death (*Patrides* 469). In his sickness, Donne describes himself as just outside 'that Holy roome, / Where...I shall be made thy Musique' (ll. 1-3). He 'tune[s] the Instrument here at the dore' (l. 4) in order to prepare himself. Donne was presumably aware that the etymology of 'psalm' was 'a twitching of the strings of the harp' (*OED*), and Helen Wilcox comments that 'Donne's devotional writing is, throughout, a tuning of the instrument at the door' (2006: 164). After this introductory stanza, the Hymn moves on to Donne's fullest development of a geographical metaphor to which he returns again and again: of the furthest west and east on a 'flat map' being the same point on a globe. He uses this metaphor in a parenthesis in *Annun* (l. 21), and comes back to it twice in his Sermons, in 1619 (2.199) and 1623 (6.59). In *Sickness* the speaker, the patient, is the flat map, lying on his bed, while his 'Physitians... are growne / Cosmographers' (ll. 6–7), poring over the map. The flat map allows Donne (the speaker) to develop his familiar metaphor: that two points apparently at the furthest remove from each other may turn out to be in fact the same: 'So death doth touch the Resurrection' (l. 15). Here Donne adds detail to his flat map, as the physicians poring over the map of his body may find his 'South-west discoverie / *Per fretum febris*, by these streights to die' (ll. 9–10). There is a pun on *fretum*, which may describe the raging of the fever, but also means 'strait'. Two stanzas later he develops the idea of straits, naming *Anyan* (the name given to the as yet merely conjectured North-West Passage; see Owens), Magellan (the South-West Passage), and Gibraltar. In naming all these straits, and speculating on which part of the globe is 'my home', Donne not only brings east and west to one point, but begins to reduce the whole globe to one geographical point. It seems not to matter whether the straits lead to the Pacific, to the 'Easterne riches' (l. 17), or to Jerusalem. And he continues this theme of geographical coincidence in the next stanza, with the typological claim 'that *Paradise* and *Calvarie*, / *Christs* Crosse, and *Adams* tree, stood in one place' (ll. 21–2). Likewise, in this moment of conjunction, Donne implores God to 'finde both *Adams* met in me' (l. 23). This geographical conjunction echoes the temporal conjunction of the feast of the Annunciation and Good Friday: at the moment of death, at the moment of transition into the next world, there is no time and no space either: the world and the self are reduced to one point.

Donne's *Father* (1623) is most celebrated for his witty punning on his own name in the refrain that ends the three stanzas: 'When thou hast done, thou hast not done, / For, I have more.' Although the 1633 *Poems* and most subsequent printed editions (including Patrides 491, l. 18) read the last line of the poem as 'I *feare* no more', important manuscript versions of the poem read this line, 'I *have* no more' (Pebworth and Summers 1987: 20–2). This seems an extreme example of the individual rather than the collective voice: only one voice could sing these lines with their full import. And yet, *Father* is in one way the most liturgical of Donne's works, since Isaak Walton says that at Donne's own request it was 'set to a most grave and solemn tune, and... often sung to the organ by the Choristers' of St Paul's Church, 'in his own hearing; especially at the Evening Service' (1658: 77–8). If the Hymn was indeed sung at evening service, it crosses a boundary between the joy that Donne (according to Walton) re-experienced every time he reheard it (78) and the communal experience of hearing the Hymn sung or even of singing it; it becomes, in a sense, public property.

The repetitive structure of the Hymn recalls the formal structure and the supplications of *Lit*, with the repeated request 'Wilt thou forgive that sinne...?' The word 'sinne' is repeated eight times in the Hymn, and the word 'done' seven times, and this heavy repetition links the sin and the sinner. Frank Kermode connects the pun on

Donne's name here with the Latin epigraph to *Deaths Duell* beneath the portrait of Donne in his shroud: *Corporis haec Animae sit Syndon, Syndon Jesu* ('May this shroud of the body be the shroud of the soul of Jesus'; translation by Shawcross in Donne 1967a: 394), finding a similar pun in the repeated 'Syndon' (Kermode 1971: 148). Helen Wilcox observes that the poem's rhetorical tour de force is in the changing of one letter—from 'sinne' to 'sonne', or, in the manuscripts, 'sunne'; damnation to salvation (2006: 164; 1994: 13). And yet the Hymn's alternating rhyme-scheme of -unne and -ore means that the 'sonne'—the redemption—of the last stanza is predicted, and primed, by the tight rhyme scheme itself and even by the repetition of 'done'. Thus while 'done' seemed inextricably linked to sin through repetition, its sound turns out to link the self with the possibility of redemption. His last 'sinne of fear' is a fear about the disintegration of the self: that after death he will 'perish on the shore'. Rather than asking forgiveness for this sin, Donne's speaker defiantly asks for assurance of salvation after death, asking God to 'sweare by [him]selfe' that (in the manuscripts) his 'Sunne / Shall shine as it shines now'. 'Having done that', he concludes 'Thou haste done, / I have no more' (ll. 15–18). As Pebworth and Summers point out, this significantly different manuscript reading 'recapitulates the final lines of the first two stanzas' while 'feare no more' recapitulates only the opening of the third stanza (1987: 22). 'I *have* no more' is a neater reversal of the preceding refrains, and not only closes the poem but erases the speaker. Once assured of salvation, he has no more need to speak, or to be. Like the speaker of *Christ*, he 'goes out of sight', because once he knows for sure that there is a life of the world to come the speaker of the poem has no more need for words.

Donne's religious poetry contains until the end a struggle between the individual and the collective voice. His speakers resist the dissolution of the self that seems to be implicit in surrendering to the collective, liturgical voice. There is a kind of peace promised in the self's 'goe[ing] out of sight' in *Christ*, but Donne's speakers reiterate the fear that the self will 'perish on the shore' and be 'no more'. From the 'ego trip' of *Goodf* to the 'thou hast not done' of *Father*, Donne's speakers continue to assert their individuality. He has to find a way to reconcile the self with both the communal expression of the liturgy and the hope of life after death that is implied by the liturgy, and ultimately he finds that in the simultaneously individual and communal voice of the Psalms. *Sidney* remains his ideal vision of the liturgical voice and resolves the fissure between the individual and the collective: 'when hence we part' we will each individually 'sing our part' and thus become subsumed in God's 'Extemporall song' (ll. 55–6, 51).

CHAPTER 17

THE PROBLEM

MICHAEL W. PRICE

The generic history of the 'problem' began with ancient Greek problemata literature, including various collections descending from the school of Aristotle, to whom traditionally are attributed books of problems: questions *cum* answers about health, physiognomy, and numerous other puzzlements, including moral and legal issues, possibly used as schoolbooks for medical and other kinds of education. Along with many Peripatetic traditions, including the related genre of the dialogue, this form of questions and answers was preserved through late antiquity and into the Christian era, mainly for education. By the twelfth century, at European universities, this variety of the problem had developed a subgenre, the 'disputed question', an exercise in dialectic for medical, theological, or philosophical training. In this form, the problem continued in use for sixteenth- and seventeenth-century university disputations (*Problems* xxvii–xxxi).

Another strain of generic development stemmed from Plutarch, whose *Moralia* included several books of questions and answers, some based on academic exercises, but also *quaestiones convivales*, table-talk with a diverting twist, extending the genre as matter for discussion of various wonderful curiosities at dinner parties and other social gatherings. A related form of recreational problem, devolving from more serious academic pursuits, was described by Aulus Gellius as having been part of student life in Greece. Later examples of this subgenre occurred in Macrobius' *Saturnalia* and in Giovanni Boccaccio's *Il Filocolo*. In the sixteenth century collections of problems mixing the academic and social subgenres began to appear in Italy: for example, Hieronimo Garimberto's *Problemati naturali, e morali* (1549); and, with a more pointedly comic flair, Ortensio Landi's *Quattro libri de dubbi con le solutioni* (1552). These writers took all knowledge for their province, displaying marvellous erudition in sparkling prose (*Problems* xxxi–xxxviii).

In Tudor England related entertainments were embedded within dramatic and other works by Robert Greene, Thomas Lodge, and notably by John Heywood, Donne's grandfather. In particular, Heywood slyly embedded elements of the generic tradition of the problem in his court entertainments, plays, and poems, including politically charged debates about seemingly innocuous topics, such as the weather, or whether wit or witlessness contributes more to happiness. But Donne himself was the first to write, after the example of Landi in Italian, numerous Problems in delightful English prose. Donne's nineteen Problems, written during the first Jacobean decade, are a satirical, subversive version of the genre, using irony and dissimulation, providing both entertainment and opportunities to collaborate on those occasions when Donne met with certain friends (lawyers and other wits) at the Mermaid and Mitre taverns. Donne's Problems were likely designed for oral performance at these or similar gatherings.

Donne's correspondence with one member of this circle, Sir Henry Goodere, included some revealing remarks about Problems that he enclosed in Letters. In one Letter Donne requested, 'I pray read these two problemes: for such light flashes as these have been my hawkings in my sorry journies' (*Letters* 88). This characterization of the Problems in part trivializes them ironically, but Donne conveys a more serious subtext when he compares his own 'hawkings' to Goodere's intense obsession with falconry: both occupations connote a hunt for prey. In a Verse Letter to Goodere, Donne elaborates a similar analogy, both chiding Goodere for being 'too indulgent to your sports' and commending to him the example of high touring birds (*HG* l. 20). The topic connotes both the trivial and the serious, ambiguously signifying, in the social circle of Donne and Goodere, both recreation and ratiocination; similarly, Ben Jonson's epigram 'To Sir Henry Goodyere' portrays hawking as a recreation yet also nuances it as more seriously related to learned discourse: the birds 'instruct men' that they 'to knowledge so should toure vpright, / And neuer stoupe, but to strike ignorance' (Jonson 8.55, ll. 7–8). These men understood both falconry and Donne's Problems as more than trifling pursuits.

Other Letters include similar references to the Problems. In one Donne speaks of riding on horseback as one of his two 'forges' for writing to Goodere (the other was his library), again suggesting that the Problems, though written in passing, were of more than 'light' or trivial mettle (*Letters* 137). In yet another Letter to Goodere, Donne encloses a Problem (now lost) 'which was occasioned by you, of women wearing stones; which, it seems, you were afraid women should read, because you avert them at the beginning, with a protestation of cleanlinesse' (*Letters* 108). This joking slur on women's prurience cannot now be compared to the Problem itself to check whether a more serious subtext is also conveyed; probably the points made are about jewellery worn by court ladies. In any case, the series of transactions outlined here demonstrates that, far from regarding Problems as trifles, Donne and Goodere were willing to spend considerable time and effort on them. Goodere's words had first prompted this Problem and Donne's having written and sent it to him; whereupon Goodere returned it after adding the 'protestation of cleanlinesse'; and now Donne, having studied Goodere's augmentation and again revised the Problem, again returns it for Goodere's further delectation. This sort of collaboration may be present also in Problems still extant and may have been part of their rehearsals at the tavern dinners Donne, Goodere, and their witty friends enjoyed.

In this same Letter Donne closes with a request that Goodere 'let goe no copy of my Problems, till I review them. If it be too late, at least be able to tell me who hath them' (*Letters* 108). Here he refers to the Problems as possibly circulating but nonetheless his own; again his tone indicates a sense of pride or concern about his writings, testifying to a seriousness he felt about them, perhaps even protectiveness and anxiety. In a later Letter Donne concludes by enclosing another Problem, 'whose errand is, to ask for his fellowes. I pray before you ingulfe your self in the progresse, leave them for me, and such other of my papers as you will lend me till you return' (*Letters* 99). Donne's pleading for the return of his Problems, along with his emphasis on the constraints of timing implied in his terms, 'before you ingulfe your self', sounds again a note of urgency. These were not writings that Donne regarded slightly or thought unworthy of his care; above all, he did not want them disseminated at court or on royal progresses.

In fact, all of Donne's Problems either focus satirically on, or are easily applicable to, criticism of the royal court. An example will show why Donne was so careful of them: 'Why Venus starre onely doth cast a Shadowe?' begins as a traditional Problem of astronomical science but at once blithely shifts attention from planetary to mythological significations, arguing that not Venus but Mercury would seem the more likely to be in need of shadow or disguise or dissimulation. Mercury's occupation is not love but eloquence, which 'is all shadowes and colours', because it 'must perswade people to take a yoake of Soveraignty and then beg and make lawes to tye them faster, and then give more monny to the Invention, repayr and strengthen it'. This obligation of Mercury, Donne argues, 'needes more shadowes and colourings then to perswade any man or woman to that which is naturall', as do the persuasions of Venus (*Problems* 33–5). For Donne and his coterie of wits, several of them former or current Members of Parliament, this discussion of eloquence evoked the early Jacobean debate over supply for the King's government, including issues of sovereignty, legislation, and taxation, issues that had been a main feature of parliamentary sessions from 1604. Donne's implication is that the task of eloquence in the service of the King is to establish an unnatural sovereignty, get the people to enforce it through law, and moreover get them to pay taxes to support it, all through the use of dissimulating speech. This construction of the matter fairly approximates the view of parliamentary opponents to Crown policy, who were reluctant to subsidize the extravagance of King James (see Ch. 30.II).

In his opening speech to the Parliament of 1604 James himself had given Donne and other writers an opening pointedly to use this comparison of royal policy to the glozings of Mercury, when he concluded: 'That as farre as a King is in Honour erected aboue any of his Subiects, so farre should he striue in sinceritie to be aboue them all, and that his tongue should be euer the trew Messenger of his heart: and this sort of Eloquence may you euer assuredly looke for at my hands' ([James I] 1604: 280). Donne, in his Problem, disputes James's promise to speak with sincerity, even going so far as to depict the Crown's rhetorical strategies (especially when the King or his spokesmen are negotiating with Parliament) as 'all shadowes and colours' (*Problems* 33). Moreover, Donne implies, when the King had cited the eloquence of Mercury the messenger god, he had actually betrayed the falseness of his speech, since Mercury, as well as for eloquence, was known as the patron of thieves and liars. Like Mercury, according to this Problem, Crown policy can only with difficulty be discerned 'creeping into our understanding in our darkenesse' (34). The Problem is a daring and dangerous piece of work, entrusted to a friend only with misgivings that copies must not be made or much circulated for fear of provoking disapproval or even reprisal.

Another striking example of such dangerous writing is 'Why are Statesmen most Incredible?'(*Problems* 44–5), based on passages in the *Annals* of Tacitus (4.125–7), who questioned the emperor Tiberius' pretensions to privileged *arcana imperii*, implying that these were used to legitimize immorality and corruption. *Arcana imperii* is translated variously as 'mysteries of state' or 'royal secrets'. In theory, it suggests that the sovereign is entitled (by his kingship) to a royal privilege, the prerogative to cloak himself in godlike inscrutability and inaccessibility. Indeed, it signifies that the sovereign is categorically separated from and impervious to his subjects (Kantorowicz 65–6). King James, a proponent of divine-right kingship, claimed that an aura of mystery and secrecy shrouded him, an aura that elevated him above all others and hid his royal prerogative. In a word, no subject might presume to fathom his mind.

James had stressed this idea—that people could not approach him—in *Basilikon Doron* (1603), where he had spoken of the king's 'secretest drifts' and 'need to vse secrecie in may [*sic*] things' (James I 1994: 5, 44). Thus again, it was King James himself who had given Donne and others entrée for satire. Ironically, it was not Jacobean malcontents who revived Tacitus in Renaissance England but James himself, rescuing the historian from obscurity by foregrounding learned allusions to him in *Basilikon Doron* (Schellhase 159). Once again, James chose language so ambiguous that it enabled critics to craft a double-voiced message. On the surface, one could compliment James by citing Tacitus (just as James had hoped); beneath the surface, however, some writers could use Tacitus' political scepticism and cynicism to criticize James.

Donne was treading deliberately on dangerous ground when he selected Tacitus as his source and Tiberius as his topic. Ben Jonson had staged the story of Tiberius in *Sejanus* (1603) and struck a nerve. The Privy Council immediately summoned and interrogated him on grounds of suspected treason. Critics have conjectured that the play caused such an uproar because Jonson might have implied analogies between characters and events in the play and those in contemporary England, specifically implicating King James and his ministers in the portrayal of a dissembling Tiberius (see work by Wikander; K. W. Evans; Hill; Barish; and A. Patterson 1984).

In his Problem Donne, more frankly than Jonson, suggests the extent to which Jacobean governance has debased royal privilege. He exposes this abuse simply by asking a question: 'are those (as they call them) *Arcana Imperii*, as, by whome the Prince provokes his lust, and by whome hee vents it, Of what cloth his socks are, and such, so deepe and so unreveald, as any error in them is inexcusable?' (*Problems* 45). Contrary to James's grandiose claims, the *arcana imperii* here consist merely of three rather ordinary matters: the names of the King's sexual interests; the names of those who assist in his sexual satisfaction; and the type of cloth James's tailors select for sewing his socks. James has debased the *arcana imperii* by reducing them to 'tools for parody, revelations of insubstantiality beneath the dazzling show' (Goldberg 1989: 69).

Donne intensifies the discrepancy between lofty claims and base actualities by contrasting theologically laden terms, terms all the more ironic because the King claimed his mystification derived in large part from theology. Donne's question suggests that 'lust' and 'error' (*Problems* 45) define the *arcana imperii*, rather than unfathomable truths illuminated by divinity, as James claimed. In fact, Donne's word 'deepe' alludes to a number of the royal deficiencies decried by various voices in the opposition: the magnitude of James's government's corruption, the excessive costs of his lifestyle, and the drinking and gaming associated with his court. More importantly, 'deepe' (along with Donne's implied reference to Tiberius) reinforces the perception of James and his ministers as dissimulators, signifying profound subtlety and craft, exhibiting the qualities of cunning, artfulness, and slyness.

Critical attention to this sort of danger and daring in the Problems has been scant, usually ignoring their subversive dissimulation, accepting as if literal Donne's ironic trivialization of them and passing over them mainly as bridges to discussions of *Biathanatos*, *Pseudo-Martyr*, or *Ignatius His Conclave*. Like the Paradoxes, the Problems have been treated as mere *jeux d'esprit* since their earliest editors (perhaps themselves dissimulating) described them as '*Iuvenilia*' and as things of little weight or significance. A notable departure from the rule has been Arthur Marotti's perception that the Problems are 'sophisticated iconoclastic pieces' (1986: 181), not only 'recreatively witty' but also sceptical, satiric, and resentful, so much so that they 'express...political opposition, disappointment, and alienation' (182–3). Otherwise, widespread censure and neglect of the Problems has proceeded from a failure to situate these writings in the coterie context for which they were originally designed and performed, or written and circulated.

'Why Venus starre onely doth cast a Shadowe?' has been treated simply as a parody of classical and medieval educational Problems, taking up traditional kinds of subject matter (*Problems* xxxviii–xxxix, 104–7), without notice of its orientation in regard to Jacobean politics or its particular meaning for some of Donne's parliamentary colleagues. It can hardly be ignored that other Problems insistently convey the demoralized and demoralizing tone of life at court: 'Why are Courtiers sooner Atheists then men of other Condition?' (23–4), 'Why have Bastards best Fortune?' (31–3), and 'Why are New Officers least oppressing?' (42–3) all frankly portray the striving for court office as an unscrupulous, dog-eat-dog struggle in the 'forge where fortunes are made, or at least the shopp where they are sold' (33), an immoral effort in which men have 'clamberd above competitions and oppositions' (42). These themes are often dismissed, mainly in relation to Donne's biography, as trifling expressions of his envy as a disappointed outsider obsessively ambitious for court advancement, rather than daring, deft, and accurate descriptions of political reality. Their connection to Donne's circle of friends—literary men, courtiers, and lawyers—has not been much noted; instead, the Problems have been seen as contemporaneous but otherwise unrelated to Donne's more serious prose works. However, to recover the particular social setting chosen for writing and performing the Problems makes their relation to Donne's prose tracts of political, not merely chronological, significance.

An illustration of the point may be seen in the Problem 'Why doth the Poxe so much affect to undermine the nose?' (*Problems* 40–2). As in several other Problems, Donne here lambastes court corruption by comparing it to venereal disease. Ostensibly writing in the tradition of the medical Problem, Donne begins with references to Paracelsus and anatomy but quickly shifts his focus to the royal court by observing that syphilis is 'begot and bredd in the obscurest and secretest corner' (40). Moreover, because the 'Serpentine crawlings, and Insinuations' of the disease through the male body are 'not suspected nor seene, hee comes sooner to greate place, and is abler to destroy the worthyest Member then a disease better borne' (40). This language compares contraction of the disease through the furtive activity of the penis to the bawdy advent of base-born court favourites, who subsequently rise to 'greate place' and then 'destroy the worthyest Member' (40) as pox destroys the nose. Continuing in this manner, Donne cites the Roman emperor Heliogabalus' practice of choosing 'his Minions in the Bath', according to the size of their noses, as an indicator of the size of their penises (41). The reference alludes to King James's penchant for merely handsome young men, who were successfully used by scheming politicians to exploit the King's fancy. This corruption debilitated the well-being of the Crown and worsened the King's political relationships with Parliament, reluctant to fund such royal excesses as the elevation of vulgar and vacuous upstarts.

To conclude, Donne reinvented the genre of the Problem, crafting a double-voiced message: superficially innocuous recreations of curious import, in actuality they ambiguously plant subtexts that carry a much less innocuous message, for example, criticizing King James's abuse of the *arcana imperii* privilege (though the Problems include other messages than this). The Problems thus contain, in Marotti's words, a carefully encoded 'political dimension that would not have been missed'

(1986: 184), a dimension that can be recovered by contextualizing them in the political realities of King James's court and issues of the Parliaments of 1604 to 1610. This might explain why some did not appear in the earliest editions of Donne's writings; it certainly helps explain why Sir Henry Herbert, the original licenser, was hauled before the Star Chamber to explain 'why hee warranted the booke of D. Duns paradoxes to bee printed' (*Problems* lxxxii).

CHAPTER 18

THE CONTROVERSIAL TREATISE

GRAHAM ROEBUCK

Few inhabitants of Europe from Luther's time to the Thirty Years War and the British Civil Wars were unaffected by the confessional turbulence of Christendom. Popes, emperors, monarchs, religious orders, secular governments, legal institutions, scholars: these initiated, or were drawn into, both wars of words and of military engagement. It is appropriate that the opening sentence of Donne's dedication of *Pseudo-Martyr* to King James I introduces a martial simile: 'As Temporall armies consist of Press'd men, and voluntaries, so doe they also in this warfare, in which your Majestie hath appear'd by your Bookes' (*Pseudo-Martyr* 3; on textual problems with this edition, see Ch. 5 above). Donne cannot exempt himself from 'this Battaile'. The figurative military language continues with reference to 'your strong and full Garisons, which are your Cleargie, and your Universities', indicating Donne's acute awareness of his status as a layman involving himself in theological controversy. Yet his book aspires also to join a 'conversation' (4). Thus Donne signals that, in this unsettled time, historical exigency has refashioned the genre of the controversial treatise as a polemical instrument, one, however, that will not forsake the expected manners of civilized, witty discourse, of 'conversation'. Into this wide ambit the treatise draws a number of genres, subgenres, and modes found elsewhere in Renaissance imaginative literature.

The controversial treatise, a serviceable genre since antiquity, disputes any body of knowledge for which there exists a more or less acknowledged orthodoxy: scientific, philosophical, theological, political, ethical, and so on. This genre flourishes where competing bodies of belief confront each other. Its fundamental characteristic is to demonstrate superior, corrective knowledge, or belief, and to denigrate flawed or misleading understanding. Its tone can register everything from the satirical jeer through the quietly reasonable to the irenical embrace. Among the most potent influences on Donne, masters of the genre in the humanist tradition, were Erasmus and Thomas More. Both occur in interesting guises in *Pseudo-Martyr*. In the self-revelatory Preface, with playful irony, Donne remarks, 'Since *Erasmus*... is called by *Bellarmine* a Halfe-Christian, these men will certainly be more rigid and severe upon me' (12). More is invoked not specifically as Thomas More, martyred for refusing an oath that denied papal supremacy, but rather as one who, although firm in his Catholic faith, sought to *'deliver the world from superstition, which was crept in under Religion'* (94). To this end, he translated Lucian, thus mocking those who invent fables of saints and of damnation that *'make an olde woman weepe or tremble'* (94). Thus, Donne's persona in *Pseudo-Martyr* imbues the tincture of satirical scepticism. Erasmus's personal aversion to martyrdom—'if strife were to break out, I shall behave like Peter' (Erasmus 1988: 259; Letter 1218 to Richard Pace)—fits well with the agenda of *Pseudo-Martyr*, as does his irenical reputation. More is problematic, for many would remember Cardinal Pole's (Mary Tudor's chief theologian) vivid image, that in the deaths of More and Fisher the finger of God had written his book of 'very holy martyrs of God... not with ink but with blood' (qtd. in Duffy 2009: 36). Roman Catholic apologists had gone some way, also, to eliding More's role as an avid persecutor of heresy (Dillon 183)—not an aspect of his celebrated ancestor that Donne had any need to emphasize.

Did the controversial treatise bring with it generic expectations anything like as specific as those associated with more 'literary' productions such as the sonnet sequence or the epic? Given categories of 'central' and 'peripheral' genres (Fowler 1982: 11–12), *Pseudo-Martyr* as Controversial Treatise must belong to the latter category. To the list of genres of ambiguous literary status, such as histories, essays, philosophical, and scientific treatises, the controversial treatise might, without much objection, be appended. Indeed, several examples from the sequence of treatises to which Donne's belongs, those contesting the Jacobean Oath of Allegiance, are various bundles of all the ambiguous genres in this list.

Like the Renaissance humanist encyclopedic anatomy, also derived from classical antiquity, *Pseudo-Martyr* reorders what Raspa calls 'a universe of ideas' to address a particular issue of great moment (*Pseudo-Martyr* xii). This formulation would not have surprised Donne's contemporaries. They would have recognized the structure of this Treatise as including, for instance, the lineaments of church history from the Fathers to their own time, even though that aspect might be subsidiary to their immediate reception of the text as contentious journalism arguing up-to-the-minute issues. Even so, its 'uniqueness' lies in harnessing humanist scholarly method to its treatment of contemporary concerns (xiv). With this aim and this method comes the spirit of humanist scepticism, the dominant mode of the controversial treatise as handled by Donne. His account of himself in the Preface also serves to epitomize his preparation for *Pseudo-Martyr* and to establish his credentials: 'I...survayed and digested the whole body of Divinity, controverted betweene ours and the Romane Church' (13). Thus Donne acknowledges the intellectual continuity of his Treatise and gestures towards a potential generic affinity between the component parts of that extensive controversy—of which he has made a digest, or systematic condensation—in the phrase 'body of Divinity'. Simultaneously, as one who has 'digested' all, he raises an anticipation of going beyond the established bounds of the controversy, thus testing the reader's expectations of the genre.

The organization of *Pseudo-Martyr* strongly suggests also the presence of the 'disputed question' genre, especially in chapter headings such as that of chapter 2, an argument: '*That there may be an inordinate and corrupt affectation of Martyrdome.*' This 'question' had been continuously in play in England since the Marian burnings of the 1560s, when Roman Catholic apologists denied that heretics who went 'gladly...to the fyre' were genuine martyrs (Duffy 2009: 89 and *passim*). The 'cause', not the 'suffering', was the touchstone of authenticity. In other headings the tone set is that of dispassionate scholarly inquiry, as in chapter 6: '*A comparison of the Obedience due to Princes, with the severall obediences requir'd and exhibited in the Romane Church*' (*Pseudo-Martyr* 130), which then attacks '*blind Obedience, and stupiditie*' and other evils. The heading itself constitutes a compressed polemic. We are close here, too, to Donne's Problems, a related genre in which he worked even as he composed *Pseudo-Martyr* (see Ch. 17 above). Of particular interest is the Problem 'Why Doe young Laymen so much study Divinity?' (*Problems* 27–8), which glances at the recent, general neglect of such study, either because English clergy were busy only with preferment—a charge made also in one of Donne's Letters connected with *Pseudo-Martyr* (*Letters* 160)—or because Rome was impregnable until 'the Lutherans broke downe theyr uttermost stubborne dores and the Calvinists pick'd theyr inwardest and subtillest locks' (*Problems* 27). Here Donne expresses metaphorically his interpretation of the sources, and the course, of this polemical warfare, and goes on to express his *saeva indignatio*, not only at the multiplicity of heresies, but even more so at 'a dull and stupid security in which many grosse things are swallowed', which aids the Devil more than 'debating religion' does (27).

From the times of the early Christian Church, sectarian controversy arose out of disputes over authority and legitimacy, both scriptural and ecclesiastical, from which flowed bitter disputes over articles of faith and of heresy. These matters form the vast, detailed, scholarly, and historical disquisition that is *Pseudo-Martyr*. But the central issue is the papal claim of supremacy, specifically the power to depose heretical rulers and, necessarily, the authority to determine what is and is not heresy—a claim clashing with the English Crown's assertion of its complete independence from papal pretensions. Thus a great irruption of the ancient contest of church and state ensued. This is the master narrative of Christendom from which arise the numerous contentions in the form of histories that the later controversialists deploy in their causes.

The Reformation (or reformations) set in motion by Luther's opening salvo took many courses, but did nothing to diminish the intensity of the contest between church and state, notwithstanding the emergence of cults that repudiated both temporal and spiritual authorities. On the contrary, it intensified and complicated the narrative. Thus the Oath of Allegiance controversy can profitably be read in the context of the longer-running controversy over martyrdom following Henry VIII's break with Rome. The phase was initiated by John Foxe's *Book of Martyrs*, as it was popularly known, which exerted enormous influence from its first English edition in 1563 into the late seventeenth century. Foxe was, of course, not alone in the enterprise of constructing, or recovering, a church of the elect that pre-dated the Reformation (see Questier 1996: 23–30). The pathway to this vision required demonstrating the validity of the reformed religion by heavy emphasis on its own roll of martyrs, many of recent memory, celebrated in passages that have been dubbed 'pyre-side' narratives (Duffy 2009: 83). Foxe's most notable English opponent, the greatly admired polemicist, Robert Persons, SJ, counter-attacked in numerous publications, some pseudonymous, that *inter alia* disputed the question of valid martyrdoms in England. As Foxe claimed for the Reformers the recovery of the pure primitive church, so Persons aimed to demonstrate that only in the Roman Church did the true faith continue undefiled. His *A Treatise of Three Conversions* (1603–4) denounces Foxe's list as pseudo-martyrs (Houliston 2007: 96–103). He was to be one of Donne's most formidable opponents. As leader of the ultramontane Catholics who called on fellow religionists to reject the Oath of Allegiance, enacted into law in June 1606 directly after the Gunpowder Plot, Persons actively encouraged martyrdom. Yet he was careful to distinguish the reasonableness and steadfastness he regarded as essential to authentic martyrdom from the fanatical disposition he attributed to Protestant heretics (Clancy 134–5). Persons succeeded in re-centring English Catholicism on the papacy after the relative indifference to papal claims of the Marian regime (Duffy 2009: 196, 190). This achievement, however, caused a split in the Roman Catholic community that King James's Oath of Allegiance sought to exploit.

The historical actions arising from the struggle between the papacy and independently minded national churches of north-western Europe—Scottish, English, French (or Gallican, as it was known), and Swedish, for example—flourish in scholarly inquiry. In the case of England, the execution of Mary, Queen of Scots, the defeat of the Spanish Armada, the excommunications of Elizabeth I and James I, the St Bartholomew Day massacre, the assassination of the French king Henri IV, and the Gunpowder Plot all continue to resonate in both the popular and the scholarly imagination. So do some of those celebrated as martyrs—the Protestants commemorated by Foxe, notably bishops Latimer and Ridley and Archbishop Cranmer, and such Roman Catholics as Edmund Campion, SJ, Robert Southwell, SJ (the poet), Fr William Harrington, and Henry Garnett, SJ. The memory of Thomas More—who refused an oath—remains fresh. But the methods and conventions of dispute on canon law and political theory by which the legality of such events was contested are far removed, the disputants themselves largely forgotten. Except for Donne. But, it is not for his mastery of canon law or for *Pseudo-Martyr* that he is celebrated.

The reign of Elizabeth saw religious controversy issue forth in violent, satirical language, and frequently in pamphlet form, most notably in the 'Martin Marprelate' exchanges of the late 1580s. These satires—Puritan rejections of episcopal governance—witty and scurrilous, are related to such popular genres as balladry. They are not controversial treatises, having no pretension to careful, protracted, and documented exposition. But they, and their rejoinders, are rich in wit and invective. A similar linguistic vigour marks the deprecations and reproofs the controversialists lay on their opponents, frequently in the guise of Christian charity. It is likely that the spirit of the Marprelate pasquils, and Thomas Nashe's salty responses, flavours the controversy to which *Pseudo-Martyr* belongs.

In the shorter reign of James, although many more controversies were published they display a greater 'richness and mellowness', reflecting the developing 'patristic and even scholastic learning' in the established church (Milward vii–viii). *Pseudo-Martyr* plays a part in that development, though it should not be thought that satirical thrusts, even vituperation and railing, were suddenly eliminated from the genre or the expectations of readers. Neither Donne's writing nor, especially, the responses it elicited supports such a view. Yet the practice of refuting Rome's or Canterbury's positions principally by citing the other's own apologists and theologians in a scholarly, forensic manner, for the most part, controlled the moral high ground.

But any moral advantage gained could be easily forfeited by simply neglecting the cardinal rule of polemics: 'leaving an attack unanswered.' Chief Justice Sir Edward Coke's failure to answer an attack by Persons created a vacuum that Donne called attention to without actually writing in Coke's defense (Clancy 121). Given the 'fact that the rival polemical arsenals were equally matched', as it may appear from a much later historical perspective (Questier 1996: 33), anxiety about possible defeat in controversy—which certainly afflicted the English Protestant establishment at the time of the Oath of Allegiance controversy—persisted. It was a reality, just as changes of mind and conversions, which were remarkably numerous, were attributed to the persuasiveness of controversial writers. The achievement of persuasiveness was a key goal of the genre, and to this end a number of characteristics typical of the genre can be observed.

The ground selected by the controversialist had to be of central importance. Often Roman apologists argued the apostolic continuity of their church and, from that, the authority of the See of Rome. English Protestant apologists, increasingly in the seventeenth century, elaborated an argument for their church's continuity from the primitive church, from which line, it followed, Rome had at crucial junctures departed. When argument was joined, therefore, historiography was the most contested site, calling upon readings of the Fathers and of church councils, and interpretations of historical accounts of heresies and schisms. Learning that could accomplish such tasks—learning of a high order, requiring fluency in classical and

Renaissance Latin, in classical and scriptural Greek, as well as (to a lesser degree) Hebrew—and its carefully annotated display are indispensable to the genre. Rejoinders to controversial gambits were, necessarily, obliged in some measure to respond point by point to their opponents while attempting to wrest the initiative away by highlighting lacunae and, often, dismissing allegedly major claims of their opponents as no more than matters indifferent. The latter argument against necessary articles of Roman faith became a staple of the genre in Protestant treatises and is especially well honed by Donne.

In *Pseudo-Martyr* Donne assures the reader that his scholarly method is scrupulous, thus inviting generic identification of the book as a scholarly treatise and toning down the polemical imperative. Although not bound 'precisely and superstitiously' to the text, he has 'no where made any Author, speake more or lesse, in sense, then hee intended' (10). Perhaps Donne would be spared Francis Bacon's general censure of 'controversies of religion, which have so much diverted men from other sciences', and their 'fury...wherewith the church laboureth' (F. Bacon 1857–74: 3.477, 481). Indeed, the Dean of Canterbury praised Bacon and *Pseudo-Martyr* for discrediting schoolmen's learning (Bald 1970, quoting John Boys, the Dean of Canterbury, who in 1610 commends Donne on catching a 'shipfull of their [the canonists] fooleries', 226; Keynes 1973: 6).

Pseudo-Martyr's array of learning, in addition to theology and mastery of languages, includes document-based historiography (anticipating seventeenth-century advances), political theory, literary criticism (for instance, catching Bembo straying into 'prophane elegancies' [81], or Bellarmino 'mutilating' a Latin sentence [71–2]), and textual criticism in identifying doctrinal intrusions into key texts ('this rage of detorting scriptures' [82]). Donne draws on his familiarity with the sciences, especially medicine, mathematics, and navigation—Raspa's 'universe of ideas' (xii)—to invigorate complex arguments with vivid figures. His mastery of jurisprudence, especially of canon law, is seen throughout. So provided by his Inns of Court studies, and his 'Hydroptique immoderate' reading (*Letters* 51) (perhaps one should add to these strengths the professed inspiration of King James), he engages with, and often sets against each other, the most prestigious proponents of papal supremacy: cardinals Bellarmino, Baronius, and Du Perron; the Jesuits James Gretser and Robert Persons. Perhaps with the 'Appellants controversy' in mind, Donne refers to Persons as an 'ordinary'—that is, one with jurisdiction—instrument of the devil whose books have 'drawne more of that bloud, which they call Catholique, in this Kingdome, then all our Acts of Parliament have done' (9).

The Appellants were Roman Catholic priests who objected to the 1598 papal appointment of an archpriest rather than a bishop to govern English Catholic clergy. Catholic opinion was deeply divided by the Appellants controversy, so bitterly that one appellant priest denounced Persons, who, at that juncture, supported the archpriest appointment, as an instrument of the devil. The secular clergy, following the Archpriest George Blackwell's initial acceptance of the oath, argued that they were loyal subjects of the King, although many baulked at the theology of the oath

(Pritchard 193). Neither the Jesuit mission, controlled by Persons, nor Rome would allow any such compromise. Cardinal Bellarmino's letter to Blackwell of September 1607 admonishes the archpriest that he risks losing 'an eternal weight of glory' for fear of a 'light & momentarie tribulation'. He reminds Blackwell that Thomas More 'led the way to *Martyrdome* to many others, to the exceeding glory of the English nation'. This application of 2 Corinthians 4:17 to martyrdom is also employed by Protestants. Bellarmino's valediction is: 'Quite [*sic*] you like a man, and let your heart be strengthened' (James I 1918: 84–5). King James includes the Cardinal's letter in his *Triplici Nodo.... Or An Apologie for the Oath of Allegiance*, and undertakes a brief 'Answere' but does so with 'no desire of vaine-glory by matching with so learned a man' (85). It fell to Donne to undertake a full response.

But James's own response, although brief, laid down certain markers that Donne took up. However brilliant a controversialist Bellarmino might be, his arguments are 'guilded pilles, as full of exterior eloquence, as of inward vntrewthes' (James I 1918: 85), and James catches out Bellarmino manipulating his citations—'detortion', as Donne labelled the practice—and even goes so far as to call the Cardinal a liar. A necessary element in the controversial genre, of course, is to discredit the credentials of the most potent opponent. This is clearly important to him, but James also makes surprisingly clear the purpose of the oath: to divide 'ciuilly obedient Papists' from 'peruerse disciples of the Powder-Treason' (85). It becomes Donne's task to dissuade English Catholics from hearkening to the siren call of martyrdom—which he understood only too well—not with the chimera of religious toleration, which he is in no way able to offer, but with extensive and grounded reasoning that locates the decision of each Catholic in conscience, rather than hope of political expediency.

In dramatic language Donne arraigns the Jesuits before the court, and on the stage, of history:

you excell in... kindling and blowing, begetting and nourishing jelousies in Princes, and contempt in Subjects, dissention in families, wrangling in Schooles, and mutinies in Armies; ruines of Noble houses, corruption of blood, confiscation of States, torturing of bodies, an anxious entangling and perplexing of consciences.... you are in your institution mixt and complexioned of all Elements, and you hange betweene Heaven and Earth, like *Meteors* of an ominous and incendiarie presaging. (*Pseudo-Martyr* 106)

Such language would not be out of place in Shakespeare. This dramatic denunciation of the corrosive effects of Jesuits on the fabric of society at every level is Donne's vivid reworking of a central theme of the controversial genre. Just as Roman Catholic polemicists railed against the social destruction wrought by Reformist heresy, so Protestants returned the accusation with equal or greater opprobrium.

Throughout *Pseudo-Martyr*, as legal brief, the case for the defence, 'lawyerly finesse' controls the argument (Houliston 2006: 477). Satirical and mocking tones, Menippean in spirit as befits an anatomy, sound frequently alongside earnest exhortation and personal confession in the mode of spiritual autobiography, or disarming acknowledgement of a digression. In short, tonal suppleness and verbal dexterity, delight in paradox and conceit, play their parts in creating the unique Donnean texture.

To do battle over such a broad territory requires organized argument, and the fact of its having been organized according to exacting, systematic, scholarly standards needs to be displayed. The subtitle of *Pseudo-Martyr*—'Wherein out of certaine Propositions and Gradations, This Conclusion is evicted. That Those which are of the Romane Religion in this Kingdome, may and ought to take the Oath of Allegeance'—manifests scholarship in a tone of reassuring reasonableness and measured reflection, notwithstanding its deliberately infuriating effect on opponents. Donne is well aware of the propensity of controversy to provoke or inflame violence, as he denies any intention in his own work of continuing a 'Booke-warre' that might provoke exasperation, 'to draw out the civill sword in causes, which have some pretence and colour of being spirituall' (*Pseudo-Martyr* 12). Yet the tone of the genre is established from the outset between the parameters of violence and subtlety, striking a note that, although clearly heard in *Pseudo-Martyr*, often modulates into tones of scholarly distress at the gross credulity of so many interpreters and proponents of Roman doctrine.

There are instances on virtually every page of *Pseudo-Martyr* of 'these tumors, & excresences, with which it [the Roman Church] abounds at this time, and swelles daily with new additions' (*Pseudo-Martyr* 191). In this way Donne, without denying the spiritual validity of the Roman Church, undermines any confidence that in the current dispute papal edicts are infallible. Such proceeding suggests the importance contemporary readership accorded the entertainment, instruction, or truth-bearing quotients of a sequence of controversial works such as those arising from the Oath of Allegiance. It is probably vain to discriminate between these qualities when, in all likelihood, readers sought all three and more—including the agile, witty deployment of vast learning so admired across the whole spectrum of written and spoken language. Style, in short.

The persistence of qualities that make up style in treatises of many varieties, long after their freight of knowledge or information became irrelevant, promotes generically peripheral works to literary or almost literary status. Examples from the age of Donne are plentiful. Persons has been described as 'one of the best writers of Elizabethan prose, natural and easy, admired by Swift' (Rowse 41). It is possible, then, for a controversialist to live on as a stylist. Yet of Donne's prose works *Pseudo-Martyr* is probably the least likely to be found on a curriculum of literary studies, despite its being, perhaps, the most interesting treatise in the Tudor and Stuart phases of religious controversy in English, not only because of its contribution to the debate surrounding the Oath of Allegiance, but also for its place in the Donne canon and its relevance to understanding Donne's life and thought.

For example, one section of the 'ADVERTISEMENT TO *the Reader*', containing the well-known passages on Donne's family, his education, and his having 'beene ever kept awake in a meditation of Martyrdome' (8), is of exceptional interest in the quest for the 'real' Donne who might be concealed behind his public masks. So is a passage in the second Preface addressed to 'Priestes and Jesuits', describing his spiritual *agon* prior to settling his religious convictions: 'I had a longer worke to doe then many other men; for I was first to blot out, certaine impressions of the Romane religion, and to wrastle both against the examples and against the reasons, by which some hold was taken; and some anticipations early layde upon my conscience' (13). This strenuous exercise, with its grave effects upon his fortunes and his reputation, conjures up heroic mental strife and might be regarded as the prose equivalent of striving to reach Truth standing on a 'huge hill, / Cragged, and steep', about which 'and about must goe' the seeker of *Sat3* (ll. 79–81).

Such spiritual and intellectual athleticism is interestingly in tension with his expression in the same Preface of his 'naturall impatience not to digge painefully in deepe, and stony, and sullen learnings' (*Pseudo-Martyr* 12). For many readers the vast body of the work that follows from this 'declaration of my selfe' (13) is indeed 'stony and sullen'. The avalanche of scholastic learning that descends on the would-be reader quickly drove modern scholars from *Pseudo-Martyr*, leaving behind them pronouncements on its dullness and on the monomania of any reader determined to make it through. The same might be alleged of virtually every controversial treatise of the time. A desert of 'unrelieved somberness, allusiveness, and tight argumentation', in the words of Robert H. Ray, whose *John Donne Companion* (1990) has probably guided some readers into other paths. 'If Donne had written nothing but this work', Ray concludes, 'he and it would be virtually unknown today' (265). Yet the fact that this is Donne's work obliges commentators to find a niche for it in the edifice of his widely admired productions, a place in the canon. The editor of *Ignatius His Conclave*, for instance, writes that 'even the most devoted of Donne students will not want to spend much time on his controversial prose works. These can only be of serious interest in their relation to his poetry and the sermons' (*Ignatius* xxxviii).

Although by its nature the controversial treatise is ephemeral, some scholars have discerned more durable properties in *Pseudo-Martyr*. As A. L. Rowse declares, it is 'mistakenly little read by literary scholars, though it is Donne's most important prose work and of acute historical significance' (70). Moreover, as Peter Milward points out, it is of interest to a 'student of literature and its religious background' in what has been termed the age of Shakespeare, Donne, and the young Milton (ix–x). There is also its delayed effect to take into account. Donne was a potent influence on the Erasmian circle of Great Tew when it was composing religious tracts and histories, and commemorative verse in the 1630s just before the Civil War, as was Thomas Nashe for laughing the Marprelate sectaries off the stage (Roebuck 1999: 23–5). This suggests that major controversial treatises enjoyed some afterlife as both ecclesiological-theological and literary products, and further suggests the mixed nature of the genre.

That *Pseudo-Martyr* plays a role in political history, defending the validity of the Oath of Allegiance, and thus contributes to the shape of the modern nation state, is an unexceptionable assumption. How to assess that role's distinctness from the imperatives of Donne's own career ambitions is contested territory. Thus, Donne's presumed intention in writing *Pseudo-Martyr* is a question central to recent scholarship. Dedicated to James I in words adapted from the Queen of Sheba to King Solomon—'happie are those thy Servants, which stand before thee alwayes'—and with the claim to have 'your Majesties permission' (*Pseudo-Martyr* 4), the work has been taken as pro-government propaganda—a bid for royal favour and preferment. Izaak Walton's account of this stage of Donne's career has King James, as the instigator of the task, commanding Donne to draw arguments into a method (1675: 35). The proposed contents of his treatise—the 'heads' or topics—Donne circulated for suggestions and criticisms. In undated Letters to Sir Henry Goodere, his familiar friend, he asks for the return of a document in question as well as his papers and books (*Letters* 225–6, 68–9), and it appears from the 'ADVERTISEMENT TO *the Reader*' of *Pseudo-Martyr* that some Roman Catholics were included in this circulation, who 'having onely seene the Heads and Grounds handled in this Booke' have traduced him as 'an impious and profane under-valuer of Martyrdome' (8). Other requests of the reader to correct with his pen printing errors (a list of errata follows; Donne 1610: sig. ¶2^v) and to take note that the two advertised final chapters (13 and 14) are omitted because in the many months of circulation these were 'quarrelled by some, and desired by others' (*Pseudo-Martyr* 8–9) draw attention to his punctilious procedure.

Donne's contribution to defending both the oath and King James's *Triplici nodo, triplex cuneus* ('A triple wedge for a triple knot')—James's own apology for the oath, first published in Latin and English editions in 1607—brought him academic recognition with an honorary master's degree from Oxford in 1610. Further honour—the Cambridge Doctor of Divinity degree—was conferred only after Donne's ordination in 1615, and, it seems, against the university's inclination (Chamberlain 1.589). *Pseudo-Martyr* no doubt also helped to repair his reputation, damaged by his ambivalence in religion that lay him 'open to many mis-interpretations' (*Pseudo-Martyr* 13). It did not, however, succeed in winning for him state employment. *Pseudo-Martyr* is, therefore, accounted a failure according to that view of Donne's theological writing as essentially opportunistic flattery of the King—an expectation raised by the dedicatory letter.

For example, according to John Carey: 'When Donne put forward this medley of superstition and assertion, which tallied so conveniently with James I's theory of the divine right of kings, he was using, at best, only half his mind'. This, the most denigrating of modern criticisms, goes on to propose for it a (mock?) genre: 'an uproarious saga of sanctified buffoonery' (1981a: 33–4). Others, likewise troubled by Donne's apparent political alignment, read *Pseudo-Martyr* as a pseudo-Controversial Treatise: a work that in the guise of a conventional, closely documented apology for the establishment position reveals to the close reader an intellectual declaration of independence, especially marked in his many assertions of the importance of reason in theological debate. The portmanteau genre of the treatise, on this account, carries elements of other discourses, evidently in tension with it. Freedom of thought is allowed by such 'paradoxical and satirical modes' (Houliston 2006: 486). Thus the more familiar and more agreeable Donne, whose verse can hold in play simultaneously a number of contradictions, can appear in *Pseudo-Martyr* 'jauntily, if not self-destructively, *subversive of* as well as contritely *deferential toward* the Establishment' (Marotti 1986: 182). Such duality of intention may be at work in the irony with which Donne infuses the Controversial Treatise, making possible a reading of *Pseudo-Martyr* in conjunction with Letters to like-minded friends, as expressing 'a point of view of apparent scepticism toward both sides' (Flynn 1973: 66).

Other critical approaches have investigated the suspicion of subversion by demonstrating that some parts of Donne's argument against the theoretical basis of Rome's claims to temporal supremacy might just as readily be turned against James's claims for the divine sanction of monarchy. This point, characterized as Donne arguing against James, rather than in his favour (A. Patterson 1991: 262), hinges principally on a brief passage in *Pseudo-Martyr* discussing, hypothetically, the most primitive occurrence of political authority:

if...a company of Savadges, or men whom an overloaded kingdome had avoided [i.e. cast out]...should create a *King*, and reserve to themselves a libertie to revenge their owne wrongs, upon one another, or to doe any act necessary to that end, for which a King hath his authority, this liberty were swallowed in their first acte, and onely the creation of the King were the worke of rectified reason, to which God had concurr'd, and that *reservation* a voide and impotent act of their appetite. (*Pseudo-Martyr* 133–4)

Donne characterizes 'rectified reason' as 'Nature', and argues that God duly 'instils such a power as we wish' in the person chosen (132). This opens the possibility of the chosen person being pope, or doge of Venice, or other elected magistrate. Hence arises the suspicion of democratically inclined subversion in the treatise, or of Donne stumbling upon his own republicanism (Stevens 67).

Brief though this passage is, it suggests continuity of Donne's thought with passages in *Biathanatos* where he probes the idea of the law of nature, finding that the term 'is so variously and vnconstantly deliuer'd, as I confesse I read it abundant tymes, before I vnderstood it once' (*Biathanatos* 40). But what it boils down to is, '*Fly Euill, Seeke Good*. That is, Do according to Reason' (46). Donne seems less concerned to dig for the anthropological roots of politics than to underline the supreme importance of peaceable and religious tranquillity—a theme to which he often turns in *Pseudo-Martyr*. Indeed, he deliberately abstains from speculation on the endlessly debatable theory of origins (*Pseudo-Martyr* 131) in favour of the proposition, '*Nature* teaches him to obey him that can preserve him' (175).

Perhaps uncertainty—virtually a principle in Donne's thinking on matters of faith and doctrine—rather than subversion, colours this discussion in *Pseudo-Martyr*.

Again and again Donne questions the grounds of doctrines promulgated by the Council of Trent and subsequent papal pronouncements, arguing that in many instances they change, even reverse, the simpler, fewer necessary beliefs agreed upon by the Fathers and the early church. Some of these, carefully compiled from Catholic commentaries, come about as results of copyists' errors in Latin, such as the ludicrous declaration of Pope Adrian VI that '*al Poetry was Hereticall*' (196). Misled by an error in a copy of Gratian's *Decretum*—*Hereticus versibus* for *Heroicis versibus*—this Pope showed himself as fallible as any other person. Gratian (with numerous subsequent commentaries) is a rich source of error for Donne's purposes, but not unique. Indeed, Donne generalizes on the unreliability of canons—their fictions—and warns Roman Catholics against being drawn by them into self-murder and treason (196). He plays many variations of this theme announced in the 'Preface to The Priestes, and Jesuits, and to their Disciples in this Kingdome', cautioning those who are 'hungerie of poison…Ambitious of ruine…pervious and penetrable to all meanes of destruction' (23).

Deeply immersed in studies, of which *Pseudo-Martyr* is the fruit, Donne conveys in a Letter to Goodere his acute critique of the formation of dogmatic truth: just as litigious men, tired out by lawsuits, and princes, tired out by war, agree to terms they are soon ashamed of, 'so Philosophers, and so all sects of Christians, after long disputations and controversies, have allowed many things for positive and dogmaticall truths which are not worthy of that dignity' (*Letters* 12–13). Here is the humanist scepticism of *Pseudo-Martyr*. Yet, far from expressing a thoroughly Pyrrhonist attitude, *Pseudo-Martyr* is as much concerned with good and safe grounds of faith as with demonstrating the self-contradictory and, as Donne depicts it, absurdly emphatic dogma emerging from Trent, from proponents of papal supremacy, and from the Jesuits and Franciscans.

This same Letter to Goodere—like an essay—ranges through Western medicine from Hippocrates to the present as an analogue to debates over grace and free will and theories of the nature of the soul. Donne concludes by acknowledging the danger of unrestrained sceptical probes, 'such as shake old opinions, and do not establish new as certain, but leave consciences in a worse danger then they found them in' (*Letters* 18). Yet his scepticism signals his quest for reasonableness in religion, thus anticipating a major intellectual project of the seventeenth century (Shell and Hunt 67).

Several Letters from the period leading up to publication of *Pseudo-Martyr* provide candid testimony of his further wrestling with religion. This struggle includes his profound misgivings about the controversy he was preparing himself to join. The most important of these Letters is again to Goodere, probably from May–June 1609 (*Letters* xix). It starts with a sharp animadversion on the churchmen involved in controversy: 'the Divines of these times, are become meer Advocates, as though Religion were a temporall inheritance; they plead for it with all sophistications, and illusions, and forgeries.… They write for Religion, without it' (*Letters* 160).

The heart of the matter, the 'perplexity'—Donne stresses this is his provisional view, 'as farre as I see yet'—is that 'both sides may be in justice, and innocence; and the wounds which they inflict upon the adverse part, are all *se defendendo*' (ibid.). The oath is a necessary protection of the kingdom against treason, yet it limits the Roman supremacy, which may be no less valid than the prerogative of kings. This is a critical moment: 'the watch is set, and every bodies hammer is upon that anvill' (161). The Church of England side of the protracted, complex, and widening controversy has stumbled badly. Donne's judgement of Bishop William Barlow's response of early 1609 to Robert Persons's attack on *Triplici nodo* is scathing. Not only is Barlow (whom Donne does not name in the Letter) guilty of 'miscitings, or mis-interpretings', but also his tone, notwithstanding pleasant literary ornaments, divine and profane, is 'extremely obnoxious' (161–2). By this term Donne means a condition of weakness, 'apter to admitte...poisonous ingredients' (*Pseudo-Martyr* 100). He applies it also to his own 'humane infirmities' in which he is 'obnoxious enough' (12). It is, therefore, a sharp criticism of Barlow's misuse of the genre. The unscholarly work is full of falsifications of words, sense, facts, and of contradictions, of triviality and flattery and suspect doctrine. Moreover, it fails to defend the King, neglecting 'some enormous advantages which the other gave' (*Letters* 163). He concludes the Letter on the ecumenical note he sounds frequently in his correspondence: despite its fractured condition, Christianity is 'still one Corporation'. Care is to be taken not to draw 'misconclusions' from disunity (164).

This extensive critique is a useful guide to Donne's understanding of the controversial treatise: a list of errors to avoid. By the date of this Letter to Goodere, Donne was evidently well versed in the intricacies of the controversy. A case in point, very significant to English Protestant sensibilities, and contemporaneous, was the dispute between Venice and Pope Paul V which led to the excommunication of Venice and to vigorous disagreement between Roman Catholic controversialists: on the one hand, those supporting the papacy; on the other, those defending the right of the Venetian Republic to oppose clerical intrusion. Fra Paolo Sarpi defended Venice against papal claims advanced most powerfully by Cardinal Bellarmino. His manner of argument, displayed in several treatises swiftly translated and published in English, is similar to Donne's. Donne may have met him in Venice (Bald 1970: 151). The strength of his argument in, for instance, *A Fvll and Satisfactorie Answer to the Late Vnadvised Bull, thundred by Pope Paul the Fift, against the renowmed State of Venice* (1606) depends on the solidity of his learning: 'Hee that will but read all the foresaid Canons, may be fully instructed, that he need no whit to doubt' (72). The certainty here, based on documentary evidence, is in studied contrast to the sceptical doubt with which he treats papal claims to temporal power in Venice. 'By 1610 the whole argument was familiar to Donne's English readers' (*Pseudo-Martyr* 276).

It is a disputed conjecture that for several years Donne had collaborated with his mentor and benefactor, Thomas Morton, Dean of Gloucester, the most learned and able Church of England controversialist of the day, preparing *A Catholike Appeale for Protestants, out of the confessions of the Romane Doctors*, the manuscript of which he read eighteen months before its publication in late 1609 (see Chs. 31.I and 32.I). *Pseudo-Martyr* adopts some of the key strategies of *Catholike Appeale*, especially its generally irenic approach and its concern to realign the term 'Catholic' with its pre-Trent meaning (Shell and Hunt 73–6). Indeed, *Pseudo-Martyr* throughout makes the case that the English Church—'ours' (*Pseudo-Martyr* 13)—is the true catholic church. Part of the title of *Catholike Appeale* points to Donne's determination in *Pseudo-Martyr* to use Catholic writers to make his case. Copious knowledge of, and exact quotation from, opponents' literature had now become a touchstone of controversy. (For the sequences and changing styles of Elizabethan–Jacobean controversy see James I 1918: xlix–lxxx; Clancy *passim*; Bald 1970: 200–36; Milward *passim*; Shell 1999: *passim*.)

Whether or not Donne's prose works, principally *Pseudo-Martyr*, which reveals his most fundamental thought on religion, are his enduring monuments (Sommerville 2003: 73), he writes to deliver his former co-religionists from a crippling, life-threatening restraint. To do this he re-conceptualizes martyrdom, 'across genres... [with] a careful, intellectually rigorous attempt to formulate a moderate response to the powerful contemporary martyr-complex linking suffering with religious confidence' (Monta 132). *Pseudo-Martyr* is therefore a nationalist text, important to the emerging nation state (Stevens 61–7). If this is its principal historical moment, the book also embodies a timeless truth, a penetrating view of the impulse to self-destruction. Donne must be writing from personal experience. Is this what he gestures to in those 'anticipations layde upon my conscience' (*Pseudo-Martyr* 13)? A generic component of *Pseudo-Martyr*, as previously suggested, is spiritual autobiography. In this light, *Pseudo-Martyr* testifies to what Donne succinctly captures in the invocation of the Martyrs in *Lit*: 'begge for us, a discreet patience / Of death, or of worse life: for Oh, to some / Not to be Martyrs, is a martyrdome' (ll. 88–90).

Thomas Fitzherbert, SJ, saw none of this in his jeering riposte of 1613. He complains of Donne's method, his citing 'euery meane, and obscure Catholick writer, to find somewhat to iest at' (F[itzherbert] 96), thus acknowledging, grudgingly, that he is reading a Treatise. Likewise his mocking allusions to Donne's sceptical attitude— 'how bold and confident he is still to speak *without doubt*' (87)—suggest Donne's success, as does his effort to paint *Pseudo-Martyr* as a malicious 'Lucianicall and Atheisticall' pasquil (106). In similarly mocking vein, John Floyd in 1613 depicts Donne as a mere sensualist, known to have a picture of his mistress in his chamber to which he prays '*Lighte[n] my darknes deare Lady*' (Floyd 17). That he had such a picture we might doubt, but he did possess a portrait of Paolo Sarpi which was hanging in his parlour at the Deanery of St Paul's at his death. It was important to him: he bequeathed it in his will.

Although he expected one, Donne never received a full response to his work, and may be regarded as having had the last word (Bald 1970: 226). Perhaps it 'was too closely reasoned and written with too studied a moderation to admit of a reply being easily framed (Keynes 1973: 5). One wonders how Persons would have responded, but he died in Rome in 1610. Nevertheless, *Pseudo-Martyr* became a sure foundation for all Donne's later religious thinking, underlying much of the thought of the Sermons. It transcends the moment, demanding a serious intellectual response. Simpson's pronouncement—'the subject has lost its interest for modern readers' (1948: 189)—does not completely hold true, although the genre that kept seventeenth-century booksellers in business subsequently lost its appeal. Certainly, no modern scholars or critics have sought to enlist Donne's method or argument in ecclesiastical debate, as did the Tractarians of the 1830s and 1840s Oxford Movement, some of whom thought *Pseudo-Martyr* Donne's most important work (Haskin 2006: 237–8). But in recent times scholarship of a historical turn has reassessed *Pseudo-Martyr* on other grounds—work made possible by a historically contextualized edition, a landmark in Donne studies. The detailed, painstaking editor's introduction and indispensable commentary, identifying the disputants to whom Donne refers and alludes, and their works, justify the claim that *Pseudo-Martyr* is 'not a failed piece of literature': 'it is a difficult monument in the literature of the history of ideas' (*Pseudo-Martyr* xiii, l).

CHAPTER 19

THE ESSAY

JEFFREY JOHNSON

MONTAIGNE: THE ESSAY INVENTED

When Michel de Montaigne published *Essais* (two volumes in 1580, and a third in 1588), he effectively established a new literary genre. The late Renaissance was not an era lacking literary ingenuity, nor one bereft of literary genres, and Montaigne's contemporaries realized that meaning is determined as much by style as by matter. So, the question that the appearance of *Essais* raises is this: why would Montaigne, in an age so genre-rich and genre-conscious, reject the established genres and instead create a new one? In addressing this question, we identify the defining characteristics of the essay and thus the criteria for evaluating John Donne's *Essayes in Divinity*.

The first point to note is Montaigne's statement of his intention in *Essais*, namely, 'I have proposed unto my selfe no other than a familiar and private end,...for it is my selfe I pourtray' ('The Author to the Reader'; 1.12). In short, Montaigne's purpose throughout *Essais* is to examine himself as subject matter, and thus, the genre is characterized primarily by its subjectivity, that is, by the 'I' who is both the author and the topic. This subjectivity not only provides the familiar essay with its meditative quality, but it also justifies the need for a distinct genre.

The expectation in Montaigne's era was that authors would choose genres based on their level of accomplishment and expertise, for only by establishing their literary credibility could they claim literary authority. Montaigne, however, avows no expertise and offers his personal reflections as an educated amateur; he selects his own particular ideas, preferences, and opinions as his subject matter, and he fashions himself within a literary style that he labels 'essay', the definition of which is 'a trial', 'a proof', 'a testing' of some topic. Montaigne, therefore, responds to the challenge of literary authority not only by writing about 'so frivolous and vaine a Subject' as himself, but also by labelling his work with a word that by definition suggests an ongoing process of intellectual inquiry.

In addition to subjectivity, Montaigne's invention is also characterized by a pervasive scepticism. This term refers not to a cynical dismissal of ideas, but rather to the thoughtful engagement *with* ideas and the correctives afforded by the exercise of both reason and experience. Montaigne reminds us that this world is full of ambiguities and contradictions (see 'Of the inconstancy of our actions' [Book 2] and 'Of profit and honestie' [Book 3]), and all of us are nothing 'but a botching and party-coloured worke', as evidenced by the opinion of painters, 'that the motions and wrinkles in the face, which serve to weepe, serve also to laugh' ('We taste nothing purely'; 2.410). The vagaries of life and the dappled realities of human nature call forth Montaigne's scepticism, which for him *is* epistemology; informed doubt becomes his method for knowing.

This formal scepticism can be recognized in the stylistic features of *Essais*, which consist of a rambling composite of quotations, digressions, anecdotes, and apparent contradictions, a montage of subjects that shift abruptly without transitions, that include more topics than the one announced in the title (or that move far afield from the title), and that offer a closure that is more suggestive than emphatic because the topic is almost always open for further exploration. Thus, stylistically, Montaigne prefers writing that avoids the affected use of rhetorical ornament, writing that moves quickly from point to point and employs loosely structured sentences.

Montaigne's tastes in reading-matter, as well as the models influencing his style, align him more with the author-oriented approach of Plutarch and Seneca than with the subject-oriented approach of Cicero, and thus the writings that Montaigne finds 'fittest' for him are those that 'ammuse and busie themselves more about counsels than events, more about that which commeth from within, than that which appeareth outward' ('Of Bookes'; 2.104). Montaigne's preference for the inner workings of persons might be read as an expression of self-fashioning, of late Renaissance individualism. The occasions that give rise to the subjects explored in *Essais* are matters of particular import to the author, whose inner life is realized in these personal expressions. Yet, in spite of Montaigne's introspective subjectivity, the intention of *Essais* is not the promotion of individualistic identity through a radical opposition to society.

Montaigne's aim throughout *Essais* is the development of virtue, the concern for which always extends beyond the self to the community. A civic-mindedness thus pervades *Essais*. Yet as Montaigne articulates in his provocative 'Of custom' (Book 1), the common good that can result from those who have been properly trained in virtue does not remove the tensions between individual liberties and state regulations. In contemplating these tensions, Montaigne concludes that the benefit resulting from study and private meditation is primarily 'to prove better, wiser, and honester' in the commerce of communal interactions ('Of the institution and education of Children'; 1.157).

THE ENGLISH ESSAYISTS

There is evidence that in England Montaigne was read in French and also that translated portions of *Essais* (by John Florio and possibly by others) may have circulated in manuscript before Florio's text became the first published English translation (1603). One English reader of Montaigne is William Cornwallis, who published his own *Essayes* in 1600, and then a year later added twenty-four pieces to the original set of twenty-five (with three more included in the 1606 edition). While Cornwallis's work is not a slavish imitation of Montaigne's, there are distinct similarities. The topics, the manner of treatment, and the titles of Cornwallis's essays echo Montaigne's, even to the point of Cornwallis's insistence that if his pieces stray from the topic, he will not mend their course ('Of Essaies and Bookes' [1946: 202]). More substantively, however, Cornwallis's *Essayes* display the same characteristic subjectivity as Montaigne's, the same scepticism (including a complementary tone of stoicism), and the same concern for virtue. The two thus share a similar civic-mindedness, which for Cornwallis entails not only training the soul in virtue, but also healing the soul by opening one's private contemplations for the common weal (see 'Of Life, and the fashions of Life').

Yet the manner in which Cornwallis discusses the exercise of virtue distinguishes his writing from Montaigne's. In such essays as 'Of Advise', 'Of Ambition', and 'Of Feare', Cornwallis exhibits the idealism and assurance of the 22-year-old youth that he was at the time. Because of his relative inexperience, it is not surprising to discover a young moralist whose vision is much more prescriptive and far less ambiguous than Montaigne's. In addition, Cornwallis redefines the genre by stating that Montaigne's writings and Plutarch's short pieces are not proper essays, by describing himself as a 'newly bound Prentise to the inquisition of knowledge', and by offering the apology that his attempt in the genre is '"But an Essay", like a Scriuenour trying his Pen before he ingrosseth his worke' ('Of Essaies and Bookes'; 190).

In spite of Cornwallis's brash youthfulness, and the complications of literary credibility accompanying it, his *Essayes* are readily acknowledged as genuine expressions of the genre that afford him a legitimate claim to being the first English essayist. Even though Francis Bacon published a volume titled *Essayes* in 1597, this collection poses certain problems of genre that complicate any challenge Bacon may have to precedence. The 1597 *Essayes* consists of only ten very short pieces, and because transitions are virtually non-existent, the thought resides at the sentence level, each piece presenting itself more like a formal, though loosely grouped, series of maxims offered by a counsellor than the personal, familiar essays Cornwallis developed in the tradition of Montaigne.

Of further note is Robert Johnson's *Essaies, or, Rather Imperfect Offers* published in 1601. This volume of sixteen pieces is essentially a conduct book in which Johnson discusses each topic rather briefly, using an approach dominated by precepts and aphorisms regarding rules for governing oneself in civic life. A much stronger representation of the genre is found in Daniel Tuvill's *Essaies Politicke, and Morall* (1608) and his *Essayes Morall and Theologicall* (1609), containing nine and twelve pieces, respectively, all of which are more substantially developed than Johnson's. While both of Tuvill's volumes show a penchant for the precept, the pieces include a wide range of learning (from Latin, Greek, and Hebrew writers, to the Church Fathers, as well as to Montaigne) that Tuvill combines, in loosely structured discourses, with his own experiences and observations. Finally, the sixteen pieces in Nicholas Breton's *Characters vpon Essaies: Morall, and Divine* (1615) rely on the witty manner of the character to present each topic as an extended definition, and are notable more for Breton's dedication of the volume to Bacon than for their development of the genre.

Because Bacon's 1597 volume and those by Johnson, Tuvill, and Breton are works characterized by their aphoristic advice rather than their subjectivity and scepticism, none of them fully articulates the tradition established by Montaigne and reaffirmed by Cornwallis. However, with the appearance of Bacon's substantially revised *Essayes* in 1612, which were further expanded and refined in 1625 to fifty-eight selections, the English essay emerges in its most recognized form. The dedications of these two later editions, to Prince Henry and to King James's favourite (George Villiers, Duke of Buckingham), respectively, and the expanded title of 1625, *The Essayes or Covnsels, Civall and Morall*, underscore Bacon's abiding concern for civil business, as well as his desire to demonstrate his abilities as a counsellor.

Along with this central focus, it is also Bacon's style that accounts for the more formal, and much less familiar, tone of these later renditions. Bacon uses parallelism, aphorism, symmetry, and vivid and concrete language to create his highly individual style. It is a style that, on the one hand, complements his intellectual habit of classifying, dividing, and labelling knowledge into ordered expressions of reality. On the other hand, Bacon's style suits his method of setting what he refers to as the broken language of maxims, proverbs, and *sententiae* in opposition as a means for assaying their contradictions. Thus, the experience of reading Bacon's *Essayes* is one in which the reader becomes consistently unsettled by the absence of emphatic closure, and this purposefully unfinished mode of inquiry establishes Bacon's scepticism.

Donne's *Essayes in Divinity*

This overview of the essay prepares us for Donne's expression of the genre. Far more is unknown than is known about the historical circumstances surrounding *Essayes in Divinity*. At the initiative of Donne's son, John Jr., *Essayes* first appeared in print in 1651, twenty years after Donne's death. Donne's son states that at the time of writing *Essayes* his father *'was obliged in Civill business, and had no ingagement in that of the Church'* (*Essayes* 3). Because both Donne and his son indicate that *Essayes* was written prior to Donne's taking holy orders, the *terminus ad quem* for its composition is 1615, and 1611 is the date typically given for when Donne began the work. Even though we lack a precise date of composition, the range of dates still situates *Essayes* as one of the earliest examples of the genre in English. Also problematic is the title, *Essayes in Divinity: Being Several Disquisitions, Interwoven with Meditations and Prayers*; it is not known whether Donne or his son created this title. The words '*Disquisitions*' and '*Prayers*' also raise questions related to the work's genre, the former indicating a long, elaborate written account (in contrast to the brevity of early English essays), and the latter appearing altogether out of place since no other early collection of essays contains prayers.

Beyond these matters, the purpose and audience of *Essayes in Divinity* are difficult to determine. In 'To the Reader', Donne's son describes his father's work as 'the voluntary sacrifices of severall hours, when he had many debates betwixt God and himself, whether he were worthy, and competently learned to enter into Holy Orders' (5). This statement indicates that Donne conceived the work as a private endeavour for demonstrating his fitness for ministry. In addition, Donne adds to the difficulties of purpose and audience by further complicating the identification of the work's genre when he refers to it as 'these Sermons', explaining that they 'lack thus much of Sermons, that they have no Auditory' (47–8).

The early essayists, as noted above, cultivate a meditative quality in their work as they contemplate the exercise of morals and virtue. However, while religion at times provides a context for such meditations, none of the early essayists, except for Donne, makes Christian religion the matter and the style, the object and the wit. In fact, *Essayes in Divinity* is a work of biblical hermeneutics, and this exegetical intention affects the subjectivity of the work. While it is true that 'I' is the first word of *Essayes*, the stated focus is not Donne, but rather the opening verse of each of the first two books of the Bible, Genesis and Exodus. Furthermore, the titles of the individual pieces within *Essayes* share the topicality and occasional aspect of the early essayists. However, the individual pieces by Donne are not reflections on distinct topics, but a portion of a strictly ordered analysis, one linked to and building upon the next, so that the work is structured as two 'Sermons' divided into various sections as the Scripture texts demand and accompanied with prayers. These issues, therefore, raise initial doubts about the extent to which Donne's *Essayes* properly belong to the genre tradition created by Montaigne. Nevertheless, Donne displays various conventions of the essay that reveal him working within, even as he redefines, the parameters of the genre.

There is very little scholarship on *Essayes*, and among those who have written on it there is little agreement about the intention and accomplishment of the work. Edmund Gosse calls *Essayes* 'scholastic exercises and no more', complaining that the text reads 'more like the notes of a theological professor' than 'the outpourings of a man who is trembling on the threshold of the Holy of Holies' (2.63). Arthur Marotti describes the work as 'a piece of mock- or comical-scholarship, parodying the methods of scriptural exegesis and mystical writing' (1986: 261), while Evelyn Simpson characterizes *Essayes* as 'the kindest, the happiest, the least controversial of Donne's prose works' (Donne 1952*b*: xii). Michael Hall, the only scholar to analyse *Essayes* fully within its generic context, argues that Donne's work shares 'many of the essential qualities' of the essay in that Donne, like Montaigne, employs 'rhetorical techniques which are subtly subversive, which purposely confound the reader and lead to active and cooperative inquiry' (425). Hall contends that Donne may have considered these pieces to be 'essays' in the late Renaissance sense of 'tentative efforts in an area in which the author is not an authority or expert, has not perfected his ideas and opinions, but is merely a beginner or an apprentice' (424).

The text shows that Donne was acutely aware of his non-authoritative status as a biblical interpreter. Donne begins *Essayes* with an apology that someone such as himself, one who had earned no degree in divinity nor had taken holy orders, should engage in the practice of scriptural interpretation. He thereby addresses the problem of credibility in the opening paragraph of the work by imagining himself sitting 'at the door' and meditating 'upon the threshold' of a 'well provided Castle', that is, the Holy Scriptures (*Essayes* 7). He confesses that he is not one of the 'reverend Divines, who by an ordinary calling are Officers and Commissioners from God', and who may, therefore, undertake biblical exegesis without apology. However, Donne also states that he is not situating himself in this liminal position because he 'may not enter further', but because, by the examples of Jesus and Daniel, he chooses to exercise humility in his 'Search of those Secrets of God, which are accessible' (7). Further, Donne describes each individual essay to follow as a 'stone of this threshold' (8). With that, Donne responds to the problem of authority by purposefully locating himself in a humble, liminal position, as well as by the scriptural injunction, *Scribes ea in limine* (Ezek. 46:2), that he cites as the principle for his exegesis.

Donne returns to this question of credibility on two occasions in *Essayes*. The first appears in the final part of the 'Sermon' on Genesis, in which Donne aligns himself with those 'who are but Interlopers, not staple Merchants, nor of the company, nor within the commission of Expositors of the Scriptures' (38) so that in this portion of the work he will limit himself to surveying the thought of established scriptural interpreters. The second instance occurs in the essay 'Variety in the Number' (62–8), and in considering the number seventy and its sacred meaning

Donne describes himself as 'a vulgar Christian' (66). He immediately offers a parenthetical disclaimer, explaining that the phrase is not one 'of Diminution or Distrust', but instead one that acknowledges that to push the matter further would be to move 'above that which serves our particular consciences'. In other words, Donne's discretion in remaining humbly on the threshold speaks to his credibility.

Donne's style in *Essayes* complements his insistence that he is not writing with the expertise of those 'reverend Divines' by insisting on continuing exploration and reconsideration rather than emphatic closure. Thus, Donne's style further signals that he is working within the tradition of the essay. In certain respects, Donne's *Essayes* shares various stylistic features with the works of his fellow countrymen, such as the precepts and literary anecdotes he includes that are associated with such early English essayists as William Cornwallis, Robert Johnson, and Daniel Tuvill (see esp. *Essayes* 73–4). In addition, Donne makes such aphoristic assertions as '*Propagation* is the truest Image and nearest representation of eternity' (76), and offers such analytical categorizations as:

For God delights not so much in the exercise of his *Power*, as of his *Mercy* and *Justice*, which partakes of both the other: For *Mercy* is his *Paradise* and garden, in which he descends to walk and converse with man: *Power* his *Army* and *Arsenel*, by which he protects and overthrows: *Justice* his *Exchequer*, where he preserves his own Dignity, and exacts our Forfeitures. (93)

These passages echo the intellectual penchant for classifying knowledge into ordered expressions of reality found in Francis Bacon's *Essays*.

While such writing is comparable to Bacon's, Donne's style is closer overall to Montaigne's. Donne, like Montaigne, prefers the loosely structured Senecan sentence, and the progression of his thought is primarily associative. In the essay 'Of Moses' (*Essayes* 12–16), arguably the most dense and purposefully confusing piece in the book, Donne writes a single sentence spanning sixteen lines of printed text ('Therefore, as in violent tempests,... *Moses* had the primacy'; 15). The purpose of the sentence, and of the essay overall, is 'to unentangle our selves' from the debate over whether or not Moses is the author of Genesis. Donne begins with an elaborate metaphor, applies it to the consideration of authorship, and adds an allusion to Aquinas, before ending with his assertion that '*Moses* had the primacy'. This unwieldy sentence makes the larger point: that Donne's stylistic method seeks to demonstrate the complications of biblical interpretation through a hermeneutic of exploration and inquiry rather than a hermeneutic of resolution and conclusion.

One other example, from 'Variety in the Number', will have to suffice in illustrating Donne's style:

Nothing therefore seems so much to indanger the Scriptures, and to submit and render them obnoxious to censure and calumniation, as the appearance of Error in Chronology, or other limbs and members of Arithmetick: for, since Error is an approbation of false for true, or incertain for certain, the Author hath erred (and then the Author is not God) if any

Number be falsly delivered; And we erre, if we arrest our selves as upon certain truth (as we do upon all the Scriptures,) when there is sufficient suspicion of Error, (abstracting the reverence of the Author,) and a certain confession and undeniablenesse of uncertainty. (62)

This densely worded sentence opens with a statement that at first reads as an assertion that errors in numbering call into question the veracity of the Scriptures. Donne, however, thoroughly complicates the matter. To begin with, the assertion is qualified by the words 'seems' and 'apparance', by which Donne insinuates not only that there may be greater dangers to the Scriptures than errors in numbering, but also that the perceived errors may not be errors at all, if we only knew more. This qualification informs the remainder of the sentence as Donne inserts three parenthetical statements modifying what precedes them; offers a definition of 'error' in a subordinate clause in which he equates 'false' with 'incertain' and 'true' with 'certain'; and specifies the errors of the author and the reader even as he subtly implies a distinction between the authorship of God and some human agent, and between the readers of *Essayes* and of the Scriptures (perhaps including ecclesiastical authorities from differing confessions). The method of the sentence and our struggle to untangle it reflect Donne's point regarding the uncertainty, the scepticism as it were, one should have, not about the Scriptures themselves, but about their interpretation, and about our need to be ever vigilant in avoiding the myriad paths leading to misinterpretation.

Donne's sceptical style, which characterizes his epistemological approach and thus his hermeneutic, is everywhere apparent in *Essayes*. In the Genesis 'Sermon', Part 4, Donne states that the words of the creation have been 'so abundantly handled, by so many, so learned' that he 'will expositorily say nothing, but onely a little refresh, what others have said' (38). Before proceeding, however, Donne delineates three types of interpretive approaches that he sees as limited and misleading: first, those 'supple and slack' interpreters who are 'miscarried with the streame and tide of elder Authority' (the Roman Catholics); second, those 'too narrow and slavish' interpreters who are 'coasting ever within the view and protection of Philosophy' (natural philosophers); and third, those 'too singular' interpreters who, 'disdaining all beaten paths, may fall within one of these expositions' (religious separatists) (38). Donne thus rejects any interpretive method that promotes a prescriptive, or otherwise delimiting, scriptural hermeneutic.

In *Essayes* Donne draws eclectically upon a varied array of classical, Jewish, patristic, and scholastic writers. As a complement to his scepticism, Donne practises a hermeneutics of dilation. Quite simply, Donne indicates in *Essayes* that a wide range of learning is preferable in explicating the Scriptures because no single person and no single exegetical practice can fully account for the complexities of the text. As a result, Donne's interpretive method reflects his belief that truth can be achieved only through the commerce of ideas, and herein lies the civic-mindedness of *Essayes*.

The communal interests Donne addresses are, not surprisingly, those of the church, so that the virtue he argues for is ecclesiological. He urges the church to abandon its sectarian divisiveness and instead be shaped by a propagating dialogue consisting not only of words, but also of the intercourse of charitable practices. As a means of focusing this message within the dialogic ecclesiology that he wishes to promote, Donne includes in *Essayes* a series of 'Prayers'. While the inclusion of prayers resides completely outside of the essay tradition, these prayers nevertheless complete Donne's '*Disquisitions*'. Thus, Donne asks God in one prayer to let his soul '*produce Creatures, thoughts, words, and deeds agreeable to thee*' (43), and in another he thanks God, who '*hast multiplied thy children in me, by begetting and cherishing in me reverent devotions, and pious affections towards thee*' (104). The dialogic here is all-encompassing, as Donne addresses himself to God (in a metaphysical interchange of human and divine), as he communicates both with and for his (silent) auditory (in a moment of liturgical conversation), and as he meditates on the workings of his own soul (in an act of subjectivity).

There is no question that Donne, pushing hard as he does against the tradition, challenges our conceptions and expectations of the essay. By doing so, however, he reinvents the genre even as he practices the idiosyncratic scepticism of his exegesis.*

---

* I wish to thank the graduate students from my seminar on the Renaissance essay for their insights and intellectual curiosity: Christopher Blankenship, Elizabeth Bowman, Michelle Eisenberg, Sarah Erickson, Sharon Hekman, and Lise Schlosser.

CHAPTER 20

THE ANNIVERSARY POEM

GRAHAM ROEBUCK

The literary record of the life and death of Mistress Elizabeth Drury might have been a very dull affair, soon forgotten by all but members of her family. Dead shortly before her fifteenth birthday, unknown to the world for any notable action or attribute, having lived a quiet, conventional life in an agreeable English rural setting, her passing might have been lamented in the conventional terms of pastoral elegy, decorously applied to her private condition. Instead, her poetic monument, made public in print, instantly, by its extravagant strangeness shook the literary firmament, readers, patrons, and poets.

Elizabeth had been buried on 17 December 1610; the first edition of *An Anatomy of the World* appeared in 1611. This title provides a broad suggestion of its generic affiliations: literary 'anatomies', usually in prose, were by no means uncommon in those times. Yet 'anatomy' as a Renaissance 'metaphorical label' is 'vague, formally, by comparison with the classical genre terms' (Fowler 1982: 131). However, it generally brings a satirical tone to the dissection or analysis of its subject, treating erudition ironically (N. Frye 311, 365), often figuring it as pedantry, even while exhibiting a wide mastery of disparate ideas. The volume's subtitle, *Wherein, By Occasion of the vntimely death of Mistris Elizabeth Drvry the frailty and the decay of this whole world is represented*, considerably extends, and complicates, generic expectations.

The title poem, *FirAn* (*Variorum* 6.7–17), consisting of 474 lines in rhyming couplets, is preceded by a commendatory poem of forty-eight lines, also in rhyming couplets and generally thought to be by Joseph Hall, entitled 'To the Praise of the Dead, and the Anatomy' (6.5–6). This is followed by a second Donne poem, *FunEl*

(6.18–20), its title declaring its genre, consisting of 106 lines in couplets. In this arrangement *FunEl*, which reads as if it were the prelude to *FirAn*, seems logically and chronologically out of position.

The title page of *An Anatomy of the World* is enclosed by a quite elaborate architectural motif of two classical pillars in Corinthian mode, mounted on plinths with geometrical ornaments, rising to capitals with acanthus motifs supporting a semicircular ornamented arch. This title-page design suggests that a decorous, traditional elegiac lament resides beyond the arch. Hall's commendatory poem supports such an expectation in its commonplace figure of the Egyptians expending more effort on their tombs than on their modest homes of clay ('To the Praise of the Dead, and the Anatomy', ll. 27–9).

What the reader finds, however, is not a reassuring continuation of the pastoral elegy in the Tudor manner, which tends to sententiousness and to making the poetic voice, by being conventional, secondary to the subject being commemorated. Dennis Kay states succinctly the aversion of Tudor elegists to anything but matter and sentence: 'The notion that funeral verse might constitute a showcase for a poet's personal talents would have seemed indecorous to them: none indulges in self-display' (27). In contrast, the new voice of Donne in *An Anatomy* is unmistakably that of a personality delineated by persistently and restlessly witty turns of mind, a penetrating gaze, and a thoroughly sceptical outlook.

The generic indicators of Donne's two titles, their kinds—'anatomy' and 'funeral elegy'—do not, however, account for the poems' intellectual reach; nor have these terms satisfied critical inquiry into their generic ingredients. To achieve his goal—although what that goal may have been continues to be disputed—it is clear that Donne employs a great many literary resources that suggest a rich assembly and mixture of the genres, and echoes of genres, known to the early modern world.

This elaborate confection was further enhanced with the 1612 re-publication of *FirAn*, its 1611 subtitle retained on a new title page under the rubric *The First Anniuersarie*, in a volume containing also *SecAn* in 528 lines of rhyming couplets, a companion piece subtitled on a second title page, *Of the Progres of the Soule. Wherein: By Occasion Of The Religious Death of Mistris Elizabeth Drvry, the incommodities of the Soule in this life and her exaltation in the next, are Contemplated*. This third poem (*Variorum* 6.25–37) was doubtless composed in France while Donne accompanied the Drurys on their extensive travels. (The '*Conclusion*' of *SecAn* locates the author in a place of 'mis-deuotion' [l. 511] where bogus saints are invoked.) In this volume are reprinted Hall's 'To the Praise of the Dead, and the Anatomy' and, also presumed to be Hall's work, 'The Harbinger to the Progres' (6.23–4; cf. Donne 1978*b*: xxx-xxxi). *FunEl* in the 1612 volume stands between *FirAn* and *SecAn*—the slighter middle of a triptych. There is also an errata slip with corrections to both Anniversaries (reproduced in Keynes 1973, facing 172) probably added by Donne to unsold copies when he returned from France in September 1612. It could be inferred, therefore, that Donne did not object to the order of the volume's contents. The 1611 *FirAn*, although it was described as the poet's 'first yeares rent' (l. 447), invites being read as thematic amplification of the *FunEl*. In 1612 it assumes a further dimension as the first in a promised series of poems. With 'take this, for my second yeeres true Rent' (*SecAn* l. 520), the genre of the anniversary poem, as a term that can contain both an 'anatomy' and a 'contemplation', seems here to be strongly affirmed. There were to be, however, no more links in that chain.

The question of the *Anniversaries*' genre is perhaps best approached by distinguishing it from epicedes and obsequies. *FunEl* was no doubt the first of Donne's three poems to be composed, probably in December 1610. It is possible that the poem was delivered at the actual funeral, which would warrant seeing its original generic state as epicede. Being well received by Sir Robert and Lady Drury, it probably led to Donne's composition of a Latin epitaph for Elizabeth's monument. This monument can be seen on the south chancel wall of the parish church, Hawstead, Suffolk. Major themes of the Anniversary poems appear here, condensed and epigrammatic, such as, 'Thou liest here thyself, if thou art virtuous; for indeed here lies Virtue herself' (for the Latin, *Variorum* 8.175, with Milgate's translation on 429–30).

As a printed work, what originated as Epicede became a Funeral Elegy. Fowler observes the tendency of many subgenres—such as epicede, anniversary, and epitaph—carefully distinguished in classical theory and practice, to collapse into the encompassing genre of elegy (Fowler 1982: 141). Elegy, the 'quintessential Renaissance kind', a 'form without frontiers', is characterized by generic variety (Kay 6–7)—the perfect vessel for Donne's endeavour.

Were *FunEl* Donne's sole poem on Elizabeth Drury, it would be notable for the elegance of its construction, which so well houses the consolation indispensable to Christian funeral lament, as well as for expressing the difficulty for mourners to see and understand that consolation:

> May't not be said, that her graue shall restore
>   Her, greater, purer, firmer, then before?
> Heauen may say this, and ioy in't; but can wee
>   Who liue, and lacke her, here this vantage see?
>
> (ll. 45–8)

The concluding movement of the poem, in proper elegiac mode, employing legal and theatrical concepts, celebrates the joyful, restored harmony between the divine and mundane that, paradoxically, Elizabeth's death makes possible through the example and memory of her virtues:

> For future vertuous deeds are Legacies,
>   Which from the gift of her example rise.
> And 'tis in heau'n part of spirituall mirth,
>   To see how well, the good play her, on earth.
>
> (ll. 103–6)

The controlling metaphor of the poem is architectural. The simile of the deceased as a fair building ruined is a commonplace of the lamentation genres. Donne rings a dramatic change at the outset of the poem: figuring a tomb, a magnificent one, richly ornamented, infinitely wonderful as if 'euery inche were ten escurials' (l. 8)—referring to the Escorial, recently completed, one of the most lavish buildings of its age (Donne 1963: 170)—as hopelessly inadequate to contain Elizabeth. She so outshines the precious gems, 'Chrysolite…Pearles, and Rubies' (ll. 4, 5), and if the two Indies were joined in this tomb, the whole would be but 'glas' (l. 6) compared with her. With sudden directness, 'Yet shee's demolish'd' (l. 9), Donne banishes this phantasm of hyperbolical excess to consider the next overriding challenge: can she be kept in 'workes of hands, or of the wits of men?' (10). What possibility is there for 'these memorials, ragges of paper' (10–11) to endure? She herself, 'a Tabernacle', to be wrapped in paper (ll. 16–17)? Readers expecting the familiar topos of the immortality of verse and its superiority to the greatest works of hands—'Not marble nor the gilded monuments / Of princes shall outlive this pow'rful rime', as Shakespeare's Sonnet 55 expresses it—receive instead a Donnean surprise: they, the readers, imagined as mourners at this funeral oration, shall themselves, by their actions imitative of Elizabeth's virtue, become the missing leaves of Elizabeth's book, leaves torn out by premature death.

In these passages Donne prefigures certain themes in the *Anniversaries* and the manner of their treatment. How can elegy express her virtue? In manner, there is the extravagant imaginative energy—deft, sudden shifts of perspective and reversals of attitude. In *FunEl*, after the eighteen-line opening conceits of tombs and elegies, passionately engaged as if a guiding truth might be wrung from them, the speaker throws it all away: 'But 'tis no matter' (l. 19). The decrepit world will not long survive the wound her death has inflicted. There follows a swift anatomy in satirical tones, listing what the world contains—'The Rich for stomachs, and for backes the Pore' (l. 24), for instance—as a minimalist version of the *contemptus mundi* responding to the 'sicke world' of *FirAn*.

Paul A. Parrish offers this judgement on the success of Donne's engagement with the elegiac genre: 'The "Elegie" is a poem built solidly on a tradition but, more than that, it is a poem that transforms conventional motifs into poetic experiences unique to Donne and the Anniversaries' (57). The poem as building, and the challenges inherent in the poetic presumption to build a fit temple, are close to the surface in this poem. It is a fit repository for ideas brought to fruition in the greater Anniversary poems.

Elegies by Donne written prior to the *Anniversaries*, private and personal though they purport to be, nevertheless employ the tone of public epigrammatic wit, as a single couplet from *Mark* (1609) exemplifies: 'Nothing but man, of all envenom'd things, / Doth worke vpon it self with in-borne stings' (*Variorum* 6.112, ll. 13–14). General truths, wittily turned, are applied to the subject of the Elegy: 'Shee sinn'd but Iust enough to lett vs see / That Gods word must bee true, all sinners bee' (ll. 43–4). Neither here nor in the *Anniversaries* do such lines paint idiosyncrasies of individual character or particularities of the subject's conduct. However, they do not pertain to Elizabeth Drury: rather, they apply to the readership of the poems, the whole human condition since the Fall. They do not confine their attention to the personal circumstance, but restlessly shift the readers' perspectives back and forth between the macro- and microcosms, drawing attention to the poet's intellectual agility to a greater degree than was usual in the genre of elegy. His not having known Elizabeth Drury allows the poet to impart a more public voice and, at the same time, a greater freedom to exploit his own distinct voice.

Donne's tone, however, does not imply an abandonment of the traditional, three-part structure of the elegy—lament, panegyric, and consolation, in roughly equal proportions. In *Mark*, consolation and praise are reversed, allowing Donne in the concluding lines to touch upon a theme he opens out in the *Anniversaries*, making it part of the generic repertoire, namely the 'excellence of women'. This theme, arising from an ancient gloss on Gen. 2:7 and 2:22, and given revived energy by Cornelius Agrippa's 1509 treatise, Englished as *Of the Nobilitie and Excellencie of Womankynde* (1542 and subsequent printings), influenced a number of treatises likely to have been known to Donne (Roebuck 1996a: 178–80). Here, in a minor key, it is to reform a 'forward heresie, / That women can noe parts of friendship bee' (*Variorum* 6.113, ll. 57–8). Throughout the *Anniversaries* Elizabeth is associated with light—she has 'shut in all day' (*FirAn* l. 73), leaving this world in twilight. Her ghost is but a 'glimmering light' (*FirAn* l. 70), an image repeated as a taper that Death, a groom, brings to lead forth the soul (*SecAn* 85–7). Elizabeth is thus identified as *Foemina praecellentia*—the excellent woman—in the philosophical tradition Agrippa expounded: she is 'apt and mete...to receyue the heuenly light and bryghtnes, and is ofte replenyshed therwith.... the clere brightnes of goddes visage naturallye sette in thinges' (Agrippa Bii–Bii^v).

In the Funeral Elegies, as elsewhere in his oeuvre, Donne's voice is argumentative, working out fine or unsuspected distinctions, picking up a new idea, sometimes glossing it, sometimes casting it away as inadequate to the gravity of the topic. Yet the grave topic is by no means always treated gravely: 'How witty's ruine?' (*FirAn* l. 99). Wit is the oxygen the poems breathe. The reader is conscious of the poet in the act of assembling, or reassembling, a world from the fragments to which a death has reduced God's ordering of things. We are witness to Herculean intellectual labour. In the *Anniversaries* we readers, defective, lethargic though we are—'thou, sicke world, mistak'st thy selfe to bee / Well, when alas, thou'rt in a Letargee' (*FirAn* 23–4)—are required to enlist in the morally strenuous project of reanimating the world. In this way, as Kay puts it, Donne 'challenged decorum and fashion in creating an innovatory non-pastoral mode'. His new register is 'appropriate to conversation, satire, and the dramatic expression of inner turmoil' (Kay 95).

But of course the *Anniversaries* are a completely different matter from Donne's other funeral poems. Indeed, that such a genre as the anniversary ever existed has been doubted by, among others, W. M. Lebans, who writes of 'a supposed tradition which, if known at all, was not practiced in English up to this point'. Lebans refers to Ausonius' *Parentalia* as a possibly relevant classical model (Lebans 1972a: 549). The fourth-century *Parentalia* is a collection of short poems, or dirges, mostly in the versatile elegiac metre that Ovid used for love poetry, in memory of deceased relatives—nothing like the scope of Donne's *Anniversaries*.

Nor have the *Anniversaries* led to further examples. If the anniversary as an English formal genre was short-lived, the influence of the three constituent poems, especially on occasional commemorative verse, is striking. The death of Prince Henry, heir to the throne, on 6 November 1612 provided an early instance. Josuah Sylvester's collection *Lachrymae Lachrimarum* was rushed into print before the prince's funeral. A second edition appeared before the end of the year, and a third, dated 1613, in which Donne's *Henry* saw print (Bald 1986: 268–9). One striking feature of the *Anniversaries*, which has a bearing on the matter of genre—intellectual complexity—was remarked negatively by Jonson who, quoting Donne's words, told Drummond that Donne's poem for Prince Henry was written 'to match Sir Ed: Herbert jn obscurenesse' (1–2.136).

In the first book of his *The Art of English Poesy* George Puttenham addresses the subject of 'The form of poetical lamentations' (135–7). Although he does not identify an anniversary genre, the following remarks on funerary practice, in an unspecified period of antiquity, have been taken as a warrant for its existence: 'the lamenting of deaths was chiefly at the very burials of the dead, also at month's minds and longer times, by custom continued yearly, whenas they used many offices of service and love toward the dead, and thereupon are called obsequies in our vulgar' (137). Puttenham provides no instances of annual poetic memorializing, but seems to allow for such works as a species of obsequy.

It is widely accepted that the *Anniversaries*, along with Donne's Epicedes and Obsequies, are influenced, in some degree, by classical forms, adapted to his purposes. Lebans's researches into the classical models lead him to conclude that they are the most likely formal influences on

> Donne's funeral elegies and [his] preoccupation with the problems which characterize the works of the classical theorists. The mere existence of a considerable body of classical funeral elegy and rhetorical works dealing with funeral orations and consolations, a body which was easily accessible and widely known, makes such influence difficult to deny. (Lebans 1972b: 129)

As Lebans argues, the direct influence of classical models and classical theory is most probable for the Epicedes and Obsequies, but is not so evident for the *Anniversaries*. He goes on to express a view that most readers of the *Anniversaries* would endorse: 'knowing Donne's practice, who would assume that he would tamely quote or rely on the conventionally beautiful or approved classical authors?' (ibid. 137). The intellectual scale of Donne's poems puts them beyond such putative classical forms. Although eclectic influences may be discerned, the *Anniversaries* are *sui generis*.

Dennis Kay supports Lebans's judgement: 'There was no "tradition of anniversary" as some have supposed. Puttenham had merely recorded ancient obsequies' (Kay 105). The *Anniversaries*, then, may justly be considered Donne's generic innovation: a great structure comprising allusions to, adaptations of, and borrowings from the repertoire of literary modes available from antiquity to his own time. But above any such considerations is the force of Donne's intellectual, theological energy striving to make sense of things, outdoing any classical precedent. He needed no model or textbook.

It is very likely that Donne's repertoire included materials not considered then as literary, or purely literary in an aesthetic sense, such as liturgical and ecclesiastical forms. Louis Martz (1954: 354) draws attention to the following passage from Thomas Blount's *Glossographia* (London, 1656): 'Those were of old called *Anniversary days*, wheron the martyrdoms or death-days of Sts. were celebrated yeerly in the Church; or the days whereon at the yeers end, men were wont yeerly to pray for the souls of their deceased friends according to the continued custom of Roman Catholiques' (T. Blount C8). This practice illustrates the continuity since antiquity of concern for the dead as essential (perhaps *the* essential element) to realigning the living according to the revived memory of those who had gone before—especially recollection of their virtues, fashioned as exempla. Memory in this sense is the agent of a coherent pattern of the future rather than the more modern connotation of memory as recovered sense impressions (see Quinn 99). In early modern thought overwhelming respect for the ancients, though this tradition was showing signs of fracture, prevailed. Several topoi in the *Anniversaries* arise from this mentality. Reverence for the dead, like respect for the authority of the ancients, naturally involves denigration of the present: 'We're scarse our Fathers shadowes cast at noone' (*FirAn* l. 144) laments the poet in the section designated 'Smalnesse of stature'.

In his thoroughly humanist way, Donne's habit of mind is inclusivist, as Rosalie Colie's masterful analyses remind us, which explains the poems' 'hospitality to multiple readings' (Colie 1972: 193). Thus, following J. C. Scaliger's observation that complex, inclusive utterances require mixture of kinds (*genera mixta* or *mista*), which may underlie Sidney's similar argument (Colie 1973: 28), Colie points out how pervasive mixed genre works are in Renaissance literature, with particular application to Shakespeare (Colie 1972: 194). This inclusivism is the timbre of one driven, or diverted, by 'an Hydroptique immoderate desire of humane learning and languages', as Donne depicts himself in a private Letter of September 1608 to Sir Henry Goodere (*Letters* 51). The typical mode of Donne's thought is paradox. Thus a witty inversion turns this disease into health in *SecAn*, where the speaker's 'insatiate soule' makes the only 'Health, to be Hydropique' (ll. 45, 48).

It should be no surprise, then, that such work provoked at its first appearance, and continues today to provoke, great critical interest, ingenuity, disagreement—sometimes acrimonious—and a bewildering array of propositions about its generic lineaments. It is not possible within the bounds of this chapter to discuss more than a sampling of this range. Such a sampling, however, will suggest the validity of just about the sole agreement among the many commentators, namely that—here, in the words of Edward Tayler—'the text, brought into alignment with any number of topics or abstract categories, becomes almost infinitely malleable' (78).

Accounts of the formal structure of the text—as distinct from topics or categories—present no consensus. Donne's own side notes, seemingly symmetrical with ten for each Anniversary (none in *FunEl*), are both formal and topical. The entrance and conclusion sections are signalled in each poem. Between them the subject of discussion is given: for example, 'Weaknesse in the want of correspondence of heauen and earth' and 'Of accidentall ioyes in both places', the penultimate side notes in the first and second poems respectively (*Variorum* 6.15, 35). Dr Johnson's pronouncement on the 'performances of art' being impossible to reduce 'to any determinate idea' suggests that, in the end, the situation is as it should be, and must be: there is 'scarcely any species of writing, of which we can tell what is its essence, and what are its constituents; every new genius produces some innovation, which, when invented and approved, subverts the rules which the practice of foregoing authors had established' (1969: 300; qtd. in Fowler 1982: 42).

Untimely death provides the occasion of Donne's poetic performance, thus prompting critical debate on the question of the work's functions. Are the functions of the work best explained in terms of the patronage relationship of Donne to the Drurys, for example, or by Donne's disinterested passion for philosophical-religious inquiry, or his thirst for immortality, or any other possible ways in which poetic function may determine form? Certainly the fact that Donne was unacquainted with the girl whose praise he sings in such absolute terms—she was the 'forme and frame' of the now decaying world (*FirAn* l. 37), for instance—provoked much criticism of the poet's supposedly cynical opportunism. Yet his intense playing with the idea of the metaphysical significance of the individual child and the world itself—it occurs in the context of an extended conceit on baptism and naming—in the introductory section, 'The entrie into the worke', suggests a much more ambitious journey of exploration. The elegiac anatomist expresses his sense of embarking on a daring venture that no other poet—such as one better situated socially than he in relationship to the Drurys—has attempted. Elizabeth has been dead some months, 'yet none / Offers to tell vs who it is that's gone' (*FirAn* ll. 41–2).

As the two *Anniversaries* perform different functions, so their generic characteristics differ. Their extended titles provide clues. The 'Anatomie' is written on the 'occasion' of the 'vntimely' death of Elizabeth Drury, and is therefore an elegiac lament for that death and an extended treatment of the world's decay. As in a proclamation, five times her death is announced, like a refrain: 'Shee, shee is dead; shee's dead: when thou knowest this...' (ll. 183, 237, 325, 369, 427). Although its dominant tone is lamentation, intensified beyond that in any likely elegiac model by the hyperbolic praise of Elizabeth and the matching hyperbolic condemnation of 'frailty' and 'decay' in all earthly things, it does not neglect the duty of consolation—but the anticipated performance of that duty is dramatically delayed.

Before the apostrophe to the 'blessed maid' heralding the final thirty-line section, the poet's anatomical demonstration concludes with a striking and disconcerting synaesthesia, 'Nor smels it well to hearers, if one tell / Them their disease' (*FirAn* ll. 441–2), suggesting the poet's restraint in not driving home the culminating point of the anatomy lesson, namely the identification of the audience with the decayed corpse. Instead he offers the consolation of a therapeutic 'best concoction' drawn from Elizabeth's virtue, and verse that, like the Song of Moses, dictated to him by God (Deut. 32:1–43), will be remembered. Yet, as we readers are 'hearers' of the song, we cannot avoid smelling our 'disease'. The consolation of the poem, like Moses's Song to Israel, permits no forgetting what we are. It also 'discovers' the poet, who initially, not knowing who he is, 'Offers to tell vs who it is that's gone' (l. 42), as one fit to sing a sacred song, 'Of the Progres of the Soule'. Thus representations of the poet as singer, and in 'Progress' as 'Trumpet' of the 'Proclamation' of the 'Immortal Maid' (*SecAn* ll. 516–28) reveal a species of spiritual autobiography inhering in the elegy.

'I ame / The Trumpet, at whose voice the people came' (*SecAn* ll. 527–8) concludes the *Anniversaries*. The trumpet image is richly and variously suggestive in relation to Scripture. Perhaps its leading allusion is to the trumpet in Revelation, thus inviting a correspondence between *FirAn* as 'Old Testament' and *SecAn* as 'New Testament', according to the conventional Christian construction of scriptural hierarchy. In its revelation of the author's ambition, now the visionary prophet (a corrective to Dante's figure of the poet as visionary prophet; Frontain 2003*b*: 119–21), it completes the spiritual journey on which the poet initially embarks.

FirAn sows the seeds of the consolatory structure of *SecAn* in its first lines: 'When that rich soule which to her Heauen is gone, / Whom all they celebrate....' (ll. 1–2). The second poem's title, 'Of the Progres of the Soule. Wherein: By Occasion of the Religious Death of Mistris Elizabeth Drvry, the incommodities of the Soule in this life and her exaltation in the next, are Contemplated', serves notice of its essentially consolatory and contemplative functions. Thus a further generic aspect of the *Anniversaries*, revealed at the end of *FirAn*, is affirmed: that of sacred verse. Yet it by no means neglects 'A iust disestimation of this world', as a side note signals (*SecAn* l. 45). Now, however, the trope of forgetfulness is radically redirected: we are reminded that 'All haue forgot all good, / Forgetting her' (*SecAn* ll. 28–9), but the work of *FirAn* has been fruitful in that its 'song' will now, inspired by the chaste copulation of Elizabeth (dramatically figured as 'Father') with the singer's (female) 'Muse', bring forth progeny, 'Hymes', both from this poet and 'future wits' (ll. 34–7), 'As till Gods great Venite change the song' (l. 44). This greatly admired line—Saintsbury pronounced it 'the finest line of English sacred poetry', a '*Dies Irae* and a *Venite* itself combined' (*Variorum* 6.466)—announces the vision of the poem and its liturgical dimension. To forget is now imperative:

> Forget this world, and scarse thinke of it so,
> As of old cloaths, cast of a yeare agoe.
> To be thus stupid is Alacrity;
> Men thus lethargique haue best Memory.
>
> (ll. 61–4)

Thus Donne brilliantly manages to achieve a new direction in *SecAn* as well as continuity with *FirAn*. A nicely controlled element of pastoral elegy's consolation is suggested in the return of fertility, 'fathered' by Elizabeth. This reminds us that the decayed world of *FirAn*, to be cast off like old clothes, as the body is cast off by the soul's departure, can from this vantage point be seen as a version of pastoral—an extreme version. The death of the lamented subject causes nature to droop and languish in traditional pastoral. In Donne's treatment, characteristically, the effect is far more dire, not confined to the vegetable realm, but spread throughout the universe and, crucially, into human ability to comprehend the world. All is called into doubt by man's futile intellectual systems, especially 'new philosophy' in a famous, much-quoted passage (*FirAn* ll. 205–18: 'And new Philosophy cals all in doubt...'). The sceptical catalogues of what we don't know ring out through both poems, like encyclopedias in a grimly comic or Menippean vein.

In *SecAn* this satirical note is less frequent, as befits the regenerative mood of the whole and the redirection of the speaker's and readers' minds to the 'religious death of Mistris Elizabeth Drury' and the 'exaltation' of the soul. The sceptical cast of mind is vividly displayed in an extended passage on the inadequacy of human knowledge that interrogates, 'Poore soule in this thy flesh what do'st thou know' (l. 254) from a section side-noted as 'Her ignorance in this life and knowledge in the next' (*SecAn* l. 252). Notwithstanding the personal pronoun of the side note, the passage rapidly expands its application to all: 'Haue not all soules thought / For many ages, that our body'is wrought / Of Ayre, and Fire, and other Elements?' (ll. 263–5). This passage on the human energy expended in 'Pedantery' (l. 291) reads as a companion piece to the 'new philosophy' passage of *FirAn*, suggesting again the architectural and philosophical symmetry of the poems. Whereas in *FirAn* the catalogue of ignorance invites despair, for she, who alone could be the 'new compasse' (l. 226) for the lost human voyage, is dead: 'Shee, shee is dead; shee's dead' (l. 237); in *SecAn* the catalogue concludes with the command, 'vp vnto the watch-towre get, / And see all things despoyld of fallacies' (ll. 294–5).

The side notes and the catalogues suggest that the poems mimic the learned-treatise genre. Scientific treatises are seldom accorded literary status before their information is obsolete, yet here Donne's treatise on knowledge provides aesthetic pleasure as well as philosophical wisdom. Donne's learning is paradoxical. He is genuinely learned in numerous fields necessary to know and express the limitations—even the futility—of knowledge. For this Donne had notable examples in Erasmus' *The Praise of Folly* and Agrippa's *Of the Vanity of Arts and Sciences*, and others in the humanist tradition that Rosalie L. Colie explores in *Paradoxia Epidemica* (1966). The depth and extent of his knowledge—scientific, historical, legal, theological, and philosophical, to name a few regions of his intellectual inquiry—has received scholarly attention. To these might be added a growing awareness of Donne's familiarity with another 'commerce' in addition to that 'twixt heauen and earth' (*FirAn* 399), namely economics, which finds expression, and connection with the satirical vein, in *FirAn*. Donne's familiarity with the emerging mercantilist thought, which underwrites a line of social criticism in the poems, has seldom been remarked but requires to be taken into account (Solomon 59–74).

The discursive mode of the *Anniversaries* sorts well with the meditative components, especially given the tension engendered between the this-world and the next-world perspectives they present. Since Louis L. Martz powerfully argued for Ignatian spiritual exercises as the organizing and structuring genre of the poems—an argument developed in several stages and most fully presented in *The Poetry of Meditation*—scholarly focus on generic questions has spawned many intensive and extensive studies, seeking to contextualize these poems in their early modern milieu and its classical antecedents. Barbara Lewalski's detailed reading of the poems in a contrary Protestant context as primarily in the epideictic genre, explored earlier by O. B. Hardison, required a different structural account of the poems from Martz's—a subject revisited by Tayler, whose reading of the poems places Donne in a tradition of thought from Plato, Aristotle, Augustine, and Aquinas. These studies, though differing in their choices of context and critical emphases, agree on the greatness of the *Anniversaries* and the variety of genres that may be perceived at work in them. Celebration is added to the possibilities by Dennis Quinn, who concludes that it is a 'high and ambitious genre, always written in high even extravagant style and on a grand scale' (105).

Given the extravagant display of intellect and invention of the *Anniversaries*, it is perhaps surprising that Dr Johnson did not treat these productions to the *reductio ad absurdum* Milton's pastoral elegy, *Lycidas*, received. It is not difficult to imagine Johnson's feigning ignorance of the generic conventions of the poems: Elizabeth as having 'Guilt the West Indies, and perfum'd the East' (*FirAn* l. 230) or 'all Libraries had throughly red' (*SecAn* l. 303), or any other items in the great blason of her virtuous achievements. Rather than demolishing the poems as vessels of elaborate insincerity, he is moved to pronounce that lines from *SecAn*—'Thinke in how poore a prison thou didst lie... thinke thy Soule hatch'd but now' (ll. 173–84)—express the 'sum of humanity' (S. Johnson 2006: 1.211).

Wesley Milgate writes that 'no limiting conception of genre or structure breaks the flow of this discursive and meditative verse' (Donne 1978*b*: xl). He also observes that the ideas and materials that make up the discourse of the poems were commonplaces but are distinguished by pointed and coherent organization (xxxvii). Such well-worn jeremiads as the decay of the world are in Donne's handling startlingly fresh and urgent. Yet Milgate directs attention to the 'only "genre"' that can accommodate all the qualities of the *Anniversaries*—the Sermons (xl). This insight, further developed by Jeanne Shami, reveals the patterning of anatomy and progress in the Sermons. Donne at sermon typically dramatizes the religious lives of ordinary people, such as Elizabeth Drury might have been. This poses a problem of the apparent disjunction in the poems between the elevated language and the ordinary subject (Shami 1984*a*: 222–4). Perhaps such considerations lay behind the 'censures' of his book, to which Donne responded that he had written the best that he could conceive (*Letters* 75; see also 238–9).

The poems as therapies applied to counter *timor mortis*, a recent study argues, are shown to achieve ambivalent results. For elegy to succeed as literature, rather than as effective consolation of those who are grieving, makes it necessarily subject to the laws of poetry, which 'need not respect the truth' (K. A. Craik 2007: 73–87). Thus arises the suspicion of the emotional insincerity of the *Anniversaries*, which unsettled some of the first readers, unconsoled by the poems (ibid. 75). But what of the *Anniversaries* as therapies for the poet's *timor mortis*? When read in the light of modern generic expectations shaped by psychoanalytic insights, the poet's anxieties about his own annihilation come into focus (R. N. Watson 1994: 164). The immortalizing function of poetry, an ancient theme in vogue again in early modern practice, may be one more object of the poet's scepticism, as a recent study arguing Donne's scepticism regarding literary conventions shows (Sherman 40–64). For the elegists who celebrate Donne's genius in the 1633 *Poems By J. D.*, Donne is immortalized as having exhausted the resources of literature by his unparalleled wit and invention. The *Anniversaries*, displaying those powers at their fullest, may justly be labelled the 'finest long poems written in English between *The Faerie Queene* and *Paradise Lost*' (Donne 1978*b*: xxxiv).

Ill. 20.1. Elizabeth Drury's tomb, All Saints Church, Hawstead, Suffolk. Elizabeth Drury died and was buried in December 1610. Donne's epitaph for her is carved and painted into the black stone tablet above the alabaster relief sculpture depicting her reclining figure. The designer and sculptor of this tomb are unknown. (Photo, Paul Parrish.)

CHAPTER 21

THE EPICEDE AND OBSEQUY

CLAUDE J. SUMMERS

EPICEDES and obsequies are funeral poems. They are distinguished from each other by the fact that epicedes are generally spoken over a body that has not yet been buried, while obsequies are usually spoken later and tend to emphasize consolation rather than lament (Colie 1972: 199).

Although there have been some recent efforts to rehabilitate the Epicedes and Obsequies (see e.g. R. C. Evans 1989*a*; Kolin; Lewalski 1973; Maurer 2007; Donne 1978*b*; Pebworth 1992; Pebworth and Summers 2000; Sherwood; Summers 1992; and Tourney), they remain among Donne's least read and least appreciated work, variously seen as strained exercises in flattery, clumsy attempts to win patronage, and unedifying expressions of the poet's personal anxieties about death. While the poems are deeply implicated in the patronage system and are often extravagant and idiosyncratic in their conceits, they are distinguished by their rhetorical agility and their innovativeness. Indeed, not only are they characteristically Donnean in their imaginative leaps, restless thought, disturbing images, ingenious ideas, and powerful accents, but they also reveal Donne's persistent awareness of audience and occasion and his bold transformation of the traditional English elegy. In them, Donne pioneers the development of a new kind of funeral elegy and a new rhetoric of grief.

Although the publication of the *Anniversaries* established him as an acknowledged (though sometimes derided) master of the funeral poem in seventeenth-century England, Donne was a reluctant elegist, apparently moved to write Funeral Elegies only in order to please patrons or to capture the attention of prospective patrons. Despite his own preoccupation with death, he wrote relatively few funeral poems, memorializing only a handful of individuals. Except for his wife, he did not mourn family members or close friends in verse. Indeed, his only surviving poems that seem occasioned by deep personal loss are the Latin Epitaph for his wife and the Holy Sonnet *HSShe*.

As David Novarr remarks, Donne exhibited a 'lifelong disinclination' to write mourning verse (1980: 195–6). He declined, apologizing profusely, Henry Goodere's plea that he commemorate the death of an old friend, Richard Martin; and he wrote no Elegies for figures whom he might have been expected to mourn, such as Spenser or Shakespeare or Sir Thomas Egerton or the Countess of Bedford or King James or, indeed, his close friend Goodere. (In contrast, Ben Jonson memorialized dozens of individuals, including two of his children, in a variety of poetic forms.) In 1625 Donne remarked in the Prose Letter to Sir Robert Ker that accompanied *Ham* that he was 'loth' to fulfil the request for a memorial poem, asserting that he would have preferred to preach a funeral Sermon than write an Elegy. In another Letter he complained that the Countess of Bedford rewarded him insufficiently for his Obsequies on her brother, Lord Harington. Since virtually all of his funeral poems were occasioned by or implicated in the pursuit of patronage, Donne may well have associated the genre with mercenary motives and have resented the necessity to mourn individuals whom he knew only slightly or to praise public figures whose policies he did not support.

The fact that Donne likely felt little personal sympathy for the subjects of his Epicedes and Obsequies may have contributed to the coldness and distance that many critics have noted in them. His lack of personal grief for his subjects probably also prompted his creation of a Funeral Elegy that is more philosophical and abstract than either the classical models he imitated—especially the elegies of Ovid, Propertius, and Statius—or the English elegies of contemporaries such as Ben Jonson and Henry King. W. M. Lebans, who has most fully studied Donne's indebtedness to the classical elegy, has noted that the Epicedes and Obsequies employ some of the conventions of non-pastoral elegy that Donne derived from his knowledge of classical models and from the prescriptions of classical rhetoricians, especially the requirement that funeral elegies include three basic elements: lament, eulogy, and consolation. Yet, Lebans concludes, the real significance of this debt to classical models lies not in the borrowing of classical structure or subject matter, but in Donne's original manipulation of classical conventions as he adapted them to the needs of his individual style (1972*a*: 547; see also 1972*b passim*). That is, Donne's funeral poems achieve originality by means of their rhetorical agility and poetic imagination. Combining Roman form with Christian doctrine, he employs a recognizably Donnean idiom in his Elegies, which are argumentative, conversational, and dramatic.

As Rosalie Colie and Lebans have demonstrated, the question of genre in the seventeenth century is slippery. Moreover, as Dennis Kay and others have observed, charting the development of the funeral elegy is especially difficult. As a genre, the elegy is not like a sonnet, which is distinguished by formal properties as well as subject matter, which one can monitor and place on various scales, such as changes in the rhyme scheme or employing an octet–sestet division or achieving effect by omitting the final couplet or by using a form associated with erotic love to sing of religious devotion or by linking sonnets together to create a sequence that tells or implies a story. Rather, the elegy developed in England by accretion. The term itself was used very loosely, referring at first to a metrical form, and only gradually coming to refer to mourning poems rather than love poems, and then to many different kinds of mourning poems, sometimes being used as an umbrella term to embrace various subgenres from the obsequy to the lament to the epitaph.

While Donne's Epicedes and Obsequies fulfil the requirements of both the classical non-pastoral funeral elegy and the traditional English elegy to include passages of mourning, praise, and consolation, and seem occasionally to reflect the influence of continental Latin elegists such as Marino, they go far beyond the work of Donne's contemporaries in the genre to explore large theological questions. Donne's attempt to create what Kay has described as a non-pastoral Latinate elegy 'that could be both domestic and serious' (95) entailed slighting the traditional elegy's characteristic emphasis upon the personal. In the traditional English elegy, praise for the deceased is often the most important element of the poem and is usually accomplished by rehearsing biographical details (A. L. Bennett *passim*), but Donne typically praises his subjects in such a way as to efface their individual qualities and rarely does more than allude to biographical details. While the traditional elegy typically attempts to create an illusion of intimacy and to convey a sense of personal loss, particularly when written to mourn a private individual, Donne's Epicedes and Obsequies typically speak in a communal voice and mourn the deceased as an exemplar rather than an individual. As Matthew Greenfield observes: 'Where a private elegy like Henry King's "Exequy" attempts to work through the poet's grief over the death of a loved one, a public elegy responds to the death of a stranger or a casual acquaintance and attempts to console a patron or community' (75–6). Although not all of them are written for public figures, Donne's Elegies are public poems rather than private communications of condolences.

Donne is hardly the first poet to mourn by placing death in a theological perspective. Indeed, the search for religious consolation in the face of death is so much a staple of the elegy, both classical and contemporary, as to be almost a formal requirement. From the early modern period hundreds of elegies for public and private figures survive in which the poet versifies religious commonplaces and platitudes, discovers consolation by meditating on the prospect of an afterlife, or uses the occasion of death to make (often partisan) theological points. However, Donne is arguably the first serious theological thinker who was also a major poet. Hence, his theological ruminations have an interest that goes beyond the recitation of standard dogma or the repetition of platitudes. They often raise serious and difficult, sometimes arcane, theological points, such as the relationship of body and soul after death and the association of faith and reason in a fallen world, and express them in conceits that are startling and intellectually challenging. In the Epicedes and Obsequies, Donne typically explores the divide between the transient and the eternal and does so by means of imaginatively daring images and sometimes by reference to obscure points of theology.

Donne was also not the first poet to portray deceased subjects (especially monarchs and other powerful public figures) as exemplars of virtue and objects of philosophical or theological contemplation. But, as Barbara Lewalski has noted, Donne's poetry of praise is 'radically different from the epideictic poetry of his contemporaries' by virtue of its wit and audacity (1973: 43). 'Specifically,' she concludes, 'the unique elements of Donne's poetry of compliment are the speaker's meditative stance and the symbolic value he discovers in the person addressed' (44). His practice in the Epicedes and Obsequies of portraying the deceased person as an exemplar of the regenerate soul or as a symbol of transfiguration not only licenses his neglect of his subjects' individual qualities but also adds intellectual and philosophical weight to poems that had their origin in social obligations and the pursuit of patronage. Donne's funeral poems typically find in the death of an individual an opportunity to explore questions of religious or philosophical truth, while also fulfilling the epideictic obligations of the elegiac mode. As Kay points out, Donne created

a new form of English elegy whose canons of decorum were based not on external, formal details but on an imaginative coherence whose purpose was consolatory and panegyric, and on a dramatized performance by the speaker that both demonstrated, and advocated, meditating on the essential, ideal, spiritual qualities of the subject rather than on more tangible attributes. (100–1)

But despite Donne's interest in theology, he was more of a rhetorician than a philosopher, and the Epicedes and Obsequies are not merely philosophical or theological meditations on death. Like much of Donne's poetry, including especially the Verse Letters, the Epicedes and Obsequies are at once local and transcendent. They may aspire to the timelessness of art and their ideas may soar beyond the immediate circumstances that led to their composition, but they are also very much implicated in their occasions. Their poetic strategies are to a large extent dictated by the nature of the audiences conceived for the individual poems. Although they contain abstract philosophizing about the nature and meaning of death, they are also coterie performances carefully tailored to particular circumstances. They are shaped by political and social considerations, especially the imperatives of the patronage system, as well as by their philosophical perspectives (on the Jacobean patronage system, see R. C. Evans 1989a).

Although Donne wrote eleven funeral poems in all, his Epicedes and Obsequies are generally considered to consist of seven poems, most of which were grouped together under the heading 'Epicedes and Obsequies Upon the Deaths of Seuerall Personages' in two late manuscripts and, with some modifications, in the 1635 and subsequent editions of Donne's *Poems*. The Verse Letter to Lucy Russell, Countess of Bedford, *BedfShe*, consoling Lady Bedford on the death of her kinswoman Lady Bridget Markham, is sometimes grouped with the Epicedes and Obsequies, as by John Shawcross in his 1967 edition of Donne's poetry. (Another Verse Letter to Lady Bedford, *BedfCab*, contains an 'Epitaph on Himself', which Joshua Scodel [1991: 113] regards as a significant mourning poem. Conversely, in some modern editions *Sorrow* is sometimes included among the love Elegies, where it appears in several manuscripts.) The other funeral poems—the two Anniversaries and *FunEl*—are also related to the Epicedes and Obsequies and may even be said to extend many features of the earlier Epicedes and Obsequies to their logical and most ambitious extremes, especially the adoption of a 'symbolic mode' in which the ostensible subject, Elizabeth Drury, is rendered as a universal figure; but because they enjoy a separate place in the history of Donne's reception, they will not be discussed here (see Ch. 20; on 'symbolic mode', see Lewalski 1973; but see also Tayler).

Sorrow, Donne's earliest surviving Funeral Elegy, was probably written in the 1590s. Because so little is known about its subject and occasion, it remains the most mysterious of these poems. The least developed of the Epicedes and Obsequies, *Sorrow* is unusual among them for its emphasis on the dead body of the subject. The poem is most interesting for its presentation of an anthropomorphized sorrow and its depiction of the deceased's surviving children as 'Pictures of him dead, senseles, cold as hee' (*Variorum* 6.103, l. 24). The poem's brevity, bleakness, and lack of consolation are puzzling. Since the poem circulated in manuscript with some love Elegies, it is possible that *Sorrow* was not composed to mourn a particular individual but to fulfil a classical convention that includes a Funeral Elegy among collections of love Elegies.

Much more impressive are Donne's next four funeral poems—those occasioned by the deaths of Lady Bridget Markham and Cecilia Bulstrode, two friends and kinswomen of Donne's patroness Lucy, Countess of Bedford, in May 1609 and August 1609 respectively. Donne probably knew these women only slightly as members of Lady Bedford's court circle and Bulstrode as mistress of his friend Sir Thomas Roe, but by 1609 he had forged a deep but complex relationship with Lady Bedford that was important to both of them: it was not the friendship of equals that permits familiarity (after all, at this time Bedford was one of the most powerful women in England and Donne an impoverished and disappointed office-seeker), but it was characterized by mutual respect, intellectual intimacy, and social ease. These poems, including Donne's Verse Letter to Lady Bedford *BedfShe* and Lady Bedford's 'Death bee not proude, thy hand gaue not this blowe', constitute a dynamic sequence of grief and comfort, yoked together by their self-referentiality, their linked images, and their common goal of discovering meaning in the face of death. Seen together, the poems are highly complex social transactions between Donne and Lady Bedford (see Summers 1992: *passim*).

The sequence begins with two companion poems mourning the death of Lady Markham: the Verse Letter to Lady Bedford (*BedfShe*) and the Funeral Elegy on Lady Markham (*Mark*). The first poem, addressed directly to Lady Bedford and developing the familiar paradox of two-in-one, is tenderly personal, and was probably meant to be read only by the Countess herself. It celebrates the friendship of the two women and consoles Lady Bedford on the loss of her close friend. The Elegy, on the other hand, like the other Epicedes and Obsequies, is a more public poem, perhaps not meant to be published but certainly intended to be shared with friends and acquaintances of the deceased. It is addressed not to an individual but to a community of mourners, and the poet speaks in the first-person plural. The two poems reach similar conclusions about death, but their tones and arguments are quite different. In the Verse Letter the consolation is personalized, while in the Elegy it is generalized.

The Elegy opens with the lament, emphasizing the reaction provoked by the death of Lady Markham, for though God 'hath sett marks, and bounds' between our world and death's ocean, yet the latter 'breakes our banck when ere it takes a friend' (ll. 4, 6). Consequently, we vent our passions in tears, which 'Take all a brackish tast, and funerall, / And euen these teares which should wash sin, are sinne' (ll. 10–11). In this gentle remonstrance against weeping, Donne reveals himself as a moderate rigourist in the Renaissance debate about the appropriateness of mourning: he sides with those who, like Erasmus and Thomas Wilson, saw excessive expressions of grief as evidence of weakness, irrationality, and lack of faith, but he nevertheless allows moderate expressions of mourning (on rigourism, see Pigman 1985: esp. 16–19). Although he does not ally himself with the extreme view that mourning should be avoided altogether, he expresses uneasiness with immoderate grief, and translates lamentation into consolation.

Donne is able to console Lady Markham's mourners by explaining the significance of her death and defining who she really was, declaring that her grave is an alembic that purifies and transforms:

> As men of China after an ages staye,
>   Doe take vp Purslane, where they buried clay;
> So at this Graue, her Limbeck, which refines
>   The Diamonds, Rubies, Saphirs, Pearles, and mynes,
> Of which this fleash was; her Soule shall inspire
>   Fleash of such stuff; as God, when his last fire
> Annulls this world, to recompence it, shall
>   Make, and name then the Elixar of this All.
>
> (ll. 21–8)

Thus, in the mysterious alchemy of God's covenant with man, corporal death is defined as a means of freeing the soul; and even the body, which on earth is subject to decay, will be purified and restored at the Judgement Day.

Having lamented Lady Markham's death, and found consolation for her mourners, Donne ends his poem on a note of panegyric, lauding the deceased as one in whom Grace was 'extreamly diligent, / That kept her from sinn, yet made her repent' (ll. 39–40). Typical of the Epicedes and Obsequies generally, the poem asserts a proposition ('Man is the world, and Death the Ocean'; l. 1) only to discover consolation by reversing the argument. Also typical of the mourning poems, it presents Lady Markham as an exemplar rather than as an idiosyncratic individual. It places her demise in a theological context that diminishes the power of Death, thereby reducing its temporary triumph to a pyrrhic victory.

The consolation that Donne offered in the Markham Elegy may have seemed too facile when Lady Bedford's friend Cecilia Bulstrode died a scant three months later. Hence, Donne opens *BoulRec* by recanting the premise on which the Markham Elegy concluded: 'Death I recant, and say, vnsaid by mee / What ere hath slipt, that might diminish thee' (ll. 1–2). Whereas in the Markham Elegy Death was an ocean constantly encroaching on and eroding the (separate) land that is man, in the Bulstrode Elegy man lives in a universe of death. Referring to the consolation he offered in the Markham Elegy, Donne now asks: 'Howe could I thinke thee nothing that see nowe / In all this All, nothing els is, but thou' (ll. 25–6). Even the knowledge that Death is a 'mighty Bird of prey' constrained by God to 'laye / All that thou kill'st at his feet' fails to offer much comfort, for God reserves 'but fewe, and leaues the most to thee' (ll. 31, 32–3, 34).

Structured like a masque, the Elegy opens with an antimasque of despair that is reversed only through the contemplation of Cecilia Bulstrode as one of the 'few' reserved by God. From this new perspective, the speaker recovers his confidence. He now realizes that Death has captured only 'her lower roome' (l. 38), that is, her body; and even that victory is only temporary, for 'Her soule is gone to vsher vpp her coarse / Which shalbe'almost another soule; for there / Bodies are purer then best soules are here' (ll. 46–8). Moreover, by killing Bulstrode while she is still young, Death has deprived himself of the opportunity of winning her through the vices of age. Death's last hope lies in the 'immoderate grief' (l. 70) felt by the young woman's mourners; yet, Donne says, 'wee may scape that sin' (l. 71) if we weep not because she has gone, but because we are not as good as she was. The poem ends by acknowledging loss even in an assertion of victory: 'Some teares that knott of friends her death must cost, / Because the Chaine is broke, though noe linke lost' (ll. 73–4). Donne's uneasiness with excessive expressions of grief is apparent even in this legitimation of Lady Bedford's tears for her friend.

BoulRec divides into two approximately equal parts: the first thirty-six lines argue the supremacy of Death, while the final thirty-eight lines dismantle the argument by referring to the example of Cecilia Bulstrode's triumph over death. Despite this reversal, however, the powerful and heterodox first half of Donne's poem seems to have disturbed its primary reader, Lady Bedford, perhaps because its emphasis on the universality of Death might be seen as insufficiently congruent with the Calvinist principle of predestination to which she subscribed and because its assertion that immoderate grief is sinful may have struck her as an impertinent criticism of her reaction to Bulstrode's death. In response, she wrote her own poem, the 'Elegie' beginning 'Death bee not proude, thy hand gaue not this blowe'. Lady Bedford's interesting but predictable couplets dispute Donne's contention that 'In all this All, nothing els is but [Death]' (l. 26). Most pointedly, she rejects Donne's warning against immoderate grief, justifying tears not as the human response that Donne grudgingly permitted, but as a manifestation of God's grace. She tells Death:

> Glory not thou thy selfe in these hot teares
> Which our face, not for her, but our harme, weares,
> The mourning livery giuen by grace, not thee
> Which wills our soules in these streames washd should be.
>
> (ll. 23–6)

Donne may have been stung by the implicit rebuke in Lady Bedford's elegy. In response, he wrote yet another poem on Cecilia Bulstrode, *BoulNar*. The topos of inexpressibility with which the poem opens functions as an oblique apology to Lady Bedford not only for the inevitable inadequacies of the present work, but also for the failure of the previous Elegy. It begs forgiveness by establishing the fiction that the poet was too moved by the death of the subject to find adequate language to comfort her survivors. While Donne never explicitly acknowledges the Countess's 'Elegie', the new poem, in its more orthodox piety and in its specific adoption of Lady Bedford's imagery and terms of reference, reveals its author's awareness of her objections.

In *BoulNar* Donne not only gives Bulstrode an apotheosis similar to that in the Countess's poem, but he also adopts Lady Bedford's view of the efficacy of tears, conceding what may have been a major point of contention between them:

> God tooke her hence, least some of vs should loue
>   Her, like that plant [i.e. the Tree of Knowledge], him, and his lawes aboue,
> And when we teares, hee mercy shed in this
>   To raise our minds to heau'en, where nowe shee is.
>
> (ll. 39–42)

Then, in the most unconvincing lines of the poem, Donne celebrates Bulstrode's saintliness in hyperbolic terms, probably suggested by Lady Bedford's reference to the 'crowned Saynts in heauen' (l. 10). In Donne's poem, Bulstrode's death is declared a 'Holi-daye' (l. 44), for

> Her heart was that strange Bush, where sacred fire
>   Religion, did not consume, but inspire.
> Such Pietie, soe chast vse of Gods daye
>   That what wee turne to feasts, she turn'd to praye.
> And did prefigure here in devout tast
>   The rest of her high Sabäoth, which shall last.
>
> (ll. 45–50)

This description of a woman that Ben Jonson derided as the 'Court Pucell' (but later retracted in an epitaph; see J. Lee *passim*) may be intended to expose the entire poem as an exercise in insincerity, or it may simply be another way of idealizing Bulstrode by rendering her an abstraction, a symbol of piety.

Donne offers consolation to Lady Bedford by addressing one of the central concerns of her poem, the state of Bulstrode's body after death. He returns to the idea he had advanced in the Markham Elegy, the grave as alembic:

> The rauenous earth, that nowe wooes her to bee
> Earth too, will bee Lemnia and the tree
> That wrapps that chrystall in a woodden tombe,
> Shall bee tooke vp spruce, fill'd with Diamon.
>
> (ll. 57–60)

As an alembic, the earth will transmute the crystal of Bulstrode's body into a diamond; and her 'woodden tombe', her coffin, will be transmuted into a 'spruce', that is, a wooden 'coffer or chest' designed to contain and protect valuables (see *OED*, 'Spruce', *sb* 2.a). This rich image of transmutation hearkens back to the equally suggestive idea in the Markham Elegy and signals the conclusion of the sequence directed to console the 'sad glad friends' who grieve at losses that 'would wast a Stoicks heart' (ll. 60–1). The reference to stoicism here functions to emphasize both the greatness of Lady Bedford's bereavements and the corresponding necessity to relax the restrictions against mourning urged by stoics. Hence, although Donne responds to the Countess's defence of tears by abandoning his own rigourist position about excessive grief, he does so without sacrificing his integrity, for even stoics would be staggered by the losses sustained by Lady Bedford.

The death of Henry, Prince of Wales, the elder son of King James I, on 6 November 1612 occasioned not only Donne's next Epicede, but also a national outpouring of grief, especially from Puritans, who saw the Prince as more sympathetic to their cause than his father and who had hoped that he would complete the Protestant reformation begun by his namesake Henry VIII, as expressed in a couplet by Sir John Harington of Kelston: *Henry the eighth pull'd down Monks and their Cells. / Henry the ninth should pull down Bishops, and their Bells* (Harington 1653: A1). In his Elegy on Prince Henry, Donne pushes the strategies of idealization and abstraction that he employed in the second Bulstrode poem even further, as he moves from the private to the political sphere. The problem for Donne in mourning Prince Henry was that the poet was unsympathetic to the Prince's political position. He shared King James's reluctance to make war and his distaste for radical Protestantism. He resolved the problem of mourning Henry by refashioning the Prince in his father's image. (On Donne's religio-political stances, see Cain 2006, who points out that King James and Donne shared a commitment to peace and an irenic approach to religious differences. See also Chs. 34.II, 35.I, 35.II, 36.II, and 37.)

The Elegy for Prince Henry opens with a powerfully worded statement on the consequences of the Prince's death, one that forcefully co-opts the reader into acquiescence. Donne announces the loss of his two '*Centres*', reason and faith, and proceeds with an extended consideration of the relationship of one to the other (ll. 1–16). Finally, at line 18, identifying the cause of his intellectual and spiritual dislocation as the loss of 'the PRINCE wee misse', Donne moves into the first-person plural as he expands his personal confusion into a universal dislocation caused by Henry's death (ll. 19–24). In the next passage (ll. 25–42), its two halves each introduced by the inclusive question, 'Was it not well believ'd' (ll. 25, 35), intended to effect a universal assent, Donne defines his former faith—now shaken by death—as belief not in the young Prince's accomplishments, but in his potential: first in using his strength to aid his father in achieving '*Peace* through[out] CHRISTIANITIE' (l. 34) and then in sustaining that '*general Peace*' until it should 'th'eternall ouertake' (l. 36). In contrast to what might have been, in the next passage (ll. 43–54) Donne 'now' sees this former faith as '*Heresie*' and human life reduced to such a state that ''twere an *Ambition* to desire to fall' (l. 50).

Donne's portrayal of the bellicose Henry as a champion of his pacific father's policies is not merely the kind of exaggeration endemic to the elegiac mode; it is also a blatant distortion of the Prince's politics: whereas King James carefully cultivated his image as peacemaker on the European stage and as one who endeavoured to avoid English entanglements in the continent's religious wars (see Ch. 34.II), the Prince was associated with the extreme wing of Puritanism and a more aggressive foreign policy, especially towards Catholic Spain (see J. W. Williamson *passim*; Strong 52–4, 71–85). At the same time, however, the poet's refashioning of the Prince in the image of his father is a deft solution to the dilemma Donne faced in having to praise a political figure whose positions were counter to official policy. In a strategy designed to please the King, whom he was actively lobbying for support via his favourite Robert Carr, Viscount Rochester (later Earl of Somerset), Donne praises the Prince by imagining how he might have evolved in the future under his father's tutelage (see Pebworth and Summers 2000: *passim*).

The Prince Henry Elegy finds consolation by joining the Prince in bonds of love with the '*Shee-Intelligence*' to create '*Two mutual Heauens*' (ll. 90, 97). Although much ink has been spilt trying to identify the '*Shee-Intelligence*' as a real person, the figure should more properly be associated with the angelic intelligences controlling the heavenly spheres of the Ptolemaic universe. At the point in the poem where she appears, the Prince has been rendered thoroughly abstract; indeed, he has become the Platonic 'idea' of a prince rather than the actual flesh-and-blood Henry. The appropriate consort for him in that state, then, is not an actual woman but an angelic guide who has acted as his '*Conscience*' and has thereby 'mov'd' his '*Sphear*' (ll. 92, 90). The imaginative joining of the Prince with such a creature in mutual bonds of love consoles the poet and makes him wish to be 'an *Angel singing* what *You* were' (l. 98).

The death of John Baron Harington, the younger brother of Lady Bedford and close companion of Prince Henry, on 27 February 1614 occasioned Donne's *Har*. Feeling obligated to mourn in verse Lady Bedford's brother, who, like Prince Henry, was associated with extreme Puritanism and the war party, Donne found himself in a situation similar to that which had occasioned the Prince Henry Elegy: he felt obliged to praise a person whose political and religious positions he disliked and which were inimical to those of the King, whose patronage he continued to seek even as his relationship with Lady Bedford had cooled. Interestingly, the strategy Donne designed for this poem differs from that of the Elegy for Prince Henry.

As Ted-Larry Pebworth has observed, *Har* is 'extraordinary for its silences' (1992: 31): it pointedly fails to idealize its subject or to praise his public accomplishments. The poem mourns the passing of the young nobleman, and it ultimately offers consolation in its vision of the entry of Harington's soul into heaven. But Donne's principal method of praise is by means of negative formulas and indirection, and this practice (coupled with the poem's accusatory tone) subtly reveals the poet's deep-seated ambivalence about Harington's accomplishments. The praise of Harington is deliberately focused away from potentially controversial public issues to celebrate his private virtues of chastity and learning.

The most overt acknowledgement of Harington's accomplishments is couched in two questions that are afforded no specific answer: 'where can I affirme, or where arrest / My thoughts on his deeds? which shall I call best?' (ll. 41–2). The young man was unquestionably virtuous, Donne admits, but he died before his virtues could be differentiated and enumerated. Harington conquered his 'owne Affections', but these were only those resulting from 'the heate / Of youths desires, and Colds of Ignorance' (ll. 194–5). Rather than listing his accomplishments, Donne focuses on what Harington might have become had he lived longer. Significantly, however, the young man's failure to live longer argues against his being allowed an early triumph, no matter how promising he might have seemed (ll. 186–91). Although his 'Fayre soule' (l. 1) is finally granted a triumphal entry into the New Jerusalem, that triumph is effected solely through the exercise of God's 'absolute / Prerogatiue' and is in fact ''Gaynst Natures Lawes' (ll. 240–1, 242).

The poem ends with Donne fulfilling the generic expectation of an obsequy in an imagined graveside rite. Pleading the precedents of 'Saxon wiues', 'French soldurij', and 'Great Alexanders greate Excesse' at the deaths of husbands and comrades (ll. 250–2), the poet offers a 'sacrifice' to the soul of the young nobleman: 'in thy Graue I do interre my Muse / Which by my greefe, greate as thy worth, beeing cast / Behind hand; yet hath spoke, and spoke her last' (ll. 255, 256–8). In interring his muse here, Donne in effect expresses his discomfort with the poetry of patronage. As Pebworth has noted: 'The muse that Donne inters with Harington is ... not the muse of poetry in general or even the muse of secular poetry, but the muse of the poetry of patronage. He had labored long in that vineyard and had found himself facing increasingly demanding tests of his integrity and ingenuity with only niggardly rewards' (1992: 42).

Although Donne interred his muse in the grave of Lord Harington, he in fact wrote another funeral poem, *Ham*. Among the last poems Donne was to write, this Epicede was apparently composed at the request of Sir Robert Carr to commemorate a man Donne apparently knew casually, if at all. Hence the poem, like the other Epicedes and Obsequies, evinces little personal grief, but rather uses the demise of an individual to pose larger questions about death and salvation. Through some references to Hamilton's offices and the beauty of his person, as well as to rumours about the gruesome details of his death and allegations that he had experienced a deathbed conversion to Catholicism (see Maurer 2007: *passim*), the subject is personalized and his loss lamented, but the bulk of the poem is consolatory, finding in Hamilton's reception into heaven hope for all sinners.

As with several of the other Epicedes and Obsequies, the Hamilton poem poses questions about the relation of body and soul. Here, however, the poem opens with Hamilton's soul entering heaven, attempting to claim an appropriate place among the orders of angels. It acknowledges his earthly remains only in terms of his soul's having left them, but subtly alludes to reports that Hamilton's body putrified unusually quickly after his death (Maurer 2007: 6). Indeed, the poem may best be appreciated as an ingenious meditation on the relationship of body and soul as seen from the perspective of scholastic theology, a meditation prompted by the peculiar circumstances of Hamilton's death.

The larger point that the poem makes, however, is the efficacy of repentance. Rather than idealizing Hamilton the man, Donne celebrates him as an exemplar of the penitent who in heaven wishes his fellow sinners to join him there: 'let it bee / Thy wish to wish all there, to wish them cleane / Wish Him a Dauid, Her a Magdalene' (ll. 40–2). This conclusion, which may tactfully acknowledge Hamilton's reputation as a womanizer, has the effect of moving away from hyperbolic idealization to an acknowledgement of the universality of human unworthiness juxtaposed with a celebration of the miraculous effects of God's grace.

Donne's Epicedes and Obsequies illustrate the poet's innovativeness and rhetorical agility. In these distinctive poems, Donne imaginatively fulfilled the obligations of the patronage system even as he created works that transcend their occasions. By making it a more intellectual and supple genre than he found it, and by imposing on it his own distinctive idiom, he considerably expanded the traditional English elegy. Mourning individuals whom he did not know intimately and for whom he felt little personal grief, Donne focused not on creating an illusion of private loss or on evoking emotion, but on exploring larger issues, presenting the deceased as exemplars and symbols whose deaths not only witness to the common human fate but also serve to illustrate different aspects of the Christian hope for eternal life.

CHAPTER 22

THE EPITHALAMION

CAMILLE WELLS SLIGHTS

Today Renaissance epithalamions or wedding songs appear distinctly odd and John Donne's odder than most. Although weddings are social events rather than purely private experiences, our culture valorizes weddings as individualized expressions of personal romantic love. By contrast, early modern wedding poems seem conventional and impersonal. While poetic or musical compositions produced for particular weddings are now relatively rare and almost invariably gifts from family or close friends, in early modern England most serious poets produced epithalamions for the weddings of social and economic superiors from whom they sought patronage. Although the tradition of wedding poetry reaches back to biblical and classical literature and flourished in sixteenth-century Italy and especially in France among the Pléiade, the vogue for the epithalamion in England began with Edmund Spenser (for useful summaries of the epithalamic tradition in general see Greene, and Tufte; on the English epithalamion see McGowan, and Dubrow 1990). After the publication of Spenser's *Epithalamion* in 1595, a long list of English poets, including Ben Jonson, George Chapman, and Robert Herrick as well as John Donne, wrote epithalamions. These poems honouring aristocratic and noble weddings were modelled on classical epithalamions, especially Catullus 61, which, according to Virginia Tufte, is 'almost a catalogue of scenes, themes, actions, and images for the epithalamic tradition' (24). Typically the epithalamion celebrates a significant communal event rather than depicting a marriage of true minds. As Thomas M. Greene observes, it is 'a ritualistic *public* statement, unconcerned with the actual intimate experience undergone by individuals' (221). Since social institutions of marriage, patronage, gender, and class intersect with literary traditions in Renaissance epithalamions, our readings of them, even more than of most other contemporary texts, depend on and contribute to our understanding of how cultural and literary structures interact.

The ceremonial praise of the marriage of strangers seems an unlikely genre to attract the talents of John Donne, whose poetic lovers often claim to constitute a world separate from and superior to ordinary society. Nevertheless Donne's three wedding poems exhibit the general characteristics of the Renaissance epithalamion. None of the three celebrates the marriage of a close friend or family member. The first (*Variorum* 8.87–9) was probably written in about 1595 when Donne was a law student, although the participants have not been identified. The other two were occasioned by important weddings at court, that of Princess Elizabeth and Friedrich, the Elector Palatine, on 14 February 1613 (8.108–110), and that of Frances Howard and Robert Carr, the Earl of Somerset, on 26 December 1613 (8.133–9). Each, like Catullus 61, is organized chronologically through the events of the wedding day narrated from the point of view of the poet-speaker who presents himself as a member of the community celebrating the wedding.

But while Donne's wedding poems signal their connection with the traditional epithalamion, they simultaneously transform generic conventions. The wedding poem variously entitled 'Epithalamium', 'Epithalamion on a Citizen', and 'Epithalamion made at Lincolnes Inne' in extant manuscripts is the most puzzling. In fact, scholarly opinion is divided over whether it is an epithalamion at all. On one hand, it draws explicitly on epithalamic tradition. The poet-speaker directs the events of the wedding day, from the morning, when he summons the bride to rise from her solitary bed, until evening, when he instructs her to undress in preparation for the marriage bed and assures the other wedding guests that she 'at the bridegroomes wish'd approch doth ly' (l. 88). The eight twelve-line stanzas include such traditional motifs as adornment of the bride with jewels and flowers, instructions in their duties to the bride's and groom's attendants, invocation of the church, banishment of such threats to the marriage as infidelity and infertility, bedding of the bride, and anticipating offspring. A refrain is repeated with variations at the end of each stanza. The imagery too draws on the store of traditional material. Consonant with Heather Dubrow's observation that epithalamions typically 'effect and celebrate the harmony of the natural and civilized worlds' (1990: 73), the opening lines connect the wedding with the natural world: 'The Sun-beames in the East are spred / Leaue leaue fayr bride your solitary bed' (ll. 1–2). In Stanza 5 the speaker, impatient with the long daylight hours of the summer wedding, complains that the sun 'flyes in Winter, but now he stands still' (l. 55), but in the next stanza nature again provides a pattern to be followed: 'The amorous euening Star is rose / Why should not then our amorous Star enclose / Herselfe in her wish'd bed' (ll. 61–3). And in the final stanza the speaker urges the sun to rise early on the following morning, but the bride is now 'This Sun', who, he predicts, 'will love so dearly / Her rest, that long, long, we shall want her sight' (ll. 93–4).

In point of view, structure, and several topoi and poetic strategies, then, Donne's poem alludes to epithalamic traditions. On the other hand, in important ways it is decidedly unconventional. The bride receives unusual emphasis but conspicuously little praise. She figures prominently in every stanza, the speaker addresses her but not the groom, and the refrain that rings minor changes on the line, 'To day put on perfection and a womans name', pertains solely to the bride. Although the speaker anticipates the bride and groom becoming 'but one' when 'mistically ioynd' (l. 39), the repeated refrain locates the significance of the wedding not in union but in the bride's fulfilment. She gladly relinquishes virginity because 'She a Mothers riche Stile doth prefer' (l. 87). The claim that a woman becomes truly a woman only through heterosexual sex and motherhood, unacceptable today, would not have been offensive in early modern England, and Donne insists that the implication is that sex is not a therapeutic correction for a defect but a miraculous paradox by which she who is not imperfect becomes perfect: 'Wonders are wrought, for She which had no maime / To night puts on perfection and a Womans name' (ll. 95–6). Apparently the best that can be said for the bride is that she is not maimed. While Spenser praises his bride's outward and inward beauties at some length, Donne's speaker offers no details to support his claim that the Lincoln's Inn bride is 'the best bride, best worthy of prayer and fame' (l. 47). He directs the bridesmaids to dress her so that she will be 'fayre, rich, glad, and in nothing lame' (l. 23) for the occasion, but her sexual and reproductive capacity is her only noted attribute.

The Lincoln's Inn Epithalamion also differs from generic tradition in presenting the wedding of a law student and a London merchant's daughter rather than a noble or aristocratic union. Admittedly Spenser provided a precedent for a middle-class epithalamion, but, while the bourgeois setting of Spenser's *Epithalamion* contributes to a tone of tenderness and delicate humour in celebrating his own wedding, the attitude towards the middle-class milieu in Donne's poem is less respectful and the humour more satiric. As Greene points out, the merchants' daughters in Spenser's poem 'render the bride more brilliant' (223). In Donne's, the bride's attendants who will bring with them 'Thousands of Angels on [their] mariage dayes' (l. 16) implicate the current bride and groom in the mercenary dimension of marriage. Furthermore, while the bridesmaids are notable only for having rich fathers, the groom's attendants, 'Sonnes of these Senators, wealths deepe Oceans', include 'painted Courtiers, Barrells of others witts' and 'Cuntrymen, who but your Beasts, love none' (ll. 26, 27, 28).

Even more disruptive of generic expectations than the images of money and bestiality are morbid images of death and mutilation. Having called on the church to unite the couple by enfolding them in its bosom, the poet-speaker continues:

> Then may thy leane and hunger sterved wombe
> Long time expect their bodyes and ther tombe
> Long after ther owne Parents fatten thee.
>
> (ll. 40–2)

Praying for the couple's long life is conventionally appropriate, but figuring the church as hungering for their deaths and feeding on the anticipated deaths of their parents seems tactless and disturbing. Yet more grotesque is the description of the bride waiting for defloration 'Like an appointed Lambe, when tenderly / The Priest comes on his knees to'embowell her' (ll. 89–90).

Citing these and other instances of epithalamic indecorum, David Novarr (1980) has argued persuasively that the appropriate social context for understanding the poem is not early modern weddings but Inns of Court revelry. Designed for a mock-wedding performed at Lincoln's Inn, it is, he proposes, a mock-Epithalamion that parodies Spenser's recently published *Epithalamion*. If we imagine a mock wedding performed by law students with a young man in drag in the role of bride, the concentration on the bride's gender and sexuality, the mockery of young men's financial motives, and the death imagery, even the disembowelling priest, become sources of humour rather than crass and morbid intrusions into a poem intended as compliment and celebration. Building on Novarr's argument, John Shawcross suggests that editors should group this poem with Donne's Epigrams rather than his Epithalamions, because grouping it with other Epithalamions 'does not lead the reader to a contextual reading of parody' (1986: 121). Novarr's argument, however, has not been accepted universally. Heather Dubrow, for example, objects tellingly that, if Donne were writing a parody, we would expect 'a bolder and funnier one' (1990: 158), and concludes that the poem results from Donne's ambivalence between writing an epithalamion and a parody (160). Perhaps the most important conclusion we can draw from the scholarly controversy over the Lincoln's Inn Epithalamion is the humbling one that, although appropriate literary and scholarly contexts are necessary for reading well, they are more complicated and less easily recoverable than we sometimes imagine.

The occasion for *EpEliz* (*Variorum* 8.108–10) presents no mysteries comparable to those surrounding the Lincoln's Inn Epithalamion. The marriage of King James's daughter to the Elector of the Palatine was a major social and political event celebrated at court with magnificent spectacles. Almost inevitably, Donne, who in 1613 was actively trying to secure patronage that would provide him with a position in the church or at court and who a few months earlier had composed an Elegy mourning the death of Princess Elizabeth's brother, took advantage of this happier opportunity to display again his wit, learning, verbal skill, and loyalty.

Unsurprisingly Donne's poem for the wedding of the King's daughter does not subvert the values and forms of the traditional epithalamion with a salacious reference to the bride's thigh, flippant remarks about the groom's friends, tactless musing about death, or images of violent sexual initiation. The occasion called for a poem of courtly compliment and John Donne obliged. An epithalamion for a royal wedding requires the integration of the general with the particular, at once honouring marriage as a social and religious institution, paying tribute to the political structure the marriage participates in, and complimenting two specific people. Donne met this challenge deftly. An opening invocation to Bishop Valentine, the saint on whose feast day birds legendarily mated, places the wedding in the temporally and spatially inclusive contexts of Christian tradition and of the natural world. Bishop Valentine's diocese comprises *all* the air, his parishioners *all* the birds, and he marries them *every* year. The poet-speaker's reference to Noah's ark (ll. 20–1), his comparisons of the wedding guests to fairies and to satyrs (ll. 68, 104), and his appeal to the authority of 'Antiquity' (l. 69) connect the wedding to Christian, folk, and classical traditions. Recurrent images of birds, stars, sun, and moon link it with nature. Yet the poem also localizes and particularizes the event. The title and the opening line, 'Hayle Bishop Valentine whose day this is', identify the poem as not a merely generic epithalamion but a response to a specific wedding on a specific date, Valentine's Day, 14 February, a date subtly echoed throughout in fourteen-line stanzas each ending 'Valentine'. By substituting the Christian saint for the more usual classical Hymen and by introducing into the congregation of birds such familiar English sights as 'The houshold bird with the redd stomacher' (l. 8) and 'The Husband Cock' whose wife 'brings her feather bedd' (ll. 11–12) Donne localizes literary traditions. This integration of the immediate and local with the universal and timeless represents the wedding of Elizabeth and Friedrich as present participation in an ancient ritual that links human activity with the rhythms of nature.

By adapting the conventions of the epithalamion to the immediate occasion Donne demonstrates his political sensitivity and social tact. He displays his exceptional talents more strikingly by transforming literary conventions. The phoenix is the central image that enables him to combine the innovative with the traditional. The legendary phoenix is unique, a mythical bird that lives several hundred years until it burns on a funeral pyre and rises reborn from its own ashes. Figuring the bridal pair paradoxically as two unique phoenixes whose mating will produce yet more young phoenixes adds mutuality and sexual ardour to the phoenix's traditional attributes of beauty, faith, constancy, and imperishability. This union, the poet-speaker claims, produces something totally new: 'What the Sunne never sawe, and what the Arke…Did not contayne' (ll. 20–2), and it transforms the future, making Valentine's day last 'the whole yeare through' (l. 28).

The generically conventional praise of the bride is not, like Spenser's, a blason of her beauties but rather a celebration of the transcendent and transformative powers of the 'fayre Phænix-Bride' (l. 29). Instead of calling on her to awake because the sun has risen, the poet-speaker calls on her to 'frustrate the Sunne' (l. 29). She is self-sufficient, taking 'warmth enough' (l. 31) from her own affection and providing from her eyes warmth and light for 'All lesser birds' (l. 32). The speaker celebrates her power and brilliance by urging her to transform her jewels into a blazing constellation of stars and to make herself into a new star on her wedding day. He also insists that such splendour has consequences, meanings for others to read. The blazing constellation would signify 'That a Greate Princesse falls but doth not dye' (l. 38). The 'new Starre' would presage wonderful consequences, and he urges the princess to fulfill that promise, 'bee thou those ends' (l. 40).

While the poet-speaker's instructions to the bride envision self-sufficiency and power, the following stanzas emphasize interdependency and mutuality. The bride is in the process of becoming part of an inseparable union, which 'diuers wayes / Must bee effected' (ll. 52–3). The church has its part to play: 'the Bishop stayes / To make you one, his way' (ll. 51–2). But, if others help to create the union, they also obstruct it. After Bishop Valentine and the bishop of the church have united the bride and groom 'by harts and hands' (l. 54), they have, the speaker reminds Elizabeth, 'one way left your selues to entwyne' (l. 55), and that private entwining is delayed by the wedding festivities. The speaker's complaint that the sun is slow to set and the guests slow to leave is traditional, but his impatience is especially pertinent to the royal wedding when he chastises the bridal couple themselves:

> And why doe you two walke
> So slowly pac'd in this Procession?
> Is all your care but to bee lookd vpon
> And bee to others Spectacle and talke?
>
> (ll. 61–4)

King James had instructed Prince Henry that kings are 'publike persons...set...vpon a publike stage, in the sight of all the people'. Apparently Elizabeth recognized that she too had a responsibility 'to glister and shine' before her father's subjects (James I 1994: 4, 13).

Finally, however, the tedious formalities end, and Donne imagines the princess's wedding night with a surprising frankness reminiscent of *ElBed*. The groom arrives and 'passes through Spheare after Spheare / First her Sheetes, then her Armes, then any where' (ll. 81–2). Instead of a conventionally modest and sexually reluctant bride he finds sexual enthusiasm equal to his own:

> They quickly pay theyr debt, and then
> Take no Acquittances, but pay agen.
> They pay, they giue, they lend, and so let fall
> No such ocasion to bee liberall.
>
> (ll. 93–6)

Through the sexual consummation of their marriage the couple becomes one flesh and thus resolves the paradox of two unique phoenixes: 'Nature agayne restored is / For since these two are two no more / Theres but one Phænix still as was before' (ll. 100–2). The natural order is restored through the private act of the bride and groom, but they remain figures on a public stage, objects of people's gaze. As a member of the community, the poet-speaker warns that 'we' also exercise effective agency. We will wait up and watch until morning, some guests eagerly anticipating the bride's radiance, others placing bets on whether the bride or the groom will emerge from bed first.

The Epithalamion for Elizabeth and Friedrich, then, performs the traditional generic function of reconciling sexual energy with social order, and it does so with

Donne's characteristic extravagance and precision. Hyperbolic praise is tempered by bold eroticism and playful but pertinent acknowledgment of the responsibilities and inconveniences entailed by rank and position. By adapting literary conventions to the particularities of the marriage of the King's daughter the poem both performs the necessary tribute to the royal wedding and avoids a self-defeating appearance of excessive and insincere flattery.

The royal marriage posed the challenge of showing respect for established social hierarchy and traditional literary forms while also demonstrating exceptional talent, and readers have found that Donne's Valentine Epithalamion meets the challenge with ingenuity and grace. The marriage of Lady Frances Howard and Robert Carr, Earl of Somerset, presented more difficult problems, and Donne's solution continues to trouble his critics. The marriage followed shortly after the nullification of Frances Howard's first marriage to the third Earl of Essex. The nullification trial was marked by sensational allegations of impotence, witchcraft, and poisoning, and the controversial marriage occasioned much prurient gossip. In spite of the scandal, there were strong motivations to contribute to the wedding celebrations. Robert Carr was the most powerful man at court, the King's favourite through whom royal favours and court positions were dispensed. In addition, King James promoted the marriage and the enabling nullification in order to gratify Carr and to effect an alliance between powerful political factions (see Lindley for a comprehensive account of the social and political background and consequences of the Howard/Somerset marriage).

Donne, who had received patronage from Somerset and at the time of the wedding was hoping to secure a position through him, was apparently eager to serve Somerset but reluctant to write an epithalamion. He wrote to a friend, 'I deprehend in my self more than an alacrity, a vehemency to do service to that company', mentioning the possibility of writing a legal defence of the annulment and stressing his preference to serve 'in a more serious fashion, then an Epithalamion', although he acknowledged, 'by my troth, I think I shall not scape' (*Letters* 180–1). (Milgate speculates that the addressee is Donne's friend Henry Goodere [Donne 1978*b*: 118]. On the ambiguous evidence concerning Donne's relations with Carr, see Chs. 32.I and 32.II.) Much of the scholarly reaction to his Epithalamion has been regret that he did not escape connection with the lurid sex scandal and indignation that he wrote poetry to solicit favour from the King's favourite. The unsavoury reputation of the Somersets was intensified by their conviction in 1616 for the murder of Sir Thomas Overbury, who had been imprisoned in the Tower when he opposed the marriage. Lindley argues that these subsequent events have retrospectively tainted reactions to the poetry honouring the marriage. McClung and Simard note the suppression of Somerset's homoerotic behaviour and suggest that displaced homophobia has distorted criticism. (The *Variorum* edition gives a helpful sampling of nineteenth- and twentieth-century comments on the Epithalamion.) Only recently have scholars shown less interest in judging Donne's motives and morals than in analysing the complex interplay between the text and its cultural contexts (see Dubrow 1990; Hodgson; McClung and Simard; Pinka; and A. V. Scott).

The most interesting feature of the poem is that a conventionally organized Epithalamion is embedded in the framework of a pastoral Eclogue that radically destabilizes it. While R. C. Bald claimed that the introductory Eclogue functions merely to excuse the poem's not arriving until several weeks after the wedding, and dismissed it as 'an extravagant admission of the extremes to which court flattery obliged Donne to stoop' (1970: 274), recent critics have interpreted it as Donne's representation of his internal struggle within the constraints of the patronage system. In the prefatory *Eclog* (*Variorum* 8.133–5), Allophanes (one sounding like another) remonstrates with Idios (a private man) for withdrawing from court where 'all is warmth and light, and good desire' (l. 32) to the cold solitude of the country. In Allophanes' account, the fires that warm and light the court are the 'Zeale to Prince and State' and 'Loues desires' that burn in Somerset's breast, but the ultimate source of creative energy at court is the King: 'The Princes fauour, is diffusd o're all / From which all fortunes names and natures fall' (ll. 18, 23–4). Idios counters that, since princes animate not only their court but 'all theyr state' (l. 42), he is virtually already at court and that, since kings, like God, bestow not only blessings but the capacity 'to feele and see / And comprehend' them (ll. 46–7), a recluse may see and understand more than a worldly man. Allophanes picks up Idios' emphasis on individual responsiveness: just as 'Stuff well disposd' can become gold only when exposed to the sun, so well-disposed men achieve 'Wisedome and honour from the vse of kings' (ll. 62, 68). For Idios' claim that he is already at court Allophanes offers his own paradox: 'Angels, though on earth employd they bee / Are still in heauen: so is hee still at home / That doth abrode to honest Actions come' (ll. 70–2).

In one sense, then, the Eclogue fulfills generic expectations of a debate on the relative merits of court and country, action and contemplation. Idios endorses quiet contemplation in the country and Allophanes active engagement at court. From another, biographical, perspective Allophanes can be seen to represent Donne's private and Idios his public persona, or Allophanes embodies Donne's attraction to the court and Idios his 'reluctance to participate in that world' (Dubrow 1990: 196). Yet despite these contrasts, Idios and Allophanes share fundamental values. Allophanes' final speech praises the court, 'where All affections doe assent / Vnto the Kings' and 'the Kings are iust' (ll. 76–7), and explains that this harmony is achieved through a patronage system in which the King's favours are channelled through a man who rewards virtue. Right now, moreover, this wise man, the King's confidant, is in love. Idios agrees completely: 'I Knewe / All this' (ll. 91–2). Admitting the futility of knowing and feeling without means for making individual understanding public, he explains that he fled to the country because he could not find words to express his perceptions of the wedding celebrations. Like Donne, however, he found that he had 'scap't not' (l. 97): 'Full of the common Ioye I vttered some', and invites Allophanes to read his 'Nuptiall song' (ll. 98–9).

Eclog, then, is not a departure from Donne's real concerns into uncongenial territory but a working through of the tensions between private retirement and public engagement that absorbed him throughout his life. Idios, who believes that 'reclus'd Hermits often times doe knowe / More of heauens Glory then a worldling can' (ll. 48–9) yet describes himself as 'dead and buryed' (l. 101) in the country, recalls the Satires, where retired privacy is both 'wholesome solitarinesse' (*Sat4* l. 155) and associated with the grave: 'in this standing woodden chest, / Consorted with these few bookes, let me lye /...and here be coffin'd, when I dye' (*Sat1* ll. 2–4). When Idios, who withdrew from court, nevertheless finds words to participate in the 'common Ioye', he anticipates Donne the preacher's warning: 'Almighty God ever loved *unity*, but he never loved *singularity*' (*Sermons* 5.113).

Idios' wedding song, the embedded Epithalamion (*Variorum* 8.135–9), enacts this merging of the individual with the collective. It follows the traditional chronological organization, but the speaker does not act as master of ceremonies, the role Greene calls 'one of the most distinctive' conventions (219–20). Idios, in the country imagining the wedding, calls attention to the effort involved with phrases such as 'let mee heere contemplate thee', 'first let mee see', and 'it is some wrong / To thinke' (ll. 129, 130, 138–9). He rebukes his 'vndiscerning Muse' for the refrain ending the first stanza, 'The fire of these inflaming eyes, or of this louing hart' (ll. 116, 115), which seems to assume the conventional figures of irresistible bride and desiring groom when on reflection he knows that 'his eye as enflaming is / As hers, and her heart loues as well as his' (ll. 118–19). When he shifts his attention from the bride and groom themselves to their public appearance, he shifts from first-person singular to plural, merging his individual point of view with that of the community. But, even as he speaks as a representative of the social group, he emphasizes its perceptual weakness, requesting the bride to tone down her brilliance for 'our ease' (l. 146) and confessing that 'wee' think of the bride and groom as two although, 'By the Church rites, you are from thenceforth one' (ll. 160–5).

The merging of Idios' individual perceptions with those of the community and the merging of the imperfect perceptions of the community with that of 'The Church Triumphant' that 'made this Match' (l. 166) act out recognition of the Epithalamion's dominant idea, the merging of the bride and groom into one. Even gender differences are dissolved since on the basis of beauty the 'Bridegrome is a Mayd' and judged on courage the 'Bride / Becomes a man' (ll. 121, 123–4). In brief references to the opposition to the marriage—'vniust opinion' (l. 123), 'chance or enuyes Art' (l. 124), the striving of the church militant (l. 167)—Idios acknowledges forces that attempt to divide them, but insists that 'Loues strong Arts' can transform 'Indiuiduall parts' into 'Ioyes bonfire', 'One fire of 4 enflaming eyes, and of 2 louing harts' (ll. 223–5).

Since Donne did not write a legal opinion about the nullification, we have no external evidence for the cause of his expressed reluctance to write an Epithalamion for Frances Howard's second marriage. The poem itself does not suggest insincere flattery undercut by coded signals of disapproval but the precarious balance of individual and group identity in the interests of social unity. Frances Howard needs to dim her dangerous brilliance for the common good, and Idios must learn that the public has a claim on the nuptial song inspired by the communal celebration. The process by which divergent views become one is not without strain, even coercion. In the final ten lines, when Idios announces his intention of burning his song as a sacrifice, Allophanes refuses to return it since, 'Whatever celebrates this Nuptiall / Is common, since the Ioye thereof is so' (ll. 231–2). Maintaining the image of the court of James I as one 'where all Affections doe assent / Vnto the Kings' (ll. 76–7) would have required similar strain and pressure or a leap of faith akin to maintaining that husband and wife are one flesh.

Much of Donne's poetry deals with male/female relations being negotiated in a world fraught with complications of power imbalances and public scrutiny. In many of his most familiar poems a pair of lovers is in dynamic tension with the outside public world. *SunRis*, for example, begins by rejecting the sun and everything under it as irrelevant to the lovers and ends by inviting the sun's gaze to the lovers' bed that is an epitome of the entire world. Similarly, *Canon* begins by defining a private world of love against the outside world and ends with a communal hymn in which 'all' petition the lovers for 'A patterne of [your] love' (l. 45). In the Epithalamions Donne examines this pull between the privacy of love and the collectivity of community from the other side, assuming the voice of outsider rather than lover. When he outrageously refers to the bride's attendants as 'Our golden Mines and furnish'd Treasuree' (*EpLin* l. 14), reminds Princess Elizabeth and Elector Palatine that they are 'to others Spectacle and talke' (*EpEliz* l. 64), and admonishes Frances Howard to subdue her brilliance to accommodate 'our Infirmity' (*Eclog* l. 149), he represents the demands of the community on individuals. When he calls on those 'Daughters of London' to praise 'These rites which allso vnto you grow due' (*EpLin* l. 18), he suggests that since Elizabeth 'dost this day in new glory shine / May all men date Records from this thy Valentine' (*EpEliz* l. 42), and prays that Howard and Somerset will produce heirs who will serve the King's heirs 'to the worlds end' (*Eclog* l. 177), he reminds the community of its dependence on the private, intimate act of love. As Donne later said in a marriage Sermon, 'both of *Civill* and of *Spirituall* societies, the first roote is a *family*; and of families, the first roote is *Mariage*' (*Sermons* 2.336).

In his Epithalamions, then, Donne uses a fashionable genre to fulfil its traditional function of celebrating the intersection of the personal and the communal even as he bends conventional forms to register the disjunctions and difficulties of merging the individual into the collective in his own social, financial, and political world. Although they are not among Donne's most popular or moving poems, they are complex and fascinating instances of his characteristic concerns and poetic strategies. All three exhibit the energy, the arresting speaking voices, the unexpected images, the ingenious, paradoxical arguments, the intellectual agility, and the transformation of literary traditions and conventions that mark the Songs and Sonets and Holy Sonnets, and they have a similar capacity to puzzle, delight, and outrage readers.

CHAPTER 23

THE DEVOTION

KATE NARVESON

A 'devotion' generally consisted of meditation and prayer. The term was used loosely during the seventeenth century and had no stable referent in terms of form, but devotional writing had developed a number of characteristic features. Its structure reflected the purpose of meditation: to awaken the heart to sin, repentance, and desire for God. A devotion therefore moved from considerations that unfolded the spiritual implications of a topic to fervently felt responses. Its voice was generic: because it was assumed that any particular Christian's experience conformed to a general godly pattern, devotions did not offer immediate self-expression but rather voiced the meditator's experience in well-established theological terms, in which readers also found their own experience expressed.

For a picture of how devotion was understood by Donne's contemporaries, we can turn to Joseph Hall's *The arte of divine meditation* (1606). By meditation, Hall explained, we 'get more light to our knowledge, more heat to our affections, more life to our devotion' (3). Meditation begins with 'a bending of the mind vpon some spiritual obiect…vntill our thoughts come to an issue' (7), but any 'labour of the brain' (150) is useless unless it touches the heart and shapes desire. Thus meditation must also stir up the emotions, and indeed, an affective response should follow naturally, for 'we can not knowe aright but wee must needes bee affected' (151). Meditation, then, culminates in prayer. Hall also distinguishes meditation into two types, extemporal, 'occasioned by outward occurrences', and deliberate, on a theological topic (7).

Within this general pattern were many meditative modes. The Protestant reformations and Roman Catholic renewals stimulated the development of systematic devotional disciplines. Ignatius of Loyola's *Spiritual Exercises* (1524) contributed to the period's sense of devotion's trajectory from thought to affect, and a conception of devotional psychology was broadly shared across confessional lines even while there was a perceived sense of difference, reflected primarily in uses of Scripture. While devotion gave renewed attention to Scripture even before 1517, English Protestants, committed to the principle of *sola scriptura*, rooted their works in ample biblical quotation and citation whereas English Catholic works included relatively less scriptural reference. John Roberts notes that in response to Protestant scripturalism, 'Catholics began to stress tradition and to de-emphasize the role of Scripture' (J. R. Roberts 1966: 11). Further diversity was created by the concern among late Elizabethan Protestants to create native resources and to root meditation in doctrinal understanding, a concern that caused a proliferation of subgenres providing aids to devotion: treatises on affliction, manuals for the sick, arts of dying well, guides to prayer, and so forth. Yet across these subgenres and across the confessional spectrum, as a body of literature, early Stuart devotional writing was unified by a shared theological anthropology with its own terminology for articulating human experience vis-à-vis God.

Features of this anthropology inform the genre. First, devotional affect was to be based on right understanding, with a resultant blurring of the line between expression and instruction. Just as devotional treatises sought to arouse emotion, teaching about (for instance) sin and hellfire in order to spur repentance, so meditation and prayer rehearsed a doctrinal understanding of the believer's condition even as they expressed devotion. A meditator understood experience through the lens of doctrine, especially as it explained the twists and turns of spiritual psychology. That approach, along with the belief that spiritual experience conformed to a general pattern, contributed to the characteristic voice and style of the genre. Most early Stuart meditations shifted easily between some combination of the first-person singular of the Everyman and the more didactic first-person plural, so that the voice is generic and exemplary even when it expresses penitence or joy. Devotions also tended to adopt a plain style similar to that of the Puritan sermon, though there was room for stylistic variation: the eloquent meditations of a notable Christian could serve as inspiration and example, and some devotions employed a fervent, rhetorically elaborate style. A feature especially characteristic of Protestant style was the way it foregrounded its scripturalism. Devotional writers quoted passages, worked phrases from the Bible into the fabric of their meditations, and developed their points by means of collation, or the collection of supporting verses from throughout the Bible, a process felt to show the tenor of God's ways and to demonstrate, as Grace Mildmay put it in her meditations, 'euery poynt of doctrine confirmed and approoued by the Scriptures' (Mildmay 5). In contrast, Catholic works generally include citations to a figure or event, or to a point that is summarized rather than quoted, so that the prose is less thoroughly imbued with direct biblical quotation.

In characterizing any feature as Protestant, of course, it is important to recognize the degree to which Catholic and Protestant works borrowed from or responded to each other (R. V. Young 2007: 378–80). One of the most influential Elizabethan works was the *Resolution*, by a Jesuit, Robert Persons. The *Resolution* was quickly revised by the Protestant Edmund Bunny, whereupon Persons responded with outrage that Bunny made him 'speake after the phrase of Protestantes' (Persons 1585: 11r). He similarly attacked Thomas Rogers for his 1580 translation of the *Introduction to the Devout Life*. Rogers had typographically emphasized Scripture references, a choice he explained in another translation, of *A pretious booke of heavenlie meditations*, attributed to Augustine: 'me thought were the places of Scripture annexed in the margine, it would be a quick spur... unto the true Christians zealouslie to read this ancient and godlie Father, when they should see al his sentences in a maner to be nothing but verie Scripture' (Rogers 1604: A7r). Most Catholic devotions were less persistently scripturalist even when in Protestant translations, such as Francis Meres's version of Luis de Granada's meditations. The same holds true in Catholic manuscript devotional notebooks such as Huntington Library HM 104 and BL MS Lansdowne 322. Most citations in Catholic works, except in prefatory matter that engaged in controversy, are to the Psalms, the wisdom books, and the gospel accounts of the life of Christ, rather than to the more theological books of the Pentateuch, prophets, and epistles. Further, in Catholic works there tends to be more organization around traditional categories such as the seven virtues, eight beatitudes, five bodily senses, and so forth, and more discussion of good works, using a vocabulary (e.g. degrees of perfection, corporal acts of mercy) rarely found in Protestant devotional works. Catholic works also tend to assume the distinction between the religious and the laity. These differences were matters of emphasis and degree and were not essential to the vision of what a disciplined devotional life involved, as witnessed by the numerous Protestant versions of Catholic works. But they registered the strong sense most believers had of confessional identity.

The fervent style and the scripturalism united in a devotional subgenre based on medieval meditations or 'soliloquies' attributed to Augustine and Protestantized by Thomas Rogers, who announced on his title page that his work, *A right Christian Treatise entituled S. Avgvstines Praiers*, was 'purged from diuers superstitious points; and adorned with manifold places of the S. Scripture'. Imitated by men such as Sir John Hayward in his best-selling *Sanctuarie of a troubled soule* (1604), the soliloquy offers one of the closest formal parallels to Donne's work. The rhetoric was highly affective, with apostrophe, exclamation, expostulation, and rhetorical questioning of God or the soul (Narveson). Two other subgenres are also particularly relevant, the occasional meditation and the spiritual autobiography. The occasional meditation had as its focus a striking event or sight, the meditator drawing out its spiritual significance as a stimulus to prayer. In most collections of occasional meditations, each is discrete, a collection of assorted observations. While the sights prompting the meditation have a kind of particularity (a hog eating acorns, a clock-tower), the voice is still generic. Since Donne's *Devotions* are not only occasional but are linked as stages in a particular passage in his life, his work also bears some relation to the genre of spiritual autobiography, exemplified by Augustine's *Confessions*, which seeks to see God's hand and purposes in the events of one's life (Frost 15–38).

The 'devotion' in early Stuart England, then, had forebears reaching back to St Augustine as well as a flourishing immediate family, with varied offspring linked by common familial traits. Donne's *Devotions*, while of that family, is remarkable among them. The work exhibits many features of contemporary meditation and prayer: its structural dynamic; easy shift from singular to plural voice; display of the self as exemplary; scripturalism; and rehearsal of spiritual truth merging with affective expression. But Donne's particular aims led him to innovate on these features and to recombine features from various subgenres, resulting in a work that reinvents the genre, giving it an unprecedented intellectual and emotional intensity. It is distinctive as well in seeming more personal and spontaneous than other such works.

The most immediate context for the *Devotions* was a grave illness that confined Donne to his bed from November 1623 through the winter. The illness, possibly typhus fever, was severe enough that Donne felt the need to prepare for death. Then, still on his sickbed, Donne readied the resultant Devotions for print and in January 1623/4 published the *Devotions upon Emergent Occasions*. Since Donne's only previous published works had been connected to a patron or issue of public concern, it is striking that he sought publication of what might seem to be a private work. His sense of calling provides one explanation. Figuring illness as exile, Donne questions God: 'Why callest thou me from my calling?' He confesses that 'thine *Apostles* feare takes hold of mee, *that when I have preached to others, I my selfe should be a cast-way*' (17). We can, then, see the *Devotions* as a preaching from the sickbed (Mueller 1968: 7–8). Another context may have been the publication in 1621 of a work recounting the alleged deathbed conversion to Catholicism of Bishop John King (Levy-Navarro 2000: 481–3). In the *Devotions*, Donne fears '*ill interpretation*' (27) and prays for defence against that person who would 'defame me, & magnifie himselfe, with false rumors of such a victory, & surprisall of me, after I am dead' (28). Consciousness of the public eye seems also to have motivated publication. Finally, Donne seems to have aimed to model Devotions that reflect his irenic theology so that they give a 'local form attuned to the national aspirations of Reformation England' and yet avoid 'the more controversial religious issues of the early seventeenth century' (R. V. Young 2007: 380, 373).

These contexts have implications for Donne's choices about genre. The first, his choice to write Devotions, is the most significant. While Donne's conception of sin and sickness was influenced by treatises on illness and affliction, when it came to genre he chose to write meditations such as Hall described (Goldberg 1971: 507–8). His work's formal division of each Devotion into Meditation, Expostulation, and Prayer, while distinctive to Donne, reflects the trajectory from consideration to affective response to prayer. Further, Donne's voice reflects the way meditation saw the personal in light of the general. He states, for instance, 'I stand in the way of tentations, (naturally, necessarily, all men doe so...)' (*Devotions* 8), and he confesses to God that 'Thou hast imprinted a *pulse* in our *Soule*, but we do not examine it' (9). He therefore moves easily between first-person singular, 'this minute I was well, and am ill, this minute', and plural: 'We study *Health*, and we deliberate upon our *meats*...But in a minute a Cannon batters all, overthrowes all' (7). And in line with contemporary meditation, his work roots godly emotion in doctrinal understanding. In Meditation 6, for example, Donne anatomizes the state of a man possessed by fear. He realizes that, 'As the ill affections of the *spleene*, complicate, and mingle themselves with every infirmitie of the body, so doth *feare* insinuat it self in every *action*, or *passion* of the *mind*' (29), and the Expostulation gives his emotional response as he breaks into vehement questioning—'*O my God*, can I doe this, and *feare* thee; come to thee, and speak to thee, in all places, at all houres, and *feare* thee? Dare I ask this question?' (31). The Expostulation's doctrinal resolution of this question generates the relief and gratitude voiced in the Prayer.

The style, then, is highly affective, licensed by the aim to arouse as well as instruct, yet Donne applies the licence in a distinctive way. Rather than adopting a generic voice, Donne crafts a voice that conveys the urgency of a particular individual. In its attempt to arouse emotion, it is closer to the voice of the preacher than to the voice of most published meditations, and yet it is more personal than a homiletic voice, and gives the impression that the sentences emerge from the heat of passionate thought (B. Nelson 2003: 247). This impression is the result in part of Donne's use of Scripture. In two ways, this scripturalism is similar to that in other devotions. First, he uses Scripture to remind God of precedent, because God is 'ever constant to [God's] owne wayes' (*Devotions* 49). For example, he points out that: 'Thy corrections may go far, & burn deepe, and yet not leave me spotles: thy *children* apprehended that, when they said, *From our former iniquitie wee are not cleansed, untill this day*' (69). Second, Donne's Prayers weave in phrases from Scripture as his own. But a third characteristic, an extravagant use of metaphor, innovates dramatically. Donne justifies his practice as scriptural, pointing out that in God's Word there is 'such a height of *figures*, such *voyages*, such *peregrinations* to fetch remote and precious *metaphors*' (99) as surpasses all prophane authors. Yet the remoteness of the metaphors and remarkable associative leaps set his work apart from other devotional writing. One of the most striking features of the *Devotions* is the way that each thought is subject to further angles of vision that cumulatively capture the riddling nature of human experience. We can see this process in Meditation 3: finding himself flat on his sickbed, Donne begins with the commonplace that Man is not, 'as others, groveling, but of an erect, of an upright form, naturally built, & disposed to the contemplation of *Heaven*' (14–15). Yet 'what state hath he in this *dignitie*? A fever can fillip him downe' (15). Donne's mind then leaps to the posture of Adam before his animation, 'flat upon the ground', and thus to our posture when breath leaves us, 'flat upon [the] bed' (15). On this bed Donne is a prisoner, paradoxically manacled by the weakness of his sinews: 'Strange fetters to the feete, strange Manacles to the hands, when the feete, and handes are bound so much the faster, by how much the coards are slacker' (15). Shifting metaphors again, on his sickbed he is 'mine owne *Ghost*, and rather affright my beholders, then instruct them' (15). Inhuman posture, Donne concludes in one final associative leap, 'where I must practise my lying in the *grave*, by lying still, and not practise my *Resurrection*, by rising any more' (16). Ostensibly imitating Scripture's voyages to fetch remote and precious figures, Donne's restless, associative heaping of figures gives his work much of its remarkable energy.

Donne's use of Scripture in the Expostulations involves another innovation. Where most meditations weave in phrases from the Bible in a way that assimilates Scripture to their own voice, Donne treats Scripture as the voice of an Other that can correct and expand his limited human perspective (Mueller 1968: 3). Faced with the questions that have arisen in the Meditations, Donne finds answers in God's words, printed in italics and cited in the margins. In the Fourth Expostulation, for instance, having raised the question whether it is legitimate to consult physicians, Donne tells God that he finds 'It is the voyce of thy Sonn, *Wilt thou bee made whole*? That drawes from the patient a confession that hee was ill, and could not make himselfe wel. And it is thine owne voyce, *Is there no Phisician*? That inclines us, disposes us to accept thine *Ordinance*' (*Devotions* 21). In this way, Donne conveys the impression of genuine discovery. Where in most devotions the writer joins Scripture quotations with his or her own words to build a monologic utterance, Donne developed a new, dialogic way of representing how the believer's interaction with Scripture resolves perplexity: confronted with Scripture verses, Donne protests and resists what he sees as God's ways, until the 'voices' that he finds in Scripture finally break through and reorient his perspective. In the Fifth Expostulation, finding himself isolated by his sickness and finding that the Bible represents solitude as a curse, he protests: 'Have I such a *Leprosie* in my *Soule*, that I must die alone; alone without thee?' (27). He notes verses that might mitigate his fear, such as Exodus 24:2, where '*Moses was commaunded to come neere the Lord alone*', and Genesis 32:24, where God came to Jacob when he found him alone. Yet he does not accept that solution, instead searching the Bible further till he finds another voice in Ecclesiasticus 6:16, '*a faithfull friend is the phisicke of life, and they that feare the Lord, shall finde him*' (28). This verse eases Donne's fear by allowing him to see both healing and divine presence in the attendance of his physician.

Donne's remarkable style can, then, be attributed in part to his departures from convention in the way he used Scripture. But the style of the Meditations, which rarely quote Scripture, also conveys intellectual ferment. Questions, exclamations, apostrophes, and asyndeton all communicate the force of Donne's thoughts, while asymmetrical parallelism, abrupt openings, and incomplete sentences unbalance the prose (Webber 1963: 144–7). These features of Donne's style reflect the way he drew on three devotional subgenres. First, Donne's affective style resembles that of holy soliloquies such as the pseudo-Augustinian *Soliloquium animae*, Hayward's

Sanctuarie, and the meditations of Luis de Granada, translated in 1598 as *Granados Spirituall and heavenlie Exercises*, in which the soul passionately addresses itself and God. Still, soliloquies use a fervent style without giving the impression of a distinctive, individual voice. One reason that Donne created a more individual voice than the norm is that he looked not only to pseudo-Augustinian meditation but to the *Confessions* themselves, and built on Augustine's assumption that a particular person's interrogation of experience may be exemplary. In the dedication Donne declares that 'Examples of Good Kings *are* Commandements; *And* Ezechiah *writt* the Meditations *of his* Sicknesse, *after his* Sicknesse'. Donne follows Hezekiah's example by allowing readers to observe God's hand in Donne's life, to 'their owne spirituall benefit' (*Devotions* 24). In Expostulation 16 Donne notes that 'a man extends to his *Act* and to his *example*; to that which he *does*, and that which he *teaches*' (84). Donne's Meditations perform something like the confession as homiletic self-display that Donne describes in a Sermon: 'when I accuse my selfe, and confesse mine infirmities to another man, that man may understand, that there is, in that confession of mine, a Sermon' (*Sermons* 5.51). Donne added to the passionate but non-individualized rhetoric of the soliloquy the particularity of self-display.

Donne also drew on the tradition of spiritual autobiography in other ways. The *Devotions* regularly cites the *Confessions*. Yet here too, even as he adapts some features of a genre Donne departs significantly from it. He does not situate his illness within a narrative of his life, and thus where Augustine considers events as causes of his distinctive development, in the *Devotions*, events are occasions for meditation, each confronting Donne with the problem of interpreting his illness as beneficial affliction. The debt to the *Confessions* shows in other ways. Donne draws on Augustine's understanding of confession as a means to edify others and as a duty whereby one acknowledges one's relationship to God. True, God can see the heart directly, but '*O my God*, there is another way of knowing my sins, which thou lovest better then any of these; To know them by my *Confession*' (*Devotions* 54), and 'thou knowest them not to my *comfort*, except thou know them by my telling them to thee' (54–5). The Devotions thus address God rather than their human audience, even while devotional writing is an act directed to the community. But while Donne borrowed from Augustine's *Confessions* ways of conceiving his project, he did not adopt its structure. Augustine explored a linear path from confusion and error to spiritual understanding, whereas Donne structures his work around the always necessary, recurrent exercise of transcending the perspective of a natural man. A collection of Devotions was thus better suited to Donne's ends than autobiographical narrative.

While the *Devotions* incorporates elements of spiritual autobiography, holy soliloquy, and scriptural devotion, the title links the work most explicitly with occasional meditation, and here too, Donne innovates in ways that help to explain his work's urgency. Whereas most collections of occasional meditation offer discrete meditations, Donne created a series of linked Devotions, so that the occasions are 'emergent' not simply in presenting themselves to him but as developments in a larger event. Donne highlighted this narrative by prefacing the work with a Latin hexameter poem that details the 'stationes' or stages of his sickness. The line describing each stage reappears as a headnote to the Devotion that reflects on that stage, so that the whole collection recounts an unfolding drama (Papazian 1991). This adaptation transforms the genre. No longer merely a collection of observations, the Devotions address a critical episode in the speaker's life, and because the occasions emerge in time, a compelling plot links them.

The question of why Donne combined elements from so many devotional modes returns us to the work's context. Donne's anxiety about the way he will be 'read' by the public indicates that he was concerned about the responsibility of the Christian, and in particular of the preacher as public figure, to proffer an edifying example not only in his work's sentiments but in its method, modelling how to read God's hand in the life of a believer aright. His illness calls for interpretation, and therefore the reader must be shown where and how to look for truth. A hermeneutic lies behind the writing of any work of devotion, because in so far as the genre begins with consideration of spiritual truth in order to create a devout response, the writer's sense of what that consideration involves will inform the focus and structuring of the movement from thought to affect. Donne's innovations in the devotional genre can be seen as the product of a hermeneutic far more sophisticated than is usual in devotional works.

The challenge in the *Devotions* is to find a way to read illness as consonant not with judgement but mercy. Donne grounds his effort by invoking the simultaneity of sin and grace. He finds comfort in God's decrees: though sin persists, God need only refer him to the promises written in Scripture and he will be healed (*Devotions* 49). He must watch for sin while at the same time he is 'establish'd, both in a constant assurance, that thou wilt speake to me...and that, if I take knowledg of that voice then, and flye to thee, thou wilt preserve mee from falling, or raise me againe, when by naturall infirmitie I am fallen' (10). Donne can confront his infirmity because God's voice awakens him, and God can prevent or overrule sin.

The situation therefore dictates the form. It first requires self-examination. Aware of his melancholic temperament, Donne chides himself for the sorts of 'vaine imaginations' that 'this suspicious, & jealous diligence will turne to an inordinate dejection of spirit, and a diffidence in [God's] care & providence' (10). The historical context is significant here. Anti-Puritan sentiment characterized the scrutiny of the heart as egocentric self-concern. In focusing devotions around self-examination, Donne might seem to align his excursion into the genre with the hotter sort of Protestant. However, in another reimagining of the genre, he balances self-scrutiny with scrutiny of communal and divine evidence. He models a combination of self-examination and attention to God's promises, to the experience of believers in all times, and to outward signs, for 'meanes are not meanes, but in their *concatenation*, as they *depend*, and are *chained* together' (102). Donne thus avoids the solipsism of which Puritans were accused. In each Devotion he achieves assurance as the product of strenuous interpretive efforts in tracing the concatenation of God's signs.

Structurally, then, the twenty-three Devotions are the main formal units, each representing a complete movement from fallen human perspective to spiritual clarity. Each Devotion is then divided to reflect the trajectory of thought and affect involved. Reflecting the need to connect the signs of God's hand, Meditations and Expostulations display the speaker's associative habit of mind. Donne makes an observation and then follows a chain of associations, generally secular in the Meditations and biblical in the Expostulations, that cumulatively allow new insight. Donne's starting points are often commonplaces—sickness awakens us to sin, makes us call on God, weans us from the world—but his associations bring them into unexpected focus. For instance, Donne states that 'This *Resurrection* of my *body*, shewes me the *Resurrection* of my *soule*'. But the idea spurs him to ask why God has not called him, as Lazarus, '*with a loud voice*, since my *Soule* is as dead as his *Body* was?' (112). Scripture reveals that God's voice is heard in winds, chariots, thunders, floods. Donne's sins cry aloud, and why does God's voice not overwhelm them? Indeed, there are scriptural precedents that 'even they that are *secure* from danger, shall perish; How much more might I?' (114). Nonetheless, Donne concludes, 'let me bee content with that…which thou declarest in this *decaied flesh*', that he must attend God with faith (114). From body to Scripture and back, this train of associations leads to new insight into how God uses illness to 'declare' spiritual truth.

Within each Devotion, Donne's hermeneutic proceeds in stages enacted in the sequence of Meditation, Expostulation, and Prayer. The Meditations show the speaker as observer of his condition. He must confront not only the collapse of his body but its opacity to understanding. Donne conveys this opacity by developing the parallel between the nature and diagnosis of physical and spiritual illness, drawing on current medical thought, which spoke of the 'indications' that call for yet resist interpretation (Pender 230–48). Thus, in Meditation 10 Donne reflects that 'The *pulse*, the *urine*, the *sweat*, all have sworn to say *nothing*, to give no *Indication* of any dangerous *sicknesse*' (*Devotions* 52). So, too, sin works in secret. The Meditations model the way a believer must proceed by observation and inference yet remember that truth is elusive, confronting us only with a fuller sense of 'how manifold, and perplexed a thing, nay, how wanton and various a thing is *ruine* and *destruction*' (46).

The Expostulations are Donne's unique contribution to devotional writing, in which he developed an intermediate stage to represent the soul seeking to resolve the problems raised in the Meditations. Donne models how a believer, anxious about how to view his condition, must range through the books of Scripture and Nature for signs and evidences. Indeed, God speaks 'not onely in the *voice* of *Nature*, who speakes in our *hearts*, and of thy *word*, which speakes to our *eares*, but in the speech of *speechlesse Creatures*, in *Balaams Asse*, in the speech of *unbeleeving men*, in the confession of *Pilate*, in the speech of the *Devill* himselfe' (89). Therefore, Donne uncovers a multitude of signs. God has 'imprinted a *pulse* in our *Soule*...; a voice in our conscience' (9). In the funeral bell the church preaches a *'repetition Sermon'* (84). Even through the *'seale'* of so common a thing as sleep, God offers *'evidence'*, *'testimony'*, and *'Argument'* (79). As Donne searches these signs, he reasons with God, voicing dissatisfactions and fears yet arriving ultimately at the greater wisdom of God's dispensation.

The Expostulations dramatize the stance of the soul impatient for delivery. For Donne, when a devout person seems to be questioning God, he is in fact making a doctrinal statement and calling for its confirmation:

when [David] sayes, (in apparence) by way of expostulation, and jealousie, and suspition, *Will God shew wonders to the dead? shall the dead arise and praise him?*...All these passionate interrogatories, and vehement expostulations may safely be resolved into these Doctrinall propositions, Yes, God will shew wonders to the dead. (*Sermons* 4.67)

Expostulation is the manner in which God's people voice their distress and yet reveal their faith. Whatever fears Donne's illness may inspire, each Devotion brings him to the point where he can state, 'I clog not... my *prayers* to thee, with any limited conditions', and can pray, 'relieve me, in thy way, in thy time, and in thy measure' (*Devotions* 29). Expostulation allows the simultaneous experience of sin and grace, and by making it the crux of each Devotion, Donne adapted towards even greater expressivity a genre that allowed confession of sin and doubt as well as faith.

Each Devotion culminates in a Prayer whose balanced clauses reflect achieved insight. Most Prayers use the governing metaphors of the Devotion they conclude so that, although the Prayers are the most traditionally conceived component of Donne's work, they provide a closure that is effective in literary as well as devotional terms, giving each Devotion a unity that is Donne's final contribution to the genre.

CHAPTER 24

THE SERMON

JEANNE SHAMI

1

We read Donne's Sermons today for a variety of reasons, many of them accidents of history. Only six of Donne's Sermons (preached on important occasions, between 1622 and 1627, before eminent auditories) were published during his lifetime. Donne's eldest son arranged for the printing of his father's Sermons in three great folios in the seventeenth century (see Ch. 5), but they were not revived until the nineteenth century (Haskin 2007), when Henry Alford published most of them in his six-volume edition of Donne's works. In the 1920s Donne's Sermons were examined—and dismissed—by T. S. Eliot as the egocentric rantings of a 'religious spellbinder, the Reverend Billy Sunday of his time' (292), but Eliot's judgement was not sufficient to quell enthusiasm for Donne's Sermons once rediscovered, and in 1962 Evelyn Simpson completed the ten-volume scholarly edition of Donne's Sermons begun with George Potter in the 1940s, making Donne's 160 surviving Sermons available in their entirety for the first time to scholars.

We *ought* to read Donne's Sermons because they were important to him: the culmination of his intellectual life, the repository of his moral and political thought, and, at their best, his finest literary creations. When Donne entered the pulpit in 1615 at the age of 43, he had been apprenticing for this position for some time. As early as the Satires (*c*.1593–7) Donne had contrasted the satirist's moral and rhetorical authority with that of Preachers, who are 'Seas of Wit and Arts' (*Sat4* l. 238) capable of drowning the sins that the satirist can only attempt to wash away. In *Lit*, Donne had urged interpretive independence from the potentially oppressive authority of Doctors of the Church, who in their zeal may have 'misdone' or 'mis-said' (A. Patterson 2002:

42–3). The *Essayes in Divinity*, tentatively dated c.1611–15, practise exegesis in a private forum, referring to themselves as sermons without auditories (see Ch. 19). When Donne delivered his last Sermon, *Deaths Duell* (published 1632), contemporaries believed he had preached his own funeral sermon, thereby fulfilling his ambition to die in the pulpit and completing his lifelong fascination with the pulpit's transformative power and authority.

Moreover, we ought to read Donne's Sermons because they were important cultural events that established his considerable contemporary reputation as a preacher in their own day. His professional gifts were so eminent that within a year of his ordination he had been offered fourteen clerical positions. Izaak Walton, one of Donne's parishioners, his first biographer, and 'his *Convert*' (Donne 1633b: 384, l. 76), wrote that Donne was 'a Preacher in earnest, weeping sometimes for his Auditory, sometimes with them' (Walton 1670: 38). Constantijn Huygens, Dutch statesman and secretary to King James's son-in-law, King Friedrich of Bohemia, praised Donne in this way: 'From your golden mouth,' his verse states, 'whether in the chamber of a friend, or in the pulpit, fell the speech of Gods, whose nectar I drank again and again with heartfelt joy' (Bald 1970: 442). The commemorative verses accompanying Donne's *Poems* consolidate his reputation as England's 'golden Chrysostome', the great preaching Father of the early church (c.347–407), whose reputation for powerful rhetorical delivery, earnestness of conviction, and practical moral wisdom made him—like Donne—a preacher who 'Could charm the Soule' (Donne 1633b: 379, l. 17), 'divide the heart, and conscience touch' (395, l. 62).

Donne's Sermons are a lens through which to understand his culture, not because they are representative but because they are unique. His Sermons reveal clearly the hotly contested matters of his day, articulate the crises on which they comment in their most complex forms, and expose the fault-lines of their religious and political contexts. Donne is so helpful in understanding his culture's anxieties because he brings all of these to the forefront, often engaging his hearers in a self-conscious reflection on how these crises ought to be interpreted. In him, we encounter a passionate intellect, prompted to great efforts of moderation and negotiation between hard-line extremes threatening religion, the state, and individual consciences. His capacious imagination envisaged—and then modelled—ways of dealing with these crises, ways that resisted the pressure to adopt uncompromising positions, although his Sermons betray the stress of remaining whole. In his Sermons, Donne developed a professional and personal identity that confronts in all its complexity the contentious temper of the Renaissance.

While other preachers were using the pulpit to deliver 'position papers', then, Donne the preacher, like the poet, saw its potential as a place of conversion. Through his emphasis on teaching the processes of moral decision-making rather than enforcing blind obedience or dogma, Donne links the most private of arbiters—conscience—to the most public of media—the sermon. More important, his Sermons use all the resources of language to wring assurance of salvation from the rich but mysterious ambiguities of Scripture. Among early seventeenth-century sermons, Donne's stand out for their inclusive reach, their accommodating rhetorical gestures, and their imaginative interpretive strategies. His Sermons present him as an ethical model of integrity and a force of cohesion in an institution—the English Church—that was fractured by religious debate and polemic.

2

As Erasmus indicated in his translation of John 1:1 as 'In principio erat sermo' (a famous and controversial departure from the Vulgate's 'In principio erat verbum' (Remer 47), a sermon is a kind of 'conversation' in imitation of God's originary Creation by his Word. Donne thus sees the sermon as a continuation of God's conversation with men initiated in Scripture (M. A. C. Johnson 280), in which the preacher's role is to paraphrase or dilate the biblical text (e.g. *Sermons* 4.45, 8.115, 9.298). The homiletic tradition Donne inherited was made up of complex strands, which he wove to create an interpretive and rhetorical template uniquely his own. Donne knew the precise value of each development of the generic tradition, and he deliberately made each development new using his unique resources in wit, learning, eloquence, and penetrating insight into human sinfulness and motivation—all in the service of edifying and ultimately converting his congregations to a personal experience of Christianity in a uniquely reformed English Church. Donne's professed aim in all of his Sermons is what he calls 'nearnesse', the recognition by the audience that the preacher 'speaks to my conscience, as though he had been behinde the hangings when I sinned, and as though he had read the book of the day of Judgement already' (3.142). Such an aim required the exercise of 'discretion', an active and strenuous principle that enabled Donne through careful calibration of doctrine, tone, preaching occasion, and the needs of his audience to uncover sin both zealously and charitably and to move his hearers to a personal application of the Bible to their own lives (Shami 1980).

It has been argued that early modern sermons 'are best understood as full-scale classical orations adapted through centuries of tradition to a Christian purpose' (McCullough 2006: 167). Donne's Sermons, however, derived more directly from a rich and complex network of traditions of preaching, homiletic theorizing, and biblical interpretation that included Augustine and the Church Fathers; Aquinas and the scholastic theologians; Erasmus and the humanists; and Reformers including Luther, Calvin, and Melanchthon. Donne selected from these traditions eclectically and idiosyncratically, making it difficult to classify his preaching, but demonstrating once again the range of his imagination—and his constantly reiterated position to discard nothing that is useful to salvation, to edification, and that contributes to his goal of *conversion* through 'nearnesse', no matter what its source.

The two authorities whose thought on sermons was most congenial to Donne were Augustine and Erasmus. What they had in common, despite the hundreds of years that separated them, was their overtly biblical focus, their emphasis on the character and motive of the preacher, and their end of not only *instructing* their hearers in Christian doctrine, but of *moving* them to apply that doctrine to their lives—to live in conformity with Christ. Augustine's *De doctrina christiana* assumes that the Bible is a divinely revealed, internally coherent, sacred text containing all essential articles of the Christian faith. As Donne's practice of reconciling apparently contradictory scriptural texts further indicates, following Augustine he believed that the Bible brought its own interpretive key—to interpret obscure passages in light of clearer passages elsewhere to recover meaning. Such an interpretive practice mitigates partial readings that 'agree to thy particular tast and humour', 'for the Scriptures are made to agree with one another' (*Sermons* 5.39). Such a practice also facilitates the assurance that comes from understanding the whole of God's promise of salvation. These assumptions subsume all exegesis within an interpretive context that Augustine calls the rule of faith, meaning that all interpretations must be consistent with fundamental articles of the Christian faith, but charitably flexible where the articles are not in dispute.

Donne's debt to Augustine both as theorist and practitioner of scriptural exegesis is much more thorough and complex than previously understood. A forthcoming volume by Katrin Ettenhuber will demonstrate that Donne's views on the sermon as a genre, as well as his preaching practice, derive from an intimate and complex encounter with many more Augustinian texts than hitherto recognized, the most important of which Donne knew by direct access, and some of which were transmitted through various mediating channels such as handbooks of theology, polemical tracts, Scripture commentaries, ecclesiastical histories, collections of excerpts, and compilations (see Vessey, Raspa's Introduction to *Pseudo-Martyr*, and Stanwood 1996 for foundational, but preliminary, work in this field). Trained in the humanist practices of annotation, compilation, and excerption, Donne emerges in Ettenhuber's analysis as one of Augustine's most complex readers, one who reinvents Augustine for a multitude of purposes through citational practices that were well established in Donne's writings before his ordination and that run the gamut from accurate and fully contextualized reference to deliberate misquotation for pastoral or, occasionally, polemical purposes.

Erasmus is the pre-eminent sixteenth-century theorist of the sermon, although neither his preparatory work as a translator nor his irenic stance in controversy recommended him to zealots of any denomination—Protestant or Catholic. His interest in making Scripture available both in the original languages and the vernacular was crucial to his theory. Towards his work on sermons, his unique achievements in religious writing were masterful editions of biblical texts based on state-of-the-art textual and philological principles; paraphrases of these biblical texts; and important editions of Church Fathers, themselves placing Scripture at the crucial centre of all Christian concern. From time to time Erasmus also had written pastoral, polemical, or educational treatises, always presenting the Scriptures as a way towards peace amidst political and religious conflict. By 1535 these preliminaries had sometimes interrupted his work on the preaching of sermons, begun before 1523; but the book was finished, the last major work he published.

Erasmus's *Ecclesiastes, sive de ratione concionandi*, running through ten editions during its first decade in print (O'Malley 1985: 2), was the most important theoretical work on preaching since Augustine's *De doctrina*. In tandem with the Protestant rejection of scholastic preaching techniques (even though some scholastic elements persisted even in Protestant sermons for some time), the *Ecclesiastes* 'destroyed at a blow' hundreds of years of adherence by Catholic preachers to the dominant *ars praedicandi* tradition (on this tradition see Kneidel forthcoming). After 1535 the scholastic sermon was never again advocated in a treatise on preaching (O'Malley 1985: 12–13). Moreover, the *Ecclesiastes* was the first treatise on preaching to show command in its exposition not only of classical rhetorical traditions but of the entire history of Christian preaching, including the scholastic tradition, which Erasmus not only ridiculed but also understood and sometimes treated with 'unaccustomed gentleness' (13).

An estimated 3,600 copies of the *Ecclesiastes* were in circulation by 1545, but by the same time the general reputation of Erasmus had begun to decline sharply among both Protestants and Catholics (McGinness 93–5). A series of developments led to these results, including on the one hand 'his altercation with Luther in 1524–25' over the freedom of the will; and on the other hand a series of bannings and prohibitions leading to 'the placing of his *Opera* on the Roman *Index librorum prohibitorum* of 1559' (O'Malley 1988: xiii). Nevertheless, 'although the authors of works on preaching after 1535 almost without exception give him no credit, and some surely were unaware that his was the model they were ultimately following', the *Ecclesiastes* 'established a new model for one of the most important genres of the age, treatises on preaching' (xxxi).

Of particular interest for the student of Donne's Sermons is the first book of the *Ecclesiastes*, devoted to the preacher's piety as the most essential requirement for preaching. Immediately, Erasmus defines the Christian preacher's role in relation to the social order, in accord with which princes have responsibility for establishing peace in the world, while bishops have responsibility for peace in people's souls. In this division of concerns, Erasmus asserts, princes have been far better trained than their ecclesiastical counterparts, a problem he addresses by focusing on training the clergy for their task (Kleinhans 253). Neither the pressure of authority nor disputes of theologians, Protestant or Catholic, can avail unless the preacher strives for holiness, employing his eloquence with scriptural, classical, and patristic learning (Weiss 107).

The balance of the lengthy first book of *Ecclesiastes* precedes discussions in the second to third books on practical details of preaching. But primarily and fundamentally, Erasmus gives preaching a foundation in theology and spirituality, arguing in summary that: 'The essence of Christian eloquence consists in the piety that renders the heart docile to the imitation of Jesus Christ' (Fumaroli 107, qtd. in translation by O'Malley 1985: 15). Preaching should then be imbued not with controversy but with didactic and moral concerns. All subsequent writings on how to preach were 'indebted directly or indirectly to Erasmus' great work' (O'Malley 1985: 17).

3

In Donne's time sermons satisfied appetites for news, entertainment, social interaction, politics, and, of course, religious edification. They were the mass media of their day, fulfilling the role that newspapers and television occupy today in reporting breaking news or debating politics, religion, and cultural values. But, sermons also satisfied a high cultural appetite such as that provided by the theatre. Their rhetorical and spiritual power was intense, and, in fact, the reward of reading Donne's Sermons today partakes of this residual performative power (McCullough 2006; Shami 2003a: 168).

The audience they reached, an audience that extended even to the illiterate, was substantial. In the seventeenth century attendance at Sunday service in the Church of England was mandatory—those who recused themselves (recusants or separatists) incurred fines and other penalties—and sermons were a prominent feature of the service. The sermons these audiences heard worked towards a sense of social cohesiveness (largely through the experience of having heard the same things in the same place). Additionally, sermons provided the locus and moment of intellectual force and moral direction in the service, and, as the practice of 'gadding' (wandering from one sermon to the next) indicates, they were intellectually stimulating, entertaining, educational, and moving. People *attended* them, *took notes* at them, *repeated* them at home to families and servants, *debated* them, *read* them, *reread* them, *collected* them, and *bequeathed* them. Understandably, early modern sermons have been touted as their age's most influential organ of public opinion.

More important than that, however, in this age of religious conflict and uncertainty, knowing how to interpret Scriptures assuaged doubt and exercised devotion. Donne's Sermons (1615–31) and those of his contemporaries inhabited a peculiarly equivocal position in the post-Reformation English Church, providing moral education and guidance for people engulfed by the scepticism, fragmentation, political and religious division, and controversy resulting from the Reformation break with Rome and the Roman Church's counter-move to define (and, crucial for Donne, to add to) the articles of faith. In his comments on adiaphora (doctrinal matters indifferent in that they were not necessary to salvation), Erasmus had said that:

> The sum and substance of our religion is peace and concord. This can hardly remain the case unless we define as few matters as possible and leave each individual's judgment free on many questions. This is because there is great uncertainty about very many issues, and the mind of man suffers from this deeply ingrained weakness, that it does not know how to give way when a question has been made a subject of contention. (Erasmus 1989: 252, ll. 232–7)

Donne agreed, lamenting that the Council of Trent had arbitrarily increased the number of articles of faith required for salvation (*Sermons* 3.369; 6.300; 3.132). Despite such debates, all Christians, including Catholics, believed that the Scriptures were the revealed word of God and necessary for salvation. Audiences of all denominations were hungry for the assurance of salvation and knowledge of how to achieve it.

4

In the pursuit of assurance, Donne's audiences were treated to a bracing intellectual and emotional experience, one that took theological differences seriously into account but often rested in paradoxes rather than dogmas. Donne was self-conscious about what a sermon might be, careful to distinguish the preacher's words (the sermon) from God's words (the Bible). With Augustine, Donne calls preachers *vehicula Spiritus*, 'The chariots of the Holy Ghost' (*Sermons* 5.37), conveying the word of life unto men. 'It is not Many words, long Sermons, nor good words, witty and eloquent Sermons that induce the holy Ghost, for all these are words of men; and howsoever the whole Sermon is the Ordinance of God, the whole Sermon is not the word of God' (5.36–7). The word 'Ordinance' is congenial to Donne for its dual meaning (both something ordained by God and an army in battle order or ranks): 'All the Sermon is not Gods word, but all the Sermon is Gods Ordinance, and the Text is certainly his word. There is no salvation but by faith, nor faith but by hearing, nor hearing but by preaching' (7.320).

In the post-Reformation debate on the relative precedence of preaching and the sacraments, Donne does not choose sides. Consistently, he refers to both preaching and the sacraments as elements of God's ordinance (8.220):

> then does God truly shine to us, when he appears to our eyes and to our ears, when by visible and audible means, by Sacraments which we see, and by the Word which we heare, he conveys himself unto us…They are a powerful thunder, and lightning, that go together: Preaching is the thunder, that clears the air, disperses all clouds of ignorance; and then the *Sacrament* is the lightning, the glorious light, and presence of Christ Jesus himself. (4.105)

In one Sermon Donne transcends the preaching–sacrament dichotomy entirely by referring to 'the Word preached' as 'the Sacrament of faith' (5.262).

However, Donne does distinguish sermons from other genres of public speech: the oration, the lecture, and the satire or libel. In each case he does so by identifying what makes a sermon a sermon: application of the scriptural text and focus on moving and persuading hearers to spiritual conversion. A sermon is not, first of all, an oration, despite its similarities in structure and elevated language. Donne uses the term 'oration' when he wants to refer to sermon discourses that 'over-praise men, and never give God his due praise' (4.307), or to pulpit utterances that use 'more then convenient ornament' (10.147). Erasmus makes the point in *Ecclesiastes*, contrasting use of classical rhetoric for merely human purposes by human orators to the preacher's use of God's word, embodied in Christ and the Bible (1991: 5.4.38–9).

Neither is a sermon a lecture:

for, as that's a difference betweene *Sermons* and *Lectures*, that a Sermon intends *Exhortation* principally and *Edification*, and a holy stirring of religious affections, and then *matters of Doctrine*, and points of *Divinity*, occasionally, secondarily, as the words of the text may invite them; But *Lectures* intend principally *Doctrinall points*, and matter of *Divinity*, and matter of *Exhortation* but *occasionally*, and as in a *second* place. (8.95)

In *Ecclesiastes* Erasmus had made the same distinction, emphasizing the preacher's focus on the emotions of his congregation, even above instructing them (1991: 5.4.274). Merely instructive lectures might be appropriate for teaching, but Donne recognizes that 'A man may teach an Auditory, that is, make them know something that they knew not before, and yet not preach; for Preaching is to make them know things appertaining to their salvation' (*Sermons* 4.202).

Equally, a sermon ought not to descend into satire or libel, either when the 'wit' or 'malice' of the congregation makes 'a Sermon a libel against others, and cannot find a Sermon in a Sermon, to our selves' (3.56), or when the preacher makes 'a Sermon, a Satyr' or 'a Prayer, a Libel' (4.91). As Erasmus argues in *Ecclesiastes*, the preacher, in order to move and persuade his congregation, must accommodate to, rather than rail against, the nature of man, using calm and gentle words rather than furious attack (1991: 5.4.58 and 174–6).

One can infer Donne's views on the role of the sermon and the function of the preacher from the metaphors he uses to describe them in those Sermons particularly devoted to these subjects. Although it is true that not all of Donne's Sermons are equally intense, Donne's metaphors to describe preachers emphasize their disruptive, transformative, and illuminating functions. As Erasmus in *Ecclesiastes* saw the preacher as the herald of God's word, as Christ's ambassador (1991: 5.4. 36–8), so for Donne preachers are *speculatores* or watchmen who discern and denounce sin (*Sermons* 2.168), *tubae* (trumpets) to bring people to a sense of their sins (2.168), voices and songs (2.172–74), *Sagittarius dei* (the deliverer of God's arrows) (2.68), a thunder-clap (4.105), stars (4.192, 209), military ordinance (5.37). Donne stresses the instrumentality of 'the testimony of... the *preacher*, crying according to Gods ordinance, shaking the soule, troubling the conscience, and pinching the bowells, by denouncing of Gods Judgements, these beare witnesse of the light, when otherwise men would sleep it out' (4.211).

Frequently, he reminds us that sermons ought to avoid or transcend doctrinal wrangling, although Donne himself occasionally quarrelled polemically with expositors, especially those who advanced particular doctrines he believed were not supported by Scripture. One such doctrine was purgatory (including the prayers for the dead that were its foundation and the indulgences that were its consequence). In studying the genealogy of indulgences, therefore, Donne identifies the 'Grandmother Error' (prayers for the dead), the 'Mother' error (purgatory), and the 'children' of this error (indulgences) (7.168). Sometimes Donne disagreed with particular authors (even those such as Augustine whom he generally admired) when he believed they were in error, and he reserved a special animosity against the Roman Church's Council of Trent for its designation of certain doctrines as 'new' articles of faith. For the most part, however, Donne, like Erasmus in *Ecclesiastes* (1991: 5.4.64), favoured adaptation to particular circumstances and toleration, even of doctrinal differences (Remer 52). Although Donne himself, like Augustine and Erasmus, occasionally disputed particular doctrines and scriptural interpretations, he generally preached in accord with the principle implicit in Richard Hooker's claim that sermons are as 'keyes to the kingdom of heaven, as winges to the soule, as spurres to the good affections of man' (Hooker 2.87).

5

Even within the rich and sophisticated sermon culture of the early seventeenth century, Donne's Sermons can be distinguished by several strategies. First among these are his strategies of biblical interpretation, in particular his skill in applying biblical texts to particular audiences on particular occasions. Of course, it is important to recognize that we don't know *exactly* what Donne said on particular occasions, because he spoke from notes rather than reading his Sermons, and because he did not write up his sermon notes immediately after the Sermons were preached (Sparrow 1930: 163–7). The majority of Donne's surviving Sermons were written out in full in 1625 (when he removed from London to Chelsea on account of the plague) and again in 1630 (when he was visiting his daughter, Constance, at her home at Aldborough Hatch, and recovering from illness: Bald 1970: 523). What we *do* know, finally, is not what Donne said, but how Donne re-presented what he had said on a particular occasion when he wrote up his Sermons, sometime later, and, at that key moment of transcription, adapted what he had said for a new audience, the readers in posterity for whom he was writing.

Nonetheless, Donne's Sermons as they have been transmitted to us demonstrate principles of decorum suitable to the physical and congregational character of specific occasions. Donne preached Sermons to a wide variety of audiences 'in the Mountaine' (to the courtly and learned) and 'in the plaine' (to the simple country parishes) (*Sermons* 7.330–1). The interpretive and rhetorical demands of Sermons preached at diverse pulpits (Paul's Cross, Lincoln's Inn, St Paul's, St Dunstan's in the West, at court), on various liturgical occasions (Christmas, Easter, Whitsunday, the conversion of St Paul), and at marriages, funerals, and churchings were influenced by Christian and humanist traditions of 'accommodation' articulated by commentators such as Augustine and Erasmus.

Like Augustine and Erasmus, Donne reflected often on the preacher's role, and, in particular, on the example of Paul, whose epistles Donne admired (2.49). And with these thinkers, Donne adopted Paul as the model of the preacher whose goal of 'nearnesse' required him to be 'all things to all men'. Donne as preacher follows a *via Pauli* underwritten by the recognition that Paul's paradoxes and struggles are not merely psychological but rhetorical and communal, problems of an audience in a church made up of Gentiles and Jews, and part of the communal context in which God's word is understood (Kneidel 2001: 229). Crucial for Donne's exegetical strategies, his *via Pauli* sanctions rhetorical adaptability of character, thus stressing pastoral as well as confessional emphases, the biblical Word as expressing communal values and doctrine rather than the absolute opinion of a single exegete.

Even Donne's choice of scriptural text is significant, and one can infer several things from his selections. In some cases, the text chosen was part of the day's liturgical readings. In others—and these are the most interesting—Donne reveals a contrarian notion of how a text could be suited to its occasion. Perhaps the most famous—though not necessarily the most provocative—pairing of text and occasion was Donne's choice of text for a Sermon at the Paul's Cross pulpit defending James I's *Directions to Preachers* (1622), thought by contemporaries to be intended to silence political preaching. Although he does not specify his meaning, contemporary newsletter-writer John Chamberlain commented on the strangeness of Donne's text, perhaps voicing a popular impression regarding the fitness of the text to the much-anticipated occasion of defending pulpit censorship (Chamberlain 2.451; see also Shami 2003a: ch. 4). Taking as his text Judges 5:20, but citing it in the Vulgate as well as the Authorized version ('De Coelo Dimicatum est contra Eos: Stellae Manentes in Ordine, & Cursu suo Adversus Siseram Pugnaverunt. They fought from Heaven; The Stars in their Courses Fought Against Sisera'), Donne's equivocal choice enabled a spirited defence of preaching as God's 'ordinance' bolstered by an equally spirited defence of 'orderly' pulpit speech. Balancing the scriptural imperative that the gospel should be preached in and out of season with the imperative that all things should be done decently and in order (2 Tim. 4:12 and 1 Cor. 14:40) (Morrissey 168), Donne is trying to quell anxieties precipitated by the occasion. Perhaps the strangeness Chamberlain observed resided in the choice of an ambiguous text, one in which the application was not transparent or preordained. Gosse, for one, assumed that Donne was aligning James with Sisera (Gosse 2.161), a misperception suggesting how little control a preacher had over the interpretations opened by his text.

The effect on Donne's auditory when he began by announcing a text that was counter-intuitive must have been riveting, engaging hearers precisely to the extent that they were unable to predict how he would unfold its meanings and apply it to the present moment. Many of Donne's texts are challenging in precisely this way. Donne's first Sermon preached before King Charles I following the death of his father King James I, for example, focuses provocatively on the politically and ecclesiastically sensitive questions arising from this regime change by speaking on Psalm 11:3 ('If the Foundations be Destroyed, What can the Righteous doe?'). Ultimately, Donne denies that foundations have been destroyed, but in order to make that claim, he must first define foundations in such a way that the word is not synonymous with the person of either dead king or heir, but with the structures of authority by which each king is created and supported: God, the church, the law, and the conscience. These foundations, in other words, are the underlying structures that unify the English Church and transcend historical change during this difficult time of transition.

In sum, Donne continually uses his chosen text—taken from across the Scriptures—to provoke, surprise, and engage his audiences, deliberately avoiding in his Christmas Sermons, for example, reference to the babe of Bethlehem and opting, instead, for texts that allowed him to convey his more equivocal attitudes to this festival than his contemporaries—and certainly his modern readers—might expect (Haskin 1992: 152), and that take these hearers on a circuitous journey of reading that needs to be plotted out in relation to the map of the entire Bible.

Donne's Sermons can also be distinguished by their ability to model and teach how to think about complex moral and political issues, individually and in intellectual collaboration with—or opposition to—the great Christian thinkers and interpreters. Donne thinks of sermons as places for exploration more than for dogma (something handled more properly in church councils and synods rather than in the pulpit: *Sermons* 4.305; 7.204). What was important for Donne was imagining a church that was not bound finally to 'over-precise' doctrinal positions, but that was continually engaged in a public and open process of adjudication, negotiation, and consensus, and whose aim was salvation rather than correctness. This collaborative impulse demonstrates his acute insight into his age's compelling controversies.

The starting point for Donne—and the surest way to avoid dispute—was to respect the literal sense of the Bible. Donne's exegesis is founded primarily on the literal sense, supported by the Reform emphasis on figurative meaning as a dimension of the literal text. For Donne, however, 'many times by altercation and vehemence of Disputation, the truth of the literal sense is indangered' (*Sermons* 4.114). For this reason, the primacy of the literal sense must be supported by a definition that rescues it from absurd literalism while eschewing mystical readings of historical events: 'The literall sense is always to be preserved,' Donne says, 'but the literall sense is not always to be discerned: for the literall sense is not always that, which the very Letter and Grammer of the place presents, as where it is literally said, *That Christ is a Vine*, and literally, *That his flesh is bread*' (6.62). Donne justified the scope of his interpretive reach, however, by adding that the literal sense is 'the principall intention of the Holy Ghost', but an intention that might be to express things 'by allegories, by figures; so that in many places of Scripture, a figurative sense is the literall sense' (6.62). Capturing the right sense of the literal is enabled by the 'Rule...which is, Not to admit figurative senses in interpretation of Scriptures, where the literall sense may well stand' (7.193). Donne attacks the Roman Church for its interpretive excesses: either too literal (as in debate over transubstantiation) or too figurative (as in debate over purgatory) (Shami 2008b: 110–11, 324). Donne's literal sense, in the end, while a guiding principle, is determined by the rhetorical demands of accommodating his text to his hearers for their conversion and edification.

Donne's use of secondary sources to explicate his texts also exemplifies his accommodating religious imagination and clarifies the preacher's responsibility not to interject his personal opinions into sermons in place of Christ's doctrine. Any authority receives Donne's respect if he can avoid what Donne sees as the greatest obstacle to religious reform: 'personal revilings' and 'vehemency against his present adversary' (*Sermons* 7.203). Calvin is cited in one of Donne's Sermons for his willingness to compromise for the sake of confessional unity, even on important matters that had not been determined, such as how the Eucharist ought to be administered. Donne explains that Calvin believed the sacrament might be administered in prisons, but departed from his own opinion because the church in Geneva thought differently, thus supporting Donne's view that national churches might develop very different interpretations of such important disciplinary questions. In this respect, Calvin becomes Donne's authority against what he calls '*Morositatem*':

> a certain peevish frowardnesse, which, as he calls in one place *deterrimam pestem*, the most infectious pestilence, that can fall upon a man, so in another, he gives the reason, why it is so, *semper nimia morositas est ambitiosa*, that this peevish frowardnesse, is always accompanied with a *pride*, and a *singularity*, and an ambition to have his opinions preferred before all other man, and to condemn all that differ from him. (10.175)

For Donne, no expositor can claim an absolute authority. Each must be judged on the merits of his biblical interpretations in particular cases. Even Augustine, Donne thought, went too far in his 'vehemency' against his doctrinal adversaries, the Pelagians and the Manicheans (7.203). Donne calls these occasions when in the 'heat of disputation' expositors become transported against their doctrinal enemies a 'disease that even some great Councels in the Church, and Church-affaires have felt', occasioned by 'collaterall and occasionall, and personall respects' (7.203). Although it is undeniable that Donne's habits of quotation, citation, and interpretation are occasionally polemical, they generally eschew name-calling, heated disputation, and personally pointed vehemence against perceived adversaries. The complexity of his engagements with these authorities cannot be overestimated, and demonstrates a range of interactions from faithful and full quotation to deliberate misquotation (almost always for some pastoral end). In every case, authorities are used to enable scriptural interpretation that moves hearers to apply that Scripture to their own spiritual and earthly lives.

Donne's Sermons can also be distinguished by the confidence they demonstrate that the saving religious knowledge and experience of the Scriptures is accessible to each audience member (although mediated through the preacher as spokesperson for the established church), and that fundamentally these are 'matter without controversie' (3.206–24). Donne's catechizing impulse expresses itself in the ways in which he frames his interpretations within the Augustinian context—the rules of faith and charity (see Ettenhuber 146–7 on charity in particular; Shami 2009). Donne's Augustinian rule of faith is 'That wee admit no other sense, of any place in any Psalm, then may consist with the *articles* of the *Christian faith*' (*Sermons* 2.72). A 1629 Sermon expresses the rule of charity clearly: 'Where divers senses arise, and all true, (that is, that none of them oppose the truth) let truth agree them. But what is Truth? God; And what is God? Charity; Therefore let Charity reconcile such differences' (9.94–5). These rules of faith and charity, for Donne, contain all of the elements required for a

right exposition of Scripture; which are, first, the glory of God, such a sense as may most advance it; secondly, the analogie of faith, such a sense as may violate no confessed Article of Religion; and thirdly, exaltation of devotion, such a sense, as may carry us most powerfully upon the apprehension of the next life; and lastly, extension of charity, such a sense, as may best hold us in peace, or reconcile us, if we differ from one another. (9.95)

Donne's interpretive framework also treats the Bible as profoundly typological, a unified, coherent, poetic text requiring close reading to recover its full meaning and to reveal the individual's place in sacred history. Such a strategy was potentially assuring in that it emphasized the coherence of God's plan, repeated throughout human history. This way of understanding the Christian's place in salvation history worked by showing how even scriptural texts from remote historical circumstances could be digested by or accommodated to present readers. This complex reading code was based on three fundamental principles: that types and antitypes were historically real; that the imperfect order of the law prepared for the more perfect order of grace; and that the New Testament was 'more perfect' than the Old Testament, because Christ fulfilled all of the biblical prophecies (Dickson 260). Typology was, in fact, established by Paul to defend the early Christians, transforming Jewish history into a universal history of Christianity in which Christ's coming was foreshadowed by the Old Testament. Donne inherits and advances this Christian universalist reading of the Old Testament/Hebrew Bible, contributing to Catholic/Protestant and Jewish/Christian textual and religious polemic (Goodblatt 223). Despite an expansive sense of God's inclusiveness that sometimes extends even to some ancient Jews who lived before Christ (*Sermons* 6.162), they are always subsumed by Christian history and denied any current theological significance.

Lewalski (1979: 31–144) has claimed, misleadingly and yet influentially, that this typological application of the Scripture to the self is particularly Protestant. R. V. Young, however, demonstrates that a focus on private interpretation and application to the self also describes Catholic engagements with the Bible from the earliest Christian periods through Erasmus and the Catholic humanists, in the biblical commentaries of figures such as Cardinal Roberto Bellarmino, and in Renaissance Catholic continental writers (R. V. Young 2000*a*: 85–8; 2000*b*: 223–34). Not to recognize that Renaissance biblical engagements reflected a long tradition of Christian, and specifically Catholic, exegesis oversimplifies and weakens their resonance for Donne, whose scriptural commitments are filtered through the Catholicism into which he was born as well as the English Church in which he matured. Donne modifies his inherited generic template to produce Sermons whose structure and language recognize, discover, and apply spiritually transformative truths to his audiences.

Finally, Donne's Sermons distinguish themselves by the interpretive strategies he employs and models for his hearers for dealing with controversial matters—whether theological or political. These strategies reveal Donne's sensitivity to the complexity of his audience. Many, like him, had been born and baptized as Catholics and yet regarded themselves as continuing members of the Church of England. Still others had been born into the Reformation and baptized in one of its denominations. Some—church papists—conformed only outwardly to avoid religious persecution, but retained their Catholic beliefs and their longing for Catholic sacraments and ceremonies. It is safe to say that as the only Reform church in which the Head of State was also Supreme Governor of the Church (i.e. the monarch), the Church of England, more than any other, found itself constantly balancing, redefining, readjusting the terms of its constitution or identity, either irenically in efforts to integrate the sectarian impulses that threatened it, or polemically in an effort to expel those Christians who did not adhere to the English Church's Thirty-Nine Articles (of doctrine) or worship according to its Book of Common Prayer. Although capable of polemical attacks (particularly against those he deemed extremists—i.e. the current generation of Roman Catholics, nonconforming Puritans, and Separatists), Donne in his Sermons adhered more closely to the irenic than to the controversial arm of the clergy.

6

Probably the most impressive feature of Donne's Sermons—what has earned him his reputation as a successful preacher (one who not only explains doctrine—whether plainly or elegantly—but one who moves his hearers to life-changing transformations)—is his rhetorical skill: the dramatic, performance-driven oral intensity of his Sermons, still evident even in their printed forms, and their dazzling rhetorical sophistication and variety. It is important to realize that rhetoric—as Donne understood the term—was not mere verbal deftness but was tied closely to concepts of 'decorum' (suiting his language to the needs of the hearers) and 'accommodation' (explaining and applying the language of the Bible and the interpretations of commentators to the doctrinal and moral needs of his hearers).

Donne's rhetorical concerns are evidenced first by his careful preparation of his Sermons for delivery and his revision of some Sermons for printing. Walton says that Donne began preparing for his next Sermon immediately after delivering the last, first selecting his text and determining the heads of his division, then searching the Scriptures and his library for pertinent cross-references, interpretations (especially conflicting ones, which he used to educate his audiences in moral decision-making), and authorities (Walton 1675: 59). Like the best contemporary preachers (and in direct contrast to Puritan preachers who, convinced that they were inspired by the Holy Ghost, delivered their sermons extemporaneously), Donne spoke from notes, which he amplified in the pulpit moment, thereby exercising oratorical skills of *memoria*, *pronuntiatio*, and *actio* to kindle the hearts of his hearers (Sparrow 1930). With Augustine, Donne believed that lengthy preparations enabled participation in the emotional power of the moment (*Sermons* 8.149; 10.174). It was important, however, that the sermon, although thoroughly prepared, not be memorized lest the cold recitation of the discourse fail in emotional appeal.

Of course, the relationship between the Sermon as delivered, copied in manuscript, or printed remains elusive to scholars (Donne 1996*b*). British Library MS Royal 17.B.XX—a copy of a Sermon commanded by the King for immediate inspection but never published in Donne's lifetime—is the only example of a Donne Sermon linked directly to the author (through his holograph corrections) and to its preaching occasion. The circumstances surrounding this Sermon suggest that the manuscript is closer to what Donne preached at Paul's Cross on 5 November 1622 (the anniversary of the Gunpowder Plot) than the version eventually revised for *Fifty Sermons* (1649). The most marked differences are clearly authorial, including one passage where the manuscript's cryptic statement that princes who act through others 'are therefore excusable' in their actions is revised in the printed version to say that princes 'may be excusable; at least, for any cooperation in the evil of the action, though not for countenancing, and authorizing an evil instrument; but that is another case' (1996*b*: 31). This example and others show that

Donne was wary in 1622 of criticizing the King as openly as he did when he revised the Sermon for posthumous publication. Moreover, the two versions of the Sermon suggest that Donne revised his Sermons not only for stylistic and rhetorical reasons (as Potter and Simpson suggested) but for political ones as well.

For Donne, Scripture is salvific not only because it is God's revealed word, but also because of its literary qualities: 'the Holy Ghost in penning the Scriptures delights himself, not only with a propriety, but with a delicacy, and harmony, and melody of language; with height of Metaphors, and other figures, which may work greater impressions upon the Readers, and not with barbarous, or triviall, or market, or homely language' (*Sermons* 6.55). The eloquence of the Holy Ghost extends beyond musical cadence, tropes, and figures, including even 'wit' (Doerksen 2004: 155), a source of 'holy delight' (*Letters* 249) for his hearers. For Donne, as for Augustine and Erasmus, it is a model of rhetorical decorum, perfectly fitted to its audience.

Donne's respect for rhetorical eloquence is everywhere apparent in the variety of his tropes, images, and figurative devices as well as in his supple, evocative rhythms

Ill. 24.1. John Donne as Dean of St Paul's, said to have been painted by Cornelius Johnson (oils, 1620, St Paul's Cathedral, London, hanging in the deanery). (Reproduced by permission of the Dean and Chapter of St Paul's Cathedral, London.)

(Schleiner; Webber 1963; B. Nelson 2005; Guffey). He conceives of the sermon as both thunder and music, expressing both power and order simultaneously:

> The sentences are copious, nervous, meditative, and rhythmic. The metaphors are insistent, overzealous, strongly controlled. The texture is tremulous, legalistic, macabre, witty, exalted, and, above all, literary. Things became words, and words came alive when Donne erected for his congregation a gorgeous palace that would subside into print after the hour's end. (Webber 1963: 182)

Donne warned his congregation, however, not to respect the minister more than the ministry, or his manner of delivery more than his message, calling '*Invention*, and *Disposition*, and *Art*, and *Eloquence*, and *Expression*, and *Elocution*, and *reading*, and *writing*, and *printing*' 'secondary things, accessory things, auxiliary, subsidiary things' (*Sermons* 6.103).

However, just as Donne acknowledged the Bible as the eloquent repository of saving truth, he also understood that the Holy Ghost's intentions were mediated through fallible human translators. Consequently, Donne consulted Aramaic, Syriac, and Arabic Bibles, the Septuagint, the Greek New Testament, and the Latin Vulgate (*Sermons* 10.295–328). Typically, Donne compares texts, selecting the reading he judges to be most accurate linguistically, historically, or etymologically, but reserving the discretion to choose readings that are edifying, even if not doctrinally foundational. In choosing his text for a Sermon on Psalm 2:12, for example, Donne finds that the King James and the Vulgate texts differ dramatically. Rather than dismissing the Vulgate (which reads 'Embrace knowledge' rather than 'Kisse the son'), Donne garners support for it in other translations before choosing the wording of the Authorized Version, which rightly follows the Hebrew.

7

Fundamentally, Donne's strategies of scriptural engagement apply the Bible to individual Christians as a salvific instrument. A true searching of the Scriptures is 'to finde all the *histories* to be *examples* to me, all the *prophecies* to induce a Saviour for *me*, all the *Gospell* to apply Christ Jesus to *me*' (*Sermons* 3.367). 'This is *Scrutari Scripturas, to search the Scriptures*, not as though thou wouldest make a *concordance*, but an *application*; as thou wouldest search a *wardrobe*, not to make an *Inventory* of it, but to finde in it something fit for thy wearing' (ibid.). The Bible's radically figurative language as well as its exemplary historical characters can kindle the devotion and salvation of willing hearers who are not 'Sermon-proofe' (6.219).

Donne's interpretive and rhetorical impulses were all directed to what he saw, arguably, as his most important task, correcting the perspectives of his hearers (Shami 2003*a*: 142, 262). 'All error consists in this,' he says, 'that we take things to be lesse or more, other then they are' (*Sermons* 6.230). Sometimes Donne corrects perspectives by exercising his hearers in avoiding singular interpretations, or by distinguishing between fundamental and secondary matters. In this respect he mirrors Erasmus, who strove for consensus and probable certainty about the many controversial matters he considered matters 'indifferent' (Remer 59–68). Sometimes he showed his audience how to 'ruminate' (to translate Augustine's term 'ruminatio') over Scripture, to reconcile conflicting passages, and to digest them. Sometimes he redefined controversial terms, divesting them of their more polemical baggage and showing how they could be renewed. The terms 'glass' and 'spectacle' permeate the fabric of Donne's Sermons, emphasizing the extent to which fallen human vision required corrective lenses, not to mention hearing-aids, both of which sermons could provide.

The spiritual vision of early modern congregations was most challenged by the vexed question of election: the extent to which God predestined salvation for some (and not others) and the place of grace and repentance in the active Christian life. Donne interpreted their dilemma as a failure of assurance rather than faith, and his Sermons frame his comments accordingly to emphasize the experience rather than the doctrine of election. Sometimes, however, Donne requires his hearers either through paradox, or through rhetorical pivoting, to hold the contradictions together imaginatively so as to experience their combined effects. In a Sermon preached on 24 February 1626 Donne counters the 'singularity' of strict predestinarian doctrine by figuring it as hearing with only one ear. The metaphor is brilliant in figuring interpretation as something requiring not only two ears, but also the capacity to hear—and comprehend—the whole meaning resonating in a mind between them. Donne says that expositors of his text sometimes hear only one thing, 'wee must perish' (*Sermons* 7.74). Hearing with this single Calvinist ear preserves God's honour ('we our selfes, and not *God*, are the cause of that desperate irremediablenesse': 7.74) but leaves souls desperate. Those who hear with two ears extend the text 'fairely', Donne says, to suggest that 'There is no necessitie that any Man, any this or that Man should perish' (7.74). This stereophonic interpretation clearly mitigates the rigours of God's absolute decree of reprobation while maintaining an entirely mainstream notion of election. The point Donne stresses, however, is not what God has done (a mystery irresolvable through discourse or dispute) but what we can experience. So Donne says 'That, not disputing what *God*, of his *absolute* power might doe, nor what by his *unreveald Decree* hee hath done, God hath not allowed *me*, nor *thee*, nor *any* to conclude against our selves, a necessity of perishing' (7.85).

Donne's 18 April 1626 Sermon on John 14:2 continues his focus on the experience rather than the doctrine of election. As Donne expresses it: 'conditionall salvation is so far offered to every man, as that no man may preclude himselfe from a possibility of such a performance of those Conditions which God requires at his hands, as God will accept at his hands, if either he doe sincerely endevour the performing, or sincerely repent the not performing of them' (7.127–8). The result is not simply a series of statements that balance or contradict one another, or the elaboration of justification as a temporal process, but a metaphorical figuring of the elements of salvation as links in a chain, a gem set in a precious ring, or a stamp made all at once in eternity. Donne's Sermons dealing with election, then, animate spiritual conversion through paradoxes that suspend contradictions in an imaginative activity of the whole person that heals the fragmentation and contradiction of merely literal minds.

While Donne uses many rhetorical means to achieve nearness by making abstract theological doctrines familiar to his audiences, all of Donne's familiarizing strategies are offset by defamiliarizing techniques that make his audience see differently, by wearing spectacles, or hear differently, by using two ears, or speak differently by rethinking controversial labels. Doing so rouses them from their spiritual lethargy, their deadness to God's grace. Donne asks subjects to look on the King with 'little and dark spectacles' so that his 'errors are to appear little, and excusable to them', thereby exposing the interpretive charity due to figures of authority that these 'spectacles of obedience, and reverence, to their place, and persons' provide. But he is able to recommend this deliberate alteration of perspective precisely because God's 'perspective glasse' will hold Kings accountable, 'and through that spectacle, the faults of Princes, in Gods eye, are multiplied, farre above those of private men' (6.172). Here, as Donne stresses on many occasions, we see as through a glass, darkly, but the glass is at least an instrument of sight, and one that—however faulty—can be used to approach God. (See discussion below of Donne's Easter 1628 Sermon on 1 Cor. 13:12.)

The renovation of controverted terms allowed Donne to divest them of their polemical baggage, or, perhaps more accurately, to deploy them polemically against those whose perspectives were restricted by negative labels. Whereas opponents hurled labels at each other, Donne proclaimed: 'I am a Papist, that is, I will fast and pray as much as any Papist, and enable my selfe for the service of my God, as seriously, as sedulously, as laboriously as any Papist... [and] I am a Puritan, that is, I wil endeavour to be pure, as my Father in heaven is pure, as far as any Puritan' (9.166). Similarly, Donne removed scandal from the names of 'clergy' and 'layetie' by merging them as two callings with 'an equall interest in the joyes, and glory of heaven' (4.371).

8

One rhetorical strategy—in my view the most effective, although Donne does not use it in every Sermon—is to end his Sermon by contrasting worldly perspectives (even the most enlightened) with the heavenly, eternal perspective in a move that inspires his hearers with desire for that eternity. These perorations are the emotional complement to the rational exercise of scriptural interpretation that forms the bulk of the Sermon, and transcend, as faith must, the world of earthly values and perspectives.

As Donne says in a Lincoln's Inn Sermon, the heavenly sight of God will end religious controversy. Then, 'I shall see all problematicall things come to be dogmaticall, I shall see all these rocks in Divinity, come to bee smooth alleys; I shall see Prophesies untyed, Riddles dissolved, controversies reconciled' (*Sermons* 3.111). This pattern is reiterated throughout Donne's Sermons, often in grand perorations that not only inspire his hearers with a vision of eternal life, but indicate how precisely he understands and values worldly things. Donne's rhetorical perorations carry his hearers to contemplate a time and place, then and there, that are radically different from their present occasion (see 4.129–30; 8.191).

Donne's most famous peroration occurs in a Sermon preached before the Earl of Carlisle, Donne's friend and patron, where he asks his hearers to imagine with him a thing even more fearful than falling into the hands of the living God: that is, falling *out* of the hands of the living God, 'a horror beyond our expression, beyond our imagination'. As Donne contemplates this horror, he structures it rhetorically in a breathtaking periodic sentence that ends with the congregation 'secluded eternally, eternally, eternally from the sight of God'. The passage builds both in suspense and horror as the clauses pile one upon another for over a page—six long and complex dependent clauses—before the sentence comes to rest in what, for Donne, is the ultimate horror:

That God should let my soule fall out of his hand,... That of that providence of God, that studies the life and preservation of every weed, and worme, and ant, and spider, and toad, and viper, there should never, never any beame flow out upon me;... That that God should loose and frustrate all his owne purposes and practises upon me, and leave me, and cast me away, as though I had cost him nothing, that this God at last, should let this soule goe away, as a smoake, as a vapour, as a bubble, and that then this soule cannot be a smoake, nor a vapour, nor a bubble, but must lie in darknesse, as long as the Lord of light is light it selfe, and never a sparke of that light reach to my soule; What Tophet is not Paradise, what Brimstone is not Amber, what gnashing is not a comfort, what gnawing of the worme is not a tickling, what torment is not a marriage bed to this damnation, to be secluded eternally, eternally, eternally from the sight of God. (5.266–7)

Even at a distance of 400 years we can feel the ponderous weight of that possibility, and cling all the more desperately to the hope that we will fall into God's correcting hands rather than slipping entirely out of them.

9

Three Sermons can serve to exemplify the rhetorical, doctrinal, and political pressures brought to bear on Donne's Sermons on particular occasions and Donne's characteristic responses to these pressures. These Sermons do not necessarily represent Donne's most famous, most engaging, or most memorable achievements, but they present opportunities to explore some typical strategies, as well as to show the range and variety of his accomplishments in this genre.

On 26 April 1625 Donne preached at Denmark House, some few days before the body of King James was removed for burial. Taking as its text Canticles 3:11: 'Goe forth ye daughters of Sion, and behold King Solomon, with the crown, wherewith his mother crowned him, in the day of his espousals, and in the day of the gladnesse of his heart', the Sermon handles the valedictory imperatives of this sad occasion with sombre dignity and restraint as Donne bids farewell to his mentor and friend, King James.

Available to Donne from his text was the biblical typology of Solomon, James's own biblical exemplar which he appropriated to emphasize his self-styled role as Europe's peacemaker. The possibilities of this comparison, in fact, suffuse—and indeed structure—the *official* sermon preached for him by John Williams, Bishop of Lincoln and Lord Chancellor, culminating in the portrait of James as a statue or monument to the legacy of Solomon, a pattern to his son, the new king, Charles, and an idealized 'image' of the dead monarch whose happy life, happy reign, and happy death that sermon celebrates. Donne's treatment of the Solomonic typology, however, and his choice to portray James as a 'glass' rather than an 'image', reveal the thrust of this Sermon, which is to emphasize James's exemplary though sinful humanity. The absolute monarch of Donne's Sermon, his Solomon, is pre-eminently Christ, the Head of God's church, and his most extravagant claims of kingship accrue to *that* Solomon, who was more perfect than the Old Testament one, rather than to the broken, sinful, and humiliated body of James, whom Donne invokes as an 'abridgement' of the Solomon of the text, of Christ himself.

The command of Donne's chosen text to 'behold' could invite contemplation of an idealized, monumental Solomon memorialized in Williams's funeral sermon for James, but it invites Donne to focus on the multiplicity of perspectives that the typological 'glasses' of his text—Christ and his abridgement James—offer to the congregation. Appropriately for a sermon delivered over the body of his dead king, Donne chooses to focus on the humiliation of Christ in this text as the best glass by which to achieve salvation. This picture of Christ at his crucifixion, in his passion, crowned with the thorns of his humiliation, leads to Donne's meditation on King James, another glass in which his congregation can see themselves. James, says Donne, is a better glass in which men can see themselves, because he is like us in sin.

Christ as he was a pure *Crystall* glasse, as he was *God*, had not been a glasse for us, to have seen ourselves in, except he had been *steeled, darkened with* our *humane nature;*...Those therefore that are like thee in all things, subject to humane *infirmities*, subject to *sinnes*, and yet are translated, and *translated* by *Death*, to everlasting *Joy*, and *Glory*, are nearest and clearest glasses for thee, to see thy self in; and such is this glasse, which God hath proposed to thee, in this house. (*Sermons* 6.289)

James's authority as the 'better' glass inheres precisely in the stain of humanity and imperfection that makes him more 'exemplary' to Donne's sinful congregation than Christ.

The Sermon also allows Donne to model rhetorically for his audience that aspect of James's religion that he deemed most exemplary: James's strenuous policy of defining the English Church as a middle ground between papist and Puritan extremes, a policy that contributed to a unity of belief and practice founded on a wide-reaching and inclusive definition of that ground. Anticipating uncertainties about new directions in the English Church with the transition to Charles I, Donne explains the duties of the congregation, especially those with authority to shape that institution in their home parishes, figured by the text's 'daughter of Sion'. These daughters are asked to go forth, but 'it is not to go so far, as *out* of that Church, in which God hath given us our station'. With obvious reference to the Puritans or papists seeking the church across the sea, Donne advocates something closer to home, even as he acknowledges the imperfections of that institution. The church of God is not so far away that it must be sought 'either in a *painted Church*, on one side, or in a *naked Church*, on another; a Church in a *Dropsie*, overflowne with *Ceremonies*, or a Church in a *Consumption*, for want of such Ceremonies, as the primitive Church found usefull, and beneficiall for the advancing of the glory of God, and the devotion of the Congregation' (6.284). Using James's language of inclusion (Fincham and Lake 1993), he warns against straying towards '*Idolatrous Chappels*' or '*schismaticall Conventicles*', but exhorts his audience to follow a path on which some have gone before. Donne's suggestion is that, following these ceremonies of burial, many will go forth in their several ways, some 'to the service of their *new Master*, and some to the enjoying of their Fortunes conferred by their old; some to the raising of new *Hopes*, some to the burying of old, and all; some to new, and busie endeavours in Court, some to contented retirings in the Countrey', but that the example of James will continue to unite 'all we that have served him' (6.291).

The ending of the Sermon, while it rests in Christian consolation and faith in the afterlife, is marked by restraint. Its caution to his hearers, that 'none of us, goe so farre from him, or from one another, in any of our wayes, but that all we that have served him, may meet once a day' (6.291), registers Donne's anxieties for the church lightly. Equally, Donne's final words, in which 'to see that face [James's] againe, and to see those eyes open there, which we have seen closed here', will be '*an addition*, even to the joy of that place, as perfect as it is, and as infinite as it is', are suffused with personal intimacy. The Sermon as a whole reveals the difficulties of joining these earthly and heavenly perspectives, but the necessity of doing so.

Donne's 1628 Easter Sermon exemplifies how he uses the *image* of the 'glass' (found in his scriptural text) as well as *structure* to establish the discourse of perspective at the heart of his rhetorical method. In this Sermon, Donne awakens his audience's desires not simply through passionate delivery and eloquence, but at the most basic level of invention, 'in the cognitive and affective structures he finds both in his text and in the circumstances of his congregation "in the world"' (B. Nelson 2005: 75). Rhetorically, Donne is asking his hearers to 'court' things superior to their quotidian earthly experiences but found and understood only there, and he does so using Augustine's familiar text for treatment of the beatific vision.

The Sermon is preached on 1 Corinthians 13:12, 'For now we see through a glasse darkly, but then face to face; Now I know in part, but then I shall know, even as also I am knowne', a text that Donne frequently uses to contrast this world and its corruptions with the perfections of the next (see 1.189; 2.266; 3.111; 3.362; 4.73; 4.129; 4.177; 5.168; 7.254; 7.342; 9.127). The Sermon's exordium establishes the terms of the contrast: '*Nunc* and *Tunc*, Now and Then, Now in a glass and in part, Then face to face and knowing as we are known'. The Sermon builds on this contrast as its principal structure of development, appealing to the *memories* of its hearers (in the repetitions of the logical structure predicated on these contrasts) even as its forward momentum in this world advances the congregation's meditations to the sight and knowledge that characterize the next. The Sermon is first divided into half: here and now, there and then. Each half is further subdivided so that we consider the *theatre* (or place), the *medium*, and the *light* by which we first see and then know God in this world and in the next. So that the theatre for our sight of God is the whole created world, the medium is the Book of Creatures, and the light is natural reason, and the theatre for our knowledge of God is the church, the medium is God's ordinances (preaching and sacraments), and the light is faith. For our sight of God there and then, in heaven, our place is heaven, our medium is God's revelation of himself to us, and our light is the light of glory. For our knowledge of God there and then, in heaven, 'God himself is All' (8.220): the place, the medium, and the light.

Having established the structure, Donne considers theatre, medium, and light for each of the four parts derived from the words of his text, so that the progression from this world to the next builds, and hearers are encouraged to see the contrast between earthly and heavenly perspectives not in terms of binaries, but of a scale that ascends by degrees from earthly to heavenly sight and knowledge. Central to all parts of the structure is Donne's interpretation of the glasses provided by God that enable this progress to occur.

Accordingly, the light of reason, focused on the Book of Creatures, in the theatre of this world allows humans to see God, at least to see that there is a God. This sight of God, although only a reflection, is 'a true sight of God, though it be not a perfect sight' (8.223). At this very basic natural level, Donne says, every created thing is a glass wherein we may see God.

> There is not so poore a creature but may be thy glasse to see God in. The greatest flat glasse that can be made, cannot represent any thing greater then it is: If every gnat that flies were an Arch-angell, all that could but tell me, that there is a God; and the poorest worme that creeps, tells me that...and whatsoever hath any beeing, is by that very beeing, a glasse in which we see God, who is the roote, and the fountaine of all beeing. (8.224)

Similarly, we take our degrees of knowledge of God in the university of the church through the medium of his ordinances of preaching and the sacrament, and by the light of faith. This section of the Sermon confirms Donne's view that while it is possible to be enlightened by God outside of that institution (just as it is possible to grow learned outside the university), the normal place for such illumination is the church, through the Scriptures mediated through the instrumental means of preaching, through the seal of the sacrament, and in the presence of competent witnesses, the congregation. These are the glasses that enable the congregation to see God when illuminated by the light of faith. Even this light, however, is but darkness 'in respect of the vision of God in heaven' (8.230), a perspective intended to stimulate the desire of his congregation beyond even faith: 'Faith is infinitely above nature, infinitely above works, even above those works which faith it self produces... But yet faith is as much below vision, and seeing God face to face' (8.230).

The second half of the Sermon—focused on the sight and knowledge of God in heaven—moves more quickly, in part due to audience anticipation of the repeated structure. So the theatre, medium, and light are God's essence, manifested to his faithful, there and then, an ineffable light of glory to which 'the light of honour is but a glow-worm; and majesty it self but a twilight; The Cherubims and Seraphims are but Candles; and that Gospel it self, which the Apostle calls the glorious Gospel, but a Star of the least magnitude' (8.232–3).

The most moving moment in Donne's Sermon pivots on what it means to know God as we are known, a knowledge surpassing human imagination. 'A comprehensive knowledge of God it cannot be... Our knowledge cannot be so dilated, nor God condensed, and contracted so, as that we can know him that way, comprehensively.' In fact, this most difficult and beautiful concept turns on a single word: 'It is not *quantum*, but *sicut*; not as much, but as truly.' So the perfect knowledge that humans will experience in heaven *inverts* all merely human perspectives. The heavenly reward is not the acquisition of more and more knowledge—something that the steady and laborious intellectual path of the Sermon might have predicted—but the ineffable experience of being truly known: 'So then, I shall know God so, as that there shall be nothing in me, to hinder me from knowing God... And so it shall be a knowledge so like his knowledge, as it shall produce a love, like his love, and we shall love him, as he loves us' (8.235). That the beatific vision is underwritten by and enacted through charity (or love) is consistent with Donne's understanding—enabled by his reading of Augustine—of charity as interpretive, rhetorical, and theological principle (see Ettenhuber for application of the Augustinian concept of charity to certain Lincoln's Inn Sermons). Donne's achievement is to have transformed the potentially arid and schematic structure of the Sermon (with its programme of divisions and subdivision) into a vehicle to transport his audience inevitably towards that sight and knowledge of God that surpasses, but paradoxically is only achievable by, the ascending imagination. The perspectives of his hearers, gradually corrected through the course of the Sermon as much by the Sermon's moving inspiration to love as by its logical structure, are the instruments by which this spiritual vision is both understood and experienced.

Donne's Lenten court Sermon for 12 February 1629/30 was preached before the King at Whitehall on Donne's 'old constant day' (Walton 1670: 70), the first Friday in Lent. The Sermon, preached on Matthew 6:21 ('For, where your treasure is, there will your heart be also'), is a sustained meditation on and exegesis of the relationship between 'treasure' and 'heart', and exemplifies many characteristic features of Donne's best homiletic practice. If the Easter 1628 Sermon expresses features of Donne's engagements with Augustine, this Sermon may owe something to Erasmus' 'philosophy of Christ', in particular his efforts to Christianize the classical concept of decorum by endowing Christ with the qualities of a superior orator /preacher (Remer 76–9), and especially his discretion in accommodating his message rhetorically to his hearers. Donne's text for his Sermon—taken from Christ's Sermon on the Mount—explicitly invokes this occasion, as does Donne's discreet adaptation of the text to his courtly audience.

The Sermon opens with an exordium (from the Latin 'to move forward') that engages the audience immediately in contemplating this text 'as through a glass' (*Sermons* 9.173). The 'glass' of Donne's opening is not the perspective glass, the mirror, or the spectacles evoked in other Sermons, but a glass that measures time, analogous to the hourglass that will measure his Sermon. Nonetheless, the exordium arrests the audience with an exercise in perspectival adjustment that will be necessary preparation for distinguishing worldly from godly treasures—the subject of the Sermon. A short-lived minute-glass, Donne says, would be sufficient to preach to the worldly man how quickly his treasures (and his heart) are spent, while a 'Glass that would run an age' would not be enough to tell the godly man what his treasure is. The two are entirely disproportionate. Worldly treasure (and worldly vision) is contrasted with godly seeing, the former revealed as superficial and false only by placing the two experiences of time at opposite ends of a spectrum ranging from a minute to eternity. Ironically, the minute-glass tells the shallow worldly man all he needs, while the age-glass is insufficient to tell the godly man what he needs. Already, Donne is establishing that the major terms of his exegesis depend for their impact on the agile interpretations of the hearers.

If auditories will be challenged by this exercise in discernment, the preacher's task is equally difficult. The exordium also pits two speakers—a parrot and the most respected preachers of the primitive Christian church, Ambrose and Chrysostom—against one another, saying that the parrot will have an easier time describing worldly treasure (here depicted, dismissively, as the 'wisdom of a Council Table') than a great preacher will have describing heavenly treasure. Both are suited to their tasks (the preachers have 'Gold and Honey in their names', fitting to express the 'Treasure' and 'Sweetness' of Heaven, while the parrot, a bird of 'pregnant imitation' can presumably repeat what he hears at the Council Table). Donne's strategy in this opening statement is complex: on the one hand diminishing worldly treasure, including the wisdom of his audience of courtiers, and on the other, engaging their desire for the riches and sweetness, the gold and honey of heavenly treasure.

Immediately, then, Donne has established the difficulty of his task of making worldly men, particularly those in the courtly audience, understand and savour the sweetness of the treasures of heaven. He has made it clear that he is neither parrot nor golden-tongued orator, but that he aspires to the example of the greatest preacher, Christ, and that his Sermon on the treasures of the heart is modelled on the ideal sermon, thus provoking his hearers to remember the entire Sermon on the Mount, from which this fragment has been drawn.

Typically, Donne divides his exegesis into logical parts that assist his hearers in understanding the scope of his entire Sermon, but in the *divisio* of *this* Sermon Donne uses an unusual device, the symbolical letter Y, that has a stalk or stem and two beams. The stalk is the word 'For': 'Take heed where you place your Treasure: for it concerns you much, where your Heart be plac'd' (9.174), a small particle that, nonetheless, becomes the foundation of the exegesis as well as the foundation of the treasure of both the worldly and the godly man. The two branches, though not equally broad, denote worldly treasures and heavenly treasures. The pastoral significance of this symbolic or 'Hieroglyphical Letter' inheres in its 'catechetical' function, something that Donne emphasizes in this unusual structure—at once verbal and visual—designed to appeal to the memories of the auditory.

Donne's exegesis of the 'heart' as the foundation of this text reinforces his intention to probe its workings, to distinguish one heart from another, and, paradoxically, to move the changeable heart to a condition of firmness and fixity. As Donne's rhetorical anatomy of the human heart shows, man must be called upon and excited to fix his heart upon a worthy object:

And yet truly, even this first work, to recollect our selves, to recapitulate our selves, to assemble and muster our selves, and to bend our hearts intirely and intensly, directly, earnestly, emphatically, energetically, upon something, is, by reason of the various fluctuation of our corrupt nature, and the infinite multiplicity of Objects, such a Work as man needs to be called upon, and excited to do it. (9.175)

The insistence of Donne's adverbs dramatizes rhetorically the processes of spiritual rumination, gathering, and bending that the preacher must induce in his congregation.

For the heart to fix itself upon a godly treasure requires powerful incitement. The fallen human heart that Donne describes suffers from several impediments that prevent its holy 'fixation' on the proper object of its desire, the heavenly treasure. Too often, Donne says, we give God an eye or an ear rather than the whole heart. Donne explains such partial response to God's call for man's 'entire' heart as the failings of the natural man (who contemplates God only in his works) or of the so-called religious man (who counts his sermons as superstitiously as the papist counts his rosary beads). Neither gives God 'the heart, the whole man, all the faculties of that man' that God requires.

Donne continues his anatomy of the fallen human heart in the next section of the Sermon—still the stalk or stem of the Y—by outlining three impediments to this holy 'fixation' of the heart: 'a meer Heartlesness, no Heart at all'; 'a doubtful, a distracted Heart'; and finally a 'wandring, a wayfaring, a weary Heart: which is neither Inconsideration, nor Irresolution, but Inconstancie' (9.176), wittily described as a trinity of enemies against the goal of unity that God loves. Each of these hearts, as the heart is the foundation of this text, poses a danger to the godly man, making him value worldly rather than heavenly treasures. Donne's meditation on each of these hearts is masterful, distinguishing between corrupt and regenerate versions of each kind. The 'idle' heart that does not think or consider, like the body that does not eat, starves and evaporates while its soul breathes and smokes through the body. Good nullification of the heart, as when its coldness or lukewarmness is overcome, is a pouring out, an 'evacuation' and a 'glorious annihilation of the heart'. Worldly evidence of this sinful nullification of the heart is to know our age only by the baptismal register and not by our actions, or to know religion only by its convenience or the preferments it offers, and is the enemy of the firmness and fixation without which we have no treasure.

The second heart, the irresolute or perplexed heart, is equally dangerous. This spirit of contradiction is a 'rack and torture', and a 'sickly complexion of the soule'. This disposition, 'to be able to conclude nothing, resolve nothing, determine nothing, not in my Religion, not in my Manners, but occasionally, and upon Emergencies', which might appear to be a 'wise circumspection, or wariness', he says, is a 'sickly complexion of the soul, a dangerous impotencie, and a shrewd and ill-presaging *Crisis*' (9.179), in fact, a 'vertiginous giddiness'. The third heart, wandering and wayfaring, is the final threat to firmness. Even if we conquer the first two in our consciences, these do not resolve in action. 'Except the Lord of Heaven fix our Resolutions, of our selves, we have *Cor vagum*, a various, a wandering heart; all smoaks into Inconstancie' (9.181).

As this probing of the human heart reveals, however, and as the words of the biblical text expose, all hearts—even these lethargic, irresolute, and wayward hearts—fix themselves upon some objects, desire some treasure. And it is to these that Donne directs the remainder of the Sermon. As with the Easter 1628 Sermon, Donne returns here to the exploration of the heart focused on worldly treasures in the here and now, and the heart focused on the everlasting treasures of heaven there and then.

Donne spends the rest of the Sermon examining treasures, first bad and then good, that accrue to men's hearts. The treasures of wickedness are the earnest of our sins, and Donne probes very near to his courtly audience in this section to expose their treasures: the supplantations and misrepresentations of the court, oppression of the poor in the country, extortions in Westminster, collusion and circumvention in the City, hypocrisy in the church, national and imported sins, sins of our age as well as those of former ages. Even the wretchedest beggar in the street contributes to this treasure, the treasure of sin (9.183), and in this respect, Donne says, 'is a Subsidy man' (9.183)—that is, a man of means or substance. Despite all of the 'many helps' that England enjoys, including 'the power of a vigilant Prince, executed by just Magistrates;... [and] the Piety of a Religious Prince seconded by the assiduity of a laborious Clergy' (9.182), this treasure of sin multiplies, to be answered by the treasury of God's displeasure here and indignation hereafter.

In the final portion of the Sermon Donne examines the earthly treasures of 'Grace and Peace' and the heavenly treasures of 'Joy and Glory'. The earthly treasures are in 'Vessels that may be broken; Peace that may be interrupted, Grace that may be resisted, Faith that may be enfeebled, Justification that may be suspected, and Sanctification that may be blemished' (9.187). The grand rhetorical flourish of the final lines invites his courtly hearers to see and love the treasures of heaven and value the treasures of earth, even those of the godly, as infinitely inferior to these. The transformation of these treasures into heavenly riches is the theme of the Sermon's peroration, ending in a sustained, cumulative accretion of treasures, expressed in the hyperbolic language of eternity:

Where all tears shall be wip'd from mine Eyes; not onely tears of Compunction for my self, and tears of Compassion for others; but even tears of Joy, too: for there shall be no sudden joy, no joy unexperienced there; There I shall have all joys, altogether, always. There *Abraham* shall not be gladder of his own Salvation, then of mine; nor I surer of the Everlastingness of my God, then of my Everlastingness in Him. (9.188)

10

As the examples discussed in this chapter have demonstrated, in his Sermons Donne alters perspective in a variety of ways, but always to achieve nearness. Most of these exercises in perspective are accomplished structurally and syntactically. The Sermon on seeing through a glass darkly alternates between here and there, now and then, using the corrective lens of structure to illuminate Donne's contrasts, and modify the perspectives of his hearers. The Sermons ending in grand perorations contrast by repetition and accumulation—using rhetorical figures of multiplication and amplification—this corrupt, time-bound, sinful earth with the incorruptible eternal world of glory. We experience these appeals as rhythms, such as those created by repetition and refrain in the perorations of his Sermons. We experience them as metaphors that transform temporally bound linear and hierarchical thinking (that contributed to doctrinal controversy and undermined assurance) into spiritually transformative moments that transcend these limits (such as Donne's discussion of election as a series of links in a chain or as the setting of a precious ring: 7.228; 3.377).

Donne's resistance to overworked ideas, structures of thought, language—what William Minto called his 'invincible repugnance to the commonplace' (862)—can help to explain all of his writings, from his love lyrics (so compellingly discussed in Dayton Haskin's essay above, Ch. 13) to his Sermons. What distinguishes Donne's Sermons from his love poems, in the end, is the intended audience. Donne's love poems, Haskin demonstrates, are deliberately difficult, unaccommodated to the many, and Donne expected generous cooperation from the best-knowing sort of readers to understand them. That is not to say that Donne's Sermons are *straightforward*, however. He consistently challenged his listeners to alter their perspectives, to see, hear, and speak differently in ways that would rouse them from spiritual lethargy and awaken them to God's grace. Ultimately, though, Donne's Sermons are more 'accommodating' than his poems, and to a much more diverse range of readers and hearers, in accord with his goal of enabling for *this* audience ongoing spiritual transformations or conversions, inspired by God's word and the desire for eternity.

Donne's treatment of the scandalous and controversial terms 'clergy' and layetie' in the Sermons by merging them as two callings with 'an equall interest in the joyes, and glory of heaven' (*Sermons* 4.371), for example, demonstrates this accommodation to his congregation even as it jars with his use of the same terms in poems such as *ValMourn* or *Canon*. Both of these poems distinguish between the lovers of the poems—whose two souls are one—and those 'Dull sublunary lovers' (*ValMourn* l. 13) or 'layetie' (l. 8) who find this joyously physical yet spiritual love incomprehensible or inimitable. In *ValMourn* the gap between the two kinds of lovers—as between two kinds of readers—is so great that the very expression of this refined love to the 'layetie' constitutes a 'prophanation' (l. 7) of these joys. More optimistically, *Canon* imagines future lovers (though likely none in the present age) who will be able to read the poem's lovers as a 'pattern' (l. 45) and invoke them as canonized saints of love (ll. 35–7).

Donne's Sermons can also be distinguished from his poetry in other ways that highlight their generic differences. In heaven, the Sermons suggest, the sharp distinctions epitomized by the perspectives of clergy and laity on earth (and underwritten by the religious and political controversies of his time) are utterly broken down. The Sermon as Donne uses it anticipates time and again the heavenly situation where the joys of earth are a foretaste of those in heaven, the lights of this world an anticipation of heavenly light, but there comes a point in the Sermon where Donne can no longer stress the continuity or progression between these states of being, but must evoke the perspective of the eternal that dissolves earthly conflicts and controversies, and makes the 'rocks' of this world into the 'smooth alleys' of heaven, or, as in the great Easter 1628 Sermon, dissolves the perceptions of the dark glass into the blaze of understanding that is 'knowing even as I am known'. In that spectacular instance we see most clearly how Donne's practice in his Sermons differs from that of his poems. It is not the reader who works hard to understand and becomes knowing who is saved in this Sermon; it is the reader who opens himself/herself to be known. The broken speaker of *HSBatter* who pleads to be ravished by God (*Variorum* 7.1.25, l. 14), the broken-hearted subject and reader of the *Devotions*, and most surely the speaker of *Ecst* are all engaged in seeking this ineffable experience of being truly known that is the hard-earned promise of that Sermon.

In the end, Donne's Sermons illustrate his most sustained and creative engagement with a literary genre. The Sermons as printed are the glass through which we glimpse—through the distortions of almost 400 years of history—the imaginative efforts of a person committed to speaking both for and through a public institution—the Church of England—to the consciences of his congregations. While we cannot experience the immediacy of Donne's pulpit utterances, except at several removes, we can envision that 'nearnesse'—and our understanding of it—as at least a partial and earthly achievement of Donne's desire to know as he is known.

CHAPTER 25

THE PROSE LETTER

MARGARET MAURER

Most of John Donne's Prose Letters survived through the agency of others. Thirty-eight are preserved in his hand; the rest were transcribed in manuscripts or committed to print within decades of his death. Until the appearance of the forthcoming Oxford edition (undertaken in the 1920s by I. A. Shapiro, significantly advanced by him, and now moving towards completion under the editorship of M. Thomas Hester, Ernest W. Sullivan II, and Dennis Flynn), the only collection of them attempting to be comprehensive (though it often inaccurately copies and mistakenly dates them) will remain Edmund Gosse's *The Life and Letters of John Donne* (1899).

Gosse's work, as Dayton Haskin explains, can be seen as the logical extension of a tradition, increasingly the dominant one as the nineteenth century progressed, of reading letters as 'personal expressions', for 'details about the experience of someone whom [the reader of them] already knew by reputation', rather than as 'artifacts', for their inherent beauty (2007: 68). Many of Donne's Letters, however, illustrate all too clearly the hazard of assuming that any biographical information they might convey can be understood without attention to the nuances of language, style, and thought that are as characteristic of Donne's Letters as of his poems and Sermons. Most of the Letters, in fact, probably owe their preservation to the elegant intricacy of their design. The early modern fascination with familiar letters as a genre or kind of writing, which doubtless inspired many of those who collected Donne's Letters to do so, promoted the value of letters as conveyors of the self but not without appreciation for the art of doing so.

The first of Donne's Letters to be published appeared in a context emphasizing their art. They were published with Donne's poems, a circumstance that H. J. C. Grierson, Gosse's contemporary, thought 'rather odd' (Donne 1912: 2.xci). In addition to two that are prefaces to particular occasional poems and printed with them, nine 'Letters', one in Latin, are placed after 'Poëms' and 'Satyres' and before 'Elegies upon the Author' in *Poems, By J. D. With Elegies On The Authors Death* (1633). None of these Letters includes any mention of practical affairs or news, such concerns, Donne says, as drive his correspondent's (Sir Henry Goodere's) 'often, long, and busie letters' (1633*b*: 359) or that oppress Sir Henry Wotton so that he writes seldom, 'under the oppression of businesse or the necessity of seeming so' (360). Two refer to themselves as meditations (368, 372). Donne calls friendship his 'second religion' (359); letter-writing is its piety, a piety he says he practises obsessively: 'no mans letters might be better wanted then mine, since my whole letter is nothing else but a confession that I should and would write' (360). Letters themselves (351, 353, 359, 362), literary 'problems' (358, 361), and verses (360, 366, 367) are recurring subjects. Goodere is the addressee of all but one, a Letter to the Countess of Bedford requesting a copy of verses the Countess had shown him (367). One hypothesis is that the 1633 editor included these Letters as 'examples of epistolary elegance' (R. E. Bennett 1941: 126); but whatever the motive, the effect of their appearing in *Poems* is to suggest that Donne's Letters reward the attention to style and structure that his poetry demands (Maurer 1982: 183 ff.).

Five Letters were then added to this section in the substantially rearranged 1635 *Poems*: three to George Garrard, one to Garrard's sister, and one (in Latin verse) to Richard Andrews. In the one to Martha Garrard, Donne's wit is again on display, as he makes something, a graceful compliment, out of virtually nothing; but the new Letters also include personal details. Two describe their ageing author's ailments (to which the Verse Letter also alludes). Another defends his Anniversaries and denies rumours that he will return from France to pursue a career in law and that Sir Robert Drury attended a Mass. R. E. Bennett suggested that this Letter was fabricated out of two separate Letters to cast its 'businesse' in a particular light (1940: 72–4). Whether or not this conjecture is true, a more purely biographical motive seems to have been behind the inclusion of additional Letters in the 1635 *Poems*.

The next group of Letters to see print are in publications associated with Izaak Walton, whose influence may also explain the additional Letters in the 1635 *Poems* (Novarr 1958: 38–48). The first version of Walton's 'life and death of Dr. Donne', prefaced to *LXXX Sermons* (1640), includes a Letter from Donne to Garrard, an edited version, judging from another version of it that has survived. Subsequent issues of Walton's life added and removed parts of Letters (R. E. Bennett 1937: 31), and four Donne Letters to Magdalen Herbert were printed in Walton's life of her son George (1670: 24–6, 141–6).

Donne's son John may, like Walton, have been concerned with the character of the writer conveyed by the 129 Donne Letters he printed as *Letters to Severall Persons of Honour* (1651). He says the volume's contents had been '*scattered, more then Sibyls leaves, I cannot say into parts, but corners of the World*' (A3ᵛ); and he praises its dedicatee, Bridget Dunch, for helping to protect '*that part of* [Donne's] *Soul, that be left behinde him, his* Fame *and* Reputation' (A4). This collection reprints Letters from the 1633 and 1635 *Poems*. Some of the newly included Letters are assigned to a wider range of his father's acquaintances than their content will admit (Shapiro 1931: 294–301), either mistakenly or to convey Donne's association with more 'persons of honour' (R. E. Bennett 1941: 120, 139–40).

Cabala, Mysteries of State, in Letters of the great Ministers of K. James and K. Charles…Faithfully Collected by a Noble Hand (1654a), brings two more Letters to light as part of its project of '*present*[ing] *naked*' '*the great* Ministers *of* State…*their* Consultations, Designs, Policies' (A3). Both of the Donne Letters in this collection are to George Villiers, Marquis and then Duke of Buckingham. One thanks Villiers for exercising his influence on Donne's behalf, and the other presents him with a copy of *Devotions*.

After *Letters* (1651), the other large group of Letters printed within decades of Donne's death is in a collection initiated by Sir Tobie Matthew. Matthew acknowledges his principle of selection and admits to suppressing elements of the letters he includes. Describing letters as '*Casuall and Contingent Things*' (*TMC* B2ᵛ), he promotes those he has collected as of a particular kind:

These Letters were, for the most part, written upon a sudden, and à la volée; *and therefore you must not wonder, if they all be not so very exact. Nor shall you expect Clinches or Knacks, of that kind of Wit, which uses to play wantonly with Words.…many of them are not void of conceit; and they express themselves naturally, and nobly enough; considering, that they are not written, but in the familiar way.* (*TMC* B1ʳ⁻ᵛ)

Donne's son, presiding over this collection's publication in 1660, added seventeen letters written to his father and twenty-five of Donne's Letters (Feil 276–7), two of which—one to Sir Robert Ker (*TMC* 312–13) and one to Robert Carr, Viscount Rochester (*TMC* 318–19) and later Earl of Somerset—he had already included in a slightly different form in *Letters* (299–300, 290–1), and another of which (300–2), possibly printed from Donne's own copy of it, is one of the two included in *Cabala*. That Donne himself saved copies of at least some of his Letters is also suggested by other Letters in this group that are printed alongside replies to them.

Intended to describe the eight Donne Letters he himself included in his collection, Matthew's phrase '*written…in the familiar way*' is an invitation to consider Donne's letter-writing style in relation to the humanist concept of the familiar letter. The humanists invented the genre of the familiar letter to distinguish their letters from those categorized in the medieval letter-writing formularies by analogy to rhetorical modes. The concept originated with Petrarch, who, imitating Cicero, ordered and prepared to publish his own letters under the titles *Epistolae familiares*, *Epistolae seniles*, and a later group, which he apparently did not complete (E. H. Wilkins 16–17). In a letter to his friend Ludovico, whom he calls Socrates and apostrophizes as 'my Idomeneus, my Atticus, and my Lucilius' (Robinson 150), alluding to the correspondents of Epicurus, Cicero, and Seneca, Petrarch places his *Epistolae familiares* in the tradition of classical letter-writers:

You will find no great eloquence or vigour of expression in them. Indeed I do not possess these powers.... I chose a new name, and entitled the volume *Letters of Familiar Intercourse*, letters, that is, in which there is little anxious regard to style, but where homely matters are treated in a homely manner. Sometimes, when it was not inappropriate, there may be a bit of simple narration or a few moral reflections, such as Cicero was accustomed to introduce into his letters.... If ever I put the last touches to this work, I will send you, not a Phidian Minerva, as Cicero says, but an image, in some sort, of my mind and character, hewn out with great labour. (Robinson 135, 145)

Petrarch acknowledges the ancient models of familiar letters, but after him this kind of letter became new again and fashionable as humanists recovered it to displace the formulaic understanding of letter-writing that had been the basis of medieval rhetorical education. His expression—'If ever I put the last touches to this work... hewn out with great labour'—concedes the artfulness involved in conveying 'an image, in some sort, of [the] mind' of the letter-writer; and 'when it was not inappropriate' allows that some ornamentation ('simple narration or a few moral reflections') is not out of place in familiar letters. Petrarch also admits to adjusting his letters for publication (Robinson 140). His letters, written in Latin, relegate questions of business to now-lost vernacular footnotes.

An early imitator of Petrarch in English was Joseph Hall, publishing his epistles in six collections of ten ('decades'), four in 1608, two more in 1611. Dedicating his first book to Prince Henry, Hall describes his epistles as *'a new fashion of discourse... new to our language, vsual to others... more free, more familiar. Thus, we do but talke with our friends by our pen, and expresse our selues no whit lesse easily; somewhat more digestedly'* (1608: A7^v). His epistles are discourses on discrete topics, entitled accordingly: *'Expostulating for his* [correspondent's] *departure, and perswading his returne'* (1), *'A report of some Obseruations in my trauell'* (35).

Donne's Letters in *Poems* (1633), more intricately conceited than Hall's, apologize for their discursive quality: 'this letter... being intended for a letter is extended and strayed into a Homily' (1633*b*: 355); 'But I must not give you a Homily for a letter' (358); 'I meant to write a letter, and I am fallen into a discourse' (372). Nonetheless, Hall's practice may have influenced the editor of *Poems* (1633), where the 'Letters' section follows one labelled—as distinct from the 'Poëms' preceding it—'Satyres', another genre Hall practised. Hall's verses accompany Donne's Anniversaries in *Poems* as they had when they were printed in 1611, 1612, 1621, and 1625; and the suggestion of a connection between the literary endeavours of the recently deceased Dean of St Paul's and those of Joseph Hall would be even more apt in 1633, when Hall had been Bishop of Exeter for six years.

With the phrasing *'more free'* and *'easily'* qualified by *'some-what more digestedly'*, Hall negotiates the paradox that familiar letters embody: their cultivated style should seem artless. Humanist letter-writing treatises make similar prescriptions. The most influential of them, Erasmus' *De conscribendis epistolis* (1522), is the basis of Angel Day's *The English Secretorie* (1586), which discusses the traditional categories (demonstrative, judicial, deliberative) taken over from rhetorical treatises and adds a fourth, familiar (B3), specifying an unadorned style for letters of this type, 'Seeing an Epistle hath cheeflye his definition hereof, in that it is termed the familiar and mutuall talke of one absent friend to an other…' (18). Donne often echoes Day's description of letters as 'mutuall talke', conversation with someone who is not present.

Justus Lipsius' *Epistolica Institutio* (1591), less widely disseminated but, in England, known because it influenced John Hoskins's *Directions for Speech and Style*, defines a letter as '*A message of the mind to someone who is absent or regarded as absent*'. Quoting Turpilius, Lipsius says a letter can make the 'absent present' (9); and he emphasizes the connection between letter-writing and talk (*sermo*), as distinct from speech-making. For Lipsius, all of the possibilities of a letter's content can be confined 'within these three terms: serious, learned, familiar': 'I call a letter "serious" *which pertains to public or private matters, but also treats them fully and carefully*.… I call a letter "learned" *which appertains to knowledge or wisdom; it dresses up a non-epistolary subject in the garment of a letter*.' Learned letters, says Lipsius, can be literary, philosophical, or theological.

> Finally, I call 'familiar' *a letter which touches our affairs or the affairs of those around us, or whatever is unremitting in life*. That is the proper and most common subject of a letter and, if we are willing to admit the truth, the only one belonging to it. The two previous kinds—I refer to *serious* and *learned*—are often mixed with the familiar letter; but truly mixed, so that the content is varied and not plain. (21)

Lipsius thus supplies a useful term for describing many of Donne's Letters, notably those in *Poems* (1633). They are 'truly mixed', learned and familiar; and Donne acknowledges that the mixture is not as proper to a letter as more purely personal matters would be. He tells Goodere that only letters that have 'a convenient handsome body of news' are 'Letters'; those 'spun out of nothing', such as might describe almost all the Letters in *Poems* (1633), are 'ghosts' (*Letters* 121).

There is no evidence that Donne knew Lipsius' *Epistolica Institutio*, though it is likely he did; nor, though they knew one another, would he necessarily have known how Hoskins makes what he incorporates from Lipsius' treatise into his never-published *Directions* an occasion to disdain a protestation Donne often uses, that friendship is the business of a letter. As Hoskins puts it,

> But sometimes men make business of kindness, as:… My business is no other than to certify my love towards you and to put you in mind of my willingness to do you all kind office. Or: Have you leisure to descend to the remembrance of that assurance which you have long had in me, and upon your next opportunity to make me happy with any employment you shall assign me, or such like words, which go a-begging for some meaning and labor to be delivered of a great burthen of nothing. (4)

Ben Jonson incorporated this passage into his commonplace book, *Timber, or Discoveries Made upon Men and Matter* (8.629).

Donne frequently describes his Letters' office as a substitute for speech disabled by separation: 'Sir, I kisse your hands; and deliver to you an intire and clear heart; which shall ever when I am with you be in my face and tongue, and when I am from you, in my Letters, for I will never draw Curtain between you and it' (*Letters* 69); 'If you were here, you would not think me importune, if I bid you good morrow every day; and such a patience will excuse my often Letters' (*Letters* 105); 'this Letter shall but talke, not discourse; it shall but gossip, not consider, nor consult, so it is made halfe with a prejudice of being lost by the way' (*Letters* 143); '(for our Letters are our selves) and in them absent friends meet)' (*Letters* 240). His preoccupation with a Letter's capacity to make the absent present, however, leads him to just the excess Hoskins deplores. At times, even when transacting something that might be considered business, Donne's Letters profess their business to be kindness.

For Matthew, this is just the quality that makes letters valuable. The letters he has collected exhibit the special quality of the English:

Withall, our very Bowells yerne, to be spreading our selves upon our friends...our Pulse beates towards our Friends in the dark; and our heart doth, as it were pant, and gaspe, till it be even opening, and powring it self out, upon others, for the very pleasure of the thing it self, till our Friends be even lockt up, with us, in those very hearts. (*TMC* B3^v)

Prefacing each letter with '*a word or two, by way of Argument*' (*TMC* B2^v), Matthew often describes one or both parties as 'a friend'. He labels three of Donne's Letters in his collection this way: 'Doctor Dunne, *in kindnesse to an absent Friend*' (*TMC* 63), '*Of the same to the same, upon the like occasion*' (*TMC* 64), and '*Doctor* Dunne, *with a kind of labour'd Complement, to a Friend of his*' (*TMC* 67). The heading of this last, marking it as extreme within its kind, accurately acknowledges how its ending concedes that the purpose of its laboured argument has been, in Hoskins's terms, to convey a 'great burthen of nothing'. In its single-minded protestation of friendship as its only concern, however, it nonetheless reflects, like many other such Donne Letters, complexities of the world Donne and his correspondent inhabit.

This Letter of '*Complement*' professes Donne's desire to resume communication with his correspondent (doubtless Matthew himself):

I therefore, who could do nothing towards the begetting, would fain do somewhat towards the breeding and cherishing of such degrees of friendship, as formerly I had the honour to hold with you. If Letters be not able to do that office, they are yet able, at least to testifie, that he, who sends them, would be glad to do more, if he could.

Donne is reopening a correspondence that has lapsed. In characterizing his action of writing the Letter as 'breeding' and 'cherishing' what he could not beget, Donne employs distinctions used in the competing theologies of his day to understand human agency in relation to the dispensation of God's grace. A sentence in which he anticipates a meeting likewise has religious overtones: 'I have a great desire, not without some hope, to see you this Summer there; and I have more hope and more desire, to see you this next Winter here; and I have abundantly more of both, that, at least, we shall meet in Heaven'. That he and his correspondent differ in religion emerges now explicitly, though once articulated it can be seen to have shaped the Letter's manoeuvring throughout:

That we differ in our wayes, I hope we pardon one another. Men go to *China*, both by the Straights, and by the *Cape*. I never mis-interpreted your way; nor suffered it to be so, wheresoever I found it in discourse. For I was sure, you took not up your Religion upon trust, but payed ready money for it, and at a high Rate. And this taste of mine towards you, makes me hope for, and claime the same disposition in you towards me.

The Letter concludes by denying its concern with any business, referring his correspondent to others for news: 'For it is but earlie daies with me here; and I see not things so distinctlie yet, as to lay them under such eyes as yours. This Letter doth therefore onely aske your safe conduct, for those others of mine, which are to follow, as the most constant testimonies of my love' (*TMC* 68–9). Donne's concern for the 'safe conduct' of future Letters reasserts his willingness to allow his correspondent to set the term of their continuing intercourse.

The extension of the self in a letter entails more than an emotional risk. The correspondent must be willing to arrange messengers; and the writer must trust his correspondent's discretion in sharing the sentiments the letter conveys with others. The possibility of a letter's being mistaken, misconstrued, shared unwisely, or intercepted (Stewart and Wolfe 147–53) seems to have been a present danger for Donne in many of the circumstances in which he wrote Letters (A. Patterson 1982; see also Ch. 43 below). A reference in one of his Letters to the techniques of discovering invisible writing—'all the experiments of pouders, and dryings, and waterings to discover some lines which appeared not' (*Letters* 77)—is facetious; but a genuine anxiety about the security of his Letters is reflected in his preoccupation with the practicalities of letter-writing: the distinctiveness of his hand; a resort to ciphers or the inclusion of 'a schedule to burn, lest this Letter should be mis-laid' (*Letters* 185); concern about his Letters' reception and subsequent treatment by their recipients; the conduct of his own and others' letters through agents and messengers.

In some of the earliest of his surviving Letters the concern is especially prominent: 'y^o will p[ar]done me if I write nothing ernest' (E. M. Simpson 1948: 304); 'except I receue by y^r next lett^r an assurance vpō the religion of y^r frendship y^t no coppy shalbee taken for any respect of these or any other my compositions sent to y^o, I shall sinn against my conscience if I send y^o any more. I speak y^t in playnes wch becomes (methinks) o^r honestyes; & therfore call not this a distrustfull but a free spirit' (316). One especially memorable formulation reverberates with particular irony for the unintended reader: 'if words seald vp in letters be like words spoken in those frosty places where they are not heard till ye next thaw they haue yet this advantage y^t where they are heard they are herd only by one or such as in his iudgment they are fitt for' (310). Even more mysteriously than Donne's printed Letters, these Letters were saved from what Donne's son calls '*the fate of most* Letters' (*Letters* A4) by someone whose motives are unknown. Transcribed probably in Donne's lifetime, with no indication beyond what can be gleaned from evidence internal to them to whom, by whom, or when they were written, they owe their survival to the very circumstances Donne professes in them to fear.

Donne fears the security of the self his Letters expose in the 1651 collection as well: 'I dare say nothing by a Letter of adventure' (*Letters* 231); 'I would you could burn this letter, before you read it, at least do when you have read it' (219—a fearfulness Goodere either took for an over-reaction or chose to ignore); 'I [do not] discern by [your letter] that you have received any of mine lately; which have been many, and large, and too confident to be lost' (*Letters* 148). At one point, in a postscript to a long Letter to Goodere recounting the 'story' of an aborted duel between Robert Cecil, Earl of Salisbury, and Edward Seymour, Earl of Hertford, Donne presumes familiarity in the service of security: '*You know me without a name, and I know not how this Letter goes*' (*Letters* 217). Another Letter begins by expressing mild alarm that Goodere has misconstrued something he wrote in a 'postscript... which (so God help me) was so little, that I remember not what it was, and I would no more hear again what I write in an officious Letter, then what I said at a drunken supper'. Mild alarm becomes a sense of betrayal as Donne recounts how he realizes that Goodere, reading Donne's postscript in light of a letter from Garrard, has attributed some knavish motive to Donne: 'for I might think by this, (if I had not other testimony) that I have been little in your contemplation. Sixteen letters from M. *Gherard*, could not (I think) persuade a *Middlesex* Jury of so much dishonesty...' (*Letters* 182–4).

Yet in many of the Letters in *Letters* (1651), all of those added to Matthew's collection, and the several that survive in state papers and private collections, anxiety about being misunderstood is less prominent. Perhaps this is because many are, to use Lipsius' categories, more serious or learned than purely familiar. Donne may even have written such Letters with the expectation of readers beyond their addressee. As a letter-writer, after all, Donne was a professional. He sued to be a secretary, a position that would involve drafting letters for others to send over their own signatures, as he did for Sir Robert Drury and his wife (Bald 1970: 249, 258–9). Andrew Gordon's chapter (Ch. 29.II) suggests that 'managing Egerton's correspondence networks' may have been some part of the duties Donne performed for the Lord Keeper. There is evidence that he wrote Letters for Goodere (S. M. Johnson 1948) and, at Goodere's direction, for some 'house' (*Letters* 192–4). Moreover, as priest, Donne wrote Letters of consolation as he would have delivered a public funeral sermon (*TMC* 106–8). Even the Letter '*to his Mother: comforting her after the death of her Daughter*' (*TMC* 323–7) is not purely familiar, though the identity of the addressee gives it an aura of intimacy.

Though the style of them is consistently his, Donne's more purely familiar Letters also differ in tone, reflecting a distinctive relationship with each correspondent. The three largest groups are to Goodere, Garrard, and Sir Robert Ker.

For some time, Donne wrote 'Every tuesday' to Goodere (*Letters* 48). While his concern that someone else might read these Letters is not entirely absent—

When it shall not trouble you to write to me, I pray do me the favour to tell me, how many you have received from me, for I have now much just reason to imagine, that some of my Pacquets have had more honour then I wished them: which is to be delivered into the hands of greater personages, then I addressed them unto. (*Letters* 126)

—a feature of this correspondence is that Donne sometimes appears to expect that Goodere will share his Letters with another. Letters to Goodere are often warm and intimate, but they are seldom easy or playful. It is chiefly in Letters to Goodere that Donne meditates on letter-writing itself, developing the implications for a courtier that a familiar letter can convert absence into presence. In one Letter Donne uses this trope to confess a courtier's fear: 'SIR, That which is at first but a visitation, and a civill office, comes quickly to be a haunting, and an uncivill importunity: my often writing might be subject to such a misinterpretation, if it were not to you' (*Letters* 120). 'Importunity', improper familiarity, is a word that recurs in more anxious letters to a more powerful patron Donne seems to have been ambivalent about cultivating (*TMC* 318). Jeanne Shami's chapter on Donne's vocation (Ch. 32.I) is a sensitive reading of this correspondence with Robert Carr, Viscount Rochester and later Earl of Somerset.

Reflections on letter-writing in Letters to Goodere are often memorable. One rehearses a conceit of his poetry: letter-writing is 'a kind of extasie, and a departure and secession and suspension of the soul, wch doth then cōmunicate it self to two bodies' (*Letters* 11). Another makes it analogous to a sacrament, as 'it seems a kinde of resisting of grace, to omit any commodity of sending into *England*' (*Letters* 73). In another, letter-writing enables friendship on another plane: 'In the History or style of friendship, which is best written both in deeds and words, a Letter which is of a mixed nature, and hath something of both, is a mixed Parenthesis' (*Letters* 114). Donne's distinction, mentioned above, between letters that convey news and 'ghosts' that do not (*Letters* 121) collapses in a Letter to Goodere where he lets his ironic imagination play with what is probably an actual event, as he converts what he has heard about a large fine the Crown has decided to collect to 'newes': 'I give you (I think) the first knowledge, of two millions confiscated to the Crown of England.' As he considers how various people might sue for a share of the windfall, he does not forget himself: 'I pray make a petition in my name for as much as you think may be given me for my book [*Pseudo-Martyr*?] out of this...If I get no more by it, yet it hath made me a Letter' (*Letters* 54–6).

The familiarity of Letters to Garrard, fewer in number and less intricately constructed, is usually laced with business. Donne, writing from France in 1611–12, chides Garrard jokingly for not writing (*Letters* 262–3, 264–5), urging him, at one point, not to delay writing until he has something to report: '[telling me I am still your friend] shall be the gold of your Letter: and for allay, put in as much newes as you will' (264). Letters to Garrard are also preserved from a later period of Donne's life. Among the last Donne Letters that we have, these are considerably more dignified and restrained in tone.

What remains of Donne's correspondence with Sir Robert Ker (created Earl of Ancram in 1633) is usually preoccupied with the business that united them: Ker was an intermediary for Donne with the former's more powerful cousin, Robert Carr, and he also served as a go-between for Donne in his relationship to kings James and Charles. These Letters contain indications of the deep affinity that connected Donne and Ker. Ker seems to have appreciated Donne's writing to a degree unmatched by anyone else. Donne sent him *Biathanatos* (*Letters* 21–2) and wrote occasional poetry at his request (Donne 1633b: 162–4; Novarr 1980: 192–205). Letters to Ker in *Letters* (1651) and *TMC*—pressing him to assure King Charles or his advisers of Donne's loyalty in the face of rumours that a sermon had violated propriety, declining an invitation to dine before he preaches (*Letters* 307–10 and 311)—convey Donne's gratitude for Ker's support. Donne's Letters to Ker can be startlingly personal:

Sir, Perchance others may have told you, that I am relapsed into my Fever: but that which I must intreat you to condole with me, is, that I am relapsed into good degrees of health ... I am fallen from fair hopes, of ending all; yet I have scaped no better cheap, then that I have paid death one of my Children for my Ransome. Because I loved it well, I make account that I dignifie the memorie of it, by mentioning of it to you, else I should not be so homely. (*Letters* 273)

The loss of the full extent of this correspondence between two men who esteemed each others' character and gifts so highly seems particularly great. A beautiful letter from Ker to Donne (Ker 1.46–7) survives, only because Ker kept a copy.

The uncertainties that attend Donne's Letters preserved in print or through transcriptions make the few Donne holograph Letters especially valuable. One to the Lady Kingsmill consoling her on the loss of her husband permits the comparison of it to printed versions in both the 1651 *Letters* (7–10) and *TMC* (106–8). Letters preserved in state papers exhibit Donne's habit of writing even a purely 'businesse' letter with the taut conceitedness of a poem, beginning where he begins so as to end there. Holographs are also reassuring evidence that, with allowance for some loss of nuance, what seems to be true about Donne's epistolary style as conveyed in printed letters is not false to the impulses of his epistolary style as warranted by his hand. An official Letter to Dudley Carleton, ambassador to the Hague, opens with an image of its writer writing the letter: 'I present to yor Lp: here a hand w^{ch}, I thinke, you never saw, and a name wch carryes no such merit w^t yt, as that it should be well known to yo^u: but yet yt ys the hand, and the name of a person very much devoted to yor Lps service.' Its closing then represents its business as nothing more than the occasion to remind the recipient of the devotion its opening protests:

Yt ys so generall a busines that even so low and poor a man as I, have a part in yt and an office to do for yt, wch ys to promove yt w^t ye same prayers, as I present for myne own soule to y^e

ears of allmighty god. In wch I shall never be defective, nor in any thinge, wherein I might declare in particular, my desire to be esteemed by y^r Lp: Yo^r Lps most humble servant in chr: Jes: J: Donne. (TNA, SP 84/91/236R)

The holograph, preserved among state papers, renders the Letter's opening particularly apt. The hand Donne says he thinks Carleton never saw and now dedicates to Carleton's service is as distinctively elegant as the style of the Letter.

Among the Loseley manuscripts now in the Folger Shakespeare Library are eight Letters dated from around the time of Donne's marriage. These are particularly intense manifestations of the advantages and hazards of his epistolary style; and their holographic condition conveys additional dimensions to that style. Further, the Loseley papers include Donne Letters to Egerton and to Wotton as well as to members of the More family, suggesting that the family had access to Letters to others on matters that concerned them. The circumstances of that access must be imagined as an aspect of appreciating the various occasions and accidents that preserved Donne's Letters.

The neat penmanship of the first Letter to Sir George More (2 February 1602), written after Donne's secret marriage became known, contrasts with the looser writing of the 13 February Letter to Egerton, the former suggesting a level of deliberation at odds with the plainness and directness it protests. Donne pleads that 'my sicknes, as that I cannot stir', prevented the 'boldness' of doing 'the Office of this letter, by wayting upon yow my self: To have given yow truthe, and clearnes of this Matter between your Daughter and me; and to show to yow plainly the limits of our fault'. Explaining his decision to act in secrecy, Donne professes to be 'deal[ing] with the same plainnes that I have usd'. The profession of a plain style is an affectation of familiarity that must have been an affront. The holograph suggests further that, in his claim that he and Anne acted 'having those honest purposes in our harts', 'honest' seems inserted above the line. Donne signs the Letter several inches below his closing to register a humility the Letter does not really convey (*Marriage Letters* 35–6, 67–8). In the more apparently contrite Letter to Egerton, his signature is as far down in the lower corner of the sheet as it could possibly be (73).

The three Letters addressed to Donne's brother-in-law Sir Robert More are not Donne's most intimate surviving Letters, but they focus with extraordinary clarity the questions that attend any consideration of his Letters. Familiar in the most literal sense of that word, they convey homely matters, yet Donne's peculiar wit and style emerges in them nonetheless.

A Letter to Sir Robert from Amiens with news from Paris is 'my second letter to yow; that ys, my second fault' (*Marriage Letters* 54). Where is the first? Did it not arrive? Or did Sir Robert not preserve it? More suggestive is this letter's conveyance, after the bulk of its news, of Donne's anxiety that he has

had no returne from [the Isle of Wight, where his pregnant wife was staying] of any letter, since my comminge out of England. And thys silence, especially at thys tyme, when I make

Map 25.1. Detail from Map of Surrey taken from *Surrey described and divided into hundreds* by John Norden/ John Speed (1610). British Library Maps C.7.c.5 (44). This detail shows important Donne locations including Pyrford, Mitcham, Twickenham, Loseley, and Croydon (© The British Library Board, BL Maps C.7.c.5(44).)

account that your sister ys near her paynfull and dangerous passadge, doth somewhat more affect mee, then I had thought any thinge of thys world could have donne. (55, 95)

In a second Letter, writing to return a horse Sir Robert had lent him, Donne fills the whole of one side of a sheet and part of the reverse with his exasperation that the unexpected visit of King Christian of Denmark has 'put my little Court busines out of the way': 'I ame so angry at theyr comminge, that I have not so much as inquir'd why they came. But they are even with mee; for, in truthe, they came for nothing. Statesmen, who can finde matter of state, in any wrinckle in the kings socks, thinke that he came for the busines of Cleve' (57, 97). Did Sir Robert preserve this for its wit?

In the latest of the three, written two weeks later, Donne is again returning a horse 'by thys carryar of Gilford'. What saved this Letter from being destroyed is even more mysterious—perhaps this passage, which Sir Robert may have deemed, knowing the circumstances, memorably put:

We are condemnd to thys Desart of London for all thys sommer: for yt ys Company, not houses which distinguishes between Cityes, and Desarts. When I began to apprehend, that even to myselfe, who can releive myselfe upon books, solitarines was a litle burdenous, I beleevd yt would be much more so, to my wyfe, if shee were left alone. So much company therefore, as I ame, shee shall not want: and wee had not one another at so cheape a rate, as that we should ever be wearye of one another.

A postscript, directing Sir Robert to 'give thys note enclosed to my lady, your mother. It ys of some parcells which she commanded my wyfe to buy for her...' (59, 100), suggests a detail of Donne's life with Anne. While it is now thought that some Letters in the Burley ms. may have been ones Donne wrote to Anne during the period of their courtship (I. Bell 1986; see also Ch. 30.I), no Letters survive from their married life, though it is clear that he wrote them and Anne must have sometimes replied.

Donne's Letters are so finely constructed, and they intimate so much that is rich and interesting about his life, his times, and his other writing, that it is easy to regret the loss of the many others that he must have written; but Donne's view of posterity's interests in his correspondence may have been different. A Letter to Goodere, acknowledging with a touch of playfulness the enduring value of the letters of long-dead famous or learned men, distinguishes them from such Letters as he exchanges with friends: 'the papers of any living now, (especially friends)' we read 'with how much desire,' but 'we would scarce allow [them] a boxe in our cabinet, or shelf in our Library, if [their authors] were dead' (*Letters* 107). It is a remark that reads ironically, addressed as it is to the recipient of most of his surviving Letters. Goodere may have taken it wholly for what in part it is, a flourish of Donne's exploration of the humanist concept of the familiar letter as a species of dialogue, essentially disabled by the death of one of the interlocutors. Yet, since Goodere predeceased Donne, it must be allowed that he may have intended but was unable to honour Donne's implicit wish that his Letters be destroyed at his death.

What may have been Donne's impulse to protect the privacy of familiar correspondence is supported by another Letter written to Goodere on the eve of Donne's departure abroad. He is 'surveying and emptying my Cabinet of Letters', presumably destroying them in anticipation of the possibility that he will not return. (One, in verse, from an unnamed correspondent, Donne does not destroy. He sends it to Goodere in place of a verse composition of his own.) Donne's Letter wishes Goodere 'such a reparation in your health, such an establishment in your estate, such a comfort in your children, such a peace in your conscience, and such a true cheerfulnesse in your heart, as may be strong seales to you of [God's] eternall gracious purpose upon you' (*Letters* 223–4). Four centuries later, readers eavesdropping on the affection this Letter expresses, cannot wish undone the acts and accidents that have preserved some of Donne's Letters; but they must notice as well that he writes in the act of disabling such exposure of those who corresponded with him.

PART III
BIOGRAPHICAL AND HISTORICAL CONTEXTS

INTRODUCTION

DENNIS FLYNN AND JEANNE SHAMI

PART 3 gives equal place to paired essays, by biographers and by historians. These pairs work as teams, for the most part maintaining their distinct disciplinary approaches: talking to each other; creating perspective on what is known about Donne's life; showing how Donne's life and writings epitomized and affected important controversial issues of his day; and bringing to bear on Donne studies some of the most stimulating and creative ideas developed in recent decades by historians of early modern England, ideas that have been too often ignored in literary studies and are thus unfamiliar to many students of Donne. These historical ideas suggest reasonable conjecture about Donne's biography and imply the need for reconsideration of many fundamental assumptions underlying the work of Donne critics. To this end, Part 3 essays supply readers with conceptual tools for removing obstacles and developing new paths towards an understanding of Donne's life and writings.

Patrick Collinson and Dennis Flynn review Donne's family background and early years in the context of earlier Tudor, and especially mid-Elizabethan, religious reform. The importance of this approach is highlighted by Flynn's conclusion that 'Donne's first biographer Izaak Walton (whose influence in Donne studies remains incalculably great) expressed little interest in most of the details discussed in this essay'; Collinson emphasizes the recent insights of historians of the period, who have explored complications newly discovered in misleading binary concepts such as 'Protestant' and 'Catholic', 'conformist' and 'recusant', and 'apostasy' and 'conversion'.

Alexandra Gajda surveys the ordinary educational options available to a boy of Donne's background, noting that 'in the confessional conflicts that divided Christendom, education—and education of youth in particular—was seen as a vital tool for the propagation of true religious belief, and an essential weapon in the fight against the false'. Observing prevalent obscurity about Donne's later childhood and adolescence, Dennis Flynn invites refutation, conjecturing that, in view of the boy's background and the neglected evidence of his prentice-work in poetry (his lost Latin Epigrams known only in posthumous translations), he likely rejected all standard alternatives, enrolling (*pace* Walton and later biographers) only briefly at Oxford and instead travelling to the continent in early 1585, in conjunction with the deportation of his uncle, the Jesuit Jasper Heywood.

Reviewing Donne's participation in the Cadiz raid and the Azores voyage during 1596–7, Albert C. Labriola notes that 'Donne's references to these expeditions emphasize life at sea and maritime warfare, not assaults overland. If, therefore, Donne saw action on the ground at Cadiz, he did not write graphically about his experiences. He may have been in the rear guard, not the vanguard'. Paul E. J. Hammer places Donne's combat experience in the context of larger political events, especially the rise and fall of Robert Devereux, second Earl of Essex, regarded by Walton and following biographers as the courtier/soldier towards whom Donne gravitated in the late 1590s. Hammer points out, however, that while service as a gentleman volunteer 'offered young gentlemen the prospect of adventure, new social contacts through military comradeship, the possibility of plunder, and first-hand knowledge of war', on the other hand, gentlemen volunteers 'attached themselves to a military commander—often a colonel or another senior subordinate officer, rather than directly with the general himself—and served at their own expense as private soldiers in order to acquire the personal experience of war which was expected of their class'; this was 'an expensive business, especially as gentlemen soldiers were expected to live as befitted their rank and the costs of food and other essentials were often exorbitantly high in a war zone'.

Steven W. May starts from the perception that Donne returned from the Azores 'aware that he was no "swordsman", despite the belligerent aura of the portrait he had commissioned in 1591'. Yet, as May admits, Donne's employment by Lord Keeper Thomas Egerton remains something of a puzzle: no evidence tells us what this work entailed. Oddly inflecting the puzzle is Donne's attitude towards the royal court, the arena for a large part of Egerton's work, but a place Donne seems nowhere to mention except with the bitterly 'negative sentiments of a court outsider', surpassingly expressed in *Sat4*. Andrew Gordon's discussion of the court mentions its 'atmosphere of suspicion and intrigue' during the later 1590s. Gordon concludes that, unlike friends such as Henry Wotton, Donne 'confidently avoided factional allegiance', in particular allegiance to the ill-fated Earl of Essex. Donne's work for Egerton, Gordon conjectures, may have involved his careful rhetoric, performing 'some junior role' in connection with the Lord Keeper's correspondence.

Dennis Flynn tells the story of Donne's wedding to Anne More, showing that it was 'carefully planned, not a reckless adventure of love', but instead the product of a scheme including intricate timing and litigation. He stresses our need to know more about Anne More's personality and active agency in this matter, and in the marriage as a whole, dismissed or minimized as these have been by Donne's biographers since Walton. During the earliest years of the Jacobean reign, while Donne and his new family stayed with Anne's cousin Francis Wolley at Pyrford, Donne regarded the developing political scene at considerable distance from London and the court. Concerning this period, Anthony Milton describes the outlook of Catholics and Catholic sympathizers as one of hope that King James would grant toleration to Catholics, hope that was disappointed by 1604. In particular, Milton observes that 'Donne's patron Northumberland, who had urged James before his accession that "it weare pittie to losse so good a kingdome for the not tolerating a messe [sic] in a cornere" soon lost favour (at least temporarily) when he pleaded for a full toleration now that James was on the throne'. Milton extends his discussion of Donne's political attitudes in these years to considerations that culminated in the publication of *Pseudo-Martyr* (1610).

Johann Sommerville looks back at Donne's Mitcham years from the vantage of the May 1612 death of Robert Cecil, Earl of Salisbury, maintaining that during this period Donne agreed with Cecil on matters of political principle. Reviewing Donne's *Pseudo-Martyr* and *Ignatius His Conclave*, as well as Cecil's writings, all regarding implications of the Gunpowder Plot and the Oath of Allegiance, Sommerville finds that Donne and Cecil both distinguished between the general culpability for the plot of English Catholics as a whole and the particular responsiblity of the Jesuits and other hard-line papists. Further, Donne agreed with Cecil that certain practices and teachings of the latter could not be tolerated, although Catholics who did not subscribe to these should be treated with mercy. Donne and Cecil agreed, for example, about the papal deposing power, an issue controverted between Venetian and Gallican writers on one hand and Jesuit and other Roman Catholic writers on the other. Concerning this same period in Donne's biography, Dennis Flynn argues that Donne's attitude towards the plot and the Oath was more complicated than has been thought, citing the work of Michael Questier concerning the effects of the Oath on English Catholic consciences. Reviewing events connected to Donne's puzzling travel on the continent in 1605–6 and features of Donne's relationship to Catholic friends, such as Toby Matthew and Ben Jonson, Flynn argues that while Donne did conform to the general lines of government policy in regard to the plot, attacking Jesuit controversialists and advising English Catholics to swear the Oath, he was careful (while publicly identifying himself as a member of the Church of England) to preserve space for traditional Catholicism within this kind of conformity: 'He repeatedly contested the notion that the only Catholicism was the Roman Catholicism propounded by the Council of Trent; and he continued to express fundamental sympathy and concern to accommodate traditional English Catholics, intending help to secure for them some limited toleration within the English Church.'

Chapters by Jeanne Shami and Alastair Bellany probe the years just prior to Donne's decision to take orders in the Church of England, especially Donne's murky relations with the royal favourite Robert Carr, Earl of Somerset. Bellany's essay maps 'the multiple centres of power and the complex articulation of influence at the Jacobean court', contextualizing Donne's movements within the factionalized politics that emerged in 1612–13, factions 'fluidly composed and never ideologically homogeneous', culminating in Carr's decline and the rise of George Villiers as the King's powerful favourite. Shami's essay steps back from the events and forces depicted in Bellany's account to focus primarily on Donne's extant correspondence as it illuminates his uncomfortable relations with Carr, and the pressures exerted by that relationship as well as by Donne's relationships with his friends, family, in-laws, and other patrons in 1614, but concludes that 'it is likely that in 1616 Donne and his mother shared the same religion, if not the same church', and that Donne's ordination as a divine was a career choice 'not only tolerated but approved by his closest family members'.

Peter McCullough and Kenneth Fincham combine to consider the complexities and 'hazards' of serving as court chaplain first to King James and then to Charles I. McCullough points out that the 'explosion' of court-centred preaching, leading to an 'exponential growth' in the number of court chaplains appointed by James, cannot explain the unprecedented effort that James put into Donne's creation and clerical promotion: 'Donne went from laity to clergy, from no degree to doctorate, from unemployment to royal chaplaincy, in no more than a few weeks'. Further, Donne's appointment as chaplain to the embassy of James Hay, Viscount Doncaster, read as an extension of his court chaplaincy, again shows an 'extraordinary degree' of royal favour, esteem that carried over into the reign of Charles, although Donne's position became more tentative by 1627, in part because of disfavour by Bishop William Laud. Fincham's account of the character of ecclesiastical politics during this period—especially the role of George Abbot, Archbishop of Canterbury—confirms that the extraordinary arc of Donne's promotion—especially as Dean of St Paul's—was a signal mark of royal favour in line with James's pattern of personal religious patronage in the period. Donne's ability to avoid being drawn into the turmoil of emerging religious factionalism appears all the more remarkable in Fincham's account, although he concludes that Donne's ties with evangelical Calvinists were strong.

Emma Rhatigan and Malcolm Smuts handle the years 1616–20, during which Donne was made Reader at Lincoln's Inn and subsequently chaplain to Doncaster, on his diplomatic embassy to mediate between James I's Protestant son-in-law, Friedrich of the Palatinate, and the Catholic Prince Ferdinand, soon to become Holy Roman Emperor. Rhatigan's essay focuses on Lincoln's Inn as a formative institutional context for Donne's development within the English Church during the first years of his ministry. His rhetorical and diplomatic skills also fitted him, as James's chaplain, to act on the state's behalf on the delicate political and religious matters boiling over on the continent. Malcolm Smuts's essay focuses primarily on this international context for understanding Donne's churchmanship and theology in the early years of his ministry. This essay provides students of Donne with a fascinating window onto James's 'intricate middle path' between most of the period's oppositions—Catholic/Protestant; English/continental—thus illuminating Donne's own conflicting allegiances. Moreover, Smuts's essay offers a paradigmatic example of how important it is to distinguish—in Donne's writings as well as those of other public figures, including James's—between rhetorical formulations of problems and beliefs and their pragmatic expressions in times of crisis. Smuts thinks Donne is best understood as a 'moderate Calvinist royalist' trying to 'preserve a middle ground on which British and European evangelicals might remain united against their common foes'. He cautions scholars to resist the impulse to align Donne with players in various contests of religion, thinking of him instead as one 'struggling to prevent such contests from developing'.

Chapters by Clayton D. Lein and Simon Healy cover the crucial years—the 1620s—during which Donne established his churchmanship first as James's and subsequently as Charles I's royal chaplain, one who maintained amiable relations with people at entirely opposite ends of the political and ecclesiastical spectrums (e.g. William Herbert, Earl of Pembroke, and George Villiers, James's favourite and Duke of Buckingham). Donne's key pulpit performances—defending James's *Directions to Preachers*, preaching the first Sermon before King Charles, and a 1627 court Sermon that offended William Laud, Bishop of London—are interpreted within this complex network of relationships, allegiances, and circumstances to reveal a Donne who, while not a major political player, was nonetheless influential in defining and maintaining his vision of the English Church among those increasingly in competition in the 1620s. Lein's essay provides insight into what is emerging as a key issue in understanding Donne as divine—the dizzyingly complex character of late Jacobean and early Caroline religious and political factionalism, and Donne's characteristically Erasmian moves to resist such divisions while still maintaining the official orthodoxy of the English state church. Healy expands the picture of domestic politics within which Donne operated in these years, characterizing Donne's own position as one of intelligent and well-informed caution, unlike that of more politically ambitious figures such as John Williams, with whom Healy contrasts Donne. Donne's topical pulpit utterances are woven into the web of his allegiances and associations involving church (and thereby state) matters. Donne's glancing comments on matters being debated in Parliament, including his essentially 'non-partisan' remarks on many current controversies, confirm for Healy that Donne was preaching in the eye of the hurricane, amid increasingly factionalized parties who fought against or sought to profit by alterations of the status quo.

The final chapters of Part 3 mark Donne's death in 1631, but look forward to the moment historically even as they resonate with the full weight of Donne's passing. Arnold Hunt gathers up the historical threads that have woven the narrative of Donne's ascendancy in the English Church at the same time as they have marked the evidence of Donne's growing alienation from some features of that institution's development. Hunt's crucial conceptual insight is that 'climate change, however profound, is not always obvious to those living through it'. So while it is clear, in retrospect, 'that the accession of Charles I in 1625 was indeed a critical turning point in religious and political affairs', Donne's prominence as a court preacher 'was a visible symbol of continuity between the two reigns'. In Hunt's reading, 'Donne did not negotiate the transition to the reign of Charles I entirely smoothly or seamlessly, and the Sermons preached in the final years of his life often betray a mood of ambivalence, looking back to the reign of James as well as forward to the political and religious changes of the 1630s'. Donne's appropriation after his death by both Laudians and Catholics for their own purposes leads Hunt to conclude that at his death Donne's style of piety 'seemed to belong to an earlier generation', a conclusion shaped by the weight of evidence adduced in this essay. This view of Donne's last days in the pulpit is enriched by Alison Shell's essay on 'The Death of Donne', which examines 'how Donne used his consciousness of mortality and his own deathbed to forge bonds with family, friends, and mankind in general'. Working from the perception that, for Donne and his contemporaries, 'death was a public matter', Shell's insight into the communal effects of death, its impact on the kinship bonds within a religious community, leads her to dissociate Donne from the 'Puritan instinct to consort only with the elect and pull away from the wider community', and to see him paradoxically as one of the age's most individual voices articulating 'the limits of religious individualism'. In his poems, Sermons, and even in his seal, Shell traces a pattern common in Donne's writings, whereby real-life experiences 'could act as a foretaste of heaven'. Strikingly, the essay evokes 'Donne's consciousness of the excitement of death', imbued with the Christian hope that death is not 'an end in itself, but a journey towards a new beginning'. Shell's concluding words provide a fitting conclusion to this section of the Handbook: 'Few can have been as concerned as he was to give directions to future voyagers'.

CHAPTER 26.1

THE ENGLISH REFORMATION IN THE MID-ELIZABETHAN PERIOD

PATRICK COLLINSON

In the traditional perspective (now largely superseded) of the Church of England and its historians, the English Reformation had come to its conclusion and consummation in the first regnal year of Queen Elizabeth I. The Elizabethan Settlement of Religion had been defined by Elizabeth's first Parliament in 1559, a historic watershed. The alleged aberration of the return to Catholicism in the reign of Mary Tudor (1553–8), 'the Marian reaction', had been reversed, the essence of that reversal contained in two Acts of the 1559 Parliament: the Act of Supremacy, which acknowledged the Queen to be Supreme Governor of the Church of England (not Head, as is often suggested), in terms reasserting the exemption of that church from any foreign jurisdiction, meaning Rome, a statute still in force today; and the Act of Uniformity, which replaced the Mass and other Catholic rites with a Book of Common Prayer that was the second and more radically Protestant Prayer Book of Edward VI (1547–53); albeit with a few, significant adjustments in a more conservative direction, the essence of what some scholars have called the Elizabethan compromise. This essentially Protestant Prayer Book was legally no more than a schedule to an Act of Parliament requiring all adult inhabitants of the land, not having a reasonable excuse, to be present in church twice on Sundays and holy days, on pain of a fine; and to use the Prayer Book rites and no others when they married their spouses, baptized their children, and buried their dead. The greatest philosophical defender of these religious developments, Richard Hooker, insisted that membership of the Church of England and citizenship within the realm and commonwealth of England were virtually one and the same thing.

This was Hooker's pipe dream. When he wrote in the 1590s, and even more so thirty or forty years earlier, most English subjects and citizens can best be characterized as dissenting 'Catholics', of one kind or another (Duffy 1992). 'Of one kind or another' requires some comment. What should we intend if we label this or that Elizabethan a Catholic? Should we include all those (of the older generation especially) who were accustomed to the religion in which they had been brought up, and who had neither learned, understood, nor accepted the tenets of Protestantism? Or should we restrict its application to those, defined by the law as 'recusants', who on grounds of conscience absented themselves from Protestant services, and, in the case of the diaspora of exiled scholars and clergy, from the country, while continuing to participate in the Catholic sacraments? Catholic historiography in the past favoured the narrower definition. All Catholics either were, or ought to have been, recusants. Protestants were not too concerned about fine distinctions, and called all those whom they knew or suspected to be 'of the old religion' 'papists'. Modern historians distinguish between recusants and 'church papists', those whose private religious convictions did not prevent them from conforming, outwardly, by attendance at some church services. But, as we shall see, there were in reality many points on the spectrum between these two positions; and individuals constructed their lives differently, at different times in a life-cycle, and in different circumstances.

Politics was a major issue: whether to be some kind of Catholic was compatible with obedience to the Protestant monarch, Elizabeth I. In 1570, after Pope Pius V excommunicated Elizabeth and absolved her subjects from their natural obedience, the last time in history that any pope presumed to depose a reigning sovereign, there might seem to have been no choice for Catholics. But in practice there was, just as choices in marital and sexual conduct continue for modern Catholics beyond the promulgation of Pope Paul VI's encyclical *Humanae Vitae*. A kind of patriotism was as strongly felt among Elizabethan Catholics as among Protestants, and that could translate into a degree of accommodation with the Protestant regime. The idea that the English nation was an exclusively Protestant construct is a piece of national mythology. Catholics with a sense of history argued that England owed its very Christian identity to Roman evangelism, not to speak of the special patronage extended by the Virgin Mary. Closely connected with that issue of political obedience, and identity, was another choice: between the new and, in the perception of some, foreign Catholicism, the Catholicism of the Counter-Reformation enshrined in the canons of the Council of Trent, and more traditional ways, which valued outward observances, the rhythm of feasts and fasts. These were divisive issues throughout the period with which we are concerned (Walsham 1999; Questier 2006; Shagan; Highley).

From the outset, the Elizabethan Settlement was a less than wholly successful compromise. It was challenged from opposite sides of the fence, as Sir Nicholas Bacon, Elizabeth's Lord Keeper, anticipated it would be in a speech at the close of the 1559 Parliament. He had words of warning for, 'aswell those that be to swifte as those that be to slowe, those, I say, that goe before the lawe or beyond the lawe, as those that will not followe' (Hartley 51). The religious situation remained fluid, prone to more change, change that was more than likely in the event of the Queen's marriage to a Catholic consort, or of her death from natural or unnatural causes, and the probable succession in those circumstances of her Scottish cousin, Mary Stewart.

A dynastic change would probably have entailed a reactionary change, back to the Catholicism that was never far below the topsoil of the Elizabethan Protestant Settlement. A change in the opposite direction, towards what those sometimes called 'the hotter sort of Protestants' demanded, a 'further Reformation', had strong support, and was regularly demanded in successive Parliaments by vociferous and well-organized members of the Elizabethan House of Commons. A fissure in the Protestant Settlement began to open up over certain ceremonies required by the Act of Uniformity, the Prayer Book, and the Royal Injunctions of 1559: in particular, the stipulation that the clergy wear vestments and the outdoor dress associated with the old religion. The Vestments Controversy of the mid-1560s found the bishops obliged to enforce things that they, or some of them, deplored. The consequence was that the bishops began to look more like the problem than the solution to the scandal of a church only half reformed. And so the fault developed into a chasm, as some of those now often nicknamed 'Puritans' were radicalized, denouncing episcopacy itself as popish and anti-Christian, and the Prayer Book as full of popish 'dregs'. Here were the beginnings of presbyterianism on the model of Calvin's Geneva.

What put steam into an organized Puritan movement was the support of powerful figures in the politics of court and country, not least the Queen's favourite of favourites, Robert Dudley, Earl of Leicester; together with the scandalous fact that a church but half reformed still lacked what was called a 'godly preaching ministry', with a majority of parish clergy in most parts of the country poorly educated, unable or unwilling to preach, and arguably not 'godly' in the Protestant sense (Collinson 1967). This state of affairs was thought to threaten not only the salvation of those left in ignorance but the security of the realm, which was held to lie in an informed and conscientious obedience. Elizabeth's second Archbishop of Canterbury, Edmund Grindal, told her: 'Where preaching wanteth, obedience faileth' (Collinson 1979: 240).

In Norfolk, in 1575, it was said that the state could not 'longe stand thus; it wold ether to Papistry or Puritanisme' (A. H. Smith 204). But the challenges from both extremes failed and the centre held, mainly because Elizabeth neither married nor died but reigned for more than forty years; and because for all of that time she rejected all demands for further religious change. The Settlement was also competently defended by a succession of apologists and polemicists, by Hooker more than competently. But these apologists were perhaps less decisive in securing conformity to the Settlement than laws, increasingly draconic, which imposed a graduated scale of penalties for Catholic recusancy and the mission to regain England for the Faith. To a considerable extent these pressures were counter-productive, inciting a religion of resistance and martyrdom; and the same could be said of the efforts to repress Puritan nonconformity. The result was an Established Church that stood firm on the basis of the Elizabethan Settlement, but which would never again embrace the whole nation.

Until late in the twentieth century, historians of the English Reformation thought their task all but complete when they reached 1559. That year all but marked the conclusion of a book hailed in 1964 as a nearly definitive account of its subject, *The English Reformation* by A. G. Dickens. At about the same time, the leading ecclesiastical historian of his day, Owen Chadwick, published a history of the Reformation containing a confessional map of Europe in 1600. England was given a distinctive shading all of its own: neither Catholic nor Reformed, but 'Anglican'.

That was misleading. 'Anglican' was used as a point of geographical reference, as in '*Ecclesia Anglicana*', but it was not a word much used before the nineteenth century to define a distinct position on the ecclesiastical map, as it might be halfway between Rome and Geneva. The Church of England was a part of the Protestant polity of churches, as defined by its formularies, including the official statement of its doctrine, the Thirty-Nine Articles of Religion, leaning more towards the Reformed (or, in vulgar parlance, Calvinist) tendency than the Evangelical (or Lutheran). However, Elizabeth saw to it that the Church of England retained its own peculiar features, which went with monarchy: in particular, a hierarchical ministry headed by diocesan bishops, with all the traditional trappings of cathedrals and cathedral worship, together with orders of service that in form and structure, if not in doctrinal content, bore a closer resemblance to the traditional, pre-Reformation liturgy than to the simpler forms adopted in other Reformed churches. These were some of the stumbling-blocks for Puritans.

Moreover, in respect of the infrastructure of the English Church, ecclesiastical laws and institutions, there had not been, nor would there be, any profound change. The outward appearance of the church was in these many respects unaltered. The ministry in parish churches was maintained, as it always had been, by tithes, a payment of one-tenth on the products of the soil. Order and discipline, in matters concerning marriage and sexual morality, but also the making and validation of wills and the inheritance of property, were taken care of, as they always had been, by courts held in the name of the bishop, or of his deputy, the archdeacon. These procedures contrasted with what other Reformed churches regarded as 'discipline', which was often more severe and placed in the hands of officers of the local congregation, while other matters of social regulation were secularized. This system of church governance was what presbyterian Puritans wanted to see in England. They insisted that nothing else was consistent with certain biblical texts.

Such things were not thought to compromise the emphatically Protestant position adopted by the English Church in the religious and ecclesiastical politics of the mid-sixteenth century. The doctrine of the church was repeatedly defined in contradistinction to Catholicism, a faith widely, but not universally, held to be not only mistaken but profoundly anti-Christian. The only sermons that were ordered to be preached in the early Elizabethan church were anti-Catholic sermons, denouncing the Pope and all 'popish' superstition. The most public statement made in defence of the church was by Bishop John Jewel: *Apologia Ecclesiae Anglicanae*. That title may properly translate not only as an apology *for* the Church of England but as the apology *of* the Church of England for a faith shared with other Protestant churches. Speaking of the burning of radical heretics, among them Michael Servetus in Geneva, Jewel boasted: 'We burnt them' (J. Jewel 3.188).

There are two fundamental respects in which our perspectives have changed in recent decades, decades of 'revisionism' so far as English Reformation history is concerned. That Dickens brought his story to a close with Elizabeth implied his belief that by the end of Edward VI's reign England was already an essentially and irrevocably Protestant nation. The Marian reaction was doomed from the start, and the Catholicism that survived Mary's reign was, at first, little more than 'survivalism'. Professor Sir Geoffrey Elton, who dominated Tudor history for four decades, was of much the same opinion. But that diagnosis of a Catholicism that had had its day, and of a Protestantism whose idea had come, has been challenged by the recognition that the old religion was in a healthy condition on the very eve of Henry VIII's Reformation, strongly supported by the English people, who (literally) invested heavily in their religion (Duffy 1992; 2001). And there has been a profound change in our appraisal of the Marian episode. It is now seen as a significant chapter in the burgeoning Catholic Counter-Reformation, of which Mary and her Archbishop of Canterbury, Cardinal Reginald Pole, invented many features (Duffy 2009). Under Elizabeth, English Catholicism picked itself up, dusted itself down, and started all over again. John Bossy found profound irony in the fact that it was the once-dominant Catholics who now became the first of the minority nonconformities that would disturb and enrich English history for the next 400 years (Bossy 1975).

The second shift in our thinking concerns the Reformation itself. The moment we turn our attention from Acts of Parliament and other orders from on high to the grassroots of religion in the towns and villages of Elizabethan England, we are forced to admit that in any more than a formal sense the Reformation, as the

Protestantization of a nation accustomed to the old ways and beliefs, had in 1559 hardly begun. A radical critic of the Elizabethan church wrote ironically: 'All this people, with all these manners, were in one daye, with the blast of Queen Elizabeth's trumpet, of ignorant papistes and grosse idolaters made faithfull Christianes and true professors' (Barrow 1962: 283). Dickens regarded East Anglia as precociously and almost uniformly Protestant. But the dissemination of Protestant belief depended on a preaching ministry, and in East Suffolk there was, in the early years of Elizabeth, only one preacher, who happened to be a layman, itinerating like a precursor of John Wesley (MacCulloch 189–90). Dickens knew that Catholicism, as 'survivalism', continued to hang on in the north of England. But there seem to have been as many Catholics, or crypto-Catholics, in East Anglian Norfolk as anywhere else (A. H. Smith 201–2). Historians have begun to write about a 'long Reformation', a Reformation that took time to get properly under way: a Reformation that found a new head of steam in the revolutionary circumstances of both the 1640s and 1680s, maintaining its momentum well into the eighteenth century (Tyacke 1998). This is consistent with the perceptions of Jean Delumeau in France and John Bossy in England, that profound religious and moral change in Western Europe was a protracted process, not adequately or usefully labelled 'the Reformation' (Delumeau; Bossy 1985, 1998). But it appears that it was in the mid-Elizabethan years, the 1570s especially, that Protestantism began to make significant headway in the localities, and in hearts and minds. That was down to the political clout and patronage of the Protestant elite, magnates like Leicester, and to the ruling gentry in, yes, East Anglia; and to the preaching ministers they brought in, in increasing numbers, from the universities, especially Cambridge. Credit is also due to the more evangelically minded of Elizabeth's first batch of bishops, Archbishop Edmund Grindal especially (Collinson 1979).

Whether England in 1600 could be called a Protestant nation in any meaningful rather than purely legal sense, it certainly had all the appearance of an anti-Catholic nation, or at least of a nation that increasingly defined and constructed itself in contradistinction to Catholicism. From the early 1570s the Catholic mission mounted from seminaries in the Low Countries, Spain, and Rome, by both members of the Society of Jesus and secular priests, products of the new Tridentine seminaries, interacted in a vicious circle with an ever-heightened penal legislation based on the premise that these were not spiritual men but traitors, agents of a global conspiracy. It became treason to be one of those priests, or to harbour such a priest, or to convert to Catholicism with a subversive intent. These offences were punished by the obscene cruelty of hanging and disembowelment. Mere recusancy was rewarded with punitive fines, after 1581 £20 a month—say, £2,000 in modern values. In a debate carried on in print, Catholic apologists insisted that the victims of the penal legislation were not traitors but true martyrs for their faith, who had nothing to do with matters of state. However, it is clear that without regime change the Catholic mission probably made no sense; while Catholicism needed its martyrs fully as much as Protestants, readers of John Foxe's 'Book of Martyrs', needed the validation of their own martyr stories (Dillon).

As the Elizabethan state moved towards hostilities with Catholic Spain, the Catholic threat became the guiding principle of English foreign policy: something that anyone having lived through the Cold War or the more recent 'War against Terror' can well understand. This ideologically motivated mentality belonged especially to Sir Francis Walsingham, in effect Elizabeth's Secretary of State for foreign affairs. It is not irrelevant that Walsingham had been present as ambassador in Paris and had witnessed the St Bartholomew massacres in 1572, atrocities celebrated in Rome with a *Te Deum*. Protestant Elizabethans believed themselves to be engaged in a kind of cold, but eventually hot, war against an ideological foe, a war motivated, like most such conflicts, by fear, but also by religious zeal. And they confronted a similar mentality on the other side, a mirror image.

All this concerned the young John Donne deeply. As Dennis Flynn's essay (Ch. 26. II) explains in detail, he was descended from the spiritual aristocracy of English Catholicism, the kith and kin of the proto-Catholic martyr, St Thomas More. His mother, who guided his early upbringing, was the granddaughter of John Rastell, More's brother-in-law, and was resolutely recusant to her dying day, even when her son was dean of St Paul's Cathedral. Donne's close relations included Jesuits. His uncle, Jasper Heywood, was briefly head of the Jesuit mission in England, and it is likely that the 12-year-old Donne was taken by his mother to visit Heywood in the Tower before he was forced into exile. It is certain (cf. *Pseudo-Martyr* 163) that Donne was an eyewitness to some of those grisly executions.

When Donne was 22 his brother Henry died of the plague in prison, where he was incarcerated for harbouring a seminary priest who was executed, following Henry's admissions made under torture. There were later unsubstantiated allegations that the priest, William Harrington, had been betrayed by a Jesuit. His death, and—as it were, incidentally—the death of John's brother, have been seen as an aggravation of growing hostility between the Jesuits and the secular Catholic clergy that later came to boiling point in the imprisonment they shared in Wisbech Castle, the so-called 'Wisbech Stirs'; and which would culminate in the late Elizabethan Archpriest Controversy, when some of the secular clergy appealed to Rome against the appointment over their heads of an archpriest, a Jesuit scheme. In any case, charges about a Jesuit 'betrayal' of Harrington did not emerge until 1601, when some of this party collaborated with the bishops (notably Bishop Bancroft of London, later Archbishop of Canterbury) and the government, who were glad to exploit Catholic divisions. There was more to these quarrels than the issue of loyalty, including internal matters of organization and discipline, but unhappiness with the politics of violence and regime-change, with which many Jesuits were connected, may have been part of the scenario of division. In so far as John Donne was personally involved, through the death of Henry Donne, all this may shed light on the nature and quality of his residual Catholic leanings and loyalties, and above all why he became such a bitter critic of the Society of Jesus (Morris; Cain 2004; Shami 2000; Marotti 2005).

It is understandable that John Carey made the issue of 'apostasy' the centrepiece of his anatomy of Donne (Carey 1981a). And Donne's was arguably a rather extreme case. But the choices that Donne made, the questions that tormented him and perhaps never went away (Truth standing on a huge hill, and 'hee that will / Reach her, about must, and about must goe': *Sat3* ll. 80–1), need to be placed in their proper context. Bishop John Jewel can help us. He wrote: 'Truth and falsehood are nigh neghbours, and dwell one by the other; the utter porch of the one is like the porch of the other; yet their way is contrary; the one leadeth to life; the other leadeth to death' (J. Jewel 4.1167). We used to think that the Elizabethan age was one of stark, incompatible binary opposites: Catholic versus Protestant, Anglican versus Puritan. And so it should have been, if Truth were blindingly obvious and non-negotiable. But in practice very many Elizabethans inhabited a porch located somewhere between Jewel's two contrary porches, or in the course of their lives shifted from one porch to the other.

To return to recent and current historiography, we now find ourselves in a climate of post-revisionism, or of revisionism beyond revisionism. This historiographical climate entails a more drastic deconstruction of the elements, and defining labels, of Elizabethan religious history than anything we have hitherto seen. Even revisionist historians of the English Reformation supposed that they were dealing with more or less fixed and defined categories, Protestant and Catholic; and 'Puritan' too, although it has long been acknowledged that this was a slippery category, depending on its spiteful application as a nickname by anti-Puritans, one half of a vicious interaction (Collinson 2008). But now the whole religious landscape is changing before our eyes, becoming altogether more complex and confused.

This complexity particularly concerns our understanding of what constituted the continuing Catholic constituency. For centuries, the history of post-Reformation English Catholicism was a history of a religious ghetto, written for Catholics still living in a kind of ghetto. The themes were, overwhelmingly, resistance and fidelity, priest-holes in country houses, torture, martyrdom, and the craving for martyrdom, a hagiographical history. In 1975 John Bossy published a ground breaking book, *The English Catholic Community, 1570–1850*, more sophisicated, less confessional, and more cultural and sociological, in that it investigated from the inside what it was to be a Catholic in the post-Reformation world.

But that very phrase, 'the Catholic community', leaves out of account a plurality of Catholic communities of different sorts, and at varying levels of intensity, together with Catholics of no community, but still connected in various ways, through kinship, neighbourhood, wealth and property dealings, even public office, to the majority community (Questier 2006; A. Milton 1999). The type of person nicknamed 'church papist' has been rediscovered, especially by the book on that subject published in 1993 by Alexandra Walsham. 'Church papist' was a derogatory label in the mouths of Protestants for people condemned as 'schismatics' by the Jesuits and other Catholic hardliners. These were partial, or occasional, conformists, who attended services in the parish church, but often absented themselves, or put their fingers in their ears, or their hats in front of their faces, when the minister mounted the pulpit; and who avoided taking communion. In many cases, in gentry families, the husband, with property to safeguard and the need to play his proper social and political role, would conduct himself as a semi-conforming church papist, while his wife might be a recusant. It used to be thought that church papistry was a transient, pre-1570 phenomenon. But when John Earle, in his book of character studies called *Microcosmographie*, depicted the church papist as 'one that parts his religion betwixt his conscience and his purse, and comes to church not to serve God but the king... he loves popery well, but is loth to lose by it', he was writing not in the 1560s but in the 1620s (J. Earle 41–4).

Michael Questier (2006) has updated John Bossy. It now appears that even the dichotomy of recusant and church papist is too crude. Absence from church was not something that attracted an automatic penalty, like speeding, or parking on a double yellow line. People were identified and prosecuted as recusants for reasons that often need to be explored. Many recusants probably got away with it. And not all recusants were recusants all the time; and certainly not after death. There are many surviving tombs of Catholic grandees, erected in the most demonstrative part of the parish churches to which their families had been linked, sometimes for generations. Within extended families there were often relatives of both religions, and even, to all intents and purposes, of none.

Questier has some striking case studies to support this more nuanced anatomy of Elizabethan Catholicism: among them the Sussex gentry family of Caryll, who in some respects conformed, but who were linked to a network of Catholic families, and who had Jesuit friends. Most striking of all is the case of Anthony Browne, first Viscount Montagu. Montagu was the only lay peer to vote against the Supremacy Bill in the 1559 Parliament. You could not get more Catholic than that. He was connected with Catholic families all over England. Yet Montagu was a conformist, and he was employed by the government in diplomatic missions. He continued to sit in the House of Lords, even on a committee of both Houses to consider a bill to enforce church attendance more strictly. In 1591 he played host to the Queen at his seat of Cowdray in Sussex. By contrast, Browne's wife Magdalen, a former Maid of Honour to Mary Tudor, was a stalwart recusant who fashioned a 'little Rome' in the Sussex countryside (Highley 9–10).

Among Montagu's closest friends was Sir William More of Loseley, an archetypical godly Protestant magistrate—if you like, a Puritan—and a neighbour to some of Montagu's lands in Surrey. It was More's granddaughter whom John Donne married. Her father's indignation (the marriage was immeasurably unwelcome) may have had to do not only with the irregularity and social inequality of the match but

Ill. 26.I.1. Donne's sheaf of snakes seal (Folger Shakespeare Library, L.b.534). This red wax seal was used by Donne for Letters sent throughout his life. The sheaf of seven snakes was a charge in the arms Donne claimed, indicating his paternal descent from Welsh gentry. (Reproduced by permission of the Folger Shakespeare Library.)

also with Donne's well-known Catholic background. But it was not the case that the Mores had no Catholic friends.

So far, this revisionist account of how religion often worked out in Elizabethan England may suggest an almost cynical pragmatism, a tongue-in-cheek dishonesty which, however, the priests who heard the confessions of these people were prepared, with their casuistry, to condone, whatever the Jesuits and other hardliners might have had to say in their published polemics. Things were said in private, the ultimate privacy of the confessional, that could not be said publicly. But there were Elizabethans who, for principled reasons, either chose not to take confessional sides or believed that it was possible to combine loyalty to the Queen and the state with a non-political Catholicism, or with a politic disinclination to be anything but a mere Christian. This was Donne's position after his 'apostasy'. And this was the essence of the debate about the Jacobean Oath of Allegiance, to which Donne's *Pseudo-Martyr* contributed.

A good example of this kind of conscientious fence-sitting is provided by Thomas Sackville, Lord Buckhurst and later first Earl of Dorset, a long-serving privy councillor (Zim 2007). We know that Sackville conformed to the religious status quo. But we are entitled to our suspicions about his private religious beliefs. He sent his four sons to be educated at Hart Hall in the University of Oxford, a well-known bolt-hole for Catholics. Sackville married the daughter of a prominent Marian Catholic; and his mother was arrested and imprisoned in 1562 for hearing Mass. Sackville tolerated the diversity of his family's religious beliefs, but condemned all nonconformists, be they Jesuits or Puritans, anyone who threatened the established religious and political order. Sackville's own conduct, wherever he had clout, was even-handed. As a fully qualified lawyer he had his justified doubts as to whether all recusants were even potential traitors. Like the later Donne, he saw no point in martyrdom. His watchword was moderation. There were more Elizabethans who resembled Sackville, or Donne, than the old, embattled historiography acknowledged.

But when all this nuancing is said and done, there were still what we may properly call conversions, from the old religion to the new, or, indeed, in the opposite direction (Questier 1996). Some of these were significant and identifiable punctuation points in lives. But many other changes of faith went without public notice or formality, conversion by a kind of osmosis, or by simple conformity over the years to the status quo: in Michael Questier's word, 'unscripted'. Such changes must have happened to very many of those born in the 1530s or 1540s and dying in the early years of the next century, or even to the generation after that. There has been much debate, most of it inconclusive, about the religion of William Shakespeare, whose plays contain so many resonances of the pre-Reformation world. It appears most likely that the dramatist's father, John Shakespeare, the glover and burgess of Stratford, was some sort of Catholic, although not necessarily or always a recusant. With Shakespeare, as with Donne, there were many connections, through family and school, to committed, hard-line Catholics, even Jesuits. But the evidence of the Shakespearean canon suggests someone who in early life had been exposed to the official Bishops' Bible, heard in church, but who later, like so many of his contemporaries, became a reader of the more evangelical Geneva Bible, the family Bible most in use before the appearance of the Authorized Version of 1611, and indeed for some time after that (Collinson 1994).

Simply to attend the parish church ought not to be taken as conversion. That was 'an essentially negative act and had virtually no connection with a person's actual religious beliefs' (Questier 1996: 100). Attempts by the bishops to enforce participation in the communion, which might have been more purposeful, repeatedly failed. But there were also conversions that were formalized and scripted, and which had clear-cut political and financial consequences. Indeed, the process by which known and convicted recusants obtained a discharge from that status (and its financial penalties) were rigorous, an explicit act of abjuration: 'I confess and acknowledge that I have grievously offended God in contempning her Majesty's godly and lawful government and authority, by absenting myself from church' (ibid. 104).

This drawing of hard lines was, pronounces the authority on these matters, 'a world away from church papistry' (ibid.). Certainly, John Donne underwent no such process. Nor, on the evidence available to us, can we even say that his past was that of a church papist. His ultra-Catholic genes and inheritance are not in doubt. How far he made them his own is subject to interpretation. Questier speaks of him as 'loftily detached in his religious opinions' (ibid. 56). Until—what signalled full conversion in his case—he took holy orders in the Church of England. But what we can say of Donne, and not of others who 'fluctuated in and out of vague shows of conformity' (ibid. 116), is that he had thoroughly, even exhaustively, researched all the issues at stake.

CHAPTER 26.II

DONNE'S FAMILY BACKGROUND, BIRTH, AND EARLY YEARS

DENNIS FLYNN

1

OUTSTANDING in Donne's family background was a history of opposition to Tudor religious reform. 'It was a family that adhered to Catholicism as an unflinching principle of existence, without regard for persecution, exile, or death' (May 1998: 52). Extensive evidence of the family's Catholicism has been well known: the bonds of family tradition and the sense of solidarity uniting the various and distinguished members of the maternal family in their religion; and the feeling of 'almost aristocratic exclusiveness as well as a specific pride' in their descent from Thomas More (Bald 1970: 22–6; see also Reed 1–93 and 184–240; B. W. Whitlock 1959: 258–60; and Bang 238–48). Less well known has been Catholicism in Donne's father's family (but see Davidson 299–300). In a Letter to his mother Donne referred to his father as 'my most dear and provident father' (*TMC* 324). Scion of the traditionally Catholic Dwnns of Kidwelly, Carmarthenshire, he had made his way in London as an apprentice and journeyman of the strongly Catholic Ironmongers Company; and at least until his early death in 1576 he had also been able, with some cunning, to protect, against total loss to the Crown, some of the English lands of his exiled father-in-law, John Heywood (Flynn 1995c: 67–8; Reed: 237–8; Bald 1970: 20–3 and 31–4; B. W. Whitlock 1959: 260–2 and 348–9).

In all, Donne could look back at three generations of principled resistance, articulated with the occasionally exasperating satire for which his mother's family especially was well known. Having heard an early example, Edward Hall, Under-sheriff of London, disapproved of the style in which Sir Thomas More conveyed principle, spoiling the decorum of his own beheading on 6 July 1535: 'I cannot tell whether I shoulde call him a foolishe wyseman, or a wise foolishman, for undoubtedly he beside his learnyng, had a great witte, but it was so myngled with tauntyng and mockyng, that it semed to them that best knew him, that he thought nothing to be wel spoken except he had ministred some mocke in the communicacion' (E. Hall 2.265–6). Listed by Hall among other offensive witticisms on this occasion was More's last request, head already on the block, that the axe-man take careful aim to keep from striking off his prison-growth of beard, because unlike his head it had given the king no offence. Despite More's incongruous concern, the axe did its work neatly enough for his whole head to be parboiled intact and stuck up on a pike on London Bridge.

For the rest of the sixteenth century, under the impact of Tudor reform, Donne's family continued to express scruple and distinction, leading to nonconformity and imprisonment as well as exile and death. Symbolic of the family's Catholic heritage is the story that was later told about one of More's teeth, loosened from his skull. It was kept as a relic and eventually given to Donne's uncles, Ellis and Jasper Heywood. They were once to part company, but both were loath to part with what each considered his right to the tooth, when spontaneously it '*fell asunder and divided of it self*' (Wood 1. fo. Dᵛ). So did the religion of this family express itself repeatedly in witty separations during the course of the religious conflict. Mindfulness of More endowed them with a fractious notion of honour, reaching Donne through two branches of the family—Rastells and Heywoods—while spreading through parallel branches of the More circle, generations of Mores, Ropers, and Clements. The family's enduring sense of More's legacy was a peculiar mixture that included a natural pride in his renown as humanist scholar and officer at the court of Henry VIII, overshadowed by awe and understated irony about his martyrdom.

Before and after More's death, various members of the family established high positions of their own, their learning and intelligence allowing them some knowledge, and in some cases direct experience, of the ways of the Tudor court (Flynn 1995c: chs. 1–4; Bald 1970: 23–6). This experience coloured their outlook on events, particularly on the development of religious reform.

Among relatives at the point of More's resignation from office, only his nephew William Rastell had appreciated how fully and irrevocably this stroke would prove

Ill. 26.II.1. Loseley, Guildford, Surrey. Built by Anne More Donne's grandfather Sir William More in 1569, this was the house in which he (not her father) raised and educated her. It is still the residence of direct descendants, the More–Molyneux family (Photo, Loseley Park Estate Office.)

a turning point in the life of the family. Rastell also had clearly perceived the radical implications of More's danger in relation to Tudor religious reform by parliamentary statute. Within a few months he exchanged an already successful business, publishing religious controversy, for a new career in the law: at 25 he began professional studies at Lincoln's Inn, the law school More had attended. Called to the Bar, he prospered as a Lincoln's Inn bencher and, before the end of King Henry's reign, married Winifred Clement, daughter of Margaret Giggs Clement (More's adopted daughter) and of John Clement, a tutor of More's children. Into the reign of King Edward VI, Rastell continued the practice of traditional Catholicism until Parliament imposed the English Book of Common Prayer in place of the Latin Breviary and Missal. In 1549 he abandoned a second successful career, along with life in England, for religious reasons. With his wife, her parents, and other members of the More circle, he emigrated to Bruges, continuing there his work in progress on a biography of More (Flynn 1995c: 24–5; Reed 86–7).

After More's beheading, Rastell had in this work integrated his own expert notes on More's trial with various documents given to him by Margaret Roper. Along with his 1557 edition of More's English writings, his biography was designed to set the record straight about the late Lord Chancellor's wise–foolish life and death (Harpsfield 219–52; R. W. Chambers 20–3, 34–7). Rastell also published in 1557 his

A Colleccion of All the Statutes, containing the texts of all parliamentary legislation still enforced from the time of Magna Carta, indispensable for legal research in England until well into the seventeenth century. With leisure for such scholarship, Rastell did not suffer much materially; his life at Bruges and later at Louvain was an intellectual one, centred in the academic community of English émigrés at the University of Louvain. Though outlawed in England, they enjoyed their exile as an inconvenience, prudently prepared for, only until England returned to a more reasonable practice of Christianity (McConica 1965: 128–33; Bossy 1975: 12–13). Widowed and childless, Rastell returned from exile when the Mass was restored to England under Queen Mary.

Less uncompromising in opposition to early Tudor reform was Donne's grandfather, John Heywood, who from early in the reign of Henry VIII enjoyed intermittent celebrity as a musician, comic entertainer, and poet serving the courts of all the Tudor princes. Because he was a poet, Heywood's ways of dealing with the problem of being a Catholic are particularly instructive for the biographer of Donne. Heywood's connection to More had begun before the time of Luther's schism, of *Utopia*, and of early friendship between More and Erasmus. Though not himself a classical scholar, Heywood had become a member of the More circle and shared its humanist ideas about literature, law, education, and religion even before he had married William Rastell's sister Joan in the 1520s. In these years were forged the many links in business, religious conviction, and law that tied him to the complex of families surrounding More. But while More's and William Rastell's attitudes towards religious reform underwent change in the late 1520s and early 1530s, Heywood, like the rest of More's family and friends, continued to hold a confused attitude of approval—even up to the time of More's beheading—towards governmental reform of the church (McConica 1965: 264–5; Carpinelli 1–10).

Such attitudes had changed by 1543, when several members of the More circle began to think they finally understood what he had died for. In that year Heywood, with other friends and relatives of More (though these did not include the wary William Rastell), joined in a hapless conspiracy to resist the Crown's supremacy over the church by accusing Archbishop Thomas Cranmer of heresy. King Henry had no intention of allowing Cranmer to fall. Heywood, with co-conspirators, was imprisoned, convicted, and sentenced to a common traitor's death. Cruelly allowed to think he would die with the others, Heywood was taken from the Tower of London and laid on the wicker hurdle used to drag traitors to execution at Tyburn. Only after this rough journey, a grisly joke on the court jester, at the gallows he was granted a pardon. As a condition of his reprieve the shaken convict agreed to don a white robe at Paul's Cross precisely on the ninth anniversary of More's beheading and there and then introduce an anti-Catholic sermon by reading out a humiliating public recantation (Foxe 1838: 5.528–9).

Heywood's recantation can be understood in light of his circumstances. Like More he had five children, all still of school age, whom he was careful to support.

The oldest of these were at university, the youngest (Donne's mother, Elizabeth) just beginning her schooling. In consequence, Heywood presumably felt he could not afford to be as uncompromising as Rastell about religion. Instead of choosing exile, he remained in England to raise his children with such advantage as his court connection could provide. He had for years taught music to the children of members of the court and had produced entertainments in which the children, his own and others, performed. Jasper Heywood, for example, before he went to Oxford, had studied with a group of students including Princess Elizabeth (ARSI, Anglia 30/I, fo. 292^v). Among these children were some who remained friends of the Heywoods in later life: for example, Mildred Cooke, one of the learned daughters of King Edward's tutor Sir Anthony Cooke; and the Earl of Warwick's son, Ambrose Dudley.

In the reign of Edward VI, when Rastell and other members of the More circle first became religious refugees, John Heywood maintained his court associations despite the prevalent anti-Catholicism of government policy in the nation at large. A striking feature of the court early in Edward's reign was the atmosphere of comparative toleration inherent in educational and other associations. The reign of King Henry, and subsequently the reigns of Queen Mary and especially of Queen Elizabeth, saw more stringent confessional restrictions on the religious education of noble children. But under King Edward, during the years of the Protector Somerset, radical Protestant reform at court (whatever violence occurred in the cathedrals, the universities, the Inns of Court, or parishes within or outside London) was carried on without persecution (Jordan 1932: 68–9 and 1968: 206–9; Lecler 2.343–4). In this climate of relative toleration, Heywood could remain a Catholic yet receive appointment (in 1552) as an honorary Sewer of the King's Chamber (Reed 44).

At the death of King Edward in the summer of 1553, Catholics felt their time had finally come. For those of the More circle still in England and for exiles alike, the accession of Queen Mary was an answer to their prayers and a confirmation of their faith. To them it seemed that a brief interval of heresy and turmoil had been quelled forever, so that traditional Catholicism could be restored to its former strength in England. Detested homilies directed against Catholicism would cease; statuary, paintings, candles, and music would again become acceptable elements of worship; bells would be rung again for the angelus and during Mass; the use of holy water, rosaries, fasting, and abstinence would openly resume. Among Heywood's co-religionists joyful celebration exploded. People 'made great and many fires...with settinge tables in the streates and banketting allso, with all the belles ringinge in every parishe church in London till x of the clock at night'. When, a few weeks later, the new queen was on her way to Westminster to be crowned, she was greeted in St Paul's churchyard by John Heywood, returning to the site of his public recantation of Catholicism, this time in a pageant among children (probably including some of his own), sitting under a green vine and making 'an Oration in Latin and English' (Wriothesley 617). Soon William Rastell returned from Louvain with other friends and relatives, and the members of the More circle were reunited with the coming of better times.

Rastell resumed the practice of law as a bencher at Lincoln's Inn and contributed to the general sense that the Catholic past could be re-created. From the wealth he had retained and augmented in exile, Rastell now furnished a new altar to repair the destruction in Lincoln's Inn chapel, with 'a greate image or picture in a table of the taking down of Cryste from the Cross'. He also requested collects for the soul of his late wife and for their parents and friends, which the Masters of the Inn ordered to be said at every Mass in the chapel (Reed 88). Rastell was appointed serjeant-at-law in the autumn of 1555 (*CPR Philip and Mary* 2.59), and for the next months he sat at the northern assizes, twice a year riding circuit through the northern counties. In one of Queen Mary's last official acts she promoted Rastell to Justice of the Queen's Bench (ibid. 3.457); but with the accession of Elizabeth his position was, he soon saw, untenable. Although all of Queen Mary's judicial appointees were confirmed in office at the outset of the new reign, the Privy Council quickly determined that the judges of the realm were to be a main instrument of political and religious reform. Beginning in 1561, Rastell and his colleagues were given the job not only of enforcing the Acts of Uniformity and Supremacy but of purging Catholic magistrates from the local Commissions of the Peace (Cockburn 23–4, 40).

Rastell's resistance to carrying out such actions is reflected in the complaint of the Bishop of Carlisle, John Best, who wrote to Principal Secretary William Cecil that Rastell and his associate, Serjeant-at-Law Nicholas Powtrell, made a show of religion when giving their charge to the Justices of the Peace but that all their other talk and doings opposed Protestantism, 'which the people moche marke and talke of' (*HMC Salisbury* 1.310). Presumably Rastell was given to understand this was unsatisfactory service in the council's view. In any case, in January 1563 he again chose the life of an émigré, absconding to Louvain, a felony in a Justice of the Queen's Bench. Twice choosing exile for the sake of conscience, Rastell took a less drastic course than More, whose choice of imprisonment led to execution. But this choice was, no less than More's, an uncompromising rejection of Protestantism in England. The Louvain exiles generally husbanded their wealth, withholding both it and their service from their native country. This carefully prepared exile represents one choice among several undesirable alternatives variously faced by members of the family before Donne's time.

In contrast, John Heywood's four years at the Edwardian court had made a difference in his outlook. His attitudes had been shaped not only by the change of religions but also by the continuity of his relationships and habits at court. Prior to the reign of Queen Elizabeth he defined confessional lines less drastically than the exiles, especially their implications for policy and social behaviour. This difference is suggested by his long poem *The Spider and the Flie* (1556), in which Heywood made use of the real issues and personalities he had known as a witness to events of the past thirty years in England. The poem includes what appears to be a lengthy allusion (J. Heywood 1967: 416 ff.) to the 1553 trial and execution of Heywood's patron, John Dudley, Duke of Northumberland, who recanted on the scaffold his consistent support for evangelical Protestantism (Jordan and Gleason 1 ff.). In Heywood's poem such confession apparently signified neither the comforting miracle it seemed to English and other Catholics abroad, nor the cynical scandal it seemed to Protestants. In fact, throughout the poem we glimpse an ambiguous and kaleidoscopic array of topical references to the law courts and legal processes, enclosures, arbitrations, conspiracies, popular rebellions, pitched battles, battlefield carnage, death sentences, and executions. Along with these are many palpable references to particular events and personalities, translated into Heywood's imagined dispute between spiders and flies. Strikingly omitted, however, are partisan references to the terms of religious controversy. This characteristic of Heywood's poem should be of particular interest to Donne scholars, for the Catholic Heywood nowhere argues the Catholic point of view.

Instead, Heywood seems at pains to prevent the reader's natural presumption that, since the poet was a Catholic, the flies are Catholics and the spiders are Protestants. Thus it is the flies, not the spiders, who try to hang a captured ant on 'their tree of reformacion' (Heywood 1967: 222). Many such passages, however one interprets them, provide no consistent pattern of references by which to identify Protestants and Catholics in the poem. As Heywood's editor, A. W. Ward, accurately observes (xiv), Heywood refuses to articulate the religious conflict in the apologetic terms already becoming conventional in the 1550s. Instead, he assumes at the outset, in his 'Preface', a stance above confessional differences, implying that to read his poem as taking sides for or against either faction is to read it superficially and to miss its point. Readers should not simply 'scan' the book: 'scanning who is the spider: who the flie.' Unless they apply the parable inwardly to themselves, reading the book becomes a 'vaine exersise'. Heywood disowns such readings of his work: 'Who that this parable doth thus define, / This parable thus, is his and not mine' (5). The reader is instead challenged (in a manoeuvre later often repeated by Donne) to heed the nearness of the parable and not to evade the point by misinterpreting it.

Contrary to the unsupported assertions of critics, summarized in Ward's introduction (vii, xiv), Heywood avoided partisan polemic; nevertheless he did build into *The Spider and the Flie* a recurring pattern alluding persistently to the conflict of religions from a personal point of view. At the beginning of the poem a fly in a cobweb is threatened with death by a spider, who enunciates a narrowly drawn legal argument (35). Throughout most of the poem the fly remains trammelled in the spider's web, his life in jeopardy. In the end the spider's responsibility for the fly's suffering is highlighted as a ground for his own execution. Thus the individual conscience in the merciless hands of authority emerges as a central theme of the poem, Heywood's indirect comment on the religious conflict. Similarly, the ant awaiting execution on the flies' 'tree of reformacion' is a creeping insect who, simply because of his nature, grows wings in the course of the poem. Suspected at various points by both spiders and flies, he is accused of treasonous double-dealing and required to explain his seeming duplicity: 'Thant: having to this demaund: good answer, none, None answere made he: but stoode still silently' (265). Both Thomas More and Thomas Cranmer in Heywood's experience had halted without speaking when put in a similar position. As the ant stands silent on a ladder, hosts of flies shouting for him to be turned off and hanged, Heywood reflects on the horror of such executions for the victim, in a deeply felt rejection of successive Tudor governments' attempts to force conscience with the threat of death. The plight of conscience, later felt variously throughout the writings of John Donne, descended as a theme in part from the writings of his grandfather.

In the early enthusiasm of the entire More circle for Erasmian reform, in their subsequent opposition to Protestantism in England, in their deliberate emigration or temporary acquiescence, in their rejoicing at the Catholic restoration, as in their subsequent exile under Elizabeth, are exhibited the continuity, discontinuity, and pathos of traditional Catholicism in Tudor England. Inclined to ameliorate conflict and deepen the spirituality of England through humour, controversy, and poetry, members of the More circle were unprepared to resist effectively the forces mobilized by the nascent modern nation state, which had its own very different programme of reform.

2

In the harshly wrenched careers of the next generation of Heywoods occurred a related pattern of frustrated, irenic hopes turning into futile opposition to Protestantism in England. Both of John Heywood's sons, Ellis and Jasper, after receiving early education at court, studied at Oxford. During the reign of Edward VI, Ellis was elected a fellow of All Souls College in 1548 and graduated as a Bachelor of Canon Law in 1552. Shortly afterwards, in principled expression of his family's politics and religion, he left England for Italy in order to serve as a secretary to the exiled Cardinal Reginald Pole. Heywood's broken academic career and adherence to Pole suggest his distress, shared with Pole, over the course taken by the Council of Trent's hardening of confessional lines by adopting dogmatic formulations. Heywood's *Il Moro*, the first book ever published about Thomas More, appeared at Florence in the mid-1550s, dedicated to Pole, in the context of what has been called 'the war of the saints', the competition between Pole and Gian Pietro Carafa for dominance of the Counter-Reformation Catholic Church (E. Heywood ix–x). Cardinal Carafa had headed the Roman Inquisition in the 1540s and, attacking his fellow cardinal as a heretic, had torpedoed Pole's candidacy for the papacy in the consistory of 1550 (Fenlon 269–79). Five years later Carafa himself was elected Pope Paul IV.

Published at Florence by the official printer of Grand Duke Cosimo I, *Il Moro* seems to have been used in a programme designed to enhance the prestige of Florence, in part by defying the pretensions of the Carafa papacy. This publishing programme featured a large number of religious books in the vein of Erasmus and Marsilio Ficino, all evincing Florentine Academy thinking, out of step with the Pope's style of Catholicism. *Il Moro* was probably written in English and then translated into Tuscan by one of the members of the Academy. An English manuscript copy of the book apparently once existed, as is suggested by an entry in the Stationers' Register, on 7 November 1601, of 'a booke Called the English Academy A dialogue between Sir Thomas Moore and others' (see the introduction by the editor of *Il Moro*, Patrizia Grimaldi Pizzorno, in E. Heywood xiv–xxiii). Donne may or may not have been aware of this intended volume, no copy of which is known to have survived.

By the time *Il Moro* was published, Ellis Heywood had returned to England, and with Cardinal Pole's support appointed a prebendary in Lichfield Cathedral, where he served David Pole, the vicar-general of the diocese and a relative of the Cardinal. From this position Heywood viewed the course of affairs with dismay. Cardinal Pole died before Elizabeth's accession; David Pole became Bishop of Peterborough, but was deprived of his see along with all the persistently Catholic bishops under the new regime. By 1563 Ellis Heywood was preparing to vacate his prebend and leave again for the continent, this time with his parents (Flynn 1995c: 61; Bald 1970: 25). To the Heywoods, Elizabeth's reign, though still relatively peaceful for most Catholics, did not seem reassuring in prospect.

Jasper Heywood, having studied with Princess Elizabeth at court, went to Oxford in 1547, graduated with a BA on 15 July 1553, and was elected a fellow of Merton College, gaining repute as a 'quaint poet' (Wood 1. fo. R). In 1558 his promising career at Merton ended when, in customary conflict with authority, he had to resign his fellowship after repeated admonitions by the college's warden. Nevertheless, Heywood gained an MA on 10 June 1558, and in November was elected to a fellowship at All Souls College, following in his brother Ellis's footsteps. Although at All Souls Jasper Heywood gave impetus to the development of Elizabethan tragedy, producing three ground breaking translations of plays by Seneca, his tenure ended when, refusing to comply with Elizabethan religious reform, he abandoned his Oxford career to stay briefly at the Inns of Court with his uncle William Rastell, soon going into exile at Louvain and then Rome, where he became a Jesuit on 21 May 1562. In Rome Heywood taught and studied for the priesthood until he was sent to teach at the University of Dillingen, Bavaria, in March 1564 (Flynn 1995c: 41–52).

John Heywood's youngest child, Elizabeth Heywood, was about 20 when she married John Donne the elder in the spring of 1563; her husband was just over 30. Soon after his youngest daughter's marriage John Heywood seized the opportunity to leave England. His older daughters had married earlier, and his sons, Ellis and

Jasper, were both priests. For the most part, Heywood had prospered under three Tudor monarchs; at 67 he was beginning to fill a role at the court of a fourth. But the prospect of royal favour was not enough to hold him in England. Heywood handed over management of his properties to his new son-in-law, joining William Rastell and the other members of the More circle already in exile. Thus, by the time Elizabeth Heywood Donne had married, two generations of Heywoods, Rastells, Clements, Ropers, and Mores were already represented among the exiles in Brabant, Flanders, and elsewhere on the continent, several of the younger generation entering religious orders there. These relatives had dedicated their lives, at considerable sacrifice, to perseverance in the Catholic religion despite political and religious developments in England. Another group of relatives stayed at home, most of them also determined to persevere in their religion (Flynn 1995c: 60–1).

3

Before his flight John Heywood had designated his son-in-law John Donne to manage his estate, including valuable land in Kent at Romney Marsh and also in Hertfordshire; Donne had collected rents in England that, for the next few years, he would be forwarding to Heywood on the continent. He had established himself as a member of the Ironmongers Company, serving as apprentice and then journeyman in the 1550s. In 1561 Donne had received a bequest from the widow of his former master, along with the lease of a house next to the Mitre Tavern in Bread Street Hill. This inheritance had enabled him to establish a business of his own and to marry John Heywood's daughter. Through the early 1560s, retaining a retail trade in Bread Street Hill, Donne diversified his business into more extensive trading, including the wholesaling and factoring of raw materials. His property grew with his prosperity, and in 1566 he was selected from among yeomen of the company to take part in arranging the inauguration of a new Lord Mayor of London, a fellow ironmonger. In the following year Donne was admitted to the company's livery and began to serve regularly in an official capacity (Flynn 1995c: 62–3).

Against the grain of this worldly prosperity came the last will and testament of William Rastell, who died on 27 August 1565 at Louvain. Rastell's will provided rings for Donne's mother and aunt, but his sizeable bequests went to exiles, principally to Ellis Heywood, who as the eldest male of his generation inherited from Rastell the nominal leadership of the More circle in exile. Rastell had no children, and Heywood was chosen as principal heir over another exile, Bartholomew More, a grandson of the late Lord Chancellor. But Bartholomew More's inheritance, a relatively small annuity, was made conditional on his 'not passing over to live in England until

England is reconciled fully to the Catholic faith and church'. Moreover, if More does not remain in exile, or if (as Rastell further stipulates) he 'declines into some heretical opinion', his annuity is to be given to charity by Heywood (Bang 246–8). Since Heywood stood eventually to inherit his father's properties as well, although a celibate priest unwilling to extend his lineage, Ellis in effect held most of the assets of both the Rastell and Heywood families.

The logic behind Rastell's will is evident in Ellis Heywood's actions about a year later: by the end of 1566 he had begun to implement a plan that would rule out the possibility that his family's wealth in England could ever become a cause of weakening religious resolve. Having seen to the provisions of Rastell's will, shortly before Christmas 1566 the now-wealthy Ellis Heywood showed up unannounced at Dillingen in Bavaria, where his Jesuit brother Jasper had been teaching for two years at the university. Ellis himself was now admitted to the Society of Jesus, simultaneously deeding all his inherited wealth, annuities (later including the deceased Bartholomew More's annuity), and lands to Francisco de Borja, the Superior-General of the Jesuits, and to his successors in office forever (Bang 241–2).

In England, John Heywood's son-in-law continued to care for the property Heywood had left behind; and in 1569 the crushing of the Northern Rising made clearer to the government than ever before that traditional Catholicism was not going to expire without a struggle. The Privy Council now resolved to stiffen the statutory penalties for practising Catholicism, viewed from this time forward as an act of political disloyalty directly connected to the promotion of Mary Stewart's succession to the throne. Among several anti-Catholic Bills proposed for the convening Parliament of 1571 was 'An Acte agaynst Fugytyves over the Sea', which bore directly on Heywood and on management of his properties by Donne. Within three months of this Bill's passage Donne would have to make a complete report on the role he had played in Heywood's affairs. Should this reveal him involved in secret dealings with a fugitive, he would be prosecuted. Moreover, if Heywood himself did not return to England, all his property would be forfeit to the Crown (*Statutes* 4.531–4; see also Flynn 1995c: 68–9).

Forewarned, Donne stopped forwarding Heywood's rents, turning over their collection to his sister-in-law, Heywood's daughter, the widow Elizabeth Marven, a smaller and much less tempting target for prosecution (Reed 70). At the same time Donne contrived a way to hold on to the Romney Marsh lease, by far the most valuable of Heywood's properties. Donne managed affairs so that the Crown's commissioner investigating Heywood's holdings in Kent himself (corruptly, or perhaps unwittingly) purchased the lease from Heywood and then sold it to Donne, thus veiling Donne's culpability in having dealings with a fugitive and at the same time keeping the property in the family (Flynn 1995c: 68). At some point during these months Ellis Heywood, at risk of arrest as a fugitive, quietly returned to England, attempting to secure his inherited properties as well as his father's properties in Hertfordshire against the threat of commissions appointed to confiscate them.

Unsuccessful, he had returned to the continent by 1573; by 1574 commissioners had determined that all the Heywoods' Hertfordshire properties were forfeit to the Crown (Bang 236).

During his stay in England Ellis had probably visited the Donnes, since he had not seen his sister Elizabeth Donne for eight or nine years. Another priest in the family, with whom the Donnes probably had contact in these years, was Thomas Heywood, who had been a monk until the dissolution of monasteries. At that time he had subscribed to the Crown's supremacy over the church in England, receiving in consequence a small pension on the understanding that he would thenceforth serve as a parish priest. He seems to have done so during the next two reigns and to have been one of the many Marian priests who continued to administer the Catholic sacraments clandestinely after the accession of Elizabeth (Reed 34–5). On Palm Sunday 1574, following orders from the Privy Council, London magistrates cracked down on papists in and around the city. In raids on four homes they interrupted or prevented Catholic Masses. Fifty-three people were arrested, among them a dozen or so in the immediate neighbourhood where the Donnes lived. Just north of the city wall Thomas Heywood was arrested and imprisoned for saying Mass (Flynn 1981: 325–7; *APC* 8.218, 270, 287).

The child John Donne was only 2 years old, as yet too young to be aware of these events, although his mother and her household must have been affected profoundly. Of these, Donne's earliest years, we know almost nothing else directly. He wrote of his mother much later that the childbearing years of her first marriage had been the happiest time in her life. We have also his brief recollection that his parents 'would not give mee over to a Servants correction' (*TMC* 324–5; *Devotions* 13).

4

To conclude, it is worth reflecting on the fact that Donne's first biographer Izaak Walton (whose influence in Donne studies remains incalculably great) expressed little interest in most of the details discussed in this chapter. Outstanding among these were the imprisonment and judicial murder of Sir Thomas More and the death in exile of William Rastell; consistent on the part of generations of Donne's family was resistance to religious repression, often leading towards fatality. A descendant of a group directly afflicted by enormous and penetrating social developments, Donne's personality stemmed from a family experience that influenced virtually everything he wrote. We should connect Donne's birth and early years, as well as his subsequent life and writings, to his family's religious persecution, imprisonment, exile, and death, as we connect the writings of Solzhenitsyn or Wiesel to theirs.

CHAPTER 27.1

EDUCATION AS A COURTIER

ALEXANDRA GAJDA

'Wherefore if thou looke for any favour or preferment in our Court, nay if thou looke for any seate or resting place in the Court of heaven, seeke for it by learning' (Kempe E^v). Sixteenth-century writers hymned the dynamic between the pragmatic and ideological utility of education. Learning might advance the public career of the socially aspirant young man, but also the fortunes of the commonwealth, which—ideally—was supported and governed through the talents and virtues of wise counsellors and magistrates. Humphrey Gilbert urged Elizabeth to revitalize the education of 'the youth of nobility and gentlemen' so that 'the Cowrte of England shall become for ever an Achademy of *Philosophie and Chiualrie*', her reign blessed with 'everlasting honnour' (Gilbert 10–12).

Humanists of the early sixteenth century had deemed the secular and religious ends of education inseparable. In post-Reformation Europe this ideal was seized upon by Protestant and Catholic reformers: in the confessional conflicts that divided Christendom, education—and education of youth in particular—was seen as a vital tool for the propagation of true religious belief, and an essential weapon in the fight against the false. Also reflecting their humanist legacy, sixteenth-century authors wrote repeatedly that education was a holistic process, which developed a student's reason and understanding of moral philosophy and therefore virtuous conduct. Educational instruction was offered to cover all aspects of external behaviour and social interaction as well as intellectual edification—appropriate manners or 'carriage', and recreations and pastimes suitable for virtuous living. For the would-be courtly gentleman there was a particularly strong seam of this kind of instructive advice.

Even Roger Ascham's *Scholemaster* (first published in 1570), famous for its detailed description of the course of classical study to be undertaken by young scholars, outlined 'exercises' and 'pastimes that be fitte for Courtlie Gentlemen', and directed his readers towards Castiglione's *Book of the Courtier*, which could be 'aduisedlie read, and diligentlie folowed' in Sir Thomas Hoby's English translation (Ascham fo. 20^v).

1

In 1530 Thomas Elyot (with some rhetorical and polemical edge) complained that 'to a great gētilman, it is a notable reproche to be well lerned, and to be called a great clerke' (Elyot fo. 43^r). By the seventeenth century a scholarly education was a central and assumed element of noble and gentle culture. Lawrence Stone (1975) might have exaggerated the extent of an educational revolution in sixteenth- and seventeenth-century England, but growing educational provision in the form of private and grammar schools, and swelling numbers of undergraduates at the universities and Inns of Court, reflect the increasing importance of learning to elites. In 1584 an estimated 48 per cent of Members of Parliament had been educated at university or the Inns of Court: by the Long Parliament of 1640–2 this number had increased to 70 per cent (Jewell 32).

There also developed a vast pedagogic literature covering all aspects of education, from the manners of children to entry into adult life. Thomas Elyot's *Boke named the Governour*, which itself drew on the educational writings and example of More, Erasmus, and Vives, expounded 'the education of them, that hereafter may be demed worthy to be gouernours of the publike weale', making explicit the association between education and the role of the wise would-be magistrate (Elyot A2^v). Elyot's treatise was reprinted seven times in the sixteenth century (the final edition in 1580). Roger Ascham's *The Scholemaster* was similarly influential, printed five times between 1570 and 1589.

The humanist injunction that active participation in public life required a thorough and carefully supervised education was, by Elizabeth's reign, a commonplace. Donne's friend Henry Wotton, in his (unfinished) *Philosophical Survey of Education*, explained that 'the Nerves or Ligaments of humane society' were not laws, as was commonly held, but 'the rules of good Nurture' (Wotton 1938: 4). The relationship between education and the *vita activa* was shored up by the pre-eminence of Cicero and Quintilian in the educational curricula generally prescribed for the 'governour' or courtier in Elizabethan England, and followed in private and grammar schools. The deep impact of the humanist educational ideal, which had at its heart the study of the liberal arts—rhetoric, poetry, history, and moral philosophy—is evident in the repeated emphasis laid on the public and practical utility of eloquence, 'in preaching, in Parliament, in Cownsell, in Comyssion, and other offices of Common Weale' (Gilbert 2). Writing in the early Jacobean period, Henry Peacham included eloquence as one of the essential qualities of true nobility which defined the 'Compleat Gentleman' (Peacham 8).

Skill in foreign languages, too, was of increasing utility to would-be courtiers. Henry Wotton, a younger son of a family that had prospered through diplomatic service, deliberately cultivated his linguistic abilities through travel and private study. Engaged in the 1590s as the Earl of Essex's secretary with special responsibility for German affairs, he enjoyed a distinguished diplomatic career under James, as ambassador to Venice and to the Hague, before returning to the field of education as Provost of Eton in 1624 (L. P. Smith).

Knowledge of the common law was esteemed by gentlemen as enhancing their capacities as local governors and informing their understanding of the laws of land-ownership and inheritance. The massive increase in the judicial business of the developing state, however, could also open career opportunities in central and royal administration, significantly increasing the attractions of a legal education.

The ideal that public magistrates should be the wisest and most virtuous of men created tension in attitudes to the relationship between education and social advancement. Thomas Elyot's ideal that education of the 'governour' perpetuated and strengthened the existing social hierarchy tended to be repeated in later discussions of true nobility and gentility; in late sixteenth-century Europe increasing economic and social polarization sharpened the rhetorical disdain of elites for those of lower birth. But education was clearly seen by many as a means to improve social fortune, especially when gentility was a nebulous status, dependent on the recognition of others (Heal and Holmes 244–5).

But educational achievements did not clear an immediate path to success in public life. Francis Bacon's Elizabethan career instructively demonstrated that political advancement was ever-dependent on the successful negotiation of patronage networks centred on the royal court. Bacon's scholarly credentials won him the support of the Earl of Essex, who unquestioningly accepted the political and public importance of the virtue of learning, and Bacon's training in the common law fitted him for a public career in administration. But Bacon's progress stalled under Elizabeth, partly because of the Queen's dislike of an ill-conceived speech he made in Parliament against the subsidy in 1593, and because his relationship with Lord Burghley, his uncle, was often difficult and strained. Despite widespread recognition of his intellectual gifts, and Essex's most energetic efforts on his behalf, Bacon's suits to be made Attorney-General, Solicitor, and Master of the Rolls failed (Jardine and Stewart 119–262).

2

As contemporaries insisted on the public utility of learning, some endorsed Aristotle's injunction that education be organized and regulated by public powers: Sir Henry Wotton noted that 'anciently the best composed Estates did commit this care more to the Magistrate then to the Parent' (Wotton 1938: 3). Unlike the promising Henrician precedents, however, in Elizabethan England new educational foundations in the late sixteenth century were the result of private endeavour rather than royal patronage. State involvement in education increased most significantly in a regulatory capacity, shaped by the concern of the Protestant ruling elite to enforce conformity to the Religious Settlement. From 1563 schoolmasters were required to subscribe to the Thirty-Nine Articles and the Royal Supremacy, while the 1571 canons attempted to limit teaching to schoolmasters and private tutors licensed by the bishops, and prescribed the grammar and catechism to be taught in schools (Jewell 4, 32). Purges of Oxford and Cambridge academics in the 1560s were followed by tightened regulations over students. In 1580 Oxford's Convocation ordered that all students reading for degrees be formally matriculated in a college or hall, whilst Oxford's matriculation statute of 1581 imposed subscription to the Religious Settlement and Supremacy for all matriculating students over the age of 15 (McConica 1986: 50–1). The government recognized that the persistence of Catholicism depended on the religion of the next generation. In the early 1580s Burghley drew up a memorandum recommending the forcible education of the children of recusants, while similar proposals were discussed in Parliament in 1593 (Beales 58–62).

These measures and attitudes obviously restricted parents who rejected the state religion: Puritans who objected to the Settlement and, most obviously, Catholics. Nevertheless, one outlet for Catholic education was the foundation, by William Allen and Robert Persons, of schools on the continent to train English seminary priests, but also scores of English Catholic laymen; Robert Persons's foundation at St Omer was established in 1593 specifically for the education of the latter. The 1571 Act 'against fugitives over the sea' made it a legal requirement that those who wished to travel on the continent must first seek a licence from the Privy Council. A. C. F. Beales has found evidence of a handful of Catholic schools that survived illegally in Elizabethan England, especially in the north, even into the 1580s: but Catholic families, especially gentry, preferred to employ unlicensed Catholic tutors—often priests (Beales 74–5).

The 'secular' content of post-Tridentine Catholic education, however, was largely humanist. That the Jesuits adopted a humanist curriculum in their famous educational strategies shows the widespread acceptance of the centrality of the liberal arts in European education by the mid-sixteenth century. Jesuits, like Elizabethan Protestants, recognized that the propagation of true religion was dependent on the education of the next generation of civic officials, and praised the relationship between learning and the active civic life. The humanistic emphasis on the capacities of man for self-improvement corresponded appropriately to a doctrinal belief that nature was ultimately perfected by grace (O'Malley 1993: 200–42).

3

Educational manuals covered the earliest years of childhood as well as the formal structure of schooling. Very young children were often referred to as empty vessels, to be filled with right learning, but dangerously receptive to harmful influence—which of course included spiritual influence. Discerning parents were therefore instructed to be wary of the companions, servants, and especially nurses chosen to bring up their children: 'For as some aunciet writers do suppose, oftentimes the childe soukethe the vice of his nouryse [nurse], with the milke of her pappe' (Elyot fo. 16^v). The importance of proper eloquence and speech was even reflected in instruction for infants of this young age: William Kempe warned parents that children must be removed from 'barbarous nursses...and all rusticall persons' as soon as they began to speak, so that they 'vse none other companie, then such as are both honest and ciuill, as well in behauiour, as in language' (Kempe E3^v).

Mothers, as well as female servants, appear to have played a significant role in the early education of children. Male writers of educational treatises were often suspicious of the dominance of female influence in early childhood. However, the example of Cornelia, whose eloquence nurtured the rhetorical skills of Tiberius and Gaius Gracchus, and the biblical example of Timothy, whose faith was instilled by his grandmother and mother, Lois and Eunice, were wheeled out with stale familiarity to defend the significant role that mothers played in the teaching of basic literacy and the religious instruction of children in both Protestant and Catholic households.

Behavioural example, though, was to be provided by fathers, who were constantly urged to take a more active role in their children's education. Donne's ancestor, Thomas More, was frequently cited as a model, although most authors recognized that fathers were unlikely to undertake such close personal supervision of studies as More had done and must instead secure the best possible tuition for their offspring.

The other chief educational responsibility of fathers was the enforcement of household obedience. Donne famously observed that 'Children kneele to aske blessing of Parents in England, but where else?' (*Sermons* 9.59). The writings of contemporaries confirm that the forms of respect paid by children to parents were particularly restrictive and elaborate. Educational manuals instructed children to be silent, to bow when spoken to, to stand or kneel in the presence of their parents, and, if male, to remain bareheaded at all times (Heal and Holmes 248–51).

Patriarchal discipline had a heightened political significance. Aristotle's comparison of the relationship of a father to his children with that of a ruler to his subjects (*Politics* 1.12) underscored patriarchal theories of the obedience owed by subjects to the monarch or magistrate. Emphasis on the enforcement of parental obedience has been described as a particularly Protestant, even Puritan, obsession (Stone 1977: 162–3). Nowell's catechism (translated into English by Thomas Norton), the catechism prescribed by the Elizabethan state, explicates the Fifth Commandment, to 'honour thy father and mother', as an injunction to obey all those in positions of authority: parents, but also 'all those, to whom any authoritie is geuen, as magistrates, ministers of ye chirch, scholemasters' and all those of 'reuerend age, or of witte, wisdome, or learning' (Nowell fo. 13^v). Laurence Vaux's English catechism, the text used by Catholic households for basic instruction after its first publication in 1567, was (understandably) much more vague on forms of secular obedience to magistrates. It discussed the Fourth Commandment, and parental authority over children, instead as evidence of the obedience owed to *spiritual* authorities, to 'our prelats, bishops and spiritual governours in Christes Church…comyng lineally from the Apostles', and as an injunction to 'take hede, that we be not caried away with any strange heretical doctrine' (Vaux 46^v).

Educationalists were agreed that basic vernacular literacy, the foundation for all further study, must be properly mastered before the serious business of learning classical languages could commence; it was a requirement of entry to most grammar schools. After learning the alphabet, students were to read first the Catechism and Primer in English, combining literacy and religious instruction. The importance of the vernacular was expressed with increasing vehemence in the later sixteenth century. Humphrey Gilbert imagined that a lecturer in rhetoric should also teach 'politique and militaire' discourse in English, because 'in what language soueuer learninge is attayned, the apliaunce to vse is principally in the vulgare speech' (Gilbert 2).

The suitable age for progression to secondary education was usually estimated at around 7, although this varied according to the proficiency of the child. For most, this secondary education began with proper instruction in Latin grammar, to be followed with Greek and possibly Hebrew. The state prescribed the use of William Lyly's Latin grammar, although private tutors would have had more leeway than masters in schools to use alternative educational texts, and to vary the curriculum followed by their charges.

Ascham, whose intensive methodology was best suited to private tuition, popularized the practice of double translation, advocated by Vives before him as a most perfect way of teaching proficiency in classical languages. Students would translate a passage of Latin or Greek into English, then turn their English translation back into the ancient language. This final translation could be compared to the original text, bringing students to a 'trewe vnderstanding and right iudgement, both for writing and speaking' (Ascham fo. 34^v). The foundations of grammar would lead to the study of rhetoric, poetry, and history, with the expectation that the student would be able to imitate classical authors before moving on to the creation of original compositions.

Well into the seventeenth century, the bedrock of classical literary studies was the study of Cicero's letters and his treatises *De Oratore* and *De Officiis*, prized for their moral and philosophical content as well as their style, as 'no mā be an excellent poet, nor oratour, vnlasse he haue parte of all other doctrine, specially of noble philosophie' (Elyot fo. 52ᵛ). Most educational treatises emphasized the moral utility, however, of a wide range of classical literature, even the racier poets and playwrights, such as Ovid and Terence. The study of history was deemed especially worthy for the man of public affairs. Tacitus of all Roman historians gained fashionable status in the later sixteenth century, but Caesar, Sallust, Livy, Xenophon, and Thucydides were praised for the exceptional insight they afforded into politics and war. Conversely, the growing market for printed books in foreign languages demonstrates that familiarity with foreign tongues, especially French—but also Spanish and Italian—was growing more common.

Ascham's humanist snobbishness about elements of the traditional quadrivium, arithmetic, geometry, astronomy, and music, warned tutors that these disciplines 'sharpen mens wittes ouer moch', and should be pursued only if they might be 'applied to som good vse of life' (Ascham fo. 5ᵛ). However, the study of cosmography, arithmetic, and geometry were highly recommended to gentlemen and would-be courtiers by other writers for their practical utility in shaping understanding of foreign terrain, or of architecture, fortifications, and engineering works useful in warfare. Following Castiglione, Ascham and Elyot both devoted a surprising amount of space to the value of painting and the composition of poetry as part of the more general education of a student, Elyot foreshadowing Sidney in his appraisal of poetry as 'the first philosophy that euer was knowen', teaching 'maners and naturall affections, but also the wonderfull werkes of nature' (Elyot fo. 49ʳ⁻ᵛ). Suitable exercises to strengthen physical and mental agility excluded wrestling and other indecorous sports but allowed tilting, running, swimming, tennis, and leaping, the latter 'very commendable, and healthfull for the body, especially if you vse it in the morning' (Peacham 180).

4

After leaving the care of the schoolroom and the tutor, an increasing number of young men chose to continue the formal process of education at Oxford or Cambridge. Lawrence Stone describes the swelling numbers of students and graduates at Oxford from 1560 to 1629 as 'by far the fastest increase in the output of graduates in the whole history of the university' (Stone 1975: 1.21). It is difficult to determine numbers of admissions precisely, but the sixteenth century solidified the transformation of the medieval universities from religious foundations of mainly graduate fellows to institutions dominated by the endowed college, which maintained large numbers of undergraduate students studying for the degree of Bachelor of Arts.

State intervention in university regulations enhanced the authority of the colleges and halls over the welfare and discipline of the undergraduate. The requirement of 1581 that all matriculated students subscribe to the Religious Settlement and Act of Supremacy had been preceded by regulations which demanded that all scholars in the town be bound to and formally matriculated in a college or hall. Undergraduate students were assigned college tutors, responsible for overseeing the welfare—educational and pastoral—of young scholars. These regulations were motivated by a well-founded fear of a persistent Catholic presence in the scholarly community (McConica 1986: 49–51). The Oath of Supremacy was usually offered to students of 16 or over, but boys as young as 12 could be required to swear. It was to avoid this greater test of probity that Donne and his brother Henry pretended to be one year younger than their respective ages of 12 and 11 when they enrolled at Oxford in 1584. The choice of Donne's college, Hart Hall, was probably determined by his Catholic background. Hart Hall, unlike the newer collegiate foundations, did not provide a chapel, so attendance at Church of England services could be more easily avoided. The principal, Philip Rondell, was sympathetic to the old religion (Flynn 1995c: 131–2). Catholics in the 1570s included the future Jesuit Richard Holtby, who tutored at Hart Hall beginning in 1574 (before sweeping off to Douai with a group of young scholars), and Francis Throckmorton, later executed for his part in the assassination plot that bears his name, who matriculated in 1572 (Hamilton 20–1).

Historians have been critical of the education received by undergraduate students in the arts at English universities in the sixteenth century. The statutory curriculum of the Faculty of Arts was revised considerably at Cambridge, where from 1488 the syllabus was reformed to require two years' study of humane letters. At Oxford, however, changes to the official statutory curriculum for the undergraduate have been described as 'gestures' that 'did little more than modify the traditional programme' (J. M. Fletcher 159). In this respect Oxford lagged behind many continental and Scottish universities, which drastically revised or reformulated their curricula in the sixteenth century. The degree of Bachelor of Arts at Oxford was a four-year course, taught in the traditional format of the lecture and academic disputation. The Elizabethan Statutes of 1564–5 continued the scholastic adherence to the division of knowledge into the seven liberal arts, ignoring, for example, the study of history and geography. Although humanistic texts were formally adopted for the teaching of rhetoric and grammar, those governing logic, geometry, and astronomy remained primarily medieval works (ibid. 154–99).

The growing pre-eminence of the college and hall, however, rectified the undergraduate experience. Founders of colleges at Oxford and Cambridge in the early sixteenth century had intended their endowments to become seats of humanist learning. Undergraduates received an increasing amount of instruction within the colleges themselves, in lectures and disputations, and there is evidence of a much wider range of teaching in arts subjects outside of the formal curriculum, in Greek and Hebrew, history, geography, mathematics, and even modern languages, represented in the increasing richness of the book collections of college libraries. Gabriel Harvey famously remarked that the modish works of contemporary political thought and history, especially Bodin and Machiavelli, crowded students' desks in sixteenth-century Cambridge (G. Harvey 79). However, Edward, Lord Herbert of Cherbury, explained that it was *despite* rather than *because* of his residence at Oxford that he did, 'without any master or teacher, attain the knowledge of the French, Italian, and Spanish languages', learned to sight-sing, play the lute, and generally to make himself 'a citizen of the world' (E. Herbert 1906: 23).

The inadequacy of the English universities prompted Humphrey Gilbert to propose his scheme for 'Queen Elizabeth's Achademy', which would provide an education for the Queen's wards and other young nobles and gentlemen that far outstripped in practical utility and variety the fare on offer at Oxford and Cambridge. Gilbert stipulated that this academy should maintain lectureships and education in the traditional arts subjects, and in divinity and Roman law. In addition, though, there should be a lecturer of equal status in the common law, who would 'teache exquisitely the office of a Iustice of peace and Sheriffe', as well as stipendiary lecturers in French, Italian, Spanish, and High Dutch. Cosmography and astronomy would be taught alongside navigation, the use of weaponry, and practical engineering skills necessary for an understanding of fortifications. Gilbert also sought to rectify the sterility of English scholarship itself by insisting that the salaried lecturers in arts and laws publish original books, and language tutors produce English translations every six and three years respectively (Gilbert 9).

Why, then, were the universities an increasingly popular destination for the children of the English gentry? The content of the arts curriculum was, in fact, probably of less interest to parents and students than it has been to historians. Around half of undergraduates never proceeded to take the BA degree itself. However, the social polish and contacts that could be acquired at university were particularly valued. Frequent warnings against neglect of studies indicate that many young men indulged in gentlemanly pursuits of the non-scholarly variety—hunting, dancing, and drinking (Heal and Holmes 268; Prest 1972: 28). Links between university and court in the late sixteenth century grew ever stronger, and not entirely because of the state's fear of popery. The Earl of Leicester, and his political heir, the second Earl of Essex, were noted patrons of university scholars. Henry Cuffe, Regius Professor in

Greek at Oxford, left Merton College to act as Essex's secretary in 1595. This was a career path that took him to the scaffold, when he was executed for his part in the Earl's rising in 1601, the most extreme reminder for contemporaries of the contrast between the scholarly *otium* of the academic cloister and the dangers of the court (Hammer 1994).

Gilbert criticized the education provided by the universities, but not the institution sometimes referred to as England's 'third university'—the Inns of Court. The progression from Oxford and Cambridge to the Inns was an increasingly frequent, if not inevitable, passage. By 1600 nearly half the entrants at the Inns had been educated at the universities (compared with only 13 per cent in 1561) (Jewell 70). Over the course of the sixteenth century the four Inns of Court—Gray's Inn, Lincoln's Inn, Inner Temple, and Middle Temple—had increased their eminence at the expense of the older Inns of Chancery, and by Elizabeth's reign qualification for pleading in the higher courts of law depended on being called to the Bar at one of the greater Inns. Donne studied for at least a year at Thavies Inn, one of the Inns of Chancery, apparently as preparation for his admission to Lincoln's Inn in 1592, and it was at Thavies Inn in 1593 that the priest William Harrington was found in his brother Henry's rooms.

Study of the labyrinthine common law was a painful process for many students. Although Edward Coke believed that the difficulties of the English common law cultivated the superior intellectual powers of the common lawyer, students who had absorbed the humanist valuation of literary style and eloquence frequently decried the 'barbarous' language of law-French (Prest 1972: 141–2). Men called to the Bar were deemed to have attended and participated successfully in the formal legal exercises and lectures provided by the Inns: the moot, or mock trial, and the reading (or lecture course) devised around a statute or part of a statute, with associated case discussion, as well as debates over points of law (case-putting), which were conducted at mealtimes. Students were also expected to supplement formal aural instruction with private study, facilitated by a growing number of printed textbooks, and to attend and observe real trials in the central law-courts.

The attractions of a legal career were obviously pecuniary. But the Inns of Court have been better known to scholars for their role as finishing schools for men of gentle birth. W. R. Prest estimated that between 1590 and 1640 88 per cent of entrants to the Inns were drawn from the gentry, squirearchy, and peerage (1972: 28–30). As with the universities, many members of the Inns had no intention of progressing to the Bar itself, and the extent to which the student developed a thorough legal education depended heavily on personal inclination.

In the late fifteenth century John Fortescue remarked that the expense of membership of the Inns prohibited the education of anyone 'excepte hee bee a gentleman borne, and come of a noble stocke' (Fortescue fo. 114^v). These expenses, which grew even steeper as the sixteenth century progressed, were compounded by the sophisticated lifestyle that members felt pressure to adopt. Nevertheless, the expense was deemed worthwhile, especially because of the social and cultural advantages available to young students along with the formal legal education that the Inns offered. Young members refined their pursuit of courtly graces and manners. Those who could afford to do so employed private tutors in dancing, singing, and fencing. Nor was more serious extra-legal activity ignored. The ambitious timetable of study of one 'Mr Langford', a member of Gray's Inn in the seventeenth century, set aside an hour in the morning to ensure that he 'Forget not Academique learning, Logick, Rhetorick'. This followed an hour of Scripture and praying; three hours of reading law; and an hour of '*harmless acts of Manhood*, Fencing, Dancing, &c'. After a two-hour (much-needed) lunch break, he visited friends in the afternoon, before reading history, poetry, and romances before dinner (Waterhouse 151–2).

The geographical position of the Inns also attracted students. The concentration of youths near London's theatres, brothels, alehouses, even scriveners' shops and networks of news and court gossip attracted inevitable censure. As with the universities, students at the Inns were known targets of Catholic priests. From the 1580s onwards the authorities governing the Inns attempted to regulate the religious orthodoxy of members and students more thoroughly by instituting compulsory annual communion, denying promotion to the Bar of suspected Catholics, and launching sporadic inspections and visitations of student chambers (Prest 1972: 174–86).

Fortescue remarked that one of the merits of the Inns was location 'nighe to ye kinges courtes' (Fortescue fo. 112^v). The proximity of the royal residence at Whitehall, too, was advantageous to those gentlemen who hoped that their sojourn at the Inns might help them to advance a political and/or judicial career. Even more than at the universities, social networks and useful contacts were built and reinforced at the Inns. Peers enrolled in increasing numbers, whilst the overlap between the judicial administrative capacities of the Crown, and the administrative and courtly roles of royal servants, cemented ties between lawyers and the court. The appointment of Sir Christopher Hatton as Lord Chancellor in 1587 offended many practising lawyers, who decried his lack of legal experience. But Hatton was a member of the Inner Temple, and it appears that he first came to the attention of the Queen at an Inner Temple entertainment in 1561 or 1562.

The significance of the literary culture of the Inns in Elizabethan England has long been recognized, as has the engagement of this literary and legal culture with the weightiest of 'high' political matters. The revels held between All Saints and Candlemas, often attended by members of the royal court or presented at the court itself, involved lawyers in the writing and performance of masques and dramatic works that sometimes operated as a form of fictionalized counsel. The most famous of these, the performance of *Gorboduc* in 1562, dramatized the horrors of civil war threatened by an unsettled succession, an abiding Elizabethan political concern still echoed in lawyers' entertainments at the end of the reign, in the *Gesta Grayorum* of 1594–5. At Christmas the lawyers also erected their own imitation of the royal court, electing a prince who chose officers mirroring those of the monarch, and who presided over mock versions of embassies, trials, and courtly rituals (Axton 2–10 and 38–60 *passim*). To orchestrate entertainments at the Inns a Master of the Revels was appointed, an office occupied by Donne himself at Lincoln's Inn in 1592–3 (Bald 1970: 56–7).

5

Broader educational opportunities were offered by continental travel. Philip Sidney's travels in the 1570s glamorized the appeal of the continental voyage. In the mid-1590s the Earl of Essex styled himself as a patron of travellers, circulating in manuscript letters of travel advice to the Earl of Rutland, written with the assistance of Francis Bacon and perhaps others of his secretariat. Essex's advice to Rutland outlined the practical benefits of touring the continent. Rutland's 'strength of mind' would be rigorously improved. He would gain understanding of the constitutions, ruling elites, and military and financial powers of other European states, would master foreign languages, and enhance his understanding of geography. All of this observational knowledge would be of benefit to the English commonwealth, most obviously in the realm of foreign affairs (Hammer 1995).

Travellers sought access to methods and materials of scholarship unavailable in England. Anthony Bacon, who travelled on the continent between 1579 and 1592, stayed in Geneva in 1581–2, where he lodged with Theodore Beza and attended lectures at the Genevan Academy (Jardine and Stewart 82). Henry Wotton trawled the library of the imperial court at Vienna, copying manuscripts, sending books back to his patron, Lord Zouche, before travelling to Prague, where he wrote home to Lord Burghley with eyewitness information about the activities of the English alchemist Edward Kelley (Curzon 33–5).

The Elizabethan government made significant use of information provided by English travellers. The distinction between the gathering of observational knowledge and spying was blurred in the early modern period: the phrase 'intelligence-gathering' conveniently encapsulates both ideas. Anthony Bacon maintained a stream of intelligence and news to his brother Francis, and to Francis Walsingham. On his return in 1592 he used the many contacts he had made on the continent to help the Earl of Essex establish a large intelligence service of his own (Hammer 1994).

The thick webs of intrigue—real and imagined—that characterized Elizabethan foreign relations and confessional politics necessitated and glamorized this pursuit of 'intelligence'. Knowledge of the activities of Catholic powers, and the intrigues of English Catholics abroad, were crucial to the English Protestant state. But for these very reasons the moral and spiritual dangers of travel were frequently sounded. Burghley bluntly warned his son Robert Cecil: 'suffer not your sonnes to passe the *Alpes*: for they shall exchaunge for theyr forraine trauell...but others vices for theyr owne vertues, *Pride, Blasphemy*, and *Atheisme*, for *Humility, Reuerence*, and *Religion*' (W. Cecil 9).

To many English Catholics, the 'dangers' of which Burghley warned were the advantages of travel. Although English travellers were required to seek a licence to leave English shores after 1571, many Catholics found pretexts and means of leaving England—to seek their education abroad, or merely to travel to foreign states where they might worship freely. By the 1590s the dubious confessional identity of the English traveller was recognizable enough to form part of the literary strategies of English Catholic polemic. Richard Verstegan's condensed version of the famous tract by Andreas Philopater (almost certainly a pseudonym for Robert Persons), *Elizabethae Angliae Reginae haeresim Calvinianam propugnantis saevissimum in catholicos sui regni edictum*, was published in 1592 as *An Advertisement written to a secretarie of my L. Treasurers by an Inglishe intelligencer as he passed throughe Germanie....* Persons's tract of 1593, *Newes from Spayne and Holland*—a description of the dreadful political and economic condition of late Elizabethan England as well as the cruel persecution of Catholics—also purported to be the reports of an English traveller in the Low Countries, writing to an acquaintance in London.

In many ways John Donne's own education represents a template of the conventional paths open to young Elizabethans. Donne's journey from private tutoring in the schoolroom to Oxford and the Inns of Court, punctuated by continental travel, mirrors the experiences of Wotton, or the Bacon brothers. But Donne's education was, of course, shaped by his Catholicism. For an ambitious youth, Catholicism made the educational process, deemed so integral by contemporaries to social advancement and a public career, a much more complicated, difficult, and even potentially dangerous experience.

CHAPTER 27.II

DONNE'S EDUCATION

DENNIS FLYNN

1

LITTLE is recorded about Donne's education before the age of 12, apart from a few comments he himself made. He thanked his mother in a Letter of 1616 for having been 'so carefullie and so chargeablie diligent' (*TMC* 325) in providing him with expert and formative early schooling, under circumstances no doubt difficult and expensive. Disturbing are his recollections of a Catholic upbringing: his 'breeding, and conversation, with Men of a suppressed and afflicted Religion'. As Donne recalled it, from boyhood into adult life, the 'hunger' of his teachers for their own execution by the Elizabethan regime led to his being 'ever kept awake in a Meditation of Martyrdome' (*Pseudo-Martyr* 8). Their enthusiasm for martyrdom suggests that his teachers had been Roman Catholic missionary priests, something confirmed by Donne's further observation that subsequently he had had 'to blot out, certaine impressions of the Romane religion' gained from these teachers, 'who by their learning and good life, seem'd to me justly to claime an interest for the guiding, and rectifying of mine understanding' (ibid. 13).

With ironic indignation, Donne cited an example of such impressions: 'I have seene at some Executions of Traiterous *Priests*, some bystanders, leaving all old Saints, pray to him whose body lay there dead; as if hee had more respect, and better accesse in heaven, because he was a stranger, then those which were familiar, had' (ibid. 163). Among such bystanders, and even among the executed, may well have been teachers who had held Donne in 'conversation' about the immediate sainthood of martyred missionary priests. He recalled also more strenuous and radical efforts 'to wrastle both against the examples and against the reasons, by which some hold was taken; and some anticipations early layde upon my conscience', influence exerted not merely by teachers but by family members, 'who by nature had a power and superiority over my will' (ibid. 13).

One priest who shared Donne's 'breeding' may have taught him, and almost certainly exerted an important influence on his education: his mother's older brother, Jasper Heywood, SJ. Heywood himself, one of the children of the entertainer and music teacher John Heywood, had been extraordinarily well educated at the royal court under his father and other royal tutors, a schoolmate to children of the English nobility, including the Princess Elizabeth Tudor, whom Jasper was said to have served as a page (unaddressed, unsigned letter from England, 6 March 1584, ARSI, Anglia 30/I, fo. 292^v; Flynn 1995c: 28). Heywood was also an outstanding student at Oxford, where (following in the footsteps of his brother Ellis) he attained a fellowship at All Souls College shortly before the death of Queen Mary in 1558. For three years at All Souls he studied and wrote, a poet and translator of Senecan tragedies, until the Act of Uniformity, the banning of the Missal, and other effects of the Elizabethan settlement of religion drove him into exile. He was welcomed into the Society of Jesus at Louvain and in May 1562 entered the Jesuit novitiate at Rome, where he studied theology for two years (McCoog 1992: 2.351–2; on Heywood's university education through the doctorate, see Flynn 1995c: 41–53 and 64–6). Later, assigned to teach and preach at Dillingen, training Bavarian boys from impoverished noble families to be priests, he unhappily missed the intellectual stimulation he had enjoyed at Oxford and at Rome (Heywood to Jèronimo Nadal, SJ, 6 June 1572; ARSI, Germ. 134/I, fo. 140; on Heywood's teaching in Germany, see Flynn 2004b: 183–90). At his university in Dillingen Heywood wrote a Hebrew grammar in Latin and acquired his doctorate in theology, along with a reputation as a maverick in the Erasmian vein and a tendency towards disdain for some of his German superiors, who after seventeen years' working with him were pleased to have the Pope send him back to England (Paul Hoffaeus, SJ to Oliver Mannaerts, SJ, 17 November 1580, quoted in Duhr 231; and Claudio Acquaviva, SJ, to Wilhelm Wittelsbach, Duke of Bavaria, 30 April 1581, ARSI, Germ. Sup. I, fo. 56^v; on Heywood's later career in Germany and departure for England, see Flynn 2004b: 194–208). After nearly two decades of religious exile (in Belgium, Italy, and, mainly, Germany) Heywood came into the life of Donne's family in the summer of 1581, when the boy was 9 years old.

Landing in the north near Newcastle, like other missionary priests Heywood planned to rejoin family members and friends on returning to England (Examination of William Holt, SJ, 1 and 2 March 1583, Bodleian, MS Tanner 79, fo. 187; on Heywood's return to England, see Flynn 1995c: 101–3). Coming home to visit his sister in London, he encountered for the first time the precocious learning of his nephew, said by Walton, if we can believe him, to have been already fluent in both Latin and French and to have been called by someone at this time '*another* Picus Mirandula' (1675:

11–12). Although other opportunities would later occur, the hunted Jesuit cannot immediately have had much time to take professional interest in Donne's further education. Heywood's colleague, Edmund Campion, SJ, had recently been captured and imprisoned, and was soon to be executed; and their Superior, Robert Persons, SJ, left for France unexpectedly, so that Heywood was alone and in charge of the English mission (Heywood to Acquaviva, n.d., ARSI, Anglia 3/I, fo. 120^v; Flynn 1995c: 104–5). His workload was soon overwhelming, taking a fearful toll on his health and effectiveness (Cardinal William Allen to Acquaviva, 6 August 1583, printed in Catholic Record Society [CRS] 1911: 9.101; Robert Persons, SJ, 'Punti per la Missioni d'Inghilterra', CRS 1907: 4.109–13; on Heywood's activities as an underground missionary, see Flynn 1995c: 106–8, 112, and 115–17). At length he was recalled to France for consultations, but on his way was captured, indicted for treason, and put in the Tower of London for months of solitary confinement, during which he was tortured (Persons to Alfonso Agazzari, SJ, 8 March 1584, CRS 1942: 39.200; on Heywood's capture and time in prison, see Flynn 1995c: 123–5, 127–30). Donne laconically recalled visiting him there in the winter of 1584, 'at a Consultation of *Jesuites* in the *Tower*, in the late Queenes time' (*Pseudo-Martyr* 56). To arrange this consultation, Heywood's successor, William Weston, SJ, had contacted Donne's mother, through her exchanged letters with Heywood, and then entered the Tower with her under the pretence of a family visit (Weston 10–11; on this visit and issues surrounding it, see Flynn 2007: 244–7), made more plausible by their bringing Donne too into the fortress prison.

The main focus of the Jesuits' consultation in the Tower was the Privy Council's reported intention, rather than continuing to execute missionary priests, to deport all those in custody and to put new legislation through Parliament making it treason for such men to set foot in the realm again and making it a felony to harbour them if they did. The measure was part of a broader initiative by the council not only to get rid of the priests but to direct pressure on Catholic families who hid them, families unable to flee from one place to another, burdened with concern for children and property. Already, during the summer of 1584, intensification of persecution had been apparent, as the council authorized officials and pursuivants to organize concerted raids in London on identified Catholic households, some not far from Donne's home, where suspected persons were routed out of bed at night and dragged off for interrogation or to prison (Certificate of Richard Topcliffe *et al.*, TNA, SP 12/172, fos. 102–15; Flynn 1995c: 126–7).

To counter these measures and the contemplated legislation, Heywood had worked with other Catholics inside and outside the Tower to prepare a petition boldly appealing to Queen Elizabeth herself, his former schoolmate, to implement a policy of toleration for Catholicism. The Catholics planned to present this petition to the Queen before Parliament convened. Weston, having learned of the plan through his correspondence with Heywood, relayed word of it to Persons in France, recognizing immediately that this petition might compromise the entire political design of the mission as Persons had conceived it (Manning 1962: 270; Flynn 2007: 244–7).

2

In Michaelmas term 1584 Donne, as a stop-gap measure, had misrepresented his age as 11 (he was 12) and matriculated at Hart Hall, Oxford, a refuge for Catholic students. As Heywood had earlier written to Rome, the Privy Council intended to step up the pressure on Catholic families exerted from the outset of the reign through the Oxford matriculation statute, which required that all students subscribe to the Thirty-Nine Articles and swear the Oath of Supremacy at the age of 16, thus acknowledging the Queen as supreme governor of the Church of England. To avoid this requirement, Catholic students had long been careful to enrol at Oxford colleges by the age of 12. But the council now resolved to question selected 12-year-old students and to require some of them to swear the Oath (Heywood to Acquaviva, n.d., ARSI, Anglia 30/I, fo. 118^v; Flynn 1995c: 131–2). Those who refused were to become 'school Hostages', their parents forced to surrender them to live and be educated under 'Good schoolmasters' (Beales 58 n. 2), an arrangement at once preventing their further Catholic education and ensuring their families' good behaviour.

Heywood understood the council's policy initiative as partly a result of his successful efforts, especially at Oxford and Cambridge, to recruit likely candidates for study in exile at continental seminaries and thus to make the two universities 'perpetual aqueducts' through which would pass English scholars bound to finish their studies at such schools as the English seminary in Rheims (Heywood to Acquaviva, n.d., ARSI, Anglia 30/I, fo. 118^v; Flynn 2007: 241). As a result of Heywood's work, twenty English students had come from English universities to Rheims in November 1582; and fifty more arrived in August 1583, a group including several 'sons of noblemen' (Allen to Agazzari, 5 November 1582 and 8 August 1583, CRS 1907: 4.73 and 115; Flynn 2007: 241). When resources at Rheims were strained by this dramatic influx of defectors, various solutions to the problem were implemented, including transfer of some students to the English College at Rome and creation of new Jesuit colleges such as those at St Omer and Eu in France, endowed for several purposes by Henri de Lorraine, Duke of Guise (A. L. Martin 65–7). Not all these young fugitives were intent on becoming priests, and with or without Heywood's knowledge seminary education leading to ordination was not the only enterprise his aqueducts were feeding. Plans for military recruitment were part of Guise's design, and he had been in touch about this matter with both the Spanish ambassador Bernadino Mendoza (with whom Heywood also had conferred) and Catholic noblemen in England (ibid. 70–3; on Heywood's relations with Mendoza, see Mendoza's dispatches to King Felipe II, on 20 October and 11 December 1581, as well as the King's reply on 18 December 1581, promising 2,000 crowns to support activities of the English Jesuits: *CLSP Simancas* 3.195–6, 236, and 242).

The Privy Council had learned enough about Heywood's missionary activities, especially at Oxford and Cambridge, to suspect his involvement in English Catholic plans, negotiated by Persons in France, Spain, and Rome, for an 'Enterprise' or invasion of England. While Guise sponsored the new college at Eu, he was also (without the approval of the French government) cultivating a related plan. Beginning as early as 1578, Guise had tried through the Spanish ambassador at Paris to negotiate King Felipe's support for such an invasion. By 1582 these plans had crystallized: Spanish forces were promised for a landing in Scotland, whence an effort could be launched southwards into England to free Mary Stewart and restore Catholicism. One element of the plan was to organize fugitive gentry and nobility as officers for companies of English soldiers, to be attached temporarily to the Spanish and allied forces fighting Dutch Protestant rebels. Raw materials for such an English unit had been on hand at least as early as the summer of 1582, when 400 unpaid English soldiers, sent by the council to fight for the Dutch, deserted to the Spaniards and were received and paid by Alessandro Farnese, Duke of Parma, leader of the Spanish forces in the Netherlands (*CLSP Simancas* 3.398; Flynn 2007: 242). Without well-trained and reliable English Catholic officers, these troops were not fit for combat, but could at least serve as decoys to attract further English deserters. And here Guise's plan could put to use Heywood's increasing flow of young nobility and gentry designated for study at the seminaries. During the summer of 1583 Persons had met with Guise to help coordinate a military effort (Bossy 2007: 191–2).

Meanwhile in England, emigration for Guise's military training, rather than education for the priesthood, required careful administration by some powerful Catholic or Catholic sympathizer, counterpart to Guise in France. Likeliest to have been coordinating Heywood's perhaps unwitting participation was Henry Percy, Earl of Northumberland, under whose auspices Heywood had landed at Tynemouth (Examination of William Holt, SJ, 1 and 2 March 1583, Bodleian, MS Tanner 79, fo. 187), and who was one of those Heywood termed 'big fish', that is, English noblemen he had engaged in reconciliation to Catholicism during the spring of 1583 (Heywood to Allen, 16 April 1583, printed in *CRS* 1911: 9.91; identified by Persons in 'Punti', *CRS* 1907: 4.93). By July 1583 Guise's troops were already poised to move, but Northumberland's position had been weakened by the Privy Council's discovery of some of his connections; ongoing contacts with Heywood, with Guise, with Mendoza, and with fellow Catholic nobles and gentry in both England and French exile had tended to suggest Northumberland's leadership role. Moreover, word of Persons's meetings with Guise had reached the council and been passed on to King

Henri III, who quickly thwarted Guise's plan for the use of ports in Normandy. In December, as Heywood was arrested trying to return to France for consultations with Persons and Cardinal Allen, the council discovered hard evidence of Northumberland's involvement in the plot for an 'Enterprise'. He was at once interrogated (Interrogatories for Northumberland, 17 December 1583, TNA, SP 12/164/36; Flynn 1995c: 117–23) and then put into the Tower, where he and Heywood were both held throughout the following year. By the end of 1584 the council had gained considerable intelligence about their activities.

3

Heywood had been scheduled for deportation before the end of January and, among other problems, he and his sister now had to consider his nephew's continuing education. Donne's vulnerability to the threat of the Oath of Supremacy at Oxford may have been an additional reason why he was brought by his mother and Weston to what was intended to seem a family meeting in the Tower. It was plain to Heywood that Donne's return to Oxford for Hilary term 1585 was too dangerous, because he was an obvious target of the Privy Council's new policy; instead, Donne would have to continue his studies elsewhere. The same situation was faced by other Catholics, from this time taking extraordinary steps to provide for the education of their children. Among the group of imprisoned priests slated for deportation with Heywood was his fellow prisoner, the Jesuit James Bosgrave, who would later spend his first weeks of exile trying to satisfy his family's urgent request that his adolescent niece and nephew somehow be transferred covertly to Catholic schools at Louvain or Rheims. Bosgrave sought to contact Catholics or Catholic sympathizers among the English merchants trading at Calais, who might be willing for a price to stow away his cherished cargo (Bosgrave to Odon Pigenat, SJ, 1 May 1585, ARSI, Gallia 92, fo. 7; Flynn 1995c: 133–4).

To take ship without licence was a dangerous course, given ongoing hostilities in the Netherlands and close supervision of ports by Privy Council agents under orders to thwart just such illegal transporting of Catholic children as Bosgrave was trying to arrange. Heywood had helped organize this risky procedure during his time at large, but under heightening tensions it would be even riskier. A possible solution for Heywood's dilemma appeared in the scheduled departure for France of Henry Stanley, Earl of Derby, as extraordinary ambassador to the court of Henri III, to invest the King with the Order of the Garter. Derby was the most prominent among those noblemen and noblewomen with whom Heywood had been tutored at court during the reign of Henry VIII. Among the first of Heywood's initiatives on returning to England in the summer of 1581 had been to secure from Derby and many other nobles and gentry their pledges of financial support for his missionary work (on Derby's pledge, see a report by the Privy Council's spy, P. H., to Sir Francis Walsingham, n.d. [but datable on internal evidence between mid-spring 1582 and midwinter 1582–3], TNA, SP 12/168, fo. 31; Flynn 2007: 240). Derby was reported to be another of the noblemen ('big fish') whom Heywood had been engaged in reconciling to Catholicism (Persons, 'Punti', *CRS* 1907: 4.93; the third nobleman Heywood had contacted was Philip Howard, Earl of Arundel).

Mindful of the danger to Donne if he returned to Oxford, and seizing the unique opportunity presented by his own deportation, Heywood could call again on his old court friend Henry Stanley to place his nephew in the ambassadorial suite, and thus convey the boy safely to France, out of range of the Oath of Supremacy. Heywood would certainly not have been the only Catholic who considered altering the size and composition of his friend's retinue. At a time when bureaucratized religious persecution extended where it never had before, when ordinary passage out of England was scrutinized with unprecedented care, and when unlicensed travel was strictly forbidden, the Earl ambassador readily gave his consent to a host of avid fellow travellers, pliancy that eventually occasioned pointed comment by the Privy Council. Although the official list of members of his suite had contained only forty-five names ('The noble mene Knights and Esquires and Gentlemene geving their Attendance one the Right Honorable the Earle of Darby', Bodleian, MS Rawlinson 146B, fo. 67; Flynn 1995c: 134–5), in the event 220 persons, most of them unofficial hangers-on, had taken advantage of the Earl ambassador's liberality (Coward 33). When the Earl at length departed Paris for England on 10 March 1585, his train had been considerably and suspiciously depleted, many of his fellow travellers having remained behind on the continent, to the dismay of the council. Implicitly reprimanding a peer of the realm, as years later they recalled his 1585 embassy, they noted that on this occasion 'divers evill disposed personnes had intruded and thrust themselves into the company of his Lordship's traine and followers, purposing under collour thereof to convey themselves beyond the seas' (Privy Council to Derby, 17 February 1588, *APC* 15.378).

4

Available evidence prompting conjecture at this point is *A sheaf of Miscellany Epigrams Written in Latin by J. D. Translated by J. Main D. D.* These poems, published by Humphrey Moseley in 1652 and for the first time since the seventeenth century by the Donne *Variorum* (8.255–69, in a special appendix not endorsing the translations' authenticity), remain the most significant, though still widely unacknowledged, problem facing students of Donne's education. Their treatment by

Donne scholars up to 1995 is summarized in the *Variorum* (8.472–80), mainly detailing a controversy about whether the poems are spurious, mere forgeries by Jasper Mayne ('*J. Main D. D.*'); or instead are Mayne's actual translations based on lost Latin originals by Donne.

The signal facts are these:

(1) Donne, in a Latin Letter to Sir Henry Goodere, asked for the return of '*epigrammata mea Latina*', listing these among writings he had sent to Goodere but intended to revise or destroy as he thought about his return to public life in the new reign of James I (Donne 1633*b*: 353);

(2) Humphrey Moseley, on 15 March 1650, applied for a licence to publish '*Fasciculus poematum & Epigramatum miscellaneorum*, by Dr Jno Donne late Deane of St Pauls' (*Stationers Register* 1.423), presumably the Latin originals we now have only in Mayne's English;

(3) in the 1652 issue of Donne's *Paradoxes, Problemes, Essayes, Characters*, Moseley published Mayne's translations (Donne 1652: 88–103); in 1654 Moseley published a catalogue bound in at the ends of books he was then publishing (as in a Harvard University, Houghton Library copy of Philip Massinger's *Three New Playes* [London: Humphrey Moseley, 1655]), listing Mayne's translations among his stock of titles already for sale (A2ᵛ) and also, in a separate section of the catalogue headed 'Books I do purpose to print very speedily', advertising imminent publication of Donne's Latin originals, '*Fasciculus Poematum & Epigrammatum Miscelaneorum Authore Iohanne Donne*' (A8ᵛ);

(4) a 1656 version of this catalogue (found in a Harvard University, Houghton Library copy of Thomas Blount's *Glossographia* [London: Humphrey Moseley, 1656]) not only again listed Mayne's translations in *Paradoxes, Problemes, Essayes, Characters* among his stock of titles for sale (a2ᵛ), but also made a separate listing of the *Fasciculus* under the heading 'Bookes lately printed for Humphrey Moseley' (a8);

(5) in 1658 William London published a '*Catalogue of The most vendible Books in England*', listing not only Mayne's translations in the 1652 edition (V2ᵛ) but also (in a separate section headed 'Hebrew, Greek, and Latin Bookes') 'D. *Donn Fasciculus Poematum & Epigrammatum Miscelaneorum*' (Gg1ʳ)—moreover, London's preface claims that for his list of Latin books in particular 'I only take such as come in my way…to my own knowledg usually sold in most places of repute in the Country' (C1ʳ); and

(6) a 1660 version of Moseley's catalogue (found in a University of Pennsylvania, Van Pelt Library copy of Massinger's *Three New Playes*), in addition to reprinting the material appearing in earlier catalogues (cf. a2ᵛ and a8), added another section of 'Bookes now in the Presse, and to be Printed', listing for imminent availability a third, combined edition of the Latin poems accompanied by

Mayne's translations: '*Fasciculus Poematum et Epigramatum Miscelaneorum Authore Johanne Dome* [sic] D. D. and Englished by *Jasper Maine*, Doctor in Divinity' (B7ᵛ).

These facts offer compelling evidence that Donne did write Latin Epigrams and that, even though no copy of them is extant, except purported translations by Mayne in *Paradoxes, Problemes, Essayes, Characters* (1652), Moseley not only had obtained authorization to publish Donne's Latin originals but also advertised them for sale in three different editions by 1660. These advertisements, along with London's independent advertisement, indicate that Mayne's translations were based on Donne's Latin originals, unfortunately themselves not extant (Flynn 1984: 126–7).

Further, important internal evidence sharpens the relevance of these poems to the period of Donne's education, since a number of them refer to the 1585 siege of Antwerp by the Duke of Parma, describing unmistakably, with detail and precision, unique features of the siege works at Antwerp and events that had taken place there by May 1585 (on the conduct of this siege see Motley 1.157–60). Five of Mayne's translations testify that Donne's Latin must have described Parma's encampment at Calloo, with the construction of a town where on high ground a forest had stood (*Variorum* 8.260). A second group of five Epigrams describe the artificial creation of a river, undoubtedly the twelve-mile canal Parma had dug from Calloo to his source of supplies at Steeken (8.261). A third series of five Epigrams suggest that Donne's Latin had described the general inundation caused by the defenders of the city, who had spectacularly opened sluices near Saftingen, inundating the fertile plain nearly to the gates of Antwerp, with the idea of hampering, if not preventing, a successful siege, so that only steeples, treetops, and castle turrets rose above the waters, while whole villages of ordinary houses disappeared (8.261–2). And a fourth group of five Epigrams describe the meadows surrounding Calloo, where Spanish forces had tented while building the encampment, now covered over by the flood (8.262–3). These phenomena, unique to the siege of Antwerp, are all clearly described in Mayne's translations of Donne's Latin Epigrams. It is far-fetched to suppose that Mayne fabricated this pattern of arcane details in translations made after Donne's death; more likely they were included first in Donne's Latin. While it is conceivable that Donne's descriptions were based on someone else's written account, no such basis is apparent; more likely (as with most of Donne's later, English Epigrams about military occurrences) they testify to his eyewitness experience.

Mention must be made of a peculiarity of Mayne's translations that has prompted much misguided critical conjecture. While they make no direct mention of the Spanish siege of Antwerp, in poems that describe distinctive features of that 1585 siege, some of them do mention a few much later events, mainly a Dutch siege of 'Dukes-Wood', evidently referring to the 1629 siege of s'Hertogenbosch (or Bois-le-Duc). By 1629 Donne was the 57-year-old dean of St Paul's and unlikely to have been

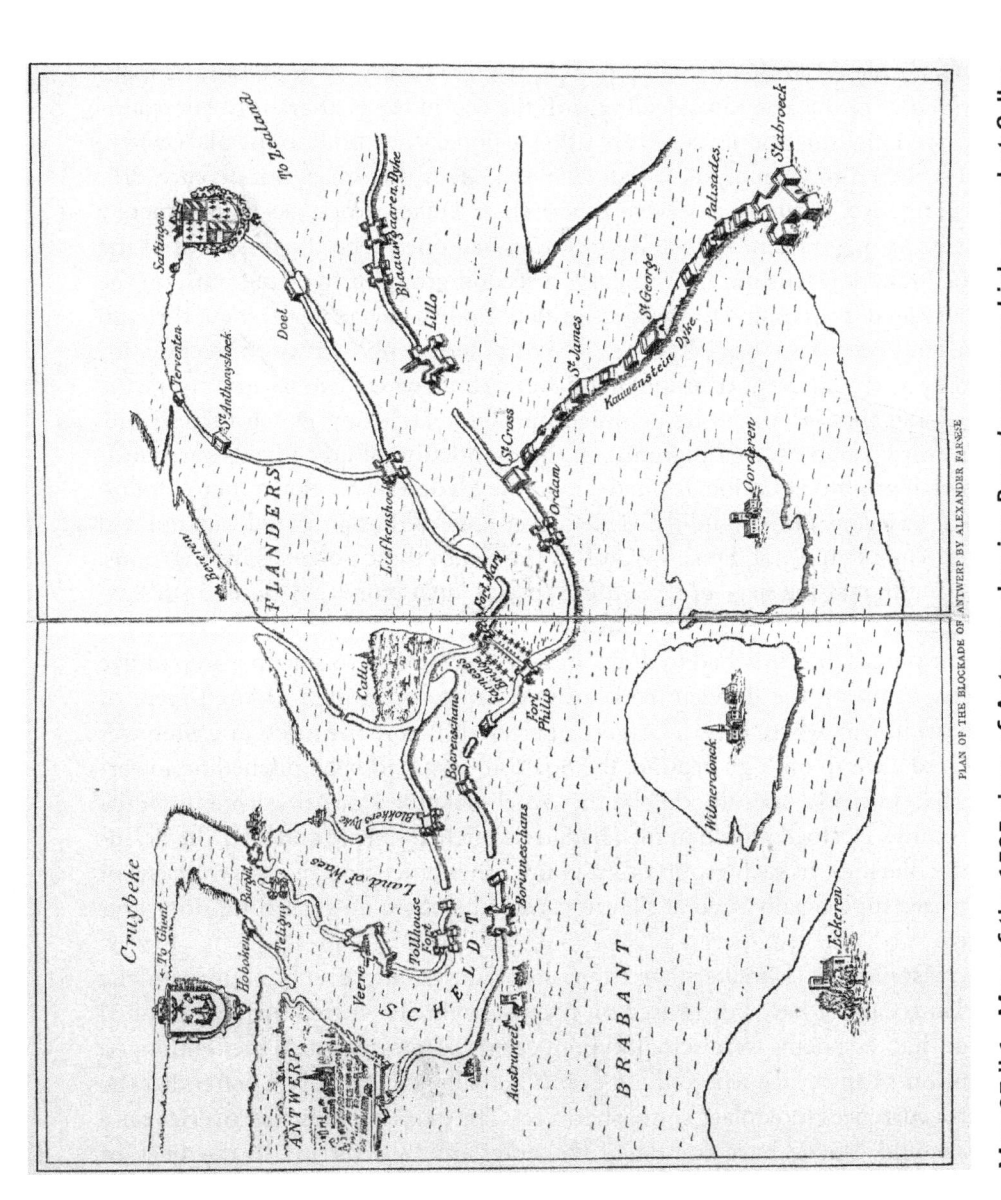

Map 27.II.1. Map of the 1585 siege of Antwerp, showing Parma's camp on high ground at Calloo, the surrounding flooded plain, and the canal dug between Calloo and Steeken, all described in the translations of Donne's Latin Epigrams. (Back endpaper of Jervis Wegg, *The Decline of Antwerp under Philip of Spain* [London: Methuen, 1924].)

present at a siege or still to have been writing Latin Epigrams. In any case, we know that Donne spent 1629 in England. Since Donne cannot have been in the Netherlands at the siege of s'Hertogenbosch, scholars have reasoned that Mayne's translations must be spurious (see e.g. scholarship summarized in *Variorum* 8.473–7).

However, these references to the siege of s'Hertogenbosch, though some are prominently placed in the titles of a few poems, are clearly unrelated to the main subject matter of the Epigrams dealing with the war in the Netherlands. For example, the five Epigrams about Calloo are titled 'Upon a town built in the place where a wood grew; From whence 'tis called *Dukes-Wood*, or the *Burse*'. But no such dramatic change ever occurred at s'Hertogenbosch or 'Dukes-Wood', so-named merely because of its magnificent park and forest that had once been the residence of the dukes of Brabant (Heinsius 27). Similarly, a second group of five Epigrams, on the canal excavated from Calloo to Steeken, is titled 'Upon a navigable River cut through a Town built out of a Wood'. But the siege of s'Hertogenbosch was in fact distinguished by a very different triumph of art over nature, where two natural rivers, the Dommel and the Aa, had to be dammed up by the attacking Dutch forces (ibid. 50–1). A third group of five Epigrams, on the inundation of green fields surrounding the high ground at Calloo, is titled 'Upon the Medows over-flown there'. But no terrain at s'Hertogenbosch, unlike Calloo, ever appeared as an island, surrounded by water. The mention of 'Dukes-Wood' in the last of these poems is incongruous, considering that at the siege of s'Hertogenbosch Dutch pioneers laboured successfully to prevent the flooding of their siege works, founded not on verdant fields but on swampy areas they first had to drain and fill (ibid. 48–53). A fourth group of five Epigrams, again on the flooded fields around Antwerp, is titled 'Upon a piece of ground ore-flown, where once a Leaguer quartered'. Before the forest at Calloo was turned into a camp on high ground, the Spanish tents had been pitched on lower-lying, adjacent fields, later flooded by the Dutch defenders of Antwerp; but Dutch tents around s'Hertogenbosch in 1629 had to be pitched during and after the draining of the marshes. In each group of Epigrams, phenomena peculiar to the siege of Antwerp are superficially sited at s'Hertogenbosch, where no such conditions ever occurred.

The reasoning of scholars, that translations describing events of 1629 in the Netherlands cannot have been based on poems originally written by Donne, failed to notice that the poems were actually about events of 1585, although they contained no mention of the place where these events actually occurred, but pretended the unique occurrences took place somewhere else. The question these discoveries raise is: why would Mayne have translated the Epigrams by referring to the siege of Antwerp as some other battle?

A possible answer to this question is suggested by another bibliographical fact, a listing by Anthony à Wood among Donne's publications, following his brief biography of Donne in *Athenae Oxoniensis*: '*Fasciculus Poematum & Epigrammatum Miscellaneorum*. Translated into English by *Jasp. Mayne*, D. D. with this title, *A sheaf of miscellany Epigrams*. Lond. 1632. oct.' (Wood 1.475). No copy of such a 1632 edition is known to be extant. But Wood's 1632 dating of the translations makes sense in relation to those events of 1629 that Mayne evidently referenced, inserting them into poems actually about events of 1585. These references to the siege of s'Hertogenbosch would still have been current in the minds of the translator and his readers in 1632. In fact, the history of the siege of s'Hertogenbosch had then just been written and published by Daniel Heinsius at Louvain in 1631. It seems unlikely that Mayne would have included these topical references twenty years later, when they had no currency and their import would have been obscure. Moreover, in 1632 Mayne and John Donne the younger were students together at Christ Church College, Oxford. Mayne would certainly have been more likely to translate Latin Epigrams in 1632 at Oxford than in 1652, when his career as a poet was finished and he had directed his literary energies to the writing of pamphlets and sermons. On the whole, we have reason to credit Wood's dating of the translations in 1632 for all these reasons, but especially because it begins to make sense of the allusions to s'Hertogenbosch. Mayne's motive for replacing Antwerp with s'Hertogenbosch, and replacing 1585 with 1629, may involve the awkwardness of publishing at London in 1632 poems by the late Dean of St Paul's that might have revealed to informed and careful readers Donne's presence among Spanish forces in the camp of the Duke of Parma at the siege of Antwerp in 1585.

5

While Donne's translated Latin Epigrams provide evidence of his presence at Antwerp in the spring of 1585, they are significant too in providing some insight into the nature of his education prior to his twelfth year. The poems dealing with the siege of Antwerp must have been written after the events they report, but others may well have been written earlier, while Donne was still in England. In any case, the Latin Epigrams may also reflect the influence of Jasper Heywood and the Jesuits on Donne's early schooling. The connection is supported not only by the tradition in Donne's family of writing epigrams, but also by the particular way in which sixteenth-century Jesuit education was infused with humanist pedagogical values. The Jesuits were like other humanist educators in stressing the study of Greek and Latin. But the *ratio studiorum* of the Jesuits included a uniquely strong emphasis on the writing of Latin epigrams, often imitations or translations of poems from the *Greek Anthology* (Hutton 16–18). Prior to entering Donne's life, Heywood as a Jesuit had been a teacher of pupils studying this curriculum for a considerable portion of his nearly two decades in Germany, from 1564 until 1581.

The first nineteen translations, preceding the poems about Antwerp, constitute a distinct group among the entire 'sheaf of Miscellany Epigrams'. Based on classical topics common in the *Greek Anthology* (Hutton 64), they may represent work designed by Heywood or done under Heywood's tutelage before Donne's twelfth year; they were certainly the sort of exercises Heywood had assigned his students in Germany. Or they may, like those poems dealing with Antwerp, be products of the period just after the spring of 1585. In any case, even in translation, these Epigrams suggest that in his earliest poems Donne could already combine considerable learning and skill with a satirical sense of humour common to the members of his family, in line with the practice of Sir Thomas More, probably the first to compose such epigrams in England (Flynn 1995c: 184–91). Dramatic effects in the grouping of the epigrams, as well as complex metaphoric structures, are organized here by an overarching thematic consistency foreshadowing the more ambitious work of Donne's poems in the 1590s.

That Donne evidently wrote Epigrams about the siege of Antwerp also prompts us to consider prospects available for his continuing education away from Oxford after the end of Michaelmas 1584. For a descendant of the Catholic humanist Sir Thomas More, religious persecution at Elizabethan Oxford was not the only reason to study on the continent rather than at an English university, particularly in view of Walton's plausible mention that Donne already knew French and Latin by the early 1580s (1675: 11). While More himself had spoken no French, and had written satirically of the penchant among young Englishmen for aping French manners and speech, it was always true that religious, political, and general cultural considerations made experience of things French a near requirement for anyone who would frequent a sixteenth-century royal court.

More had also criticized hidebound scholasticism at the universities; and to a visitor from the French court the Elizabethan university seemed shallow compared with continental universities and academies. This view of Oxford was shared by young English aristocrats such as Philip Sidney and Fulke Greville, as well as by such a cosmopolitan scholar as John Dee (Yates 239). (Alexandra Gajda details similar criticisms by Gabriel Harvey, Edward Lord Herbert, and Humphrey Gilbert; see Ch. 27.I.) Many promising English students had become fugitives or perennial travellers after the change of religions, partly for religious reasons but also simply to take up more desirable careers in various continental centres of learning. By the 1580s it had become more and more fashionable to sojourn at such universities and also in the more elite aura of the academies established in various places after the example of the Medici court's Florentine Academy. Catherine de' Medici had encouraged the formation of such academies as adjuncts to French universities, and these schools acted as magnets to attract nobility and gentry who sought the best in educational opportunity.

For Elizabethan fugitives and travellers, one of the most attractive, though rather old-fashioned, features of the French academies was their inclination towards religious toleration. In the experience of Donne's family, the early court of Edward VI had practised toleration within its own ambit, though this was before promulgation of the decrees of the Council of Trent. Nevertheless, the French academies likewise served to test whether some rapprochement was still possible across hardened confessional lines. At the Palace Academy of Henri III, as at the academy founded in emulation by the Huguenot prince Henri de Navarre, Catholic and Protestant savants and students mingled in an atmosphere of latter-day Erasmian toleration. This feature of the French academy movement, ridiculed by adherents of the Holy League, was widely known in England after 1577 through successive editions of Pierre de la Primaudaye's *L'Academie Françoise*, which reported the supposed conversations of four young noblemen who form an academy designed to open a door to pacification in a time of civil and religious conflict. Despite the Council of Trent, the Massacre of St Bartholomew's Day, and the founding of the Holy League, the French academies represented this irenic tradition into the mid-1580s. Concerned about his nephew's education and cognizant of these things, Heywood may have made arrangements for Donne to study in France or Belgium. Several writers (e.g. Sparrow 1931: 140–51; Bald 1970: 52) have conjectured that in this period occurred Donne's early travels to Spain and Italy, mentioned but obviously misdated by his first biographer (Walton 1675: 14–15).

6

Archival records yield no trace of Donne's activities between the spring of 1585 and his admittance to Thavies Inn in the spring of 1591. There is nothing to suggest that he ever returned to Oxford after Michaelmas term 1584. Our only evidence about his life in these years is his earliest portrait (a portrait miniature, probably early work by Isaac Oliver), dated 'anno dni. 1591. aetatis suae 18' and extant only in the form of a posthumous frontispiece engraving for the 1635 edition of his *Poems*. The engraving shows Donne dressed in a long-breasted doublet in an Italian style, cut from soldierly plain cloth, with a plain band. His earring, like other features of his dress and bearing, again evokes the military but also the Catholic: a cross hanging from his ear. Devotional yet impudent, unthinkable in the portrait of a Protestant, this earring has the cavalier style of Spanish and French *ligueur* captains, those 'hard riding, loose tongued, yet devoted' adherents to 'the religion of the swordsmen of Europe' (Mathew 356). Donne's ensemble in the portrait thus speaks not of the fashionable foppery some have described (e.g. Walton 1675: 73–4), but of a 'language of the sword', an idiom Tudor Catholic Englishmen used to express dissident political and religious commitment (M. James 4; Neuschel 65). He stands in military posture and costume, with a sword not hung as a fashionable adornment but rather held up by its hilt as an emblem of honour. This posture, together with his motto, *Antes muerto que mudado* ('Rather dead than changed'), suggests the swearing of an oath, an effect enhanced by the further inclusion of a coat of arms designating Donne an eldest son of descent on his father's side from the Dwns of Kidwelly, Carmarthenshire, a family that had borne swordsmen time out of mind (Bald 1970: 20–1).

The date inscribed on the portrait roughly coincides with the date of Donne's admission to Thavies Inn. This date and Donne's motto in the miniature together provide a context for his accompanying military image, a context suggesting that the image refers retrospectively to earlier experience rather than to the present and future student at the Inns of Court. The motto quotes words spoken by someone about to do the opposite of what has recently been pledged. The line of verse is re-gendered from Jorge de Montemayor's *Diana* (a romance much read at European courts), where it appears as the oath of a shepherd's mistress, ironically quoted by the shepherd after her marriage to someone else (Montemayor 1–3). So the eager swordsman, holding up his sword, swears an oath of steadfastness. But Diana was not faithful.

The subsequent capstone of Donne's formal educational experience was the period he spent enrolled at law schools. Thavies Inn was an Inn of Chancery, a preliminary school offering a year-long programme preceding entry into Lincoln's Inn, an Inn of Court. The records of Thavies Inn are lost, so that all we know about Donne's time there is the indication, in his Lincoln's Inn admission record of 6 May 1592, that he had come from Thavies Inn (Bald 1970: 55 n. 1).

For the following two years he attended some required sessions of moots and readings at Lincoln's Inn, held during the three 'learning vacations' or intervals between sessions of the courts each year (Shapiro 1930: 833). However, these years were marked by repeated suspensions of ordinary activities at the Inn. In mid-August 1592 a serious outbreak of the plague had shut down the courts and many law-school functions, a state of affairs lasting until 6 February 1593, when, at the first meeting of the Lincoln's Inn council in eight months, Donne was appointed for one year, retroactively from November 1592, a Master of the Revels (Bald 1970: 56). By the time of this appointment, however, it was too late for Donne to perform his office, which was mainly an assignment for Christmas 1592. A letter written from Rome to Jasper Heywood at Naples, on 13 February 1593 (ARSI, Neap. 4/II, fo. 450^v), suggests that Donne at the time of his appointment may have been in Italy (Bald 1970: 56–7 n. 1). Donne had reached the age of 21 at about this time; and, although he did not acknowledge receipt of any inheritance until June 1593, he may have begun immediately to act with some independence. He did not attend Lincoln's Inn during the Easter vacation (7–27 April) of 1593, following which, the plague appearing even worse than the preceding year, the Inn practically shut down again; so that for more than half the period of Donne's enrolment Lincoln's Inn was actually closed or he was otherwise occupied.

Moreover, despite his appointment as Steward of Christmas in November 1594, Donne again failed to perform his office and was fined for not doing so (Bald 1970: 57). A disaster for Donne's family may help explain his desultory attendance and even perhaps his incurring a fine for never acting as Steward in 1594: in May 1593 his brother Henry had been arrested and imprisoned for harbouring William Harrington, a priest, in his chamber at Thavies Inn. Henry was committed to the Clink prison, where under questioning he admitted that Harrington had heard his confession; within a month, in plague-ridden Newgate, Henry Donne died, having been transferred there from the Clink. Harrington was hanged, disembowelled, and quartered on 14 February 1594.

All told, Donne is listed as having attended only three of the six vacations law students were required to attend during their first three years at Lincoln's Inn (Shapiro 1930: 833). According to Walton, while at Lincoln's Inn Donne spent considerable time studying other subjects than the law: 'His Mother and those to whose care he was committed, were watchful to improve his knowledge, and to that end appointed him Tutors both in the *Mathematicks*, and in all the other *Liberal Sciences*', as well as 'Principles of the *Romish Church*' (1675: 12–13). Whatever Donne actually did while he was enrolled, he clearly cannot have studied law with any hope of passing the Bar; however, in his later publications and Letters he demonstrates more than a passing interest in and acquaintance with various legal matters. In any case, his absence from Inn records after 1594 suggests that his formal connection to Lincoln's Inn lapsed until his appointment there as Divinity Reader in 1616.

7

One conclusion to be drawn from this survey of Donne's education is that the role in it of Jasper Heywood, SJ, warrants further research and consideration. Considerable attention has already been given to a possible Jesuit influence on Donne's writings, but such study has not yet incorporated awareness of achievements in English history beginning, for example, with the work of John Bossy in the 1970s; nor important advances in the history of Jesuit education and Jesuit spirituality of the late sixteenth century, reflected, for example, in the work of John O'Malley, SJ. To gain a better sense of what Donne's education involved, these topics need also to be treated in the perspective of Donne's family traditions in Renaissance humanism, going back to Sir Thomas More.

CHAPTER 28.1

DONNE'S MILITARY CAREER

ALBERT C. LABRIOLA

DONNE's military career spans 1596–7, including two expeditions against Spain: the former a maritime assault and landing at Cadiz; the latter an ill-fated venture in the Azores, often called the Islands voyage. For both expeditions Donne was a voluntary or gentleman volunteer who served with the Earl of Essex, a sometime favourite of Queen Elizabeth I and a courtier whose vibrant personality, impulsive behaviour, and headstrong manner elicited a following of young men. Though a soldier, Donne spent most of his time on board a vessel. He may have landed at Cadiz and engaged in combat against Spanish defenders of the city, also participating in its capture and despoliation. But Donne's references to these expeditions emphasize life at sea and maritime warfare, not assaults overland. If, therefore, Donne saw action on the ground at Cadiz, he did not write graphically about his experiences. He may have been in the rearguard, not the vanguard.

Early in 1596 England was planning an assault against Spain and assembling a force that would be launched by April. The fleet commander was Lord Charles Howard of Effingham, Lord High Admiral of England; the vice-admiral was Sir Walter Ralegh; and the Lord General of the ground expedition was Robert Devereux, second Earl of Essex. Some young gentlemen from the Inns of Court and various social circles joined the ground expedition to serve with Essex, whose colourful manner was a source of appeal; others joined to serve with Ralegh or Effingham; still others represented magnates not even sailing with the expedition. It seemed of some importance to be involved, no matter what one's political faction or standing may have been. In his biography of 1640 Walton indicates that Donne 'waited upon'

Essex (1658: 12). By that assertion, he may mean that Donne, then 23 years old, served directly with the Lord Commander, perhaps as a member of his staff. Other commentators are more circumspect, for they interpret 'waited upon' to mean that Donne presented himself to Essex for service in the land force. Still others, who deem Walton to be an unreliable biographer, argue that there is no evidence that Donne even sailed on the same vessel with Essex. Perhaps Donne was emboldened to volunteer because of friendships. He possibly knew Henry Wotton, whose time at Oxford overlapped with Donne's. Or he may have known Henry Cuffe, whose brother was with Donne at Lincoln's Inn. Wotton and Cuffe were serving Essex as secretaries (Bald 1970: 80; Flynn 1995b: 193–201).

Actually Donne's inclination to military service is manifested in the earliest portrait of him, taken when he was 18 years old. The lost portrait miniature of 1591 was engraved by William Marshall for the 1635 edition of *Poems, by J. D.* The portrait shows Donne with his right hand holding the hilt of a sword pointed downward. His earring resembles a cross. And in Spanish, the motto of the portrait reads *Antes muerto que mudado* ('Rather dead than changed'), an affirmation of militant and military honour (Flynn 1995c: 2). Perhaps Donne is pledging himself as a swordsman to uphold the honour of England against Spain. But Donne's motives as a gentleman volunteer were probably more diverse. Typically, commentators cite his Verse Letter *Calm*, which may have been addressed to Christopher Brooke, his lifelong friend:

> Whether a rotten state, and hope of gaine,
> Or to disuse mee from the queasie paine
> Of being belov'd, and loving, or the thirst
> Of honour, or faire death, out pusht mee first,
> I lose my end.
>
> (ll. 39–43)

The foregoing passage indicates a depleted financial state, an expectation of plunder and booty, the wish to escape the emotional upheaval or social pastime of loving and being loved, a quest for personal honour on the battlefield, and an honourable reputation for having died gloriously in war. With other gentlemen of his social circle in the early 1590s, Donne may have sought to test his mettle and to claim trophies and prizes of martial victory, thereby proving himself a gallant not only in arts of loving but also in acts of soldiering. And the patriotic motive is cited in the Verse Letter *Storm*, definitely written to Christopher Brooke: 'England to whom we'owe, what we be, and have, / Sad that her sonnes did seeke a forraine grave' (ll. 9–10). In what follows—'From out her pregnant intrailes sigh'd a winde' (l. 13)—Donne may be ironically undercutting patriotic sentiment, or he may be suggesting that Mother Nature sighs because of the death of her progeny. In *Calm* and *Storm*, which were written during the 1597 expedition against the Azores, Donne may have been iterating motives not fully realized during the 1596 campaign at Cadiz.

Various events caused postponement of the expedition to Cadiz. Because Spanish forces captured Calais, there was uncertainty about whether this threat nearer to home would redirect the English expedition away from Spain and into northern France. The Queen, to the point of prolonged hesitancy, was uncertain about the objective of the expedition. Eventually sailing orders were issued, directing the expedition to Cadiz after more than 300 volunteers, including Donne presumably, had waited in readiness for several weeks before embarking in early June 1596. In two weeks the expedition arrived within view of Cadiz, where it remained for a few days before attacking the Spanish fleet in the harbour. Entering the inner harbour, the English fleet encountered four galleons blocking the narrow entrance. Barrages of cannon-fire between the English and the Spanish lasted for hours, until the English fleet concentrated on the *San Felipe*, the Spanish flagship. Ralegh recounts how his and other vessels sought to gain control of the Spanish flagship by grappling it. Because of high winds the effort miscarried; and the *San Felipe*, ablaze from English fireships, foundered, many of its soldiers and crew severely burned. They and most of the other Spaniards on board drowned unless first slain by bullets from Englishmen, chiefly from Ralegh's *Warspite*, and from the Dutch, allies whose vessels accompanied the English fleet. This gesture of mercy under the circumstances put the Spanish out of their misery (Bald 1970: 82–3).

Donne composed a six-line Epigram, *Ship*, probably from his observations of the burning vessel, whose damage may have been intensified by secondary explosions of its own powder kegs and by fires ignited by its own crew to prevent the capture of their ship. He also observed the Spanish soldiers and crew who, though suffering painful burns, tried to swim to safety:

> Out of a fired Ship, which by noe waie
> But drowning, could bee rescued from the flame,
> Some men leapt forth, and euer as they came
> Neer the foes ships did by their shott decaie.
> Soe all were lost, which in the Ship were founde
> They in the Sea being burnt, they in the burnt ship drownd.
>
> (*Variorum* 8.10)

The Epigram ostensibly supports the view that Donne was an eyewitness, though it is unclear whether he was in a squadron commanded by Essex, Ralegh, or Lord Thomas Howard. If this was not the account of a first-hand observer, then the reports of Donne's compatriots, who were eyewitnesses, generated the vivid details in the poem. Generically and tonally, however, this poem adapts features of Greek proverbial and Roman satirical epigrams. By such literary means Donne, ironically, may be commemorating the Spanish victims rather than celebrating the English victors. If, on the other hand, he is exulting in the consummate English victories—sinking the Spanish flagship and slaying most of the men on board—then he may

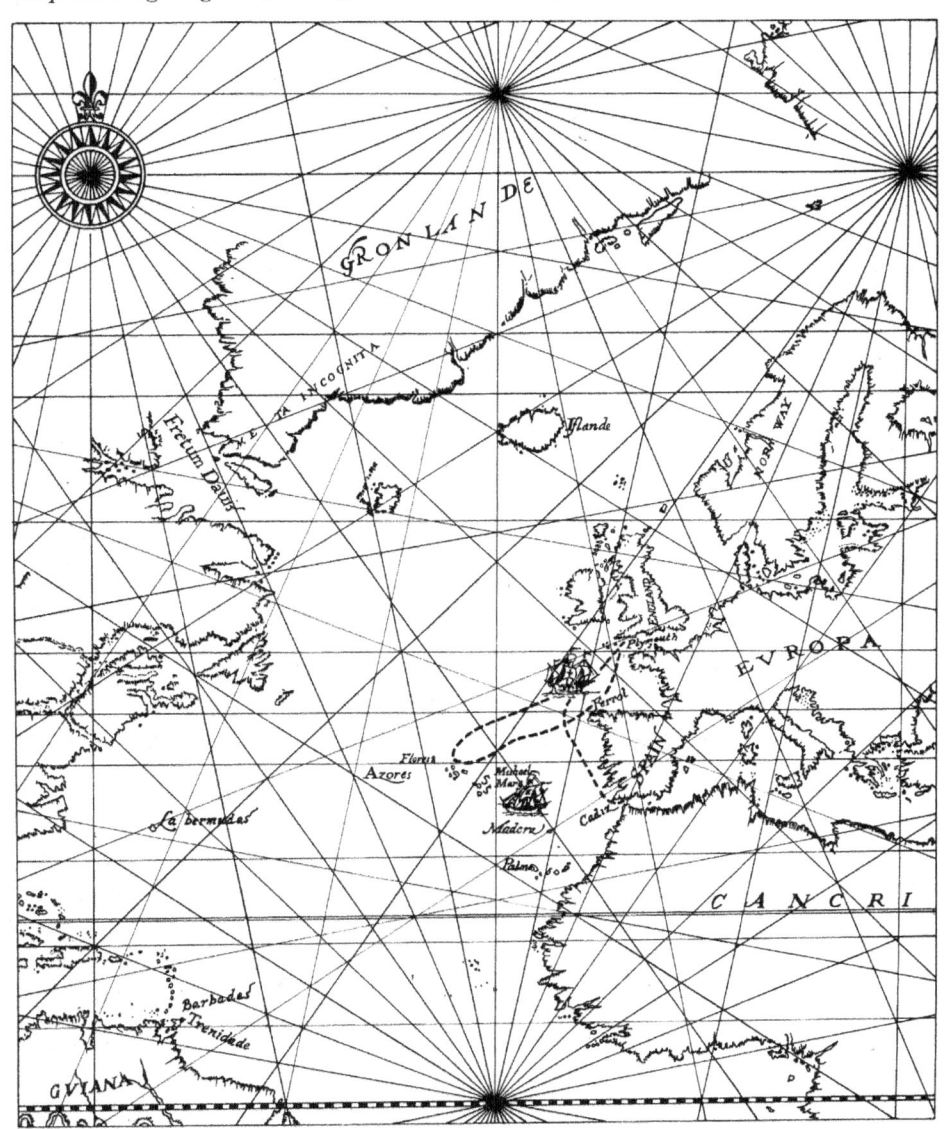

Map showing England, Cadiz, Ferrol and the Azores.

Map 28.I.1. Map of England, Cadiz, and the Azores, showing Donne's destinations in 1596 and 1597. (James Winny, *A Preface to John Donne* [Pearson Education Limited, © Longman Group Limited 1970,1981],19.)

be emphasizing his presence, perhaps participation, in just reprisal meted out to the hated Spaniards (see Ch. 8 for further discussion of this Epigram).

Landing on the peninsula under the headstrong leadership of Essex, approximately 800 soldiers moved towards the walls of Cadiz, but a Spanish military force blocked their entrance to the city. Rather than engaging the enemy in a frontal assault, the English forces executed a feint, whereby 200 of them under the command of Sir John Wingfield pretended to storm the gates of the city. Afterwards, feigning retreat in order to draw the Spanish defenders away from the entrance to the city, the 200 English soldiers unexpectedly reversed direction, this time augmented by the main body of 600 troops, who had been concealed. As he charged the gates of the city, Sir John Wingfield thrust his pike into a Spanish commander. Aided by small parties that had surmounted the walls, the English breached the entrance to the city and eventually also claimed the castle. Wingfield was immobilized by a leg wound; but having mounted a captured horse, he joined the battle in the plaza of the city where Essex and Sir Francis Vere had forged ahead. Atop the horse, Wingfield was a target of opportunity, dying from a bullet-wound to the head. Five days later he was interred at the cathedral of Cadiz (Bald 1970: 83-4). In memory of the heroic commander, Donne composed a six-line Epigram (*Wing*):

> Beyond th'old Pillers many'haue trauailed
> Towards the Suns cradle, and his throne, and bed.
> A fitter Piller our Earle did bestow
> In that late Iland; for he well did know
> Farther then Wingefield no man dares to go.
>
> (*Variorum* 8.8)

In the ancient world the Pillars of Hercules, the two mountains on either side of the Strait of Gibraltar connecting the Atlantic and the Mediterranean, signified the portal to discovery, to places uncharted and unknown. Adventurers exceeded these limits at their own peril. In commemorating Wingfield, Donne contends that a new pillar, that of heroism, has been established, a veritable limit unlikely to be exceeded. And because Felipe II of Spain presided over an empire whose imperialistic motto was *Plus Oultra* accompanied by a picture of the Pillars of Hercules, Donne may be taunting the Spanish, whose homeland Essex and Ralegh had pillaged. Simultaneously, Donne may be praising Wingfield, Essex, and Ralegh as exemplars of English national pride (Hester 1979: 203; 1986: 84; 1990*b*: 9). In the Epigram, 'the Suns cradle, and his throne, and bed' may signify, respectively, the East Indies, Africa, and the New World over which Spain sought hegemony, an enterprise that the English were counteracting (Flynn 1995*b*: 204).

In extolling Wingfield's heroism, however, Donne may be lionizing this English nobleman over Essex and Ralegh, both of whom he may have viewed as being enmeshed in political intrigue, ingratiating themselves with Elizabeth I, and projecting panache and self-aggrandizing heroics more staged than authentic. At the same time, Donne may be punning on the word 'pillar', inquiring, ironically, whether the English or the Spanish established the 'pillars' of 'pillaging'. Who are the greater pillagers, the conquistadors or the sea-dogs? In the Roman tradition of Martial, Donne's Epigram may be satirizing 'martial' pillaging, so that the so-called heroes suffer deflation by becoming comic caricatures (Hester 1986: 82–4; see also Ch. 8). At Cadiz, on the day after Wingfield's funeral, more than sixty men were dubbed knights, at least two of whom were possibly Donne's friends either at that time or afterwards, Sir Maurice Berkeley and Sir Edward Conway.

Though the attack on Cadiz was successful, Essex, who may have been impelled by the quest for personal glory, disregarded the plan that he and Sir Thomas Howard had devised for a later landing of the troops. When Howard followed Essex ashore and thereby abandoned the naval action, attention was diverted from the rich merchant fleet near Puerto da Santa Maria (Hammer 1997b: 199). Had it been plundered, the booty would have exceeded beyond measure what was acquired from the city. The Spanish, however, burned the merchant fleet on the evening of the English attack against Cadiz (ibid. 193–4).

When Cadiz was captured, looting at first was indiscriminate. Afterwards a more orderly process was established, whereby houses and districts were allocated to the officers and to the men. Items were plundered, or ransom was negotiated. By early July the English had departed from Cadiz, leaving it in flames. Shortly thereafter they landed at Faro, but the town was deserted; it was plundered and burned. Essex transported the bishop's library ('39 chestes of books... & certayne pictures'), which he granted to the Bodleian (Hammer 1997b: 199 n. 88), from that city. Two other towns, Corunna and Ferrol, which showed no evidence of shipping, were bypassed. Though Essex wished to redeploy the fleet towards the Azores, hoping to encounter the Spanish fleet laden with treasure from the West Indies, other officers demurred and the fleet headed home, eventually to Plymouth.

Despite the success at Cadiz, the plunder disappointed the Queen, who expressed concern that the booty fell chiefly into private hands. Ordering an investigation by Lord Burghley and Sir Robert Cecil, Elizabeth sought to learn how extensively the officers in the expedition prospered and why an inordinately high number of knighthoods had been awarded. The investigation exacerbated tensions and rivalries among the various noblemen and factions in several ways. For example, mariners complained that their booty was slight because the Spanish fleet was not captured. And reports after the victory at Cadiz divided the noblemen, especially Essex from Ralegh, rival claimants for the lion's share of the glory. Indeed, reports of the expedition, presumably exaggerated, recalled Sir Francis Drake, who had died about six months before the assault on Cadiz. In 1587 he had attacked the harbour of Cadiz. For this exploit and countless others he became the prototype of the Elizabethan sea-dog, to be emulated by successors (Hammer 1997b: 182–3).

If Donne himself were enriched by the expedition, there is no known historical record of his financial gain. Certainly, he was not knighted. After his return he continued to write poetry, composing *Sat4*, which may be dated to this period by internal evidence: 'Guianaes rarities' and 'the losse of Amyens' (ll. 22, 114). The former refers to Ralegh's journey to Guiana in 1595 and his record of travel there, *A Discoverie of the large, rich, and bewtiful Empire of Guiana* (1596); the latter refers to the 1597 Spanish capture of Amiens.

Early in 1597 an attack was being planned against Ferrol, where another Armada was being assembled and equipped for an invasion of England. A pre-emptive strike under the command of Essex was launched, and Lord Thomas Howard and Ralegh served as vice-admiral and rear-admiral, respectively. Many of the gentleman volunteers from the expedition to Cadiz served again, including Donne, but newcomers swelled the ranks of the land force to approximately 500. Like the volunteers for Cadiz, who lingered in port for weeks before the fleet embarked, the gentlemen endured long delays while vessels joined the fleet. Near mid-July the fleet, totalling more than 100 vessels, sailed from the harbour at Plymouth. Immediately, however, the weather turned foul, the fleet disintegrated, and gradually ships returned to port. Many men, seasick and dispirited, abandoned the enterprise (Bald 1970: 86–7).

Two of Donne's works—and a Prose Letter probably composed in August 1597—recount his experiences during and after the storm. In *Storm* Donne's description is richly graphic:

> The South and West winds joyn'd, and, as they blew,
> Waves like a rowling trench before them threw.
> Sooner then you read this line, did the gale,
> Like shot, not fear'd till felt, our sailes assaile;
> And what at first was call'd a gust, the same
> Hath now a stormes, anon a tempests name.
>
> (ll. 27–32)

Continuing, Donne writes of the disorientation, anxiety, and illness suffered by the men on the vessel:

> Sleepe is paines easiest salve, and doth fulfill
> All offices of death, except to kill.
> But when I wakt, I saw, that I saw not;
> I, and the Sunne, which should teach mee'had forgot
> East, West, Day, Night, and I could but say,
> If the'world had lasted, now it had been day.
> Thousands our noyses were, yet wee 'mongst all
> Could none by his right name, but thunder call:
> Lightning was all our light, and it rain'd more
> Then if the Sunne had drunke the sea before.

> Some coffin'd in their cabbins lye,'equally
> Griev'd that they are not dead, and yet must dye.
>
> (ll. 35–46)

Donne adds that the men on board noted:

> the ships sicknesses, the Mast
> Shak'd with this ague, and the Hold and Wast
> With a salt dropsie clog'd, and all our tacklings
> Snapping, like too-high-stretched treble strings.
>
> (ll. 53–6)

Chiefly descriptive, the foregoing passage nevertheless hints at the proliferating analogies or witty resemblances for which Donne is best known in his amatory and divine poetry.

Though a soldier, Donne's experiences as a voyager were more exciting and vividly recounted than his service on land. Having returned to Plymouth, Donne composed a Prose Letter, probably in August 1597, to an unknown recipient. In the Letter Donne indicates that he was among '150 land soldiers', whose 'stinke' was oppressive over '20 dayes of so very bad wether'. During the storm at sea Donne himself overheard one of the 'marriners' pray 'god help vs'. In the same Letter Donne laments the dishabille of the gentleman voluntaries, whose plumage and gaudy accoutrements were 'much melted' by the storm (E. M. Simpson 1948: 304). The 'bad wether' to which Donne refers may indicate that he was in Sir Thomas Howard's squadron, for most of the vessels in the squadrons of Essex and Ralegh arrived back at Plymouth or Falmouth nine days after they had embarked on or about 10 July. Only Howard's squadron spent sufficient time at sea, twenty-one days, to experience the long-term 'bad wether' to which Donne refers (R. E. Bennett 1942: 603).

Despite the setback, Essex and Ralegh sought the Queen's approval to attack the Spanish Main rather than Ferrol, but she refused. Donne's four-line Epigram *Cales*, the first word in the title referring to Cadiz, reflects the jaunty expectations of a strike, fuelled by reports from Ralegh, Lawrence Keymis (his lieutenant), and Sir Anthony Shirley (another Elizabethan sea-dog), against the Spanish settlements in South America, most notably Guiana, or the Spanish vessels laden with treasure as they were returning to the homeland:

> If you from spoyle of th'old worlds fardest end
> To the new world your kindled valors bend
> What brave Examples then do prove it trew
> That one things end doth still begine a new.
>
> (*Variorum* 8.7)

After such high expectations were dashed, Donne recounts his disappointment in a Verse Letter to Rowland Woodward, a friend:

> Guyanaes harvest is nip'd in the spring,
> I feare; And with us (me thinkes) Fate deales so
> As with the Jewes guide God did; he did show
> Him the rich land, but bar'd his entry in:
> Oh, slownes is our punishment and sinne.
> Perchance, these Spanish businesse being done,
> Which as the Earth between the Moone and Sun
> Eclipse the light which Guyana would give,
> Our discontinu'd hopes we shall retrive.
>
> (*RWSlumb* ll. 18–26)

Departing in August with a force of soldiers and vessels fewer than for the attack mounted against Cadiz, Essex and his fellow commanders suffered misfortune, notably turbulent weather that dispersed the fleet and damaged several of its vessels, including the flagships of Ralegh and Essex. The planned attack at Ferrol was interrupted; but Essex, wrongly believing that the Spanish fleet had abandoned the harbour and then sailed to the Azores, hastily travelled to the islands.

Not locating the Spanish fleet there, the English vessels, however, lapsed into a standstill, becalmed for approximately two days in the extreme heat. Donne's Verse Letter *Calm* laments that the 'ships rooted bee' (l. 10). The soldiers, having removed their 'trimme', not unlike actors divesting themselves of their costumes after 'ended playes', were on deck amidst 'Feathers and dust' or their discarded plumage (ll. 13, 14, 18). Placed out to dry on the 'tackling' were the washed clothes of mariners and soldiers alike, 'seamens ragges' (ll. 16, 15). Donne's poem likens the heat inside the vessel to 'hot Ovens', and walking on the deck was like being 'on the coales to burn' (ll. 28, 32). Some of the men, suffering from tropical delirium, jumped overboard but died 'in great fishes jawes', whereas others dived into the sea for relief, but found it was a 'brimstone Bath' (ll. 24, 30).

Essex, who had instructed Ralegh to proceed after him to the Azores, waited off the islands for the other English squadron to rendezvous with him. Passages in *Calm* may indicate that Donne was in Ralegh's squadron during the lull, because 'those Iles which wee / Seeke, when wee can move' are obviously not yet within view (ll. 9–10). Separated from 'friends' and 'foes', Donne by such language may be indicating that he was with the flotilla outside contact with English allies and Spanish adversaries alike (l. 21). Within a week of the lull, however, Ralegh did rejoin Essex at Flores. Remaining there to resupply his fleet with fresh water, Ralegh and his forces were again separated, because Essex sailed ahead to another island. To rendezvous again with Essex, whom he thought was at Fayal, Ralegh travelled there. Unsuccessful in locating his compatriot, he nevertheless landed and marched his contingent of 500 soldiers approximately four miles to the city. Because of staunch resistance that demoralized the English soldiers the Spaniards maintained control until they ceased defending Fayal, which fell to the attackers. Soon after the fall of the city Essex arrived, and the two fleets were reunited. There were some other successes during this expedition—Essex captured Villa Franca, and some Spanish vessels with treasure were captured—but the English failed to engage the main Spanish fleet, which evaded one encounter after another by moving swiftly and stealthily (Bald 1970: 91–2). There is no record in Donne's writings of the assault overland at Fayal, of the capture of Villa Franca, or of Essex's knighting of warriors after that enterprise, most notably the younger Thomas Egerton, whose father was the Lord Keeper of the Great Seal, Master of the Rolls, and a Privy Councillor, and who became the Lord Chancellor. For Egerton the elder Donne was to serve as secretary. This appointment, late in 1597, marked the end of Donne's military career.

Though Donne's military experiences were limited, his accounts of such service, whether in prose or poetry, are graphically descriptive, rich with near-journalistic detail. The poems, especially *Storm* and *Calm*, resemble the Satires in their harsh cadences and use of heroic verse. From these accounts one may infer that Donne was not in the forefront of action, whether at sea or on land. At least, his writings do not suggest the immediate dangers of combat, of firing a weapon or being fired upon; and the anxieties that derive from life-threatening circumstances, except the storm at sea, do not suffuse his works. But he was proximate enough, in the rearguard or in the reserve force on land or on a troop transport as a voyager, to see and hear battles and to converse with the mariners and soldiers who were more fully involved in the fighting during these expeditions of 1596 and 1597. More than likely Donne travelled on different vessels during these attacks, whether in a squadron under Essex, Ralegh, or Lord Thomas Howard. From his writings one may gather that Donne's attitudes towards each of these noblemen are ambivalent; or, if not ambivalent, then at different times in his life Donne may have favoured one nobleman over others, changing his preferences for reasons not fully known or documented. At one point Donne may have favoured Ralegh and the prospect of piracy along the Spanish Main, whereas on other occasions he may have supported Essex, who advocated strikes against the Spanish homeland. Both Essex and Ralegh, of course, eventually fell from power. And Donne, even as a young man observing their self-serving motives, may have appraised these noblemen as unduly ambitious warmongers. Not to be overlooked is the possibility that Donne may have been chastened by his view of war and its toll on combatants, English and Spanish alike. Disillusioned, he may have abandoned any wish to garner the spoils of war and to enhance his reputation by military exploits. At the same time, he may have rejected the use of war, the quest for glory, and the distribution of booty as manifestations of struggles for preferment at court.

Donne's negative views of the ravages of war may date back to his earlier years, when, as an adolescent in April or May 1585, he apparently viewed the siege works constructed around Antwerp by the Duke of Parma. Latin Epigrams by Donne, though the originals are not extant, were translated by Jasper Mayne. These detailed observations suggest first-hand knowledge of the siege (Flynn 1995c: 140–5; see Ch. 27.II).

After his participation at Cadiz and in the Islands expedition Donne may have rejected the acts of war to return to the arts of love. *ElWar*, though commentators disagree on a date of composition, was probably written before the attack on Cadiz, or so the weight of historical and bibliographical evidence suggests (*Variorum* 2.LXV–LXVII). Donne may be celebrating his return to the amatory relationships and to the pastime of composing poems, the social life that he had abandoned in order to go to war (*Variorum* 2.648–9; DiPasquale 2007: 341). The opposite, however, may be true: *ElWar* is a leave-taking from social life to mark his entrance into battle. Riddled with allusions to martial enterprises, the poem, as its title indicates, wittily likens love to war. For example, the speaker celebrates the capture of Spanish treasure: 'And Midas ioyes our Spanish iourneys giue, / We touch all gold, but find no food to liue' (ll. 17–18). Moreover, the speaker laments: 'Long Voyages are long consumptions / And Ships are carts for executions' (ll. 25–6). Specifically, he enumerates military weapons, whether for breaching walled fortifications or for close combat: 'There Engines farr off breed a iust trew feare, / Neere thrusts, pikes, stabs, yea bullets hurt not here' (ll. 37–8). Contrasting 'there', the site of war, with 'here', the loving relationship on the home front, the speaker includes himself among the men who 'stay swords, armes, and shott / To make at home' (ll. 44–5).

The contrast in *ElWar* drives home the point that war slays men, whereas lovemaking begets them. If war is a destructive act, then lovemaking is rich with procreative potential. The one kind of experience offsets or complements the other. Whether *ElWar* derives from direct experience on land and at sea, or adapts accounts by adventurers who accompanied or preceded Donne, we cannot be sure. Nor can we be sure whether this Elegy is serious or wittily mock-serious, because the poem provokes many questions that cannot, at present, be answered with certainty. But Donne's military career, though brief, may have impelled him towards a safer life as a civil servant while making him keenly aware that war and its aftermath do inform affairs at court and incite political intrigue.

CHAPTER 28.II

THE EARL OF ESSEX AND ENGLISH EXPEDITIONARY FORCES

PAUL E. J. HAMMER

ELIZABETHAN England's war with Spain between 1585 and 1604 is commonly perceived as a predominantly naval war. The most famous event in Elizabeth's reign undoubtedly remains 'the defeat of the Spanish Armada', while many of the Queen's most historically famous subjects—Sir Francis Drake, Sir Walter Ralegh, the Earl of Essex, Sir John Hawkins, and others—are similarly associated with specifically naval derring-do. In reality, however, Elizabeth's war with Spain was largely fought upon land and involved a series of long and costly campaigns in the Low Countries, France, and Ireland. Ultimately, it was these hard-fought land campaigns that brought England its greatest strategic successes by buying precious time for its Dutch and French allies to rebuild their strength and, in the final years of the reign, by ensuring English military domination over the whole island of Ireland. By contrast, major naval operations usually proved disappointing and sometimes disastrous (Wernham 2006).

This balance between land and sea operations did not reflect what was expected when Elizabeth formally committed herself to open military action against Spain in alliance with the Dutch States General in August 1585. Elizabeth's basic objective was to prevent the Spanish reconquest of the Low Countries and force Felipe II into making a negotiated settlement there that would both protect Dutch Protestants and remove Spain's main army from its current dangerous proximity to her own realm. To this end, England adopted a military strategy that sought to minimize the vulnerability of its land forces and exploit what were believed to be Spanish vulnerabilities at sea. The army sent to the Low Countries under the Earl of Leicester over the winter of 1585–6 was therefore required to adopt a largely defensive posture, much to the frustration of officers such as Sir Philip Sidney and the young Earl of Essex, who dreamed of striking a decisive blow against Spain and winning glory on the battlefield. At the same time a fleet was dispatched under Sir Francis Drake to sail along the Spanish coast before heading across the Atlantic in the hope of plundering Spain's settlements in the Caribbean. This aggressive naval strategy reflected ideas that had been developed in privateering voyages of the 1560s and 1570s, and especially in Drake's circumnavigation of the globe between 1577 and 1580. The latter proved to be enormously lucrative, and seemed to demonstrate that Felipe's world-spanning empire was vulnerable to attacks on its maritime lifelines. The plan was that, while Leicester's army prevented further Spanish progress in the Low Countries, Drake's expedition would capture enough booty to cover its own costs and subsidize Leicester's campaign. Elizabeth hoped that the resulting combination of military stalemate in the Low Countries and heavy losses to Drake—whose voyage would also demonstrate the vulnerability of Spain itself to future English expeditions—would convince Felipe to negotiate some kind of compromise peace that would allow Dutch Protestants to retain their faith and liberties, ensure the repayment of her war costs, and remove the threat of a future Spanish invasion of England.

As in so many wars, the optimistic calculations that were made at the outset of the conflict quickly went awry once actual military operations began. Leicester's campaign was soon soured by bitter rivalries among his officers, spiralling costs, and political tensions both with the Dutch leadership and between Leicester and Elizabeth. Drake's expedition also proved at best a partial success in financial terms, but conclusively proved to Felipe that English naval expeditions—even those, like Drake's, which were really glorified privateering ventures—could not be permitted to continue. The twin goals of protecting his empire from further maritime incursions and removing the chief prop for the Dutch now impelled Felipe to tackle these problems at their root, by initiating the 'enterprise of England'. Instead of forcing Felipe into peace talks, England's entry into open war with Spain in 1585 therefore drove Spain into preparing the very invasion of England that the war had been intended to prevent (S. Adams 1998). The result was the famous clash in 1588, when Felipe's *Gran Armada* sailed up the English Channel and, after being dispersed by fireships off Calais, was heavily pounded by cannon-fire from English warships and utimately forced to limp home by sailing around the north of Scotland and down the west coast of Ireland. Felipe's hugely expensive 'enterprise of England' had proved to be a disaster, and the blows to his finances and international prestige were substantial.

Felipe's failed attempt to invade England also transformed the nature of the war between the two states. Almost until the moment the *Gran Armada* was sighted in English waters, Elizabeth continued to hope that she could strike a deal with Felipe to settle the problem of the Low Countries and resolve the various points of dispute between England and Spain that had accumulated over the years. Felipe and his commander in the Low Countries, the Duke of Parma, deliberately encouraged her in this belief. Despite the refusal of the Dutch to participate, the doubts of most of her own council, and even the lack of an agreed meeting place, Elizabeth dispatched a high-powered delegation to meet the Spanish in February 1588—although it was not until May that they actually met with the enemy at Bourbourg. It was only as the Armada was ready to sail from Spain and Parma's army prepared for the fleet's imminent arrival in northern waters that it emerged that these representatives lacked the appropriate authority from Felipe to make any kind of agreement. Elizabeth never trusted Felipe again, and the memory of this duplicity would weigh heavily against subsequent consideration of peace with Spain. English celebrations of their subsequent victory therefore trumpeted their success as proof that God not only supported the justness of their own cause, but had also punished the pride and treachery of the Spanish.

The shattering of the *Gran Armada* in July and August 1588 left Spain's naval power in the Atlantic critically weakened, and many in England were determined to take advantage of this golden opportunity. Elizabeth hoped to confirm England's naval advantage by destroying the battered remnants of the Spanish fleet before they could be repaired. She was also determined to pursue the greatest prize of the age—capturing the annual treasure fleet that sailed from the New World back to Spain via the Azores. The wealth carried by such a fleet was equivalent to several times Elizabeth's entire annual income. Given the alarming escalation of costs involved in sustaining a substantial army in the Low Countries, this seemed an irresistibly appealing prospect. Moreover, the loss of such a fortune would devastate the highly leveraged financial system of Felipe's global empire. Unfortunately, Elizabeth's ships needed repair and her treasury was virtually empty after the exertions of confronting the Spanish fleet. This meant that the English counter-strike would need to rely heavily upon private resources, and especially ships and money provided by merchants in the City of London. The result was that the expedition grew larger in scale and its departure was delayed until April 1589. By the time it finally sailed it had swelled in size sufficiently to make it an English equivalent of the *Gran Armada*. More importantly, its commanders, Drake and Norris, were forced to promise their investors they would accomplish multiple and incompatible objectives. While Elizabeth demanded that the force destroy the surviving ships from the *Gran Armada* that had found shelter in Spain's northern ports before turning its attention to the incoming treasure fleet, most of those involved in the venture were chiefly focused upon sailing to Portugal and challenging Felipe's hold over the Portuguese crown by stirring rebellion there in favour of a native-born (but illegitimate) claimant, Dom Antonio. The latter had been in foreign exile since 1581 and had made extravagant promises of financial rewards and commercial concessions in return for English support.

The prospect of huge financial benefits, the involvement of so many different interests, and wild optimism about the venture's likely success all helped to fuel its growth in scope and scale. The fleet ultimately included some 102 vessels of all sizes carrying 3,700 seamen, while the army supposedly peaked at 17,400 soldiers in early April before declining to 12,300 before the expedition's departure (Wernham 1988: 341, 346–50). Like most expeditionary forces sent out by the Elizabethan regime, the bulk of the army consisted of men who had been conscripted by county authorities according to quotas set by the Privy Council. Since the best men were strictly reserved for national defence as members of the 'trained bands'—the portion of each county's militia that received regular training and modern equipment (Hammer 2003: 99–101, 141–3, 256–7)—levies for service overseas usually consisted of poor-quality conscripts drawn from the bottom end of society. Local authorities sometimes even met their quotas by emptying town gaols, thereby saving the cost of feeding inmates. Such men were also least likely to complain about the very dubious legality of compulsory conscription for military service overseas. However, the poor quality of most of these reluctant recruits meant that military efficiency in Elizabethan armies largely depended upon experienced officers and small numbers of veteran soldiers. The latter were soldiers who served in the English forces based in the Low Countries, whose units were withdrawn from service there in order to provide stiffening for the raw levies being sent abroad. Norris's Portugal army included 1,800 English veterans transferred from the Low Countries, in addition to six weak companies of Dutch troops (Nolan 135).

Given the conflicting pressures upon the expedition, it is not surprising that the fleet made no serious effort to destroy Spain's surviving warships (although it did spend two weeks besieging Corunna) before heading to Portugal. After being landed by the fleet, the army made a six-day march inland through the summer heat to Lisbon. Despite Dom Antonio's promises, there was no local support for him and the English lacked the numbers and heavy weaponry needed to besiege the city, even if they chose to risk a prolonged stay in enemy territory. There was no option but to retreat. Over the next few weeks soldiers and seamen began to succumb to disease in large numbers. By early June the expedition's third objective—to seize the Azores, the vital node for Spain's transatlantic shipping—was beyond the capacity of the weakened force, and more and more ships started drifting home. Although Norris burned the Spanish town of Vigo and Drake unsuccessfully tried to sail for the Azores, the last survivors of the great expedition returned to England by early July. Between a third and a half of those who had set out in April failed to return, and none of the expedition's objectives had been achieved (Wernham 1988; Hammer 2003: 159–60).

The Portugal expedition had huge implications for the Elizabethan war with Spain. Most importantly, its failure meant that England lost its one great opportunity to strike a strategically damaging blow against a weakened Spain. Left untroubled in their northern ports, the surviving ships of the *Gran Armada* were speedily repaired, while Felipe ordered a crash programme of fresh naval construction that resulted in a class of huge and heavily armed warships—the 'Apostles'—that could theoretically outmatch even the best of Elizabeth's vessels. Reports about this naval construction encouraged a fresh English attempt to intercept the incoming Spanish treasure fleet in 1590 by mounting a so-called 'double blockade', in which English warships hovered between Spain and the Azores with the dual aims of preventing Spanish ships putting to sea and of intercepting the treasure fleet returning from the New World. The English threat forced the treasure fleet to stay in Havana in 1590, prompting a fresh English attempt at a 'double blockade' of Spain the following year. In 1591 the strategy again failed and the English fleet almost found itself trapped off the Azores by a larger Spanish fleet that included several of the new 'Apostles'. Thanks to the rashness of its captain, Sir Richard Grenville, one of the Queen's best warships, the *Revenge*, became caught up in a prolonged battle with Spanish ships, including at least two 'Apostles'. In the end most of the crew were killed and the battered ship was finally surrendered, although it sank a few days later (P. Earle). Sir Walter Ralegh subsequently tried to put the best possible gloss on the actions of his cousin Grenville and the loss of the *Revenge* in a famous piece of propaganda (Ralegh 1591), but the reality was that the clash at the Azores had been a serious defeat. England's previous naval superiority in the Atlantic was now open to serious challenge, and Elizabeth insisted thereafter that her fleet should be retained in home waters to defend against the renewed threat of seaborne invasion from Spain.

The Portugal expedition was also significant because it saw the first major impact on military affairs of Robert Devereux, second Earl of Essex. Although Essex had served under his stepfather Leicester in the Low Countries in 1585–6 and during the Armada mobilization of July 1588, his rapid ascent to become Elizabeth's new favourite at court in 1587–8 left him discontented at the prospect of being denied the chance to continue his military career while his country's fate seemed to be in the balance. When Elizabeth refused him permission to join Drake and Norris in 1589, Essex secretly left the court and set sail for Portugal anyway (Hammer 1999: 82–3). There he demonstrated his boldness by plunging into the surf to lead the army ashore at Peniche and dramatically thrusting a lance into the city gates at Lisbon before the army began its retreat. He also threw away his own expensive belongings to provide transport for sick soldiers. Such gestures—in addition to his open defiance of the Queen by joining the expedition—proclaimed Essex's commitment to being seen as a soldier and his desire to take a leading part in the war against Spain. The expedition also marked the rise of Essex as a great patron of military men: he later claimed he had secretly arranged the appointment of seven or eight of the colonels and at least twenty of the captains in the Portugal army (Devereux A3^r).

Essex was finally able to exercise military command in his own right in June 1591, when Elizabeth appointed him general of an expeditionary force sent to join the siege of Rouen in Normandy. This campaign was the result of another great turning-point in the war that had followed closely upon the failure of the Portugal expedition. The Protestant Henri de Navarre's succession as Henri IV of France in mid-1589 triggered civil war and prompted Felipe II to divert Parma and his Army of Flanders into France to reinforce the Catholic League. This lessened the pressure on the Dutch, but effectively expanded the Anglo-Dutch war against Spain into France and forced Elizabeth to send troops to aid the embattled Henri IV. Essex's mission in 1591 was to join with Henri in besieging Rouen with an army of 4,000 men, including 600 veterans from the Low Countries. Unfortunately the French king failed to arrive as agreed, and Elizabeth's doubts about the trustworthiness of her ally prompted her to demand the immediate return of Essex and his army. Such a move would have been disastrous, and Essex was twice forced to return home to persuade Elizabeth to grant him extensions. He was even forced to pay the whole army out of his own purse while the Queen made up her mind. Essex also had to battle Elizabeth's demand that he return to court while his army stayed in France. Aside from being personally humiliating, such a move would have destroyed the effectiveness of the army. While the common soldiers regarded Essex as their talisman, his recall would also have demoralized the gentlemen volunteers who constituted a crucial element in the army's fighting power: 'the most men of quality, being drawn into the action by me, wold be loth to be left unto another whom they wold never have followed owt of England' (TNA, SP 78/25, fo. 104^r).

Along with veteran soldiers from the Low Countries and experienced officers, small numbers of gentlemen volunteers played a critical role in giving élan to Elizabethan armies that largely consisted of raw conscripts. These young 'men of quality' attached themselves to a military commander—often a colonel or another senior subordinate officer, rather than directly to the general himself—and served at their own expense as private soldiers in order to acquire the personal experience of war that was expected of their class (Manning 2003: 103–38). On land campaigns, such as in Normandy in 1591 and in Ireland in 1599, these young gentlemen usually served among the cavalry, which was regarded as more prestigious (but also more expensive) than serving on foot. Essex himself was a magnet for large numbers of such volunteers, but he was also happy to see his friends and followers bring along gentlemen volunteers from among their own social circles. Many of those men who are described by modern scholars as 'Essexians' were therefore really followers of friends of Essex and had only an indirect connection to the Earl himself.

Serving as a gentleman volunteer offered young gentlemen the prospect of adventure, new social contacts through military comradeship, the possibility of plunder, and first-hand knowledge of war. Essex himself urged a young protégé (probably the Earl of Rutland) to serve as 'an adventurer...to propound to yourself 2 things, honor and the learning of thatt art by whose violent arguments all the greatt questions of the world att this day are disputed' (BL, Add MS 81592, fo. 1^{r-v}). Similarly, John Harington, who joined his Markham cousins in serving as a volunteer on

Essex's expedition to Ireland in 1599, reckoned 'the knowledge I have gotten here worth more than half the three hundred pounds this jorney hath cost me; and as to warr, joyning the practise to the theory, and reading the book you so prays'd, and other books of Sir Griffin Markham's, with his conferences and instructions, I hope at my coming home to talk of counterscarpes, and cazamats, with any of our captains' (Harington 1930: 74). Although they lacked military rank, their social status and desire to win honour often made the gentlemen volunteers the boldest soldiers in the army, and their example was expected to galvanize the common soldiers, echoing the paternalistic ideal of domestic society: 'those gentlemen and adventurers thatt serve withowt pay shall do more service in any fight then the whole trowpes besides, for where good men leade they will all follow' (TNA, SP 78/25, fo. 366^r). As Essex told his protégé, 'to win honor in the warres... yt is necessary for you to hazard. Thatt is when ether you are commaunded by him under whom you have putt yourself, when the troope you are ranged in goes to fight, or when you see such extremity as the common sort by ther fearfull lookes do begg a virtuous paterne of men of most note and accompt' (BL, Add MS 81592, fo. 2^r).

Serving as a private volunteer was an expensive business, especially as gentlemen soldiers were expected to live as befitted their rank, and the costs of food and other essentials were often exorbitantly high in a war zone. As we have seen, John Harington estimated the cost of his few months in Ireland at £300, while John Bargar complained in 1601 that he had 'served her Majesty as a voluntary in four actions under him [Essex], which had cost me well near a brace of thousand pounds' (*HMC Salisbury* 11.30). In return for such expense and danger, gentlemen volunteers hoped for some reward for their service, including future patronage by the commander to whom they attached themselves. Although Bargar claimed he only received smiles that promised future recompense from Essex, Harington gained the most prized form of recognition for honourable service by being knighted by Essex. In many ways this was the ultimate reward that a general could bestow, and was all the more desirable because the distinction gave its recipient higher social standing for the rest of his life. Whereas Elizabeth regarded knighthoods as rewards that should be dispensed very sparingly and reserved for only the wealthiest and best-connected gentlemen, Essex viewed them as an essential tool for sustaining morale among the officers and gentlemen volunteers of his armies. When the army at Rouen seemed on the point of despair over his impending return to England, Essex dubbed twenty-four new knights before his departure. This steadied the army and reinforced Essex's own standing as England's greatest private patron of soldiers, but infuriated the Queen (Hammer 1999: 223).

For all Essex's efforts, the Rouen campaign proved a disappointing failure by early 1592, and the bruising experience of command there encouraged the Earl instead to focus his efforts on establishing himself as a leading member of the Privy Council over the next few years. Essex succeeded in this effort and constantly worked to buttress Elizabeth's faltering commitment to joint military action with the Dutch and the French. By 1595, however, it became increasingly clear that Elizabeth no longer saw any need to send fresh troops to France and regarded Henri IV with grave suspicion. Instead of promoting further campaigns in northern Europe, Essex therefore argued that England should again carry the war to Spain itself, especially as his intelligence suggested a new Armada was being prepared. This suggestion provoked fierce debate between Essex and Lord Burghley, but the Earl's case seemed to be proved when four Spanish galleys raided the small Cornish towns of Mousehole and Penzance in July 1595. This showed that England remained vulnerable to seaborne attack and convinced Elizabeth and the council that the best means of defence would be to destroy the Spanish ships in their home ports. The result was the readying of the first large expedition to Spanish waters since 1591. At the same time a long-delayed voyage by Drake and Hawkins to seize the Spanish settlement at Panama was finally permitted to head for the Caribbean.

What would become the Cadiz expedition finally set sail on 30 May 1596, its departure being seriously delayed by Spain's capture of Calais in April and news of the disastrous failure of the Panama expedition, in which both Drake and Hawkins died (Andrews). Originally, the expedition to Spain was planned as a largely naval operation commanded by the Lord Admiral, Lord Howard of Effingham. Early in 1596, however, the army was greatly increased in size and Essex was installed as co-commander. Dutch ships and troops were also added. This transformed the venture and generated serious tensions between the two commanders, which were exacerbated by rivalries among the many followers of each lord who joined the expedition. Howard's men dominated the fleet, while the army reflected Essex's extensive military patronage. The Earl also promised to reduce the Queen's expenditure on the expedition by paying 2*d* a day for 1,000 infantry, providing armour for 1,500 men and paying the entire cost of 100 lancers. When Elizabeth hesitated over permitting the force to sail, Essex briefly paid for the whole army out of his own purse, just as he had done in 1591. Essex's pulling power as a general also meant that the swelling army attracted large numbers of gentlemen volunteers. One of those sailing with the expedition wrote that 'we have 300 grene hedded youthes couvered with fetthers, golde and sylver lace', as well as 10,000 soldiers 'as tall handsome men as ever I caste eye on' (LPL, MS 659, fo. 1^r). Essex wanted such a large force because he secretly planned to use the expedition to forestall a new Armada, not by attacking Spanish ships in their harbours but by seizing a Spanish port and forcing Felipe to concentrate all his resources—including troops withdrawn from France and the Low Countries—to try to recover it. In a letter to the council deliberately delivered after the fleet had sailed, he stated that he sought to establish 'a continuall diversion and to have lefte (as it were) a thorne sticking in his [Felipe's] foote' (Hammer 1999: 250). This ambitious development of the old 'double blockade' strategy was why the fleet sailed directly for Cadiz.

The arrival of the Anglo-Dutch fleet off Cadiz on 20 June caught the Spanish completely by surprise. Essex hoped to capitalize on this surprise by attacking the city (which is located at the end of a peninsula) from its seaward side. Unfortunately the

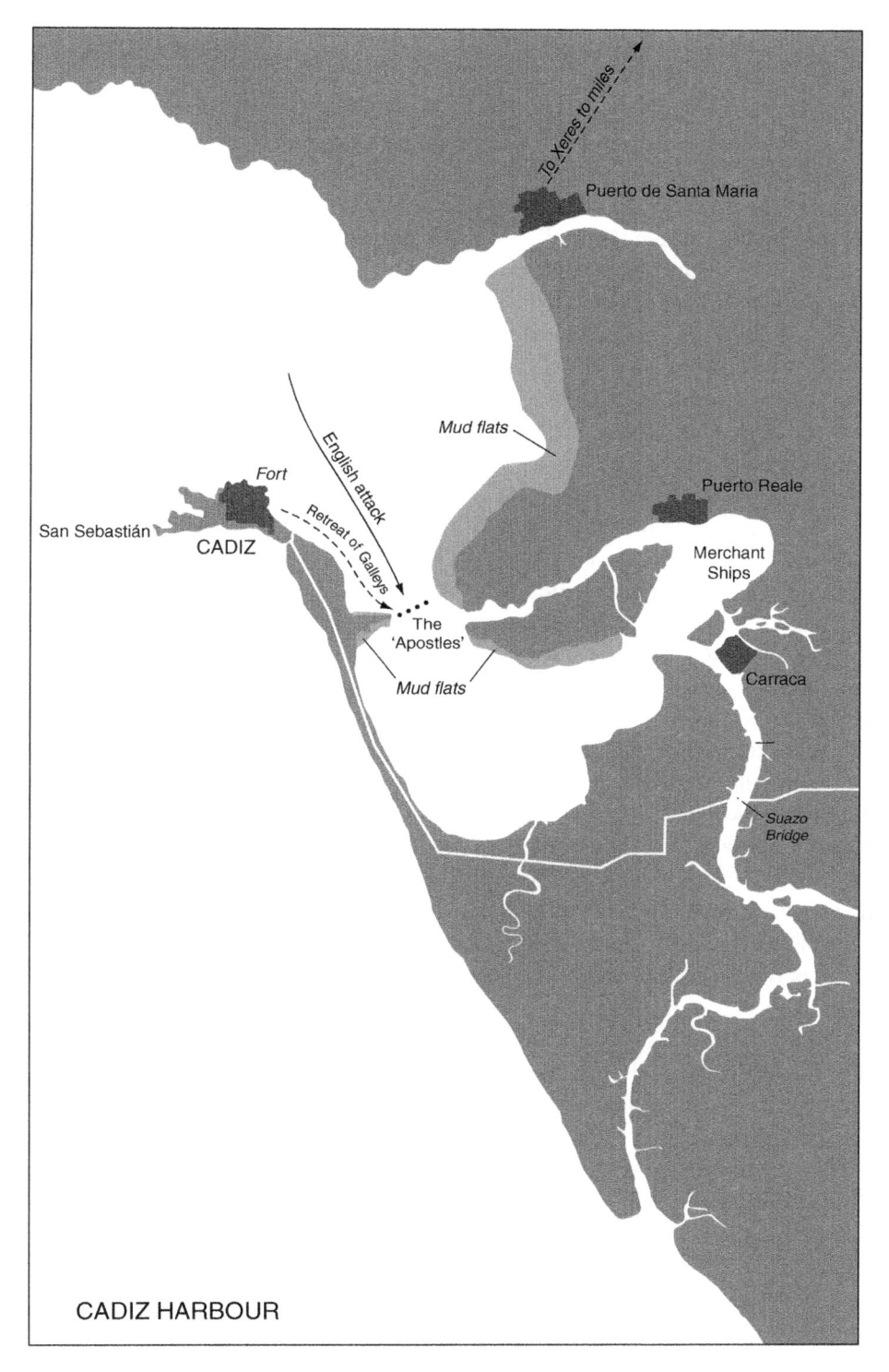

Map. 28.II.1. Map of the '1596 raid on Cadiz, showing the line of the English attack in the harbour' From *Sir Walter Raleigh* by Raleigh Trevelyan (Penguin Books, 2002). Text © Raleigh Trevelyan, 2002. Map © Penguin Books Ltd, 2002. Reproduced with permission.

heavy seas made landing difficult, and the operation had to be abandoned when several boats were swamped. This failure allowed the Spanish to withdraw the large and rich merchant convoy which was poised to sail for the New World into the furthest reaches of Cadiz Bay. Next morning the English fleet entered the narrow channel into the bay, where the leading ships found their path blocked by a substantial Spanish fleet, including numerous galleys and four great 'Apostles'. The English advance was led by Sir Walter Ralegh in the *Warspite*, hotly followed by others, including Essex on the *Due Repulse*. As the tide rose, the English warships slowly gained more room to manoeuvre and their firepower finally overwhelmed the Spanish ships, resulting in a very lopsided distribution of casualties. The *St Felipe* and *St Thomas* were set on fire, while the *St Matthew* and *St Andrew* were run aground and eventually captured. With the naval victory secured, Essex immediately began landing his troops to attack Cadiz from its harbour side. Once on the beach, Essex and his men chased the panicky Spanish defenders back to the city and promptly followed them over the walls and into the city itself. Soon only the castle remained in Spanish hands, and that surrendered the next day. However, Essex's storming of the city meant that the Lord Admiral and Ralegh felt obliged to follow him, which left the rich merchant fleet uncaptured in the bay. Rather than let the English capture their precious cargoes, the Spanish subsequently burnt the ships, knowing that many of the goods were actually owned by Dutch merchants anyway. Instead, the English had to be content with sacking Cadiz, resulting in huge windfalls for army officers and dismay among the fleet. Some semblance of balance was restored by a mass dubbing of new knights by Essex and the Lord Admiral. Nevertheless, the very richness of the goods taken helped to undermine Essex's plan to hold the city. While the Lord Admiral complained that the Queen had not approved such an action, those who had profited from the plundering were eager to get their loot safely home. In the end Cadiz was burned and abandoned (Usherwood; Hammer 1997b).

Essex responded to his failure to hijack the Spanish expedition in 1596 by trying to publish a 'True relation' of the victory that claimed the lion's share of the credit for himself. Although its printing was stopped, Essex succeeded in making himself the chief hero of Cadiz by other means. He also penned a long (and ultimately unfinished) paper arguing for a second and more elaborate attempt to implement his strategy of seizing a Spanish port (Hammer 1997a; 1999: 255–61). At first it hardly seemed likely that Elizabeth would give him this opportunity, because England experienced a new 'Armada crisis' in October and November when news came that Felipe had responded to his humiliation at Cadiz by ordering a fleet to sea. In fact the Spanish fleet was shattered by autumn gales only days out of port, and its target was Brest, rather than England or Ireland. Nevertheless, the fright caused by this new Armada ensured that Essex would be sent back to Spain to neutralize the threat in 1597.

Essex's 1597 force was even more impressive than that of 1596, and included 'manie shipps which gentilmen furnished on ther owne charges' (BL, Add MS

72407, fo. 16ʳ). The chief objectives were to destroy the enemy fleet in Ferrol harbour and then to intercept the incoming treasure fleet from Havana, but Essex's commission also permitted him to implement his strategy of seizing and holding a Spanish port. Unfortunately, almost everything that could go wrong with the expedition did so. When it set sail in July 1597 half of the fleet was driven back home by a storm. By the time the reunited (and hastily repaired) fleet set sail again in mid-August, Essex had had to discharge most of his army. Allegedly 2,000 volunteers also abandoned the voyage, although another 500 persisted (BL, Add MS. 72407, fos. 16ᵛ–17ᵛ). These losses made an attack on Ferrol marginal, and the plan fell apart completely when the two captured Spanish galleons (*St Matthew* and *St Andrew*) that were to lead fireships into Ferrol harbour failed to arrive. Receiving intelligence that the Spanish fleet had already left Ferrol to meet the incoming treasure fleet off the Azores, Essex resolved to give chase in the hope of intercepting the latter. As a result, this new counter-Armada aimed at Spain was transformed into what became known as the Azores or Islands voyage. In effect, Essex's desperation to achieve something concrete with his force—and perhaps win the chance to try again the following year—led him to undertake precisely the sort of expedition that he had condemned the previous autumn: 'idle wanderings upon the sea' (Hammer 1999: 257). During the course of this frustrating voyage, tempers among the expedition's leaders became increasingly frayed (some of Essex's subordinates even urged him to court-martial Sir Walter Ralegh for landing troops at Fayal without permission), and the incoming Spanish treasure fleet managed to reach the safety of harbour by the narrowest of margins. To restore morale, Essex dubbed a handful of new knights and planned to dub many more, 'but the wind growinge faire in the night, ancor was wayed and the gale grew so stronge as the fleete was seuered and the Generall not seene vntill all mett in Plimouth sound, wherby manie lost ther expectation' (BL, Add MS. 72407, fo. 21ʳ). Many of the gentlemen volunteers had borrowed heavily to finance their participation, and the expedition's failure to meet the lofty expectations raised by the previous year's success hit them hard. One observer noted how the fear of encountering angry creditors subsequently kept many away from London: 'the gallants I think be gotten into Crannies with the flies, for here hath not been any since their return' (*HMC Salisbury* 7.392). Even worse, the Spanish Armada at Ferrol had not sailed for the Azores as Essex had believed, but instead set sail for England in early October. Its goal was to do at Falmouth what the English had done at Cadiz the previous year. With many of the Queen's best warships still with Essex's fleet straggling back from the Azores, it was only another autumn gale in the Channel that spared the trained bands of Cornwall and Devon from facing a major Spanish landing.

    The near-disaster of 1597 put paid to Essex's Atlantic strategy. The following spring France's making of a separate peace with Spain and Elizabeth's subsequent insistence upon renegotiating the terms of her alliance with the Dutch also scotched the Earl's lingering hopes of major new military initiatives on the continent. This left him only the unwelcome prospect of fighting in Ireland, where a catastrophic English defeat in August 1598 threatened the total collapse of English control. Essex gambled that he could succeed where others had failed and sought command of the largest military expedition of the reign in the hope of reviving his fading political fortunes with a quick victory in 1599 over the chief Irish leader, Hugh O'Neill, Earl of Tyrone. Famously, this was a gamble that Essex lost. Although he re-established English control over southern Ireland and ensured the protection of Dublin and the Pale, the effort proved so exhausting that he lacked the strength to confront Tyrone in the north. As in his previous expeditions, Essex relied heavily upon the enthusiasm and fighting effectiveness of large numbers of gentlemen volunteers to bolster his army, and consequently resorted to mass knightings in an attempt to stem their departure. John Harington was one of some eighty new knights made by Essex in Ireland, as was Henry Goodere, who subsequently became a friend of Donne. However, the political price of this strategy proved disastrous for his relationship with Elizabeth, who was infuriated by such extravagant gestures when Tyrone remained unchallenged in Ulster. Moreover, like Richard II in 1399, Essex had taken so many of his friends and followers with him to Ireland that he found himself dangerously lacking in supporters who could protect his interests in England. When Essex rushed home to explain his actions in person in September 1599, the initial warmth of his reception by the Queen quickly turned to iciness and he found himself under arrest. Although the tragic sequel would take another eighteen months to unwind, Essex's political career was effectively destroyed by his failure in Ireland.

Ironically, one of the lessons about fighting in Ireland that Essex belatedly learned during his campaign in 1599 was that victory could not be achieved there by expeditionary warfare. The key to success in Ireland would be a long and sustained effort to win victory by slowly grinding down the Irish. Essex's successor in Ireland, his friend Lord Mountjoy, would pursue this brutal attritional strategy from 1600 until Tyrone was finally forced to make his submission to the dying Elizabeth in March 1603. The price for this war in the last years of the reign was enormous, both in human and financial terms, but it was only the eventual victory in Ireland that made it possible for James I to conclude a peace with Spain in August 1604 (Hammer 2005: 261–2). However, when critics of James's later pro-Spanish policies sought to change the King's course by mobilizing public opinion, it was not to memories of the war in Ireland that they appealed, but to the defeat of the *Gran Armada* in 1588 and the expeditions associated with Essex in the mid-1590s. This reflected not only the nostalgia that had grown up around Elizabeth's reign by the late 1610s, but also the impact of propagandists for the Elizabethan maritime lobby such as Richard Hakluyt and the extraordinary success of Essex's own cultivation of his public image as a patriotic military hero—an image that even his execution for treason in February 1601 failed to tarnish. The result was a myth of Elizabethan naval achievement that Charles I disastrously failed to live up to in the 1620s and that subsequently became the core of the great 'national myth' of English sea power (Hammer 1997a: 640–2; Rodger).

CHAPTER 29.I

DONNE AND EGERTON: THE COURT AND COURTSHIP

STEVEN W. MAY

THE autumn of 1597 marked a turning-point in John Donne's career. By then he had spent more than five years as an Inns of Court gentleman in London, participating in the social life and entertainments of the metropolis, all of which he is reputed to have enjoyed. Neither frivolity nor legal training occupied all his time, however. As he recalled in a Letter to his friend Sir Henry Goodere late in 1608, his study of law 'was diverted by...immoderate desire of humane learning and languages' (*Letters* 51). Along with his extra-legal studies, he had widened his circle of friends and written both verse and prose for their entertainment. He had sailed as a gentleman volunteer on both the 'Cadiz raid' (1596) and the 'Islands voyage' (1597), but had he still entertained thoughts of a military career, he returned from the latter expedition aware that he was no 'swordsman', despite the belligerent aura of the portrait he had commissioned in 1591. (This portrait, the original of which is lost, survives in an engraving by William Marshall. For a discussion of the portrait see Flynn 1995*c*: 1–11, and Ch. 27.II.) Lord Admiral Howard and the Earl of Essex had commanded these two anti-Spanish expeditions and between them had knighted at least seventy-three of the gentlemen volunteers. Donne's Lincoln's Inn associate Thomas Egerton was among the honorees, but Donne returned to England untitled.

By late 1597, then, economic necessity had brought Donne to a turning-point: his studies, he wrote, might serve as 'beautifull ornaments to great fortunes; but mine needed an occupation' (*Letters* 51). His remaining options included training for a career in the church, medicine, or at university. Alternatively, he might aim for a government post, although that would mean either purchasing it or securing it through the good offices of a patron. Better-qualified wits before him—men such as George Peele, Christopher Marlowe, and Thomas Nashe—had discovered that university degrees and literary talent could not guarantee employment in Elizabethan London. John Lyly and Edmund Spenser had, on the other hand, parlayed their university educations into secretarial posts with titled patrons. Donne managed the same transition with no degree at all, for late in 1597 or early the following year he was appointed secretary to Sir Thomas Egerton, Master of the Rolls and Lord Keeper of the Great Seal. Donne wrote to Egerton in 1602 that he had obtained the post through 'your good Sonns love to me' (*Marriage Letters* 47). Both of Egerton's sons, Thomas and John, were members of Lincoln's Inn, and while the elder son, Thomas, was not in residence during Donne's tenure, he had also served in the 1597 'Islands voyage'. Either or both of them might have preferred Donne to their father's service. (See Ch. 30.I for the suggestion that Donne's reference might have been to Egerton's stepson Francis Wolley.) And, certainly, Egerton was in great need of many kinds of assistance during this very tumultuous period in his public and private career.

Egerton's duties by the mid-1590s were critical to the operation of the central government and entailed an overwhelming workload. Elizabeth had appointed him Lord Keeper on 6 May 1596, at which time he was also sworn to her Privy Council. In addition to supervising the entire Chancery bureaucracy, Egerton as Lord Keeper presided over the House of Lords in Parliament, where he represented the Queen's interests and literally spoke for her on occasion. He supervised the foremost expressions of royal power by controlling applications of the Great Seal to all letters patent. Egerton also sat as judge in the Court of Chancery, a tribunal that met year-round and not just during the four annual law terms. In term time, however, Egerton presided as well over the Court of Star Chamber by virtue of his membership on the Privy Council. This court averaged about sixty meetings per year. In addition, as Lord Keeper, Egerton presided over meetings of the Privy Council. Ordinarily, the council met once-weekly during Egerton's tenure, but oftener, even daily, in times of crisis. Egerton also sat on the Court of High Commission, the nation's foremost ecclesiastical court.

In addition to the regular duties of these offices, Egerton also undertook an ambitious (if only partially successful) campaign to reform the practices of the central law-courts regarding bureaucratic delays, voluminous paperwork, and excessive fees. Donne justified this campaign in *Sat5*, which he addressed to Egerton. Critics have associated the poem with courtiers and the scramble for patronage at court, an activity, however, reliant on the Queen's prerogative and wholly unregulated by the law. The officers and suitors Donne describes in *Sat5* are associated only with the law-courts. Granted, the poem opens with a sneer at courtiers (ll. 3–4), but after this aside neither courtiers nor the royal court is mentioned again. Donne's officers 'Adulterate lawe' (l. 26), sell justice (ll. 36–7), and wrest 'controverted lands' from 'the strivers hands' (ll. 41–2). These cannot be lands sought through royal patronage because sovereigns only bestowed lands within their gift, and it was the sovereign, not judges, who bestowed them. Donne also personifies the law (ll. 68–78), and overtly attacks judges and pursuivants, neither of whom were courtiers nor involved with court patronage. Finally, the masses of paper Donne's wretched suitor accumulates (ll. 83–5) were a normal by-product of lawsuits, and Egerton took specific actions to reduce their volume (Jones 82–4). Win or lose, however, suitors for court favour accumulated little if any paper in the process. *Sat5* has everything to do with Egerton's attempt to reform legal procedures, but nothing to do with court patronage, and it says nothing about courtiers after line 4.

The burden of Egerton's public responsibilities was compounded by a series of upheavals in his private life. Between 1597 and 1602 the family celebrated four weddings and two funerals. On 9 June 1597 Egerton's daughter was married at York House, the Lord Keeper's London residence. By mid-September of that year Egerton had purchased a gold wedding ring, and shortly thereafter wed as his second wife Elizabeth Wolley, widow of Sir John Wolley and daughter of Sir William More. She soon took over the task of checking and signing the weekly household accounts, for her name first appears in place of Egerton's for the week of October 6 (Bodleian, MS Rawl. D.406, fos. 41^v, 45). Elizabeth died in January 1600, and in the following October Egerton married Alice, Countess of Derby. His son, John, married the Countess's daughter, Frances, in 1601. Meanwhile, Egerton's eldest son, Thomas, died while serving with the Earl of Essex in Ireland. On 19 August 1601 Egerton suffered a great loss outside his immediate family in the death of William Lambard, his deputy in the Rolls office.

During the years of Donne's employment with Egerton, the Lord Keeper undertook several other responsibilities that no doubt placed many demands on all his gentleman attendants. The disgraced Earl of Essex was imprisoned at York House from September 1599 into May of the following year. Within months of Essex's arrival, Egerton complained 'that his house is made a prison of so long continuance' (*HMC De L'Isle* 2.434, Rowland White to Sir Robert Sidney, 24 January 1600). Essex and his retainers created, in effect, a household within a household that must have complicated the duties of Egerton's staff at all levels. In addition, the Queen paid a heretofore unnoticed visit to her Lord Keeper (at a house owned by Lady Egerton) during her summer progress in 1599. On 25 August Rowland White informed his patron, Sir Robert Sidney, that Elizabeth was en route 'to Hampton Court and so to Purfleet, my Lord Keeper's' (*HMC De L'Isle* 2.385). Purfleet, far down the Thames from London and opposite Dartford, is clearly an error for Pyrford, Lady Elizabeth Egerton's estate some ten miles south-west of Hampton Court. Donne's role in this

Ill. 29.I.1. Elizabeth Wolley, damaged funeral monument, now standing (with the even more severely damaged sculpture of her second husband, Sir John Wolley) in the crypt of St Paul's Cathedral, London. From the early 1590s a Lady of Queen Elizabeth's privy chamber, she had been part of Donne's court connection as Anne More's aunt and Egerton's wife during his employment by the Lord Keeper. The two statues of Elizabeth and John Wolley are all that remain of the original monument, blackened and partly destroyed by the catastrophic fire of London in 1666. The monument was executed by an unknown artist, in accord with the will of Elizabeth Wolley's son, Sir Francis Wolley, who died in 1609. (Reproduced by permission of the Dean and Chapter of St Paul's Cathedral.)

royal visit is unrecorded but highly probable, given that receiving the Queen placed notoriously high demands on all of her hosts' resources.

Accordingly, and well before 1598, Egerton was delegating as many of his responsibilities as he could. He had, for example, appointed Lambard, a Lincoln's Inn lawyer with Chancery experience, as his deputy at the Rolls on 27 March 1597 (BL,

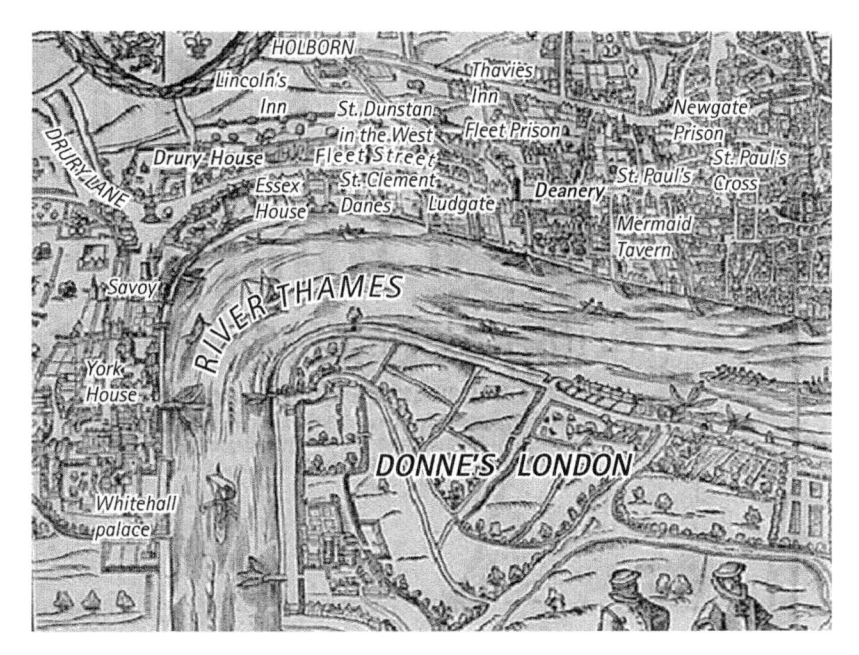

Map 29.I.1. 'Londinium Feracis' printed in Sebastian Münster's *Cosmographey* (Basel, 1598). In his 18 April 1626 Sermon at Whitehall, Donne condemned Münster for circumscribing the dimensions of hell (*Sermons* 7.137). The details reproduced here show London neighbourhoods relevant to Donne's biography. (© The British Library Board, Shelfmark 569.h.l.)

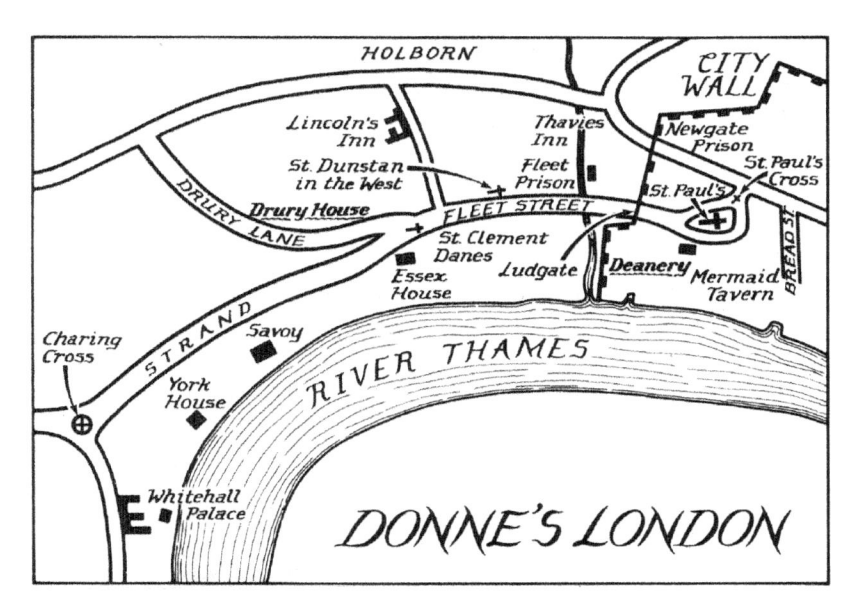

Map 29.I.2. Map of Donne's London, a schematic drawing reprinted from *A Preface to Donne*, James Winny, Pearson Education Limited, © Longman Group Limited 1970, 1981, 182, corresponding to those on the Münster map (above), but including landmarks relevant to Donne.

Add MS 46410, fo. 238). The puzzle is not that he hired John Donne, but how he employed him. Donne's title in Egerton's service was specifically that of secretary. Pleading to be restored to Egerton's service in 1602, for instance, Donne described himself as '4 years your lordships Secretary' (*Marriage Letters* 47). Yet his secretarial duties for Egerton remain obscure. Louis Knafla (2003) proposed a broad range of duties Egerton might have assigned to Donne, but we lack evidence that Donne performed any of them. There is no reason to believe, for example, that he penned any of Egerton's official correspondence as out-letters. Donne's cursive italic hand, even at its most legible (for example, in his Letters to Egerton and Sir George More following the discovery of his marriage), lacks the regularity and definition appropriate to the Lord Keeper's station. For the same reason it is unlikely that Egerton employed Donne to transcribe even marginally important Chancery records. As Lord Keeper, he had at his disposal more than sixty professional clerks in the Chancery secretariat plus his own senior secretarial staff headed by George Carew and Gregory Downhall, who were assisted by Henry Jones and John Panton (Knafla 2003: 51). Donne, the junior secretary, wrote well enough to copy ordinary business and household accounts, yet his hand has to date been found only once in Egerton's extensive surviving papers. Our one clue to the kind of duties he performed is Dennis Flynn's discovery of Donne's signature with that of John Philips of Lincoln's Inn on the dorse of a bond drawn up under Egerton's auspices 30 August 1599 (Flynn 1983). This document suggests that Donne acted in some capacity as a clerk, at least in this instance. On another occasion, however, Egerton had employed Jones and Panton to sign a legal document as witnesses, clearly a secretarial function (Collier 1840: 203–4). But as Flynn notes, Donne's signature on the bond's verso argues for some purpose other than attestation. For lack of evidence, Donne's secretarial duties for Egerton remain unknown.

As Egerton's secretary, whatever his duties, Donne probably did gain some experience at court, experience he almost certainly lacked up to that time. Indeed, all of Donne's references to the court in verse or prose before the accession of King James express the negative sentiments of a court outsider. Courtiers were rarely so bitter about the institution. Donne's most concentrated attack on the Elizabethan court occurs in *Sat4*, but what he meant by 'the court' is ambiguous. It could refer to the entire royal household, although contemporaries often distinguished the household from *the* court, meaning the sovereign's place of residence (May 1991: 12–13). As the social centre of national power and patronage, the court concerned only the chamber, the household 'above stairs' as opposed to the household service departments that operated 'below stairs'. Persons of respectable appearance and bearing could enter the great chamber of an Elizabethan palace while the Queen was in residence, stroll through the hall as far as the presence chamber, and say they had been to court (E. K. Chambers 1.14). The latter room's title is misleading, however, for the sovereign presided there only on ceremonial occasions such as the receiving of ambassadors or titled visitors. Suitors might waylay courtiers in the presence as they passed through it going to or from the adjacent suite of rooms, the privy chamber. This was the specific chamber location that could accurately be termed the royal court during Elizabeth's reign. Access to the sovereign is the *sine qua non* of courtiership, and the Queen and her immediate entourage spent most of their time in the privy chamber. The social assembly of queen and courtiers was, in fact, the only court, wherever it happened to be, that comprised the locus of royal authority and bounty.

Some have supposed that Donne attended Elizabeth's court (that he actually penetrated the privy chamber), during his Inns of Court days. R. C. Bald, for example, states that Donne 'presented himself at court' early in his career at Lincoln's Inn (1970: 53). No evidence supports this claim; it is a product of what may be termed the 'Puss in Boots' myth, a belief widely held even in scholarly circles that citizens of Donne's rank could simply go up 'to London to visit the Queen'. Elizabeth, however, instructed the guard at her privy chamber door to admit only those who were either her sworn servants or recognized, established courtiers (May 1991: 19). Donne fell into neither category, and could no more 'present himself' at court in Elizabeth's privy chamber than promising graduate students today can present themselves to her royal namesake in her private chambers at Buckingham Palace. Moreover, Donne's name fails to appear in the primary records indicative of courtiership: it is missing from extant courtier correspondence of the last decade of the reign, from accounts of the royal household, and from the surviving New Year's gift rolls, which cover the ceremonies for 1597–9, 1600, and 1603.

Whatever degree of autobiography attaches to *Sat4*, its narrative recounts the proximity to *the* court (the privy chamber) that a gentleman of Donne's standing could manage on his own recognizance. He never mentions entering the privy chamber, nor does the Queen make so much as an innocent, cameo appearance in the poem. He first describes how he 'went to Court' (l. 8), but then ran from the place when he saw 'All the court fill'd with more strange things' than the man who first accosted him there (l. 152). However, the outlandish, shabbily dressed beggar who calls the poem's speaker by name is clearly no denizen of the privy chamber. A principal victim of the satiric attack, he is merely a court hanger-on, a fantastic 'thing' who haunts the hall and the presence. Yet Donne's narrator terms the place where he met his interlocutor the court. On a second visit, the narrator refers twice to the 'Presence' (ll. 171, 199), indicating that these trips to 'court' brought him only as far as the presence chamber. But are courtiers satirized as well in *Sat4*? The speaker denigrates one class of court personnel as 'they / Which dwell at Court' (ll. 15–16). This phrase seemingly refers to genuine courtiers, many of whom, Lord Keeper Egerton among them, enjoyed bouge of court and resided in the royal palaces, at least on occasion. If so, Donne's attacks on 'courtiers' condemn two very distinct social entities: he levelled his most vivid satire at the courtier would-bes with whom he mingled in the presence. But if 'they / Which dwell at Court' refers to the Queen's actual privy chamber associates, then *Sat4* also attacks courtiers, the privileged elite he describes as 'prone to'all ill' (l. 13). 'Courtier' is as uncertain a term as 'the court' in Donne's usage and in Elizabethan discourse generally.

To what extent was Donne brought closer to the court circle as Egerton's secretary? His Verse Letter to Henry Wotton in July 1598 closed with the satiric observation, 'I end… / At Court; though From Court, were the better stile' (*HWNews* ll. 26–7). Clearly, his attitude towards the court had not mellowed after a few months in Egerton's service. The Lord Keeper had chambers at court, and Donne no doubt carried out some of his duties there. He may even have lodged at court in Egerton's service, but he remained a courtier's servant, not a courtier in his own right. If he entered the privy chamber, it was as his lordship's attendant—a gentleman attendant, to be sure, eligible to meet and talk with his betters at court were they inclined to recognize him. But Donne still could not have entered the privy chamber on his own recognizance, and it is understandable that he maintained his outsider's contempt for the institution.

Instead of hobnobbing with courtiers during his years in Egerton's service, Donne's Letters in Prose and Verse suggest that he maintained and extended his friendships with Inns of Court gentlemen. Several of these friendships are traceable back to the early 1590s. Donne may have composed his Verse Letter to Everard Guilpin (*EG*), for instance, as early as the summer of 1593. In addition, he shared some or all of his verse Satires with Guilpin, who echoed several of them in his *Skialethia* (1598) (R. E. Bennett 1939; Hester 1984). Between mid-1598 and about 1599 Donne sent two Verse Letters to his friend Henry Wotton (*HWNews* and *HWKiss*), and received Wotton's ''Tis not a coate of gray' in return (Pebworth and Summers 1984: 361). Donne certainly maintained his close friendship with the brothers Christopher and Samuel Brooke and with Rowland and, probably, Thomas Woodward during these years. He may also have met Henry Goodere (a Middle Templar since 1589) and a cluster of town wits such as John Roe, John Hoskins, Benjamin Rudyerd, Francis Bacon, and Francis Davison.

One of his friendships during his years with Egerton has, however, been underestimated, if not doubted altogether. I believe that he was well acquainted with William Cornwallis the younger (1579–1614), later Sir William, who is remembered principally for his *Essayes* (1616). Some six years Donne's junior, he was also somewhat Donne's social superior, being the son of the ambassador Sir Charles Cornwallis. His was a landed family with viable court connections. William no doubt looked up to Donne for his wit and learning, and as an Inns of Court man now launched on a promising career.

Donne's friendship with William Cornwallis has been largely ignored because Donne never mentions him (Bald 1970: 118), yet Cornwallis dedicated two works to his friend with protestations of love that echo Donne's similar assurances in his Verse Letters to others. Moreover, William cultivated many of the same genres in prose and verse—problems, paradoxes, essays, and verse letters—that were popular with Donne and his circle. Two manuscript copies of Cornwallis's paradoxical 'Encomium of Richard III' preserve the dedication to Donne. The dedicatory letter in these copies affirms that 'our loue is now of some Continuance', and reveals an attitude towards the court in harmony with Donne's views: 'let Courtiers haue Loue still in their mouthes, and none in their hartes' (W. Cornwallis 1977: iv, 1). Cornwallis also sent Donne a verse letter to accompany the four 'himnes' he enclosed as a further gift to his friend. Grierson printed the letter (Donne 1912: 2.171–2), but made no mention of the poems enclosed with it, works that Cornwallis seems to have crafted specifically to allude to Donne's service with Egerton.

Cornwallis sent these three bifolia as a packet to Donne between 1598 and the end of 1601, for they are endorsed 'To my ever to be respeckted freand Mr Iohn Done Secretary to my Lorde keeper giue these'. To this leaf part of Cornwallis's seal is still attached. The first stanza of the poem clearly identifies its function as a covering letter for the enclosed present:

> As in tymes past the rusticke sheapherds sceant [sent]
> thir tideast lames or kids for sacrefize
> vnto thir gods, sincear beinge thir intent
> thowghe base thir gift, if that shoulde moralize
> thir loues, yet noe direackt discerninge eye
> Will iudge thir ackt, but full of piety.
>
> (Bodleian, MS Tanner 306, fo. 237.
> I am grateful to Dr Bruce C. Barker-Benfield for
> examining this manuscript with me and
> helping me arrive at these conclusions)

The enclosed 'sacrefize' was filed away with these further endorsements: 'Will Cornwaless his himnes' (fo. 234^v) and 'Will. Corn Waleis himnes' (fo. 236^v). The first poem on these folios is entitled 'The Contrition of a Convertite' (fo. 233), wording that resonates in tantalizing fashion with one aspect of Egerton's affairs that Donne must have known about in some detail.

The House of Convertites (*Domus Conversorum*) was founded by Henry III in what is now Chancery Lane as a home for Jews who had converted to Christianity. Its church became the storehouse for the rolls of Chancery. The Six Clerks, the 'largest and most crucial department within the Chancery', were housed directly across the lane from the Domus (Jones 120). As Master of the Rolls, Egerton administered the foundation from 1595 (ibid. 59, 66). A stray bundle of Exchequer receipts shows that Donne's fellow secretary, Henry Jones, paid the resident convertites their pensions on the Lord Keeper's behalf at various dates between 1596 and 1600 (TNA, E 101/255/16). Perhaps Donne was never entrusted with these payments, yet he undoubtedly knew that the House of Convertites was one of Egerton's responsibilities, closely tied by physical proximity to the workings of Chancery.

Cornwallis's seventy-two-line 'The Contrition of a Convertite', the longest of the 'hymns' he sent to Donne, exhorts the reader to join him in soul-saving repentance:

> Leaue, leaue at length thy sportes, and pleasing mirthe
> And weepe w{th} mee, and bee wth mee ashamed:
>   Weepe in this life, for feare thou weepe for ever,
>   And doe not still in sinfull actes persever.
>
>   (Bodleian, MS Tanner 306, fo. 233^v)

'Convertite' is an unusual word in the penitential tradition. Donne uses it only once in his poetry, not in his devotional verse but in the Verse Letter to Lady Carey and Essex Rich (*Carey* l. 7). Convertites are converts from one religious faith to another, but nothing in the lament Cornwallis sent to Donne, nor in the poems that follow it, deals with religious conversion. The title of the first hymn is apparently Cornwallis's attempt to tailor his gift to Donne's immediate circumstances, alluding to, and purporting to be something of a prosopopoeia for, the convertites who occupied Egerton's house.

During these years Donne's social life was not restricted to his male friends. He also became acquainted with Egerton's niece by marriage, Anne More, whom he married late in 1601. When news of their elopement reached her family, her father pressured Egerton to dismiss Donne from his service (Walton 1658: 18). Our reconstruction of this courtship relies on the always-suspect testimony of Izaak Walton's *Life of Donne*, Donne's authentic, apologetic Letters after the marriage, and four Letters in the Burley manuscript (LRO, MS Finch DG.7, Lit. 2) that he presumably wrote to Anne. She was the third of Sir George More's five daughters and something of a favourite with his sister, Egerton's second wife Elizabeth, who left her an inheritance of £100. Presumably Lady Egerton made Anne a regular guest in the Lord Keeper's household, or it is difficult to imagine how Donne found occasion to meet and woo her. They perhaps met as early as the Christmas season of 1597–8, assuming that Donne had entered Egerton's service by then. He was nearly 26 at the time, Anne not yet 14. Their assocation continued, no doubt intermittently, for two years at most until Lady Egerton's death in January of 1600. Afterwards it is unlikely that Anne continued as a regular guest in the Lord Keeper's household, particularly after the dowager Countess of Derby became its mistress in October 1600.

Assuming that the four undated and unattributed Letters in the Burley manuscript are indeed Donne's Letters to Anne, they record four crises in the courtship (I. Bell 1996: 123). In one, written 'at this tyme of ye yeare (when the sun forsakes vs)', Donne affirms that the heart she melted during the summer they spent together, 'no winter shall freise' (E. M. Simpson 1948: 321). He then explains that he has been sent out of town and has thus been unable to visit her since her return (presumably) to London. Another Letter reveals that the couple has been corresponding regularly, for he laments that by not writing to him, she deprives him 'of the happines I was wont to haue in yr letters' (ibid. 328). A third Letter, written in sickness and despair, has the writer protesting that 'I should accompt even sorrow good payment if by myne yrs were lessoned'. As Simpson notes, the general circumstances of this Letter—the writer's sickness, his misery, and her sorrow—coincide with the couple's plight after their marriage became known in February 1602 (ibid. 318). These are, in any event, genuine love letters, with eloquent professions of devotion, but nothing to connect any of them specifically to John and Anne.

The fourth Letter, however, describes a serious crisis incorporating details with specific links to Donne's circle. The narrative relates, in brief, that Lord Latimer has informed the woman's father that a Mr Davies slandered her, and that the writer both heard this insult and slandered her himself. If the principals here are Donne and Anne More, then Mr Davies was no doubt the Lord Keeper's protégé, John Davies of the Middle Temple. Donne probably knew him as another Inns of Court poet and wit, but more importantly, Davies's connection with Egerton makes his acquaintance with and alleged remarks about Anne plausible. In 1601 Sir Thomas was instrumental in getting Davies readmitted to the Middle Temple after his expulsion in 1598 for assaulting a colleague. In 1602 Egerton commissioned Davies to compose the poetic lottery with which he entertained Queen Elizabeth and her ladies-in-waiting during her progress visit to Harefield. Regarding Davies, Donne assures Anne that 'I durst vpon my conscience acquit him of ever conceaving vnworthyly of you' (E. M. Simpson 1948: 320–1). His impassioned defence of Davies befits a member of Egerton's circle.

Although the writer also protests 'my loue to' Lord Latimer, this title was claimed by the conspirator Edmund Neville who, only in 1598, had been released from more than thirteen years imprisonment for suspected disloyalty to the Crown. Donne may well have known him through his family's network of Catholic friends (Flynn 1996: 146). What Neville hoped to gain by denigrating Davies and Donne with Sir George More is unclear. The exact nature of the supposed slander is also left vague, although it clearly compromised the woman's honour. If it concerned revealing to More that Anne was romantically involved with John Donne, that revelation created exactly the sort of embarrassment to have elicited Donne's *Curse*, with its condemnation of the man who told 'his mistress' name'. Ilona Bell has shown, moreover, that Neville's biography coincides to a remarkable degree with the traits of Donne's victim in *Curse* (1996). The Letter states, however, that 'yr father hath taken it [the revelation] for good fuell of anger against mr davis & perchaunce me to' (E. M. Simpson 1948: 320). Donne would be awfully naive to imagine Sir George's wrath visited more sharply on Davies the gossip than on himself as Anne's wooer. The Letter may refer to an embarrassment Donne suffered as a result of Neville's tattling to Sir George, but one unrelated to *Curse*.

Did Latimer's accusations cause More to whisk Anne back home to Loseley (as Walton affirms that he did upon learning of Donne's interest in his daughter)? If so, the quarantine proved futile. Late in 1601 the lovers were secretly married by Donne's friend Samuel Brooke, in a ceremony witnessed by his brother, Christopher. In so doing they probably took advantage of the session of Parliament convened from 27 October to 19 December. Both Donne and Anne's father were members of this assembly and, presumably, Sir George brought his family to London for all or part of that time (Bald 1970: 128). Donne informed Sir George of the match in style, with a Letter delivered personally by Henry Percy, ninth Earl of Northumberland. In the aftermath, Donne and the Brookes were imprisoned for some weeks, and Donne lost his position as secretary to the Lord Keeper (cf. Ch. 30.I).

Why did Anne and John risk a clandestine marriage at this time? First, they knew that Sir George would never agree to the match because Donne's social and economic status did not measure up to the More family's expectations; the husbands of Anne's four sisters were (or became) knights. In 1601 Donne's most likely career path was as secretary to the Lord Keeper or some equally prestigious official. Jones, Panton, and Downhall followed this course, for example, as did Lord Burghley's long-serving secretaries Michael Hicks and Henry Maynard. A secretaryship at this level of government was quite a respectable post—Hicks was in fact dubbed knight by King James. Yet it was also a rather subservient career, and few secretaries' wives could hope to become ladies. Donne's marriage to Anne had to be kept from her family.

As for the timing, a very practical incentive to marriage for John and Anne occurred in July 1601 when Donne gained a lease by letters patent to two-thirds of the manor of Uphall, Carleton, Lincolnshire. The Crown had enforced the anti-recusancy laws to seize the property from Donne's first cousin, John Heywood, only the April before. Bald doubted that Donne saw much profit from the grant, since he held it for only four years. When Heywood died in 1605, Uphall reverted to his eldest son, who had not been convicted of recusancy (1970: 116–17). In 1601, however, Donne must have welcomed the lease as a promising new source of income. The letters patent made him the sole legal recipient of all proceeds from the specified portion of the estate while in the Queen's gift. He not only secured the lease, but it moved with astonishing speed through the cumbersome bureaucracy of the various seal offices to the Great Seal. The one-time entry fine to the lease was only 20 shillings, leaving as clear profit all that the estate brought in over and above the annual rent of £40. Although no records of the proceeds are known to survive, records of Donne's payments of the rent argue strongly that he enjoyed the grant's financial benefits for as long as they lasted (Bald 1970: 117; LaRocca 3). This lease, like his membership in Parliament that autumn, testifies to Egerton's high regard for his youngest secretary. It was the kind of reward Donne could expect from time to time as the employee of a major state officeholder. It was not enough land or income to turn him into a viable son-in-law for Sir George More, but with his income as Egerton's secretary it must have seemed adequate to allow the newlyweds to reside in London, where he would continue his secretarial duties. Clearly, Anne married Donne for love, nor was he a legacy-hunter. Anne brought no dowry to the marriage, of course, and while she might hope eventually to receive a legacy from her father, she was not an heiress and there was a good chance that she might be disinherited entirely.

Donne's position as Egerton's secretary was of critical importance to his career hopes. Upon losing the income from this post, and despite collecting his wife's £100 inheritance from her aunt Elizabeth, Donne abandoned his lodgings in London. The couple moved in with Anne's relatives, the Wolleys of Pyrford. This country estate was no doubt a pleasant site for the honeymoon, but in practical terms it lay some twenty miles from the capital and Donne's best hope for securing patronage and a new position. Again, he found himself unemployed, lacking substantial income, but with the added responsibility of a wife and (before long) children. In his 1608 Letter to Goodere, Donne lamented his failure at both law and as Egerton's secretary. Of the latter appointment he wrote, 'I submitted my self to such a service, as I thought might [have] imployed those poor advantages, which I had. And there I stumbled too' (*Letters* 51). As late as 1612 he recalled in a Letter to Wotton the catastrophic effect of his dismissal from Egerton's service: 'though I dyed at a blow then when my courses were diverted, yet it wil please me a little to have had a long funerall' (ibid. 122). From the beginning of this ebb in his fortunes early in 1602, a successful future as Dr Donne, Dean of St Paul's would have seemed to him, I think, remotely improbable.

CHAPTER 29.II

DONNE AND LATE ELIZABETHAN COURT POLITICS

ANDREW GORDON

> Haue wee not kept our guards, like spie on spie
> Had correspondence when the foe stood by?
> Stolen (more to sweeten them) our many blisses
> Of meetings conference, embracementes kisses[?]
> *(ElPart* ll. 45–8)

In his examination of constancy under pressure in *ElPart*, Donne reaches for the imagery of courtly intrigue to dramatize both the excitements and the dangers of a secret affair. Anti-court complaint had long been a poetic commonplace, but the heady mix of apprehension and opportunity, of mingled fear and desire, that Donne conjures in this Elegy and in others such as *ElJeal* and *ElPerf*, is particularly evocative of the later 1590s when an atmosphere of suspicion and intrigue characterized perceptions of the court. Donne's lovers seek to accommodate their illicit pleasures within a semblance of courtly modesty, demonstrating mastery in 'all these secrets of thie art' (l. 53); an art of courting, framed as an art of courtiership. In the same poem, however, the poet signals his awareness of the limits of accommodation and the precarious position of those on the outskirts of influence: 'soe blinded iustice doth when favorites fall / Strike then their house, their frinds, their followers all' (ll. 33–4), he wrote. Donne was well aware that courtly intrigues affected not only the principal players but an extended cast allied in fortune to the courtiers and power-brokers of the Privy Council.

The dangers of such alliances feature prominently in the literature of social advancement that emerged from the Inns of Court environment at the close of the sixteenth century. Francis Bacon's contemporary essay 'Of Faction' distinguishes between the dependent condition of 'Meane Men' who 'must adhere' and those 'Great Men, that have Strength in themselves', whom he observes 'were better to maintain themselves Indifferent and Neutral' (Bacon 1625: 296–7). William Cornwallis, whose friendship with Donne is explored in Steven W. May's contribution to this volume (Ch. 29.I), describes the challenging situation of those seeking advancement for whom 'euery way appeares danger', in his essay 'Of friendship and faction'. The dilemma of the potential follower is epitomized in Cornwallis's remark: 'Hee that stands without, stands naked and subiect to euery storme, who vnderpropped, so long safe, but no sooner loosened, but ruined' (W. Cornwallis 1600: E6^{r-v}). Both volumes of essays, like Donne's Elegies, were products of the 1590s, and their careful calculation of risk and advantage is a testament to both the uncertainties and the opportunities of a court in transition.

The prospect of change and upheaval loomed large in the final decade of Elizabeth's reign. The sovereign's refusal to countenance any talk of the succession had been an effective method of consolidating her own authority, but as she reached her sixties without confronting the issue, speculation increased. Potential claims were rehearsed in a number of illicit publications issuing from the presses of Europe, whilst various potential power-brokers made covert contact with the Scottish court and initiated correspondence with James VI, a dangerous and potentially treasonable act. After Queen Elizabeth's more than thirty years on the throne, the 1590s saw a changing of the guard in the Privy Council, the principal forum in which the policies of her reign were determined. The deaths of the Earl of Leicester in 1588, Sir Walter Mildmay in 1589, Sir Francis Walsingham in 1590, and Sir Christopher Hatton in 1591 had removed four of the principal architects and enforcers of Elizabethan policy. Only William Cecil, Lord Burghley, remained as a presence from amongst the figures who had shaped Elizabeth's rule and helped maintain its course in the preceding generation.

Amongst the new faces drafted into the Privy Council in the early 1590s were Burghley's second son, Robert Cecil, and the young Earl of Essex, Robert Devereux. Between them these two figures would come to dominate court life at the close of the sixteenth century. As testimony of his talents, the younger Cecil had made European visits in the company of ambassadors, served as an MP, and authored an anonymous defence of the trial of Mary Queen of Scots, before Burghley saw him promoted to the Privy Council in 1591 at only 28. Robert Cecil was adept at the politics of clientage and a shrewd strategist in the service of the Crown. Gradually earning the confidence of the Queen, he increasingly took on responsibilities in place of his weakening father in addition to discharging the duties of his own expanding portfolio.

Essex, whose upbringing as an orphaned ward of court had been overseen by Burghley, was altogether different in character. Acceding to the earldom at the age of 10, he was addicted to the pursuit of honour and cut a dashing figure at court from the late 1580s, when he was promoted as the protégé of his stepfather, Leicester. His thirst for martial glory made him an eager participant in Leicester's operations in the Low Countries, and his first command came early with the troubled 1591 campaigns in France in support of an embattled Henri de Navarre. The Essex ideal of service placed a high value on military valour, and in the field his disregard for his own safety often bordered on recklessness. Politically he advocated an aggressive, interventionist stance in foreign policy throughout the 1590s, seeking to commit Elizabeth to large-scale and costly military operations against the Spanish in mainland Europe.

The figures of Essex and Cecil presented a clear contrast in terms of both style and policy: the glamorous military service of Essex exhorting Protestant war made for a more potent popular image than the behind-the-scenes diplomacy of the less prepossessing Cecil, whose caution in matters of policy was matched by a financial prudence inherited from his father, whose hands had held the purse-strings of governance as Lord Treasurer. Cecil's service was rewarded by Elizabeth with positions of financial responsibility and significant political patronage. As for Essex, the Queen 'alwaies was both a Favourer and an amplifier of *Essex* his honour' (Camden 1635: 476), but although she rewarded him with titles she concentrated his influence in military affairs. In 1587 he had succeeded Leicester as Master of the Horse and had become a Knight of the Garter shortly thereafter. In 1597 he was made Master of the Ordnance, a key post for the exercise of military patronage that also lent his voice some weight in policy, and later that year he was appointed Earl Marshal, an ancient office with responsibility for care of the monarch and oversight of disputes of honour, which fed his desire to fashion a role for himself at court combining martial authority with a ceremonial lustre.

Whilst careful of his martial charisma, Essex did make a calculated bid in the early 1590s to build up his credit as a power-broker in diplomatic relations by seeking to develop his own intelligence networks across Europe (Hammer 1999: 152–98). This was part of Essex's attempt to put himself forward as the natural successor to Burghley in the role of principal counsellor to the Queen and as a potential Secretary of State—an office that had lain vacant since Walsingham's death. Elizabeth delayed the appointment for six years, during which time Robert Cecil was able to demonstrate to the Queen his own qualifications for the job. Cecil had taken on an immense workload, becoming heavily involved in parliamentary committee work as well as the management of council business, while bearing much of the burden of his father's offices. The case for Essex was not helped by his growing popularity beyond the court, which unwisely he appeared to cultivate. Nor was his passionate advocacy when making the case for sustained support of Henri IV and war with the Spanish in his favour. His tendency to overbearing displays when pressing the suits of his clients also did little to advance either their causes or his own, as figures such as Francis Bacon, serially overlooked for office under Elizabeth despite the Earl's forceful striving on his behalf, came to realize. It was in July 1596, while Essex was abroad on the Cadiz expedition (with Donne in the company), that Elizabeth finally committed herself over the Secretaryship, breaking her word to Essex in the process. Receiving evidence of the Earl's attempts to sidestep her orders and his intention to orchestrate a publicity campaign to celebrate his actions, she awarded the post to Cecil. The appointment in effect consolidated the transition in influence within the council from the ageing Burghley to his son, and with his subsequent appointment as Chancellor of the Duchy of Lancaster, Cecil's powers of patronage were increased still further. By the time of Burghley's death in August 1598 the succession of a *Regnum Cecilianum* looked assured (Croft 1991b: 46–7).

The death of Burghley, whom Essex had held in high regard despite disagreements, exposed the limitations of the Earl's influence, and increasingly he came to define his interests in factional terms. Strategic collaboration between Essex and Cecil over policy was now a rarity. Cecil's appointment in succession to his father as Master of the Court of Wards, a highly influential post for the development of client relationships, confirmed Elizabeth's continued faith in him and was another blow to Essex's hopes. Essex appeared an increasingly isolated figure on the Privy Council as noble representation within its ranks declined amidst a more general narrowing of the membership (Peck 1995: 91–2). Only Essex's uncle, Sir William Knollys, appointed Comptroller of the Household and a privy councillor in 1596, could be firmly classified as an Essex ally, but all the major offices went either to overt rivals or to those cultivated by Cecil and not bound in obligation to the Earl. As Natalie Mears puts it: 'Cecil's "faction" was, in fact, the Court itself' (Mears 58). The death of the tenth Baron Cobham brought the advancement of his son, Henry Brooke, with whom Essex had a long-standing animosity that was all too evident in his effort to secure for Robert Sidney the post of Warden of the Cinque Ports rather than see Cobham succeed his father in the post (S. Adams 2002: 85). Elizabeth further undercut Essex by bestowing the earldom of Nottingham, a title superior in dignity to that of Essex, upon his rival the Lord Admiral Charles Howard, a close friend of Cecil. The letters patent exacerbated the affront to Essex by playing up Howard's role at Cadiz although Essex had the joint command—an oversight widely attributed to the Cecils (*HMC De L'Isle* 2.305). The resulting dispute was resolved only by bestowing a revived Earl Marshalcy upon Essex, an ingenious device that salved his wounded honour without strengthening his hand. Lord Buckhurst, who succeeded to Burghley's office of Lord Treasurer, was another whose ties were to the Cecils. With their support he had obtained the chancellorship of Cambridge University in 1591, to the chagrin of Essex, who had Cambridge connections and had coveted the appointment (Hammer 1999: 301). Buckhurst's management of the crown purse as Lord Treasurer would later prove a source of contention as Essex felt his efforts in Ireland undermined by shortage of funds.

Also brought into the council at this time was the career lawyer Sir Thomas Egerton, on an accelerated path through the principal legal offices. From Solicitor-General he was promoted to Attorney-General in 1592, and to Master of the Rolls in 1594, before his appointment as Lord Keeper in 1596. Egerton has sometimes been identified as an Essex ally, but this is to misread the progress of Egerton's political career and the balancing of interests it involved. M. A. R. Graves has located Egerton's rise in the context of a number of legal and parliamentary men-of-business who 'were the Council's men before they were appointed Councillors' (Graves 199), having worked under Burghley's direction managing debates and committee work in the House of Commons before being appointed to higher office. Egerton was appointed while Essex was abroad on the Cadiz voyage, during a select meeting of privy councillors that comprised all the Earl's principal opponents at court. Although Essex's secretary was persuaded that Egerton had been the Queen's independent choice, he appears to have had the backing of the Earl's enemies (Flynn 2001: 109–10). Egerton was too astute an operator to be narrowly bound in allegiance to any single figure. From the surviving correspondence it is clear he worked hard to cultivate a close working relationship with Burghley's son while preserving good relations with Essex. The Lord Keeper could write to Essex from his estate at Pyrford in praise of the country life, echoing the complaints of courtly corruption that ran throughout the Earl's own correspondence of the period: 'It seems to me the way to heaven is in the country, where there be no rubbish of Court nor State affairs to stop' (*HMC Salisbury* 9.25). Two days later he struck an altogether different note in replying to a letter from Cecil that urged his presence in council: 'this brought me double joy', he wrote, 'in recalling a prisoner to liberty and an exile from banishment' (ibid. 9.26). The letters were written in January 1598, only a few months after Donne had entered the Lord Keeper's service, and the paradoxical positions they express illustrate the demands of maintaining good relations with all sides in the tense climate of Elizabeth's final years.

Egerton's role extended well beyond his responsibility for the exercise of justice. As Lord Keeper he continued his parliamentary activity, acting now as Speaker in the House of Lords—Donne's service as an MP in the Parliament of 1601 was no doubt connected to the need to maintain influence in the Lower House. Egerton was an essential member of the Privy Council, and his diplomatic skills were recognized with employment in negotiations with France, the Netherlands, and Denmark (Knafla 1977: 34). His skill in negotiating competing influences at the Elizabethan court put Egerton in a good position to play a mediating role when matters reached an impasse. This was the case in July of 1598, when a dispute over the appointment of a military commander to be sent into Ireland got out of hand. The Queen favoured Sir William Knollys; but Essex, fearing to lose a close ally, proposed a friend of Cecil, Sir George Carew, 'so that he might ridde him from the Court'. When Essex, exasperated at the rejection of his arguments, turned his back on the Queen she 'gaue him a cuffe on the eare' for his impertinence, and Essex stormed from the court, refusing to return (Camden 1635: 493). In the aftermath it was Egerton who wrote a lengthy formal letter, pointing out to Essex the dangers of his course of action and advising him that 'pollecie dutie and religion enforceth you to yeild, and submit to yor souerainge' (BL, MS Royal 17.B.L., fo. 5^r). The letter, a set piece of rhetorical argument, failed to persuade Essex, who took the opportunity to pen a reply setting out his own vision of noble service, in opposition to the base requirement of presence at court: 'The dutie of attendance is noe Indissoluble dutie', he wrote 'I owe her ma^{tie} the office of an Erle, and of a Marshalle of England, I have ben contented, to doe her the office of a Clarke but I can never serue her as a slave, or a villaine' (BL, MS Royal 17.B.L., fos. 8^v–9^r). Essex had this manifesto of honour and duty circulated amongst his followers along with Egerton's letter, and both the text and its dissemination would later be used against him (Gordon 325–8). Such letters were not private documents, despite their evocation of personal friendships, and as a member of the Lord Keeper's secretariat Donne may well have been privy to the devising of Egerton's text, of which no holograph copy is known.

The nature of Donne's employment for Egerton has been the subject of much speculation, as May shows (see Ch. 29.I), but one possibility worth considering is that he was taken on with a view to performing scholarly services of the kind tendered by his friend Henry Wotton to the Earl of Essex. Wotton had offered to his patron the abilities of a 'pragmatic reader', prepared to place his skills in languages, his knowledge of the European political scene, and his training in analytical method at the disposal of the ambitious Earl in order to supply him with 'knowledge profitable to the enterprise of government' (Jardine and Sherman 102). Desperately seeking readmission to Egerton's employment in February 1602, Donne recalled the connections that had first brought him to attention, noting that it was 'by the favor which your good Sonns love to me, obteind' (*Marriage Letters* 47) that he secured a place in Egerton's service. Yet Donne possessed skills that would have recommended him to a Lord Keeper now taking on diplomatic negotiations with European powers. Walton praises his language abilities, claiming that at 11 Donne already possessed 'a good command both of the French and Latine tongue' (1670: 12), and he himself later boasted in a Letter to Buckingham that he had read widely amongst Spanish writers 'in any profession, from the Mistresse of my youth, Poetry, to the wyfe of myne age, Divinity' (Bodleian, MS Tanner 72/3*, fos. 305–06).

In 1603 Donne was consulted by Sir Robert Cotton over Diego de Valdes's *De dignitate regum regnorum Hispaniae*, a work bearing on the dispute over precedence between France and Spain that had been pursued through the diplomatic circles of

Europe and, with an Anglo-Spanish peace treaty imminent, was likely to raise its head in England (Bald 1970: 142). The Letter Donne wrote to Cotton (BL, MS Cotton Cleopatra F.vii., fo. 293) is a highly detailed report on the book that demonstrates the techniques of a pragmatic reader: assessing Valdes's argument, analysing his use of sources, and highlighting material supportive of the French claims that the author had overlooked. That Donne had performed similar work for Egerton is suggested by a Letter to Cotton of 20 February 1602, in the wake of the furore over his marriage, where he requests the loan of 'some of the French negotiacons' in order, as he puts it, 'to ease my imprisonm'' (BL, MS Cotton Julius C.III, fo. 153). While Bald interprets the request as a desire 'to lighten the tedium' (Bald 1970: 137), the subject matter suggests that Donne is still intent on studying for service with the Lord Keeper, with whom he would once more 'seek preferment' (*Marriage Letters* 47) in the celebrated petitioning Letter of March 1. Donne's scholarly habits are suggested by the 'Extract of near Fifteen hundred Authours' (Walton 1670: 2) found amongst his papers at his death, as well as the known contents of his library (Keynes 1973: Appendix IV), which principally reflect Donne's researches for that later work of applied scholarship, *Pseudo-Martyr*, but also include a smattering of texts on precedence and procedure in the courts of Europe (L1, L5, L29)—the subject on which Cotton had sought his opinion.

The opening of his *Sat1* also suggests the kind of techniques and training that Donne could place at Egerton's disposal, with his depiction of an Inns of Court persona surrounded by the materials of a wide-ranging reading programme focused upon acquiring a breadth of learning for application: the work of statesmen is to 'teach' lessons in governance (l. 7), the value of chronicles is their 'gathering' (l. 9) of information for a pragmatic reader to render instrumental; even Aristotle appears in the pragmatic guise of service as 'Natures Secretary' (l. 6). Donne's secretarial duties may, then, have combined targeted research work with services drawing upon a broad programme of reading such as that outlined in the Satire, including more mundane tasks such as commonplacing: providing authorities and citations for use. Should Egerton have needed any help in the matter, Donne was more than able to supply the kind of Senecan maxims that punctuate the Lord Keeper's letter to Essex.

Letter writing was a vital aspect of the business of court life, and it is possible that Donne played some junior role in managing Egerton's correspondence networks. The accomplishment of Donne's letter writing later in life, attested to by the posthumous popularity of his Letters, which appeared in such important collections as *Cabala, Sive, Scrinia Sacra* (1654b) and *A Collection of Letters made by Sir Tobie Matthew* (1660), as well as the *Letters to Severall Persons of Honour* (1651), might suggest his likely involvement in this aspect of courtly service (see Ch. 25). There is no manuscript evidence of Donne's hand in the correspondence of Egerton, however, and Donne's own Letters from the period actually show him still exploring the arts of letter writing, including the careful negotiation of social relations that was a vital function of the familiar letter in court society. The Letter to Sir George More, announcing Donne's clandestine marriage to More's daughter Anne, was vitally important to the couple's future prospects and carefully planned. But despite securing the services of the Earl of Northumberland to present it, Donne badly miscalculated in the adoption of a frank tone and a playful shortage of deference (Mack 122–3)—the grovelling humility of his subsequent Letters could not repair the damage.

Donne maintained an active letter-writing network of his own, and his Letters to Sir Henry Wotton demonstrate the younger man's diligent efforts to cultivate a correspondence. The verse epistles of the two men are of particular interest for the way they explore the vicissitudes of courtly employment. Wotton's verse epistle to Donne, 'Worthie Sir', is one of a series of poems that considers the challenges of a virtuous life—a classical convention of the verse epistle, as Margaret Maurer's chapter in this volume (Ch. 14) makes clear. Rejecting the rhetoric of courtly corruption, Wotton comes down on the side of *negotium* over *otium*, since 'every where wee may doe good or ill' (Pebworth and Summers 1984: 368–9, l. 23). In doing so, however, Wotton not only offers a contribution to the poetic debate with Donne, but also provides a careful critique of the intemperate behaviour of his patron the Earl of Essex. Advising that 'the mynd of passions must be free' (l. 7), and warning that 'desires that on extreames are bent / Are frends to care and traitors to content' (ll. 11–12), Wotton provides an insight into the frustrations of an unheeded counsellor.

While Pebworth and Summers put forward a plausible chronology for the letters and the verse epistles, the sequence is still open to debate (Scodel 1993: 503). One of the verse epistles is dateable, however, by virtue of its topicality. Donne's *HWNews* is commonly dated 20 July 1598 in manuscripts, reinforcing its association with the period of Essex's self-imposed exile from court in the aftermath of the Privy Council contretemps in which Elizabeth had boxed his ear for his insolence. The Verse Letter offers Wotton, absent from court along with his patron Essex, a condemnation of courtly machinations and intrigues, from one obliged to observe them. The poem's depiction of a court at war, with the defeat of a party inappropriately armed for such battle, and fated 'in'the Courts Squadron to marshall their state' (l. 12) before annihilation at the hands of more worldly enemies, evokes the spectre of the outmanoeuvred Earl Marshal, with his proud and forthright championing of military service ineffective in the face of courtly schemes and rumour-mongering. If Camden's account of the original incident reflects what was known at the time, Donne's humorous play on court ears, 'Tender to know, tough to acknowledge wrongs' (l. 18), looks to rub salt on the Earl's wounded honour. The Verse Letter concludes with a poetic subscription in which he appropriates epistolary convention to amplify the rejection of courtly corruption: '*At Court*; though *From Court*, were the better stile' (l. 27). While Donne puns on the scene of letter writing, his words also raise the idea of a literary style associated with absence from court. No one was more associated with such a style at this moment than Essex himself. In his response to the Lord Keeper from exile, the Earl had drawn attention to the self-consciousness of his own epistolary style: 'I must crave yor Lo^{ps} patience to give him Leave that hath a Crabbed fortune, to use a Crabbed stile' (BL, MS Royal 17.B.L, fo. 10^v; Gordon 325–6). Dennis Flynn has pointed out the error of identifying Donne wholly with the followers of Essex (Flynn 1995*b*), however, and if Donne echoes the Earl here, it is with a barbed reflection that the opposition is after all a false one, since in epistolary formulae, '*At Court*' and '*From Court*' are equivalents differing only in title. Far from being apart from the world of the court then, Essex's anti-court rhetoric is a court-centred styling after all.

Essex's literary and political positioning of himself as a discontented outsider was a strategy fraught with risk. Absence from the court left the Earl vulnerable to the machinations of those surrounding the Queen, and part of his cultivation of a crabbed style in letters and poems circulated at court was to maintain a rhetorical presence in court affairs. This style did not persuade all about him, however. While Essex continued in his obstinate course after Burghley's death, an exasperated William Knollys, the Earl's only reliable ally in the Privy Council, complained that his absence at this critical moment was 'very unseasonable both ffor the co*mm*on good (manye wayghtye causes now dependyng) & your Lo:^{shipps} owne pryvat', leaving him unable to influence directly the redistribution of patronage (WRO, *Devereux Letter Book*, fo. 44). By the time of his return to court in September the situation in Ireland had grown more urgent, but Essex rejected all candidates for the command, although in such a manner 'as hee seemed to point with the finger to himselfe' (Camden 1635: 503). In this, Essex was egged on both by his own followers and those whom Camden termed 'a subtill kinde of enemies' that 'wished him rather absent than present' (504).

When Essex eventually set off as Lord Lieutenant of Ireland in March of 1599 it was with expectations at fever-pitch and accompanied by huge outpourings of popular support, but the reality of a situation far worse than anticipated confronted him almost immediately. Setbacks in the campaign were exacerbated by adverse conditions, lack of supplies, and serious illness on Essex's part, which led him to negotiate a treaty with Tyrone against Elizabeth's orders. In September 1599 Essex secretly left Ireland and raced back to London, staking everything on a private audience with the Queen at which he might explain his actions. While he obtained his audience by bursting in upon a monarch *déshabillé*, the aftermath was house arrest at the Lord Keeper's residence in York House, where Donne would have had an opportunity to observe the Earl as he languished in poor spirits and ill health while the Queen and council decided what action to take.

Donne may also have gained access to the eventual hearing in June 1600, also in York House, where the Earl's conduct in Ireland, and his notorious letter to Egerton, were raised before a commission of councillors and an audience of 'Noble men about London, or the Court, many Knight[es] bo of the best account & other Choise menne both Courtiers & others that were about the Towne' (FSL, MS V.b. 41: 287). The principal part of the day was taken up with the censure offered by each of the lords, beginning with the Lord Keeper himself, who 'amplified to the vttermost all the Earles contempts and disobediences, that her Maiesties great mercy might appear the more cleerely' (Morrison, part 2.74). Essex was suspended from office as a privy councillor, as Master of the Ordnance, and as Earl Marshall, and placed under house arrest at Essex House. This was the end of Essex's career as courtier and councillor, but he would still have a role to play in events.

Since Essex's ability to influence proceedings in council and effectively channel patronage had faltered in the late 1590s, he and his followers had played increasingly to an audience beyond the court. Essex's *Apologie* putting the case for war against Spain was circulated in manuscript, as were the Egerton–Essex letters and a body of poetic works ranging from those attributed to the Earl himself (e.g. 'it was a time when sillie Bees could speake') to more explicit libels that lambasted the growing list of those identified as the Earl's enemies at court. In February 1601 he made a disastrous attempt to capitalize on this paper campaign, leading a few hundred of his supporters to the city in the hope of securing popular support that, in the event, failed to materialize. The result was trial for treason and execution within the month.

Whilst a number of Essex associates were imprisoned and interrogated, the more politic of his friends had either dissociated themselves already from his following or moved swiftly to do so. Francis Bacon had been seeking other patrons since shortly after the Earl's return from Ireland, and now assisted the prosecuting team. Lord Mountjoy had taken the Earl's place in Ireland, and Cecil's letter informing him of events enabled him to confirm his allegiance to Queen and council. Lord Henry Howard had quietly cultivated a connection with Cecil and now built on his contacts with James VI to transfer his allegiance. Wotton too contrived to be out of the way.

In the aftermath of the trial a major propaganda offensive was undertaken to publicize the Earl's treachery via the pulpit and the press, but the heavy-handedness of these attempts backfired. Libels continued to circulate in praise of 'Him Cankred Cecill slew', blaming the Secretary for engineering Essex's death, and condemning the now unopposed authority of 'Little Cecill [who] Rules bothe Court & Croun' (Bellany and McRae A12 and A13). Donne registered his own distaste in *The Courtier's Library* (see Ch. 12 above), where he pilloried for their part in the affair both Francis Bacon, author of the official account of the trial, and William Barlow, who gave the infamous sermon at Paul's Cross in condemnation of the executed Earl (*Courtier's Library* 36–7, 51–2). Donne's contempt for those who bent with the prevailing wind was no doubt sharpened by his own sudden fall from favour in February of the following year. As a servant to the Lord Keeper, one of those 'great men' who had scrupulously observed Bacon's own advice to 'maintain themselues indifferent and neutrall', he had confidently avoided factional allegiance. As he wrote to his former patron: 'I had, (and I had understandinge inough to valew yt) the sweetnes and security of a freedome and independency' (*Marriage Letters* 47). But Donne's independence was an indulgence for one of the mean men; in Cornwallis's words, he found himself 'no sooner loosened, but ruined'. The author of *ElServ*, with its witty distinction in duty applied to courtly service in love, 'Oh let not me serve so, as those men serve' (l. 1), now found himself able to aspire no higher than 'Fauorit in ordinary' (l. 10).

CHAPTER 30.1

DONNE'S WEDDING AND THE PYRFORD YEARS

DENNIS FLYNN

1

WHEN Donne first met Anne More is still unclear. Many writers have assumed their first acquaintance dated from the time Donne came to work for Lord Keeper Thomas Egerton at York House, in late 1597 (e.g. Bald 1970: 96). By this time Anne's grandfather, Sir William More, had arranged her continuing education under the careful eye of his favourite child, Anne's aunt Elizabeth (widow of Sir John Wolley, late the Queen's Latin Secretary), whom Egerton had married by early October, when the new Lady Egerton took over signing his household accounts (see Ch. 29.I). Elizabeth Egerton brought Anne More, not yet 14, to York House as an accustomed companion to her son Francis Wolley, a year older than Anne.

The possibility that Donne already knew Anne by this time is suggested by his important and well-known, but still puzzling, information in a Letter of 1602 that it had been through the Lord Keeper's 'good Sonns love' that he had obtained his employment as Egerton's secretary (*Marriage Letters* 47). The only son of the Lord Keeper with whom we know Donne had any close friendship was Egerton's stepson Francis, who took the newlywed couple in after their wedding and gave them a house at his Pyrford estate (for alternative suggestions see Ch. 29.I); for their part, the Donnes named their fourth child Francis, after his godfather. If Wolley was the son whose 'love' obtained for Donne a post with the Lord Keeper, then he and Donne must have had some association previous to late 1597. In this case, Donne may also have had earlier acquaintance with Wolley's cousin and schoolmate, Anne More.

In any case, at least after 1597 this trio must have been frequently in each other's company, not only at York House but at Pyrford, the favoured resort of the Lord Keeper and Elizabeth Egerton (who had inherited in dower the lease formerly held by Sir John Wolley), especially after she contracted smallpox at York House late in 1598. Until the death of Lady Egerton in January 1600, the Lord Keeper spent increasing time at Pyrford with his wife, bringing staff members there with him in order to keep up with the press of London business. Pyrford thus was a place where Donne and Anne More spent time together, if not before, then surely after his employment by Egerton began. At some point not much later than Lady Egerton's death, Anne's father removed her from Egerton's household to Loseley (Walton 1675: 16), a few miles south of Pyrford, reportedly thwarting the growing intimacy between Donne and his daughter, who was by this time nearly 16 years old. Despite the couple's consequent separation, they may have exchanged some letters that heightened desire, as has been argued by Ilona Bell (1986: 27–45), interpreting three letters in the 'Burley manuscript' (LRO, MS Finch DG.7, Lit. 2) as Donne's letters to Anne More.

Moreover, if these letters are authentic, during the summer of 1601 John and Anne shared passionate time together somewhere, possibly at Pyrford: 'in all that part of this sommer which I spent in your presence you doubled the heat and I loved under the rage of a hott sunn and your eyes' (LRO, MS Finch DG.7, Lit. 2, fo. 295). Donne apparently sent this exciting, dangerous letter to Anne at Sir George More's house in Blackfriars late in October 1601, after More had brought her with him to London, preparing to represent Surrey at the convening Parliament. By this time Donne had taken lodgings at the Savoy rents, in addition to accommodations no doubt still available to him at York House. He and Anne met somewhere several times in London during October and November 1601 and were married in the first week of December, probably at the Savoy chapel, later notorious for clandestine weddings held there (Bald 1970: 128–9). Presiding clergyman at the ceremony was Samuel Brooke; his brother, the barrister Christopher Brooke, Donne's close friend at Lincoln's Inn, took the place of Sir George More in giving away the bride; and three still-unidentified witnesses were also present.

The wedding was carefully planned, not a reckless adventure of love. In his arrangements before and after the wedding Donne must have drawn on his legal learning and/or some astute legal advice. Fortunately, his lodgings in the Savoy rents had been chosen within one of the London 'liberties', districts exempt from the jurisdiction of the London sheriffs. The Savoy chapel, constructed between 1490 and 1512, was a 'free' or 'peculiar' church, belonging to the Crown rather than to any bishop. The chapel's operations were outside the jurisdiction of the diocese of

London, supervised not by diocesan courts but by a court of original jurisdiction for the province of Canterbury, the Court of Audience. Within weeks of the wedding Donne had prepared to bring suit in this court, where two lawyers appeared, one (named Price) representing Anne, the other (named Milbery) representing Donne. At some point in January 1602 these two lawyers presented evidence and argued before a judge of the court, Dr Richard Swale, concerning the validity of the wedding. Having heard their arguments, Swale undertook to decide as a matter of law whether the couple were bound by any other marital contracts or arrangements, and whether they were in consequence lawfully man and wife (*Marriage Letters* 49–52).

During the two months following the wedding, before a hearing was concluded and these proceedings developed, Donne and Anne More kept their marriage a secret from the rest of the world. After the Parliament dissolved on 19 December 1601 Anne remained at home with her father, telling him nothing. Only in a Letter of 2 February 1602 did Donne—knowing that his legal position was secure, that his case was under consideration by Swale, and that he probably could expect a favourable judgement—reveal glimpses of the full truth to Sir George More in a Letter reportedly delivered by Henry Percy, ninth Earl of Northumberland (Walton 1675: 17). Nothing suggests that More would have been favourably influenced by this choice of a messenger. He and Northumberland had no known association (despite the unfounded suggestion of Bald 1970: 133–4). Beyond the notion, impressive in itself, that Donne had enlisted an Earl as a letter carrier, his choice of this particular earl would seem, perhaps unintentionally, startling and provocative. Northumberland was one of the principal members of the peerage, but he was a scion of executed Catholic traitors (as such regarded with suspicion by all who, like More, were fervent supporters of Tudor government and the established religion) and was held in line uncomfortably throughout his adult life by the close supervision of the Privy Council. That Northumberland carried Donne's Letter implied noble sponsorship of Donne and his wedding. Nevertheless, Donne should have expected More would receive such a message, from such a messenger, with dismay. One of his Letters to Anne More before the wedding had demonstrated Donne's awareness not only that her father was prone to taking 'good fuell of anger' when he was crossed, but that this anger could strike unreasonably and with irrational prejudice (LRO, MS Finch DG.7, Lit. 2, fo. 296).

Nevertheless, in accord with his choice of messenger, Donne's Letter to Sir George More was in effect a brazen, covertly defiant disclosure, provoking the notorious anger of the unknowing father-in-law, for whom Donne reviewed only some of the insulting and amazing details of the plot. Then, with cool insolence, Donne advised More to accept the inevitable and even to extend a dowry: 'yt ys irremediably donne' (*Marriage Letters* 36). This mischievous wrap-up is as close as he came to saying anything concerning the impending judgement by Swale. After reading this Letter the enraged More immediately urged the Lord Keeper to dismiss Donne from his service and to imprison him, something he came to regret and tried to reverse without success.

Likely surprising Donne, Egerton reluctantly complied with More's request, dismissing his secretary. Simultaneously, More petitioned the Court of High Commission, of which Egerton was a member *ex officio*, for annulment of the marriage; and by 10 February Donne had been committed by the court to the Fleet prison, whence he wrote dejected appeals for mercy to both More and the Lord Keeper, altering the brash tone of his initial Letter. The High Commission by the end of Elizabeth's reign routinely accepted cases of clandestine weddings, although decisions on the validity of such ceremonies were always left to the jurisdiction of the ordinary's ecclesiastical courts. When the High Commission acted not merely against accessories but against principals in a marriage case, this was usually because of a claim involving nonconformity, especially of Catholic recusants. It is not possible to say whether More's claim against Donne was of this kind, since the records of High Commission cases are not extant. Donne's Letters after the wedding do reveal his impression, however, that More suspected Donne was a crypto-Catholic (*Marriage Letters* 35, 36, 37, 40, and 45). In any case, claims concerning marriages without parental consent also were heard by the High Commission as matters within its sphere (Carlson 89–92 and 97–8). On one or both of these grounds, the court agreed to consider Sir George More's complaint against Donne.

However, Donne was out of prison and back in his quarters near the Savoy by 13 February, although he was to remain under house arrest in his chamber for a few days. Donne's release may have been caused by the fact that his prudent legal arrangements had ruled out any real warrant to hold him; the January hearing before Swale, and its predictably favourable verdict, had probably come to the court's attention. On the other hand, Christopher Brooke, as a practising barrister, and his brother Samuel, as a minister, were imprisoned by the court at its session on 18 February for their respective violations of common and canon law in assisting the marriage of a minor without parental consent and in procuring a licence for marriage without banns. Preliminarily, the High Commission found no justiciable objection to the marriage of John and Anne More Donne, neither as to nonconformity nor as to the absence of parental consent; instead, the court apparently ruled that the case should be decided through Donne's prior suit in the Court of Audience, whose jurisdiction it deemed more appropriate for determining the validity of this wedding.

In a Letter to Sir Henry Goodere on 23 February Donne accordingly interpreted the High Commission's deference to the provincial church court as an implicit endorsement of his wedding's validity: 'The Commissioners by Imprisoning the wittnesses and Excommunicating all us have implicitlie justified our Marriage' (GL, MS CF56). By the late Elizabethan period the mere penalty of excommunication was incurred so commonly and harmlessly that it was regarded as indefinite postponement of any disciplinary action that might be taken (Price 111). Donne's confidence in this Letter was expressed in terms suggesting that Goodere already knew a great deal about the wedding. At the same time, the Letter was phrased in a way that could not have implicated Goodere.

The crucial day in the High Commission's process was 'Mitigation Day', 25 February, on which the court convened to remit or lighten sentences rendered earlier in the term. Evidently, by that day the commissioners were inclined to lift penalties previously imposed on Donne and his accomplices. Christopher Brooke was in the Marshalsea prison; his brother Samuel was in yet another prison. From the Marshalsea, prior to Mitigation Day, Christopher had written his own appeal for release to the Lord Keeper, explaining that he had never been told by Donne that the bride's father was an important Surrey official and landowner, nor that More was Egerton's former brother-in-law. He pleaded innocence based on ignorance of these facts: '(as unwise as I am) I would have chosen rather to have undergone for master Donne some other more apparant daunger'. Nevertheless, Brooke showed no resentment towards Donne: 'And pardon me a word for him my Lord, were it not now best, that every one, whome he any way concerns, should become his favourer or his frind, whoe wants (my good Lord) but fortunes handes and tonge to reare him upp, and sett him out'. Brooke also asked that £1,100 he had been required to post as a bond (a sum estimated at more than £150,000 today) be restored to him and his bondsmen (*Marriage Letters* 43–4). Probably also on Mitigation Day, Donne paid or was required to pay the cost of all three prisoners' charges, amounting to £40—estimated at over £5,700 today—something he reported having done in his Letter to More on 1 March (ibid. 46).

On 27 April Dr Richard Swale's decree (ibid. 49–52) issued from the Court of Audience, 'deposited and promulgated…at the Court of Common Pleas, London'. It declared that Swale, as a lawfully constituted judge, had heard 'this case in the month of January' and assessed the circumstances of the wedding, its procedures, and the relevant points of law made by lawyers for both parties in the case, 'Donne v. Donne alias Moore'. Without specifying the arguments of either party, Swale decided in favour of Donne, whose case he deemed 'well founded and proved', so that 'nothing effectual from the party or through the party of the aforesaid Anne Moore alias Donne in this case has been or may be excepted, argued, proposed, alleged or proved that would negate the accusation of the said John Donne in this case, or in any way weaken it'. Swale concluded by declaring 'in effect a true and pure marriage between them to have been contracted, and solemnized and brought about and a marriage true and pure to have been and to be between the said Anne Moore alias Donne and John Donne duly initiated and also solemnized by a priest suitable and competent for that purpose and in the presence of trustworthy witnesses' (ibid. 52). All contemporary dispute regarding the date or validity of the wedding appears to have been definitively settled by this document, whose contents apparently had for weeks been anticipated and were accepted by all the principals.

2

Despite this general acceptance of the 'marriage true and pure' of John and Anne Donne, various issues in Donne studies have arisen, some of them crucial problems for our understanding of Donne's life and writings. Leaving aside largely misconceived issues of alleged immoral conduct (LeComte 168–9; Milgate 66–7; I. Bell 1986: 25–6), undoubtedly the most crucial and fundamental problem has been our inability to discern clearly the personality of Anne More; we have had no coherent sense of the part she played prior to the wedding nor in subsequent years, from the spring or summer of 1602 until early 1605, during which time the newlywed couple began to raise a family in a house on Francis Wolley's estate at Pyrford. Walton described her simply as a 'young Gentlewoman' (1675: 15), and proceeded, without supplying much personal detail, to develop two partly contradictory themes.

On the one hand, he noted that she 'had been curiously and plentifully educated' (19); that husband and wife had a close and loving 'sympathy of souls' which he compared to the concordance of 'two Lutes, being both strung and tun'd to an equal pitch' (31); that Donne wrote for her and gave to her one of his love poems, *ValMourn* (33); and that Donne and his wife shared 'mutual and cordial affections', being neither of them 'dull and low-spirited people' (52). On the other hand, Walton offered no hint of Anne Donne's own agency or responsibility in the marriage, but instead stressed her consequent loss of social status, as well as her suffering in childbirth and child-rearing, often citing Donne's uneasiness that he had been the cause of her losses (20, 25, and 30). Walton's final word on the subject was spoken with a glibness of patriarchy: that Donne's marriage had been 'the remarkable error of his life' for which 'he would occasionally condemn himself' (52); while there is little evidence of Donne's self-condemnation for having married in error, much that is extant contradicts Walton's conclusion. More to the point, Walton never mentions what Anne Donne thought about it all, something he probably did not know. He had never known her, a fact that cannot in itself explain how little he says about her but which does tend to make the more remarkable his specific information about her having been an educated and high-spirited soulmate to Donne. On the whole, Walton's version of her character may seem inconsistent.

Donne's later biographers, opting for consistency, have all ignored or dismissed Walton's striking comments about Anne Donne's curious, plentiful education or her sympathetic and equal-poised spirits. To mention only a few influential examples, Augustus Jessopp, in several publications on Donne (e.g. his 1897 biography), never referred to Walton's testimony nor offered any characterization of Anne Donne. Edmund Gosse, without mentioning Walton's comments on her education, called her a 'shadowy' person and denigrated her intellect (1.118). R. C. Bald conceded she 'must have had' intelligence, but made no mention of her reputed learning and placed greater emphasis on her 'steadiness and dependability' (1970: 326). John Carey repeated Gosse's word 'shadowy' and then, like Gosse and Bald, unaccountably contradicted Walton's point without even acknowledging it, instead offering the opinion that Anne More was 'virtually uneducated'. With this especially influential canard, Carey bolstered his notion that Donne 'soon grew tired of being cooped up with her' and the succession of children she bore. Carey went on to opine that Donne must have preferred witless and ignorant women. He concluded, in tones of disgust, that 'all we know for certain about Donne's wife is that she was generally pregnant, and that no one recorded for posterity any clear impression of her character' (1981a: 74). While these last two points are in part true, they hardly support Carey's other judgements of Anne Donne, or those of earlier biographers, for which there simply is no evidence.

However, among the Loseley manuscripts collected and preserved by Anne More's grandfather, Sir William More, there is contrary evidence to show that she (with other women of her family) did in fact receive from him the careful education Walton mentions: for example, a deed of 1587 signed by her father, providing funds for Anne's and her sisters' education by their grandfather (SHC, LM/348/178); and references to tutors Sir William More hired to give lessons in music, rudimentary Greek, and Latin poetry to children residing at Loseley (SHC, LM/COR/3/106; SHC, 6729/7/122; FSL, MS L.b.548–9). The furnishings at Loseley included virginals, lutes, and gitterns for the children, as well as a library including hundreds of books (J. Evans 289 and 290–2; FSL, MS L.b.550). Following the death of Anne's mother in 1590, when George More remarried, built his own house at Ewhurst, Surrey, and moved away from Loseley (English 54), he took his son Robert with him but left his daughters to be raised by their grandparents. By the mid-1590s Sir William More had assigned Anne for mentoring to his oldest daughter and favourite child, Elizabeth Wolley, whom he had earlier raised as one of the best-educated women of her time, one of the Queen's Ladies of the Privy Chamber (McCutcheon 1999: 43). It was Elizabeth Wolley who first brought Anne More to London to continue the tutoring and companionship she had enjoyed at Loseley with her cousin Francis Wolley. Further evidence of Anne More's educated intellect may be seen in the letters in the Burley manuscript that Ilona Bell has argued were written by Donne to Anne More prior to their wedding (LRO, MS Finch DG.7, Lit. 2, fos. 295, 296, and 299^v), letters not only mentioning exchange of earlier letters but also expressing Donne's appreciation and admiration of her learning (I. Bell 1986: 26–46). Such evidence about Anne More suggests her 'active agency' (Slights 1996: 86) as the lover and later the wife of John Donne, and contributes to our understanding of their courtship and early married life.

3

At some point later in 1602 Donne and his wife were united and lived for three years at Pyrford, occupying one of the property's two manor houses inherited by Francis Wolley from his mother. A map at Cambridge University Library illustrates these houses and other features of Wolley's Pyrford estate *c.*1614. Set among fields and streams, near a deer park and adjacent medieval ruins, Wolley's estate was situated on former abbey lands, time out of mind a favoured country home for abbots of Westminster, until the dissolution of the monasteries. By 1602 the abbots' old house may have been largely destroyed, as was nearby Newark Priory. In the 1570s Pyrford had been conveyed by a royal grant into the hands of Edward Clinton, Earl of Lincoln. His wife Elizabeth, Surrey's 'Fair Geraldine', was a lady of Queen Elizabeth's privy chamber; as a friend of Sir William More, she had taken part in grooming Elizabeth Wolley for a similar position (McCutcheon 1999: 38–40). Making Pyrford one of their country homes, the Earl and Lady Lincoln had restored the medieval manor house or built a new one, hosting the Queen there in the spring of 1576 on the occasion of William More's knighthood, conferred in a formal garden. Shortly afterwards Pyrford passed into the hands of John and Elizabeth Wolley, who in turn built a second house there, both houses surrounded by brick walls also enclosing old orchards, where they too entertained the Queen on several occasions. The one enduring structure from this period is a two-storey brick banqueting house, traditionally known as 'Queen Elizabeth's summer house', once set into the orchard wall, commanding views of the monastic orchards and of a field sloping down to the River Wey, along which at a distance were also visible the ruins of the priory (Alexander 339–60). For Anne and for her husband, living at Pyrford involved memories of their growing intimacy in the late 1590s.

Donne's activities through the remainder of 1602 are almost entirely unknown. Probably he remained quietly at Pyrford most of the time. On 6 July he came to London to receive, through the Lord Keeper's man, a legacy for Anne of £100—a sum that today might amount to £14,000—from her late aunt (*Marriage Letters* 53). The death of Queen Elizabeth in the following spring, with the succession of King James I, did not stir Donne to noticeable activity, although many of his friends and acquaintances swarmed about the new king. For example, John Davies the poet, who had frequented York House during Donne's employment, immediately rode north seeking preferment, as did Edmund Neville, the self-styled baron of Latimer. A few days later Toby Matthew rode north, bearing a letter from his very good friend Francis Bacon, offering service to the King, already en route towards London (Chamberlain 1.189 and 192). Matthew joined his father Tobie, the Bishop of Durham, in Berwick, where on 6 April Matthew the elder preached the first sermon James heard on English soil. Toby the younger took advantage of this connection for Bacon's sake, and for his own part took careful note of all that transpired at

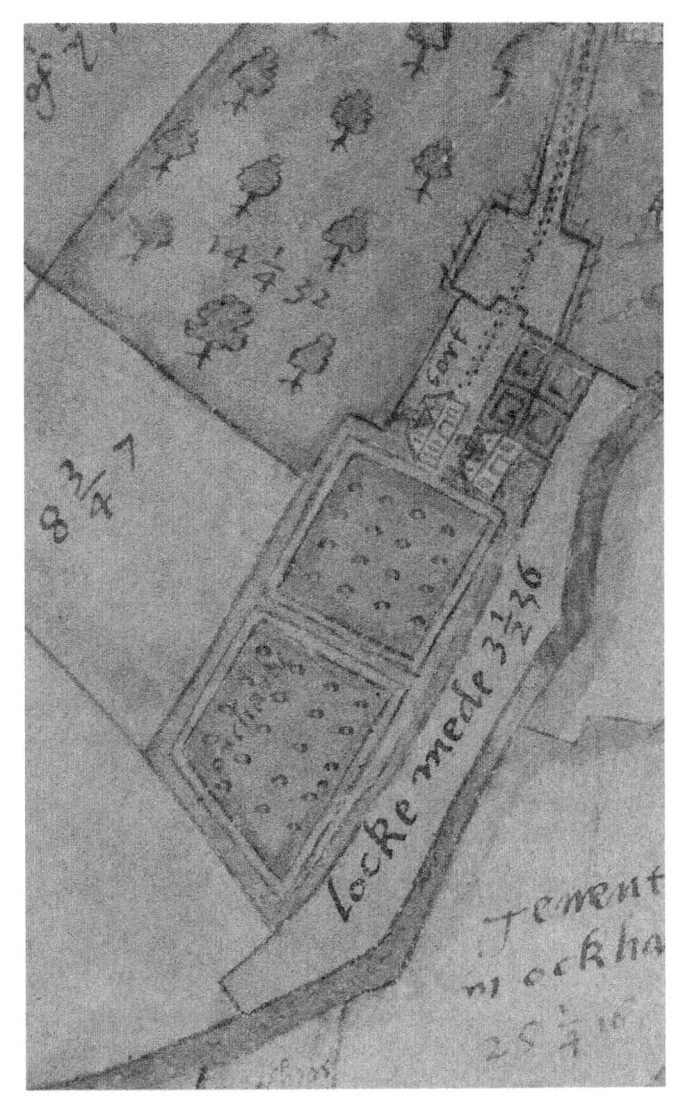

Map 30.I.1. Map of Pyrford, detail (CUL Maps MS Plans 759a). Map of Pyrford showing the estate of Sir Francis Wolley after his death in 1609. To the left of a deer park appears a long lane lined with elms, leading to the two houses owned by Wolley, in one of which the Donnes lived during the first years of their marriage. (Reproduced by kind permission of the Syndics of Cambridge University Library, Maps.Ms.Plans.758–9a.)

Berwick and all that had transpired since the King had left Edinburgh. When the King departed towards London two days later, Matthew trailed along with his father to Newcastle, where the Bishop again preached to the King on Sunday, 10 April. Thence, on 13 April, the royal party travelled to Durham, where the Bishop hosted a lavish reception. His son left Durham with the King next day to track his progress all the way to London (Firth 21–4).

From his travel Matthew did not gain more than the material he would publish as a journalist's narrative about the King's progress from Edinburgh to London; but other friends and acquaintances of Donne were knighted during the journey, including Walter Chute and Basil Brooke at Belvoir Castle, and Richard Baker at Theobalds. Sir Henry Goodere, as a client of Queen Anne's favourite Lucy Russell, Countess of Bedford, was appointed a gentleman of the privy chamber, along with other friends and acquaintances of Donne, including Sir William Cornwallis and Sir Charles Percy, brother of Donne's friend Henry Percy, ninth Earl of Northumberland. Northumberland himself, enjoying sudden favour, had been sworn a member of the Privy Council in April; in May he was appointed captain of the gentlemen pensioners, the official royal bodyguard. He took advantage of this ascendance to proffer the new king a petition from English Catholics advocating toleration of traditional Catholicism. From this point on Northumberland's advantage ceased to grow.

On 7 May the King arrived at London, travelling first to the Charterhouse for four hectic days of feasting and entertainment, amid uncontrolled throngs of people. Plague had broken out in London during the previous few weeks, adding a touch of chaos to the King's advent in the capital. Among those who died was Donne's brother-in-law William Lyly, come to London seeking preferment in the new reign. Donne, perhaps with Anne, was present at least at the climax of the Charterhouse visit on 11 May to witness the knighting of Francis Wolley in a crowd, along with other friends including Robert Cotton. Donne later recalled this occasion sarcastically as one on which King James became 'a Knight-wright', turning out titled gentleman like 'ware at 100l. 150l. and 200l. price' (Donne 1929a: 415). Wolley and other commoners (all who could clear a designated threshold in annual income from their lands) were apparently required to compound with royal commissioners and pay fees for knighthood on a sliding scale.

The local prominence of Donne's in-laws continued to afford him brief access to the court, but he did not take any active advantage. Following the coronation late in July, the King and Queen went on progress through the southern counties, staying first at Sir Francis Wolley's house in Pyrford on 10 August, followed by two nights at Loseley with Sir George More. Donne and Anne would likely have attended both these visits; and at Loseley, Goodere, apparently on his own initiative, approached Queen Anne's secretary William Fowler about the prospect of Donne's possible service in the Queen's court. This initiative led nowhere, except to provide Donne with grounds for later satirical comment (*Letters* 81). For the most part, having abandoned his London residence Donne lived at Pyrford without evident ambition during these years, isolated from the court and the other scenes of his late employment by the Lord Keeper.

Nevertheless, his interest in some of the legal and diplomatic work he had been doing evidently continued. At midsummer 1603 he had borrowed from his friend Sir Robert Cotton a book by Diego de Valdés, recently published at Granada, *De dignitate regum regnorumque Hispaniae*. Donne undertook to write an opinion of the book for Cotton, with whom, while still in the Lord Keeper's employ, he had done similar work (cf. an earlier Letter to Cotton, BL, MS Cotton Julius C. III./153). The focus of all this work was diplomacy, in connection with which Donne could use his language skills, legal study, wide reading, and experience as a traveller. But detachment from the practical application of such skills to career pursuits is implied in the laconic close of his Letter to Cotton about returning the Valdés book: 'sir I haue both held your booke longer then I ment, and held yow longer by thys letter, now I send it backe. But yow that are a reall and free doer of benefits, I presume are also an easy pardoner of vnmalicious faults' (BL, MS Cotton Cleopatra F. vii./293). The last phrase may allude to Donne's not having been pardoned by the Lord Keeper for an earlier 'vnmalicious' fault, conveying wry aloofness (to a friend who agreed Donne had been unfairly dismissed) from the business of place-seeking in the early years of the new reign.

That Donne had settled fairly comfortably into an attitude of observant indifference at Pyrford is made clear by his exchange of several letters with Matthew between December 1603 and May 1604. The first of these letters, from Matthew, discussed the trial of Sir Walter Ralegh. In the summer of 1603 Ralegh, with others, had been arrested on charges of treasonous conspiracy; in November he and the others had stood trial for treason at Winchester. Matthew reported on it as a journalist in a pamphlet published at London (M[atthew] 1603). In the letter to Donne he recounted Ralegh's stout conduct of his own defence (*TMC* 283). Three weeks after Ralegh's trial came the executions of two priests and of Cobham's brother, accused of minor roles in the conspiracy. Subsequently, the King's last-minute reprieve of Ralegh, Cobham, and two others convicted with them occurred, communicated only after three of them successively had been led past their coffins to the scaffold, the executioner standing by with whetted edge. Ralegh alone was not treated to this cruel charade but was told later in his cell that he had been spared. Donne's reply to Matthew's letter, written with careful terseness from Pyrford, shares the implied opinion that the political ruin of Ralegh was the central 'event' in the whole proceeding at Winchester (*TMC* 74–5).

Northumberland had written to the King vouching for Ralegh at the time of his arrest; he had also gone to court to plead for Ralegh's life before the reprieve, enlisting the support of Queen Anne. Northumberland's early favour with the Queen was shown in January 1604, when at her initial masque at court he was honoured with selection in the 'taking out' of noblemen, a part of the masque performed by twelve women dressed as goddesses, one of them the Queen (Barroll 95). But such favour could not alter the downward curve traced by Northumberland's political career in the early months of the new reign. Although a member of the Privy Council, he was given no specific task and soon was not regularly attending. He was not involved in the negotiation of peace with Spain in 1604, in which otherwise he might have employed Donne and/or his secretary Dudley Carleton, nor did he play much part in the 1604 debate in the House of Lords on the King's proposal for union of his kingdoms. Northumberland held no state office and was the butt of a telling contrast by Gilbert Talbot, seventh Earl of Shrewsbury, in a 1604 letter to Robert Cecil, Baron of Essendon, commenting on Northumberland's well-known hobby: 'he muste never leave planttynge, dyggynge, weedynge', whereas 'you have no leasure to becum a garrdyner' (Hatfield, MSS Salisbury 107/136). Increasingly, for various reasons, Northumberland saw little prospect of meaningfully contributing to English government.

Donne seems to have shared Northumberland's attitude. As Matthew wrote in a letter of March 1604, 'Your friends are sorry, that you make your self so great a stranger'. He went on to advise Donne to come to court as soon as possible, because 'the places of Attendance, such as may deserve you, grow dailie dearer', and 'the King's hand is neither so full, nor so open, as it hath been' (*TMC* 288–9). Two months later Donne still had not come to the court or to London, as Matthew wrote again, recalling his last visit to Pyrford, during the Christmas season of 1603–4. He lamented not having seen Donne for months and complained that Donne had not left Pyrford for many more months (probably not since his visit to the Charterhouse). He recalled having urged Donne to be more active, to come to court or to London not only for the sake of business but for friendship. Admitting that his persuasion had not so far been effective, Matthew chided Donne gently: 'I trust, it shall be no offence to interrupt your melancholly, in which soever of the fair walks it shall possesse you.' Going on to review parliamentary and other gossip of the day, Matthew concluded pointedly by regretting that Anne's pregnancy (her second child, John, had recently been born) had not come to term somewhat earlier, because then Donne might have been able to tear himself away and benefit from the spurt of largesse then experienced at court, the result of a number of gifts sent to the King and Queen by other European sovereigns (*TMC* 290–5). But several more months would pass before Donne would bestir himself for business.

CHAPTER 30.II

NEW HORIZONS IN THE EARLY JACOBEAN PERIOD

ANTHONY MILTON

1

THE succession of James VI of Scotland to the throne of England, Wales, and Ireland seemed to offer new hope to all those who had felt marginalized in the latter years of the previous regime, which had been coloured by the fiscal pressures created by war with Spain and rebellion in Ireland, a crackdown on Puritans and Roman Catholics alike, social unrest, more fractious relations between Crown and Parliament, and the putting down of the Essex revolt. James was certainly happy to encourage hopes for change, and the early years of his reign undoubtedly brought some, in the shape of peace with Spain (and eventually Ireland), an easing of socio-economic distress, an end to uncertainties regarding the succession, and a new court entourage, with the royal bedchamber dominated by Scots. There were new patronage opportunities, not just for Scots: Lord Buckhurst was favoured and the Howards made a major political comeback. James dubbed 906 knights in the first four months of his reign (more than Elizabeth had created in the forty-five years of her own), and over his first four years in England he handed out monetary gifts of over £68,000 and pensions worth nearly £30,000 a year. There was good news for some of Donne's friends amid this bonanza of knighthoods, gifts, and appointments (Bald 1986: 141–6). James remarked in 1607 that 'my first three yeeres [in England] were to me as a Christmas' (James I 1994: 166), and James had certainly acted as Santa.

Donne made little initial attempt to gain the favour of the new regime. He was no longer in the Lord Keeper's employ and did not attend the new court—perhaps wisely, as the King had clearly been primed regarding the irregular circumstances of Donne's marriage and remembered him for this several years later. Nevertheless, James's initial munificence was not quite the bonanza that it might have appeared. As with any new regime, hopes soon fell far short of the reality. While many marginalized people gained knighthoods, political power still remained in the hands of Cecil in particular. For many, the story of James's early reign was of a series of hopes faded, of a revolution that did not happen. The apparent new dawn of royal relations with Parliaments did not last very long, and conflicts over finance became an endemic problem for James's government.

This failed revolution was especially apparent in matters of religion. James kept people guessing about his religious policy, at least initially (even in 1606, in Heidelberg, there were rumours that he was planning to convert to Lutheranism during the visit of his brother-in-law, Christian of Denmark). James's accession attracted petitions for toleration and religious reform from all religious minorities—Roman Catholics, Anabaptists, and Puritans. Puritan hopes that the new regime would finally institute the church reforms that they had demanded for so long were to be frustrated at the Hampton Court Conference. James heard their objections to the church's discipline and ceremonies and concluded that they were astonishingly feeble, and determined that the Settlement should remain essentially as it was, bolstered by Convocation's canons of 1604. The renewed drive for conformity led to the expulsion of between seventy-three and eighty-three beneficed nonconformist clergy over the next five years (most in the early months of 1605). Nevertheless, the concern that James had expressed in his *Basilikon Doron* to distinguish between the radical, politically turbulent presbyterians on the one hand, and the more moderate Puritans who were nevertheless opposed to many of the ceremonies of the Church of England as 'the outward badges of Popish errours' on the other, partly underwrote the manner in which conformity was exacted (James I 1994: 7). Puritans who were prepared to offer limited conformity, and to negotiate discreet private mitigations of royal policy while publicly acknowledging the King's authority, could still be absorbed within the Jacobean church. Especially where they could rely on the support and protection of more evangelical bishops, Puritans could secure a flexible treatment of ceremonial conformity, and were relatively free to pursue their godly aspirations. For many of them, the Jacobean church, for all its faults, appeared to be going essentially in the right direction. While the King made no specific concessions to Puritans, he did initiate a number of piecemeal reforms of the church after Hampton Court, and sounded the right confessional note sufficiently often to keep moderate Puritans on board (Fincham and Lake 1985; Lake 2000).

2

This combination of a discourse of partial tolerance, private indulgence of individuals, yet concern above all else to assert the authority and dignity of the royal office, to extract proof of loyalty, and to hunt down those who opposed it, is also evident in James's treatment of Roman Catholics. Just as with the Puritans, there had been rumours that James would grant full toleration to Roman Catholics at his accession. Certainly, Catholics had special hopes for the accession of the son of Mary Queen of Scots (Watkins). James's accession was celebrated in the English College at Rome by a solemn Mass 'wishing him long life and a happy reign' (Dodd 634). William Barclay, an anti-papal theorist and erstwhile close advisor to James's mother, returned after thirty years in France. The Jesuit lay brother Thomas Pounde, after thirty years in prison, was pardoned and released at James's accession and professed himself to the King 'one of your pupills in temporall power' who was ready to debate his beliefs, 'beinge but an Ideot to anie learned man' (Tutino 2007: 87–92). The Earl of Northampton later provided a public reminder of the tangible change of atmosphere for Roman Catholics on James's accession. In contrast to the reign of Elizabeth, Northampton observed, Catholics were knighted, allowed free access to James's court and person, and were employed on embassies abroad; the 'chiefe Catholicks' were permitted to petition the Privy Council for redress of their grievances; and well-behaved recusants were allowed to 'liue in their own Countries, dispose of their Estates and Tenants, and enioy their pleasures, without any other mulct then the former Lawes had layd on them', while anti-recusant informants were chastised, and priests and Jesuits included in the general pardon issued at the end of the parliamentary session (Anon. 1606: Ff1^v–Ff2^v). Small wonder that it was reported of northern Catholics in November 1603 that 'it is hardly credible in what jollity they now live' as they observed the restoration of Catholic noblemen (Questier 1998a: 24).

James also toyed with ecumenical talk of a general council to reunite Christendom, and declared in a speech to Parliament in March 1604 that 'I acknowledge the Romane Church to be our Mother Church' (which English clergymen then struggled to gloss appropriately) (James I 1994: 139; A. Milton 1995: 141, 276–7; see also [Broughton] 1607: 14–15). Nevertheless, this was not intended to suggest that Roman Catholics were no different from Protestants and should be formally tolerated. Rather, the point was being made that there was no reason why Catholics should not be happy within James's church. Occasional conformity was a sign of their acceptance of royal authority. For some Catholics at least, this would appear to have made sense. As Michael Questier has observed of the manner in which many northern Catholics became newly prepared to offer compliance with James's regime, 'the conformity extorted by an Elizabethan regime which was anathema to nearly all Catholics could be much more willingly conceded by many papists to the Jacobean

State'. Outward conformity could be construed, then, as an assertion of allegiance to the new dynasty (Questier 1998a: 25). By contrast, straightforward requests for formal toleration were not dealt with kindly, and Roman Catholic pamphlets that appealed for toleration on the model of the Edict of Nantes were given short shrift. Those not prepared to 'give but ane outward obedience to the law' (as James put it) were soon in trouble: Barclay returned to Paris (reportedly because an offer of preferment was conditional on his conformity to the Church of England), and Pounde was pilloried and condemned again to life in prison for writing a memorial attacking the persecution of Lancashire Catholics (McCoog 2008). Donne's patron Northumberland, who had urged James before his accession that 'it weare pittie to losse so good a kingdome for the not tollerating a messe [sic] in a cornere' soon lost favour (at least temporarily) when he pleaded for a full toleration now that James was on the throne (James I 1861: 56; M. Nicholls 2008). Recusant fines, having been initially imposed, were remitted in July 1603, but then imposed again in November 1604, as James found it necessary to appease Parliament.

Yet even in his royal proclamation of 22 February 1604, in which James ordered all priests and Jesuits to leave the kingdom within less than a month, he was anxious to reassure those who thought that this might 'presage a greater seueritie towards that sort of our Subiects, who differing in their profession from the Religion by Lawe established, call themselves "Catholikes", then by our proceedings with them hitherto we haue giuen cause to expect'. He even acknowledged himself 'personally so much beholding to the now Bishop of Rome for his kinde offices and priuate temporall cariage towards vs in many things, as wee shall be euer ready to requite the same towards him (as Bishop of Rome in state and condition of a Secular Prince)' ([James I] 1604).

If this official language of moderation and toleration mingled with condemnation had a somewhat schizophrenic feel, this was significantly exacerbated by the Gunpowder Plot, and especially by the Oath of Allegiance that followed. James was anxious to emphasize that moderate Roman Catholics should not be punished. On one reading, the Oath of Allegiance gave the opportunity for some Roman Catholics to make a case for their political loyalty and to distance themselves from forms of disloyal—especially Jesuit—Roman Catholicism. James himself would claim that the introduction of the oath was 'an Acte of great fauour and clemencie towards so many of Our Subiects, Who though blinded with the superstition of Poperie, yet caried a dutifull heart towards our Obedience' ([James I] 1610: 4). There is a danger, however, in assuming that the oath necessarily 'meant' to others (either Protestant or Catholic) what James may have intended it to mean, and that therefore Roman Catholics who rejected the oath were merely being 'intransigent'. James may have genuinely intended the oath to distinguish loyal from disloyal Roman Catholics, but his own reading of these categories was coloured by Protestant assumptions, and Roman Catholic professions of loyalty were required to be framed according to James's template. The crucial problem with the oath was that the papal deposing power was declared to be not just 'impious' but 'heretical', which implied that signatories to the oath departed from the communion of those who believed in the deposing power, and hence could be read as accepting religious conformity (Questier 2008). Roman Catholics were genuinely troubled by the wording, while Protestants themselves were divided in their view of the oath and its purpose: some expressed fears of Roman Catholics who rejected the oath, while others were equally afraid that those who took it had thereby cynically bought themselves immunity from prosecution. James himself sent mixed signals, remarking in the aftermath of the plot that, while 'many honest men, seduced with some errors of Popery, may yet remaine good and faithfull Subiects: So upon the other part, none of those that trewly know and believe the whole grounds, and Schoole conclusions of their doctrine, can ever prove either good Christians, or faithfull Subiects' (James I 1994: 152). While James's written defence of the oath stressed that it did not encroach into matters of religious belief, the second edition of this work was prefaced by a demonstration that the Pope was Antichrist.

Nevertheless, there were Roman Catholics prepared to take the oath—temporarily, and especially in northern England, those approving the oath were those who had already been supporters of James's accession (Questier 1998a: 28–9). For the theorist John Barclay, the crypto-catholic MP John Good, and the aristocrat Lord William Howard, the oath provided a perfect means to demonstrate their secular loyalty to the monarch and to solicit the support of the Jacobean regime (Questier 2008: 1146). For Protestants too, who were happy to condemn Jesuits and papal secular ambitions, the controversy over the oath offered a valuable chance to show support for the monarch. Donne's first published piece of extended writing would address this situation, and entered the world of anti-papal polemic.

3

James's accession had inaugurated a golden age of theological controversy. Continental scholars would complain that the King was entirely absorbed with theology and gave no attention to classical learning. Grotius commented, on returning from England, that 'theologians are there the reigning authorities', and Sarpi observed that 'the king of England was become a doctor of divinity' (Pattison 286). It was controversial divinity in particular that occupied the royal interest. The report that James had his chaplains read through Cardinal Bellarmino's complete *Disputationes* to him at dinner (Peters 302) is undoubtedly an exaggeration, but some aspects of the controversial works of Bellarmino and others undoubtedly engaged his interest, and it was Catholic–Protestant controversy that James found increasingly absorbing. He had already published some of his own: he had identified the Pope as Antichrist in a meditation on the Book of Revelation which he wrote in 1588, and in the first decade of his English reign he published further controversial works against Rome, in his own name and through intermediaries such as Isaac Casaubon. Not surprisingly, his accession to the English throne was greeted by two extensive works on the papal Antichrist (by Robert Abbot and George Downame—the former of whom published part of the King's own commentary within the second edition of his treatise in 1609), and over the following years most prominent Jacobean divines found themselves writing anti-papal polemic, either at the King's behest or with an eye to securing his favour. James's patronage of anti-papal controversy was encapsulated in his support for the founding of Chelsea College as an institution for the systematic production of anti-papal polemic that would rival the resources deployed by the Pope's agents abroad. James himself laid the college's foundation stone in May 1609 (A. Milton 1995: 32–3, 94–5). But the college did not simply give a licence for anti-papal ranting. The King insisted on making his own appointments to the fellowship, and these included a number of divines who were notable more for their intolerance of more extreme forms of anti-Catholicism, namely John Howson, John Overall, William Covell (the defender of Richard Hooker), and even the imminent Roman convert Benjamin Carier (T. Fuller, bk. 10, p. 52).

In recent years Peter Lake has coined the term 'avant-garde conformists' for this new breed of apologists for the established church, who can be distinguished from earlier conformists by their distaste for high Calvinist divinity and churchmanship, and by their enhanced view of the importance of the church's worship, and of the positive 'signifying' value of its ceremonies. Among these divines there was enthusiasm for a more moderated view of the Roman Church. Some (such as Overall) explicitly denied that the Pope was Antichrist, while William Covell—in his semi-official defence of the work of Richard Hooker (published in 1603)—made a number of remarkable concessions regarding the Church of Rome, maintaining that those who lived and died in that church could be saved, that the doctrinal differences separating Protestants from Catholics had been much exaggerated and misunderstood, and that the 'hote spirits' who denied Rome to be a true church levelled the same accusation against the Church of England (Covell 39–40, 42, 46, 66–8, 74, 75, 76–7; A. Milton 1995: 111, 147, 162–3, 212–13). Roman Catholic controversialists were happy to capitalize on these writings, using the works of Covell and others to demonstrate divisions and inconsistencies within the English Protestant position, and in order to argue not just that such writers endorsed many of the Catholic Church's positions, but also that their distance from Puritans was so great that Roman Catholics should more justifiably be given toleration than Puritans (e.g. 'Brereley' 1604; [Broughton] 1607). However, these 'avant-garde conformist' divines were not particularly well disposed towards the Church of Rome as such. Their concern was more with the manner in which more extreme forms of anti-Catholicism could serve to undermine the doctrine and discipline of the Church of England, either by imputing extreme Puritan beliefs to the English Church, or by attacking as 'popery' the true ceremonies and doctrines of the same church (A. Milton 1995: 47–50, 147 and *passim*). Their worries about such extremes did not mean that they themselves avoided all anti-papal controversy. The Oath of Allegiance controversy provided scope for several prominent 'avant-garde conformist' divines—such as Lancelot Andrewes and John Buckeridge—to launch sustained attacks on the secular pretensions of the Pope, the nefarious activities of Jesuits, and various errors of the present Roman Church. This was still compatible with their continuing reservations over the drift of some contemporary anti-Catholicism, while also being a means of retaining the King's support. James would certainly seem to have been convinced that this breed of divines might be capable of a shrewder and more nuanced approach that might win over Roman Catholic opponents—this was presumably why the King saw fit to dictate the presence of such unlikely figures as Covell and Carier among the fellowship of Chelsea College. Moreover, the King's strategy concerning the written defence of the Oath of Allegiance was partly directed towards securing a cross-confessional alliance against the Pope's claims to universal jurisdiction and the deposition of rulers. In James's own writings, and in Buckeridge's massive *De potestate pape in rebus temporalibus* (1614), this took the form of appeals to Roman Catholic as well as Protestant princes to join the royal campaign. James's attempts to support Gallican theorists in France such as Émond Richer (with whom Donne conferred in the spring of 1612, during his visit to Paris with Sir Robert Drury; Bald 1986: 255–6), and the state of Venice during the time of the papal Interdict, also required a tactical and inclusive approach to the divisions within Roman Catholicism.

The need for subtlety in the engagement with Roman Catholicism, and for careful official scrutiny of anti-papal writings, was therefore something that avant-garde conformists could urge with some confidence of royal support. John Overall had argued in particular, in the aftermath of the Gunpowder Plot, that it was necessary that the Roman Church should be tackled with care and learning, and that it was dangerous to allow people to refute papists from their own private ideas, rather than according to the public doctrine of the church. He therefore urged the divines of Convocation to undertake collective action when responding to Roman Catholic writings (A. Milton 2006: 162).

It is important to bear this multifaceted nature of Jacobean anti-Catholic controversy in mind when studying Donne's first involvement in it. Crucial here was the figure of Thomas Morton. Morton was one of the first fellows of Chelsea College, and he was a close associate of Donne in the years prior to the college's founding. Morton had already been engaged in more sophisticated tactical engagement with Roman Catholic writers in the form of his *Apologia Catholica*, which had copied the relatively new mode of polemical exchange deployed by the Roman Catholic controversialist 'John Brereley' (probably the Clerk of the Court of Common Pleas at

Ill. 30.II.1. Samuel Ward's 'Double Deliverance' ('Deo Trin-vni Britanniae bis ultori...') Interest in the Gunpowder Plot revived at times of political crisis throughout the seventeenth century. This print, 'invented' by Samuel Ward and printed at Amsterdam in 1621, was one of the first pictorial representations circulated in England. Although Ward insisted that the drawing had not been intended as an intervention in the Spanish Match negotiations, he was arrested and questioned after the Spanish ambassador complained. The engraving was immensely popular, enjoying reprints until 1689 and serving as a pattern for several surviving pieces of needlework. (© The Trustees of the British Museum.)

Lancaster, James Anderton) in which one's opponents were quoted selectively in support of one's own position. Another work in this style was Morton's *A Catholike Appeale for Protestants* (1609), which was itself a reply to 'Brereley's' *The Apologie of the Romane Church* (1604). While this was a style of argument that was more nuanced than others, it should not be implied that it necessarily reflected a more moderate doctrinal position. It is true that Morton was capable of conducting civil exchanges with Roman Catholics—he had done so while abroad, as well as engaging in formal public disputations with them in York after his return (Baddeley and Naylor 12–14, 17–19). Even amid the volatile content of his post-plot *Exact Discoverie of Romish Doctrine in the case of Conspiracie and Rebellion*, Morton had emphasized that he considered his Roman Catholic countrymen to be his 'beloued brethren' (Morton 1605: A2ʳ). Nevertheless, the style of argument of *Apologia Catholica* and *A Catholike Appeale* was a matter of polemical tactics—and in the case of *A Catholike Appeale* this was a tactic imposed on Morton by his opponent's arguments. His deployment of such sophisticated styles of anti-papal controversy no more reflected an irenical disposition towards the Church of Rome than did the Puritan William Perkins's similar tactic of discussing in detail the elements of doctrine that Rome and the Protestants shared in his *Reformed Catholike* of 1598 (A. Milton 1999: 90–1). Morton himself was a prolific and often acerbic anti-Catholic polemicist of Calvinist views, emphatic that the Pope was Antichrist and that 'we may aswell expect grapes from thornes, or a white Aethiopian, as loyall subiection from this [Roman Catholic] Religion' (Morton 1609: 142–62; 1605: 51–2). He emphatically was not one of the 'avant-garde conformist' group of divines. Moreover, *A Catholike Appeale* was not entirely Morton's work. In fact, it was initially intended to be the creation of a panel of divines (in the manner that Overall had recommended), and although it was ultimately the work of Morton, Overall was allegedly closely involved in the production of the text, which was reportedly completed by Morton in the library of Overall's deanery house at St Paul's, where Morton then resided (Baddeley and Naylor 35–6). While this might be interpreted as friendly hospitality on Overall's part, it is just as likely that it reflected his characteristic determination to exercise surreptitious control over the content of a semi-official publication of the Church of England, of which there are several other examples from this period (A. Milton 2006). John Howson, too, reportedly imposed a number of 'corrections' on Morton's text—an intervention that Archbishop Abbot was still complaining about some years later (Cranfield and Fincham 337–8).

Morton's *Catholike Appeale* is also notable, of course, for the apparent involvement of Donne in reading over the text, at least eighteen months before publication. It would be dangerous, however, to attempt to detect Donne's contributions in a text in which the avant-garde conformist divines Howson and Overall (both significantly senior to Morton) had already recommended changes (allegedly with the King's support). Surprisingly moderate remarks on auricular confession and absolution, eucharistic doctrine, and the possibilities of salvation in the Roman Church may well reflect their intervention. Moreover, there is no evidence to suggest that Donne was acting as a full-time secretary or research assistant to Morton in preparing his text, even though Walton and others attest to the close personal relationship between the two at this time. The one contemporary allusion that survives involves Donne asking his friend Goodere for a copy of the work by 'Brereley' to which Morton's book (which Donne had read) was a reply (*Letters* 66). Donne would surely have been supplied with a copy of the work already if he had been acting in this more formal capacity for Morton. There is also a danger in attributing too much significance to Donne's involvement in a volume that adopted the tactically moderate approach of the *Catholike Appeale*. We have already noted that the 'moderation' of this work was more of a tactical ploy on Morton's part, and it is notable that Donne's relations were generally with more emphatic anti-Catholic divines such as John King and others. There is no real evidence that Donne was close to 'avant-garde conformists' at this time, or indeed later, although his friend Samuel Brooke would embrace a violently anti-Puritan Arminianism in the later 1620s (Tyacke 1987a: 57). Brooke's treatise on predestination (written 1630–1) survives at Trinity College Cambridge (TCC, MS B.15.13). Donne may conceivably have had dealings with Overall during the final stages of the work on the *Catholike Appeale*, but there is no direct evidence for this, although Overall's secretary John Cosin displayed a notable enthusiasm for Donne's Sermons in later life: his copy of Donne's *LXXX Sermons*, which he had with him during his exile in France, is copiously annotated (DUL, Cosin Library, C.II.5). Donne's contacts with Morton may have initially been prompted by overlapping circles of patronage, but there is nothing to suggest that Morton's vigorous reformed anti-Catholicism ever created divisions between them.

While Donne had clearly been an informed observer of anti-Catholic controversy for some years, his first public entry into this field came with his *Pseudo-Martyr*, completed in late 1609. Donne was undoubtedly anxious for preferment at this time, and can hardly have been unaware of the King's overwhelming concern with the matter of the Oath of Allegiance. Casaubon commented despairingly that the King was 'now so entirely taken up with one sort of book, that he keeps his own mind and the minds of all about him occupied exclusively on the one topic. Hardly a day passes on which some new pamphlet is not brought him, mostly written by jesuits, on the martyrdom of *Saint* Garnett, the sufferings of the english catholics, or matters of that description. All these things I have to read and give my opinion upon' (Pattison 286–7). Donne would certainly seem to have secured James's permission for publishing the work and dedicating it to the King (Bald 1986: 221). He would also seem to have been partly prompted by his negative response to the recent contribution to the controversy by William Barlow, Bishop of Lincoln, in his *An Answer to a Catholike English-man* (1609). Writing to his friend Goodere, probably in the late spring of 1609, Donne attacked Barlow's work as 'full of falsifications in words, and in sense, and of falsehoods in matter of fact, and of inconsequent and unscholarlike arguings...of contradiction of himself, and of dangerous and suspected Doctrine in Divinitie' (*Letters* 163). Donne had personal reasons for disliking Barlow, but he needed to be cautious in expressing such views: two Roman Catholics had to defend themselves in Star Chamber against accusations that they had attacked Barlow's work (Questier 2008: 1136 n.17). Donne's basic concern, however, was that Barlow was a careless and dishonest disputant. A distaste for poor strategy and inferior learning, rather than an avant-garde conformist's concern that anti-popery was undermining the doctrine and worship of the Church of England, seems to lie at the root of Donne's displeasure with Barlow's work. Ironically, Barlow had in the past been ready to condemn the 'wilde-fire zeale of some vniuersitie men, who pronounce euery position to be Popish, which is not within the verge of their paper booke common places', and he was closer to the avant-garde conformists in his churchmanship, although his credentials are somewhat mixed (Fincham 1990: 279–88; Barlow 1601: A3^r).

Donne may have had a genuine sense of the need to appeal to a Roman Catholic readership in the matter of the Oath of Allegiance. After all, his mother and her husband had returned to England in May 1606, and his stepfather would be imprisoned for not taking the oath (Bald 1986: 214, 267–8). Most Roman Catholics seem to have adopted an awkward middle position between accepting and rejecting the oath (Questier 2008: 1150). Donne's surprisingly balanced musings on the oath in his Letter to Goodere—'I think truly there is a perplexity (as farre as I see yet) and both sides may be in justice, and innocence'—may therefore reflect a sympathetic recognition of many Roman Catholics' sincere confusion in seeking to marry their religious and political loyalties in the manner specified by the authorities (*Letters* 160). In the text of *Pseudo-Martyr* he recalls discussions with Roman Catholics over the oath, and notes appeals for the oath to be rephrased (*Pseudo-Martyr* 245–6, 253, 255). Nevertheless, there was of course no hint in this book that 'both sides may be in justice, and innocence'. Not only was Donne anxious to ensure that Roman Catholics take the oath so that they avoided punishment by the authorities, but also his decision to have his arguments printed as a public defence of the oath with a dedication to the King meant that there was no room for balance or ambiguity in his exposition. The argument is black and white: the oath is 'no more but an attestation of a morall truth' which Roman Catholics have been tricked into rejecting, despite the King's manifold favours in moderating the form of the oath in the face of Parliament's hostility towards Catholics after the Gunpowder Plot (164–5, 234, 253).

Donne insists on the essential unity of all Christians. In *Pseudo-Martyr* he draws attention to 'My easiness, to affoord a sweete and gentle Interpretation, to all professors of Christian Religion, if they shake not the Foundation, wherein I have in my ordinary Communication and familiar writings, often expressed and declared my selfe'. His only objective was 'the unity and peace of...[Christ's] Church' (12). This was no mere rhetorical ploy: in the same private Letter in which he attacked Barlow's book, Donne invoked his same commitment to the unity of the church and declared 'for, whether the Maior and Aldermen fall out, (as with us and the Puritans; Bishops against Priests) or the Commoners voyces differ who is Maior, and who Aldermen, or what their Jurisdiction, (as with the Bishop of *Rome*, or whosoever) yet it is still one Corporation' (*Letters* 164). In another famous private Letter written the same year, Donne declared: 'You know I never fettered nor imprisoned the word Religion; not...immuring it in a *Rome*, or a *Wittemberg*, or a *Geneva*; they are all virtuall beams of one Sun...They are not so contrary as the North and South Poles; and...they are connaturall pieces of one circle. Religion is Christianity...' (*Letters* 29). However, such sentiments did not feed into any conspicuous moderation in Donne's treatment of relevant doctrinal points in his *Pseudo-Martyr*, which is ultimately a conventional assault on the secular pretensions of the papacy and the doctrines and practices of the Jesuits. Essentially, Donne focuses on the negative side of his inclusive view of Christianity, attacking in vehement tones the exclusivity of the Church and court of Rome. His sense of the genuine unity of all individual Christians on a personal level may have been profoundly felt, and expressive of his cross-confessional friendships and family background, but there is no evidence that these sentiments drove the arguments of his anti-papal controversy at any point. Ultimately, *Pseudo-Martyr*'s appeals to Roman Catholics misled by the abhorrent and subversive doctrines of Rome are no different than Thomas Morton's appeals to his 'seduced brethren' in his *Exact Discoverie*. When Donne declares that 'It becomes not me to say, that the Romane Religion begets Treason', he immediately adds, 'but I may say, that within one generation it degenerates into it' (*Pseudo-Martyr* 25). In the Jacobean church Donne's confessional identity was clear: he never implied that there was more than one legitimate local religion, and all his known theological contacts were with those of an emphatically Protestant confessional orthodoxy. Donne was deeply involved in Protestant–Catholic debates that were saturated with Roman Catholic protestations of political loyalty and appeals for religious toleration, but Donne made no positive responses (or even allusions) to any of these appeals. Whatever the theoretical unity of all Christians, or the agreeableness of civil friendships with individual Roman Catholics, Donne made no overt allusion to any justification for formal religious toleration in the Jacobean church.

Donne's vague sense of a broader unifying Christian identity, combined with hostility towards the Pope's supremacy, the Jesuits, and the superstitions and exclusive claims of the Roman Catholic religion, were views that were compatible with a broad swathe of Jacobean churchmanship, embracing avant-garde conformists and Calvinist conformists alike. Most of all, they chimed in closely with the attitudes of the King himself. It was in the following decade that Donne's relationship with the King would flourish, but a happy conjuncture between his own instincts and the political and religious rhetorics and realities of James's regime was already evident, and would ensure a successful career for Donne in due course.

CHAPTER 31.1

THE DEATH OF ROBERT CECIL: END OF AN ERA

JOHANN SOMMERVILLE

ROBERT Cecil, Earl of Salisbury, died on 24 May 1612. The news soon reached John Donne, who was travelling on the continent with Sir Robert Drury. In July Donne penned a lengthy Letter, expressing surprise at the number of libellous attacks on Salisbury that had appeared after his death. These libels, he said, were 'so tastelesse and flat, that I protest to you, I think they were made by his friends' for the specific purpose of boring the public with diatribes against the deceased Earl. Donne contended that libelling dead men was 'ignoble, and uselesse', but he argued that there can be good reasons for writing and circulating anonymous criticisms of the living, 'For, where a man is either too great, or his Vices too generall, to be brought under a judiciary accusation, there is no way, but this extraordinary accusing, which we call Libelling' (*Letters* 89–91). This remarkable Letter requires us to consider in some detail what Donne's attitude to the most important English politician of the day was before May 1612. The Letter is ambiguous, probably by intention. One possible implication of these remarks is that Donne was not among the Earl's friends. Another is that he thought that Salisbury's power had been too great during his lifetime, and that libels against him would then have been justified. He did, however, praise Salisbury's handling of foreign policy: 'in the chiefest businesses between the Nations, he was a very good patriot' (89).

Salisbury's death ended the era of Cecil hegemony. For more than half a century William Cecil and his son Robert had served in turn as the Crown's leading minister.

Some scholars have linked the rise in Donne's fortunes to the decline in power of the Cecils (e.g. Cain 2006: 90). There are a number of connections between Donne and rivals of the Cecils, including the Earl of Essex and Sir Walter Ralegh, and later the Howards and Somerset. Perhaps Donne's attitudes towards Salisbury were coloured by his membership in a political faction opposed to the Earl. Factional strife often centred not only on personal rivalries but also on ideological commitments. It has been suggested that Donne held more tolerant and less intransigent views than Salisbury towards Catholicism (e.g. Tutino 2004: 1316 and n. 38). Certainly, Jacobean Catholics commonly regarded Salisbury as one of their worst enemies. It is arguable that Donne sided against Cecil politically because the poet endorsed liberal views on questions of religion and church–state relations—questions on which he wrote and published at length in Salisbury's last years. But the evidence is also open to another interpretation, which de-emphasizes the political and religious differences between the poet and the lord. In the first section below we shall investigate Donne's connections to Salisbury's rivals for power, as well as to Salisbury himself. We will see that it is not easy to link Donne and his friends with any single political grouping. The second section examines the ideas of Donne and of Salisbury on church–state relations and Catholicism, concluding that they agreed more than they differed. The key documents here are Donne's *Pseudo-Martyr* (1610) and *Ignatius his Conclave* (1611; first published in a Latin edition earlier in the same year, and soon republished on the continent in Latin), and Cecil's *Answere to Certaine Scandalous Papers* (1606).

1

In the 1590s Donne took part in the Cadiz and Islands expeditions led by the Earl of Essex and Sir Walter Ralegh. He became a friend of Henry (later Sir Henry) Wotton, who in 1594 became one of Essex's secretaries (just when and how closely Donne and Wotton were friends remain disputed: Flynn 1995*b*). By 1599 Essex was fast sliding from royal favour, and in 1601 he was convicted of treason and executed. Wotton's worries for his own safety are reflected in his correspondence with Donne at around this time (Summers and Pebworth), and Wotton left for the continent before the execution of Essex. There is no conclusive evidence that Donne himself was ever an especially warm supporter of Essex (Flynn 1995*b*: 197–201), but he had friends who were; in addition to Wotton, they arguably included Sir Henry Goodere and Sir William Cornwallis. Before Essex's fall his political faction had been the main rivals for power of the Cecils and their adherents. But the collapse of Essex's position left the Queen's secretary, Sir Robert Cecil, in almost total control of Elizabeth's government. Donne's poem *Metem*, dated 16 August 1601, tells of the progress of a 'great soule' that first inhabited the apple that corrupted Adam and Eve, and then passed through a variety of bodies until it ended in that of a male 'here amongst us now'; currently, the soul 'moves that hand, and tongue, and brow, / Which, as the Moone the sea, moves us' (ll. 61–3 and Epistle l. 32–5). The soul represents corruption, vice, and innovation. Perhaps the most persuasive reading of the poem suggests that it also represents Cecil, while Elizabeth is the moonlike body (M. Smith 143; at p. 144 Smith attributes a critical account of Salisbury to Donne's friend Wotton, but it is in fact by Edward Hyde: see L. P. Smith 2.414).

After James I succeeded to the throne in 1603 Cecil remained important, but the new King counterbalanced the secretary's power by entrusting others, and especially members of the Howard family, with key positions. At first Donne's friend the Earl of Northumberland also did well under the new regime, becoming a privy councillor and commander of the King's bodyguard (for valuable material on Northumberland, see Ch. 30.I). A series of blunders led to his lengthy imprisonment (M. Nicholls 2008). Cecil has sometimes been blamed for this, but the persons responsible were arguably the King and Northumberland himself. In 1606 Northumberland's brother declared that if Cecil were to fall, the imprisoned Earl's position would worsen (Gardiner 1883: 1.93). Again, Cecil has sometimes been blamed for the fall of Ralegh in 1603, but his role in that affair remains debated, as does the question of what links (if any) there were between Donne and Ralegh. (A judicious discussion of Cecil's role in Ralegh's fall is in Nicholls 2008; Donne is connected with Ralegh e.g. in Summers and Pebworth 35 n. 27; links between Donne and Ralegh are discussed in M. Smith 145–6, and are downplayed or ignored in Colclough 2007 and 2003.)

Early in James's reign a number of former Essex supporters became reconciled with Cecil and profited from his patronage. Cecil let Wotton's brother know that Henry would be welcome to return to England. Henry wrote warmly to Cecil, proclaiming 'my perpetual fidelity and observation towards you'. He came back to England, was knighted, and gained office as ambassador to Venice. He had a close working relationship with Cecil, and enjoyed his 'favour and friendship'. On his deathbed Salisbury recommended Wotton as his successor in the secretaryship (L. P. Smith 1.318, 44).

Other friends of Donne profited from Cecil's favour. In 1604 Goodere was elected a Member of Parliament for West Looe in Cornwall, probably through Cecil's influence (Considine). Sir William Cornwallis won Cecil's 'favourable notice' and became a member of the King's Privy Chamber (Kincaid). Sir William's father, Sir Charles, pursued a career at court, where 'he had a meteoric rise under the patronage of Robert Cecil, earl of Salisbury' (Kyle). In 1604 Sir Charles was appointed ambassador to Spain. Sir William joined him there in the following year, and it is possible that Donne too travelled to Spain at about this time. While Donne was abroad he left his wife at home in England. Her father was Sir George More, who benefited from Cecil's patronage throughout the first decade of the seventeenth century. In 1610 Salisbury appointed More treasurer and receiver-general to Henry, Prince of Wales (Knafla 2008*b*). As a member of James I's first Parliament, More was an active participant in debates in the Commons, for instance on the anti-Catholic legislation of 1606 that included the Oath of Allegiance that Donne defended in *Pseudo-Martyr*. Donne expended considerable effort on winning the friendship, and patronage, of Lucy, Countess of Bedford. Lucy's own patron was Salisbury (Payne).

It has recently been suggested that 'Donne was an intellectual associate of the courtier and controversialist Sir Edward Hoby', and certainly the Jesuit John Floyd grouped the two together (Shell 2003: 121–2). Hoby was Salisbury's first cousin, and he rose to high favour at Elizabeth's court through the good offices of Salisbury's father. He consolidated his position under James, who made him a gentleman of the privy chamber (Knafla 2008*a*). Writing against Floyd, Hoby drew on Salisbury's *Answere to Certaine Scandalous Papers* (Hoby 67).

Scholars sometimes link Donne with the prolific controversialist Thomas Morton, who rose to prominence in the church during Salisbury's years at the centre of power. It has been suggested that Morton and Salisbury were among the bitterest critics of Catholicism in the aftermath of the Gunpowder Plot (Tutino 2004: 1316 n. 38). Morton became Dean of Gloucester in June 1607, and was later promoted to a bishopric. Izaak Walton says that when Morton was appointed to the deanery he offered to make over to Donne another benefice in his possession, but that at this point Donne was not yet convinced that the church was the right career path for him (1670: 23–7). Walton's account is often unreliable, but in this case Morton's biographers Richard Baddeley and Joshua Naylor tell substantially the same story, and supply a number of details that Walton does not record. There is little reason to doubt the accuracy of what they say. They state that the benefice in question was the valuable rectory of Long Marston in Yorkshire, worth some £200 a year. They also relate that on one occasion Morton gave the unemployed Donne 'a good quantity of Gold', quipping that gold was restorative (or health-giving), to which Donne wittily riposted that he doubted whether he would ever restore it. Again, they record that Donne wrote to Morton from Amiens—presumably when he was there with the Drury family in 1611–12—asking if he should take a doctorate of laws (that is to say, of civil and canon law) with a view to practising ecclesiastical law in the Court of Arches—the court of the Archbishop of Canterbury. Morton replied that it would be 'safer, and fitter for him' to become a minister, which Donne eventually did (Baddeley and Naylor 98–104).

More recently, some scholars have argued that Donne collaborated with Morton in at least one of the latter's many anti-Romanist writings, namely *A Catholike Appeale for Protestants*, first published late in 1609. The evidence for this claim is a Letter of 5 March 1607/8 from Donne to Sir Henry Goodere, in which Donne reminds the knight to send him '*the Apology*' as '*by occasion of reading the Deans answer to it,*

I have sometimes some want' of the book (*Letters* 66). These words have been seen as compelling evidence that '*the Apology*' was the Catholic *Apologie of the Romane Church* of 1604, that the dean was Morton, and that the answer was Morton's *Catholike Appeale*. 'It is clear', said R. C. Bald, 'that Donne was reading portions of the manuscript of *A Catholike Appeale* a full eighteen months before that work was published' (Bald 1970: 212). But there were many books with 'apology' or 'apologia' in the title, and more that could be described as apologies because of their content. And there were many deans, in England and elsewhere. In 1596 Matthew Sutcliffe, Dean of Exeter, published *The examination of M. Thomas Cartvvrights late apologie*, which answered *A brief apologie* by the Puritan Thomas Cartwright. Donne possessed at least one book by Sutcliffe (Bald 1970: 223), and he satirized that dean's wide-ranging and prolific output in his *Courtier's Library* (37, 52). In 1604 George Abbot, Dean of Winchester, published *The reasons vvhich Doctour Hill hath brought, for the vpholding of papistry*, in which he answered the priest Edmund Hill's *A quartron of reasons of Catholike religion*. Perhaps Donne meant the book of one of these deans. If Morton *was* the dean, it is possible that the book was his *Apologia Catholica* of 1605 (followed by a second part the following year), which 'was directed against' the *Apologie of the Romane Church* (Quintrell 2008a). However, Morton's book can be seen as a response to the earlier *Apologie* only in a very general way. It is *not* a point-by-point refutation of the Catholic work (unlike the later *Catholike Appeale*), and it is therefore difficult to see why reading Morton's *Apologia* would have led Donne to want to consult the Catholic volume. In a Letter of 1609 Donne referred to Morton not as 'the Dean' but as 'D. Morton' (*Letters* 162). Elsewhere in Donne's Letters 'the Dean' and 'the Deanery' refer to St Paul's (ibid. 168, 199). The Dean of St Paul's in 1608 was John Overall. His chaplain John Cosin later said that Overall was the main author of the *Catholike Appeale* (Quintrell 2008a). Perhaps 'the Deans answer' means 'the deans' answer', and both Morton and Overall are intended. Baddeley and Naylor state that Morton wrote the book with the help of others and completed it at the deanery house of St Paul's where his friend Overall was dean (Baddeley and Naylor 35–6).

It is perfectly possible that Donne was one of those whom Morton, or Overall, consulted in preparing the *Catholike Appeale*. Others included Thomas James, an Oxford scholar and Bodley's first librarian (Baddeley and Naylor 35). In his *Treatise of the Corruption of Scripture* (1611), James repeatedly and approvingly cited Donne's *Pseudo-Martyr*, and endorsed points that Donne 'wisely obserued out of' the writings of the Catholics, and to their discredit (T. James pt. 3, p. 55; pt. 4, pp. 6, 9). The *Catholike Appeale* likewise deployed Catholic sources to undermine the Roman religion and support Protestantism. *Pseudo-Martyr* was published with a dedication to the King, who clearly permitted, and likely encouraged, both the dedication and the publication. The King was highly sensitive about hostile criticism towards his own writings and those of his defenders, such as Donne. He certainly would not have permitted the printing of *Pseudo-Martyr* unless he had received expert testimony of the book's high scholarly standards, and of the congruence of its arguments with those of other defenders of the Oath of Allegiance, including Morton. Morton himself took charge of licensing the original (Latin) version of *Ignatius* for the press early in 1611—a job normally left to less exalted figures, though Morton had helped to license one of his own books in 1609 (*Ignatius* 172; a discussion of the question of Donne's collaboration with Morton is at 168–73). It made sense for the various polemicists who defended the oath to collaborate with each other, since doing so reduced the chances that they would contradict their colleagues in print and lay themselves open to embarrassing Catholic attack. They did indeed consult each other. When, in debate with Morton, the Catholic priest Richard Broughton accused Sutcliffe of holding a certain opinion, Morton simply asked Sutcliffe what he thought (Morton 1606: 119). A good reason for conferring with Donne in particular was that he had an extraordinary knowledge of Catholic writers on canon law and casuistry, as well as a keen eye for the comic potential of their less guarded remarks. His bitter critic the priest Thomas Fitzherbert, agent at Rome for the Catholic clergy, and later Rector there of the English College, rightly noted how 'curious and diligent' Donne was 'in seeking, and sifting of the *Decretalls, Extrauagants*... all sorts of Canonists, yea euery meane, and obscure Catholick writer, to find somewhat to iest at' (F[itzherbert] 96). Broughton similarly attacked Morton for citing 'so many, not vsuall Catholike Authors' and thus disclosing 'his inueterate malice against vs' (Broughton 1606: a1^r). Donne ultimately decided not to become a professional civil or canon lawyer, though the rumour circulated in 1612 that he was planning to do so (*Letters* 238), but in the same year he was confident enough of his abilities to offer his advice to the celebrated Gallican theorist Émond Richer, Syndic of the Sorbonne. Richer had written an anti-papalist defence of the liberties of the Gallican Church, for which he was called to account by the French ecclesiastical authorities. In Paris, Donne wanted to meet him and tell him that he could justify every proposition in the Syndic's book from medieval Catholic writings (*Letters* 130–1).

The defenders of the Oath of Allegiance commonly benefited from the patronage of the higher clergy and sometimes from that of the King himself. This does not, of course, mean that they were in any sense political opponents of Salisbury. The best-known political rivals of Cecil in the early years of James's reign were the Howards, or perhaps more correctly, the senior figure in that family, namely the Earl of Northampton. Another important member of the clan, the Earl of Suffolk, was one of Salisbury's closest friends—and rumour had it that Suffolk's wife was still more intimately associated with Cecil. Salisbury's eldest son married their daughter Catherine (Croft 1991a: 784–5). Donne sent a copy of *Pseudo-Martyr* to Northampton (Bald 1970: 221 n.3), but otherwise there seems to have been little connection between them. The record suggests that Donne's failure to acquire office in the early years of James's reign stemmed not from Salisbury's hostility, or from his connections with rivals of the Cecils, but from memories of his unorthodox marriage and of his subsequent dismissal by Lord Keeper Egerton. When Lord Hay lobbied the King on

Donne's behalf around the end of 1608, James remembered Donne for what the poet termed 'the worst part of my historie, which was my disorderlie proceedings, seaven years since, in my nonage' (*TMC* 330). Perhaps we could hypothesize that Salisbury poisoned the King against Donne. But there is little evidence of that. If Donne really was deeply hostile to Salisbury, it was not, apparently, for reasons of personal animus or factional commitment. There remains the possibility that the two men differed on key matters of principle, and that is the subject of the next section.

2

It is sometimes said that the Oath of Allegiance, enacted by Parliament in 1606, was a subtle instrument for the persecution of Catholics. The oath required Catholics to renounce the Pope's claims to be able to intervene in the affairs of states by means that included deposing their rulers and to condemn anyone who enforced a papal deposition by killing a king. King James and other defenders of the oath argued that its purpose was to secure the state in the wake of the Gunpowder Plot—when a group of zealous Catholics had conspired to blow up Parliament, the King, and most of the royal family. But this was a mere pretext for religious persecution, it is sometimes said, since the King and his advisors well knew that the deposing power was an obsolete doctrine that the Pope would never put into practice, and that good Catholics would never try to kill the King (a discussion of these and other points connected with the oath is in Sommerville 2005; a recent statement of the view that the papal deposing power was obsolete is in Houliston 2006: 480). In fact, the State Papers, and Salisbury's correspondence, are full of reports of plots by Catholics to assassinate James and other notables.

After the Gunpowder Plot, Cecil entered into negotiations with the papacy through intermediaries such as the papal nuncio in Flanders and the Spanish ambassador (e.g. Frangipani 581–2; Loomie 70–1). He offered to halt the persecution of Catholics if the Pope would command them to be loyal to the King. The Pope preferred to keep alive the prospect that he himself would take action against James, and so encourage the King to pursue a moderate policy towards Catholics. Parliament proceeded to debate new laws against Catholics, including the oath, and these were enacted in May 1606. Before the laws were passed, Salisbury received a letter (so he said) purporting to come from five Catholics. The five had heard that Cecil was planning to introduce 'some more cruell and horrible Lawes against Catholicks' in the next Parliament. So they resolved to shoot Salisbury unless he abandoned his 'tragicall Stratagems'. None of the five knew who the others were, so if one failed in his assassination attempt he could not inform on the rest. Two of the five were terminally ill and had nothing to lose, while the others were also in great distress (R. Cecil B3^r–4^v; a fine analysis of Cecil's religious views is Croft 1991a). Whether the five really existed is impossible to prove, and they failed to make good their threat, but the letter (real or concocted) gave Cecil an opportunity to write a reply setting out his attitudes towards Catholics in the wake of the Gunpowder Plot. This *Answere to Certaine Scandalous Papers* appeared in both English and Latin in 1606, and perhaps it was intended largely for a continental audience. Sir Charles Cornwallis informed Salisbury that many reports of the plot of the five were spread in Spain (Winwood 2.193).

It has been said that Salisbury and Morton blamed the Gunpowder Plot, and all earlier attempts against the state, on Catholics as a whole rather than on the Jesuits in particular; Donne, by contrast, distinguished carefully between the Jesuits and the rest, blaming the plot on the former and thus opening the way for toleration of the latter (Tutino 2004: 1316 and n. 38). In fact, Salisbury stressed that he knew 'with what obedience and applause' Catholics as well as Protestants had welcomed James's accession, and 'how little assistance' they had given the plotters (R. Cecil F1^{r-v}). He distinguished between those Catholics who differed from the King only 'in point of conscience' and others upon whose 'fidelitie, in ciuil obedience' the king could not rely (C2^v–3^r). In the wake of the plot, many people had been 'inflamed' 'against the generalitie of the Papists', but the authorities had ensured that no 'acte of blood or crueltie' was committed against the innocent, and the King rightly made clear 'how farre he was from the condemnation of the generall for particulars' (D1^v). Queen Mary had shed more Protestant blood in five years than her sister Elizabeth had shed Catholic blood in forty-five, and James had been still more merciful than Elizabeth (D1^r).

Alluding to his own diplomatic overtures to the papacy, he remarked that if the Catholic authorities wanted to persuade the world that Catholics as a whole were scrupulously loyal to non-Catholic governments in purely civil matters, then it would make sense to issue 'some publike and definitiue sentence' to that effect (C2^v). Salisbury emphasized his own preference for mercy, but made it clear that the teachings of some Catholics could not be tolerated. One of these was the doctrine that popes can depose secular rulers if they deem this beneficial to Christians generally. In early times the ecclesiastical authorities had exercised the spiritual power of excommunication, by which sinners were excluded from the church, but it was only much more recently that popes had usurped the authority to employ temporal penalties against monarchs (C3^r). Another objectionable Catholic principle was the doctrine of equivocation and mental reservation, according to which in some circumstances it is permissible to deceive people we are talking to by using words ambiguously or by keeping some words silently in our minds while we outwardly voice others. Cecil strongly condemned the practice, claiming that it tears 'in sunder all the bondes of humane conuersation' (C3^v). His *Answere* objected to the papal deposing power, to conspiracies, rebellions, and assassinations perpetrated by Catholics, and to equivocation. It had very little to say about other, more purely religious Catholic doctrines. He did express the hope that religious uniformity would one day prevail in England. But his work makes it plain that he thought Catholics should be mercifully treated as long as they did not adopt principles that encouraged treason.

Donne and Morton likewise argued especially against Catholic justifications of the papal deposing power, theories of legitimate resistance to heretical rulers, and equivocation. The leading Jesuit Robert Persons attacked Cecil's *Answere* in his *Treatise tending to Mitigation* (1607)—a book largely written in reply to a work by Morton (Persons 1607: 19–20). Morton's response was dedicated to Salisbury. Donne's *Pseudo-Martyr* also attacked Persons frequently. Morton drew extensively on French and Venetian Catholics who rejected the deposing power, such as William Barclay and Paolo Sarpi (e.g. Morton 1610: 7). Donne treasured pictures of Sarpi and his anti-papalist colleague Fulgenzio Micanzio, and in *Pseudo-Martyr* he drew approvingly on the *Tractatus de Interdicto* (1606) they co-wrote with some other Venetian theologians against papal claims (Flynn 2000b: 349; *Pseudo-Martyr* 176). Wotton sent Salisbury a portrait of Sarpi in 1607 (Flynn 2000b: 350). Donne was keenly interested in French as well as Venetian Catholic attacks on the claims of the Pope and the Jesuits. *Ignatius* is addressed to the two opposed guardian angels of the Pope's consistory and of the Sorbonne—the bastion of Gallicanism (*Ignatius* 5).

In *Pseudo-Martyr* Donne used the disagreements between Gallican and Venetian Catholics on the one hand, and papalists on the other, to show that there were radical divergences of opinion among Catholics about such issues as the papal deposing power, and that dying in defence of such doubtful doctrines could not constitute martyrdom, since martyrs were people who died rather than renounce some clearly essential Christian principle. *Pseudo-Martyr* was to a large extent a fairly conventional defence of the Oath of Allegiance, rehearsing many of the same arguments as those employed by James I, Morton, the anti-papalist Benedictine Thomas Preston, and others. It was unusual only in that it was written by a layman, and that it was not targeted against any single papalist work (though it assailed many in passing), but rather intended to confirm the thesis that those who died after refusing the oath were not true martyrs. By the time Donne wrote *Ignatius* Gallican themes had acquired added topicality with the assassination of Henri IV of France by a Catholic fanatic in May 1610, and the subsequent renewed assault on Jesuit thinking by the French anti-papalists' 'two great *Gyants*, *Gog* and *Magog*, their Parliament of *Paris*, and their *Colledge* of *Sorbon*' (*Ignatius* 57). *Ignatius* is a learned satire that uses Catholic writings to poke fun at the ambition and duplicity of the Jesuits. Like *Pseudo-Martyr* and the *Catholike Appeale*, it employs the words of Catholics to undermine their own claims, but in a much more imaginative and humorous way. To some degree, it is reminiscent of the notorious Catholic prose satire *Pruritanus* (1609), which interpreted scriptural texts eccentrically—as Catholics commonly held Protestants *did* interpret them—to suggest such things as that Anne Boleyn was Henry VIII's daughter, that Elizabeth had multiple affairs with foreigners including Ethiopians, and that the Scots swarmed over England like plagues of locusts and flies (Dolabella 10, 9, 11). Copies of *Pruritanus* were distributed in London from the residence of the Venetian ambassador, though without his knowledge. Salisbury sent the book to Wotton, who duly brought up the matter in Venice (L. P. Smith 1.472).

Pseudo-Martyr and *Ignatius* are sometimes seen as more liberal and tolerant than most works of anti-Catholic polemic, and it has been claimed that in neither does Donne call the Pope Antichrist. But in *Pseudo-Martyr* he says that it is doubtful whether a Jesuit will ever become pope, since 'it is already reveil'd by *Christ* to S. *Francis*: that *Antichrist shall come out of the family of the Franciscans*', which evidently rules out the possibility of a non-papal Antichrist (*Pseudo-Martyr* 104). Popes in *Ignatius* are treated unflatteringly, though Donne did not stress their anti-Christian qualities, for to do so would have involved upstaging the book's (anti-) hero Loyola. One of the earliest works to refer to *Ignatius* was Francis Burton's *The Fierie Tryall of Gods Saints* (1611), which classed Catholics as worshippers of 'the Beast' or 'his Image', praised the author of *Ignatius* as 'a late, but wittie Satyrist', and quoted from the Latin version of it. Burton's book was dedicated to the Earl of Salisbury (Burton title-page, 'A Post-Script' 10).

Salisbury's *Answere*, like Donne's works, distinguished between Catholics who held dangerous and anti-social principles, and those who had conscientious scruples about purely religious matters. Of course, it is possible to voice moderation but practise persecution. Perhaps Cecil's actions, if not his words, stamp him as an implacable foe of Catholicism. One point that needs making here is that there were limits to what one minister, however powerful, could do. Unquestionably, he long wielded greater authority than anyone in England, with the exception of the King himself—but James was perfectly capable of overruling him, particularly on matters that closely concerned him, such as the debate over the Oath of Allegiance. Salisbury cannot be held solely responsible for Jacobean legislation against Catholics, for lawmaking required the consent of the two Houses of Parliament, which no single person could control. To a very large degree the King's policies were his own, and in church affairs he arguably relied as much or more on the advice of the bishops as on that of Cecil. It was envy, said Salisbury, that led people to ascribe to him more power than he in fact had: I 'am onely great in the eyes of Enuy' (R. Cecil D2^v). In so far as it is possible to assign responsibility for the actions of the authorities to specific individuals, Cecil arguably acted as a moderating influence. Spanish diplomats were deeply suspicious of him, but their records suggest that they did not always have good cause. In 1608 the (crypto-)Catholic Countess of Suffolk informed the Spanish ambassador that recent executions of Catholics had not been Salisbury's fault. Two years later the ambassador reported that Cecil had spoken in the council *against* the rigorous enforcement of anti-Catholic laws, and that he opposed harassing recusants excessively. When the Benedictine John Roberts was executed in December 1610, Salisbury apologized to the ambassador, blaming the execution on Parliament and promising there would be no further killings. Nevertheless, upon Salisbury's death in 1612 the ambassador remarked that every Catholic had reason to rejoice, for the Earl had been their greatest persecutor. Not long afterwards, however, he noted that Cecil had kept his word about the executions, but that as soon as he was dead other councillors persuaded the King to allow two more priests to be killed. A little later he expressed pleasure that, since Salisbury's demise, the wicked schemes that typified him had all failed, and he gave as an example the project for a marriage alliance with the ruling house of the Palatinate (Loomie 119, 156, 160, 162, 191, 198). In fact, the marriage between Princess Elizabeth and Friedrich of the Palatinate went ahead less than a year later, and Donne wrote a poem to celebrate the occasion. It very much looks as though what annoyed Spanish diplomats about Cecil was less that he persecuted Catholics than that he outwitted Spaniards in foreign affairs.

We began with Donne's Letter about the libels levelled against Cecil after his death. In it he remarked on Salisbury's abilities in the international arena, styling him 'a very good patriot' 'in the chiefest businesses between the Nations' (*Letters* 89). He argued that there is not much point in libelling the dead, since they are beyond reforming. The purpose of those who defamed Cecil was not to get him to mend his ways. Rather, they were motivated by envy. Salisbury's loss of health, power, and perhaps wealth had seemed to Donne to render him increasingly unenviable: 'It was easily discerned, some years before his death, that he was at a defensive war, both for his honour and health, and (as we then thought) for his estate: and I thought, that had removed much of the envy' (ibid.). This was why Donne was surprised at the number of libels against Salisbury. Whatever differences of principle may have divided Donne and Cecil at the time of *Metem* in 1601, a decade or so later they were both voicing similar ideas on church–state relations. And both, seemingly, agreed on the reasons for Salisbury's unpopularity: he was great, and detested, in the eyes of envy.

CHAPTER 31.II

DONNE'S TRAVELS AND EARLIEST PUBLICATIONS

DENNIS FLYNN

In the decade between his dismissal from Lord Keeper Thomas Egerton's secretariat in 1602 and the death of Robert Cecil, Earl of Salisbury, in 1612, Donne's activities included his 1605–6 travel on the continent and the advent of his earliest publications. These activities must be understood in the context of events with large political implications: the discovery of the Gunpowder Plot in November 1605, and in 1606 the promulgation of the Oath of Allegiance as a defensive weapon against traitorous Catholics. This chapter therefore includes discussion of the oath (a significant and troubling development for some of Donne's friends, especially the Catholics Toby Matthew and Ben Jonson), as well as the fall from favour of the most significant political supporter of toleration for Catholicism early in the Jacobean reign, Henry Percy, Earl of Northumberland, another friend of Donne's (see also Ch. 30.I). Also included here is some discussion of the travels of Matthew and several others among Donne's friends, embarking for the continent in the early years of the reign. Discussion of Donne's own travel will require explanation of the true date of his Latin Letter to Sir Henry Goodere: 1605, rather than 1611 as has long been thought. In addition to Donne's 1605–6 travel, the Latin Letter also introduced Goodere to a significant change in Donne's attitude towards those manuscript writings he had earlier put into circulation.

This change in attitude will be discussed in the context illustrated by Donne's first published writing, his commendatory poem included in the first edition of Ben Jonson's

Volpone, a play produced under circumstances—Jonson's involvement in the fallout from the Gunpowder Plot and his prosecution for recusancy—that condition our understanding of Donne's earliest published writing. Finally, Toby Matthew's conversion to Roman Catholicism is discussed as a background to Donne's subsequent publications, *Pseudo-Martyr* and *Ignatius His Conclave*, expressing both his support of the oath as compatible with Catholic faith and his opposition to the Jesuits.

1

The Oath of Allegiance has been called 'the most lethal measure against Romish dissent ever to reach the statute book', and 'an oath that struck at the entire ideological basis for Roman Catholicism in England, and principally by an insistence that the religious tenets within it could not be held separately from the political ones' (Questier 1997: 313, 329). It was developed by Richard Bancroft, Archbishop of Canterbury, with the advice of a former Jesuit, Sir Christopher Perkins (Sommerville 2005: 165; W. B. Patterson 79; Feil 43), who had served English governments in various capacities since the early 1590s and had been knighted early in the Jacobean reign.

English Catholics had long been kept constantly aware of the danger inherent in their religious beliefs, liable to a range of penalties including praemunire for refusal to swear a loyalty oath selectively tendered but ever more widely threatened (on Donne's nearly having been tendered such an oath, see Ch. 27.II). In particular, the Act of Supremacy (1° Eliz. c. 1.; *Statutes* IV.1.352–3), in force for generations, had incorporated the Oath of Supremacy, determining and imprinting effects of religious persecution apparent in Donne's family history and personality (see Chs. 26.I–30.II); but now the Popish Recusants Act (3° Jac. I. c. 4; *Statutes* IV.2.1073–4) incorporated the Oath of Allegiance, more subtle and more dangerous for Catholics than the Elizabethan oath had been, because it 'forced its way into the conscience of the individual', making 'a window into men's souls in a way the Elizabethan regime had only briefly contemplated' (Questier 1997: 322). The Oath of Allegiance was devised in the last of five decades during which English government, managed by Cecils, continued through statutory and administrative measures to winnow English Catholicism with a double-edged distinction between the loyalty of traditional Catholics (i.e. wheat) and the potential or alleged treason of Romanists (i.e. chaff) who envisaged assassination or foreign invasion as ways to supplant Protestantism in England. The ways in which the government wielded this distinction necessarily and increasingly burdened the consciences of all English Catholics, attenuating their adherence to the papacy.

These conditions presented various challenges for all who had been, were, or would become Catholics in England during the early reign of James I, among them Donne himself, some of his closest friends, and some members of his family. In particular, three of Donne's friends—Toby Matthew, Ben Jonson, and Sir Henry Goodere—illustrate, in their activities and interactions with each other and with Donne, some of the tensions and problems inherent in English Catholicism or created by the plot and the oath. In late April or early May 1606 Matthew (the son of Tobie Matthew, who had been created Archbishop of York on 16 April 1606) defiantly became a Catholic at Florence (Feil 23–4); declaring this conversion on his return to England in 1607, he was imprisoned and tendered the oath, which he refused, making himself liable by a second refusal to incur the penalties of praemunire (ibid. 44), an event that would cause unavoidable embarrassment for the Church of England. Jonson had become a Catholic in prison in 1598 and was prosecuted for recusancy beginning in January 1606; six months later his admission that he had not received communion in the Church of England for over two years rendered him liable to be tendered the oath (Jonson 1.220–3). Goodere, like Donne a close friend to both men, was deeply affected especially by Matthew's example, and throughout his life was troubled by the origin of his estate as confiscated church property. He had agreed with Matthew to take part in certain financial arrangements connected to the latter's conversion; these arrangements were sometimes a topic of Donne's correspondence with Goodere during these years (e.g. *Letters* 140, 195–6, 283–4), as was controversy over the oath.

Donne's own attitude towards the oath was 'complicated' by these relationships as well as, also in 1606, after more than a decade of religious exile at Antwerp, the return to England of his mother Elizabeth and her husband Richard Rainsford (Bald 1970: 214). Rainsford would subsequently be imprisoned by early 1612 and then indicted for recusancy, shown not to have attended Church of England services for two months and thus liable to be tendered the oath (ibid. 115–16). These and other complications related to Catholicism between 1602 and 1612 formed a background for Donne's travel and his earliest appearances in print.

Donne began these years living at Pyrford in a house belonging to his wife's cousin, the newly knighted Sir Francis Wolley. His friends visited him in Surrey (cf. Ch. 30.I), Sir Henry Goodere and Toby Matthew urging him to join them, at court and in London, taking advantage of opportunities offered by the accession of a king. Goodere, having been appointed a gentleman of the privy chamber, tried unsuccessfully to arrange for Donne the reversion of William Fowler's secretaryship to Queen Anne (*Letters* 81–2; Bald 1970: 141, 160); Matthew, serving in Parliament through the patronage of Sir Francis Bacon, wrote letters of friendly complaint that Donne was wasting his opportunities, secluded in the country for the most part in what Matthew characterized as melancholy isolation, walking country lanes and reading about religion (*TMC* 288, 290; Bald 1970: 143–4).

During the summer of 1604 Matthew obtained licence to travel for three years and, following prorogation of Parliament, left England for France in July (Feil 15). Also in July 1604 other friends were travelling: another new knight, Sir Henry Wotton, had been appointed ambassador for Venice and departed, soon joined by Rowland Woodward who served as a member of his staff (L. P. Smith 1.45, 48). Later in 1604, or early in 1605, Donne himself considered an opportunity to travel with yet another acquaintance who had been knighted in the first weeks of the new reign, Sir Walter Chute; Donne and Chute were licensed to travel for three years on 16 February 1605 (TNA, SP 38/8; Shapiro 1967: 76; Bald 1970: 148). Just at this point Matthew briefly returned to England to make financial arrangements (some involving Goodere) for a longer stay on the continent. Remaining in England from February until 1 May, Matthew then departed again, this time with a secret purpose, to Italy and the ultimate intention, perhaps not yet fully conscious, of becoming a Roman Catholic (Feil 16–17). Others of Donne's acquaintance (including Sir Robert Drury, Sir William Cornwallis, and Dudley Carleton) also left England in the spring of 1605 to attend the embassy of Charles Howard, Earl of Nottingham, promulgating at Valladolid the Treaty of London, concluding nearly two decades' hostilities with Spain. Yet another friend who travelled at this period was Goodere, who left England in April 1605 for Brussels and Antwerp, appointed to attend the embassy of Edward Seymour, Earl of Hertford, to the Archdukes Albert and Isabella. Donne thus was arranging to leave England, as were a number of his friends, at a time when the state of war with Spain was ending in a spate of diplomacy and when tensions over religious differences seemed diminished, given the widespread perception that King James might extend some form of toleration to Catholics (see Ch. 30.II), although by 1604 that perception was evidently mistaken (Questier 2006: 271–2).

Additional information about Donne's decision to travel in 1605–6 is available through consideration of his Latin Letter addressed to Goodere (Donne 1633*b*: 351–2), discussing among other matters a new opportunity for travel. Donne wrote confidentially but without elaboration that a new occasion to go see other countries ('*occasio extera visendi regna*') had arisen, something on which he wanted Goodere's advice. He described this opportunity as neither unseasonable nor unsuitable, though perhaps a little less distinguished than he would have liked ('*paulò quam optaram fortassis magis inhonora*'), but he made no mention of any particular business connected to the trip; and he regretted that, if he took the opportunity, he would be leaving his wife and children for some years ('*aliquot ad annos relinquendi*').

The Latin Letter seems to have been written before February 1605, although it has been dated 1611 by several writers (e.g. E. M. Simpson 1948: 150; Bald 1970: 241–2) who have asserted that it refers to Donne's 1611–12 travel with Sir Robert and Anne Drury to France and Germany, designed to further Donne's disappointed aspiration for secular preferment (for some, the default and summary explanation for everything Donne did before he was ordained). Without published dispute, the 1611 dating of this Letter has been widely accepted; but Simpson, Bald, and other Donne scholars have been unaware of a persuasive though unpublished case, dating the Latin Letter in 1605, made by the late I. A. Shapiro (UB, Shapiro Papers, Folder S16, part of Shapiro's commentary for his unfinished edition of Donne's Letters). Shapiro suggested that Donne's characterization of his opportunity for travel, a little less distinguished than he might wish, more likely referred to Donne's prospective travel in 1605–6 with Chute than to his travel with the Drurys in 1611–12.

As Shapiro noted, Donne's Letters written from France and Germany in the first half of 1612 suggest that he would not likely have thought this travel undistinguished: he and the Drurys reported on important events to various readers in England (e.g. Donne's Letter to Sir Robert More on 28 January [7 February] 1612, *Marriage Letters* 54–5); they met and conversed in the course of their travels with numerous English and continental European nobles, diplomats, and other government officers (cf. *Letters* 75–8, 122–5, and 127–32; for overviews of this trip, cf. Bald 1959: 90–103 and 1970: 241–60); and Donne himself undertook at least one diplomatic initiative usefully connected to policies of the English government, approaching the Syndic of the Sorbonne, Émond Richer, to consult with him about Gallican principles in conflict with the Jesuits of Paris (*Letters* 129–31; Bald 1970: 255–6). To emphasize the implications of these activities, Shapiro highlighted passages in a letter written to Drury on 12 May 1612 by Sir Walter Cope in his capacity as administrative secretary for Robert Cecil (Cope had earlier for many years also served Salisbury's father): 'although Mr. Dun, and you haue noe place of Ambassadors yet I trust you haue, that canne and doe obserue as much as the best that have imploiement from the State'. Cope went on to commend explicitly Donne's activities on the continent for 'inriching his Treasury, for his Countries better service' (qtd. by Bald 1959: 99–100, and 1970: 259). Drury himself had engaged in official diplomacy and expected to do more, a view apparently shared by Cope. Moreover, Drury's wife Anne lent further distinction to the travel Donne anticipated in 1611: she was a highly educated daughter of Sir Nicholas Bacon and a sister to Anthony and Francis.

In contrast, comparatively little importance has been discerned in the travel licence issued to Donne and Chute on 16 February 1605; Shapiro reasoned that the Latin Letter to Goodere must have been written before the date of that relatively undistinguished arrangement. His argument was based on several features of the Letter itself as well as on certain biographical facts unnoticed by Bald or others. For example, he dwelt on a passage about Goodere's London quarters, in the house of Sir Thomas Bartlett. Donne stresses here that he would like to meet and discuss with Goodere his travel opportunity, but he would prefer this not happen at Bartlett's house. The reason he gives for staying away is the embarrassment he feels in having acted there recently on more indiscreet impulse than accorded with a friendship neither long-established nor close ('*Amicitiæ enim nec veteris, nec ita strictæ munera paulò quam deceat imprudentiori impetu mihi videor ibi peregisse*'). Simpson and Bald did not dwell on this passage, although Bald did mention certain unspecified 'other references in Donne's letters [to] Sir Thomas and Lady Bartlett' (1970: 241 n. 4). These other references in Letters left unexplained by Bald were a basis for Shapiro's dating the Latin Letter earlier than 1611, because in them Donne's closer acquaintance with the Bartletts and visits to their house can be seen to have begun by at least March 1608, and very likely some years earlier.

Shapiro thought that Donne had probably met the Bartletts through Goodere, whose own acquaintance with them was certainly earlier than Donne's and may have begun before the Bartletts moved from Gloucestershire to London. Goodere must have maintained a London residence, at some point at the Bartlett house, at least as early as the start of his service as a gentleman of the privy chamber in the autumn of 1603. Donne, for a couple of years before 1605 ensconced without London lodgings in familial isolation at Pyrford, may well at this period have regarded his relations with the London Bartletts as neither long-established nor close. In contrast, by the time of his travel with the Drurys in 1611 Donne had himself commuted to London lodgings continually for the past five years; moreover, he had frequented and even himself become a lodger at the Bartlett house, to which he also planned to return when, writing from Belgium in the summer of 1612, he referred to 'my Ladie *Bartlets* my lodging' (*Letters* 252). Subsequently, when Donne moved his family to Drury Lane in 1613 Lady Bartlett visited them there (ibid. 181). Given these facts, late 1604 or early 1605 seems more likely than 1611 to be a date when Donne, in a Letter concerning prospective travel, would cautiously refer to his relations with the Bartletts in the unfamiliar, distant, and uncertain terms used by the Latin Letter.

Shapiro thought it 'inconceivable' that in 1611 Donne would have consulted Goodere about the wisdom of going abroad with the Drurys. Goodere's appointment as a gentleman of the privy chamber, his early preferment at the Jacobean court, his election to the Parliament of 1604, and his selection to serve on the Hertford embassy may all have led Donne at first to overestimate Goodere's influence and judgement. Moreover, Goodere at this time was someone who commonly travelled far from home in order to serve the royal court, as Donne knew and mentioned in many Letters. By 1611, however, Lady Goodere was dead and Goodere's career as a courtier/diplomat had ended. After 1607 Goodere ignored repeated advice from Donne, who saw his friend run steadily into debt and disfavour (Considine). Thus, for various reasons, by 1611 Donne would have been less likely to consult or allude to Goodere's experience in these matters, as he does in the Latin Letter. From this perspective, the Letter seems out of place amidst Donne's acknowledged correspondence in 1611, when he had established himself independently on a new footing through his first published writing and was about to engage in unofficial public service with the Drurys. For example, in a Letter undoubtedly of 1611 (*Letters* 93–5), addressed to Goodere just before Donne's departure with the Drurys in the autumn of 1611, Donne sounds relatively experienced, more assured, with none of the anxieties or deference to Goodere's experience that occur in the Latin Letter.

Finally, further evidence for dating the Latin Letter before February 1605 is Donne's reference to the house of a man named Tincomb, where he was staying at the time he sent the Latin Letter to Goodere. As Shapiro noted, Donne probably rented these quarters as a short-term measure near the beginning of 1605, after he moved his family from Pyrford to Peckham, where relative proximity to London made a commute to city lodgings for the first time feasible. There is no evidence that Donne ever had lodgings at Tincomb's after returning to England in early 1606; instead, with a residence at Mitcham, he began also to room at an unnamed house in the Strand and at some point began to room (where Goodere had roomed) at the Bartlett house, until at length he moved his family to a London residence in Drury Lane. If, as the case seems to be, Donne rented lodgings at Tincomb's house only *before* his 1605–6 travel (and there is no evidence of his having resided there after 1605), then dating of the Latin Letter in 1611 is surely mistaken.

Dating the Latin Letter in early 1605, in addition to illuminating the circumstances of Donne's travel, lends altered significance to another passage in it, a well-known request we can now see Donne addressed to Goodere apparently six years earlier than has generally been thought (Donne 1633b: 351–2). This passage asked that Goodere return quickly (presumably before Donne departed England for the continent) a number of holograph manuscripts Donne had sent to him; Donne named among a larger group of unspecified writings his Latin Epigrams ('*epigrammata mea Latina*') and his satirical booklist, *Courtier's Library* (*Catalogus librorum satyricus*). Without exception Donne clearly was concerned to recover and revise or destroy all of these literary works—probably including Paradoxes, Epigrams, Elegies, and Satires, not merely the examples he named—intending to subject all of them to their Last Judgement ('*extremum iuditium*'). Some of these holographs, Donne wrote, he planned to send to purgatory, to come forth chastised through revision; others that had been copied without his knowledge would witness that they had been condemned to hell by his burning their originals; finally, the remainder, either virgins (except that many had had their hands on them) or so unfortunately barren that no copies of them had been engendered, were to be burned and to pass away into complete annihilation.

Donne stipulated in the Latin Letter that all the manuscripts requested had been received by Goodere with the promise that they would quickly be returned ('*chartulas meas, quas cum sponsione citæ redhibitionis*'), a promise Goodere obviously had not yet kept. In fact, not only had Goodere not returned any of the promised manuscripts, but Donne's words imply the possibility—and he seems resigned to it—that Goodere may have lost some of them or lent them to someone else ('*Inter quas, si epigrammata mea Latina, & Catalogus librorum satyricus non sunt, non sunt*'). It is not clear whether Donne here named the Epigrams and *Catalogus* mainly because these seemed particularly to need their Last Judgement; or mainly because, having earlier discussed their return, Donne already understood that Goodere might no longer have them in his possession. Perhaps Donne meant to express both these concerns.

One interpretation of this passage in the Latin Letter has been that Donne 'was in the course of revising some of his writings for the press', perhaps with the 'intention in 1611 of publishing a selection of his poems and shorter prose pieces' (Bald 1970: 241–2). This conjecture, whatever force it may have had as a scenario occurring in 1611, seems comparatively unlikely as an occurrence of 1605. In fact, there was no point during Donne's lifetime when he could prudently have contemplated printing either his Latin Epigrams or his *Catalogus*, not to mention several of his other dangerous writings. Many of these writings expressed views on religion, politics, and sexuality that could be penalized by the English government or society. Rather than a planned edition, what Donne more likely had in mind was to call back these writings from Goodere in order to maintain better control of them, or perhaps to leave himself less exposed to criticism for having written them. Donne's extraordinary request of Goodere suggests that, as he thought about travelling in 1605, he was beginning to have reservations about the way he had disseminated his writings in the past and already at this point intended to revise and abridge his work embodied in manuscripts that he feared had already to some extent passed beyond his control. Accordingly, on a new footing during the next few years, while he would continue more carefully permitting some new writings to circulate in manuscript, he would also initiate the series of his publications, in a way even more daring than his dissemination of manuscripts.

2

Although Donne obtained his licence to travel in February 1605, like Matthew he remained in England for nearly three months, as is shown by a Letter with enclosure that Donne himself delivered to Goodere's lodgings at the Bartlett house while Goodere was still absent abroad with the Hertford embassy, not to return until 15 May 1605. Accomplishing a promised, last-minute errand before Donne himself crossed the Channel in early May, this undated Letter (*Letters* 146–7) refers to Anne Donne's labour in childbirth throughout the previous night, conjecturally identified by a series of biographers as the birth of Donne's fourth child, Francis, in early January 1607 (e.g. Jessopp 93–4; Gosse 1.154–5; Bald 1970: 157–9). However, as Shapiro pointed out (UB, Shapiro Papers, Folder S14), this newborn son must instead have been George, the third child, born in early May 1605. That this son was George, not Francis, is indicated by the fact that the Letter Donne delivered was again written and signed at Tincomb's house.

Donne and Matthew, each awaiting his departure between February and early May 1605, were still close friends and would naturally have discussed their planned itineraries. Such conversations would also have included their mutual friend Goodere, before he left to serve the Hertford embassy in April. Whether Sir Walter Chute also waited nearly three months to depart after his licensing for travel is not known. In fact, nothing is known of Donne's association with Chute after their joint licence was issued; and nothing is known about their destination (if indeed they travelled together). No record at all remains of Chute's activities while abroad, and nothing in his background or subsequent career suggests what purpose he and Donne would have had for travelling together. Evidence does show that at least Donne himself went to Paris: in a Letter of 1612, written during a subsequent trip to Paris, he recalled that earlier, 'when I was last here', the young King Louis XIII, born in 1601, had been at a 'more childish age' (*Letters* 124–5; Shapiro 1967: 76; Bald 1970: 149).

Other evidence suggests that Donne also went to Venice, inevitably visiting there with Wotton and Woodward. Bald quotes Henry King's letter prefaced to Izaak Walton's *Life* of Donne, in which King presents his understanding that the friendship of Donne and Wotton had been 'continued in their various Travels' (Walton 1675: 2–3; Bald 150). For the most part, however, Donne and Wotton, though practised travellers, did not leave England during the same periods; and when they did so they failed, despite their plans, to meet while they were both abroad. Except during 1605–6 at Venice, there appears no occasion on which such a meeting abroad could have occurred. Bald also quotes Walton's suggestion that the two portraits Donne bequeathed to Henry King, of Venetian Servite priests Paolo Sarpi and Fulgenzio Micanzio, were acquired after he met these men in Italy (Walton 1675: 61; Bald 1970: 150 and, for the bequests in Donne's will, 563); there again appears no occasion but a visit to Venice in 1605–6 on which such a meeting could have occurred.

More puzzling evidence of Donne's travel to Venice in 1605 is a letter Toby Matthew wrote from Italy to Donne in England in August 1606, expressing his disappointment at having 'received a young Letter' from Donne (unfortunately not extant) 'dated as out of *England*'. Matthew explains further his belief, until he had recently received this letter, that Donne had been in Venice and had intended travelling on to Florence, where Matthew was staying (*TMC* 274–5; Feil 306–7; Bald 1970: 151–2). Whether Matthew came by his expectation, that Donne was to come to him from Venice in 1606, through conversation or through correspondence with Donne himself is not clear. He and Donne might have discussed their impending itineraries before they both left England in May 1605; or shortly thereafter at Paris, where Matthew stayed until about mid-May (Feil 17), when Donne too arrived, staying for an undetermined period before travel to Italy. It is also possible that Matthew had read or heard someone else's report of Donne's intentions, or had conceived a misunderstanding. But in any case, Matthew's letter states not only his firm belief that Donne would be travelling from Venice to join him at some point in 1606 in Florence, but also Matthew's perplexity after having received Donne's belated notice that he had been back in England for some time. Deprived of the letter Donne wrote Matthew from England, we can only conjecture about this turn of events. Despite the terms of Donne's travel licence, and contrary to the expectation he expressed in his Latin Letter, he chose not to remain abroad for a period of years. For some reason he instead returned to England from Venice, and did not take time in advance to inform Matthew of this apparent change of plans.

Donne must still have been at Venice when word arrived there near the end of 1605 that the Gunpowder Plot had been exposed. He then would have heard the news possibly from Wotton, who had received, 'besides private letters, a very large and particular dispatch from my Lord of Salisbury' (Wotton to Edward Barrett, 31 December 1605; L. P. Smith 1.339). Even as, earlier in the year, Donne was getting his licence to travel and planning his trip, excavation of a tunnel under Westminster had been attempted by Catholic conspirators; subsequently, as Donne travelled the continent, rumours had caused arrests and examinations of Catholics on suspicion of revolutionary plotting. By November rumour was confirmed in the discovery and arrest of Guy Fawkes, minding barrels of explosives in a leased cellar of the palace of Westminster, leading to the pursuit and killing or capture of Fawkes's numerous associates, including Thomas Percy, estates officer and a distant cousin of Donne's friend Henry Percy, Earl of Northumberland, whose sympathy with traditional Catholics Donne shared. By the end of November Northumberland had been arrested, as had his former secretary Dudley Carleton, and other friends of Donne who were personal associates of Percy, including Edmund Whitelocke and Thomas Harriot. All were held for questioning about possible ramifications of the plot, their belongings and papers searched energetically, and their recent associations and activities scrutinized with suspicion.

Donne's immediate response to this sort of news evidently was, without informing Matthew who expected him at Florence, to cut short his travelling and return to England at some point in the first part of 1606. Matthew's August letter to Donne suggests that, if (as was hard for Matthew to believe) Donne had indeed written to him not from Venice but from England, then he had left Italy in great haste: 'what wind, or water could drive you back so soon?' (*TMC* 274)—a question expressing Matthew's puzzled conjecture that Donne may have journeyed home not by any leisurely, overland route but by sea or river, much quicker methods of travel. Reasons for Donne's haste are again matter of conjecture: he may have had urgent concerns about his imprisoned friends; he may have been worried about other friends, and above all about his family; and he may have thought of possible disasters beyond the plot not so fortunately to be averted.

3

Following his return to England from Venice, Donne resumed contact with friends, among them Ben Jonson, whose work for several years had illustrated how dangerous writing in early modern England could be. Jonson had been in and out of prison from the summer of 1597, initially on account of collaborating with Thomas Nashe in writing a play, *The Isle of Dogs*, 'contanynge very seditious & sclandrous matter', according to the Privy Council. In or out of prison, Jonson believed, he was thereafter kept under surveillance by what he called 'spies', agents of the council. In consequence of his killing a fellow *Isle of Dogs* player in a duel, he had been again imprisoned for two weeks in autumn 1598 and was released only after he had been branded with a 'T' (i.e. destined for Tyburn) on his thumb. During this imprisonment he became a Catholic. After his release he continued to incur censorship of his writings, a series of defiant plays resulting in a summons to testify before the Privy Council about a charge of 'popery and treason' in connection with his *Sejanus* (1603) and imprisonment again for his part in the composition of *Eastward, Hoe* (1604). After release from this latest imprisonment, while Donne was abroad, Jonson in October 1605 had shared a supper party with several of the Gunpowder conspirators (Jonson 1–2.217–20; Dutton 13–19; Flynn 2004*a*: 383–4).

Having learned that Jonson had attended this supper, Cecil within two days of the plot's discovery used this incident and Jonson's other brushes with the law to enlist his cooperation with the Privy Council's investigation and public relations in the wake of the plot's discovery. A council warrant dated 7 November directed Jonson to contact a certain priest and offer him the council's assurance of safety if he will 'do good service to the state'. Jonson's letter to Salisbury, written a few days later, shows that he himself was intent on proving his loyalty, despite his Catholicism (Jonson 1–2.202–3). Jonson's apparently cooperative attitude continued through the first weeks of 1606 (just as Donne must have been leaving Venice), partly because he and his wife were presented on 10 January before an ecclesiastical court and charged with recusancy (Dutton 22–4). Although Salisbury took no known step to influence these proceedings, Jonson experienced them in a context that included his particular vulnerability to Salisbury in relation to the October dinner and its implications. He was certainly under pressure not to write anything that commented on Salisbury's effort to establish an official explanation of the Gunpowder Plot, concerning which the government's initial reports, including explanation of the arrest of Northumberland, were regarded by Dudley Carleton and other friends of the Earl as a fable—'but ignis fatuus or a flash of some foolish fellowes brayne, to abuse the world' (Carleton to John Chamberlain, 13 November 1605; TNA, PRO SP 14/16/69).

Yet, later in 1606, when Donne returned from Venice, Jonson was not only trying to deal with his prosecution for recusancy but also at the same time writing *Volpone*, a play about a fox in Venice, whose topical focus also evoked 'the religio-political situation in the early years of James I's reign; specifically the Gunpowder Plot; and even more specifically the role in these of Robert Cecil, the Earl of Salisbury' (Dutton 7). When Jonson specified in prefatory material for the first edition of *Volpone* that the play had been written during a five-week period and within the two months preceding its first performance (on some date before 24 March 1606), he confirmed that it was written during the prosecutorial and propaganda campaigns directed against those held under arrest or under prosecution for the plot. *Volpone*'s first edition also included in its front matter a Latin poem by Donne—*Amic*—praising Jonson's daring as a poet. In view of Jonson's political and personal circumstances, the daring required to write and produce this play was remarkable.

Moreover, the striking topicality of *Volpone* can hardly have been based entirely on printed sources (Dutton 94–8; Flynn 2004a: 375). For example, material in the play that parallels quotidian detail of Sir Henry Wotton's propensities and activities in Venice (presented through the character Sir Politic Would-be) may well have come to Jonson through personal reports, such as Donne's stories about his recent visit with Wotton. Would-be and Wotton had a number of remarkable resemblances: at the time of the play's completion, both had been at Venice for fourteen months; both were inveterate gossips and diarists; both indulged in ingenious inventions (including their similar schemes for preventing fire in powder magazines); both were notoriously in debt to Venetian Jews for the costs of furnishing their lodgings; and both were fascinated by plots and intrigues witnessed or imagined at Venice or other Italian cities, both also keeping notes for many 'projects' and intrigues of their own (Flynn 2004a: 375–6).

Jonson's use of detail about the Privy Council's representative at Venice seems intended to comment on the policies of the government, policies whose leading proponent was Salisbury (Dutton 61–6; Flynn 2004a: 375–82). As Dutton remarks, there does seem to be 'something of Robert Cecil, or at least of the policies over which he presided, offered in refracted form through Sir Pol' (Dutton 63). But neither Jonson nor Donne would have been concerned maliciously to caricature the plot-sniffing ambassador to Venice himself, nor could such an intention have been effective on the London stage, whose audiences would hardly have found Would-be's proclivities recognizable as Wotton's. On the other hand, these things would be 'undoubtedly more readily intelligible to a close coterie of Jonson's own circle, such as those who contributed the commendatory verses' published before *Volpone* (ibid. 7); these were people several of whom were personally acquainted not only with Jonson and Donne but also with Wotton, in some cases quite friendly with him, although not necessarily aligned politically with the policies he served. For example, among the contributors of verses was Sir Thomas Roe, both Wotton's and Donne's friend and correspondent, who contributed two of the eleven prefatory poems. Perhaps even more to the point was the contribution of Edmund Bolton, the Catholic poet and historian, summoned by the Privy Council in January, together with Jonson and his wife, for questioning about their religion. Bolton's poem, like Donne's, was distinct from the nine others in having been written in Latin; moreover, Bolton's and Donne's poems had pride of place, first and second among the commendatory contributions and alone among them emphasizing in Latin the daring of Jonson's play (ibid. 38; Flynn 2004a: 380–1).

Donne's prefatory poem was his earliest publication, initiating the series of his publications and public authorship. Until 1607 strictly a manuscript writer, Donne had designed his early poems and prose works as rhetorical transactions between individuals or with relatively small groups, maintaining some (perhaps illusory) sense of control over dissemination of these writings, with a relatively clear sense of his particular, intended audience. By the time he wrote the prefatory poem published with *Volpone* he had in some ways begun to think of himself as also a publishing author, whose audience would intentionally encompass larger numbers of readers unknown to him. There followed the series of his disparate initial publications (more fully discussed in Chs. 12, 18, and 20): *Pseudo-Martyr* (1610); *Ignatius* (1611), published in Latin editions at both London and Hanau and in an English edition at London; panegyric verses prefacing Thomas Coryate's *Crudities* (1611); *FirAn*, including also *FunEl* (1611); reprintings of these bound with *SecAn* (1612); and *Henry* (1613)—to mention only those writings he published prior to taking orders in the Church of England, when his publications became those of an official voice in the preaching hierarchy, however unique or distinctive.

The impulse towards this activity is in part traceable to the Latin Letter written at the time Donne was contemplating travel in 1605–6, when he recalled from Goodere a number of his until then exclusively holograph writings, intending either to revise or to burn them. Whether these plans materialized or not, soon after returning from travel Donne was preparing to augment his authorship with a new element: publication. Whatever risks he felt he previously had taken in writing for a particular, intended audience, from this time forward he sometimes wrote with greater daring, emulating the boldness of Jonson, whose artistry deliberately intended the wide dissemination of politically charged work not designed for certain eyes only, but made freely available in print, even to the eyes of censors. By this decision Donne became, like Jonson, something of a controversialist, a status he had earlier avoided. Not that Donne had been unfamiliar with political and religious controversy even in the Elizabethan period. His manuscript writings—Epigrams, Elegies, Paradoxes, Satires, *Metem*, and the *Courtier's Library*—had shown awareness of controversy, though without his ever engaging in it as more than a confidential and aloof observer. But after his 1605–6 travel he adopted a new and more active posture, resulting eventually in his various published writings of the next twenty-five years, from the prefatory poem to Jonson's *Volpone* through the Sermons.

Matthew, Jonson, Goodere, and Donne, until and probably even after discovery of the Gunpowder Plot, had shared a position of sympathy and toleration for traditional Catholics, in opposition to the dominant policy of Robert Cecil, who practised sympathy without toleration (Croft 1991a: 782–4). In his private life Salisbury was friendly with many Catholics, and his correspondence includes Catholics writing and thanking him for favours. However, in the matter of opposition to toleration for Catholics, Salisbury's chief political opponent until the winter of 1605–6 had been the Earl of Northumberland. Compared to Salisbury or his father, Northumberland had never been much of a politician. The Cecils had defeated him and his family time after time during a period stretching back before his birth. Nevertheless, Catholics and Catholic sympathizers favouring toleration could look for a political advocate to no one else on the early Jacobean scene but a handful of Catholic peers, such as Northumberland; Edward Somerset, Earl of Worcester; or Anthony Browne, Viscount Montagu (Questier 2006: 270–1). Among these the most eminent, if least effective (especially after he approached the King early in the reign with a petition asking toleration for Catholics; see Ch. 30.I), Percy held title to one of the three ancient English earldoms; he was regarded as a figure of importance by the King, as well as by the Gunpowder conspirators and many other people. Whatever his self-admitted personal incapacities, his lineage alone was well recognized and in itself, even in 1605, made him a political factor, though practically ineffective.

Following discovery of the plot, Northumberland had immediately been placed under guard in his own home; later he was examined at great length and then transferred to the Tower of London for further, more intense interrogation. These proceedings were meant to lead to a trial at which the government could show that the plot had been another of the ancient Catholic nobility's traditional revolts against the Crown. Salisbury expressed this intention in a letter to his ambassador at Brussels, stressing that Percy's inclusion among those 'divers noblemen' taken into custody could be justified because he was one whom the conspirators in their arrangements had been 'very careful to preserve'. Northumberland deserved prosecution because he had acted as an advocate for English Catholics, having 'upon the death of the queen and after...declared often to the king that the Catholics had offered themselves to depend upon him in all their courses so far' (Cecil to Sir Thomas Edmondes, 2 December 1605; qtd. by Questier 2006: 281). Salisbury and other officers of the government tried to identify Northumberland as that nobleman intended by the conspirators to have served as protector of the realm had the Jacobean regime collapsed in the ruins of Westminster palace.

Although no conclusive evidence ever pointed to Northumberland, clearly the government was trying to obtain evidence that would implicate him as a leading figure in the plot. Robert Cecil took a keen interest in the investigation, reading and annotating transcribed testimony for use at a trial (M. Nicholls 1991: 70). Especially after the capture of Henry Garnett in February 1606, questioning of the Jesuit included as a salient element the topic of noble Catholics and Catholic sympathizers, especially Northumberland. 'The investigators' persistence here is instructive, for much the same question had been asked over and over for two months'. Any piece of tantalizing testimony tending further to implicate Northumberland 'only made the investigators hunger for more substantial results' (ibid. 73).

Salisbury, immediately in November 1605, had begun gathering testimony about Northumberland and the plot. His professional informers supplied various reports still extant in the Hatfield papers (ibid. 180–1, 184) but nothing that could clinch a case against the Earl. Meanwhile, Cecil's attitude towards Northumberland was consistently guarded, including some ironic and politic damning with faint praise (ibid. 181). In this he repeated his treatment of Northumberland's friend Sir Walter Ralegh, whom Cecil had eliminated from their (almost equally unequal) rivalry through discovery of an earlier plot. Donne's correspondence with Matthew suggests that both men believed Ralegh had been framed (see Ch. 30.I).

In April 1606 Garnett was convicted of conspiring with the plotters; he was hanged, drawn, and quartered in the churchyard of St Paul's Cathedral on 3 May. Donne shared the harsh opinion held by his uncle, the late Jesuit Jasper Heywood, about the political intrigues of some English Jesuits, especially Robert Persons (Ch. 27.II). He may also have connected the conviction of Garnett to developments at Venice, where the Jesuits, who had supported the papacy in various disputes with the *Signoria*, were expelled from the republic. These events reinforced his impression, later expressed throughout *Pseudo-Martyr* and *Ignatius*, that the Jesuits had become a malign force in the hands of the Pope, directed for the cause of Roman religion towards the disruption of both English and Venetian civil order, as well as other mischief.

Through the early spring of 1606 Northumberland remained under suspicion in the Tower, tentatively scheduled for trial in Star Chamber as soon as the Crown's case was ready. Here matters had stood when Jonson began to write *Volpone*. The government could not convict Northumberland of having shared in the conspiracy as designated protector of the realm, although they had repeatedly asked Garnett about this matter before he was executed. In default of this more serious charge, at the end of June Northumberland was finally convicted of encouraging Catholics to look to King James for toleration (which the King had plainly written to him he would not grant); misprision of treason (i.e. knowing about a planned treason but not revealing it); and secretly sending his messengers north after the fleeing conspirators (deemed tantamount to sending them a warning, a 'watche word'). He was stripped of court office; condemned to imprisonment during the King's pleasure, which lasted for fifteen years; and fined £30,000. This fine has dispassionately been termed 'preposterous' (Hallam 1.406), and was quite simply, as Northumberland told the King, 'the greatest Fine that ever was gott upon any Subject in this Realme' (Northumberland to King James, July 1606; Fonblanque 2.283). A copy of the 1607 first edition of *Volpone* remains at Petworth, Sussex, part of Northumberland's library; he may have read the play, and Donne's commendatory poem on it, while imprisoned in the Tower of London.

4

In June 1607 Toby Matthew returned from the continent to England. By this time he had been a Roman Catholic for over a year, although, having left Italy for Paris, he had maintained as well as he could for the benefit of English observers the fiction that he was still a Protestant (Feil 37–8). At home he was hardly believed by his father, the Archbishop of York, Tobie Matthew, who had given him futile orders to return to England by April (ibid. 39). Matthew did not leave France for England before pledging his Roman faith in a letter to Robert Persons, SJ (whom he called 'the Father of my soul'); a few days after arriving he surprised his birth father's former rival, Richard Bancroft, Archbishop of Canterbury, by confessing his Catholicism. Bancroft at first scolded, then tried to dissuade Matthew, enlisting for this purpose his helper in devising the Oath of Allegiance, Perkins, whom Matthew had known as a fellow member of Parliament and Gray's Inn. At length, after fruitless bickering between Matthew and Perkins, Bancroft, on the advice of King James, condemned Matthew's conversion and asked him to swear the Oath of Allegiance (ibid. 39–44).

When Matthew refused, on 7 July 1607, Bancroft committed him to the Fleet prison (ibid. 44), in accord with the procedure outlined in the statute. Ordinarily, someone refusing the oath was to be held in prison until the next assizes or quarter sessions, then to be tendered the oath again. But the likely prospect that Matthew would again refuse to swear would subject him to the penalties of praemunire and inevitably become a cause of embarrassment to his father, the Archbishop of York, and to Bancroft himself as primate of the English Church. To persuade Matthew to change his mind and swear the oath, Bancroft introduced him to the Catholic Archpriest George Blackwell, who had himself recently been arrested and committed to the Clink prison, sworn the oath, and urged other Catholics to do so if required. However, Matthew rebuked Blackwell for disputing and disobeying papal breves against swearing the oath (ibid. 46). Subsequently, Matthew was required to confer with Alberico Gentili and Lancelot Andrewes; but these meetings too accomplished little or nothing to sway his Roman resolution (ibid. 47–9). Several friends, including Sir Francis Bacon and Dudley Carleton, were also allowed to visit and reason with Matthew in the Fleet. But Matthew held fast, and instead of relenting began to proselytize in his cell, giving religious instruction to his visitors, including several women, some of them noblewomen (ibid. 51–2). Another of Matthew's visitors was his good friend Goodere, whose malleability he was easily able to turn towards Romanism, except that Goodere was unsteady and believed as well in what the next person told him. When visited by old friends Donne and Richard Martin, Matthew tried to win them to his Catholic views; but they both rejected these efforts, causing Matthew to term them mere 'libertines' (ibid. 54–5).

Of Donne's further conversation with Matthew in the Fleet leading to this characterization nothing is known. But clearly the Oath of Allegiance must have been an element in opening the gulf that came to exist between the two friends. By the time of their interview, nearly two years after he had met Sarpi in Venice and begun his study of the Venetian controversy, Donne was well along in an extensive course of study, reading not only Venetian and Roman but English, Gallican, and other controversialists, study that resulted in his publishing *Pseudo-Martyr* in 1610 and *Ignatius* in 1611 (cf. Chs. 12, 18, 30.II, and 31.I). In *Pseudo-Martyr* Donne demonstrated his conversance with this literature while dealing distinctively in his own way with the situation faced by English Catholics in regard to the oath. Donne expressed through the public act of *Pseudo-Martyr* his conformity to the general lines of English government policy in regard to the Gunpowder Plot and the Oath of Allegiance. Attacking Jesuit controversialists and advising English Catholics to swear the oath as a civil matter that could not compromise their spiritual integrity, nevertheless he was careful in *Pseudo-Martyr*, while publicly identifying himself as a member of the Church of England rather than a papist, to preserve space for traditional Catholicism within this kind of conformity. He repeatedly contested the notion that the only Catholicism was the Roman Catholicism propounded by the Council of Trent; and he continued to express fundamental sympathy and concern to accommodate traditional English Catholics, intending help to secure for them some limited toleration within the English Church. Unsparing in his condemnation of Trent, the Jesuits, and papal claims of temporal jurisdiction, having travelled to Venice and returned in 1606, and having begun to publish his writings as a controversialist, Donne nevertheless remained to some extent a member of the religion he was born into (cf. Chs. 32.I, 35.I, and 36.II).

CHAPTER 32.1

DONNE'S DECISION TO TAKE ORDERS

JEANNE SHAMI

THIS chapter proposes to focus on a particular moment—Donne's decision to take orders in the Church of England in 1615. No decision in Donne's life has generated such divergent accounts of his situation—economic, personal, political, social, religious, or spiritual—or raised as many questions about his motivations and inner life. In part, the diversity of biographical opinion rests on the nature of primary source evidence: Izaak Walton's *Life of Donne* and Donne's extant Letters. Walton's *Life of Donne* is a shaky foundation on which to establish biographical claims. No scholar reading David Novarr, for example, can doubt that Walton, through successive versions of the *Life*, 'increasingly drew a wealth of impression from the vaguest hint of a fact' (1958: 126). And yet, despite this fact, much in Walton's narrative—even uncorroborated elsewhere—resonates with explanatory power. The Letters, too, require reading strategies attuned to their baffling contradictions (see Ch. 25). Donne described them using the enigmatic trope of the 'conveyance' (*Letters* 105), both 'an organ or channel of communication' (a definition implying self-revelation) and 'a private or secret passage' (a definition implying self-concealment). Annabel Patterson has focused on the deeply conflicted nature of Donne's Letters, wittily expressed in self-division, and occupying a space *somewhere* between self-censorship and public statement (1982: 43). That space—at once so intimate and so impenetrable—can illuminate, but also occlude, Donne's biography.

In the years under consideration (roughly 1607–15), Donne was uncertain about many things in his life: his ability to maintain his growing family; his ability to prove useful to his society; the form that his service or usefulness would take; his health. All these factors are crucial for understanding his decision to take orders, which, whatever the motives, proved to be a life-changing consequence of these uncertain conditions: the culmination of his public and personal religious identity and the foundation of his reputation for years to come (see Ch. 24). Walton's emphasis on the priesthood as 'a new outlet for his intellectual energies, rather than a turning away from them' (Colclough 2003: 11) offers a compelling starting point for analysing this decision: 'And now all his studies which had been occasionally diffused, were all concentred in Divinity. Now he had a new calling, new thoughts, and a new imployment for his wit and eloquence. Now all his earthly affections were changed into divine love; and all the faculties of his own soul were ingaged in the conversion of others' (Walton 1658: 44–5).

As Michael Questier (2006) and Achsah Guibbory (Ch. 37 below) have cautioned, however, the word 'conversion' as applied to religious identities in the early modern period was complex, suggesting a transformation best understood as a 'return' (from the Hebrew *teshuvah*) to the former path, 'a turning away from idolatry to the path set by God' (Guibbory). Moreover, the work of Questier and other historians (see Collinson, Ch. 26.I above) has shown that religious identities in the period were fluid, and that 'flux in religion was the norm rather than the exception' (Questier 1996: 206). Finally, as Guibbory also reminds us (Ch. 37), Walton's account of Donne's 'conversion' in fact marked a transition not from Catholicism to the Church of England, but from the earthly to the spiritual, the sacred to the profane.

Elaborating, then, on Walton's central insight (that in seeking ordination Donne was translating thoughts, attention, and skills that hitherto had been 'occasionally diffused' to another 'imployment'), this chapter will trace a more nuanced path through the various considerations that complicated Donne's decision, a path that explores the central dilemma they highlight: how to act in a way that satisfies both *ambition* (to serve, to be recognized publicly and remembered for one's talents, to advance in the world) and *honour* (to serve with integrity, to be held accountable for one's principles, to contribute to the public good). As Hugh Adlington points out in Chapter 41, the majority of commentaries on Donne's choice of a course have focused narrowly on ambition as 'the zealous pursuit of employment and status at court and in the church', based on a perhaps anachronistic use of the *OED*'s primary definition of the word: 'The ardent (in early usage, inordinate) desire to rise to high position, or to attain rank, influence, distinction or other preferment'. However the terms 'conversion' and 'ambition' are understood, Donne's negotiations of the available pathways—including those offered by patrons—involved him publicly in circumstances that exposed the political and social hazards of seeking preferment, as well as the traps of self-deception and self-interest that might taint such a decision.

The Impact of Walton's *Life of Donne*

Following Walton, all accounts of Donne's decision to take orders in the Church of England in 1615 begin with the purported offer of a benefice by Thomas Morton (c.1564–1659), newly appointed Dean of Gloucester in 1607 (Walton 1658: 25–33). This episode, allegedly related to Walton by Morton himself, was added to the 1658 edition of the *Life of Donne* (and to subsequent editions) when Morton, as Bishop of Durham, was still a living witness. Walton's account has shaped the discussion of Donne's vocation for over 400 years. Yet Donne's relations with Morton remain obscure. Neither of two seventeenth-century lives of Morton mentions his collaboration with Donne, nor does Walton mention it, despite his desire to prove their close relationship (Donne 1969: 168–73). That Donne was probably acquainted with Morton from at least 1603 might justify Walton's claim that the offer was based on 'long friendship' and was prompted by Morton's recent elevation to the deanery of Gloucester (22 June 1607), but Walton's 'use of the passage as an early manifestation of Donne's talents in divinity, as foreshadowing what was to be' was Walton's own conjecture (Novarr 1958: 73).

From Walton we have also inherited several controversial half-truths masquerading as facts: the 'necessities' of Donne's 'temporall estate'; the 'irregularities' of Donne's former life; Donne's 'expectation of a State-employment'; and Donne's decision as one weighing 'Court-hopes' against 'holy Orders' (thus creating 'inward conflict'). Most influential has been the view that Donne was unable to choose between '*Gods glory*' ('holy Orders') or a '*maintenance*' ('state-employment'), a case of conscience in Walton that by 1970 had metamorphosed into R. C. Bald's view that Donne was holding out for a secular position. Moreover, Novarr's cautions against adhering to Walton's narrative have gone unheeded. Donne's ordination has consistently been read as the culmination of fruitless attempts to undo the 'remarkable errour' (Walton 1658: 74) of his life (his marriage to Anne More) by attaining court preferment, whether secular or ecclesiastical.

Some of these assumptions need to be revisited. The view that Donne's motives for pursuing divinity were primarily economic, for example, has scant evidentiary basis. That Donne by 1615 was not rich is undeniable, but that he was destitute is questionable, and requires rethinking in light of his prolonged uncertainty—during the twelve years after his marriage and consequent dismissal from the service of Lord Keeper Thomas Egerton—about the best course to pursue. We know that during these twelve years and throughout his life Donne kept a manservant, found time and resources to write frequent Letters and poems, paid rent at Drury's house in London, travelled extensively, owned numerous books, sat for and perhaps commissioned portraits by some of the period's most fashionable artists (including an Oliver miniature dated 1616), and was a connoisseur and collector of art (at some point even acquiring a Titian). We also know that during his continental trip with

Drury (1611–12) Donne did not burden his literary patron Lucy Russell, Countess of Bedford, with requests, financial or otherwise (*Letters* 95), and that he did not receive a living immediately upon his ordination; in fact, the first came a full year after that date (Ch. 33.II). Additionally, Donne seems to have been prepared to pay the sizeable sums necessary to obtain the appointments he considered after 1607. None of these activities suggests indigence, although his Letters imply that he lived on the margin of his means, as his obligations to creditors at the time of his ordination attest (*Letters* 148–9, 196–7).

That a '*maintenance*' such as might be obtained in accepting a benefice was necessarily at odds with '*Gods glory*' (thus contaminating the spiritual motive) has been another biographical consequence of Walton's powerful narrative. Walton's account of Morton's offer laid the foundation for this interpretation, but the spiritual crisis the offer supposedly induced became entangled with Donne's alleged preference for secular preferment, inferred from his participation in a complex and

Ill. 32.I.1. John Donne as a royal chaplain in 1616 (portrait miniature by Isaac Oliver in the Royal Collection at Buckingham Palace). (The Royal Collection © 2009, Her Majesty Queen Elizabeth II.)

varied network of patronage relationships, particularly those related to the Countess of Bedford, and (from 1613) King James's favourite, Robert Carr, Viscount Rochester and Earl of Somerset. Supporting this interpretation was evidence from letters written in 1614 that Donne was seeking other (secular) positions simultaneously with his professed resolution to become a divine (thus undermining the sincerity of that resolution).

Scandalized by the apparent opportunism of this moment, subsequent biographers have been highly critical of Donne's decision, in part because it appeared to contaminate the profession he entered and in part because it appeared to contaminate the writer who entered it. They have suggested that Donne removed himself from difficult circumstances, particularly those surrounding his entanglement in the Somerset fiasco (see Ch. 32.II), by abandoning this connection and achieving public respectability in the church. Unlike Walton, they have rarely credited Donne with anything as honourable as a conversion, spiritual transformation, or rebirth in making this decision. Sir Leslie Stephen was (influentially) irritated by Donne's apparently self-serving decision—not primarily, it seems, because he had become a preacher, but because he had become a preacher in the service of the government, a form of spiritual prostitution (Haskin 2007: 177–84). Stephen believed that Donne had vision, tremendous gifts, and an accommodating and irenic approach to controverted religious questions, but took the easy way out of his difficulties by becoming a spokesman for government religion and government policies, a step backward rather than forward that was occluded by Walton's ascription of this move to the workings of providence (ibid. 181). Stephen writes:

His life is as distracted and dependent as his thought. He cannot fairly decide to be the divine, and apologizes for his want of learning while he is displaying learning enough for a whole bench of bishops. The Court still charms and fascinates the strong accomplished flatterer, and he cannot help hoping that one of the great favourites to whom he can make himself so acceptable will, at last, lift him out of his troubles. All the time the poor man is 'neurotic', troubled by ill-health, weighed down by family cares, and driven to speculate upon the ethics of suicide. (A. J. Smith 1996: 2.168–9)

The recurring narrative from the nineteenth century on has been that Donne, sick, overburdened with debts and family obligations, and unable to secure the court appointment that he desperately desired, 'settled' for divinity by the end of 1614, a year in which his existential, economic, and spiritual crises peaked (Gosse 2.33, 54; Bald 1970: 301; Carey 1981a: 87). Donne's decision to take orders is described as a 'sudden resolution' (Gosse 2.22), a decision 'forced' on Donne (Bald 1970: 301), a capitulation (Carey 1981a: 88).

Some biographers have used Walton to support alternatives to the views expressed above. Robert Jackson describes Donne's state of mind before ordination as one of 'Christian worldliness' (75), a paradoxical formulation he bases on his reading of *Lit*. According to Jackson, the poem is both religious and worldly, and these two things are not incompatible. Donne just as resolutely rejects the exclusively unspiritual as he does the exclusively unworldly, and rejects 'stepladder-like, hierarchical distinctions' such as that between 'God's glory' and 'a maintenance' (79). The complexity of Donne's thinking about this decision in *Lit*, apparently reconciling polar opposites, has been richly amplified by both Annabel Patterson and Dayton Haskin. Patterson finds that the sophistication and subtlety of Donne's religious imagination in this pre-ordination poem make it unlikely that an offer of ecclesiastical preferment would have caught Donne by surprise or suggested to him an entirely new vocational direction (2002). Dayton Haskin, too, finds that the poem envisages 'continuing changes of heart' rather than a once-and-for-all conversion—that it, in fact, resists the 'category of "conversion" for explaining the remarkable course of events by which he would become a public representative of the establishment that had persecuted members of his own family'—inviting through the complex syntax of its sentences 'experimental' knowledge of repeated 'turning' to God', and thus serving as a 'prelude' to his taking orders (2002*a*: 72, 63, 72, 75). David Colclough frames Donne's search for advancement and a career as a 'search for some kind of institution—an intellectual community—where he can carry out the work of writing and the pursuit of knowledge' (2003: 4). Moreover, he notes that 'Donne's fear of being nothing, his horror of passing through the world without leaving any trace, exists in an uneasy dialectic with his skepticism about the value of worldly pursuits and institutions' (ibid.) whose deleterious effects he had previously exposed in *Sat4* and *HWKiss*. Colclough says that these years should not be seen solely or primarily as years of 'failure, marginalisation, frustrated ambition, and boredom' (8) but as years in which Donne remained active and engaged with the world (travels in 1605–6); wrote many works in prose and verse, including his first published works (see Ch. 31.II); and remained much occupied with occasional verse (see Chs. 14, 20, and 22). He concludes that 'Donne's desire to have an intellectual identity in the world—to be publicly recognised as one who searches for knowledge—knits together all his works' (16).

The evidence of the letters

The evidence of the Letters further complicates our sense of Donne's motives for deciding to enter the Church of England in 1615. Before 1607 Donne had preferred to live 'a wide distance' from the court (*Letters* 81); however, by late 1608, responding to his friends' urgings 'to awake and stare the Court in the face', he was 'content to go forward a little more in the madnesse of missing rather then not pretend' (ibid. 146), despite what he saw as the unlikelihood of success. Throughout 1607–15 Donne worried about his life's direction.

A Letter to Sir Henry Goodere (September 1608) expresses the compelling urgency of Donne's desire to 'do something', and is worth quoting at length for the authenticity of its voice and the careful distinctions and connections it draws between the personal and public imperatives of Donne's desires:

I would fain do something; but that I cannot tell what, is no wonder. For to chuse, is to do: but to be nor part of any body, is to be nothing. At most, the great persons, are but great wens, and excrescences; men of wit and delightfull conversation, but as moales for ornament, except they be so incorporated into the body of the world, that they contribute something to the sustentation of the whole. This I made account that I begun early, when I understood the study of our laws: but was diverted by the worst voluptuousness, which is an Hydroptique immoderate desire of humane learning and languages: beautifull ornaments to great fortunes; but mine needed an occupation, and a course which I thought I entred well into, when I submitted my self to such a service, as I thought might imployed those poor advantages, which I had. And there I stumbled too, yet I would try again: for to this hour I am nothing, or so little, that I am scarce subject and argument good enough for one of mine own letters. (*Letters* 50–1)

A survey of vocational options that Donne reportedly considered before 1615 reveals that in the spring of 1613 he had resolved to make his profession divinity, but that during 1614, the final year before his ordination, he was drawn, diverted, and pushed in many directions. Before 1613 alternatives included a reported vacancy in Queen Anne's household (*Letters* 81–2); a secretaryship in Ireland (ibid. 145); the secretaryship of the Virginia Company (Chamberlain 1.284); professional writer; companion to Sir Robert Drury; civil lawyer (a suggestion rejected by Donne: *Letters* 254–5). From 1613 onward, vocational options reportedly included ambassador to Venice (*TMC* 311–12); parliamentarian (in the 1614 Parliament); a 'little court business', unspecified; and, finally 'divinity', a course that he resolved to pursue, first through Robert Carr, Earl of Somerset, and, finally, through the King himself.

The story of these years is complicated by Donne's relations with patrons—especially Somerset, who proved, paradoxically, both a means and an obstacle to this decision. In Donne's own day, his long-standing patron, Lucy Russell, Countess of Bedford, was scandalized by it. Donne reported that 'she was somewhat more startling, then I looked for from her: she had more suspicion of my calling, a better memory of my past life, then I had thought her nobility could have admitted' (*Letters* 218). King James, Donne's most powerful patron, aware as he was of Donne's past indiscretions, chose to fast-track Donne's ordination and promotion to court chaplain once he had persuaded him to accept ecclesiastical preferment. Donne acknowledged James's role in his decision some years later in his dedication to the *Devotions*, where he refers to his ordination as his second birth in which King James '*vouchsafed mee his Hand, not onely to sustaine mee* in it, *but to lead me* to it' (*Devotions* 3), a circumstance Donne had inscribed on his funerary monument (*Variorum* 8.193).

Donne's patronage relationships have been only partially understood by biographers, in part because they are constructed largely through his heavily coded correspondence in prose and in verse (see Chs. 14 and 25). He has been seen, for example, as engaged in a serious literary and personal relationship with Lucy, Countess of Bedford, and the women of her circle, strained by a social—perhaps economic—need to court other noble ladies in addition to the Countess. From this point of view, Donne's Verse Letters to Sir Robert Rich's sister Lettice, to the Countess of Huntingdon (Elizabeth Stanley Hastings), and to the Countess of Salisbury (Catherine Howard); his *Anniversaries* (whose subject, Elizabeth, was the child of his patrons the Drurys); and his relationship with Magdalen Herbert (Lady Danvers), to whom he wrote several Letters and poems, are all seen as digressions from his foremost patronage relationship—and, therefore, as a kind of poetic infidelity (Bald 1970: 275–7; Marotti 1986: 230; Carey 1981a: 80; but see Maurer in Ch. 14 above).

However, the Somerset patronage has proven most challenging, and the facts that emerge from Donne's Letters to Robert Carr are more complicated than many biographical accounts suggest. Examination of Donne's five extant Letters to Carr reveals several important facts. Significantly (as Donne told the Scottish nobleman James Hay in a letter enclosing for delivery his earliest Letter to Carr), Donne first presented himself to Carr 'by this way of Letter' (*TMC* 321) only *after* he had resolved to make his profession divinity, a recurrent and explicit theme in their correspondence, broached in his first Letter to Carr: 'For, having obeyed at last, after much debatement within me, the Inspirations (as I hope) of the Spirit of God, and resolved to make my Profession Divinitie: I make account, that I do but tell your Lordship, what God hath told me, which is, That it is in this course, if in any, that my service may be of use to this Church and State' (*TMC* 319–20). Donne's coupling of ecclesiastical with political service expresses unequivocally his intentions and the compatibility of divinity and secular preferment. In fact, Donne likely timed his first approach to Somerset to coincide with this moment 'when a resolution of a new course of life and new profession, makes me a little more worthie of his [i.e. Carr's] knowledge' (*TMC* 321), following his return in mid-summer 1613, months after his visit to Sir Edward Herbert at Montgomery Castle. Guibbory (Ch. 37), while wary of biographical readings of imaginative literature, suggests that Donne's poem *Goodf*, structured by the metaphor of 'conversion'—'turning in position, direction, destination' (*OED*)—might comment 'obliquely' on Donne's own 'conversion'. Alastair Bellany (Ch. 32.II) proposes that because Donne approached Carr during a transitional period in which the favourite was recalibrating his clientage and factional networks, Carr likely recognized Donne's potential as a source of technical advice/counsel or as a pen available for religio-political polemic, but had no fixed idea of how he should be used.

The correspondence with Carr (comprising five Letters by Donne but no extant replies) shows that Donne and Carr seem to have been working at cross-purposes, Donne asking for ecclesiastical patronage (to enter the ministry), and Carr providing money and support for alternative court employments, money that Donne accepted with the requisite gratitude, but which frustrated his stated ambition of entering the ministry, and certainly compromised his efforts to remain constant to that course. Throughout this period Donne was under the impression that in approaching Carr (as he told another intermediary, his friend Sir Robert Ker), 'I should not come nearer [Carr's] presence then by a letter' (*Letters* 304); this stricture limited Donne's ability to discuss with Carr, except through the equivocal 'conveyance' of Letters, his commitment to his resolution. Donne's dilemma in this patronage relationship is expressed in a Letter of late August or early September 1613, in which Donne recalls his introductory Letter to Carr (expressing his intention of putting himself and his intention to enter the ministry wholly in Carr's hands), complicated now by the fact that Carr's purchase of Donne with 'benefits already received' had interposed 'distractions, or diversions, in the waies of my hopes' (*Letters* 290–91), thus repeating his intention to enter the ministry and his initial, specific request for Carr's 'favourable assistance' (*TMC* 320) in that matter. Carr's purchase of Donne (and Donne's inability to avoid being bought) further complicates Donne's resolution.

Over the next year, rather than advance Donne's stated goal of entering the ministry, Carr appears to have supplied Donne with more money and pressed on him several secular employment opportunities, none of them answering to Donne's original resolution or enabling it, and none of which Donne was particularly qualified to obtain or perform. One such proposal to Donne was that he instead be a candidate for a Privy Council clerkship. Two vacant clerkships had been provisionally filled by June 1613, but Donne had learned, and reported to Carr, that for their ultimate disposition Sir Henry Wotton had 'some design upon one' of them for his nephew Albertus Morton. Donne could hardly be considered a serious candidate for a clerkship, lacking the qualifications and experience of the other candidates mentioned by Bald (Francis Cottington, Dudley Norton, William Trumbull, and even Wotton's nephew Morton). By spring 1614 Somerset still had not acted to assist Donne's resolution for divinity. Reflecting on his year-long connection with Somerset, Donne could count some blessings, including the Earl's kindness to him and his family during a feverish illness that year: 'I owe unto your Lordship now all the means of my recoverie, and my health itself' (*TMC* 311). Donne also recalled with gratitude his first meeting with Somerset, evidently a result of his first Letter to the Earl in the spring of 1613, in a passage that suggests the nature and limits of the Earl's response to Donne's initial approach: 'ever since I had the happinesse to be in your Lordship's sight, I have lived upon your bread' (*TMC* 311).

Donne had met with Somerset and received unrequested money and promises from him, but none of what he had actually asked for in the spring of 1613. However, in 'obedience' to Somerset's 'commandment' that he seek out and apply for secular court posts, Donne went on to request for himself the position opened by the rumoured reassignment of Sir Dudley Carleton, ambassador at Venice: 'I humbly beseech your Lordship to pardon me the boldness of asking you, Whether I may not be sent thither' (*TMC* 312). The apologetic and questioning tone of this supplication signifies that it seemed a long shot, and conveys the awkwardness with which Donne sought this ambassadorial candidacy in lieu of his expressed wish to pursue divinity.

Donne's last Letter to Somerset followed his failed candidacies for offices he had not sought—a council clerkship and the embassy to Venice—and his realization of the futility of his original request: 'It is now somewhat more than a year, since I took the boldnesse, to make my purpose of professing Divinitie known to your Lordship' (*TMC* 314). Written in September 1614, this Letter actually came more than sixteen months after Donne's first bold profession to the Earl. His gains since then had included Somerset's 'bounty' and his 'inspiration of new hopes into me', which had made him live 'cheerfullie' (*TMC* 314). Throughout the summer of 1614 Donne once again followed the Earl's commandment, evidently nominating himself for yet another position Somerset might secure for him. This may well have been a reversion for the office of one of the Six Clerks in Chancery, a position for which Donne was somewhat qualified and which may well have been discussed with Lord Chancellor Ellesmere during the interview with him that Donne described in his Letter to Goodere on 19 August (*Letters* 172). In consideration of his ageing, his weakening health, and his continuing 'in the same degrees of honestie as I was', Donne now pleaded for a new 'commandement' from Somerset, should he be unable to secure even a position as one of the Six Clerks: 'bid me eitheir hope for this businesse in your Lordship's hand, or else pursue my first purpose, or abandon all' (*TMC* 315). As Donne concluded, these three possibilities were all that remained to him since he had become one 'who is by his own devotions and your purchase, your Lordships most humble and thankfull servant' (*TMC* 315).

Even as these negotiations were under way, Donne found himself entangled, as one of Carr's clients, in the extremely awkward 'businesse' surrounding Carr's prospective wedding to Frances Howard, whose marriage to Robert Devereux, third Earl of Essex, had been annulled, as King James wished, on 27 September 1613. Four Letters to court friends from this period reveal Donne's problematic involvement: his sense of obligation to Carr coupled with his reluctance to involve himself publicly in celebrating or defending Carr's scandalous behaviour. All these Letters express—whether openly or covertly—Donne's extreme discomfort with the situation in which this patronage relationship had landed him. In the first (addressed to Sir Robert Ker, probably November 1613), Donne raises two issues. The first is that he might be required to write an Epithalamion for the wedding, despite his assertion that his muse 'is dead, like Freewill in our Church' (*Letters* 270). The second is whether he will 'express my opinion of it [the nullity that enabled the marriage], in a more serious manner' than by an Epithalamion, something he was open to doing 'out of a generall readinesse and alacrity to be serviceable and gratefull in any kinde' (ibid.). Three weeks after the wedding Donne had not yet written the Epithalamion, though he wrote to Goodere that 'I think I shall not scape' and that his 'alacrity' had heightened to a 'vehemency' to 'do service to that company' (ibid. 180). In the event, some time after the wedding, Donne sent a belated Epithalamion, with an introductory eclogue apologizing for his absence from court on the wedding day (see Chs. 22 and 32.II). Here we see Donne at his most uncomfortable, squeezed by conflicting obligations of dependency and honour into writing what has come to be seen as one of the strangest, and most reluctant, public celebrations of a marriage ever written in the genre.

What the more serious writing might have entailed, however, remains occluded in Donne's correspondence. It has generally been assumed that, as Carr's dependent, Donne would be asked to write a treatise *defending* the nullity. Donne himself admits that he is ready to be of service in a treatise dealing seriously with 'this businesse' (*Letters* 270), although he 'deprehend[s]' (180) (or criticizes in himself) this readiness and alacrity. Certainly, *Pseudo-Martyr* had demonstrated Donne's credentials in controversial polemic and law, in performances that would qualify him to write such a piece. Commenting on 19 January 1614 to Goodere (on the rumour that 'some treatise concerning this Nullity, which are said to proceed from *Geneva*, but are beleeved to have been done within doors, by encouragements of some whose names I will not commit to this letter'), Donne wrote: 'My poor study having lyen that way, it may prove possible, that my weak assistance may be of use in this matter, in a more serious fashion, then an Epithalamion' (*Letters* 180). Donne's language indicated that he knew more about the treatise than he was able to say through the mail, and, significantly, does not indicate what specific contribution Donne might make to the nullity debate. That the treatise, though written in England, might be thought to have originated at Geneva suggests a Calvinist cast, perhaps expressing a point of view on the nullity comparable to that of the Archbishop of Canterbury, George Abbot, who as a member of the nullity commission had continued to oppose the King's will in this matter. Finally, in another Letter, written on 14 March 1614, Donne responded to Goodere's report of another 'Book of the Nullity' (*Letters* 168), this one unknown to Donne. Donne wrote that, even though 'answering of it'—that is, answering the nullity, or answering a book in support of or opposing the nullity—'be a work for some, both of better abilities really, and in common reputation also, yet I was like enough to have had some knowledge thereof' (169). Donne here describes himself as relatively less qualified to do such work, but so situated as to have been aware of work in the field.

Other sources indicate that illicit critiques of the nullity *were* circulating in unlicensed, mostly scribal, publications; that the King and the Howards were concerned enough by these to consider an official ban (or response); and that no official response was printed (although Sir Daniel Dun's treatise may have circulated scribally). When the evidence of Donne's Letters is situated in this context, it seems plausible that he was one person whom the Somerset–Howard circle might have considered using to write against the critics of the nullity; he had the knowledge, and Carr knew that Donne could write in a polemical vein for print. However, Donne seems to have escaped this quicksand.

Donne's interest in other positions, and the many strands of patronage in which he was connected (including overtures to the Countesses of Huntingdon and Salisbury, as well as the Countess of Bedford), show that his mind was not bent *solely* on divinity in 1614. His Letters for 1614 show that the costs of this year's 'business' were heavy, and included illness, near-blindness, a miscarriage and the deaths of two children, thwarted opportunities, strained friendships (in part due to Carr's stipulation, at their only known meeting in the spring of 1613, that his relation to Donne be kept secret), and difficult relations with his in-laws, who were urging him to seek court preferment. Furthermore, as Carr's client he did not escape writing an equivocal poem, although he did escape writing a defence of the nullity, and his attachment to Carr increasingly became a liability as the new favourite, Buckingham, loomed into view and appeared on Donne's radar (*Letters* 149).

The year 1614 was one of tremendous pressures. Carr's star—so powerful at the beginning of the year—had all but set (or crashed) by the end of the year, leaving Donne, as one of his dependants, to deal with the social, political, and personal fallout. Three Letters to his in-laws written in the late summer and autumn (28 July, 10 August, 3 December) show him chafing with elegant impatience at the frustration of pursuing court business. Donne's Letter of 28 July, for example, reassures his brother-in-law Sir Robert More (who has loaned him a horse to follow the court) that 'no man attends court fortunes with more impatience then I do', even as it reveals the cause of this impatience: the cost to himself and his family of these exertions. In returning More's horse, as Donne explains: 'I esteeme nothinge more inexcusable, then to attend them [i.e. court fortunes] chargeably, nor any expence so chargeable, as that of tyme' (*Marriage Letters* 57). The unexpected visit of Christian IV, James's brother-in-law, has diverted his 'little court busines', and, as Donne wittily and bitterly quips, as far as he can tell the Danes have come not for matters of state or even matters of fashion but with the sole intention of inconveniencing Donne.

This little piece of wit, however, allows Donne to handle other frustrations—the indignity of waiting on court fortunes and the pressures of Anne's family to advance himself—with *sprezzatura*. It allows Donne to insist, for example, that only his pleasure 'and the litle circumstance of my health' have been inconvenienced by the cancellation of his ride into the country. These considerations, given the illnesses and deaths of two of Donne's children that year, resonate keenly. More significantly, they justify Donne's remaining in London. Donne knows that More will not expect him to pursue this 'little Court busines' if his absence from the city might occasion rumours of 'slacknes in my busines' (*Marriage Letters* 57). Donne's witty reluctance to follow the court consistently informs the independence from his brother-in-law and family expectations epitomized in his return of More's horse. Donne assures More that he will do what is necessary with boldness when the time comes: 'If I finde yt necessary to go, I wyll be bold to ask yow', but to do so now would be a 'treason against myselfe' (ibid.). Donne's integrity, as well as the edge on which he balances it, are measured in the last phrase.

Another Letter to More on 10 August reiterates that Donne's health motivated his journey to meet the King. With bitter irony, again returning More's horse, he announces that he grows weary of this kind of 'phisick', and that he will put it off 'at least tyll the king come into these parts', preferring to relieve his wife's solitariness in 'thys Desart of London': 'so much company therfore, as I ame, shee shall not want: and wee had not one another at so cheape a rate, as that we should ever be wearye of one another'. This is a point against which More can hardly argue, and Donne ends with a trenchant instruction to Sir Robert to leave Donne to this business, which he will pursue at his own discretion and as his own circumstances demand. 'Sir,' he writes, 'when these places affoord any thinge worthe your knowledge, I shall be your Referendary', though he signs with his customary: 'Yours ever to be commanded' (*Marriage Letters* 59).

By 3 December, when Donne writes to his father-in-law, Sir George More, it is clear that Donne has gone to Newmarket to pursue his 'purpose' with the King and has been given 'as good allowance, and encouragement' as he could desire. Moreover, the Letter suggests that Donne had earlier asked More to 'speake with hys Grace' Archbishop Abbot, a matter all the more delicate now because Donne realizes that his connection with Somerset may hinder his purpose: 'they are likely to oppose one anothers dependents'. By December 1614 Donne has abandoned 'businesse' (likely the matter of the Six Clerks reversion) and achieved his resolution to make his profession divinity. During that time, as if in preparation, and despite his family's illnesses and deaths and his near-blindness, Donne had been studying with Dr Layfield, a renowned Hebrew scholar (*Letters* 171), and probably composing the *Essayes in Divinity*.

By 1616 we can measure Donne's first public steps in the world of ecclesiastical divinity: ordained minister in the Church of England, King James's royal chaplain, recipient of an honourary DD from Cambridge, and preacher (see Ch. 33.I). Donne asks his old friend Sir Robert Ker to be godfather to his daughter Bridget (*Letters* 271). Yet that patronage does not obscure Donne's commitment to family or vocation. Invited by Ker to meet Pierre du Moulin (June 1615), Donne cites a pre-contracted obligation to dine with his brother-in-law Sir Thomas Grymes and his family, and to preach in the forenoon and afternoon on that day (ibid. 295–6).

Finally, a Letter to his mother written to comfort her on the death of her daughter, Donne's sister Anne Lyly, illuminates Donne's inner world and reveals a depth of wisdom, affection, duty, and sensitivity that belies the view that his decision to take orders was marked solely by ambition or despair. Nor does it support the view that Donne had at last converted to Protestantism, if that meant rejecting the religion into which he had been born. In it, Donne speaks confidently of his mother's faith during a life experienced as a tempestuous series of calamities and, without calling her a martyr, prays 'before Almighty God, and his Angells and Saints in Heaven' that she understand these afflictions as 'assurances' of God's love for and desire for her (*TMC* 324, 326). The Letter interweaves without embarrassment the language of

Catholic religious devotion with that of Reformed election, a directness demonstrating that the correspondents share—intimately and completely—the sustaining beliefs that make life bearable. Although 'Donne was often moved to criticize the beliefs of her Church' (Bald 1970: 316), it is likely that in 1616 Donne and his mother shared the same religion, if not the same church, and that Donne's courage in making his profession divinity enabled a career choice not only tolerated but approved by his closest family members.

CHAPTER 32.II

THE RISE OF THE HOWARDS AT COURT

ALASTAIR BELLANY

1

On 24 May 1612 Robert Cecil—Earl of Salisbury, Secretary of State, Lord Treasurer, Master of the Wards, and the presiding genius of the early Jacobean Privy Council—finally succumbed to the illness that had been the talk of London and the court for months (Chamberlain 1.338, 346, 351). Cecil's death marked the end of an era at court and beyond, and the beginning of a period of intensified political flux. Major state offices had to be filled. The balance of power at court, the struggle for influence over the direction of royal policy, and the flow of patronage and reward would all have to be adjusted. And ambitious courtiers, some of whom had already begun to scramble for Cecil's offices, had to recalibrate their court connections so that they might better navigate the changes his passing would inevitably bring.

When Cecil died John Donne was out of the country, travelling with Sir Robert Drury. In mid-July, from Spa in the Netherlands, Donne offered Sir Henry Goodere what he deprecatingly termed some 'low meditations' occasioned by Cecil's death (*Letters* 89). Donne briefly noted (like others at the time) that Cecil had been in political and financial as well as physical decline for quite a while, but he praised Cecil as a manager of foreign affairs in which he had proved himself 'a very good patriot' (cf. Chamberlain 1.351). But Donne was less interested in court and international affairs than in the politics of Cecil's posthumous reputation. 'Nothing in my

L. of *Salisburies* death', he wrote, 'exercised my poor considerations so much, as the multitude of libells'—coarse, abusive poems mocking the Lord Treasurer that had circulated far and wide in manuscript copies in the wake of Cecil's demise. Donne's response to this outpouring of 'tastelesse and flat' verse was strikingly complex. Contemporary legal doctrine deemed the libelling of magistrates a type of sedition, but Donne was in principle prepared to defend the composition and circulation of abusive, personal satire against great men if the intent was to correct abuses and— most importantly—if the writing was 'witty and sharp' (cf. Bellany 2007*a*: 156–7; Flynn 1987). The poems on Cecil were so bad, Donne thought, that they would convince nobody—indeed they were so poorly written he wondered if Cecil's 'friends' had circulated them to blunt the effects of any serious criticism. In any case, since Cecil was dead, it was too late to mend him, and thus even stylish attacks would be unjustified.

Donne's Letter exposes the extent to which the politics and policies of the great Jacobean courtiers and ministers of state were subject to the crude, but never passive, judgements of a nascent political public sphere—a space constituted by a variety of communicative genres and practices that flourished despite the theoretically severe legal restrictions on many forms of political speech (Bellany 2002; O'Callaghan 2003; Lake and Pincus). Certainly the early Jacobean public sphere did not conform to Donne's idealized version of a literary-political space in which witty poets exercised a 'liberty of speaking' for moralizing ends, but, for all its shortcomings, it was an increasingly significant factor in the political culture of the age (cf. Colclough 2005). The libellous epitaphs that greeted Cecil's death circulated not only among envious courtiers and news-hungry elites, but also among men of varied stations around London, throughout the English provinces, and overseas. The libels depicted Cecil as a monster of transgression: morally, physically, politically, and religiously corrupt (Bellany and McRae D; Croft 1991*b*). The libels thus brought the high politics of the court—the pursuit of favour, office, and reward, the factional battles, the quest for access and influence, the shaping of policy, the performance of status and honour—before a growing and diverse public, framing and explaining courtly and even royal actions through resonant images of corruption.

This chapter provides an overview of court politics and its scabrous counterpoint in the political public sphere from the death of Cecil in 1612 until the ascendancy of Buckingham in 1616–17. I hope to supply useful background for scholars interested in the crucial phase of Donne's career when he drew closer to the court in search of a patron who could procure him office in—or the chance to serve—church and state (Bald 1970: ch. 11; J. Stubbs chs. 14–15; Ch. 32.I). I will map the multiple centres of power and the complex articulation of influence at the Jacobean court; describe the major individuals and groups, united by interest and by ideology, competing for power and influence; discuss the persistent political problems facing the court in the early 1610s; and narrate some of the tumultuous events that followed Cecil's death (cf. Bellany 2002: ch. 1).

2

Three days after Cecil's death, John Chamberlain wrote to Dudley Carleton, the English ambassador in Venice. Carleton needed to adjust his ways of doing business now Cecil was dead, and Chamberlain hoped to supply the relevant information and intelligence. Although Chamberlain could report only speculation on the likely successors to Cecil's offices, he had obtained useful advice from Walter Cope, one of Cecil's closest associates. 'He wisht me', Chamberlain reported, 'to perswade you to cast away a letter...now and then on the Lord of Northampton, as likewise to insinuate with the Lord of Rochester and send him some prettie advertisements'. Chamberlain urged another route, however, suggesting Carleton 'rather devise how to grow in with the Prince' (Chamberlain 1.352). This competing advice reveals the multi-centred structure of the Jacobean court and the diffusion of different forms of political power within that structure. The 'Lord of Northampton' was Henry Howard, Earl of Northampton, the elder scion of one of England's oldest noble houses, the Warden of the Cinque Ports and Lord Privy Seal, and, now Cecil was dead, the most important privy councillor (Peck 1982; Croft 2008). The 'Lord of Rochester' was an entirely different kind of political creature—he was Robert Carr (or Kerr, in the Scots spelling), a young Scotsman whose rising power rested not on inherited rank or (as yet) bureaucratic office, but on personal intimacy and favour with the King. The 'Prince' was James I's eldest son, Henry, whose household had become a court within the court, with its own aesthetic and an agenda that increasingly attracted men dissatisfied with the pacifistic and politique policies of Cecil and the King (Strong).

Power, whether measured in political influence, administrative responsibility, or access to and distribution of patronage, was widely diffused at this court, with its multiple political and cultural centres, its multiple channels of influence, and its fusion of both impersonal and personal forms of authority (see Smuts 1991; Cuddy 1987; Croft 1991c). Men competed for office—for seats on the Privy Council, for great offices of state, for ceremonial and household positions like Master of the Horse or Lord Chamberlain—and for access to the King or his intimates. Court offices carrying seemingly menial responsibilities—like cup-bearer or sewer in the privy chamber, or groom and gentleman of the bedchamber—were in fact immensely important, offering constant, informal, and immediate access to the King at his palaces in and around London or at the hunting lodges to which he so often fled (Cuddy 1987). The courts within the court—of both Prince Henry and Queen Anne—offered still more opportunities to collect office, influence, and reward (Strong; Barroll).

3

At the time of Cecil's death James and his councillors faced a number of stubborn political problems. Money was the most pressing and intractable (Dietz chs. 7–8; Prestwich chs. 3–4; Cramsie ch. 5; Thrush 2002). The Crown was deeply in debt— £500,000 in 1612, £600,000 two years later, with an annual deficit of £160,000 (Dietz 149; Rabb 174 and n. 1). In 1609–10 Cecil had attempted a deal with Parliament—the so-called 'Great Contract'—to solve the financial crisis, but scepticism, mistrust, and outright opposition within both court and Commons had wrecked the plan (Cramsie ch. 4; Rabb ch. 6; Cuddy 1987: 206–8; Croft 1991c: 146). The Crown's options were limited: the King could work with Parliament to secure tax revenue, or he could look to new extra-parliamentary sources of income, or he could do both. By 1610, however, James seems to have soured on Parliament—the Great Contract's failure compounded his bitterness at the defeat of the Anglo-Scots Union, and he suspected some MPs of political insubordination (Thrush 2002: 84, 97–102; Cramsie 122). Extra-parliamentary sources of revenue enhancement and debt management thus became increasingly attractive. Customs duties known as impositions were one potentially lucrative source of income, but they were constitutionally suspect and might provoke opposition if Parliament were recalled (Croft 1987; Sommerville 1986: 151–5). Extra-parliamentary direct taxation (loans or benevolences) was also legally dubious and politically risky. Loans from the City might help, but London might not always remain convinced that the loans were safe. Retrenchment—cost cutting by administrative reform and trimming expenses—could significantly lessen royal expenditure, but curbing James's liberality was difficult. Another option was what contemporaries labelled 'projects', which used royal prerogative powers of economic regulation to establish ventures and monopolies that in theory would plough some of their profits back into the Crown's coffers. Finally, there was the possibility that the marriage of the King's son to a foreign princess would bring a large infusion of cash as a dowry.

The lure of a large dowry ensured that the conduct of foreign affairs in the 1610s was inextricably connected to the Crown's fiscal and parliamentary policies, further complicating an already delicate area of royal activity (Thrush 2002, 2003). Marriage alliances for James's children could not only add gold to the royal coffers, but could also tip the precarious balance of power in a divided Europe teetering on the edge of renewed religious war (S. Adams 1973; Parker et al.). Late in 1612 James finalized a marriage alliance between his daughter Elizabeth and Friedrich V, the Calvinist Elector Palatine, thus tying the English to the recently formed Union of German Protestant Princes. The big prize, however, was a marriage alliance for the heir to the throne. Prince Henry had spurned overtures from Tuscany, Spain, and Savoy, had participated enthusiastically in the negotiations with the Palatinate, and seemed likely to insist on his own marriage to a Protestant bride. His death in November

1612, however, left his brother Charles heir to the throne and returned the initiative to James. There were three leading candidates for the Prince's hand—France, Spain, and Savoy—all of them Catholic, and all offering different strategic and financial headaches and compensations. Changing events on the continent, as much as shifting domestic pressures, would shape the way James explored his options.

The court was divided over all these questions of financial, parliamentary, and foreign policy, and in the years after Cecil's death a number of identifiable factions shaped the political manoeuvring. These factions cohered in multiple ways: men might be united by official position, by family connection, by patronage relationships, by personal ambition, by friendship, by shared history, by ethnicity, by religio-political ideological inclination, or by short- or long-term policy goals. Unsurprisingly, these factions were also unstable. They were fluidly composed and never ideologically homogeneous. Individuals drifted in and out of alliance. Even ideologically attuned allies quarrelled over personal matters, while short-term alliances to pursue short-term goals sometimes united members of hitherto competing blocs.

For all their fluidity, we can identify two major clusters. One significant faction, with deep social and institutional power bases, cohered around the Howard family. The faction was led by Henry Howard, Earl of Northampton, and by his nephew, Thomas Howard, Earl of Suffolk, a leading privy councillor and, as Lord Chamberlain, the possessor of the most important ceremonial office at the court (Croft 2004, 2008). Both Northampton and Suffolk tended to think Parliaments were more trouble than they were worth, and advocated a projects-based, non-parliamentary fiscal policy to solve the Crown's financial woes. In foreign affairs the Howards were pro-Spanish, favouring the Infanta of Spain as a bride for Prince Charles. In Northampton's case Hispanophilia was reinforced by a crypto-Catholic religious sensibility that was the subject of fairly widespread rumour (Bellany 2002: 203–6).

A second, more fluid, faction, revolved around a number of leading aristocrats with very different policy objectives from the Howards (ibid. 43–4; S. Adams 1973). The faction included men committed to a parliamentary solution to the Crown's fiscal problems, who believed that advance planning and negotiation would foster a better working relationship with the Commons. Many of these men were also committed to a more militantly Protestant foreign policy that would rule out a Catholic bride for the heir to the throne. A number of these men had cut their political teeth in the circle of the late Earl of Essex, and before November 1612 many of these 'patriots' (as one of their followers termed them) gravitated towards Prince Henry. After Henry's death the patriot bloc's leading courtly and aristocratic members were Henry Wriothesley, Earl of Southampton, the most prominent of the old Essexians, and William Herbert, third Earl of Pembroke (Cuddy 1993; Stater). Southampton lacked major court office, but Pembroke was a gentleman of the privy chamber, a personal favourite of the King, and, since September

1611, a privy councillor. The patriot group also included other key figures: Robert Sidney, Viscount Lisle, Pembroke's uncle and governor of Flushing; Sir Henry Neville, a former Essexian and ambassador to Paris; and Sir Ralph Winwood, Neville's secretary in Paris, and, in 1612, ambassador to the United Provinces. George Abbot, Archbishop of Canterbury since 1611, also belonged to this group, which also had patronage and ideological ties to leading MPs, including Sir Edwin Sandys and Sir Robert Phelips.

Ethnic divisions at the Jacobean court complicated factional and political ones. Bedchamber offices were virtually monopolized by Scotsmen, some of whom were important (if shadowy) political actors with a strongly pro-French perspective on foreign policy. Their monopoly on informal access to the King provoked the envy of English courtiers, and their influence gave rise to widely articulated resentments. Both MPs and, in their cruder fashion, verse libellers caricatured Scots courtiers as semi-barbaric carpetbaggers who had descended from the north like a plague of strangely garbed locusts to plunder English wealth (Cuddy 1987, 1989; Bellany 2002: 170; Bellany and McRae E).

4

The deaths of Cecil in May 1612 and Prince Henry six months later profoundly shook the structure of court politics. But an equally, if not more, momentous shift had already begun in 1611, picking up speed in 1612 and 1613 and soon changing the whole political dynamic of the court. The emergence of Robert Carr as a monopolistic court favourite—sustained by the King's affection, institutionally based in the bedchamber, but now accumulating household, ceremonial, and administrative office and an unparalleled influence over patronage and policy—changed the rules by which factions and interest groups at (and outside) court could operate (Bellany 2002: ch. 1; Braunmuller; Seddon). Carr had been brought up at the Scottish court and came south in 1603, probably in the household of George Home, later Earl of Dunbar, one of the most powerful Scots in James's entourage. In the summer of 1604 Carr was made groom of the bedchamber—a close body servant of the King—giving him much-coveted informal access to the monarch. Carr's relationship with James transformed and intensified in the years that followed. After a tiltyard accident in 1607 left Carr with a broken leg, James helped nurse him back to health, the prolonged intimacy deepening the two men's bond. By late 1607 Carr's fortunes were visibly ascendant: knighted and promoted to gentleman of the bedchamber, he was identified confidently by Chamberlain as the 'new favorite' (Chamberlain 1.249). Carr did not, at first, completely monopolize royal favour or aggressively pursue additional office or political influence. Instead, he translated favour and access into personal reward and patronage power: he accepted land from the King and brokered deals for clients and suitors, often in exchange for significant financial compensation.

In this early phase Carr thus fit the profile of the other two bedchamber servants considered especially favoured by the King—his fellow Scot James, Lord Hay, and Philip Herbert, Earl of Montgomery, Pembroke's brother and the only Englishman to hold prominent bedchamber office. But James's attachment to Carr was different in quality and intensity. Their relationship was complex and shifting, and the two played multiple roles: Carr became the King's intimate friend, his confidant and servant, protégé and pupil; he had constant access to the King's person, both in the palaces around London and during James's frequent hunting expeditions; the King praised and caressed him in public; he shared the King's bed and may have been his lover.

Beginning in 1611, Carr's ambitions broadened and his relationship with James became increasingly monopolistic. In March 1611 James created Carr Viscount Rochester, and in May installed him as Knight of the Garter. In April 1612 Carr became a privy councillor. By June 1612 the Scotsman Viscount Fenton, groom of the stole and thus chief gentleman of the bedchamber, believed Carr was 'exceeding great with his Majestie, and if I shuld saye trewlye, greater than onye that ever I did see' (*HMC Mar & Kellie* 41).

Clearly, James was responsible for this shift in Carr's role; in the wake of Cecil's political and physical decline, James was probably experimenting with different modes of rule. But James was not the sole architect of Carr's new political assertiveness. As Carr first began to flex his political muscles at court, Thomas Overbury, whom he had met in Edinburgh in 1601 or 1602, played the role of the favourite's favourite. Overbury was Carr's closest advisor and secretary, brokering suitors' access, and helping anglicize his political connections. Both Overbury and James would later insist to Carr that they had, in effect, 'made him', and it is tempting, given the lack of evidence for his political and religious opinions, to reduce Carr to a cipher—the passive instrument of others' political desires. If Carr's own preferences remained opaque in 1612, it was nevertheless apparent to anyone hoping to find office, shape debates, or secure patronage, that the favourite was the best and quickest way of reaching the King.

5

By the time of Cecil's death John Donne had established multiple connections to friends and patrons occupying a variety of institutional and ideological positions in the multi-centred Jacobean court. His intimate friend and regular correspondent Sir Henry Goodere was a gentleman of the King's privy chamber (Considine). Through Goodere, Donne had developed connections with one of Queen Anne's favourites, Lucy Russell, Countess of Bedford, the leading lady of the Queen's bedchamber, and one of the more politically active women at court (Lewalski 1993: ch. 4; Payne). Goodere also seems to have introduced Donne to James, Lord Hay, a favourite of the King, gentleman of the bedchamber, and Master of the Robes (Schreiber 1984, 2004). Donne also had ties by 1613 at the latest to Sir Robert Ker, gentleman of the King's privy chamber, who became a leading gentleman of the bedchamber in Prince Charles's household (Stevenson; Strong 32). Donne also had connections among the great Crown lawyers: Sir Edward Phelips, Sergeant at Law and Master of the Rolls, secured Donne a seat as MP for Taunton in the 1614 Parliament (R. S. More). Other connections, however, had lost their utility. Late in the previous reign he had asked for the help of Henry Percy, ninth Earl of Northumberland and privy councillor, but Northumberland was by 1612 a prisoner in the Tower, ruined by his implication in the Gunpowder Plot of 1605 (M. Nicholls 2008).

Thus Donne had multiple points of contact at court with figures, both English and Scots, occupying different places on the contemporary ideological spectrum. Goodere seems to have been relatively apolitical. Hay was known more for his extravagance than for his politics, but his long-standing connections with France made him an ideal extraordinary ambassador in 1604 and 1616, and he was presumably part of the Francophile Scottish bloc in debates about marriage alliances. Of all Donne's early Jacobean connections, Lucy Russell is politically the most interesting. She was an intimate of Queen Anne, who had a well-known antipathy to Carr. Lucy's brother John Harington (d. 1614) was an important member of Prince Henry's circle, and her parents, who had overseen Princess Elizabeth's education, accompanied the Princess to Germany after her marriage in 1613—Lucy would be a strongly pro-Palatine figure at court during the crisis that befell Elizabeth and her husband after the Bohemian revolt of 1618. Lucy was also a kinswoman of Pembroke and became increasingly close to him politically as the reign progressed. It seems likely that she shared many of the political sentiments of the patriot bloc, and she may also have shared Pembroke's personal and political antipathy towards both Carr and the Howards (Lewalski 1993: ch. 4; Payne; Strong 42–4; Barroll 43–5 and *passim*; J. Bacon 128–9).

6

Cecil's death not only removed the *de facto* head of the King's Privy Council, but also vacated two of the most significant offices of state—those of Lord Treasurer and Principal Secretary. In June 1612 James put the Treasury into commission, with Northampton and the Chancellor of the Exchequer, Sir Julius Caesar, at the helm, and including Lionel Cranfield and Arthur Ingram, major London financiers connected to Northampton and known to Donne (Cramsie 128). The position of Principal Secretary, however, remained open for nearly two years, and the office became the hotly pursued quarry of the court's main factions (Bellany 2002: 44–50). Working (often uneasily) with leading patriot courtiers, Overbury urged Carr to lobby for candidates favoured by Pembroke and Southampton—either Sir Henry Neville or Sir Ralph Winwood, or perhaps both, one charged with domestic and one with foreign affairs. Both Neville and Winwood had clear policy agendas. Neville had a plan to manage and conciliate Parliament to secure financial support for the Crown and mend the frayed relationship between King and subjects. Winwood was a vigorous Protestant internationalist, strongly pro-Dutch, pro-Calvinist, and anti-Spanish (Greengrass). Other factions and individuals pushed other candidates. The Howards urged the appointment of Sir Thomas Lake, while the Queen and Prince Henry suggested Donne's old friend Sir Henry Wotton. Perhaps suspicious of some of the candidates, and eager to assert his personal control, James chose none of these options. Instead he acted as his own secretary, using Lake and then, more consistently, Carr as his assistant. Although he continued to promise help for Neville and Winwood, Carr now worked closely with the King as *de facto* secretary, and, in part because of these responsibilities and in part because of Northampton's persistent wooing, he maintained an increasingly cordial working relationship with the Howards. But if Carr was any man's creature in 1612, he was the King's.

The death of Prince Henry in November 1612 left many of the more militaristic Protestants at court adrift, while simultaneously allowing the King to ease his financial woes by eliminating expenses associated with Henry's household (*HMC Portland* 34–8; *CSPD* 1611–18: 161–2). The events of 1613 reshaped court politics still further. On 21 April 1613 Thomas Overbury was imprisoned in the Tower for an open show of contempt in refusing a diplomatic appointment (Bellany 2002: 50–6). Overbury initially assumed that Carr would calm James's ire and secure his quick release, but he misjudged both the extent of James's personal dislike and Carr's own willingness to act. As his confinement dragged on, Overbury became convinced that Carr had betrayed him. Overbury blamed the break on their quarrels over Carr's relationship with Frances Howard, Suffolk's daughter, and, since 1606, the unhappy wife of Robert Devereux, third Earl of Essex (Lindley). Carr's affair with Frances had probably begun some time in 1612; as the relationship deepened,

Overbury had become increasingly hostile. Undoubtedly he worried that the closer Carr became to Frances, the more the favourite would be pulled towards the Howards, and the harder it would be for Overbury to maintain a relationship between Carr and Essex's friends Southampton and Pembroke.

On 17 May 1613, a little less than a month after Overbury's imprisonment, a permanent Carr–Howard alliance became likelier still when Frances petitioned a specially erected ecclesiastical commission to annul her marriage to Essex. The ground for annulment was non-consummation caused by the Earl's sexual impotence. By June 1613 Frances's attachment to Carr was common knowledge, and both observers and participants assumed that if the nullity were granted, the subsequent marriage would transform the political balance at court and definitively scotch the patriots' political ambitions. The nullity was not, however, a foregone conclusion—proof of both the Countess's virginity and the Earl's impotence was difficult and embarrassing to ascertain, and some of the attempted face-saving compromises (especially the claim that Essex was only selectively impotent, perhaps because of witchcraft) raised more legal and theological problems than they solved. Archbishop Abbot vocally opposed the nullity, and, as the case dragged on, a number of courtiers, including Pembroke and the Queen, also manoeuvred against it. When the commission eventually granted Frances Howard her nullity on 25 September 1613, it did so only because James had intervened to pack the commission with clerics willing to vote in the affirmative.

The period between April and September 1613 thus marked another crucial watershed. Overbury's imprisonment and the Essex nullity severely damaged whatever political relationship Carr had developed with the court patriots in 1612. During the summer of 1613 Carr and Northampton pressured the imprisoned Overbury to commit himself in writing to a closer alliance with Suffolk. But even after an abject letter promising to submit to the new order of things, Overbury remained in the Tower. By early September, convinced that Carr had betrayed him, Overbury threatened that he would reveal to the world 'you sacrificeing me to your Woman, your holding a firm Friendship with those that brought me hither and keepe me heare, and not mak[ing] it your first Act of any good Termes with them to set me free and restore me to your self againe' (Winwood 3.478–9). A few days later, on 15 September 1613, Overbury died, his corpse so foul that it required a hasty burial. Some whispered of poison, but most held that Overbury had succumbed to some particularly nasty disease. Few mourned his passing (Bellany 2002: 71–2).

With Overbury dead and a Carr–Howard marriage pending, the King again augmented his favourite's institutional power and social status. In October 1613 James put Carr on the Scottish Privy Council; in December he made him Lord Treasurer of Scotland, with Carr delegating responsibilities to a deputy. On 4 November James created Carr Earl of Somerset and Baron Brancepeth, the latter title acknowledging the favourite's acquisition of a sizeable amount of land in the north-east of England.

On 26 December 1613 Carr married Frances Howard in a spectacular court wedding. For the next two years Carr's personal and political fortunes were wedded tightly to those of his wife's family. When Northampton died in June 1614 Carr replaced him as Lord Privy Seal and Warden of the Cinque Ports. A month later he succeeded his father-in-law, Suffolk, as Lord Chamberlain, an office openly coveted by Pembroke, while Suffolk was appointed Lord Treasurer. Between March and October 1614 Howard clients or kin secured appointments to the Privy Council, the Chancellorship of the Exchequer, and the lucrative Mastership of the Wards (Bellany 2002: 56–8).

7

John Donne was undoubtedly one of many men who sought to hitch their fortunes to Carr's rising star in 1613 and 1614. Using Hay as his intermediary, Donne first sought the favourite's patronage in mid-summer 1613—after the fall of Overbury. Donne presented himself as 'an independent, and disobliged man, towards any other person in this State', and sought Carr's assistance in obtaining a position in the church, having resolved 'to be a houshold-servant of God' (*TMC* 320, 322). Although Carr was rumoured to have been instrumental in the appointment of Abbot as Archbishop of Canterbury in 1611, the favourite was not known as an ecclesiastical patron and perhaps did not acquire substantial patronage in church affairs until his appointment as Lord Chamberlain (*CSPV* 1610–13: 142; Fincham 1988: 40 and n. 21; McCullough 1998: 115). Presumably Donne approached Carr not because he was an independent ecclesiastical patron, but because he was the best available point of access to the King. Whatever the case, Carr appears to have done nothing immediately to realize Donne's ambitions. He did, however, accept Donne's approach, and for over a year, it seems, provided him with much-needed material assistance (*TMC* 311, 314, 318–19). At one interview Donne discussed secular offices with his new patron. By 23 September 1613, the two men discussed a clerkship of the Council (*TMC* 317; Chamberlain 1.467; cf. Bald 1970: 289–90). In March and April 1614 Donne tentatively inquired after positions as ambassador in Venice or at The Hague (*TMC* 312; *Letters* 297–8). Writing to Carr again 'somewhat more than a year' after his initial approach, Donne alluded, with some frustration, to the continual dashing of the 'new hopes' of secular office the favourite had instructed him to entertain, and he asked Carr to 'bid me either hope for this businese in your Lordship's hand [a secular appointment of some sort], or else pursue my first purpose [divinity], or abandon all' (*TMC* 314–15). In July and August 1614 Donne was once more about 'my little Court busines', though what it involved is not clear, and mentioned to Goodere a potential audience with the Lord Chamberlain to advance 'my businesse' (*Marriage Letters* 57; *Letters* 171–4). At the end of 1614, having declared to James his determined intention to enter the church, Donne was still seen as Carr's client—the Earl was 'more open[ly] avowinge' Donne than before and had promised him the reversion to an office (probably in the legal bureaucracy) 'when my Sonne, or any for mee may have profit therby' (*Marriage Letters* 60–1).

In his unlikely request for an ambassadorial position, Donne had described the post as an opportunity to perform 'services' to the favourite. What 'services' might Carr have imagined he would get in return for his patronage? He clearly knew of Donne's polemical writing on the Oath of Allegiance and may have considered him a potentially useful source of counsel and prose (*TMC* 317). Donne was not a likely candidate to replace Overbury, but Carr might have considered him as a potential expert advisor in the mould of Robert Cotton. We might also remember that Donne approached Carr during a period of rapid adjustment in the favourite's factional ties, political reach, and patronage obligations—it could very well be that Carr never actually decided how best to use him. Donne did perform some of the standard duties of a literary client—writing a belated Epithalamion for Carr's wedding, and in December 1614, 'as a valediction to the world, before I take Orders', thinking he might recompense Carr by 'printing my Poems' and 'addressing them to my L. Chamberlain' (*Letters* 196–7).

More interesting are the fragments of evidence suggesting Donne's potential involvement in discussions about a printed defence of the Essex nullity, a project that can be understood only in light of the public hostility the nullity had aroused. Newsletters and documents concerning the case had circulated in manuscript throughout the summer and autumn of 1613 (Bellany 2002: 94–5). Verse libels openly mocked the bishops supporting the nullity, while hurling nasty sexual accusations at Frances Howard (Bellany and McRae F). The official response to attacks on the nullity was hamstrung by ambivalence: supporters of the nullity were torn between their desire to defend Frances Howard's reputation and the proceedings' legality on the one hand, and their distaste for engaging in public debate with anonymous, popular opinion on the other (Bellany 2002: 133–4; Lindley ch. 4; O'Callaghan 2003: 64–7). George Chapman's poem *Andromeda Liberata*, an allegorical defence of the nullity and assault on its unruly critics, was rushed into print and licensed for the press by four privy councillors. As early as September 1613 one well-informed politician had heard that an official printed legal defence was in the works. By December news circulated that attacks on the nullity, possibly sponsored by disaffected English courtiers or churchmen, had been printed on the continent. 'There bee twoe bookes owt against it from calvenests beyond see & the one from Geneva', reported a Catholic newswriter on December 26, '& some think that the puritans have procured thease boakes' (Questier 1998*b*: 260). It was this news that prompted Donne to think he might be of 'use in this matter', presumably as a writer of—or advisor on—an official defence (*Letters* 180). Rumours of an official response persisted until at least the middle of March 1614, when Henry Goodere heard them (ibid. 168–9). In fact, no official defence of the nullity ever appeared in print. Daniel Dun drafted a legalistic defence that may have originally been intended for the press, but it circulated only in scribal copies. In the end, one contemporary speculated, the authorities decided that any further publication would only stimulate a debate that was better left to die down of its own accord.

8

Whether (and how) to defend the annulment was, in any case, not the most pressing political problem facing the King, the favourite, and his new Howard in-laws early in 1614. Once again, the Crown's financial straits had become too desperate to ignore, and whether or not to recall Parliament dominated political discussion (Bellany 2002: 59–62; Moir; Russell 1992; Rabb ch. 7; Prestwich 136–57; Colclough 2005: 159-68; Cramsie 135–7). The Privy Council was divided, Pembroke urging Parliament's recall and Northampton opposing it. Both Suffolk and Carr eventually agreed to the summons, but it is difficult to establish what they and the openly sceptical Northampton expected from the forthcoming session. Andrew Thrush has argued that Suffolk, at least, was prepared to agree to a Parliament out of fear that the King's money troubles would compel him to conclude a marriage alliance with the French. To keep alive the possibility of a Spanish Match, Suffolk was willing to roll the Parliamentary dice once more (Thrush 2003: 29–32). In the run-up to the session Carr renewed his old contacts with key patriot politicians, helping secure Ralph Winwood's appointment to the long-vacant Secretaryship (albeit without control of the seals) and securing a seat in Parliament for Sir Edwin Sandys. Yet teasing fragments of evidence suggest that, before and during the session, Carr and at least one of the Howards were engaged in murky surreptitious manoeuvres intended to sabotage the Parliament's chances of success (cf. ibid, 30–1; Peck 1982: 205–10; Bellany 2002: 59–61). Ultimately, as Linda Peck has pointed out, sabotage was strategically superfluous—the Commons were combustible enough without further incitement. The session, in which Donne sat as MP for Taunton, was a disaster, roiled from the start by suspicions of plots to manage the House covertly and by constitutional questions about impositions. Attempts to quell debate on impositions triggered fights about parliamentary privilege. For James, the final straws were the provocative speeches (including one by Donne's friend, John Hoskins) pointing a threatening finger at the court Scots as the root of the Crown's chronic financial woes. The dissolution of the 'Addled' Parliament compelled the Crown to turn again to 'projects' and other forms of extra-parliamentary revenue enhancement (Prestwich ch. 4; Cramsie 137–50). On Northampton's death, in June 1614, the direction of fiscal policy was left to Suffolk, who was appointed Lord Treasurer in July.

In the run-up to the Addled Parliament the very real prospect of an imminent deal for a French marriage alliance had strongly influenced political calculations at court. The alliance was strongly supported by the Francophile court Scots, but it faced opposition not only from those committed to a Protestant match, but also from Carr, the Howards, and the Queen, who all favoured a match with Spain (Thrush 2002: 88–89; Bellany 2002: 62–5). Early in 1614, with an official French offer imminent, Carr—on whose initiative we cannot determine—had approached the Spanish ambassador, encouraging him to urge his master to pre-empt the French with a quick and attractive counter-offer. By the dissolution of the Addled Parliament James—assured by Northampton and the Spanish ambassador that the Infanta's dowry would more than compensate for a break with Parliament—was willing to talk seriously to the Spanish. From the beginning Carr played a crucial role in the negotiations: in 1614–15, with Robert Cotton as his advisor, he conducted high-risk, back-channel talks with the Spanish ambassador, while Sir John Digby opened official negotiations in Madrid.

9

Carr's apparently intensifying monopolistic power, put to the service of the Howards' political agenda—non-parliamentary politics, fiscal projects, and a Spanish, rather than a French or Protestant, marriage alliance—inevitably provoked opponents to attempt new ways to influence the King (Lockyer ch. 1; Bellany 2002: 65–71). Their preferred solution was to find a new object for the king's affections—'one nail...being to be driven out by another', as Abbot put it (Firth 347). The new nail was George Villiers, the handsome younger son of a decayed Leicestershire family, who was introduced at court during the summer progress of 1614 to immediate success. Villiers's promotion was sponsored by a broad coalition of courtiers with a wide variety of political, ideological, and personal grievances with Carr and the Howards. The coalition included key figures from the patriot faction at court (Southampton, Pembroke, Winwood, Abbot); temporarily discontented former Howard clients like Lake; powerful bedchamber Scots like Fenton; and Carr's perennial enemy, Queen Anne. If the interregnum historian William Sanderson can be trusted, the group also included Donne's literary patron, Lucy Russell (Barroll 144–5). By the autumn of 1614 signs of

Villiers's ascendance were the stuff of court and London gossip. Unsurprisingly, Donne was as eager as others to read the signs. He and Goodere discussed Villiers's preparations for his first court masque in December 1614, and Donne was aware that his attachment to Carr might hurt his church career, given Abbot's increasingly public opposition to the favourite (*Letters* 149, 198; *Marriage Letters* 60–1). Villiers's ascent was rapid—appointed cup-bearer in the privy chamber late in 1614, in April 1615, he was knighted and promoted to gentleman of the bedchamber. Perhaps, as some contemporary observers believed, James was contemplating a system of multiple favourites, deliberately balancing Anglo-Scots power in the bedchamber. But Villiers's rise produced neither balance nor harmony, instead ushering in a bruising factional battle. Carr felt profoundly threatened and lashed out at James with tirades and threats. Carr's 'strange frenzy', compounded by his refusal to sleep in the royal bedchamber, provoked James to send him a remarkably passionate letter of rebuke (Akrigg 345–50). By the spring of 1615 the situation at court had become particularly nasty. 'Never', opined Winwood, 'was the court fuller of faction' (BL, MS Stowe 175, fo. 310). The rival favourites and their allies clashed over offices and suits, with the balance of power see-sawing throughout the summer. Somerset initially persuaded James to sign a pre-emptive general pardon to protect him from his enemies' machinations, but on the Lord Chancellor's advice the King reversed his decision. Over the summer and again in September 1615 the Privy Council seriously considered recalling Parliament to deal with the Crown's financial problems—a move that threatened to reverse the policies in place since the end of the Addled Parliament—but Suffolk headed off this initiative (Thrush 2002: 90). By then, however, the Howards' dominance had already been fatally undermined.

10

The agents of destruction were Winwood and Thomas Overbury's ghost (Bellany 2002: 71–3). In June 1615 the Lieutenant of the Tower, Sir Gervase Elwes, had told Winwood of a plot to poison Overbury that, Elwes claimed, he had discovered and thwarted back in the spring of 1613. Winwood kept this intelligence to himself until September 1615, when, perhaps fearing Carr's fortunes' resurgence, he informed the King. James demanded a written statement from Elwes, who now claimed to have learned recently that the plot against Overbury had not, in fact, been thwarted; instead, Elwes said, unbeknownst to him, Overbury had been murdered, the *coup de grace* delivered as a poisoned enema. Elwes's statement implicated Overbury's keeper, Richard Weston; the courtier and Howard client Thomas Monson; and Anne Turner, a confidante of Frances Howard. Perturbed, James ordered further investigation, and in late September/early October 1615 established a prosecutorial commission led by Edward Coke and Lord Chancellor Ellesmere. The investigation soon targeted Carr and Frances, and on 17 October 1615 they were placed under house arrest.

Over the next six months the Overbury affair developed into a spectacular and damaging court scandal (Bellany 2002: chs. 2–5). Allegations of sexual, gender, and sartorial transgression, of witchcraft and popery, of deception and betrayal, of rampant ambition, social climbing, and the perversion of royal favour were carried to a news-hungry, socially heterogeneous public by street gossip and fast-moving rumour, by printed pamphlets and manuscript letters and trial reports, by verse libels, ballads, and songs. Five conspirators were brought to trial, and four of them were publicly executed. Carr and Frances were moved to the Tower as family and close political associates were questioned and arrested (ibid. 193–4). After lengthy delays, and talk of a treason charge, Carr and Frances stood trial for murder on 24 and 25 May 1616. Found guilty by their peers, both were sentenced to die.

Some observers hoped a new political dawn was imminent. A parliamentary recall was debated anew (Thrush 2002: 90–1). As William Trumbull, a long-time adherent of the patriots, told Princess Elizabeth, now was the time for 'Good men and faithful servants' to take office; all corruption and abuses would end, and royal finances would be restored with the help of a cooperative Commons (*HMC Downshire* 386). As the murder investigation began to expose evidence of possibly treasonable secret negotiations with Spain, men like Trumbull also hoped for an imminent reversal of pro-Spanish foreign policy. Pembroke at last won major court office, replacing Carr as Lord Chamberlain in December. But there was to be no patriot revolution in 1616 (Bellany 2002: 193–9, 239–45; Jardine and Stewart ch. 13). Parliament was not recalled until 1621; royal financial policy continued to rely on intermittent retrenchments, short-term expedients, City loans, and projects (Cramsie 146 ff.). Suffolk narrowly survived the scandal and remained Lord Treasurer until the summer of 1618. And, after a temporary hiatus, marriage negotiations with Spain resumed in 1616–17, dragging on until 1624 (Thrush 2002: 93–4). Neither Carr nor Frances Howard was executed—James had almost certainly decided well in advance of the trials that he would show them mercy.

The future of court politics lay neither with the Howards, nor with Pembroke and the patriots, but with the King and with George Villiers, who quickly left behind the men who had sponsored his rise, becoming a far more powerful favourite than Carr had ever been. Between January 1616 and February 1617 Villiers became Master of the Horse, Knight of the Garter, Baron Whaddon and Viscount Villiers, Earl of Buckingham, and privy councillor. By the time he was elevated again, in January 1618, as Marquis of Buckingham, Villiers was also tightening his political grip on patronage and policy. By the summer of 1618, in the wake of Suffolk's unsuccessful attempt to displace him with another handsome young man, Villiers was able to destroy the Earl and the last vestige of the Howard hegemony of 1613–15 (Lockyer 25–38). All the grave political problems that had faced James in 1612 remained essentially unresolved—how to finance the Crown, whether and how to work with Parliament, how to navigate religious conflict in Europe. And while Villiers showed promising commitment to retrenchment and fiscal reform at court, far away in Bohemia disaster was looming.

CHAPTER 33.1

DONNE AND COURT CHAPLAINCY

PETER McCULLOUGH

NEXT to ordination itself, nothing shaped Donne's clerical career more than his status as chaplain-in-ordinary to Kings James I and Charles I. Ordination and royal chaplaincy were, uniquely in the period, coeval for Donne, and the latter was the platform from which he emerged as a preacher of national status and fame.

Donne's experience of royal chaplaincy, however, did not wait for ordination and appointment as chaplain to James I in 1615. For an aspiring young man like Donne, with an evident interest not only in some kind of professional preferment, but also in confessional politics and controverted theology, as well as later attachment to figures like the Earl of Essex and Sir Thomas Egerton, attendance at services and sermons in the Chapel Royal of Elizabeth I and James I would have been de rigueur (McCullough 1998: 25–7, 47–9). Donne's intellectual and cultural nursery c.1592–4, the Inns of Court, was tied inextricably to the royal court at Whitehall, not least by well-worn paths of patronage and preferment. The spirit of intellectual inquisitiveness that informed life at the Inns also included both religious conviction and scepticism, and the 'Inns-men' were some of London's most discriminating connoisseurs of the early modern spectator sport that was attending sermons. Their diaries burst with evidence of their appetite for hearing—and criticizing—the products of the leading pulpits of the day, whether in their own chapels, in London parish churches, at St Paul's, or (at the top of the London preaching circuit) in the pulpits of the royal palaces. It seems inescapable that Donne would himself have kept just such a young wit's preaching itinerary in the chapels and churches of London. Even if artfully exaggerated, first-hand experience of Elizabethan court religion certainly informs the keen observation by the speaker in *Sat4* (titled in some manuscripts 'Of the Courte') of the 'immaculate clothes' and 'such nicetie' worn when a hopeful 'young Preacher at his first time goes / To preach' (ll. 208–10). And when the satiric persona leaves the court in moral disgust at the end of the poem, he leaves it to 'Preachers which are / Seas of Wit and Arts' to 'Drowne the sinnes of this place' (ll. 240–1, 237–9). Although thoughts of doing so himself might hardly have crossed Donne's mind in the 1590s, preaching was a role to which he would indeed bring his own 'Seas of Wit and Arts' twenty years later.

Still, Donne counted as some of his most trusted friends and counsellors men who themselves held royal chaplaincies. One even may have been influential in his journey from Roman Catholicism to conformity to the Church of England. Donne told readers of *Pseudo-Martyr* (1610) that integral to his conversion was having 'survayed and digested the whole body of Divinity, controverted betweene ours and the Romane Church' (13). Izaak Walton expands this brief statement to Donne's having shown to 'the then *Dean of Glocester*' (1658: 11) his critical annotations on Cardinal Bellarmino's *Disputationes de Controversiis* (1586–93). In the absence of further documentary evidence, scholars will continue to debate Walton's chronology, and even the exact identity of the alleged dean in question (Colclough 2007). One entirely plausible candidate, Anthony Rudd (d. 1615), was known in the 1590s as one of the 'theologian[s] of distinction' to whom the Privy Council referred noted recusants for 'conferences...on matters of faith and doctrine' (Bald 1970: 69). But the cadre of divines entrusted with the delicate business of reducing Catholics to Protestant conformity were not merely theologically distinguished, but usually royal chaplains. And Rudd's 'distinction' was indeed as one of Elizabeth's favourite royal chaplains and preachers. If Donne sought out Rudd, he would have done so in full knowledge of Rudd's status as one of the Queen's chaplains chosen as such both for his Protestant orthodoxy and court pulpit eloquence.

Upon appointment *c*.1597 as secretary to Lord Keeper Egerton, Donne would have found the fabric of his life interwoven with those of two other men who would precede him as Jacobean court chaplains: John King (d. 1621) and Samuel Brooke (d. 1631). King had established credentials as a zealous and eloquent preacher in the household of the Archbishop of York, and his subsequent recruitment *c*.1595 as Egerton's household chaplain heralded the start of a London career advanced by royal favour. As both chaplain to the Lord Keeper and Rector of St Andrew's Holborn, King was in the thick of the London legal world's religious culture. From at least 1598 he was appointed to preach before Queen Elizabeth during Lent; Archbishop Whitgift appointed him the delicate task of preaching the first court sermon on the Sunday after her death and then endorsed his appointment as chaplain-in-ordinary to James. King was to continue throughout his life high in the favour of both James and his queen, Anne of Denmark. Similarly, Donne's intimacy with the King family continued unbroken into the next generation through the sons Henry (d. 1669) and John (d. 1639), both themselves canons of St Paul's. And it would be none other than

John King, as Bishop of London, who, on 23 January 1615, ordained Donne deacon and priest. But for nearly twenty years before that date Donne would have observed in the former Egerton chaplain's career an epitome of evangelical, anti-Catholic Calvinism inimitably tied to royal favour and prominence as a court preacher.

The other future royal chaplain in Donne's young adult life played a less fortuitous role. Samuel, younger brother of Donne's lifelong friend from student days at Lincoln's Inn, Christopher Brooke, was the—perhaps naive—clergyman recruited to officiate at Donne's clandestine marriage to Anne More in December 1601. All three men were briefly imprisoned, but the Brookes's careers recovered more quickly than that of the prime offender. Samuel returned to take further degrees and his chaplaincy at Trinity College, Cambridge, and in 1610 was appointed chaplain to the heir-apparent, Prince Henry, and successively the same to King James and King Charles. So, just as Donne's appointment as Reader at Lincoln's Inn (1616) returned him in clerical guise to a society and culture with which he was secularly already very intimate, so too his appointment as a royal chaplain to James I catapulted him not into foreign territory so much as into an office he had already observed closely as both spectator and friend.

Before considering the somewhat vexed question of exactly when Donne was sworn a royal chaplain to King James, it will be helpful to sketch the duties of the office, especially as they had evolved since 1603. Doing this requires an understanding of several separate, but somewhat overlapping, institutions within the royal household. First, chaplains had no formal affiliation with the household department known as the Chapel Royal, a fact that somewhat stymied Bald's attempts to understand Donne's royal chaplaincy (1970: 307 n. 2). The Chapel was an independent body, modelled on a cathedral chapter, governed by the Gentlemen of the Chapel (adult choirmen, some of them ordained) and a dean. Its responsibilities related only to 'choir service' in the chapel, that is, the routine choral liturgy. Preaching, although it occurred physically in the court chapels, was not the responsibility of members of the Chapel Royal, but of the so-called chaplains-in-ordinary—'in-ordinary' because fully tenured in the post. Supernumeraries, whether honorific or waiting for fully tenured appointments, were 'chaplains extraordinary'. Chaplains were appointed by the monarch and sworn as household servants by the Lord Chamberlain, the senior court officeholder in charge of all staff 'above stairs'. Like many 'above stairs' appointments, service as chaplain-in-ordinary was not paid. Much more lucrative, however, was not only the prestige that came with royal chaplaincy (with its access not only to monarch but also to other potential courtier-patrons), but also the special exemption from rules against pluralism (the holding of more than one clerical benefice). This was a loophole of which Donne availed himself fully when, even after promotion to St Paul's, he received or retained his livings at Keyston, Sevenoaks, and St Dunstan's.

Chaplains served, or 'waited', at court on a regular rota, with a group of chaplains (usually four to six) each attending one month of each year. Donne's 'month of waiting' from the time of his appointment until his death was April. The chaplains' duties were primarily preaching, which under James and Charles occurred on every Sunday and Tuesday of the year (the latter custom instituted by James in commemoration of his deliverance from the Gowrie Plot). Moreover, the chaplains on these days had to provide two sermons in the chapel royal—one early in the morning for the household 'below stairs', and one immediately before the main midday meal for the King and household 'above stairs'. Unless titled as preached 'before the King', it is almost impossible to distinguish between court sermons preached for these two very different auditories. In fact, Donne's Sermon 'Preached to the Houshold at White-hall, April 30. 1626' (*Sermons* 7.141–63) is the only known example of a sermon from the period the title of which identifies it as having been preached to court staff rather than to monarch or courtiers. Evidence of any further routine duties belonging to royal chaplains is sparse, but a Letter of Donne's from 1627 makes clear that as attending chaplain he also had some responsibility to lead daily morning or evening prayer in chapel (ibid. 7.40).

But in addition to routine service and sermons in chapel, royal chaplains could be deployed by the monarch for other duties. We have already seen the Elizabethan practice of deputing them to 'counsel' recusants. Under James I, however, royal chaplains had an even higher profile. The new king was known for his lively and active interest not just in theology and church government, but also in debate (albeit controlled) about them. Escaping from what was to him the irritant of Scots presbyterians, with their often-critical attitude towards the royal prerogative in church matters, James revelled in his English inheritance of eloquent royal chaplains who were as committed to Protestantism as they were to episcopacy and a high view of the monarch as supreme governor of the church. Royal chaplains therefore figured prominently among those assembled at the Hampton Court Conference of 1603. Even more deliberately, four royal chaplains (John King among them) were deployed at the 'second' Hampton Court Conference (1606) as official royal spokesmen to browbeat Scottish presbyterian ministers from the pulpit.

In fact, James's enthusiasm for recruiting royal chaplains knew almost no bounds. An avid and acute sermon-goer, James doubled the number of sermons preached at court every week and presided over the introduction of two new national feasts that were also annually observed with sermons at court: the anniversaries of the Gowrie conspiracy (5 August), and, after 1605, of the Gunpowder Plot (5 November). This explosion of court-sponsored preaching accounts for the exponential growth in the number of chaplains under James—from just twelve in Elizabeth's time, to over sixty by James's death in 1625. James appointed chaplains with something approaching abandon and glee, but he was always guided in his choices by an acute eye for one thing in particular—talent in the pulpit. He even sponsored what could be called auditions for aspiring Cambridge University clergy by requiring heads of colleges there to provide him with young pulpit talent when on his frequent hunting sojourns at nearby Royston and Newmarket (McCullough 1998: 125–7).

In this context, James's pursuit of ordination for Donne makes perfect sense, for Donne was, in fact, the epitome of what King James looked for in a chaplain-in-ordinary. Allegedly impressed by Donne's table talk about the royal allegiance owed by English Catholics, James had accepted the dedication of one of Donne's few published works, *Pseudo-Martyr* (1610). And there is something inevitable about Donne's journeying to Royston for his presentation to the King of a dedication copy, because Royston was where James was most used to scrutinizing new clerical talent. Although Donne himself may have been galled, it was then and there that James, perhaps for the first time, saw Donne not as a failed courtier, but as a brilliant—and therefore useful—religious rhetorician. He forthwith set about persuading Donne to take holy orders (Bald 1970: 227). When he finally came to implement his resolution to enter the ministry in November 1614, it was to Cambridgeshire that Donne again turned his horse. The location—Newmarket, James's other hunting retreat-cum-clerical recruitment enclave—was highly apt as the place where, in Donne's own words, he 'receyved from the kinge, as good allowance, and encoragement to pursue my purpose, as I could desire' (*Marriage Letters*, 60).

John King, by now Bishop of London, ordained his friend deacon and priest in the chapel of the episcopal palace adjacent to St Paul's on 23 January 1615. Donne published the news to court friends on the day, and they in return sent their compliments, including a new 'vesture' (probably the statutory black gown and white surplice) from Lord Hay (later Doncaster). And within days Donne was again heading north to Newmarket to present himself to the King, this time as an ordained minister. Although the documentary evidence is fragmentary, it seems likely that at this audience the King presented Donne with his plans to secure for him an honorary doctorate from Cambridge during his formal visit there early in March. What also seems highly likely is that during the Newmarket visit James also saw Donne sworn as his chaplain-in-ordinary, perhaps after a probationary sermon, since newsletters rumoured that Donne was a chaplain by February (Bald 1970: 305 n. 1 and 307 n. 2).

Donne also soon received instructions to attend the King's March visit to Cambridge—something that would have been highly unlikely had he not been a sworn member of the royal household (Bald 1970: 302–7; McCullough 2003*b*: 181). Donne's degree was only grudgingly granted by the Cambridge heads after some heavy royal arm-twisting. (In contrast, the now royal chaplain who had married Donne, Samuel Brooke, received applause for his pastoral comedy *Melanthe*.) But by the time of his departure from Cambridge, John Donne was just as King James wanted him to be—priest, probably royal chaplain, and doctor of divinity. The effort that James put into creating Donne thus, and in such rapid succession, is without precedent in the period as an example of royal promotion of a clerical career. James could make chaplains impulsively, but those were always appointments given to men who had laboured for years at university, and who had experience as either chaplains to nobles or as parish priests. But Donne went from laity to clergy, from no degree to doctorate, from unemployment to royal chaplaincy, in no more than a few weeks.

Small wonder, then, that John Chamberlain reported Donne's reputation in Cambridge as '*filios noctis et tenebriones* [one of the sons of night and tricksters] that sought thus to come in at the windowe' (Chamberlain 1.591). The notion of thieves entering through windows was of course proverbial. But the Cambridge dons' acid comment played on the even darker Pauline prophecy (1 Thess. 5:2–5) that Christ's second coming 'as a thief in the night' would spell disaster for all those who were not 'children of light, and the children of day: we are not of the night, nor of darkness' (*filii lucis estis… non sumus noctis neque tenebrarum*). They clearly considered Donne to be of the latter party. But James's investment in John Donne proved to be a very sound one. If the reassignment of Donne's first surviving Sermon (dated 30 April 1615) from Greenwich parish church to Greenwich palace is accepted, Donne obliged his creator-king almost immediately (McCullough 2003*b*: 180–2). Moreover, a Letter from Donne to Goodere, tentatively dated March 1615, reveals Donne anxiously attending to court chapel routines: 'I had destined all this Tuesday, for the Court, because it is both a Sermon day, and the first day of the Kings being here' (*Letters* 217–21). We might infer the immediate appointment in 1615 of April as Donne's official month of waiting at court. And the financial fruits of royal chaplaincy also shortly followed—the King presented him with the Crown living of Keyston in January 1616, to which his old employer, Lord Keeper Egerton, added the sinecure rectory of Sevenoaks in July. With his election as Reader of Lincoln's Inn in October, his place was secure as a comfortably employed divine and court chaplain—a radical transformation indeed in less than two years.

George Potter and Evelyn Simpson (*Sermons*) strove to see in Donne's early preaching career a kind of apprenticeship, during which his powers only gradually emerged. But scrutiny of his very early appearances at court and elsewhere allows little room for seeing Donne as a nervous apprentice in the pulpit, but rather as a preacher skilled at composing Sermons that were from the beginning deftly suited to the different auditories in which he was appointed to preach. He had been listening to sermons for decades before ordination, and his skills in both epideictic and forensic rhetoric were—as his poems and prose tracts brilliantly displayed—finely honed. And as a man of 42, he had for an already ripe lifetime immersed himself in both practical and academic divinity. In terms of the composition of Sermons, then, Donne would have had very little to learn, the actual delivery of a Sermon being the main aspect of preaching that was entirely new to him as a practitioner of the form.

The surviving texts suggest that he adapted his skills quickly and appropriately, for the early court Sermons are confident pieces that compare very favourably with any of those by his more experienced fellow chaplains. The two earliest, in their use of individual words of the chosen biblical texts for the divided parts of the Sermon, and in their asyndetic, often apothegmetic syntax, perhaps show a faint imitation of the then towering influence of Lancelot Andrewes. But even in these early Sermons, thematic concerns (the causes and effects of sin, the role of reason, the redemption purchased by Christ), habits of argument (logic, paradox, antithesis), and image systems (precious metals, the law) familiar from his later work are already prominent. He also deftly adjusts his vocabulary and exempla to fit the station of his auditory, as in the Greenwich Sermon's court-specific injunction, 'Let no man present...his Maces, or his Staves, or his Ensignes of power and Office, and say, call you all this nothing?', or the introduction of his text at Whitehall in November 1617 with the wry observation that, 'as Princes are Gods, so their well-govern'd Courts, are Copies, and representations of Heaven; yet the Copy cannot be better then the Original' (*Sermons* 1.161, 223).

No Sermon survives from Donne's presumed service at court in April 1617, but this gap may be explained by James's absence from Whitehall on his progress to and from Scotland (March–September). During that hiatus Donne did, however, preach a Sermon at Paul's Cross on the King's accession day (24 March). In some important ways this appearance at the Cross could be seen as a displaced, or transferred, court Sermon, for at the same time Sir Francis Bacon had taken advantage of the King's absence from London to revive the Elizabethan custom of privy councillors attending the annual Easter Monday sermon at St Mary's Hospital (McCullough 1998: 131). There is something strikingly similar, then, in the unusually detailed title for Donne's *Sermon Preached at Pauls Cross to the Lords of the Council, and other Honorable Persons, 24. Mart. 1616. [1616/17] It being the Anniversary of the Kings coming to the Crown, and his Majesty being then gone into Scotland*. The lords of the Privy Council had, as Bacon recognized, been shunted by new Jacobean custom from traditional attendance at City sermons to attendance at court instead. Their presence at the Cross to hear Donne suggests that the lords' remove from court to City sermons during the King's absence might not have waited for Easter Monday (21 April), but have included accession day as well. Given the results of his trip to Cambridge one year before, Donne was in no need of the absent King's approval, but may have been so in the eyes of the combined City and court elites whom he found himself addressing in March 1617. By simply declaiming his text (Prov. 22:11), he issued a remarkable piece of self-justification of the royal trust placed in him: 'He that loveth pureness of heart, for the grace of his lips, the king shall be his friend'. James's choice of Donne as priest in his church and chaplain to him and his household was to be defended by Donne's demonstration of 'pureness of heart', and—more to the point—'the grace of his lips', that is, his preaching. For as Donne boldly summarized his text: 'God will make an honest man acceptable to the King, for some ability, which he shall employ to the publike.... God will bless and prosper, and he will seal this blessing to him, even with that which is his own seal, his own image, the favor of the King' (*Sermons* 1.183).

Donne was too polite to say explicitly that he was talking about himself; he knew that letting the auditory draw that conclusion would be far more effective. He also deployed, in his closing peroration, another stroke of tactful, and tactical, genius: to praise James, but also to evoke the revered memory of his predecessor, 'that Queen, unmatchable, inimitable in her sex' (1.217). The strategy worked, for Chamberlain, the same reporter of Donne's bad odour upon leaving Cambridge in 1615, now wrote that at the Cross Donne had preached 'a daintie sermon…and was excedingly well liked generally, the rather for that he did Quene Elizabeth great right, and held himself close to the text without flattering the time too much' (Chamberlain 2.67).

There then ensued two deviations from Donne's routine of preaching service as a court chaplain. The 2 November 1617 Whitehall Sermon (*Sermons* 1.223–35) was perhaps delivered as a substitute for an absent fellow chaplain, or as service delayed by James's springtime progress to Scotland. Donne was then also invited to preach before Queen Anne in December of the same year (1.236-51). Delivered two days after the Queen's birthday, and perhaps arranged by his friend John King (a personal favourite of Anne's), the Sermon managed to combine a beautiful encomium to divine love with pointed warnings to the Queen (rumoured to be a closet Catholic) about the dangers of popery (McCullough 1995). Sermons like these were no mere apprentice pieces, but the work of a preacher confident in his ability to work the maximum possible effect in an elite auditory. They are also evidence of how integral court chaplaincy was to Donne's rapid consolidation of a reputation worthy of the trust placed in him by his king.

So secure was Donne's favour with James, and so quickly prominent his reputation as a court chaplain, that his appointment in February 1619, by the King himself, to attend as chaplain the embassy to Germany and Bohemia by Viscount Doncaster should come as no surprise. He was the King's chaplain, just as Doncaster was the King's ambassador, and both were on an international mission in royal service. Here James was showing wisdom, for, from the ranks of royal chaplains-in-ordinary, none was as well suited as Donne, given his earlier interest as a layman in civil and foreign service and his sympathy for embattled continental Protestants. Donne, we know, preached before James's daughter Elizabeth and her husband, the Elector Palatine, at Heidelberg, in what must have been, for her, a nostalgic reminder of sermons at her father's court (although there are doubts about the attribution to the occasion of the surviving text [*Sermons* 2.250–68; Bald 1970: 352 n. 1]).

Even at home, routine service as a royal chaplain could put Donne in some remarkable situations. Queen Anne's death (March 1619) had been swiftly followed by a scare over the King's own possible death. London courtiers rushed to his bedside at Newmarket. Among them was Lancelot Andrewes, who was commanded to deliver his appointed Easter sermon to the King in his chamber. But worship in the Chapel Royal had to go on even without the King and much of the court. Donne was on duty, so, with very little notice, he prepared and preached a Sermon '*to the Lords upon Easter-day, at the Communion, The King being then dangerously sick at New-Market*'. It deployed resurrection themes to allay the court's real and present fears of mortality (*Sermons* 2.197–212). But a royal death did eventually come to pass—James's, on 27 March 1625—which again impinged directly on Donne's service as a royal chaplain. Almost the entirety of James's lying-in-state at Denmark House fell during Donne's month of waiting, during which the sealed royal coffin had to be attended by the members of the household. The chaplains not only kept constant vigil in the makeshift chapel, but continued to preach their Sunday and Tuesday sermons there. Donne eulogized James, and looked forward to heaven where all might 'see those eyes open there, which we have seen closed here' (6.291). It was a fitting end to the Jacobean phase of Donne's career as a royal chaplain (see Ch. 24 for a more detailed analysis of this Sermon).

A second type of court sermon needs to be distinguished from those so far discussed, that is, those preached as part of the annual court sermon series for Lent. The custom dated to early Tudor times and was a part of the court calendar at least as prominent as the Christmastide and Shrovetide revels. Beginning on Ash Wednesday, by appointment of either the Lord Chamberlain or Clerk of the Closet, distinguished preachers addressed the court on every Tuesday, Sunday, and Friday until Easter Sunday. Bald and others long ago noticed that Donne's court Lent fixture was the first Friday in Lent (the Friday after Ash Wednesday), from 1618 until his death, and texts survive for all except 1626. However, Bald relied upon a later (1672) summary of the rank of preachers chosen for the different days, leading him to infer mistakenly that Donne's appointment to a Friday was a distinguished variation upon the (much later) custom of reserving Fridays for cathedral deans (Bald 1970: 313). In fact, in 1618 all Friday preachers were, like Donne, doctors of divinity (not deans), with bishops given Ash Wednesday and Sundays, and other doctors and sometimes deans the Tuesdays. The preachers who were not bishops were royal chaplains. Thus the Lent rota in Donne's first year on it included episcopal grandees like George Abbot, James Montagu, Arthur Lake, John Buckeridge, Richard Neile, and Donne's friend John King, counterpointed on weekdays with younger rising stars from the royal chaplaincies of James and Prince Charles. The Lent list was not just a map of who was, and who soon would be, powerful in the Church of England, but was also a core sample of the different layers of Jacobean conformity that would buckle and bend the church with increasing violence over the next quarter-century (McCullough 1998: 64–70, 111–15).

Donne's Lent Sermons constitute some of his most memorable pulpit performances (not least, of course, *Deaths Duell*). But they are also his most self-consciously 'courtly', if we mean those Sermons that most explicitly acknowledge the status of their royal and courtly auditory. They are also explicit about their place in the liturgical year. Both of these aspects seem to flow from Donne's keen awareness of the prominence of the court Lent Sermon series itself. Donne's April court Sermons are, by comparison, markedly 'ferial', to use the correct liturgical term meaning 'ordinary' or 'routine' (as opposed to for a seasonal or feast day). And in this respect, and for his time, Donne is not typical. Since the Lent sermons were free-standing sermons not preached as part of any liturgical service (they were, in modern terms, more comparable to a lecture), most court Lent preachers delivered sermons that could not be identified as Lent sermons, since few made Lent the subject, or even the frame, of their Lent sermons. But Donne consistently did so.

For his very first Lent Sermon (1618) Donne took as his text the words of the penitent thief crucified with Christ (Luke 23:40). Donne apologized that it was not from the Lenten exemplar of Christ's fasting in the wilderness, but from his Passion, and expressed the hope that the auditory did not only 'meditate upon the passion' on Good Friday. He then used another liturgical season to explain the logic of Lent and its relationship to Good Friday and Easter: 'As the Church celebrates an Advent, a preparation to the Incarnation of Christ...so may this humiliation of ours in the text, be an Advent, a preparation to his Resurrection' (*Sermons* 1.253). In every subsequent Lent Sermon Donne registers an urgent belief that the whole of the court sermon series in which he participated should be not a pastime or diversion, but a discipline, an arc of devotion, meditation, penitence, and hope that stretched from Ash Wednesday to Good Friday and Easter. It was, of course, to be an arc plotted across the six weeks by the sermons in the court Lent series, and again, the eye Donne keeps on the whole rota is unusual. And, in spite of Easter's being the obvious consummation of Lent, it is often Good Friday to which Donne most looks forward, perhaps savouring the parallel between the first and last Fridays in Lent.

We know that courtiers and City sermon-goers knew in advance who would be preaching on which days, and many avidly followed the series. Donne engaged his court auditory's interest by recalling them to consider the cumulative meaning of the Lent series. Hence, in 1621 he used sharp, parallel syntax to give what is almost a diagram of a minister's ascent from ordination, to royal chaplaincy, to a place on the Lent list ('bill'): 'We have a Calling in our Church; that makes us Preachers: and we have Canons in our Church; that makes us preach: and we bring a Duty, and finde favour; that makes us preach here: There is a power here, that makes bills of Preachers: But in whose power is it to make bills of Believers?' (*Sermons* 3.220). The *gradatio* ends in a rhetorical question that throws the weight of responsibility for a sermon's success away from the man in the pulpit, and onto the man or woman in the pew. He then drives the point home: 'how far do you deceive your selves, if you come not half way, if you be hearers, and not believers?' (3.220).

He was even capable of turning on its head the ostensible comfort of having a whole six-week sermon series as a preparative to Good Friday and Easter communions. Sarcastically mimicking a complacent sermon-goer who delays repentance, Donne said in 1628, 'we shall have preparatives enough, warnings enough, many more Sermons before it come to that [Good Friday], and so it is too soon yet'. Then, in his own own voice, came the devastating reminder of just how suddenly even court sermon-goers might die: 'you are not sure you shall have more; not sure you shall have all this; not sure you shall be affected with any' (*Sermons* 8.174). Donne could even pander to the crowd's taste for star preachers, as in his deft, punning compliment in 1623 to the Bishop of Lincoln and Lord Keeper, John Williams, who, as Dean of Westminster, preached the court sermon on Good Friday. Here Donne is of course endorsing a famously crowd-pleasing preacher (and yet another former Egerton chaplain). But he does so in terms that inscribe the importance of the Lenten arc that stretches from his own humble series-opener about Christ's 'Compassion' on the *first* Friday in Lent, to the 'great personage' who will address the greater matter of Christ's 'Passion' on the *last* Friday in Lent—Good Friday itself (McCullough 2006: 177–8).

Not unlike Lancelot Andrewes in his feast-day court sermons, Donne used his Lent Sermons to warn against sermons as mere 'entertainment' (*Sermons* 2.166), stressing instead not just the need for auditors to add belief to listening, but also to leave the Sermon prepared to act on the combined fruits of preaching and faith. In the very challenging auditory that was the court, Donne exemplified what Jeanne Shami has so accurately studied as 'Donne's vocation...imbued with a pastoral ethos that remains as sensitive to the needs of his audience as to the demands of his text' (Shami 2003*a*: 226).

This chapter has focused primarily on the institutional structures of royal chaplaincy that not only defined Donne's service at court, but also shaped his very path to priesthood and early preferment. As such the chapter has dealt most with the years, primarily in the reign of James I, that saw those patterns established. As I have discussed elsewhere, the accession of Charles I brought new pressures to bear on the old patterns of Donne's service at court. Not least, Donne was shown a degree of favour early in the reign of Charles that rivalled even that shown him by James. But, by 1627, he was complained of by the new Dean of the Chapel Royal, William Laud, for precisely the kind of prophetic engagement with the court auditory for which he had earlier received praise (McCullough 2003*b*: 198–202). But in spite of even that brush with disfavour, Donne's Sermons as a royal chaplain not only continued to define the progress of each preaching year that remained in his life, but were also the engagements that (even compared to decanal ministry at St Paul's) were of the greatest importance to him as preacher.

As his health faltered in the winter of 1630–1, Donne was grieved to decline the Lord Chamberlain's invitation from the King for Donne to preach at court on Gunpowder Day, 'a service which I would not have declined, if I could have conceived any hope of standing it'. Conserving what strength he had left, he delegated his statutory St Paul's Christmas Day Sermon to another, but kept Candlemas, and looked forward to the first Friday of Lent at court, rallying to insist that 'except my Lorde Chamberlaine beleeve me to be dead, and leave me out; for as long as I live, and am not speechlesse, I would not decline that service' (*Letters* 241, 243–4). Donne kept his promise, and presented himself at Whitehall on Friday, 25 February 1631, to preach before Charles and his court. That Sermon would, of course, later be published with the title *Deaths Duell, or, A Consolation to the Soule, against the dying Life, and living Death of the Body*. We do not know if, like Donne's staging of his own deathbed scene, he also prepared the Sermon with the title under which it was published.

But the violence of the title's first epithet, '*Deaths Duell*', for all its later fame, sits ill with the content of the Sermon itself, for which '*A Consolation to the Soule*' is perhaps more accurate. And the Sermon is strangely different from the previous twelve Sermons Donne had preached as royal chaplain on the same occasion. Absent is any view forward across the coming series of court Lent sermons. Muted, too, is any self-conscious reference to the court context. This latter feature, so unusual in Donne's other Lent Sermons, is here distilled perhaps only into the first part's concluding paradoxes about death as a leveller that makes '*children* of *royall parents*, and the *parents* of *royall children*' the incestuous corrupters of each other in the grave; makes 'the *poorest*…*equall* to *Princes*'; makes 'the *Mats* and the *Carpets*' and 'the *State* and the *Canapye*' of a royal presence chamber into the dust and worms that '[*cover*] *them and is spred under them*'; and, in a touching farewell allusion to the King whose coffin he had attended as chaplain, makes 'that *Monarch*, who spred over many nations alive…in his dust lye in a corner of that *sheete of lead*' (*Sermons* 10.238–9). But if the Sermon seems to lack any of the usual self-conciousness about the Lent series itself, it is because Donne has in fact magnified it to a point that at first makes one unaware of its presence. Instead of asking his first-Friday-in-Lent auditors to wait patiently for the sermonic and theological climax that will come on Lent's last Friday, he sweeps across time and ages to take them there himself: 'Take in the *whole day* from the *houre* that *Christ received* the *passeover* upon *Thursday, unto* the *houre* in which hee *dyed* the *next day*. Make *this* present *day* that *day* in thy *devotion*, and consider what *hee did*, and remember what *you have done*' (10.245). And with that begins one of Donne's longest, and most unforgettable, perorations. Using a meditative strategy that Louis Martz long ago identified in Donne's poetry as 'Ignatian', Donne carries his auditors step-by-step through each event in Christ's last hours, pausing at each to ask how the listeners' own thoughts and actions compare to Christ's. It is a haunting, compelling combination of *improperia* and Stations of the Cross that ends with the '*voluntary emission*' of Christ's soul 'into his Fathers hands' with '*no breach* or *battery*'—and no duel either (10.248). Donne has arrived calmly at Good Friday, at what was always for him the epicentre of Lent. He has leapt over the intervening weeks that would be travelled by his auditory, but, as he seems to have anticipated, not by him. He would be buried in St Paul's on Palm Sunday, the third day of the month (April) in which he would have served again as chaplain-in-ordinary. His Good Friday vision on the first Friday in Lent was to be his last. The speaker of *Goodf* famously could not face the crucified Christ: 'Restore thine Image, so much, by thy grace, / That thou may'st know mee, and I'll turne my face' (ll. 41–2). Not so the speaker on the first Friday in Lent, 1631, who brought King, court, and crucially, self to the very cross itself: 'There wee leave you in that *blessed dependancy*, to *hang* upon *him* that *hangs* upon the *Crosse*' (*Sermons* 10.248).

CHAPTER 33.II

THE HAZARDS OF THE JACOBEAN COURT

KENNETH FINCHAM

The relative stability of the early years of Jacobean court politics ended in 1610–12, and was followed by a period of intensified factional fighting and alliance-building as rivals jostled for power and place. Following the accession of James I, Robert Cecil had emerged as the King's principal adviser, and by 1608 had acquired all three major offices of state, as Secretary of State, Master of the Court of Wards, and Lord Treasurer. Although pre-eminent among English politicians, Cecil was obliged by James I to work quite closely, although not always harmoniously, with Henry Howard, Earl of Northampton and Lord Privy Seal. The other seat of power, alongside the Privy Council, was the bedchamber, highly influential in the distribution of royal patronage, overwhelmingly Scottish in composition, and headed by George Home, Earl of Dunbar. The most important of an expanding group of court clerics was Richard Bancroft, Archbishop of Canterbury since 1604 and a privy councillor since 1605.

In 1610–12 all this was to change. While Robert Cecil seemed to have recovered politically from the failure of the Great Contract in Parliament in 1610, his health began to crumble and he died in May 1612 (see also Chs. 30.II, 31.I, 31.II, 32.II). Predeceasing him were Bancroft, in November 1610, and Dunbar, in January 1611, while Northampton was to die in the summer of 1614. A major realignment of political power followed. Before Cecil's death a new Scottish favourite had emerged from the bedchamber: Robert Carr, created Viscount Rochester in 1611 and Earl of

Somerset in 1613, and a privy councillor from 1612. On Cecil's death James I declared that he would be his own secretary, but in practice used Carr as his assistant for the next two years. Thrust into the thick of political administration, Carr began making alliances with Englishmen outside the bedchamber, most notably with the Howard family, led by Northampton and his nephew Theophilus Howard, Lord Treasurer from 1614. This alliance was cemented by Carr's marriage to Frances Howard, Suffolk's daughter, in 1613 after Frances secured an annulment of her first marriage with the third Earl of Essex, on grounds of non-consummation. James I supported her suit, appointed a commission of bishops, councillors, and lawyers to investigate her claims for a nullity, and pressured them into releasing Howard from her marriage with Essex so she was free to marry Carr.

Competition to fill the vacuum left by the deaths of Dunbar and Cecil was sharpened by ideological tensions over three related issues. Should the chronic financial weakness of the Crown be addressed through parliamentary subsidy or by exploiting prerogative taxation? Should the King's children—Prince Henry and Princess Elizabeth—marry into Catholic or Protestant foreign houses? How acceptable was the presence of a number of conformist Catholics, such as Northampton and Worcester, in court and council, representing a broader constituency in the wider country? Staunch Protestants such as the earls of Southampton and Pembroke, the latter appointed a privy councillor in 1611, Ralph Winwood, Secretary of State 1614–17, Donne's old master Sir Thomas Egerton, now Lord Chancellor Ellesmere, Lord Zouche, and Archbishop Abbot all tended to favour a reliance on parliamentary support to solve the King's financial problems and to underwrite a robustly confessional approach to foreign affairs and effective action against crypto-Catholicism within the country. Their opponents, such as Northampton and Suffolk, were less enamoured of Parliament, especially after the debacle of the Addled Parliament of 1614, which Northampton probably helped to scupper, and looked to prerogative revenues, and rapprochement with foreign Catholic powers, as the way to stabilize the King's position at home and abroad.

Archbishop Abbot proved willing to stoke the fires of ideological conflict. Abbot's elevation to the see of Canterbury in March 1611 surprised many observers since he was the most junior bishop on the bench, having been consecrated as recently as 1609, although he had been promoted to the senior see of London in 1610 and groomed for the succession by Archbishop Bancroft, who was becoming increasingly alarmed at crypto-Catholicism at court and in the universities. Abbot recommended himself to Bancroft and to James I as an implacable enemy of Roman Catholicism and a tireless investigator of the activities of Catholic priests, spies, and embassies.

Abbot joined the Privy Council in June 1611 and immediately began to press for enforcing the Oath of Allegiance on prominent Catholic nobility, such as Lord Vaux and Viscount Montagu, who turned to the crypto-Catholic Northampton for protection. The failure of the Addled Parliament, and the pro-Spanish drift in diplomacy, deeply alarmed Abbot: as he wrote, 'we are inchanted by the false, fraudulent and siren-like songs of Spaine', and he feared that 'Almighty God' would punish the nation for its ingratitude (BL, Add MS 72242, fo. 33ʳ). Abbot was also the zealous champion of Calvinist orthodoxy and abandoned his predecessor's attempts to hold together the senior ranks of the clergy by openly opposing a group of more liberal or anti-Calvinist court clerics, regarding them as purveyors of popish beliefs and practice. In the winter of 1610–11 Abbot persuaded Ellesmere, Chancellor of Oxford University, to complain to James I about William Laud's candidature for the vacant presidency of St John's College. Behind Laud were two more senior figures, his patron Bishop Neile of Coventry and Lichfield, and his former tutor, Bishop Buckeridge of Rochester, and, more distantly, the King's favourite preacher and royal Almoner, Bishop Andrewes of Ely. On the fringes of this circle was Benjamin Carier, a canon of Canterbury and royal chaplain, whose decision to join the Roman Church in 1613 vindicated, in Abbot's eyes, the claim that English anti-Calvinists were little more than closet Catholics. Ironically, Abbot's hostility towards them probably had the effect of binding the group more closely together under the direction of Bishop Neile. Abbot's chief allies among the court bishops were two evangelical Calvinists—John King, Donne's old stablemate from York House and Abbot's successor as Bishop of London, and James Montagu, royal intimate and Bishop of Bath and Wells.

Abbot was one of several bishops appointed to judge the Essex annulment case in 1613. While Neile, Buckeridge, Andrewes, and Bilson of Winchester yielded to royal pressure, Abbot, backed by King of London, stuck to his guns and declared he was unconvinced that the marriage had not been consummated, which his enemies presented as a politically inspired anti-Howard manoeuvre masquerading as principled opposition to court corruption. As a result, his standing with James I was damaged, and he made an enemy of the favourite, Carr.

Into this increasingly polarized politics came John Donne in a renewed and belated search for preferment, first secular and then ecclesiastical. By 1613 he had acquired three patrons, all Scottish and all connected with the royal bedchamber: James Hay, later Viscount Doncaster and Earl of Carlisle, whom Donne reported as 'having spoke like a Courtier, but who did like a friend' (*Letters* 145); Sir Robert Ker, future Earl of Ancrum, and through Carr's influence a gentleman of Prince Charles's bedchamber (ibid. 149); and finally the royal favourite himself, Robert Carr Viscount Rochester (ibid. 290–1). None, in the event, found him a post in 1613–14, and in truth Donne was something of an outsider at court, whose thoughts were turning towards a career in the church. Donne in fact had long considered ordination. While friends such as Thomas Morton had urged him to take holy orders, the decisive voice was that of James I, who in December 1614 at Newmarket '*vouchsafed mee his Hand, not onely to sustaine mee* in it, *but to lead mee* to it' (*Devotions* 3). Just how much James had promised, and exactly what Donne's career prospects were on ordination, are worth revisiting.

Donne was ordained as deacon and priest on Sunday 23 January 1615 by Bishop John King in a private ceremony in his chapel in London palace, within the precincts of St Paul's Cathedral. The venue itself is unremarkable, since King habitually held ordination services in London palace, in his chapel at Fulham House, or in the parish church there, but never in St Paul's Cathedral (GL, MS 9532/2, fos. 178^r–223^r). Donne came armed with a dispensation from Archbishop Abbot to allow him to be ordained *extra tempore* or out of the usual ordination times, and to receive both orders of deacon and priest at the same ceremony. But according to canon 33 of 1604 he would have also needed evidence of a title, or proof of prospective employment within the church.

Was the Newmarket agreement with James I enough for Bishop King, who was an old friend of Donne and presumably privy to Donne's expectations of royal preferment? Or perhaps what served as Donne's title was a chaplaincy to his patron in Prince Charles's bedchamber, Sir Robert Ker. Four days after ordination Donne signed a Letter to him, 'ever your servant, to the addition of *Your poor Chaplaine*'. In the body of the letter Donne states his intention to return to the court at Newmarket and via 'my Lord' (probably Carr) 'procure the Kings Letters to *Cambridge*', in other words, the degree of doctor of divinity that James I had evidently promised him at their earlier meeting in December (*Letters* 289). A royal chaplaincy soon followed. As Peter McCullough has demonstrated (Ch. 33.I), Donne was quickly installed as chaplain-in-ordinary and took up his preaching duties at Greenwich the very next month, April 1615.

This was a signal mark of royal favour. Royal chaplaincies were invariably conferred on talented and well-connected clergymen who had served their time in the lower reaches of the ecclesiastical hierarchy: Laud became a royal chaplain ten years after ordination, John Williams after eleven years, Morton after twelve years. Donne, in contrast, had to wait a few weeks. His royal chaplaincy gave Donne easy access to court, the centre of ecclesiastical patronage. He was now a member of a preaching elite, from whom many senior clergy—deans and bishops—were regularly recruited. As a royal chaplain he was also eligible to hold livings in plurality, and through the pulpit of the Chapel Royal could win golden opinions from patronage brokers and the King himself. Donne's new status was underlined by the award of a Cambridge doctorate that gave him the academic title most commonly possessed by court chaplains. But a problem still remains that needs explaining: why did Donne have to wait a year for an ecclesiastical cure? In the spring of 1615 Donne possessed a university doctorate, a royal chaplaincy, perhaps even a chaplaincy to Ker, but these did not amount to a sufficient competency to survive on, especially with Donne's large family to support.

Walton implies that Donne was responsible for this situation because he turned down fourteen livings in 1615 since all were situated outside his 'beloved *London*', which he was loathe to leave. This large number sounds scarcely plausible and has left no paper trail. In any case, when Donne accepted two benefices in 1616 both were country livings: Keyston in Huntingdonshire and Sevenoaks in Kent (Walton 1658: 51). Each was granted by the Crown, the first directly in the King's gift, the second a royal living, worth under £20 a year and therefore in the patronage of the Lord Chancellor, and Donne's former employer, Thomas Egerton, Lord Ellesmere. In the same year he became divinity Reader at Lincoln's Inn, with a handsome salary of £60 per year. But if we put Walton's explanation aside, why else might Donne have had to tarry a whole year for remunerative office?

In a Letter to Sir Henry Wotton shortly after his ordination, Donne implied that he was patiently awaiting advancement from the King: 'I do not so much as enquire of myne owne hopes what the K. will do wth me' (E. M. Simpson 1948: 334). Possibly the promise of a richer prize had been dangled before Donne in December 1614, which in the event he did not secure. The newsletter writer John Chamberlain described the furore in March 1615 surrounding the award of degrees at Cambridge to outsiders, including Donne, and then stated the rumour that Donne had been promised the reversion of the deanery of Canterbury, which was in the Crown's presentation. The present incumbent was Thomas Neville, Master of Trinity College Cambridge and one of James I's hosts. Both Gosse and Bald dismiss this suggestion out of hand: 'no such grant was, or could ever have been made' and the story reflects 'Chamberlain's credulity' (Chamberlain 1.586–9, 591; Gosse 2.84; Bald 1970: 309). Yet Chamberlain was a seasoned purveyor of gossip, in Cambridge for the royal visit, so his testimony should not be lightly discounted; moreover, reversions to office, both ecclesiastical and secular, were granted fairly frequently by the Crown. The following year, for example, the controversialist Richard Field was offered the bishopric of Oxford in reversion, although the aged bishop, John Bridges, actually outlived him, only for the reversion to be reassigned to John Howson, who succeeded Bridges in 1619. Without the promise of reversions, according to Lord Keeper Williams in 1621, 'I shall have noe men of breeding or qualitie that will long continew in my service' (Field 16; Chamberlain 2.118; Gardiner 1871: 167). Rumours in March 1615 of a reversion for the deanery of Canterbury were timely, since Thomas Neville was ageing and unwell, and was to die just two months later. In the event the deanery went elsewhere, to Charles Fotherby, a man with good Kentish connections.

It is true that had Donne landed the deanery of Canterbury so soon after ordination it would have been regarded as an unprecedented and unjustifiably rapid promotion. But nothing about the circumstances of Donne's ordination was conventional: Donne is the only man James I is known to have coaxed into ordination, the only man in his reign to become a chaplain-in-ordinary within weeks of his ordination. So we should allow for the possibility that Donne was offered the prospect of a reversion, perhaps at his momentous meeting with James I at Newmarket in 1614, even if in the event the deal was not clinched. That further preferment had to wait until 1616 may also be the result of Donne's having hitched his fortunes to a waning star, the Earl of Somerset, who had to contend with the emergence of George Villiers as a key court player in the summer months of 1615, before dramatically falling from power that October. But on the other hand, even in his pomp Somerset had delivered nothing for Donne in 1613–14.

George Villiers had been introduced to the court in 1614 by a group of anti-Howard courtiers led by Pembroke, Southampton, and Abbot, with the aim of supplanting Carr in the king's affections which would lead, they hoped, to a change of policy and greater influence for Villiers's backers. The plot worked spectacularly well, as James fell in love with Villiers, while Carr was simultaneously implicated in the murder of Sir Thomas Overbury and was arrested in October 1615. The Earl of Pembroke earned his reward, taking over as Lord Chamberlain from Somerset, although the Howards were not wholly displaced, with Theophilus Howard, for example, remaining as Lord Treasurer until 1619. All were quickly overshadowed by Villiers, the new and dominant big beast of the Jacobean court. Villiers's rise was meteoric: a gentleman of the bedchamber (1615), Master of the Horse and Viscount Villiers (1616), Earl of Buckingham (1617), Marquess of Buckingham (1618), and finally Duke of Buckingham (1623). Although initially he took little role in politics, from very early on Villiers established a firm grip on the levers of royal patronage. In 1617 Sir Dudley Carleton, ambassador in the United Provinces, was angling for the secretaryship of state following the death of Ralph Winwood and was advised by Abbot to write to Villiers to know the King's wishes. Carleton enlisted the support of the earls of Pembroke and Arundel, but Villiers declared himself against Carleton's candidature and the post went instead to his client, Sir Robert Naunton (TNA, SP 105/95, fos. 13–15, 17^v, 23^v). Villiers's influence was also patent in ecclesiastical patronage. In October 1616 John Chamberlain reported that Villiers was responsible for the two latest appointments to the episcopate: one was 'an obscure fellow', Robert Snoden, who was given the bishopric of Carlisle, overcoming a strong rival, George Carleton; the other was Lewis Bayly, who received the see of Bangor despite being 'opposed and articled against' by Archbishop Abbot, a fellow Calvinist but evidently no friend to Bayly and perhaps backing an alternative Calvinist candidate (Chamberlain 2.29–30). Many other bishops, among them Theophilus Field, William Laud, and Valentine Carey, owed their elevation to Villiers. As these examples suggest, Villiers advanced both Calvinists and anti-Calvinists, evidently observing his master's wish for a broad range of Protestant opinion on the episcopal bench. On occasion James I listened to other voices when senior positions fell vacant. In 1617 Donne's friend Pembroke earned the see of Worcester for John Thornborough after the King had vetoed Villiers's choice of Robert Beaumont (Fincham 1990: 31). But Villiers had become effectively the King's patronage secretary, and Donne, were he to progress further in the church, needed to make his mark with him.

The struggle between Abbot and his anti-Calvinist opponents reached a turning-point in the summer of 1615, when the Archbishop felt confident enough to carpet William Laud and John Howson, a former Vice-Chancellor of Oxford, before James I on charges of heterodoxy. To Abbot's embarrassment the King acquitted both, though he warned Howson to preach more often against Roman Catholicism.

Howson duly did so, and within four years had become Bishop of Oxford. Abbot was still influential enough in 1615 to land the bishopric of Salisbury for his brother Robert, but also saw his old enemy Bilson of Winchester promoted to the Privy Council through the influence of Abbot's opponent Somerset.

Abbot did not profit much from the switch of favourites that he had helped to engineer. He objected both to Villiers's dominance over patronage and his expectation that clients rely exclusively on him, and complained in 1619 that 'no man goeth free that doth not stoope saile to that castle' (TNA, SP 14/171/59). At the same time James I became increasingly sceptical of the Archbishop's invocation of an international Catholic threat as the prospect of a Spanish match rose up the royal agenda. In 1617 official marriage negotiations opened, from which Abbot and Winwood were excluded 'as openly opposite' (Chamberlain 2.66). Abbot's enthusiasm for a pan-Protestant crusade on the outbreak of the Thirty Years War was also inimical to a king anxious to find a peaceful settlement and avoid a recall of Parliament. The Archbishop's position at court became more vulnerable with the deaths of his longstanding allies Ralph Winwood (1617), Bishop Montagu (1618), and Bishop King (1621). The clerical beneficiaries of this diplomatic turn were anti-Calvinist bishops, such as Neile, who received the powerful see of Durham in 1617, and Lancelot Andrewes, promoted to the Privy Council in 1616 and then to the wealthy bishopric of Winchester in 1618. Unlike Abbot and other staunch Calvinists, both were comfortable with the propriety of a royal match with Catholic Spain. Durham House in the Strand, Neile's residence in London, became the headquarters for an expanding anti-Calvinist clerical network that included William Laud, Augustine Lindsell, and John Cosin.

Donne avoided being drawn into this religious factionalism. Indeed, there is no evidence of any personal links between Donne and the Durham House set. On the other hand, there is a long line of evangelical Calvinists, all of them eventually bishops, to whom Donne was close: John King, once a fellow servant with Donne to Egerton in the 1590s; Thomas Morton, who tried to nudge him towards ordination; and Joseph Hall, once protégé to Donne's friend Sir Robert Drury. A possible fourth was Anthony Rudd, with whom Donne may have conferred on religion in the 1590s, although Walton is our only source for this episode. Rudd later became Bishop of St Davids, and in 1604 publicly urged that Convocation accommodate tender Puritan consciences over ceremonies, to the anger of hard-line bishops such as Bancroft of London. King and Morton were both members in the 1610s of a circle of evangelical bishops centring on Lambeth palace, home of Archbishop Abbot. Each was an active preacher, committed to building up the preaching ministry and encouraging a learned laity through the provision of effective catechizing, and indulgent towards moderate Puritan scruples over official ceremonies (Fincham 1990: 250–68). Was Donne part of the same network?

It is an unfortunate fact that Donne's own ties with Abbot are not well documented. It has been suggested that the two were probably closer than we can presently demonstrate in view of a diplomatic cipher of c.1616 that included Donne's name alongside those of Abbot, Secretary Winwood, Isaac Wake, and William Trumbull, the latter pair in overseas postings, all of them committed to the defence of Protestant interests abroad, a cause to which Abbot in particular was remarkably devoted throughout the 1610s. Nor was Donne's inclusion the result of a passing fancy: as late as January 1623 he was sent a copy of a larger cipher, from Venice, which makes little sense unless Donne was in fairly regular receipt of diplomatic correspondence (Bald 1970: 315). In short, it has been suggested that 'Donne must have been working directly under Abbot in this service' (Shami 2003a: 78).

Clear evidence of Donne's personal relationship with Abbot is slender. He was unknown to Abbot on the eve of his ordination in 1615, but we learn from a Letter of 30 August 1621 that Donne had been at Lambeth and Croydon several times that summer to see the Archbishop. This certainly implies some sympathy for Abbot, who was in political difficulties following his manslaughter of a gamekeeper that July (*Letters* 158); we also know that Donne dined with Abbot at Croydon in 1622 (Bald 1970: 439). But shards of other evidence, some of it negative, imply that the two were not especially close. The only extant exchange of letters between them is in c.1622, relating to a package of books, and the tone of both is fairly formal (*TMC* 309–10). Donne's name never crops up in Abbot's voluminous correspondence at home or abroad; and it may also be significant that there is no record of any gift from Donne to Abbot in the Archbishop's detailed account book for 1614 to 1623. Those wishing to acknowledge ties of friendship, connection, or clientage sent presents to Abbot, at Christmas or other times of year; but Donne was not one of them (LPL, MS 1730). Nevertheless, as Dennis Flynn observes, the regular gifts to Abbot from Donne's father- and brothers-in-law point to important familial connections linking Donne and the Archbishop.

The international knowledge and contacts implied by Donne's inclusion in the cipher, in addition to his long-standing hopes of a foreign posting, help explain his appointment in 1619 to accompany his old patron Lord Hay, now Viscount Doncaster, on a mission to mediate in the rising tension between the Austrian Habsburgs on the one hand and the German princes and the Bohemian estates on the other. Donne was going not as Doncaster's chaplain, but on the direct orders of the King as a royal chaplain: 'It is true', Donne wrote in March 1619, 'I had that commandment from the King signified to me by my L. [Doncaster]' (*Letters* 174). The choice of a churchman was unusual but not unknown. After the Reformation lay diplomats had largely superseded clerical envoys, although in 1600 Bishop Bancroft of London had been sent on an embassy to Emden to confer with Danish ambassadors, while in 1616 it was rumoured that Bishop Andrewes might head a mission to Spain in pursuit of the royal match (Chamberlain 1.101; Birch 1848: 1.447). Doncaster's embassy of 1619–20 achieved little, having been overtaken by events, but its failure did not seriously damage Doncaster's position at court, while for Donne it may have enhanced his prospects for further preferment.

That after receiving a brace of Crown livings in 1616 Donne had to wait another five years for further promotion from the Crown may well be because it took time for him to win Villiers's (Buckingham's) backing. Perhaps, as with Carr, the intermediary was Doncaster. What seems clear is that on his return from Germany in early 1620 Donne was in line for higher preferment. It appears that Buckingham had promised him the deanery of Salisbury, but Donne missed it in a promotion round of March 1620, and then had his hopes dashed in April 1621 when unexpectedly it failed to fall vacant. Two months later the gossip was that he had gained Gloucester deanery (Chamberlain 2.296, 360, 382). There was a major reshuffle that summer, as the bishoprics of London, Lincoln, Carlisle, St Davids, Salisbury, and Exeter all fell vacant, and deaneries too, as deans were elevated to the episcopate.

Donne wrote to Buckingham on 8 August 1621, reminding him of the promise of Salisbury deanery, and expressing (just as Buckingham liked to hear) his total dependency on him: 'I ly in a corner, as a clodd of clay, attendinge what kinde of vessel yt shall please you to make of your lordships humblest and thankfullest and devotedst servant' (Gardiner 1871: 158). The reminder was perfectly timed. On 26 August the Bishop of Exeter died and was succeeded by Valentine Carey, who resigned his deanery of St Paul's. By 13 September Donne was writing to thank Buckingham for the promotion to the deanery. Years later it was claimed by

Ill. 33.II.1. Old St Paul's, engraving by Wenceslaus Hollar. BL Maps 3545 (4). This cathedral, remodelled by Inigo Jones in the 1630s, was gutted in the Great Fire of London (1666) and reconstructed according to the design of Sir Christopher Wren. (© The British Library Board, BL Maps 3545 (4).)

John Hacket that John Williams, the Lord Keeper, was a successful suitor for Donne. Williams, it is true, was often free with his recommendations to Buckingham, and certainly suggested two names (including Carey's) for Exeter, but there is no contemporary evidence that he did the same for Donne. If he did so, then it was surely in collaboration with Buckingham, just as they had acted together earlier that year to acquire the bishopric of St Davids for Laud (Gardiner 1871: 160, 162; Hacket 1.63–4).

Ultimately, of course, Donne's promotion needed the royal seal of approval. As no mean theologian and an active promoter of Protestant unity, James never wholly delegated ecclesiastical patronage to Buckingham, and it may be, ever since the rumour of Donne being promised the reversion of Canterbury deanery in 1615, that the King had considered his learning and talents befitted the rank of dean (Fincham 1990: 31). Indeed, Donne's reward of St Paul's fits a wider pattern in the Jacobean church: of deaneries sometimes conferred on those who had close personal ties to James I, such as his son's tutor Adam Newton, who was lay dean of Durham 1604–20; his Scottish servant John Gordon, who was given Salisbury in 1604; or John Young, son of James VI's own tutor, who received Winchester in 1616. In 1621, by approving Donne's elevation to St Paul's, James was perhaps finally discharging the personal undertaking made to Donne at Newmarket in 1614.

CHAPTER 34.1

DONNE'S READERSHIP AT LINCOLN'S INN AND THE DONCASTER EMBASSY

EMMA RHATIGAN

In 1616 Donne was appointed preacher to the Society of Lincoln's Inn. The Society had, of course, already been influential in his biography as the location of his first entrée into the literary milieu of the capital; it was now to provide the dominant institutional context for an equally formative period of his life, his first years in the ordained ministry.

On his mother's side, Donne had extensive family connections with Lincoln's Inn. His great-uncles William Rastell, Justice of the Queen's Bench, and Richard Heywood, prothonotary of the Queen's Bench, were members of the Society, as was Richard Heywood's son, John. Thomas More, Donne's mother's illustrious great-uncle, had been a particularly distinguished member of the Inn, acting as Governor in 1511–12 and 1514–15. More's brother, John, and his son-in-law, William Roper, were also members. More recently, Donne's brother-in-law, Avery Copley, first husband of his sister Anne, was a member. It is thus hardly surprising that both Donne and his brother Henry were entered as members of the Society in 1592.

George Potter and Evelyn Simpson speculate that Christopher Brooke, Donne's long-standing friend, was the influence behind Donne's return to the Society in 1616 (*Sermons* 2.1). Brooke had acted as a surety for Donne when he entered the Society in 1592, and the men subsequently shared chambers. Donne dedicated *Storm* and a Verse Letter (*CB*) to his friend; both men are listed as members of the Mitre and Mermaid Tavern circles in the anonymous Latin poem *Convivium Philosophicum* and in Thomas Coryate's letter to the group from India in 1615; and Christopher Brooke and his brother Samuel were also, of course, complicit in Donne's wedding. Donne and Brooke remained friends throughout their lives, Brooke bequeathing two of his paintings to Donne in his will. By 1616 Brooke was an important member of the Society; he had become a bencher in 1610 and was Autumn Reader in 1614 and would thus have been in a strong position to recommend Donne to his fellow benchers.

Donne could, however, also have been beholden to Lord Chancellor Thomas Egerton. Egerton was yet another prestigious member of Lincoln's Inn, having acted as Treasurer to the Society in 1587. Donne had been Egerton's secretary from late 1597 or early 1598, apparently giving satisfaction until 1601, when he secretly married Anne More and Egerton acquiesced to the request of Anne's father, Sir George More, for his dismissal. Sir George More eventually appealed to Egerton to take Donne back into his service, but Egerton refused, because, according to Izaak Walton, he was reluctant to undermine his own authority by publicly changing his mind (1658: 21–2). If Walton is correct, then it makes sense that Egerton, a keen patron of Calvinist conformist clergy, would have welcomed the opportunity to further Donne's new religious career.

Brooke and Egerton were not, however, Donne's only friends in the Society. Donne was, for example, acquainted with William Hakewill, who was called to the Bar in 1606 and was to become a bencher in 1618. Hakewill and Donne had known each other as students together at Lincoln's Inn. They both sat in the 1601 Parliament, and their names are mentioned together in Thomas Coryate's letter from India. In 1612 Donne refers to Hakewill in a Letter to Goodere (*Letters* 55). Donne was also on close terms with Henry Hobart, who was admitted to Lincoln's Inn in 1575 and called to the Bar in 1584. He was Governor of the Society in 1591 and hence would have been an important figure during the period when Donne was a student at Lincoln's Inn. Donne mentions his friendship with Hobart in a Letter to Goodere in 1621, writing that he has been very often at '*Highgate*, where that very good man my Lord *Hobard* is' (*Letters* 158).

In taking on the role of preacher at Lincoln's Inn Donne was to become part of an illustrious preaching tradition at the Society, which had been initiated with the employment of the Society's first permanent preacher, William Charke, in 1581, and went on to include Richard Field (1594–6), John Aglionby (1596–?), Richard Crakenthorpe (?–1599), William Pulley (1599–?), Thomas Gataker (1602–11), and Thomas Holloway (1613–16). Of particular interest to Donne scholars here is Richard Field, the preacher in residence while Donne was at Lincoln's Inn as a student. If we follow Walton (admittedly not always accurate) and take Donne's student years as those when he first started to embark on extensive theological reading, in his own words, surveying 'the whole body of Divinity, controverted betweene ours and the Romane Church' (*Pseudo-Martyr* 13), then it is entirely possible that Donne would have met with Field for pastoral support. That the preacher did have such a pastoral role is suggested by Simonds D'Ewes, a student at the Middle Temple during the 1620s, who describes seeking reassurance from Thomas Master, the preacher at the Temple, on the subject of his theological doubts and scruples (D'Ewes 1845: 1.185). Not only was Field's theological perspective comparable with that of Thomas Morton in whom, according at least to Bald, Donne did confide (Bald 1970: 202–13), but Field would at that time have been working on his magnum opus, *Of the Church* (1606) (V. G. Wilkins 2008; on Field see also A. Milton 1995). This huge volume, which stands alongside Richard Hooker's *Of the Laws of Ecclesiastical Polity* as a highly influential work of theological polemic, sought to defend the Church of England against the claims of Catholic theologians such as Bellarmino and was precisely the sort of text Donne would have been drawn to as he pursued his study of points of controversy between the Catholic and English churches. Field would surely, then, have been an obvious candidate for Donne to turn to amid his theological explorations. Field seems, moreover, to have been especially open to such discussions. In his biography of his father, Nathaniel Field recalls how he regularly received theological queries from around the country. Nathaniel Field emphasizes, however, that essentially his father wished to avoid controversy. He writes that, 'In Points of such extreme difficultie he did not thinke fit to be too positive in defining any thing, to turne Matters of Opinion into Matters of Faith' and that 'He was one which laboured to heale the Breaches of Christendome, and was readie to embrace Truth wheresoever he found it' (Field 11–12, 21–2). Intriguingly, these are precisely those attributes that Jeanne Shami identifies in Donne's preaching (Shami 2003a). Field could well be an important and, as yet, unnoticed, influence on Donne's theological development.

The preaching tradition at Lincoln's Inn has usually been characterized as distinctly Puritan, and it is not difficult to see why (Prest 1972: 204). The Society's first preacher, Charke, was a highly controversial presbyterian, and Gataker, their longest serving preacher before Donne's appointment, has been described by Anthony Milton as a 'puritan luminary' (Greaves; A. Milton 1995: 397–8; Usher). However, the presence of Field, Aglionby, and Crakenthorpe means that it would be inaccurate to describe the tone of preaching at the Society as predominantly Puritan. Rather, during the 1590s the benchers were careful to employ preachers whose churchmanship was consistent with John Whitgift's drive for conformity. Indeed, while the benchers seem not to have been averse to Puritan preachers, their preference appears to have been for Calvinist conformists who held a sympathetic attitude towards Puritans. This corresponds precisely with what we can ascertain about the religious sympathies of the benchers. Although the Society brought together men from a broad spectrum of religious belief, ranging from William Noy, a supporter of William Laud, to William Prynne, the notorious Puritan, at the heart of the Society there was a core of Calvinist conformist or Puritan benchers. Such men included Edward Atkins, Samuel Browne, Edward Clarke, Randolph Crew, Thomas Egerton, Robert Eyre, William Hakewill, Thomas Hitchcocke, Henry Hobart, James Ley, Henry Sherfield, Thomas Richardson, Thomas Thornton, Rowland Wandesford, and Thomas Wentworth (for biographical details on these lawyers see Prest 1986, especially Appendix E, 'Biographical Notes on Benchers'; see also Rhatigan 2006: 32–8). These benchers' decision to appoint Donne is thus highly significant in our understanding of Donne's churchmanship at the very start of his ecclesiastical career. Clearly, in 1616 Donne's theological reputation was such that the benchers did not see him as out of place in the evangelical preaching tradition they had hitherto maintained at Lincoln's Inn.

When mounting the Lincoln's Inn pulpit, Donne faced an elite, highly educated, and politically attuned congregation. Walton's rhetoric may sound hyperbolic when he claims that Donne and the benchers existed in a state of 'love-strife of desert and liberality' (1658: 57), but there can be little doubt that Donne would have been addressing a particularly congenial auditory, many of whom would have been known to him personally since the 1590s. Broadly speaking, the congregation would have consisted of two distinct, yet overlapping constituencies. First, there were the lawyers: the benchers, barristers, and those working to be called to the Bar. Then there were the students, mostly graduates of one of the universities, who were at the Inns to complete their education. This may well have involved some study of the law, but gaining a legal training was not their primary focus, and they could be as interested in studying music, dancing, and fencing as they were in common law. The actual Society of Lincoln's Inn was not, moreover, the only source of Donne's auditory in the Lincoln's Inn pulpit. Rather, the congregation would have been relatively fluid. Members would frequent other pulpits and students from other Inns would come to the sermons at Lincoln's Inn. Thus the benchers' orders for the seating arrangements in the new 1623 chapel specifically leave seats free for 'other persons of eminent quality, as shall att any tyme resort and repaire to the Chappell' (LI, *Black Books* 2.242).

Donne was appointed to preach on the same terms as his predecessors in the pulpit. He was to preach twice every Sunday in term, once in the morning and once in the afternoon, once on each Sunday before and after each term, and once on each of the Grand Days (Candlemas, Ascension Day, St John the Baptist's Day, and All Saints' Day), which were observed as holidays in the Inns of Court and Chancery. He would also preach during the legal Readings, which were held twice each year. Of these Sermons twenty-two are extant, with at least three more for which a strong case can be made for their having been preached at Lincoln's Inn (Rhatigan 2006: 51–9; the canon of Lincoln's Inn Sermons as it is defined in *Sermons* will be completely reconsidered in the forthcoming *Oxford Edition of John Donne Sermons*, General Editor Peter McCullough). Donne's Sermons at Lincoln's Inn tended to form parts of a series. A series of sermons, usually dedicated to a particular biblical text or a logical biblical unit, was a common preaching practice in the period. At Lincoln's Inn, however, Donne took an especially creative approach to his Sermon series, preaching not only a series on Psalm 38, but also one devoted to a discussion of the doctrinal errors of Catholicism, one constructed around apparently contradictory texts, and one dedicated to the persons of the Trinity. None of these series has survived in its totality.

Donne's Sermons are always notable for their sensitivity to the specific occasion and location of preaching, and the Sermons he preached at Lincoln's Inn are no different. Throughout his Sermons to the Society it is possible to see him shaping and adapting his sermon oratory to the particular congregation before him. To use his own words, he drew on his first-hand experience of life in the Society 'in making the easier entrance, and deeper impression of Divine things' to his congregation (*Sermons* 4.143). For example, preaching on the second verse of Psalm 32 ('For thine arrows stick fast in me, and thy hand presseth me sore'), Donne deliberately shapes his exegesis of the psalm to speak directly to the Lincoln's Inn students, wittily transforming the arrows that afflict David into the temptations to which the young men of the Inn would be regularly exposed. He describes how: 'A fair day shoots arrows of *visits*, and *comedies*, and *conversation*, and so wee goe abroad: and a foul day shoots arrows of *gaming*, or *chambering*, and *wantonnesse*, and so we stay at home (2.62). Later in the same series he focuses on the students' vanity and their preoccupation with the latest fashions:

> Thou seemest, in the eye of the world, to walk in *silks*, and thou doest but walke in *searcloth*; Thou hast a desire to please some *eyes*, when thou hast much to do, not to displease every *Nose*; and thou wilt solicite an adulterous entrance into their beds, who, if they should but see thee goe into thine own bed, would need no other mortification, nor answer to thy solicitation. (2.83)

According to Thomas Overbury's *Characters*, an Inns of Court student could be 'distinguished from a Scholler by a paire of silke stockings, and a Beauer Hat', and was 'ashamed to bee seene in any mans company that weares not his clothes well' (Overbury 1628: K4[r]–K5[r]). Although this is obviously a caricature, Overbury was evoking a widely held image of an Inns student. Donne's vivid deconstruction of a fashionable young gallant was a well-aimed jibe at the youthful Lincoln's Inn students in his congregation.

Donne was equally adept at drawing on his legal knowledge to address the lawyers in the congregation. Thus he often deliberately sought out biblical texts with a particularly legal theme, such as the pair of Sermons on John 5:22 ('The Father judgeth no man, but hath committed all judgement to the sonne') and John 8:15 ('I judge no man'). And within the Sermons themselves, he develops specifically legal analogies. For example, in the Sermon on John 5:22, God's all encompassing judgement is explored in terms of legal jurisdictions. Donne asks, 'who hath divided heaven into shires or parishes, or limited the territories and Jurisdictions there, that God should not have and exercise *Judicium discretionis*, the power of discerning all actions, in all places?' (*Sermons* 2.316). The analogy would, no doubt, have created a witty, self-conscious moment in the Sermon, playing to the lawyers' pride in their collective professional identity. Later in the Sermon, in a more dramatic example, the Last Judgement is imagined as an apocalyptic court scene, complete with God as the Lord Chief Justice, handing out irreversible, eternal judgements:

> Wrangle as long as ye will who is Chief Justice, and which Court hath Jurisdiction over another; I know the Chief Justice, and I know the Soveraign Court; the King of heaven and earth shall send his ministring Spirits, his Angels to the womb, and bowels of the Earth, and to the bosome, and bottome of the Sea, and Earth and Sea must deliver, *Corpus cum causâ*, all the bodies of the dead, and all their actions, to receive a judgement in this Court: when it will be but an erroneous, and frivolous Appeal, to call to the Hils to fall down upon us, and the Mountains to cover, and hide us from the wrathfull judgment of God. (2.317)

Once again the analogy works as a compliment to the lawyers, although this time it is also accompanied by the sharply ironical reminder that those who spend their lives sitting in judgement will, on the last day, be placed in the dock themselves.

Donne's concerns in the Lincoln's Inn pulpit were not, however, limited to the specific social and vocational preoccupations of his congregation of students and lawyers. As Malcolm Smuts's chapter has demonstrated, the tensions and strains that characterized international relations in Europe during James's reign were never far from the surface, and Donne was soon to find himself directly involved in the political and religious turbulence that was overshadowing the continent (see Ch. 34.II). In April 1619, only two and a half years after he had been appointed preacher to the Society, he was ordered by James I to join the Doncaster embassy, which was travelling to Europe in order to mediate between James's son-in-law, Friedrich of the Palatinate, and the Catholic Prince Ferdinand, soon to become Holy Roman Emperor. James's choice of Donne is intriguing and provides a vivid insight into his political identity at this stage in his career. As Paul Sellin has shown, James's decision seems to have been part of an extremely pragmatic diplomatic strategy (Sellin 1988: 9–31). Donne not only had previous experience of continental travel, but he had also been involved in secret correspondence about continental affairs, as indicated by his named presence on an official cipher. The cipher dates from 1615 or 1616, but the presence of a number to designate the King of Bohemia suggests that it was still in use in this later period (Bald 1970: 340, 314–15, 569–70). Together with his rhetorical abilities and linguistic skills, these qualifications would have made him the perfect candidate for such a post. Donne's position at Lincoln's Inn would also have been significant: Lincoln's Inn was his main employment in this period, and he would presumably have had a specifically legal identity, as opposed to being connected with a parish, diocese, or university. A legal chaplain would be a clear asset to a diplomatic entourage, especially if James wished to revive the pre-Reformation tradition of using clerics on ambassadorial missions. Pre-Reformation clerical ambassadors held the distinct advantage that their knowledge of civil law equipped them with an understanding of international law. Equally, through their religious ties they had access to a network of contacts throughout Europe. Donne, however, would have held similar advantages in an early seventeenth-century context. He not only brought together a Catholic background with a firm commitment to continental Protestantism, but he also moved within the circle of English divines such as Joseph Hall and George Abbot, who were committed to strengthening ties with their brethren in Europe. His position at Lincoln's Inn meant he balanced a knowledge of civil law, through his clerical background, with a clear engagement and association with English common law. Donne was an ideal choice, and the embassy was going to call upon him to draw on a wide variety of skills and knowledge.

Donne was an important figure in the embassy, standing third in rank behind Doncaster and Francis Nethersole, who acted as secretary to the mission. When Nethersole was called back to England, Donne appears to have taken on some of his duties. His participation would thus have brought him into the centre of the religious and political issues surrounding the Palatinate. The presence of their preacher at the heart of diplomatic developments on the continent would also, of course, have brought the affairs of the Palatinate far closer to home for the Society of Lincoln's Inn, not least through the correspondence they received from Doncaster himself. Writing to the benchers to excuse Donne's continued absence, Doncaster explains:

Since therefore I am a continual witness of his desire to return to the service of your society, I thought it fittest for me to give you this signification of the reason of his absence, with an undoubted assurance that he shall suffer no prejudice in your good opinions thereby, because he is not altogether absent from that society now whilst he is with me, who, by your favour, have the honour of being a member of your society. (Gosse 2.135)

Doncaster's reference to his own membership at Lincoln's Inn, drawing on an image of the Society's corporate identity, is precisely the sort of rhetoric that would have gone down well with the benchers. Indeed, when the receipt of the letter is noted in the *Black Books* on 14 October 1619, it is stated 'With which letter the whole Bench stood well satisfied' (LI, *Black Books* 2.212). Doncaster's rhetoric, however, also has the effect of drawing Doncaster, Lincoln's Inn, and Donne into a reciprocal relationship. Donne is with the Society through Doncaster and, by implication, so too is the Society present and involved in the diplomatic negotiations through Donne and Doncaster. Such rhetoric is, moreover, similar to that used by Donne at the close of his Valediction Sermon, preached on 18 April, just under a month before he departed for the continent on 12 May. Donne tells his congregation: 'And soe as your eyes that stay here, and mine that must be farr off, for all that distance shall meet every morning in looking upon the same sun, and meet every night in looking upon the same Moone, soe our harts may meet morning and evening in that God who sees and heares alike in all distances' (*Sermons* 2.389). Meeting in God through mutual prayer, Donne and the members of Lincoln's Inn will not truly be apart while Donne travels abroad. Rather, their faith and shared religious commitment will mean that the Society is as present to Donne on the continent as he is to them back in Lincoln's Inn. Hence not only Donne himself, but also the members of Lincoln's Inn, must have felt particularly close to and involved in the events that were unravelling in Bohemia and the Palatinate.

Donne, however, appears to have been a reluctant diplomat-divine. Writing to Goodere in March, he complains, 'I leave a scattered flock of wretched children, and I carry an infirme and valetudinary body, and I goe into the mouth of such adversaries, as I cannot blame for hating me, the Jesuits, and yet I go' (*Letters* 174–5). If these misgivings stemmed from a degree of scepticism about James's enthusiasm for a diplomatic solution to the dispute, then Donne's doubts were fully justified. The embassy was far from a success. Departing on 12 May, they went first to Brussels for an audience with the Archduke, then to Heidelberg to meet with Friedrich and Elizabeth, before travelling east to consult with Ferdinand. It became clear, however, that Ferdinand had little interest in entering into negotiations with Doncaster. Shortly after their meeting all hope of a compromise was lost when Ferdinand was elected Holy Roman Emperor and the Bohemians offered the crown to Friedrich. There was little else that Doncaster could do. He was left to travel to Graz to offer his congratulations to Ferdinand, before returning to England via The Hague. Back at court Doncaster made a vigorous, if ineffectual, attempt to promote the Palatinate cause. Donne, however, returned to guide his Lincoln's Inn congregation through the political and religious upheavals of the next two years.

Recent scholarship has drawn attention to Donne's clear continuing emotional and intellectual engagement with the political and religious developments in Europe, especially as it was manifested in his preaching in the 1620s (Shami 2003a). It is, moreover, noticeable that Donne chose to dwell on these issues with particular frequency at Lincoln's Inn. This, though, is not, perhaps, surprising. Not only would Donne undoubtedly have found a receptive audience in the Lincoln's Inn congregation, who were both highly politically aware and in many cases of an evangelical Calvinist leaning, but the Lincoln's Inn pulpit was also outside the jurisdiction of the Bishop of London, meaning that Donne would have been exposed to less censorship than in other pulpits. Consequently, Lincoln's Inn constituted a safe and privileged sphere in which Donne allowed himself to speak more explicitly about 'those kingdomes, where ambition on one side and a necessary defence against imminent persecution on the other side hath drawne many swords' (*Sermons* 2.389; Rhatigan 2006: 141–81). We can see clear examples of this more politically overt voice in a pair of Sermons on Matthew 18:7 ('Wo unto the world, because of offences'), preached most likely in 1620. This year had seen both the arrival of the Spanish ambassador to pursue negotiations for the marriage of Prince Charles to the Spanish Infanta in

March and the defeat of Friedrich of the Palatinate's forces at White Mountain in November, leaving many convinced of the imminent victory of the Catholic Antichrist over the true Protestant faith in England. Donne addresses these events and his congregation's anxieties directly, warning his auditory against the man who is merely a religious 'time-server' and who:

> stays not to give God his leasure, whether God will succour his cause to morrow, though not to day. Hee stays not to give men their Law, to give Princes, and States time to consider, whether it may not be fit for them to come to leagues, and alliances, and declarations for the assistance of the Cause of Religion next year, though not this. But...as soon as a *Catholique army* hath given a blow, and got a victory of any of our forces, or friends, or as soon as a *crafty Jesuit* hath forged a Relation, that that Army hath given such a blow, or that such an Army there is, (for many times they intimidate weake men, when they shoote nothing but Paper, when they are onely *Paper-Armies*, and *Pamphlet-Victories*, and no such in truth)...yet with these forged rumours, presently hee is scandalized. (*Sermons* 3.178–9)

This strategy of approaching the issue of the Palatinate through a discussion of the various discourses that surrounded it, the 'forged rumours', the pamphlet warfare, and the godly's existential questioning about the fate of Protestantism is typical of Donne's approach to preaching on matters of foreign policy in his Lincoln's Inn Sermons. His main aim is to educate his congregation on how best to respond to the proliferation of news and gossip. Clearly, the implication of the passage is that Donne is sympathetic to the Palatine cause. It is significant that while apparently defending James, criticizing those men who have rushed to criticize their monarch without allowing him 'time to consider', he speaks not of whether God and princes will take action, but of when they will take action. He does not give any space to the idea that the prince may not wish to take action at all. James is given a respite to consider, but ultimately Donne is unequivocal that the only godly decision is to aid the cause of religion. Assuming James will take action is a powerful, if cautious, rhetorical strategy. It also, however, fits into Donne's broader approach to the issue, whereby he leaves aside the detail of the political decisions in order to devote his Sermon to instructing his auditory on how they should respond to these decisions.

Donne is equally willing to address the issue of James's changing policy on toleration for English Catholics. Thus he advises his Lincoln's Inn congregation:

> wo unto him that is so free, so unsensible, so unaffected with any thing in this kinde; for, as to bee too inquisitive into the proceedings of the State, and the Church, out of a jealousie and suspicion that any such alterations, or tolerations in Religion are intended or prepared, is a seditious disaffection to the government, and a disloyall aspersion upon the persons of our Superiours, to suspect without cause, so, not to be sensible that the Catterpillars of the Roman Church, doe eat up our tender fruit, that the Jesuites, and other enginiers of that Church, doe seduce our forwardest and best spirits, not to be watchfull in our own families, that our wives and children and servants be not corrupted by them, for the *Pastor* to slacken in his duty, (not to be earnest in the Pulpit) for the Magistrate to slacken in his, (not to be vigilant in the execution of those Laws as are left in his power) *væ mundo, væ immuni*, woe unto him that is unsensible of offences. (3.166–7)

On the one hand, in this passage we hear Donne's characteristic insistence that ordinary citizens should not busy themselves with government affairs that do not concern them. Yet, to a certain extent, just by mentioning these fears of alterations and tolerations in religion, an unambiguous reference to James's foreign policy, Donne is legitimizing them. Moreover, Donne's temperate warning against mistrust of government gives way to more emotive language in the second half of the argument. If to begin with he is arguing that concerns about a toleration of Catholicism are seditious when based only on 'suspicions', by the end of the passage he seems to be insisting that such concerns are based on fact. The sin becomes not being 'sensible' of reality, rather than being overly concerned with fictitious suspicions. The clichéd imagery of the Jesuits as caterpillars, destroying the crop of English Protestants, captures precisely the contemporary sense of the Jesuits as an insidious influence, destroying the English state from the inside. The imagery of 'tender' English youth being eaten away would, moreover, have been especially resonant in an Inns of Court setting where the young had long been a specific target of the Catholic missionaries (Prest 1972: 174–86).

Amid the challenge of guiding an anxious congregation through the political and religious disturbances of the early 1620s, Donne's energies would also, however, have been taken up by the project that was to dominate the Society for the next five years,

Ill. 34.I.1. Interior, Trinity Chapel, Lincoln's Inn, London. The altar, pulpit, and altar rails all date from after Donne's time. (Image © John N. Wall. Reproduced by permission.)

the building of the new chapel. Plans for a new chapel at Lincoln's Inn were first aired in May 1616, initiating a lengthy period of strenuous fund-raising which resulted in the dedication of the new chapel in May 1623. The building project was thus concurrent with the period of Donne's employment as the Society's preacher, and it seems highly likely that Donne played a pivotal role. Indeed, his Sermons preparing the Society to build the chapel and at the consecration indicate both his practical and emotional involvement; he speaks movingly of his role 'as an often refresher of it to your memories' and 'a poore assistant in laying the first stone' (*Sermons* 4.371–2). There is, moreover, firm, though previously unnoticed, evidence in the Saunderson papers at Lincoln's Inn that Donne was present at at least one discussion about the chapel. A dispute had arisen between John Browne, a joiner, and Lincoln's Inn, the details of which survive in the Saunderson papers. In Thomas Saunderson's statement he claims that he discharged Browne in August 1621 'upon my Lord Hobart's conference with me and D. Dunn at the reading then' (LI, Saunderson Papers, A1d1/3). Given the dates, D. Dunn must refer to Dr John Donne. Clearly on at least one occasion Donne was aware of the practical arrangements for the new chapel.

Donne's involvement is of especial interest given the churchmanship that is reflected in the building's architecture. In perfect accordance with the Calvinist conformist sympathies of the benchers, it was designed as an evangelical theatre for preaching (Rhatigan 2006: 38–51). Crucially, the layout was not the collegiate style of seating used in the Chapel Royal and college chapels. In this tradition there would be pews on each side of the chapel, facing each other across a wide central aisle. Rather, the layout chosen by Lincoln's Inn is far closer to parochial pewing. According to the benchers' seating orders, there were three blocks of seating in the main body of the chapel, facing east towards the chancel. There appear also to have been seats on all three walls of the chancel, along with the preacher's seat and the chaplain's seat. This arrangement, combined with the positioning of the pulpit in the centre of the chapel, in front of the communion table, places the main focus on the word preached, rather than on liturgical ceremonies. We have here, then, crucial evidence about Donne's churchmanship in the early years of his ordained ministry. While Donne's position on doctrinal Calvinism remains hotly debated, it is clear that he was committed to a churchmanship that was sermon- rather than sacrament-centred and that dovetailed perfectly with the godly preaching tradition that the lawyers were maintaining at Lincoln's Inn (McCullough 2003*b*: 190–202).

The only other aspects of the furnishing of the Lincoln's Inn chapel about which we have details are the stained-glass windows (Lane). The fashion for stained glass had been started by Robert Cecil and had quickly become a widespread enthusiasm (Gapper, Newman, and Ricketts 88–9). Richard Butler and the Dutch immigrant Van Linge brothers, whose fame and popularity were on the rise (Bernard van Linge had completed the east window in the Wadham College chapel, Oxford, and Abraham van Linge was to complete schemes in a number of other Oxford colleges),

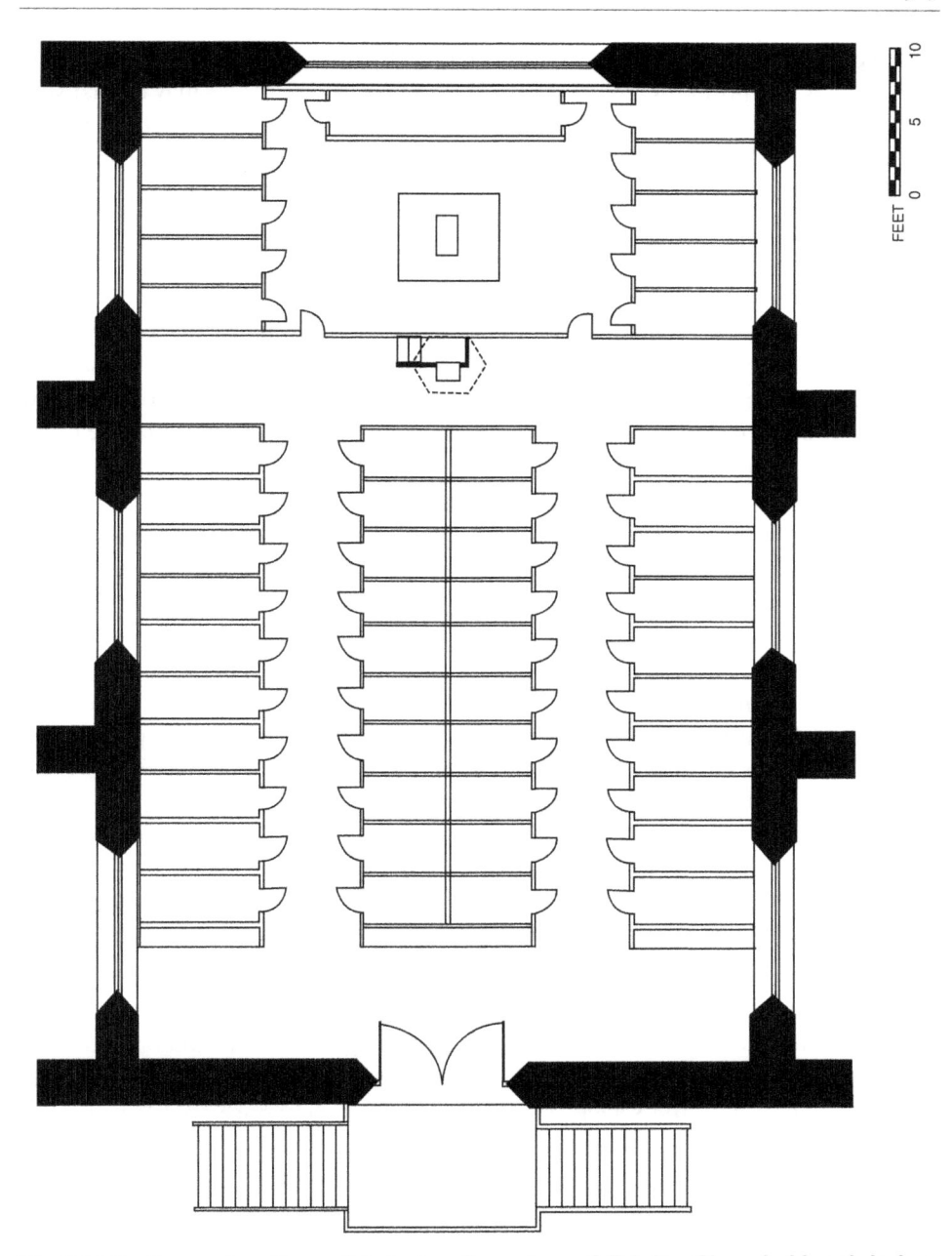

Ill. 34.I.2. Reconstruction of interior floorplan of Trinity Chapel, Lincoln's Inn, 1623, showing disposition of pulpit, communion table, and seating arrangements. Subsequent renovations frequently make it difficult to visualize the space of early modern churches, but in the case of Trinity Chapel, extensive records have enabled scholars to make a provisional reconstruction of the design of the building in the early seventeenth century. (Drawing by Eugene W. Brown, AIA, reproduced with his permission [cf. Wall 2007])

undertook the work at Lincoln College, Oxford, filling the windows with images of the apostles and prophets (Newman 167–9). A first reaction to this may be that such church beautification was a perfect example of proto-Laudian architectural preferences. It should be noted, however, that the Puritan-minded benchers seem to have had no problems with the windows in Lincoln's Inn. For example, Henry Sherfield, notorious for his iconoclasm in breaking a window in St Edmund's Church, Salisbury, appears to have had no qualms of conscience about the Lincoln's Inn windows (Cobbett and Howell 3.519–64). Indeed, Sherfield was among those benchers who paid to have their coats of arms included in the west window of the chapel (LI, *Black Books*: 2.450). Rather, as this case shows, the issue of stained glass was complex. Sherfield was distinguishing between the cautious scheme of images of the apostles and prophets portrayed in the Lincoln's Inn windows, which he found acceptable, and an image of the Trinity in St Edmund's, which his conscience found to be idolatrous. In fact, stained glass was widely accepted by both moderates and Laudians, and the benchers' choice of windows demonstrates their desire to keep up with the latest fashions, whilst remaining relatively cautious in their choice of images (Cannon 106–17).

By the time the chapel was dedicated in 1623, however, Donne had already left the Society. On 20 November 1621 he had been appointed Dean of St Paul's. This date fell just eight days before the end of Michaelmas term, and Hilary term was to start on 23 January. Since this left the benchers insufficient time to appoint a new preacher, Donne continued preaching in the Society during Hilary term and did not resign until 11 February 1622. There is every indication that the Society was sad to see Donne leave their pulpit and that Donne, in turn, was sad to go. The entry in the *Black Books* that records Donne's resignation is unusually detailed, and notes Donne's gift of six volumes of the Bible to the Society and the benchers' decision to make him an honorary bencher 'to th'end it may appear that,... they are glad of his preferm^t, yet being loath wholly to part wth him, and that he may at his pleasure and convenient leisure repair to this House' (LI, *Black Books*: 2.229–30). Donne's gift and the benchers' response indicate an extremely high level of mutual respect. The benchers' desire that Donne would be 'no stranger' was clearly sincere, and Donne returned to preach to the Society at least twice after he left: once on Ascension Day 1622 and once at the important celebration of the dedication of the new chapel. Donne's time at Lincoln's Inn was clearly crucial in terms of the development of both his religious and political identity. But, as this strikingly warm entry in the otherwise sparsely official *Black Books* suggests, it seems also to have been a personally rewarding period, in which Donne was able to exercise his ministry amid a congregation to whom he was bound not only by his role as a preacher, but also by the ties of friendship, and a shared institutional past.

CHAPTER 34.II

INTERNATIONAL POLITICS AND JACOBEAN STATECRAFT

MALCOLM SMUTS

APART from the notorious episode of the Spanish Match, Jacobean foreign policy has attracted much less attention than religion or domestic politics. This reflects the insular nature of work on early Stuart history and the ways in which the King's relations with Parliaments and issues figuring prominently in parliamentary debates have dominated treatments of his English reign. And yet James was a king with a wide British and European outlook, while many of his subjects also felt intense concern for events beyond England's borders. This was certainly true of John Donne, who counted several diplomats among his close friends and aspired to a diplomatic career before his ordination in 1615 (Adlington 2008a: *passim*). In his role as a preacher, too, Donne's horizons remained European, since many religious issues transcended national boundaries. To recover the historical contexts of Donne's life during the 1610s and 1620s we need to situate English religious politics within a wider European environment.

Shortly after his arrival in London, James told a French ambassador that the greatest source of conflict in contemporary politics was 'the diversity of opinion in religion that extends through all nations and the interest of the popes in taking advantage of it by inciting wars' (BL, MS Kings 123, fo. 327). He knew this to be a partisan statement that ignored both his own negotiations with the papacy over accommodating religious differences in Britain and the disruptive potential of radical Protestantism. But his words reflected long and bitter experience of the destruction caused by religious passions and self-seeking politicians who exploited confessional hatreds. Apart from a brief episode in the north in 1569, Elizabethan England escaped civil wars of religion on its own soil. Scotland was less fortunate. From infancy James had grown up first as a pawn and then a protagonist in violent factional conflicts inflected by religion. He had been libelled, hectored in public sermons, kidnapped, and threatened with physical harm, as he struggled to assert his authority as an 'absolute' king, 'indifferent' to noble faction and independent of his overbearing English neighbour (BL, MS Cotton Caligula C VII, fos. 266, 321).

These early experiences had taught James to keep his own counsel as he played different religious factions and foreign states against each other, turning him into an early master of the princely art of misleading others, a 'cunning King who dissimulates above everyone else in the world', as a French diplomat once put it (BN, Fonds Français 15989, fo. 61; BL, MS Cotton Caligula C VII, fo. 60). They also made him acutely aware of the power of ideas in politics. A royal scholar, 'who willingly talks of letters and above all theology' (L. P. Smith 1.315), he was the only contemporary monarch to publish both poetry and prose. Far more than a hobby, these literary and intellectual pursuits reflected his knowledge that theological arguments can have deadly practical consequences (Rickard *passim*). Even before the Gunpowder Treason he made it clear that 'he hated the Jesuits...as his personal enemies' for their willingness to defend the Pope's right to depose heretical kings (Sully 3.142). Despite Britain's peace with Spain after 1604, he remained wary of potential Catholic adversaries abroad and Catholic conspiracies within his own dominions. His Protestant subjects shared these concerns. Anti-popery and antipathy towards the Jesuits and Spain provided perhaps the single most powerful common bond uniting most English and Scots (Lake 1989: *passim*). Donne endorsed but also gently mocked this attitude in *Ignatius His Conclave*, by portraying the founder of the Jesuits as a master of subversion so adept that Satan, fearing his presence at the Court of Hell, sent him off to enlist the inhabitants of the moon in a new order of Catholic Lunatics (see Ch. 12 above).

James's peaceful accession, which removed the long-dreaded prospect of a civil war after Elizabeth's death, followed by peace with Spain, created a respite that allowed the Crown to concentrate on consolidating its domestic authority. But these events did not end English and Scottish participation in European conflicts. As David Trim has shown, the number of English volunteers fighting in the Dutch army actually increased, with James's connivance, after 1604, while two Scottish regiments also remained in Dutch service (Trim 288). Donne knew several of these mercenaries, including his close friend Robert Drury and his Scottish patron Thomas Erskine, first Earl of Kelly (Sellin 2003: 152). No one expected the European peace to last indefinitely, and James and his Privy Council knew better than to let down their guard. Ireland, with its mainly Catholic population and recent history of rebellion, seemed especially vulnerable to Spanish meddling: a fact that always lurked in the background of foreign policy calculations. Although England and Scotland, with their mainly Protestant populations, were far less vulnerable to subversion, the survival of Catholic minorities that included influential peers caused concern, especially after the Gunpowder Plot (1605) and the assassination of Henri IV of France by a Catholic extremist had underlined the dangers posed by fanatics and conspiracies. Most British Catholics wanted accommodation with the regime, and James, who had sheltered Catholic peers against Protestant vendettas in Scotland, showed some sympathy with their position. But it was not always easy to distinguish peaceful Catholics from irreconcilable adversaries, who sometimes found shelter in the households of moderate recusant families (Questier 2006: 155–68). Most British Protestants believed that a significant popish threat still existed, justifying the execution of priests and legal harassment of lay Catholics through fines and other measures. Many also justified persecution on religious grounds, arguing that tolerating an idolatrous and anti-Christian religion risked offending God (Walsham 2006: 88–9; A. Milton 1995: 31–5, 93–6; but cf. ibid. 1999: *passim*).

James attempted to follow an intricate middle path through these issues, agreeing in principle that the Pope was Antichrist, while admitting privately that he had found His Holiness a courteous gentleman with whom he had conducted fruitful negotiations; denying that he wanted to force consciences, but insisting that in present circumstances he needed to enforce the Elizabethan statutes against Catholicism. Above all, he attempted to differentiate spiritual issues, on which he professed himself tolerant, from attempts by the Roman Church to meddle in secular politics. In 1606, following the Gunpowder Plot, Parliament adopted an Oath of Allegiance requiring Catholics to abjure belief in the Pope's authority to depose monarchs. As Catholic writers on the continent attacked this measure, James organized a campaign in its defence and published an *Apology for the Oath of Allegiance* under his own name (James I 1918: 71–109). When the Pope placed Venice under interdict in 1607 James's ambassador, Donne's friend Henry Wotton, sprang to the Republic's defense and attempted to distribute James's treatise and attract Venetians to English Protestantism by instructing his chaplains to preach their sermons in Italian rather than English. (L. P. Smith 1.462, 465–6; *CSPV* 11.16; Bouwsma 392–3). In 1614 the Third Estate of the French Estates General provided James with another opportunity to seek European Catholic allies when, in reaction to the murder of Henri IV, it introduced a measure modelled after the English Oath of Allegiance. Successful efforts by the French clergy to defeat this proposal provoked another pamphlet by James excoriating the papacy. It was against the background of this international controversy that Donne wrote *Pseudo-Martyr* and *Ignatius His Conclave*, and impressed the King, during interviews described in this Handbook by Peter McCullough (see Ch. 33.I), with his talent for religious controversy.

Some contemporaries complained that James failed to back up his anti-papal words with action, preferring to cultivate Spain in a quixotic search for peace. Modern historians have echoed this view, contrasting the King's pacifism with the more robust Protestant militancy of his two eldest children, Prince Henry and

Princess Elizabeth (e.g. Strong 71–3). Although it contains elements of truth, this picture is far too simple. James preferred to avoid war if he could, and he often employed a pacific and irenic rhetoric, in which he undoubtedly believed at some level (W. B. Patterson *passim*), when discussing European affairs. But he remained more deeply suspicious of Spain and militant Catholicism than historians have commonly recognized. Historians have underestimated James by taking his pacifist rhetoric at face value, a dangerous procedure in evaluating any politician, but especially one as adept at verbal sleight-of-hand as the British Solomon. Recent work has taught us to appreciate the subtlety and complexity of James's ecclesiastical policies; we need to add similar nuance to our view of his relations with European states.

For the first several years of his English reign, James provided underhanded support to the Dutch in their war against Spain, while maintaining generally cordial relations with Henri IV, who was steadily rebuilding French power in anticipation of a future contest with the Habsburgs. In 1610 James encouraged Henri to go to war in Germany in a dispute over the Duchy of Julich-Cleves, with nebulous promises of English assistance (TNA, PRO 31/3/41, unpaginated dispatches of 17 October 1609, 14 February, 16 August 1610). These policies not only supported continental Protestants; they also helped drain the Spanish treasury, while allowing Britain to shelter behind resurgent French military power. But Henri IV's murder dramatically altered the situation, reviving fears that assassination had again become a secret instrument of Habsburg diplomacy, while threatening to neutralize France in European power politics during the long minority of Louis XIII. It also empowered Henri's pro-Spanish widow, Marie de'Medici, who as regent promptly concluded a double marriage treaty with Madrid. 'The effects of the mischief [are] not yet seen', James warned an English Parliament shortly after Henri's death: 'we may pray that quiet may continue but he is a fool that looks for it.... If France be made *campus martius* by a league we are far interested and must provide for such a danger' (TNA, SP 14/54/65). Although speaking partly for effect, in hopes of winning a more generous grant of taxation, his alarm was genuine.

James responded to pro-Spanish policies of French ultra-Catholics by encouraging Princes of the Blood to challenge the supremacy of Marie de'Medici (Birch 1749: 358, 359; BL, MS Stowe 173, fos. 79–80, 80–1, 129; TNA, PRO 31/3/48, fos. 26, 31; TNA, SP 77/11, fo. 64). He began communicating more actively with Huguenot leaders, such as the Dukes of Bouillon and Rohan, urging them on as they contemplated armed protests. Both dukes sent emissaries to London to confer over strategy (TNA, PRO 31/3/41, La Boderie dispatch of 8 February 1611; SP 78/62, fo. 246), and James may have secretly permitted them to recruit volunteers and obtain supplies in England (TNA, PRO 31/3/52, fos. 28^v, 278^v; BN, Fonds Français 15989, fos. 101, 393; BL Add MS 27962 B, fos. 102^r, 136^v, 169^v, 180^v–181; Anon. 1617: *La déscente*). He negotiated for a possible marriage of Prince Henry to a French princess, hoping that in addition to bringing him a fat dowry this alliance might strengthen the Huguenots and other French groups sympathetic to England, as Bouillon argued it would (TNA, SP 78/62, fo. 11). He also explored the possibility of a marriage alliance with Savoy, a Catholic state strategically located between France and the Spanish territory of Milan. The 1613 marriage of Princess Elizabeth to the Calvinist Elector Palatine, Friedrich V, and James's entry into a defensive alliance with the princes of the German Protestant Union, represented another effort to assure that he would not be isolated if attacked by Spain or Catholic France (Pursell 2003: 23–8). English diplomats had been alarmed in the years preceding this match by reports that Catholic and possibly Lutheran states within the Empire were uniting against German Calvinists. Friedrich's alliance with England helped him counter this threat. Spain's ambassador to London, Gondomar, feared that even the Turks might soon join the Protestant Union (Gondomar 109).

James wanted these alliances not to fight a new European war of religion—a prospect he dreaded—but to strengthen his hand in dealing with Madrid and Paris. He continued to develop his relations with Savoy and Venice, both of which had become antagonistic towards the Habsburgs and willing to consider alliances with the Protestant states. But he also welcomed opportunities to improve relations with Spain, a project helped along after 1613 by two highly skilled ambassadors: Felipe III's representative in London, Gondomar, and James's ambassador in Madrid, John Digby. James thus consolidated his position as the political leader of Protestant Europe, while simultaneously maintaining reasonably good relations with the major Catholic powers. This allowed him to adopt the role of broker and mediator, burnishing his credentials as *Rex Pacificus*. But although he did sometimes seek to restrain states like Savoy from provoking dangerous conflicts, his policies reflected the dictates of prudence at least as much as principled pacifism. He knew he had an empty treasury, which future Parliaments were unlikely to replenish, and that his poverty diminished Spanish respect for his military power. It therefore made sense to cultivate Spain, while at the same time encouraging other European states to challenge Habsburg hegemony, provided they stopped short of provoking wars they were unlikely to win. In this way he might keep Spain on the defensive, eager to cultivate British help. The policy never fooled Felipe III's government, but Madrid had its own reasons for avoiding war and therefore tolerated James's equivocations, while trying to draw him gradually into the Habsburg orbit by promising not to interfere in Ireland, playing upon his irritations with the Dutch, and exploiting his desire for friendship with Europe's greatest dynasty. Gondomar was attempting to play on this last motive when, in 1617, he suggested negotiating a marriage between Prince Charles and a daughter of Felipe III.

In several ways, the King's diplomatic balancing act complicated his role as a secular ruler and Supreme Governor of the British churches. In domestic as in foreign affairs, he sought to maintain tolerably good relations with moderate Catholics while also satisfying Protestants who saw compromise with Rome as treasonous. His negotiations with Madrid and professed dislike of religious persecution served the former purpose, while his verbal salvoes against Jesuits and alliance with Friedrich assisted in the latter. But it was a difficult balancing act to maintain convincingly. The ambiguities of his policies were reflected in his Privy Council, on which staunch Protestant internationalists like the Earl of Pembroke, Archbishop George Abbot, and several Scottish courtiers, sat alongside church papists and Spanish pensioners like the Howard earls of Northampton (d. 1614), Suffolk, and Arundel (Gondomar 86–7, 128–35 for the pensions).

A spectrum of attitudes towards Catholicism existed among British churchmen (A. Milton 1995). The dominant view remained thoroughly hostile. Especially in Scotland, but also in England and elsewhere in Europe, anti-Catholicism had given rise in the late sixteenth century to apocalyptic speculations that looked forward to a climactic battle between the true Church and Antichrist in the near future. James had written a paraphrase of the Book of Revelations during his Scottish youth, and as Peter McCullough has shown, he continued to allow the preaching of strongly anti-Catholic sermons at his court in London, although mainly in the households of his children (McCullough 1998: 189–201). James's tolerance and even encouragement of such sermons may have reflected a calculation that one way to mollify bellicose Protestants without having to take action was to focus their hopes on the future. On the other hand, James also promoted more even-handed sermons, especially on anniversaries of the Gunpowder Treason, that drew parallels between Jesuits and 'Puritans' as equally abhorrent extremists (Ferrell 80–9, 103–9). By the mid-teens he had cooled towards apocalyptic thought, which he specifically criticized in a tract published in 1616 (Smuts 2002: 383–4). Overly bellicose Protestants threatened to become an embarrassment.

In the period immediately after Donne received ordination and took up appointments as a royal chaplain and Reader at Lincoln's Inn, rifts partly rooted in European religious politics therefore began to widen within the English Church. Conformist clergy less hostile to Rome and less sympathetic to European Reformed churches than most English Protestants attempted to play upon the King's suspicions of militant Calvinism to reorient his ecclesiastical policies (A. Milton 1995: 46–60, 146–72). Most recent accounts have given James considerable credit for papering over these fissures (Collinson 1982: esp. chs. 2 and 3; Fincham 1990: *passim*), but tensions remained, and the King was highly sensitive to anything that threatened to damage his credentials as leader of the Reformed churches of Europe.

For several reasons, it therefore proved impossible to isolate potential sources of conflict within the churches of England and Scotland from developments abroad. The hotter sort of British Protestants sympathized keenly with their co-religionists on the continent and resented James's dalliance with Spain. At the same time, a two-way traffic in theological ideas between British and European Reformed churches made it easy for disputes on the continent to contaminate the British churches. James intervened to pressure the Dutch to suppress the heterodox views of Vorstius before they could spread to England and Scotland (Smuts 2002: 380, 383). Bitter controversies within Reformed churches also threatened to cause political divisions that might play into the hands of Catholic adversaries. In the late 1610s a dispute between orthodox Calvinists and Arminians who denied the doctrine of predestination came close to igniting civil war in the Dutch Republic, just as the nine-years' truce concluded with Spain in 1609 was about to expire. James sent delegates to the Synod of Dort, called to resolve the controversy, not only to restore consensus but to preserve his influence in Dutch politics. The support given by the English delegates to a moderate Calvinist formula was broadly consistent with the prevailing theological climate within the Church of England; but it also reflected awareness that the Arminians' secular allies were a pro-French party unsympathetic to England that favoured accommodation with Spain (TNA, SP 84/85, fos. 37, 72, 74, 113, 130, 190; SP 84/86, fos. 53, 108^v; cf. Shami 2003c: 48–56).

The diplomatic and ecclesiastical balancing act that James had conducted with a fair degree of success since 1603 depended on the absence of a great polarizing conflict. Localized wars, such as the Dutch contest with Spain before 1609, did not pose insuperable challenges and indeed sometimes played into his hands by increasing his leverage with the contending parties. But James would have a very hard time maintaining his ambiguous policies if a new major war of religion erupted. Most observers of European politics during the generally peaceful 1610s thought it likely that such a contest would soon break out in the Holy Roman Empire. In 1618 the Estates of the kingdom of Bohemia triggered a crisis by rejecting the candidacy of the Habsburg Archduke Ferdinand. Although once elective, the Bohemian crown had been held for several generations by the Habsburgs who regarded it as a hereditary possession, and since Bohemia's ruler possessed a potentially deciding vote in the college that elected the Emperor, the Habsburgs faced possible loss of the imperial title as well. But since Ferdinand had a reputation as 'a stirring prince...ruled by the Jesuits' (Gardiner 1865: 93) German Protestants had every reason to fear him.

As tensions mounted James offered to mediate. Gondomar discounted James's professions of goodwill and advised Madrid that the King would seek his own advantage, but he thought that accepting the offer 'cannot do any harm' and might flatter James's vanity enough to benefit Spain (ibid. 30). The Spanish therefore officially welcomed the mission entrusted in April 1619 to the Scottish courtier and diplomat James Hay, Viscount Doncaster. Donne was appointed as Doncaster's chaplain, almost certainly, as Paul Sellin has argued, because of his prior involvement in diplomacy and his reputation as an astute thinker and able preacher with evangelical sympathies (Sellin 1988: 11). At Lincoln's Inn, as Emma Rhatigan's chapter (Ch. 34.I) has stressed, Donne had been preaching to a community of strong Protestants acutely aware of European politics; he also had ties to active supporters of international evangelical causes at court, like George Abbot and Thomas Egerton. Doncaster himself and the embassy's secretary, Francis Nethersole, were also known supporters of European Protestants. Despite James's professed neutrality, he had therefore appointed a team whose sympathies leaned decidedly in one direction.

Even if Doncaster's courtly skills, Nethersole's experience, and Donne's intellectual stature made them in some ways an ideal team for an embassy of mediation, they were unlikely to adopt a strictly neutral stance. In fact, once in Germany, Doncaster encouraged Friedrich and his allies to stand their ground and sent back dispatches urging James to send military assistance. He also attempted to foment opposition to Ferdinand's candidature as Holy Roman Emperor (TNA, SP 81/16, fos. 56^{r-v}, 61^v, 63, 97^v).

This state of affairs makes it unsurprising that Ferdinand found Doncaster's arguments for compromise unconvincing. Doncaster blamed his intransigence on Spain, whose acceptance of James's offer to mediate, he now suspected, was little more than a ploy to keep Britain from aiding the Protestant side (BL, Add MS 36444, fos. 102^r, 110; TNA, SP 81/16, fos. 170–1). But Friedrich was also becoming more militant: although he denied wanting to make a war of religion, not only did he express the 'desire to be an Instrument of God's glory' in supporting the Bohemian cause (TNA, SP 94/23, fos. 115^v–16; LPL, MS 665, fo. 133); in other expressions he evidently believed and/or gave the impression that under the circumstances his election was a divine mandate (TNA, SP 84/29 fo. 206^v; BL, Add MS 27962 A, fo. 253^v). In late September, after receiving private encouragement from Abbot and other English Protestants (Pursell 2003: 77), he accepted an offer of the Bohemian crown. Doncaster may also have encouraged this decision, as the Spanish came to believe (García Oro 1997: 307). With the benefit of hindsight, most historians have assumed that from this point forward the British mission to Germany became an exercise in futility, as James pursued his naive quest for peace while Spain mobilized for war and Friedrich moved inexorably towards catastrophe. But this is not how Bohemian supporters saw things at the time. In November Doncaster reported hopefully that the King of Sweden, the Marquess of Brandenburg, and the Hungarian Calvinist Bethlehem Gabor had all offered to lend Friedrich their assistance; the latter was reported to be marching on Vienna with 30,000 men (BL, Add MS 36444, fos. 114^v–15). In England the Tuscan ambassador remarked in March on the intensified drilling of London militias in response to rumoured Spanish preparations for war. In October he commented on the prayers and sermons supporting Friedrich preached in London churches and the passionate talk of Bohemian affairs heard daily in the streets, although he noted in November that Puritans displayed more partisan feelings than moderate Protestants or British Catholics (BL, Add MS 27962 A, fos. 179^v–180^r, 217^r, 220^v, 229^r). Courtiers and diplomats became caught up in the mood of anticipation. Prince Charles's Scottish secretary, Thomas Murray, expressed hope that 'God will work that in the public cause of Germany and Bohemia, which great princes do neglect' (Birch 1848: 2.187). The French ambassador reported that Donne's friend, Wotton, had gloated over events before a Catholic diplomat, saying he hoped the new King of Bohemia would soon beat down the horns of the Pope and the time was come to make a sacrifice of the Beast of the Apocalypse and ruin Babylon. When the diplomat protested that talk of this kind would lead Catholic princes to rally behind the Emperor, Wotton shot back that the King of France wouldn't dare, and if he did 'we have a hundred thousand swords in France that will fight for our service', a reference to the Huguenots (TNA, PRO 31/3/53, fo. 59).

James publicly dissociated himself from this belligerent talk, angrily denouncing Friedrich's decision to accept the Bohemian throne and expressing horror at the prospects of a new war of religion. Modern historians have mostly taken him at his word, unlike the Spanish government and the French and Tuscan ambassadors in London at the time, who all suspected *Rex Pacificus* of playing his usual tricks, proclaiming his desire for peace while secretly encouraging his son-in-law's behaviour and waiting to take advantage of the ensuing confusion (TNA, PRO 31/3/53 fos. 35, 104, 107; BL, Add MS 27962 A, fo. 229^v; Garciá Oro 1997: 307–8, 311–16). The evidence available today suggests that while this judgement exaggerated James's duplicity, it did have some foundation. In May of 1619 the royal favourite, Buckingham, told the French ambassador in London that James wanted to transfer the imperial title to the Duke of Savoy, an aggressively anti-Habsburg proposal (TNA, PRO 31/3/53, fo. 4), and the King's correspondence with Doncaster and Friedrich V also suggests that he hoped to deprive the Habsburgs of the imperial title or at least to exploit the Habsburg's anxieties on this score to win concessions elsewhere (TNA, SP 81/16, fos. 61^v, 63). James had recently backed the war party in Dutch politics and encouraged a military alliance between the Netherlands and Venice, a state that recognized Friedrich's title as King of Bohemia. At the very least, he had kept his options open, and would almost certainly have welcomed a successful campaign by Friedrich and his allies to undermine the Habsburgs' hold on the Empire.

But there is also clear evidence that James grew alarmed as he realized that the escalating crisis threatened to drag him into a major war. To a degree that historians have not adequately appreciated, he found himself embarrassed by his defensive alliance with the Protestant Union, which he had only recently renewed. If they were attacked, his treaty obligations, as well as his paternal duty to his daughter and his position as Europe's leading Protestant king, bound him in honour to go to war. But as he told Friedrich in a remarkably frank letter, if this happened he would have to ask the German princes to lend him the money to come to their assistance, since he had no spare funds himself. The only way to save his honour, while avoiding a war he knew he lacked the resources to fight, was to blame his Protestant allies for provoking Catholic retaliation, thus absolving himself of the responsibility to come to their defence. In July James attempted to put up a caution flag by criticizing his allies' military preparations and warning them that he would not support them in an offensive war (TNA, SP 81/16, fos. 101, 102). Doncaster disapproved of the King's message and may have blunted its impact (TNA, SP 81/16, fo. 119^v).

As Paul Sellin has shown, on his way back to London Doncaster encouraged the Dutch to intervene in Germany, with vague assurances of British support that turned out to be misleading (Sellin 1988: 97–104). In doing so he exceeded his instructions, while overlooking a warning from his superiors to be careful about supporting Friedrich's cause too aggressively (ibid. 148–9). But it is difficult to see James—who once told the Duke of Bouillon 'that it is the fashion of princes, when they deceive their neighbors, first to deceive their own ambassadors', and who allegedly once remarked that 'he is the greater and deeper politic that can make other men the instruments of his will and ends, and yet never acquaint them with his purpose'—as an entirely innocent victim of his ambassador's evangelical enthusiasm (Birch 1749: 359; James I 1627: 100–01). As Sellin has also shown, James failed to respond to Doncaster's requests for precise instructions about what he should tell the Dutch (Sellin 1988: 98–9), just as he had earlier delayed in advising Friedrich during the brief period when he was deciding whether to accept the Bohemian throne (Pursell 2003: 77). Although James did not lie to Doncaster, by withholding detailed guidance he made it easier for his ambassador to deceive himself, and therefore also his Dutch interlocutors, about the future direction of British policy.

It is very difficult to know for certain whether this was a deliberate strategy on the King's part or the result of muddle and hesitation. What seems clear is that James now became the victim of his own past equivocations. Doncaster's militancy and that of figures on the Privy Council like Abbot probably misled Friedrich and his allies into discounting the warnings James attempted to send them, until the crisis had escalated to a point at which a peaceful resolution had become impossible. The King's past record of duplicity and the acts of some of his diplomats also caused Spain and other Catholic states to doubt the sincerity of his professed neutrality. James may have calculated that Spain would be unable or unwilling to fight a major war and Ferdinand too weak to do so without Spanish help, so that vague threats of British intervention, along with the recent alliance that he had promoted between Savoy, Venice, and the Protestant rulers, would drive the Habsburgs to the bargaining table (see e.g. the anonymous policy memoranda SP 81/16, esp. fo. 307 and BL, Add MS 72396). Two previous crises over the disputed succession to the German principality of Julich-Cleves had, after all, ended more or less in this way. But without British leadership states like Savoy and Denmark were unwilling to enter the conflict, while the new Olivares ministry in Spain mobilized for war. As the military balance tilted against Friedrich and his allies in 1620, the British Solomon ran out of room to manoeuvre. His policies led to catastrophe, not because of his ideological sympathy for Spain and pursuit of the chimera of European peace, but because he had been too clever by half in trying to manage a crisis spinning dangerously out of control.

From this point on James found himself facing the stark alternatives of entering a major European war on the losing side with an empty treasury or negotiating for a Spanish marriage alliance in hopes of securing his own kingdoms and possibly salvaging something from the wreckage for Friedrich and Elizabeth. Every Catholic military victory in central Europe further undercut his bargaining position, but even limited and indirect aid to the tattered remnants of the Protestant Union risked antagonizing Madrid. He was therefore effectively trapped. The foreign-policy crisis affected his handling of secular politics and the church, obliging him to strengthen the position of pro-Spanish and crypto-Catholic figures on the council and anti-Calvinist bishops in the church, who felt less solidarity with European Protestants and therefore less outrage at the King's failure to come to their aid. Spain also demanded and got de facto toleration for English Catholics as the price for advancing negotiations over the Match. These developments intensified tensions that had long existed within the church and the political nation, arousing fears of a Catholic resurgence within Britain, while fostering serious doubts about the long-term commitment of the King, Prince Charles, and an influential group of churchmen to European Reformed Protestantism. By doing so they provoked vociferous criticism of royal policies, by outraged clergy and their lay allies, of a sort that James had always equated with religious demagoguery.

There seems little doubt that Donne felt distressed at the directions royal policies had taken after his and Doncaster's return to England in early 1620. But by temperament and training he remained enough of a European diplomat to realize that growing divisions among British Protestants and shrill attacks on the King's behaviour would only play into the hands of Spain and British Catholics, church papists, and anti-Calvinists who hoped to exploit the foreign-policy debacle to dilute the evangelical character of the English Church. He is best seen, in the early 1620s, as a preacher and ecclesiastical politician striving simultaneously to resist the growth of Roman Catholicism in England and to preserve a middle ground on which British and European evangelicals might remain united against their common foes. This would explain his consultations with figures like Abbot and the Earl of Carlisle (as Doncaster had now become); the tendency that Jeanne Shami has detected in his Sermons of the period, of seeking a middle ground between the extremes of Puritanism and popery; and Hugh Adlington's observation that Donne's Sermons use 'techniques of rhetoric and persuasion drawn from the methods and language of diplomacy' in advocating religious moderation (Shami 2003a: 79, 99; Adlington 2008a: 189). It might also explain why he was selected to defend the King's controversial *Directions to Preachers* in September of 1622 (Shami 2003a: 75) and as prolocutor of the Canterbury Convocation of 1626 (ibid. 35–6). Rather than trying to align him with one side or the other in contests between Puritans and Arminians, or Stuart royalists and 'patriots' in Parliament, we should see him as a man struggling to prevent such contests from developing. We might perhaps characterize him as a moderate evangelical royalist: a clergyman who believed in a strong Protestant monarchy and an inclusive Reformed ecclesiology and theology capable of facilitating the broadest possible alliance against Spain and Rome. It is notable, for example, that Donne's strongest criticisms of parliamentary behaviour brought forward in Debora Shuger's chapter in this volume (Ch. 39) all involve instances where Parliament had appeared to weaken the Crown's power and prestige in Europe, and thus its ability to defend international Protestant interests. It is a consistent pattern, even if one that consistently cuts across the fault-lines that historians have detected in the politics of the period.

CHAPTER 35.1

DONNE: THE FINAL PERIOD

CLAYTON D. LEIN

DONNE had departed for Germany in 1619, fearful he might die abroad (*Letters* 22, 25; *Sermons* 2.248; Bald 1970: 343); he returned to England with James Hay, Viscount Doncaster, at the beginning of 1620, flush with success, for he carried with him a precious gold medal presented to him by the delegates of the Synod of Dort (Bald 1970: 364–5). Donne treasured this medal to the end of his life. He doubtless knew that only his friend Joseph Hall had been so honoured by the States General: even the other British delegates to the Synod had received silver versions. Donne cherished its value and pointedly regarded it as a personal tribute, bequeathing it to his 'welbeloved' friend Henry King as 'that Medall of gold of the Synod of Dort which the States presented me wth all at the *Hague*' (Huntley 109; Bald 1970: 563). Having served as third in rank in Doncaster's entourage, as advisor and acting secretary for much of the embassy, and also as public supporter for the mission, Donne could genuinely hope for advancement in the near future (Sellin 1988: 9–11, 109, 168, 171; 1983: 10; Bald 1970: 370). The King had advanced every member of his delegation to the Synod of Dort (W. B. Patterson 280–1, 290–1). The honours and gifts proffered by the States General to Doncaster and Donne indicated that they regarded this mission as satisfactory as well (Sellin 1988: 150–5).

Donne had now, moreover, many well-placed patrons. Of particular interest at this juncture of his career are Donne's under-studied friendships with Archbishop Abbot and William and Philip Herbert, the third Earl of Pembroke and the Earl of Montgomery, respectively. Though formed as much as a decade earlier, Donne's friendships with the two earls flourished during his years in the ministry (Novarr

Ill. 35.I.1. Gold Medal of the Synod of Dort by Jan van Bylaer, awarded to Donne by the Staaten-Generaal at the conclusion of the Doncaster embassy to the Netherlands. (Reproduced by permission of the Syndics of the Fitzwilliam Museum, Cambridge.)

1980: 154–5; Bald 1970: 351). Philip's wife had heard him preach shortly before his departure with Doncaster, and, at her request, he had presented her with a manuscript copy of the Sermon (*Letters* xxi, 24–6; Flynn 2000: 80). Donne's friendship with William Herbert, meanwhile, had deepened as a result of his service at court. As Lord Chamberlain, Pembroke was directly responsible for the royal chaplains, as well as for the Lenten rota of sermons before the King (McCullough 1998: 115), and his affection for Donne is revealed in a letter to Doncaster during the 1619 embassy, where he requested Doncaster to 'com[m]end my best loue to Mr Doctor Dunn' (Novarr 1980: 154–6; Bald 1970: 351, citing BL, MS Egerton 2592, fo. 81).

Donne's relationship with Archbishop Abbot, meanwhile, which can be traced as early as 1616, is vital to an understanding of his activities, pulpit stances, and advancements (Shami 1995*b*: 8–10; 2003*c*: 38; 2003*a*: 78, 147, 194–5; Lein 2004: 221–2; Fincham, Ch. 33.II). Donne met, dined, and corresponded with the Archbishop (who subscribed himself Donne's '*ever loving friend*') throughout the years following Donne's return. The friendship remained steady even after the Archbishop's disgrace, and Donne continued to work with Abbot on committees until at least 1629 (*Letters* 158 [misdated]; *TMC* 309–10; W. Young 2.249; Bald 1970: 373, 545). The combination of Abbot and Pembroke at this time is, moreover, highly suggestive, for the two had formed an alliance (together with Donne's friend Lucy Russell, Countess of Bedford) promoting the international Protestant cause (S. Adams 1978: 142–4; Malcolmson 1999: 15–19, 226–7; Healy, Ch. 35.II). Such alliances offer support to the proposition that upon his return Donne shaped his religious identity in reference to international Protestantism (Shami 2003*b*: 146; Papazian 2000). Donne's immortal passage in the *Devotions*—'No Man is an *Iland*, intire of it selfe; every man is a peece of the *Continent*'—rings with international implications (Papazian 2007: *Devotions* 87; see Ch. 35.II), and late Sermons insist that the King, too, must consider religion in international terms: '*David* maintains Religion at home; but he assists, as much as he can, the establishing of that Religion abroad too' (*Sermons* 8.117).

Despite powerful patronage, however, Donne's progress to the Deanery of St Paul's was decidedly wayward. Donne returned to London with Doncaster on 1 January 1620 (Chamberlain 2.280; Sellin 1988: 157). By March rumours flew about that he was being considered for a deanery. The deanery in question, however, was that of Salisbury, and Donne was passed by. Chamberlain's comment ('poore Dr. Dun is cast behind hand and fallen from his hopes') records at least *his* sense (and probably the gossip making the rounds) that Donne had anticipated advancement (Chamberlain 2.296). Rumours of Donne's becoming Dean of Salisbury arose once again in April the following year, while in June gossip suddenly surfaced that he was being advanced to the deanery of Gloucester (ibid. 2.360, 382).

Donne was obviously under serious consideration for promotion, and he broke his pattern of leaving London in the summer to remain there in order to muster support (Novarr 1980: 156–7; Bald 1970: 372). Buckingham, it seems, had promised him the deanery of Salisbury, and as late as August Donne had written him, 'Ever since I had your Lordship's letter, I have esteemed myselfe in possession of Salisbury' (Bodleian, MS Add. D111, fos. 133–4; printed in Bald 1970: 371). Again he was disappointed, but by September he learned that he was being considered for the deanery of St Paul's (*Letters* 165).

More than one figure was involved in this final negotiation. On 13 September Donne wrote to Buckingham to thank him for his favour (*Cabala, sive, Scrinia sacra* 314; printed in Bald 1970: 374–5). But, according to John Hacket, Bishop John Williams also claimed a role in the promotion (Hacket Pt. 1.63). Hacket's reliability has been challenged, yet his testimony concerning Williams's advancement and support of George Herbert, John Davenant, and William Laud has been accepted and validated (ibid., Pt. 1. 63, Pt. 2. 42; A. Charles 112–18; M. Fuller 129–35; Carlton 29). The immediate circumstances, moreover, make the claim credible. Williams was deeply involved with King James throughout the summer of 1621: in June James appointed him Lord Keeper and made him a member of the Privy Council; and throughout the spring and summer Williams was bargaining hard for his own ecclesiastical settlement, negotiations that concerned at least two other deaneries (Westminster and Gloucester) and the bishoprics of London, Lincoln, and St David's (Quintrell 2008*b*; Bald 1970: 370–1). As the new Lord Keeper (and petitioner), Williams undoubtedly enjoyed conversations with the King about various promotions—his own were finally settled in August—and he may well have spoken on Donne's behalf. As Hacket noted, Williams and Donne shared strong connections with Lord Keeper Egerton; they also shared numerous acquaintances, and Williams had doubtless heard Donne preach (Bald 1970: 375–6). On his part, Donne wittily alluded to Williams in a Lent Sermon at court in 1623, and in 1626 thanked him for 'manifold fauors to me' (McCullough 1998: 133–6; Shuttleworth 36; qtd. in Bald 1970: 487). The association begs for further exploration.

Equally significant, Donne probably wrote his poem *Sidney* shortly following the Countess's death on 25 September, in part to engage her son, the third Earl, on behalf of his advancement (Novarr 1980: 157). Donne's ability to sustain amiable relations with men and women who found themselves on opposite sides of the political fence, personalities he truly valued and enjoyed, is nowhere more apparent. Pembroke and Buckingham led different factions in Parliament and at court. Williams was Pembroke's parliamentary ally; Doncaster, with whom Donne had just served on an embassy, was one of Buckingham's chief advisors (Cogswell 78, 103, 129). Donne thus enjoyed support from members of both of the leading factions within the court. On 20 October he formally resigned the rectory of Keyston, and on 19 November he received the royal nomination to the deanery. He was elected by the chapter three days later (Bald 1970: 381, 387; Le Neve 5). Izaak Walton informs us that King James had promised Donne to 'take a particular care for his preferment' (1670: 38), and the promotion was an unmistakable sign of the King's favour. It also set Donne firmly on track for the highest ecclesiastical advancement: the classic path from royal chaplain to cathedral dignitary to a bishopric (Cranfield 120–47; Fincham 1990: 24–5, 305–6).

Donne marked his major change in circumstances, as was his habit, by fashioning a new seal for himself, and from this point he used more than one seal for documents in his hand (Wall 2004: 258–62, 286–95). He faced delays in moving to new quarters. The chapel in the deanery apparently needed repairs, and the transition was costly—Donne noted that he was poorer by £400 at the end of his first year as Dean (*Letters* 135; Walton 1670: 46). Part of that expense probably involved moving his five underage daughters (and perhaps one of his sons, George) as well as his impoverished mother, still firm in her adherence to the Old Religion. Donne officially resigned his Readership at Lincoln's Inn on 11 February 1622, at which time he presented the Inn with a six-volume edition of the Vulgate Bible with glosses by Nicolas de Lyra. By 9 May he was finally settled and could write to a friend from 'my house at S: Pauls' (Houghton Library, MS Eng 930; printed in Bald 1970: 388), although he continued to preach at Lincoln's Inn for some time (Bald 1970: 382–5). Not until 29 November 1624 did he relinquish his chambers there (LI, *Black Books* 2.254–5; pace Bald 1970: 385, who misdates the event). Donne assumed his preaching responsibilities at St Paul's immediately upon his election, for he preached there the following Christmas Day (*Sermons* 3.348). His preaching obligations at the cathedral were rather light: by statute the Dean was required to preach only at the great festivals of Christmas, Easter, and Whitsunday (ibid. 4.4–5). Those duties increased upon his becoming a prebend in 1622 (Bald 1970: 382). Each of the thirty prebends was required to recite a portion of the Psalter daily (Wall 2005: 77–8).

As Prebend of Chiswick, Donne was responsible for reading the sixty-second through sixty-sixth Psalms; he was also, as prebend, required to preach an annual sermon, several of which survive (Donne 1971b: 5–6). Donne was not content with these occasions, however, and preached on a variety of others. A unique dimension of his ministry at St Paul's consists of Sermons he delivered on the feast day of the Conversion of St Paul. The Elizabethan church had abandoned this feast (Cressy 1989: 7), but Paul's (like Augustine's) conversion, 'spirituall Regeneration', and rhetorical strategies became increasingly significant to Donne, and as Dean he increasingly shaped his persona in Augustinian and Pauline terms (Hughes 255–62; Donne 1971b: 1-2; *Sermons* 6.205). At St Paul's on Sundays and on the great festivals of the church Donne was for the first time regularly able to address a large, diverse urban audience, and in the pulpit there his fervour, eloquence, and moderate, inclusive churchmanship rapidly increased his reputation (Bald 1970: 408–9; *Sermons* 4.4).

Donne's responsibilities at St Paul's also involved the supervision of a large ecclesiastical establishment (Bald 1970: 389–90; Wall 2005: 65–6, 77–9). He formed deep attachments to the residentiary canons. One, Henry King, he had doubtless known for years, and Donne appointed him his confidante and literary executor. He likewise formed friendships with the cathedral's talented musicians, some of whom were preparing a monumental collection of English cathedral music, the first of its kind (Lein 2004: 225–35, 244–7).

Donne seems to have been a very responsible steward of the cathedral's finances and dealt honourably with such church properties as came his way, yet he was not a reforming dean and did not challenge habitual ways of doing business (Bald 1970: 396–401). Members of the cathedral continued to garner leases on church property for themselves and family members and to speculate in cathedral property (ibid. 401, citing GL, *Register Donne*), a practice Laud pointedly enquired into in his Visitation Articles in 1636 (Fincham 1994–8: 2.114). The organist and members of the choir regularly left to undertake duties in the royal chapel or other institutions, another practice Laud abhorred and tried to stop (D. Scott 15–16). Equally serious are the citations in a report submitted shortly after Donne's death of 'abuse and profanation' of the cathedral attributed to 'the neglect and sufferance of the Deane and Chapter in tymes past': that children from neighbouring parishes frequented the cathedral and played so loudly that 'many tymes' the preacher could not be heard in the choir; that foreigners and strangers 'of greater sorte and qualitie' were permitted to roam and talk in the church during divine service (a practice the Attorney-General affirmed the Dean and Prebends 'in their proper persons and habits' should stop); and that unnamed persons were carrying 'burthens through the church', a practice already forbidden but insufficiently restrained (W. S. Simpson 131–2). King Charles issued a proclamation the following year forbidding all of these practices, a development suggesting strong Laudian disapproval (ibid. 133). Donne did, however, make attempts to enforce proper reverence during divine service (B. W. Whitlock 1954: 374–5; Bald 1970: 404–5). And he paid attention to the strict fulfillment of prebendal responsibilities and ceremony: the afternoon sermons were duly delivered by the Dean and residentiaries or their deputies; and, as required, the clergy at St Paul's were properly dressed in gowns, surplices, and copes (Wall 2005: 82).

More problematic is the issue of the cathedral's repair. As early as 1608 King James had termed the condition of the cathedral a 'scandal'. In March 1620 he made a special visit to the cathedral, following which he attended a sermon at Paul's Cross, where Donne's friend, Bishop John King, urged a renewal of efforts to repair the cathedral. A survey was begun in April; in November, the King appointed a royal commission to enquire into required repairs; and a national campaign to raise funds was begun (Higgott 174; Carpenter 156–8). Money was received and a 'large quantity' of stone was purchased by Bishop Mountain (Higgott 174), but there things stalled. Even though the 1620 survey indicated that the south side of the choir, including the 'Dean's Chappell', was 'most in need of repair', there is no evidence that Donne stirred himself at any point on behalf of the repair (ibid. 175; Bald 1970: 402). By 1627 one benefactor was permitted to withdraw his funds and reinvest them in the East India Company (Keene, Burns, and Saint 57). Even before Donne's death, Laud, who became Bishop of London in 1628, instituted new mechanisms leading to rebuilding, circumventing the Dean and Chapter entirely (Higgott 175).

Ill. 35.I.2. Signatures and seals of Bishop Mountain, John Donne, and Sir Anthony Browne, 1622. Detail from Essex County PRO MS D/DBg1/27. In a 2004 article, John N. Wall, who located the seals, notes that this is the only occasion, as far as we know 'in which Donne's legal training was of direct use in his career subsequent to his loss of his job as secretary to Sir Thomas Egerton'. (*John Donne Journal*, 23 [2004]: 257.) (Reproduced by courtesy of Essex Public Record Office.)

As Dean, Donne was drawn into new activities. In 1622 he attended to the drafting of a new charter for Brentwood School, a task left uncompleted by previous deans (Wall 2004: 263–86). Further evidence of Donne's interest in the international Protestant cause came that May, when he was made an honorary member of the Virginia Company. A great many of his acquaintances and friends were subscribers—Pembroke was the second-largest investor in the Company, and over twenty were active in the Company's affairs (Bald 1970: 435–6; Cain 2001: 443; Sandler 272–3; Stater 742). The July following Donne became a member of the council, joining his close friends Christopher Brooke, Sir John Danvers, and Sir Thomas Roe (S. M. Johnson 1947: 128, 130; Sandler 272–3). Donne had known, of course, about the interest of his friends in the Virginia Company for a good many years, in some cases perhaps as early as the formation of the Company (Cain 2001: 442–4). Donne, in the event, supported the Company's efforts energetically, attended numerous meetings of the council, and, in November 1622, delivered a subtly nuanced Sermon at the Company's annual feast, one renegotiating reigning colonialist rhetorics and redirecting common assumptions about the Company's mission (Cain 2001; Sandler 280, 286–7; Shami 2004). He strongly supported the Company's current leaders (among them Sir Edwin Sandys and Nicholas Ferrar), urging them 'to continue a good worke' even in difficult times, and insisted upon the Company's 'Apostolicall' (not commercial) mission in the New World, one respecting the humanity of the native Virginians. The real wealth to be obtained in Virginia, he reminded his auditors, was a 'glorious harvest' of souls: 'O, if you would be as ready to hearken at the returne of a *Ship*, how many *Indians* were converted to *Christ Iesus*, as what Trees, or druggs, or Dyes that Ship had brought, then you were in your right way, and not till then' (Sandler 277–80, 286–7; *Sermons* 4.269, 280–2).

A more stressful assignment came his way that summer. Early in August 1622 the King issued *Directions for Preachers* and chose Donne to explain and defend them at Paul's Cross. The *Directions* marked a major shift in government policy. Protestant military defeats abroad at the hands of Catholic Habsburg forces and James's manoeuvres to arrange a Spanish match for his son, which led to a relaxation of punitive actions against recusants, alarmed English Protestants and had led to heated criticism of James's policies in the pulpit (Cogswell 18–20, 24–31, 52). At the same time, violent anti-papist sermons and, following the Synod of Dort, mounting disputes between Puritans, conforming theologians, and emerging Arminian theologians over issues of predestination and grace were also fuelling rancorous pulpit oratory (White 203–14; Shami 2003a: 64–6). The *Directions* were intended to curb such 'abuses and extravagancies' leading to 'schisme and dissention', and to silence 'bitter invectives... against the persones of eyther papists or puritans'. James would control the pulpits by restricting the content of sermons and by controlling the nature of pulpit discourse (Cogswell 27–33; Fincham 1994: 211–14).

Donne's job was to make the King's new policies palatable, particularly in light of the unexpected favouritism granted Catholics, the alarming numbers of conversions to Catholicism, the audacious recent behaviour of Catholics in Westminster, and widespread fears that the King himself would turn Catholic (Cogswell 31–4, 44–5, 138, 284; White 210; Questier 1993: 348–9; Shami 2003a: 98–9, 102, 104, 106, 106 n.14, 108–9; 1995b: 26–7). Matters were indeed tense: Thomas Winniffe, Donne's close colleague at St Paul's, had been committed to the Tower in April for strong anti-Catholic remarks concerning the Palatinate (Chamberlain 2.432). Donne most likely was chosen because he was not overly identified with any party, and his Sermon was much anticipated (Norbrook 22; Shami 1995b: 25). On 15 September Donne delivered his Sermon before (he wrote to Sir Henry Goodere) 'as great a Congregation as ever I saw together' (*Letters* 231). His complexly structured and carefully nuanced Sermon on a strange text was a masterful presentation defending the King's person and policies while preserving his own conscience through subtle phrasings and allusions to contrary material (Morrissey 167–71; A. Patterson 1984: 106–7; Shami 1995b: 28–31). Not everyone was satisfied, but the King was delighted with the performance and ordered Donne to print the Sermon (Chamberlain 2.451; *TMC* 303–4). It was the first of his Sermons to be published, and it was dedicated, at Doncaster's advice, to Buckingham. Interest in the Sermon was intense, and it ran to three issues (*Sermons* 4.33–4).

Securing the Deanery of St Paul's provided Donne with a handsome financial base such as he had probably never known (Bald 1970: 319, 424–7), but that foundation was periodically threatened by sickness. Donne was afflicted throughout his final years by severe bouts of illness. He was attended at such times by some of the finest physicians of the age, among them Sir Theodore Turquet de Mayerne and Simeon Fox, a great admirer of the Dean, and one who later generously paid for his funeral monument (Walton 1670: 74, 79–80; *TMC* 342, 350; Bald 1970: 452, 533). An attack of 'relapsing fever' at the end of November 1623, lasting several months, brought him to the edge of death. Concerned for the future, Donne quickly completed negotiations for a marriage between his daughter Constance and the actor Edward Alleyn, who married at Camberwell early in December. The marriage had been brokered by Donne's brother-in-law, Sir Thomas Grymes, and must have been sought by Constance herself (Bald 1970: 448–50; J. Stubbs 407–16).

The life-threatening experience also drove Donne to intense literary activity. The result was entered in the *Stationers' Register* on 9 January 1624 as *Devotions upon Emergent Occasions*, one of his finest creations. Donne also turned to poetry, both in Latin for a poem composed specifically for the *Devotions* (Webber 1968: 19–20; Novarr 1980: 161–75; Papazian 1991) and in English for *Father*, and, quite possibly, *Sickness*. Here, as throughout his life, an 'emergent occasion' electrified his imagination. Donne also pondered the meaning of his illness acutely, and he exploited the analogy of King Hezekiah in the *Devotions* to express his sense of divine preservation. God still wished to employ his talents, and he returned to his ministry with vigour.

Effort was required. Shortly after receiving printed copies of the *Devotions* in February 1624 he must have learned of the failing health of Dr Thomas White, one of the residentiaries living in the cathedral precincts (Bald 1970: 389, 391). White was also vicar of the parish of St Dunstan-in-the-West, whose patron, the Earl of Dorset, had evidently promised the living to Donne some time before (Walton 1670: 47). Donne had probably known Dorset for well over a decade, for the Earl and his brother became the friends of Edward Herbert as well as Donne; by 1617 Dorset was also on intimate terms with Philip Herbert, Doncaster, and the Countess of Bedford (E. Herbert 1976: 60, 81–2; Clifford 60). Once again we encounter long associations possibly originating in the Herbert households (Bald 1970: 184–5, 294–5, 318, 324). Donne may also have prepared for his upcoming efforts through presentation copies, for Buckingham received a copy of the *Devotions* and Dorset may have received another (*TMC* 296–7, 300–3; Bald 1970: 455).

Time was of the essence. The Earl was ill, and Donne clearly roused himself to secure the presentation to St Dunstan's and to prepare for his future duties as vicar. On 4 March he had a meeting with the parish's churchwardens. His official dispensation to hold two cures, his right as a royal chaplain, was pushed through on 9 March, 'by the order of the Lord Duke of Buckingham', and he gained possession of his new benefice on 18 March, ten days before his patron's death (Bald 1970: 455–8). Donne's health, meanwhile, rebounded by the end of March, and he returned to the pulpit with joy. On 28 March he preached on Easter at St Paul's, and within a month he had preached at least twice more at his new parish of St Dunstan-in-the-West (Bald 1970: 455; *Sermons* 6.81, 95).

Donne now entered his most vigorous period as a minister, and his most lucrative one. Exact figures are not available, but R. C. Bald estimated that the combined incomes of Donne's various positions (including St Dunstan's and the prebend of Chiswick) meant that Donne probably now earned more than £2,000 annually, a sizeable income for his time, and Donne indeed died a wealthy man (Bald 1970: 382, 426, 524). But Donne had not rushed to gain St Dunstan's for income. Years later he affirmed that he made 'not a shilling profit of S. *Dunstans* as a Church man'. The Earl of Dorset had bargained hard, and gave Donne 'the lease of the Impropriation, for a certain rent, and a higher rent, the[n] my predecessor had it at' (*Letters* 318). Following his near-fatal illness Donne sought a more personal care of souls, broader pastoral connections than his service at St Paul's and brief visits to his rural benefices could supply. So he announced in his first Sermon at St Dunstan's that his service was to be 'a *personall* service, not to be done always by *Proxy*, and *Delegates*'; that his duty was to root the congregation in God's 'holy obedience, and his rich, and honourable service'; and that 'the sinnes of *this Parish*, will ly upon my shoulders, if I be *silent*, or if I be *indulgent*, and denounce not Gods Judgement upon those sinnes' (*Sermons* 6.83–5). Imagining a parishioner at the edge of death, he averred, 'If he be not able to make a good account, he and I are in danger, because I have not enabled him; and though he be for himself able, that delivers not me, if I have been no instrument for the doing of it' (ibid. 6.86). Donne sought interaction on a deep personal level, and St Dunstan's fulfilled his wish. He entered the activities of the parish enthusiastically, worked closely with the vestrymen, and oversaw two major building campaigns involving the repositioning of the pulpit and the installment of new pews (B. W. Whitlock 1955a and b; Bald 1970: 458–63, 483, 489–90, 497, 504).

Donne was, in fact, at full stretch as a preacher, although much remains vague concerning specific times and locations. Walton, who knew Donne in his final years, asserted that he 'usually preached once a week, if not oftner', and provided a detailed description of his weekly preparations (1670: 61). Donne was unquestionably busy in the pulpit, with responsibilities at St Paul's, at St Dunstan's, at court as a royal chaplain, and at his country parishes in the summers, not to mention the miscellaneous Sermons preached at Paul's Cross by the Bishop's command or at the request of numerous friends and patrons. Preaching in this period of heated controversy, however, was always a delicate matter. In general, Donne's discreet handling of controversial issues kept him free from trouble; but once, in early 1627, he badly miscalculated his message. Bishop Laud, the newly appointed Dean of the Chapel Royal, detected matter offensive to King Charles (and himself) in a Sermon at court, and Donne spent several anxious days before the King forgave him 'certain slips'. Thereafter Donne was even more careful, and this seems to have been his only brush with his superiors (Bald 1970: 401–4; McCullough 2003b: 198–202).

The printed Sermons provide merely the barest indication of Donne's pulpit appearances, and a number of assumptions made about those activities are inaccurate or partial. Donne's Sermon for All Saints' Day in 1623 has survived. Donne's editors maintain that it was delivered at St Paul's (*Sermons* 10.7), but the diary of Sir Simonds D'Ewes contains the entry: 'All Saints Day [1623] falling upon this saturday, I did little, only I heard Doctor Dunne in the morning at Lincolns Inn' (D'Ewes 1974: 168). In fact D'Ewes did hear Donne at St Paul's later that month, on the twenty-third, an otherwise unrecorded Sermon (ibid. 171). The first entry also calls into question the assumption that Donne's preaching at Lincoln's Inn terminated in early 1622 (Bald 1970: 383). It suggests instead that Donne may well have continued to preach there irregularly throughout his final period. Contemporary jottings by John Burley reveal that in 1625 Donne delivered Sermons at Chelsea, possibly at Chelsea College, perhaps an extended series upon the Penitential Psalm 6 (Stanwood 1978). And although few of Donne's Sermons at St Dunstan's survive, Donne insisted in a Letter to a friend at the end of his life that 'my witnesse is in heaven, that I never left out *S. Dunstans*, when I was able to do them that service; nor will now' (*Letters* 317–18). It is clearly time to reinvestigate Donne's preaching, and such work will necessarily involve the redating and reconsideration of numerous Sermons (Lein 2004: 216–17; Matar; McCullough 2003b: 180–2, 183–6; 2003a: 193–4; Sellin 1983).

Donne's Letters, activities, and Sermons also reveal the extraordinary breadth of his social world during these years. Donne was a prized visitor in numerous aristocratic households. He could count the earls of Bedford, Bridgewater, Carlisle, Dorset, Exeter, Huntingdon, Kent, Montgomery, and Pembroke and their wives among his good acquaintance, and many of his occasional Sermons were delivered at private occasions for them. He could number bishops and future bishops such as John King, Thomas Morton, and Joseph Hall as good friends. Donne was likewise intimate with numerous members of the households of the kings and queens of England, men such as Sir Robert Ker. To these figures we can add numerous titled friends, many of them legal figures, such as Sir John Hoskins, Sir Henry Marten, Sir Julius Caesar, now Master of the Rolls, and Sir Henry Hobart, Lord Chief Justice of the Common Pleas, as well as numerous diplomats, native and foreign, preeminently Sir Henry Wotton, Sir Thomas Roe, Sir Robert Killigrew, Sir Walter Aston, and Constantijn Huygens, with whom he had a particularly influential friendship in the early 1620s (Bachrach; Daley 1991; Larson 1992; Sellin 1982).

In some of these families, particularly those of Sir Robert Killigrew and Magdalen Herbert, Donne was now a common household guest (Bald 1970: 441). Donne enjoyed a particularly vibrant friendship throughout these years with Magdalen Herbert, her husband, Sir John Danvers, and her sons Edward and George (A. Charles 34–5, 46, 56, 64–5, 118–19). Danvers, a dedicated member of the council of the Virginia Company, was doubtless instrumental in interesting Donne in the Virginia Company, and was one of those sent by the council to persuade Donne to deliver his Sermon in 1622 (Powers-Beck 193–211; Bald 1970: 435–6). When the plague struck London in 1625, Donne lodged with Magdalen and her family (including George) in Chelsea, using the occasion to copy out many Sermons for future printing (TNA, SP 16/10/28. fo. 47; Bald 1970: 471–6). Edward and George Herbert were both Donne's poetic disciples, and Donne and George may have exchanged poems in these years (Bald 1970: 184; Malcolmson 2004: 25–30). When Magdalen died in 1627 Donne was the family's firm choice to preach her funeral Sermon.

Donne's service at St Dunstan's advanced a quite different range of friendships. From the outset Donne strove to deepen his associations with members of the parish. He made concerted efforts to attend vestry meetings, where closer relations were formed with leaders in the parish community, particularly at the tavern celebrations where he was found following these meetings (B. W. Whitlock 1955a and b). Service at St Dunstan's likewise allowed Donne to remain on easy, intimate terms with the region's lawyers, a large group including those whom he had cared for as Reader at Lincoln's Inn, friends from his youthful days, such as Christopher Brooke and Sir Robert Rich, and more recent acquaintances such as John Selden whom he also met when visiting the Earl of Kent at Wrest (Bald 1970: 438). Donne was already known to many of the stationers in the parish, which, with the exception of the region about St Paul's, could boast the largest concentration of printers and booksellers in the capital (Bald 1965: 69–80). Among the most important figures here are the printer John Marriot, who after Donne's death would see most of Donne's works through the press, and Izaak Walton, the tradesman who became the friend of Donne and of many of Donne's own friends and penned the first biography of the Dean, one of the monuments of seventeenth-century literature.

Donne's activities and social interactions were thus complex and far-ranging, particularly after his return to London following the plague, early in 1626. His professional stature then is conveniently documented by his selection to serve as Prolocutor in the Convocation that met a month after his return (Bald 1970: 481–3; Shami 2003c: 35–41). Several responses to Donne's election and subsequent oration at the opening of this Convocation have recently been recovered and reveal the high regard in which he was held. Leonard Mawe, the Master of Peterhouse, Cambridge, introduced Donne on that occasion as a man 'endowed with all the gifts of genius' and pronounced him to be 'the Chrysostom of his age'. Elaborating on his qualifications, Mawe praised Donne first as a poet ('Versus pangit? nemo felicius'), then celebrated his capabilities as an orator, controversialist, and artful preacher. Samuel Harsnett, the Bishop of Norwich, speaking next, contended that when Donne left the university, 'all the muses, all the artes, all learning did accompeny him thence' (Bawcutt and Kelliher 443). Such reactions by eminent clerical contemporaries confirm that Donne was widely recognized by his peers for his learning and eloquence. Prolocutors, furthermore, were chosen by the bishops (Bray 8: 3, 91, 5, 142, 160). The lavish praise extended to Donne by Mawe (a future bishop of Bath and Wells) and Harsnett indicates that Donne was clearly seen as an eminent candidate for a bishopric himself. In fact, service as Prolocutor made that future quite likely. As Donne must have known, men elected to that office in the early seventeenth century customarily advanced to bishoprics (Bray 8.3, 91, 5, 142, 160). It hardly seems accidental in this light that in his virtuoso Latin oration Donne, following Mawe's lead, considered bishops as 'stellas maioris magnitudinis', though an eyewitness noted that he did not go so far in his hyperbolic praise of bishops as did Mawe (Bawcutt and Kelliher 443). Donne may have been ambitious, desirous to help his church in contentious times (Bald 1970: 482–3), yet we should recollect Kenneth Fincham's observation that '[a]mbition and piety need not be regarded as strange bedfellows', and recall his examples of bishopric-hunters who subsequently supplied model pastoral and spiritual leadership (1990: 33–4). Donne's reputation for learning, respect for sober consultative debate, and distaste for personal attacks, moreover, were doubtless critical in moderating issues threatening to divide the delegates during the session (Shami 2003c: 37–59).

Additional recognition came Donne's way in 1626 when he was chosen one of the governors of Charterhouse. The group that elected Donne included Archbishop Abbot; Thomas Coventry, Lord Keeper of the Privy Seal; George Mountain, Bishop of London; Donne's friend, Sir Henry Marten, Dean of the Arches; and the Earl of Pembroke (R. C. Evans 1989b: 134–5). Donne became a dedicated and energetic governor until the very end of his life, serving continuously on committees of the Charterhouse (Bald 1970: 424, 528; R. C. Evans 1989b: 138–46). Pembroke and the Archbishop doubtless played a role in Donne's election, and Donne's steady service at Charterhouse and at court again highlights his sustained association with Pembroke and his family throughout his final period. Philip Herbert succeeded his brother as Lord Chamberlain in 1626, so Donne's activities as a royal chaplain regularly brought them together. In 1627 Donne, William Herbert, and Philip Herbert all served as judges on the High Commission at the Bishop of London's palace in the complicated, sensational case of Lady Frances Purbeck, where all three voted with the majority to convict her of adultery (Bald 1970: 419–22; Bowen 398–410, 529–31; J. Stubbs 430–1). A few months later Philip himself was elected a governor of Charterhouse, where Donne worked with both brothers until the end of his life (R. C. Evans 1989*b*: 142–6). That Philip, like William, much appreciated Donne's Sermons is made certain by Donne's repeated appearance on the Lenten rota; as Lord Chamberlain he alone appointed the Lenten preachers, many of them distasteful to Laud (Fincham 2000: 72, 74–5).

Prominent in the compliments lavished upon Donne at Convocation was recognition of his superlative command of civil, canon, and common law, learning likewise singled out by Bishop Richard Corbett in his epitaph for Donne (Corbett 89). Donne had demonstrated his mastery of this very learning as early as 1610 (*Pseudo-Martyr* xxxi–xxxvii; Adlington 2008*b*). During his final years he had reason to make use of it constantly. Donne was repeatedly appointed to serve on various ecclesiastical commissions. Bald supplies a meticulous account of these 'judicial activities', noting that 'it is not generally realized how much Donne himself needed the legal knowledge that he possessed and how often, after he became Dean, he had to act in a judicial capacity' (1970: 414–23; J. Stubbs 428–31). Bishops in Donne's time had a distinct need for such knowledge, and a note in the State Papers shows that Donne was indeed being considered for a bishopric during the summer before his death (Fincham 1990: 149 ff., esp. 157, 159; Bald 1970: 515, citing TNA, SP 16/172/114, Charles I/172, no. 114).

As for Donne the man, although some changes in his activities and behaviour emerge in this period, more things remain constant. His love of learning never wavered. '*He was earnest and unwearied in the search of knowledge*', Walton reports, observing further that the 'latter part of his life may be said to be a continued study' (1670: 81, 61). But Walton also stressed Donne's sociability, his habit of spending Saturdays visiting friends (ibid. 61; *TMC* 341). Among them were many women. Sir Richard Baker recorded that Donne, his 'old acquaintance', was 'a great visiter of Ladies' as a young man (Baker 156). Donne's interactions with the Countess of Bedford, Magdalen Herbert, and the Countess of Huntingdon (*Letters* 155, 176, 224–5, 236–7) confirm that Donne cultivated the company of women to the end of his life. He particularly enjoyed the conversation of Anne Clifford, the wife of his patron Richard Sackville, and later of Philip Herbert, professing '*That she knew well how to discourse of all things, from Predestination, to Slea-silk*' (*Sermons* 1.129–30; Rainbowe 38). It comes as no surprise, then, given Donne's inclinations, that Edward Alleyn recalled that at the deanery negotiations for his marriage were interrupted because Donne was 'cauld away by ye Coming off som Ladyes' (B. W. Whitlock 1955*c*: 367). Donne's Letters in his final decade to his '*noblest and lovingest Sister*', Ann Stanhope

(Mrs Cokayne), whom he had known for many years and had often visited at Ashbourne, are among his most intimate (*Letters* 316–18; *TMC*: 338–56; Bald 1970: 508–11; J. Stubbs 448–9).

Donne, Walton likewise observes, '*was by nature highly passionate*' (1670: 81), but he had learned to master and redirect his emotions. Walton stresses his assiduous balancing of contrary impulses: 'The melancholy and pleasant humor, were in him...contempered' (ibid. 80). He was a brilliant conversationalist: even decades later Constantijn Huygens recollected his 'golden words...Uttered among friends' (Bachrach 116), and he was generally amiable. 'His aspect *was chearful*', says Walton (1670: 80). Rarely do we find Donne erupting with violent emotion, 'being inflamed', as he was in 1625 during a wild altercation with Alleyn (J. Stubbs 411–13). For the most part Donne channelled his emotions into a passionate style of delivery for his Sermons: 'weeping sometimes for his Auditory, sometimes with them' (Walton 1670: 38). Still, we constantly sense tensions, ambiguities, contradictory impulses and motivations, conscious and unconscious ironic interplay in his life and writings, so that we never feel entirely certain of his opinions or feelings. Nonetheless, Donne strove to perfect a religious self, a self at peace with itself (at least in public), assured of its future (Papazian 1992: 610, 613–15).

There was a new element, however, to this persona, new perhaps from the period of the *Devotions*, an element born out of his experience, suffering, and recent affluence. Donne focused increasingly upon the Christian's need to extend charity whenever possible (R. C. Evans 1989*b*: 147–8). He supported poor ministers and poor students at the universities; he made loans to needy friends; he made periodic gifts to unfortunates in London prisons, freeing 'many' who languished there because they could not afford to pay 'their Fees or small Debts' (Walton 1670: 65). Donne's service as governor of Charterhouse, a charitable institution dedicated to the care of destitute men and young boys, must, in this light, have been profoundly satisfying (Shami 2003*c*: 58). But Walton notes an equally important aspect of Donne's charity. Donne paid 'a cheerful and frequent visitation [to] any friend whose mind was dejected, or his fortune necessitous' (1670: 65), a point substantiated by Donne's comment to Sir Thomas Roe in 1622, that he had 'assisted in the tyme of sicknes, and now attended at the funeralls' of Lady Jacob and Sir William Killigrew (TNA, SP 14/134, fo. 134^v). The biting elitism that found expression in Donne's earlier years (the contemptuous scorn of citizens and their wives, of country labourers, of the Lord Mayor, of men 'arm'd' with 'seely honesty' at court, and of the court itself, contaminated with 'th'extremitie / Of vice'), the mocking voice of *Metem*, which rejects all 'such Readers as I can teach', is gone, replaced by a rich and deep compassion. The resultant emphasis on charity in his Sermons and in his behaviour is a notable feature of his final years (*Sermons* 5.278–9; 8.155, 241–2, 246, 277–9, 289).

Donne's greatest achievement in his final years was the forging of an extraordinarily complex, 'almost unique brand of churchmanship', one not ascribable to any faction (George and George 68–9; J. Johnson 1999*b*: 10, 12, 39–40, 50, 146; McCullough 2003*a*: 191; Shami 2003*a*: 2). Again and again Donne struggles to define a 'middle way' between extremes, not simply between Roman Catholicism and extreme forms of Calvinism (Scodel 1995: 64–5), but equally between extreme factions within the Church of England itself (Shami 2003*b*: 157; 2003*c*: 53–6). Attempts to classify Donne as an absolutist have been met with demonstrations of Donne's extensive friendships with opposition leaders in Parliament and his insistence on the priesthood of all believers and the 'Christian liberty' men have 'to read the Scriptures at home' (A. Patterson 1990: 38–9, 56–7; Shami 2003*a*: 77; McCullough 2003*b*: 199–201; *Sermons* 7.401; but see Shuger, Ch. 39). Attempts to settle Donne within the Arminian camp have been strongly met by discussions of Donne's long friendships with leading Calvinists and by meticulous demonstrations of Donne's conformist Calvinist leanings in numerous crucial matters (Doerksen 2003: 12–27; Shami 2003*a*: 246; Sellin 1983: 6–7, 11–15; Narveson). Instead of denigrating Calvin, as was the practice of the anti-Calvinists, Donne, like other moderate English Calvinists, cites him as 'that great professor, and reader in Divinity' and praises 'his religious wisdome'; moreover, direct and favourable references to Calvin actually increase in the printed Sermons surviving from the reign of Charles (A. Milton 1995: 416–17, 424, 428–32; *Sermons* 7.210, 432; also 7.149, 160, 379, 430; 8.111, 143, 197, 316, 365; Reeves 2.47–8; Norbrook 22; Doerksen 2003: 23). Whereas anti-Calvinists like Richard Montague attacked and belittled the Synod of Dort (A. Milton 1995: 428, 430), Donne found in the 'blessed sobriety' of the Synod a method of dealing with doctrine and religious controversy that he deeply admired (*Sermons* 7.127, delivered before King Charles; Sellin 1983: 27–34), and discussions during the Synod contributed to his interest in the larger Protestant cause (Doerksen 2003: 23; Shami 2003*c*: 43, 48–9, 54, 56–7). Like many moderate English Calvinists, he moved away from extreme Calvinist concepts of predestination (see Shami, Ch. 24), and like British delegates to the Synod, he, too, openly rejects the 'rigid' positions of Piscator (A. Milton 1995: 535–6; 2005: xlvi–xlvii; *Sermons* 8.144, 151–2). He resists to the end, furthermore, the Roman Church's attempt to splinter the Protestant cause as well as Laudian efforts to isolate the English Church (A. Milton 1995: 446–7, 525–8). Instead of opposing Lutherans and Calvinists, he, like his friend Joseph Hall, regularly links these Reformed traditions to affirm a united, international Protestant cause (A. Milton 1995: 377–8, 389–90, 392; *Sermons* 2.206; 4.370, 373; 9.198–9, 363; 10.184).

Donne devoted himself to fashioning a theology for his church that would allow it to embrace the broadest range of Protestant believers, while preserving for himself a certain critical distance (Shami 2003*b*: 155–6; Scodel 1995: 67–70). Disliking 'singular' interpretations of Scripture, he likewise fashioned a scriptural theology based on conscientious and rigorous cross-referencing of Scripture and embracing the broadest range of Christian commentators, refusing to grant final authority to any one: 'no Scripture is of private interpretation' (Shami 2003*a*: 82, 87, 141; *Sermons* 3.210). The breadth of his friendships matched the breadth of his vision for his church. No faction could claim him entirely, and he staunchly repudiated the use of labels and 'personal revilings' (Shami 2003*b*; 2003*c*: 47–8). He insisted upon the necessity of communal worship—separatists were the true enemies of his church (Shami 2003*a*: 30, 92, 140), and he firmly maintained that within that church preaching the Word and the sacraments were equally necessary for salvation (*Sermons* 2.319–20; 3.210; 5.90; J. Johnson 1999*b*: 131–2). Nonetheless, certainly in comparison with Andrewes and Laud, it was preaching that fired Donne's imagination (Norbrook 23; McCullough 2003*a*: 197; 2003*b*: 192–3). 'Who but my selfe can conceive the sweetnesse of that salutation, when the Spirit of God says to me in a morning, Go forth to day and preach', he cried in 1626 (*Sermons* 7.133). '[I]f there be a discontinuing, or slackning of preaching', he pronounced, 'there is a danger of loosing Christ' (ibid. 7.157). Preaching is a debt a pastor owes to God, he informed his congregation at St Dunstan's, and the pastor must 'condemne himself' before the Bar in the court of Heaven 'if hee pay not this debt, performe not this duty, as often, as himself, knowes himselfe, to bee fit, and able to doe it' (ibid. 6.93). This was the code that governed his behaviour to the end of his life. If he had strength to deliver a sermon, though it meant his death, it was an obligation owing to God.

CHAPTER 35.II

DONNE, THE PATRIOT CAUSE, AND WAR, 1620–1629

SIMON HEALY

> No man is an *Iland*, intire of it selfe; every man is a peece of the *Continent*, a part of the *maine*; if a *Clod* bee washed away by the *Sea*, *Europe* is the lesse, as well as if a *Promontorie* were, as well as if a *Mannor* of thy *friends*, or of *thine owne* were; Any Mans *death* diminishes *me*, because I am involved in *Mankinde*: And therefore never send to know for whom the *bell* tolls; It tolls for *thee*.
>
> (*Devotions* 87)

DONNE's most famous lines were written as part of a spiritual meditation inspired by his own brush with death, but they also adumbrate a clear strategic viewpoint—that the survival of English Protestantism was threatened by Catholic enemies at home and on the continent, a position Donne maintained to the end of his life (Ch. 35.I; Simms 9-10; Papazian 2007).

At the time Donne wrote these lines (1623/4), this view was espoused by Prince Charles (dedicatee of the *Devotions*), the Duke of Buckingham (the royal favourite), and supporters of the 'patriot' cause, in opposition to the irenic, pacific, and largely pro-Spanish policy King James had pursued since 1604 (Gray and Shami 343–4). However, in politics and diplomacy, as in literature, words cannot always be taken at face value. In the autumn of 1623 Charles and Buckingham were very recent converts to the anti-Spanish cause, having hitherto supported James's quest for a negotiated settlement of the German war provoked by the Bohemian revolt of 1618 (see Ch. 34.II). Nor, of course, had James intended to become a Spanish dupe; but the collapse of the German Protestant Union in 1620–3 wrecked his over-ambitious plans to uphold the status quo in the Holy Roman Empire.

Englishmen who viewed domestic politics and international diplomacy in religious terms were particularly alarmed by the keystone of James's diplomacy, his plan to marry Prince Charles to a Habsburg princess. The price for such a match was widely (and correctly) assumed to be toleration for English Catholics, whose freedom of worship was circumscribed by recusancy laws draconian in their intent, though inconsistently enforced. Matrimony was the most intimate of royal prerogatives, and it was difficult to discuss Charles's marriage publicly—James dismissed the 1621 Parliament for doing so. But criticism of Jacobean statecraft poured almost unchecked from press and pulpit in the early 1620s. The most vituperative pieces were published anonymously, while those (such as Donne) who enjoyed a prominent public profile were generally more circumspect in expressing their views; but the very name of 'patriot' adopted by James's critics implied that a pro-Spanish policy was unpatriotic.

However, it should be remembered that not all of those who disagreed with royal policies shared the apocalyptic fears voiced by extremists, and many who were neither Catholic sympathizers nor pro-Spanish had reservations about the likely cost, duration, and outcome of a war against the Catholic powers of Europe. The obvious solution to this problem was an alliance with Catholic France, vigorously pursued by Charles and Buckingham in 1624–6; Donne's Sermons supported this initiative, and his links to the Herbert affinity reinforce the possibility of his having pro-French sympathies. Nevertheless, it is hard to be definitive about Donne's views on diplomacy. Although many of his public pronouncements came to the attention of the court and the City of London, particularly the Sermons he preached from St Paul's Cross, Donne did not aspire to mould or lead public opinion—probably more from choice than fear—except when that role was thrust upon him, in his Sermon of 15 September 1622 (see Chs. 35.I and 24). He was always an intelligent and well-informed commentator, but his cautious approach stands in contrast to that of his less literary-minded but more politically ambitious counterpart, John Williams, Dean of Westminster.

The Bohemian crisis, 1618–1621

King James's widely publicised quest for peace in Western Europe suited the temper of the times during the middle of his reign as king of England, coinciding with the twelve years' truce between the Spanish and Dutch (from 1609), while the assassination of Henri IV of France in 1610 reduced the likelihood of French aggression.

James seized the opportunity to forge links with both sides of the confessional divide, marrying his daughter Elizabeth to Elector Friedrich V of the Palatinate, leader of the German Calvinist princes, and seeking a commensurate match between his surviving son Charles, and a Catholic bride from Spain, France, Tuscany, or Savoy.

Peace was, however, very much the exception in early modern Europe, and the twelve years' truce was punctuated by a series of crises, one of the most acute being the Arminian controversy in the Netherlands, which began as a theological quarrel about predestination, with Jacobus Arminius, professor of theology at Leiden University, maintaining that Calvin's successors were unwise to reject any role for human free will in the pursuit of salvation. This prompted a broader debate about church/state relations in the United Provinces, which was abruptly terminated in 1618 with the overthrow of the pro-Arminian peace party in the province of Holland. James, rather uncharacteristically, supported the Dutch hawks, particularly in upholding Calvinist doctrine at the Synod of Dort (1618–19), which was attended by an English delegation. James could not afford to see the United Provinces disintegrate only a few years before the expiry of the truce with Spain; and theologians in the Church of England had their own differences about predestination, which the King did not wish to exacerbate (Ch. 34.II; Sellin 1988; A. Milton 2005; Nobbs).

While a resumption of war was expected upon the expiry of the twelve years' truce in April 1621, hostilities actually commenced almost three years earlier, in May 1618, with a rebellion by the largely Protestant nobility of Bohemia against their new king, Archduke Ferdinand von Habsburg, who initially struggled to suppress this insurrection. Following the death of the Emperor Mathias in March 1619, the Bohemian estates deposed Ferdinand as king and offered the crown to Elector Friedrich of the Palatinate. This constituted a massive provocation to the Habsburgs, particularly as it took place only two days before Ferdinand was elected emperor. To James's dismay—he never acknowledged his son-in-law as King of Bohemia—Friedrich accepted this offer in September 1619, thus turning a local upheaval into a German crisis (Wilson 269–85; Pursell 2003: 66–80).

By this point James had already sent the diplomat Viscount Doncaster to Germany (Donne, his chaplain, preached before Friedrich and Elizabeth at Heidelberg), where he secured little more than empty promises of cooperation from Ferdinand and Friedrich (Pursell 2003: 82; Sellin 1988; Bald 1986: 351–2). Back in England, many endorsed the Dutch view that 'it is better to begin the change with advantage than disadvantage' (Carleton to Chamberlain, in Carleton 271); in 1619–20 around 4,000 English volunteers journeyed to Bohemia and the Palatinate on their own initiative and at their own expense; voluntary contributions solicited by the Palatine agent in England from March 1620 may have raised as much as £70,000 (Pursell 2003: 80–3, 102, 109). With no funds for an army of his own, James's diplomatic initiatives amounted to little more than ostentatious sabre-rattling, as his domestic critics were quick to observe. In the best-selling pamphlet *Vox Populi*, the cleric Thomas

Scott credibly portrayed James as a Habsburg dupe, talking peace while his enemies prepared for a renewal of hostilities. The military situation came to a head on 29 October/8 November 1620, when Habsburg and Bavarian forces routed Friedrich's army at the battle of the White Mountain outside Prague. Meanwhile, Spanish forces, operating under Imperial instructions, entered Friedrich's lands on the Rhine (the Lower Palatinate), where they confronted German and English troops (Wilson 294–307, 314–16; Pursell 2003: 105–6, 113).

Even before news of the disaster in Bohemia reached England, the Spanish incursion into Friedrich's hereditary lands persuaded James to call a Parliament, the first since the ill-fated 1614 session. This summons offered the prospect of a more aggressive stance against the Habsburgs, although a proclamation forbidding public debate on matters of state—which Donne endorsed in a Sermon preached at this time—suggested otherwise (Larkin 1.495–6; *Sermons* 3.166–7). Most unusually, the Commons swiftly voted two subsidies (£140,000) at the start of the session, a sum insufficient to raise a fresh army but adequate to support the existing English and German garrisons in the Palatinate. The price for this timely infusion of cash was an investigation into courtiers holding lucrative monopoly patents, initially focusing on Buckingham's relative Sir Giles Mompesson, who fled to France and was impeached by Parliament *in absentia*, the first prosecution of this kind since 1459 (Russell 1979: 89–91, 105–7).

Donne offered his own warning about Mompesson's abuses in a Sermon at court two weeks after the impeachment: 'do not drink the cup of Babylon, lest thou drink the cup of God's wrath too' (*Sermons* 3.239; Shami 2003*a*: 91). Meanwhile Buckingham, taking Dean Williams's advice to 'swim with the tide', quickly disowned Mompesson; but after Easter the Commons claimed a much bigger scalp, that of Lord Chancellor St Alban (Francis Bacon), who was impeached, fined £40,000, and banished from court. Everyone knew that Buckingham lay at the centre of the web of court patronage from which these corrupt practices sprang, but at this stage even James struggled to restrain his parliamentary critics. The tide finally turned on 1 May, when the former Attorney-General, Sir Henry Yelverton, under investigation before the House of Lords, compared Buckingham to Edward II's odious favourite Hugh Despenser. Prince Charles, outraged by the suggestion that his father governed in a manner likely to cost him the crown, interrupted Yelverton, whose disgrace soon followed, leading Buckingham (somewhat prematurely) to pronounce himself 'Parliament-proof' (Hacket 1.49–50; Zaller 73–90, 117–20; Chamberlain 2.374). The entire court breathed a sigh of relief, as did Donne, whose quest for ecclesiastical preferment may have been delayed by this political crisis; he remained in London over the summer, soliciting Buckingham and possibly Williams (Bacon's successor as Lord Keeper of the Great Seal), and was eventually appointed Dean of St Paul's in November (Bald 1986: 374–81; BL, MS Egerton 2594, fo. 109; Ch. 35.I).

Meanwhile, on the continent the battle of White Mountain destroyed the Protestant cause in Bohemia. The 'Winter King' and his Queen fled into exile at The

Hague, while in January 1621 Ferdinand placed Friedrich under an Imperial ban, by which he forfeited his lands and titles. However, the Spanish inability to disengage from the Palatinate, and the death of Felipe III of Spain on 21/31 March 1621, meant that Spain resumed hostilities with the Dutch without a grand offensive (Wilson 314–20, 331–2). During this military hiatus English diplomats helped to arrange a ceasefire that preserved part of the Lower Palatinate in Protestant hands, while at Westminster the Commons, chafing at their impotence, victimized a Catholic lawyer who had rejoiced at the news of White Mountain. More positively, on 4 June, before they rose for the summer, MPs passed a motion, widely distributed abroad as propaganda, promising their 'lives and estates' to the Palatine cause (TNA, SP 84/101, fo. 141^v; Zaller 104–14, 136–7; Russell 1979: 117–20). The military tempo picked up in September, when Friedrich's last field army, commanded by Count Mansfeld, was ejected from the Upper Palatinate, and the Spanish attacked the Dutch on the Lower Rhine (Wilson 331–3; Pursell 2000). James, justifiably alarmed, recalled Parliament in November in pursuit of a further vote of cash, although he confided to the Spanish ambassador, Gondomar, that it would be dissolved if debate strayed beyond the relief of the Palatinate—as (with Buckingham's connivance) it did. The arrest of three MPs and the dissolution of Parliament that followed (February 1622) sent a clear message to Madrid that James intended to resolve this crisis by diplomatic means (Russell 1979: 135–6, 142–3; Lockyer 109).

The Spanish Match and the 'Blessed Revolution', 1622–1624

At the start of the 1622 campaign season Friedrich rejoined Mansfeld's army in the Lower Palatinate; but Spanish and Bavarian forces chased them out of the area in June, and set about reducing the three remaining Protestant strongholds. Following heavy casualties, the Anglo-German garrison of Heidelberg surrendered on 5/15 September, and that of Mannheim on 23 October/2 November (Wilson 333–9). James was furious with his son-in-law for undermining his plan for a negotiated settlement; he intended that Prince Charles should marry the Spanish Infanta Maria, whose brother, Felipe IV of Spain, would then withdraw his troops from the Lower Palatinate and persuade Emperor Ferdinand to remove the Bavarians from the Upper Palatinate.

Donne was deeply attached to Princess Elizabeth, to whom he sent copies of his works throughout the 1620s, and it seems likely that his *Lam* was composed in response to the fall of Heidelberg (Daley 1991; Papazian 2007: 284–5; Bald 1986: 327 n. 1). Donne's Letters and Sermons from this period also contain numerous references to military affairs (*Sermons* 4.157; 5.75; *Letters* 154–9, 165–7, 211–12, 229–32), and in February 1622, as Dean of St Paul's, he contributed £15 to the benevolence promoted among taxpayers as a gesture of support for the Palatine cause; while controversial, this levy raised almost £89,000, a sum equal to the subsidy James had lost by dissolving Parliament (TNA, SP 14/156; Cust 157).

James's decision to pursue a Spanish Match provoked rancorous protests from many quarters, particularly the London pulpits and presses, prompting much private speculation about likely developments (Cogswell 20–35). In August 1622, in order to prove his good faith to Felipe IV, James declared an amnesty for at least 170 English Catholic prisoners and ordered the recusancy laws against lay Catholics suspended (Questier 2009: 32–3, 150–3). At the same time, to avert some of the inevitable storm of protest, Archbishop Abbot issued a set of directions barring all clergymen under the rank of dean from debating matters of political or theological controversy, or using 'bitter inuectives' against 'either Papist or Puritan' (Abbot). Donne was selected to endorse these directions in a Sermon at Paul's Cross on 15 September, partly because this task came within his purview as Dean, and partly because he had always stressed that preachers should avoid courting controversy for its own sake (see Ch. 35.I; for a full discussion of this Sermon's context, see Shami 2003*a*: 75–101). This task would probably have been simpler for a cleric more sympathetic to the Spanish Match, such as Lord Keeper Williams, but Donne's links to pro-French courtiers such as Doncaster, Pembroke, and the Herberts sent an important message: his public endorsement of a policy that cut across his personal inclinations demonstrated that James would brook no disputation over this point (for an explication of Donne's rhetorical handling of this complex moment, see Shami 2003*a*: 107 n. 17, and Ch. 35.I).

Donne turned in a creditable performance, freely admitting that 'to take away preaching were to disarm God', but warning that 'when there is not an uniform, a comely, an orderly presenting of matters of faith…preaching in the church comes to be as pleading at the bar, and not so well'. Stressing that the King had acted after consultation with the bishops, Donne insisted that preachers would still be able to engage in responsible debate using the fundamentals of faith: the catechism, the Thirty-Nine Articles, and the Homilies (*Sermons* 4.192, 195, 197, 200–8). However, neither this Sermon nor Abbot's preaching directive staunched the flow of debate about the wisdom of Jacobean diplomacy.

For all the public clamour, royal policy over the match was decided by James, Charles, and Buckingham, and so long as this triumvirate remained in agreement there was little anyone else could do to effect a change. Negotiations with Spain were further complicated on 13/23 February 1623, when Emperor Ferdinand granted Friedrich's electoral title and most of his lands to Duke Maximilian of Bavaria, making an amicable resolution of the Palatine question almost impossible. The Spanish ambassador to the Empire, fearing the rise of Bavaria as a threat to the House of Austria, boycotted the transfer ceremony, and James took advantage of this tension by ordering the English garrison at Frankenthal to yield to Spanish, rather than Bavarian, forces in March 1623 (Wilson 340, 355–6; Pursell 2003: 201–10; Redworth 56–7, 73).

By this stage Charles, believing that his marriage treaty was almost concluded, had seized the initiative from his father by departing incognito for Madrid to collect his bride, arriving in March 1623, accompanied only by Buckingham and five gentleman servants. Many Spaniards, as well as the English ambassador, John Digby, Earl of Bristol, initially assumed that Charles would announce his conversion to Catholicism in the congenial surroundings of the Spanish court. This was never Charles's intention, even though various courtiers back in England, including Buckingham's wife and mother, did convert, presumably in hopes of securing places in the Infanta's household. Charles's sojourn forced Felipe IV to declare his intentions, but even though James signed a secret agreement in July 1623 conceding further toleration for English Catholics, Felipe declined to assist Friedrich in securing the restitution of the Palatinate and his electoral title. Realizing that they would never achieve the main aim of the negotiations, Charles and Buckingham left Madrid at the end of August; the Prince's arrival home just over a month later provoked widespread and spontaneous rejoicing (Redworth 73–133; Cogswell 6–12, 60–2; W. B. Patterson 328–30).

On their return, Charles and Buckingham persuaded a reluctant king to halt the marriage negotiations, but James did not share their new-found desire for a 'Blessed Revolution' that would place England at the head of the pan-European Protestant cause. In order to force his hand, the Prince and Duke secured the summons of a fresh Parliament, which convened in February 1624. They laid the groundwork for a successful session by assembling a 'patriot' coalition of anti-Spanish courtiers and MPs, men whose opinions James had striven to ignore for the past two years (Cogswell 77–105). James realistically (but unhelpfully) warned Parliament that war would require a grant of £750,000, but when MPs voted £300,000 for defensive preparations—fortifications, the navy, the defence of Ireland, and an alliance with the Dutch—he broke off negotiations with Spain. Further pressure brought him to order the full enforcement of the recusancy laws, a significant obstacle to the resumption of marriage negotiations with Spain, while Dutch representatives were invited to London to discuss a military alliance (ibid. 114–21, 166–226).

The strains of war, 1624–1626

The breach with Spain met with widespread domestic approval, but James stopped short of direct hostilities. In the summer of 1624 an English force of 6,000 troops was sent to the Netherlands, but only as auxiliaries under Dutch command.

Meanwhile, the French were offered a marriage alliance with Prince Charles in return for a joint expedition to reconquer the Palatinate: early in 1625 an Anglo-French army commanded by Count Mansfeld gathered in the Netherlands, but this force was not permitted to intervene in the Spanish siege of the Dutch stronghold of Breda. For all that the French wished to see the Habsburgs weakened, they could hardly concede a marriage treaty without securing concessions for English Catholics, and thus the recusancy laws were relaxed as quickly as they had been reimposed—a consequence many of the patriots had overlooked in their enthusiasm for a French alliance (Cogswell 265–81; Lockyer 198–210).

Open war with Spain became possible only following the death of King James in March 1625. Perhaps in anticipation of this, the Sermon Donne preached before the new King Charles on 3 April (the first Sunday of the reign) was notably anti-Catholic, although, as the *Directions* required, it did not descend to personal abuse. Donne conceded that matters of state should be debated only 'In those Councells, where Lawes are made or reformed'—in other words, in a Parliament such as Charles had already resolved to summon (Shami 2003*a*: 269–71; *Sermons*, 6.253, 259). The arrival in England of Charles's French bride, Henrietta Maria, shortly before Parliament convened, raised justifiable suspicions of a secret agreement over toleration for Catholics. This suspicion, and a growing threat from the plague, led the Commons to vote only two subsidies (£128,000), a deliberately miserly contribution towards a war. Charles undertook to enforce the recusancy laws—a promise he kept—and Buckingham worked hard behind the scenes to secure more money, but the Commons' repeated refusal to increase their initial offer led to a swift dissolution of Parliament in August (Russell 1979: 204–59). In fact, the immediate financial crisis was swiftly rectified with the arrival of £120,000 from France—half the new Queen's dowry—and an amphibious force set sail for Spain in October.

Against all the odds, the English achieved tactical surprise with a landing near Cadiz, but failed to press home their attack and returned home with little to show for their efforts; the Spanish retaliated by unleashing their privateers on English shipping. English plans to reconquer the Palatinate also evaporated: Mansfeld's forces, lacking both funds and an operational base, were crippled by desertion; while Anglo-French relations were complicated by Charles's marital difficulties, disputes over the treatment of English Catholics and French Huguenots, and a trade embargo (Lockyer 222–9, 274–85; Russell 1979: 260–8). In any case, further English offensives against Spain required a huge infusion of cash. Buckingham's efforts to pawn the crown jewels in Amsterdam in November 1625 raised only £47,000, and loans demanded from wealthy taxpayers were slow to yield fruit. Careful preparations were laid for another Parliament: several troublesome MPs were appointed sheriffs to render them ineligible for election; Lord Keeper Williams, Charles's only pro-Spanish minister, was sacked and denied a writ of summons to Parliament; while the Earl of Bristol, whose account of Buckingham's negotiations in Madrid in 1623 differed sharply from the Duke's, was kept under house arrest.

For all these careful preparations, the 1626 Parliament began in acrimony and ended in disaster. At the instigation of the French ambassador, the earls of Arundel and Pembroke fomented trouble among their clients in the Commons, particularly William Coryton and Dr Samuel Turner (TNA, SP 16/523/77). Buckingham retaliated early in March 1626, having Arundel arrested (thus removing the last prominent Hispanophile from the Lords) and requiring Pembroke and Archbishop Abbot to endorse his attempts to rebuild the French alliance. However, one of Pembroke's clients in the Commons (Samuel Turner) filed charges against Buckingham, and thereafter a generous vote of supply (ultimately £340,000) was linked to the Duke's impeachment. After Easter news of an improvement in Anglo-French relations arrived from Paris, but this news was overshadowed by impeachment charges brought against each other by Bristol and Buckingham. Charles made it clear that he would not abandon his favourite, but behind the scenes Buckingham was urged to surrender his military responsibilities as Admiral and Warden of the Cinque Ports. Negotiations over this point broke down by the end of May, and when the Lords signalled their intention to give Bristol a fair trial, Charles dissolved the Parliament, thereby losing the funding for his war (Russell 1979: 286–322; Lockyer 325–31).

Theological controversy and confessional diplomacy

The fluid diplomatic situation in the mid-1620s had important repercussions within the Church of England. The Elizabethan church was dominated by a 'Calvinist consensus', but dissenting views about predestination, similar to those of the Dutch theologian Jacobus Arminius (see above), had some impact in England—a group of Cambridge dons publicly expressed misgivings about predestination in the mid-1590s, but their views were swiftly censured by Archbishop Whitgift, who ensured that their careers were wrecked thereafter (Porter 277–429). Jacobean clerics who were sceptical of Calvinist doctrines were often stigmatized as Arminians by their enemies—a categorical insult after the Synod of Dort—but many simply avoided public discussion of the vexed question of predestination. Donne's Sermons during the 1620s suggest that he had misgivings about Calvinism: he rarely discussed soteriology at length, and declined to identify the Pope as the Antichrist, reserving his bile for the Council of Trent (1545–63), which had laid down the doctrinal blueprint for Counter-Reformation Catholicism (Guibbory 2001; McCullough 2003*b*: 189–201; Shami 2003*a*: 208–10, 242–6).

Views sceptical of a hardline Calvinist, anti-Catholic religious orthodoxy became useful to James once he had resolved to pursue the Spanish Match. The vociferous outrage many clerics expressed at the prospect of a Catholic Queen of England, and a toleration for her English co-religionists, made Felipe IV understandably reluctant to conclude a treaty. However, anti-Calvinists offered a less vituperative and more reasoned critique of Rome, allowing James to reassure Philip that his sister would not be abused and humiliated at the English court (Questier 2006: 390–400). This development was exploited to particularly telling effect by one clique, the Durham House group, named after the London residence of its leader, Richard Neile, Bishop of Durham. In 1623 William Laud, a member of this group, in sparring with the Jesuit who had converted Buckingham's mother to Catholicism, discarded the conventional argument that the Pope was the Antichrist, opting to discuss the relative merits of Rome and Canterbury in a reasonable way. In the following year Richard Montague's book *A New Gagg for an Old Goose*, another anti-Catholic polemic, used the same tactic, and dismissed Calvinist doctrine as mere Puritanism, an insult for which he was investigated by the 1624 Parliament (Tyacke 1987a: 147–51).

Donne rehearsed similar arguments in a Sermon preached before William Cecil, second Earl of Exeter, in June 1624, when he stressed that neither Rome nor sectarian conventicles offered a certain path to salvation; in fact, he insisted, Antichrist was not to be identified as any individual or denomination, but as 'that opposition to the kingdome of Christ, which is in our selvs' (*Sermons* 6.151). While such statements allowed Montague's arguments to be read in a positive light, the conclusion Donne reached was decidedly non-partisan, and his remarks may have been chiefly intended to foster negotiations for a papal dispensation to allow Henrietta Maria to marry Prince Charles (Guibbory 2001: 417–24; Shami 2003a: 241–5; Ch. 35.I).

Montague, meanwhile, responded to his parliamentary critics with another book, *Appello Caesarem*, which restated his earlier position, but was published with royal approval. MPs summoned him to answer for his contempt in July 1625, but Charles made his views clear by claiming parliamentary privilege for Montague as a royal chaplain. In the same session a bill was apparently drafted to incorporate the decrees of the Synod of Dort as part of the doctrine of the Church of England, although it never reached the floor of the Commons. At the start of the 1626 Parliament Buckingham convened a theological conference at which he threw his weight behind the Arminian views of the Durham House group, but shortly before the dissolution a bill was tabled in the Commons to adopt the Irish Articles of 1615 in England, which would have rendered Montague's Arminian views untenable. MPs also revived their investigation of Montague, but decided to leave the clergy to judge his offences (Russell 1979: 240–1, 298–9; Tyacke 1987a: 147–55). This put Donne at the centre of the controversy, as he had been chosen to chair the lower house of Convocation—the legislative body for the clergy of Canterbury archdiocese, which met alongside Parliament. Few details of Convocation's debates survive, but plans to silence Montague probably existed, even if they were never carried into effect. Convocation was also expected to vote clerical taxation, but the abrupt dissolution to the session meant that no clerical supply bill reached the Commons (Bawcutt and Kelliher 441–3; Bald 1986: 481–3; Tyacke 1987a: 155–7).

'New Counsels', 1626–1628

From the start of his reign Charles's readiness to consider alternatives to constitutional norms, including Parliament and the common law, alarmed many of his subjects. James had advocated royal absolutism as a bulwark against the international pretensions of the papacy, but in his native Scotland, where a weak monarchy had been further enfeebled by decades of civil and religious strife, claims for the prerogative constituted a bargaining position rather than a normative statement. In England, however, where Charles had grown up, the Crown had always enjoyed a stronger constitutional position, and Charles was generally less prepared to compromise than his father had been.

In Scotland the new reign began with a sweeping resumption of Crown lands that threatened the estates of many noblemen (Macinnes 49–97). Meanwhile, in England, the threat of a Spanish invasion in July 1626 was used to promote the collection of a benevolence equal to the sum lost at the recent dissolution of Parliament, under the pragmatic maxim 'necessity knows no law'. However, the Spanish threat was widely discounted, and the benevolence raised less than £1,000, with taxpayers from numerous counties responding that 'the parliamentary way of raising money was most equal and indifferent' (Gilmore 107–8; Cust 94). The Privy Council learned from their mistakes, and in calling for a fresh 'loan' of five subsidies (£300,000) in October, they built up momentum by soliciting payment from judges, bureaucrats, and courtiers, and then sent councillors into every shire to promote its collection (Cust 13–58, 94–9).

This levy, known to historians as the Forced Loan, would probably have failed too, but for changed diplomatic circumstances. Following the Franco-Spanish Treaty of Monzón (27 February/8 March 1626) the French abandoned the English alliance and Mansfeld's army, turning away to resolve their longstanding domestic difficulty with the Huguenots. The English had been unofficial guardians of their French co-religionists since the 1560s, and thus Anglo-French relations spiralled downwards after news of Louis's ratification of the Monzón treaty reached England in early July (Wilson 383–4; Lockyer 296–7, 347–52, 360–2). By early 1627, as the French army blockaded the Huguenot stronghold of La Rochelle, the English prepared a rescue mission. Charles's determination to fight for the Huguenots caught the imagination of many of those rated to pay the Forced Loan for two reasons: along the south coast of England, where troops had been quartered without pay for eighteen months, Loan receipts were devoted to paying billeting arrears; while in the rest of the country, where the Loan yielded an average of 72 per cent of its quota, it seems that the cause to which it was to be assigned appealed to many taxpayers (Healy 446).

Despite its success as a fiscal device, the Loan met with significant resistance: around one hundred gentry refusers were harangued by the Privy Council, and if they remained obdurate, imprisoned or exiled to shires far from their homes. Some humbler refusers were conscripted, and in a half dozen shires where the collection went awry, local officeholders were sacked: in Bedfordshire Donne's patron, Henry, Earl of Kent, was one of those dismissed (Cust 102 n. 13). However, Catholics, normally excluded from public office, welcomed the opportunity to prove their loyalty to Charles, and many paid a cash composition in lieu of recusancy fines, an important step towards a toleration. Anglican clergymen were also enjoined to support the Loan in a set of instructions (drafted by Laud) issued in September 1626, but those who rose to the occasion were largely Arminians (Cust 47–50; Reeve 66–7, 70). In February 1627 an ambitious cleric, Robert Sibthorpe, assured the assize judges at Northampton of the King's right to demand obedience even in the case of an unjust tax, and insisted that anyone 'that resisteth the Prince resisteth the power and ordinance of God, and consequently shall receive damnation'. Archbishop Abbot refused to license this sermon for printing, for which he was suspended from office and his functions consigned to members of the Durham House coterie, while Sibthorpe was appointed a royal chaplain (Sibthorpe 3, 13; Cust 71–2; Fielding). Laud, newly appointed Dean of the Chapel Royal (and privately assured of his eventual succession at Canterbury), encouraged court preachers to follow this absolutist line, and in July Roger Maynwaring, echoing Sibthorpe, held that subjects who refused to pay any tax imposed without parliamentary consent risked damnation (Snapp 217–20; Cust 62–5).

In this context, Donne's court Sermon of April 1627 appeared lukewarm in its endorsement of the prerogative. He justified the Loan as a counsel of necessity, not of right: 'If you heare him [the King] not in his *Lawes*, heare him not in his *Proclamations*, heare him not in the *Declarations* of his wants and necessities, you are none of his'. Donne urged his hearers to exhibit 'Obedience to Superiours, and charity to others', warning (using the analogy of King Saul) that 'not to have contributed to his present wars, and his present wants, this occasioned...jealousie'. He also warned against slandering the King: 'The cursing of the King, and the cursing of God, the Prophet *Esai* hath joyned them together'; but he suggested that everyone was entitled to his private opinion, and failed to follow Sibthorpe's line that refusers faced damnation. Finally, he courted trouble in a passage about 'Very religious Kings' with wives 'that may have retained...some impressions of errour...from another Church'. Charles, acting on Laud's information, scrutinized the Sermon personally and may have been displeased, as he declined to have it printed (*Sermons* 407–9; Guibbory 2001: 434).

For all Sibthorpe's claims for the prerogative, the Forced Loan was a political gamble. The relief of La Rochelle would probably have given Charles's war effort the credibility to secure funding from a new Parliament, but in late October the gruelling four-month siege of a key fortress on the Île de Rhé—where Donne's second son George served as a captain—ended in a withdrawal which turned into a bloody rout (Lockyer 378–404; Bald 1986: 501, 552). When news of the disaster reached London in November, Sir Simonds D'Ewes saw 'sadness and dejectedness almost in every man's face' (D'Ewes 1845: 2.361). The financial news was even worse: in December it was estimated that the war effort urgently required a further £600,000, while receipts from the Forced Loan dried up following the defeat at Rhé.

In the face of these problems Charles contemplated desperate measures, notably a test case for the Forced Loan, in breach of his undertaking at its inception that it would not become a precedent (Larkin 2.111). At the end of October 1627 five Loan refusers were granted writs of *habeas corpus*, which revealed no more than that they had been detained 'by his majesty's special commandment' (Cust 61). This made the case a test of the royal prerogative rather than the Forced Loan, but the judges wisely avoided giving a definitive verdict, remanding the prisoners until the start of the next law term. The Attorney-General tried to alter the record to provide a better precedent, but the Privy Council released all refusers during the Christmas vacation (Kishlansky 1999: 60–7). Many assumed that a Parliament would automatically follow, but in the two and a half months before it met, its fate hung in the balance. Meanwhile, the Crown resolved its severest financial problems by raising £125,000 from the City of London through land sales, and a further £100,000 by anticipating customs receipts. Additional revenues were sought from Privy Seal loans of £200,000, knighthood fines, and an excise tax on beer, none of which was ever implemented. During the elections Charles briefly opted to delay the start of the session to allow for collection of Ship Money, a provocative order he was swiftly persuaded to rescind (Cust 72–7, 83–7).

THE CRISIS OF PARLIAMENTS, 1628–1629

At the start of the 1628 parliamentary session Sir Benjamin Rudyerd warned, 'This is the crisis of Parliaments; by this we shall know whether Parliaments will live or die...whether we shall be a kingdom or no' (*Commons* 2.58–9). While he was an inveterate doomsayer, Rudyerd's words rang true on this occasion: if the safeguards of Magna Carta (1215) could be overridden, did the law have any meaning? In the face of rather half-hearted ministerial opposition, the Commons quickly voted to condemn arbitrary imprisonment, offering five subsidies (£300,000), payable in a single year, to secure Charles's cooperation. The King agreed, amid rumours of a Franco-Spanish invasion, and lacking any other source of funds for the relief of La Rochelle (*Sermons* 7.25; Lockyer 405), but when MPs drafted a Petition of Right condemning prerogative taxation, arbitrary imprisonment, billeting, and martial law, courtiers in the Lords attempted to qualify these sweeping concessions. The Commons stood their ground, but Charles then offered no more than conditional assent to the Petition (2 June); this provoked wild rumours of a *coup d'état*, which were silenced only by a second answer on 7 June, which endorsed the Petition without reservations (Russell 1979: 342–84).

Although the Petition helped to allay the fears of men like Rudyerd, other major tensions between Parliament and the Crown remained unresolved. Chief among these was the dispute over customs duties, which had been collected without statutory authority since the beginning of the reign. Legislation was tabled in 1628, but news of proposals to increase customs rates without consulting Parliament outraged MPs, and the bill remained incomplete at the end of the session (ibid. 384–8). Meanwhile, Maynwaring provoked the Commons by recapitulating his absolutist views in a sermon in early May 1628, which led to his being impeached, fined £1,000, suspended from the ministry for three years, forbidden to preach at court forever, and barred from holding any office thereafter (ibid. 375; Snapp 220–9). Finally, while Buckingham had long since concluded an agreement with his court rivals to avoid being impeached, towards the end of the session the Commons, provoked by the first answer to the Petition of Right, recapitulated many of the 1626 impeachment charges in a remonstrance—which Charles ostentatiously chose to ignore (Russell 1979: 326–7, 377–85).

Agreement over the Petition of Right offered some opportunity for reconciliation, a fact Buckingham recognized in the ministerial reshuffle that commenced shortly after the end of the parliamentary session. With the French war now overshadowing the dispute with Spain, one Hispanophile, Sir Richard Weston, was appointed Lord Treasurer, while another, Sir Thomas Wentworth, a Loan-refuser who had played a key role in promoting the Petition, became a privy councillor. Meanwhile, in the church Montague was appointed Bishop of Chichester and Laud promoted to the bishopric of London, although preferments for Arminians were partly counterbalanced by Abbot's reinstatement to his ecclesiastical functions (Lockyer 448–9; Russell 1979: 391; Reeve 62–3). However, before the realignment was completed Buckingham was killed on 23 August by a disgruntled former army officer, as he prepared to lead another expedition to relieve La Rochelle. Most of the nation rejoiced, but Charles was overwhelmed with grief; the emotional void left in his life was ultimately filled by Henrietta Maria. Buckingham's death delayed a final relief effort for La Rochelle, which was repulsed in October; the town was starved into surrender only weeks later (Russell 1979: 392–3). Yet the international situation remained salvageable: a dynastic crisis in Italy provoked a fresh confrontation between France and Spain, giving Charles the opportunity to approach both his enemies with peace overtures (Lockyer 450; Wilson 438–40, 443–6). Parliament was thus recalled for January 1629 in the hope that a harmonious session would allow Charles to negotiate from a position of strength. Preparations included a pardon for various Arminians, including Maynwaring, who had been recalled to court and given a rich benefice, in open defiance of the sentence imposed upon him by Parliament; Montague's *Appello Caesarem* was finally proscribed; and twelve Jesuits were released from prison, lest the Commons clamour for their execution (Snapp 229–30; Reeve 33–62; Larkin 2.218–20).

The 1629 session began with an acrimonious clash over the printing of the Petition of Right that Parliament had ordered in June 1628. The day after the 1628 session ended Charles had the copies pulped and a fresh batch printed, accompanied by his first (unsatisfactory) response, and a commentary expaining that the prerogative could not be bound by Parliament (Russell 1979: 401–2). At least two privy councillors, Weston and Laud, hoped to undermine the 1629 session (Reeve 81–3), with good reason, as some MPs almost certainly aimed to destroy them. Since the previous autumn customs officials had been impounding the goods of merchants who refused to pay customs, one of whom, the MP John Rolle, quickly complained to the Commons. Many MPs would have been happy to settle the issue quietly, but a vociferous group led by Sir John Eliot insisted on censuring the customs officials for implementing laws that were not actually in force. Meanwhile, godly MPs, led by John Pym and Francis Rous, revived earlier attempts to have Arminian soteriology outlawed in the Church of England, and began impeachment proceedings against Neile and other members of the Durham House group (Russell 1979: 404; Reeve 73–7; C. Thompson). Charles might have been able to defend either of these interests by abandoning the other, but he declined to compromise (Reeve 80–5).

Donne preached a court Sermon in the middle of these controversies, delivering one of his most complex performances. Recalling the proclamation against controversial preaching, he asked: 'who will offer to dispute unnecessary things, especially where Authority hath made it necessary to us, to forbear such Disputations?' Yet, despite Charles's increasingly apparent inclination towards arbitrary government, Donne also reminded his audience that 'godliness is, to believe that God hath given us a Law, and to live according to that Law', advice that, if applied to the political forum, constituted a direct criticism of the Caroline regime. Donne served his King, but he also spoke his conscience (*Sermons* 8.344–5, 349–50; Harland 28, 32; see also Ch. 39). Whatever discussions Charles had with his critics behind the scenes had broken down by 2 March, when Eliot and five other MPs restrained the Speaker while the Commons passed a protestation condemning popery and Arminianism, and declaring collectors and payers of customs to be in breach of the law. Eight days later Charles dissolved Parliament and began his eleven-year Personal Rule (Reeve 89–95).

Conclusion

'No man is an *Iland*'—the troubles the Stuart dynasty encountered during the 1620s arose because many English subjects regarded religion, politics, and diplomacy as intimately related topics. The prospect of Prince Charles's marriage to a Catholic altered the factional balance in both church and court, threatening the end of the pan-Protestant alliance that had formed the keystone of English diplomacy since Elizabeth's accession. Thus it is hardly surprising that beneficiaries of the status quo fought against this alteration, that others sought to profit from it, or that war raised the stakes for all concerned. The advent of peace with France (April 1629) and Spain (December 1630) reduced tensions (Lockyer 460; Reeve 255), while Weston's revenue reforms, many of which had first been mooted in 1626–8, dispensed with the need for Parliament, and thus closed off an important forum for criticism of the Caroline regime. Yet the 'Personal Rule' constituted an uneasy truce, with Catholics enjoying unprecedented influence at court via the Queen, and a partial toleration in the provinces; with Laud and his Durham House allies in charge of the church; and with Gustavus Adolphus of Sweden, rather than Charles, as the saviour of Protestant Europe.

CHAPTER 36.1

THE ENGLISH NATION IN 1631

ARNOLD HUNT

'In the seventeenth century', Kevin Sharpe has written, 'the succession of a new monarch was still the fundamental change in the political climate—the event which decided who would grow in the sun of royal favour and who would wither in the cold of obscurity' (Sharpe 1987: 226). But climate change, however profound, is not always obvious to those living through it. In retrospect, it is clear that the accession of Charles I in 1625 was indeed a critical turning-point in religious and political affairs. Yet many familiar faces and features of Jacobean court culture still lingered on, not least Donne himself, whose continuing prominence as one of the stars of the court preaching rota was a visible symbol of continuity between the two reigns. Even by the time of Donne's death, six years later, the new pattern of politics was by no means clear even to well-informed observers. Sharpe writes that while some historians have been tempted to underplay the importance of the succession, 'to those at court...things quite rapidly looked different'. With regard to the monarch's personal style of government this may be true, but with regard to the broader direction of policy it is more questionable. To modern historians the accession of the new king marks a natural break, but at the time it may have been the continuities rather than the differences that stood out.

There are several reasons why this was so. Sharpe's main point—that monarchical government at this period was highly personal, so that a change of monarch had far-reaching effects on the nature of government—is well taken. But Charles's intentions were not easy to read. As one observer at court remarked in 1632, while awaiting the appointment of a new Secretary of State, 'the King...is very secrett & retired in discouering which way hee inclineth' (BL, Add MS. 33936, fo. 15). Moreover, this was a culture in which any change tended to be referred back to an earlier precedent. Many of Charles's departures from his father's style of government could plausibly be presented as a reversion to an older Elizabethan way of doing things; in 1638, for example, when the reform of the royal household was being canvassed, Donne's friend George Garrard informed his patron Thomas Wentworth that the proposals 'look back to Henry the Seventh, Henry the Eighth and Queen Elizabeth's time' (Sharpe 1987: 235). This invariable appeal to precedent tended to muffle the effects of change, and made it less natural for contemporaries than it may seem to us to identify a distinctively 'Caroline' style of government. Even Donne, who with his court connections was well placed to know what was going on, seems to have had considerable difficulty in gauging the temper of the times—which, as we shall see, led to several embarrassing missteps in his later court Sermons.

The assassination of the Duke of Buckingham in August 1628 is seen by many historians as marking the decisive break between the old reign and the new. The implications, though, were not immediately obvious. Buckingham's death did not precipitate a sudden change in royal policy, and only gradually did it become clear that it had brought about a shift to a new style of government—'a new spheare of courtship', as Sir Robert Ker described it in a letter to Donne—in which Charles was more directly involved and, rather than delegating power to a single favourite, divided power among a circle of leading courtiers. The system of government by or through a single minister-favourite had existed in England since 1612, first with Robert Carr, Earl of Somerset, as the reigning favourite, and then after 1615 with Buckingham as his successor. In departing from this system, Charles was reverting to an older Elizabethan model in which no single favourite held a monopoly of patronage. The 1630s saw the rise of a group of privy councillors, including Thomas Wentworth, Earl of Strafford (President of the Council in the North and later Lord Deputy of Ireland), Richard Weston, Earl of Portland (Lord Treasurer), and Francis Cottington (Chancellor of the Exchequer), none of whom was allowed to monopolize patronage in the way that Buckingham had done. The resulting style of personal monarchy that has led to this period being labelled the Personal Rule was, arguably, not so much about Charles's ruling without Parliament as about his ruling without a leading favourite.

The death of Buckingham, closely followed by the military failure at La Rochelle, also brought about a shift in foreign policy. Donne would have followed this closely, as his younger son George had accompanied Buckingham on his naval expedition to the Isle of Rhé in 1627, the first of several unsuccessful attempts to protect the Huguenot garrison at La Rochelle against the French. The fall of La Rochelle in October 1628 left England with no credible strategy for military involvement in the Thirty Years War. Peace treaties with France and Spain followed soon afterwards, and the maintenance of peace became the governing theme of English foreign policy for the next decade, summed up in Charles's declaration after the dissolution of Parliament in 1629, in which (echoing the description of Israel's peace under the rule of Solomon, 1 Kings 4:25) he invited his subjects to consider 'whether, in respect of...the great peace and quietnesse which every man enjoyeth under his owne vine and figtree, the happinesse of this Nation can be paralleled by any other of our neighbour Countreyes' (Charles I 45). Nowhere is this better summed up than in Rubens's painting *Minerva Protecting Pax from Mars*, now in the National Gallery in London, in which the blessings of peace, symbolized by marriage and fertility, are contrasted with the horrors of war. Rubens had been sent to London in 1629 to begin the negotiations for the Anglo-Spanish peace treaty, and presented the painting to Charles in 1630 when the treaty was successfully concluded.

In reverting to a more pacific foreign policy, Charles could plausibly claim to be returning to the Jacobean status quo. The image of the king as *Rex Pacificus*, the royal peacemaker, had been one of the keynotes of Jacobean politics, and many of the funeral elegies for James I had expressed hopes of a continuing peace under his successor. George Morley's elegy, for example, declared that James would be remembered not only for his own 'two and twenty years long care' but also

> For providing such an heire
> Which to the Peace he had before
> May add twise two, and twenty more.

> (Camden 1657: 393)

To many observers—not least Donne himself, who commemorated James in a Sermon of May 1626 as 'he who was in his desire and intension, the Peace-maker of all the Christian world' (*Sermons* 7.166)—the peace treaties of 1629–30 must have seemed like a welcome return to Jacobean business as usual. Charles certainly perceived the advantages of cultivating an impression of continuity with his father's reign. Rubens's other great work for Charles, the ceiling of the Banqueting House at Whitehall, depicts James I borne to heaven amid the symbols of plenty and prosperity, not only a compliment to James's peacemaking skills but also a deft piece of propaganda for the new *Pax Carolina* of the 1630s, which would later come to be celebrated, particularly by royalists looking back after the Civil War, as a halcyon decade of peace and stability (Parry 32–7; Sharpe 1992: 608–11.)

Yet English neutrality was also a result of military weakness and, to some, a humiliating reminder of the failure to secure the Palatinate or come to the aid of fellow Protestants in Europe. Many of the confident assertions of the blessings of peace that turn up so frequently in poems, masques, and other court-sponsored texts of the 1630s have an unmistakably defensive tone to them. In December 1632, for example, one of Donne's successors in the court pulpit, Robert Skinner, had the difficult task of preaching at Whitehall just after the news had reached England of the death of Gustavus Adolphus, King of Sweden, at the battle of Lutzen. This was a disastrous blow for the Protestant cause in Europe, yet Skinner blandly turned it into a reminder of the exceptional blessings bestowed on England:

> If in ye map of ye Xian world ye can discover a people that are in peace and prosperitie when others mourne; that turne speares into pruning hookes when the nations about y^m turne plowshares into speares, beware of overlooking it; stand still awhile, behold, admire and be thankfull ... let the righteous rejoyce, and give thankes, and confesse with the *prophet*, Happie is ye people that be in such a case, yea happie is ye people whose god is the Lord. (BL, Add MS. 20065, fo. 33^v)

Like much of the official rhetoric of the 1630s, this is defiantly insular, in marked contrast to the pan-European rhetoric that had characterized James I's efforts at international peacemaking.

The other great political event of the late 1620s was the failure of the 1628–9 Parliament and its dissolution in March 1629 in an atmosphere of mutual distrust between King and Commons (see Ch. 35.II). Again, however, the implications were not immediately clear. Charles was careful to stress that he was not opposed to Parliaments on principle; in his view, the collapse of the 1629 session was due to 'some ill-disposed persons' who had seized control of the Commons against the wishes of the wiser majority, and he continued to believe that his intentions had been misunderstood. In a proclamation issued shortly after the dissolution he reiterated his 'Love to the use of Parliaments', ending with a slightly ambiguous pledge 'to meete in Parliament againe, when Our People shall see more cleerely into Our Intents and Actions' (Larkin 2.226–8). There was certainly no reason to believe in 1629 that more than a decade would pass before Parliament was summoned again. Indeed, it seemed very likely that Charles's need for money would oblige him to call a new Parliament sooner rather than later. As Sharpe has shown, there were several occasions in the later 1630s when Charles seriously considered entering the war in Europe, much to the dismay of some of his advisers, particularly William Laud and Wentworth, who did all they could to dissuade him. Had he done so he would almost certainly have had to recall Parliament, as there was little prospect of financing a war without parliamentary subsidy.

In the absence of parliamentary subsidy Charles was forced to turn to other financial expedients such as Ship Money, which had already been tried unsuccessfully in 1628 but was then reintroduced in 1634. The situation would not have been unfamiliar to Donne, who in his poem *LovGrow* commented ironically on the way that emergency taxation might be used to effect a permanent increase in the monarch's ordinary revenues: 'As princes do in times of action get / New taxes, and remit them not in peace' (ll. 26–7). Ship Money was certainly a case in point. As Sharpe has shown, it was used for its stated purpose of financing the navy, rather than simply being absorbed into the royal exchequer (Sharpe 1992: 594), but it appears that Charles regarded it as a way of strengthening his bargaining position in the event of a new Parliament. This was made explicit in a position paper presented by Sir John

Melton, secretary to the Council of the North, to Thomas Wentworth in 1635, at a time when it seemed that a Parliament might soon be summoned to fund a European war. Melton feared that a new Parliament would be 'of no better Temper than those we have had lately', but argued that it would be better to have a Parliament sooner rather than later, 'when there is but a tacite Necessity, and while the current of his Majesty's Prerogative is strong, and the People sensibly apprehending his Power to subsist without a Parliament' (Knowler 1.419). This is probably close to Charles's own thinking. He did not intend to govern permanently without parliament, but he was determined that any future Parliament was to be a Parliament on his terms, one that would vote him the money he needed without imposing awkward conditions.

It is not easy to tell where Donne might have stood on these matters. Paul Harland has argued that he allied himself with the parliamentary opponents of the royal prerogative, basing this argument on the Sermon preached by Donne at Whitehall on 20 February 1629, less than a fortnight before the disastrous end of the 1629 Parliament. Donne's text on this occasion was James 2:12, 'so speak ye, and so do, as they that shall be judged by the law of liberty', and Harland argues that in choosing this text Donne was deliberately echoing the language used in the House of Commons about law as the crucial safeguard of liberty (Harland). However, as Debora Shuger argues elsewhere in this volume (Ch. 39), it is not at all clear that this Sermon can bear the weight of interpretation that Harland wishes to place on it. Much of the Sermon, indeed, can be read as an indirect reproof of the parliamentary opposition. In a key passage, Donne criticizes those who take the liberty to pass judgement on matters of state: 'every conjecturing person, that is not within the distance to know the ends, or the ways of great Actions, will Judge the highest Counsels, and execution of those Counsels' (*Sermons* 8.337). He goes on to lay down some rules for counselling the monarch: the king, he declares, 'will always be well pleased' to receive advice, but only when it is spoken by those 'to whom it belongs to speak it' (i.e. those who occupy 'the great places of power, and Councel') and in a suitably 'humble and reserved manner' (8.340). Donne may, as Harland suggests, be addressing a perceived 'crisis of counsel', but this is hardly the voice of an outspoken defender of parliamentary liberties; rather, it is the voice of a court insider for whom the solution to any crisis of counsel was to be found at Whitehall rather than Westminster.

There is some evidence to suggest that Donne, in private, was far more critical of royal policy. A copy of Thomas More's *Utopia*, now in the library of the University of San Francisco, bears Donne's signature and motto on the title page, and contains a running commentary on the text in the form of marginal notes drawing parallels between the abuses of monarchical power evoked by More and the political situation in England under Charles I. In one passage More refers to royal counsellors who advise the king to declare 'a make-believe war, under pretext of which he would raise money, and then when he thought fit make peace with great solemnity, to throw dust in the eyes of the people'. This is annotated in Latin: 'all these things have happened in our time'. Another passage, in which More refers scathingly to 'judges who will in every case decide in favour of the royal prerogative', prompts the succinct remark: 'ship-monie'. John B. Gleason, who first discovered and published these annotations, argued that they revealed a sharp and troubling discrepancy between Donne's private thoughts and public utterances, exposing him, in effect, as a smooth and accomplished sycophant whose court Sermons bore no relation to his real convictions (Gleason). There are, however, some grounds for suspecting that the annotations may not be by Donne but by a later owner. First, this pungent style of annotation is very unusual for Donne, who often marked up his books with marginal lines and emphases but rarely added comments of his own. Secondly, the remark on Ship Money would seem to belong more naturally to the later 1630s, after Donne's death, when the legality of Ship Money had been tested in the courts. All that can be said at present is that if these annotations are by Donne, they offer a highly important insight into his political opinions, representing, in Tom Cain's words, 'the most private and unguarded form of his discourse that survives' (Cain 2006: 97–8). But rather than exposing Donne as a hypocrite, and his court Sermons as skilful exercises in flattery, this should cause us to read the Sermons with greater political sensitivity, looking for hints of the same concerns expressed in a more oblique and indirect form.

Peter McCullough has argued that Donne's late Sermons are conspicuous for their lack of political engagement. 'The nine surviving sermons that Donne preached at court after 1627', he writes, 'are striking as a group for their complete avoidance of the politically charged opinions that Donne expounded so confidently in the first two years of the new reign'. Donne, he suggests, found himself increasingly out of step with the Caroline regime, but rather than signalling his disagreement from the pulpit, chose to turn away from political preaching altogether (McCullough 2003*b*: 202). Yet there are political statements to be found in these Sermons, though they are brief and often heavily coded. Preaching before the King in April 1630, Donne observed that even kings were subject to 'mis-interpretation', and gave three examples of what he saw as unwarranted criticism of royal policies, relating to fiscal policy, domestic policy, and foreign policy respectively. Some people, he remarked, will reason as follows: 'Treasures are empty, therefore there are unnecessary wastes', 'Discontented persons murmure, therefore things are ill carried', 'our neighbours prosper by Action, therefore we perish by not appearing'; but all these, he went on, 'are hastie conclusions in State affaires' (*Sermons* 9.215–16). In another Sermon, probably of the same year, he pleaded for an attitude of passive obedience, arguing that in the mysteries of both religion and politics we should be content to accept things as they are, without inquiring how they come to be so. 'It is enough for a happy subject to enjoy the sweetnesse of a peaceable government, though he know not *Arcana Imperii*, The wayes by which the Prince governes' (9.246).

Whatever we may make of these remarks (and their intended application is very far from obvious), it is clear that they are very carefully weighed. They employ what by the early 1630s had become a standard rhetorical ploy in court preaching, drawing an analogy between God and the King in order to argue that the ways of heavenly and earthly monarchs are alike unsearchable, and thus to reprove unnecessary speculation both in matters of divinity and in affairs of state. In another of his late court Sermons, preaching on 'God said, let us make man' (Gen. 1:26), Donne draws attention to God's use of the royal we—the 'royal plurall' as he calls it—and goes on to develop the analogy with earthly kings. Kings, he declares, are 'Images of God', and we must therefore kneel to God in church just as we would kneel before the King in his presence: a neat comparison that enables Donne to defend both religious conformity and political obedience (9.58–9). Donne, it appears, was making a determined effort to fit in with the prevailing mood of court preaching, and very largely succeeding. In doing so, however, he was also very conspicuously refraining from the court preacher's traditional task of offering advice or admonition to the monarch. These Sermons rarely address the King directly; instead, the emphasis falls very heavily on the task of preaching obedience to the subject. Only in his remarks on the 'mis-interpretation' of royal policy and the murmurings of 'discontented persons' did Donne betray any awareness of political tensions in the world beyond Whitehall, or offer any hint or warning to the King that his policies were not universally popular.

Another passage in one of the late court Sermons is also worth pausing over. In Donne's Sermon of 20 April 1630—the same Sermon in which he comments on the 'mis-interpretation' of royal policy—he draws an analogy between God's judgement and the King's, and illustrates this with an extended metaphor moving up through a rising series of different types of court. 'I shall not be tried by an arbitrary Court, where it may be wisedome enough, to follow a wise leader, and think as he thinks. I shall not be tried by a Jury...Nor tryed by Peeres...But I shall be tried by the King himselfe, then which no man can propose a Nobler tryall' (9.229–30). The implication is that kingly justice is as far removed as possible from the merely 'arbitrary' justice to be expected from a lower court. Donne may simply be using the term 'arbitrary' in the sense of arbitration—certainly the phrase 'arbitrary government' was not as loaded in 1630 as it would become in the later seventeenth century—but his use of the word is strikingly different from the way it would be used by another court preacher the following year. Preaching before the King at Whitehall on 27 December 1631, Robert Skinner declared that our life and death depend on the will of God, 'but in an Arbitrary, not in a Peremptory way' (BL, Add MS. 20065, fo. 8^v). It is not clear that Donne intended any criticism of the King by his use of the word 'arbitrary'; what is clear, however, is that it did not come naturally to him to equate royal power with arbitrary power, or to make the exalted claims for the royal prerogative that other preachers in the 1630s were increasingly willing to make.

This shift in the tone of court preaching was only one aspect of the religious changes that were taking place in the late 1620s and early 1630s under the leadership of William Laud (appointed Bishop of London in 1628 and Archbishop of

Canterbury in 1633) and the clergy of the so-called 'Durham House group', notably Richard Neile (appointed Bishop of Durham in 1617, Bishop of Winchester in 1628, and Archbishop of York in 1632), Richard Montague (appointed Bishop of Chichester in 1628 and Bishop of Norwich in 1638), and John Cosin (appointed Master of Peterhouse, Cambridge, in 1635). Laud's determination to enforce Prayer Book ceremonies such as kneeling at communion, which had been widely neglected in many parishes, has led some historians to argue that he was chiefly concerned with the maintenance of order and uniformity in public worship (Sharpe 1992: 289). However, the writings of Laud and his circle are also characterized by some very novel and distinctive theological priorities, including a general aversion to religious controversy, a special distaste for the Calvinist doctrine of predestination, and a shift away from the harsh anti-Catholic polemic that had been the norm in the Jacobean church (A. Milton 1995). It seemed to many observers that this was part of a concerted strategy to realign the Church of England by detaching it from other Protestant Reformed churches and moving it closer to the Roman Catholic Church. While this would have been controversial at any time, it appeared especially threatening in the 1630s because it reinforced fears of a pro-Spanish foreign policy designed to resist the calling of a new Parliament and to keep England out of the war in Europe.

An important insight into Laud's thinking can be found in a series of letters written to him in 1637–8 by the English ambassador in Paris, Viscount Scudamore, a man very much in sympathy with Laud's religious agenda. In these letters Scudamore reported on the discussions he had held with the Dutch diplomat Hugo Grotius on the possibility of an ecclesiastical union between England and Sweden, which he hoped could pave the way to a broader union between the three British churches of England, Scotland, and Ireland and the three Scandinavian churches of Sweden, Denmark, and Norway. Grotius believed that such a union was feasible for three reasons: first, because both churches possessed episcopal government; secondly, because neither imposed the doctrine of predestination as a necessary point of belief; and thirdly, because they had adopted many of the same ceremonies, 'as uncovering the head and bowing at the name of Jesus' (Tighe). Laud, it would seem, shared the interest in ecumenical union that had been such a prominent part of Jacobean religious policy, but with the crucial difference that whereas James's ecumenical hopes had been focused on the Calvinist churches of France and Holland, Laud's were focused on the Lutheran churches of Scandinavia. His enemies were not mistaken, therefore, in supposing that he wished to bring about a realignment of the Church of England, even if they mistook its nature. Laud was not a crypto-Catholic; rather, he saw in the Lutheran churches a model of how to break away from the predestinarianism of the French and Dutch Reformed churches, and to promote a greater emphasis on religious imagery and ceremony, without compromising the Church of England's credentials as a Protestant church.

The new drift of religious policy would have been very visible to Donne through his links with the royal chapel at Whitehall. One of Laud's first acts on becoming dean of the Chapel Royal in October 1626 was to ask the King to attend public prayers as well as the sermon on Sunday. On securing Charles's approval, he penned a triumphant note in his diary: 'This had not before been done from the beginning of King James's reign to this day. Now, thanks be to God, it obtaineth'. The effect of this change was to upgrade the role of public prayer while dethroning the sermon from its position as the sole focus of the service (Laud 3.197; McCullough 1998: 155). The use of the Chapel Royal as a laboratory for Laud's religious reforms was to continue through the 1630s. It was reported in March 1635 that the King had given order 'that all his servants should receave the Communion three tymes in the yeare', and that anyone who refused to do so, or who failed to deliver a certificate to the dean of the Chapel Royal showing that they had received communion elsewhere, 'shall be suspended from their offices, and other men shall bee put in' (Bodleian, MS Carte 77, fo. 40ᵛ). This is again very revealing of Laud's priorities, in that it affirmed the importance of regularly receiving the sacrament, in a way which Laud may well have hoped would make the royal chapel more attractive to Roman Catholics at court, while at the same time giving no encouragement to Catholics who wished to remain outside the communion of the Church of England.

However, Donne seems to have been slow to adapt to the new religious agenda. In May 1626 he preached a Sermon at Paul's Cross in which he argued that it was time to resume theological controversy against the papists. He admitted that only a few years earlier, in the 1622 *Directions to Preachers*, James had given orders for a 'discreet and temperate forbearing' of religious controversy, but argued that this had only been a temporary measure while the Spanish Match negotiations were under way. '[T]hings standing now in another state, and all peace, both Ecclesiasticall and Civill, with these men, being by themselves removed, and taken away...since wee heare that Drums beat in every field abroad, it becomes us also to returne to the brasing and beating of our Drums in the Pulpit too' (*Sermons* 7.166). Once again, Donne seems to have expected a return to Jacobean business as usual. As it turned out, his timing could hardly have been worse. Only a month later Charles issued a proclamation, drafted by Laud, 'for the establishing of the Peace and Quiet of the Church of England', declaring that the 'sharpe and indiscreete handling' of some points of religious controversy, 'at first onely being meant against the Papists', had now got out of hand. All clergy were ordered to follow a 'Rule of sobrietie' in handling matters of controversy, and not to maintain any opinions that were not clearly grounded on the doctrine and discipline of the Church of England (Larkin 2.90–3). Donne appears to have been completely wrong-footed by this proclamation; certainly his Sermon of May 1626 gives no hint of any move to damp down the flames of religious controversy.

The Laudian religious reforms also extended to Donne's home territory of St Paul's Cathedral. The building had been in a poor state of repair for decades, and the constant traffic of workmen, tradesmen, and casual passers-by, not just in the churchyard but inside the cathedral itself, disrupted the services and often made it difficult for the preacher to be heard. In the 1630s Charles and Laud mounted a major campaign to raise funds for the restoration of St Paul's. In 1632 Charles wrote to the Lord Mayor urging the City of London to set a good example by contributing to the restoration; then in 1633 the appeal went nationwide, and commissions were issued to local JPs to raise money on a county-by-county basis. The response was spasmodic, in part because many people seem to have felt that the City of London ought to pay for its own cathedral church, but also because of fears that Charles might be using the appeal as a pretext to raise money for other purposes. Nevertheless, the appeal raised £30,000 by 1634 and continued to bring in substantial sums for the remainder of the decade, its major legacy being the new classical portico added to the cathedral by Inigo Jones, which survived until the Great Fire of 1666 (Sharpe 1992: 322–8; Atherton 110–19; Crankshaw 57–60). In 1633 St Paul's was also caught up in a controversy over the placing of the altar, not in the cathedral itself but in the adjoining parish of St Gregory by St Paul's, which was under the jurisdiction of the dean and chapter. This became a test case for the Laudian campaign to promote greater reverence in the receiving of the sacrament by railing off the communion table and setting it 'altarwise' at the east end. Donne was dead by this time, but the order to rail off the communion table in St Gregory's was signed by two of his close friends, Henry King, his executor, and Thomas Winniffe, his successor as dean (Fincham and Tyacke 193).

The modern editors of his Sermons took it for granted that the beautifying of St Paul's Cathedral was 'a cause which Donne had much at heart' (*Sermons* 9.8-9). Yet the evidence leaves room for doubt. In the last few years of his life Donne certainly began to push for higher standards of religious observance in the cathedral. Preaching there on Christmas Day 1629, he complained that 'there come some persons to this Church, and persons of example to many that come with them', who, 'excepting some few', had never knelt during the service or required their servants to kneel with them; and in March 1630 he pursued this complaint by prosecuting a member of the congregation who had refused to kneel when ordered to do so (9.152; B. W. Whitlock 1954). But these belated efforts do not seem to have made much impression on Laud, who described St Paul's in 1631 as 'a disgrace to our Country, and the Cittie, and a common imputat[i]on and scandall laid vpon o[u]r Religion' (qtd. in Crankshaw 58). Giles Fleming, preaching there in 1634 in support of the restoration appeal, bluntly described the state of the cathedral as 'scandalous' (ibid.; Fleming 47). These criticisms clearly reflected badly on Donne, who, as Dean of St Paul's, had presided over this state of affairs. The same could be said of King and Winniffe, both of them long-serving members of the cathedral chapter; they may have put their names to the order to move the communion table in St Gregory's, but as Kenneth Fincham and Nicholas Tyacke drily remark in their study of the case, 'By 1633 it was a little late in the day for either of them to denounce the profanity to which they had been party over the years' (Fincham and Tyacke 193). The real pressure for reform was clearly coming from elsewhere.

Given the guarded and often heavily coded language that pervades Donne's later Sermons whenever they touch on controversial matters, it is not surprising that scholars have had difficulty in pinpointing his precise theological position. One of the most detailed and informed attempts to locate Donne theologically has come from Achsah Guibbory, who argues that he moved sharply away from his earlier Calvinism, and towards the strident anti-Calvinism associated with Richard Montague and other Laudian divines (Guibbory 2001). Yet there is a passage in one of the later Sermons, not noted by Guibbory, which suggests that Donne was keeping his distance from the views of Montague and other anti-Calvinists. Preaching at St Paul's on Easter Day 1629, he entered into a curious digression on the sixth-century Saracen king Alamandurus, who resisted the attempts of some bishops at his court to convert him to heresy. The moral of this story, Donne explained, was that

> a pious and religious King should not easily be suspected of that levity, to hearken to impious and hereticall motions, though there were good evidence, that that were practised upon him; much lesse, when the feares in himself, and in those which should practise upon him, are but imaginary, and proceed, (as by Gods grace they doe) rather out of zeale that it may not be so, then out of evidence that it is so. (*Sermons* 8.363)

If, as seems likely, Donne intended his audience to apply this to Charles and some of his religious advisers, then his careful choice of words is worth noting. While casting doubt on the likelihood of 'impious and hereticall motions' among Charles's circle of divines, he does not rule the possibility out completely. He also appears remarkably sympathetic to concerns about the King's religious orthodoxy, suggesting that they arise from 'zeale' (albeit, as he adds, 'zeale distempered') rather than disloyalty. This is hardly the language of a card-carrying anti-Calvinist in the mould of Montague or Laud.

Guibbory is right, however, to point to a change in theological emphasis in the Sermons of the later 1620s. Nowhere in these Sermons does Donne specifically reject the key Calvinist doctrines of election, assurance, and final perseverance, yet he repeatedly directs his audiences away from unnecessary speculation on the mysteries of predestination and urges them towards a more practical form of religion solidly grounded on the evidence of good works. In his Sermon at Whitehall on 20 February 1629 he stressed the need to avoid matters of controversy in religion. 'Who will offer to dispute unnecessary things, especially where Authority hath made it necessary to us, to forbear such Disputations?' This, he went on, required his audience to turn their attention away from 'the object of Election' (man predestined by the eternal decree of God) to 'the subject of Execution' (man judged by the law but redeemed by Christ), about which there could be 'no controversie'. 'Let no man make you afraid of secret purposes in God, which they have not, nor you have not seen; for, that by which you shall be judged, is the Law' (8.345–6). This warning against futile speculation into God's secret purposes recurs in a later Sermon, preached at St Paul's on Easter Day

1630, where Donne reproves those who 'pant after high and un-understandable Doctrines of the secret purposes of God' while neglecting 'the fundamentall point of Doctrine', the resurrection of Christ (9.205). This is very much in line with the pattern we have already seen in Donne's handling of political matters. It suggests a willingness to adapt to the new mood of court divinity, but only up to a point, stopping well short of the extremes to which other preachers were prepared to go.

The extent and limits of Donne's progress in an anti-Calvinist direction are clearly spelled out in his final Sermon, *Deaths Duell*, preached before the King on 25 February 1631. The popular view of this Sermon as a dying man's deeply personal meditation on mortality makes it easy to overlook the care with which Donne stakes out his theological position. The first section of *Deaths Duell* addresses itself to the question of how far we may obtain assurance of our own election. Donne argues

Ill. 36.I.1. Frontispiece for *Deaths Duell* (1632), line engraving by Martin Droeshout. (© National Portrait Gallery, London. Reproduced by permission.)

that we should ground our assurance on God's purposes and decrees, but—with a crucial caveat—not upon 'such as are *conceived* and imagined in our selves', but upon those 'which he hath declared and manifested' by outward signs. He then offers a carefully nuanced and qualified doctrine of assurance as resting not merely on faith, but on faith as manifested in good works, and consisting of a '*holy certitude and a modest infallibility*' rather than an absolute certainty of salvation (10.237). This was an implicit rebuke to some Calvinist theologians who, in Donne's view, had gone too far in pressing the need for assurance without a corresponding insistence on the need for a holy life. In this Donne was entirely in agreement with the new school of anti-Calvinist divines. Yet he was very careful not to deny the possibility of assurance altogether—just as, in another court Sermon preached a few months earlier, he had been careful not to deny the possibility of a 'finall perseverance, grounded upon the eternall knowledge of God', arguing that there 'may be' such a thing even though it was not easily discernible (9.230–1).

In these late Sermons Donne was aligning himself with a moderate Calvinism that would have been acceptable to Laud while still remaining within the bounds of Reformed orthodoxy. But by the early 1630s it was becoming increasingly difficult to find this middle ground, as other preachers were making similar remarks about the dangers of theological speculation, or the necessity of good works, but without the saving clauses that Donne had been so careful to put in. Again, the sermons of Robert Skinner provide a useful point of comparison. Preaching at court in December 1631, Skinner rebuked those who inquired into 'remote mysteries afore ye foundation of the world, as p^{re}destination, election, reprobation, and the like', implying that all discussion of these matters was off-limits. He also took an openly anti-Calvinist line on free will, declaring that God's decree of election was 'conditionall...according to his p^{re}science and foreknowledge of the meanes, which may be taken or left, accepted or refused' (BL, Add MS. 20065, fos. 10–11). Sir William Drake, whose commonplace books have recently been analysed by Kevin Sharpe, was one of many observers who felt that the sermons at court had taken on a more aggressively confrontational tone since the beginning of Charles's reign. 'In King James's time', he wrote in 1633, 'the court preachers chose texts for peace, as follow peace etc [Heb. 12:14]...but now they see that the times incline to superstition they preach for the outward pomp and glory of the church, the splendour and outward beauty of the church they much advance' (Sharpe 2000: 140).

It is not surprising, therefore, that after his death Donne was appropriated by Laudian writers who wished to turn him into one of themselves. Anthony Stafford's *The Femall Glory* (1635), which sought to promote a higher sense of reverence for saints and angels, includes a passage urging its female readers to kneel down before the Virgin Mary, 'the Grand white Immaculate Abbesse of your snowy Nunneries' (Stafford 148), an obvious allusion to Donne's lines in *Lit*: 'The cold white snowie Nunnery, / Which, as thy mother, their high Abbesse, sent / Their bodies backe againe to thee' (ll. 100–2). Three years later the Durham clergyman William Milbourne, a protégé of John Cosin, published a sermon collection entitled *Sapientia Clamitans* (1638) in which Donne's 'Sermon of

Valediction at his Going into Germany' appeared alongside two sermons by the Arminian divine Thomas Jackson. The 'Sermon of Valediction', preached at Lincoln's Inn in 1619, was a classic expression of moderate Calvinism in which Donne criticized the high-Calvinist or supralapsarian position which, he believed, put the divine decrees in the wrong order, placing 'decrees of reprobation, decrees of condemnation, before decrees of creation' (*Sermons* 2.246). In the context of *Sapientia Clamitans*, however, and taken in conjunction with Jackson's anti-Calvinist arguments, the sermon was open to a radically different interpretation, in which Donne's remarks could be read not simply as a criticism of a particular type of predestinarian doctrine but as a rejection of the entire concept of predestination.

While it is not surprising to find Laudians appropriating Donne for their own purposes, it is considerably more unexpected to find Catholics doing the same. Yet Michael Questier has recently discovered a remarkable position paper written by two English Catholic clergy in the mid-1630s in which Donne is cited in support of a proposal to restore the Catholic episcopal hierarchy in England. The writers, probably John Southcot and George Leyburn, argued that 'the wisest and most moderat of the Protestant clergy' did not object to Catholics being governed by a bishop of their own, 'and as a learned Protestant, sometime deane of St Paules in London, tould a Catholick that was his freind, hee wondred to see so many provincialls, rectours and other superiours of regular orders in England, and yet noe bishop to governe the clergy' (Questier 2005: 239). This is almost certainly a reference to Donne. (It is possible that it refers to John Overall, one of Donne's predecessors as Dean of St Paul's, but if Southcot and Leyburn had Overall in mind it would have made more sense for them to refer to him as Bishop of Norwich.) It is a striking illustration of the changed religious climate of the 1630s that the proposal to restore the Catholic hierarchy could plausibly be defended as likely to find favour with leading members of the Church of England. That Donne should be mentioned in this context suggests that he was remembered after his death not as the anti-papal polemicist of *Pseudo-Martyr* and *Ignatius His Conclave* but as a divine of a notably moderate and irenic temperament.

After his death, of course, Donne's writings were more widely circulated than they had been in his lifetime, with the publication of the *Poems* in 1633 and the first volume of his collected Sermons in 1640. It is arguable that his reputation stood higher in the 1630s than it had ever done before. Yet, as I have argued here, Donne did not negotiate the transition to the reign of Charles I entirely smoothly or seamlessly, and the Sermons preached in the final years of his life often betray a mood of ambivalence, looking back to the reign of James as well as forward to the political and religious changes of the 1630s. It may be significant that the Newcastle manuscript of Donne's poems, probably copied in the early 1630s—its existence testifying to the fact that Donne's writings continued to be widely read and circulated—should have described the Holy Sonnets as 'written. 20. yeares since' (BL, Harleian 4955, fo. 138^v). It suggests that Donne's style of poetry, and perhaps his style of piety as well, now seemed to belong to an earlier generation.

CHAPTER 36.II

THE DEATH OF DONNE

ALISON SHELL

THE early modern era can be thought of as one of pervasive honesty about death, in contrast to our own times. It was certainly one in which intensive preparation for death bulked largely in the life of anyone who took the Christian faith seriously, and where the ideal of the *bona mors*, or good death, directed moral discourse at every intellectual level (Watt; Beaty ch.17, esp. 389–93). Human skulls acted as a focus for contemplation, in themselves or pictured in conjunction with other emblems of mortality—hourglasses, skeletons, and bubbles—in a number of visual media: oil paintings, woodcuts, tombstones, and funeral monuments. Commemorative inscriptions, epitaphs, funeral elegies, and funeral sermons can be numbered among the ways that death shaped the literary culture of the time, while biographical writing in a broader sense can hardly be detached from death's gravitational drag. Texts and physical artefacts alike can be placed under the heading of the memento mori, a call to remember the inevitability of death. Just as the dance of death proverbially united all degrees of society, so the memento mori contained a universal message; and this chapter will examine how Donne used his consciousness of mortality and his own deathbed to forge bonds with family, friends, and mankind in general.

Like many pious individuals of his era, Donne kept a memento mori about him: in his will he bequeaths 'the Picture call'de the Sceleton wch hanges in the Hall' to his friend Thomas Winniffe (Bald 1970: Appendix II [ref. on 563]; see Llewellyn 1991: 13). But his poems suggest that he hardly needed his memory to be jogged on the subject. Even at their most rakish, they fulfil the era's basic moral obligation to keep death constantly in mind. In *Relic*, for instance, the speaker speculates upon the moment

> When my grave is broke up againe
> Some second ghest to entertaine,
> ...
> And he that digs it, spies
> A bracelet of bright haire about the bone.
>
> (ll. 1–2, 5–6)

The reader acts as sexton, participating in the process of unearthing the speaker's remains, while the bracelet of hair, less subject than flesh to decay and hence a reminder of life in death, sets up a provocative tension with the notion of memento mori (Targoff 2006: 222; see also Gittings 111). *Will*, another of the Songs and Sonets, is a satirical take on the whole idea of preparing for death. Some of the speaker's imaginary legatees receive bequests that satirically undermine the notion of worldly possessions:

> To him for whom the passing bell next tolls,
> I give my physick bookes; my writen rowles
> Of Morall counsels, I to Bedlam give;
> My brazen medals, unto them which live
> In want of bread ...
>
> (ll. 37–41)

Others stand in all too much need of what he is relinquishing:

> My constancie I to the planets give,
> My truth to them, who at the Court doe live;
> Mine ingenuity and opennesse,
> To Jesuites; to Buffones my pensivenesse;
> My silence to'any, who abroad hath beene;
> My mony to a Capuchin.
>
> (ll. 10–15; see Hunt)

Striking in the first poem is the idea of being picked over by spectators; in the second—for all its flippancy—the way in which the dying person acts as an exemplar for the living. For Donne and his contemporaries, after all, death was a public matter. In a relentlessly teleological world, where a good death was the crown of life, the behaviour of the dying was scrutinized to see whether they departed as peacefully and cheerfully as Christians should (Cressy 1997: 390–3). In his *ValMourn*, Donne gives us a glimpse of this thronged deathbed:

> As virtuous men passe mildly away,
> And whisper to their soules, to goe,
> Whilst some of their sad friends doe say,
> The breath goes now, and some say, no.
>
> So let us melt, and make no noise,
> No teare-floods, nor sigh-tempests move,
> T'were prophanation of our joyes
> To tell the layetie our love.
>
> (ll. 1–8)

Though presented as a simile, this is not comparing like with like. The tension here between the public arena of the virtuous deathbed and the lovers' private ecstasy is picked up in the notion that it is profane to 'tell the layetie' of their shared death. Contemporary cautions to the bereaved about avoiding excessive grief are parodied in the speaker's caution about climaxing too loudly—like many other early modern writers, Donne is capitalizing on the sexual pun whereby 'die' stands for experiencing orgasm (Cressy 1997: 393–5; Phillippy 7–16, 66–9, 128–9). The lines may also pick up on those notions of pagan sacerdotalism epitomized by the sibyl's words in Book 6 of the *Aeneid*, '*Procul, o procul este, profani*' (line 258). Either way, the erotic injunction towards privacy gains added piquancy for being set against the highly public, didactic spectacle of the good man's deathbed. *Relic* makes similar use of a defiant sexual privacy in the face of death, this time set against a background of the resurrection of the body and the Last Judgement. From the passage quoted earlier, it continues:

> Will he not let'us alone,
> And thinke that there a loving couple lies,
> Who thought that this device might be some way
> To make their soules, at the last busie day,
> Meet at this grave, and make a little stay?
>
> (ll. 7–11)

At a time when it was widely believed that all one's remains would be collected together at the general resurrection, this conceit was not just a conceit (Cressy 1997: 387–8; Houlbrooke 42; Targoff 2008: 166–7).

Given the large number of women who died in childbirth at this time, the linkage of sexual love and death that characterizes so many of Donne's poems may have gendered overtones. Given his family history, Donne would have recognized these all too well. Anne Donne, his wife, died in August 1617 after giving birth to a stillborn twelfth child (Walton 1675: 30–1; J. Stubbs 283–5), and the poem that pays tribute to her (*HSShe*) has, like so many of the other Holy Sonnets, violent sexual connotations:

> Since She whome I lovd, hath payd her last debt
> To Nature, and to hers, and my good is dead
> And her Soule early into heauen rauished,
> Wholy in heauenly things my Mind is sett.
> Here the admyring her my Mind did whett
> To seeke thee God.
>
> (*Variorum* 7.1, ll. 1–6)

Anne Donne has been 'rauished' by death—a word with overtones of both rape and abduction—and so has forcibly turned Donne towards aspirations modelled by Christian Neoplatonism. She first kindled desire that has since become a desire for God, as yet unslaked: 'A holy thirsty dropsy melts mee yett' (l. 8). Picking up on the common comparison of desire for God to thirst, famously expressed in Psalm 42:2—'My soul thirsteth for God, for the living God: when shall I come and appear before God?'—dropsy is also a disease that swells the body in a manner similar to pregnancy. If one follows this train of thought, then for a woman, the idea of discharging a debt to nature can be seen as having overtones of Eve's curse, 'In sorrow thou shalt bring forth children' (Gen. 3:16). Perhaps one is to detect a pun on 'heirs' in the poem's unidiomatic phrase 'to hers', which has often troubled editors (*Variorum* 7.1. 446–7).

Donne's father, who died when Donne was a small child, is commemorated in another Holy Sonnet (*HSSouls*):

> If faythfull Soules be alike glorified
> As Angels, then my fathers Soule doth see
> And ads this even to full felicitee,
> That valiantly'I hells wide mouth orestride.
>
> (ll. 1–4)

'Alike' is ambiguous, meaning both that faithful souls may be glorified in the same way angels are, but also injecting an element of conditionality into the idea that all of them will be glorified in the same way. One may be justified in reading into this a nervous acknowledgement of John Donne senior's Catholicism, similar to that which appears in *Sat3*: 'shall thy fathers spirit / Meete blinde Philosophers in heaven, whose merit / Of strict life may be'imputed faith...?' (ll. 11–13). When he pondered the death of family members, Donne had a particular interest in how the parameters of salvation might be extended, but also a heightened awareness of what might lie between them and salvation. A similar uncertainty would surely have accompanied the death of Donne's mother Elizabeth, a lifelong recusant. This did not long precede Donne's own; as R. C. Bald has said: 'It must not be forgotten that the death of his mother, as well as his own approaching end, hangs over Donne's last sermon' (Bald 1970: 524–5; see also Bevan). Certainly, this Sermon, later entitled *Deaths Duell*, is heavy with metaphors of pregnancy and stillbirth, collapsing the distinction between birth and death.

Our very *birth* and entrance into this life, is *exitus à morte*, an *issue from death*, for in our mothers *wombe* wee are *dead so*, as that wee doe *not know* wee *live*, not so much as wee doe in our *sleepe*, neither is there any *grave* so close, or so *putrid* a *prison*, as the *wombe* would be unto us, if we stayed in it *beyond* our time, or dyed there *before* our time....In the wombe the dead *child* kills the *Mother* that conceived it, and is a murtherer, nay a *parricide*, even after it is dead. (*Sermons* 10.231–2)

With a chilling glance at the doctrine of predestination, Donne describes the womb as a nursery for corruption: 'wee are taught *cruelty*, by being *fed with blood*, and may be *damned*, though we be *never borne*' (10.232). The unfilial behaviour of the foetus finds a correlative in the unwholesome family relations that must ensue from juxtaposition with one's family in death—by implication, in the same grave or vault—and being consumed by the same worm:

When those bodies that have beene the *children* of *royall parents*, and the *parents* of *royall children*, must say with *Iob*, to corruption thou art my father, and to the Worme thou art my mother and my sister [Job 17:14]. Miserable riddle, when the *same worme* must bee *my mother*, and *my sister*, and *my selfe*. Miserable incest, when I must bee *maried* to my *mother* and my *sister*, and bee both *father* and *mother* to my *owne mother* and *sister*, *beget*, and *beare* that *worme* which is all that *miserable penury*. (10.238; see Targoff 2008: 64–5, 165)

Deaths Duell was preached on the first Friday of Lent 1631—a doubly penitential date—at the King's chapel in Whitehall, at a time when Donne's final illness was leaving its marks on his body. Writing to an unnamed recipient, Donne had declared: 'It hath been my desire...that I might die in the Pulpit; if not that, yet that I might take my death in the Pulpit, that is, die the sooner by occasion of my former labours', and when he delivered *Deaths Duell* it seemed that his wish was on the point of being granted (*Letters* 243). His first biographer, Izaak Walton, describes how:

when to the amazement of some beholders he appeared in the Pulpit, many of them thought he presented himself not to preach mortification by a living voice: but, mortality by a decayed body and a dying face...[H]is strong desires enabled his weak body to discharge his memory of his preconceived meditations, which were of dying: the Text being, *To God the Lord belong the issues from death*. Many that then saw his tears, and heard his faint and hollow voice, professing that they thought the Text prophetically chosen, and that Dr. Donne *had preach't his own Funeral Sermon*. (1675: 68; see also J. Martin)

Certainly, it appears to have been an impossible act to follow; in the printed edition of *Deaths Duell* the epistle to the reader tells us that 'This *Sermon was, by Sacred Authoritie, stiled the Authors owne funeral Sermon*' (*Sermons* 10.229; see also Bevan). The stratagem was all the more appropriate as Donne had wished for a private interment, though Walton tells us his funeral was, in fact, very well attended (Walton 1675: 76–7; see also Bald 1970: 530–1). The funeral elegies affixed to his posthumously published *Poems* (1633*b*) gave his contemporaries a formal chance for epideictic commemoration, not least of *Deaths Duell* itself. But as Henry King declared, even this had its difficulties. Implicitly praising Donne for passing up the opportunity to display his powers by writing his own elegy, he nevertheless admits that he would have done it best of all:

> Thou, like the dying Swanne, didst lately sing
> Thy Mournfull Dirge, in audience of the King;
> When pale lookes, and faint accents of thy breath,
> Presented so, to life, that peece of death,
> That it was fear'd and prophesi'd by all,
> Thou thither camst to preach Thy Funerall.
> O! hadst Thou in an Elegiacke Knell
> Rung out unto the world thine owne farewell,
> And in thy High Victorious Numbers beate
> The solemne measure of thy griev'd Retreat;
> Thou mightst the Poets service now have mist
> As well, as then Thou did'st prevent the Priest;
> And never to the world beholding bee
> So much, as for an Epitaph for thee.
>
> (Donne 1633*b*: 374, ll. 29–42)

It is not surprising that King should have turned to the metaphor of the passing bell as a comparison for Donne's last words. Bells were a prominent part of London's soundscape, and here, as across the rest of England, they lent themselves well to being moralized (B. R. Smith 53, 60). Calling parishioners to church, they asked one to put aside one's worldly concerns and worship God; marking the passage of time, they were a ready-made invitation to consider one's latter end. But of all the occasions for bell-ringing, the passing bell—rung when a member of the parish was dying or dead, and sometimes too at their burial—lent itself best to imaginative meditation (Cressy 1997: 421–5; Gittings 133–5). Donne's *Devotions* show how highly he regarded bells as an aid to meditation on death. Addressing God, he scoffs at those who dare to object 'when in the voice of thy *Church*, thou givest allowance, to this *Ceremony* of *Bells* at *funeralls*' (*Devotions* 83). Though the charge is general, Donne is probably thinking of commentators like the separatist Henry Barrow, who criticized bells, together with fonts, church organs, and vestments, as 'popish idolatrous reliques'

Ill. 36.II.1. Donne's funeral monument, sculpted by Nicholas Stone and stored for over 200 years after the 1666 fire of London in the crypt of St Paul's Cathedral, London. In the nineteenth century it became the only example of sculpture from the old St Paul's to be restored for display on the main floor of the cathedral. (Reproduced by permission of the Dean and Chapter of St Paul's Cathedral.)

(Barrow 1591: 40; see Cressy 1997: 423). This would partly have derived from the popular notion of bell-ringing as apotropaic, something to drive demons away (Thomas 34–5, 56, 59, 65, 303, 588). Refuting the criticism by engaging with it, Donne declares: 'Is that enough, that their ringing hath been said to drive away *evill spirits*? Truly, that is so farre true, as that the *evill spirit* is vehemently vexed in their ringing, therefore, because that action brings the *Congregation* together, and unites *God* and his *people*' (*Devotions* 83). As this implies, Donne sees the passing bell as emblematic of how Christianity requires one to recognize not only the bond between God and man, but the kinship within a religious community; in the same meditation on the topic, perhaps with another blow at the separatists, he implores: 'Lord let us not breake the

Communion of Saints, in that which was intended for the *advancement* of it' (84). It may be helpful to read in this light the most famous piece of Donne's prose, also from the *Devotions*:

No Man is an *Iland*, intire of it selfe; every man is a peece of the *Continent*, a part of the *maine*; if a *Clod* bee washed away by the *Sea*, *Europe* is the lesse, as well as if a *Promontorie* were, as well as if a *Mannor* of thy *friends*, or of *thine owne* were; Any Mans *death* diminishes *me*, because I am involved in *Mankinde*; And therefore never send to know for whom the *bell* tolls; It tolls for *thee*. (87)

This and surrounding passages display a complex interplay of spatial and acoustic stimuli that can fruitfully be read not only onto Donne's physical situation as an inhabitant of a London parish, but onto the sectarian shiftings of his day. Among a church bell's other significations was that it defined a parish unit; basic to the Established Church in England, parishes were seen as being undermined not only by those of separatist tendencies, but by the Puritan desire to go beyond the boundaries of one's parish if better spiritual nourishment was to be found further afield. Hence, in contrast to the Puritan instinct to consort only with the elect and pull away from the wider community, Donne can be seen as affirming the diverse, even motley, gathering who only have in common their position within parish boundaries. The knell was a way of letting those in a parish know that someone was dead: a death that, even in London, was likely to affect one personally. This affirmation of community makes Donne's injunction 'never send to know for whom the *bell* tolls' startlingly paradoxical; because one's interests are so closely identified with one's neighbour's, it can be seen as the acme of neighbourliness not to try to find out who is dying. From one of Tudor and Stuart England's most individual voices, this articulation of the limits of religious individualism has particular force.

As this famous passage also implies, one function of the knell could be seen as its invitation to the hearers to consider their own mortality rather than ruminating on someone else's life. Hence, it is not surprising that Donne is the primary addressee of his own exhortations.

My *God*, my *God*, Is this one of thy waies, of *drawing light out of darknesse*, To make *him* for whom this *bell* tolls, now in this dimnesse of his sight, to become a *superintendent*, an *overseer*, a *Bishop*, to as many as heare his *voice*, in this bell, and to give us a *confirmation* in this action? Is this one of thy waies *to raise strength out of weaknesse*, to make him who cannot rise *from his bed*, nor stirre *in his bed*, come *home* to *me*, and in this sound, give mee the strength of *healthy* and vigorous *instructions*? (*Devotions* 87–8)

Instructed by God, Donne is empowered to convey instruction to his immediate circle, and Walton takes up the tale: Donne,

being sensible of his hourly decay, retired himself to his bed-chamber: and, that week sent at several times for many of his most considerable friends, with whom he took a solemn and deliberate farewell; commending to their considerations some sentences useful for the regulation of their lives, and then dismist them, as good *Jacob* did his sons, with a spiritual benediction. (Walton 1675: 74–5)

Walton's descriptions of Donne's deathbed and the harbingers of death that preceded it are copious and specific, running to just over half the text, which gives a good idea of the topic's importance for his implied readership. His record of the monument that Donne commissioned for himself, and that still stands in St Paul's Cathedral, has attracted much scholarly attention (Gardner 1979: 29-44; Foxell; Llewellyn 2000: 235, 289). For those interested in the interplay between text and artefact in early modern religious practice, another of the most fascinating passages concerns the commemorative seals commissioned by Donne. Not long before his death Donne

> caused to be drawn a figure of the Body of Christ extended upon an Anchor, like those which Painters draw when they would present us with the picture of Christ crucified on the Cross: his, varying no otherwise then to affix him not to a Cross but to an Anchor (the Emblem of hope) this he caused to be drawn in little, and then many of those figures thus drawn to be ingraven very small in *Helitropian* Stones, and set in gold, and of these he sent to many of his dearest friends to be used as *Seals*, or *Rings*, and kept as memorials of him, and of his affection to them. (Walton 1675: 54–5; J. Martin 190)

They are not mentioned in Donne's will, though the cathedral officials Robert Christmas and Thomas Roger were bequeathed £5 apiece for mourning rings (Bald 1970: 523).

The device on these seals, adopted by Donne around the date of his ordination, takes on an added resonance in the context of death, and crucial to its meaning is the kind of semi-precious stone that Donne specified (see E. M. Simpson 1965; Donne 1978a: Appendix G; cf. Crawley-Boevey 42). A heliotropian stone, or bloodstone, is a green variety of quartz with spots or veins of red jasper, described by Pliny the Elder as refracting the sun's rays when put in water in such a way as to make the water appear bloody (*Natural History* 2.627). Donne may be drawing on this well-known source to give an apocalyptic cast to his gift, asking his friends to see in his death the prefiguration of the sun's and world's demise.

At the very least, the connotations of the names 'heliotrope' and 'bloodstone' would not have escaped him (*OED* under 'heliotrope', 'heliotropian', bloodstone'). 'Heliotrope', as with the flower of the same name, figures a turning towards the sun, which in contemporary emblematics was often compared to the Christian soul's turn towards God (e.g. in Drexel). The penitential cast to this continuing process of conversion shapes the ending of *Goodf*:

> O thinke mee worth thine anger, punish mee,
> Burne off my rusts, and my deformity,
> Restore thine Image, so much, by thy grace,
> That thou mayst know mee, and I'll turne my face.

(ll. 39–42)

If the notion of blood draws one's attention to issues of life and death, and the red spots and veins of bloodstone emblematize the human anatomy that so often transfixed Donne, these stones were also credited with the virtue of staunching blood. Hence, the dialogue of the stone with the figure of Christ would have been a complex one: Christ, by shedding his blood, caused others to live. Finally, the anchor on which Christ is shown crucified has multiple connotations: as Walton observes, it is an emblem of hope, but it also figures steadfastness in mortal life and the stasis of eternity. Several of the device's broader connotations are teased out in Donne's poem *GHerb*, and Herbert's response, 'In Sacram Anchoram Piscatoris' (Donne 1978a: 52–3, 111–12 and Appendix G, 138–47; G. Herbert 1991: 450–1; E. M. Simpson 1965; Frontain 1984: 285–9; H. Kelliher 1974: 46).

As Walton's account suggests, the seals could have formed part of mourning rings, which throughout the early modern era were a common parting gift from the dying to the living (Llewellyn 1991: 19, 86, 95–6). But however they were set, seals would have had powerful affective overtones, thanks to the Song of Songs' injunction, 'set me as a seal upon thine heart, as a seal upon thine arm: for love is strong as death' (S. of S. 8:6a). Walton's account also suggests the importance they would have had beyond the immediate occasion, an iconic quality that would have been enhanced as they were passed from hand to hand (Strickland 254–5; cf. Crawley-Boevey, and Donne 1978a: Appendix G). Walton may have been a recipient of a memorial seal himself, and if so, it would have been one reason why his *Life* reads as if it is written to repay an insupportable debt of friendship (but see Donne 1978a: 140). The introduction ends: '*And if the Authors glorious spirit, which now is in Heaven; can have the leasure to look down and see me, the poorest, the meanest of all his friends, in the midst of this officious duty, confident I am, that he will not disdain this well-meant sacrifice to his memory...*' (Walton 1675: 10). Like Donne in *Lit*, Walton is evoking the communion of saints and expressing pious hopes in relation to them. But in Protestant England the church militant had to keep some distance from the church triumphant, since praying to saints or for souls was forbidden as popish. *Lit* goes as far as it can, and further than most Protestant writers would have gone, in petitioning the prophets 'in common pray for mee', while immediately adding: 'That I by them excuse not my excesse / In seeking secrets, or Poëtiquenesse'; similarly, the speaker asks the doctors of the church, 'pray for us there / That what they have misdone / Or mis-said, wee to that may not adhere' (ll. 70–2, 113–15). The pronouns, sliding from second to third person, evoke Donne's own confessional shift, and express a more general difficulty: how could the intuition that those in heaven were concerned about the welfare of those on earth be reconciled with the requirement that God alone should be the addressee of one's prayers?

That was not a question to which Protestants of Donne's time had any clear answer, but they could at least try to bridge the gap between earth and heaven. Public services were a standard means of evoking and aspiring towards heavenly prayer and praise, and in a Sermon preached at St Paul's on Easter Day 1627, in keeping with the day's theme of resurrection, Donne does everything a Protestant could to console the bereaved for the loss of purgatory:

if the dead, and we, be not upon one floore, nor under one story, yet we are under one roofe. We think not a friend lost, because he is gone into another roome, nor because he is gone into another Land; And into another world, no man is gone…the dead, and we, are now all in one Church, and at the resurrection, shall be all in one Quire. (*Sermons* 7.384; see also Cressy 1997: 388)

As this suggests, real-life choirs could act as a foretaste of heaven, and as Dean of St Paul's Cathedral Donne had the power to personalize their repertoire. Of the poem now known as *Father*, Walton writes:

he caus'd it to be set to a most grave and solemn Tune, and to be often sung to the *Organ* by the *Choristers* of St. *Pauls* Church, in his own hearing; especially at the Evening Service, and at his return from his Customary Devotions in that place, did occasionally say to a friend, *The words of this* Hymn *have restored to me the same thoughts of joy that possest my Soul in my sickness when I composed it. And, O the power of Church-musick! that Harmony added to this hymn has raised the Affections of my heart, and quickned my graces of zeal and gratitude;* and I observe, *that I always return from paying this publick duty of* Prayer *and* Praise *to God, with an unexpressible tranquillity of mind,* and a willingness *to leave the world.* (1675: 54)

This anecdote may be somewhat enhanced; as deployed in versions of the *Life* from 1658 onwards, it makes an anti-Puritan point about the devotional efficacy of church music, and all those who use Walton's *Life* of Donne as a source have to contend with what Jessica Martin has described as his 'extrapolation' of biographical detail (J. Martin 180, 186, 190, 314). Still, a contemporary musical setting of the poem by John Hilton survives, and the story would be a surprising one to invent in an age when original verses, as opposed to settings of scriptural texts or translations of Psalms and office hymns, did not typically form part of public worship (Souris x, xvii–xix, 18–19; Donne 1965: 246–7; J. R. Watson 69–70). In some ways, Donne's initiative is a remarkable anticipation of the highly personal, confessional hymns associated with early Methodism. But if the conversational musings reported by Walton bear any relation to what actually happened, Donne's affective designs were principally directed not towards the conversion of others, but towards soothing and elevating his own thoughts. Certainly, even leaving aside Donne's signature onomastics—'And, having done that, Thou hast done, / I feare no more' (*Father* ll. 17–18)—the poem's blend of abjection and self-display does not obviously lend itself to communal acts of worship (see Chs. 16 and 4.I on the disputed reading of the text of this line: 'I feare' or 'I have'). Though the poem long figured within the Anglican Church's English Hymnal, the fact that it was eventually dropped by the revisers suggests as much (Donne 1985: 490).

Sickness, also quoted by Walton in his *Life*, again demonstrates a disconcerting blend of private meditation and public chorus, but this time with an awareness that heavenly harmony may transform individuality:

> Since I am comming to that Holy roome,
> Where, with thy Quire of Saints for evermore,
> I shall be made thy Musique; As I come
> I tune the Instrument here at the dore.
>
> (ll. 1–4)

The poem's dating has proved a scholarly headache; Walton gives the date of 23 March 1630/1, six days before Donne died, but a contemporary manuscript of the poem dates it to another illness of Donne's in 1623 (Donne 1978a: 132–5; Walton 1675: 58; see also J. Martin 191–3). Donne may have returned to it on his deathbed, or Walton may have streamlined events to improve the story, but the possibility of elision and confusion has its origin in Donne's own awareness that one cannot know in advance which illness will be one's last. The poem undoubtedly lends itself well to being regarded as among Donne's last words, and while this may be deceptive from the biographical point of view, it testifies to how every illness could be regarded as a rehearsal for death, a time to 'tune' the instrument of the soul. The next stanza runs:

> Whilst my Physitians by their love are growne
> Cosmographers, and I their Mapp, who lie
> Flat on this bed, that by them may be showne
> That this is my South-west discoverie.
>
> (ll. 6–9)

Generations of commentators have, rightly, been struck by how these lines exploit two of the age's most imaginatively potent concerns, anatomies and travel to the New World. Still, one must not neglect the most obvious feature of the map metaphor used here. Maps are a schematic representation of how to get somewhere: in this case, the destination is death. The speaker—whom one need not be afraid to identify as Donne—places himself in the position of one who is instructed by the physician-cosmographers, but maps display knowledge as well as needing interpretation, and the speaker's body maps mortality just as Donne's did on the later sickbed that actually proved his deathbed: 'as his soul ascended, and his last breath departed from him, he closed his own eyes; and then, disposed his hands and body into such a posture as required not the least alteration by those that came to shroud him' (Walton 1675: 76; J. Martin 202). But the word 'discoverie', in a line that is omitted by Walton, points to what readers of Walton's life might miss elsewhere too: Donne's consciousness of the excitement of death. Most memento moris of Donne's time emphasize the transience and fragility of life; in *Sickness*, Donne demonstrates the Christian hope that death should not be an end in itself, but a journey towards a new beginning. Few can have been as concerned as he was to give directions to future voyagers.

PART IV

PROBLEMS OF LITERARY INTERPRETATION THAT HAVE BEEN TRADITIONALLY AND GENERALLY IMPORTANT IN DONNE STUDIES

INTRODUCTION

DENNIS FLYNN

The purpose of Part 4 is to survey, for students and Donne scholars, major critical debates affecting the reception of Donne from the seventeenth to the twenty-first century. To direct these discussions the editors chose seven questions:

- Do Donne's writings express his apostasy?
- Do Donne's writings express his misogyny?
- Do Donne's writings express his political absolutism?
- Are Donne's writings harsh, obscure (or merely witty), and unrhythmical?
- Do Donne's writings express his desperate ambition?
- Do Donne's writings reveal two Donnes?
- Are Donne's writings in part or in whole so dangerous (in one way or another) that, as Donne himself and particular critics in every generation have thought, they should never have been published?

All these legitimate critical questions about Donne's writings were *foreseen and raised by Donne himself*; they have continued—indeed are continuing—to provoke debate in succeeding generations. As they are conceived, these questions do not represent mere straw men or myths that modern readers have accepted or rejected. One way or another, they underlie a good deal of valuable criticism—from Donne's time to our own—and the editors foresaw that articulation of them in seven essays would allow complex, multifaceted response and redefinitions of the problems of interpretation they raise. All seven essays, then, are prisms refracting much the same materials in seven different ways; they cast up focused accounts of Donne's life and writings, panoramas each seen from a different angle. The goal here has been both to give a historical overview of Donne's reception and to pose the central questions anew without necessarily resolving them.

Part 4 is generally intended to present various conjectures and refutations, not to establish a consensus about Donne by refuting influential points of view the editors or authors consider erroneous. First, Achsah Guibbory's 'Donne and apostasy' provides equable review of what has been perhaps the most contentious of all perennial disputes in Donne studies. In Donne's world, and in our own, such matters could (and still can) end lives or glorify deaths; from our vantage-point today, as Guibbory observes (quoting the historian Michael C. Questier), we can see that in Donne's time '"flux in religion was the norm rather than the exception"'. She finds generally in Donne's writings 'an emphasis on seeking, on process, and a corresponding suspicion of rigidity and divisive dogma'. Donne's writings question 'the rigid assumptions that might lie behind such terms as "apostate" or even "convert"'.

Theresa M. DiPasquale's 'Donne, women, and the spectre of misogyny' notes that, while Donne's misogyny has been 'an enduring focus of critical inquiry in Donne studies', there is 'no single proof-text' to indicate 'whether Donne revered women, reviled them, or judged them on a case-by-case basis, as he did—sometimes quite harshly—persons of the male sex'. Quoting John R. Roberts, she deprecates a frequent tendency: 'Too often, what critics most desire is to make Donne's works "lie down quietly on...prefabricated Procrustean beds"', whereas 'the challenge is to resist that desire in favour of attentive response to the range of different tones and perspectives Donne can employ'.

A partial exception to the rule not to refute erroneous views is Debora Shuger's 'Donne's absolutism', which, after characterizing much previous critical work as in some degree based on a misunderstanding, sets forth a pioneering discussion of Donne and political theory, informed by wide-ranging and detailed study of technical particulars and putting our apprehension of Donne's politics on a new footing.

Albert C. Labriola's 'Style, wit, prosody in the poetry of John Donne' poses large questions to organize the history of controversy over these topics: 'What is the relationship between art and experience in Donne's works? When is the author also the speaker in a poem? Or when is the author distanced from the speaker, who becomes a character in his own right? How may a composition be artful and finely wrought, both structurally and verbally, but still convey the semblance of spontaneity? May a poem be "sweet" if it is not metrically rhythmic or melodious? How may irregular prosody still be poetic?' To such questions Labriola's answers emerge through a focused history of decline in esteem for Donne's prosody and wit, leading eventually to the nineteenth- and twentieth-century Donne revival.

Looking at shifting 'social and cultural connotations of ambition' since the seventeenth century, Hugh Adlington directly asks the question 'Do Donne's writings express his desperate ambition?' in order to determine where 'this widely held notion of Donne's restless ambition' comes from. His analytic survey of received opinions concludes with innovative discussion of Donne's opinions on the topic, a 'valuable source of evidence' that has been paid 'little or no attention', although Donne's own attitudes can help us to develop 'one possible response to the oft-made but rarely answered call for increased historical contextualization of Donne's life and writing'.

Judith Scherer Herz, in '"By parting have joyn'd here": the story of the two (or more) Donnes', identifies among salient and various critical contributions concerning this issue those of Izaak Walton, Samuel Johnson, Samuel Taylor Coleridge, Edmund Gosse, and John Carey, all best understood in relation to Donne's own 'doublings' of his personality in poetry and prose. Herz concludes that in these Donne in different ways joins the company of Walt Whitman, Fernando Pessoa, Robert Schumann, and Bob Dylan.

Rounding out Part 4, with the last word in the *Handbook*, Lynne Magnusson's 'Danger and discourse' amplifies perhaps the least-appreciated ground tone in and between the lines of Donne's poetry and prose, as well as in critical studies of them. Magnusson explores Donne's own thoughts about 'the dangers associated not only with linguistic interaction but also with the circulation of written texts'; and she emphasizes how Donne's 'early lessons in communication related to his positioning within the Catholic minority at a time when persecution aimed at enforcing uniformity in religion and eradicating Catholicism in England'. She shows that these large and momentous social contexts determined Donne's habitual practices in communication, including a sense of danger that 'inflects his imaginative writing'.

Together, these seven essays provide for twenty-first-century Donne studies what the entire Handbook aims at: both summaries of achievement in major areas of scholarship and directions for further work.

CHAPTER 37

DONNE AND APOSTASY

ACHSAH GUIBBORY

What do we call someone who changes from one religion or confessional allegiance to another? A 'convert'? An 'apostate'? The word we choose is not neutral.

'Convert' suggests the person has turned away from a former belief, practice, or nature (now assumed to be erring) and embraced what he now considers a true faith or belief. 'Conversion' suggests transformation (from classical Latin *convertere*—to turn altogether). It is a Christian revision of the Hebrew notion of *teshuvah*, which in Deuteronomy and the Hebrew prophets signifies a change that is a 'return' to the former path, a turning away from idolatry to the path set by God. Paul (in Acts) is the archetypal convert, having experienced a transforming encounter on the road to Damascus, which changed him from a Christian-persecuting Jew to a Christian, anxious to mark his difference from his past by divorcing himself from past beliefs and practices (now seen as false, erroneous, incapable of saving him), renouncing Jewish Israel even while holding out hope that some, if not 'all', of his Jewish 'brethren' would be saved by recognizing Christ as saviour.

But an 'apostate?' 'Apostasy' signifies 'Abandonment or renunciation of one's religious faith or moral allegiance'—'By extension: The abandonment of principles or party generally' (*OED*). The *OED* defines an 'apostate' as a 'pervert', 'turncoat', 'renegade', and 'infidel'. The very word labels the person a traitor, someone who lacks principles or loyalty, who is faithless. The term 'apostasy' characterizes a person who has abandoned the true religion, who, indeed, has rejected God. The term demonizes the person it is applied to. Satan is, in Milton's *Paradise Lost*, an 'Apostate' (*PL* 5.852).

But what if there is political pressure to change confessional identities? In late fifteenth-century Spain and Portugal, Jews were forced either to convert to Catholicism or to face death or exile. There were no such forced conversions for Roman Catholics in post-Reformation England, which, after the accession of Elizabeth I, was officially a Protestant nation. Religious beliefs did not suddenly change, and Catholic and Protestant traditions continued to coexist. Still, attendance in the Church of England was coterminous with being considered fully English. There was pressure to convert—or at least (as a 'church-papist'; Walsham 1999) to conform outwardly to the English church—if one wanted to take a university degree or hold office. Acts of Uniformity and Supremacy passed under Elizabeth, as well as increasingly vigilant efforts to enforce them, created an oppressive environment intended to encourage English Catholics to convert.

Suspicion dogs the convert. A convert may be suspected of not being a 'real' believer. The Spanish Inquisition was intended to ferret out 'new Christians' (Jewish converts to Catholicism) who were suspected of still being secretly Jewish, whose Christian public practices hid a private Jewishness, which might reside in the conscience or be expressed in the home. Some Catholics in England attended the English Church but privately remained Catholic. Others, particularly those wealthy enough to pay the fines for non-attendance, continued to practice the faith, even though it was outlawed and though harbouring the priest needed for performing the sacraments might lead to imprisonment or even death.

This was the situation that Donne grew up with in England. Born in 1572 into a traditional Catholic family, he attended Oxford University but left before taking a degree, which would have required him to subscribe to an oath declaring England's monarch (rather than the Pope) his supreme authority. More than twenty years later, in 1615, he was ordained as a priest in the Church of England. We do not know when he 'converted' or, perhaps better, 'conformed' to the Established Church, and later biographers and readers have speculated on his motives for conversion. Pragmatism? Ambition? Conviction? Accommodation? Genuine spiritual change? We can never know what he 'really' believed, but that has not stopped scholars from trying to determine that belief and label him. Convert? Apostate? Conformist?

COMMENTS BY DONNE IN HIS PROSE (LETTERS, *PSEUDO-MARTYR*, SERMONS)

Pseudo-Martyr (1610) contains some of Donne's most explicit statements about his 'religion', but we must remember that these remarks were published, intended for a public audience, and part of a polemical tract. Shaped by contingencies and multiple motives, these statements cannot be read simply as transparent expressions of Donne's beliefs. In *Pseudo-Martyr* he chose a generic, inclusive definition of his religious identity, hoping to convince Roman Catholics that they could in good conscience take the Oath of Allegiance to England's Protestant monarch while remaining loyal to their Catholic beliefs. Having described his own Catholic background, acknowledging the many members of his extended family who had suffered either 'Martyrdome' or exile for their faith, the many nights in his youth when he was 'kept awake' by fear of and obsession with martyrdom (*Pseudo-Martyr* 8), Donne now identified himself as one who 'dares not call his Religion by some newer name then *Christian*' (14)—as if he had matured from an earlier sense of being part of a vulnerable, persecuted religious group towards an inclusive, ecumenical identity. Insisting on the antiquity and continuity of Christian religion, Donne offered a self-description that defies the label of either 'apostate' or 'convert'. He has simply expanded, not changed—a description that revises but does not contradict the motto of Donne's 1591 portrait ('sooner dead than changed').

Even as he retained a sense of connection to the devotion of his past, Donne was critical of the post-Tridentine Catholic Church, aspects of which seemed to him to oppress the individual conscience or to place believers in unnecessary physical danger in a Christendom split by confessional differences and conflict. The Church of Rome, after the Council of Trent, added new principles and obligations for Catholics. As he put it in *Pseudo-Martyr*, 'to cal every pretence of the Pope, Catholique faith, and to bleede to death for it, is a sickenesse and a medicine, which the Primitive Church never understood' (19; for more on *Pseudo-Martyr* in context, see Chs. 18 and 30.II).

Donne's relatively inclusive view of the Christian church is evident in *Essayes in Divinity*, written before his ordination but not published. Here he defended his allegiance to the Church of England but also suggested that the Church of Rome was part of the 'universal, Christian, Catholick Church' (*Essayes* 54–9). This assertion contradicted the view of 'hotter' Protestants, who believed that Roman Catholics were cut off from salvation: 'Synagogue and Church is the same thing, and of the Church, *Roman* and *Reformed*, and all other distinctions of place, Discipline, or Person, but one Church, journeying to one *Hierusalem*, and directed by one guide, Christ Jesus' (58). Donne here insists that God's church may have more than one name, and that labels are divisive—an insight we might keep in mind when we think about what to 'call' Donne's spiritual or confessional change.

Generously inclusive statements—critical of the contemporary atmosphere of religious dissension—appear in more private moments, in Letters to friends. Writing to Sir Henry Goodere, Donne insists that he has 'never fettered nor imprisoned the word Religion' by 'immuring it in a *Rome*, or a *Wittenberg*, or a *Geneva*; they are all virtuall beams of one Sun' (*Letters* 29). On the other hand, there is a limit to his inclusivity. 'Religion' for Donne meant 'Christianity' (29). But his tendency to define Christianity broadly diminished the differences between 'Roman' and 'Reformed' 'religion'. Another Letter to Goodere speaks of both churches as 'the sister teats of his [God's] graces'—'the channels of Gods mercies run through both fields' (102). The metaphors make it clear that, though neither is perfect ('both [are] diseased and infected'; 102), salvation can be had in either.

Balancing that inclusiveness, and perhaps in part explaining it, is Donne's revealing comment to Goodere that it is virtually impossible to erase one's 'former habits' in religion. You may try to 'remove' the early 'marks' but it is, as with a 'Coyne, upon which the stamp were removed, though to imprint it better, but it looks awry and squint' (*Letters* 101–2; discussed in Shell and Hunt 78–9).

A Letter to Sir Robert Ker asserts, 'My Tenets are always, for the preservation of the Religion I was born in, and the peace of the State, and the rectifying of the Conscience' (*Letters* 306–7). The statement is intriguing. What religion does Donne mean he was 'born in'? Roman Catholicism? An English Catholicism that, from at least the 1530s through the 1560s had been largely independent of Rome (Macek; Wooding)? Pre-Tridentine Catholicism? Christianity, generally? How does his dedication to preserving that religion fit with his concern with 'the peace of the State'? What if one's religion might seem a threat to the state? And what about the relation between conscience and matters of state? What takes precedence if religion, state, and conscience are not all in harmony? What's important here is Donne's expressed sense of his loyalty, his faithfulness in preserving, not turning away from, that religion even as he follows his conscience and works for the peace of the state.

We need to be careful how we interpret Donne's statements about religion in these texts—some are public, even polemical, and are shaped by political and historical contingencies; others, in Letters to friends, are more private, what Donne might call communications of his 'soule' to a friend (see the Verse Letter to Henry Wotton on letters mingling souls: *HWKiss*). After his ordination, Donne preached numerous Sermons that, while they avoided polemic (Shami 2003a: 139–65), were decidedly public pronouncements. Although he sometimes refers in these Sermons to 'Rome' (i.e. the Church of Rome) as 'our Adversaries' (*Sermons* 6.245; 7.190) (a designation that was political as well as religious), we often see an ecumenical position similar to that expressed both in *Pseudo-Martyr* and his private Letters, particularly in Sermons preached after 1624 as the church became more sharply divided between those clergy who favoured ceremony and were anti-Calvinist, and 'Puritans' who believed that the English Church was becoming too much like that of Rome. Donne's God in these Sermons is a generous God whose embrace is universal: he 'desires to have his kingdome well peopled; he would have *many*, he would have *all*' (6.151). God's 'house' has '*many mansions*' (6.152). Donne attacks those who 'so farre abridge the great Volumes of the mercy of God...as to restrain this salvation, not only in the effect, but in Gods own purpose, to a few, a very few soules' (9.267). A 1626 Sermon delivered on the anniversary of the Gunpowder Plot speaks of the 'Universality' of Gods grace (7.247). In a Sermon at Paul's Cross on 22 November 1629 Donne criticizes the 'over-pure' who are 'loth that Christ should spread his armes, or shed his bloud in such a compasse, as might fall upon *all*. Men that think no sinne can hurt them, because they are *elect*, and that every sin makes every other man a *Reprobate*' (9.119). These are public pronouncements, often with an obliquely anti-Puritan edge. But Donne's sharp critique of those who would draw the boundaries of the church too narrowly, or of ardently predestinarian Calvinists who would limit God's grace, may also reflect a personal desire or need to assure himself of a continuing connection with his Catholic family and ancestors, believing they would all be saved.

The debate about Donne's religion—and to what extent he might be said to have embraced the Church of England, conformed, or remained somehow still Catholic—has affected how different scholars read Donne's religious prose after his ordination. Jeanne Shami (1995a; 2003a) sees in the Sermons a Donne who strives for consensus; Joshua Scodel (1995) similarly finds Donne seeking a middle ground between opposing positions, seeking the 'mean'; Daniel Doerksen (1997), Paul Sellin (1983) and others have written about a 'Calvinist' Donne; while Richard Strier and Achsah Guibbory (2001) have found in Donne an affinity for the Arminian theology and ceremonialism that was becoming increasingly influential and divisive in the mid- to late 1620s. There remain, that is, many ways of understanding the changes (or continuities) in Donne's religion.

THE CRITICAL DEBATE: HOW BIOGRAPHERS AND SCHOLAR-CRITICS HAVE DESCRIBED DONNE, AND THE IMPLICATIONS

Donne's first biographer, Izaak Walton, who affixed his 'Life of Dr. Donne' to the first edition of Donne's *Sermons* in 1640, presented Donne as following the pattern of St Augustine, who more than a thousand years earlier had converted from paganism and a life of sensuality to Christianity and the life of the spirit. Walton's revisions between 1640 and 1675 increasingly portrayed 'Dr. Donne' as a figure of piety to be venerated. Artfully manipulating dates and sources (Novarr 1958), Walton made Donne into a pillar of the English Church that seemed, to contemporary Puritans, insufficiently reformed from Catholicism, and would later be called the 'Anglican' Church. In his 'hagiography' or 'saint's life', Walton downplayed Donne's Catholic background, even as he mentioned his descent from Sir Thomas More on his mother's side and the formative example of his 'pious Parents' (1675: 13). We see, not a Catholic Donne, but a studious, serious Donne who in 'the nineteenth year of his age,... being then unresolv'd what Religion to adhere to', put aside 'all study of the Law' and began to 'survey and consider the Body of Divinity, as it was then controverted betwixt the *Reformed* and the *Roman Church*' (ibid.). Donne's search for religious 'truth' continued into 'the twentieth year of his age' (14). Walton states that Donne had come to recognize the truth of the English Church by that time, though he observes that Donne continued studying the controversy between the Roman Catholic and Reformed churches. Walton then remarks that Donne wrote *Pseudo-Martyr* (1610) at the King's request to persuade Catholics to take the Oath of Allegiance, and that James tried to persuade Donne to become a priest in the English Church. Collapsing the five years between *Pseudo-Martyr* and Donne's ordination (1615), as if they were but a matter of a few months, Walton presents Donne's 'modesty' (not doubts) as the cause of his apparent 'unwilling[ness]' to take holy orders and compares it to the 'strifes' 'St. *Austine* had, when St. *Ambrose* indeavoured his conversion to Christianity' (1675: 35, 38). That 'conversion' is the basic principle of Walton's biography of Donne is clear when Walton translates the Spanish motto in Donne's 1591 portrait (*antes muerto que mudado*, properly translated 'sooner dead than changed') as 'How much shall I be chang'd, / Before I am chang'd' (Flynn 1995c: 1–16). Walton thus changes Donne's assertion of unwavering loyalty (perhaps to the traditional, Catholic faith?) into a prognostication of, first Donne's inconstancy, and then his conversion. Significantly, in Walton, Donne's 'conversion' is *not* from Roman Catholicism to the reformed English Church but from a secular life (and from youthful witty poems) to a ministerial and 'penitential' one in a church that Walton assumes to be the true orthodox church. For Walton, Donne's ordination marks a neat conversion from secular to sacred, from earthly to spiritual concerns: 'now all his studies which had been occasionally diffused, were all concentred in Divinity. Now he had a new calling, new thoughts, and a new imployment for his wit and eloquence: Now, all his earthly affections were changed into divine love; and all the faculties of his own soul, were ingaged in the Conversion of others' (1675: 38)—like St Paul. Indeed, Walton invokes the parallel when he describes Donne preaching at Lincoln's Inn: he became 'a *Paul*' in the very place where in his 'irregular youth' 'he had been a *Saul*', quick to 'deride' Christianity with his wit (1675: 44).

Walton's Donne (converted from a profane to a sacred life, rather than from Catholicism) fits comfortably into an English Church whose spirituality and practices Walton sees stretching back to Augustine. Walton makes Augustine's lament about the profanation of churches by 'enemies of Christianity' resonate as an attack on contemporary Puritans who would strip the English churches of '*Publick Hymns* and Lauds', such as the 'hymns' Walton describes Donne as writing late in his life (1675: 53–4). Redefining Donne's conversion in a way that minimizes the Catholic/Reformed divide and erases Donne's early Catholicism, Walton praises Donne as a 'most dutiful Son to his Mother, careful to provide for her supportation,...who having sucked in the Religion of the *Roman Church* with her Mothers Milk, spent her Estate in forraign Countreys, to enjoy a liberty in it, and died in his house but three Moneths before him' (64). It is Donne's mother (not Donne) who sucked in the Roman religion 'with her Mothers Milk'. (As Dayton Haskin points out, Walton 'said nothing about his [Donne's] father's religion': 2007: 84). Filial loyalty to his mother remains even as he is devoted to the Church of England, his spiritual faith uninfluenced by his mother's Roman Catholicism. Walton leaves Donne buried in St Paul's, as if that is where he had always belonged.

Haskin has shown that Walton's account dominated the nineteenth-century view of Donne, the 'convert' (2007: 84). The 1796 edition of Walton's *Life of Donne*—the first new edition in over a hundred years—helped establish 'the priority of Walton's *Life of Donne*' in shaping the idea of 'Donne' (ibid. 20). Henry Alford's 1839 edition of *The Works of John Donne, D.D.*, building on Walton, 'emphasized' that Donne had converted 'on purely rational grounds' (ibid. 59). Donne's late nineteenth-century editor A. B. Grosart also made the idea of 'conversion' central to his picture of Donne, but, unlike Walton, he attended to Donne's 'early life', his 'having been bred a Catholic' (ibid. 131), and focused on Donne the love poet. In Grosart's narrative, Donne gave up Catholicism, fell into 'moral turpitude', and was redeemed not by studying religious controversy but by Anne More's love (Haskin 2006: 238; cf. Haskin 2007: 131–9). Grosart's narrative thus romanticized and secularized the idea of Donne's 'conversion'. At the end of the nineteenth-century Edmund Gosse, in *The Life and Letters of John Donne Dean of St. Paul's*, returned to the idea that Donne's 'conversion' was religious, but suggested it happened two years after his ordination, with the death of his wife, Anne: Donne 'dedicated himself anew to God with a peculiar violence of devotion, and witnessed the dayspring of a sudden light in his soul' (Gosse 1899: 2.99). Gosse pictured the earlier, Catholic Donne as self-serving and 'enslave[d] to the flesh'—as his sensual poetry supposedly revealed. In contrast to Walton's pillar of the church, Gosse's Donne came to a principled religious life very late (Haskin 2007: 173–7).

In the early twentieth century, for Sir Herbert Grierson and T. S. Eliot, Donne was, primarily, a poet. 'New Criticism', as it developed after World War II, was interested in the formal qualities of poetry, not politics or religion. But questions about Donne's religion and the authenticity of his movement from the Roman to the English Church would resurface in the mid-twentieth century, with Helen Gardner's 1952 edition of *The Divine Poems* and R. C. Bald's *John Donne: A Life* (1970), to become, in the half-century since, some of the most intensely debated and controversial issues in Donne studies, particularly as scholars and critics have come to view literary texts as culturally, historically situated, the products of their times, not something transcendent, free-floating, universal.

Helen Gardner's dating of Donne's Holy Sonnets as having been written well before his ordination dismantled Walton's notion of a neat conversion from secular to sacred. Moreover, she suggested a Catholic continuity when she noted that Donne's 'devotional temper is Catholic', though she added: 'his devotion is a "rectified devotion"; his theological position is Protestant' (Donne 1952a: 131). While rejecting any suggestion that Donne was intellectually dishonest, she did remark that 'Donne never speaks as if he felt any direct inward call to the ministry' (131; see Shell and Hunt 68). Her discussion of Donne's religion thus implicitly raised questions about his 'conversion' and about his spiritual commitment to the Church of England—questions that would be given more weight, first by Bald's, and then by John Carey's biographical accounts of Donne's life.

Bald added new elements to the picture. In contrast to Walton, Bald emphasized Donne's early, formative experience in coming from a Catholic family. He described in sympathetic detail the difficult position of being a Catholic in Elizabethan England, hampered by legalized disabilities, subject to discrimination, persecution, even death for keeping the faith. Where Walton erased Donne's Catholic past, Bald attended to it. Bald described a protracted, more complex (indeed ambiguous) conversion as he charted the different stages of Donne's life. Reaffirming Gardner's revisionist dating of Donne's Holy Sonnets as having been written while Donne was living at Mitcham (1608–10), Bald depicts those years as a time of sickness, despair, and depression, a period during which Donne was quite uncertain about whether he would be saved. But Bald insists that this extended 'spiritual crisis' (1970: 235) did not result in conversion. Rather, Donne moved on to another struggle: whether to continue seeking political position and patronage, or whether to enter orders in the English Church, both of which Bald presents as solutions to the pressure Donne felt to support himself and his family economically. While Bald praises Donne's reluctance in the years following *Pseudo-Martyr* (1610) to enter the church as a matter of 'scruples' that we 'must respect' (i.e. Donne wanted to be convinced 'he had a genuine call'; he was conscious of 'sins in his past life' that might seem to diminish his ability to perform 'the holy offices of priesthood', and maybe he was still uncertain of his own salvation: 1970: 207), Donne's 'steps to the Temple' (title of ch. 11) seem in Bald's account to be inspired by concerns less spiritual than economic. Bald's language describing Donne's 'begging letters' (276, 280) and 'complimentary verses' to patrons and patronesses, and his remark that the 'note of financial stringency is heard more often in the letters of this period than in any of the earlier ones' (279–80), present a Donne motivated by necessities and ambition rather than by conscience or faith (see Ch. 41 below on the division over the question of 'Donne's ambition'; see also Ch. 32.I for a detailed and nuanced account of that decision). The year before his ordination has Donne making 'his supreme and final effort to secure state employment' (Bald 1970: 289) but, finding his hopes dashed, 'he deliberately set about making an end to his old way of life. First, however, he sought assurances that the King would be as good as his word to provide for him in the Church' (293). Bald leads us to expect conversion, but that expectation (or at least the spiritual legitimacy of Donne's conversion) is immediately undermined by his intimation of Donne's practical and financial motives, and Bald remarks that Donne's Letters from this time show 'little sense of spiritual issues' but rather 'one who had mastered at last the arts of the courtier' and intended 'to rise by them' (301). Indeed,

Donne's 'conversion' is, for Bald, again postponed—located not in a movement from Catholicism to the English Church, nor in his becoming a priest, but rather in the death of his wife Anne, two years later (1617). In this, Bald amplifies Gosse's earlier suggestion. 'The death of his wife marked a turning-point... and produced something much closer to a conversion than the feelings which had prompted him to enter the Church' (328).

Bald's picture of an ambitious Donne has made a deep mark on scholarly and critical studies of Donne, not only because Bald's remains the authoritative biography (though called into question by Dennis Flynn's work) but also because this picture was colourfully developed by John Carey in his controversial, powerfully written *John Donne: Life, Mind, and Art* (1981a). Even more than Bald, Carey emphasized the role of ambition in Donne's 'conversion'. Carey defined 'two vital factors' as influencing Donne's poetry: 'his desertion of the Roman Catholic Church and his ambition' (14). Carey's first chapter begins boldly: 'The first thing to remember about Donne is that he was a Catholic; the second, that he betrayed his Faith' (15). The statement defines Donne's essential quality as treachery, faithlessness. Chapters on 'Apostasy' and 'Ambition' link Donne's apostasy with his self-seeking ambition, 'a constant element in Donne's life' (90). Carey, with his alliterative twin topics, was responsible for changing the terms in which Donne's shifting confessional allegiance was seen. No longer was Donne's change a result of rational, intellectual inquiry, or his love of Anne More, or even her death. Rather, it was fuelled by the persecution Catholics experienced and by Donne's own ambition. One could say that Carey was not so much following Walton, as reversing Walton's idea of a spiritual conversion/redemption.

Carey insisted he was presenting a 'sympathetic' picture of Donne (14)—despite such comments as Donne 'chose hell. That is to say, he deserted the Catholic God.... He was an apostate' who 'committed a mortal sin against the Faith' (25)—but some subsequent scholars have not thought so. Having seen Carey as calling Donne's integrity into question, they have responded in several ways. Literary scholars, for much of the decade following Carey's book, built on his understanding of Donne's ambition, even if they did not concern themselves with whether Donne was a convert or apostate. Arthur Marotti presented Donne the 'coterie poet', concerned with advancement and patronage. For Marotti, not just the Verse Letters but also many Songs and Sonets express Donne's desire for socio-economic success. Jonathan Goldberg found Donne's figurative language mirroring and reinforcing James I's absolutist ideology. Debora Shuger also saw Donne embracing absolutist 'habits of thought'. These readings implicitly raised questions about his spiritual integrity.

If the idea of Donne as a place-seeker less concerned with faith or principle than getting ahead has had an effect on how people read his writing, there have also been dissenting voices who have presented a different Donne—a person of honour, faith, principle. Dennis Flynn suggested we think of Donne as a 'survivor' (rather than 'apostate'), characterized by 'survivor's' guilt at having escaped Catholic persecution and martyrdom (Flynn 1986). Flynn's book *John Donne and the Ancient Catholic Nobility* (1995c) and several articles have continued to attack the view of Donne promoted by Bald and Carey. Flynn has marshalled evidence suggesting that Donne was 'not' ambitiously pursuing positions or advancement during certain crucial years (Flynn 2000b). Moreover, he places the early Donne in the context of his descent on his mother's side from Sir Thomas More and his family's long association with 'the ancient Catholic nobility'. Where Walton ignored Donne's Catholic associations, Flynn studies Donne's 'Catholic heritage' (Flynn 1995c: 19; see also Ch. 26.II above on the 'history of opposition to Tudor reform' in Donne's family background). Where Bald and Carey presented an ambitious Donne, Flynn instead stresses a code of 'honour' particularly associated with the Catholic nobility. The effect is to reject the notion that Donne was an 'apostate', and to emphasize his integrity and loyalty. Adding to the controversy about Donne the 'convert', some literary critics have insisted on the residual Catholic elements in his writing, which suggest he never fully turned away from his past (Martz 1954; Donne 1952a: 131; Carey 1981a: 51; Young 1987a; Hester 1990a; Guibbory 2001; Shami 1995a, 2003a; but cf. Lewalski 1979).

Others, too, have presented a sympathetic, or at least a less negative, view of Donne's religious change, though they are not of one mind. Tom Cain has remarked that 'The recklessness of the marriage suggests Donne was not as ambitious as most biographers assume' (Cain 2006: 90). Cain suggests that the 'betrayal' (possibly by Jesuits) of Donne's brother Henry for hiding a Catholic priest and Henry's subsequent death in prison might have been a 'determinant for John's move away from Roman Catholicism, a motive more than strong enough to counter the construct of ambitious but tortured "apostate" offered by John Carey' (86). Jeanne Shami has emphasized the place of conscience and principle in Donne's Sermons. Shami's *John Donne and Conformity in Crisis in the Late Jacobean Pulpit* (2003a) identifies Donne during the years after his ordination, not as a controversialist or careerist, but as a person of 'integrity' (20), supportive of 'conformity' with the established English Church, and using 'casuistical discourse and habits of thought' to help his 'audience' 'resolve cases of conscience' (21). Shami's view of Donne the preacher, flexible, conscientious, striving for consensus, avoiding divisive polemic—Donne the 'conformist'—might cast a retrospective light, allowing us to see Donne as having 'conformed' rather than 'converted' to the Church of England (Shell and Hunt 68; see also Maltby).

Recent work by historians as well as literary scholars has given us a better sense of the complexity of early modern religious identities (see Ch. 26.I above). The English Reformation was not simply 'a struggle between two tightly consolidated blocs, Roman and Protestant' (Questier 1996: 9). Not only was there no neat opposition between English Protestant and Catholic identities, but those identities were in flux. English Catholicism was in the process of adapting to political and cultural changes (Macek 83). From the 1530s, when Henry VIII broke with Rome, until at least the beginning of Elizabeth I's reign in 1558, many English Catholics could feel loyal to their English monarch while also maintaining their traditional beliefs and practices (Wooding 5; Macek). Moreover, English Catholicism had a 'habit of independence from Rome' (Wooding 227). It was only about when Donne was born—after Elizabeth I was excommunicated by papal bull in 1570—and more so in the 1580s that it became difficult for English Catholics to maintain loyalty to their faith and allegiance to the Queen. Elizabethan measures cast Catholics as 'rebels' (ibid. 234–5), and seemed to be forcing a choice. Now English Catholics were more likely to defer to the authority of Rome and the Pope (12). The English Church itself was far from stable in its Reformed identity. The reigns of James I and Charles I witnessed changes in worship and doctrine: a movement towards more ceremony, challenges to Calvinist orthodoxy, and a softening of its oppositional stance towards the Church of Rome (A. Milton 1995: esp. 229–373, 529–46). In light of the complexity of the religious situation, it is not surprising that Michael Questier has concluded that 'flux in religion [even conversion, or "change of religion"] was the norm rather than the exception' (Questier 1996: 206; Cain 2006; Shell and Hunt).

Donne, then, lived at a time when religious identities were fluid. For Donne, conformity might be seen as a way of surviving, being true both to England's church and to his Catholic family and ancestors. The Church of England in 1615, when he was ordained, might have seemed a more hospitable home. In assessing Donne's 'conversion', above all it is important to remember Questier's insistence that movement 'to and from Rome' was almost never simply politically or materially motivated, and that '[c]onversion is as much a declaration of freedom from institutions as a pledge of allegiance to them' (1996: 75).

Donne's poetry: the preoccupation with faithfulness, truth, change, conversion

It is precarious to link Donne's poetry directly to his religious trajectory, since we do not know when individual poems were written—with the notable exception of the *Anniversaries* on the death of Elizabeth Drury (1611 and 1612) and *Goodf*. Even the date of the Holy Sonnets is uncertain. Gardner, followed by Bald and most later critics, assumed these poems (with the exception of the three 'late' Sonnets appearing only in the Westmoreland ms.) were written while Donne was at Mitcham, suffering from a despair that the Holy Sonnets seem to echo (Stachniewski).

> I dare not moue my dimme eyes any way,
>   Despaire behind, and Death before doth cast
>   Such terrour, and my feebled flesh doth wast
> By sinne in it, whch it t'wards Hell doth weigh.
>   (*Variorum* 7.1, *HSMade* ll. 5–8)

'Oh, I shall soone despaire, when I shall see / That thou lou'st Mankind well, yet wilt not chuse me' (*HSDue* ll. 12–13). 'Oh my blacke Soule' (*HSBlack* l. 1). But, the recent Donne *Variorum* edition refutes Gardner's argument for the Mitcham years and suggests the Sonnets could have been written earlier.

Regarding the Holy Sonnets' relation to Donne's conversion, we might note that these Sonnets follow the Italian sonnet rhyme scheme in which the 'volte' or turn from the first eight lines (octave) to the final six (sestet) signifies the moment in the poem where the speaker turns to God, usually addressing God. Formally, therefore, the Holy Sonnets enact a 'conversion', in the sense of turning from a state of sin towards God. Their form symbolically embodies what they contemplate: a turn from false beliefs (or lack of faith) to a true faith. Perhaps this conversion also signifies Donne's contemplating or reflecting on a conversion to the reformed Church of England. Yet these Sonnets, while expressing a desire for salvation, do not end with assurance; and they take place in the speaker's soul, not in a church (on Holy Sonnets, see Ch. 15).

One Donne poem directly addresses the problem of how one might seek 'true Religion' and the related question of what is the true church: *Sat3* ('Of Religion' in some manuscripts), probably written when Donne was in his early twenties. *Sat3* suggests that all the confessional options available (Rome, the Calvinist church in Geneva, the fairly recently established English Church, the indiscriminate acceptance of all Christian churches, or the rejection of all) are flawed. Still, the speaker insists that God demands each individual arduously 'seeke true religion' (l. 43), searching for spiritual truth (Donne, by his own account as well as Walton's, engaged in such intellectual inquiry); that the search is oblique and that even 'To stand inquiring right, is not to stray' (l. 78); that the full truth (the summit of the 'hill', l. 79) will be attained only after death; and, finally, that despite the threat of persecution and even death at the hands of earthly authorities, one must choose allegiance to God, rather than to any human being, whether one's monarch or the head of a religious institution (English or Roman). Donne's Satire itself presents a powerful argument against any who might accuse him of apostasy: it is not the continuing search for God's presence but rather faithfulness to an imperfect church or a human being—king ('Harry') or pope ('Gregory') or theologian Luther ('Martin') who claims religious authority/'Power'—that is the true apostasy (ll. 96–7, 110).

A witty, paradoxical argument for inclusivity appears in *HSShow*, written after Donne's ordination, where he asks Christ to 'show' him the true church, the 'spouse' (*Variorum* 7.1, l. 1). Sceptical about the imperfection of earthly churches, each of which presumes to be the exclusive site for the soul's salvation, Donne concludes that Christ's spouse is the church 'open to most Men' (l. 14)—that is, most promiscuously loving and accepting. In its near-blasphemous use of the trope of the church as bride, this poem offers a theological position but also a psychologically satisfying solution to the fear of not being chosen that appears in Donne's devotional poetry, even in what is probably his final poem (*Father*)—'I have a sinne of feare, that...I shall perish on the shore' (ll. 13–14).

Another aspect of his poetry relates to the debate over Donne's apostasy or conversion: Donne's obsession with inconstancy, unfaithfulness in both his religious and secular love poetry. *HSVex* expresses Donne's worry that his very changeableness may be the sin that damns him, and the Holy Sonnets chart that inconstancy. His 'profane' love poetry is also preoccupied with constancy and inconstancy. Many Elegies, but also some Songs and Sonets, feature speakers who reject constancy as unnatural (*ElVar*, *Ind*, *WomCon*), or who flaunt their promiscuity or adulterous affairs (*ElVar*, *ElPerf*, *Commun*). Yet other poems, expressing a love that is immutable and enduring, present an image of exceptional constancy in an imperfect world (*Anniv*, *ValMourn*). Donne's poems, that is, oscillate between exalting constancy or exalting freedom, sometimes even in a single poem. Witness *ElChange*. The speaker begins condemning the presumed promiscuity of his mistress whose 'Apostasee' (*Variorum* 2, l. 3) he fears, but, after expressing his revulsion at her expected 'change', he ends by discriminating between her promiscuity and the serial monogamy he will embrace: the river that 'leau[es]' one 'banke' and 'Neuer looke[s] backe' as it moves to another is 'purest' (ll. 33–5): 'Change is the Nurcery / Of Musicke, Ioye, Life, and Eternity' (ll. 35–6). The speaker in *ElServe* declares his constancy in serving his mistress, but refuses a service that either fails to reward him or destroys him (like the 'careles flowers strawd on the waters face' who are 'drowne[d]' by the 'embrace' of the 'whirlepooles': ll. 15–17). At the end he threatens to leave, to 'renounce thy dallyance' (l. 44), though we do not see him actually choose another mistress.

Donne's speaker struggles with ideas of change, trying to distinguish good 'change' from unfaithful 'apostasy'. Carey claims that 'Donne, in the fantasy world of the poems, rids himself of his disloyalty by transferring it to women, and directing against them the execrations which he could be seen as meriting' (1981a: 38). But there are other ways of seeing Donne's obsession with being 'true'. The words 'true' and 'false' often occur in his poems exploring questions of faithfulness in love, the attractions of variety or promiscuity, the inconstancy that seems to mark human experience and nature, even the heavens. Those words had strong religious meanings in Donne's time. In Spenser's *Fairie Queene*, 'Una' represents truth but also the true 'faith', faithfulness. Donne in his poetry uses the word 'true' to mean 'faithful', and 'false' to mean 'unfaithful', voicing an analogy between sexual and religious fidelity that goes back to the Old Testament, where the prophets describe the covenant between Israel and God as a marriage and Israel's idolatrous defection from God as adultery. The last book of the New Testament, Revelation, further develops the analogy, contrasting the Whore of Babylon with the final marriage of the Lamb with 144,000 virgins. Donne draws on these analogies in *HSShow* when he paradoxically describes Christ's faithful spouse—the true Church—as open to most men (false). The ideal church mirrors a God who expects fidelity (and denounces adultery) from his people but who himself (as Donne says in his Sermon) wants to 'have' or embrace '*all*' (*Sermons* 6.151).

We see in Donne's poetry, whether erotic or devotional, an attraction to flexibility, an emphasis on seeking, on process, and a corresponding suspicion of rigidity and divisive dogma—all of which might be seen as variations on ideas expressed in his Sermons and Letters. Donne's own writing, that is, calls into question the rigid assumptions that might lie behind such terms as 'apostate' or even 'convert'. We will end with the devotional poem, *Goodf*, Donne's guilty meditation about being engaged in business rather than devotion on a specific holy day, but also perhaps a poem obliquely about his own 'conversion'. We need to be wary of biographical readings of poetry, which is 'fiction', imaginative. Yet the metaphor structuring the poem is 'conversion'—'turning in position, direction, destination' (*OED*). The narrative of the poem first expresses anxiety about going the wrong way but then concludes that what seemed to the speaker to be a movement away from God (or specifically Christ, the instrument of salvation) is actually a movement towards Christ. Donne assures himself that going the seemingly wrong way is actually going the right way. It is significant that he is travelling 'westward'—away not just from the site of the crucifixion but away from Rome. Donne's description of his westward journey works on literal and metaphorical levels, suggestive of his leaving the Roman Church, in which he could indeed 'see' (l. 11) the crucifix and pictures of Christ on the cross, which now (in a reformed church) he can only see in his 'memory' (l. 34) and imagination. In the poem, memory and contemplation lead him both back and forward to God as he imagines coming face to face with Christ at death. His westward movement will lead him full circle to Christ, to the place on the physical and spiritual map where east touches west. We see here Donne's hope that, for those who truly desire or seek God, many roads (or churches) all lead to the same place, to salvation.

CHAPTER 38

DONNE, WOMEN, AND THE SPECTRE OF MISOGYNY

THERESA M. DiPASQUALE

The narrator of Donne's *FirAn*, who loudly identifies himself as the poem's author, blames Eve and her daughters for human mortality: the 'first mariage was our funerall', he says; 'One woman at one blow, then kill'd vs all, / And singly, one by one, they kill vs now' (*Variorum* 6, ll. 105–7). Sweeping indictments of the female sex also appear in *Metem*, which traces the soul of the Forbidden Fruit as 'she' transmigrates through various vegetable and animal incarnations. This pernicious *anima*, having accumulated a range of vices, at last knows 'treachery, / Rapine, deceit, and lust, and ills enow / To be a woman'. The soul of sin itself thus makes its human debut as '*Themech*... / Sister and wife to *Caine*' (ll. 507–10). This misogynous dilation of Genesis remains incomplete, however; in the next stanza, which brings his work to a sudden end, the poet-narrator addresses his reader: 'Who ere thou beest that read'st this sullen Writ, / Which just so much courts thee, as thou dost it, / Let me arrest thy thoughts' (ll. 511–13). What do these lines mean, and to whom are they addressed? Given the topical nature of the text—with its allusions to the downfall of Essex and the authority of the ageing Queen—Donne's original manuscript audience for the poem no doubt included friends such as Henry Wotton and Henry Goodere, courtiers with whom Donne corresponded in prose and verse and to whom he confided his views on a wide range of political, social, and religious topics.

Is Donne hinting that his poem can persuade such urbane readers to accept sexist fables only if they are already inclined to believe them? Perhaps. But the narrator seems to care less about determining what his readers believe than about challenging those beliefs. Whatever the trajectory of readers' 'thoughts', whether towards approving the previous stanza's slur on woman, or towards rejecting the satire the poet is about to abandon, the narrator insists on 'arrest[ing]' them; he redirects those thoughts, inviting meditation on 'Why plowing, building, ruling and the rest, / Or most of those arts, whence our lives are blest, / By cursed *Cains* race invented be' (ll. 514–16). In another work, such an 'arrest' might have led to a new perspective on the curse of Eve as well as that of Cain, prompting reflection on how much men owe the members of the sex they blame for their fall. For this narrator, however, the only alternative to misogyny is weary relativism: 'Ther's nothing simply good, nor ill alone, / Of every quality comparison, / The onely measure is, and judge, opinion' (ll. 518–20). With this generalization *Metem* ends, and the reader is left to recall Donne's warning in the work's prefatory epistle: 'I would have no such Readers as I can teach' (26). Donne's brusque refusal to guide the reader of *Metem* is not entirely typical; as Lynne Magnusson points out in Chapter 43, Donne often expresses concern that his writings may be 'misinterpretable' and takes various steps to prevent misreading. Here, however, Donne rejects a Spenserian poetics that would attempt to mould readers into something better than they were before. Whatever our current level of moral judgement, we will have to rely upon it in forming our 'opinion' of the poem and the subjects it covers, including the subject of woman.

But the speakers of Donne's erotic poems are less chary of didacticism. Many of the Songs and Sonets are lectures on women and sex, and more than a few of the speakers—including those of *LovAlch*, *Ind*, and *Commun*—demonstrate deep-seated contempt for females. Several of the speakers in Donne's erotic Elegies also preach disrespect for women; *ElComp*, for example, employs a range of misogynous rhetoric in an effort to convince a male addressee that the woman he loves is disgusting. Even the noblest part of the woman's body, her head, is the epitome of disorder and mutability; kissing her is 'as filthy and more / As a worme sucking an envenomd sore'; and the man who has sex with her is like 'a Plough' rending 'stony ground' (*Variorum* 2, ll. 43–4, 48). As several twentieth-century scholars have pointed out, moreover, the speaker's allegedly contrasting praises of his own beloved are nearly as disturbing as his attacks on the addressee's mistress. The speaker's lady has a head round as the Apple of Discord or the Forbidden Fruit; her vagina is a wound that the lover, as 'surgeon', gently probes (l. 51). These tropes blend clinical anxiety with revulsion; could Donne have invented them without experiencing the feelings they evoke? The poet may be ventriloquizing gynophobia, repeating some creep's offensive jokes only to parody his offensive language; the last lines of the poem encourage such a reading: 'Leaue her, and I will leaue comparing thus / She, and comparisons are odious' (ll. 53–4). (See Dayton Haskin [Ch. 13 above] on some pre-nineteenth-century readers' classifying as 'satirical' many of Donne's short love poems and erotic Elegies.) But how often can you enact such 'odious' attitudes before you become the creep you meant to mock?

Questions like these, posed by readers who find misogynous rhetoric offensive, have made the issue of misogyny an enduring focus of critical inquiry in Donne studies. The poet himself raises the issue by articulating negative beliefs about women in memorable terms that invite any reader inclined to do so to 'sweare' that 'No where / Lives a woman true, and faire' (*SGo*, ll. 16–18). At the same time, however, Donne confounds any easy attempt to classify his attitude, for he is also the author of many a passage that may be read as reflecting ironically on misogyny rather than expressing it unequivocally. The passage from *FirAn* quoted above is a case in point; the speaker does not simply assert that *mulier est hominis confusio*; rather, he asks, 'How witty's ruine?' (*Variorum* 6, l. 99), and then proceeds to explore the deep ironies of fallen existence, finding fault both with women and with 'vs', the normatively male and radically imperfect 'mankinde' that responds to its own 'ruine' by insisting that 'they' are to blame. As Graham Roebuck notes in his chapter on the *Anniversaries* (Ch. 20 above), 'Wit is the oxygen the poems breathe'. A similarly equivocal quality informs *Metem* and several of Donne's prose Paradoxes and Problems, which mock women, but also demonstrate the inconsistencies and absurdities of male attitudes towards women. (See also Camille Wells Slights [Ch. 22 above] on the critical debate over Donne's *EpLin*, in which the images of the bride's defloration are particularly disturbing; scholars are divided on the question of whether this poem is a genuine Epithalamion or a parody written for a mock-wedding.)

Less obviously playful are Donne's anti-feminist remarks in the Sermons, texts designed neither to entertain readers nor to satirize miscreants, but to save souls. 'God forbid', Donne says in a 24 March 1616/17 Sermon preached at Paul's Cross, that 'any should say, That the Virgin *Mary* concurred to our good, so, as *Eve* did to our ruine'. The point of this declaration, made by a former Catholic in the most public of preaching venues, is perhaps to display his Protestant convictions or perhaps to hint, through ironic hyperbole, that anti-Marian rhetoric is as excessive as Mariolatry. Certainly, the rhetoric grows more extreme as Donne continues:

It is said truly, *That as by one man sin entred, and death* [Rom. 5:12], so by one man entred life. It may be said, *That by one woman sin entred, and death*, (and that rather then by the man; for, *Adam was not deceived, but the woman being deceived, was in the transgression* [1 Tim. 2:14]). But it cannot be said...that by one woman innocence entred, and life: The Virgin *Mary* had not the same interest in our salvation, as *Eve* had in our destruction; nothing that she did entred into that treasure, that ransom that redeemed us. (*Sermons* 1.200)

Here, the preacher reverses publicly what the poet had said privately in such poems as *Goodf*, in which Mary furnishes 'Halfe of that Sacrifice, which ransom'd us' (l. 32) and *Lit*, in which the Blessed Virgin is 'That she-Cherubin, / Which unlock'd Paradise' (ll. 38–9). Yet Donne supports the Reformed Mariology of his Sermon with some exegetical sleight of hand that undermines the Protestant ideal of *sola scriptura*; he interpolates between Romans 5:12 and 1 Timothy 2:14 his own, misogynous revision of Romans 5:12. Indeed, he uses Paul's remarks in 1 Timothy about Eve's having been deceived to *correct* Romans 5:12, claiming '*That by one woman sin entred*...(and that rather then by the man...)' (*Sermons* 1.200). Is the auditory meant to notice that Donne is inventing and 'quoting' a deliberately warped version of Holy Writ? They had ample leisure to do so, for the preacher's comments on the Blessed Virgin are part of a lengthy digression in which he contrasts the worthy but corruptible love that man feels for woman with the 'noble and incorruptible affection of Love' that, according to Scripture, the righteous man feels for 'pureness of heart' (1.206). The point of the digression—which includes not only Donne's remarks about Mary but also a detailed exploration of the scandal caused by St Jerome's friendship with a pious woman named Paula—is thus not to vilify women. On the contrary, Donne stresses that the Virgin Mary, 'and many other blessed women since, have done many things for the advancing of the glory of God, and imitation of others; so that they are not unfit for spiritual conversation; nor for the civil offices of friendship' (1.200). The only peril in such friendship, the preacher concludes, is that 'an over-tender indulgence towards such women, that for other respects they were bound to love, [has] inclined' far too many men 'to do such things, as otherwise they would not have done' (1.203).

Why does Donne devote so much time to this digression in a Sermon for the 24 March 1616/17 anniversary of Queen Elizabeth's death and James's accession? Later in the Sermon he praises the deceased Virgin Queen as a martial maid who managed all the wars of Christendom with manly ability and the living King as a peacemaker seeking to end those wars. One observer, John Chamberlain, noted that the Sermon 'was excedingly well liked generally, the rather for that he did Quene Elizabeth great right, and held himself close to the text without flattering the time too much' (Chamberlain 2.67). Perhaps when Chamberlain says that Donne did not flatter the time, he means that the preacher's digression about the problems caused by uxoriousness might be a warning to the King about the dangers of seeking a match between Prince Charles and the Spanish Infanta. By 1617 the English ambassador to Spain had been working for several years to hammer out the terms of such an alliance, and James had asked the Privy Council to authorize 'more formal negotiations' only a few weeks before the Sermon was preached (Redworth 17); many members of the Council were present at Paul's Cross, though the King had left on a trip to Scotland. In short, Donne's point in bringing up woman trouble was more likely religio-political than misogynous.

In the less politically charged atmosphere of a 1621 wedding Sermon, Donne explicitly condemns misogyny: 'To make...[women] Gods is ungodly, and to make them Devils is devillish; To make them Mistresses is unmanly, and to make them servants is unnoble; To make them as God made them, wives, is godly and manly too' (*Sermons* 3.242).

Many of Donne's Verse Letters insist, moreover, that it is women who have made and 'refin'd' him, rather than vice versa (*BedfRef* l.1). Donne sometimes praises the noblewomen he addresses—as he does Elizabeth Drury in the *Anniversaries*—by defining them as exceptions that prove the rule of female weakness and inferiority. (On the *Anniversaries* as exploring the ancient theme of *Foemina praecellentia*, see Ch. 20; and on the interpretive challenges posed by Donne's Verse Letters to noblewomen, see Ch. 14.) But is Donne falling into the misogynous Madonna/whore dichotomy that prevails in Western culture, or is he self-consciously invoking it in order to engage savvy female readers in intellectually challenging discourse? One verse epistle to the Countess of Huntingdon (*c.*1609) begins with an archly sexist rendering of Genesis 2 and a cheeky reminder that the Countess's sex is excluded from positions of authority:

> Man to Gods image, *Eve*, to mans was made,
>   Nor finde wee that God breath'd a soule in her,
> Canons will not Church functions you invade,
>   Nor lawes to civill office you preferre.
>
> *(HuntMan* ll. 1–4*)*

These lines introduce a compliment singling out Elizabeth Stanley Hastings, a woman Donne has known since her 'yonger dayes' (l. 69), as astoundingly exempt from the norm that makes 'milde innocence' uncommon in women, 'but active good / A miracle' (ll. 9, 10–11). Then, lest the addressee think that he means her to swallow whole either the insult or the compliment, Donne declares,

> If you can thinke these flatteries, they are,
>   For then your judgement is below my praise,
> If they were so, oft, flatteries worke as farre,
>   As Counsels, and as farre th'endeavour raise.
>
> (ll. 49–52*)*

This passage addresses a reader capable of complex thought, not a prima donna looking for worshippers. Similarly intricate are the conceits informing Donne's Verse Letters to other ladies, including the Countess of Bedford, the Countess of Salisbury, and Magdalen Herbert. Thus, just as one must ask how often one can play a misogynous role before one becomes a misogynist, so one must ask how often one may claim that certain women are exceptions to the rule before one demonstrates one's actual rejection of the rule. A considerable number of Donne's extant Prose Letters are respectful and intellectually challenging texts addressed to women, including the Countess of Bedford, the Countess of Montgomery, Lady Kingsmill (Bridget White), Ann Cokayne, Martha Garrard, and his own mother. And as Claude Summers explains in Chapter 21 above, Donne's elegies on the 1609 death of Cecilia Bulstrode not only respond to the Countess of Bedford's grief at the death of her friend, but also reflect Donne's engagement in a serious literary and theological debate with the Countess over the power of death and the appropriateness of mourners' tears.

For generations of readers, moreover, many of Donne's love poems have appeared as beacons of egalitarian desire in a world oppressed by hierarchy. Some of the most famous Songs and Sonets celebrate heterosexual love that finds its fulfilment neither in Petrarchan self-abasement nor in the hierarchical union of Pauline marriage, but in perfect parity: 'Let us possesse one world, each hath one, and is one', a lover cries in *GoodM* (l. 14). Another claims that he and his beloved have transcended gender difference: 'so, to one neutrall thing both sexes fit, / Wee dye and rise the same, and prove / Mysterious by this love' (*Canon* ll. 25–7); another theorizes that the love between a man and a woman 'Interinanimates two soules' (*Ecst* l. 42). Even more startlingly, the lesbian love Elegy *Sappho* may be read as extending Donne's sympathy for female sexuality and female subjectivity beyond the boundaries of heterosexual desire. Yet this work has also been interpreted as designed to silence, marginalize, contain, or nullify the Sapphic voice it ventriloquizes.

The question of misogyny in Donne's writings cannot, in short, be easily resolved. No single proof-text can answer the question of whether Donne revered women, reviled them, or judged them on a case-by-case basis, as he did—sometimes quite harshly—persons of the male sex. The issue is clouded by Donne's tendency to contentiousness (evoked by Ben Jonson, who praises Donne in an epigram by marvelling at his 'language, letters, arts, best life, / Which might with half mankind maintain a strife' (Jonson 8.34, ll. 7–8). But was the 'half' of 'mankind' with whom Donne was most clearly 'at strife' the female half?

No commentary explicitly describing Donne's attitude towards women is extant from the period of his own lifetime, though the subject does arise indirectly. In 1612, shortly after the *Anniversaries* were published, Donne responded to negative criticism of the poems in a Letter to his friend George Garrard. Noting the objections of certain female readers who feel he has 'said too much' in his celebration of Elizabeth Drury, he says: 'If any of those Ladies think that Mistris *Drewry* was not so, let that Lady make her self fit for all those praises in the book, and they shall be hers' (*Letters* 239). Donne also seems to have discussed the *Anniversaries* with Ben Jonson; according to William Drummond, Jonson 'told Mr Donne, if it had been written of ye Virgin Marie it had been something to which he answered that he described the Idea of a Woman and not as she was' (Jonson 1–2.133). It is unclear whether the phrase 'not as she was' implies a negative assessment of actual women as contrasted with the exalted 'Idea' the *Anniversaries* celebrate; certainly, the challenge Donne issues to those 'Ladies' who dislike his work may be read as hinting at a cynical assessment of their potential for virtue. But any tendency towards misogyny in the *Anniversaries* themselves was lost on another of Donne's contemporaries, John Webster, who alludes to the poems repeatedly in *The Duchess of Malfi* (first performed in 1613). The play includes many misogynous speeches by villainous male characters, but none of these quotes Donne; instead, the playwright draws on the *Anniversaries* in constructing the loving and passionate exchanges between the courageous Duchess and her husband. Nor is a Donne-quoting Jacobean noblewoman merely the stuff of fiction.

One of the most complimentary allusions to Donne's love poetry during the period flows from a female pen; Lady Mary Wroth's 1621 'sweetest love returne againe' (100–1) gives voice to the female addressee of Donne's *SSweet*, interpreting Donne's poem as inviting the woman's reciprocal self-expression.

The next generation of poets, including Thomas Carew, John Suckling, Abraham Cowley, and William Habington, took Donne's erotic verse as their point of departure for various exaggerated attitudes towards women, ranging from disdainful disillusionment to pornographic lust and chivalrous compliment. Given the range of different speakers Donne employs, the Cavalier poets could find whatever they were looking for, either by echoing Donne or by rebuking him. Particularly indebted to Donne-as-male-supremacist is Carew's 'A Rapture', which reads like a blatant attempt to match and exceed the aggressive, possessive masculinity of *ElProg* and *ElBed*. Also recognizably Donnean in their flippant remarks about women are the personae of many Suckling lyrics, such as the sporting Epicurean of 'sonnet II' and the weary libertine of 'sonnet III'. But a Donne persona could also serve as a straw man for a Cavalier intent on gallantry; Habington's *Castara* includes a poem 'Against them who lay Unchastity to the Sex of Women', which begins by threatening that only 'unwholesome Springs', 'infectious' summers, and fruitless encounters with mermaids and falling stars are in store for 'Who ever dare, / Affirme no woman chaste and faire' (1870: 80).

One Caroline reader with the initials 'G. O.' (probably the clergyman Giles Oldisworth) does annotate a copy of the 1639 edition of Donne's poems with sober rhyming annotations, including an approving paraphrase of the most misogynous passage in *Metem* (see A. J. Smith 1975: 128–9). But most writers of Charles I's reign find in Donne's secular poetry nothing more serious than raw material for witty conceits. Donne's contemporary Richard Baker, writing in 1643, describes the late poet in terms that make him sound like a Cavalier. Baker recalls his 'old acquaintance' during their days at the Inns of Court neither as a cynical Don Juan nor as the locker-room comedian of the Elegies, but as a man of fashion: 'not dissolute, but very neat'—which is to say, not a spendthrift, though elegantly dressed within his means—'a great visiter of Ladies, a great frequenter of Playes, a great writer of conceited Verses' (Baker 156). Baker's brief catalogue evokes a gentleman who, far from being inclined to use and abuse women, seeks out their company in order to read them clever compositions. As Ernest W. Sullivan II has demonstrated, this urbane and stylish Donne continued to be quoted and transcribed throughout the seventeenth century. The spunky Lady Ward in Margaret Cavendish's 1662 play *The Second Part of the Lady Contemplation* calmly quotes *Storm* when accused of madness, and selected passages from Donne's poetry were featured in self-help books for people in search of fine expressions (see Ch. 2 above). The 1684 edition of John Gough's *The Academy of Complements*, specifically intended 'for the use of *Ladies* and *Gentlewomen*', includes lines 15–18 of *Break*, in which the female speaker pronounces business and love incompatible (Sullivan 1993: 35–6 and 44).

Ill. 38.1. Portrait of Donne, by an unknown artist (oil on panel, c.1595, National Portrait Gallery 6795), known as the 'Lothian portrait' since its discovery in 1959 at Newbattle Abbey. (© National Portrait Gallery, London; reproduced by permission.)

In 1693, however, John Dryden would censure Donne for taxing female readers: 'He...perplexes the Minds of the Fair Sex with nice Speculations of Philosophy, when he shou'd ingage their hearts, and entertain them with the softnesses of Love' (Dryden 1956– : 4.7). Dryden's opinion, reinforced by Samuel Johnson's largely negative assessment of metaphysical wit, exerted a powerful influence in the eighteenth century. Donne's rough versification, outlandish conceits, and occasional gross indelicacy are the foci of much commentary throughout the period; but it does not occur to any Augustan writer to detect in Donne, as Johnson does in Milton, a 'Turkish contempt of females' (2006: 1.276). In fact, women—apparently resistant to Dryden's assessment—appear to have been among Donne's greatest admirers. In a March 1710 issue of *The Female Tatler*, a writer using the pen name 'Emilia' (probably the playwright Susanna Centlivre) describes a tea at which she and four other 'Ladies of Thought and Conversation' discuss many serious topics; when they consider love, they consult 'the Oracles of that Deity', among whom none are 'more expressive than those left us by the memorable Dr. Donne'. A long quotation from *Ecst* and the complete text of *Anniv* follow, as do Emilia's comments on the 'exalted' and 'convincing' sincerity of 'the Doctor', to whom she refers as 'my charming Author' (qtd. in Rude 155–9).

Like their eighteenth-century predecessors, most Romantic and Victorian commentators ignore the question of misogyny in Donne's writings, instead deploring vulgar language and questionable morality in the amatory verse or waxing misty-eyed at the tale of Donne's marriage and the adversities he and Anne endured for love's sake. By the late nineteenth century, however, a few writers began to explore the poet's attitude towards women in general, some characterizing Donne as hostile towards females, and others praising his deep understanding of and sympathy for women. William Minto notes in 1880 that the fragmentary *Metem* 'breaks off abruptly and unworthily, with a commonplace scoff at the wickedness of women' (862). Edmund Gosse, in his 1899 biographical reading of Donne's corpus, interprets the libertine poems as the effusions of an 'impudent' young poet who lacks any 'sense of the dignity of womanhood' and who, after a sordid affair with a morally bankrupt woman, is driven by 'exhausted cynicism' to declare 'all women…vile' (1.64–5, 74). Arthur Symons, however, writes in 1899 that no other poet has 'known as much of women's hearts and the senses of men, and the interchange of passionate intercourse between man and woman' (Symons 742). In his love lyrics, Symons asserts, 'Donne shows women themselves…; they know that he finds nothing in the world more interesting, and they much more than forgive him for all the ill he says of them. If women most conscious of their sex were ever to read Donne, they would say, He was a great lover; he understood' (743).

Some references to Donne by nineteenth-century women writers corroborate this generous assessment; George Eliot uses passages from *Under* and *GoodM* as epigraphs for chapters in *Middlemarch* dealing with the heroic love of Ladislaw and Dorothea; and in 1889 Sarah Orne Jewett writes to a female friend that she has 'been reading an old copy of Donne's poems with perfect delight' (Jewett 60). But others are less certain; in 1892 Agnes Repplier, the first woman to accuse Donne of misogyny in a print publication, characterizes him as having 'united a great devotion to his fond and faithful wife with a remarkably poor opinion of her sex in general' (Repplier 45). The hyperbolic praises of female addressees in some of Donne's poems seem to Repplier to go hand in hand with his disdain for women as a group: he 'pushed his adulations to the extreme verge of absurdity', she says, quoting the line 'The whole world vapors with thy breath' from *Fever* (l. 8), and remarking: 'After which ebullition, it is hardly a matter of surprise to know that he considered females in the light of creatures whom it had pleased Providence to make fools. "Hope not for minde in women!" is his warning cry; at their best, a little sweetness and a little wit form all their earthly portion' (45–6). Repplier's assessment of Donne's attitude depends upon her conflation of the speaker with the poet in both

Fever and *LovAlch*; it requires, further, that she find the poet cynically insincere in the complimentary poem addressed *to* a woman, yet completely without irony in the one that speaks scathingly *of* women. Repplier's assessment is by no means the product of simple naivety, however; in Chapter 42 below Judith Scherer Herz explores the ways in which the poet himself encouraged readers to believe that there were 'two Donnes'.

Many readers, however, can see only one or the other; for, as George Saintsbury observed in 1896, Donne polarizes his audience: 'It is almost necessary that those who do not like him should not like him at all; should be scarcely able to see how any decent and intelligent human creature can like him. It is almost as necessary that those who do like him should either like him so much as to speak unadvisedly...or else curb and restrain the expression of their love for fear that it should seem on that side idolatry' (Saintsbury xi). This tendency either to be repelled by Donne or in awe of his powers continues in twentieth- and twenty-first-century criticism and is nowhere more evident than in scholars' discussions of Donne's attitude towards women.

The most prominent early twentieth-century critic to voice distaste for that attitude is C. S. Lewis, who argues, in an oft-reprinted 1938 essay, that Donne's love poetry is vastly overrated; not least among the poet's faults is his medieval perspective on women and sexuality, which prevents him from attaining what Lewis characterizes as the healthy, enlightened Protestant views of Spenser and Shakespeare. Rejecting the argument of *Ecst* as nastily disingenuous, Lewis concludes, with a dry disgust worthy of the poet he so disparages, that it would be difficult to imagine 'What any sensible woman would make of such a wooing...if we forgot the amazing protective faculty which each sex possesses of not listening to the other' (76). This remark elicits a pointed reply from Joan Bennett, who—grouping Lewis with Dryden—marvels that such 'distinguished critics' could fail to grasp Donne's appeal. While 'it may be that "any sensible woman" would' prefer lavish descriptions of her beauty to Donne's frank expressions, Bennett muses, 'I am not sure...It may interest her more to know what it feels like to be a man in love' (J. Bennett 1938: 85–6). Bennett proceeds to argue that 'Donne did not think sex sinful, and that contempt for women is not a general characteristic of his love poetry'. But she does not exclude the possibility that he was a misogynist: 'Is it so strange to be contemptuous of many, or even of most women and to love and reverence a few?' (102, 104).

Though Bennett prudently avoids referring either to her own sex or to that of the scholarly Alpha-males she challenges, reception-oriented criticism of the later twentieth century often stresses the importance of gender in shaping Donne's sense of audience. George Klawitter (1986, 1987), Dennis Flynn (1989), and Arthur Marotti (1986) explore how Donne's poems cater to or challenge various male and female coteries; and in this volume, Dayton Haskin's essay on the love lyrics (Ch. 13) emphasizes the problematic consequences of assuming 'that Donne wrote only or chiefly for men'. Scholars underscoring other aspects of Donne's religious, social, and political circumstances also consider his portrayal of women. John Carey (1981a) portrays Donne's attitude towards women as reflecting the deep insecurities of a recusant who abandoned his religion for ambition's sake. Margaret Maurer (1976, 1980) attends to the courtly protocols that Donne observes and analyses in his Verse Letters to the Countess of Bedford. Ilona Bell (1996, 1997) rereads seemingly misogynous passages in Donne's love poems in the context of his clandestine courtship of and marriage to Anne More. And Achsah Guibbory stresses the Elizabethan political milieu in which the Elegies were written, arguing that 'the misogyny evident in many of these poems' reflects 'tensions over submission to female rule' (1990: 812, 813). Guibbory's 2006 essay on Donne's erotic poetry reaffirms this reading of the Elegies, while noting the 'more diverse range of attitudes towards women' to be found in the Songs and Sonets (136).

The question of Donne's misogyny is also illuminated by formalist analysis that stresses the distinction between the poet and the speakers of the poems, as well as by criticism emphasizing genre or intertextuality. Richard Hughes argues that Donne distances himself from the speakers of the Satires, Elegies, and erotic lyrics by basing them on well-established types in the works of Horace, Martial, Ovid, and the Petrarchans (38). See also Dayton Haskin's essay (Ch. 13) on how the 1635 edition of Donne's poems signals the distance between the poet and the speakers of the love lyrics by grouping them under the subtitle 'Songs and Sonets'. Stella Revard finds that the voice of Sappho in Donne's *Sappho* owes more to Sappho herself than to the Ovidian heroical epistle on which the poem is in part modelled; and Janel Mueller (1992) finds Donne's representation of Sappho to be a proto-feminist achievement more progressive than any to be found in Sappho poems by his humanist forebears and contemporaries. Ronald Corthell (1981) analyses *Metem* as a Paradox that, like Donne's prose works in the genre, invites reader resistance; and Heather Dubrow interprets Donne's erotic Elegies in the context of the Petrarchan 'ugly beauty' topos (1995: 233–44).

Donne's portrayals of women have been studied, too, in light of Judaeo-Christian theology, with attention to Donne's application of scriptural exegesis, as well as the influence of liturgy, typology, kabbalistic thought, and Pauline doctrine on his work. Theologically informed studies dealing with Donne's idea of woman include Frank Manley's introduction to Donne's *Anniversaries* (1963) and critical studies by Lindsay Mann (1981, 1987), George Klawitter (1995), Maureen Sabine (1992), Jeffrey Johnson (1999a), Elizabeth M. A. Hodgson, Roberta Albrecht, and Theresa M. DiPasquale (2008).

Feminist critics are divided on the question of misogyny in Donne's writing. Ilona Bell (1983, 2006a), Barbara Estrin, and Camille Wells Slights (1990, 1996) argue that Donne's poems embrace a complex and sometimes empowering image of woman; Janel Mueller (1989) finds that Donne's approach to women and the feminine varies depending on the genre in which he is writing. H. L. Meakin, who finds the treatment of gender in most Donne criticism to be deeply under-theorized, reads Donne in light of Luce Irigaray, and finds that his constructions of gender often reinforce but sometimes challenge repressive cultural norms. Other feminist readers—including Thomas Docherty, James Holstun, Janet Halley, Elizabeth Harvey (1992), and Stevie Davies—are largely concerned to demonstrate that Donne's writings silence, confine, subjugate, colonize, and exploit the female Other or the feminine voice. For these scholars, Donne's misogyny is indisputable; they seek to shatter the icon of Donne as sensitive male and to demonstrate the insidious workings of his prose and poetry. Stanley Fish endorses this negative assessment, diagnosing Donne as pathologically obsessed with the masculine power of his own language.

In his 1997 critique of twentieth-century critical jargon, Stanley Stewart mounts a challenge to such studies; his chapter 'Donne Among the Feminists' takes the form of a dialogue in which he attempts to voice the feminist position he opposes. No dialogue, however, can unite those convinced of Donne's misogyny with those determined to deny it. As Deborah Aldrich Larson points out in surveying twentieth-century assessments of the question (1989: 137–43), critics' conclusions depend upon which works they emphasize. Readers' perceptions of whether Donne was a misogynist are also shaped by their historical circumstances, their theoretical orientations, and—as Ben Saunders argues in his sceptical anatomy of Donne criticism through the centuries—their desires (B. Saunders 2006).

Too often, what critics most desire is to make Donne's works 'lie down quietly on...prefabricated Procrustean beds' (J. R. Roberts 1990: 57); the challenge is to resist that desire in favour of attentive response to the range of different tones and perspectives Donne can employ even within a single short poem. As Judith Scherer Herz (2001, 2007), Maureen Sabine (1995), Jonathan Post, Raymond-Jean Frontain (2007), and Helen Brooks (2007) have found by tracing Donne's 'voiceprint' in the twentieth century and beyond, poets and fiction writers continue to produce some of the most revealing responses to those tones and perspectives. Particularly powerful are the echoes of and answers to Donne in such feminist works as Adrienne Rich's 'A Valediction Forbidding Mourning' (1971) and A. S. Byatt's *Possession* (1990), neither of which takes a stand on the question of Donne and misogyny, but each of which illuminates the ongoing repercussions of Donne's words to, for, and about women.

CHAPTER 39

DONNE'S ABSOLUTISM

DEBORA SHUGER

LIKE many questions, that of Donne's absolutism hinges on definition. If one adopts the strong version favoured by Glen Burgess (29, 69, 90) and Conrad Russell (1990: 150–3), for whom it means royal legislative sovereignty—the position that the king can himself make law and impose taxes without Parliament—then it seems unlikely Donne was an absolutist. Absolutism so defined attracted little support in early Stuart England; even James abjured it once south of the border (G. Burgess 18; Christianson 1991: 72). Moreover, those who did betray absolutist sentiments rarely fared well. King Charles disallowed publication of Filmer's *Patriarcha* in 1632, but most professed absolutists ran afoul of Parliament: Cowell in 1610, Sibthorpe and Maynwaring in 1627–8. Given the high-profile pulpits from which Donne preached, his absolutist claims, had he made any, would scarcely have escaped, at the very least, hostile comment. That no offence was taken strongly suggests that he had given none, raising the possibility that this chapter treats a non-issue.

Yet it is scarcely a non-issue in Donne criticism, where 'absolutism' has been a fighting word since 1981, when John Carey invoked 'Donne, the absolutist', echoed two years later by Jonathan Goldberg. Neither scholar, however, was interested in political theory. In Carey's book, the influence of which would be hard to overestimate, politics is swallowed up by psychodynamics: Donne's absolutism becomes either the product of 'resolute self-deception', revealing his obsession with 'unlimited power', or a tactic to curry favour with James, revealing his self-interested careerism (Carey 1981a: 115–16).

Carey's picture of Donnean absolutism as a mix of self-seeking ambition and self-deluded mystification inspired a series of rebuttals documenting Donne's ties to leading figures among both Calvinist and parliamentary opposition (A. Patterson 1991: 257; Shami 1995b: 7–10). However, as Richard Strier pointed out in 1996, the attempts to locate anti-absolutist strains in Donne's prose have 'not been notably successful' (93), in part because, with a single exception, these seek to deny Carey's conclusions regarding Donne without challenging his premises regarding absolutism; like Carey, that is to say, his critics treat absolutism not as a political theory but as more or less equivalent to sycophancy and the worship of power. David Norbrook's influential response to Carey thus equates absolutism with the 'naked exercise of power...mystified by dazzling images' (Norbrook 5, 8). Most studies of Donne's politics similarly end up reproducing Carey's notion of absolutism even as they attempt to rebut his claims by showing that Donne 'was firm in his rejection of tyranny', not 'a sychophantic [sic] supporter of divine right', not a 'royalist puppet' or 'careerist' (D. Nicholls 52; Harland 22; Shami 1995a: 381; 1995b: 1). As this language implies, these studies accept Carey's view of absolutism as morally and rationally untenable, which is why, one assumes, their focus is not on absolutism but on exculpating Donne from its taint.

The first significant break with this line of argument comes in Strier's 1996 essay on the politics of Donne's *Devotions*, which pointed out that Donne might have a '*principled* loyalty to the established church and state' (Strier 94). Strier's insight did not, however, spur inquiry into what views a principled *absolutist* might have held, since the same essay went on to argue that Donne's political convictions were ecclesiological rather than constitutional: that the *Devotions* were political *because* they emphasized sacraments and ceremonies. Over the past ten years scholarship on Donne's post-ordination writings has followed Strier from court to church, although not always to the same one.

Yet alongside this current interest in Donne's political theology, one notes a reluctance to let go of the oppositional Donne or to rethink the premises on which this is based, among them the view of absolutism as fur-gowned dictatorship. It is a view that both Carey and Norbrook presupposed, as did Paul Harland's essay on a Donne Sermon preached as the 1629 Parliament entered its final crash-and-burn phase. Harland sketched this background by explaining that 'Parliament [was] determined to assert the liberties of the subject' in the teeth of Charles's high-flying claims for 'the royal prerogative', in which crisis, Harland continued, Donne supported Parliament, cautioning 'the king against arbitrary rule' (Harland 21). Most modern studies of Donne's politics take as self-evident the antithesis between 'royalist puppet' and 'defender of the legal rights of subjects against illegal oppression by the monarch' (22; Shami 1995a: 381). Yet this final quotation, describing a picture of early Stuart history that remains current in Donne scholarship, comes from Wormuth's 1939 critique of what he, like others, terms 'the Whig view': a view that 'assumes that Parliament rather than the court was in the right in specific disputes as to the power of the king...a contention which Parliament itself was unable to prove conclusively and which was disputed with considerable success by the court lawyers' (Wormuth 3). Moreover, Wormuth is just one of a parade of historians, from Figgis's 1896 *Theory of the Divine Right of Kings* to Russell's *Causes of the English Civil War*, doing battle with Macaulay's ghost (Plucknett 50, 195–6; Russell 1990: 132–50). Yet very little of this historiography seems to have crossed the literary divide into Donne studies, with the exception mentioned above: a 2003 essay by Johann Sommerville which points out that King James was scarcely 'further to the right than his opponents', given that '[t]hose opponents were staunch defenders of individual property rights and reduced taxation, while James wanted to subordinate individual rights to the welfare of the community. Many of those opponents were Christian fundamentalists, of rigidly puritanical moral views'. Why literary scholars have felt it 'pessimistic to suppose that Donne sided against them is', Sommerville concludes, 'mysterious' (2003: 87). If, as the foregoing suggests, a respectable case can be made for the Crown vis-à-vis Parliament, if Charles was not conspiring to destroy 'the fundamental liberties of all subjects' (Harland 22–3), then consideration of Donne's politics can turn from battling suspicions of careerist fawning and mystified power-lust to address the rather more fruitful question of what Stuart absolutism was.

STUART ABSOLUTISMS

Although Donne's politics were not those of Sibthorpe and Maynwaring, whether he was an absolutist remains a live question because the definition of absolutism also remains a live question. For our purposes, the long-standing debate over the true definition can be set aside in favour of Michael Mendle's showing that there was more than one definition operative during the period. While the exact number is up for grabs, the existing scholarship points to the existence of three historically distinct conceptualizations of absolute power. These do not, it should be noted, include two positions that are often mislabelled absolutist. As Glen Burgess has convincingly argued, active resistance to a legitimate ruler was so uniformly disallowed (no one, however, disallowed passive resistance to a command against divine or natural law) that if this prohibition constituted absolutism, most members of the Long Parliament would be absolutists (G. Burgess 19–25, 40, 95). The divine right of kings was likewise affirmed by political thinkers of diverse stripes and primarily against the papacy. This claim that the king's power derived from God alone concerns the *source* of royal authority, whereas absolutist theory centres on its *extent* vis-à-vis both positive law and Parliament (94–5, 121; Christianson 1991: 72–3; Russell 1990: 150; Wormuth 43; Mendle 1993: 99).

The most sweeping formulation of absolutism—the strong absolutism of Burgess and Russell—derives from Bodin's 1576 *Les six livres de la république* (English trans. 1606). For Bodin, the marks of sovereignty are indivisible; that is to say, the key powers of government, including making laws and imposing taxes, must be lodged in one person or body, since their division does not yield a workable system of checks and balances, but a suicidal gridlock of competing interests (Mendle 1993: 100; Franklin 298–9, 307). Moreover, Bodin holds that 'a soueraigne prince'—or the corresponding sovereign body in a non-monarchic state—'cannot be subiect to his owne lawes', but must instead have 'power to giue lawes to all his subiects in generall, and to euerie one of them in particular... without consent of any other'. The sovereign is thus not only unconstrained by positive law, but may himself make law, for 'the names of Lords and Senators, which wee oftentimes see ioyned vnto lawes, they are not thereunto set as of necessitie to giue thereunto force or strength' (Bodin 92, 159–60). Bodin thus rejects the two main pillars of traditional (i.e. Aristotelian) political theory: the mixed constitution and the supremacy of law. His sovereign is limited by divine and natural law alone, although, it should be added, Bodin makes these real limitations; for example, he holds that, except in dire public emergencies, the sovereign cannot avail himself of his subjects' money without their consent, since both God and nature prohibit stealing (108–9).

Bodin did not draw a large English following, although, as we shall see, Donne briefly joined on. Far more typical of English 'absolutist' thought were formulations derived from the medieval civil-law distinction between *gubernaculum* and *jurisdictio*, but often associated with the Senecan tag-line: 'To princes belongs government; to private persons, property'. The classic English statement of the distinction occurs in Chief Baron of the Exchequer Thomas Fleming's 1606 verdict in Bates's Case, which concerned the king's right to tax imports. The Exchequer found for the Crown on the grounds that 'the government of the realm and his people' had been committed to the king, along with the requisite 'power to govern'. For the 'Kings power', Fleming explained,

is double, ordinary and absolute.... That of the ordinary is for the profit of particular subjects... and with us, [called] common law: and these laws cannot be changed, without parliament.... The absolute power of the King... is only that which is applied to the general benefit of the people and is *salus populi*...and is most properly named Pollicy and Government. (qtd. in Oakley 324)

So too Francis Bacon held that the king has no 'power to alter the laws, which is the subjects' birthright', yet 'his sovereign power, which no judge can censure, is not of that nature', but since it concerns '*matter of government and not of law*, must be left to his managing by his Council of State' (qtd. in G. Burgess 88; italics mine). As late as 1621, even Coke held that the monarch has both 'a Prerogative disputable and a

Prerogative indisputable, as to make warre and Peace; the other concerns *meum et tuum* and are bounded by Lawe' (Wormuth 56).

This *gubernaculum/jurisdictio* distinction associated Parliament with local government and also, in conjunction with the courts, with private property rights. In regards to the latter, the king was clearly under the law. Some matters of state, however, were *arcana imperii* and thus outside both the jurisdiction of the courts and the competence of Parliament (Kantorowicz). On several occasions both Elizabeth and James thus warned Parliament that they 'should do well to meddle with no matters of state' unless specifically called upon to do so (Wormuth 56, 74; Guy 322–5). As these warnings imply, although the Commons did not *reject* the Crown's absolute prerogative regarding state matters until a very late date, it did not rest unchallenged (Wormuth 76–7). The challenge was made overt in the Commons' Protestation of 1621, which asserted their right to debate freely all 'affairs concerning the King, State, and defence of the realm and of the church of England', at which point James personally tore the offending document out of the Commons' Journal and dissolved Parliament. Eleven years earlier, in response to James's warning not to debate his prerogative to levy impositions, John Hoskins had vehemently objected that 'we may dispute [the prerogative]... And as to the phrases of infinite and inscrutable... he that looks for them here upon earth, may miss them in heaven'. Donne dwelt within earshot of these disputes, having been himself a Member of Parliament as well as Hoskins's long-time friend (A. Patterson 1991 [quoting Hoskins]: 257). He could not have been unaware that the 'absoluteness' of the royal prerogative respecting state matters was in dispute, that the Commons' claim to liberty of speech hinged on denying that the 'government of the kingdom... pertained to the King alone' (Oakley 328). That Donne knew the political stakes involved in the distinction between matters of state and law means that when he invokes this distinction in his Sermons a political subtext may be presumed.

As Francis Oakley has shown, the dominant model of absolutism under the Stuarts derives from the theological distinction between the ordinary and absolute powers of God. The king, on this model, ordinarily governs according to the positive law of his realm, just as God ordinarily governs the world by natural law. However, as God retains the power to work miracles above and against natural law, so too the king has a reserve authority to mitigate or suspend positive law; for, Sir John Davies writes, the king 'doth imitate the Divine Majesty, which in the Government of the world doth suffer things for the most part to passe according to the order and course of Nature, yet many times doth shew his extraordinary power in working of miracles above Nature' (J. Davies 32). 'Many times', but not very many; miracles are unusual events. Analogously, as Strafford noted in 1641, the king's absolute prerogative 'must be used, as God doth his omnipotency, at extraordinary occasions'; Stuart absolutism, that is, generally concerned the king's 'extraordinary power'—the power to do what was needed *pro bono publico* in exceptional or emergency situations—'not a system of ordinary, normal or perpetual government' (Oakley 336–7; Pocock 389).

This power, however, is capable of being understood in two ways, ways that are not always easy to distinguish, and it is in the slippery area between them that the road—or at least *a* road—to civil war lay (Mendle 1993). On the one hand, the king's absolute prerogative could be viewed as operating within legally defined parameters. So, for example, Davies notes that 'the King doth not condemn all Malefactors, but by the rule of the positive Law; but when the Malefactor is condemned by the Law, he giveth him a pardon by his absolute Prerogative' (J. Davies 31; G. Burgess 198–9). This is *not* absolutism. Most heads of state have some discretionary (i.e. absolute) authority, but as long as the scope of that authority remains itself a matter of law, there is nothing absolutist about it (D. Nicholls 58–9; see Art. II, sect. 2 of the US Constitution). A distinguished cadre of historians, moreover, has argued that the Stuarts viewed their absolute prerogative as operating within such legal limits. Thus, in 1610 James answered Parliament's challenge regarding impositions with a warning not to 'dispute my prerogative and call in question that power which I have in possession, confirmed by law, derived from my progenitors and which my judges have denounced [i.e. pronounced]' (Christianson 1991: 78; G. Burgess 31, 48–9; Russell 1990: 132, 138). James's appeal to law and precedent suggests that we are dealing here not with absolutism but with 'constitutional monarchy created by kings' (Christianson 1991: 72), a view strongly corroborated by the fact that, in the key prerogative cases of the early Stuart period, the Crown lawyers rested their claims not on the king's being above the laws but, like James, on positive law and precedent. Russell concludes that the royalists were not 'champions of arbitrary government' nor 'one whit less attached to the principles of the rule of law than their Parliamentary opponents' (Wormuth 57, 71–2; Russell 1990: 132, 138, 149; Kishlansky 1999).

Yet a majority of MPs clearly thought otherwise, and with reason. As Mendle has shown, Crown apologists gave a counter-intuitive twist to Fortescue's constitutionalist model of England as a *dominium politicum et regale* by equating this distinction with the king's ordinary and absolute prerogative, thus producing what Mendle terms 'Fortescuean absolutism'. Proponents of this view 'showed a proper respect for the municipal law of the kingdom... [but argued that] there were times... when the *dominium politicum* had to yield to the *dominium regale*—instances of general emergency and "reasons of state"'. Moreover, although the law might recognize the existence of such prerogative powers, it could not define or limit them, since one reason for having a king was so there would be someone able to take extraordinary measures when the *salus populi* required it (Mendle 1993: 101–6; J. Davies 29). James repeatedly promised to rule according to law and almost always did so; but he also insisted upon his prerogative to make whatever exceptions he thought necessary (Wormuth 89), and, in Carl Schmitt's famous dictum, '[s]overeign is he who decides on the exception' (Schmitt 5). This is an absolutist model.

Yet its grounds, as Mendle points out, are not Bodinian. Fleming's verdict in the 1601 Case of Monopolies and the royalist judges' in the 1637 Ship-Money Case do not argue for the sovereign powers inherent in kings qua kings, but for the Crown's authority to 'provyde for the benefit and safety of the Realme...as the occurents and affaires of the state require'. The judges do not say that the king had a right to Ship Money, but that, as the 'executor of the common good', he was bound in conscience to collect it, since in times of danger, 'equity (the "exception" made by the laws of God and nature to "the law of man") justified otherwise illegal charges upon the subject' (G. Burgess 83–4; Mendle 1989: 517–19). Prior to the 1620s most MPs would probably have accepted this view of royal authority. There was 'good common law basis for something very like an indisputable prerogative', one exempt, that is, from challenge in the courts or Parliament (Wormuth 54–7). This was Coke's view as late as 1621. Yet by the time of his death in 1634 he, along with many of his fellow MPs, had come to hold that 'the King has no prerogative but that which the law of the land allows him' (Coke 6.299), by which Coke means the specific enumerable powers (granting pardons, summoning Parliament, proclaiming war) explicitly recognized by the common law, and not the 'infinite and inscrutable' discretionary authority, which already in 1610 so troubled Hoskins, to suspend, under extraordinary circumstances and for the common good, the ordinary legal rules, which mostly protected private property rights (Wormuth 54–7; G. Burgess 201; Bacon 1826: 4.302–3; Mendle 1993: 103).

The political crises leading to 1641 hinged on the question of whether the king had only the specific prerogatives allowed by law or, in addition, a reserve of discretionary authority to act outside or even against ordinary law. After 1621 these two positions become increasingly polarized. Yet even then the distinction between them often proves murky, since both sides appealed to common law and both found considerable support there. In turning to the question of Donne's absolutism, one needs to keep in mind both that the relevant distinctions are often between shades of grey and also that against certain backgrounds some shades of grey clash.

The politics of the preacher

The discussion thus far points to three strands of early modern absolutism: Bodinian (indivisible sovereignty, principally legislative); governmental (the medieval *gubernaculum/jurisdictio* distinction); and, to borrow Mendle's suggestive label, 'casuistical' absolutism, where, on a 'case by case' basis, 'general adherence to the rule of law...[is] superseded by an emergency or exception' (what Mendle terms

Fortescuean absolutism but also Oakley's *potentia absoluta* disclosed in the miracle that suspends the law) (qtd. in G. Burgess 50 n. 129). While these are not Platonic Ideas, they allow us to approach Donne's prose with some sense of what might count as absolutist. The focus will be on the late works, on Donne's response to Caroline absolutism, but I want to begin with the early *Pseudo-Martyr* (1610), since this contains Donne's most explicit passage of Bodinian absolutism.

Like most anti-papal political argument, *Pseudo-Martyr* is primarily a defence of divine-right kingship, not absolutism. Its assertion that the supreme magistrate(s) in every body politic receive power immediately from God does not challenge 'the rule of law or the rights of Parliament' but affirms the autonomy of temporal power against papal claims (*Pseudo-Martyr* 132–3; Cain 2006: 93). Yet Donne incorporates elements that imply such a challenge (Sommerville 2003). Against the traditional idealization of mixed or constitutional monarchy, he defends Bodin's position on the indivisibility of sovereign power, for 'God inanimates every State with one power, as every man with one soule' (*Pseudo-Martyr* 133; see also *Sermons* 4.240–1). Somewhere in every regime must reside 'that *soveraignty*, which is a power to doe all things availeable to the maine ends' for which political order exists. Donne, however, says nothing about royal legislative sovereignty. This omission of the hallmark of Bodinian absolutism suggests that *Pseudo-Martyr*'s understanding of sovereignty belongs rather to the ambit of casuistical absolutism, as does its claim that, since political order exists so that we might live peaceably and religiously, God endows rulers with the '*power to use all those meanes, which conduce to those endes*' (133). As the 'all' implies, sovereign power is *solutus legibus*; the ruler is accountable to God for the welfare of his realm, but he is not accountable to its laws. It was precisely this view of the prerogative as an *undefined* reserve of extra-legal power, and not Bodinian assertions of royal legislative sovereignty, that constituted 'the central tenet of early Stuart absolutist thinking' (Sommerville 2003: 89).

There no longer seems much doubt that Donne's 'commitment to the crown was unimpeachable' (McCullough 2003*b*: 192; A. Patterson 1997: 18, 26; Shami 2003*a*: 11). His preaching is suffused by a sense of the divinity hedging those 'anointed of the Lord', of kings as 'Images of God', of God as 'the Type of *Monarchy*' and monarchy as the '*Type of Heaven*' (*Sermons* 4.239–41, 243; see also 7.357, 8.336). As he proclaims in a Paul's Cross Sermon of 1627, 'God and Kings are at a near distance, All *gods*; Magistrates, and inferiour persons are at a near distance, all *dust*', and later that same year he preaches that 'in the Kings lawfull working upon his Subjects, God works, and the Kings acts are Gods acts' (7.425; 8.115). The word 'king' or 'kings' appears 879 times in the Sermons, only once in a negative sense: in a Sermon preached to King Charles in April of 1626. However, the Sermon directs against the papacy, not against kings (7.126), its criticism of those who govern by 'a secret judgement in one breast' instead of 'by a knowne, and constant Law'; one finds a similar critique (and, moreover, argued on strikingly conciliarist-republican grounds) in William

Laud's *Conference with Fisher* (Laud 2.221–2, 234–35, 252–3). In neither case does it seem warranted to treat such anti-papal rhetoric as implicitly anti-monarchic.

References to 'Parliament' in Donne's Sermons, by contrast, are thin on the ground, a word count yielding only seven citations. More often (but not much more often) he refers to it obliquely. One suspects that he preferred such indirect mention because his point is almost always critical. A week after Charles's angry dissolution of the 1626 Parliament to prevent Buckingham's impeachment, Donne thus blasted its members for having 'retard[ed] publique businesse' by their 'hunt after... [a] particular person'; by 'unseasonable pressing of present remedies', they have shown themselves willing to 'evacuate the blessed and glorious purpose of the whole Councell', and thus to risk becoming God's 'instrument to destroy, or farther to punish us' (*Sermons* 7.204; cf. Laud 3.192). Sermon after Sermon addresses what was, from a royalist perspective, the fundamental political issue of the age: Parliament's failure to vote subsidies sufficient for governing a nation, much less for fighting a continental war. Donne's 1622 Gunpowder Plot Day Sermon reminds his congregation that kings are 'to be preserved... by *support* and *supply*', for 'it is the service of God, to contribute to *the King*' (*Sermons* 4.239, 262). Preaching during the 1626 Parliament, which refused to vote subsidies until they had avenged themselves on Buckingham, Donne goes so far as to imply the king's *right* to such support *maugre* Parliament, pointing out that 'Customes, and Tributes, and Impositions were due to the Kings of *Jewry*, due in natural right, and due in legal right, fixed and established by that Law in *Samuel*' (7.149; see James I 1994: 64–70). His harshest censure comes a year later in a passage that is hard not to read as a defence of the Forced Loan, to which Charles turned after the 1626 Parliament yielded nothing despite the fact that England was at war with both Spain and France. In an explicit 'civill application' of the Gospel to the matter of 'obedience to Superiours', Donne warns his congregation: 'If you [do not] heare [the king]... you are none of his. If you heare him not... in the *Declarations* of his wants and necessities, you are none of his, that is, you had rather you were none of his.' Moreover, when a people 'will not believe their Civill dangers', God 'will depart first, as he is the *Angel of the great counsell*, and not enlighten their understandings, that they might see their dangers'. The great council is, of course, Parliament, on whose intransigence Donne blamed the current and impending crises, for 'not to have brought *Saul presents*, not to have contributed to his present wars, and his present wants, this occasioned the jealousie' (*Sermons* 7.404). Through the final weeks of the disastrous 1628–9 session Donne continued to urge Parliament to offer 'a reall supply in Deeds... [and] so do good to God, in reall assisting his cause' by doing 'good to them, whom God hath called Gods' (8.342–3; see also 8.218, 244). None of these passages, except perhaps that of 1626, is absolutist, since Parliament's obligation to vote supplies does not entail that the Crown may demand them willy-nilly, but they do indicate an unambiguous, even defiant, royalism.

The apparent absence of corresponding glances at royal policies cannot be put down to prudent reluctance to awaken the wrath of power. One need not find 'subtly oppositional stances' in the Sermons to counter suspicions of careerism. Donne preached regularly to an audience of common lawyers and Parliament men. His own experience in the Parliament of 1614 would have left him with no illusions about the Commons' punitive reflex when dealing with clerics whom they viewed as having spoken too slightingly of their role or too highly of the prerogative. Donne's friend Richard Martin suggested hanging them, and he was only half joking (Foster 2.328). The Commons' pursuit of Cowell, vicar-general to Archbishop Bancroft, in 1610 for a law dictionary; of Bishop Neile in 1614 for an alleged slur made in passing during a debate in the Lords; of Maynwaring in 1627 for a sermon; and of Montague from 1624 to 1629 for 'Arminianism'—the actual charge being considered was treason—suggest that Donne's criticisms of Parliament carried considerable personal risk (Cobbett and Howell 2.865–70, 3.335–58; for a different view see Shuger 2006: 239–50, 269–72; A. Patterson 1991: 267).

Criticism of Parliament does not, however, make Donne an absolutist any more than criticism of royal policy would disqualify him. While his post-ordination writings do not use the language of Bodinian absolutism, they regularly affirm the governmental model, which was a standard Tudor position, although, as the Protestation of 1621 makes clear, it had begun to strike some MPs as granting the Crown dangerously broad power to determine policy on such vital matters as impositions, the Bohemian crisis, and the Spanish Match. Donne, however, assigns the domain of *gubernaculum* to the Crown alone. It is the king's office, he thus avers, to deal with 'publick and general dangers', and ours to 'rely upon that *Wisdome*, in civill affaires, affaires of State', for 'the *care of all*, appertaineth unto him' (*Sermons* 4.238, 260–1). Unless the fundamentals of Christianity are at stake, private persons are to remain quiet, since 'they cannot possibly discerne the *Ende*, to which their *Superiours* goe', God having entrusted the running of things into the '*hand* of the *Magistrate*', an assertion that effectually dismissed the possibility or desirability of a public sphere (6.245; see also 1.255; 4.263). Furthermore, among public persons, it is the king alone who 'propose[s] Directions' for God's glory and the public good; the rest serve the state by executing 'those gracious Directions received from their royall Master' (8.245).

Some of Donne's theological analogies likewise invoke governmental absolutism. In these, the *arcana Dei* do not concern predestination, but rather such high policy matters as the timing of the Incarnation and the Second Coming. And God has revealed these 'secrets of his State, and of his government' to no one, they being (and here Donne sounds amazingly like King James's warnings to Parliament) 'acts of his Regality, and of his Prerogative; and as Princes say of their Prerogative, *nolumus disputari*, wee will not have it disputed, nor called into question' (8.153) A Sermon reproving over-refined theological speculation suddenly breaks into a similarly resonant analogy: '[i]t is enough', Donne proclaims, 'for a happy subject to enjoy the sweetnesse of a peaceable government, though he know not *Arcana Imperii*, The wayes by which the Prince governes' (9.246). The comparison may be just a comparison, but not if Potter and Simpson are right in dating the Sermon to the first year of Personal Rule (9.30–1).

In declaring it blasphemy to dispute what a king could do at the height of his powers, James upheld the general principle of casuistical absolutism, but since he also promised to rule according to settled law, and rarely, if ever, actualized his supralegal *potentia*, royal absolutism remained a fairly abstract issue up to 1626, when the failure of parliamentary supply led Charles to such expedients as the Forced Loan—measures that Heath, his Attorney-General, defended on the grounds that '"there be *Arcana Dei, et Arcana Imperii*"' (qtd. in Christianson 1985: 71). Christianson goes on to note that Heath thought these arcana 'unfit for the prying eyes of subjects', who are to 'trust kings when they take unusual actions for the good of the commonwealth' (ibid.). Heath denied such actions violated 'the law of the land' (79), a claim vigorously rejected by the common lawyers in Parliament, for whom law meant fixed rules *as opposed to* discretionary powers.

Hence, with respect to Donne's post-1626 Sermons, the key issue is casuistical absolutism: does he view the prerogative as limited by known law or does he acknowledge an undefined reserve of emergency powers in the Crown, whose exceptional operation corresponds to the role of miracles vis-à-vis natural law in God's administration of the universe? There are passages in these Sermons that bear upon this question. These passages, however, present two problems. First, they are almost all theological analogies; and second, they appear to give contradictory answers.

Those that seem to endorse casuistical absolutism are sufficiently alike that a single example from the 1629 Easter Sermon will suffice to indicate the difficulty with a political reading. Donne affirms that: 'Generally we are to receive our instructions from Gods established Ordinances.... But yet, we are not so to conclude God in his Law, as that he should have no Prerogative, nor so to bind him up in his Ordinances, as that he never can, or never does work by an extraordinary way of revelation' (*Sermons* 8.366). The passage concerns God's prerogative, but does it simultaneously intimate a like power in Charles I? It seems hard to disagree with Jeanne Shami that Donne's 'analogies, including analogies to government and state power, can register something of the political valences of a work' (1995*b*: 52); yet it also seems fair to say that registering something of a valence does not qualify as stating a political position. Donne's fondness for such analogies suggests that his political instincts were absolutish, but their referent is too specifically theological to prove him an absolutist.

The passages that point in the opposite direction—those that seemingly advocate governing according to known law and affirm the inseparability of law and liberty (both parliamentary watchwords)—are trickier to decode. There are not many such passages, but they have, for obvious reasons, drawn critical attention. The most striking comes from a St Paul's Sermon of late 1628 on the duty of almsgiving, in which Donne suddenly veers off topic to argue that:

as the Law is our Judge, and the Judge does but declare what is Law, so the Scripture is our Judge, and God proceeds with us according to those promises and Judgements... [Hence,] if I come to thinke that God will call me in question for my life, for my eternall life, by any way that hath not the Nature of a *Law*, (And, by the way, it is of the Nature and Essence of a Law, before it come to bind, that it be *published*) if I think that God will condemn me by any *unrevealed will*...this is to reproach God. (8.281–2)

As before, we are dealing with a theological analogy, and one, moreover, comparing God to a judge, not a king. However, it clearly associates God with the rule of law, and if God governs according to fixed and known law, which his 'unrevealed will' never overrides, it seems no great leap to conclude that Donne here sides with the common law and its parliamentary champions against Caroline absolutism.

Yet the passage is an analogy, and the point of the analogy is to condemn Calvinist predestination. The point is characteristic of Donne's Sermons during this period, which never mention habeas corpus or the other constitutional issues of the age, but instead repeatedly and explicitly address the theological ones. As Achsah Guibbory and others have noted, Donne consistently takes the High Church position, defending bowing at the name of Jesus, the use of 'altar' and 'sacrifice'; denying the irresistibility of grace, the perseverance of the elect, and double predestination (Guibbory 2001; McCullough 2003*b*: 193–5; Strier 101, 109). These are the controversies that inform his preaching, not the constitutional ones—and yet they are intimately linked.

The modern division of disciplines has made this link hard to see. Scholarship on the political conflicts of the Caroline era does not treat theology; histories of the Stuart church do not comment on impositions or Darnel's Case. Yet one need only skim the Commons Journals from the late 1620s to realize that the same members defending law and liberty against the Crown's prerogative claims were also spearheading the attack on Montague and, by the end, demanding that the hard-line Calvinism of the Lambeth Articles be imposed under penalty of death. The Protestation that the parliamentary leadership read to wild cheers during the final chaotic moments of the 1629 session is three sentences long, the first of which states: '[W]hosoever shall bring in innovation in Religion, or by favor or countenance, seek to extend or introduce, Popery or Arminianism or other opinion disagreeing from the true and orthodox Church, shall be reputed a capital enemy to this Kingdom and Commonwealth' (Shuger 2006: 271). Donne's Sermon, which only three months earlier had praised the rule of law as part of an argument against this 'true and orthodox' doctrine, is clearly up to something. But what? Why use the political vocabulary of the parliamentary opposition to defend a theological position they abhorred? If Donne's real point is the anti-Calvinist one, as would seem to be the case, then he is using the Commons' politics against their theology (like defending gun control with right-to-life arguments). He borrows the Commons' political watchwords to associate predestination with prerogative rule (government by 'unrevealed will'), Scripture's universal promise of salvation to all believers with the law-based polity of the ancient constitution, but his point is theological, not constitutional.

A Sermon preached at Whitehall just days before the collapse of the 1629 Parliament adopts a similar strategy. Its foregrounding of the loaded phrase (from James 2:12), 'the law of liberty', has led Paul Harland to interpret the Sermon as censuring Caroline absolutism on the grounds that by 1628 every Englishman who was not a fool or knave 'associated the king and extended prerogative with lawless rule, Parliament and its privileges with the rule of law' (J. H. Hexter, qtd. in Harland 22). As he rightly notes, the Sermon consistently uses 'theological language that had political overtones'. The defence of law and liberty—of law as the sole guarantee of liberty—was, in fact, the central plank of the Commons' platform, the ideological ground for its resistance to prerogative claims.

In a parliamentary context, 'law of liberty' would refer to the common law's enforcement of the property rights that distinguish a free man from a serf (Peck 1993: 91; Sommerville 1986: 148–60). In Donne's Sermon, however, 'law of liberty' never has anything remotely close to that sense. Rather than extending the Commons' political watchwords in a theological direction, as the 1628 Sermon did, the 1629 Sermon reappropriates them for theology alone. The Sermon consistently defines its key terms so as to mute their political overtones, at one point equating law with the scriptural commands to feed the hungry and clothe the poor (*Sermons* 8.348), at another defining 'Evangelical liberty' as the courage to examine one's conscience with honesty and rigour (8.352), at a third explaining that the Gospel is a law of liberty because it 'restores us to liberty, after we are falne...into Gods displeasure for sin' (8.350). The Sermon continues in this vein up to the concluding summation of the law of liberty as that which 'delivers us, upon whom it works, from the necessity of falling into the bondage of sin before, and from the impossibility of recovering after, if we be falne into that bondage', and then ends with a final clinching sentence: 'And this is liberty enough' (8.354). The last five words drive home the point implicit throughout: that the law and liberty demanded by the Commons are not, for Christians, essential or even principal goods. Donne's use of parliamentary language may signal his acknowledgement of the members' concerns, yet the overall tone is critical, exposing the awkward gap between the Commons' political agenda and their religious commitments, mostly by insisting on the primacy of the latter—this being the role of a preacher, which Donne was.

He was not, however, a political thinker, and throughout his ministry made a point of not using his pulpit for editorializing on emergent occasions (4.202, 276). *Pseudo-Martyr* flirts with Bodinian absolutism, but this was an anti-papal work, a genre conducive to high-flown royalism. In the Sermons one finds a consistent strain of governmental absolutism, a position that, although becoming increasingly contentious, had been Tudor orthodoxy and was still widely accepted. Donne's stance on casuistical absolutism, the terrain on which the constitutional struggles of the Caroline era were fought, is less clear. As noted above, virtually all the relevant passages in the Sermons concern God's Kingdom, which, having an inerrant ruler and no Parliament, cannot without further showing be taken as Donne's model for English politics. One suspects that statements like that from Donne's Christmas Sermon of 1627—'in extraordinary distresses, wee pray for extraordinary reliefes, though extraordinary helps...bee Reserved cases, and acts of his Regality, and Prerogative' (8.155)—were meant to gesture support for royal emergency powers. Yet the passage expresses the hope that God will aid the Protestant cause; it does not say whether Charles might aid it by invoking the prerogative to raise troops. For some in Caroline England the two sorts of 'extraordinary relief' probably seemed related; for others, not.

How are we to understand such ambiguities? They are certainly consistent with Shami's view of Donne as seeking a rhetoric that eschewed 'partisan or factional' assertion (1995b: 10). This judicious and, for Shami, laudable refusal to take sides is, however, more or less what Peter Lake means by 'fudge': the empty compromise 'masking very different visions...that must sooner or later come into conflict' (2000: 195). If Shami's account idealizes Donne, Lake's betrays the easy cynicism of hindsight, given its entailment that if two visions eventually collide, any earlier attempt at mediation can be dismissed out of hand. A more promising approach is suggested by Burgess, who observes that evasiveness with regard to absolutism is typical of Stuart divines, who almost never detail the implications of their divine-right theories or how they bear upon the conundrums of law and prerogative. There is thus nothing particularly *Donnean* about the ambiguities noted above, nor was such reticence confined to the pulpit. Early modern Englishpersons, Burgess notes, betray a 'habitual evasion of the question of sovereignty' (G. Burgess 132–3, 113–14). Yet he does not view this as spineless pussyfooting. Rather, drawing on the work of Michael Foley, he raises the possibility that all constitutions, written and unwritten, rest on 'habits of wilful neglect, protective obfuscation, and complicity in non-exposure' in order to defer conflict and contain insoluble disagreements (Foley, qtd. in G. Burgess 133). It is precisely by this 'silence of constitutions', in Foley's enchanting metaphor, that 'the sleeping giants of potentially acute political conflict are communally maintained in slumber'—or as Wentworth urged the Commons during the 1621 session, '[let it] never be stirred here whether the king be above the law or the law above the king' (Foley 82, 34).

CHAPTER 40

STYLE, WIT, PROSODY IN THE POETRY OF JOHN DONNE

ALBERT C. LABRIOLA

1

IN the most unlikely places, whether Sermons, poems, or Letters, but not formal critical commentary, Donne provides brief remarks on poetry. From such piecemeal disclosure one must infer or interpret what the author's poetics may have been. At times the process of inference and interpretation is not unlike reading one of Donne's poems. Considerations of figurative language, irony, paradox, the use of a persona that may or may not be autobiographical, tonal range, and the like—all come into play even when engaging Donne's remarks on poetry. In a Sermon on the Book of Psalms, for instance, Donne likens 'the whole frame of the Poem' to 'a beating out of a piece of gold…' (*Sermons* 6.41), an image similar to one he uses in *ValMourn*, where he speaks of the souls of the speaker and his beloved that are '[l]ike gold to ayery thinnesse beate' (l. 24). Whatever else such comments mean, surely Donne specifies painstaking craftsmanship: the poet who figuratively hammers gold into a finished artefact (namely the poem) is likened to a metalsmith who literally hammers malleable gold into foil or a leaf.

In the same Sermon Donne also emphasizes that the force or impact of a poem issues largely from the 'shutting up', by which he means closure. For him, 'the last clause' is 'as the impression of the stamp' (6.41), a reference to the use of gold or silver in mintage, when a blank or planchet of precious metal is pressed between two dies, then hammered so that the metal becomes attenuated. Both sides bear the impressions of coinage. Much as those final impressions designate the worth of a coin, so also the hammering art of the poet leads to closure, to the final verse(s) stamping the significance of the contents. The author's emphasis on the endings of poems spurs the reader to recall works like *Fun, Air, SGo, Ecst*, and some of the Divine Poems, including the Holy Sonnets, where the last lines emphasize, retract, modify, or undercut what preceded them. In their last lines, some of Donne's poems exemplify a dramatic turnabout, basically a *tour de force*, which results in surprise and laughter at one's naivety as a reader for having been drawn into an argument, sentiment, or point of view, only to be jerked unexpectedly in the opposite direction. When Donne's endings include couplets or triplets, they become aphoristic in their wry and satirical wit in the secular poems or in their ironic and reverential wit in the Divine Poems.

A comment by Donne to Sir Robert Ker, in a brief Letter (1627) prefixed to *Ham*, appraises the quality of his poems in inverse proportion to the truth that they contain. Donne argues that he 'did best when [he] had least Truth for [his] subiect' (*Variorum* 6.219). If interpreted seriously, not ironically, such a comment fosters the perspective that in some poems the speakers do not articulate the author's own views; nor do the speakers who become involved in particular situations or dramatic encounters reflect autobiographical experiences. Relevant here is the critical viewpoint that likens Donne to a ventriloquist, who creates and manipulates a character with views different from his own. But in the poem eulogizing Hamilton, ironically, Donne may be more subtle than his foregoing statement indicates. Confronted with scandals in Hamilton's life and in the manner of his death, Donne may be speculating on Hamilton's presence or status in the community of saints or, more likely, in an afterlife short of saintly bliss. Donne engages the emotions of survivors whose perceptions of Hamilton differ significantly. The poet, therefore, acknowledges the loss of Hamilton, encourages mourning, but resists judgement on the disposition of the soul of the deceased. The voice of the poet simultaneously accommodates multiple perceptions so that any one does not exclude another (Maurer 2007: 15–16). In the end, Donne may be urging the readers of his poem to weigh Hamilton's imperfections against those of certain biblical figures, who repented and are deemed saintly.

In one of his Sermons Donne similarly argues: 'Poetry is a counterfait Creation, and makes things that are not, as though they were' (*Sermons* 4.87). Accordingly, one may infer that Donne creates a scenario and invests its principal character, the speaker, with reasoning and emotions different from his own, but still lifelike. One may contend that the verisimilitude of some poems lures the reader into thinking that he or she is entering Donne's own self. But Donne may be delineating a speaker who in some instances is being satirized for his hubris. Overconfident in his 'words masculine persuasive force' (*Variorum* 2.246, *ElFatal* l. 4), a force characterized by complex allusions, overpowering emotion, and formidable reasoning or even sophistry, the speaker may have underestimated the silent but discerning female listener in the poem. Such is the case in *Flea*, when the woman, though silent, still renders a judgement on the would-be seducer by crushing the insect. Reading or listening to dramatic recitations of Donne's works, coteries of sophisticated men or women—or men and women—would have been amused by the speaker's adroitness in plying his wit.

Or Donne, when alleging that his best writing has 'least Truth'—that it is a 'counterfait Creation'—may be referring to the *Anniversaries*, in which inordinate adulation of a deceased adolescent, Elizabeth Drury, becomes hyperbolic idealization. Writing from Paris in April 1612 to George Garrard and then to Sir Henry Goodere, Donne reacted to censures of his epideictic poetry that he had received while abroad. He acknowledged that since he 'never saw the Gentlewoman, [he] cannot be understood to have bound [him] selfe to have spoken just Truth' (*Letters* 255). And having 'received so very good testimony of her worthinesse', he wrote 'the best that [he] could conceive' and 'the best praise that [he] could give' (75). In 1619 Ben Jonson recounted for William Drummond of Hawthornden his own objections to the rhetorical excesses of *FirAn*: that the poem 'was profane and full of Blasphemies'. If, however, 'it had been written of ye Virgin Marie it had been something'. Concerning these objections, Jonson comments that Donne 'answered that he described the Idea of a Woman and not as she was' (Jonson 1–2.133).

If Donne distances himself from the speakers of some poems, or acknowledges that fulsome praise deviates from the truth, he affirms in the Letter to Robert Ker (cited above) that '[i]n this present case there is so much Truth as it defeats all Poetry' (*Variorum* 6.219). In fact, 'this present case' is his hymn to the deceased Hamilton, which is intended to be overheard by the Marquess of Hamilton and the survivors of the nobleman. The language of the poem, while laudatory, is certainly more measured and less fulsome than what appears in *FirAn*. In this Elegy commemorating Hamilton perhaps Donne's own voice is heard through the speaker in the poem. In other instances, as well, Donne's own voice may prevail, notably in the Sonnet on his deceased wife or in some Divine Poems that may constitute spiritual autobiography, including his Sonnet on the Church of England, the church to which Donne conformed after having been reared a Catholic.

In another Letter (1627) to Sir Robert Ker, Donne, while acknowledging that Charles I read some of his poems, likens his meticulous technique of constructing Sermons to that of composing poetry: '[T]he King who hath let fall his eye upon some of my Poems, never saw, of mine, a hand, or an eye, or an affection, set down with so much study, and diligence, and labour of syllables, as in this Sermon…' (*Letters* 308). In the Sermons and the poems Donne exhibits extraordinary craftsmanship in selecting words, even syllables. Indeed, artful composition belies the spontaneity that Donne evidently manifested in the oratorical performances of his Sermons. In the same Letter to Sir Robert Ker, Donne adds that he heard the

King say 'of a good Sermon, that he thought the Preacher never had thought of his Sermon, till he spoke it; it seemed to him negligently and extemporally spoken' (*Letters* 309). Despite their rehearsed presentations, the apparent spontaneity that characterizes the Sermons likewise informs the conversational, sometimes dramatic, rhythms of speakers in the poems and perhaps the imagined gestures that may accompany their utterances.

Finally, in a Sermon, Donne extols the Psalms for manifesting a 'limited, and a restrained form; Not in an *Oration*, not in *Prose*, but in *Psalms*; which is such a form as is both curious, and requires diligence in the making, and then when it is made, can have nothing, no syllable taken from it, nor added to it'. And the 'words are numbered, and measured, and weighed' (*Sermons* 2.50). Related to the foregoing comments is Donne's poem *Sidney*, in which the author commends the Sidneys' 'sweet learned labours' (l. 54) to render the Psalms into English. These comments in a Sermon and in a poem on the Psalms emphasize the 'curious' or carefully wrought form, the 'labours', and the economy of composition (nothing can be added or subtracted) that Donne admires and presumably emulates. And the adjective 'sweet' may mean '[p]leasing to the ear' and 'melodious' (*OED* 4.a.), but it may also mean 'persuasive' and 'winning' (5.c.) and '[e]asily managed, handled, or dealt with' (6.c.). What may one infer from Donne's use of 'sweet' to praise how the Sidneys rendered the Psalms into English? Does the word mean melodious or rhythmically regular; or persuasive and winning because of effective adaptation to English; or handled and executed with apparent ease despite the erudite labour involved? Or in Donne's mind do the various meanings of 'sweet' all converge to describe the work of the Sidneys? Furthermore, Sir Lucius Cary (1610–43), in an elegy on John Donne, comments that his '[p]oetrie' was 'oftentimes divinity'. Focusing on '[t]hose Anthemes', called 'almost second Psalmes' and composed to 'make us know the Crosse' (Donne 1633*b*: 390, ll. 40–2), Cary refers presumably to Donne's *Cross*, which, to him, is no doubt 'sweet' in one or more of the senses mentioned above.

2

The currents and cross-currents of Donne's views on poetry provide a context for understanding whether his writings are harsh, obscure or merely witty, and unrhythmical. That is, Donne's own views raise the very enquiries that have engaged his readers from his own era to the present: what is the relationship between art and experience in Donne's works? When is the author also the speaker in a poem? And when is the author distanced from the speaker, who becomes a character in his own right? How may a composition be artful and finely wrought, both structurally and verbally, but still convey the semblance of spontaneity? May a poem be 'sweet' if it is not metrically rhythmic or melodious? How may irregular prosody still be poetic? When refined to their essence, the foregoing enquiries emanating from Donne's own comments highlight three topics—style, wit, and prosody—and their interrelationship. These same topics provide the framework in which to chart Donne's literary reputation in three major stages: his own era, the eighteenth century, and the nineteenth century to the present.

Among the most significant early comments on Donne's style, wit, and prosody are Ben Jonson's. A friend and fellow author, Jonson, in an epigram 'To John Donne' (c.1610), focuses on the wit in the early poems, probably the Songs and Sonets or the Elegies. Though brief, the epigram stresses that Donne's wit was an 'example' still unsurpassed. Jonson contends that the wit of Donne's poems is '[l]onger a knowing, then most wits doe live' (Jonson 8.34, l. 5). In these two passages 'wit' refers to Donne's 'great mental capacity; intellectual ability; genius, talent, cleverness; mental quickness or sharpness, acumen' (OED 5.a.); his 'lively fancy' intended to 'amuse' others (10); and his 'quality of…writing which consists in the apt association of thought and expression, calculated to surprise and delight by its unexpectedness' (8.a.). The 'wits' are the other poets who would strive vainly across a lifetime to comprehend, never to match or exceed, Donne's wit. Jonson also argues that 'Phoebus' and 'each *Muse*' inspiring Donne 'all other braines refuse' (Jonson 8.34, l. 1). Not only do the very sources of Donne's inspiration refuse to abide in other authors, but also other poets' brains could not sustain, and thereby 'refuse', the profound inspiration visited upon Donne. Such inspiration signifies Donne's overly active and fanciful wit.

To be added to the foregoing comments are Jonson's conversations with William Drummond in 1619 that include the following remarks: that Donne 'for not keeping of accent deserved hanging', that he was 'the first poet in the World jn some things', and that he 'for not being understood would perish' (Jonson 1–2.135, 138). By such verbal shorthand, Jonson calls attention to Donne's irregular prosody or metrical irregularity, unique style, and sometimes incomprehensible wit, culminating in the prediction that because of such traits his poetry will be forgotten. Counterbalancing these remarks, however, Jonson sent his own epigrams to Donne for appraisal. In a poem accompanying the manuscript, he invited his fellow poet, who 'hast best authoritie' (Jonson 8.62, l. 6), to praise or censure them freely. With Donne's approbation, Jonson would acquire 'great glorie, and not broad' (l. 12), an acknowledgement that Donne's reputation was limited primarily to the *literati* and *cognoscenti* and that his poems were not intended for the general populace. And Jonson, who sent Lucy, Countess of Bedford, copies of Donne's Satires, affirmed in an introductory poem to the noblewoman that these works '[b]e of the best' of their kind (Jonson 8.61, l. 14).

Numerous elegies after Donne's death in 1631 echo Jonson's appraisals concerning the style, wit, and prosody of his friend and fellow poet. In 1632 Henry King, for instance, struggled to compose an elegy that would befit Donne, who 'liv'd eminent, in a degree / Beyond our lofty'st flights', a poet whose 'excesses finde no Epitaph' (Donne 1633b: 373, ll. 1–2, 4). By 'excesses' King presumably means departures from custom (*OED* 1.b.), sometimes described as 'glorious' (2), an excess of mind that astonishes others (1.c.), and an excellency that surpasses others (6.a.). In short, King is celebrating Donne's wit. He adds, moreover, that '[a]t common graves we have Poetique eyes' that '[c]an melt themselves in easie Elegies' (Donne 1633b: 373, ll. 5, 6), a reference to metrically regular or conventional elegiac verses flowing smoothly (*OED* 4.b.), an unfit means by which to memorialize Donne's unique and iconoclastic poetry. Immobilized, therefore, by the daunting duty of eulogizing Donne with a work '[r]ich...of wit, and language' (l. 10), a work befitting his memory, King futilely concludes that '[w]idow'd invention' will visit no author after Donne (l. 13).

In his 1633 elegy, Izaak Walton, Donne's first biographer, describes Donne's sonnet sequence *Corona* composed 'in harmonious-holy-numbers' (Donne 1633b: 384, l. 34), an acknowledgement that Donne could and did write in metrically regular verse when he believed that such prosody suited the topic, the tone, and the artistic intention. Such is true, moreover, of some of Donne's secular poems, notably *Bait*, which is metrically regular: seven stanzas, each a quatrain composed of couplets in tetrameter verse. Parodying Christopher Marlowe's 'The Passionate Shepherd to His Love', Donne's poem appropriates the content and form of conventional love poems. Walton, in *The Compleat Angler*, cites *Bait* as proof that Donne 'could make soft and smooth Verses, when he thought them fit and worth his labour' (1653: 184).

Most memorable and frequently cited, Thomas Carew's elegy echoes King's anxiety that no appropriate epitaph for Donne can be composed, none that approximates Donne's unique wit, which revitalized poetry when '[t]he Muses garden with Pedantique weedes / O'rspred, was purg'd by thee' and the 'lazie seeds / [o]f servile imitation throwne away; / And fresh invention planted' (Donne 1633b: 386, ll. 25–6). The commonplace meaning of 'weedes' is undesirable vegetation overtaking a garden, and the word '[p]edantique' signifies strict, indeed schoolmasterly, adherence to custom and tradition, particularly repetitious academic exercises (*OED* B. 1. 2.). Ironically, to substantiate these meanings of 'pedantique', the *OED* cites the use of the word in Donne's *SunRis* and in Carew's elegy. By implying that Donne weeded the garden and cultivated 'the flowers of rhetoric', a common Renaissance term for discourse freshly grown by the power of inventiveness or wit, Carew recognizes Donne as a potent and seminal force in poetry. He adds that Donne's style, wit, and prosody liberated English poetry from its dependence on, not to mention imitation or adaptation of, classical sources and analogues: the writings of Anacreon, Pindar, and others of 'the Greeke, or Latine tongue' (l. 36). Celebrating Donne for his 'rich and pregnant phansie' (l. 38), 'masculine expression' (l. 39), and 'imperious wit' (l. 49), Carew denigrates the traditional metrical regularity of other poets: their 'tun'd chime / More charmes the outward sense' (ll. 46–7). Instead, 'phansie', 'masculine expression', and 'imperious wit' enabled Donne to prevail so that '[o]ur stubborne language bends' and is 'made only fit' as 'her tough-thick-rib'd hoopes' do 'gird about' the author's '[g]iant phansie', a faculty 'too stout' to be accommodated by more traditional 'soft melting Phrases' (ll. 51–3). More than other elegists, Carew, while emphasizing the hallmarks of style, wit, and prosody, provides a comparative critical commentary on Donne's poetry and that of his contemporaries.

Though Carew is a major spokesperson of the seventeenth-century critical viewpoint on Donne's poems, other commentators of that era may be cited for their insightful observations. In his elegy of 1633 Jasper Mayne, a poet and a Church of England divine like Donne, comments on his colleague as a preacher, whose words 'could charme [his] audience' so that 'eare was all our sense' (Donne 1633b: 395, ll. 55–6). Mayne adds that Donne in the pulpit exemplified by 'looke, and hand' (l. 58) how preachers should comport themselves. Terms such as 'speaking action', 'carriage', and 'gesture' (ll. 59–61) suggest that sermons, while appearing to be 'negligently and extemporally spoken' (echoing Charles I's observations cited above), were well rehearsed to the degree that a performative self emerged. Though these observations pertain to the Sermons, one may argue that they may also apply to the speakers in various poems, speakers and enactors whose impact aurally and visually is tantamount to dramatic performance.

Even Donne's admirers acknowledged that his prosody was harsh and rugged, but they recognized that his innovations in verse served a larger purpose, the creation of dramatic lyrics and dramatic personae as speakers. They recognized, moreover, that in his extraordinary exercise of wit Donne necessarily pressured the English language beyond metrical regularity so that it might encompass his ever-widening imagination. The upshot was an iconoclastic style of poetry that challenged traditional verse forms.

3

The numerous elegies praising Donne imply that his poems were unique among English authors. While citing his iconoclastic style of composition, singular wit, and irregular prosody, the elegists note that Donne's talent is not only singular but also inimitable. The fertility to which Carew refers—the 'fresh invention' that Donne 'planted' in the realm of poetry—affected some seventeenth-century poets often classified in the 'school of Donne': George Herbert, Andrew Marvell, Thomas Traherne, Henry Vaughan, John Cleveland, and Abraham Cowley. Some of them imitated Donne but stopped short of his extravagant style, wit, and prosody. In doing so, they practised restraint, thereby acknowledging Donne's uniqueness while tempering his influence on them. Others, like Cleveland and Cowley, sought to imitate his extravagant style, wit, and prosody; but their works are cited, especially by twentieth-century literary historians, as evidence of the decline or decadence of the so-called 'school of Donne'. Their works became unwitting parodies of Donne's extravagances. They did not heed the admonition of Donne's elegists: that his unique achievements were inimitable.

The most radical change in outlook on Donne's poetry occurred later in the seventeenth century, when John Dryden appraised the satires of Donne and Cleveland. In *An Essay of Dramatick Poesie* (1668) Dryden contends that Donne couches 'deep thoughts in common language, though rough cadence', while Cleveland frames 'common thoughts in abstruse words' (Dryden 1956– : 17.30). And in *A Discourse Concerning the Original and Progress of Satire* (1693), Dryden asserts that Donne 'affects the Metaphysicks, not only in his Satires, but in his Amorous Verses, where Nature only shou'd reign; and perplexes the Minds of the Fair Sex with nice Speculations of Philosophy, when he shou'd ingage their hearts, and entertain them with the softnesses of Love' (4.7). This sentiment is echoed in the letter to Mistress Arabella Fermor that introduces Alexander Pope's *The Rape of the Lock* (1714). Pope highlights 'how disagreeable it is to make use of hard Words before a Lady', when 'the Concern of a Poet [is] to have his Works understood, and particularly by your Sex' (Pope 217).

Such remarks typify how the predominant literary sensibility concerning love poetry had changed since the era of Donne and his followers. By 'Nature' Dryden means the phenomenal world as a source of imagery in traditional love poetry: flowers, fruits, the climate, the seasons, precious metals, luminaries in the firmament, and the like. For Dryden, the felicitous comparisons of a woman's characteristics, physical and psychological, to the realm of Nature was the appropriate means by which to examine loving relationships. But Donne had juxtaposed the *visibilia* and the *invisibilia*, or the natural world and the Platonic, spiritual, or metaphysical realm. These two spheres interacted synergistically in his poems, so that abstruse and rarefied speculations proliferated. For these reasons, Dryden and Pope expressed dissatisfaction with Donne's works, presuming also to speak on behalf of women who, they contended, would be displeased by this kind of love poetry. Strikingly, there is a counter-current among some eighteenth-century women concerning Donne's poetry. An essay in *The Female Tatler* (1710), purportedly reflecting the views of sophisticated women, provides a biographical reading of two of Donne's poems, *Ecst* and *Anniv*. For these readers, Donne is 'a model lover whose poems expressed an ardent and sincere ideal of love and who had no counterpart among the beaux of the Augustan Age' (Rude 154; see Ch. 38 above). Even in the era immediately after the Restoration, Donne's verse was incorporated into poems and dramas with or without attribution. In her drama called *The Second Part of Lady Contemplation* (1662), Margaret Cavendish, Duchess of Newcastle, refers to Donne in a speech by one of the characters, Lady Ward, who says, 'I remember a witty Poet, one Doctor *Don*', after which she quotes two verses (ll. 35–6) from *Storm* (Sullivan 1993: 35–6).

In their critiques of Donne's poetry Dryden and Pope typically find fault with the erudite language, irregular prosody, and muscular expression: what Carew called the 'tough-thick-rib'd hoopes' (Donne 1633*b*: 387, l. 51) that struggle to encompass the range of Donne's inventive wit. The same traits of Donne's poetry, in other words, are viewed positively by Carew and negatively by Dryden and Pope. Demonstrating how Donne's verses might be regularized, thereby conforming to the eighteenth-century preference for heroic couplets (or rhymed iambic pentameter verse), Pope rewrote the second and fourth Satires. Though regular versification was achieved by such redaction, what was lost? Donne's Satires and love poems generally manifest emotions beyond what regular verse can project. By his accentual, not metrical, stresses, the speaker in Donne's poems enacts dramatic intonations, whereas the impersonal voice of Pope's regular verse narrates. Pope reflects the literary sensibility of the Augustan era of Queen Anne, King George I, and King George II in the first half of the eighteenth century. Socially, politically, and aesthetically, the tone of that era included a calm dignity, regular rhythm, and orderliness in poetry beneath which conflicts were suppressed or subtly expressed.

In Donne's poems, moreover, the personalized speaker, often distinguished by dramatic flair, projects self-characterization. An attentive reader discerns that the speaker sometimes becomes the butt of the humour and satire of the poem. Additionally, Donne's unique conceits defy Pope's definition of wit in *An Essay on Criticism*: '[w]hat oft was *Thought*, but ne'er so well *Exprest*' (Pope 153, l. 297). Clearly, Donne and his admiring, even adulatory, contemporaries perceived 'wit' differently than Pope.

In the late eighteenth century Dr Samuel Johnson vigorously disapproved of Donne's poetry. In the *Life of Cowley* (1779) Johnson names 'a race of writers that may be termed the metaphysical poets', among whom are Donne, Cowley, and a few others. Citing imperfect 'modulation', Johnson highlighted the irregularity of the metaphysical poets' lines (2006: 1.199–200). In defining 'modulation' the *OED* (6) cites Johnson at least twice to illustrate the following meaning: '[h]armonious treatment of language'. Differing from Pope in the definition of wit, Johnson perceives it in the following light: that 'which is at once natural and new, that which though not obvious is, upon its first production, acknowledged to be just; if it be that, which he that never found it, wonders how he missed; to wit of this kind the metaphysical poets have seldom risen'. Instead, '[t]heir thoughts are often new, but seldom natural; they are not obvious, but neither are they just; and the reader, far from wondering that he missed them, wonders more frequently by what perverseness of industry they were ever found'. Johnson contends that 'abstracted from its effects on the hearer', wit is a 'kind of *discordia concors*; a combination of dissimilar images, or discovery of occult resemblances in things apparently unlike'. In addition, '[t]he most heterogeneous ideas are yoked by violence together'. Though the metaphysical poets were learned, the 'modulation' of their works was 'imperfect'. And 'they were not successful in representing or moving the affections' (1.200).

Citing poems and specific passages by Donne, Cowley, and Cleveland, Johnson highlights the extravagant and unnatural wit that does not, in his view, convey or engender emotion. He concludes his account by referring to the last four stanzas of *ValMourn*, which elaborate the witty conceit whereby the lover and his beloved are compared to 'a pair of compasses'. Johnson ponders whether 'absurdity or ingenuity' is the more appropriate judgement for such an analogy (1.213).

Dr Johnson's magisterial comments issue from a literary sensibility in many ways akin to Pope's. As an author and a critic, Johnson represented the eighteenth-century attitudes towards poetry that resulted in disapproval of Donne. Significantly, Johnson's critique was the medium through which many readers learned of Donne's poetry. Because the critique was largely unfavourable, there was little incentive to read Donne's poems beyond the excerpts that Johnson quoted.

4

Having fallen into disrepute because of his iconoclastic style in poetry, ingenious wit, and irregular prosody, Donne remained in the shadows for almost a century. Samuel Taylor Coleridge, however, brought Donne again to the forefront of admiration. His Notebooks (1795–1804) contain many entries on Donne. A measure of Donne's rehabilitation is Coleridge's commentary on the very poem that Dr Johnson debunked, *ValMourn*. For Coleridge, '[n]othing were ever more admirably made out than the figure of the Compass' (1984: 223). In addition to his Notebooks, Coleridge in 1811 made marginal notes in Charles Lamb's copy of Donne's poems, comments that were published in his *Notes Theological, Political, and Miscellaneous* (1853). In one note on prosody he compares Dryden and Pope, on the one hand, with Donne, on the other. To read the former, he says, one 'need only count syllables'; but 'to read Donne [one] must measure *Time*, & discover the *Time* of Each word by the Sense & Passion' (1984: 216, emphasis in the original). Here Coleridge diminishes the pre-eminence, for conventional criticism, of metrical stress in order to emphasize the accentual stress of heightened or unfolding passion in the speaker, which is conveyed, in turn, to the reader, a view that counteracts Johnson's belief that Donne's poetry manifests an excess of wit at the expense of emotion. Since the poems are neither metrically stressed nor pointed for accentual stress and intonation, a reader cannot know the emotions, emphasis, and tonal range of the speakers. But when engaging a poem, a reader has the latitude to interpret the work dramatically. Whereas Pope and Johnson faulted Donne's excess of wit, which to them resulted in ingenious but unnatural resemblances between disparate things, Coleridge contravened their eighteenth-century appraisal by redefining alleged vices as corresponding virtues. In 1829 he made notes on Donne's poems in a volume of Chalmers's *The Works of the English Poets*. The notes include the following accolades: 'Wonder-exciting vigour, intenseness and peculiarity of thought, using at will the almost boundless stores of a capacious memory, and exercised on subjects, where we have no right to expect it—this is the wit of Donne!' (1984: 17).

Because Coleridge read Donne's poems and much of the prose, notably the Sermons, over many years, his critical appraisal was independent of Johnson's. Coleridge, indeed, celebrated Donne's wit, rather than debunking it in the manner of Johnson. Unlike the latter, Coleridge praised Donne as a logician, whose unique power of reasoning was informed by vigorous energy, thereby generating witty conceits that elicited both admiration and awe (Haskin 2007: 52–8).

Even more than Coleridge, however, Thomas De Quincey anticipated the very features of Donne's poetry that elicited approval in the early twentieth century. Writing in *Blackwood's Magazine* in 1828, he affirmed that Donne 'combined—what no other man has ever done—the last sublimation of dialectical subtlety and address with the most impassioned majesty'. In Donne's poetry, the convergence of thought and passion appealed to literary audiences in later eras. De Quincey, moreover, contends that rhetoric, rather than regularity and rhyme, is the measure of Donne's successful style and wit: '[t]he artifice and machinery of rhetoric furnishes in its degree as legitimate a basis for intellectual pleasure as any other.' More to the point, he challenges Johnson's adverse criticism of Donne, arguing that '[e]very species of composition is to be tried by its own laws' and alleging that Johnson's model of poetry is unduly prescriptive largely because it underestimates the power of rhetoric and overestimates metrical regularity. De Quincey contends that '[m]etre is open to any form of composition', especially for a poet, like Donne, who is *sui generis* (A. J. Smith 1975: 346). By his rhetorical style, which is poetically unconventional, Donne achieves a level of poetic expression, dialectical subtlety, and passionate expression lacking in eighteenth-century poetry.

Like Coleridge and De Quincey, Robert Browning admired Donne's poetry, citing it often in his letters to Elizabeth Barrett, most notably the verses concerning the compasses from *ValMourn*. In a letter of 11 September 1845 Browning incorporates Donne's witty conceit to personal use, suggesting that when Barrett was in Italy, while he remained in England, they would 'lean and harken' towards each other (Browning: 1.189). For Browning, unlike Johnson, the most renowned conceit in metaphysical poetry must have been redolent with emotion, for he integrated it into a love letter that was the prelude to an explicit avowal of love after Barrett's return to England. So widely known was his admiration of his literary forebear that Alexander B. Grosart could dedicate his edition of Donne's poems (1872–3) to Browning, whom he calls 'the poet of the century for thinkers', implying intellectual kinship with Donne (A. J. Smith 1975: 349). Furthermore, as a poet who often focused on the interior life of characters, Browning may have been intrigued by Donne's speakers, whose emotional intensity or languor he emulated in the accentual stress and rhetoric of his dramatic monologues. For Browning, thought and feeling were fused in Donne's poetry and in his own. Like Donne's poems, Browning's were obscure, challenging to read, and harsh and rugged. Inevitably, readers drew comparisons between the two poets (Haskin 2007: 120–1).

5

Grosart's edition and Browning's admiration of Donne intensified interest in metaphysical poetry on both sides of the Atlantic (Haskin 2007: 151–2). This interest increased with the 1912 edition of Donne's poems by Herbert J. C. Grierson. In his Introduction, called 'The Poetry of Donne', Grierson provided influential critical commentary. Referring to Dryden, Johnson, and Coleridge, Grierson, who cites De Quincey approvingly, highlights 'Donne's peculiarity, the combination of dialectical subtlety with weight and force of passion' (Donne 1912: 2.xxxi). Grierson elaborates on this so-called combination: 'the strain of dialectic, subtle play of argument and wit, erudite and fantastic; and the strain of vivid realism, the record of a passion which is not ideal nor conventional, neither recollected in tranquillity nor a pure product of literary fashion, but love as an actual, immediate experience in all its moods, gay and angry, scornful and rapturous with joy, touched with tenderness and darkened with sorrow' (2.xxxiv). In the religious poetry, moreover, Grierson senses that 'passionate penitence' is the channel for the speaker's emotions (2.liii).

Elaborating on his previous views, Grierson in *Metaphysical Lyrics and Poems of the Seventeenth Century from Donne to Butler* (1921) situates Donne historically in a manner not unlike that of Johnson. But Grierson's critical judgements are very positive. Whereas Johnson decries 'a race of writers that may be termed the metaphysical poets', Grierson extols the same authors, whose 'greatest achievement' is 'the peculiar blend of passion and thought, feeling and ratiocination'. He adds that 'Donne is the great master of English poetry in the seventeenth century' (Grierson 1921: xvi), and among his triumphs is 'the expression in unconventional, witty language of all the moods of a lover that experience and imagination have taught him to understand—sensuality aerated by a brilliant wit' (xix). Accordingly, Donne in his Satires, Elegies, and love lyrics was 'bending and cracking the metrical pattern to the rhetoric of direct and vehement utterance' in order 'to find a rhythm that will express the passionate fullness of his mind, the fluxes and refluxes of his moods'. He cites Donne's use of stanzas or verse paragraphs in which the discordances of individual verses 'are resolved in the complex and *rhetorically effective* harmony of the whole group of lines' (emphasis mine), thereby echoing De Quincey's appraisal (xxiii). By methodically rebutting Johnson's assessment of Donne and the metaphysical poets, Grierson, in effect, provided a critical framework in which to admire the same features of Donne's poetry that displeased most eighteenth-century commentators.

The most influential twentieth-century critic of Donne's poetry was T. S. Eliot, whose review of Grierson's anthology of metaphysical poems appeared in the *Times Literary Supplement* (20 October 1921: 669–70). The review was reprinted among Eliot's essays as 'The Metaphysical Poets'. Challenging Johnson's negative critique, Eliot, who appropriates Grierson's comments, frames (what he calls) 'a theory': that '[t]he poets of the seventeenth century, the successors of the dramatists of the sixteenth, possessed a mechanism of sensibility which could devour any kind of experience' (Eliot 247). Crediting the Elizabethan dramatists and the metaphysical poets with a unified sensibility that fuses thought and feeling, Eliot perceives 'a direct line' or tradition across two centuries of dramatic verse in plays and quasi-dramatic verse in poems (248). By likening playwrights and poets, Eliot implies a style and prosody akin to the rhythms of speech with accentual stress. Eliot laments the dissociation of sensibility in the late seventeenth century, attributable in large measure to the powerful influence of Milton and Dryden, whereby thought was overemphasized at the expense of feeling, or vice versa.

In sum, Eliot's magisterial pronouncement claimed Donne as a poet whose so-called unified sensibility was attuned to the modern era. The Elizabethan dramatists and the metaphysical poets became atavistic forebears of Eliot's own works and of the writings of many others. Subject to a myriad of critical perspectives and poetic practices after Eliot, the style, wit, and prosody in Donne's poetry were adapted in the modern and postmodern eras. The hallmarks of Donne's vestigial presence in these eras include untraditional and irregular style, conversational rhythm, dramatic intonation, accentual stress, inflected emotion, tonal range, erudite or arcane images, and even *vers libre* that relegates metrical regularity, at one time the sine qua non of poetry, to insignificance.

Not to be overlooked, however, are the allusions to, and appropriations of, Donne in manifold ways in poetry, prose, painting, playwriting, and song lyrics. Among British and American poets of the twentieth century, such as Herbert Read, Hart Crane, and William Empson, allusions to Donne abound. Joseph Brodsky carried a copy of Donne's poems when he departed the Soviet Union for England in 1972, professing to have learned English in order to read the works. Novelists like Virginia Woolf read Donne carefully and assimilated references to him and his writing in the voices of her characters. In 1911 Stanley Spencer painted *John Donne Arriving in Heaven*, which hangs in the Fitzwilliam Museum at Cambridge (Herz 2001: 29–32). In 1996 the American dramatist Wallace Shawn wrote *The Designated Mourner*, a play that explores what may be called the 'phenomenon' of Donne—as biographical personage, poet, and sermonist—in the present era (Haskin 2000: 182–209). And in 1999 Margaret Edson composed a Pulitzer Prize-winning drama, *Wit*, on suffering, death, and dying, in which she integrates Donne's meditations on those very topics in his Holy Sonnets. Whether engaged profoundly or superficially, Donne is an abiding presence and influence not merely in literature but in the arts and culture of our era.

CHAPTER 41

DO DONNE'S WRITINGS EXPRESS HIS DESPERATE AMBITION?

HUGH ADLINGTON

For over four centuries the question of Donne's ambition has divided critics. Even when most narrowly conceived—as the zealous pursuit of employment and status at court and in the church—the extent and nature of Donne's social and professional aspirations hold a peculiar fascination for his readers. A brief survey of bibliographies of criticism, covering the period 1598–2008, turns up over a hundred essays, articles, and books that touch on the disputed role played by desire for preferment in Donne's life and work (J. R. Roberts 1973, 1982a, 2004; A. J. Smith 1975, 1996). The majority of these commentaries understand ambition according to the *OED*'s primary definition of the word, that is: 'The ardent (in early usage, inordinate) desire to rise to high position, or to attain rank, influence, distinction or other preferment'. A handful of critics have also looked beyond Donne's efforts at social and professional advancement to consider his artistic and spiritual aspirations more generally (Carey 1981a; B. Nelson 2005). Why critical interest in Donne's ambition should be so acute, and what forms the arguments take, are the main questions this chapter aims to address. Most commentary in this area clusters around a relatively limited canon of texts: the *Anniversaries* (1612), the Verse Letters, the Somerset Epithalamion (1613), *Pseudo-Martyr* (1610), and the Sermons (1615–31). The relationship of life to work, therefore, and the material transmission of that work are central to this enquiry. To that end, this chapter takes seriously the recent assertion that any reception history must attempt to integrate 'textual, critical, and biographical perspectives' (Haskin 2007: xxi).

The chapter's first and longest section offers an analytic survey of the debate over Donne's motives, paying particular attention to influential interventions by Edmund Gosse (1899), R. C. Bald (1970), and John Carey (1981a). Analysis aims to bring to light the salient critical assumptions—epistemological, methodological, and political—underlying competing strands of thought, while locating such preoccupations within their historical and dialectical contexts. How have the social and cultural connotations of ambition shifted over time (in relation to social attitudes to place-seeking, social and literary patronage, and the emerging concept of 'profession')? Is there a difference between 'acceptable' and 'desperate' ambition? And why does it matter whether Donne is perceived as ambitious or not? What is at stake in drawing such psycho-biographical inferences from Donne's writings? The final section considers future directions in the study of this topic and includes a review of Donne's own references to ambition in his poetry and prose, a crucial source that has been almost wholly neglected in previous commentary. How far does Donne's attitude to aspiration—whether for erotic conquest, for secular or ecclesiastical preferment, or for Pauline union with God—tally with that of his peers? Merely to ask this question is to begin to recast the inadequately binary terms of the historical debate over Donne's 'desperate' ambition.

Donne's reception

'Donne's art (both his poems and his sermons) expresses [his] personality – self-advancing, anxious, unsatisfied' (Carey 1981a: 94). Carey's vivid portrayal of Donne as a brilliant, idiosyncratic, but recognizable type of the Renaissance overreacher has played a provocative and influential part in recent debates over the connection between Donne's life and work. But where does this widely held notion of Donne's restless ambition come from? In what sense is Carey merely reiterating, in the lexicon of late twentieth-century psychology, a long-standing critical axiom that runs through the history of Donne's reception?

A central strand of that history begins with Donne's friend and fellow aspirant, Ben Jonson (1572–1637), and his well-known response to Donne's *Anniversaries* (1611–12). In *FirAn* Donne had elevated 14-year-old Elizabeth Drury, a girl he had never even seen, to the status of a cosmic principle: 'she to whom this world must it selfe refer, / As Suburbs, or the Microcosme of her' (ll. 235–6). Visiting Drummond of Hawthornden in 1619, Jonson reportedly remarked 'that Dones Anniversarie was profane and full of Blasphemies', adding that 'if it had been written of ye Virgin Marie it had been something' (Jonson 1–2.133). Clearly Jonson's charge of profanity reflects his distaste at the religious and rhetorical extravagance of Donne's poetic conceit. Later commentators, however, objected less to Donne's use of Elizabeth Drury's death as an inspiration for political, social, and theological rumination, and more to Donne's motives in writing the *Anniversaries*, decrying what they perceived as the corrosive moral effects of writing to order. Nineteenth-century critics were particularly explicit in their indictments. In 1822 historian and memoirist Lucy Aikin deplored the 'abuses' of the patronage system and its effect in producing an art of flattery (Aikin 1.75–6). Augustus Jessopp observed of Donne's *Anniversaries* that: 'The compliment was too delicate, and the flattery too eloquent not to be appreciated very highly' (Donne 1855a: xxxviii); and, at century's end, a host of critics and opinion-formers in Great Britain and the United States, including Charles Eliot Norton, Leslie Stephen, and John White Chadwick, drew explicit attention to Donne's 'mercenary' aim in writing the *Anniversaries* (Donne 1895 2.262). Underpinning such remarks was a shared Victorian repugnance for Donne's apparent servility, toadying 'about the crowded ante-chambers of the rich, in the common but vain expectation of Court preferment' (Anon. 1861: 82). That nineteenth-century critics of Donne should prefer to see him in post-Revolutionary, post-Romantic colours should come as no surprise, nor is it remarkable that such a tendency should continue to manifest itself among later commentators (Sheavyn 22; E. N. S. Thompson 1924: 112); even historicist criticism is invariably shaped by the preoccupations of its own time. Less well recognized, however, is how nineteenth-century defenders of Donne also set the terms for later debate. In 1811 Samuel Taylor Coleridge debunked 'the fashionable outcry about Patronage', arguing that no one ever thought less of the work of Renaissance artists such as Michelangelo, Raphael, or Titian because it was produced for patrons (1984: 235). Later scholars echoed Coleridge's call for greater historical sensitivity and sought to judge Donne by the social mores of his day instead of by those of their own. Henry Alford observed that Donne's 'manners were the manners of the court and the society in which he lived' (Donne 1839: 1.xxiv); Herbert Grierson declared Donne's *Anniversaries* to be 'in the manner of the time' (Donne 1912: 2.xxix); and Donne's bibliographer, Geoffrey Keynes, asserted that Donne's encomia were acceptable in his age (1951: 2). Twentieth-century critics of the *Anniversaries* also questioned the monocular vision of some earlier commentary: after all, why shouldn't a poet's motives be diverse, that is, simultaneously worldly and ideal (Leishman 1962: 242–3; Carey 1981a)? And why couldn't poems be written to order, yet nonetheless be transformed in the writing (Donne 1963: 6)?

Other early sources for the debate over Donne's ambition also instigated lasting critical traditions. John Chudleigh's elegy for Donne, for example, asks: 'Did not his sacred flattery beguile / Man to amendment?' (Donne 1635: Cc7ᵛ), providing the model for Izaak Walton's later account of Donne pulpit oratory, 'enticing [his auditory] by a sacred art and courtship, to amend their lives' (1640: B2). The composite picture is of a preaching eloquence so honeyed, so courtierlike, as to bring its own sincerity of utterance into doubt. Almost four centuries on, the same doubts over sincerity continue to fuel wide-ranging arguments over Donne's rhetorical 'discretion' in his Sermons (Harland 2; Shami 2003a) and remain central to allied disputes over Donne's politics, religion, and innovations in literary art. With regard to the latter, Donne's novelties in poetic form, tone, and content, Samuel Johnson famously remarked of the poet and his followers that: 'Their wish was only to say what they hoped had been never said before' (2006: 1.201). This striving to be original, Johnson argued, was indissolubly linked to a want of proper feeling: 'Their courtship was void of fondness, and their lamentation of sorrow' (ibid.). Johnson's remarks echo those of Chudleigh in setting up powerful binary oppositions—authenticity versus insincerity, and genuine poetic feeling versus mere wit and learning—that came to form the conceptual poles of the subsequent debate over Donne's ambition. Early nineteenth-century critics, too, in their insistent emphasis on the opposition of nature and artifice, shaped the binary terms of later discussion. Commenting on a Verse Letter in which Donne transforms the Countess of Bedford into a goddess, 'M. M. D.' deplores Donne's 'perversion of moral sentiment', and complains that in such works Donne unites a 'prostrate servility of adulation to a total abandonment of nature, whose modesty [he] left at an immeasurable distance behind' (108–12). Literary criticism and biography shade into one another in such caustic remarks, but it wasn't until 1899, and the publication of Edmund Gosse's *The Life and Letters of John Donne*, that the disparate attitudes to Donne's literary and social ambitions recorded above were, for the first time, wrought into a unified and highly influential portrait.

The Life and Letters, Gosse declared, would be 'a biographical and critical monograph on Donne in his full complexity' (Gosse 1.xvi). In contrast to earlier partial accounts, Gosse aimed to compass 'the vast curves of [Donne's] extraordinary and contradictory features': 'He [Donne] was not the crystal-hearted saint that Walton adored and exalted. He was not the crafty and redoubtable courtier whom the recusants suspected' (2.290). Yet ultimately, Gosse confessed, Donne 'eludes us' (2.290). Despite this frank admission of the limitations of the biographer's art and the implied provisionality of his findings, Gosse's factual errors and the vicissitudes of reception history would combine to reinforce and sharpen the existing division between the two sides of the ambition debate, rather than challenging the framework of the debate itself. On most of the familiar areas of controversy Gosse is relatively muted, even permissive, in his judgements. The *Anniversaries* are 'somewhat venal' (1.317), a missive to the Countess of Huntingdon is a 'begging letter' (2.77), the Funeral Elegy for Prince Henry is described as unanimated by 'by one touch of sincere emotion' (2.6), and Donne's petition to become the ambassador to Venice is dismissed by Gosse as an 'uncouth application' (2.39). Taken alone, or even in sum, these are hardly damning revelations—neither particularly provoking nor emollient. In fact, the most telling of Gosse's contributions to the ambition debate was in another area altogether: namely, in his treatment of Donne's relations with the King's favourite, Robert Carr, made Viscount Rochester in 1611 and Earl of Somerset in 1613.

Sometime in 1613 Donne used his prior connection to James Hay (then Baron Hay of Sawley, later to become Viscount Doncaster, and Earl of Carlisle) to present himself in a Letter to the powerful royal favourite, Rochester. In the Letter Donne declared his resolution to 'make my Profession Divinitie' and sought Rochester's 'favourable assistance' in this new course of life (*TMC* 320). Gosse suggests that Donne's resolution probably met with discouragement from Rochester, and for that reason, 'Donne seems to have dropped it as abruptly as he adopted it, for we meet with no further suggestion that he should enter the Church until three years later' (Gosse 2.22). The implication is stark, that pragmatic self-interest lay at the root of Donne's desire to seek ordination. Our sensitivity to such an interpretation of events is only heightened by Gosse's histrionic disclaimer, at the end of his account: 'Are we, then, to say that when Donne accepted the profession of the Church he was an insincere and ungodly man? A thousand times, no!' (2.99). Leslie Stephen (1898–1902: 66–7), Sidney Dark (57), and others followed Gosse in questioning the extent to which Donne's resolution to enter the ministry was driven by godly motives. Gosse's most damaging allegation, that Donne devilled for Somerset (acted as junior legal counsel) in the notorious scandal of his marriage to Lady Frances Howard, Countess of Essex, was shown soon thereafter to be groundless, based largely on Gosse's confusion (and Jessopp's before him) of John with the jurist Sir Daniel Donne (Dun) (Bald 1970: 273–4; Haskin 2007: 173). Gosse, nevertheless, characterized Donne's relations with Somerset as 'ignominious' and 'degrading to his judgment and conscience' (2.54), and contemporary critics were swift to pass judgement. 'The Victorian is not the Jacobean conception of the social hierarchy', observed an anonymous reviewer in 1899, 'yet it goes against the grain to find Donne...doing dirty work for so poor a wretch as the Earl of Somerset' (Anon. 1899a: 646). The further ignominy of Donne's Epithalamion for Somerset and his bride, who would later be indicted and imprisoned for the murder of Sir Thomas Overbury, was met by Gosse with 'repulsion' (2.31), a response shared by many of his Victorian readers. J. W. Chadwick, in his review of Gosse, remarked acidly: 'He [Donne] set out to write an Epithalamion for the "blest pair of swans" while the woman's divorce had not yet been decreed. And still his condition was that of the countryman who mistook some lesser light for Whitefield, and "rolled himself in the dirt for nothing"' (Chadwick 31–48).

Echoing Gosse, early twentieth-century defenders of Donne's character and moral integrity also chose to foreground the 'full complexity' of his personality, though with mixed results. Richard Garnett, for instance, concurred with Gosse that such a character as Donne's could not be comprehended in a formula. Garnett proposed instead that Donne be regarded as 'not merely a problematic but a daemonic man', a figure who 'lived entirely in the circumstance of the hour'. Thus: 'When engaged in Somerset's service, he [Donne] could think of nothing but the obligations which he owed him' (Garnett 583). Later developments in Donne studies take their cue from this depiction of Donne as consummate role-player, not least the resourceful self-fashioning of the new historicist's Renaissance gentleman, and the picture of 'professional Donne', a figure simultaneously active in, and shaped by, overlapping social and institutional codes and practices (Colclough 2003). The 'daemonic Donne' theory certainly proved popular in the years immediately following its introduction. W. M. Sinclair's 1909 evaluation typifies a strand of pre-First World War thinking when he asserts: 'To whatever influence he [Donne] surrendered himself it absorbed him for the time' (Sinclair 202). As a defence against the charge of time-serving, however, it was hardly adequate. The portrait of Donne as a man of intense, but temporary, preoccupations shaded all too easily into that of a man of facile conscience, the trimmer, 'whose subtlety, one knows, will make any cause that he takes up seem for the moment unimpeachable, but of whose moral genuineness in the different phases he assumes...one has incurable doubts' (Arnold 203). To forestall such pejorative judgements, defenders of Donne were all too often driven to ingenuity or special pleading: 'so speculative a brain...could allow itself to be guided by no fixed rules; and to a brain so abstract, conduct must always have seemed of less importance than it does to most other people' (Symons 738). The resulting portrait of Donne, as 'always the casuist, always mentally impartial in the face of a moral problem' (738–9), only served to excite further distrust and suspicion; it treated Donne too reverently, cutting off his life and work from the irregular pulse and imperfect reality of everyday life at precisely the moment when the mainstream of literary criticism, following Gosse's lead, sought to place 'the frailties, the worldliness, the morbidities' of Donne's character (Anon. 1899b: 723) in direct relation to his 'frustrated circumstance' and 'bread-and-butter needs' (Danby 522).

The willingness to find explanations for Donne's conduct in his frustrated circumstances, rather than in his character per se, lies at the heart of the next landmark publication in the debate over Donne's ambition, that is, R. C. Bald's *John Donne: A Life* (1970), completed and edited by Wesley Milgate. Like Gosse, Bald examines the basis of Donne's decision to enter the ministry, and his efforts to win patronage to further that end, and clearly dislikes what he finds: 'In spite of his [Donne's] disclaimers, he appears as one who had mastered at last the arts of the courtier, and it is clear, even when he finally turned to the Church, that he did not intend to abandon those arts, but to rise by them. At no period in his life does he appear less unselfish, more self-seeking' (1970: 301). Crucially, though, Bald chooses not to see Donne's self-interest at this juncture as 'essential and permanent traits of his character; rather, they were symptoms of his despair—not the despair of one who feels that he has been denied salvation, but that of one whom success eludes in spite of all his efforts' (ibid.). The distinction is an important one, reflecting Bald's biographical method of construing Donne's psychology through the prism of documented events. The appeal of such a method to subsequent scholarship was far-reaching. Echoing Bald, Arthur Marotti sought to relate the *Anniversaries* to Donne's 'social, economic, and political failures' (1981: 228), while Annabel Patterson gave fuller expression to the rationale of such an approach: 'more than any other Renaissance poet, Donne challenges us to conceive of subjectivity in environmental terms, to see how socioeconomic and political circumstances interact with a particular temperament to produce the historical person, who is both partly conscious of the rules by which he must play and partly director of all his roles' (1991: 251). Recent accounts of Donne's life also continue to reflect Bald's reading of Donne's psychology in socio-political terms (Colclough 2004).

In the decade between the appearance of Bald's biography and that of John Carey's *John Donne: Life, Mind and Art* (1981a) two further developments were particularly significant for the debate over Donne's ambition. The first was the challenge posed to the accuracy of Bald's scholarship, and to Bald's consequent emphasis on Donne as an ambitious place-seeker (Flynn 1975). Calls for interpretation to be more securely tethered to matters of documentary record were not, of course, new in Donne studies: Gosse's many errors of fact, and consequently of evaluation, were justifiably reprehended by contemporary reviewers; and Henry Beeching had inveighed against Leslie Stephen's interpretive prurience, arising from his cavalier handling of the material evidence (Beeching 89–123). Nevertheless, Dennis Flynn's call, post-Bald, to return *ad fontes* marked the beginning of a sustained re-evaluation of the documentary sources for all previous commentary on Donne's ambition. The second notable development in the 1970s was a renewed focus on the place of rhetorical convention in Donne's poetry and prose. John Shawcross, for example, sought to demonstrate Donne's use in his lyrics of different modes of oratory suitable to each poem. Adopting the forensic mode in *Mess*, Donne thus becomes 'prosecuting attorney in iambic'. Arguments about Donne's sincerity in such poems were therefore 'meaningless and beside the point' when his works were viewed in this way, as primarily rhetorical rather than autobiographical artefacts (1974: 24, 35). Other commentators in the period also presented Donne as the master rhetorician, skilfully generating ambiguities in poems such as the 1613 *Eclog* for the marriage of the Earl of Somerset. Such ambiguities enabled Donne to reconcile private scruples with a pursuit of patronage, allowing him to make both a 'bid for royal largesse and yet to register his knowledge of courtly corruption' (Goldberg 1979: 391). As with the 'argument from the sources', the 'argument from rhetoric' would become a recurring feature of subsequent debate over the nature of Donne's character and moral identity.

Unquestionably, John Carey's 1981 depiction of Donne as the self-advancing apostate raised the temperature of exchanges in the debate over ambition, but did it add anything new? Perhaps Carey's most distinct contribution was to find the explanation for Donne's ambition in his desire to overcome his outsider status, first as a Roman Catholic adrift from the currents of power in English society, and latterly as an exile even from the religion of his birth. Closely linked to this external form of separation, in Carey's account, is the powerful internal tension between Donne's egotism and self-absorption on the one hand, and his sense of his own incompleteness on the other. According to Carey, this tension gave rise to an 'insatiability of the soul', and to a lasting sense of isolation from some greater earthly or transcendent whole (1981a: 60–130). Carey's theme of intellectual alienation and internal turmoil, published at a moment of fierce ideological struggle within literary studies, and amid a climate of severe pressure on institutional funding for university research in the humanities in both the United States and the United Kingdom, immediately found its full complement of supporters and detractors. Those who shared Carey's vision saw Donne's internal contradictions and dissatisfaction as both cause and consequence of his thirst for worldly success. David Aers and Gunther Kress, for example, echoed Carey in claiming that, '[t]he life of an alienated intellectual was not one Donne could embrace' (1981: 74); they argued that by entering the church Donne found that 'the way to establish his self identity was exactly the one he had always wanted—incorporation in the establishment' (ibid.). Pushed to its most extreme and abstract realization, in Jonathan Goldberg's depiction of Donne's 'absolutist' self-constitution, almost all internal agency was lost: 'He [Donne] is fully made—or unmade—in relation to the powers of society' (1983: 219). Arthur Marotti, too, echoed Carey by finding in Donne's poems the constant expression of his social and political ambitions: '[his] metaphorics of love reflect the dynamics of suit, service, and recompense characteristic of a society that tied advancement to patronage' (1981: 212). Marotti's depiction of Donne as a coterie poet (1986)—the key to whose work was the codes of paradox and irony shared by the social circles that he inhabited—further enhanced the image of Donne as manipulator of powerful social connections for the purposes of self-advancement. Other critics too, in different ways, lent further weight to Carey's thesis. Focusing on the way in which Donne used the scribal medium to control the distribution of his works, Harold Love conferred upon Donne the title of '[t]he best and most ambitious example of author-publication' in the period (1987: 138). Even the Satires, which seemed ostensibly to attack the affectations and corruptions of court life, were construed by critics of Donne's alleged careerism as simply gambits, or calling-cards, used by Donne in 'an attempt to transcend his social estrangement' (Corthell 1982: 156). Donne's Sermons, too, came to be regarded by some critics as extended exercises in justifying his own social ascent via the patronage system (Donnelly; Oliver).

Carey's detractors, on the other hand, typically charged his account with three besetting sins: psychological oversimplification, historical myopia, and selective and prejudicial use of evidence (Gardner 1981; Shami 1987; A. Patterson 1991; Flynn 2000b; Edwards). In Donne's defence, scholars held up his injudicious marriage as proof of his impulsive, passionate nature (I. Bell 1986; Stubbs), and urged a more precise historicism in engaging with the social and rhetorical conventions that shaped the writing of the past (DeStefano; Cain 2006). Helen Gardner's critique of Carey's decontextualizing method is typical of the larger wave of opposition. For Gardner, Carey's book lacks 'historical imagination and imaginative sympathy with its subject', and its tone is 'too confident in the reduction of the complexity of the poet who wrote "doubt wisely"' (1981: 53). Annabel Patterson and others argued that Donne's personal Letters, treated by Carey merely as contextual documents rather than texts in themselves, showed that Donne did not 'sell out in the crudely ambitious way suggested by Carey' (1982: 51). Above all, Carey's critics echoed Coleridge's plea that Donne's life and work should be understood according to the standards of his time. Thus J. W. Saunders claimed, *pace* Carey, that Donne's career was 'that of a normally ambitious wit' (1983: 39), and Graham Parry sought to show how Donne's ministry was not simply the vehicle for his social and political elevation: 'When Donne preached, the priorities of the spirit were upheld in the Chapel Royal' (Parry 240).

This first wave of responses to Carey, pro and contra, was followed, perhaps inevitably, by a second wave more notable for its focus on mediation between competing views. Such deliberative efforts detected, in poems such as the Somerset Epithalamion, '[n]either the humiliating sycophancy that most readers have found in this lyric nor the tact and integrity that others claim for it' (Dubrow 1988: 201). Instead, critics sought to show how Donne's responses to the problems of patronage variously ranged along an entire spectrum, from uncritical adulation to uncompromising criticism (Shami 1987; Norbrook 1990; A. Patterson 1990). Such approaches thus complemented the work of revisionist Reformation historians in the period, which emphasized the fluctuation and instability inherent in early modern politico-religious identity and allegiance (Lake 1988; Tyacke 1987*b*). The new-historicist assumption, that the only alternative to careerism and sycophancy was criticism and opposition, was dismissed as a false dichotomy (Felperin 249). Instead, the possibility of Donne's *principled* loyalty to the established church and state was mooted (Strier 109), and a host of similar formulations was generated by the marked turn to religion in Donne studies in this period, and in literary studies more broadly. Thus, in his Holy Sonnets, Donne 'developed a rhetoric of supplication that could record at once the sincere desire for submission and the lingering ambitions of the self' (Schoenfeldt 86); in churchmanship, Donne's independent vision of a proper religious mean allowed him 'to embrace the English church without wholly relinquishing his commitment to the individual's quest for religious truth' (Scodel 1995: 45); and in his Sermons, Donne's principled adjustment of 'the law of conscience to the laws of political authority' marked the limits rather than the 'beginnings of [his] ambitions' (Shami 1995*a*: 404, 390). In methodological terms at least, each of these disparate commentaries on the topic of Donne's public and private motives was distinguished by its precise historical contextualization of Donne's writing. Each sought to be sensitive to the finely graduated rhetoric of Donne's moral reason, while remaining wary of taking the controversial vocabulary of seventeenth-century religious and political polemic at face value; each aimed to be alive to Donne's habit of engaging deliberately not only with the resonances of his sources, sacred and profane, but also with the prevailing expectations of his readers and auditors. Arguments from history and rhetoric were thus united.

Three quite different recent approaches to the question of Donne's ambition complete this brief reception history. The first concerns the ambitious biographical project of Dennis Flynn, which aims 'to present new facts...that...imply the need for reconsideration of a whole range of assumptions underlying the work of critics' (1995c: 16). In a series of publications based on archival evidence, Flynn has sought to show the crucial role played by the concept of honour in Donne's life and work and thus to propose an alternative thesis to that of Bald and Carey; that 'Donne's contemporaries apparently regarded him not as a desperately ambitious, place-seeking, social-climbing son of a hardware salesman, but as a person of remarkable honor' (1995a: 35). In an important article on Donne's prose writing of 1601–15, Flynn also argued against the 'myth', propagated by Bald, Carey, and Marotti, that works such as *Pseudo-Martyr* (1610) were motivated chiefly by Donne's 'desperate ambition' for worldly success (Flynn 2000b). In fact, the evidence shows that Donne was involved in relatively few attempts, between 1602 and 1610, to secure a government appointment: these included half-hearted dealings in 1607, through the mediation of Henry Goodere, with William Fowler, Queen Anne's secretary; and 'some offer for the place' in 1608 of the deceased Geoffrey Fenton, Secretary in Ireland (347–9). In accord with Annabel Patterson and David Norbrook, therefore, Flynn suggests that the motives for Donne's engagement with public life in this period, or the lack of it, derive more from his relation to political developments (in particular the 'loosening of Salisbury's [Robert Cecil's] grip on English politics') than from his personal ambition (335–7).

In sharp contrast to Flynn's biographical approach, both Peter DeSa Wiggins and Brent Nelson focus their recent studies of Donne's writing on his adoption of rhetorical modes of courtship. In Wiggins's account, Donne wrote 'a poetry of ambition designed to advance his political interests' (2), and in so doing used Thomas Hoby's 1561 translation of Baldassare Castiglione's *Libro del Cortegiano* as his principle guide to mastery of the skills valued at court. Wiggins's account disregards 'biographical particularization', advocating in its place a 'more discourse-oriented approach to his [Donne's] life, mind, and art' (3). In censuring the 'positivism' of writers who attempt to explain Donne's writing by contextualizing it, Wiggins echoes earlier post-structuralist admonitions in a similar vein (Docherty 1–11). Contrary to its expressed 'discourse-oriented' approach, however, Wiggins's study offers, in conclusion, a psychological portrait of Donne's life and work almost indistinguishable from the picture painted by John Carey: 'Donne's poems and sermons are still alive for us, possibly because they are so frankly compromised by his ingenious opportunism, are so much the product of it, and exhibit so much tormented consciousness of the fact' (20). Brent Nelson's study, although confining itself to the Sermons, represents a potentially more fruitful mode of enquiry. Unlike virtually all other commentators on the nature of Donne's moral identity, Nelson pays attention to the remarks of Donne himself on earthly and spiritual forms of courtship and ambition. For Donne: 'Worldly ambition and holy ambition are substantially the same: the former is lower in the scale of perfection, but a starting point on that scale nonetheless' (2005: 135). Thus, even worldly ambition may contain an 'inchoation of virtue', in that it 'sets men in the right direction of desiring something better' (ibid.). Despite confining historical contextualization of Donne's attitudes to ambition to a footnote (124 n. 335), the significance of Nelson's study lies in his focus on Donne's own words and in the richly variegated and flexible idea of ambition that emerges from them. Such an approach suggests a way out of a perceived critical impasse—that arguments over motive are doomed to a perpetual binarism, between those who 'admire Donnean desire' and those who 'repudiate it' (B. Saunders 2006: 21)—and prompts further (if brief) exploration in this chapter's concluding section.

In Donne's words

More than forty direct references to social, political, and religious ambition and its cognates in Donne's writing reveal a varied yet coherent pattern of attitudes to the concept. Thus far, however, little or no attention has been paid to this valuable source of evidence; nor to where and how Donne's views might be located in the history of ambition as a social idea. To that end, Anthony Esler's *The Aspiring Mind of the Elizabethan Younger Generation* (1966) still provides a useful set of categories by which social attitudes to the concept of ambition might be understood. Esler argues that 'a Marlovian mood of high aspiration' grew up among Elizabethan courtiers of Donne's generation, rooted in the social mobility of Tudor society (Esler xxiv). Wary of the perils of unrestrained ambition, the period's literature of moral instruction laid 'particular insistence' on overweening ambition as a social, religious, and political sin (24–50; R. N. Watson 1984: 1–10). Each of these admonitory senses can be found in Donne's writing. Thus Donne warns Sir Henry Wotton of the social and political unwholesomeness of 'Courts hot ambitions' (*HWKiss* l. 60), and castigates the religious transgression of those with 'a wretched ambition, to be usurpers upon damnation' (*Sermons* 2.240). Donne's censure of ambition in its various forms thus appears to be of a piece with similar attitudes expressed in the writing of his contemporaries. Thomas Nashe, in *Christs Teares ouer Ierusalem*

(1593), decries careerism, asserting that 'Ambition is any puft vp greedy humour of honor or preferment' (fo. 40ᵛ); Mark Anthony's eulogy, in Shakespeare's *Julius Caesar* (1601), famously plays upon popular disapprobation of lust for power: 'If it were so, it was a grievous fault' (III. iii. 2); and John Fletcher in *The Island Princess* (1621) depicts desire for worldly success as a principal source of man's moral undoing: 'Love and Ambition draw the devils coach' (III. i). Each of these writers, in his different way, acknowledges the immoral and subversive nature of ambition; a view encapsulated in the Elizabethan 'Homily Against Disobedience and Wilful Rebellion' (1570), in which ambition is defined as 'the unlawful & restles desire in men to be of hygher estate then God hath geuen or appointed vnto them' (Anon. 1570: Giiiiiᵛ).

Yet merely to say that Donne echoes contemporary attitudes to ambition is grossly to underplay the scope and specificity of his references to the concept, in varying literary genres and on diverse occasions. In at least two of his Sermons, for example, Donne places ambition in a favourable light, employing the term to illustrate the limitless love of God for mankind. In a Whitsunday address Donne describes the Holy Ghost as having 'an extraordinary, a perverse ambition, to goe downewards, to inlarge himselfe, in his working, by falling' (*Sermons* 5.36); and this same divine impulse, to effect salvation through communion with men, is identified elsewhere by Donne as the basis for a liberal soteriology (hypothetical universalism): 'the *Ambition*, that God hath, to have us all' (6.161). Human aspiration to artistic achievement is also regarded favourably in Donne's work: in *SecAn* and in the Verse Letter *MHPaper* a poet's desire for literary inspiration is depicted, respectively, as 'chast' and 'noble' (*Variorum* 6, *SecAn* l. 35; *MHPaper* l. 35). And in a characteristically paradoxical formulation in a Whitehall Sermon, Donne declares the spiritual virtue of humility, or lowliness, to be the 'highest ambition' (*Sermons* 8.185).

That Donne's writings should both praise and disparage ambition, finding it worthy or insidious according to circumstance, accords not only with wider literary usage of the concept in Donne's lifetime but also with the broad traditions of classical and Christian attitudes informing that usage. Francesco Guicciardini's *Ricordi* (1512–30), for instance, makes explicit the distinction between the different kinds of ambition that Donne implies: 'Ambition is not to be condemned, nor should one revile the ambitious man's desires to attain glory by honourable and worthy means. [Yet] ... Ambition is pernicious and detestable when its sole end is power' (1965: 13). Thomas Hoby's translation of Castiglione also endorses the notion of a just or worthy fame: 'And I beleaue euen as it is an yll matter to seke a false renoume ... so is it also an yll matter to defraude a mans self of his due estimation' (Castiglione Miᵛ). This dual focus of Renaissance writers on the instrumentality and extent of ambition—the end to which it is put and the manner in which it is exercised—finds a classical root in Aristotle's *Nicomachean Ethics*: 'We blame ... the ambitious man [*philotimos*] as aiming at honour more than is right and from wrong sources' (Aristotle 2.1776); and Donne himself, in a Whitehall Sermon of 1628, renders a Christianized version of the Aristotelian notion of an acceptable or median level of ambition. In this Caroline court address, Donne makes the crucial distinction between moderate and excessive desire for high office, exhorting his auditory to follow St Stephen's example and strive to be 'humble servants of his [Christ] without inordinate ambition of high places' (*Sermons* 8.187).

In common with many other writers in the period, Donne's poems and prose also place immoderate ambition within the sphere of Renaissance concepts of virtue and vice. In at least six different Sermons, and twice in *Devotions Upon Emergent Occasions* (1624), inordinate desire for honour keeps close company with lust, envy, anger, and covetousness or greed in lists (*systrophe*) of cardinal sins: 'fire in your Chymney grows pale, and faints, and out of countenance when the Sun shines upon it; so whatsoever fires of lust, of anger, of ambition, possessed that heart before, it will yeild [*sic*] to this, and evaporate' (*Sermons* 4.109). Out of this catalogue of vice, ambition is identified by Donne as particularly a sin of maturity: 'when thy heats of youth are not overcome, but burnt out, then thy middle age chooses ambition, and thy old age chooses covetousness' (2.245). Francis Bacon, in his essay 'On Ambition', echoes Donne's association of ambition with the classical Greek element of fire and with the dry heat of middle age (connected in humoural theory with yellow bile), remarking that, '*Ambition* is like *Choler*; Which is an Humour, that maketh Men Actiue, Earnest, Full of Alacritie, and Stirring, if it be not stopped' (1625: 218). Marlowe's Tamburlaine, too, explains the motivation for his own ambition in terms of the humours: 'Nature, that fram'd us of four elements / Warring within our breasts for regiment, / Doth teach us all to have aspiring minds' (Part 1, II. vii. 18–20). Two issues—those of degree and consequence—recur throughout the corpus of Donne's references to aspiration. Where ambition itself is neutral, inordinate ambition is not. What flows from excessive desire is disorder: 'My *God*, my *God*, the *God of Order*, but yet not of *Ambition*' (*Devotions* 106). Whether alluding to Jesuit 'ambition of Martyrdome' (*Biathanatos* 148), or to venal pursuit of ecclesiastical preferment, 'some Preachers, vile ambitious bauds' (*Sat3* l. 56), Donne's pattern of references reflects both the sociological and psychological charge carried by the concept of aspiration in the period and the abundance of disparate attitudes to it.

This brief survey may, therefore, suggest one possible response to the oft-made but rarely answered call for increased historical contextualization of Donne's life and writing. Gleaning more documentary evidence from the archives remains a primary goal, but further consideration might also be given to Donne's attitudes to ambition in relation to a web of associated early modern terms and discourses. Relevant terms include social and ethical precepts such as honour, courtesy, and civility; the interrelated Platonic and Ciceronian concepts of *honestas* (moral goodness) and *utilitas* (profit); sixteenth-century Italian ideals of courtiership, such as *sprezzatura* and *grazia*; moral-philosophical categories of virtue and vice; and the much-debated extent to which an ethos of individualism emerged in England in the period in conflict with, or as a complement to, existing notions of commonwealth and service (Richards; Whigham). Moreover, this combined approach, an integration of both social and intellectual history, might usefully be extended to consideration of attitudes to ambition in the eighteenth, nineteenth, and twentieth centuries, and thereby build on, and contribute to, the growing body of scholarship on Donne's reception.

CHAPTER 42

'BY PARTING HAVE JOYN'D HERE': THE STORY OF THE TWO (OR MORE) DONNES

JUDITH SCHERER HERZ

JACK and the Doctor...that phrase has reverberated through literary history, although at the very least there should probably be three terms, since it was a third Donne, that is John, keeping a bit of distance from his character, who set the formulation in motion. He did it in 1619, just before setting out for Germany on the Doncaster mission. In entrusting the manuscript of *Biathanatos* to his friend Sir Robert Ker (he also gave him copies of his poems at that time), he described it as 'written by me many years since; and because it is upon a misinterpretable subject, I have always gone so near suppressing it, as that it is onely not burnt.... Keep it, I pray, with the same jealousie; let any that your discretion admits to the sight of it, know the date of it; and that it is a Book written by *Jack Donne*, and not by D. *Donne*' (*Letters* 22). Yet he tells Ker to 'Keep it', indeed let others see it, so long as those two separate, although not necessarily separable, identities are maintained.

That 1619 Letter, however, was not the first occasion of his writing to a friend with the aim of representing a particular version of the self or selves to his correspondent and, possibly, to himself. As early as 1605, before any work of his had been published, he had written to Sir Henry Goodere requesting the return both of his Latin Epigrams and *The Courtier's Library* for either subsequent revision or destruction (see Ch. 31.II for an argument dating the Letter). Dr Donne was then not yet on the horizon (or at least not in view), but in 1614, just before taking orders, he explained in another Letter to Goodere (perhaps with a more ambivalent sense of self-representation) how he was 'brought to a necessity of printing my Poems... By this occasion I am made a Rhapsoder of mine own rags... for I must do this, as a valediction to the world, before I take Orders' (*Letters* 196–7). In the event, he did not publish the poems, although the project is interestingly paradoxical: the potential public calling up of Jack (even if 'not for much publique view, but at mine own cost, a few Copies') at the moment of his extinction. Indeed it was only months earlier, in the concluding lines of *Har*, that he had anticipated that valedictory gesture:

> Doe not, fayre Soule, this sacrifice refuse
> That in thy Graue I do interre my Muse
>   Which by my greefe, greate as thy worth, beeing cast
>   Behind hand; yet hath spoke, and spoke her last.
>   (*Variorum* 6, ll. 255–8)

It is not clear how seriously he intended these last words, other than possibly implying the end to the poetry of patronage-seeking (a much-debated phrase, as Chs. 41 and 32.I suggest), which is so complexly enacted in the Epicedes and Obsequies. But they do provide one further mark of that dividing of the self that a few years later he was to name as Jack and the Doctor.

For Donne, the impulse to dismiss the past, to repudiate it, was strong. In *Christ*, written close to the time of the 1619 Letter to Ker, and possibly, as David Novarr has suggested (1980: 127), included among the poems Donne sent to Ker along with *Biathanatos*, Donne asks Christ in the concluding stanza to

> Seale then this bill of my Divorce to All,
> On whom those fainter beames of love did fall;
> Marry those loves, which in youth scattered bee
> On Fame, Wit, Hope (false mistresses) to thee.
>   (ll. 25–8)

Thus did the Doctor divorce Jack, indeed all worldly preoccupations: 'To see God only, I goe out of sight: / And to scape stormy dayes, I chuse / An Everlasting night' (ll. 30–2). And yet, it is worth emphasizing that he did not ask Ker to destroy Jack's work: 'Reserve it for me, if I live, and if I die, I only forbid it the Presse and the Fire' (*Letters* 22). Some of the tensions in both the Letter and the Hymn are also audible in another poem written at about the same time, *Tilman*, but resolved in that poem in an embracing of 'that profession, / Whose joyes passe speech' (ll.26–7). Replaying the language he had used in much of his poetry (lodestone, Indian ware, kings' faces on coins, astronomers, and new-found stars), he applauds Tilman's choice in ways that reflect his own sense of vocation as an angel/preacher speaking out of pulpits/

clouds, bringing 'man to heaven and heaven againe to man' (l. 48), the preacher as 'a blest Hermaphrodite' (l. 54), uniting these separate realms. Indeed, that last phrase offers a provocative figure for the relationship between Jack and the Doctor, both as Donne imagined it and as literary history has fashioned and refashioned it.

Nonetheless, it is not a figure that Izaak Walton, the first of the Donne historian/biographers, would have used, since his Donne did not combine opposites so as to create a new unity. If Donne's letter to Ker proposed a divided self, it also kept both terms in play. However, Walton's Donne absolutely repudiates that earlier self with all its 'infirmities'. Walton uses the models of saints Augustine and Ambrose, the angel wrestling with Jacob, and the transformation of Saul to Paul to structure the conversion story that his *Life of Donne*, first written to accompany the 1640 publication of a selection of Donne's Sermons (*LXXX Sermons*), tells. There the earlier self is disavowed. The poems of his youth were 'facetiously Composed and carelessly scattered [although Walton does recognize their skill, but]...in his penitential years...he was no friend to them' (1675: 52–3). Walton did contribute to the 1635 edition of the *Poems* in the form of an epigram beneath Donne's portrait, but there, too, he emphasizes the transformation, for that book contained the Divine Poems as well as those 'facetiously composed': 'Witness this Booke, (thy Embleme) which begins / With Love: but ends, with Sighes, and Teares for sins'. Indeed, mistranslating Donne's early motto, 'Antes muerto que mudado' (sooner dead than changed), as '*How much shall I be changed / Before I am chang'd*' (1675: 74), Walton makes change, the transformation of Jack to the Doctor, the point: '*His great and most blessed change was from a temporal to a spiritual imployment*: in which he was so happy, that he accounted the former part of his life to be lost' (ibid.).

Of course, a double Donne would have existed without that anxious remark in the Ker Letter (his family history, his move from Catholic to Protestant, would have assured that). And it would also have existed without Walton's story, for Donne *was* double, even if not either divided or divisible, and even if *multiple* is possibly the more accurate designation. Many of the funeral elegies accompanying the 1633 edition of the poems speak to both aspects, Thomas Carew's most memorably: '*Here lie two Flamens, and both those, the best, / Apollo's first, at last, the true Gods Priest*' (Donne 1633*b*: 388, ll. 97–8). And Sir Lucius Cary used nearly the same language in his: 'And as he was a two-fold Priest; in youth, / Apollo's; afterwards, the voice of Truth, / Gods Conduit-pipe for grace' (389, ll. 7–8). Indeed, what seems like a random arrangement of the poems in this edition might be construed rather as almost intended to blur that divide, to present a more unified textual representation of Donne in so far as it avoids any chronology, Jack and the Doctor changing places throughout with possibly a framing function given to the Doctor since the religious poetry is placed near the start, at the centre, and at the end. The volume begins with *Metem*, followed by *Corona* and the Holy Sonnets; at the centre *Goodf* and *Lit* are placed before many of the Songs and Sonets; and it ends with *Father*, itself immediately preceded by *Sats 1–5*. The Letter section begins on the page facing the

Hymn with the 1605 Latin Letter to Goodere that asks for the return of both the Latin Epigrams and *The Courtier's Library* ('*Catalogus librorum satyricus*'). Thus placed, the Letter almost serves as an editorial comment for the undertaking, as it points to the relative accomplishment of the poems included. The John Donne presented in *Poems 1633* is at the same time both Jack and the Doctor, with the Doctor possibly keeping a vigilant eye on Jack; in 1635, however, the Walton trajectory is the one followed, as the 'facetious' scatterer of verses yields place to the transformed divine.

Through the mid-seventeenth century both Donnes remain in play. In George Daniel's poem (*c*.1640) he is both 'the Reverent Donne, whose quill soe purely fil'd' and 'a Poet.... [of] Shadow, Light, the Ayre, & Life of Love' (12). But towards the end of the century both the love poet and the Doctor are less prominent, and the poet of the Satires comes forward, as well as the poet who is, if truth be told, not a very good poet. As Dayton Haskin argues, 'Dryden 'sent [Donne's] poems packing on a road headlong to oblivion' (2006: 235), even if this was not his intention, since, as A. J. Smith observes, Dryden both admired and imitated him (1975: 13). However, Dryden's emphasis on Donne's 'rough cadence' (Dryden 1956– : 17.30) in his critical writing, his remark that Donne was 'the greatest Wit, though not the best Poet of our Nation' (3.233), and his preference for the Satires set the terms for much of what little response there was to Donne in the eighteenth century. There was only one edition of his poems between 1669 and 1779. If there was a Donne to be read, it was Pope's, who at least prevented Donne 'from perishing, by putting his thoughts and satire into modern verse' (A. J. Smith 1975: 235). He remained as something of a Jack, who did not really know how to construct a poetic line, and who, in Samuel Johnson's view, could be profound, but, like Cowley and others of that 'race' of metaphysical poets, was the writer 'of thoughts so far-fetched as to be not only unexpected' (2006: 1.199, 204), but sometimes 'grossly absurd, and such as no figures or licence can reconcile to the understanding' (ibid. 1.209).

A wit but not a very good poet—these constitute the two Donnes of the eighteenth century, a division that held for much of the nineteenth century as well, although the harsh/conceited division was sometimes replaced by unschooled versifier/profound thinker. George Henry Lewes offers a good example in an unsigned 1838 article: 'That Donne's "poems" are not poems at all, may be very readily granted; but they are a very pleasant repertory of thought, wit, fancy and conceits' (375). Donne as thinker is the central point made by Robert Bell, journalist and compiler of a twenty-four-volume edition of English poets, who noted in his life of Cowley that Donne, 'To profound and extensive erudition... united a subtle intellect, and a vivid imagination', but along with these came a 'heaping up [of] a fatiguing quantity of distant and startling analogies' (50). Nonetheless, in 1839 the Doctor re-enters the story: for Henry Alford, Donne showed the mark of great genius in his poetry, but most especially in his Sermons. However, the same habit of mind is visible in both: 'scholastic learning and divinity are constantly to be found showing themselves in his poems'. Alford published Donne's Sermons in six volumes that also included the

Devotions, Prose Letters, and some of his poetry. Alford's Donne is essentially Dr Donne, but although Alford follows Walton's outline of Donne's life he argues against finding moral depravity in the 'licentiousness of some of his poetical pieces', suggesting that they were merely reflective of 'the court and society in which he lived' (Donne 1839: xxiv). To be sure, his lines can be 'harsh and unpleasing', but there is no strict division in his understanding of Donne, even though the figure chiefly presented is the Doctor whose eloquent Sermons poured 'forth from the fullness of his heart' (xxi). Certainly, once the Sermons were published it was the Doctor who was to be the primary figure. Even as late as the 1888 *Dictionary of National Biography*, as Kathleen Tillotson has noted (Tillotson 29), there was only cursory reference to Donne as a poet in its twenty-column entry. The Walton narrative of Jack's transformation into the Doctor and the understanding of Walton's *Life* as 'Donne's surpassing monument' (Haskin 1996: 46) remained in place until the end of the century, even as some readers, such as Coleridge and, somewhat later, Browning, were far less quick than Walton to dismiss the early poetry.

However, the conception of Donne as two in one did begin to take hold by the middle of the century. In America, as Haskin points out, Evert Duyckinck 'remarked on the basic compatibility of Walton's two Donnes' (1985: 229), but in ways that are essentially against the Walton grain: to read Donne's life 'as an illustration of the converting power of religion, is to misunderstand not only Donne, but the spirit of Christianity itself. If Donne had not been a very devoted lover, he would not have been the same zealous Dean of St. Paul's' (Duyckinck 26). However, earlier in the century Coleridge's careful, close, and often profound reading of Donne's poems, Sermons, and Prose Letters laid the groundwork for an essentially unified understanding of Donne. He had been reading and citing Donne as early as 1795. In his 1811 marginalia on Lamb's copy of Donne's poems he responded to many of the Songs and Sonets, observing how vigorous, or admirable, or noble many of the lines were. Of *WomCon*, a poem that explicitly dramatizes a self-division between the he and she, he noted that '[a]fter all, there is but one Donne' (1984: 218). As Haskin has argued, that assertion 'was not so much an answer to those who sought to reconcile Donne's youth and maturity as it was a recognition of Donne's utterly unique individuality and a denial that the parts of Donne's life could be separated' (2007: 44). It was with equal attention, care, and engagement that Coleridge annotated his copies of *LXXX Sermons*, something he did at two very distinct periods of his life, as George Whalley shows. Annotations in Copy A 'were probably written in 1809–10', in Copy B in 1830–1 (Coleridge 1984: 244, 250). He often argued points of theology but also noted passages 'that peculiarly pleased or struck me—and opposite to which, in the margin, I have written R. i.e. recollige' (261)—as well as those he found wanting. He was keenly attentive to the struggle he observed in Donne's thinking: 'it is most affecting to see the Struggles of so great a mind to preserve its inborn fealty to the Reason under the servitude to an accepted article of *Belief* which was, alas! confounded with the high obligations of *Faith*' (267).

For Coleridge, the two Donnes are one. In a conversation recorded during an 1833 visit to Cambridge, he remarked that 'the prose works of this admirable Divine, are Armouries for the Christian Soldier.... Donne's poetry must be sought in his prose; yet some of his verses breathe an uncommon fervency of spirit... The following poem [*SSweet*], for sweetness and tenderness of expression, chastened by a religious thoughtfulness and faith, is, I think, almost perfect' (Wilmott 15). It should be emphasized that, despite the comment on needing to seek the poetry in the prose, Coleridge was a very attentive reader of Donne's poetry, of both metrics and language, arguing that although '*all* Donne's Poems are equally *metrical*... in Poems where the Author *thinks* [italics in original] & expects the Reader to do so, the Sense must be understood in order to ascertain the metre' (1984: 221). Of lines 65–9 of *Sat3*, he observes that they offer an 'instance of free, vehement, verse-disguising Verse. Read it as it ought to be read; and no Ear will be offended' (227). A few years later George Craik, describing Donne's poetry in *Sketches of the History of Literature and Learning in England* (1844–45), also quoted *SSweet*. He responded to the delicateness of its execution, although he found many other poems difficult in their mingling of the harsh and the harmonious, as 'the pious and the profane meet and mingle in the strangest of dances' (G. Craik 169, 171). Lacking Coleridge's ear, Craik was still able to hear in Donne's poems 'a deep and subtle music of their own'. But he also was able to sense a connection between the two Donnes, even though the dance between them might be strange.

Of course, there could hardly be one Donne or two without Donne in print, especially when new editions of Walton's *Lives* were becoming rarer. Thus A. B. Grosart's 'bungling' (Haskin 1985: 247) edition, published in 1872–3, marks an important stop along the two-Donne narrative track. His desire to see (if not accept) Donne whole certainly framed his understanding of Donne. There were still two Donnes, in so far as Grosart followed the larger outline of the Walton narrative; nonetheless, he tried to 'reconcile the extraordinarily licentious character of much of the verse with the well-known story in which Doctor Donne had been an exemplary Jacobean clergyman' (Haskin 2006: 238). 'I deplore that Poetry, in every way almost so memorable and potential,' Grosart wrote in the preface, 'should be stained even to uncleanliness on sorrowfully too many places' (Donne 1872–3: 1.ix). In the 'Essay on the Life and Writings of Donne' that prefaced his second volume, Grosart writes that he must 'make the supremest claims for Donne as a Thinker and Imaginator... the light of his imagination lies goldenly over his thinking' (2.xxxvii, xxxix). He hears in the poetry 'an indefinable something suggestive of Shakespeare', but he remains uneasy with Donne's language, with his mode, for his Donne was 'an Artist of ideas rather than words in verse' (2.xliv–xlv). Nonetheless he is far from dismissive of the early Donne, reading him in large measure as Coleridge had and appreciating, as well, the moral force of the Satires. Grosart thus marks an important shift in the two-Donne construct. For him, as Haskin has argued, Donne's conversion from Catholicism, his fall into moral turpitude, and his rescue by marriage (Haskin 2006: 238–9) are the crucial events, and not, as Walton had it, his taking holy orders in the English Church. In this way Grosart's two Donnes follows in part the trajectory that Anna Jameson had marked out in her 1829 *Loves of the Poets*, which made Donne's marriage the crucial redeeming event (Haskin 2007: 127). However, most important for this account, Jack the poet is, for Grosart, as profound a thinker as the divine doctor, and he is a poet whom we must learn to read.

More editions followed Grosart's, certainly more textually competent ones. By 1895 in the United States there was Norton's revision of Lowell's 1855 edition, and in Britain the Chambers edition of 1896. Then came Gosse's 1899 *Life and Letters*, with its explicit intent to see Donne whole even while noting the divisions and revisions that constituted his life. But what Gosse wanted to find in the poems and Letters was the life. 'There is hardly a piece of his genuine verse which, cryptic though it may seem, cannot be prevailed upon to deliver up some secret of his life and character' (1.62). That life, however, was not the Walton story, which for the most part erased biographical detail, replacing it with the exemplary—Augustine and Ambrose, Saul and Paul—even as it made the life its main subject. However, as Haskin (1996: 18) shows, using *Canon* as his example, Walton's *Life* placed constraints on the poem's interpretation and yet ultimately inspired biographical readings. Gosse reconstructed Donne's 'life', methodically and ingeniously, even if often absurdly, creating what 'now appears more like a late nineteenth-century novel than a biography designed to enhance a reader's pleasure with Donne's poetry' (Haskin 1985: 248). However, the biographical imperative can, curiously enough, be traced back to Donne himself in the Jack and the Doctor remark that started this hare from its hiding place in the 1619 Letter. For through that formulation he identified himself with his writing in the very act of distancing himself, and to the degree that it was picked up it sends the reader back to the life, 'desiring m/More'.

That imperative, as Deborah Larson has argued, remained constant in twentieth-century criticism: 'With Donne's love poetry...it is often difficult if not impossible for a number of critics to separate the *persona* of the poems from John Donne himself' (1989: 70). Using the debates over the dating of *Noct*, she argues that 'basing...[the dating] on Donne's supposed attitudes toward women in general, Lucy or Anne in particular, or his ministry continue in more sophisticated form the division of his character into libertine and dean' (78–9). Indeed, because the voice in the poems seems so particular, so rooted in time and place, one wants—or so the strong biographical emphasis in so much Donne criticism down to this moment would suggest—to locate it in the person, too. And this is despite another of Donne's remarks in a Letter to Ker some six years later, accompanying his poem *Ham*, that 'I did best when I had least Truth for my subiect' (*Variorum* 6.219). Yet since this is the Doctor speaking, what did he mean by 'truth', or 'best', for that matter?

Thus, do we hear truth or fiction, confession or imagination, when we read Donne's poetry? Is it person or persona speaking? To attempt an answer, one 'about must, and about must goe', a circling made the more difficult by the multiple binaries that descend from, even though they do not precisely correspond to, that initial Jack and the Doctor formulation, which still remains a useful shorthand for all of them: Jack/John, sinner/saint, Catholic/Protestant, apostate/survivor, careerist/man of integrity, rake/husband, courtier/divine, poet of the carnal/poet of the sacred—the list could go on and on. For many of these pairings, as the critical tradition reveals, it is often an issue of both/and rather than of either/or, although the more historicized and biographically situated a critic's reading is, the more likely the commitment to one or another of the terms. Hence John Carey's apostasy thesis in his 1981 *John Donne: Life, Mind and Art*, where the opening sentence sets the terms for the entire study: 'The first thing to remember about Donne is that he was a Catholic; the second; that he betrayed his Faith' (1981a: 15). This claim is offered as totally explanatory of Donne's life and art, so that doubling is necessarily understood as duplicity: Donne 'led a double life, his poetry supplying a covert outlet for impulses which his public self refused to recognize' (70). Carey does allow, it should be noted, that 'the more we read the poems and sermons the more we can see them as fabrics of the same mind, controlled by similar imaginative needs' (11); the difficulty lies with Carey's suspicions about that mind. As well, as much recent research has shown, Donne could have been interested in a career without the negative implications of 'careerist', indeed could have sought a career *as* a man of integrity. Similarly, more linguistically oriented critics often play on the carnal/erotic binary by showing its essential unity in Donne's imagination, Jack in the Doctor, the Doctor in Jack, picking up the earlier emphasis on wit as the crucial term or, like Coleridge, seeing the same linguistic daring in his prose as in his poetry.

Certainly doublings are a Donne specialty, often enacted in his poems and sometimes given names. A master ventriloquist, he often stages one Donne speaking to another, or he sets up an implicit dialogue where he answers for the other (*WomCon*, *Flea*, *Canon* come immediately to mind). Sometimes the one addressed seems to merge with the speaker, as in the opening line of *Sat1*. Who is the 'fondling motley humorist' that is sent away, only to return at the last line? In the interim the speaker lets himself be led out of his chamber door by this 'wild uncertaine thee' (ll. 1, 12), and in whispered asides both assents to and criticizes, indeed often seems to become one with, this peripatetic, performing self. *Sappho* offers another example. There Donne not only has Sappho and Ovid speaking through him, but he speaks as Sappho, making her voice and body contain those of her lover, so that the two separate women become one: 'touchinge my selfe, all seemes done to thee. / My selfe I embrace' (ll. 52–3). Possibly more playful than serious, the poem offers a useful model for Donne's ability to imagine himself as other, to be other to himself and yet self-same. Another variation of the doubling process occurs in *Eclog*. The poem opens and closes with a dialogue between Idios and Allophanes, framing the Epithalamion at the marriage of the Earl of Somerset. Written at a time when Donne was still hoping for court patronage, possibly ecclesiastical, possibly not, the entire text enacts a cautious treading through a minefield of politics and gossip surrounding the Overbury affair that provides context for its ambivalences and rhetorical shifts and turns. The two speakers are traditionally understood as Idios/Donne and Allophanes/Sir Robert Ker, and on a literal level that is certainly the case. But it has also been persuasively argued that the two figures enact two aspects of Donne, Allophanes 'an alternative side of Idios, an alter ego [who] stands for the attraction to the court that motivated so many of Donne's actions', as Heather Dubrow suggests (1988: 212). Similarly, Annabel Patterson claims that the poem 'provides the most sharply delineated version in Donne's work of that formally divided self to which he apparently had recourse when attempting to deal with ambivalence, here personified as Idios ("one's own", "pertaining to one's self") and Allophanes ("appearing otherwise", or perhaps, "the face of the Other")' (1990: 52). That Donne made Allophanes/Ker the recipient of the Jack and the Doctor remark is suggestive, although possibly too neat. What is clear, however, is that Donne's habit of thought involved a stepping out of the self the more fully to step back in, and that this often involved a splitting, fictional as well as real, of that self. It is little wonder that alchemy, as it speaks to the processes of transformation, refining, and change, is so central to Donne's imagination.

The poem in which Donne confronts this double, potentially transformed self most directly is the Holy Sonnet *HSVex* (*Variorum* 7.1). It is not known whether this poem, appearing only in the Westmoreland ms., was written before or after ordination, but Jack and, at the very least, an intimation of the Doctor, each yielding place to the other, certainly participate in its riddling uncertainties:

> Oh, to vex me, contraryes meete in one:
> > Inconstancy vnnaturally hath begott
> > A constant habit; that when I would not
> I change in vowes, and in devotione.
> As humorous is my contritione
> > As my prophane love, and as soone forgott:
> > As ridlingly distemperd, cold and hott,
> As praying, as mute; as infinite, as none.
> I durst not view heauen yesterday; and to day
> > In prayers, and flattering Speaches I court God:
> > To morrow I quake with true feare of his rod.
> So my deuout fitts come and go away
> > Like a fantastique Ague: Save that here
> > Those are my best dayes, when I shake with feare.

Contrition and profane love are set in opposition, each itself unstable, then rotated around the relative conjunctive adverb, 'as', eight instances in four lines of what the *OED* identifies as the '*Comparative of Equality*'. That small word makes for a vertigo-inducing run-up to the volta as the I, constantly inconstant, seeks a point of balance, a means to compare a riddling, divided self to itself. Whether resolution is achieved or not in the last line and a half (and critics have lined up on both sides, as the

Variorum commentary makes clear), the poem certainly stages the doubling and the awareness of that doubling that the Jack and the Doctor formulation so memorably names. 'Complex, oppositional self-hood', is the useful phrase that Richard Sugg (2007: 55) offers in a recent study as an approach to reading Donne. Or, as the concluding phrase of the Epigram *Pyr* has it: 'by parting, have ioynd here' (*Variorum* 8.10), which neatly captures the two-way movement, the disjunctive conjunction enacted in the texts and biography of John Donne.

Coda: Walt Whitman, Fernando Pessoa, Robert Schumann, and Bob Dylan have the last word

'Do I contradict myself? / Very well then, I contradict myself, / (I am large, I contain multitudes)' (Whitman 246). Whitman's multitudes were not Donne's, for they are not so much parts of an interior Whitman as they are all those others who inhabit his multitudinous, yawping, composite self. One can hear Donne readily assent to the line, 'I am the poet of the Body and I am the poet of the Soul' (207), but he could not, as Whitman did, so easily have written 'My rendezvous is appointed, it is certain, / The Lord will be there and wait till I come on perfect terms, / The great Camerado, the lover true for whom I pine will be there' (241). 'Do I contradict myself? I certainly do', Jack and the Doctor, might say, possibly even with a bit of pride. For the artist as a composite, contradictory self is perhaps the truest of truisms. Fernando Pessoa, the early twentieth-century Portuguese poet, created separate, biographically distinct personae, heteronyms, distinct selves who neither knew each other nor wrote like each other, and who lived entirely separate lives. Robert Schumann imagined himself as two and gave each a name, both in his music and in his journal. Floristan was passionate, engaged, while Eusebius was pensive and quiet, Il Penseroso to the other's noisier L'Allegro. Bob Dylan does not give his selves separate names (although of course Dylan's name isn't Dylan, even if Bob stayed Bob), but he is multiple, as Todd Haynes's 2007 film, *I'm Not There*, brilliantly reveals in its simultaneous layering of Dylan selves, Woody Guthrie and Rimbaud, Christian and Jew, Jack to Jude to Billy the Kid, all melded, each distinct.

Jack and the Doctor is not the title of any film, although it is the title of Mary Clive's 1966 novelistic biography that concludes with a scene at St Paul's, tourists looking at the cluster of stone bishops and deans among whom Donne's figure stands: 'Jack is above eye-level, and not one in ten look up at him. Considering the trouble he took to design this monument it really is pathetic. One longs to whisper, Look up! There! Just above your head! There's Jack! Doctor Donne! You know, the famous Dean of St. Paul's! The man who wrote', and then she quotes *SGo* and 'I have a sinne of feare' (Clive 192). Jack and the Doctor speaking together to the end. A recent novel, *Conceit*, by Mary Novik also structures its understanding of Donne around this duality, focusing it through his daughter Margaret's attempts to know her parents, even to be them, as she attends her dying father, a scene played and replayed from multiple perspectives and times. Where might one find the true Donne, the novel asks. One answer is Walton's: '"Your father's sermons will always be revered", Walton said'. Donne's daughter agrees, but, she replies, it will be '[f]or their cleverness, their wit, but do not look there for the man, Izzy. Such mysteries are only found in poems' (Novik 313).

And mystery is exactly what remains when one has finished rotating those two little words that Donne dropped into the archive of literary history in 1619. Certainly there were distinct Donnes, but they inhabited the one Donne. They played together, they were played off one another, they served and continue to serve a vast variety of polemical ends. They might have been invented at the start as an anxious bit of disguise, but John Donne was/is one and singular and so multiple there is no counting. The 'two Donnes' construct was a means, a very clever means, of ensuring that capacious singularity.

CHAPTER 43

DANGER AND DISCOURSE

LYNNE MAGNUSSON

> Now I see many dangers
>
> (*ElJeal* l. 25)

DANGERS of all kinds, and especially the dangers inherent in many different forms of discourse and communication, were rarely far from Donne's mind. His Elegies and Satires not only abound in risk-taking language, but they also frequently intimate the danger of various situated forms of speech ('We must not as we vs'd, flout openly': *Variorum* 2, *ElJeal* l. 17) and writing ('Libells, or some interdicted thing / Which negligently kept, thy ruyne bring': *ElBrac* ll. 101–2). Even listening to loose talk by a courtier is construed as a dangerous activity in *Sat4*, where the narrator claims he 'felt my selfe then / Becomming Traytor, and mee thought I saw / One of our Giant Statutes ope his jaw / To sucke me in; for hearing him' (ll. 130–3). Frequently, from early to late in his career, we find Donne imagining and dramatizing taut speech situations like that of an accused before a 'dradd Iudge' (*ElBrac* l. 18). One of his later Sermons parses for his auditors as strictly limited the options for evasion—'To an Incompetent Judge, if I be interrogated, I must speake truth, if I speake; but to a Competent Judge, I must speak:…I may not be silent' (*Sermons* 9.162).

Donne's Letters and other prose reflections provide considerable evidence of how often his thoughts turned to the dangers associated not only with linguistic interaction but also with the circulation of written texts. In a Letter delivering a copy of his Paradoxes to a friend, he requires his addressee's assurance that he will not copy or circulate the Paradoxes, or the Elegies and Satires—for 'to my satyrs there belongs some feare & to some elegies & these [Paradoxes] p[er]haps shame' (E. M. Simpson 1948: 316). The 1599 Bishops' Ban in England, an instance of censorship involving the recall and burning of existing printed books of satires by writers like Joseph Hall, John Marston, and Thomas Middleton and the prohibition of further publication in this genre (McCabe), is often cited to explain Donne's expression of 'fear' in relation to his Satires, although his had circulated only in manuscript among friends and trusted connections.

Donne is clearly fascinated by the exercise and effects of print censorship. He goes on in the same letter to discuss the effects upon the Italian writer Pietro Aretino of a ban on books enforced by a different authority, in this case the Roman Church's *Index of Prohibited Books* authorized by the mid-sixteenth-century Council of Trent. But Elizabethan practices of print censorship can by no means account adequately for the acute apprehension, to be found in so many of Donne's writings, that linguistic interaction and practical communication are fraught with risks deriving from state or religious authority. This chapter will explore the extent to which Donne's understanding is conditioned by early lessons in communication related to his positioning within the Catholic minority at a time when persecution aimed at enforcing uniformity in religion and eradicating Catholicism in England was intensified. My emphasis here is not on Donne's religious beliefs but instead on the shaping of his linguistic *habitus* (Bourdieu)—that is, his habitual orientation in his communication practices. I am concerned with his self-reflexive analysis of this discourse habit and how his early conditioning in communication enters into and inflects his imaginative writing.

But not all danger imagined in speech or writing arises in encounters (anticipated or real) with authorities. Donne identifies at least two other agents of threat: his readers or auditors, who lay his discourse open to misinterpretation, and himself, whose free expression or sceptical discourse risks misleading others, endangering or even 'damnif[ying]' those impressionable readers or auditors not 'strong and watchfull enough' to arm their consciences against its threats (*Letters* 18–19). 'Danger' is demonstrably an insistent keyword in Donne's reflections on his communications across a range of media. This chapter takes as its point of departure Donne's own interpretive comments, whether straightforward or enigmatic, on the perils of verbal performance relating to authority, the reader, and the author. With attention to a range of genres, especially the correspondence, the Elegies and *Sat4*, and the readers' prefaces to *Pseudo-Martyr*, it considers how an apprehension of danger conditioned Donne's speech and writing. The argument falls into two parts: the first focuses on threats from authorities and the second on threats that accrue from the dialogic relation of writer and reader.

'Dradd Iudge' and 'Priviledg'd Spie': Threats from Authorities

Donne's Catholic upbringing in a family with close connections to the Jesuit English mission, during a period when statutes were enacted making it treasonous to be a Catholic priest and a capital felony to harbour one, taught him lessons about communication, both tacit and explicit, that were not part of the grammar- and rhetoric-based curriculum of the Elizabethan grammar schools. Foremost among them must have been the art and the appropriate occasions for standing mute and also some of the complicated consequences of silence. He would have come to know the importance to Catholic priests and their protectors of silence when searchers or pursuivants invaded homes and drove them to confined priest-holes or improvised hiding places to wait in dread. In *ElPerf* the wit of the narrator's betrayal by his own perfume to his mistress's father depends, in large part, on a recognition of the trifling use to which this lesson of silence for concealment has been put:

> I tought my silkes their whistling to forbeare
> Euen my opprest shoes dumb and speachles weare;
> Only thou bitter sweete whom I had layd
>   Next me, me trayterously hast betrayd.
>   (*Variorum* 2, ll. 51–4)

Helen Gardner notes in these lines an allusion suggestive of a second specialized historical context for self-silencing in response to hostile authority: the mute and 'opprest shoes' allude to '"Pressing", the *peine forte et dure*, [that] was inflicted on those arraigned for felony who stood mute and refused to plead' (Donne 1965: 123). An infamous case had followed hard upon the anti-recusant legislation against sheltering priests passed in 1585: on 25 March 1586 Margaret Clitherow was pressed to death under seven or eight hundredweight on Ouse Bridge in York, after she refused to plead when charged with harbouring a priest who had eluded capture, a frightened child having revealed to searchers the secret priests' room in her home (C. Walker). The example of silence in cases like this one, like the issue raised by charges of Jesuit equivocation under interrogation, was a controversial topic on which Donne continued to reflect and search his conscience, pronouncing in a Sermon in January 1630: 'Certainly, that standing mute at the Bar, which, of late times hath prevailed upon many distempered wretches, is, in it selfe, so particularly a sin, as that I should not venture to absolve any such person, nor to administer the Sacrament to him, how earnestly soever he desired it at his death...except he repented in particular, that sin, of having stood mute and refused a just triall...' (*Sermons* 9.162–3).

Similarly, early on Donne must have learned lessons in letter-writing not found in a standard textbook like Erasmus's *De conscribendis epistolis*. Among Catholic families and priests, correspondence was at once necessary for keeping up contacts within dispersed networks and dangerous in increasing vulnerability. Intercepted correspondence, or correspondence carried and manipulated by double agents or treacherous informers, was well known to have made for the undoing of Mary Queen of Scots and the Babington conspirators, and was a usual means of tracking or exposing Catholic practices or fugitive priests. One entry in *The Courtier's Library*, Donne's satiric book catalogue, attributes to Thomas Phelippes, the chief cryptographer at work in Francis Walsingham's intelligence system, the imaginary book, 'Quidlibet ex quolibet; *Or the art of decyphering and finding some treason in any intercepted letter*' (P. Brown 2008: 860). Even in *Pseudo-Martyr*, published in 1610, the very work that constituted Donne's public rejection of the 'meditation of Martyrdome' in which he had been 'kept awake' by 'the Teachers of Romane Doctrine' (8), he affirms the same lesson from his specialized education in epistolarity: 'in a jealous, and obnoxious state, a Decipherer can pick out Plots, and Treason, in any familiar letter which is intercepted' (10). Not only does this lesson articulate the potential threat of state authority, but it imparts the alarming message that familiar letters even on innocent or indifferent topics are vulnerable to misinterpretation; and it introduces the loathed figure of the treacherous intermediary in state oppression. This betraying figure is often alluded to in Donne's Elegies, Satires, and other works, whether in the guise of decipherer, 'search[er]' (*Variorum* 2, ElPerf l. 18), 'finder' (*ElBrac* l. 91), 'spie' (*Sat4* l. 119), or even as a guilty, self-exposing 'I'.

In Donne's own correspondence he shows familiarity with the elaborate techniques for secret writing used by Jesuits, as in the case Father John Gerard was to record in his *Autobiography* of writing with orange juice as invisible ink to help effect his escape from prison (Gerard 116–20, 129). Donne jokes about invisible ink in a Letter to Sir Henry Goodere: 'if you did not finde the remembrance of my humblest services to my Lady *Bedford*, your love and faith ought to try all the experiments of pouders, and dryings, and waterings to discover some lines which appeared not' (*Letters* 76–7). Donne's own mother, Elizabeth Syminges, endangered herself in the mid-1580s by contriving to pass letters between William Weston, a Jesuit newly arrived in England, and her brother Jasper Heywood, the English Superior at that time, imprisoned in the Tower of London (Bald 1970: 44–5; Flynn 1995c: 127; 1996: 188–90). Donne's dangerous acquaintance with such transactions is registered in *ElNat*, in a lesson in silent communication that he professes regret at having taught his married mistress:

> I had not tought thee then, the Alphabett
> Of flowers; how they devisefully beeing sett
> And bound vp, might with speechlesse secresy
> Deliuer arrands mutely'and mutually.
>
> (*Variorum* 2, *ElNat* ll. 9–12)

Crossing between different universes of discourse, between religious persecution and sexual liaison, Donne's art replays his distinctive orientation to dangerous communication in new keys that contribute to the originality of his poetic expression.

Together with such curious subterfuges, we have evidence about more everyday tactics used by endangered Catholics. In 1587, for example, the Jesuit Fathers Robert Southwell and Henry Garnett explicitly strategized about stylistic devices for safe communication, after Southwell was reproved by the Jesuit General, Claudio Acquaviva, for the potentially damaging forthrightness of his epistolary style. These included simple tactics like making only indirect allusions to individuals discussed or signing 'Rob', 'Robertus', or 'R. S.' instead of a full name (Caraman 64). More interesting, perhaps, was Acquaviva's direction that important subjects should 'to some extent be veiled in allegory', with pre-agreed vocabulary—typically economic vocabulary—providing a rudimentary code: creditors and debtors represented persecutors and persecuted, for example, merchants represented priests, and merchandise stood in for souls (Pollen 1908: 320; Caraman 63). At the same time, Southwell was alert to the risks involved in being overly cryptic: 'We are not afraid to say openly...even what can well be said secretly, for anything written obscurely, enigmatically or figuratively, is liable on discovery to more close examination and to more perverse interpretation' (qtd. in Caraman 63–4).

The seeming 'newless[ness]' (Carey 1981*b*) of much of Donne's correspondence suggests that he internalized early lessons in epistolary caution, making it a reflex to be guarded about sensitive content. Annabel Patterson (1982) has richly illuminated the self-censorship in Donne's *Letters*, while Claude Summers and Ted-Larry Pebworth (1991) and Dennis Flynn (1995*b*) have shown how they do treat politically sensitive issues, like the fall of Essex, but do so in covert or coded ways. Indeed, Donne occasionally uses precisely the epistolary tactics that Southwell and his superiors discuss. He draws on knowledge shared with his addressee to express his views on controversial books without giving titles or naming authors—citing Bishop William Barlow's *Answer to a Catholike English-man* as 'that Book in whose bowels you left me' (*Letters* 160)—or to protect his identity: '*Yours intirely. / You know me without a name, and I know not how this Letter goes*' (*Letters* 217). Furthermore, in Donne's complex poetry, especially the earlier work of the 1590s, we can find dangerous topics broached in highly inventive ways under the cover of apparently trivial subjects and economic vocabulary. Take, for example, *ElBrac*, which adapted from Thomas Kyd's *Soliman and Perseda* the situation of a lost chain (Donne 1965: 122). Here, when the speaker responds to his mistress's demand that his twelve gold coins or 'righteous angels' be melted to replace her missing gold chain, Donne ostensibly treats a trivial 'economic' loss but in a manner blown way out of proportion by the intensity of the speaker's outcry at 'the bitter cost' (*Variorum* 2, l. 8). Donne prompts the reader to ask why the speaker talks about losing money as betraying 'Martyrs' (l. 82)? Or longs to see the 'finder' (l. 91) 'fetterd, mannacled, and hangd in Chaines' (l. 95), like a tortured priest? Or imagines precious coins as angelic protectors 'which heauen commanded to prouide / All things to me, and be my faythfull guide' (ll. 13–14)? Or treats a girlfriend's demand as the 'seuere / Sentence' of a 'dradd Iudge' (ll. 17–18)? With the vehicles of the metaphors so much more potent than their ostensible tenors, this equivocating language prompts the 'deciphering' reader to hear more than the tale of a chain—to hear rather a muffled speech act of protest against an intolerable situation that makes the speaker feel part persecuted and part traitor. The indirect strategy captures the kind of bitter frustration that a young man like Donne must have felt, who had to face, with his coming of age, the dreadful episode of his own younger brother Henry's death by plague in prison, not as a shining Catholic martyr but marked instead as a Judas to the Catholic priest, William Harrington, whom he had aimed to protect (Cain 2004).

Donne would have been privy to the strategies of bold approach that characterized the zealous proselytizing Jesuit fathers like his uncle Jasper Heywood and, also, to the tactics of covert communication they practiced to mitigate risk. But beyond the direct threats from anti-Catholic authorities these methods addressed, communication was complicated and its danger intensified by the late Elizabethan proclamations aimed at dividing the Catholic community, requiring that friends, neighbours, and relatives inform against one another. Thus, Donne grew up in a context in which trust in communication among networks of friends within a surrounding community was, on the one hand, essential to survival and necessary for any political action and was, on the other hand, always contaminated by wariness about possible treachery. This is the situation of discursive paranoia that Donne captures so precisely in the stance of his satiric persona in *Sat4* as a muted conversational participant at the Elizabethan court, sweating with fear that the loosely conversing and gossiping jaws of his courtly interlocutor will suddenly clamp down with the full force and the giant bite of statute law.

In *Sat4*, the speech inhibition that must have been associated with Donne's Catholic minority positioning and tutelage is brilliantly turned to use to create an unorthodox satirical persona. Although the poem is modelled on Horace's *Satire 1.9*, where a genial satirist encounters a boor, the conversational stance and interactive dilemma of Donne's speaker, confronted by a garrulous figure while visiting the Elizabethan court, are dramatically different (*Sat4*, ll. 17 ff.; Hester 1982: 76–7). The first of his two visits to court is set up as foolishly risk-taking in a way specifically associated with endangered Catholics: he ventures into court 'as Glaze which did goe / To' a Masse in jest, catch'd, was faine to disburse / The hundred markes, which is the Statutes curse' (ll. 8–10). This prepares for an experience the speaker represents as 'suffer[ing]' (l. 17) or torture, heightened by allusion to the reprehensible methods of the loathed Elizabethan pursuivant and torturer Richard Topcliffe. Yet this torture, to modern readers, looks like nothing more threatening than a tedious conversation with a down-at-heels and newsmongering character who cultivates foreign speech and mindless social compliment. What really sets the interaction

Ill. 43.1. Frontispiece of *Poems, by J. D.* (1635), engraved by William Marshall. (Reproduced by permission of the Huntington Library, San Marino, California.)

apart is the complicated and unpredictable response (even to himself) of the speaker, positioned as, but acting entirely unlike, a satiric persona. At first, when pressed for conversation, he tries to reserve an aloof satirical distance, venturing, under pressure to engage only an opinion about 'the best linguist' (l. 53), a brief rebuttal to a critique of his 'lonenesse' (l. 67), and some deliberately obtuse responses to evade his interlocutor's quixotic agenda: 'He...askes, "What newes?" I tell him of new playes' (l. 92–3). But as his curious interlocutor blathers on, commenting on precisely the corruptions of court that one might expect the satirist to berate (producing 'Libells...'gainst each great man' [l. 120], exposing the unjust purchase or entail of court offices that closes down opportunities for worthy candidates), the poem delivers a vivid apprehension of what it might feel like to be terrified and silenced just by mundane talk. It makes one understand how such an alienating sense of fear in simple conversation could be heightened by suspicion (even without great likelihood) that one's interlocutor could be 'a priviledg'd spie' (l. 119) or that a simple misstep could spring a hidden trap: 'He with home-meats tries me; I belch, spue, spit, / Looke pale and sickly, like a Patient' (ll. 109–10). Paying a crown to bribe his interlocutor to be gone, Donne's persona feels, like the speaker in *ElBrac*, 'the bitter cost' (l. 8) to him of 'my forefathers sinne' (l. 138)—that is, the price exacted merely for being born into the family of an oppressed minority. Here the 'cost' exhibited in such a remarkable way is not the monetary penalty: it is a hideously dysfunctional positioning in communication situations.

Annabel Patterson makes the important point that in *Sat4* and elsewhere Donne responds 'to the restraints imposed on his culture by political censorship' by a 'strategy of self-division': that is, in the strange 'boor' he creates 'a socially dangerous persona to do his libeling for him' (1990: 48). But it is an equally potent indictment of the late Elizabethan court and administration as approximating that 'jealous, and obnoxious state' mentioned in *Pseudo-Martyr* (10) to show so graphically how it could turn a peaceable and talented person's everyday conversational encounters into a seeming 'hell'. Escaped home, into the low-risk refuge of 'wholesome solitarinesse' (l. 155), he feels a hell-like trance induced by the court encounter overwhelming him and struggles to come to terms with his own fear. What is it in court company, this satirist manqué asks himself, that can so intimidate and prevent him from speaking bold truths—or from speaking at all? 'Low feare', he tells himself, 'Becomes the guiltie, not th'accuser' (ll. 160–1). The poem shows a source of intimidation running deeper than rank and class, but the speaker takes assurance by reminding himself he's 'nones slave' (l. 162), raising courage to make a return appearance at court and to assume a satirist's critical voice. Now he is positioned not in courtly conversation, but, somewhat equivocally, as the 'wise' reader's 'spie', boldly but covertly exposing both court corruption and the malevolence of a system that creates people as 'spies' in the first place. Even so, he admits to fear when he finally departs, an admission coded with a covert analogy to the experience of men like Robert Southwell, imprisoned and tortured en route to execution: 'Tyr'd, now I leave this place, and but pleas'd so / As men which from gaoles to'execution goe' (ll. 229–30).

In the contamination of discourse depicted in *Sat4*, authority exerts its power indirectly over the speaker's social conversation, with the speaker never coming face to face with the Queen or other significant authority figure (see also Ch. 29.I). In this light, it is interesting to glimpse the strategy in *Sat5*, levelled against corrupt legal structures with fee-demanding officers preying pitilessly on those caught in lawsuits, of seemingly direct address to the Queen as 'Greatest and fairest Empresse' (l. 28) and to Sir Thomas Egerton, the Lord Keeper, as 'You Sir, whose righteousnes she loves' (l. 31). Most of the Satires are meant for the eyes of Donne's most trusted friends, but it is often thought that Donne had at least the Lord Keeper (if not the Queen) as reader in mind here, thinking Egerton would value the poem as support for his concerted efforts to reform the law-courts and officers under his jurisdiction. Still, it is hard to imagine Donne expecting sympathy from above for the poem's strong protest against the closing down of channels for oppressed subjects to appeal:

> Powre of the Courts below
> Flow from the first maine head, and these can throw
> Thee, if they sucke thee in, to misery,
> To fetters, halters; But if th'injury
> Steele thee to dare complaine, Alas, thou go'st
> Against the stream, when upwards:...
>
> (ll. 45–50)

Donne seems to be struggling again with the catch-22 lessons learned within his native discourse community, perhaps seeing them as more broadly applicable, as he exposes the high risks run by the injured suitors, even in speaking of their woes. In the 1580s and 1590s the English Catholics had found it virtually impossible to get a petition about their sufferings delivered to or heard by the Queen (Southwell 74–80). This poem's question to Queen Elizabeth, 'Greatest and fairest Empresse, know you this?' (l. 28), replicates the strategy of Robert Southwell's *An Humble Supplication to Her Maiestie*, playing the dangerous game of postulating the Queen's non-complicity based on her ignorance in areas where she should be knowledgeable (Southwell 1–2, 44).

My point is, then, that early lessons related to the dangers to which the English Catholic community was exposed in the last two decades of Queen Elizabeth's reign had a significant impact on Donne's own understanding and habits of communication. The pressures where linguistic interaction is so fraught with risk are likely to produce both uncontrolled responses and behaviours (like the speaker's in *Sat4*) and strategies for covert and indirect communication. Furthermore, these lessons contributed to his literary art in works like the Satires and Elegies, both to the complexity of rhetorical strategies and to the choice and handling of subject matter. Needless to say, this influence was mediated or countered by many other aspects of his formal education, his reading, his temperament, and his talent (Magnusson). And changing life experiences must have always been reshaping what Donne knew of dangerous discourse. Later in life, for example, with political conditions and his religion and situation altered, Donne had repeated occasions of direct speech with King James I, and, in his Sermons and Divine Poems, risky encounters with authority (whether monarch, God, or judge) are more often represented as direct dialogue or face-to-face conversation. But the early foundation certainly helps to explain why 'danger' remained a keyword in Donne's explicit and implicit theorizing about discourse and interpretation.

'Misinterpretable' words: the mutual 'danger' of reader and writer

Donne's strong tendency is to characterize communication as bound up with danger, but state and religious authorities are by no means the sole agents of threat in the risk-filled arena of linguistic interaction. Repeatedly, in his self-reflexive comments on the composition and circulation of his writings, he identifies as one key source of danger the reader and, as another, the author himself. At times, the reader appears to be cast as an independent source of threat, especially on the occasions when Donne leaves the protective cocoon he favours—manuscript circulation among trusted friends—having, in his own peculiar idiom, 'descended to print' (*Letters* 238). This is, perhaps, the general impression given by the distressed Letters Donne wrote from Paris in April 1612, responding to the 'many censures' of the *Anniversaries* by arguing that readers have misinterpreted. Later, in the *Devotions* (1624), when Donne addresses God as not simply a '*literall*' but also 'a *figurative*, a *metaphoricall God*', the address is accompanied by defensive action against the reader, cast as the interceptor and potential misinterpreter of his talk with God: '*Lord* I intend it to thy *glory*, and let no *prophane mis-interpreter* abuse it to thy *diminution*' (99; Baumlin 1991: 58).

The most familiar example of Donne constructing the author or the author's work as potentially injurious to an unprepared reader occurs in his comments on *Biathanatos*, the paradoxical treatise defending suicide. Travelling to Germany in 1619, many years after its composition, and requesting that his friend Sir Robert Ker preserve and guard the manuscript in his safe keeping, 'only forbid[ding] it the Presse, and the Fire', Donne pronounced it to be 'upon a misinterpretable subject' (*Letters* 21–2). His security, when he ventures into topics or methods of expression that he admits can be construed or 'suspect[ed]...of new or dangerous doctrine' (*Letters* 20), is not only in manuscript circulation to friends he trusts to protect his works from indiscriminate copying but also in their possession of the strength of mind to read wisely. There are, however, difficult moments in Donne's Letters when, in the mirror of a friend's response to his words, what he sees reflected back is a kind of Faust-cum-Mephistopheles figure, himself as both the taster of 'dangerous doctrine' and the tempter. In a moving Letter to his long-term correspondent Sir Henry Goodere (*c*.1617), he apologizes and assumes responsibility for having influenced or effected a damaging change in his friend through his own bold testing of religions:

> In my particular, I am sorry, if my ingenuity and candor in delivering my self in those points, of which you speak to me, have defaced those impressions which were in you before: if my freedome have occasioned your captivity, I am miserably sorry. I went unprofitably and improvidently, to the utmost end of Truth, because I would go as farre as I could to meet Peace; if my going so far in declaring my self, brought you where you could not stop. (*Letters* 209–10)

Writing to Goodere years earlier, Donne had reflected more speculatively about the responsibilities of the author or interlocutor who ventured boldly into novel opinions or unorthodox freethinking: 'I would not be in danger of that law of *Moses*, That if a man dig a pit, and cover it not, he must recompense those which are damnified by it: which is often interpreted of such as shake old opinions, and do not establish new as certain, but leave consciences in a worse danger then they found them in' (*Letters* 18). In this Letter, Donne had absolved himself as writer of harm-doing, declaring his case 'not obnoxious to that law', since he had taken the measure of his friend and judged 'my meditations...neither too wide nor too deep for you' (19).

While these are extreme cases, Donne's regular tendency is to send forth works with the early modern equivalent of instruction manuals, warning about risks and directing selected readers on how best to disarm them, thus constructing the author's contribution as at least potentially 'misinterpretable' and dangerous. For example, he feels the need to warn the friend to whom he entrusts the book of Paradoxes against their misleading appearance as 'enemies' to truth, defensively claiming that they can be made to 'do there [their] office' if the reader actively exercises his own ingenuity in order to 'find better reasons against them' (E. M. Simpson 1948: 316).

In trying to understand the risky dynamic that Donne takes communication to be, it may be a mistake to separate out reader and author. Even where he appears to single out the reader or the author as the party in the circuit of communication most prone to inflict injury, he is almost invariably anatomizing a two-way interaction that can, in surprising ways, expose the vulnerability of both parties. Here Donne's signature term 'misinterpretable'—the adjective rather than the noun 'misinterpretation'—may be a key for locating the potential for risk, where Mikhail Bakhtin located all discourse, at the boundary between self and other (Bakhtin 293). In Donne's critical commentaries on specific writings, the term 'misinterpretable' often seems to hover or pass between the writer and the reader, with responsibility shifting, neither definitively assigned to the fault or contrivance of the writer nor to the malice or misapprehension of the reader. This reciprocal susceptibility to risk is highlighted in the 'Advertisement to the Reader' that Donne includes in his *Pseudo-Martyr*, his entry into printed controversy in 1610 to support King James's policy by making a public argument that English Catholics 'may and ought to take the Oath of *Allegeance*'. The reason Donne gives for including an address to the reader at the outset of the work is that '*both he, and I*, may suffer some disadvantages, if he should not be fore-possessed, and warned in some things' (*Pseudo-Martyr* 8, emphasis added). To modern ears, the instructions that immediately follow, associating inadequate copy-editing with perilous danger to readers, may sound melodramatic: 'I must first intreat him, that he will be pleased, before hee reade, to amend with his pen, some of the most important errors, which are hereafter noted to have passed in the printing. Because in the Reading, he will not perchance suspect nor spy them, and so *he may runne a danger, of being either deceived, or scandalized*' (8, emphasis added). Yet it seems that Donne is entirely serious. Indeed, two of the main dangers or promptings to misinterpretation, which he tries to disarm by forewarning readers, are also ones he had condemned in a Letter to Goodere attacking Bishop Barlow's previous defence of the Oath of Allegiance: that 'Book is full of falsifications in words, and in sense', he claimed, and of 'miscitings, or mis-interpretings' (*Letters* 163, 161). Lest he as author likewise run a danger from the malice of those who, like the perverse 'Decipherer' of familiar letters, 'can spy out falsifyings in every citation' (*Pseudo-Martyr* 10), Donne forearms the reader and defends against injurious 'mis-interpretings', explaining his procedures in citing other authors: he sometimes summarizes, he claims, and sometimes cites 'Catholique Authors, out of their owne fellowes', but he 'no where ma[kes] any Author, speake more or lesse, in sense, then hee intended, to that purpose, for which I cite him' (10).

Here Donne seems to be working hard to tie meaning down, to disallow his own words anything resembling the play of signification for which twentieth-century readers have valued his language, especially in his poetry. The 'Preface' that follows the address to the general reader, addressed 'to The Priestes, and Jesuits, and to their Disciples in this Kingdome' (11), is, though in a different key, also dedicated to negotiating a mutual relation between author and reader that turns on fixing intentions in order to disarm fear of mutual injury. He offers an explanation of his early life in order to forearm against injury from those of the Roman religion who would 'put me into their danger' through 'rigid and severe' censure (12). He registers his recognition of how 'open to many mis-interpretations' (13) might have been his own irresolution and delay in declaring his religious position. Donne's procedures here are fascinating and complex, for he opens up his own vulnerability and sense of the risk in his present communication. He also opens up an account of how vulnerable both he and some of his Catholic readers were in past communications of the kind in which, he claims, '*Jesuits* and other *Confessors*' could 'bewitch by faire words, and...praise a man to death' (24), drawing men with a strong charm to the attractions of potential martyrdom. Exposing this shared vulnerability to dangers greater than either author or reader will meet in this misinterpretable treatise, to 'un-evitable dangers', even 'to be their owne executioners' (29), Donne works to disarm the Catholic reader's justifiable fear of potential harm from this author of *Pseudo-Martyr*: 'Thus much I was willing to permit, to awaken you...to a just love of your own safetie...and to acquaint you so farre, with my disposition and temper, as that you neede not be afraid to read my poore writings' (28).

To some extent, the case of *Pseudo-Martyr* is uncharacteristic, in that Donne writes this controversial prose work for print publication to a wide and many-minded audience and aims to communicate across a vast gulf or religious divide. This may make it an extreme case, but it nonetheless illustrates clearly how Donne construes interpretation as a dialogic encounter of writer and reader who must struggle to build trust and to negotiate the reciprocal dangers of 'misinterpretable' words. Despite this seemingly pessimistic view of communication, Donne is clearly committed to social conversation and the dialogic encounters of writing, or what, in *Pseudo-Martyr*, he calls the 'Offices of societie' (27; Wollman). Clearly he places a high value on the fraught negotiations of writer and reader, and he understands both textual meaning and personal identity to be significantly shaped in dialogic interaction, on the boundary of self and other.

Do Donne's own comments on the reciprocal risks of interpretation offer guidance to twenty-first-century readers of his prose or verse? When Donne instructs anticipated readers, he hardly imagines a four-century remove from the immediate moment and contextual circumstances that gave rise to his words. Donne cannot 'runne a danger' in the fullest sense he imagined from our misreadings; neither can whatever dangers we as readers run be precisely those that he imagined. Our contemporary readings of Donne are necessarily conditioned by our separate cultural frameworks, and we as readers are responsible for negotiating a new kind of relationship. To grasp the full complexity of his writings, however, it is imperative that we understand how apprehension of danger conditioned their production. Furthermore, while works like *Pseudo-Martyr* show Donne at his most earnest about the dangers of 'misinterpretable' discourse, we need to be alert to how he used this signature word across a range of contexts. This is especially true today, since modern-day readings of his poetry almost invariably exploit and celebrate the potential of his writings for ambiguity and multiple meanings. His soaring literary reputation in the twentieth century was grounded upon this openness of his language to a plurality of meanings, upon a positive understanding of its 'misinterpretable' words. The free play it afforded to the inventiveness of readers was celebrated as a chief delight, offering professors of literature trained in the New Criticism occasions for bravura classroom performances of their own ingenious interpretations and providing open-ended training vehicles for their students. Could this *jouissance* or liberating joy in free textual play be a counterpart to the dangers in 'misinterpretable' words that Donne would himself have recognized and valued? Or does it make modern-day readers 'perverse intelligencers' or 'prophane misinterpreters' of his words? Writing in 1607 to his friend and benefactress, Mrs Magdalen Herbert, in the course of a correspondence that combines serious theological reflections and amicable teasing, Donne asserted, 'I am to my letters as rigid as a Puritan, as Cæsar was to his wife. I can as ill endure a suspicion and misinterpretable word as a fault' (Gosse 1.165). One thing is clear, as we puzzle over this 'seuere / Sentence' (*Variorum* 2, *ElBrac* l. 18) and ask whether he was in earnest or jest: that Donne's word 'misinterpretable' is itself teasingly misinterpretable. However seriously Donne took the dangers of 'misinterpretable' words, he also made them his chief poetic resource.

BIBLIOGRAPHY

Manuscript sources

Roman Archives of the Jesuits (ARSI)

Anglia 30/I	Correspondence (English Jesuit Mission)
Gallia 92	Correspondence (French Jesuit Mission)
Germ.134/I	Correspondence (German Jesuit Mission)
Germ. Sup. I	Correspondence (German Jesuit Mission); supplement
Neap. 4/II	Correspondence (Neapolitan Jesuit Mission)

Bibliothèque Nationale, Paris (BN)

Fonds Français 15989	Correspondence and papers relating to the French ambassador in London in the early 1620s

Bodleian Library, Oxford (Bodleian)

MS Carte 77	Huntingdon papers
MS Eng. poet. e. 112	Early seventeenth-century verse and prose by various authors
MS e Musaeo 131	Sir Edward Herbert's copy of *Biathanatos* with Donne's autograph corrections
MS Rawlinson 146B	Collections of Richard Rawlinson (1690–1755)
MS Rawlinson D.406	Collections of Richard Rawlinson (1690–1755)
MS Rawlinson poetry 61	Collections of Richard Rawlinson (1690–1755)
MS Tanner 79	Collections of Thomas Tanner (1674–1735)
MS Tanner 306	Collections of Thomas Tanner (1674–1735)

British Library, London (BL)

MS Additional 20065	Court Sermons of Robert Skinner, 1613–41
MS Additional 27962 B	Papers of Tuscan envoys in England, 1616–91
MS Additional 33936	Letters of Peter Moreton, secretary to Sir Isaac Wake

MS Additional 36444	Correspondence of Walter Aston, first Baron Aston, while ambassador to Spain
MS Additional 46410	Collections of Sir Robert Cotton, Courts of Chancery and Requests
MS Additional 72407	Trumbull Papers
MS Additional 72242	Trumbull Papers
MS Additional 72396	Trumbull Papers
MS Additional 78423	Evelyn Papers: Sir Samuel Tuke commonplace book, c. 1655
MS Additional 81592	Robert Devereux, 2nd Earl of Essex: letter to an unnamed nobleman
MS Cotton Caligula C VI–C VIII	Privy Council Scottish correspondence, 1580–85
MS Cotton Cleopatra F. vii	Collectanea de precedentia regum Angliae Franciae, et Hispaniae
MS Cotton Julius C. III./153	Collection of Letters to Sir Robert Cotton
MS Egerton 2594	Carlisle correspondence
MS Harleian 4955	Manuscript of Donne's poems, probably copied for Sir William Cavendish, 1st Duke of Newcastle, c.1630
MS Kings 123	Transcripts of French state papers
MS Royal 17.B.XX	John Donne's Sermon on Lamentations iv. 20
MS Royal 17.B.L	Letter from Egerton to Essex
MS Stowe 173	Papers of Sir Thomas Edmondes
MS Stowe 175	Papers of Sir Thomas Edmondes
MS Stowe 962	Collection of early Stuart poetry

Cambridge University Library (CUL)

MS Plans.759a	Map of Pyrford

Canterbury Cathedral (CC)

U210/2/2	*Biathanatos* manuscript

Derbyshire Record Office (DRO)

MS D258/7/13/6 (vi)	Gell Family Papers

Durham University Library (DUL)

Cosin Library, C.II.5	John Cosin's annotated copy of Donne's *LXXX Sermons*

Folger Shakespeare Library, Washington, DC (FSL)

MS L.b.548-50	Loseley Papers

MS V. a. 241	Composite quarto manuscript containing Donne's *Metem*, six dialogues attributed to Lucian, and a brief fable entitled 'The Tale of the Fauorite'
MS V. b. 41	Contemporary account of the York House hearing of the Earl of Essex (fos. 287–90)

Inner Temple (IT)

MS 538, vol. 43	Composite volume of 480 folios with miscellaneous items by authors such as Mary Sidney

Guildhall Library (GL)

MS CF56	John Donne to Sir Henry Goodere, 23 February 1602 and 17 July 1613; and John Donne to Lady [Nethersole?], 1 February 1624
MS 9532/2	Ordinations Register for the Diocese of London, 1578–1628

Hatfield

MSS Salisbury 107/136	Letter from Gilbert Talbot to Robert Cecil

Lambeth Palace Library (LPL)

MS 659	Papers of Anthony Bacon
MS 1730	Archbishop Abbot's Account Book, 1614–23

Leicestershire Record Office (LRO)

MS Finch DG. 7, Lit. 2	Burley manuscript

Lincoln's Inn (LI)

A1d1/3	Saunderson papers

Rosenbach Museum & Library, Philadelphia (RML)

MS 239/22	Verse miscellany prepared *c.*1634

Surrey History Centre (SHC)

LM/348/178	Papers of the Mores of Loseley
LM/COR/3/106	Papers of the Mores of Loseley
6729/7/122	Papers of the Mores of Loseley

The National Archives (TNA)
[formerly the Public Record Office (PRO)]

E 101/255/16	Exchequer, accounts various
PRO 31/3	Baschet transcripts
SP 12	State Papers Domestic Elizabeth I
SP 14	State Papers Domestic James I
SP 16	State Papers Domestic, Charles I
SP 38	Signet Office: Docquets
SP 63	State Papers Ireland
SP 77	State Papers Flanders
SP 78	State Papers France
SP 81	State Papers Germany
SP 84	State Papers Netherlands
SP 94	State Papers Spain
SP 105/95	Letterbook of Sir Dudley Carleton, 1616–18

Trinity College Cambridge (TCC)

MS B 15.13   S. Brooke treatise on predestination

University of Birmingham Library, Birmingham (UB)

Shapiro papers

Warwickshire Record Office (WRO)

Devereux Letter Book

Published sources

Abbot, G. (1622). *Directions concerning Preachers*. London.
Acts of the Privy Council of England (1890–1907). J. R. Dasent (ed). 32 vols. London: HM Stationery Office. (*APC*)
Adams, J. (1699). *An Essay Concerning Self-Murther*. London.
Adams, S. (1973). 'The Protestant Cause: Religious Alliance with the West European Calvinist Communities as a Political Issue in England, 1585–1630'. Unpublished DPhil. thesis, Oxford University.
—— (1978). 'Foreign Policy and the Parliaments of 1621 and 1624', in K. Sharpe (ed.), *Faction and Parliament: Essays on Early Stuart History*. Oxford: Clarendon Press, 139–71.

—— (1998). 'The Decision to Intervene: England and the United Provinces, 1584–1585', in J. M. Millan (ed.), *Felipe II (1527–1598): Europa y la Monarquia Catolica*, vol. 1. Madrid: Parteluz, 19–31.

—— (2002). *Leicester and the Court: Essays on Elizabethan Politics*. Manchester: Manchester University Press.

ADLINGTON, H. (2008a). 'Donne and Diplomacy', in J. Shami (ed.), *Renaissance Tropologies: The Cultural Imagination of Early Modern England*. Pittsburgh: Duquesne, 187–216.

—— (2008b). '"No Rule of our Belief"? John Donne and Canon Law', in J. F. van Dijkhuizen and R. Todd (eds.), *The Reformation Unsettled: British Literature and the Question of Religious Identity, 1560–1660*. Turnhout, Belgium: Brepols, 45–57.

AERS, D. and G. KRESS (1978). '"Darke Texts Need Notes": Versions of Self in Donne's Verse Epistles'. *Literature and History*, 8/2 : 138–58.

—— —— (1981). 'Vexatious Contraries: A Reading of Donne's Poetry', in D. Aers, B. Hodge, and G. Kress, *Literature, Language and Society in England, 1580–1680*. Dublin: Gill & Macmillan; Totowa, NJ: Barnes & Noble, 49–74.

AGRIPPA, C. (1542). *A Treatise of the Nobilitie and Excellencie of Womankynde*. London.

AIKIN, L. (1822). *Memoirs of the Court of King James the First*. 2 vols. 2nd edn. London: Printed for Longman, Hurst, Rees, Orme, & Brown.

ALBRECHT, R. (2005). *The Virgin Mary as Alchemical and Lullian Reference in Donne*. Selinsgrove, Pa.: Susquehanna University Press.

ALEXANDER, M. (2000). 'Pyrford, Pyrford Place, and Queen Elizabeth's Summerhouse'. *John Donne Journal*, 19: 339–60.

ALONSO, J. C. (1996). 'Two Examples of Poetic Parallelism between John Donne and Lope de Vega'. *Sederi*, 6: 21–8.

—— (1999). 'Donne's Holy Sonnet I and Alciato's Emblem CXXI'. *Sederi*, 9: 91–122.

ANDERSON, W. S. (1964). 'Anger in Juvenal and Seneca'. *California Publications in Classical Philology*, 19/3: 127–95.

ANDREWS, K. R. (1972). *The Last Voyage of Drake and Hawkins*. Cambridge: Hakluyt Society, 2nd ser., 142.

ANEAU, B. (1990). *Le Quintil horacien*, in F. Goyet (ed.), *Traités de poétique et de rhétorique de la Renaissance*. Paris: Librairie Générale Française, 175–218.

ANON. (1570). *An Homelie against Disobedience and Wylfull Rebellion*. London.

—— (1606). *A true and perfect relation of the whole proceedings against the late most barbarous Traitors*. London.

—— (1617). *La Déscente des Anglais pour le secours des Princes, empêchés par le Marquis de Spinola; ensemble ce quis'est passé à La Rochelle sur ce sujet*. Paris.

—— (1752). *Satyre menippée de la vertu du Catholicon d'Espagne, et de la tenue des états de Paris...*, vol. 1. Ratisbon: Kerner.

—— (1861). 'Donne the Metaphysician'. *Temple Bar*, 3: 78–91.

—— (1899a). Review of Edmund Gosse, *The Life and Letters of John Donne*. *Athenaeum* (11 Nov.): 645–6.

—— (1899b). Review of Edmund Gosse, *The Life and Letters of John Donne*. *Athenaeum* (25 Nov.): 723.

—— (1935). *Dicta Catonis*, in J. W. Duff and A. M. Duff (eds.), *Minor Latin Poets*. Cambridge, Mass.: Harvard University Press, 592–639.

ARISTOTLE (1984). *The Complete Works of Aristotle: The Revised Oxford Translation*, ed. J. Barnes. 2 vols. Princeton: Princeton University Press.
ARMSTRONG, A. (1977). 'The Apprenticeship of John Donne: Ovid and the *Elegies*'. *English Literary History*, 44/3: 419–42.
ARNOLD, T. (1862). *A Manual of English Literature, Historical and Critical*. London: Longmans & Green.
ASCHAM, R. (1570). *The Scholemaster*. London.
ATHERTON, I. (1999). *Ambition and Failure in Stuart England: The Career of John, First Viscount Scudamore*. Manchester: Manchester University Press.
—— and J. SANDERS (eds.) (2006). *The 1630s: Interdisciplinary Essays on Culture and Politics in the Caroline Era*. Manchester: Manchester University Press.
AUBERLEN, E. (1984). 'Love Poetry', in J. O. Fichte, H. Ludwig, and A. Weber (eds.), *The Commonwealth of Wit: The Writer's Image and his Strategies of Self-Representation in Elizabethan Literature*. Tübingen: Gunter Narr Verlag, 34–9.
AUGUSTINE (1998). *The City of God against the Pagans*, trans. R. W. Dyson. Cambridge: Cambridge University Press.
AUSONIUS (1991). *Parentalia*, in R. P. H. Green (ed.), *The Works of Ausonius*. Oxford: Clarendon Press, 25–41.
AVELING, H. (1963). 'The Marriages of Catholic Recusants, 1559–1642'. *Journal of Ecclesiastical History*, 14/1: 68–83.
AXTON, M. (1977). *The Queen's Two Bodies: Drama and the Elizabethan Succession*. London: Royal Historical Society.
BACHRACH, A. G. H. (1976). 'Constantijn Huygens's Acquaintance with Donne: A Note on Evidence and Conjecture', in J. P. Gombert and M. J. M. ed Haan (eds.), *Litterae textuales: Essays Presented to G. I. Liftinck*, 3: 111–17.
BACON, F. (1625). *The Essayes or Covnsels, Civill and Morall, of Francis Lo. Verulam, Viscovnt St. Alban*. London.
—— (1904). *Bacon's essaies; being a facsimile reprint of the first edition*. New York: Dodd, Mead, and Company.
—— (1826). *The Works of Francis Bacon*. 10 vols. London: C. and J. Rivington, *et al.*
—— (1857–74). *The Works of Francis Bacon*, ed. J. Spedding, R. L. Ellis, and D. D. Heath. 14 vols. London: Longmans.
BACON, J. C. (2003). *The Private Correspondence of Jane Lady Cornwallis Bacon, 1613–1644*, ed. J. Moody. Madison, NJ: Fairleigh Dickinson University Press.
BADDELEY, R. and J. NAYLOR (1669). *The Life of Dr Thomas Morton, late Bishop of Duresme*. York.
BAKER, R. (1643). *A Chronicle of the Kings of England*... London.
BAKHTIN, M. M. (1981). 'Discourse in the Novel', in M. Holquist (trans.), C. Emerson and M. Holquist (eds.), *The Dialogic Imagination: Four Essays*. Austin, Tex.: University of Texas Press, 259–422.
BALD, R. C. (1959). *Donne and the Drurys*. Cambridge: Cambridge University Press.
—— (1964). 'A Latin Version of Donne's Problems'. *Modern Philology*, 61/3: 198–203.
—— (1965). 'Dr. Donne and the Booksellers'. *Studies in Bibliography*, 18: 69–80.
—— (1970). *John Donne: A Life*. Oxford: Clarendon Press.
—— (1986). *John Donne: A Life*. rev. edn. Oxford: Clarendon Press.

BALLESTEROS, A. (1998). '"The Rest is Silence": Absent Voices in John Donne's Songs and Sonnets'. *Sederi*, 8: 59–64.

BANG, W. (1907). 'Acta Anglo-Lovaniensia'. *Englische Studien*, 38: 234–50.

BARFOOT, C. C. and R. TODD (eds.) (1992). *The Great Emporium: The Low Countries as a Cultural Crossroads in the Renaissance and the Eighteenth Century*. Amsterdam: Rodopi.

BARISH, J. (ed.) (1965). *Ben Jonson: Sejanus*. New Haven: Yale University Press.

BARLOW, W. (1601). *A defence of the articles of the Protestants religion*. London.

—— (1609). *An Answer to a Catholike English-man*. London.

BARROLL, L. (2001). *Anna of Denmark, Queen of England: A Cultural Biography*. Philadelphia: University of Pennsylvania.

BARROW, H. (1591). *A Plaine Refutation of M. G. Giffardes Reprochful Booke*. n.p. [Dort].

—— (1962). *The Writings of Henry Barrow 1587–1590*, ed. L. H. Carlson. Elizabethan Nonconformist Texts, 3. London.

BAUMLIN, J. S. (1986). 'Generic Contexts of Elizabethan Satire: Rhetoric, Poetic Theory, and Imitation', in B. K. Lewalski (ed.), *Renaissance Genres: Essays on Theory, History, and Interpretation*. Cambridge, Mass.: Harvard University Press, 444–67.

—— (1991). *John Donne and the Rhetorics of Renaissance Discourse*. Columbia, Mo.: University of Missouri Press.

BAWCUTT, N. W. and H. KELLIHER (1995). 'Donne Through Contemporary Eyes: New Light on his Participation in the Convocation of 1626'. *Notes and Queries*, NS 42/4 (Dec.): 441–4.

BEAL, P. (1980). *Index of English Literary Manuscripts*, vol. 1, pt. 1. London: Mansell; New York: Bowker.

—— (1998). *In Praise of Scribes: Manuscripts and their Makers in Seventeenth-Century England*. Oxford: Clarendon Press.

—— (2002). 'John Donne and the Circulation of Manuscripts', in J. Barnard and D. F. McKenzie with M. Bell (eds.), *The Cambridge History of the Book*, vol. 4: *1557–1695*. Cambridge: Cambridge University Press, 122–26.

—— (2008). *A Dictionary of English Manuscript Terminology, 1450–2000*. Oxford: Oxford University Press.

BEALES, A. C. F. (1963). *Education under Penalty: English Catholic Education from the Reformation to the Fall of James II, 1547–1689*. London: Athlone Press.

BEATY, N. L. (1970). *The Craft of Dying: A Study in the Literary Tradition of the 'Ars Moriendi' in England*. New Haven: Yale University Press.

BEAUMONT, F. and J. FLETCHER (1982). *The Dramatic Works in the Beaumont and Fletcher Canon*, gen. ed. Fredson Bowers. Cambridge: Cambridge University Press.

BEDFORD, R. D. (1982). 'Ovid Metamorphosed: Donne's "Elegy XVI"'. *Essays in Criticism*, 32/3: 219–36.

BEECHING, H. C. (1902). *Religio Laici: A Series of Studies Addressed to Laymen*. London: Smith, Elder.

BELL, I. (1983). 'The Role of the Lady in Donne's *Songs and Sonets*'. *Studies in English Literature*, 23/1: 113–29.

—— (1986). '"Under Ye Rage of a Hott Sonn & Yr Eyes": John Donne's Love Letters to Ann More', in C. J. Summers and T-L. Pebworth (eds.), *The Eagle and the Dove: Reassessing John Donne*. Columbia, Mo.: University of Missouri Press, 25–52.

—— (1996). '"if it be a shee": The Riddle of Donne's "Curse"', in M. T. Hester (ed.), *John Donne's 'desire of more': The Subject of Anne More Donne in His Poetry*. Newark: University of Delaware Press, 106–39.

—— (1997). 'Women in the Lyric Dialogue of Courtship: Whitney's "Admonition to al yong Gentilwomen" and Donne's "The Legacie"', in C. J. Summers and T-L. Pebworth (eds.), *Representing Women in Renaissance England*. Columbia, Mo.: University of Missouri Press, 76–92.

—— (2000). 'Courting Anne More'. *John Donne Journal*, 19: 59–86.

—— (2006a). 'Gender Matters: The Women in Donne's Poems', in A. Guibbory (ed.), *The Cambridge Companion to John Donne*. Cambridge: Cambridge University Press, 201–16.

—— (2006b). 'Introduction', in *John Donne: Selected Poems*. London: Penguin Classics, xix–xxxvi.

BELL, R. (1839). *Lives of the Most Eminent Literary and Scientific Men of Great Britain*, vol. 1. London: Longman.

BELLANY, A. (2002). *The Politics of Court Scandal in Early Modern England: News Culture and the Overbury Affair, 1603–1660*. Cambridge: Cambridge University Press.

—— (2007a). 'The Embarrassment of Libels: Perceptions and Representations of Verse Libelling in Early Stuart England', in P. Lake and S. Pincus (eds.), *The Politics of the Public Sphere in Early Modern England*. Manchester: Manchester University Press, 144–67.

—— (2007b). 'Railing Rhymes Revisited: Libels, Scandals, and Early Stuart Politics'. *History Compass*, 5/4: 1136–79.

—— and A. MCRAE (eds.) (2005). 'Early Stuart Libels: An Edition of Poetry from Manuscript Sources'. *Early Modern Literary Studies*, Text Series 1 <http://purl.oclc.org/emls/texts/libels/>.

BENNETT, A. L. (1954). 'The Principal Rhetorical Conventions in the Renaissance Personal Elegy'. *Studies in Philology*, 51/2: 107–26.

BENNETT, J. (1938; rprt. 1962). 'The Love Poetry of John Donne: A Reply to Mr. C. S. Lewis', in *Seventeenth Century Studies Presented to Sir Herbert Grierson*. Oxford: Clarendon Press, 85–104; rprt. in W. R. Keast (ed.), *Seventeenth Century English Poetry: Modern Essays in Criticism*. New York: Oxford University Press, 111–31.

BENNETT, R. E. (1933). 'The Addition to Donne's *Catalogus Librorum*': *Modern Language Notes*, 48/3: 167–8.

—— (1937). 'Walton's Use of Donne's Letters'. *Philological Quarterly*, 16: 30–4.

—— (1939). 'John Donne and Everard Gilpin'. *Review of English Studies*, 15/57: 66–72.

—— (1940). 'Donne's Letters from the Continent in 1611–12'. *Philological Quarterly*, 19: 66–78.

—— (1941). 'Donne's *Letters to Severall Persons of Honour*'. *Publications of the Modern Language Association*, 56/1: 120–40.

—— (1942). 'John Donne and the Earl of Essex'. *Modern Language Quarterly*, 3/4: 603–4.

BEREZKIVA, V. I. (1984). 'Iz istorii zhanra esse v angliskoi literature XVII veka' [From the History of the Essay Genre in Seventeenth-Century English Literature]. *Sovetskaia nauka*, 6: 24–30.

BERRY, L. E. (ed.) (1969). *The Geneva Bible: A Facsimile of the 1560 Edition*. Madison, Wisc.: University of Wisconsin Press.

BEVAN, J. (1994). 'Hebdomada Mortium: The Structure of Donne's Last Sermon'. *Review of English Studies*, 45/178: 185–203.

BIRCH, T. (ed.) (1749). *Historical View of the Negotiations between England, France, and Brussels from the Year 1592 to 1617*. London.

—— (ed.) (1848). *Court and Times of James I*. 2 vols. London: Henry Colburn.

BLACKLEY, B. M. (1994). 'The Generic Play and Spenserian Parody of John Donne's "Metempsychosis"'. Unpublished Ph.D dissertation, University of Kentucky.

BLANCHARD, W. S. (1995). *Scholars' Bedlam: Menippean Satire in the Renaissance*. Lewisburg Pa.: Bucknell University Press.

BLAND, M. (2008). Unpublished lecture. John Donne Society, February, Baton Rouge, La.

BLOUNT, C. (1680). *The Two First Books of Philostratus*. London.
BLOUNT, T. (1656). *Glossographia*. London.
BOASE, C. W. and A. CLARK (eds.) (1884–9). *Register of the University of Oxford*. 5 vols. Oxford: Clarendon Press.
BODIN, J. (1606). *The Six Bookes of a Common-Weale*. London.
BØGH, K. (1979/80). 'Domprovsten, der Lovpriste Selvmord: John Donne og hans Danske Angribere fra 1675' [The Dean Who Praised Suicide: John Donne and his Danish Attackers]. *Fund og forskning*, 24: 93–118.
BOOTY, J. E. (ed.) (2005). *The Book of Common Prayer, 1559: The Elizabethan Prayer Book*. Charlottesville and London: University of Virginia Press/The Folger Shakespeare Library.
BOSSY, J. (1975). *The English Catholic Community, 1570–1850*. London: Darton, Longman & Todd.
—— (1985). *Christianity in the West 1400–1700*. Oxford: Oxford University Press.
—— (1998). *Peace in the Post-Reformation*. Cambridge: Cambridge University Press.
—— (2007). 'The Heart of Robert Persons', in T. M. McCoog (ed.), *The Reckoned Expense: Edmund Campion and the Early English Jesuits*. Rome: Institutum Historicum Societatis Iesu, 187–208.
BOURDIEU, P. (1977). 'The Economics of Linguistic Exchanges', trans. R. Nice. *Social Science Information*, 16/6: 645–68.
BOUWSMA, W. J. (1968). *Venice and the Defense of Republican Liberty: Renaissance Values in the Age of the Counter Reformation*. Berkeley: University of California Press.
BOWEN, C. D. (1957). *The Lion and the Throne: The Life and Times of Sir Edward Coke, 1552–1634*. Boston: Little, Brown & Co.
BOYCE, B. (1943). 'News from Hell: Satiric Communications with the Nether World in English Writing of the Seventeenth and Eighteenth Centuries'. *Publications of the Modern Language Association*, 58/2: 402–37.
BRAUNMULLER, A. R. (1991). 'Robert Carr, Earl of Somerset, as Collector and Patron', in L. L. Peck (ed.), *The Mental World of the Jacobean Court*. Cambridge: Cambridge University Press, 230–50.
BRAY, G. L. (ed.) (2005–6). *Records of Convocation*. 20 vols. Woodbridge, Suffolk: The Boydell Press in association with the Church of England Record Society.
'BRERELEY, J'. (*vere* J. ANDERTON) (1604). *The Apologie of the Romane Church*. n.p.
BRETON, N. (1615). *Characters upon Essaies Morall, and Divine*. London.
BROOKS, C. (1947; rprt. 1968). *The Well Wrought Urn: Studies in the Structure of Poetry*. London: Dennis Dobson.
BROOKS, H. B. (2007). 'A "Re-Vision" of Donne: Adrienne Rich's "A Valediction Forbidding Mourning"'. *John Donne Journal*, 26: 333–62.
[BROUGHTON, R.]. (1606). *A Iust and Moderate Answer, to a most Iniurious, and Slaunderous pamphlet*. [England, secret Catholic press].
—— (1607). *The First Part of Protestant Proofes, for Catholikes Religion and Recusancy*. [England, secret Catholic press].
BROWN, M. L. (1992). '"Though it be not according to the law": Donne's Politics and the Sermon on Esther'. *John Donne Journal*, 11/1–2: 71–84.
BROWN, P. (2008). '"Hac ex consilio meo via progredieris": Courtly Reading and Secretarial Mediation in Donne's *The Courtier's Library*'. *Renaissance Quarterly*, 61/3: 833–66.
—— (2009). 'Donne and the *Sidereus Nuncius*: Astronomy, Method and Metaphor in 1611'. Unpublished Ph.D dissertation, University of Toronto.
BROWNING, R. and E. B. BROWNING (1969). *The Letters of Robert Browning and Elizabeth Barrett Browning 1845–1846*, ed. E. Kintner. 2 vols. Cambridge, Mass.: Belknap Press.
BRYSON, A. (1998). *From Courtesy to Civility: Changing Codes of Conduct in Early Modern England*. Oxford: Oxford University Press.

BURGESS, G. (1996). *Absolute Monarchy and the Stuart Constitution*. New Haven: Yale University Press.
BURGESS, T. (1902). *Epideictic Literature*. Chicago: University of Chicago Press.
BURROW, C. (1993). 'Horace at Home and Abroad: Wyatt and Sixteenth-Century Horatianism', in C. Martindale and D. Hopkins (eds.), *Horace Made New: Horatian Influences on British Writing from the Renaissance to the Twentieth Century*. Cambridge: Cambridge University Press, 27–49.
BURTON, F. (1611). *The Fierie Triall of Gods Saints*. London.
BYATT, A. S. (1990). *Possession: A Romance*. London: Chatto & Windus.
Cabala, mysteries of state, in letters of the great ministers of K. James and K. Charles. (1654a). London.
Cabala, sive, Scrinia sacra: mysteries of state & government. (1654b). London.
CAIN, T. (2001). 'John Donne and the Ideology of Colonization'. *English Literary Renaissance*, 31/3: 440–76.
—— (2004). 'Elegy and Autobiography: "The Bracelet" and the Death of Henry Donne'. *John Donne Journal*, 23: 25–57.
—— (2006). 'Donne's Political World', in A. Guibbory (ed.), *The Cambridge Companion to John Donne*. Cambridge: Cambridge University Press, 83–99.
Calendar of Letters and State Papers Relating to English Affairs: Preserved Principally in the Archives of Simancas (1892–9). M. A. S. Hume (ed.). 4 vols. London: HM Stationery Office. (*CLSP Simancas*)
Calendar of Patent Rolls Preserved in the Public Record Office: Philip and Mary, 1553–58 (1936–9). M. S. Giuseppi (ed.). 4 vols. London: HM Stationery Office. (*CPR Philip and Mary*)
Calendar of State Papers, Domestic Series, Of The Reign of James I. 1611–18. (1858). M. A. E. Green (ed.). London. (*CSPD*)
Calendar of State Papers and Manuscripts, Relating to English Affairs, Existing in the Archives and Collections of Venice (1864–). 38 vols. London: HM Stationery Office. (*CSPV*)
CAMDEN, W. (1635). *Annals or the History of the most Renowned and victorious Princesse Elizabeth*, trans. R. Norton. London.
—— (1657). *Remaines Concerning Britain*. London.
CAMERON, A. B. (1976). 'Donne's Deliberative Verse Epistles'. *English Literary Renaissance*, 6/3: 369–403.
CAMPBELL, L. B. (1959). *Divine Poetry and Drama in Sixteenth-Century England*. Cambridge; Berkeley: Cambridge University Press and University of California Press.
CAMPION, T. (1909). *Campion's Works*, ed. P. Vivian. Oxford: Clarendon Press.
—— (1595; rprt. 1619). *Thomae Campiani Poemata*. London.
CANNON, J. (1998). 'The Poetry and Polemic of English Church Worship, c.1617–1640'. Unpublished DPhil. thesis, Cambridge University.
CANNY, N. (2001). *Making Ireland British, 1580–1650*. Oxford: Oxford University Press.
CANTELI, M. J. P. (1994). '"The Idea of a Woman and Not As She Was". Some Notes on the Representation of Donne's Elizabeth Drury and Quevedo's Lisi'. *Sederi*, 5: 114–24.
—— (1999). 'Sonnets, Rooms, Tears and Books: The Poetics of Physical Spaces in Donne's Love Poetry'. *Sederi*, 9: 123–8.
CARAMAN, P. (1964). *Henry Garnet 1555–1606, and the Gunpowder Plot*. London: Longmans, Green.
CAREY, J. (1981a). *John Donne: Life, Mind and Art*. London: Faber & Faber.
—— (1981b). 'John Donne's Newsless Letters'. *Essays & Studies*, 34: 45–65.
—— (1990). *John Donne: Life, Mind and Art*. Rev. edn. New York: Oxford University Press.

CARICATO, F. S. (1974). 'John Donne and the Epigram Tradition'. Unpublished Ph.D dissertation, Fordham University.
CARLETON, D. (1972). *Dudley Carleton to John Chamberlain, 1603–1624: Jacobean Letters*, ed. M. Lee, Jr. New Brunswick, NJ: Rutgers University Press.
CARLSON, E. J. (1994). *Marriage and the English Reformation*. Cambridge, Mass.: Blackwell.
CARLTON, C. (1987). *Archbishop William Laud*. London: Routledge & Kegan Paul.
CARPENTER, E. F. (1957). 'The Reformation: 1485–1660', in W. R. Matthews and W. M. Atkins (eds.), *A History of St Paul's Cathedral and the Men Associated with it*. London: Phoenix House Ltd., 100–71.
CARPINELLI, F. (1978). 'Thomas More and the Daunce Family', in M. J. Moore (ed.), *Quincentennial Essays on St. Thomas More: Selected Papers from the Thomas More College Conference*. Boone, NC: Albion, 1–10.
CASTIGLIONE, B. (1561). *The Courtyer of Count Baldessar Castilio diuided into foure bookes. Very necessary and profitable for yonge gentilmen and gentilwomen abiding in court, palaice or place, done into English by Thomas Hoby*. London.
CATHOLIC RECORD SOCIETY (1907). *Miscellanea IV*. Publications of the Catholic Record Society, vol. 4. London: Catholic Record Society. *(CRS)*
—— (1911). *Miscellanea VII*. Publications of the Catholic Record Society, vol. 9. London: Catholic Record Society. *(CRS)*
—— (1942). *Letters and Memorials of Father Robert Persons*, ed. L. Hicks. Publications of the Catholic Record Society, vol. 39. London: Catholic Record Society. *(CRS)*
CATULLUS (1988). *Catullus, Tibullus, and Pervigilium Veneris*, ed. G. P. Goold. Cambridge, Mass.: Harvard University Press.
CAVENDISH, M. (1662). *Playes*. London.
CECIL, R. (1606). *An Answere to Certaine Scandalous Papers*. London.
CECIL, W. (1617). *Certaine precepts or directions, for the well ordering and carriage of a mans life*. London.
CENTERWALL, B. S. (2003). '"Loe her's a Man, worthy indeede to travell": Donne's Panegyric upon *Coryats Crudities*'. *John Donne Journal*, 22: 77–94.
CHADWICK, J. W. (1900). 'John Donne, Poet and Preacher'. *The New World*, 9: 31–48.
CHAMBERLAIN, J. (1939). *Letters of John Chamberlain*, ed. N. McClure. 2 vols. Philadelphia: American Philosophical Society.
CHAMBERLIN, J. S. (1976). *Increase and Multiply: Arts-of-discourse Procedure in the Preaching of Donne*. Chapel Hill, NC: University of North Carolina Press.
CHAMBERS, A. B. (1992). *Transfigured Rites in Seventeenth-Century English Poetry*. Columbia and London: University of Missouri Press.
CHAMBERS, E. K. (1923). *The Elizabethan Stage*. 4 vols. Oxford: Clarendon Press.
CHAMBERS, R. W. (1935). *Thomas More*. London: Jonathan Cape.
[CHARLES I] (1628). *His Maiesties Dclaration [sic] to all his Louing Subiects, of the causes which moued to dissolve the last Parliament*. London.
CHARLES, A. M. (1977). *A Life of George Herbert*. Ithaca, NY: Cornell University Press.
CHOI, Y-S. (1990). 'John Donne eui Anniversaries: Jashin eui segae reul chiyu haryeoneun noryeok' [John Donne's Anniversaries: An attempt to heal the world and himself]. *English Studies* (Seoul National University, Korea), 14: 23–36.
CHRISTIANSON, P. (1985). 'John Selden, the Five Knights' Case, and Discretionary Imprisonment in Early Stuart England'. *Criminal Justice History*, 6: 65–87.
—— (1991). 'Royal and Parliamentary Voices on the Ancient Constitution, c.1604–1621', in L. L. Peck (ed.), *The Mental World of the Jacobean Court*. Cambridge: Cambridge University Press, 71–98.

CICERO (1971). *De Senectute, De Amicitia, De Divinatione*, trans. W. A. Falconer. London: William Heinemann.

CLANCY, T. H. (1964). *Papist Pamphleteers: The Allen–Persons Party, and the Political Thought of the Counter-Reformation in England, 1572–1615*. Chicago: Loyola University Press.

CLIFFORD, A. (1990). *The Diaries of Lady Anne Clifford*, ed. D. J. H. Clifford. Stroud: Alan Sutton Publishing Inc.

CLIVE, M. (1966). *Jack and the Doctor*. London: Macmillan.

COBBETT, W. and T. B. HOWELL. (1809–28). *Cobbett's Complete Collection of State Trials and Proceedings for High Treason and Other Crimes and Misdemeanours from the Earliest Period to the Present Time*, ed. T. J. Howell and D. Jardine. 33 vols. London: R. Bagshaw.

COCKBURN, J. S. (1972). *A History of English Assizes, 1558–1714*. Cambridge: Cambridge University Press.

COFFIN, C. (1937). *John Donne and the New Philosophy*. New York: Columbia University Press.

COGSWELL, T. (1989). *The Blessed Revolution: English Politics and the Coming of War, 1621–1624*. Cambridge: Cambridge University Press.

COIRO, A. B. (1988). *Robert Herrick's* Hesperides *and the Epigram Book Tradition*. Baltimore: Johns Hopkins University Press.

COKE, E. (1826). *The Reports*, ed. J. H. Thomas and J. F. Fraser. 6 vols. London: J. Butterworth.

COLCLOUGH, D. (2005). *Freedom of Speech in Early Stuart England*. Cambridge: Cambridge University Press.

—— (2004). 'John Donne', in H. C. G. Matthew and B. Harrison (eds.), *Oxford Dictionary of National Biography*. 61 vols. Oxford: Oxford University Press, 16.535–45.

—— (2007). 'Donne, John (1572–1631)', *Oxford Dictionary of National Biography*, online edn.

—— (ed.) (2003). *John Donne's Professional Lives*. Cambridge: D. S. Brewer.

COLERIDGE, S. T. (1853). 'Coleridgiana. Mss. Notes of Coleridge in the Books of Charles Lamb, Now for the First Time Published'. *The Literary World*, 30 Apr. 1853: 349–50; 14 May 1853: 393; 28 May 1853: 433.

—— (1836–9). *The Literary Remains of Samuel Taylor Coleridge*, ed. H. N. Coleridge. 3 vols. London: W. Pickering.

—— (1984). *Marginalia II*, ed. G. Whalley. Princeton: Princeton University Press.

COLIE, R. (1966). *Paradoxia Epidemica*. Princeton: Princeton University Press.

—— (1970). *'My Ecchoing Song': Andrew Marvell's Poetry of Criticism*. Princeton: Princeton University Press.

—— (1972). '"All in Peeces": Problems of Interpretation in Donne's *Anniversary* Poems', in P. A. Fiore (ed.), *Just So Much Honor: Essays Commemorating the Four-Hundredth Anniversary of the Birth of John Donne*. University Park and London: Pennsylvania State University Press, 189–218.

—— (1973). *The Resources of Kind: Genre-Theory in the Renaissance*, ed. B. K. Lewalski. Berkeley: University of California Press.

—— (1974). *Shakespeare's Living Art*. Princeton: Princeton University Press.

COLLIER, J. P. (1866). *A Bibliographical and Critical Account of the Rarest Books in the English Language*. 4 vols. New York: Charles Scribner.

—— (ed.) (1840). *The Egerton Papers. A Collection of Public and Private Documents*. London: Camden Society.

COLLINS, S. (2005). 'Bodily Formations and Reading Strategies in John Donne's *Metempsychosis*', in A. Fahraeus and A. Jonsson (eds.), *Textual Ethos Studies, or Locating Ethics*, Critical Studies 26. Amsterdam: Rodopi, 191–207.

COLLINSON, P. (1967). *The Elizabethan Puritan Movement*. London: Cape.

—— (1979). *Archbishop Grindal 1519–1583: The Struggle for a Reformed Church*. London and Berkeley: University of California Press.

—— (1982). *The Religion of Protestants: The Church in English Society, 1559–1625*. Oxford: Clarendon Press.

—— (1994). 'William Shakespeare's Religious Inheritance and Environment', in P. Collinson (ed.), *Elizabethan Essays*. London and Rio Grande: Hambledon, 219–52.

—— (2008). 'Antipuritanism', in J. Coffey and P. C. Lim (eds.), *The Cambridge Companion to Puritanism*. Cambridge: Cambridge University Press, 19–33.

COMBS, H. C. and Z. R. SULLENS (eds.) (1940; rprt. 1970). *A Concordance to the English Poems of John Donne*. Chicago: Packard.

Commons Debates: 1628 (1977). R. C. Johnson (ed.). New Haven and London: Yale University Press. (*Commons*)

CONSIDINE, J. (2008). 'Goodere, Sir Henry (*bap*. 1571, *d*. 1627)', *Oxford Dictionary of National Biography*, online edn.

COOPER, H. (1942). 'John Donne and Virginia in 1610'. *Modern Language Notes*, 57/8: 661–3.

COOPER, R. (1977). 'The Political Implications of Donne's *Devotions*', in G. Stringer (ed.), *New Essays on Donne*. Salzburg: Inst. f. Engl. Sprache u. Literatur, 192–210.

CORBETT, R. (1955). *The Poems of Richard Corbett*, ed. J. A. W. Bennett and H. R. Trevor-Roper. Oxford: Clarendon Press.

CORKINE, W. (1612). *The Second Book of Ayres*. London.

CORNWALLIS, W. (1600). *Essayes*. London.

—— (1946). *Essayes*, ed. D. C. Allen. Baltimore: Johns Hopkins Press.

—— (1977). *The Encomium of Richard III by Sir William Cornwallis the Younger*, ed. A. N. Kincaid; intro. J. A. Ramsden and A. N. Kincaid. London: Turner & Devereux.

CORTHELL, R. (1981). 'Donne's Metempsychosis: An "Alarum to Truth"'. *Studies in English Literature*, 21/1: 97–110.

—— (1982). 'Style and Self in Donne's Satires'. *Texas Studies in Literature and Language*, 24/2: 155–84.

—— (1997). *Ideology and Desire in Renaissance Poetry: The Subject of Donne*. Detroit: Wayne State University Press.

CORYATE, T. (1611). *Coryats crudities; hastily gobled vp in five moneths trauells in France, Sauoy, Italy, Rhetia...* London.

—— (1611). *The Odcombian Banquet: Dished foorth by Thomas the Coriat*. [London].

—— (1616). *Thomas Coriate traveller for the English wits: greeting: from the court of the Grand Mogul, resident at the towne of Asmere, in Easterne India*. London.

COTTON, R. (1651). *Cottoni Posthuma*. London.

COVELL, W. (1603). *A Ivst and Temperate Defence of the five Books of Ecclesiastical Policie Written by M. Richard Hooker*. London.

COWARD, B. (1983). *The Stanleys, Lords Stanley, and Earls of Derby, 1385–1672. The Origins, Wealth and Power of a Landowning Family*. Manchester: Chetham Society.

CRAIK, G. L. (1844–5). *Sketches of the History of Literature and Learning in England*, vol. 3. London: Charles Knight.

—— (1864). *A Compendious History of English Literature and of the English Language*. London: Charles Griffin.

CRAIK, K. A. (2004). 'Reading Coryats Crudities (1611)'. *Studies in English Literature*, 44/1: 77–96.

—— (2007). *Reading Sensations in Early Modern England*. Basingstoke: Palgrave Macmillan.

CRAMSIE, J. (2002). *Kingship and Crown Finance Under James VI and I, 1603–1625*. Woodbridge and Rochester: Royal Historical Society and Boydell Press.

CRANE, M. T. (1986). 'Intret Cato: Authority and the Epigram in Sixteenth-Century England', in B. K. Lewalski (ed.), *Renaissance Genres: Essays on Theory, History, and Interpretation*. Cambridge, Mass.: Harvard University Press, 158–86.

—— (1993). *Framing Authority: Sayings, Self, and Society in Sixteenth-Century England*. Princeton: Princeton University Press.

CRANFIELD, N. W. S. (1996). 'Chaplains in Ordinary at the Early Stuart Court: The Purple Road', in C. Cross (ed.), *Patronage and Recruitment in the Tudor and Early Stuart Church*. Borthwick Studies in History, 2: 120–47.

CRANFIELD, N. W. S. and K. FINCHAM (eds.) (1987). 'John Howson's Answer to Archbishop Abbot's Accusations at his "Trial" Before James I at Greenwich, 10 June 1615'. *Camden Miscellany*, 29 (Camden Society, 4th ser. 34): 319–41.

CRANKSHAW, D. (2004). 'Community, City and Nation, 1540–1714', in D. Keene, A. Burns, and A. Saint (eds.), *St Paul's: The Cathedral Church of London, 604–2004*. New Haven: Yale University Press, 45–70.

CRAWLEY-BOEVEY, A. W. (1896). 'Dr Donne's Memorial Seals'. *Notes and Queries*, 8th ser. 9: 41–3.

CRESSY, D. (1989). *Bonfires and Bells: National Memory and the Protestant Calendar in Elizabethan and Stuart England*. London: Weidenfeld & Nicolson.

—— (1997). *Birth, Marriage, and Death: Ritual, Religion, and the Life-Cycle in Tudor and Stuart England*. Oxford: Oxford University Press.

CROFT, P. (1987). 'Fresh Light on Bate's Case'. *Historical Journal*, 30/3: 523–39.

—— (1991a). 'The Religion of Robert Cecil'. *Historical Journal*, 34/4: 773–96.

—— (1991b). 'The Reputation of Robert Cecil: Libels, Political Opinion and Popular Awareness in the Early Seventeenth Century'. *Transactions of the Royal Historical Society*, 6th ser. 1: 43–69.

—— (1991c). 'Robert Cecil and the Early Jacobean Court', in L. L. Peck (ed.), *The Mental World of the Jacobean Court*. Cambridge: Cambridge University Press, 134–47.

—— (2004d). 'Howard, Thomas, first earl of Suffolk (1561–1626)', *Oxford Dictionary of National Biography*, online edn.

—— (2008). 'Howard, Henry, Earl of Northampton (1540–1614)', *Oxford Dictionary of National Biography*, online edn.

CROWLEY, L. (2007a). 'Cecil and the Soul: Donne's *Metempsychosis* in its Context in Folger Manuscript V. a. 241'. *English Manuscript Studies, 1100–1700*, 13: 47–76.

—— (2007b). 'Manuscript Context and Literary Interpretation: John Donne's Poetry in Seventeenth-Century England'. Unpublished Ph.D dissertation, University of Maryland.

—— (forthcoming). 'Was the Earl of Southampton a Poet? A Verse Letter to Queen Elizabeth'. *English Literary Renaissance*.

CRUM, M. (ed.) (1969). *First-line Index of English Poetry, 1500–1800, in Manuscripts of the Bodleian Library, Oxford*. Oxford: Clarendon Press.

CRUTTWELL, P. (1954). *The Shakespearean Moment and its Place in the Poetry of the 17th Century*. London: Chatto & Windus.

CUDDY, N. (1987). 'The Revival of the Entourage: The Bedchamber of James I, 1603–1625', in D. Starkey (ed.), *The English Court from the Wars of the Roses to the Civil War*. London: Longman, 173–225.

—— (1989). 'Anglo-Scottish Union and the Court of James I, 1603–1625'. *Transactions of the Royal Historical Society*, 5th ser. 39: 107–24.

—— (1993). 'The Conflicting Loyalties of a "vulgar counselor": The Third Earl of Southampton', in J. Morrill, P. Slack, and D. Woolf (eds.), *Public Duty and Private Conscience in Seventeenth-Century England: Essays Presented to G. E. Aylmer*. Oxford: Clarendon Press, 121–50.

CULLER, J. (2008). 'Why Lyric?' *Publications of the Modern Language Association*, 123/1: 201–6.

CUNNINGTON, D. (2003). 'The Profession of Friendship in Donne's Amatory Verse Letters', in D. Colclough (ed.), *John Donne's Professional Lives*. Cambridge: D. S. Brewer, 97–119.

CURIONE, C.(1566?). *Pasquine in a Traunce*, trans. W. P. Seene. London.

CURTIUS, E. R. (1953). *European Literature and the Latin Middle Ages*, trans. W. R. Trask. New York: Pantheon.

CURZON, G. (2003). *Wotton and his Worlds: Spying, Science and Venetian Intrigues*. Philadelphia: Xlibris.

CUST, R. (1987). *The Forced Loan and English Politics, 1626–1628*. Oxford: Oxford University Press.

DALEY, K. (1990). *The Triple Fool: A Critical Evaluation of Constantijn Huygens' Translations of John Donne*. Nieuwkoop: De Graaf Publishers.

—— (1991). '"And Like a Widdow Thus": Donne, Huygens, and the Fall of Heidelberg'. *John Donne Journal*, 10/1-2: 57–69.

DANBY, J. F. (1950). 'Jacobean Absolutists: The Placing of Beaumont and Fletcher'. *Cambridge Journal*, 3: 515–40.

DANDO, J. [Daniel, G.] (1595). *Maroccus Extaticus. Or Bankes Bay Horse in a Trance...Anatomizing some abuses and bad trickes of this age*. London.

DANIEL, G. (1959). 'A Vindication of Poesie', in T. B. Stroup (ed.), *The Selected Poems of George Daniel of Beswick, 1616–1657*. Lexington, Ky.: University of Kentucky Press.

DANIEL, S. (1963). 'Certain Epistles', in *The Complete Works in Verse and Prose of Samuel Daniel*, ed. A. B. Grosart. 5 vols. New York: Russell & Russell, 1.189–219.

DARK, S. (1928). *Five Deans: John Colet, John Donne, Jonathan Swift, Arthur Penrhyn Stanley, William Ralph Inge*. New York: Harcourt, Brace.

DASGUPTA, D. B. (1981–2). '"Death Be Not Proud": An Explication'. *Journal of the Department of English* (Calcutta), 17/1: 84–92.

DAVIDSON, A. (1976). 'An Oxford Family: A Footnote to the Life of John Donne'. *Recusant History*, 13: 299–300.

DAVIES, H. (1970; rprt. 1996). *Worship and Theology in England: From Cranmer to Baxter Fox, 1534–1690*. 2 vols. Grand Rapids, Mich.: William B. Eerdmans.

DAVIES, J. (1656). *The Question Concerning Impositions, Tonnage, Poundage, Prizage, Customs, &c*. London.

DAVIES, S. (1994). *John Donne*. Plymouth: Northcote House.

DAWSON, G. E. and L. KENNEDY-SKIPTON (1966). *Elizabethan Handwriting, 1500–1650: A Manual*. New York: Norton.

DAY, A. (1586). *The English Secretorie. Wherein is contayned, A Perfect Method, for the inditing of all manner of Epistles and familiar Letters*. London.

DEAN, J. S. (1997). 'Politics and Pulpit in John Donne and António Vieira'. *Luso-Brazilian Review*, 34/1: 43–55.

DEKKER, T. (1606). *Newes from hell; Brought by the Diuells Carrier*. London.

DELUMEAU, J. (1971). *Le Catholicisme entre Luther et Voltaire*. Paris: Presses Universitaires de France. (English trans., *Catholicism Between Luther and Voltaire*: London, 1978.)

DENNY, W. (1653). *Pelecanicidium: or the Christian Adviser against Self-Murder*. London.

DeSTEFANO, B. (1984). 'Evolution of Extravagant Praise in Donne's Verse Epistles'. *Studies in Philology*, 81/1: 75–93.

DEVEREUX, R. (1603). *An apologie of the earle of Essex against those which falsly and maliciously taxe him to be the onely hinderer of the peace and quiet of his countrey*. London.
D'EWES, S. (1845). *Autobiography and Correspondence*, ed. J. O. Halliwell Phillipps. 2 vols. London R. Bentley.
—— (1974). *The Diary of Sir Simonds D'Ewes (1622–1624): Journal d'un étudiant londonien sous le règne de Jacques 1ᵉʳ*, ed. E. Bourcier. Paris: Didier.
DICKSON, D. (1987). 'The Complexities of Biblical Typology in the Seventeenth Century'. *Renaissance and Reformation*, 23/3: 253–72.
DIETZ, F. C. (1964). *English Public Finance 1558–1641*. New York: Century Co.
DILLON, A. (2002). *The Construction of Martyrdom in the English Catholic Community, 1535–1603*. Aldershot: Ashgate.
DiPASQUALE, T. (2007). 'Donne's *Epigrams*: A Sequential Reading'. *Modern Philology*, 104/3: 329–78.
—— (2008). *Refiguring the Sacred Feminine: The Poems of John Donne, Aemilia Lanyer, and John Milton*. Pittsburgh: Duquesne University Press.
DOCHERTY, T. (1986). *John Donne, Undone*. London: Methuen.
DODD, A. H. (1938). 'The Spanish Treason, the Gunpowder Plot and the Catholic Refugees'. *English Historical Review*, 53/212: 627–50.
DOERKSEN, D. W. (1997). *Conforming to the Word: Herbert, Donne, and the English Church Before Laud*. Lewisburg, Pa.: Bucknell University Press.
—— (2003). 'Polemist or Pastor? Donne and Moderate Calvinist Conformity', in M. Papazian (ed.), *John Donne and the Protestant Reformation: New Perspectives*. Detroit: Wayne State University Press, 12–34.
—— (2004). 'Discerning God's Voice, God's Hand: Scripturalist Moderation in Donne's *Devotions*', in D. Doerksen and C. Hodgkins (eds.), *Centered on the Word: Literature, Scripture, and the Tudor-Stuart Middle Way*. Newark: University of Delaware Press, 148–72.
DOLABELLA, H. (1609). *Prurit—anus, vel nec omne nec ex omni. Sive apologia pro Puritanis, & nouatoribus vniuersis*, [St Omer]. [The author may have been the priest John Wilson.]
DONNE, J. (1610). *Pseudo-Martyr*. London.
—— (1611a). *Conclave Ignati*. London.
—— (1611b). *Conclave Ignati*. n.p. [Continent].
—— (1611c). *Ignatius His Conclave*. London.
—— (1624). *Devotions upon Emergent Occasions*. London.
—— (1632). *Deaths Duell, or a Consolation to the Soule, against the dying Life, and liuing Death of the Body*. London.
—— (1633a). *Ivvenilia*. London.
—— (1633b). *Poems, by J.D. With Elegies on the Authors Death*. London.
—— (1635). *Poems, by J.D., with Elegies on the Authors Death*. London.
—— (1640). *LXXX Sermons*. London.
—— (1647). *Biathanatos*. London.
—— (1648). *Biathanatos a declaration of that paradoxe or thesis, that selfe-homicide is not so naturally sinne, that it may never be otherwise*. London.
—— (1649). *Fifty Sermons*. London.
—— (1650). *Poems*. London.
—— (1651a). *Essayes in Divinity*. London.
—— (1651b). *Letters to Severall Persons of Honour*, ed. J. Donne, jr. London.
—— (1652[3]). *Paradoxes, Problemes, Essayes, Characters*, ed. J. Donne, jr. London.
—— (1660). *XXVI Sermons*. London.

——(1719). *Poems on Several Occasions, Written by the Reverend John Donne, D.D.*, ed. J. Tonson. London.

——(1779). *The Poetical Works of Dr. John Donne*, ed. J. Bell. Vols. 23–5 of *Bells Edition: The Poets of Great Britain Complete from Chaucer to Churchill*. London.

——(1793). *The Poetical Works of Dr. John Donne*, ed. R. Anderson. London.

——(1810). *The Poems of John Donne, D.D.*, ed. A. Chalmers. Vol. 5 of *The Works of the English Poets, from Chaucer to Cowper*. London: Printed for J. Johnson *et al.*

——(1839). *The Works of John Donne, D.D., Dean of Saint Pauls 1621–1631. With a Memoir of His Life*, ed. H. Alford. 6 vols. London: John W. Parker.

——(1855a). *Essays in Divinity by John Donne D.D.*, ed. A. Jessopp. London: John Tupling.

DONNE, J. (1855b). *The Poetical Works of Dr. John Donne, with a Memoir*, ed. J. R. Lowell. Boston: Little, Brown.

——(1872–3). *The Complete Poems of John Donne*, ed. A. B. Grosart. 2 vols. London: The Fuller Worthies Library.

——(1895). *The Poems of John Donne, from the Text of the Edition of 1633*, ed. C. E. Norton [and M. Burnett]. 2 vols. Rev. by J. R. Lowell. New York: The Grolier Club.

——(1896). *The Poems of John Donne*, ed. E. K. Chambers. 2 vols. London: Lawrence & Bullen.

——(1905). *The Love Poems of John Donne*, ed. C. E. Norton. Boston: Houghton Mifflin.

——(1912). *The Poems of John Donne*, ed. H. J. C. Grierson. 2 vols. London: Oxford University Press.

——(1923a). *Devotions upon Emergent Occasions*, ed. J. Sparrow. Cambridge: Cambridge University Press.

——(1923b). *Paradoxes and Problems by Iohn Donne with two Characters and an Essay of Valour. 1633, 1652*, ed. G. Keynes. Soho: Nonesuch Press.

——(1929a). *John Donne, Dean of St. Paul's: Complete Poetry and Selected Prose*, ed. J. Hayward. London: Nonesuch Press.

——(1929b). *The Poems of John Donne*, ed. H. J. C. Grierson. London: Oxford University Press.

——(1930). *The Courtier's Library*, ed. E. M. Simpson. London: Nonesuch Press. (*Courtier's Library*)

——(1931). *Poems of John Donne*, ed. H. Fausset. London: J. M. Dent.

——(1941). *Complete Poetry and Selected Prose of John Donne and the Complete Poetry of William Blake*, ed. R. Hillyer. New York: Random House.

——(1942). *The Complete Poems of John Donne*, ed. R. E. Bennett. Chicago: Packard.

——(1946). *Complete Poetry and Selected Prose of John Donne*, ed. C. Coffin. New York: Random House.

——(1952a; 2nd edn. 1978). *The Divine Poems*, ed. H. Gardner. Oxford: Clarendon.

——(1952b). *Essays in Divinity*, ed. E. M. Simpson. Oxford: Clarendon Press.

——(1953–62). *The Sermons of John Donne*, ed. G. R. Potter and E. M. Simpson. 10 vols. Berkeley and Los Angeles: University of California Press. (*Sermons*)

——(1956; rev. edn 1983). *The Songs and Sonets of John Donne*, ed. T. Redpath. London: Methuen.

——(1963). *John Donne: The Anniversaries*, ed. F. Manley. Baltimore: Johns Hopkins University Press.

——(1965). *Donne: The Elegies and the Songs and Sonnets*, ed. H. Gardner. Oxford: Clarendon Press.

—— (1967a). *The Complete Poetry of John Donne*, ed. J. T. Shawcross. Garden City, NY: Doubleday Anchor Books.

—— (1967b). *John Donne: The Satires, Epigrams and Verse Letters*, ed. C. W. Milgate. Oxford: Clarendon Press. (*Milgate*)

—— (1967c). *Selected Prose*, ed. E. M. Simpson and T. S. Healy. Oxford: Oxford University Press.

—— (1969). *Ignatius His Conclave*, ed. T. S. Healy. Oxford: Clarendon Press. (*Ignatius*)

—— (1971a). *John Donne: The Complete English Poems*, ed. A. J. Smith. Harmondsworth: Penguin.

—— (1971b). *Donne's Prebend Sermons*, ed. J. Mueller. Cambridge, Mass.: Harvard University Press.

—— (1972). 'John Donne's Holograph of "A Letter to the Lady Carey and Mrs Essex Riche"', ed. H. Gardner. Oxford: Scolar Mansell.

—— (1974). *Pseudo-Martyr*, ed. F. J. Sypher. Delmar, N. Y.: Scholars' Facsimiles & Reprints.

—— (1975). *Devotions Upon Emergent Occasions*, ed. A. Raspa. Montreal: McGill-Queen's University Press. (*Devotions*)

—— (1977). *Letters to Severall Persons of Honour*, ed. M. T. Hester. Delmar, NY: Scholars' Facsimiles and Reprints. (*Letters*)

—— (1978a). *John Donne: The Divine Poems*, ed. H. Gardner. 2nd edn. Oxford: Clarendon Press.

—— (1978b). *John Donne: The Epithalamions, Anniversaries, and Epicedes*, ed. C. W. Milgate. Oxford: Clarendon Press.

—— (1980). *John Donne Paradoxes and Problems*, ed. H. Peters. Oxford: Clarendon Press. (*Paradoxes* and *Problems*)

—— (1982). *Biathanatos*, ed. M. Rudick and M. Pabst Battin. New York and London: Garland Publishing, Inc.

—— (1984a). *Biathanatos*, ed. E. W. Sullivan, II. Newark: University of Delaware Press. (*Biathanatos*)

—— (1984b). 'Six Poèmes de John Donne', trans. and ed. S. Marandon. *Groupe d'Études et de Recherche Britanniques (GERB). Cahiers sur la poésie*, 1: 133–57.

—— (1985). *The Complete English Poems of John Donne*, ed. C. A. Patrides. London: J. M. Dent & Sons. (*Patrides*)

—— (1990). *John Donne*, ed. J. Carey. Oxford: Oxford University Press.

—— (1993). *Pseudo-Martyr*, ed. A. Raspa. Montreal: McGill-Queen's University Press. (*Pseudo-Martyr*)

—— (1995–). *The Variorum Edition of the Poetry of John Donne*, ed. G. A. Stringer *et al*. Vols. 2, 6, 7.1, and 8. Bloomington and Indianapolis: Indiana University Press. (*Variorum*)

—— (1996a). *John Donne: Selected Poetry*, ed. J. Carey. Oxford: Oxford University Press.

—— (1996b). *John Donne's 1622 Gunpowder Plot Sermon: A Parallel-Text Edition*, ed. J. Shami. Pittsburgh: Duquesne University Press. (*1622 Sermon*)

—— (2001). *Essayes in Divinity*, ed. A. Raspa. Montreal: McGill-Queen's University Press. (*Essayes*)

—— (2002). *Selected Letters*, ed. P. Oliver. New York: Routledge.

—— (2005). *The Marriage Letters of John Donne at The Folger Shakespeare Library*, ed. M. T. Hester, R. P. Sorlien, and D. Flynn. Washington, DC: The Folger Shakespeare Library. (*Marriage Letters*)

—— (2006). *Selected Poems*, ed. I. Bell. London: Penguin.

—— (2007). *John Donne's Poetry*, ed. D. Dickson. New York: W. W. Norton.

DONNELLY, M. L. (1991). 'Saving the King's Friend and Redeeming Appearances: Dr Donne Constructs a Scriptural Model for Patronage'. *Yearbook of English Studies*, 21: 107–20.

DRAYTON, M. (1612). *Poly-Olbion*. London.

DREXEL, J. (1627). *Heliotropium seu Conformatio Humanae Voluntatis cum Divina*. Munich.

DRUMMOND, W. (1711). *The Works of William Drummond of Hawthornden*, ed. J. Sage and T. Ruddiman. Edinburgh: James Watson.

DRYDEN, J. (1692). *Eleonora*. London.

——(1956–). *The Works of John Dryden*, ed. E. N. Hooker and H. T. Swedenberg. 20 vols. Berkeley: University of California Press.

DU BELLAY, J. (1984). *Œuvres Poétiques*, VII: *Œuvres Latines: Poemata*, ed. G. Demerson. Paris: Librairie Nizet.

DU BELLAY, J. (2006). *'The Regrets', with 'The Antiquities of Rome', Three Latin Elegies, and 'The Defense and Enrichment of the French Language'*, ed. and trans. R. Helgerson. Philadelphia: University of Pennsylvania Press.

DUBROW, H. (1988). '"The Sun in Water": Donne's Somerset Epithalamium and the Poetics of Patronage', in H. Dubrow and R. Strier (eds.), *The Historical Renaissance: New Essays on Tudor and Stuart Literature and Culture*. Chicago: University of Chicago, 197–219.

——(1990). *A Happier Eden: The Politics of Marriage in the Stuart Epithalamiun*. Ithaca, NY: Cornell University Press.

——(1995). *Echoes of Desire: English Petrarchism and Its Counterdiscourses*. Ithaca, NY: Cornell University Press.

——(2008). *The Challenges of Orpheus: Lyric Poetry and Early Modern England*. Baltimore: Johns Hopkins University Press.

DUFFY, E. (1992). *The Stripping of the Altars: Traditional Religion in England c. 1400–c. 1580*. New Haven and London: Yale University Press.

——(2001). *The Voices of Morebath: Reformation and Rebellion in an English Village*. New Haven and London: Yale University Press.

——(2009). *The Fires of Faith: Catholic England under Mary Tudor*. New Haven: Yale University Press.

DUHR, B. (1900). 'Die Deutschen Jesuiten im 5%-Streit des 16. Jahrhunderts'. *Zeitschrift für Katholische Theologie*, 24: 209–48.

DUTTON, R. (2008). *Ben Jonson, 'Volpone' and the Gunpowder Plot*. Cambridge: Cambridge University Press.

DUYCKINCK, E. (1841). 'Dr. Donne'. *Arcturus*, 2/1: 19–26.

EARLE, J. (1966). *The Autograph Manuscript of Microcosmographie*. Leeds: Scolar Press.

EARLE, P. (1992). *The Last Fight of the Revenge*. London: Collins & Brown.

ECKHARDT, J. (2006). '"Love-Song Weeds, and Satyrique Thornes": Anti-Courtly Love Poetry and Somerset Libels'. *Huntington Library Quarterly*, 69/1: 47–66.

——(2009). *Manuscript Verse Collectors and the Politics of Anti-Courtly Love Poetry*. Oxford: Oxford University Press.

EDWARDS, D. L. (2001). *John Donne: Man of Flesh and Spirit*. London: Continuum.

ELIOT, G. (2000). *Middlemarch: An Authoritative Text, Backgrounds, Criticism*, ed. B. G. Hornback. New York: Norton.

ELIOT, T. S. (1932). *Selected Essays*. London: Faber & Faber.

[ELIZABETh I, QUEEN OF ENGLAND] (1585). *A declaration of the causes mooving the Queene of England to give aide to the defence of the people afflicted and oppressed in the Lowe Countries*. London.

ELLRODT, R. (1984). 'Espace et poésie de Donne a Traherne', in *Espaces et Représentations dans le Monde Anglo-Américan aux xviie et xviiie Siècles*. Paris: Presses de l'Université de Paris, 1–16.
—— (trans.) (1993). *John Donne: Poésie*. Paris: Imprimerie Nationale.
ELYOT, T. (1531). *The Boke named the Gouernour*. London.
EMPSON, W. (1993). *Essays on Renaissance Literature*, vol. 1: *Donne and the New Philosophy*, ed. J. Haffenden. Cambridge: Cambridge University Press.
ENDRES, C. (1981). *Joannes Secundus: The Latin Love Elegy in the Renaissance*. Hamden, Conn.: Archon Books.
ENGLISH, J. (2002). 'George More's Other House—Baynard's Mansion, Ewhurst'. *Surrey Archaeological Collections*, 89: 53–63.
ERASMUS, D. (1515). *Moriae Encomium*. Basel.
ERASMUS, D. (1988). *The Correspondence of Erasmus: Letters 1122–1251, 1520 to 1521*, ed. and trans. P. Bietenholz and R. A. B. Mynors. *Collected Works of Erasmus*, vol. 8. Toronto: University of Toronto Press.
—— (1989). *The Correspondence of Erasmus: Letters 1252–1355, 1522 to 1523*, ed. and trans. J. M. Estes and R. A. B. Mynors. *Collected Works of Erasmus*, vol. 9. Toronto: University of Toronto Press.
—— (1991 and 1994). *Opera Omnia*. Amsterdam, New York, Oxford, and Tokyo: North Holland, vols. 5.4 and 5.5.
—— (2005). *Adages III iv 1 to IV ii 100*, ed. J. N. Grant, trans. D. L. Drysdall. *Collected Works of Erasmus*, vol. 35. Toronto: University of Toronto Press.
ESLER, A. (1966). *The Aspiring Mind of the Elizabethan Younger Generation*. Durham, NC: Duke University Press.
ESTIENNE, C. (1553). *Paradoxes ce sont propos contre la commune opinion*. Paris.
—— (1593). *The Defence of Contraries: Paradoxes against common opinion*, trans. A. Munday. London.
ESTRIN, B. L. (1994). *Laura: Uncovering Gender and Genre in Wyatt, Donne, and Marvell*. Durham and London: Duke University Press.
ETTENHUBER, K. (2007). '"Take heed what you hear": Re-reading Donne's Lincoln's Inn Sermons'. *John Donne Journal*, 26: 127–57.
EVANS, J. (1855). 'Extracts from the Private Account Book of Sir William More, of Loseley, in Surrey, in the Time of Queen Elizabeth'. *Archaeologia*, 36: 287–310.
EVANS, K. W. (1971). '*Sejanus* and the Ideal Prince Tradition'. *Studies in English Literature*, 11/2: 249–64.
EVANS, R. C. (1989a). *Ben Jonson and the Poetics of Patronage*. Lewisburg, Pa.: Bucknell University Press.
—— (1989b). 'John Donne, Governor of Charterhouse'. *John Donne Journal*, 8/1–2: 133–50.
—— (2002). 'Lyric Grief in Donne and Jonson', in M. Swiss and D. A. Kent (eds.), *Speaking Grief in English Literary Culture: Shakespeare to Milton*. Pittsburgh: Duquesne University Press, 42–68.
EZELL, M. J. M. (1999). *Social Authorship and the Advent of Print*. Baltimore: Johns Hopkins University Press.
FEIL, J. P. (1962). 'Sir Tobie Matthew and His Collection of Letters'. Unpublished Ph.D dissertation, University of Chicago.
FELPERIN, H. (1985). 'Canonical Texts and Non-Canonical Interpretations: The Neohistoricist Rereading of Donne'. *Southern Review: Literary and Interdisciplinary Essays*, 18: 235–50.
FENLON, D. (1972). *Heresy and Obedience in Tridentine Italy: Cardinal Pole and the Counter Reformation*. Cambridge: Cambridge University Press.

FERENC, G. (trans.) (1987). *John Donne: Negativ szerelerm.* Budapest: Helikon Kiadó.

—— (ed.) (1989). 'John Donne', in *Donne, Milton és az angol barokk Költöi.* Budapest: Európa Könyvikadó: 9–93, 351–4.

FERRABOSCO, A. (1609). *Ayres.* London.

FERRELL, L. A. (1998). *Government by Polemic: James I, the King's Preachers, and the Rhetorics of Conformity, 1603–25.* Stanford, Calif.: Stanford University Press.

FERRY, A. (1975). *All in War with Time: Love Poetry of Shakespeare, Donne, Jonson, Marvell.* Cambridge, Mass.: Harvard University Press.

FIELD, N. (1716–17). *Some Short Memorials Concerning the Life of the Reverend Divine Doctor Richard Field.* London.

FIELDING, J. (2004). 'Sibthorpe, Richard Waldo (d. 1622)', rev. M. Clifton, *Oxford Dictionary of National Biography,* online edn.

FIGGIS, J. N. (1896). *The Theory of the Divine Right of Kings.* Cambridge Historical Essays, no. 9. Cambridge: University Press.

FINCHAM, K. (1988). 'Prelacy and Politics: Archbishop Abbot's Defence of Protestant Orthodoxy'. *Historical Research,* 61/144: 36–64.

—— (1990). *Prelate as Pastor.* Oxford: Oxford University Press.

—— (2000). 'William Laud and the Exercise of Caroline Ecclesiastical Patronage'. *Journal of Ecclesiastical History,* 51/1: 69–93.

—— (ed.) (1994–8). *Visitation Articles and Injunctions of the Early Stuart Church.* 2 vols. Woodbridge: Boydell.

—— and P. LAKE (1985). 'The Ecclesiastical Policy of King James I'. *Journal of British Studies,* 24/2: 169–207.

—— —— (1993). 'The Ecclesiastical Policies of James I and Charles I', in K. Fincham (ed.), *The Early Stuart Church, 1603–1642.* Basingstoke: Macmillan, 23-49.

—— and N. TYACKE (2007). *Altars Restored: The Changing Face of English Religious Worship, 1547–c.1700.* Oxford: Oxford University Press.

FIRTH, C. H. (ed.) (1903). *Stuart Tracts 1603–1693.* Westminster: Archibald Constable.

FISH, S. (1990). 'Masculine Persusive Force: Donne and Verbal Power', in E. D. Harvey and K. E. Maus (eds.), *Soliciting Interpretation: Literary Theory and Seventeenth-Century English Poetry.* Chicago and London: University of Chicago Press, 223–52.

F[ITZHERBERT], T. (1613). *A Svpplement to the Discvssion of M. D. Barlowes Ansvvere To the Iudgement of a Catholicke Englishman &c interrupted by the death of the Author F. Robert Persons of the Society of Iesvs.* n.p. [St. Omer].

FLACIUS ILLYRICUS, M. (1552). *Wonderfull Newes of the Death of Paule the last byshop of Rome,* trans. W. Baldwin. London.

FLEMING, G. (1634). *Magnificence Exemplified...in a Sermon appointed to be preached at St Pauls-Crosse, but preached in the Church.* London.

FLETCHER, G. (1593). *Licia.* London.

FLETCHER, J. M. (1986). 'The Faculty of Arts', in J. McConica (ed.), *The History of the University of Oxford,* vol. 3: *The Collegiate University.* Oxford: Clarendon Press, 157–200.

FLETCHER, P. (1627). *Locustae, vel Pietas Iesuitica.* Cambridge.

FLORÉN, C. (ed.) (2004). *John Donne: A Complete Concordance of the Poems.* 2 vols. Hildesheim and New York: Olms–Weidmann.

FLOYD, J. (1613). *Pvrgatories' Trivmph over Hell, Maugre The barking of Cerberus in Syr Edvvard Hobyes Counter-snarle.* n.p.

FLYNN, D. (1969). 'Three Unnoticed Companion Essays to Donne's "An Essay of Valour"'. *Bulletin of the New York Public Library*, 73: 424–39.
—— (1973). 'Irony in Donne's *Biathanatos* and *Pseudo-Martyr*'. *Recusant History*, 12: 49–69.
—— (1973/4). 'The Originals of Donne's Overburian Characters'. *Bulletin of the New York Public Library*, 77: 63–9.
—— (1975). 'Donne's Catholicism: I'. *Recusant History*, 13/1: 1–17.
—— (1981). '"Sir Thomas Heywood the Parson" and Donne's Catholic Background'. *Recusant History*, 15/5: 325–7.
—— (1983). 'John Donne in the Ellesmere Manuscripts'. *Huntington Library Quarterly*, 46/4: 333–6.
—— (1984). 'Jasper Mayne's Translations of Donne's Latin Epigrams'. *John Donne Journal*, 3/2: 122–30.
—— (1986). 'Donne the Survivor', in C. J. Summers and T-L. Pebworth (eds.), *The Eagle and the Dove: Reassessing John Donne*. Columbia, Mo.: University of Missouri Press, 15–24.
FLYNN, D. (1987). 'Donne's *Ignatius His Conclave* and Other Libels on Robert Cecil'. *John Donne Journal*, 6/2: 166–83.
—— (1989). 'Donne and a Female Coterie'. *LIT: Literature Interpretation Theory*, 1: 127–36.
—— (1995a). 'A Biographical Prolusion to Study of Donne's Religious Imagination', in R. Frontain and F. Malpezzi (eds.), *John Donne's Religious Imagination: Essays in Honor of John T. Shawcross*. Conway, Ark.: University of Central Arkansas Press, 28–44.
—— (1995b). 'Donne, Henry Wotton, and the Earl of Essex'. *John Donne Journal*, 14: 185–218.
—— (1995c). *John Donne and the Ancient Catholic Nobility*. Bloomington, Ind.: Indiana University Press.
—— (1996). 'Anne More, John Donne, and Edmond Neville', in M. T. Hester (ed.), *John Donne's 'desire of more': The Subject of Anne More Donne in His Poetry*. Newark: University of Delaware Press, 140–8.
—— (2000a). 'Donne Manuscripts in Cheshire'. *English Manuscript Studies, 1100–1700*, 8: 280–92.
—— (2000b). 'Donne's Politics, "Desperate Ambition", and Meeting Paolo Sarpi in Venice'. *Journal of English and Germanic Philology*, 99/3: 334–55.
—— (2001). 'Donne's Most Daring *Satyre*: "richly For service paid, authoriz'd"'. *John Donne Journal*, 20: 107–20.
—— (2004a). 'Donne's "Amicissimo et Meritissimo Ben. Ionson" and the Daring of *Volpone*'. *Literary Imagination: The Review of the Association of Literary Scholars and Critics*, 6: 368–9.
—— (2004b). 'Jasper Heywood and the German Usury Controversy', in T. McCoog (ed.), *The Mercurian Project: Forming Jesuit Culture, 1573–1580*. Rome: Institutum Historicum Societatis Iesu, 183–211.
—— (2007). '"Out of Step": Six Supplementary Notes on Jasper Heywood', in T. M. McCoog (ed.), *The Reckoned Expense: Edmund Campion and the Early English Jesuits: Essays in Celebration of the First Centenary of Campion Hall (1896–1996)*. 2nd rev. edn. Rome: Institutum Historicum Societatis Iesu, 233–49.
—— (2009). '"Only in Obedience" to Whom?—The Identity of a Donne Correspondent'. *Literature Compass*, 6. http://www.blackwell-compass.com/subject/literature/.
FOLEY, M. (1989). *The Silence of Constitutions: Gaps, 'Abeyances,' and Political Temperament in the Maintenance of Government*. London: Routledge.
FONBLANQUE, E. B. DE (1887). *Annals of the House of Percy, from the Conquest to the Opening of the Nineteenth Century*. 2 vols. London: R. Clay & Sons.

Ford, A. (2006). '"Force and Fear of Punishment": Protestants and Religious Coercion in Ireland, 1603–33', in E. Boran and C. Gribben (eds.), *Enforcing Reformation in Ireland and Scotland, 1550–1700*. Aldershot and Burlington: Ashgate, 91–130.

Fortescue, J. (1567). *A learned commendaton of the politique lawes of England*. London.

Foster, E. R. (ed.) (1966). *Proceedings in Parliament 1610*. 2 vols. New Haven: Yale University Press.

Foucault, M. (1970). *The Order of Things: An Archaeology of the Human Sciences*. New York: Pantheon.

Fowler, A. (1982). *Kinds of Literature: An Introduction to the Theory of Genres and Modes*. Oxford: Clarendon Press.

—— (ed.) (2002). *The New Oxford Book of Seventeenth-Century Verse*. Oxford: Oxford University Press.

Foxe, J. (1572). *Pandectæ Locorum Communium, Præcipua Rerum Capita et Titulos Ordine Alphabetico Complectentes*. London.

Foxe, J. (1838). *The Acts and Monuments of John Foxe*, ed. G. Townsend. 8 vols. London: Sealey & Burnside.

Foxell, N. (1978). *A Sermon in Stone: John Donne and his Monument in St Paul's Cathedral*. London: Menard Press.

Frangipani, O. M. (1942). *Correspondance d'Ottavio Mirto Frangipani, Premier Nonce de Flandre*, ed. A. Louant. Brussels, Institut Historique Belge, vol. 3.

Franklin, J. (1991). 'Sovereignty and the Mixed Constitution: Bodin and his Critics', in J. H. Burns and M. Goldie (eds.), *Cambridge History of Political Thought 1450–1700*. Cambridge: Cambridge University Press, 298–346.

Freeman, A. (1970). 'An Epistle for Two'. *Library*, 5th ser. 25: 226–36.

Freeman, T. (1614). *Rubbe, and a great cast. Epigrams*. London.

Frontain, R-J. (1984). 'Donne's Biblical Figures: The Integrity of "To Mr. George Herbert"'. *Modern Philology*, 81/3: 285–9.

—— (2003a). 'Donne, Coryate, and the Sesqui-Superlative'. *Explorations in Renaissance Culture*, 29/2: 211–24.

—— (2003b). 'Donne's Protestant *Paradiso*: The Johannine Vision of the *Second Anniversary*', in M. Papazian (ed.), *John Donne and the Protestant Reformation: New Perspectives*. Detroit: Wayne State University Press, 113–142.

—— (2007). 'Registering Donne's Voiceprint: Additional Reverberations'. *John Donne Journal*, 26: 295–312.

Frost, K. (1990). *Holy Delight: Typology, Numerology, and Autobiography in Donne's 'Devotions upon emergent occasions'*. Princeton: Princeton University Press.

Frow, J. (2006). *Genre*. London: Routledge.

Frye, N. (1957). *Anatomy of Criticism*. Princeton: Princeton University Press.

Frye, S. (1993). *Elizabeth I: The Competition for Representation*. New York and Oxford: Oxford University Press.

Fuller, M. (1897). *The Life, Letters & Writings of John Davenant D.D. 1572–1641, Lord Bishop of Salisbury*. London: Methuen & Co.

Fuller, T. (1655). *The Church-History of Britaine*. London.

Gabrieli, V. (1995). 'John Donne, Thomas More e Roma'. *Rivista di Letterature Moderne e Comparate*, 48: 235–62.

Gapper, C., J. Newman, and A. Ricketts (2002). 'Hatfield: A House for a Lord Treasurer', in P. Croft (ed.), *Patronage Culture and Power: The Early Cecils*. New Haven: Yale University Press, 67–87.

GARCIÁ ORO, J. (1997). *Don Diego Sarmiento de Acuña, Conde de Gondomar y Embajador de España (1567–1626)*. n.p.
GARDINER, S. R. (1865). *Letters and Other Documents Illustrating the Relations Between England and Germany at the Commencement of the Thirty Years War, from the Outbreak of the Revolution in Bohemia to the Election of the Emperor Ferdinand II*. Camden Society Publications, os 90 (facsimile edn. New York 1968).
—— (1883). *History of England from the Accession of James I to the Outbreak of the Civil War*. 10 vols. London: Longmans, Green, & Co.
—— (ed.) (1871). *The Fortescue Papers*. London: Camden Society, NS 1.
GARDNER, H. (1979). 'Dean Donne's Monument in St. Paul's', in R. Wellek and A. Riberio (eds.), *Evidence in Literary Scholarship: Essays in Memory of James Marshall Osborn*. Oxford: Clarendon Press, 29–44.
GARDNER, H. (1981). 'The Combination of Opposites: John Donne: A New Look'. *Encounter*, 57/1: 45–53.
GARNETT, R. (1899). 'Mr Gosse's Life of Donne'. *The Bookman*, 10: 582–4.
GASCOIGNE, G. (2000). *A Hundreth Sundrie Flowres*, ed. G. W. Pigman, III. Oxford: Clarendon Press.
GEORGE, C. H. and K. GEORGE (1961). *The Protestant Mind of the English Reformation 1570–1640*. Princeton: Princeton University Press.
GERARD, J. (1951). *The Autobiography of an Elizabethan*, trans. P. Caraman. London: Longmans, Green & Co.
GILBERT, H. (1869). *Queen Elizabethes Achademy*, ed. F. J. Furnivall. London: Early English Text Society.
GILL, R. (1975). '*Musa Iocosa Mea:* Thoughts on the Elegies', in A. J. Smith (ed.), *John Donne: Essays in Celebration*. London: Methuen, 47–72.
GILMORE, G. D. (1947). 'Papers of Richard Taylor of Clapham'. *Bedfordshire Historical Record Society*, 25.
GITTINGS, C. (1984). *Death, Burial and the Individual in Early Modern England*. London: Croom Helm.
GLEASON, J. B. (1970). 'Dr. Donne in the Courts of Kings: A Glimpse from Marginalia'. *Journal of English and Germanic Philology*, 69/4: 599–612.
GOLDBERG, J. (1971). 'The Understanding of Sickness in Donne's *Devotions*'. *Renaissance Quarterly*, 24/4: 507–17.
—— (1979). 'James I and the Theater of Conscience'. *English Literary History*, 46/3: 379–98.
—— (1983; rprt. 1989 Stanford University Press). *James I and the Politics of Literature: Jonson, Shakespeare, Donne, and Their Contemporaries*. Baltimore: Johns Hopkins University Press.
GOODBLATT, C. (2003). 'From "Tav" to the Cross: John Donne's Protestant Exegesis and Polemics', in M. Papazian (ed.), *John Donne and the Protestant Reformation: New Perspectives*. Detroit: Wayne State University Press, 221–46.
GONDOMAR, D. S. (1943). *Correspondencia oficial de don Diego Sarmiento de Acuña, conde de Gondomar*, vol. 3. Madrid: Tipografia de Archivos.
GORDON, A. (2007). '"A fortune of paper walls": The Letters of Francis Bacon and the Earl of Essex'. *English Literary Renaissance*, 37/3: 319–36.
GOSSE, E. (1899). *The Life and Letters of John Donne, Dean of St. Paul's*. 2 vols. London: William Heinemann.
GOUGH, J. (1645). *The Academy of Complements*. London.
—— (1654). *The Academy of Complements*. London.

—— (1663). *The Academy of Complements*. London.
—— (1684). *The Academy of Complements*. London.
GRANADA, L. (1598). *Granados Spirituall and heavenlie Exercises*. London.
GRANQVIST, R. (1975). *The Reputation of John Donne, 1779–1873*. Uppsala: Almqvist and Wiksell.
GRAVES, M. A. R. (1989). 'The Common Lawyers and the Privy Council's Parliamentary Men-of-Business, 1584–1601'. *Parliamentary History*, 8/2: 189–215.
GRAY, D. and J. SHAMI (1989). 'Political Advice in Donne's *Devotions*: "No man is an island"'. *Modern Language Quarterly*, 50/4: 337–56.
GREAVES, R. L. (2008). 'Charke, William (d. 1617)', *Oxford Dictionary of National Biography*, online edn.
GREENE, T. M. (1957). 'Spenser and the Epithalamic Convention'. *Comparative Literature*, 9/3: 215–28.
GREENFIELD, M. (1998). 'The Cultural Functions of Renaissance Elegy'. *English Literary Renaissance*, 28/1: 75–94.
GREENGRASS, M. (2008).'Winwood, Sir Ralph (1562/3–1617)', *Oxford Dictionary of National Biography*, online edn.
GREETHAM, D. C. (1994). *Textual Scholarship: An Introduction*. New York: Garland Publishers.
GREGORY, B. S. (1994). 'The "true and zealouse seruice of god": Robert Parsons, Edmund Bunny, and *The first booke of the christian exercise*'. *Journal of Ecclesiastical History*, 45/2: 238–68.
GRIERSON, H. J. C. (ed.) (1921). *Metaphysical Lyrics and Poems of the Seventeenth Century: Donne to Butler*. New York: Oxford University Press.
GROSS, K. (2004). 'John Donne's Lyric Skepticism: In Strange Way'. *Modern Philology*, 101/3: 371–99.
GUFFEY, R. (2007). 'Parabolic Logic in John Donne's Sermons'. *John Donne Journal*, 26: 103–25.
GUIBBORY, A. (1983). 'A Sense of the Future: Projected Audiences of Donne and Jonson'. *John Donne Journal*, 2/2: 11–21.
—— (1990). '"Oh, Let Mee Not Serve So": The Politics of Love in Donne's *Elegies*'. *English Literary History*, 57/4: 811–33.
—— (2001). 'Donne's Religion: Montagu, Arminianism and Donne's Sermons, 1624–1630'. *English Literary Renaissance*, 31/3: 412–39.
—— (2006). 'Erotic Poetry' in A. Guibbory (ed), *The Cambridge Companion to John Donne*. Cambridge: Cambridge University Press, 133–47.
—— (ed.) (2006). *The Cambridge Companion to John Donne*. Cambridge: Cambridge University Press.
GUICCIARDINI, F. (1965). *Selected Writings*, ed. C. Grayson, trans. M. Grayson. London: Oxford University Press.
—— (1994). *Ricordi*, ed. G. Masi. Milan: Mursia.
GUILLÉN, C. (1971). *Literature as System: Essays Toward the Theory of Literary History*. Princeton: Princeton University Press.
GUILPIN, E. (1598). *Skialetheia*. London.
GUSS, D. L. (1966). *John Donne, Petrarchist: Italianate Conceits and Love Theory in the Songs and Sonets*. Detroit: Wayne State University Press.
GUY, J. (1988). *Tudor England*. Oxford: Oxford University Press.
HABINGTON, W. (1870). *Castara*, ed. E. Arber. London: A. Murray.
HACKET, J. (1693). *Scrinia reserata: a memorial offer'd to the great deservings of John Williams, D.D., who some time held the places of Ld Keeper of the great seal of England, Ld Bishop of Lincoln, and Ld Archbishop of York*. 2 vols. London.

HACKETT, H. (1995). *Virgin Mother, Maiden Queen: Elizabeth I and the Cult of the Virgin Mary*. London: Macmillan.
HALL, E. (1904). *Henry VIII*, ed. C. Whibley. 2 vols. London: T. C. & E. C. Jack.
HALL, J. (1597). *Virgidemiarum. The three last Bookes. Of byting Satyres*. London.
—— (1606). *The arte of divine meditation*. London.
—— (1608). *Epistles The First Volvme: Containing II. Decads*. London.
—— (1609). *Discovery of a New World (Mundus alter et idem)*, trans. John Healey. London.
—— (1949). *Collected Poems*, ed. A. Davenport. Liverpool: Liverpool University Press.
HALL, M. (1981). 'Searching and Not Finding: The Experience of Donne's *Essays in Divinity*'. *Genre*, 14/4: 423–40.
HALLAM, H. (1978). *The Constitutional History of England*. 2 vols. New York: Garland.
HALLEY, J. E. (1989). 'Textual Intercourse: Anne Donne, John Donne, and the Sexual Poetics of Textual Exchange', in S. Fisher and J. E. Halley (eds.), *Seeking the Woman in Late Medieval and Renaissance Writings: Essays in Feminist Contextual Criticism*. Knoxville, Tenn.: University of Tennessee Press, 187–206.
HAMBURGER, M. (ed.) (1985). *John Donne: Zwar ist auch Dichtung Sünde: Gedichte Englische und Deutsch*. rev. edn. Leipzig: Philipp Reclam.
HAMILTON, S. G. (1903). *Hertford College*. London: F. E. Robinson & Co.
HAMMER, P. E. J. (1994). 'The Uses of Scholarship: The Secretariat of Robert Devereux, Second Earl of Essex, c. 1585–1601'. *English Historical Review*, 109/430: 26–51.
—— (1995). 'Letters of Travel Advice from the Earl of Essex to the Earl of Rutland: Some Comments'. *Philological Quarterly*, 74/3: 317–25.
—— (1997a). 'Myth-Making: Politics, Propaganda and the Capture of Cadiz in 1596'. *Historical Journal*, 40/3: 621–42.
—— (1997b). 'New Light on the Cadiz Expedition of 1596'. *Historical Research: The Bulletin of the Institute of Historical Research*, 70/172: 182–202.
—— (1999). *The Polarisation of Elizabethan Politics: The Political Career of Robert Devereux, 2nd Earl of Essex, 1585–1597*. Cambridge: Cambridge University Press.
—— (2003). *Elizabeth's Wars: War, Government and Society in Tudor England, 1544–1604*. Basingstoke: Palgrave.
—— (2005). 'The Crucible of War: English Foreign Policy, 1589–1603', in S. Doran and G. Richardson (eds.), *Tudor England and its Neighbours*. Basingstoke: Palgrave, 235–66.
HAO, F. (trans.) (1999). *John Donne: Amorous and Divine Poems*. Beijing: China Translation and Publishing Co.
HARDISON, O. B. (1962). *The Enduring Monument: A Study of the Idea of Praise in Renaissance Literary Theory and Practice*. Chapel Hill, NC: University of North Carolina Press.
HARINGTON, J. (1653). *A Briefe View of the State of the Church of England as it Stood in Q. Elizabeths and King James his Reigne, to the Yeere 1608*. London.
—— (1930; rprt. 1977 by Octagon Books, New York). *The Letters and Epigrams of Sir John Harington. Together with The prayse of private life*, ed. N. E. McClure. Philadelphia: University of Pennsylvania Press.
—— (1962). *A New Discourse of a Stale Subject, Called the Metamorphosis of Ajax*, ed. E. S. Donno. New York: Columbia University Press.
HARLAND, P. (1992). 'Donne's Political Intervention in the Parliament of 1629'. *John Donne Journal*, 11/1–2: 21–37.

Harpsfield, N. (1932). *The Life and Death of Sir Thomas More*, ed. E. V. Hitchcock. London: Early English Text Society.

Harrison, G. B. (1929). *An Elizabethan Journal: Being a Record of Those Things Most Talked About During the Years 1591–1594*. New York: Cosmopolitan Book Corp.

Hartley, T. E. (ed.) (1981). *Proceedings in the Parliaments of Elizabeth I*, vol. 1: *1558–1581*. Leicester: Leicester University Press.

Harvey, E. D. (1992). *Ventriloquized Voices: Feminist Theory and English Renaissance Texts*. London and New York: Routledge.

—— (2007a). 'Nomadic Souls: Pythagoras, Spenser, Donne'. *Spenser Studies*, 22: 257–79.

—— (2007b). 'The Souls of Animals: John Donne's *Metempsychosis* and Early Modern Natural History', in M. Floyd-Wilson and G. A. Sullivan, Jr. (eds.), *Environment and Embodiment in Early Modern England*. Basingstoke: Palgrave Macmillan, 55–70.

Harvey, G. (1884). *Letter-book of Gabriel Harvey*, ed. E. Scott. London: Camden Society, NS 33.

Haskin, D. (1985). 'Reading Donne's *Songs and Sonnets* in the Nineteenth Century'. *John Donne Journal*, 4/2: 225–52.

—— (1989). 'New Historical Contexts for Appraising the Donne Revival from A. B. Grosart to Charles Eliot Norton'. *English Literary History*, 56/4: 869–95.

—— (1992). 'John Donne and the Cultural Contradictions of Christmas'. *John Donne Journal*, 11/1–2: 133–57.

—— (1993). 'A History of Donne's "Canonization" from Izaak Walton to Cleanth Brooks'. *Journal of English and Germanic Philology*, 92/1: 17–36.

—— (1996). 'On Trying to Make the Record Speak More about Donne's Love Poems', in M. T. Hester (ed.), *John Donne's 'desire of more': The Subject of Anne More Donne in His Poetry*. Newark: University of Delaware Press, 39–65.

—— (2000). 'When Performance Is At Odds with Narrative: *The Designated Mourner* as Wallace Shawn's Wager on John Donne'. *Narrative*, 8/2: 182–209.

—— (2002a). 'Is There a Future for Donne's "Litany"?' *John Donne Journal*, 21: 51–78.

—— (2002b). 'No Edition is an Island: The Place of the Nineteenth-Century American Editions within the History of Editing Donne's Poems'. *TEXT: An Interdisciplinary Annual of Textual Studies*, 14: 169–207.

—— (2006). 'Donne's Afterlife', in A. Guibbory (ed.), *The Cambridge Companion to John Donne*. Cambridge: Cambridge University Press, 233–46.

—— (2007). *John Donne in the Nineteenth Century*. Oxford: Oxford University Press.

Hassel, R. C. Jr. (1971). 'Donne's *Ignatius His Conclave* and the New Astronomy'. *Modern Philology*, 68/4: 329–37.

Hayward, J. (1604). *Sanctuarie of a troubled Soule*. London.

Heal, F. and C. Holmes (1994). *The Gentry in England and Wales, 1500–1700*. Basingstoke: Macmillan.

Healy, S. (2003). 'Oh, What a Lovely War? War, Taxation, and Public Opinion in England, 1624–29'. *Canadian Journal of History*, 38/3: 439–65.

Heffernan, J. J. (1998). 'John Donne and the New Universe: Retaking the Issue'. *Sederi*, 8: 71–82.

Heinsius, D. (1631). *Histoire du Siège de Bolduc*. Louvain: Ex Officina Elzeviriorum.

Helgerson, R. (1976). *The Elizabethan Prodigals*. Berkeley: University of California Press.

—— (2006). 'Introduction', in J. du Bellay, *'The Regrets', with 'The Antiquities of Rome', Three Latin Elegies, and 'The Defense and Enrichment of the French Language'*, ed. and trans. R. Helgerson. Philadelphia: University of Pennsylvania Press, 1–36.

HERBERT, E. (1906). *The Autobiography of Edward, Lord Herbert of Cherbury*, ed. S. Lee. London: Routledge.

——(1976). *The Life of Edward, Herbert of Cherbury*, ed. J. M. Shuttleworth. London: Oxford University Press.

HERBERT, G. (1991; rprt. 2004). *The Complete English Poems*, ed. J. Tobin. London: Penguin.

HERENDEEN, W. H. (2001). '"I launch at paradise, and saile toward home": *The Progresse of the Soule* as Palinode'. *Early Modern Literary Studies*, 7: 9.1–28. <URL: http://purl.oclc.org/emls/si-07/herendeen.htm>.

HERZ, J. (1994). 'Reading [out] Biography in "A Valediction forbidding Mourning"'. *John Donne Journal*, 13/1–2: 137–42.

——(2001). 'Under the Sign of Donne'. *Criticism*, 43/1: 29–58.

——(2007). 'Tracking the Voiceprint of Donne'. *John Donne Journal*, 26: 269–82.

HESTER, M. T. (1979). '*Genera Mixta* in Donne's "Sir John Wingfield"'. *English Language Notes*, 16: 202–6.

HESTER, M. T. (1982). *Kinde Pitty and Brave Scorn: John Donne's 'Satyres'*. Durham, NC: Duke University Press.

——(1984). '"All Are Players": Guilpin and "Prester Iohn" Donne'. *South Atlantic Review*, 49/1: 3–17.

——(1986). 'Donne's Epigrams: A Little World Made Cunningly', in C. J. Summers and T-L. Pebworth (eds.), *The Eagle and the Dove: Reassessing John Donne*. Columbia, Mo.: University of Missouri Press, 80–91.

——(1987*a*). 'Donne's (Re)Annunciation of the Virgin(ia Colony) in *Elegy XIX*'. *South Central Review*, 4/2: 49–64.

——(1987*b*). 'Re-signing the Text of the Self: Donne's "As Due By Many Titles"', in C. J. Summers and T-L. Pebworth (eds.), *'Bright Shootes of Everlastingnesse': The Seventeenth-Century Religious Lyric*. Columbia, Mo.: University of Missouri Press, 59–71.

——(1990*a*). '"this cannot be said": A Preface to the Reader of Donne's Lyrics'. *Christianity and Literature*, 39/4: 365–85.

——(1990*b*). 'The Titles/Headings of Donne's English Epigrams', *American Notes and Queries*, NS 3: 3/1–11.

——(1996*a*). '"Faeminae lectissimae": Reading Anne Donne', in M. T. Hester (ed.), *John Donne's 'desire of more': The Subject of Anne More Donne in His Poetry*. Newark: University of Delaware Press, 17–34.

——(1996*b*). '"Let me love": Reading the Sacred "Currant" of Donne's Profane Lyrics', in H. Wilcox, R. Todd, and A. MacDonald (eds.), *Sacred and Profane: Secular and Devotional Interplay in Early Modern British Literature*. Amsterdam: VU University Press, 129–50.

——(2008). '"a mixed Parenthesis": John Donne's *Letters to Severall Persons of Honour*'. *Literature Compass*, 5/4: 842–54.

HEYWOOD, E. (2003). *Il Moro*, ed. P. G. Pizzorno. Florence: Leo S. Olschki.

HEYWOOD, J. (1967). *The Spider and the Flie*, ed. A. W. Ward. New York: Burt Franklin.

——(1992). *Woorkes*. Cambridge: Chadwick-Healy.

HIGGOTT, G. (2004). 'The Fabric to 1670', in D. Keene, A. Burns, and A. Saint (eds.), *St Paul's: The Cathedral Church of London 604–2004*. New Haven: Yale University Press, 171–90.

HIGHET, G. (1954). *Juvenal the Satirist*. Oxford: Oxford University Press.

HIGHLEY, C. (2008). *Catholics Writing the Nation in Early Modern Britain and Ireland*. Oxford: Oxford University Press.

HILL, G. (1960). 'The World's Proportion: Jonson's Dramatic Poetry in "Sejanus" and "Catiline"', in *Jacobean Theatre*. Stratford-Upon-Avon Studies, 1. London: Arnold, 113–31.

HOBBS, M. (1992). *Early Seventeenth-Century Verse Miscellany Manuscripts*. England: Scolar Press.

HOBY, E. (1613). *A Counter-snarle for Ishmael Rabshacheh*. London.

HODGSON, E. M. A. (1999). *Gender and the Sacred Self in John Donne*. Newark: University of Delaware Press.

HOLSTUN, J. (1987). '"Will you rent our ancient love asunder?" Lesbian Elegy in Donne, Marvell, and Milton'. *English Literary History*, 54/4: 835–67.

HOLYDAY, B. (1673). *Decimus Junius Juvenalis, and Aulus Persius Flaccus Translated and Illustrated*. Oxford.

—— (1616). *Avlvs Persivs Flaccvs Persius his Satires translated into English*...Oxford.

HOOKER, R. (1977). *The Folger Library Edition of the Works of Richard Hooker*, ed. W. S. Hill. 7 vols. Cambridge, Mass.: Belknap Press of Harvard University Press.

HORACE (1970). *Satires, Epistles and Ars Poetica with an English Translation*, ed. and trans. H. R. Fairclough. Cambridge Mass.: Harvard University Press.

HOSKINS, J. (1935). *Directions for Speech and Style*, ed. H. H. Hudson. Princeton: Princeton University Press.

HOULBROOKE, R. A. (1998). *Death, Religion, and the Family in England, 1480–1750*. Oxford: Oxford University Press.

HOULISTON, V. (2006). 'An Apology for Donne's *Pseudo-Martyr*'. *Review of English Studies*, 57/231: 474–86.

—— (2007). *Catholic Resistance in Elizabethan England: Robert Persons's Jesuit Polemic, 1580–1610*. Aldershot: Co-published with Institutum Historicum Societas Iesu (Rome).

HRON, Z. (trans.) (1987). *John Donne: Komu zvoni hrana* [John Donne: For Whom the Bell Tolls]. Praha: Ceskoslovensky Spisovatel.

HUDSON, H. H. (1947). *The Epigram in the English Renaissance*. Princeton: Princeton University Press.

HUGHES, R. (1968). *The Progress of the Soul: The Interior Career of John Donne*. New York: William Morrow & Co.

HUMPHRYES, P. (1688). 'WILT thou forgive', in H. Playford, *Harmonia Sacra*. London.

HUNT, T. (1996). *Villon's Last Will: Language and Authority in the 'Testament'*. Oxford: Clarendon Press.

HUNTINGTON, J. (2001). *Ambition, Rank, and Poetry in 1590s England*. Urbana: University of Illinois Press.

HUNTLEY, F. L. (1979). *Bishop Joseph Hall 1574–1656: A Biographical and Critical Study*. Cambridge: D. S. Brewer.

HUTTON, J. (1946). *The Greek Anthology in France and in the Latin writers of the Netherlands to the year 1800* Ithaca, NY: Cornell University Press.

HUYGENS, C. (1658). *KOREN-BLOEMEN*. Graven-Hage.

IOPPOLO, G. (2006). *Dramatists and their Manuscripts in the Age of Shakespeare, Jonson, Middleton and Heywood: Authorship, Authority and the Playhouse*. London: Routledge.

JACKSON, R. (1970). *John Donne's Christian Vocation*. Evanston, Ill.: Northwestern University Press.

[JAMES I] (1604). *By the King having after some time spent in settling the politique affaires of this realme*... London.

[——] (1610). *By the King a proclamation for the due execution of all former lawes against recusants*.

—— (1627). *Flores regii. Or proverbes and aphorismes divine and morall*. London.

[———] (1861). *Correspondence of King James VI of Scotland with Sir Robert Cecil and Others in England*, ed. J. Bruce. London: Camden Society, 78.

——— (1918; rprt. 1965). *The Political Works of James I*, ed. C. H. McIlwain. Cambridge, Mass.: Harvard University Press.

——— (1984). *Letters of King James VI and I*, ed. G. P. V. Akrigg. Berkeley: University of California Press.

——— (1994). *Basilikon Doron. King James VI and I: Political Writings*, ed. J. P. Sommerville. Cambridge: Cambridge University Press.

JAMES, M. (1978). *English Politics and the Concept of Honour, 1485–1642*. London: Past and Present Society.

JAMES, T. (1611). *A Treatise of the Corruption of Scripture*. London.

JARDINE, L. and W. SHERMAN (1994). 'Pragmatic Readers: Knowledge Transactions and Scholarly Services in Late Elizabethan England', in A. Fletcher and P. Roberts (eds.), *Religion, Culture and Society in Early Modern Britain: Essays in honour of Patrick Collinson*. Cambridge: Cambridge University Press, 102–24.

JARDINE, L., W. SHERMAN and A. STEWART (1999). *Hostage to Fortune: The Troubled Life of Francis Bacon*. New York Hill and Wang.

JAVITCH, D. (1978). *Poetry and Courtliness in Renaissance England*. Princeton: Princeton University Press.

JESSOPP, A. (1897). *John Donne, sometime Dean of St Paul's: A.D. 1621–1631*. London: Methuen.

JEWEL, J. (1848). *The Works of John Jewel*, ed. J. Ayre. Cambridge: Parker Society, vols. 3 and 4.

JEWELL, H. (1998). *Education in Early Modern England*. London: Palgrave Macmillan.

JEWETT, S. O. (1911). *Letters of Sarah Orne Jewett*, ed. A. Fields. Boston: Houghton Mifflin.

JOHNSON, J. (1999a). 'Recovering the Curse of Eve: John Donne's Churching Sermons'. *Renaissance & Reformation*, 23/2: 61–71.

——— (1999b). *The Theology of John Donne*. Cambridge: D. S. Brewer.

——— (2004). 'Consecrating Lincoln's Inn Chapel'. *John Donne Journal*, 23: 139–60.

JOHNSON, M. A. C. (1970). 'Homiletic Theory and Practice in the Sermons of John Donne and Lancelot Andrewes'. Unpublished Ph.D dissertation, University of Illinois at Urbana-Champagne.

JOHNSON, R. (1613). *Essaies, or, Rather imperfect offers*. London. [Originally published 1601.]

——— (1665). *The Scholars Guide from the Accidence to the University*. London.

JOHNSON, S. (1969). *The Rambler*, ed. W. J. Bate and A. B. Strauss, 3 vols. Vols. 3–5 of the *Yale Edition of the Works of Samuel Johnson*. New Haven and London: Yale University Press.

——— (2006). *The Lives of the Most Eminent English Poets, with Critical Observations on their Works*, ed. Roger Lonsdale. 4 vols. Oxford: Clarendon Press.

JOHNSON, S. M. (1947). 'John Donne and the Virginia Company'. *English Literary History*, 14/2: 127–38.

——— (1948). 'Sir Henry Goodere and Donne's Letters'. *Modern Language Notes*, 63/1: 38–43.

JONES, W. J. (1967). *The Elizabethan Court of Chancery*. Oxford: Clarendon Press.

JONSON, B. (1925–52). *Ben Jonson*, ed. C. H. Herford and P. Simpson. 11 vols. Oxford: Clarendon Press.

JORDAN, W. K. (1932). *The Development of Religious Toleration in England from the Beginning of the English Reformation to the Death of Queen Elizabeth*. London: Allen & Unwin.

——— (1968). *Edward VI: The Young King: The Protectorship of the Duke of Somerset*. London: Allen & Unwin.

—— and M. R. Gleason. (1975). *The Saying of John Late Duke of Northumberland upon the Scaffold, 1553*. Cambridge, Mass.: Harvard College Library.

JUVENAL (2004). *Juvenal and Persius*, trans. S. M. Braund. Cambridge, Mass.: Harvard University Press.

KANTOROWICZ, E. (1955). 'Mysteries of State: An Absolutist Concept and its Late Mediaeval Origins'. *Harvard Theological Review*, 48/1: 65–91.

KARUMIDZE, Z. (1984). 'John Donne: Logic of Intuition', in N. Kiasashvili (ed.), *Poeturi Xatis Memkvidreobit' Oba: Jon Doni, Uiliam Batler Leits, Tomas Sternz Elioti* [Three Essays on John Donne, W. B. Yeats and T. S. Eliot]. Tbilisi: Tbilisi University Press, 9–61.

KAY, D. (1990). *Melodious Tears: The English Funeral Elegy from Spenser to Milton*. Oxford: Clarendon Press.

KEEBLE, N. H. (2002). 'To "build in Sonets pretty roomes"? Donne and the Renaissance Love Lyric', in A. D. Cousins and D. Grace (eds.), *Donne and the Resources of Kind*. London: Associated University Presses; Madison, NJ: Fairleigh Dickinson University Press, 71–86.

KEENE, D., A. BURNS, and A. SAINT (eds.) (2004). *St Paul's: The Cathedral Church of London 604–2004*. New Haven: Yale University Press.

KELLIHER, H. (1974). 'The Latin Poetry of George Herbert', in J. W. Binns (ed.), *The Latin Poetry of English Poets*. London: Routledge & Kegan Paul, 26–57.

KELLIHER, H. (1993). 'Donne, Jonson, Richard Andrews and the Newcastle Manuscript'. *English Manuscript Studies, 1100–1700*, 4: 134–73.

KEMPE, W. (1588). *The education of children in learning*. London.

KEMPIS, T. (1580). *Of the imitation of Christ*, trans. T. Rogers. London.

KER, R. (1875). *Correspondence of Sir Robert Kerr, First Earl of Ancram, and his son William, Third Earl of Lothian*. 2 vols. Edinburgh: R. & R. Clark.

KERMODE, F. (1971). 'John Donne', in *Shakespeare, Spenser, Donne: Renaissance Essays*. London: Collins, 116–48.

—— (ed.) (1975). *Selected Prose of T. S. Eliot*. New York: Harcourt Brace & Co.

KERNAN, A. (1959). *The Cankered Muse: Satire of the English Renaissance*. New Haven: Yale University Press.

KEYNES, G. (1951). 'Postscript', *An Anatomy of the World: A Facsimile of the First Edition 1611*. Cambridge: Printed for Presentation to Members of the Roxburghe Club.

—— (1973). *A Bibliography of Dr John Donne, Dean of Saint Paul's*. 4th edn. Oxford: Clarendon Press.

KINCAID, A. N. (2008). 'Cornwallis, Sir William, the younger (c.1579–1614)', *Oxford Dictionary of National Biography*, online edn.

KING, H. (1965). *Poems*, ed. M. Crum. Oxford: Clarendon Press.

KORKOWSKI, E. (=Kirk, E.) (1975). 'Donne's *Ignatius* and Menippean Satire'. *Studies in Philology*, 72/4: 419–38.

—— (1980). *Menippean Satire: An Annotated Catalogue of Texts and Criticism*. New York: Garland.

KISHLANSKY, M. (1999). 'Tyranny Denied: Charles I, Attorney-General Heath, and the Five Knights' Case'. *Historical Journal*, 42/1: 53–83.

—— (2005). 'Charles I: A Case of Mistaken Identity'. *Past and Present*, 189: 41–80.

KLAWITTER, G. (1986). 'John Donne and the Countess of Huntingdon: The Transformation of Renaissance Woman'. *Wisconsin English Journal*, 28/3: 10–12.

—— (1987). 'John Donne and Woman: Against the Middle Ages'. *Allegorica: A Journal of Medieval and Renaissance Literature*, 9: 270–8.

—— (1992). 'Verse Letters to T. W. from John Donne: "By You My Love Is Sent"', in C. J. Summers (ed.), *Homosexuality in Renaissance and Enlightenment England: Literary Representations in Historical Context*. New York: Haworth Press, 85–102.

—— (1995). 'John Donne's Attitude toward the Virgin Mary: The Public versus the Private Voice', in R-J. Frontain and F. M. Malpezzi (eds.), *John Donne's Religious Imagination: Essays in Honor of John T. Shawcross*. Conway, Ark.: University of Central Arkansas Press, 122–40.

KLEINHANS, R. (1978). '*Ecclesiastes Sive de Ratione Concionandi*', in R. DeMolen (ed.), *Essays on the Works of Erasmus*. New Haven: Yale University Press, 253–65.

KNAFLA, L. (1977). *Law and Politics in Jacobean England: The Tracts of Lord Chancellor Ellesmare*. Cambridge: Cambridge University Press.

—— (2003). 'Mr Secretary Donne: The years with Sir Thomas Egerton', in D. Colclough (ed.), *John Donne's Professional Lives*. Cambridge: D. S. Brewer, 37–71.

—— (2008a). 'Hoby, Sir Edward (1560-1617)', *Oxford Dictionary of National Biography*, online edn.

—— (2008b). 'More, Sir George (1533-1632)', *Oxford Dictionary of National Biography*, online edn.

KNEIDEL, G. (2001). 'John Donne's *Via Pauli*'. *Journal of English and Germanic Philology*, 100/2: 224–46.

—— (2005). 'Religious Criticism, the Verse Epistle, and Donne's Daring Discretion'. *Christianity and Literature*, 55/1: 27–50.

—— (forthcoming). 'Artes Praedicandi', in P. McCullough, H. Adlington, and E. Rhatigan (eds.), *Oxford Handbook of the Early Modern Sermon*. Oxford: Oxford University Press.

KNOWLER, W. (ed.) (1739). *The Earl of Strafforde's Letters and Dispatches*. 2 vols. London.

KOLIN, P. C. (1974). 'Donne's "Obsequies to the Lord Harrington": Theme, Structure, and Image'. *Southern Quarterly*, 13/1: 65–82.

KRUZHKOVA, G. (trans.) (1994). *Dzhon Donn: Izbrannoe iz ego elegii, pesen i sonetov, satir, epitalam, i poslanii: s dobavieniem graviur, portretov, not i drugikh illustatsii, a takzhe s predisoviem i kommentariiami perevodchika* [John Donne: Selections from his Elegies, Songs and Sonets, Satires, Epithalamions, and Letters...]. Moscow: Moskovskii Rabochii.

KULLMANN, T. (1994). 'Höfischkeit und Spiritualität: Dramatische Elemente in der "Metaphysical Poetry"'. *Literaturwissenschaftliches Jahrbuch im Auftrage der Görres-Gesellschaft*, NS 35: 121–37.

KYLE, C. R. (2008). 'Cornwallis, Sir Charles (c. 1555-1629)', *Oxford Dictionary of National Biography*, online edn.

LABRANCHE, A. (1966). '"Blanda Elegeia": The Background to Donne's "Elegies"'. *Modern Language Review*, 61/3 (1966): 357–68.

LAKE, P. (1988). *Anglicans and Puritans? Presbyterianism and English Conformist Thought from Whitgift to Hooker*. London: Allen & Unwin.

—— (1989). 'Anti-popery: The Structure of a Prejudice', in R. Cust and A. Hughes (eds.), *Conflict in Early Stuart England: Studies in Religion and Politics 1603–1642*. London: Longman, 72–106.

—— (2000). 'Moving the Goal Posts? Modified Subscription and the Construction of Conformity in the Early Stuart Church', in P. Lake and M. Questier (eds.), *Conformity and Orthodoxy in the English Church, c.1560–1660*. Woodbridge: Boydell & Brewer, 179–205.

—— and S. Pincus (2006). 'Rethinking the Public Sphere in Early Modern England'. *Journal of British Studies*, 45/2: 270–92.

LANDI, O. (1543). *Paradossi*. Lyons.

LANE, G. (2008). 'The Glazing of Lincoln's Inn Chapel'. Glaziers' Company Lecture, given in Lincoln's Inn Chapel, 3 June 2008.
LaRocca, J. J. (1997). *Jacobean Recusant Rolls for Middlesex: An Abstract in English*. Catholic Record Society, Records Series, 76. London: Catholic Record Society.
LARKIN, J. F. (ed.) (1983). *Stuart Royal Proclamations*. 2 vols. Oxford: Clarendon Press.
LARSON, D. A. (1989). *John Donne and Twentieth-Century Criticism*. London and Toronto: Associated University Presses.
—— (1992). 'John Donne and the Astons'. *Huntington Library Quarterly*, 55/4: 635–41.
LAUD, W. (1847–60; rprt. 1977 Hildesheim: G. Olms). *The Works of William Laud.*, ed. W. Scott and J. Bliss. 7 vols. Oxford: J. H. Parker.
LAUDUN d'AIGALIERS, P. (2000). *L'Art poëtique françois*, ed. J-C. Monferran. Paris: Société des Textes Français Modernes.
LAURITSEN, J. R. (1976). 'Donne's *Satyres*: The Drama of Self-Discovery'. *Studies in English Literature*, 16/1: 117–30.
LEBANS, W. M. (1972a). 'Donne's *Anniversaries* and the Tradition of Funeral Elegy'. *English Literary History*, 39/4: 545–59.
—— (1972b). 'The Influence of the Classics in Donne's *Epicedes and Obsequies*'. *Review of English Studies*, 23/90: 127–37.
LECLER, J. (1960). *Toleration and the Reformation*, trans. T. L. Westow. 2 vols. New York: Association Press.
LeComte, E. S. (1968). 'The Date of Donne's Marriage'. *Études Anglaises*, 21: 168–9.
LEE, J. (1986). 'Who Is Cecilia, What Was She? Cecilia Bulstrode and Jonson's Epideictics'. *Journal of English and Germanic Philology*, 85/1: 20–34.
LEIN, C. D. (1974). 'Donne's "The Storme": The Poem and the Tradition'. *English Literary Renaissance*, 4/1: 137–63.
—— (2004). 'Donne, Thomas Myriell, and the Musicians of St. Paul's'. *John Donne Journal*, 23: 215–47.
LEISHMAN, J. B. (1951; rev. edn. 1962). *The Monarch of Wit: An Analytical and Comparative Study of the Poetry of John Donne*. London: Hutchinson University Library.
Le NEVE, J. (1969). *Fasti Ecclesiae Anglicanae 1541–1857*, vol. 1: *St. Paul's, London*, comp. J. M. Horn. University of London: Institute of Historical Research.
LERNER, L. S. (1990). 'Golden Age Satire: Transformations of Genre'. *Modern Language Notes*, 105/2: 260–82.
Le Roy, P. et al. (1602). *Englandes Bright Honour: Shining Through the Dark Disgrace of Spaines Catholicon*, trans. T. W[ilcox?]. London (rprt. of Le Roy, P. et al. [1595]. *A Pleasant Satyre*, trans. T. W[ilcox?]. London.
L'ESTOILE, P. DE (2001). *Registre-Journal du Règne de Henri III*, vol. 5: *(1585–1587)*, eds. M. Lazard and G. Schrenck. Geneva: Droz.
LEVACK, B. (1988). 'Law and Ideology: The Civil Law and Theories of Absolutism in Elizabethan and Jacobean England', in R. Strier and H. Dubrow (eds.), *The Historical Renaissance*. Chicago: University of Chicago Press, 220–41.
LEVY-NAVARRO, E. (1988). '"Goe forth ye daughters of Sion": Divine Authority, the King, and the Church in Donne's Denmark House Sermon'. *John Donne Journal*, 17: 163–73.
—— (2000). 'John Donne's Fear of Rumors in the *Devotions upon Emergent Occasions* and the Death of John King', *Notes and Queries*, 47/245: 481–3.
LEWALSKI, B. K. (1973). *Donne's 'Anniversaries' and the Poetry of Praise: The Creation of a Symbolic Mode*. Princeton: Princeton University Press.

—— (1979). *Protestant Poetics and the Seventeenth-Century Religious Lyric*. Princeton: Princeton University Press.

—— (1993). *Writing Women in Jacobean England*. Cambridge, Mass.: Harvard University Press.

LEWES, G. H. (1838). 'Donne's Poetical Works'. *National Magazine and Monthly Critic*, 2/9: 374–8.

LEWIS, C. S. (1938; rprt. 1962). 'Donne and Love Poetry in the Seventeenth Century', in *Seventeenth Century Studies Presented to Sir Herbert Grierson*. Oxford: Clarendon Press, 64–84; rprt. in W. R. Keast (ed.), *Seventeenth Century English Poetry: Modern Essays in Criticism*. New York: Oxford University Press, 92–110.

—— (1954). *English Literature in the Sixteenth Century, Excluding Drama*. Oxford: Oxford University Press.

LINCOLN'S INN (1898). *The Records of the Honorable Society of Lincoln's Inn. The Black Books*, vol.2 *From A.D. 1586 to A.D. 1660*. W. P. Baildon and J. D. Walker, (eds). London: Lincoln's Inn. (*LI Black Books*)

LINDLEY, D. (1993). *The Trials of Frances Howard: Fact and Fiction at the Court of King James*. London and New York: Routledge.

LIPSIUS, J. (1996). *Principles of Letter-Writing: A Bilingual Text of 'Justi Lipsi Epistolica Institutio'*, ed. and trans. R. V. Young and M. T. Hester. Carbondale, Ill.: Southern Illinois University Press.

LIVELY, G. and P. SALZMAN-MITCHELL (eds.) (2008). *Latin Elegy and Narratology: Fragments of Story*. Columbus, Ohio: Ohio State University Press.

LLEWELLYN, N. (1991). *The Art of Death: Visual Culture in the English Death Ritual, c.1500–c.1800*. London: Reaktion and Victoria & Albert Museum.

—— (2000). *Funeral Monuments in Post-Reformation England*. Cambridge: Cambridge University Press.

LOCKYER, R. (1981). *Buckingham: The Life and Political Career of George Villiers, First Duke of Buckingham 1592–1628*. London: Longman.

LODGE, T. (1883; rprt. 1963). *A Fig for Momus*, in *The Complete Works of Thomas Lodge, 1580–1623*. 4 vols. London: Hunterian Club. New York: Russell & Russell.

LONDON, W. (1658). *A Catalogue of the most vendible Books in England*. London: William London.

LOOMIE, A. (1973). *Spain and the Jacobean Catholics*, vol. 1: *1603–1612*. London: Catholic Record Society.

LOVE, H. (1987). 'Scribal Publication in Seventeenth-Century England'. *Transactions of the Cambridge Bibliographical Society*, 9/2: 130–54.

—— (1993). *Scribal Publication in Seventeenth-Century England*. Oxford: Clarendon Press.

LOW, A. (1993). *The Reinvention of Love: Poetry, Politics and Culture from Sidney to Milton*. Cambridge: Cambridge University Press.

LUCK, G. (1969). *The Latin Love Elegy*. 2nd edn. Totowa, NJ: Rowman & Littlefield.

MACCOLL, A. (1972). 'The Circulation of Donne's Poems in Manuscript', in A. J. Smith (ed.), *John Donne: Essays in Celebration*. London: Methuen, 28–46.

MACCULLOCH, D. (1986). *Suffolk and the Tudors: Politics and Religion in an English County 1500–1600*. Oxford: Oxford University Press.

MACEK, E. A. (1996). *The Loyal Opposition: Tudor Traditionalist Polemics, 1535–1558*. New York: Peter Lang.

MACHADO, M. S. (2002). 'Defying Convention: The Verbalization of Eroticism in W. Shakespeare's *Othello* and J. Donne's "Elegie XIX"'. *Sederi*, 11: 195–202.

MACINNES, A. (1991). *Charles I and the Making of the Covenanting Movement, 1625–1641*. Edinburgh: J. Donald.

MACK, P. (2002). *Elizabethan Rhetoric: Theory and Practice*. Cambridge: Cambridge University Press.

MAGNION, M. (1995). 'Approches humanistes de la satire régulière: hésitations et réticences'. *Littératures Classiques*, 24: 11–28.

MAGNUSSON, L. (2006). 'Donne's Language: The Conditions of Communication', in A. Guibbory (ed.), *The Cambridge Companion to John Donne*. Cambridge: Cambridge University Press, 183–200.

MALCOLMSON, C. (1999). *Heart-Work: George Herbert and the Protestant Ethic*. Stanford, Calif.: Stanford University Press.

—— (2004). *George Herbert: A Literary Life*. Basingstoke: Palgrave Macmillan.

MALLOCH, A. E. (1956). 'The Techniques and Function of the Renaissance Paradox'. *Studies in Philology*, 53/2: 191–203.

—— (1958). 'A Critical Study of Donne's *Biathanatos*'. Unpublished Ph.D dissertation, University of Toronto.

MALTBY, J. (1998). *Prayer Book and People in Elizabethan and Early Stuart England*. Cambridge: Cambridge University Press.

MANN, L. (1981). 'Radical Consistency: A Reading of Donne's "Communitie"'. *University of Toronto Quarterly*, 50/3: 284–99.

—— (1987). 'The Typology of Woman in Donne's *Anniversaries*'. *Renaissance and Reformation*, 11/4: 337–50.

MANNING, R. B. (1962). 'Richard Shelley of Warminghurst and the English Catholic Petition for Toleration of 1585'. *Recusant History*, 6: 265–82.

—— (2003). *Swordsmen: The Martial Ethos in the Three Kingdoms*. Oxford: Oxford University Press.

MANNINGHAM, J. (1976). *Diary of John Manningham of the Middle Temple, 1602–1603*, ed. R. P. Sorlien. Hanover, NH: University Press of New England.

MARLOWE, C. (1976). *Complete Plays and Poems*, ed. E. D. Pendry and J. C. Maxwell. London: Dent.

MAROT, C. (1990). *Œuvres poétiques*, ed. G. Defaux. 2 vols. Paris: Bordas.

MAROTTI, A. F. (1981). 'John Donne and the Rewards of Patronage', in G. F. Lytle and S. Orgel (eds.), *Patronage in the Renaissance*. Princeton: Princeton University Press, 207–84.

—— (1986). *John Donne, Coterie Poet*. Madison and London: University of Wisconsin Press.

—— (1995). *Manuscript, Print, and the English Renaissance Lyric*. Ithaca and London: Cornell University Press.

—— (2005). *Religious Ideology and Cultural Fantasy: Catholic and Anti-Catholic Discourses in Early Modern England*. Notre Dame, Ind.: University of Notre Dame Press.

—— (2006). 'The Social Context and Nature of Donne's Writing: Occasional Verse and Letters', in A. Guibbory (ed.), *The Cambridge Companion to John Donne*. Cambridge: Cambridge University Press, 35–48.

MARSTON, J. (1961). *Poems*, ed. A. Davenport. Liverpool: Liverpool University Press.

MARTIAL (1993). *Epigrams*, ed. D. R. Shackleton Bailey. 3 vols. Cambridge, Mass.: Harvard University Press.

MARTIN, A. L. (1973). *Henry III and the Jesuit Politicians*. Geneva: Librairie Droz.

MARTIN, C. (2007). 'Fall and Decline: Confronting Lyric Gerontophobia in Donne's "The Autumnal"'. *John Donne Journal*, 26: 35–54.

MARTIN, J. (2001). *Walton's Lives: Conformist Commemorations and the Rise of Biography*. Oxford: Oxford University Press.

MARTZ, L. L. (1947). 'John Donne in Meditation: The *Anniversaries*'. *English Literary History* 14/4: 247–73.
—— (1954; 2nd edn. 1962). *The Poetry of Meditation: A Study in English Religious Literature of the Seventeenth Century*. New Haven and London: Yale University Press.
MATAR, N. I. (1992). 'The Date of John Donne's Sermon "Preached at the Churching of the Countesse of Bridgewater"'. *Notes and Queries*, 39/4 (Dec.): 447–8.
MATHEW, D. (1933). *The Celtic Peoples and Renaissance Europe: A study of the Celtic and Spanish Influences on Elizabethan History*. London: Sheed & Ward.
M[atthew], T. (1603). *The Copie of a Letter Written from Master T. M. neere Salisbury, to Master H. A. at London, concerning the proceeding at Winchester*. London.
—— and J. DONNE, JR. (eds.) (1660). *A Collection of Letters, Made by Sr Tobie Mathew, Kt.* London. (*TMC*)
MAURER, M. (1976). 'John Donne's Verse Letters'. *Modern Language Quarterly*, 37/3: 234–59.
—— (1980). 'The Real Presence of Lucy Russell, Countess of Bedford, and the Terms of John Donne's "Honour is so Sublime Perfection"'. *English Literary History*, 47/2: 205–34.
—— (1982). 'The Poetical Familiarity of John Donne's Letters'. *Genre*, 15/2-3: 183–202.
—— (2007). 'Poetry and Scandal: John Donne's "Hymne to the Saynts and to the Marquesse Hamilton"'. *John Donne Journal*, 26: 1–33.
MAY, S. (1980). 'Tudor Aristocrats and the Mythical "Stigma of Print"'. *Renaissance Papers*, 11–18.
MAY, S. (1991). *The Elizabethan Courtier Poets: The Poems and their Contexts*. Columbia, Mo.: University of Missouri Press.
—— (1998). Review of Dennis Flynn, *John Donne and the Ancient Catholic Nobility*. *American Notes and Queries*, 11/2: 51–3.
—— (2004). 'The Future of Manuscript Studies in Early Modern Poetry'. *Shakespeare Studies*, 32: 56–62.
MAY, S. W. and W. A. RINGLER, JR. (eds.) (2004). *Elizabethan Poetry: A Bibliography and First-line Index of English Verse, 1559–1603*. London and New York: Thoemmes Continuum.
MCCABE, R. A. (1981). 'Elizabethan Satire and the Bishops' Ban of 1599'. *Yearbook of English Studies*, 11: 188–93.
MCCLUNG, W. A. and R. J. SIMARD (1987). 'Donne's Somerset Epithalamion and the Erotics of Criticism'. *Huntington Library Quarterly*, 50/2: 95–106.
MCCONICA, J. K. (1965). *English Humanists and Reformation Politics under Henry VIII and Edward VI*. Oxford: Clarendon Press.
—— (1986). 'The Rise of the Undergraduate College', in J. McConica (ed.), *History of the University of Oxford*. Vol. 3. *The Collegiate University*. Oxford: Oxford University Press, 1–68.
MCCOOG, T. M. (1992). *Monumenta Angliae*. 2 vols. Rome: Institutum Historicum Societatis Iesu.
—— (1996). *The Society of Jesus in Ireland, Scotland, and England 1541–1588: 'Our Way of Proceeding?'*. Leiden: E. J. Brill.
—— (2008). 'Pounde, Thomas (1539–1615)', *Oxford Dictionary of National Biography*, online edn.
MCCULLOUGH, P. (1995). 'Preaching to a Court Papist? Donne's Sermon Before Queen Anne, December 1617'. *John Donne Journal*, 14: 59–81.
—— (1998). *Sermons at Court: Politics and Religion in Elizabethan and Jacobean Preaching*. Cambridge: Cambridge University Press.
—— (2003*a*). 'Donne and Andrewes'. *John Donne Journal*, 22: 165–201.

—— (2003b). 'Donne as Preacher at Court: Precarious "Inthronization"', in D. Colclough (ed.), *John Donne's Professional Lives*. Cambridge: D. S. Brewer, 179–204.

—— (2006). 'Donne as Preacher', in A. Guibbory (ed.), *The Cambridge Companion to John Donne*. Cambridge: Cambridge University Press, 167–81.

McCutcheon, E. (1999). 'Playing the Waiting Game: The Life and Letters of Elizabeth Wolley'. *Quidditas*, 20: 31–53.

—— (2005). 'Thomas More at Epigrams: Humanism or Humanisms?' in T. Hoenselaars and A. F. Kinney (eds.), *Challenging Humanism: Essays in Honor of Dominic Baker-Smith*. Newark: University of Delaware Press, 75–89.

McGinness, F. J. (2006). 'An Erasmian Legacy: *Ecclesiastes* and the Reform of Preaching at Trent', in R. Delph, M. Fontaine, and J. Martin (eds.), *Heresy, Culture, and Religion in Early Modern Italy*. Kirksville, Mo.: Truman State University Press, 93–112.

McGowan, M. M. (1972). '"As Through a Looking-glass": Donne's Epithalamia and their Courtly Context', in A. J. Smith (ed.), *John Donne: Essays in Celebration*. London: Methuen, 175–218.

McLeod, R. (2005). 'Obliterature: Reading a Censored Text of Donne's "To his mistress going to bed"'. *English Manuscript Studies, 1100–1700*, 12: 83–138.

McRae, A. (2004). *Literature, Satire and the Early Stuart State*. Cambridge: Cambridge University Press.

Meakin, H. L. (1998). *John Donne's Articulations of the Feminine*. Oxford: Clarendon Press.

Mears, N. (1995). '*Regnum Cecilianum*? A Perspective of the Court', in J. Guy (ed.), *The Reign of Elizabeth*. Cambridge: Cambridge University Press, 46–63.

Mendle, M. (1993). 'Parliamentary Sovereignty: A Very English Absolutism', in N. Phillipson and Q. Skinner (eds.), *Political Discourse in Early Modern Britain*. Cambridge: Cambridge University Press, 97–119.

—— (1989). 'The Ship Money Case, *The Case of Shipmony*, and the Development of Henry Parker's Parliamentary Absolutism'. *Historical Journal*, 32/3: 513–36.

Milani, M. (trans.) (1987). *John Donne: Poesie e traduzioni*. Pavia: Amici di via Cardano.

Mildmay, G. (1620). *Meditations*. Northampton Central Library, Northamptonshire Studies Collection.

Milgate, W. (1969). 'The Date of Donne's Marriage: A Reply', *Études Anglaises*, 22: 66–7.

Miller, H. K. (1956). 'The Paradoxical Encomium with Special Reference to its Vogue in England, 1600–1800'. *Modern Philology*, 53/3: 145–78.

Milton, A. (1995). *Catholic and Reformed: The Roman and Protestant Churches in English Protestant Thought, 1600–1640*. Cambridge: Cambridge University Press.

—— (1999). 'A Qualified Intolerance: The Limits and Ambiguities of Early Stuart Anti-Catholicism', in A. Marotti (ed.), *Catholicism and Anti-Catholicism in Early-Modern English Texts*. Basingstoke: Macmillian, 85–115.

—— (2006). 'Anglicanism by Stealth: The Career and Influence of John Overall', in P. Lake and K. Fincham (eds.), *Religious Politics in Post-Reformation England: Essays in Honour of Nicholas Tyacke*. Woodbridge: Boydell & Brewer, 159–76.

—— (ed) (2005). *The British Delegation and the Synod of Dort (1618–1619)*. Woodbridge: Boydell Press in association with the Church of England Record Society.

Milton, J. (1957). *Complete Poetry and Major Prose*, ed. M. Y. Hughes. New York: Odyssey.

Milward, P. (1978). *Religious Controversies of the Jacobean Age: A Survey of Printed Sources*. Lincoln, Nebr.: University of Nebraska Press.

Minto, W. (1880). 'John Donne'. *Nineteenth Century*, 7: 845–63.

MINTURNO, A. S. (1971). *L'Arte Poetica* (1564), facsimile rprt. Munich: Wilhelm Fink.
'M. M. D.' (1822). 'Essay on the Genius of Cowley, Donne and Clieveland.' *The European Magazine*, 84 (Aug.): 108–12.
MOFFETT, T. (1940). *Nobilis; or, A View of the Life and Death of a Sidney*, ed. and trans. V. B. Heltzel and H. H. Hudson. San Marino, Calif.: Huntington Library.
MOIR, T. L. (1958). *The Addled Parliament of 1614*. Oxford: Clarendon Press.
MONTA, S. B. (2005). *Martyrdom and Literature in Early Modern England*. Cambridge: Cambridge University Press.
MONTAIGNE, MICHEL DE (1967). *The Essays of Montaigne*, trans. J. Florio. 3 vols. New York: AMS Press.
MONTEMAYOR, J. DE (1989). *The Diana*, trans. R. Mueller. Lewiston, NY: E. Mellen Press.
MONTROSE, L. (1980). 'Gifts and Reasons: The Contexts of Peele's "Araygnement of Paris"'. *English Literary History*, 47/3: 433–61.
MORE, G. (1597). *A Demonstration of God in his Workes*. London.
MORE, R. S. (2008). 'Philips, Sir Edward (c. 1555-1614)' *Oxford Dictionary of National Biography*, online edn.
MORE, T. (1516). *Utopia*. Louvain.
——(1984). *Latin Poems. The Complete Works of St. Thomas More*, ed. C. H. Miller et al. vol. 3, pt. 2. New Haven: Yale University Press.
MORRIS, J. (1874). 'The Martyrdom of William Harrington'. *The Month*, 20: 411–23.
MORRISSEY, M. (2003). 'John Donne as a Conventional Paul's Cross Preacher', in D. Colclough (ed.), *John Donne's Professional Lives*. Cambridge: D. S. Brewer, 159–78.
MORTON, T. (1605). *An exact discoverie of Romish Doctrine in the case of Conspiracie and Rebellion*. London.
——(1606). *A Fvll Satisfaction concerning a Dovble Romish Iniqvitie; Hainous Rebellion, and more then Heathenish Æquivocation*. London.
——(1609). *A Catholike Appeale for Protestants*. London.
——(1610). *The Encounter against M. Parsons*. London.
MORYSON, F. (1617). *An Itinerary*. London.
MOTLEY, J. L. (1861). *The History of the United Netherlands*. 34 vols. New York: Harper.
MROCZKOWSKI, P. (1981). 'John Donne', in *Historia Literatury Angielskiej*. Wrocław: Zakład Naradowy Im, 217–19.
MUELLER, J. (1968). 'The Exegesis of Experience: Dean Donne's *Devotions upon Emergent Occasions*'. *Journal of English and Germanic Philology*, 67/1: 1–19.
——(1972). 'Donne's Epic Venture in the "Metempsychosis"'. *Modern Philology*, 70/2: 109–37.
——(1985). '"This Dialogue of One": A Feminist Reading of Donne's "Extasie"'. *Association of Departments of English Bulletin*, 81: 39–42.
——(1989). 'Women Among the Metaphysicals: A Case, Mostly, of Being Donne For'. *Modern Philology*, 87/2: 142–58.
——(1990). 'The Play of Difference in Donne's "Aire and Angels"'. *John Donne Journal*, 9/1: 85–94.
——(1992). 'Lesbian Erotics: The Utopian Trope of Donne's "Sapho to Philaenis"', in C. J. Summers (ed.), *Homosexuality in Renaissance and Enlightenment England: Literary Representations in Historical Context*. New York: Haworth, 103–34.
MURRAY, W. A. (1959). 'What Was the Soul of the Apple?' *Review of English Studies*, NS 10/38: 141–55.

NARVESON, K. (1998). 'Piety and the Genre of Donne's *Devotions*'. *John Donne Journal*, 17: 107–36.

NASHE, T. (1593). *Christs teares ouer Ierusalem Wherunto is annexed, a comparatiue admonition to London*. London.

NELSON, B. (2003). '*Pathopoeia* and the Protestant Form of Donne's *Devotions upon Emergent Occasions*', in M. Papazian (ed.), *John Donne and the Protestant Reformation: New Perspectives*. Detroit: Wayne State University Press, 247–72.

—— (2005). *Holy Ambition: Rhetoric, Courtship, and Devotion in the Sermons of John Donne*. Tempe, Ariz.: Medieval & Renaissance Texts & Studies.

NELSON, H. F. (2007). 'Milton and Poetry, 1603–1660'. *The Year's Work in English Studies*, 86/1: 497–531.

NEUSCHEL, K. (1989). *Word of Honor: Interpreting Noble Culture in Sixteenth-Century France*. Ithaca, NY: Cornell University Press.

NEWMAN, J. (1997). 'The Architectural Setting', in N. Tyacke (ed.), *The History of the University of Oxford*, vol. 4: *Seventeenth-Century Oxford*. Oxford: Clarendon Press, 135–78.

NICHOLLS, D. (1988). 'The Political Theology of John Donne'. *Theological Studies*, 49/1: 45–66.

NICHOLLS, M. (1991). *Investigating Gunpowder Plot*. Manchester: Manchester University Press.

—— (2008). 'Percy, Henry, Ninth Earl of Northumberland (1564–1632)', *Oxford Dictionary of National Biography*, online edn.

NICHOLS, F. (1988). 'Generating the Unwritten Text: The Case of Rabelais'. *Esprit Créateur*, 28/1: 7–17.

NICOLSON, M. (1940a). 'Cosmic Voyages'. *English Literary History*, 7/2: 83–107.

—— (1940b). 'Kepler, the *Somnium*, and John Donne'. *Journal of the History of Ideas*, 1/3: 259–80.

NOBBS, D. (1938). *Theocracy and Toleration: A Study of the Disputes in Dutch Calvinism from 1600 to 1650*. Cambridge: Cambridge University Press.

NOLAN, J. S. (1997). *Sir John Norreys and the Elizabethan Military World*. Exeter: Exeter University Press.

NORBROOK, D. (1990). 'The Monarchy of Wit and the Republic of Letters: Donne's Politics', in E. D. Harvey and K. E. Maus (eds.), *Soliciting Interpretation: Literary Theory and Seventeenth-Century English Poetry*. Chicago: University of Chicago Press, 3–36.

NORTON, C. E. (1896). 'The Text of Donne's Poems', *Studies and Notes in Philology and Literature* [Harvard], 5: 1–19.

NOVARR, D. (1958). *The Making of Walton's 'Lives'*. Ithaca, NY: Cornell University Press.

—— (1980). *The Disinterred Muse: Donne's Texts and Contexts*. Ithaca, NY: Cornell University Press.

NOVIK, M. (2007). *Conceit*. Toronto: Doubleday Canada.

NOWELL, A. (1570.) *A Catechisme, or first Instruction and Learning of Christian Religion*. London.

OAKLEY, F. (1968). 'Jacobean Political Theology: The Absolute and Ordinary Powers of the King'. *Journal of the History of Ideas*, 29/3: 323–46.

O'CALLAGHAN, M. (2003). '"Now thou may'st speak freely": Entering the Public Sphere in 1614', in S. Clucas and R. Davies (eds.), *The Crisis of 1614 and The Addled Parliament: Literary and Historical Perspectives*. Aldershot: Ashgate, 63–80.

—— (2007). *The English Wits: Literature and Sociability in Early Modern England*. Cambridge: Cambridge University Press.

O'CONNELL, P. (1986). '*La Corona*: Donne's *Ars Poetica Sacra*', in C. J. Summers and T-L. Pebworth (eds.), *The Eagle and the Dove: Reassessing John Donne*. Columbia, Mo.: University of Missouri Press, 119–30.

OLIVARES, A. (1992). *La Mirada del Desengaño: John Donne y la Poesía del Barroco*. Valencia, Venezuela: Universidad de Carabobo.

OLIVER, P. M. (1997). *Donne's Religious Writing: A Discourse of Feigned Devotion*. London: Longman.

O'MALLEY, J. W. (1985). 'Erasmus and the History of Sacred Rhetoric: The *Ecclesiastes* of 1535'. *Erasmus of Rotterdam Society Yearbook*, 5: 1–29.

—— (1988). 'Introduction', in *Collected Works of Erasmus*, vol. 66 (Spiritualia). Toronto, Buffalo, and London: University of Toronto Press, ix–li.

—— (1993). *The First Jesuits*. Cambridge, Mass.: Harvard University Press.

ONG, W. J. (1947). 'Wit and Mystery: A Revaluation in Medieval Latin Hymnody'. *Speculum*, 22/3: 310–41.

ORD, M. (2004). 'Provincial Identification and the Struggle over Representation in Thomas Coryat's *Crudities* (1611)', in P. Schwyzer and S. Mealor (eds.), *Archipelagic Identities: Literature and Identity in the Atlantic Archipelago 1550–1800*. Aldershot: Ashgate, 131–40.

ORMEROD, G. (1882). *The History of the County Palatine and City of Chester*, rev. and enlarged T. Helsby. 3 vols. London: G. Routledge.

OVERBURY, T. (1614). *A Wife Now The Widdow of Sir Thomas Overburye Being A most exquisite and singular Poem of the choice of a Wife. Whereunto are Added many witty Characters, and conceited Newes, written by himselfe and other learned Gentlemen his friends*. London.

—— (1616). *Sir Thomas Ouerbury His Wife. With New Elegies vpon his (now knowne) vntimely death. Whereunto are annexed, New Newes and Characters, written by himselfe and other Learned Gentlemen*. London.

—— (1622). *Sir Thomas Ouerbury His Wife. With Additions of New Characters, and many other Wittie Conceits neuer before Printed*. London.

—— (1628). *His Wife. With Additions of New Characters, and Many Other Wittie Conceits Neuer Before Printed*. London.

—— (2003). *Characters: Together with Poems, News, Edicts, and Paradoxes based on the Eleventh Edition of A Wife Now the Widow of Sir Thomas Overbury*, ed. D. Beecher. Ottawa: Dovehouse Editions.

OVID (1977). *Heroides and Amores*, trans. G. Showerman, ed. G. P. Goold. 2nd rev. edn. Cambridge, Mass.: Harvard University Press.

—— (1979). *The Art of Love and Other Poems*, trans. J. H. Mozley, ed. G. P. Goold. 2nd edn. Cambridge, Mass.: Harvard University Press.

—— (1988). *Tristia, Ex Ponto*, trans. A. Wheeler, ed. G. P. Goold. 2nd rev. edn., rev. G. P. Goold. Cambridge, Mass.: Harvard University Press.

OWENS, R. R. (1975). 'The Myth of Anian'. *Journal of the History of Ideas*, 36/1: 135–8.

PABLOS, J. A. P. (1999). 'John Donne's Rhetoric of Suspension'. *Sederi*, 9: 129–34.

PAPAZIAN, M. A. (= Arshagouni, M.) (1991). 'The Latin "Stationes" in John Donne's *Devotions upon Emergent Occasions*'. *Modern Philology*, 89/2: 196–210.

—— (1992). 'Donne, Election, and the *Devotions upon Emergent Occasions*'. *Huntington Library Quarterly*, 55/4: 603–19.

—— (2000). 'John Donne and the Thirty Years' War'. *John Donne Journal*, 19: 235–66.

—— (2003). 'The Augustinian Donne: How a "Second S. Augustine"?', in M. A. Papazian (ed.), *John Donne and the Protestant Reformation: New Perspectives*. Detroit: Wayne State University Press, 66–89.

—— (2007). '"No man [and Nothing] is an *Iland*": Contexts for Donne's "Meditation XVII"'. *John Donne Journal*, 26: 381–5.

PARKER, G. et al. (eds.) (1997). *The Thirty Years' War*. 2nd rev. edn. London: Routledge.

PARR, A. (2007). 'John Donne, Travel Writer'. *Huntington Library Quarterly*, 70/1: 61–85.

PARRISH, P. A. (1986). '"A Funerall Elegie": Donne's Achievement in Traditional Form'. *Concerning Poetry*, 19: 55–66.

PARRY, G. (1981). *The Golden Age Restor'd: The Culture of the Stuart Court 1603–42*. Manchester: Manchester University Press; New York: St Martin's Press.

PASQUIER, E. (1602). *The Iesuites Catechisme. Or examination of their Doctrine*, trans. W. Watson. London.

PATTERSON, A. (1982). 'Misinterpretable Donne: The Testimony of the Letters'. *John Donne Journal*, 1/1–2: 39–53.

—— (1984). *Censorship and Interpretation: The Conditions of Writing and Reading in Early Modern England*. Madison, Wisc.: University of Wisconsin Press.

—— (1990). 'All Donne', in E. D. Harvey and K. E. Maus, *Soliciting Interpretation: Literary Theory and Seventeenth-Century Poetry*. Chicago: University of Chicago Press, 37–67.

PATTERSON, A. (1991). 'John Donne, Kingsman?' in L. L. Peck (ed.), *The Mental World of the Jacobean Court*. Cambridge: Cambridge University Press, 251–72.

—— (1997). 'Donne in Shadows: Pictures and Politics'. *John Donne Journal*, 16: 1–36.

—— (2002). 'A Man is to Himself a Dioclesian: Donne's Rectified Litany'. *John Donne Journal*, 21: 35–49.

—— (2006). 'Satirical Writings: Donne in Shadows', in A. Guibbory (ed.), *The Cambridge Companion to John Donne*. Cambridge: Cambridge University Press, 117–31.

PATTERSON, W. B. (1997). *King James VI and I and the Reunion of Christendom*. Cambridge: Cambridge University Press.

PATTISON, M. (1892). *Isaac Casaubon, 1559–1614*. 2nd edn. Oxford: Oxford University Press.

PAYNE, H. (2008). 'Russell, Lucy (née Harington), countess of Bedford (1581–1627)', *Oxford Dictionary of National Biography*, online edn.

PEASE, A. (1926). 'Things Without Honor'. *Classical Philology*, 21/1: 27–42.

PEACHAM, H. (1622). *The compleat gentleman*. London.

PEBWORTH, T-L. (1981). 'Sir Henry Wotton's "O Faithles World": The Transmission of a Coterie Poem and a Critical Old-Spelling Edition'. *Analytical and Enumerative Bibliography*, 5: 205–31.

—— (1992). '"Let Me Here Use That Freedome": Subversive Representation in John Donne's "Obsequies to the Lord Harington"'. *Journal of English and Germanic Philology*, 91/1: 17–42.

PEBWORTH, T-L. and C. J. SUMMERS (1984). '"Thus Friends Absent Speake": The Exchange of Verse Letters between John Donne and Henry Wotton'. *Modern Philology*, 81/4: 361–77.

—— (1987). 'The Editor, the Critic, and the Multiple Texts of Donne's "A Hymne to God the Father"'. *South Central Review*, 4/2: 16–34.

—— (2000). 'Contexts and Strategies: Donne's Elegy on Prince Henry'. *John Donne Journal*, 19: 205–22.

PECK, L. L. (1982). *Northampton: Patronage and Policy at the Court of James I*. London: Allen & Unwin.

—— (1993). 'Kingship, Counsel and Law in Early Stuart Britain', in J. G. A. Pocock (ed.), *The Varieties of British Political Thought, 1500–1800*. Cambridge: Cambridge University Press, 80–115.

—— (1995). 'Peers, Patronage and the Politics of History', in J. Guy (ed.), *The Reign of Elizabeth: Court and Culture in the 1590s*. Cambridge: Cambridge University Press, 87–108.

PELETIER, J. (1990). *Art poétique*, in F. Goyet (ed.), *Traités de poétique et de rhétorique de la Renaissance*. Paris: Librairie Générale Française, 219–314.

PENDER, S. (2003). 'Essaying the Body: Donne, Affliction, and Medicine', in D. Colclough (ed.), *John Donne's Professional Lives*. Cambridge: D. S. Brewer, 215–48.

PERSIUS (2004). *Juvenal and Persius*, trans. S. M. Braund. Cambridge, Mass.: Harvard University Press.

PERSONS, R. (1607). *A Treatise tending to Mitigation towards Catholicke-Subiectes in England*. [St Omer].

PETERS, R. (1969). 'Some Catholic Opinions of King James VI and I'. *Recusant History*, 10: 292–303.

PETRARCH, F. (1975). *Rerum Familiarium Libri I–VIII*, trans. A. S. Bernardo. Albany, NY: State University of New York Press.

PHILLIPPY, P. (2002). *Women, Death and Literature in Post-Reformation England*. Cambridge: Cambridge University Press.

PIGMAN, G. W., III. (1985). *Grief and English Renaissance Elegy*. Cambridge: Cambridge University Press.

PINKA, P. G. (1993). 'Donne, Idios, and the Somerset Epithalamion'. *Studies in Philology*, 90/1: 58–73.

PLAYFORD, J. (1659). 'On Womens Inconstancy', in J. Wilson, *Select Ayres and Dialogues*. London.

PLINY, THE ELDER (1601). *The Historie of the World*, trans. P. Holland. London.

PLUCKNETT, T. (1956). *A Concise History of the Common Law*. 5th edn. Boston: Little, Brown.

POCOCK, J. (1993). 'A Discourse of Sovereignty: Observations on the Work in Progress', in N. Phillipson and Q. Skinner (eds.), *Political Discourse in Early Modern Britain*. Cambridge: Cambridge University Press, 377–428.

POLACHEK, D. (2007). 'Le Mécénat meurtrier, l'iconoclasme et les limites de l'acceptable: Anne d'Este, Catherine-Marie de Lorraine, et l'anéantissement d'Henri III', in K. Wilson-Chevalier (ed.), *Patronnes et mécènes en France à la Renaissance*. St-Étienne: Publications de l'université de St-Étienne, 433–54.

POLLEN, J. H. (1907). 'Notes Concerning the English Mission', in *Miscellanea IV*. Catholic Record Society, vol. 2. London: Catholic Record Society, 1–161.

—— (1908). *Unpublished Documents Relating to the English Martyrs*. Catholic Record Society, vol. 5. London: J. Whitehead & Son.

POOLE, J. (1657). *The English Parnassus*. London.

POPE, A. (1963). *The Poems of Alexander Pope: A One-Volume Edition of the Twickenham Text with Selected Annotations*, ed. J. Butt. New Haven: Yale University Press.

PORTER, H. C. (1958). *Reformation and Reaction in Tudor Cambridge*. London: Cambridge University Press.

POST, J. F. S. (2007). 'Donne, Discontinuity, and the Proto-Post Modern: The Case of Anthony Hecht'. *John Donne Journal*, 26: 283–94.

POWERS-BECK, J. (1998). *Writing the Flesh: The Herbert Family Dialogue*. Pittsburgh: Duquesne University Press.

PRAWLISCH, H. (1985). *Sir John Davies and the Conquest of Ireland: A Study in Legal Imperialism*. Cambridge: University Press.

PRESCOTT, A. L. (1987). 'Humanism in the Tudor Jestbook'. *Moreana*, 24/95–6: 5–16.

—— (1998a). 'Donne and Rabelais'. *John Donne Journal*, 16: 37–58.

—— (1998b). *Imagining Rabelais in Renaissance England*. New Haven: Yale University Press.

—— (2000). 'The Evolution of Tudor Satire', in A. F. Kinney (ed.), *The Cambridge Companion to English Literature 1500–1600*. Cambridge: University of Cambridge Press, 220–40.

PREST, W. R. (1972). *The Inns of Court under Elizabeth I and the Early Stuarts, 1590–1640*. London: Longman.

—— (1986). *The Rise of the Barristers: A Social History of the English Bar, 1590–1640*. Oxford: Clarendon Press.

PRESTON, C. (2006). 'The Jocund Cabinet and the Melancholy Museum in Seventeenth-Century English Literature', in R. J. W. Evans and A. Marr (eds.), *Curiosity and Wonder from the Renaissance to the Enlightenment*. Aldershot: Ashgate, 87–106.

PRESTWICH, M. (1966). *Cranfield: Politics and Profits Under the Early Stuarts*. Oxford: Clarendon Press.

PRICE, F. D. (1942). 'The Abuses of Excommunication and the Decline of Ecclesiastical Discipline Under Queen Elizabeth'. *English Historical Review*, 57/225: 106–15.

PRITCHARD, A. (1979). *Catholic Loyalism in Elizabethan England*. London: Scolar Press.

PROPERTIUS (1912). *Elegies*, trans. H. E. Butler. Cambridge, Mass.: Harvard University Press.

PROPRIS, F. de. (trans.) (1993). *John Donne: Perché l'Oro Non Sporca le Dita?: Paradossi e Problemi*. Rome: Castelvecchi.

PURSELL, B. (2000). 'James I, Gondomar and the Dissolution of the Parliament of 1621'. *History*, 85/279: 428–45.

—— (2003). *The Winter King: Frederick V of the Palatinate and the Coming of the Thirty Years War*. Aldershot: Ashgate.

PUTTENHAM, G. (2007). *The Art of English Poesy*, ed. F. Whigham and W. A. Rebhorn. Ithaca and London: Cornell University Press.

QUESTIER, M. C. (1993). 'John Gee, Archbishop Abbot, and the Use of Converts from Rome in Jacobean Anti-Catholicism'. *Recusant History*, 21/3: 347–60.

—— (1996). *Conversion, Politics and Religion in England, 1580–1625*. Cambridge: Cambridge University Press.

—— (1997). 'Loyalty, Religion, and State Power in Early Modern England: English Romanism and the Jacobean Oath of Allegiance'. *Historical Journal*, 40/2: 311–29.

—— (1998a). 'The Politics of Religious Conformity and the Accession of James I'. *Historical Research*, 71/174: 14–30.

—— (2006). *Catholicism and Community in Early Modern England: Politics, Aristocratic Patronage and Religion, c. 1550–1640*. Cambridge: Cambridge University Press.

—— (2008). 'Catholic Loyalism in Early Stuart England'. *English Historical Review*, 123/504: 1132–65.

—— (ed.) (1998b). *Newsletters from the Archpresbyterate of George Birkhead*. Camden Society, 5th ser., vol. 12. Cambridge: Cambridge University Press.

—— (ed.) (2005). *Newsletters from the Caroline Court, 1631–1638: Catholicism and the Politics of the Personal Rule*. Cambridge: Cambridge University Press for the Royal Historical Society.

—— (ed.) (2009). *Stuart Dynastic Policy and Religious Politics, 1621–1625*. Camden Society, 5th ser., vol. 34. Cambridge: Cambridge University Press.

QUINN, D. (1969). 'Donne's *Anniversaries* as Celebration'. *Studies in English Literature*, 9/1: 97–105.

QUINTRELL, B. (2008a). 'Morton, Thomas (*bap.* 1564, *d.* 1659)', *Oxford Dictionary of National Biography*, online edn.

—— (2008b). 'Williams, John (1582–1650)', *Oxford Dictionary of National Biography*, online edn.

RABB, T. K. (1998). *Jacobean Gentleman: Sir Edwin Sandys, 1561–1629*. Princeton: Princeton University Press.

RABELAIS, F. (1962). *Oeuvres Complètes*. 2 vols. Paris: Éditions Garnier Frères.

RAINBOWE, E. (1677). *A Sermon Preached at the Funeral of the Right Honorable Anne Countess of Pembroke, Dorset, and Montgomery*. London.

RAJNATH, A. (1979). 'From Image to Idea: A Re-examination of T. S. Eliot's Dissociation of Sensibility'. *Indian Journal of English Studies* (Calcutta), 19: 149–61.

[RALEGH, SIR W.] (1591). *A report of the truth of the fight about the Iles of Acores this last sommer*. London.

—— (1621). *The History of the World; in Five Bookes*. London.

RANKINS, W. (1598). *Seauen Satyres Applyed to the Weeke*. London.

RAY, R. H. (1990). *A John Donne Companion*. New York: Garland.

REDWORTH, G. (2003). *The Prince and the Infanta: The Cultural Politics of the Spanish Match*. New Haven: Yale University Press.

REED, A. W. (1926). *Early Tudor Drama*. London: Methuen.

REEVE, L. J. (1989). *Charles I and the Road to Personal Rule*. Cambridge: Cambridge University Press.

REEVES, T. D. (1979–81). *An Index to the Sermons of John Donne*. 3 vols. Salzburg: Universität Salzburg.

RELIHAN, J. C. (1993). *Ancient Menippean Satire*. Baltimore: Johns Hopkins University Press.

REMER, G. (1996). *Humanism and the Rhetoric of Toleration*. University Park, Pa.: Pennsylvania State University Press.

REPPLIER, A. (1892). *Points of View*. Boston and New York: Houghton Mifflin; Cambridge, Mass.: Riverside Press.

REVARD, S. (1993). 'The Sapphic Voice in Donne's "Sapho to Philaenis"', in C. J. Summers and T-L. Pebworth (eds.), *Renaissance Discourses of Desire*. Columbia, Mo.: University of Missouri Press, 63–76.

RHATIGAN, E. (2004). 'Knees and Elephants: Donne Preaches on Ceremonial Conformity'. *John Donne Journal*, 23: 185–213.

—— (2006). 'John Donne's Lincoln's Inn Sermons'. Unpublished DPhil. thesis, Oxford University.

RIBES, P. (1996). 'John Donne: Holy Sonnet XIV or the Plenitude of Metaphor'. *Sederi*, 7: 147–52.

—— (1999). 'Religious Struggle in John Donne and Ausiàs March'. *Sederi*, 9: 135–48.

RIBNER, I. (1957). *The English History Play in the Age of Shakespeare*. Princeton: Princeton University Press.

RICH, A. (1971). 'A Valediction Forbidding Mourning', in *The Will to Change: Poems 1968–1970*. New York: Norton, 50.

RICH, B. (1593). *Greenes Newes both from Heauen and Hell*. London.
RICHARDS, J. (2003). *Rhetoric and Courtliness in Early Modern Literature*. Cambridge: Cambridge University Press.
RICKARD, J. (2007). *Authorship and Authority: The Writings of James VI and I*. Manchester: Manchester University Press.
RIDGELY, B. S. (1957). 'A Sixteenth-Century French Cosmic Voyage: *Nouvelles des régions de la lune*'. *Studies in the Renaissance*, 4: 169–89.
RINGLER, W., JR. (ed.) (1992). *Bibliography and Index of English Verse in Manuscript, 1501–1558*, prepared and completed by M. Rudick and S. J. Ringler. London and New York: Mansell.
ROBERTS, D. R. (1947). 'The Death Wish of John Donne'. *Publications of the Modern Language Association of America*, 62/4: 958–76.
ROBERTS, J. R. (1966). *A Critical Anthology of English Recusant Devotional Prose, 1558–1603*. Pittsburgh: Duquesne University Press.
—— (1973). *John Donne: An Annotated Bibliography of Modern Criticism, 1912–1967*. Columbia, Mo.: University of Missouri Press.
—— (1982a). *John Donne An Annotated Bibliography of Modern Criticism, 1968–1978*. Columbia and London: University of Missouri Press.
—— (1982b). 'John Donne's Poetry: An Assessment of Modern Criticism'. *John Donne Journal*, 1/1–2: 55–67.
—— (1990). '"Just such disparitie": The Critical Debate About "Aire and Angels"'. *John Donne Journal*, 9/1: 43–64.
—— (2004). *John Donne: An Annotated Bibliography of Modern Criticism, 1979–1995*. Pittsburgh: Duquesne University Press.
—— (ed.) (1975). *Essential Articles for the Study of John Donne's Poetry*. Hamden, Conn.: Archon Books.
ROBINSON, J. H. (1969). *Petrarch: The First Modern Scholar and Man of Letters*. 2nd edn. New York: Greenwood Press.
RODGER, N. A. M. (2004). 'Queen Elizabeth and the Myth of English Sea-power in English History'. *Transactions of the Royal Historical Society*, 6th ser. 14: 153–74.
ROEBUCK, G. (1996a). '"Glimmering lights": Anne, Elizabeth and the Poet's Practice', in M. T. Hester (ed.), *John Donne's 'desire of more': The Subject of Anne More Donne in His Poetry*. Newark: University of Delaware Press, 172–82.
—— (1996b). '*Johannes Factus* and the Anvil of the Wits'. *John Donne Journal*, 15: 141–9.
—— (1999). 'Cavalier', in C. Summers and T-L. Pebworth (eds.), *The English Civil Wars in the Literary Imagination*. Columbia and London: University of Missouri Press, 9–26.
ROGERS, T. (1581). *A Right Christian Treatise, entituled S. Avgvstines praiers*. London.
—— (1604). *A Pretious Booke of Heavenlie Meditations*. London.
ROWSE, A. L. (1983). *Eminent Elizabethans*. London: Macmillan.
ROYAL COMMISSION ON HISTORICAL MANUSCRIPTS (1883–1976). *Calendar of the Manuscripts of the Most Hon. the Marquis of Salisbury, Preserved at Hatfield House, Hertfordshire*. 24 vols. London: HM Stationery Office. (*HMC Salisbury*)
—— (1923). *The Manuscripts of His Grace the Duke of Portland, Preserved at Welbeck Abbey*, vol. 9 [Harley MSS]. London: HM Stationery Office. (*HMC Portland*)
—— (1925–66). *Report on the Manuscripts of Lord De L'Isle & Dudley Preserved at Penshurst Place*. 6 vols. London: HM Stationery Office. (*HMC De L'Isle*)

—— (1988). *Report on the Manuscripts of the Marquess of Downshire, Preserved at Easthampstead Park, Berks*, ed. G. D. Owen, vol. 5. Papers of William Trumbull the elder, September 1614–August 1616. London: HM Stationery Office. (*HMC Downshire*)

—— (1930). *Supplementary Report on the Manuscripts of the Earl of Mar & Kellie, preserved at Alloa House, Clacmannanshire*, ed. H. Paton. London: HM Stationery Office. (*HMC Mar & Kellie*)

RUDD, N. (1986). *Themes in Roman Satire*. Norman, Okla.: University of Oklahoma Press.

RUDE, D. W. (1999). 'John Donne in *The Female Tatler*: A Forgotten Eighteenth-Century Appreciation'. *John Donne Journal*, 18: 153–66.

RUSSELL, C. (1979). *Parliaments and English Politics, 1621–9*. Oxford: Clarendon Press.

—— (1990). *The Causes of the English Civil War*. Oxford: Clarendon Press.

—— (1992). *The Addled Parliament of 1614: The Limits of Revision*. Reading: University of Reading.

SABINE, M. (1992). *Feminine Engendered Faith: The Poetry of John Donne and Richard Crashaw*. Basingstoke and London: Macmillan.

—— (1995). '"Thou Art the Best of Mee": A. S. Byatt's *Possession* and the Literary Possession of Donne'. *John Donne Journal*, 14: 127–48.

SAINTSBURY, G. (1896). 'Introduction', in E. K. Chambers (ed.), *Poems of John Donne*. 2 vols. London: Routledge, 1.xi–xxxiii.

SALENIUS, M. (2001). 'Kopernikaaninen vallankumous ja retoriikan reformaatio: Maailmankaikkeus Jumalan kuvana John Donnen uskonnollisessa proosassa 1600-luvun Englannissa' [The Copernican Revolution and the Reformation of Rhetoric: The Universe as an Image of God in John Donne's Religious Prose in Seventeenth-century England], in P. Mehtonenn (ed.), *Kielen ja Kirjallisuuden Hämärä* [Obscurity in Language and Literature]. Tampere: Tampere University Press, 60–86.

SALMON, J. H. M. (1975). 'French Satire in the Late Sixteenth Century'. *Sixteenth Century Journal*, 6/2: 57–88.

—— (2002). *Renaissance and Revolt: Essays in the Intellectual and Social History of Early Modern France*. Cambridge: Cambridge University Press.

SANCHEZ, R. (1999). 'Menippean Satire and Competing Prose Styles in *Ignatius His Conclave*'. *John Donne Journal*, 18: 83–99.

SANDERS, W. (1971). *John Donne's Poetry*. Cambridge: Cambridge University Press.

SANDLER, F. (2000). '"The Gallery to the New World": Donne, Herbert, and Ferrar on the Virginia Project'. *John Donne Journal*, 19: 267–97.

SARPI, P. (1606). *A Fvll and Satisfactorie Answer to the Late Vnadvised Bull, thundred by Pope Paul the Fift, against the renowmed [sic] State of Venice: Being modestly entitled by the learned Author, Considerations vpon the Censure of Pope Pavl the Fift, against the Commonwealth of Venice*. London.

SAUNDERS, B. (2000). '"Straight From Your Heart": Convention, Sincerity, and Sexuality in Donne's Early Verse Letters'. *Journal x*, 4/2: 113–32.

—— (2006). *Desiring Donne: Poetry, Sexuality, Interpretation*. Cambridge, Mass. and London: Harvard University Press.

SAUNDERS, J. W. (1951). 'The Stigma of Print: A Note on the Social Bases of Tudor Poetry'. *Essays in Criticism*, 1/2: 139–64.

—— (1964). *The Profession of English Letters*. London: Routledge & Kegan Paul; Toronto: University of Toronto Press.

—— (1983). 'John Donne', in *A Biographical Dictionary of Renaissance Poets and Dramatists, 1520–1650*. Brighton: Harvester Press; Totowa, NJ: Barnes & Noble, 39–42.
SCALIGER, J. C. (1964). *Poetices Libri Septem*; 1561 facsimile rprt. with an introduction by A. Buck. Stuttgart: Friedrich Frommann.
SCHELLHASE, K. (1976). *Tacitus in Renaissance Political Thought*. Chicago: University of Chicago Press.
SCHLEINER, W. (1970). *The Imagery of John Donne's Sermons*. Providence, RI: Brown University Press.
SCHMITT, C. (1985). *Political Theology: Four Chapters on the Concept of Sovereignty*, trans. G. Schwab. Cambridge, Mass.: MIT Press.
SCHOENFELDT, M. C. (1994). 'The Poetry of Supplication: Toward a Cultural Poetics of the Religious Lyric', in J. R. Roberts (ed.), *New Perspectives on the Seventeenth-Century English Religious Lyric*. Columbia, Mo.: University of Missouri Press, 75–104.
SCHREIBER, R. (1984). 'The First Carlisle: Sir James Hay, First Earl of Carlisle as Courtier, Diplomat and Entrepreneur 1580–1636'. *Transactions of the American Philosophical Society*, 74/7. Philadelphia: American Philosophical Society.
—— (2004). 'Hay, James, first earl of Carlisle (c.1580–1636)', *Oxford Dictionary of National Biography*, online edn.
SCODEL, J. (1991). *The English Poetic Epitaph: Commemoration and Conflict from Jonson to Wordsworth*. Ithaca, NY: Cornell University Press.
—— (1993). 'The Medium Is the Message: Donne's "Satire 3," "To Sir Henry Wotton" (Sir, more than kisses), and the Ideologies of the Mean'. *Modern Philology*, 90/4: 479–511.
—— (1995). 'John Donne and the Religious Politics of the Mean', in R-J. Frontain and F. Malpezzi (eds.), *John Donne's Religious Imagination: Essays in Honor of John T. Shawcross*. Conway, Ark.: University of Central Arkansas Press, 45–80.
SCOTT, A. V. (2006). *Selfish Gifts: The Politics of Exchange and English Courtly Literature 1580–1628*. Madison, Wisc.: Fairleigh Dickinson University Press.
SCOTT, D. (1972). *The Music of St. Paul's Cathedral*. London: Stainer & Bell.
SCOTT, M. (1614). *The Philosophers Banquet*. London.
SÉBILLET, T. (1990). *Art poétique francais*, in F. Goyet (ed.), *Traités de poétique et de rhétorique de la Renaissance*. Paris: Librairie Générale Française.
SECUNDUS, J. (2000). *The Amatory Elegies of Johannes Secundus*, ed. P. Murgatroyd. Boston and Cologne: Brill.
SEDDON, P. R. (1970). 'Robert Carr, Earl of Somerset'. *Renaissance and Modern Studies*, 14: 46–68.
SELLIN, P. (1982). 'John Donne and the Huygens Family, 1619–1621: Some Implications for Dutch Literature'. *Dutch Quarterly Review of Anglo-American Letters*, 12/3: 193–204.
—— (1983). *John Donne and 'Calvinist' Views of Grace*. Amsterdam: VU Boekhandel/Uitgeverij.
—— (1988). *'So Doth, So Is Religion': John Donne and Diplomatic Contexts in the Reformed Netherlands, 1619–1620*. Columbia, Mo.: University of Missouri Press.
—— (2003). '"Souldiers of one Army": John Donne and the Army of the States General as an International Protestant Crossroads, 1595–1625', in M. Papazian (ed.), *John Donne and the Protestant Reformation: New Perspectives*. Detroit: Wayne State University Press, 143–92.

SEMLER, L. E. (2002). 'Mannerist Donne: Showing Art in the Descriptive Verse Epistles and the Elegies', in A. D. Cousins and D. Grace (eds.), *Donne and the Resources of Kind*. Madison, NJ: Fairleigh Dickinson University Press, 40–58.

SHAGAN, E. (ed.) (2005). *Catholics and the 'Protestant Nation': Religious Politics and Identity in Early Modern England*. Manchester: Manchester University Press.

SHAKESPEARE, W. (2002). *Julius Caesar*, ed. D. Daniell. London: Arden Shakespeare.

SHAMI, J. (1980). 'Donne on Discretion'. *English Literary History*, 47/1: 48–66.

—— (1984a). 'Anatomy and Progress: The Drama of Conversion in Donne's Men of a "Middle Nature"'. *University of Toronto Quarterly*, 53/3: 221–35.

—— (1984b). Review of Troy D. Reeves, *Index to the Sermons of John Donne*. *Renaissance and Reformation*, 8/1: 59–62.

—— (1987). 'Kings and Desperate Men: John Donne Preaches at Court'. *John Donne Journal*, 6/2: 9–23.

—— (1992). 'Introduction: Reading Donne's Sermons'. *John Donne Journal*, 11/1–2: 1–20.

—— (1995a). 'Donne's Sermons and the Absolutist Politics of Quotation', in R-J. Frontain and F. Malpezzi (eds.), *John Donne's Religious Imagination: Essays in Honor of John T. Shawcross*. Conway, Ark.: University of Central Arkansas Press, 380–412.

—— (1995b). '"The Stars in their Order Fought Against Sisera": John Donne and the Pulpit Crisis of 1622'. *John Donne Journal*, 14: 1–58.

—— (2000). 'Anti-Catholicism in the Sermons of John Donne', in L. A. Ferrell and P. McCullough (eds.), *The English Sermon Revised: Religion, Literature and History 1600–1750*. Manchester: Manchester University Press, 136–66.

—— (2003a). *John Donne and Conformity in Crisis in the Late Jacobean Pulpit*. Cambridge: D. S. Brewer.

—— (2003b). 'Labels, Controversy, and the Language of Inclusion in Donne's Sermons', in D. Colclough (ed.), *John Donne's Professional Lives*. Cambridge: D. S. Brewer, 135–57.

—— (2003c). '"Speaking Openly and Speaking First": John Donne, the Synod of Dort, and the Early Stuart Church', in M. Papazian (ed.), *John Donne and the Protestant Reformation: New Perspectives*. Detroit: Wayne State University Press, 35–65.

—— (2004). 'Love and Power: The Rhetorical Motives of John Donne's 1622 Sermon to the Virginia Company'. *Renaissance Papers 2004*: 85–106.

—— (2008a). 'New Manuscript Texts of Sermons by John Donne'. *English Manuscript Studies, 1100–1700*, 13: 77–119.

—— (2008b). 'Troping Religious Identity: Circumcision and Transubstantiation as Tropes in Donne's Sermons', in J. Shami (ed.), *Renaissance Tropologies: The Cultural Imagination of Early Modern England*. Pittsburgh: Duquesne University Press, 89–117.

—— (2009). 'Donne and the Bible', in R. Lemon *et al.* (eds.), *The Blackwell Companion to Literature and the Bible*. Oxford: Blackwell, 240–53.

SHAPIRO, I. A. (1930). 'John Donne and Lincoln's Inn, 1591–1594'. *Times Literary Supplement* (16 Oct.): 833 and (23 Oct.): 861.

—— (1931). 'The Text of Donne's *Letters to Severall Persons*'. *Review of English Studies*, 7/27: 291–301.

—— (1950). 'The "Mermaid Club"'. *Modern Language Review*, 45/1: 6–17.

—— (1967). 'Donne in 1605–6'. *Times Literary Supplement* (26 Jan.): 76.

SHARPE, K. (1987). 'The Image of Virtue: The Court and Household of Charles I, 1625–1642', in D. Starkey *et al.* (eds.), *The English Court: From the Wars of the Roses to the Civil War*. London: Longman, 226–60.

—— (1992). *The Personal Rule of Charles I*. New Haven: Yale University Press.
—— (2000). *Reading Revolutions: The Politics of Reading in Early Modern England*. New Haven: Yale University Press.
SHAWCROSS, J. (1974). 'The Poet as Orator: One Phase of His Judicial Pose', in T. Sloan and R. B. Waddington (eds.), *The Rhetoric of Renaissance Poetry: From Wyatt to Milton*. Berkeley, Los Angeles, and London: University of California Press, 5–36.
—— (1986). 'The Arrangement and Order of John Donne's Poems', in N. Fraistat (ed.), *Poems in their Place: The Intertextuality and Order of Poetic Collections*. Chapel Hill, NC: University of North Carolina Press, 119–63.
—— (1991). *Intentionality and the New Traditionalism: Some Liminal Means to Literary Revisionism*. University Park, Pa.: Pennsylvania State University Press.
SHEAVYN, P. A. B. (1909). *The Literary Profession in the Elizabethan Age*. Manchester: Manchester University Press.
SHELL, A. (1999). *Catholicism, Controversy and the English Literary Imagination, 1558–1660*. Cambridge: Cambridge University Press.
—— (2003). 'Donne and Sir Edward Hoby: Evidence for an Unrecorded Collaboration', in D. Colclough (ed.), *John Donne's Professional Lives*. Cambridge: D. S. Brewer, 121–32.
—— and A. Hunt (2006). 'Donne's Religious World', in A. Guibbory (ed.), *The Cambridge Companion to John Donne*. Cambridge: Cambridge University Press, 65–82.
SHEPPARD, S. (1653). *Merlinus Anonymus*. London.
SHERMAN, A. G. (2007). *Skepticism and Memory in Shakespeare and Donne*. New York: Palgrave Macmillan.
SHERWOOD, T. (1973). 'Reason, Faith, and Just Augustinian Lamentation in Donne's Elegy on Prince Henry'. *Studies in English Literature 1500–1900*, 13/1: 53–67.
SHUGER, D. K. (1990). *Habits of Thought in the English Renaissance: Religion, Politics, and the Dominant Culture*. Berkeley: University of California Press.
—— (2006). *Censorship and Cultural Sensibility: The Regulation of Language in Tudor–Stuart England*. Philadelphia: University of Pennsylvania Press.
SHUTTLEWORTH, K. (2007). 'Autobiographical Reference in John Donne's "Nature's Lay Idiot"'. *Notes and Queries*, NS 54/1: 36–7.
SIBTHORPE, R. (1627). *Apostolike Obedience*. London.
SIDNEY, P. (1965). *An Apology for Poetry or, The Defence of Poesy*, ed. G. Shepherd. London: Thomas Nelson & Sons.
SIMEON, J. (1856–7). 'Unpublished Poems of Donne'. *Miscellanies of the Philobiblon Society*, 3: 1–31.
SIMMS, B. (2007). *Three Victories and a Defeat: The Rise and Fall of the First British Empire, 1714–1783*. London: Allen Lane.
SIMPSON, E. M. (1924; rprt. 1948). *A Study of the Prose Works of John Donne*. Oxford: Clarendon Press.
—— (1931). 'Donne's "Paradoxes and Problems"', in T. Spencer (ed.), *A Garland for John Donne, 1631–1931*. Cambridge, Mass.: Harvard University Press, 23–49.
—— (1965). 'Two Notes on Donne'. *Review of English Studies*, 16/62: 140–50.
SIMPSON, W. S. (ed.) (1880). *Documents Illustrating the History of St. Paul's Cathedral*. London: Camden Society, NS 26.
SINCLAIR, VEN. W. M. (1909). 'John Donne: Poet and Preacher'. *Transactions of the Royal Society of Literature*, NS 2/29: 179–202.

SITO, J. S. (1981). *Poeci Metafizyczni* [The Metaphysical Poets]. Warsaw: Instytut Wydawniczy Pax.

SLIGHTS, C. W. (1990). 'Air, Angels, and the Progress of Love'. *John Donne Journal*, 9/1: 95–104.

—— (1996). 'A Pattern of Love: Representations of Anne Donne', in M. T. Hester (ed.), *John Donne's 'desire of more': The Subject of Anne More Donne in his Poetry*. Newark: University of Delaware Press; London: Associated University Presses, 66–88.

SMEED, J. W. (1985). *The Theophrastan 'Character': The History of a Literary Genre*. Oxford: Clarendon Press.

SMET, I. DE (1996). *Menippean Satire and the Republic of Letters 1581–1655*. Geneva: Droz.

SMITH, A. H. (1974). *County and Court: Government and Politics in Norfolk, 1558–1603*. Oxford: Clarendon Press.

SMITH, A. J. (ed.) (1975). *John Donne: The Critical Heritage*. London: Routledge & Kegan Paul.

—— (ed.) and C. PHILIPS (intro. and ed.) (1996). *John Donne: The Critical Heritage*, vol. 2. London and New York: Routledge.

SMITH, B. H. (1968). *Poetic Closure: A Study of How Poems End*. Chicago and London: University of Chicago Press.

SMITH, B. R. (1999). *The Acoustic World of Early Modern England: Attending to the O-factor*. Chicago: Chicago University Press.

SMITH, L. P. (ed.) (1907). *The Life and Letters of Sir Henry Wotton*. 2 vols. Oxford: Clarendon Press.

SMITH, M. VAN WYK (1973). 'John Donne's *Metempsychosis*'. *Review of English Studies*, 24/93: 17–25, and 'John Donne's *Metempsychosis* (Concluded)', 24/94: 141–52.

SMUTS, M. (1991). 'Cultural Diversity and Cultural Change at the Court of James I', in L. L. Peck (ed.), *The Mental World of the Jacobean Court*. Cambridge: Cambridge University Press, 99–112.

—— (2002). 'The Making of *Rex Pacificus*: James VI and I and the Problem of Peace in an Age of Religious War', in D. Fischlin and M. Fortier (eds.), *Royal Subjects: Essays on the Writings of James VI and I*. Detroit: Wayne State University Press, 371–87.

S. N. (1678). *The Loyal Garland*. London.

SNAPP, H. F. (1966–7). 'The Impeachment of Roger Maynwaring'. *Huntington Library Quarterly*, 30/3: 217–32.

SNYDER, S. (1973). 'Donne and Du Bartas: The Progresse of the Soule as Parody'. *Studies in Philology*, 70/4: 392–407.

SOLOMON, M. (2003). 'Trafique: A Consideration of John Donne's *The First Anniversarie An Anatomie of the World*'. *John Donne Journal*, 22: 59–75.

SOMMERVILLE, J. P. (1986). *Politics and Ideology in England, 1603–1640*. London. Longman.

—— (2003). 'John Donne the Controversialist: The Poet as Political Thinker', in D. P. Colclough (ed.), *John Donne's Professional Lives*. Cambridge: D. S. Brewer, 73–95.

—— (2005). 'Papalist Political Thought and the Controversy over the Jacobean Oath of Allegiance', in E. Shagan (ed.), *Catholics and the 'Protestant Nation': Religious Politics and Identity in Early Modern England*. Manchester and New York: Manchester University Press, 162–84.

SOURIS, A. (ed.) (1962). *Poèmes de Donne, Herbert et Crashaw mis en musique par leurs contemporains*. Paris: Centre Nationale de la Recherche Scientifique.

SOUTHWELL, R. (1953). *An Humble Supplication to Her Maiestie*, ed. R. C. Bald. Cambridge: Cambridge University Press.
SPADE, P. (1973). 'The Origins of the Mediaeval *Insolubilia* Literature'. *Franciscan Studies*, 33: 292–309.
SPARGO, J. W. (1952). *Imaginary Books and Libraries: An Essay in Lighter Vein*. Chicago: The Caxton Club.
SPARROW, J. (1930). 'John Donne and Contemporary Preachers: Their Preparation of Sermons for Delivery and Publication'. *Essays and Studies*, 16: 144–78.
—— (1931). 'The Date of Donne's Travels', in T. Spencer (ed.), *A Garland for John Donne, 1631–1931*. Cambridge, Mass.: Harvard University Press, 121–51.
SPENCE, J. (1949). 'Quelques Remarques Hist: sur les Poëts Anglois', in J. M. Osborn, 'The First History of English Poetry', in J. L. Clifford and L. A. Landa (eds.), *Pope and his Contemporaries: Essays Presented to George Sherburn*. Oxford: Clarendon Press, 230–50.
SPENSER, E. (1595). *Amoretti and Epithalamion*. London.
SPENSER, E. (2001). *Faerie Queene*, ed. A. C. Hamilton. Harlow: Pearson.
STACHNIEWSKI, J. (1991). 'John Donne: The Despair of the "Holy Sonnets"', in *The Persecutory Imagination: English Puritanism and the Literature of Religious Despair*. Oxford: Oxford University Press, 254–91.
STAFFORD, A. (1635). *The Femall Glory: or, the Life and Death of our blessed lady, the holy Virgin Mary*. London.
STANWOOD, P. G. (1978). 'John Donne's Sermon Notes'. *Review of English Studies*, NS 29/115: 313–20.
—— (1979). 'Time and Liturgy in Donne, Crashaw and T. S. Eliot'. *Mosaic*, 12/2: 91–105.
—— (1996). 'Donne's Reinvention of the Fathers: Sacred Truths Suitably Expressed', in H. Wilcox, R. Todd, and A. MacDonald (eds.), *Sacred and Profane: Secular and Devotional Interplay in Early Modern British Literature*. Amsterdam: VU University Press, 195–201.
STAPLETON, L. (1958). 'The Theme of Virtue in Donne's Verse Epistles'. *Studies in Philology*, 55/2: 187–200.
STAPLETON, M. L. (1996). '"Why should they not alike in all parts touch?": Donne and the Elegiac Tradition'. *John Donne Journal*, 15: 1–22.
STATER, V. (2008). 'Herbert, William, Third Earl of Pembroke (1580–1630)', *Oxford Dictionary of National Biography*, online edn.
The Statutes of the Realm (1963). 11 vols. London: Dawsons. (*Statutes*)
STEIN, A. (1984). 'Voices of the Satirist: John Donne', in C. Rawson (ed.), *English Satire and the Satiric Tradition*. Oxford: Basil Blackwell, 72–92.
—— (1986). *The House of Death: Messages from the English Renaissance*. Baltimore and London: Johns Hopkins University Press.
STEPHEN, L. (1898–1902). *Studies of a Biographer*. 4 vols. London: Duckworth; New York: G. P. Putnam's Sons, 3.36–82.
—— (1899). 'John Donne'. *National Review*, 34: 595–613.
STEVENS, P. (2001). 'Donne's Catholicism and the Innovation of the Modern Nation State'. *John Donne Journal*, 20: 53–70.
STEVENSON, D. (2004). 'Ker, Robert, First Earl of Ancram (1578-1654)', *Oxford Dictionary of National Biography*, online edn.
STEWART, A. and H. WOLFE (2004). *Letterwriting in Renaissance England*. Seattle: University of Washington Press.
STEWART, S. (1997). *'Renaissance' Talk: Ordinary Language and the Mystique of Critical Problems*. Pittsburgh: Duquesne University Press.

STONE, L. (1966). 'Social Mobility in England, 1500–1700'. *Past and Present*, 33: 16–55.

—— (1975). 'The Size and Composition of the Oxford Student Body 1580–1909', in L. Stone (ed.), *The University in Society*. 2 vols. Princeton: Princeton University Press, 1.3–110.

—— (1977). *The Family, Sex and Marriage in England, 1500–1800*. London: Weidenfeld & Nicolson.

STORHOFF, G. P. (1977). 'Social Mode and Poetic Strategies: Donne's Verse Letters to His Friends'. *Essays in Literature*, 4: 11–18.

STRACHAN, M. (1962). *The Life and Adventures of Thomas Coryate*. London: Oxford University Press.

STRICKLAND, A. (1866). *The Lives of the Seven Bishops Committed to the Tower in 1688*. London: Bell & Daldy.

STRIER, R. (1996). 'Donne and the Politics of Devotion', in R. Strier and D. Hamilton (eds.), *Religion, Literature, and Politics in Post-Reformation England, 1540–1688*. Cambridge: Cambridge University Press, 93–114.

—— and D. B. Hamilton (eds.) (1996). *Religion, Literature, and Politics in Post-Reformation England, 1540–1688*. Cambridge: Cambridge University Press.

STRINGER, G. (1999). 'An Introduction to the Donne Variorum and the John Donne Society'. *Anglistik: Mitteilungen des Verbandes Deutscher Anglisten*, 10/1 (March): 85–95 (updated July 2007).

—— (1991). 'Donne's Epigram on the Earl of Nottingham'. *John Donne Journal*, 10/1–2: 71–4.

—— (2007). 'Some of Donne's Revisions (And How to Recognize Them)', in. D. Dickson (ed.), *John Donne's Poetry*. New York: Norton, 298–313.

STRONG, R. (1986). *Henry, Prince of Wales and England's Lost Renaissance*. London: Thames & Hudson.

STUBBE, H. (1658). *Delicae Poetarum Anglicanorum in Graecum versae quibus accedunt elogia Romae & Venetiarum*. Oxford.

STUBBS, J. (2006). *John Donne: Reformed Soul*. London: Viking.

SUCKLING, J. (1971). *The Works of Sir John Suckling: The Non-dramatic Works*, ed. T. Clayton. Oxford: Clarendon Press.

SUGG, R. (2000). 'Donne, Vesalius, and the Anatomy of Body and Soul'. *Signatures*, 1, ch. 3: 1–29.

—— (2007). *John Donne*. London: Palgrave Macmillan.

SULLIVAN, E. W., II (1981). 'The Problem of Text in Familiar Letters'. *Papers of the Bibliographical Society of America*, 75/2: 115–26.

—— (1993). *The Influence of John Donne: His Uncollected Seventeenth-Century Printed Verse*. Columbia, Mo.: University of Missouri Press.

—— (1994). '1633 Vndone'. *TEXT*, 7: 297–306.

—— (2000). 'Poems, by J. D.: Donne's Corpus and his Bawdy, Too'. *John Donne Journal*, 19: 299–309.

—— (2003). 'What Have the Donne Variorum Textual Editors Discovered, and Why Should Anyone Care?' *John Donne Journal*, 22: 95–107.

—— (2007). 'Donne and Disbelief: The Early Prose'. *Literature Compass*, 4/2: 423–32.

SULLY, M. DE BETHUNE (1810). *Memoirs of the Duke of Sully*, trans. C. Lennox. 5 vols. London: W. Miller.

SUMMERS, C. J. (1987). 'The Bride of the Apocalypse and the Quest for True Religion: Donne, Herbert, and Spenser', in C. J. Summers and T-L. Pebworth (eds.), *'Bright Shootes of Everlastingness': The Seventeenth-Century Religious Lyric*. Columbia, Mo.: University of Missouri Press, 72–95.

—— (1992). 'Donne's 1609 Sequence of Grief and Comfort'. *Studies in Philology*, 89/2: 211–31.

—— and T L. Pebworth (1991). 'Donne's Correspondence with Wotton'. *John Donne Journal*, 10/1–2: 1–36.

Symons, A. (1899). 'John Donne'. *Fortnightly Review*, ns 72: 734–45.

Tacitus (1951–2). *The Histories and Annals*, ed. C. H. Moore et al. 4 vols. Cambridge, Mass.: Harvard University Press.

Talbert, E. W. (1962). *The Problem of Order: Elizabethan Political Commonplaces and an Example of Shakespeare's Art*. Chapel Hill, NC: University of North Carolina Press.

Targoff, R. (2001). *Common Prayer: The Language of Public Devotion in Early Modern England*. Chicago and London: University of Chicago Press.

—— (2006). 'Facing Death', in A. Guibbory (ed.), *The Cambridge Companion to John Donne*. Cambridge: Cambridge University Press, 217–31.

—— (2008). *John Donne, Body and Soul*. Chicago: University of Chicago Press.

Tayler, E. W. (1991). *Donne's Idea of a Woman: Structure and Meaning in 'The Anniversaries'*. New York: Columbia University Press.

Tepper, M. (1976). 'John Donne's Fragment Epic: "The Progresse of the Soule"'. *English Language Notes*, 13: 262–6.

Theophrastus (1993). *Characters*, in *Theophrastus, Herodas, Cercidas, and the Choliambic Poets*, ed. and trans. J. Rusten, I. C. Cunningham, and A. D. Knox. Cambridge, Mass.: Harvard University Press.

Thomas, K. (1984). *Religion and the Decline of Magic*. Harmondsworth: Penguin.

Thompson, C. (1978). 'The Divided Leadership of the House of Commons in 1629', in K. Sharpe (ed.), *Faction and Parliament: Essays on Early Stuart History*. London: Methuen, 245–84.

Thompson, E. N. S. (1924). 'Familiar Letters', in *Literary Bypaths of the Renaissance*. New Haven: Yale University Press; London: Oxford University Press, 91–126.

—— (1927). *The Seventeenth-Century English Essay*. University of Iowa Humanistic Studies, vol. 3/3. Iowa City: Iowa University Press.

Thomson, P. (1972). 'Donne and the Poetry of Patronage: The Verse Letters', in A. J. Smith (ed.), *John Donne: Essays in Celebration*. London: Methuen, 308–23.

Thrush, A. (2002). 'The Personal Rule of James I, 1611–1620', in T. Cogswell, R. Cust, and P. Lake (eds.), *Politics, Religion and Popularity in Early Stuart England: Essays in Honour of Conrad Russell*. Cambridge: Cambridge University Press, 84–102.

—— (2003). 'The French Marriage and the Origins of the 1614 Parliament', in S. Clucas and R. Davies (eds.), *The Crisis of 1614 and the Addled Parliament: Literary and Historical Perspectives*. Aldershot: Ashgate, 25–35.

Tibullus (1976). *Elegies*, in *Catullus, Tibullus, Pervigilium Veneris*, trans. F. W. Cornish, J. P. Postage, and J. W. MacKail. Cambridge, Mass.: Harvard University Press.

Tighe, W. J. (1987). 'William Laud and the Reunion of the Churches': Some Evidence from 1639 and 1638. *Historical Journal*, 30/3: 717–27.

Tilley, M. P. (1950). *A Dictionary of the Proverbs in England in the Sixteenth and Seventeenth Centuries*. Ann Arbor, Mich.: University of Michigan Press.

Tillotson, K. (1959). 'Donne's Poetry in the Nineteenth Century (1800–1872)', in *Elizabethan and Jacobean Studies Presented to Frank Percy Williams in Honour of his Seventieth Birthday*. Oxford: Clarendon Press, 307–26.

Todd, R. (2002). 'The Manuscript Sources for Constantijn Huygens's Translation of Four Poems by John Donne, 1630'. *English Manuscript Studies, 1100–1700*, 11: 154–80.

Tourney, L. D. (1974). 'Convention and Wit in Donne's *Elegie* on Prince Henry'. *Studies in Philology*, 71/4: 473–83.

A Transcript of the Registers of the Worshipful Company of Stationers 1640–1708 (1913–14), ed. G. E. B. Eyre. 3 vols. London: Roxburghe Club. (*Stationers Register*)

TREVOR, D. (2000). 'John Donne and Scholarly Melancholy'. *Studies in English Literature*, 40/1: 81–102.

TRILLING, L. (1972). *Sincerity and Authenticity*. Cambridge, Mass.: Harvard University Press.

TRIM, D. (2002). 'Fighting "Jacob's Wars": The Employment of English and Welsh Mercenaries in the European Wars of Religion: France and the Netherlands, 1562–1610'. Unpublished Ph.D thesis, University of London.

TUFTE, V. (1970). *The Poetry of Marriage: The Epithalamium in Europe and Its Development in England*. University of Southern California Studies in Comparative Literature, vol. 2. Los Angeles: Tinnon-Brown.

TURBERVILLE, G. (1977). *Epitaphes and Sonnettes* (1576), in *Epitaphes, Epigrams, Songs and Sonets (1567) and Epitaphes and Sonnettes (1576)*, facsimile edn, with introduction by R. J. Panofsky. Delmar, NY: Scholars' Facsimiles and Reprints.

TUTINO, S. (2004). 'Notes on Machiavelli and Ignatius Loyola in John Donne's *Ignatius his Conclave* and *Pseudo-Martyr*'. *English Historical Review*, 119/484: 1308–21.

—— (2007). *Law and Conscience: Catholicism in Early Modern England, 1570–1625*. Aldershot: Ashgate Press.

TUVILL, D. (1971). *Essays politic and moral* [1608], and *Essays moral and theological* [1609], ed. J. L. Livesay. Charlottesville, Va.: University Press of Virginia.

TYACKE, N. (1987a). *Anti-Calvinists: The Rise of English Arminianism, c.1590–1640*. Oxford: Oxford University Press.

—— (1987b). 'The Rise of Arminianism Reconsidered'. *Past and Present*, 115: 201–16.

—— (ed.) (1998). *England's Long Reformation 1500–1800*. London. University College London Press.

USHER, B. (2008). 'Gataker, Thomas (1574–1654)', *Oxford Dictionary of National Biography*, online edn.

VAUX, L. (1568). *A catechisme, or a Christian doctrine necessarie for chyldren and the ignorant people*. Louvain.

VESSEY, M. (1992). 'Consulting the Fathers: Invention and Mediation in Donne's Sermon on Psalm 51:7 ("Purge me with hyssope")'. *John Donne Journal*, 11/1–2: 99–110.

VEYNE, P. (1988). *Roman Erotic Elegy: Love, Poetry, and the West*, trans. D. Pellauer. Chicago and London: University of Chicago Press.

VICKERS, B. (1999). Review of Donne *Variorum*, Volume 8. *Analytical and Enumerative Bibliography*, ns 102: 107–11.

—— (1996). *Francis Bacon*. Oxford: Clarendon Press.

VIPERANO, G. A. (1967). *De Poetica Libri Tres* (1579), facsimile rprt. Munich: Wilhelm Fink.

VIRGIL (1969). *Opera*, ed. R. A. B. Mynors. Oxford: Clarendon Press.

WALDRON, F. G. (1802). 'Miscellaneous Poetry', in *The Shakespeare Miscellany*. London.

WALKER, C. (2004). 'Clitherow, Margaret [St Margaret Clitherow] (1552/3–1586)', *Oxford Dictionary of National Biography*, online edn.

WALKER, D. P. (1985). 'Ficino's *Spiritus* and Music', in P. Gouk (ed.), *Music, Spirit and Language in the Renaissance*. London: Variorum Reprints, 131–50.

WALL, J. (2004). 'John Donne Practices Law: The Case of the Brentwood School'. *John Donne Journal*, 23: 257–97.

—— (2005). '"That Holy roome": John Donne and the Conduct of Worship at St. Paul's Cathedral'. *Renaissance Papers 2005*: 61–84.

——(2007). 'Situating Donne's Dedication Sermon at Lincoln's Inn, 22 May 1623'. *John Donne Journal*, 26: 159–239.

WALSHAM, A. (1999). *Church Papists: Catholicism, Conformity and Confessional Polemic in Early Modern England*, 2nd rev. edn. Woodbridge: Boydell Press.

——(2006). *Charitable Hatred: Tolerance and Intolerance in England, 1500–1700*. Manchester: Manchester University Press.

WALTON, I. (1640). 'The Life and Death of Dr Donne, late Deane of St Pauls London', in *John Donne, LXXX Sermons*. London.

——(1653). *The Compleat Angler: or, the Contemplative Man's Recreation*. London.

——(1658). *The life of John Donne, Dr. in Divinty* [sic], *and Late Dean of Saint Pauls Church London*. London.

——(1670). *The Lives of Dr. John Donne, Sir Henry Wotton, Mr. Richard Hooker, Mr. George Herbert*. London.

——(1675). *The Lives of Dr. John Donne, Sir Henry Wotton, Mr. Richard Hooker, Mr. George Herbert*. London.

WANNING, A. (ed.) (1962). *Donne*. New York: Dell.

WATERHOUSE, E. (1663). *Fortescutus illustratus*. London.

WATKINS, J. (1999). '"Out of Her Ashes May a Second Phoenix Arise": James I and the Legacy of Elizabethan Anti-Catholicism', in A. Marotti (ed.), *Catholicism and Anti-Catholicism in Early Modern English Texts*. Basingstoke: Macmillan Press, 116–36.

WATSON, J. R. (1997). *The English Hymn: A Critical and Historical Study*. Oxford: Clarendon Press.

WATSON, R. N. (1984). *Shakespeare and the Hazards of Ambition*. Cambridge, Mass.: Harvard University Press.

——(1994). *The Rest is Silence: Death as Annihilation in the English Renaissance*. Berkeley: University of California Press.

WATSON, T. (1582). *The Hekatompathia or Passionate Centurie of Loue*. London.

WATT, T. (1991). *Cheap Print and Popular Piety, 1550–1640*. Cambridge: Cambridge University Press.

WAYNE, V. (1996). 'Advice for Women from Mothers and Patriarchs', in H. Wilcox (ed.), *Women and Literature in Britain, 1500–1700*. Cambridge: Cambridge University Press, 56–79.

W. B. (1614). 'To the Reader', in M. Scott, *The Philosophers Banquet*. London.

WEBBER, J. (1963). *Contrary Music: The Prose Style of John Donne*. Madison, Wisc.: University of Wisconsin Press.

——(1968). *The Eloquent 'I': Style and Self in Seventeenth-Century Prose*. Madison, Wisc.: University of Wisconsin Press.

——(1972). 'The Prose Styles of Donne's *Devotions upon Emergent Occasions*'. *Anglia*, 79: 138–52.

WEBSTER, J. (2001). *The Duchess of Malfi*, ed. B. Gibbons, 4th edn. London: A. & C. Black; New York: W. W. Norton.

WECKHERLIN, G. R. (1641). *Gaistliche und Weltliche Gedichte*. Amsterdam.

WEINBROT, H. D. (2005). *Menippean Satire Reconsidered: From Antiquity to the Eighteenth Century*. Baltimore: Johns Hopkins University Press.

WEISS, J. (1974). '*Ecclesiastes* and Erasmus'. *Archiv für Reformationsgeschichte*, 65: 83–108.

WELLINGTON, J. E. (1971). 'The Litany in Cranmer and Donne'. *Studies in Philology*, 68/2: 177–99.

WENTERSDORF, K. P. (1982). 'Symbol and Meaning in Donne's *Metempsychosis or The Progresse of the Soule*'. *Studies in English Literature*, 22/1: 69–90.

WERNHAM, R. B. (ed.) (1988). *The Expedition of Sir John Norris and Sir Francis Drake to Spain and Portugal, 1589*, vol. 127. Aldershot: Navy Records Society.

—— (2006). 'Amphibious Operations and the Elizabethan Assault on Spain's Atlantic Economy, 1585–1598', in D. J. B. Trim and M. C. Fissel (eds.), *Amphibious Warfare, 1000–1700: Commerce, State Formation and European Expansion*. Leiden: Brill, 181–215.

WESTON, W. (1995). *An Autobiography from the Jesuit Underground*, trans. P. Caraman. Garden City, NY: Image Books.

WHIGHAM, F. (1984). *Ambition and Privilege: The Social Tropes of Elizabethan Courtesy Theory*. Berkeley: University of California Press.

WHITE, P. (1992). *Predestination, Policy and Polemic: Conflict and Consensus in the English Church from the Reformation to the Civil War*. Cambridge: Cambridge University Press.

WHITLOCK, B. W. (1954). 'The Dean and the Yeoman'. *Notes and Queries* (Sept.): 374–5.

—— (1955a). 'Donne at St. Dunstan's I'. *Times Literary Supplement* (16 Sept.): 548.

—— (1955b). 'Donne at St. Dunstan's II'. *Times Literary Supplement* (23 Sept.): 564.

—— (1955c). 'Y^e Curioust Schooler in Cristendom'. *Review of English Studies*, SN 6/24: 365–71.

—— (1959). 'The Heredity and Childhood of John Donne'. *Notes and Queries*, 204: 257–62 and 348–53.

WHITLOCK, K. (2004). 'The Robert Ashley Founding Bequest to the Middle Temple Library and John Donne's Library'. *Sederi*, 14: 153–78.

WHITMAN, W. (1994). 'Song of Myself', in J. Kaplan (ed.), *Walt Whitman: Poetry and Prose*. New York: Library of America.

WIGGINS, P. D. (2000). *Donne, Castiglione, and the Poetry of Courtliness*. Bloomington, Ind.: Indiana University Press.

WIKANDER, M. (1979). '"Queasy to be Touched": The World of Ben Jonson's *Sejanus*'. *Journal of English and Germanic Philology*, 78/3: 345–57.

WILCOX, H. (1994). '"Curious Frame": The Seventeenth-Century Religious Lyric as Genre', in J. R. Roberts (ed.), *New Perspectives on the Seventeenth-Century Religious Lyric*. Columbia and London: University of Missouri Press, 9–27.

—— (2006). 'Devotional Writing', in A. Guibbory (ed.), *The Cambridge Companion to John Donne*. Cambridge: Cambridge University Press, 149–66.

WILKINS, E. H. (1959). *Petrarch's Later Years*. Cambridge, Mass.: Medieval Academy of America.

WILKINS, V. G. (2008). 'Field, Richard (1561–1616)', *Oxford Dictionary of National Biography*, online edn.

WILLIAMSON, G. (1930). *The Donne Tradition*. Cambridge, Mass.: Harvard University Press.

—— (1969). 'Donne's Satirical *Progresse of the Soule*'. *English Literary History*, 36/1: 250–64.

WILLIAMSON, J. W. (1978). *The Myth of the Conqueror: Prince Henry Stuart: A Study of 17th Century Personation*. New York: AMS Press.

WILMOTT, R. A. (1836). *Conversations at Cambridge*. London: John W. Parker.

WILSON, P. H. (2009). *Europe's Tragedy: A History of the Thirty Years War*. London: Allen Lane.

WINWOOD, R. (1725). *Memorials of Affairs of State*, ed. E. Sawyer. 3 vols. London.

WOLLMAN, R. (1993). 'The "Press and the Fire": Print and Manuscript Culture in Donne's Circle'. *Studies in English Literature, 1500–1900*, 33/1: 85–97.

WOOD, A. (1691–2). *Athenae Oxonienses*, 2 vols. London.

WOODING, L. E. C. (2000). *Rethinking Catholicism in Reformation England*. Oxford: Clarendon Press.
WORMUTH, F. (1939). *The Royal Prerogative, 1603–1649: A Study in English Political and Constitutional Ideas*. Ithaca, NY: Cornell University Press.
WOTTON, H. (1650). *Reliquiae Wottonianae*. London.
—— (1938). *A Philosophical Survey of Education, or Moral architecture*, ed. H. S. Kermode. London: Hodder & Stoughton.
WOUDHUYSEN, H. R. (1996). *Sir Philip Sidney and the Circulation of Manuscripts, 1558–1640*. Oxford: Clarendon Press; New York: Oxford University Press.
WRIOTHESLEY, C. (1875). *A Chronicle of England during the Reigns of the Tudors, 1485 to 1559*. 2 vols. London: Camden Society.
WROTH, M. (1983). *The Poems of Lady Mary Wroth*, ed. J. A. Roberts. Baton Rouge: Louisiana State University Press.
WYATT, SIR T. (1988). *The Complete Poems*, ed. R. A. Rebholz. Harmondsworth: Penguin Books.
YAN, K. (2007). 'A Glory to Come: John Donne Studies in China'. *John Donne Journal*, 26: 311–32.
YATES, F. A. (1939). 'Giordano Bruno's Conflict with Oxford'. *Journal of the Warburg and Courtauld Institutes*, 2/3: 227–42.
YOUNG, R. V. (1987a). 'Donne's Holy Sonnets and the Theology of Grace', in C. J. Summers and T-L. Pebworth (eds.), *'Bright Shootes of Everlastingnesse': The Seventeenth-century Religious Lyric*. Columbia, Mo.: University of Missouri Press, 20–39.
—— (1987b). '"O my America, my new-found-land": Pornography and Imperial Politics in Donne's *Elegies*'. *South Central Review*, 4/2: 35–48.
—— (2000a). *Doctrine and Devotion in Seventeenth-Century Poetry: Studies in Donne, Herbert, Crashaw, and Vaughan*. Cambridge: D. S. Brewer.
—— (2000b). 'Donne and Bellarmine'. *John Donne Journal*, 19: 223–34.
—— (2000c). 'Love, Poetry, and John Donne in the Love Poetry of John Donne'. *Renascence*, 52/4: 251–73.
—— (2007). 'Theology, Doctrine, and Genre in *Devotions upon Emergent Occasions*'. *John Donne Journal*, 26: 373–80.
YOUNG, W. (1889). *The History of Dulwich College*. 2 vols. London: T. B. Bumpus.
YU, C. (1982). 'John Donne's Poetry and Modern Poetry'. *Journal of the English Language and Literature* (Chongwon, Korea), 21: 67–89.
ZALLER, R. (1971). *The Parliament of 1621*. Berkeley: University of California Press.
ZIM, R. (1987). *English Metrical Psalms: Poetry as Praise and Prayer, 1535–1601*. Cambridge: Cambridge University Press.
—— (2007). 'Religion and the Politic Counsellor: Thomas Sackville, 1536–1608'. *English Historical Review*, 122/498: 892–917.
ZUBER, R. (1986). '*Eloge du dialogue des morts*: John Donne et le pamphlet gallican', in M. Jones-Davies (ed.), *La Satire au temps de la Renaissance*. Paris: Touzot.

Index 1: Conceptual Tools

Absolutism, 626–29, 662, 690–703. *See also* DONNE, **Character traits and beliefs**
'Accommodation', *see* DONNE, **Genres**, Sermons
Act (and Oath) of Supremacy, 41, 371, 379, 388, 398, 402, 411, 413–14, 507, 665. *See also* DONNE, **Biography**, early years and education, at Oxford
Act of Uniformity, 371, 373, 388, 409
'Addled' Parliament, *see* Parliament—of 1614
Allegiance, Oath of, 5–6, 250, 252–53, 255–56, 258, 367, 486–87, 493, 498, 501, 506–08, 521–22, 567, 591. *See also* Parliament—of 1604
    controversy concerning, 5–6, 12, 67–68, 169, 249–63, 367, 380, 489, 491–94, 498–505, 522, 548, 558, 591, 666, 669, 754
'Anglicanism', 230
Antwerp, siege of, 416–18. *See also* DONNE, **Biography**, travels, military service
'Apostasy', 365, 378, 380. *See also* DONNE, **Character traits and beliefs**
Arcana imperii, 245, 637, 694–95, 700
    in Donne's Problems, 245–48
    in Donne's Sermons, 637–38, 694, 699–700
Archpriest controversy, 377, 521
Arminianism, 492, 595, 599, 606, 614, 618, 624–25, 627, 629–30, 645, 668, 699
    in Donne's Sermons, 701
Attributions, problems of, 175. *See also* DONNE, **Writings**, uncertainty of canonical, intentional, and textual attribution
Audiences, reading or listening, 4, 16, 36, 38–40, 65–66, 80, 100, 119, 124, 135, 145, 152, 154, 159, 183–84, 186–87, 262, 266–67, 276, 321, 323, 327, 333, 341, 365, 377, 381, 389, 396, 400, 405, 422, 441, 455, 465–66, 468–69, 487, 491–92, 498–99, 502, 508, 514, 517, 519–21, 578, 582, 604, 614, 625, 644, 654, 679. *See also* DONNE, **Writings**, audiences, reading or listening
'Avant-garde conformists', 488–94
    and Donne, 489, 491–92, 494

Azores ('Islands') voyage, 444–45. *See also* DONNE, **Biography**, travels, military service

Bible, 15, 155, 233–35, 268–69, 309–10, 313, 320–22, 324–35, 588, 603
Bibles, 334, 381
Bibliographies, 81, 84–85, 718
Bibliography, textual, 12–96, 141, 165–68, 210–17, 222, 247, 348–50, 357–60, 414–16, 434, 496
'Bloody Question', 109, 114
Book of Common Prayer, 223, 234–35, 331, 371–73, 385, 639

Cadiz raid, 142, 424–29, 432, 442–45, 463–64. *See also* DONNE, **Biography**, travels, military service
Calvinism, 139, 230, 292, 335, 373–75, 407, 488, 491, 494, 533, 540, 545, 548, 556, 568, 571–72, 577–79, 583, 586, 593–96, 599, 614, 618, 624, 639, 642, 645, 668, 675, 701. *See also* DONNE, **Character traits and beliefs**
    and anti-Calvinism, 488, 491–92, 568, 571–72, 577, 593–95, 614, 618, 624–25, 638–39, 642–45, 667–68, 674 *See also* DONNE, **Character traits and beliefs**
Canon law, 252–54, 261, 390, 472–75, 569. *See also* DONNE, **Biography**, early years and education
Canonical literature, 88, 94, 123, 256, 381
Casuistry, 380, 696, 700, 702. *See also* DONNE, **Biography**, early years and education
Catholicism, English, 127, 193, 219, 252, 297, 311, 331, 365–94, 398–400, 402, 405, 406–07, 409–14, 420–23, 457–58, 473, 480, 483–91, 492–93, 496, 499–504, 506–09, 515–22, 535–36, 541, 567–68, 590–91, 593–94, 596, 598–99, 616–17, 621, 622–23, 627, 631, 640, 645, 649, 663, 665–75, 744. *See also* Catholicism, Roman; DONNE, **Character traits and beliefs**

Catholicism, English (cont.)
  and anti-Catholicism, 127, 193, 252, 365–67, 369, 371, 373–94, 398, 402–05, 407–14, 420–21, 423, 457–58, 473–74, 480, 483, 486–87, 489–91, 496, 498–99, 501, 504–05, 507–08, 515, 517, 519–22, 663, 665–66, 669, 671, 673, 743–44. *See also* Catholicism, Roman, and anti-Catholicism; Loyalism, Catholic; DONNE, **Character traits and beliefs**
Catholicism, Roman, 230, 236, 251–53, 255–56, 259, 261, 323–24, 326, 329, 331, 365–69, 371–77, 379, 381, 389–94, 398, 406–14, 485–91, 493–94, 498, 500–04, 506–09, 515–16, 519–22, 535–36, 541, 561, 567–68, 571–72, 578, 580, 584–85, 590–95, 596–99, 614, 616–17, 619–20, 622–25, 639–40, 665–67, 669–70, 672–74, 677, 744. *See also* Jesuits; Loyalism, Catholic; Catholicism, English; DONNE, **Character traits and beliefs**
  and anti-Catholicism, 165, 171–72, 252, 297, 365–67, 369, 371, 374–77, 406–08, 412, 486–92, 494, 498, 500–04, 506–08, 515–16, 519–22, 606–07, 623–25. *See also* Catholicism, English, and anti-Catholicism; DONNE, **Character traits and beliefs**
Cavalier poets, 684
Censorship, 1, 13, 37, 152, 327, 516, 583, 744, 750
Ceremonialism, 668. *See also* Arminianism
Chancery, *see* Law courts
Chapel Royal, 554, 556–557, 561, 564, 569, 586, 604, 609, 627, 640, 650, 726. *See also* DONNE: **Biography**, attendance at Chapel Royal
Chaplains, royal, 554–60, 562, 564. *See also* DONNE, **Biography**, royal chaplaincy
Characters, 154, 245–46, 267, 334, 379, 517, 580, 683, 711, 714–16. *See also* DONNE, **Genres**
Children, 372, 386–88, 392–93, 394, 398–400, 403, 409–10, 413, 477, 530, 540–41, 565, 584, 591–92, 594, 648, 650. *See also* DONNE, **Biography**
Church of England, 219, 228, 230, 235, 320, 323, 328, 331, 339, 371–76, 402, 411, 484, 486, 488, 491–93, 562, 578, 594–95, 614, 624–25, 665, 674–75, 694, 710. *See also* 'Anglicanism'; DONNE, **Biography**, Church of England member
  and Catholicism, 234, 260–61, 323–24, 371–76, 382, 387, 394, 402, 411, 485–89, 508, 521, 578, 591, 594–95, 599, 614, 639–40, 645, 665–67, 672

  and Puritanism, 373–75, 594–95, 599, 614, 618, 624–26, 630, 638–39, 666, 694
'Church papists', 5, 255, 331, 372, 378–79, 381, 594, 599, 665
Civil law, 474–75. *See also* DONNE, **Biography**, early years and education
Classical traditions, see DONNE, **Writings**, classical influences on
Closure, literary, 4, 106, 117, 121, 131, 265, 267, 270, 317, 705
Common law, 403–04, 474, 579, 582, 612, 626, 693, 696, 701–02
Concordances, 11, 50, 81, 83, 86, 94
Conformity and nonconformity, religious, 127, 308–09, 321, 331, 365, 372, 374–75, 379, 381–82, 384, 398, 474, 484–89, 492, 494, 555, 562, 567, 577–79, 586, 594, 606, 638, 665, 674. *See also* 'Avant-garde conformists'; DONNE, **Biography**, conformity
Conscience, 219, 255, 260, 270, 295, 317, 319–20, 326, 328, 347, 361, 367, 372–73, 379, 381, 388, 390, 502, 504, 507, 525, 572, 588, 591, 607, 614, 666–67, 673, 690, 726, 744, 753. *See also* DONNE, **Character traits and beliefs**
Constancy, 52, 114, 123, 171, 331, 420, 487, 507, 552, 562, 686, 693, 738. *See also* DONNE, **Character traits and beliefs**
  and inconstancy, 129, 253, 265, 331, 370, 373–78, 381, 386, 388, 420, 422, 461, 491, 521, 541, 566, 577, 584, 633, 638, 645, 664–65, 674. *See also* DONNE, **Character traits and beliefs**
Conversion, 171–72, 252–53, 297, 311, 319–21, 325, 327, 329, 336, 346, 365, 376, 381–82, 455–56, 484, 488, 524, 530, 604, 606–07, 622, 625, 642, 655–56, 664–65, 668–69, 674–75, 677, 734. *See also* DONNE, **Biography**
  of Toby Matthew, 507–08, 520–21
Copy-texts, 21, 34–35, 46–55, 57–60, 67–77, 79, 137. *See also* Textual bibliography; Variants, textual
Council of Trent, 373, 376, 390, 398, 421. *See also* DONNE, **Writings**, Council of Trent in
Courts, *see* Ecclesiastical courts; Law courts; Royal courts

Decorum, see DONNE, **Writings**
Dicta Catonis, 111–12
DigitalDonne, 45, 82–84, 86, 92

Directions to Preachers, 327, 369, 599, 606, 621, 623, 640
'Divine Poems', 218–19, 233–35, 237. *See also* DONNE, **Genres**
Divine right of kings, 245, 258–59, 691–94, 697, 703
DONNE, Dr. JOHN, Dean:
Biography, 151, 182, 184, 193–96, 247, 348, 365–70, 523–28, 668–74, 677, 690–92, 719–28.
  See also **Index 2: Personal names**, Bald; Cain; Carey; Flynn; Gosse; Haskin; Jessopp; Novarr; Patterson; Sellin; Shami; Strier; Walton
  ancestry, 4–5, 99–100, 107–11, 115–18, 129, 142, 149, 243, 250, 252, 255–56, 287, 365–66, 368, 381, 383–94, 399, 408–14, 419–23, 494, 535–36, 576, 646, 648–50, 665–66, 668, 670–71, 673–74, 734, 745, 748, 750
  persecution for religion, 5, 41, 152, 165, 408–11, 413–14, 507, 748
  early years and education, 5–6, 107, 256–57, 365–66, 399, 407–11, 419–21, 535, 746, 748, 751
  at Oxford, 41, 155, 366, 402, 407, 411, 413–14, 665
  academic degrees, 368, 498, 558–59, 569–70
  at Thavies and Lincoln's Inn, 145, 150–51, 160, 209–10, 254, 299, 404, 406–07, 421–23, 425, 447–48, 453–54, 457, 466, 472, 554, 556, 576–78, 580, 684
  study of civil law, canon law, and casuistry, 12, 253–54, 299–301, 404, 406, 422–23, 425, 447–48, 452–53, 472–75, 498, 500, 556, 569–70, 582, 612, 673, 700, 702, 723
  travels, 86, 95, 161, 212, 366, 407, 481, 525, 677
  exile, 40–41, 413–21
  military service, 4, 421–22, 424–34
  at siege of Antwerp, 416–19, 433. *See also* DONNE, **Genres**, Latin Epigrams
  on Azores ('Islands') voyage, 4, 142, 366, 424–25, 427, 430–34, 447–48, 496.
    See also DONNE, **Genres**, Epigrams and Verse Letters
  in Cadiz raid, 4, 109, 112–15, 142, 146, 366, 424–32, 434, 442–45, 447, 463, 496.
    See also DONNE, **Genres**, Epigrams
  in 1605–06, 261, 367, 506, 508–18, 521–22, 525, 528
  in 1611–12, 62, 214, 216, 274, 349, 356, 489, 495, 497–98, 500, 508–11, 514, 525–26, 529, 537–38, 706, 752
  in 1619–20, 5, 155, 239, 368, 561, 573–74, 581–83, 595–602, 618, 732, 752
  secretary to Lord Keeper Egerton, 6, 15, 76, 191, 355, 366, 433, 447–59, 464–66, 469–72, 474, 500, 506, 525, 554–56, 559, 567, 570, 572, 577, 602–03, 605, 750
  leasing of a recusant's Lincolnshire manor, 458
  in Parliament—of 1601, 168, 457–58, 464, 472–73, 577, 694
  marriage to Anne More, 6, 38, 145, 193, 195, 200, 358, 366–67, 379, 452, 456–58, 466–67, 471–79, 484, 500–01, 525–26, 556, 577, 673, 686, 688, 737–38
  imprisonment, 458, 466, 473–74, 556, 650
  Church of England member, 193, 219, 228, 230, 232, 261–62, 320, 323, 328, 331, 339, 347, 367, 368–69, 382, 411, 484, 518, 522–25, 528, 535, 547–48, 554–55, 645, 651–53, 665–75, 706, 726, 738
  residence at Pyrford, 194, 359, 367, 449–50, 459, 464, 471–72, 476, 478–82, 484, 508, 511–12
  unemployment, 478, 480–82, 484, 498–501, 508–10
  residence at Mitcham and London, 164, 359, 367, 491–94, 512, 671, 674–75
  publication, 1–4, 13–17, 22–23, 25, 66, 68, 71, 101, 109, 150, 154–55, 173–74, 204, 206–07, 213–14, 216, 228, 238, 240, 273–74, 291, 311, 315, 318, 332, 367, 423, 487, 492, 493, 496, 499, 506–07, 511–13, 517–18, 521–22, 528, 548, 607, 659, 666, 683, 701, 733, 744, 754
  sickness, 12–13, 71–72, 311–17, 456, 527, 534–35, 607–08, 649–50, 656–57
  dangers faced by, 6, 129–30, 149, 152–53, 155, 165, 245–46, 260, 262, 319, 344, 354, 390, 407, 413–14, 433, 458, 461, 472, 507, 513, 607–08, 615, 663, 675, 751
  patronage and preferment, 10, 13, 15, 25, 35–36, 191, 200–01, 251, 258, 280, 286–87, 289–90, 296–97, 301, 304–05, 311, 337, 344, 356, 367–68, 433, 448–49, 459, 466, 469–70, 486, 492, 509, 524–32, 534–35, 538, 544, 547–48, 550, 554, 564, 568–70, 573–74, 577, 588, 600, 602–03, 608–09, 612, 619, 627, 671–72, 719, 720, 723–26, 730, 733, 739
  conformity, 367, 382, 384, 474, 491–94, 522, 555, 614, 637–38, 665, 668, 673, 706
  conversion, 5, 193, 382, 524, 527–28, 530, 535, 555, 654, 662, 664–66, 669–75, 677, 734, 736
  residence at Drury Lane, 451, 511–512
  Privy Council and, 245, 411, 461, 464, 467, 480, 531–32, 547, 560, 681

DONNE: **Biography** (cont.)
  in Parliament—of 1614, 529, 544, 549–50, 614, 699
  and Spain, 421, 424–26
  vocation, 218, 356, 367–68, 523–36, 564, 677, 733
  ordination, 6, 14, 193, 213, 216, 219, 228, 238, 258, 268–69, 319, 321, 367–68, 382, 509, 518, 523–36, 548, 554, 556, 558–59, 563, 568–70, 572–73, 576, 586, 589, 594, 654, 665–71, 673–75, 691, 699, 722, 733, 738, 740
  royal chaplaincy, 368–69, 529, 554–65, 569, 594, 603, 609
  attendance and preaching at the Chapel Royal, 554, 557, 559, 561, 564, 569, 609, 726
  rector of Keyston, 556, 559, 570, 603
  rector of Sevenoaks, 556, 559, 570
  Lenten preaching, 562–65, 603, 612, 650
  readership at Lincoln's Inn, 71, 327, 337, 341, 368, 559, 570, 576–88, 594–95, 603, 609–10, 645, 669
  cipher entrusted to, 573, 581
  and Synod of Dort, 600–01, 614
  as Dean of St. Paul's, 6, 13, 33, 71, 178, 240, 262, 332–33, 351, 368, 377, 415–16, 419, 459, 556, 564–65, 574–75, 588, 602–15, 617, 619, 621, 640–42, 645, 652, 654–56, 667, 670, 680, 683, 736, 741–42
  prebend of Chiswick, 604, 608
  vicar of St. Dunstan's, 327, 556, 608–10, 615
  residence at Chelsea, 326, 609–10
  prolocutor of 1626 Convocation, 599, 611
  attendance at and governor of the Charterhouse, 480, 482, 611–13
  death of, 2, 6, 13–14, 20, 25, 29, 56, 107, 118, 154, 228, 268, 286–87, 311, 319, 348, 350, 369–70, 416, 425, 466, 562, 564–65, 604–05, 607, 610, 612, 615–16, 632, 637, 643–57, 675, 677, 708
  burial, 651
  and London, 15, 100, 145, 211, 326, 367, 409, 447, 451, 456, 458–59, 469, 472, 478, 480, 482, 508, 525, 534, 554–55, 569, 602, 610–11, 619, 645, 653. *See also* DONNE, **Writings**, and London
  children of, 459, 471–72, 476–77, 482, 509, 513, 534–35, 648–49
  library of, 16, 52, 85, 243, 332, 360, 466
  mottoes of, 422, 425, 636, 666, 669, 734
  portraits of, 54, 147, 241, 262, 366, 421–22, 425, 447, 514, 525–26, 643, 666, 669, 685, 734
  seals of, 370, 380, 603, 605, 654–55

friends and friendship, 4, 13–17, 19–20, 27, 29, 43, 154–55, 173, 176, 181, 190, 192, 206, 211, 229, 236, 243, 247, 259, 277, 287, 291–92, 294, 299, 319, 349, 353, 356, 360, 366–68, 370, 429, 432, 447, 454, 456–57, 478, 480, 482–83, 494, 506, 508–10, 515, 528, 534, 538, 544, 555, 561, 588–89, 606, 609–10, 612–14, 616, 646, 654–55, 667, 744, 748, 751–52. *See also* DONNE, **Writings**, coteries; **Index 2: Personal names**: George Abbot; Sir Walter Aston; Christopher Brooke; Samuel Brooke; Cecilia Bulstrode; Sir Julius Caesar; Sir Dudley Carleton; Sir William Cornwallis; Thomas Coryate; Sir Robert Cotton; Sir John Danvers; Sir Robert Drury; Bridget Dunch; George Garrard; Martha Garrard; Sir Henry Goodere; William Hakewill; Joseph Hall; John Harington, second baron Harington of Exton; Thomas Harriot; Elizabeth Hastings (née Stanley), countess of Huntingdon; James Hay, viscount Doncaster and first earl of Carlisle; Edward Herbert, first baron Herbert of Cherbury; George Herbert; Magdalen Herbert (née Newport), Lady Danvers; Philip Herbert, first earl of Montgomery; William Herbert, third earl of Pembroke; Sir Henry Hobart; John Hoskins; Constantijn Huygens; Ben Jonson; Sir Robert Ker; Sir Robert Killigrew; Henry King; John King; Bridget Kingsmill (née White); Sir Henry Marten; Richard Martin; Toby Matthew; Thomas Morton; Henry Percy, ninth earl of Northumberland; Sir Edward Phelips; Sir Robert Rich; Sir Thomas Roe; Lucy Russell (née Harington), countess of Bedford; Anne Sackville (née Clifford), Countess of Dorset; William Stanley, sixth earl of Derby; Izaak Walton; Edmund Whitelock; Thomas Winniffe; Rowland Woodward; Thomas Woodward; Sir Francis Wolley; Sir Henry Wotton
pastoral cares, 6, 217, 321, 327, 330, 343, 564, 578, 584, 608, 611, 615
and English Reformation, 223, 365, 383–86, 492, 604, 669, 673, 677. *See also* DONNE, **Writings**, and English Reformation

Character traits and beliefs:
absolutism, 614, 638, 661–62, 672, 690–92, 694, 697–703, 725
ambition, 480–81, 524–27, 528–36, 547–49
'apostasy', 5–6, 378, 661–62, 664–77, 724–25, 739
Calvinism, 139, 335, 368–69, 494, 572, 577, 579, 583, 586, 595, 614, 642, 668, 675
  and anti-Calvinism, 230, 292–93, 614, 624–25, 642–45, 668, 701
Catholicism, 165, 219, 228, 260, 331, 336, 365–68, 377–83, 394, 402, 407–11, 413–14, 419–23, 474, 487, 491–94, 496, 499, 502–04, 507–08, 510, 517, 521–22, 524, 535–36, 555, 582, 645, 649, 663, 665–74, 737
  and anti-Catholicism, 311, 323–24, 326, 329, 331, 487, 489, 492, 498–500, 503–04, 521–22, 584, 623–24, 663, 666, 669, 671, 673–74, 677, 743–44. *See also* Catholicism, English, and anti-Catholicism; Catholicism, Roman, and anti-Catholicism; Jesuits; Loyalism, Catholic
conscience, 13, 131, 257, 262, 270, 320, 354, 409, 457, 630, 667, 671, 722–23, 745
constancy, 6, 130, 148, 197, 202, 229, 302, 312, 315, 320, 342, 354, 422, 425, 447, 460, 530–31, 562, 612, 646–47, 649, 666–68, 672, 674–77, 697, 725, 734–35, 748
  and inconstancy, 22, 73, 99, 127, 130, 137, 144, 147, 212, 225, 231, 260, 344, 370, 422, 433, 528, 584, 612, 642, 668–69, 672–74, 676, 697, 734, 740, 751–52
daring, 2, 106, 108–09, 117, 125, 190, 245–47, 280, 289, 513, 518, 739
discretion, 6, 181, 199, 262, 320, 334, 342, 354, 529, 535, 609, 640, 721, 732
fear, 1, 4, 113, 129–30, 132, 136, 139–40, 144, 152, 162, 190, 210, 212, 218, 225–26, 228–29, 232, 240–41, 245, 311–13, 317, 337, 355–56, 430, 432, 434, 460, 513, 528, 561, 585, 590, 600, 642, 651, 656, 666, 676, 687, 740, 742, 744, 748, 750, 754–55
honour, 6, 132, 174, 177–78, 258, 298, 304–05, 320, 335, 341, 350, 353, 356, 360, 422, 425, 465, 467, 505, 524, 527, 533, 535, 582, 600, 604, 608, 672–73, 691, 726–27, 729–30
loyalty, 13, 218, 301, 357, 377–78, 493–94, 507, 584, 642, 666–67, 669–70, 673, 676, 691, 726
misogyny, 6, 24, 143–44, 161, 192, 205, 661–62, 678–89
opportunism, 258, 280, 527, 727–28

Protestantism, 143, 219, 223, 227, 229, 236, 254, 315, 331, 494, 535, 555, 561, 582, 584, 595, 599, 602, 606, 614, 616, 645, 655–56, 666, 670, 680
Puritanism, anti-Puritanism, 161, 223, 294–96, 315–16, 331, 332, 336, 339, 370, 493, 599, 621, 653, 668, 755
scepticism, 100, 102, 129, 271, 282, 284, 583, 744
Genres. *See also* **Index 4: Individual works discussed**
Anniversaries, 3, 14–17, 44, 48, 53–4, 56, 99, 106, 207, 214, 216, 220, 273–85, 286, 290, 349, 351, 530, 645, 674, 680, 682–3, 688, 706, 718–21, 724, 752
Characters, 12, 39, 72, 151–52, 158, 165, 167, 175–79, 580, 762, 707–08, 732, 748–52
Controversial Treatise (*Pseudo-Martyr*), 3, 12–13, 29, 66–72, 77, 100, 152, 160, 173, 246, 249–63, 321, 356, 367, 377, 380, 408, 410, 466, 492–94, 496, 498–500, 503–04, 507, 518, 520–22, 533, 555, 558, 591, 612, 645, 665–67, 669, 671, 697, 702, 718, 727, 744, 746, 750, 753–55
'Divine Poems', 33, 44, 46, 52, 54, 94, 184, 431, 705, 734, 739, 751. *See also* DONNE: **Genres**, Liturgical Poems; Religious Sonnets
Elegies, 2, 14–15, 18, 20–21, 24, 32, 37, 44–45, 50, 52, 54–55, 58–60, 85, 94, 100, 106, 109, 134–48, 151, 181–82, 184, 187, 218, 228, 290, 434, 460–61, 512, 518, 676, 679, 683–84, 688, 708, 715, 743–44, 746, 751
Epicedes and Obsequies, 15, 25, 44, 57–58, 100, 106, 136, 173, 182, 216, 277–78, 286–97, 301, 682, 706, 721, 733
Epigrams, 2, 15, 20–21, 31, 44, 52–53, 59–60, 62, 85, 99, 103, 105–21, 182, 301, 366, 414–20, 426, 428–29, 431, 433, 512–13, 518, 732, 735, 741
Epitaphs and Inscriptions, 15, 18, 53, 228, 275, 285, 287
Epithalamions, 15, 28, 44, 49, 59, 85, 101–02, 182, 188, 298–307, 532–33, 548, 680, 718, 722, 726, 739
Essays, 12–14, 76–78, 102, 151, 228, 264–72, 319, 535, 666. *See also* DONNE, **Genres**, Characters
  as Sermons, 268–69, 271, 319
Latin Epigrams, 105, 107, 109, 117, 366, 414–20, 433, 512–13, 732, 735
Liturgical Poems, 15, 24, 50–52, 100, 216, 233–41, 527–28, 656, 669–70, 674, 676, 733, 734–35

DONNE: **Genres** (*cont.*)
  Love Lyrics ('Songs and Sonets'), 3–4, 15, 18, 23, 44, 47, 50, 52–55, 61, 85, 94, 101–03, 106, 115, 159, 173, 180–206, 210, 218, 223, 228–29, 307, 346, 476, 647–48, 657, 670, 672, 676, 679, 683–88, 709–13, 715, 724, 734, 736, 738
  Paradoxes, 2, 12, 14–15, 25, 27, 36, 39, 72–73, 100, 105, 149–57, 161, 178, 246, 512, 518, 680, 743–44, 752–53
  Biathanatos, 12–14, 25, 27, 29, 35–36, 41, 68, 74–75, 100, 153–157, 160, 204, 246, 259, 357, 730, 732–733, 752
  Problems, 12, 17, 36, 39, 72–73, 99, 156, 165, 212, 242–48, 251, 349, 680
  Prose Letters, 13–17, 25, 27–29, 35–36, 44, 78–80, 85, 95, 150, 152, 154–55, 160, 164, 184, 204, 207, 211–17, 259–61, 284, 287, 333, 348–61, 368, 380, 430–31, 452, 454, 456, 465–67, 474, 477, 508, 510–11, 523, 525–30, 532–34, 557, 564, 573, 600–03, 608–10, 612–13, 620–21, 650, 666–67, 671, 677, 682, 704, 726, 734–36, 738, 743–44, 746–47, 752
    holographs, 38, 79, 145, 155, 350, 357–58, 452, 458, 466
    letters to:
      George Abbot, archbishop of Canterbury, 573
      Sir Dudley Carleton, 357–58
      Robert Carr, earl of Somerset, 350, 356, 501, 529–32, 547, 568, 722
      Anne Cokayne (née Stanhope), 682
      Sir Robert Cotton, 466, 481
      Anne Donne (née More), 360, 456–57, 472–73, 477
      Sir Thomas Egerton, Lord Keeper, 358, 448, 452, 465–66, 470–71
      George Garrard, 15–16, 349, 355–56, 511, 514, 682–83, 706
      Martha Garrard, 349
      Sir Henry Goodere, 14–17, 27, 73, 76, 107, 136, 146, 150, 152, 164, 174, 211–13, 215–16, 235–36, 243–44, 251, 258, 260–61, 279, 287, 304, 349, 352, 354–56, 360–61, 415, 447–48, 459, 474–75, 480, 491–93, 495, 498–500, 505–06, 508–14, 518, 526, 528–29, 532–33, 535, 537–38, 548–49, 551, 559, 573, 577, 583, 607, 666–67, 706, 732–33, 735, 743–44, 746–47, 752–54
      Elizabeth Hastings (née Stanley), countess of Huntingdon, 721
      James Hay, viscount Doncaster and first earl of Carlisle, 722
      Edward Herbert, first baron Herbert of Cherbury, 155, 752
      Magdalen Herbert (née Newport), 349, 755
      James VI and I, 258
      Sir Robert Ker, 14, 27, 155, 197, 204, 287, 350, 355, 357, 531–32, 535, 548, 568–69, 667, 705–07, 732–34, 738, 752
      Bridget Kingsmill (née White), 357, 682
      Sir George More, 38, 145, 358, 452, 458, 467, 473–75, 535, 551
      Sir Robert More, 358, 360, 510, 534–35, 547–48
      Lucy Russell (née Harington), countess of Bedford, 349, 682
      Susan Herbert (née Vere), countess of Montgomery, 38, 600–01, 682
      Sir Toby Matthew, 353–54, 514
      Elizabeth Donne (née Heywood; Syminges, Rainsford), 355, 383, 408, 535–36, 682
      George Villiers, duke of Buckingham, 79, 350, 465, 602
      Sir Henry Wotton, 211, 358, 467, 570
    letters written for:
      Anne Drury (née Bacon), 355
      Sir Robert Drury, 355
      Sir Thomas Egerton, 355, 452, 466
      Sir Henry Goodere, 355
    problematic addresses of, 14, 78–79, 164, 211, 304, 350, 355, 431
    problematic dates of, 14–15, 73, 76, 78–79, 136, 164, 258, 355, 459, 506, 509–13, 601
    problematic texts of, 78–79, 349–50, 355, 357
  Religious Sonnets, 3, 15, 18–19, 21, 23, 44, 50–52, 54–55, 59–61, 64, 82, 85, 100–01, 104, 109, 137, 163, 182, 185, 216, 218–33, 239, 287, 307, 645, 649, 670–71, 674–76, 705–06, 717, 726, 734, 740
  Satires, formal verse, 2, 14, 30, 35, 46, 48, 52–53, 55, 61, 100–02, 109, 122–33, 136, 151, 179, 181–82, 188–89, 202, 306, 318, 325, 433, 453–54, 466, 512, 518, 555, 675, 688, 708, 711–12, 715, 725, 735, 737, 743–44, 746, 748–51
  Sermons, 4, 11–14, 18, 69–71, 77–78, 81, 85, 87–88, 90, 92, 100, 102–03, 175, 193, 198, 207, 217, 236–37, 240, 257, 263, 268–69, 271, 284, 287, 306–307, 314, 317–349, 355, 357, 369–70, 375, 419, 492, 518, 554, 557, 559–565, 577, 579–584, 586, 599, 601–04, 606–10, 613–615, 617, 619–621, 623–625, 627, 629–630, 633–634, 636–638, 640–645, 650–651, 655–56, 667–668, 673,

677, 680–681, 691, 694, 697–707, 710, 714, 717, 718–719, 721, 725–30, 734–736, 739, 742–743, 745, 751
'accommodation' in, 320, 325, 327, 329–30, 332, 342, 346
audiences of, 13, 320, 323–24, 326–28, 330–33, 335–37, 339–46, 557, 561, 579–81, 607, 681
conversion in, 319–21, 325, 327–29, 336, 346, 563
Council of Trent in, 324, 326
holograph corrections of, 36, 63, 332–33
influence of Augustine, 320–22, 324, 326–27, 329–30, 332–33, 335, 340–42
influence of Calvin, 320, 329, 335, 614
influence of Erasmus, 320–27, 331, 333, 335, 342
'nearnesse' in, 320–21, 327–28, 336, 345–46
predestination in, 335–36, 346
Verse Letters, 2–4, 15–18, 21, 25, 28, 44, 61–63, 85, 103–04, 106, 158, 181–82, 185, 187, 190–91, 197, 199, 201, 206–17, 220, 243, 289–91, 349, 425, 431–33, 454–56, 467, 529–30, 577, 667, 672, 678, 681–82, 688, 718, 721, 729
Writings. *See also* **Index 4: Individual works discussed**
and English Reformation, 5, 219–20, 229, 236, 311, 320, 324, 328–29, 614, 644, 666, 669, 673, 675, 677, 680. *See also* DONNE, **Biography**, and English Reformation
and London, 130, 138, 140, 142, 148, 210, 300, 307, 360, 510–12, 518, 535, 617, 643. *See also* DONNE, **Biography**, and London
and performance, 101–02, 150–52, 185, 191, 194, 197, 205, 237–238, 243, 246–47, 280–81, 289, 301, 303, 314, 323, 332, 335, 355, 366, 369, 422–23, 452, 465–66, 531, 533, 548, 562, 607, 615, 621, 630, 671, 706, 710, 739, 744, 755
and Spain, 114–15, 139, 142–43, 213, 428, 465
attribution, problems of, 20, 39, 41, 44–45, 50–52, 173–75, 220, 414–19, 472
audiences, reading or listening, 10–11, 46, 53–55, 58, 60, 63, 67, 70–71, 74, 77–79, 82, 85, 87–88, 103, 106, 111–12, 119–21, 127, 132–34, 136, 145, 154, 157, 162, 164, 169, 181–82, 185, 188–97, 199, 202, 204, 214, 232, 236–37, 239, 251, 254, 257–58, 263, 269, 271–72, 274, 276–78, 281–82, 295, 298, 301–02, 304, 307, 314–15, 318–19, 323, 327–28, 330, 337, 345–47, 348, 354, 361, 497, 523, 636–37, 649, 651, 656–57, 661, 672, 678–80, 682–83, 686–89, 705–07, 712–16, 718, 722, 726, 736–39, 744, 747–48, 750, 754–55
of the sixteenth- and seventeenth-centuries, 9–10, 13–18, 22, 24–33, 36–37, 41, 71, 87, 109, 128, 132, 140, 151–58, 163, 180–81, 183, 185, 189, 191–92, 195, 198–201, 206, 210, 212–14, 216, 229–30, 232, 243, 253, 256, 261, 273, 284, 286, 289, 291–92, 305, 308, 318–20, 323–24, 326–28, 330–33, 335–37, 339, 341–45, 346, 354–56, 360, 419, 430, 473, 481, 493, 510, 518, 554–55, 557, 559–65, 579–88, 604, 606, 613, 630, 642, 645, 647, 651, 665–66, 673, 678–79, 681, 684–85, 699, 706, 710–11, 721, 727, 730, 743–44, 751–55
authorial revisions in, 23–24, 50–53, 60, 75
Calvinism mentioned in, 251
canon of, 9, 20–21, 43, 46–47, 52–53, 78–79, 86, 100–02, 109, 182, 193, 239, 256–57, 346, 579
classical influences on, 2–3, 71, 102, 107–08, 110–12, 122–25, 128, 130–38, 142, 144–45, 148, 158, 162, 175–76, 192, 202–03, 207, 213, 215, 238–39, 246, 250, 271, 274, 278, 287–88, 290, 298, 302, 310–11, 314, 320–22, 342, 350–51, 420, 467, 709, 729–30
compression in, 106–107, 110, 115, 127, 167, 175, 178
conceits, poetic, 4, 20, 24–25, 58, 112, 137, 144, 148, 159, 170, 175–76, 178–179, 189, 192, 197–198, 202, 210, 215, 217–218, 223, 231, 236–239, 256, 276, 280, 286, 289, 350, 356, 648, 682, 684–685, 712–714, 720, 735, 742
coteries of, 4, 9, 15, 26, 37, 128, 145, 150–53, 181, 191–92, 195, 206, 214, 244, 246, 289, 672, 687, 706, 725
Council of Trent in, 260, 262, 324, 326, 367, 522, 624, 666–67, 744
dating of, 5, 9, 15, 24–25, 35, 51, 53, 57, 65–66, 69–70, 73–74, 76–79, 82, 85, 87, 161, 164, 173, 176, 184–85, 195, 220, 224, 237, 258, 261, 268, 302, 348, 358, 419, 421–22, 430, 433–34, 456, 467, 471, 475, 497, 506, 509–14, 525–26, 559, 581, 585–86, 588, 650, 654, 657, 668, 670–71, 674, 699–700, 732–33, 738
decorum in, 5, 109, 231, 273–74, 277, 289, 301, 327, 332–33, 342, 384, 401
dialogic writings, 103–04, 124–25, 130, 160, 171, 242, 272, 313, 360, 655, 739, 744, 751, 754–55
'Dubia', 21, 52, 175–77

DONNE: **Writings** (*cont.*)
  'emergent occasions' of, 201–202, 206–07, 213, 314–15, 344, 693, 695–96, 700, 702, 703.
    See also DONNE, **Writings**, occasional
  exegesis in, 77, 102, 268–69, 271–72, 319, 327–28, 331, 342–43, 580, 680, 688
  Eve, 198–99, 497, 649, 678–82
  'fresh invention' of, 2, 107, 112, 117, 121, 134, 148, 189, 201, 205–06, 228, 283–84, 709–10
  harshness of, 128, 147, 173, 188, 210, 217, 235, 661–62, 683, 698, 707, 710, 715, 735–37
  holographs, 16, 20, 34, 36, 38, 51, 56, 58, 62–63, 79, 87, 141, 155, 195, 207, 214, 217, 222, 332, 348, 357–58, 465–66, 506, 512, 518, 732
  humanism in, 102, 127, 136, 142, 145, 151, 163, 165–67, 250, 260, 279, 283, 320–21, 327, 350, 360, 419–21, 423
  imitation in, 106, 111, 134–36, 142, 145–46, 148, 151, 205, 215, 287, 313, 342, 346, 559–60, 681, 709–11, 735
  innovation in, 102–03, 106, 111, 136, 138, 145, 147, 156, 163, 167, 170, 185, 237, 277, 286–87, 297, 302, 311–15, 497, 662, 710, 721, 747
  irenicism in, 100, 227–28, 230, 250, 260, 294, 311, 331, 527, 644–45
  irony in, 111, 113–14, 118–19, 131, 134, 139–40, 144, 148–49, 152, 163, 166, 170, 176, 178–79, 183–84, 202, 218, 228, 230–31, 243, 246, 250, 259, 273, 342, 354, 356, 360, 408, 422, 425–26, 429, 535, 581, 613, 635, 680, 687, 704–05, 709, 725
  'Juvenilia', 36, 72–73, 151, 176
  libels, 495, 537–38
  literary personae of, 82, 124, 128, 130–32, 137–40, 143–48, 219, 223–25, 231–32, 250, 305, 466, 555, 604, 613, 684, 704, 710, 712, 738, 748–50
  manuscripts, 2–4, 9–10, 13–24, 27–29, 34–64, 66–76, 78–79, 82–84, 87, 92, 109, 118, 128, 135–36, 141, 150, 153–55, 161–62, 165, 177, 180–81, 183–84, 192, 199, 202–05, 207, 211, 217, 219–21, 224, 228, 240–41, 258, 290, 299, 332, 348, 456, 467, 472, 506, 513, 517–19, 555, 601, 645, 657, 675, 678, 708, 732, 744, 755
  metaphor in, 106, 111, 113, 115, 117, 143, 161, 189, 231, 233, 239–40, 251, 270, 273, 276, 312–13, 317, 325, 333–36, 345, 420, 530, 638, 650–51, 657, 667, 677, 725, 748, 752
  metre of, 43, 54, 103, 174, 187–88, 197–98, 211, 233, 235, 662, 708–10, 712–16, 737

Neoplatonism in, 192, 649
obscurity of, 21, 26, 106, 122, 125, 132, 138, 152, 160, 164, 185, 205, 207, 214, 219, 228, 236, 239, 245, 247, 262–63, 268, 278, 289, 307, 320, 339, 341–43, 346, 419, 500, 642, 655, 661, 700, 707, 715, 737–38
occasional, 4, 12–13, 15, 59, 61, 87, 103, 132, 152, 184, 188, 199, 201, 205–07, 210, 212–14, 217, 238–39, 243, 249, 273–74, 280–81, 286–87, 289–90, 294, 296–97, 299–302, 304, 314–15, 318, 320–21, 325–28, 330, 332, 336–38, 342, 344, 348, 353, 357–58, 480, 505, 528, 537, 561, 565, 580, 604, 607, 610, 636, 650, 702
on idolatry, 223, 226, 231, 339, 651, 687
on Jesuits, 12, 100, 107, 118, 129, 170–72, 177, 220, 254–55, 257, 260, 262, 366–67, 377–78, 381, 409–11, 413, 419, 423, 498, 502–04, 507, 510, 520, 522, 583–85, 590, 647, 673, 730, 745–46, 748, 754
on martyrdom, 139, 192, 251, 256–58, 262, 377–78, 381, 408–09, 503, 535, 666, 673, 730, 746–48, 754
on papacy, 100, 169–70, 174, 232, 251, 254, 256, 259–61, 336, 343–44, 367, 487, 492, 494, 500, 503–04, 520, 522, 561, 599, 621, 624–25, 640, 645, 665–66, 675, 697–98, 702
on Parliament, 140, 244–48, 254, 369, 482, 497–98, 503, 508–09, 511, 599, 623, 625, 627, 636, 690–92, 697–98, 700–03
on predestination, 139, 143, 168, 226, 292–93, 335–36, 346, 370, 535–36, 612, 614, 642–45, 650, 653, 667–68, 699, 701
on Purgatory, 170, 326, 329, 512, 655–56
Ovidian style in, 22, 106, 135, 138, 142, 144, 161–62, 187, 192, 207, 287, 688, 739
paradox in, 6, 24, 36, 76, 100, 108, 117, 150–51, 153–54, 157, 165–67, 172, 174, 212, 217, 223, 225, 227, 231, 236–39, 256, 259, 275, 279, 282–83, 291, 300, 302–03, 305, 307, 312, 324, 335–36, 341, 343, 370, 464, 527, 529, 560, 565, 653, 675, 704, 725, 729, 733, 752
parody in, 103–04, 147, 167, 219, 223, 229–31, 246, 269, 301, 679–80, 709
pastoral and non-pastoral poetry, 103, 273–74, 277, 282, 305
Petrarchism in, 104, 106, 115, 139, 188, 192, 200, 207, 218–19, 227–30, 232, 350–51, 688
  and anti-Petrarchism, 104, 106, 115, 146–47, 161, 188, 192, 200, 231, 683. *See also*, DONNE, **Writings**, Ovidian style
Platonism in, 15–16, 177, 295, 711, 730

INDEX   821

reception, 23, 41, 74, 95, 250, 290, 354, 583, 661–62, 719–28, 731
sacraments and the sacred in, 82, 104, 192, 218–19, 221, 223, 229, 231–32, 269, 281, 293, 324–25, 329–30, 340–41, 356, 586, 615, 691, 721, 727, 739, 745
saints and canonization in, 171, 192–93, 210, 217, 223, 229, 232, 235, 274, 293, 301–02, 346, 408, 535, 653, 657, 705
satire and the satirical in, 2, 41, 69, 72, 75–76, 110–12, 114, 118–20, 127, 129–34, 152, 158, 160–61, 163, 165, 167–70, 173, 178–79, 181, 192, 202, 243–46, 250, 253, 255, 276–77, 282–83, 300, 420, 429, 433, 453–54, 480, 499, 503, 512, 647, 679–80, 705, 712, 746, 748–50
scepticism in, 102, 127, 151, 167, 177, 246, 250, 259–62, 271–72, 274, 282, 583, 675–76
scholasticism, 14, 71, 165, 167, 191, 219, 257, 269, 271, 297, 320, 735
and anti-scholasticism, 167
seals in, 22–23, 144, 317, 341, 354, 361, 560, 733
sequences of, 3, 10, 18, 45–46, 51, 53, 59–62, 64, 70, 101, 106–07, 109, 113–14, 117–21, 124, 137–38, 147–48, 182, 184–86, 210, 219–28, 231, 290–91, 294, 316, 467, 709
sex and sexuality in, 23, 26, 30, 32, 118, 120, 137–38, 143, 146–47, 161–62, 167, 171, 180, 182, 185, 188–89, 192–93, 196, 218, 228–29, 231, 300–04, 513, 648–49, 662, 676, 679, 682–83, 686–87, 747
style, 69, 79, 82, 101, 107–08, 114–15, 117, 125, 130, 147, 151, 160, 176, 185, 188, 231, 268, 270–71, 283, 287, 312–14, 348–50, 355–58, 370, 458, 467–68, 613, 637, 645, 662, 708–11, 713–14, 716
treason and traitors in, 109, 114, 129, 140, 152, 167, 245, 260–61, 494, 534, 745–46, 748
typology in, 113–14, 170, 240, 330–31, 338, 688, 697
uncertainty of canonical, intentional, and textual attribution, 9, 14–15, 20–21, 24, 39, 41, 43–47, 49–54, 69–75, 78–80, 107–09, 128–31, 158, 161–64, 169–71, 173–79, 182, 220, 224, 259–63, 270–71, 277–79, 298–301, 304–07, 327–28, 336, 414–19, 472, 523, 525–36, 614, 642, 664–65, 674, 678, 744–46, 751. *See also* DONNE, **Writings**, scepticism in; paradox in
versification, 6, 15, 20, 103, 132, 211, 224, 662, 685, 708–13, 716. *See also* DONNE, **Writings**, metre

Variorum, 2–3, 10–11, 21, 24, 28, 44, 56–64, 72, 81–84, 90, 92, 94, 101, 106, 109, 132, 136–37, 141, 161, 180, 195, 205, 210, 220–24, 304, 414–15, 418, 675, 741
Dort, Synod of, 595, 600–601, 606, 614, 618, 624–625. *See also* DONNE: **Biography**, and Synod of Dort

Ecclesiastical courts, 448, 474, 494, 498, 516
  Court of Arches, 498
  Court of Audience, 473–75
  Court of High Commission, 448, 474–75, 612
Ecumenism, 230, 261, 485, 639, 666–67
Edict of Nantes, 169–486
Education, 32, 37, 95, 111–12, 126, 161, 242, 246, 322–23, 332, 351, 365, 373, 381, 385–87, 390, 395–407, 471, 476–77, 510, 544, 579, 584. *See also* DONNE, **Biography**, early years and education
Election. *See* Predestination; DONNE, **Character traits and beliefs**, predestination
Elegies, 21, 124, 134–39, 145–48, 186, 207–08, 273–76, 278, 280, 282–84, 286–88, 297, 646. *See also* DONNE, **Genres**, Elegies
  for Donne, 29, 31, 36, 145, 349, 612, 634, 651, 707–11, 720, 734
Elizabethan Settlement, 371–74, 398, 402, 409, 484
Epicedes and Obsequies, 224, 274–75, 277–79, 288, 293. *See also* DONNE, **Genres**, Epicedes and Obsequies
Epigrams, 105–21, 123–25, 128, 134, 182–83, 185, 187, 198, 207, 243, 276, 301, 429, 683, 708, 734. *See also* DONNE, **Genres**, Epigrams
Epitaphs and Inscriptions, 20, 105, 107–08, 183, 209, 538, 612, 646, 651, 709. *See also* DONNE, **Genres**, Epitaphs and Inscriptions
Epithalamions, 22, 163, 298–301. *See also* DONNE, **Genres**, Epithalamions
Essays, 154, 250, 260, 264–70, 454, 461, 730. *See also* DONNE, **Genres**, Essays
Exegesis, 41, 321, 331. *See also* DONNE, **Writings**, exegesis in
Exile, religious, 107, 116, 142, 372, 377, 383–88, 390–94, 407, 409–14, 492, 508, 619–20, 627, 665–66, 725. *See also* DONNE, **Biography**, travels

Fabliau, 116–17
Fear, 122, 124, 156, 168, 171, 255, 266, 377, 402–03, 441, 445, 456, 464, 487, 549, 551, 568, 592–93, 595, 599, 607, 617, 621, 629, 636, 639, 641. *See also* DONNE, **Character traits and beliefs**, fear

Forced Loan, 626–29, 698, 700
Friendship, 36, 38, 91, 123, 128, 142, 161, 173, 176, 178–79, 209, 277, 279, 290–92, 294, 298, 299, 301, 313, 350–52, 353, 356, 360, 379–80, 386–88, 405, 409, 414, 440, 454–57, 461, 463, 465, 469, 478, 491, 494–95, 499–500, 516, 519, 538, 541, 543, 546, 560, 573, 588, 593, 648, 653, 655–56, 681–82, 686, 748, 751–52. See also DONNE, **Biography**, friends

Galli, 119
Gallicanism, 252, 367, 489, 500, 503, 510, 521
Gallus, Gaius Cornelius, 135
Genera mixta (or *mista*), 279
Gentleman volunteers, 249, 366, 424–26, 430–31, 440–42, 445–47, 590, 592, 618
Good Friday, 237, 240, 562–65
'Great Contract', 540, 566
Greek Anthology, 107–08, 115–17, 419–20
'Greek' epigram, 110, 115
Gunpowder plot, 5–6, 36, 140, 169, 252, 332, 367, 486, 489–90, 493, 498, 501–02, 506–07, 515–20, 522, 544, 557, 564, 590–91, 594, 667, 698

Habsburgs, 573, 592–93, 595, 597–98, 606, 617, 619, 623
Hagiography, 193, 378, 668
Handbooks, 1–6, 40, 88, 180, 186, 196, 321
Heresy, 161, 164, 250–53, 255, 260, 277, 295, 375, 386–87, 390, 393, 400, 486–87, 503, 590, 642
Honour, 111, 149, 244–45, 379, 380, 383–84, 390, 400, 440–41, 457, 462–63, 465, 467, 481, 505, 524, 538, 568, 582, 597, 600, 664. See also DONNE, **Character traits and beliefs**, honour
Humanism, 76–77, 102, 115, 117, 126–27, 135, 150, 158, 165, 207, 250, 283, 320–21, 327, 331, 350–51, 360, 384–86, 395–99, 401–04, 419–21, 423. See also DONNE, **Writings**, humanism in

Idolatry, 231, 376, 524, 588, 591, 651, 664, 676. See also DONNE, **Writings**, on idolatry
Il Moro (Ellis Heywood), 390–91
Imitation, 32, 107, 116, 126, 135–36, 158–59, 184, 186–87, 208, 210, 218, 234, 266, 276, 310, 320, 323, 350–51, 401, 406, 419, 694. See also DONNE, **Writings**, imitation in

Imprisonment for religion, 39, 377, 381, 384, 386, 388, 393–94, 409–13, 423, 457, 486, 492–93, 508, 515–17, 519–20, 544, 621, 627–30, 665, 673, 746, 748, 750. See also DONNE, **Biography**, imprisonment
Innovation, 52, 94–95, 280, 701, 721. See also DONNE, **Writings**, innovation in
Inns of Chancery, 404, 422, 579
  Thavies Inn, 404, 421–23, 451
Inns of Court, 37, 105, 300–01, 387, 391, 396, 404–06, 424, 450, 521, 576, 578–80, 585–88. See also DONNE, **Biography**, early years and education; readership at Lincoln's Inn
Irenicism, 321, 331, 369, 390, 421, 491, 592, 616. See also DONNE, **Writings**, irenicism in
Irish expedition of Essex, 435, 440, 445–46, 449, 464, 468–69, 483
Irony, 75, 117, 123, 139–40, 172, 245, 375–76, 446, 492, 519, 568. See also DONNE, **Writings**, irony in

Jesuits, 107, 166, 169, 171–72, 252, 255, 262, 310, 376–77, 379–81, 391, 393, 398–99, 402, 409–13, 419, 423, 485–87, 489, 492, 494, 498, 502–03, 510, 519–22, 590, 594–95, 625, 630, 747. See also Catholicism, Roman, and anti-Catholicism; DONNE, Jesuits
John Donne Journal, 2, 40, 89–92, 94, 605
John Donne Society, 2, 89–92, 94

Law courts
  Chancery, Court of, 404, 422, 448, 450, 452, 455, 532, 579
  Common Pleas, Court of, 475, 489
  King's Bench, 576
  Queen's Bench, 388
  Star Chamber, 151, 248, 448, 492, 520
Law education, 385, 390–91, 396–97, 403–06, 461, 579. See also DONNE, **Biography**, early years and education
Lenten preaching, 555, 562–64, 601, 612. See also DONNE, **Biography**, Lenten preaching
Libels, 469, 495, 505, 537–38, 542, 548, 552, 590. See also DONNE, **Writings**, libels
Lincoln's Inn, 71, 299–301, 327, 337, 341, 368, 385, 388, 404, 406, 422–423, 425, 447–48, 450, 451–53, 472, 556, 559, 570, 576–588, 594–595, 603, 609–10, 645, 669. See also DONNE, **Biography**, early years and education; readership at Lincoln's Inn

Literary personae, 136, 144, 146, 684, 741.
　　See also DONNE, **Writings**, literary
　　personae of
Love Lyrics, 32, 36, 104, 110, 160, 163, 180, 182–89,
　　192–93, 198, 209–10, 218–19, 221,
　　227–28, 231–32, 250, 276, 288, 655, 684,
　　709, 718. See also DONNE, **Genres**,
　　Love Lyrics
Loyalism, Catholic, 13, 116–17, 218, 254, 377–78,
　　380, 393, 457, 485–87, 491, 493–94,
　　501–03, 507, 516, 627, 666–67, 674.
　　See also Catholicism, English, and anti-
　　Catholicism; DONNE, **Character
　　traits and beliefs**, loyalty

Manicheans, 330
Manuscripts, 9, 22, 42, 45, 51, 58–60, 64, 90, 101,
　　136, 141, 152, 161, 175, 209, 224, 262, 266,
　　290, 310, 391, 406, 454–56, 465–66, 469,
　　477, 498–99, 538, 548–49, 552, 719.
　　See also DONNE, **Writings**,
　　holographs; manuscripts
Marriage, 100, 120, 123, 146, 298–307, 327, 337,
　　373–74, 394, 422, 505, 532–33, 540–41,
　　544–47, 549–50, 552, 567, 568, 572,
　　583–84, 592–93, 598, 607, 612, 617–23,
　　631, 634, 676–77, 680–81, 722, 724, 733,
　　739, 746. See also DONNE, **Biography**,
　　marriage to Anne More
Martyrdom, 100, 250–52, 255, 279, 374–78, 381,
　　383–86, 388–90, 408–10, 423, 492, 503.
　　See also DONNE, **Writings**, on
　　martyrdom
Metaphor, 117–18, 125, 333, 703. See also DONNE,
　　Writings, metaphor in
Metre, 43, 54, 134–35, 186–87, 197, 207–09, 233–35,
　　278, 288, 662, 713–16. See also DONNE,
　　Writings, metre of
Miscellanies, verse or prose, 28, 34, 36–37, 39, 41,
　　44, 48, 69, 101, 181–84, 188, 203, 205,
　　414–15, 418–20
Misinterpretation, 14, 21, 25, 27, 58, 155, 165, 193,
　　204–05, 271, 356, 389, 637–38, 679, 732,
　　744, 746, 752–55
Missionary priests, 107, 366, 376–78, 398, 409–13,
　　486, 630
Mottoes, 114–15, 428. See also DONNE,
　　Biography, mottoes of

Nearness, 152, 320–21, 327, 336, 345, 347, 389
Neoplatonism, 146, 167, 192, 649. See also
　　DONNE: **Writings**, Neoplatonism in
New Criticism, 85, 194–95, 670, 755
Numerology, 163

Oath of Allegiance, 5–6, 250, 252–53, 255–56, 258,
　　367, 486–87, 493, 498, 501, 506–08, 521–22,
　　567, 591. See also Parliaments, Jacobean
　　controversy concerning, 5–6, 12, 67–68, 169,
　　249–63, 367, 380, 489, 491–94, 498–505,
　　522, 548, 558, 591, 666, 669, 754
Oath of Supremacy, see Act (and Oath) of
　　Supremacy
Oath of Uniformity, see Act of Uniformity
Obscurity, 123, 125, 128, 130, 149, 278, 287–88, 321,
　　404, 578, 747. See also DONNE,
　　Writings, obscurity of
Occasional writing, 17, 32, 184, 186–87, 208, 278,
　　308, 310, 325–26, 628. See also DONNE,
　　Writings, occasional
Ordination, 411, 569. See also DONNE,
　　Biography, ordination
Ovidian style, 126, 135–36, 208–10, 278, 401.
　　See also PetRarchism and anti-
　　Petrarchism; DONNE, **Writings**,
　　Ovidian style in; Petrarchism, and
　　anti-Petrarchism

Papacy, 127, 166, 169–72, 174, 193, 249, 252, 254–55,
　　336, 339, 344, 367, 372, 374–76, 379,
　　390–91, 394, 403, 484–86, 489, 492–94,
　　507, 516, 561, 589–91, 596, 599, 606, 621,
　　624–26, 630, 651, 655, 701. See also,
　　Catholicism, Roman, and anti-
　　Catholicism; DONNE, Catholicism,
　　and anti-Catholicism; DONNE,
　　papacy
　　of Adrian VI (Boeyens), 260
　　of Clement VIII (Aldobrandini), 486
　　of Gregory XIII (Buoncompagni), 142,
　　　　409, 675
　　of Paul III (Farnese), 171
　　of Paul IV (Carafa), 390–91
　　of Paul V (Borghese), 169, 261, 501–02, 596
　　of Paul VI (Montini), 372
　　of Pius V (Ghislieri), 372
　　authority of, 100, 142, 251, 256, 259–61, 367,
　　　　486–91, 494, 499–504, 520–22, 590–91,
　　　　665, 674, 692, 697–98, 702
　　power to excommunicate and depose, 109,
　　　　169, 250–51, 254, 367, 372, 486–87,
　　　　501–03, 590–91, 674
　　thought antichristian, 373, 487–88, 491, 504,
　　　　591, 624–25
Paradox, 108, 117, 149, 156, 159–60, 165, 259, 327,
　　351, 454. See also DONNE, **Writings**,
　　paradox in
Paradoxes, 149–51, 153–54, 157, 161, 283, 454.
　　See also DONNE, **Genres**, Paradoxes

Parlement of Paris, 503
Parliament, 176, 244, 254, 369, 371–73, 375–76, 379, 385–86, 393, 396–98, 410, 448, 462, 464, 551–53, 567, 572, 589, 593, 599, 626, 628, 633, 635–36, 690–96, 699. *See also* DONNE, **Biography**, in Parliament—of 1601; in Parliament—of 1614
—of 1601, 168, 457–58, 472–73, 577, 694
—of 1604, 140, 244–48, 482–86, 493, 497–98, 501, 504–05, 508–09, 511, 521, 540–42, 545, 566, 591–92, 694–96, 699
—of 1614, 529, 544, 549–50, 567, 699
—of 1621, 552, 603, 617, 619–21, 694, 696, 698–99
—of 1624, 622, 625
—of 1625, 623, 700
—of 1626, 623–26, 629, 698
—of 1628, 628–31, 634–36, 691, 698
Parody, 31, 219, 246. *See also* DONNE, **Writings**, parody in
Pasquil, 105, 160, 169, 171, 179, 253, 262, 287–88
Pastoral and non-pastoral poetry, 283, 558. *See also* DONNE, **Writings**, pastoral and non-pastoral poetry
Pastoral care, 322, 402, 564, 578, 611. *See also* DONNE, **Biography**, pastoral care
'Patriots', 5, 372–73, 425, 446, 495, 505, 537, 541–42, 544–46, 549–50, 552, 599, 616–17, 622–23
Patronage and preferment, 123, 145, 155, 164, 184, 245, 273, 288, 298, 368, 372, 376, 389, 395, 397–98, 403, 406, 439, 441–42, 448–49, 452, 462, 463, 465, 467–69, 478, 480, 483, 488, 497–98, 500, 508, 511, 524, 537, 539, 541–43, 552, 556, 564, 566, 568, 571–72, 575, 577, 590, 608, 619, 633, 718, 720, 729. *See also* DONNE, **Biography**, patronage and preferment
Pelagians, 330
Performance, 150, 159, 183, 186, 280, 387, 405, 481, 516, 538, 665, 683, 755. *See also* DONNE, **Writings**, and performance
Persecution for religion, 140, 152, 165, 250, 331, 383–94, 398, 407–11, 413–14, 420, 486, 501–02, 504–06, 528, 591, 593–94, 663, 665–66, 671–73, 675, 744, 747–48. *See also* DONNE, **Biography**, persecution for religion
Petrarchism, 106, 115, 126, 139, 146–47, 160, 187–88, 218–19, 227–32
and anti-Petrarchism, 127, 160. *See also* DONNE, **Writings**, Petrarchism, and anti-Petrarchism
Platonism, 110, 177, 697

Portraits and portraiture, 109, 262, 503, 514, 525. *See also* DONNE, **Biography**, portraits of
Predestination, 252, 335, 370, 492, 595, 606, 612, 618, 624, 639, 644. *See also* DONNE, **Character traits and beliefs**, predestination
Preferment. *See* Patronage and preferment
Privy Council, 245, 693. *See also* DONNE, **Biography**, Privy Council and
Elizabethan, 388, 393–94, 398, 410–14, 433, 437–38, 441–42, 448, 461–64, 468–69, 473, 516, 555
Jacobean, 245, 473, 480, 482, 485, 504, 516–17, 537, 539, 545, 547, 549, 551, 566–67, 572, 590, 594, 598–99, 602, 681
Caroline, 626–28
Problems, 242–44, 454. *See also* DONNE, **Genres**, Problems
Prose letters, 32, 35–36, 124, 152, 155–56, 165, 209, 211, 250, 255, 327, 349–55, 368, 401, 406, 409, 410–11, 422, 442, 449, 454–55, 460, 464–66, 468–69, 475, 478, 481–82, 501–02, 508, 510, 514–16, 519–21, 539, 546, 551–52, 558–59, 573, 577, 582, 590, 597, 601, 607, 633, 639, 711, 714, 746. *See also* DONNE, **Genres**, Prose letters
Prosody. *See* Versification
Protestantism, 143, 219, 223, 321–22, 331, 365, 369, 395, 489, 545, 567, 572–73, 582, 592–95, 597–99, 601–02, 606, 614, 622, 631, 634–35, 673. *See also* DONNE, **Character traits and beliefs**
Dutch, 412, 436, 614
English, 5, 100, 117, 142, 145, 219, 223, 229, 234, 236, 252–55, 261–62, 283, 294, 308–10, 315, 365, 369, 371–79, 387–90, 398–400, 407, 462, 485–88, 491, 494, 499, 502, 504, 507, 520, 535, 541, 545, 550, 555, 557, 567, 571, 575, 584–85, 589–91, 594–96, 606, 614, 616, 639, 645, 655–56, 665–66, 670, 680, 687, 703, 734, 739
French, 169, 421, 440
German, 227, 368, 540, 561, 584, 593, 595–98, 617–20, 634
Scottish, 591, 594
'Public sphere', 4, 294, 538, 699
Puritanism, 127, 253, 294–96, 309, 332, 373–75, 379, 400, 484–85, 491, 499, 572, 578–79, 588, 596, 606, 653, 667, 692. *See also* DONNE, **Character traits and beliefs**
and anti-Puritanism, 161, 315, 374, 378, 381, 398, 483, 488–89, 492, 548, 594, 606, 621,

625, 667, 669. *See also* DONNE, **Character traits and beliefs**

Ratio studiorum, 107, 419
Reception, 6, 35, 66, 122, 687. See also DONNE, **Writings**, reception
Recusancy, 114, 140, 142, 145, 148, 219, 323, 365, 372, 374, 376–77, 379, 381–82, 398, 458, 474, 485–86, 504–05, 507–08, 516–17, 555, 557, 591, 606, 617, 621–23, 627, 650, 688, 721, 745
Reformation, Catholic, 219, 323–24, 373, 375, 390, 395, 624
Reformation, continental, 170, 219, 252, 374–76, 395, 594–95, 599
Reformation, English, 129, 161, 170, 219–20, 252, 255, 294, 323, 331, 371–76, 378, 387–91, 395, 484, 492, 536, 573, 594, 639, 642, 668, 673–74, 726. *See also* DONNE, **Biography**, Reformation, English; **Writings**, and English Reformation
Revisionism, 106, 375, 378, 380, 671, 726
Royal courts, 183, 207–08, 413, 420, 422, 461, 466, 622, 647, 692, 718, 721, 727–28, 736
 of Anne of Denmark, 480–81
 of Charles I, 71, 87, 368–70, 633–34, 636–38, 640, 643–44, 730
 of Edward VI, 387–88, 421
 of Elizabeth I, 41, 71, 75–76, 114, 116–18, 129, 132, 139, 152, 165–68, 192, 211, 366, 373, 384–89, 392, 395–97, 401, 403–06, 414, 424, 433–34, 439–40, 448–50, 452–55, 460–70, 480, 498, 554, 678, 725, 728, 743, 748–50
 of Henry VIII, 126, 243, 384, 386–87, 390–91, 409, 413
 of James I, 5, 36–37, 87, 117, 173, 177, 192, 209, 216, 243–44, 246–48, 290, 294, 299, 301, 304–07, 339, 342–45, 356, 360, 367–70, 480–85, 497, 508, 511, 520, 524–25, 527–34, 537–73, 575, 583, 594–96, 601, 603, 609, 611, 613, 617, 619, 621–22, 625–27, 629–32, 671, 688, 691, 720, 723–24, 739–40
 of Mary I, 387–88
 of Prince Henry, 172
Royal prerogative, 245, 261, 296, 448, 540, 557, 567, 617, 627–30, 636–38, 691, 693–97, 699–703

Sacraments and the sacred, 82, 168, 321, 324, 331, 372, 394, 524, 586, 640–41, 651, 655, 665, 669–70, 720–21. See also DONNE, **Writings**, sacraments and the sacred in

Saints and canonization, 162, 171, 250, 390, 492, 504, 644, 655, 668, 721, 734, 739. *See also* DONNE, **Writings**, saints and canonization in
Satire and the satirical, 36, 105, 108, 111–12, 115–16, 123–26, 128–29, 147, 158–63, 165–67, 169, 171–72, 175–76, 208, 221, 245, 250, 253, 259, 273, 325, 384, 420, 426, 503, 538. *See also* Satires, formal verse; DONNE, **Genres**, Satires, formal verse; **Writings**, satire and the satirical in
Satires, formal verse, 20, 45, 122–33, 161, 179, 187, 207–09, 454, 711, 744, 748. *See also* DONNE, **Genres**, Satires, formal verse
Scepticism, 41, 46, 126, 161, 166–67, 200, 245, 265–67, 323, 540, 549, 554, 572, 624, 689. *See also* DONNE, **Character traits and beliefs**, scepticism; **Writings**, scepticism in
Scholasticism, 167, 253, 322, 402. *See also* DONNE, **Writings**, scholasticism in and anti-scholasticism in, 167, 322, 420. *See also* DONNE, **Writings**, anti-scholasticism in
Separatism, religious, 271, 323, 331, 615, 651–53
Sex and sexuality, 26, 30, 37, 116–17, 119, 123, 187–88, 195, 246, 300, 372, 374, 546, 548, 552, 561, 684–85, 687, 711. *See also* DONNE, **Writings**, sex and sexuality in
Seals, 433, 448, 455, 458, 539, 547, 549, 562, 566, 575, 611, 619, 628. See also DONNE, **Biography**, seals of; **Writings**, seals in
Septuagint, 334. *See also* Bible; Bibles
Sequences, 5, 35, 135, 183, 188, 250, 256, 262, 288. *See also* DONNE, **Writings**, sequences of poems
Sermons, 123, 125, 309, 320–23, 326, 375, 386, 469, 478, 554–55, 557, 559–60, 562–64, 590–91, 594, 596, 601, 605–06, 644, 646. See also DONNE, **Genres**, Sermons
Sexism, 24, 192, 678–79, 682. *See also* Sex and sexuality; DONNE, **Character traits and beliefs**, misogyny; **Writings**, sex and sexuality in
Sonnet sequences, 183–84, 188, 223, 231. *See also* DONNE, **Genres**, Religious Sonnets
Spanish Inquisition, 665
Spanish Match, 490, 541, 549–50, 552, 572–73, 583, 589, 592–93, 598–99, 606, 617–18, 620–24, 640, 699
Spider and the Flie, 388–90
St Bartholomew massacre, 377
Star Chamber, 151, 248, 448, 492, 520

Stemmas, 51, 53, 58, 60, 61, 131, 141, 222
Style, 101, 108, 117, 125–26, 134, 150, 160, 172, 178, 209, 256, 262, 264–65, 267–68, 309–10, 312, 351–52, 384, 391, 401, 404, 421, 462, 468, 490–91, 586, 632–33, 637, 716, 747. *See also* DONNE, **Writings**, style
Supremacy, Act (and Oath) of, *see* Act

Textual bibliography, 2, 3, 10–25, 35, 37, 42, 43–80, 82–85, 92, 101, 141, 195, 210, 220–22, 719. *See also* Variants, textual; Copy-texts
Thirty-nine Articles, 331, 374, 398, 411, 621
Thirty Years War, 230, 249, 572, 633
Toleration, religious, 169, 255, 326, 367–68, 381, 387, 410, 421, 480, 484–86, 488, 494, 496, 501–02, 506, 509, 518–20, 522, 536, 584–85, 591, 599, 617, 622–23, 625, 627, 631
Torture for religion, 114, 129, 167, 255, 344, 377–78, 410, 673, 747–48, 750
'Tottel's Miscellany', 101, 183
Transmission of manuscripts, *see* Manuscripts; DONNE, **Writings**, holographs; manuscripts
Travel and travellers, 37, 61, 86, 94, 123, 172, 175, 397–98, 406–07, 414, 420–21, 424–46, 480, 506, 657. See also DONNE, **Biography**, travels
Treason and traitors, 39, 161, 245, 255, 376, 381, 386, 390, 410, 446, 461, 469, 473, 481, 496, 503, 507, 516, 520, 552, 590, 593–94, 664, 699, 745. See also DONNE, **Writings**, treason and traitors in
Trent, see Council of Trent
Tyburn, 146, 386, 516
Typology, 77, 331. See also DONNE, **Writings**, typology in

Uniformity, Act of, *see* Act
University education, 381, 386, 390–91, 393, 396, 398, 401–04, 407, 409, 411–13, 419–21, 425, 448, 535, 556. *See also* DONNE, **Biography**, early years and education
Utopia, 153–55, 159, 176, 386, 636

Variants, textual, 18, 22–24, 34–36, 40, 46–48, 50–55, 57–58, 60, 66–67, 69–70, 72–73, 75, 77, 79, 83–84, 86, 92, 181, 752. *See also* Textual bibliography; Copy-texts
Venetian interdict, 261, 489, 503, 521–22, 591. *See also* DONNE, **Biography**, travels, in 1605–06; **Genres**, Controversial Treatise (*Pseudo-Martyr*)
Verse letters, 39, 467. *See also* DONNE, **Genres**, Verse Letters
Verse miscellanies, 28, 34, 37, 39, 41, 48, 183–84, 188. *See also* Manuscripts; 'Tottel's Miscellany'
Versification, 82, 132, 288, 708, 716. *See also* ; Metre; DONNE, versification; DONNE, metre
Vulgate, 174, 320, 327, 334, 603

Index 2: Personal Names

Abbot, George, archbishop, 368, 491, 499, 533, 535, 542, 546–47, 550–51, 562, 567–69, 571–73, 582, 594–96, 598–99, 600–01, 611, 621, 624, 627, 629
Abbot, Robert, 488
Adams, John, 154, 156
Adrian VI, pope, 260
Aglionby, John, 577–78
Agrippa, Cornelius, 166, 277, 282
Alabaster, William, 104, 219
Alamanni, Luigi, 126, 208
Alford, Henry, 45–46, 51, 70, 318, 670, 720, 735–36
Allen, William, cardinal, 398, 410–13
Alleyn, Edward, 607, 612–13
Ambrose, 342, 669, 734, 738
Anacreon, 186, 709
Anderson, Robert, 45
Anderton, James ['John Brereley'], 489–91
Andrewes, Lancelot, bishop, 230, 489, 521, 559–61, 564, 568, 572–73, 615
Andrews, Richard, 16, 217, 349
Aneau, Barthélemy, 208
Anne [of Denmark], queen of England, Scotland, and Ireland, consort of James VI and I, 480–81, 508, 529, 539, 544, 550, 555, 561, 727
Anne, queen of Great Britain and Ireland, 712
Antonio, king of Portugal ['Dom Antonio'], 438
Apuleius, 158, 159
Acquaviva, Claudio, SJ, 409–11, 747
Aquinas, Thomas [St. Thomas], 237, 270, 283, 320
Aretino, Pietro, 744
Ariosto, Lodovico, 126, 208
Aristotle, 110, 164, 167, 175, 242, 283, 398, 400, 466, 693, 729–30
Arminius, Jacobus, 618, 624. *See also* **Index 1: Conceptual tools**, Arminianism
Ascham, Roger, 396, 400–01
Aston, Sir Walter, 610
Augustine [St. Augustine], of Hippo, 125, 179, 193, 219, 223, 237–38, 283, 310–11, 314, 320–22, 324, 326–27, 329–30, 332–33, 335, 340–42, 604, 668–69, 734, 738

Bacon, Anne, *see* Drury [née Bacon], Anne
Bacon, Anthony, 406–07, 510
Bacon, Francis, viscount St. Alban, 176, 179, 254, 266–67, 270, 397, 406–07, 454, 461, 463, 469, 478, 508, 510, 521, 560, 619, 693, 730
Bacon, Nicholas, 373, 510
Baddeley, Richard, 498–99
Baker, Daniel, 30
Baker, Richard, 145, 480, 612, 684
Bald, R. C., 69, 72, 216, 305, 453, 458, 466, 473, 477, 499, 509–11, 513–14, 525, 531, 556, 562, 570, 578, 608, 612, 650, 670–74, 719, 723–24, 727
Baldwin, William, 158, 171
Bancroft, Richard, archbishop, 377, 507, 521, 566–67, 572–73, 699
Barclay, John, 158, 161, 487
Barclay, William, 485–86, 503
Barlow, William, 261, 469, 492–93, 747, 754
Barnes, Barnabe, 102
Baronius, 254
Barrow, Henry, 376, 651–52
Bartlett [née Dauntsey], Mary, 510–13
Bartlett, Sir Thomas, 510–13
Bastard, Thomas, epigrammatist, 116
Beal, Peter, 16, 18, 28, 34–35, 39–42, 55, 57, 59, 61, 66, 72–74
Beaumont, Francis, 28, 30
Beda, Noël, 165
Bell, Ilona, 26, 55, 457, 472, 477, 688
Bell, John, 45
Bellarmino, Roberto [cardinal and saint], SJ, 100, 169, 250, 254–55, 261, 331, 487, 555, 578
Bembo, Pietro, 254
Bennett, Roger E., 53–54, 56–57, 349
Bennett, Joan, 687
Berkeley, Maurice, 429
Bernard [St. Bernard], of Clairvaux, 223
Beza, Theodore, 170, 235, 406
Bilson, Thomas, bishop, 568, 572
'Bishop Valentine', *see* St Valentine, bishop
Blackwell, George, archpriest, 169, 254–55, 521
Blount, Charles, eighth baron Mountjoy, 446, 469

Blount, Thomas, 28, 279, 415
Boccaccio, Giovani, 243
Bodin, Jean, 403, 693, 696–97, 699, 702
Boleyn, Anne, 504
Bolton, Edmund, 209, 517
Borges, Jorge Luis, 168
Borja, Francisco de, SJ, 393
Bosgrave, James, SJ, 413
Bossy, John, 375–76, 378–79
Bouillon, duke of, *see* D'Auvergne, Henri de la Tour, duke of Bouillon
Boys, John, 254
Brahe, Tycho, 132–3, 169
'Brereley, John', *see* Anderton, James
Brooke, Basil, 480
Brooke, Christopher, 28, 190, 213, 425, 454, 457–58, 472, 474–75, 556–77, 606, 610
Brooke, Henry, eleventh baron Cobham, 463, 481
Brooke [Jacob], Mary, 613
Brooke, Samuel, 28, 454, 457–58, 472, 474–75, 492, 555–56, 558, 577
Brooke, William, tenth baron Cobham, 463
Broughton, Richard, 500
Browne, Anthony, first viscount Montagu, 379
Browne, Anthony, second viscount Montagu, 518–19, 567
Browne, Sir Anthony, 605
Browne, Magdalen, 379
Browning, Robert, 714–5, 736
Buckeridge, John, bishop, 489, 562, 568
Bulstrode, Cecilia, 176, 290, 292–94, 682
Bunny, Edmund, 310
Burley, John, 609
Burton, Francis, 504
Burton, Robert, 160
Butler, Richard, 586

Caesar, Sir Julius, 545, 610
Cain, Tom, 294, 637, 673
Callimachus, 135
Calvin, John, 170, 320, 329, 373, 614, 618. See also **Index 1: Conceptual tools**, Calvinism, and anti-Calvinism
Camden, William, 116, 467–68
Campion, Edmund [St Edmund Campion], SJ, 114, 252, 410
Campion, Thomas, 135–36, 182–83
Carafa, Gian Pietro, 390–91
Carew, Sir George, 452, 465
Carew, Sir Nicholas, 29
Carew, Thomas, 2s, 28, 30–31, 39, 107, 134, 145, 205, 684, 709–10, 712, 734
Carey, John, 55, 86, 146–47, 163, 258, 378, 477, 663, 671–73, 676, 688, 690–91, 719, 724–27, 739

Carey [née Rich], Lettice, 28, 30, 62, 214–15, 456, 530
Carey, Valentine, 571, 574–75
Carier, Benjamin, 488–89, 568
Carleton, Dudley, viscount Dorchester, 28–29, 357–58, 482, 509, 515–16, 521, 531–32, 539, 571, 618
Caro, Annibal, 221
Carr, Robert, viscount Rochester and earl of Somerset, 5, 16–17, 28, 35–36, 213, 295, 299, 304–07, 350, 356–57, 367–68, 496, 526–27, 529–35, 539, 542–52, 566–68, 570–571, 574, 633, 718, 722–24, 726, 739
Carr, Robert, first earl of Ancram, *see* Ker, Robert, first earl of Ancram
Carr, Sir Robert, *see* Ker, Sir Robert, later first earl of Ancram
Carter, Edward, 29, 156
Cartwright, Thomas, 499
Cary, Lucius, 29, 707, 734
Casaubon, Isaac, 171, 175, 488, 492
Castiglione, Baldassare, 396, 401, 727, 729
Catullus, 107, 110, 119, 134–35, 137, 187, 298–99
Cave, John, 122, 132–33
Cavendish, Margaret, Duchess of Newcastle, 28, 30, 684, 711–12
Cavendish, William, Marquess of Newcastle, 29
Caxton, William, 162
Cecil, Robert, baron of Essendon and first earl of Salisbury, 5, 41, 152, 160–62, 165, 167, 170, 355, 367, 407, 429, 461–65, 469, 482, 484, 495–98, 500–07, 510, 515–19, 537–45, 566–67, 586, 727
Cecil, William, first baron Burghley, 388, 397–98, 406–07, 429, 442, 458, 461–64, 468, 495–96, 500, 507, 510, 518
Cecil, William, second earl of Exeter, 625
Centlivre, Susanna, 685
Chadwick, John White, 720, 722
Chamberlain, John, 327–28, 516, 539, 543, 559, 561, 570–71, 602, 618, 681
Chamberlain, Robert, 21, 28
Chambers, E. K., 20, 34, 47, 49–50, 738
Chapman, George, 221, 298, 548
Charke, William, 577–78
Charles I, prince and, later, king of England, Scotland, and Ireland, 6, 13, 87, 328, 338–39, 357, 368–70, 446, 541, 544, 554, 556–57, 562, 564, 568–69, 583, 593, 596, 599, 604, 609, 614, 616–36, 640–42, 644–45, 674, 681, 684, 690–692, 697–98, 700, 703
Charles V, Holy Roman Emperor, 113
Christian IV, king of Denmark, 360, 484, 534
Christmas, Robert, 654

Chrysostom, [St John], 319, 342, 611
Chudleigh, John, 720–21
Chute, Sir Walter, 480, 509–10, 513–14
Cicero, Marcus Tullius, 110, 209, 265, 350–51, 396, 401, 730
Clarke, Edward, 579
Clavius, Christopher, as character in *Ignatius*, 170, 179
Clement [St Clement] of Alexandria, 154
Clement, John, 385
Clement, Margaret Giggs, 385
Clement, Winifred, 385
Clement VIII, pope, 486
Cleveland, John, 710–11, 713
Clifford, Anne, countess of Dorset, *see* Sackville [née Clifford], Anne, countess of Dorset
Clinton, Edward Fiennes de, first earl of Lincoln, 478
Clinton, Elizabeth de Fiennes, countess of Lincoln, 478
Clitherow, Margaret, 745
Cobham, *see* Brooke
Cokayne [née Stanhope], Anne, 612–13, 682
Cokayne, Aston, 30
Coke, Sir Edward, 253, 404, 552, 693–94, 696
Coleridge, Samuel Taylor, 26, 185, 189, 191–92, 194, 202, 663, 713–15, 720, 726, 736–37, 739
Colie, Rosalie, 113, 117, 279, 283, 287
Collinson, Patrick, 524
Columbus, Christopher, as character in *Ignatius*, 170
Conway, Edward, 29, 429
Cooke, Sir Anthony, 387
Cooke, Mildred, 387
Cope, Walter, 510, 539
Copernicus, Nicolaus, as character in *Ignatius*, 170, 179
Copley, Avery, 576
Corbett, Richard, bishop, 29, 612
Corkine, William, 28, 30
Cornelia Africana, 399
Cornwallis, Charles, 454, 502
Cornwallis, William, 266–67, 270, 454–56, 461, 470, 480, 496–97, 509
Coryate, Thomas, 52, 158, 168, 172–74, 176–77, 518, 577
Cosimo I de'Medici, grand duke of Tuscany, 391
Cosin, John, 492, 499, 572, 639, 644
Cottington, Francis, 531, 633
Cotton, Robert, 28, 38, 176, 465–66, 480–81, 548, 550
Covell, William, 488–89
Coventry, Thomas, 611
Coverdale, Miles, 234

Cowell, John, 690, 699
Cowley, Abraham, 28, 684, 710–13, 735
Crakenthorpe, Richard, 577–78
Crane, Ralph, 36
Cranfield, Lionel, 29, 545
Cranmer, Thomas, archbishop, 116, 235, 252, 386, 390
Croft, Pauline, 502
Crowley, Robert, 117
Cuffe, Henry, 403–04, 425
Curione, Caelio, 158, 160, 169, 171

Daniel, George, 736
Daniel, Samuel, 3, 209, 221, 231
Dante, 129, 171, 187–88, 281
Danvers, John, 199, 606, 610
Danvers, Lady, *see* Herbert [née Newport; Danvers], Magdalen
D'Auvergne, Henri de la Tour, duke of Bouillon, 592–93, 598
Davenant, John, 602
Davies, Sir John, 116, 167, 175, 457, 478, 694, 695
Davison, Francis, 20, 454
Day, Angel, 351–52
Dee, John, 167, 420
Dekker, Thomas, 28, 169
Delumeau, Jean, 376
Denny, William, 156
Despenser, Hugh, 619
Devereux, Robert, second earl of Essex, 36, 39, 109, 113, 160, 162, 213, 366, 397, 403–04, 406, 424–26, 428–33, 435–36, 439–42, 444–47, 449, 461–69, 471, 483, 496–97, 541–42, 554, 678, 747
Devereux, Robert, third earl of Essex, 304, 532, 545–46, 548, 567–68
D'Ewes, Sir Simonds, 578, 609, 628
Digby, John, first earl of Bristol, 550, 593, 622
Diogenes Laertius, 110, 160
Donne [Copley, Lyly], Anne [Donne's sister], 355, 535, 576
Donne [née More], Anne [Donne's wife], 15, 18, 21, 24, 26, 28, 30, 38, 193–94, 199, 227–29, 231, 287, 358, 360, 366–67, 379, 385, 450, 456–59, 467, 471–78, 480, 482, 497, 508–09, 513, 525, 534–35, 556, 577, 648–49, 670, 672, 686, 688, 738
Donne, Bridget [Donne's daughter], 535, 603
Donne, Constance [Donne's daughter], 326, 603, 607
Donne [née Heywood; Syminges, Rainsford], Elizabeth [Donne's mother], 355, 377, 383–84, 387, 391–94, 408–10, 413, 423, 493, 508, 535–36, 576, 603, 650, 668–70, 673, 682, 746

Donne, Francis [Donne's son], 471, 513, 534
Donne, George [Donne's son], 513, 603, 628, 633
Donne, Henry [Donne's brother], 377, 402, 404, 423, 576, 673, 748
Donne, John [Donne's father], 129, 383–84, 391–93, 422, 649, 670
Donne John [Donne's son], 28, 44, 68, 72–76, 78, 125, 151, 155–56, 160, 268, 318, 349–50, 355, 419, 482, 548
Donne, Margaret [Donne's daughter], 742
Downame, George, 488
Downhall, Gregory, 452, 458
Drake, Francis, 174, 429, 435–39, 442
Drake, William, 644
Drayton, Michael, 16, 182, 209
Droeshout, Martin, 643
Drummond, William, 2, 28, 106, 183, 207, 213, 278, 683, 706, 708, 719–20
Drury [née Bacon], Anne, 28, 30, 274–75, 280, 355, 498, 509–11, 530
Drury, Elizabeth, 273, 275–77, 280, 282, 284–85, 290, 674, 681–83, 706, 719–20
Drury, Sir Robert, 274–75, 280, 349, 355, 489, 495, 498, 509–11, 525–26, 529, 530, 537, 572, 590
Dryden, John, 26, 28, 30, 32, 125, 183, 189, 191, 685, 711–13, 715–16, 735
Du Bartas, Guillaume, 164
Du Bellay, Joachim, 135–36, 208, 210
Dubrow, Heather, 298, 299, 301, 688, 740
Dudley, Ambrose, earl of Warwick, 387
Dudley, John, duke of Northumberland, 388–89
Dudley, Robert, earl of Leicester, 373, 376, 403, 436, 439, 461–62
Dugdale, William, 28
Du Moulin, Pierre, 535
Dun, Sir Daniel, 533, 549, 722
Dunch, Bridget, 349
Du Perron, Jacques Davy, cardinal, 254

Earle, John, 379
Edward VI, king of England and Ireland, 371–72, 375, 385, 387, 390, 421
Egerton [née More; Polsted, Wolley], Elizabeth, 449, 450, 471–72s, 477–78s
Egerton [née Spencer; Stanley, countess of Derby], Alice, 449, 456
Egerton, John, first earl of Bridgewater, 448
Egerton, Thomas, Baron Ellesmere, first viscount Brackley, 6, 15, 28, 53, 118, 191, 287, 355, 358, 366, 433, 448–50, 452–59, 464–66, 468–72, 474–75, 500, 506, 525, 532, 551–52, 554–56, 559, 564, 567–68, 570, 572, 577, 579, 595, 602–03, 605, 750–51
Egerton, Sir Thomas the younger, 433, 447–48

Eliot, Sir John, 630
Eliot, T. S., 26, 85, 185, 232, 318, 670, 716
Elizabeth I, queen of England and Ireland, 39, 109, 118, 126–27, 129–30, 132, 139, 143, 160, 171, 194, 200–201, 219, 229, 252–53, 371–77, 387–88, 390–91, 394–97, 403, 404, 409–10, 424, 428–29, 435–37, 439–42, 444–46, 448–50, 452–53, 457, 461–64, 467–68, 474, 478, 483, 485, 496–98, 502, 504, 554–55, 557, 561, 590, 631, 633, 665, 674, 681, 694, 751
Elizabeth, Princess [Stuart], queen of Bohemia and electress Palatine, consort of Frederick V, 28, 299, 301–04, 307, 505, 540, 544, 552, 561, 567, 583, 591–93, 598, 618, 620
Elwes, Sir Gervase, 551
Elyot, Thomas, 396–97, 399, 401
Emanuele, Carlo, duke of Savoy, 597
Empson, William, 129, 716
Ennius, 134
Epicurus, 350
Erasmus, Desiderius, 100, 149–50, 152, 158, 163–64, 167, 171, 250, 282–83, 291, 320–27, 331, 333, 335, 342, 351–52, 369, 386, 390–91, 396, 409, 421, 746
Erskine, Thomas, viscount Fenton, 543, 550, 590
Etherege, George, 28

Farnese, Alessandro, duke of Parma, 412, 416–17, 419, 433, 437, 440
Fawkes, Guy, 515
Feilding, William, 29
Felipe II, king of England and Ireland, consort of Mary I, and king of Spain, 113–15, 142, 412, 428, 435–37, 439–40, 442, 444
Felipe III, king of Spain, 593, 620
Felipe IV, king of Spain, 620–22, 624–25
Fenton, Geoffrey, 727
Fenton, viscount, *see* Erskine, Thomas, viscount Fenton
Ferdinand II, Archduke of Austria, and Holy Roman Emperor, 368, 581, 583, 595–96, 598, 618, 620–21. *See also* **Index 1: Conceptual tools**, Habsburgs
Ferrabosco, Alfonso, 28, 30
Ferrar, Nicholas, 606
Ficino, Marsilio, 391
Field, Nathaniel, 578
Field, Richard, 570, 577–78
Field, Theophilus, 571
Figgis, [John] Neville, 692
Filmer, Sir Robert, 690
Fincham, Kenneth, 611
Fischart, Johann, 166
Fisher, John, bishop, 250

Fisher, Payne, 28
Fitzjeffery, Henry, 30
Fitzherbert, Thomas, SJ, 262, 500
Flacius Illyricus, Matthias, 171
Fleming, Giles, 641
Fleming, Thomas, 693, 696
Flesher, Miles, 29
Fletcher, Giles, 163
Fletcher, John, 729
Fletcher, Phineas, 169
Floyd, John, 262, 498
Flynn, Dennis, 38, 39, 40, 41, 178, 179, 348, 377, 409, 410, 447, 452, 468, 496, 573, 672, 673, 687, 724, 727, 747
Fortescue, John, 404–05, 695–97
Fowler, William, 480, 508, 727
Fox, Simeon, 607
Foxe, John, 252, 376–77
Frederick V, see Friedrich V, count palatine of the Rhine, elector of the Holy Roman empire, and king of Bohemia
Friedrich V, count palatine of the Rhine, elector of the Holy Roman empire, and king of Bohemia, 28, 299, 301–04, 307, 319, 368, 505, 540, 561, 581, 583–84, 593–94, 596–98, 618–22

Gabor, Bethlehem, 596
Galileo Galilei, as character in *Ignatius*, 169, 171
Gallus, Gaius Cornelius, 135
Gardner, Helen, 3, 21, 44, 50–56, 136, 220–21, 224, 226–28, 230, 670–71, 674–75, 725–26, 745
Garimberto, Hieronimo, 242
Garnett, Henry, SJ, 252, 492, 519–20, 747
Garrard, George, 15, 28, 349, 355–57, 537, 633, 683, 706
Garrard, Martha, 349, 682
Gataker, Thomas, 577–78
Gellius, Aulus, 242
Gentili, Alberico, 521
Gilbert, Humphrey, 395, 400, 403–04, 420
Gondomar, Diego Sarmiento de Acuña, conde de, 593, 595, 620
Good, John, 487
Goodere, Sir Henry, 15–17, 25, 28, 40, 76, 107, 164, 211–16, 235–36, 243–44, 258, 260–61, 279, 287, 304, 349, 352, 355–56, 360–61, 415, 446–47, 454, 459, 474–75, 480, 491–93, 496–99, 506, 508–13, 518, 521, 529, 532–33, 544, 547–49, 551, 559, 583, 607, 666–67, 678, 706, 727, 732–35, 746, 752–54
Gordon, John, 575
Gosse, Edmund, 14, 78–79, 156, 219–21, 228, 269, 328, 348, 476–77, 570, 663, 670, 672, 686, 719, 721–24, 738

Gough, John, 28, 31–32, 685
Gracchus, Gaius, 399
Gracchus, Tiberius, 399
Granada, Luis de, 310, 314
Gratian, 260
Gray, Thomas, 134
Greene, Robert, 243
Gregory XIII, pope, 142, 409, 675
Grenville, Richard, 439
Gretser, James, SJ, 254
Greville, Fulke, 420
Grey, Henry, tenth earl of Kent, 609, 627
Grierson, Herbert, 20–21, 34, 44, 47–55, 57, 59, 73, 86, 114, 191, 198, 227–28, 348, 455, 670, 715–16, 720
Grindal, Edmund, archbishop, 373, 377
Grindal, Johann, 28, 71
Grosart, Alexander B., 20, 34, 43, 45–47, 50, 56–57, 181–82, 670, 714–15, 737–38
Grotius, 488
Grymes, Sir Thomas, 535, 607
Guibbory, Achsah, 88, 138, 524, 530, 642, 668, 688, 701
Guicciardini, Francesco, 729
Guilpin, Everard, 128, 131, 454
Gustavus Adolphus, king of Sweden, 596, 631, 634
Guzmán, Gaspar de, duke of Olivares, 598

Habington, William, 30, 684
Habsburgs, *see* **Index 1: Conceptual tools**, Habsburgs
Hacket, John, 574–75, 602
Hakewill, William, 577, 579
Hakluyt, Richard, 446
Hall, Edward, 384
Hall, Joseph, 127–28, 130, 158–60, 166, 179, 273–74, 308, 311, 351, 572, 582, 600, 610, 614, 744
Hamilton, James, second marquess of Hamilton, 57, 297, 705–06
Hammond, John, 109, 114
Hare, Nicholas, 21
Harington, John, second baron Harington of Exton, 17, 213, 287, 296–97, 544
Harington, Sir John, 36, 158, 166–67, 294, 440–41, 446
Harley, Sir Robert, 28
Harrington, William, 252, 377, 404, 423, 748
Harriot, Thomas, 515
Harsnett, Samuel, 611
Harvey, Gabriel, 403, 420
Haskin, Dayton, 26, 45–46, 63, 70, 88, 235, 346, 348, 528, 670, 679, 687–88, 735–38
Hastings [née Stanley], Elizabeth, countess of Huntingdon, 15, 17, 28, 30, 215–16, 530, 534, 612, 682, 721

Hastings, Henry, fifth earl of Huntingdon, 609
Hatton, Christopher, 405, 461
Hawkins, John, 435, 442
Hay, James, viscount Doncaster and first earl of Carlisle, 5, 28–29, 239, 368, 500–01, 530, 543, 544, 547, 558, 561, 568–69, 573–74, 581–83, 595–03, 607–08, 618, 621, 722, 732
Hayward, Sir John, 310, 313–14
Healey, John, 158–59, 175
Heinsius, Daniel, 158, 167, 171, 419
Heliogabalus, 247
Henri III, king of France, 166, 170, 412–13, 421
Henri IV [de Navarre], king of France, 159, 166, 169, 170–72, 252, 421, 440, 442, 462–63, 503, 591, 592, 617
Henrietta Maria [of France], queen of England, Scotland, and Ireland, consort of Charles I, 623, 625, 629
Henry III, king of England, 455
Henry VIII, king of England and Ireland, 118, 126, 168, 252, 294, 375, 384–87, 413, 504, 633, 674
Henry Frederick, prince of Wales, 5, 28, 44, 172, 267, 278, 294–96, 303, 351, 498, 539–42, 544–45, 556, 567, 591–92, 721
Herbert, Edward, first baron Herbert of Cherbury, 28, 36, 155–56, 278, 403, 420, 608, 610, 752
Herbert, George, 28, 602, 610, 655, 710
Herbert, Sir Henry, 151, 248
Herbert (née Newport), Magdalen, 24, 28, 30, 138, 191, 199, 215, 349, 530, 610, 612, 682, 755
Herbert [née Sidney], Mary, countess of Pembroke, 234–35, 603, 707
Herbert, Philip, first earl of Montgomery, 543, 600, 608–09, 611–12
Herbert, [née Vere] Susan, countess of Montgomery, 38, 682
Herbert, William, third earl of Pembroke, 369, 542–47, 549–50, 552, 567, 571, 594, 600–01, 603, 606, 609, 611–12, 621, 624
Herrick, Robert, 298
Hester, M. Thomas, 78, 79, 89, 132, 143, 196, 233, 348
Heywood, Ellis, SJ, 384, 390–94
Heywood, Jasper, SJ, 41, 107, 110, 116, 366, 377, 384, 387, 390–91, 409–14, 419–23, 520, 746, 748
Heywood, John, 107–08, 111, 115–18, 243, 384, 386–93, 409, 458
Heywood, Richard, 576
Heywood, Thomas, 394
Hill, Edmund, 499
Hilton, John, 656

Hippocrates, 260
Hobart, Sir Henry, 577, 579, 586, 610
Hoby, Sir Edward, 498
Hoby, Sir Thomas, 396, 727, 729
Hodges, William, 29
Holland, Henry, 28
Holloway, Thomas, 577
Holtby, Richard, SJ, 402
Holyday, Barten, 125–26
Home, George, 542, 566
Hooker, Richard, 230, 326, 372, 374, 488, 578
Hopkins, John, 235
Horace, 123–26, 130, 142, 207–10, 215, 688, 748
Hoskins, John, 352–53, 454, 549–50, 610, 694, 696
Howard, Catherine, countess of Salisbury, 28, 30, 215, 530, 534, 682
Howard, Charles, second baron Howard of Effingham and first earl of Nottingham, 109, 424, 442, 447, 463, 509
Howard [Devereux, Carr], Frances, countess of Somerset, 28, 30, 299, 304, 306–07, 496, 532, 545–48, 551–52, 567, 722
Howard, Henry, earl of Northampton, 469, 485, 497, 500, 533, 539, 541, 544–47, 549–52, 566–67, 594
Howard, Henry, earl of Surrey, 183, 209, 478
Howard, Katherine [née Knyvett, *other married name*, Rich], Countess of Suffolk, 500
Howard, Philip, thirteenth earl of Arundel, 414
Howard, Theophilus, 567, 571
Howard, Thomas, first earl of Suffolk, 426, 429–31, 433, 497, 500, 533, 541, 544–47, 549–53, 567, 594
Howard, Thomas, fourteenth earl of Arundel, 571, 594, 624
Howard, Lord William, 487
Howell, James, 176
Howson, John, 488, 491, 570–72
Humphryes, Pelham, 28, 30
Hutten, Ulrich von, 165
Huygens, Constantijn, 28, 30, 35, 319, 610, 613
Hyde, Edward, 497

Infanta, *see* Maria Ana, archduchess of Austria, Infanta of Spain
Ingram, Arthur, 545
Isabella Clara Eugenia, archduchess of Austria, co-sovereign of the Netherlands, 509

Jackson, Thomas, 644–45
Jacob, Lady, *see* Brooke, Mary
James VI and I, king of Scotland, England, and Ireland, 1, 5–6, 13–14, 29, 36, 39, 68, 87, 118, 140, 165, 167, 169, 177, 219, 244–49, 252–55,

258–59, 261–62, 267, 287, 294–96, 301, 303–05, 307, 319, 327–28, 332–34, 336, 338–39, 342, 357, 367–70, 397, 415, 446, 452, 458, 461, 469, 478, 480–89, 492–94, 497–505, 508–09, 516, 519–21, 527, 529, 532–35, 539–62, 564–75, 581–85, 589–03, 605–06, 616–26, 634–35, 639–40, 644–45, 669, 671–72, 674, 681, 690, 692, 694–95, 699–700, 706–07, 710, 722, 751, 753
James II and VII, king of England, Scotland, and Ireland, 171
James, Thomas, 499
Jessopp, Augustus, 5, 77, 476, 702, 720, 722
Jewel, John, 375, 378
Johnson, Cornelius, 333
Johnson, Samuel, 30, 189, 191, 280, 283, 663, 685, 712–16, 721, 735
Johnson, Ralph, 175
Johnson, Robert, 267, 270
Jones, Henry, 452, 455, 458
Jones, Inigo, 641
Jonson, Ben, 2, 16, 26, 28, 30, 39, 52, 91, 105–06, 128, 135, 167–68, 171, 183–84, 188, 207, 213, 243, 245–46, 278, 287, 294, 298, 352, 367, 506–08, 515–18, 520, 683, 706, 708, 719–20
Juvenal, 122–27, 128, 130–31

Kelley, Edward, 406
Kempe, William, 398–99
Kendall, Timothy, 116
Ker, Robert, first earl of Ancram, 14, 25, 27, 73, 155, 204, 287, 297, 350, 355, 357, 531–32, 535, 544, 568–69, 610, 633, 667, 705–07, 732–34, 738, 740, 752
Keymis, Lawrence, 431
Keynes, Geoffrey, 12, 53–54, 69, 71, 73, 76, 84–85, 720
Killigrew, Sir Robert, 610
Killigrew, Thomas, 28
Killigrew, Sir William, 613
King, Henry, 29, 43, 287, 288, 514, 600, 604, 641, 651, 708–09
King, John, bishop, 311, 492, 555–58, 561–62, 568–69, 572, 605, 610
Kingsmill (née White), Bridget, Lady Kingsmill, 28, 357, 682
Knollys, William, 463, 465, 468
Kyd, Thomas, 140, 747

Lake, Peter, 488, 703
Lake, Sir Thomas, 545, 550
Lamb, Charles, 189, 713, 736
Lambard, William, 449–50
Landi, Ortensio, 149, 151–52, 242–43

Latimer, Hugh, bishop, 252
Latimer, Lord, *see* Neville, Edmond
Laud, William, archbishop, 5, 368–70, 564, 568–69, 571–72, 575, 578–79, 588, 602, 604–05, 609, 612, 614–15, 625, 627, 629–31, 635, 638–42, 644–45, 669, 697–98
Laudun D'Aigaliers, Pierre de, 208
Layfield, John, 535
Lee, Nathaniel, 28–30, 156
Lem, Stanislas, 168
L'Estoile, Pierre de, 166, 168–69
Lewalski, Barbara, 220, 283, 289, 290, 331
Lewis, C. S., 124, 125, 688
Lipsius, Justus, 158, 207, 237, 352, 355
Livy, 401
Lodge, Thomas, 209, 243
London, William, 415–16
Lorraine, Henri de, duke of Guise, 411
Louis XIII, king of France, 514, 592
Lowell, James Russell, 43, 45–46
Loyola, Ignatius, SJ, 72, 220, 283, 308–09, 565
 as character in *Ignatius*, 170, 171, 172, 504
Lucian, 100, 110, 158–61, 169, 171, 250, 262
Luther, Martin, 142, 167, 234, 249, 251–52, 320, 322, 374, 386, 484, 593, 614, 639, 675
 as character in *Ignatius*, 170
Lygdamus, 135
Lyly (née Donne), Anne, *see* Donne [Copley, Lyly], Anne [Donne's sister]
Lyly, John, 448
Lyly, William [Donne's brother-in-law], 480
Lyly, William, grammarian, 400
Lyra, Nicolas de, 603

Macaulay, Thomas Babington, 692
Machiavelli, Niccolo, as character in *Ignatius*, 170–71, 403
Macrobius, 159, 242
Magellan, Ferdinand, 174
Manley, Mary de la Rivière, 28, 30
Manners, Roger, fifth earl of Rutland, 406, 440
Mansfeld, Ernst Graf von, 620, 623, 626
Maria Ana, archduchess of Austria, infanta of Spain, 541, 550, 583–84, 620, 622, 681
Marino, Giambattista, 288
Markham, Bridget, 290–92, 294
Markham, Sir Griffin, 440–41
Markham, Lady, *see* Markham, Bridget
Marlowe, Christopher, 91, 136, 140, 187, 448, 709, 728, 730
Marot, Clément, 104, 208, 210, 219, 235
Marotti, Arthur, 15, 26, 35, 246, 247, 269, 672, 687, 724, 725, 727
Marriot, John, 20, 21, 24, 29, 43–44, 62–63, 610

Marriot, Richard, 76
Marshall, William, 425, 447, 749
Marston, John, 127–30, 132, 744
Marten, Sir Henry, 29, 610, 611
Martial, 107, 110–11, 115–16, 118–21, 123, 134, 429, 688
Martin Marprelate, 253, 257
Martin, Richard, 287, 521, 699
Martz, Louis, 220, 228, 233, 279, 283, 565
Marvell, Andrew, 28, 30, 710
Marven, Elizabeth, 393
Mary I, queen of England and Ireland, 116, 250–52, 371, 375, 379, 386–88, 409, 502
Mary [Mary Stewart], queen of Scots, 252, 373, 393, 412, 461, 485, 746
Mary, Blessed Virgin, 143, 223, 372, 644, 680–81
Mary Magdalen, 23
Massinger, Philip, 415
Master, Thomas, 578
Matthew, Tobie, archbishop, 478–80, 508, 520–21
Matthew, Sir Toby, 350, 353, 355, 367, 478, 480–82, 506–09, 513–15, 518, 520–21
Maurer, Margaret, 190, 201, 467, 530, 688
Mawe, Leonard, bishop, 611
Maxey, Thomas, 76
Maximilian, Duke of Bavaria, 621
May, Steven W., 35, 39, 41, 461, 465
Mayerne, Theodore Turquet de, 607
Maynard, Sir Henry, 458
Mayne, Jasper, 107, 415–16, 418–19, 433, 710
Maynwaring, Roger, bishop, 627, 629–30, 690, 692, 699
McCullough, Peter, 569, 579, 591, 594, 637
Medici, Catherine de, queen of France, 118, 166, 420
Melanchthon, Philipp, 320
Mendoza, Bernadino, 412
Menippos, 158
Melton, Sir John, 635–36
Mennes, Sir John 28
Meres, Francis, 310
Micanzio, Fulgenzio, 503, 514
Michelangelo, 720
Middleton, Thomas, 127–28, 744
Milbourne, William, 644–45
Mildmay, Lady Grace, 309
Mildmay, Sir Walter, 461
Milgate, Wesley, 44, 50, 52–53, 55, 110, 275, 283–84, 304, 723
Milton, Anthony, 578
Milton, John, 91, 134, 184, 257, 283, 664, 685, 716
Minturno, Antonio, 208
Moffett, Thomas, 208–09
Mohammed, as character in *Ignatius*, 170
Mompesson, Sir Giles, 619

Monson, Sir Thomas, 551
Montagu. *See also* Browne
Montagu, James, bishop, 562, 568, 572
Montague, Richard, bishop, 614, 625, 629–30, 639, 642, 699, 701
Montaigne, Michel de, 176, 264–70
Montemayor, Jorge de, 422
Montpensier [née de Guise], Catherine-Marie de, 166
More, Anne, *see* Donne [née More], Anne [Donne's wife]
More, Bartholomew, [grandson of Sir Thomas More], 392–93
More, Sir George, 28, 38, 126, 145, 358, 452, 456–58, 467, 472–75, 477, 480, 497–98, 534–35, 577
More, Robert, 28, 358, 360, 510, 534–35
More, Sir Thomas, 100, 107–10, 115–18, 149, 153–54, 156–57, 159, 250, 252, 255, 377, 383–88, 390, 392, 394, 396, 399, 420, 423, 576, 636–37, 668, 673
More, Sir William [Anne's grandfather], 379–80, 385, 449, 471, 477–78
More, Elizabeth, *see* Egerton [née More, Polsted, Wolley], Elizabeth
Morton, Sir Albertus, 531
Morton, Thomas, bishop, 69, 261–62, 489–92, 494, 498–500, 502–03, 525–26, 568–69, 572, 578, 610
Moseley, Humphrey, 414–16
Mountain, George, bishop, 605, 611
Mueller, Janel, 688
Munday, Anthony, 149–50, 152
Murray, Thomas, 596

Nashe, Thomas, 158–59, 253, 257, 448, 515–16, 728–29
Naunton, Sir Robert, 571
Navarre, Henri de, *see* Henri IV [de Navarre], king of France
Navarre, Marguerite de, 165
Naylor, Joshua, 498, 499
Neile, Richard, archbishop, 562, 568, 572, 625, 630, 638–39, 699
Nero, Roman emperor, 126, 161
Nethersole, Sir Francis, 582, 595–96
Neville, Edmond, 457, 478
Neville, Sir Henry, 542, 545
Neville, Thomas, 570
Newport, Francis, first earl of Bradford, 76
Newton, Sir Adam, 575
Norris, Sir John, 437–38
Norton, Charles Eliot, 46–48, 181, 720, 738
Norton, Dudley, 531

Norton, Thomas, 400
Novarr, David, 287, 301, 523, 525, 733
Nowell, Alexander, 400
Noy, William, 578–79

Oldisworth, Giles, 28, 684
Olivares, *see* Guzmán, Gaspar de, duke of Olivares
Oliver, Isaac, 421, 525, 526
O'Neill, Hugh, 446, 468
Overall, John, bishop, 488–89, 491–92, 499, 645
Overbury, Sir Thomas, 36, 175–76, 304, 543, 545–48, 551–52, 571, 580, 722, 739–40
Ovid, 22, 106, 126, 135–36, 138–39, 142, 144–46, 161–62, 187, 192, 207–10, 278, 287, 401, 688, 739

Palgrave, Francis Turner, 188–89
Panton, John, 452, 458
Paracelsus [Phillip von Hohenheim], 247
  as character in *Ignatius*, 170
Parma, duke of, *see* Farnese, Alessandro, duke of Parma
Paschal, Pierre, 210
Pasquier, Estienne, 169, 171
Patterson, Annabel, 13, 127, 128, 523, 528, 724, 726, 727, 740
Paul III, pope, 171
Paul IV, pope, 391
Paul V, pope, 169, 261
Paul VI, pope, 372
Peacham, Henry, 397
Pebworth, Ted-Larry, 241, 296, 747
Peele, George, 448
Peletier due Mans, Jacques, 208
Pembroke, countess of, *see* Herbert [née Sidney], Mary, countess of Pembroke
Percy, Charles, 480
Percy, Henry, eighth earl of Northumberland, 412–13
Percy, Henry, ninth earl of Northumberland, 170, 367, 458, 467, 473, 480–82, 486, 497, 506, 515–16, 518–20, 544
Percy, Thomas, 515
Perkins, Sir Christopher, 507, 521
Perkins, William, 491
Persius, 123–28, 130
Persons, Robert, 252–56, 261, 263, 310, 398, 407, 410–13, 503, 520–21
Pessoa, Fernando, 663, 741
Petrarch, 187–88, 207, 218–19, 350–51. *See also* **Index 1: Conceptual tools**, Petrarchism, and anti-Petrarchism; DONNE: **Writings**, Petrarchism in

Petronius, 158–59, 161
Petty, Sir William, 38
Phelippes, Thomas, 152, 746
Phelips, Sir Edward, 544
Phelips, Sir Robert, 542
Philip II, *see* Felipe II, king of England and Ireland, consort of Mary I, and king of Spain
Philip III, *see* Felipe III, king of Spain
Philip IV, *see* Felipe IV, king of Spain
'Philips', *see* Phelippes, Thomas
Philips, John, 452
Phillipps, Sir Thomas, 38
Philopater, Andreas, 407
Phrine, 109
Pico della Mirandola, Giovanni, 167, 409
Pindar, 186, 709
Pius V, pope, 372
Planudes, Maximus, 107–08, 113–14
Plat, Sir Hugh, 167
Plato, 110, 163, 179, 283. *See also* **Index 1: Conceptual tools**, Platonism; DONNE: **Writings**, Platonism in *Neoplatonism*
Plautus, 110
Playford, Henry, 30
Playford, John, 28, 30
Pliny, 654   *Plotinus/theurgy*
Plutarch, 110, 242, 265–66
Pole, Reginald, cardinal and archbishop, 250, 375, 390–91
Pole, David, bishop, 391
Poole, Joshua, 28, 32
Pope, Alexander, 132, 189, 711–13
Potter, George, 70, 87, 318, 333, 559, 577, 669–700
Pounde, Thomas, 485–86
Powtrell, Nicholas, 388
Prescott, Anne Lake, 127, 167
Preston, Thomas, 503
Primaudaye, Pierre de la, 421
Propertius, 135–36, 142, 144–45, 287
Prynne, William, 578–79
Pulley, William, 577
Purbeck, Lady Frances, 612
Puttenham, George, 105, 187, 208, 278–79
Pym, John, 630

Quarles, Francis, 30
Questier, Michael, 379, 381–82, 524, 645, 674

Rabelais, François, 158–59, 161, 165–68, 171, 173–74
Raderus, Matthew, 118–19
Rainsford, Sir Richard, 508
Ralegh, Sir Walter, 26, 39, 424, 426, 428–33, 435, 439, 444–45, 481, 496–97, 519–20

Rankins, William, 128, 163
Raphael, 720
Rastell, Joan, 386
Rastell, John, 377
Rastell, William, 384–88, 391–94, 576
Rich, Barnabe, 169
Rich, Essex, 28, 62, 456, 530
Rich, Robert, third baron Rich, later first earl of Warwick, 28
Rich, Sir Robert, later second earl of Warwick, 62, 530, 610
Richard II, king of England and lord of Ireland, 446
Richer, Émond, 489, 500, 510
Ridley, Nicholas, bishop, 252
Rintjus, Henrik, 28
Roberts, John [Benedictine], 505
Roberts, John R., 85, 89, 309
Rochester, viscount, see Carr, Robert, viscount Rochester and earl of Somerset
Roe, John, 41, 454
Roe, Sir Thomas, 28, 290, 517, 606, 610, 613
Roebuck, Graham, 173, 174, 680
Roger, Thomas, 654
Rogers, Thomas, 310
Rolle, John, 630
Rondell, Philip, 402
Ronsard, Pierre, 135
Roper [née More], Margaret, 385
Roper, William, 576
Rous, Francis, 630
Rouzee, Louis, 72
Rubens, 634
Rudd, Anthony, bishop, 555, 572
Rudyerd, Sir Benjamin, 454, 628–29
Russell, Edward, third earl of Bedford, 609
Russell, Francis, fourth earl of Bedford, 28
Russell [née Harington], Lucy, countess of Bedford, 15, 17, 25, 28, 30, 36, 53, 128, 191, 200, 215–16, 224, 287, 290–94, 296, 349, 480, 498, 526–27, 529–30, 534, 544, 550, 601, 608, 612, 682, 688, 708, 721, 746
Rutland, earl of, see Manners, Roger, fifth earl of Rutland

Sackville [née Clifford], Anne, countess of Dorset, 609, 612
Sackville, Edward, fourth earl of Dorset, 608–09
Sackville, Richard, Lord Buckhurst and third earl of Dorset, 381, 608–09, 612
Sackville, Thomas, first Baron Buckhurst and first earl of Dorset, 381, 463–64, 483
Sallust, 401
Sanderson, Sir William, 550

Sandys, Sir Edwin, 542, 549, 606
Sansovino, Francesco, 126
Sappho, 186, 683, 688, 739
Sarpi, Paolo, 261–62, 487, 503, 514, 521
Saunderson, Thomas, 586
Savoy, Duke of, see Emanuele, Carlo, duke of Savoy
Scaliger, Julius Caesar, 208, 279
Schoppe, Caspar, 169
Schumann, Robert, 663, 741
Scott, Michael, 31
Scott, Thomas, 618–19
Scudamore, John, first viscount Scudamore, 639
Sébillet, Thomas, 207–08
Secundus, Joannes, 135–36
Selden, John, 610
Sellin, Paul, 71, 581, 595, 597, 598, 668
Seneca, 110, 158, 265, 270, 350, 391, 409, 466, 693
Servetus, Michael, 375
Seyle, Henry, 151
Seymour, Edward, duke of Somerset [Protector Somerset], 387
Seymour, Edward, first earl of Hertford, 355, 509, 511, 513
Shakespeare, John, 381
Shakespeare, William, 2, 20, 39, 40, 48, 94, 145, 181, 182–83, 203, 255, 257, 276, 279, 287, 381, 687, 729, 737
Shami, Jeanne, 36, 38, 63, 284, 356, 564, 578, 599, 621, 668, 673, 700, 703
Shapiro, I. A., 78, 173, 348
Sheppard, Samuel, 28, 31–32
Sherfield, Henry, 579, 588
Shirley, Anthony, 431
Sibthorpe, Robert, 627–28, 690, 692
Sidney, Mary, see Herbert [née Sidney], Mary, countess of Pembroke
Sidney, Sir Philip, 3, 176, 178, 183, 188, 196, 208–09, 218–19, 221, 231, 234–35, 279, 401, 406, 420, 436, 707
Sidney, Robert, first earl of Leicester, 449, 463, 542
Simeon, John, 20, 46
Simpson, Evelyn, 70, 73, 75–77, 79, 87, 156, 165, 234, 263, 269, 318, 333, 456–57, 509–10, 559, 577, 700
Simpson, Percy, 165
Sinclair, W. M., 723
Skinner, Robert, bishop, 634–35, 638, 644
Slights, Camille Wells, 680, 688
Snowden, Robert, bishop, 571
Somerset, Earl of, see Carr, Robert, viscount Rochester and earl of Somerset
Somerset, Edward, fourth earl of Worcester, 519

Somerset, Protector, *see* Seymour, Edward, duke of Somerset
Southcot, John, 645
Southampton, earl of, *see* Wriothesley, Henry, third earl of Southampton
Southwell, Anne, 176
Southwell, Robert, SJ, 104, 219, 252, 747, 750, 751
Spencer, Alice, Countess of Derby, *see* Egerton [née Spencer; Stanley, countess of Derby], Alice
Spencer, Sir Stanley, 716
Spenser, Edmund, 91, 160–63, 188, 192–93, 198, 209, 230, 234, 287, 298, 300–02, 448, 676, 679, 687
St Jerome, 681
St John of the Cross [Juan de Yepes], 104, 219
St Paul, 327, 331, 559, 604, 664, 669, 681, 683, 688, 719, 734, 738
St Paula, 681
St Stephen, 730
St Valentine, bishop, 301–03
Stafford, Anthony, 644
Stanley, Henry, fourth earl of Derby, 413–14
Stansby, William, 173
Statius, Publius Papinius, 287
Stephen, Sir Leslie, 527, 720, 722, 724
Sternhold, Thomas, 235
Strier, Richard, 668, 691
Stringer, Gary A., 44, 56, 81, 82, 109, 122, 141, 221
Stubbs, Henry, 28, 30
Suckling, Sir John, 684
Sullivan II, Ernest W., 74, 85, 192, 200, 348, 684
Sulpicia, 135
Sutcliffe, Matthew, 499–500
Swale, Sir Richard, 473–76
Swift, Jonathan, 256
Sylvester, Josuah, 14, 164, 278

Tacitus, 245, 401
Talbot, Gilbert, seventh earl of Shrewsbury, 482
Terence, 401
Theophrastus, 175–76, 178
Thimelby, Katherine, 28, 30
Thornborough, John, bishop, 571
Thorney, Tom, 167, 177
Thorpe, Thomas, 173
Thornton, Thomas, 579
Throckmorton, Francis, 402
Thrush, Andrew, 549
Thucydides, 401
Tiberius, 245–46, 399
Tibullus, 134–36, 144–45, 187
Tilman, Edward, 28
Tincomb, 511–13

Titian, 525, 720
Tonson, Jacob, the younger, 43, 45–46, 48
Topcliffe, Richard, 114, 167, 748
Tottel, Richard, 101, 183
Traherne, Thomas, 710
Trumbull, William, 28, 531, 552, 572–73
Tuke, Sir Samuel, 36
Turberville, George, 183, 209
Turner, Anne, 551
Turner, Samuel, 624
Turpilius, Sextus, 352

Valdes, Diego de, 465–66
Valentine, bishop, *see* St Valentine, bishop
Van Linge, Abraham, 586–88
Van Linge, Bernard, 586–88
Varro, Marcus Terentius, 158–59
Vaughan, Henry, 28, 30, 32, 710
Vaux, Laurence, 400
Vaux, Edward, fourth baron Vaux of Harrowden, 567
Vere, Aubrey de, twentieth earl of Oxford, 29
Vere, Sir Francis, 428
Verstegan, Richard, 407
Villiers, George, marquis and first duke of Buckingham, 28, 79, 267, 350, 368–69, 465, 534, 538, 550–53, 570–72, 574–75, 597, 602–03, 607–08, 616–17, 619–25, 629, 633, 698
Viperano, Giovanni, 208
Virgil, 142, 161
Vives, Juan Luis, 396, 400
Von Habsburg, Ferdinand, *see* Ferdinand II, Archduke of Austria, and Holy Roman Emperor; **Index 1: Conceptual tools**, Habsburgs
Von Hutten, Ulrich, *see* Hutten, Ulrich von
Vorstius, Conrad, 594

Wake, Sir Isaac, 572–73
Waldron, F. G., 20, 46
Waller, Edmund, 183
Walsingham, Sir Francis, 152, 377, 406, 414, 461–62, 746
'Walsingham, Sir Francis', as essayist, 178
Walton, Izaak, 4–6, 14, 28, 33, 138, 180–81, 191, 193, 199, 204, 216, 218, 240, 258, 319, 332, 349, 365–67, 394, 409, 420, 423–25, 456–57, 465, 476–77, 491, 498, 514, 523–27, 555, 569–70, 572, 577–79, 603, 609–10, 612–13, 650–51, 653–57, 663, 668–73, 675, 709, 720–21, 734–38
as character in *Conceit*, 742
Wandesford, Rowland, 579
Watson, Thomas, 184
Watson, William, 171

Webster, John, 28, 30, 32, 101, 684
Weckherlin, Georg Rudolf, 28, 30
Wentworth, Thomas [lawyer], 579
Wentworth, Thomas, first earl of Strafford, 629, 633, 635–36, 703
Wesley, John, 376
Weston, Richard, 551
Weston, Richard, first earl of Portland, 629–31, 633
Weston, William, SJ, 410–11, 413, 746
Whetstone, George, 184
White, Bridget, 28, 357, 682
White, Rowland, 449
White, Thomas, 607–09
Whitelock, Edmund, 515
Whitgift, John, archbishop, 555, 578, 624
Whitman, Walt, 663, 741
Williams, John, archbishop and lord keeper, 29, 338, 369, 563–64, 569–70, 574–75, 602–603, 617, 619, 621, 623
Wilson, Thomas, 291
Wingfield, Sir John, 113–15, 428–29
Winniffe, Thomas, bishop, 607, 641, 646
Winstanley, William, 28
Winwood, Sir Ralph, 542, 545, 549–51, 567, 571–73
Wolley, Elizabeth, *see* Egerton [née More, Polsted, Wolley], Elizabeth
Wolley, Sir Francis, 194, 367, 448, 450, 459, 471–72, 476–80, 508
Wolley, Sir John, 449–50, 471–72
Wood, Anthony, 418–19
Woodward, Rowland, 19, 28, 137, 209–10, 221, 431–32, 454, 509, 514
Woodward, Thomas, 454
Wotton, Edward, first baron Wotton, 497
Wotton, Sir Henry, 28, 73, 169, 211, 349, 358, 366, 396–98, 406–07, 425, 454, 459, 465, 467, 469, 496–97, 503–04, 509, 514–15, 517, 531, 545, 570, 591, 596–97, 610, 667, 678, 728
Wright, Abraham, 28
Wriothesley, Henry, third earl of Southampton, 39, 541
Wroth [née Sidney], Lady Mary, 684
Wyatt, Sir Thomas, 126, 183, 208, 234
Xenophon, 401

Yelverton, Sir Henry, 619
Young, John, dean of Winchester, 575
Young, Robert V., 89, 140, 331

Zouche, Edward la, eleventh baron Zouche, 406, 567

Index 3: Place names

Aa River, 418
Africa, 428
Aldborough Hatch, 326
Alexandria, 186
All Souls College, *see* Oxford, University of
Amiens, 62, 358, 430, 498
Amsterdam, 490, 623
Antwerp, 416–420, 433, 508–509
Ashbourne, 613
Azores Islands, 4, 142, 366, 424–5, 427, 429–34, 437–9, 445, 447–8, 496

Bangor, see of, 571
Bath, 247, 432
Bath and Wells, see of, 568, 611
Bavaria, 391, 393, 409, 619–22
Bedfordshire, 627
Bedlam, *see* St Mary of Bethlehem Hospital
Belgium, 93, 135, 409, 421, 511
Belvoir Castle, 480
Berwick, 478, 480
Blackfriars, 472
Bodleian Library, *see* Oxford, University of
Bohemia, 544, 553, 561, 573, 581, 583, 595–598, 617–619
Bourbourg, 437
Bread Street, 392, 451
Brentwood School, 606
Brest, 444
Bridewell Prison, 140
Bruges, 385–86
Brussels, 509, 519, 583

Cadiz, 4, 109, 112–15, 142, 146, 366, 424–32, 434, 442–45, 447, 463–64, 496, 623
Calais, 413, 426, 436, 442
Calloo, 416–8
Camberwell, 607
Cambridge, University of, 41, 258, 376, 396, 398, 401–04, 411–12, 463, 535, 557–61, 569–70, 624, 737. *See also* **Index 1**: Conceptual tools, DONNE, **Biography**, academic degrees

Cambridge University Library, 34, 156, 478–79
  Peterhouse, 611, 639
  Trinity College, 75, 492, 556, 570
Cambridgeshire, 558
Canterbury, see of, 253, 473, 567, 570, 575, 599, 625, 627
Canterbury Cathedral, 74
Carleton, 458
Carlisle, see of, 571, 574
Carmarthenshire, Wales, 383, 422
Caribbean, 436, 442
Chancery Lane, 455
Charterhouse, 480, 611–613
Chelsea, 326, 609–610
Chelsea College, 488–9, 609
Christ Church College, *see* Oxford, University of
Cleves, *see* Jülich-Cleves
Clink Prison, 423, 521
Cornwall, 445, 497
Corunna, 429, 438
Coventry, see of, 568
Cowdray, 379
Croydon, 359, 573

Denmark, 360, 464, 484, 555, 598, 639
Denmark House, 338, 562
Devon, 445
Dillingen (Bavaria), University of, 391, 393, 409
Dommel River, 418
Douai, 402
Drury House, 451
Drury Lane, 451, 511–512
Dublin, 446
Durham, 480, 644
Durham House, 572, 625, 627, 630–631, 639
Durham, see of, 478, 525, 572, 575, 625, 639
Dutch Republic, *see* Netherlands

East Anglia, 376
Edinburgh, 480, 543
Ely, see of, 568
English Channel, 436, 445
English College, 485, 500

Essex House, 451, 469
Eu, 411–12
Ewherst (Surrey), 477
Exeter, see of, 499, 574–75

Falmouth, 431, 445
Faro, 429
Fayal, 432–433, 445
Ferrol, 429–432, 445
Fitzwilliam Museum (Cambridge), 601, 716
Flanders, 440, 501
Fleet Prison, 451, 474, 521
Florence, 390–391, 508, 514–515
Florentine Academy, 420
Flores, 432
France, 93, 126, 135, 139, 147, 166, 169, 172, 210, 298, 376, 410, 426, 435, 440, 442, 445, 462, 464–466, 485, , 492, 503, 509, 521, 541, 544, 591–593, 597, 617–619, 623, 629, 631, 633, 639, 698. *See also* **Index 1: Conceptual tools**, DONNE: **Biography**, travels, in 1611–12
Frankenthal, 622
Fulham House, 569

Geneva, 230, 329, 373–375, 406, 493, 533, 548, 666, 675
Germany, 107, 166, 234, 397, 409, 419–20, 540, 544, 573–74, 592–93, 595–98, 600, 617–20. *See also* **Index 1: Conceptual tools**, DONNE: **Biography**, travels in 1611–12 and in 1619–20
Gloucester, see of, 525, 555, 574, 602
Gloucestershire, 511
Granada, 481
Gray's Inn, *see* Inns of Court
Graz, 583
Great Tew, 257
Greenwich, 559–60, 569
Guildford, 385

Hague, The, 357, 397, 547, 583, 600, 619–20
Hampton Court, 449, 484, 557
Hanau, 518
Harefield, 457
Hart Hall, *see* Oxford, University of
Havana, 439, 445
Hawstead, 275, 285
Heidelberg, 484, 561, 583, 618, 620
Hertfordshire, 392–394   Heythrop
Highgate, 577
Holborn, 451, 555
Holland, *see* Netherlands
Holy Roman Empire, 595, 617
House of Convertites, 455–56
Huntingdonshire, 570

India, 94, 187, 577
Indies, East, 428, 605
Indies, West, 283, 429
Inner Temple, *see* Inns of Court
Inns of Chancery, 404, 422, 579
  Thavies Inn, 404, 421–23, 451
Inns of Court, 37, 105, 145, 150–51, 160, 209, 254, 301, 387, 391, 396, 404–07, 422, 424, 447, 453–54, 457, 461, 466, 554, 579–80, 585, 684. *See also* **Index 1: Conceptual tools**, DONNE, **Biography**, early years and education; readership at Lincoln's Inn
  Gray's Inn, 404–05, 521
  Inner Temple, 404–05
  Lincoln's Inn, 71, 299–301, 327, 337, 341, 368, 385, 388, 404, 406, 422–23, 425, 447–48, 450, 451–53, 472, 556, 559, 570, 576–88, 594–95, 603, 609–10, 645, 669. *See also* **Index 1: Conceptual tools**, DONNE, **Biography**, early years and education; readership at Lincoln's Inn
  Middle Temple, 404, 454, 457, 578
Ireland, 35, 93, 95, 435–36, 440–41, 444, 446, 449, 464–65, 468–69, 483, 529, 590, 593, 622, 633, 639, 727
Isle of Wight, 358
Italy, 210, 409, 421, 509, 520, 629

Jülich-Cleves, 360, 592, 598

Kent, County of, 392–93, 570, 609–10, 627
Keyston, *see* **Index 1: Conceptual tools**, DONNE, **Biography**, rector of Keyston
Kidwelly, Carmarthenshire, 383, 422
King's Bench, see **Index 1: Conceptual tools**, Law courts

Lambeth Palace, 572–73
Lancashire, 486
Lancaster, 490
La Rochelle, 626, 628–29, 633
Leicestershire, 550
Leicestershire Record Office, 38, 73
Leiden, University of, 618
Lichfield Cathedral, 391
Lincoln, see of, 492, 563, 574, 602
Lincoln College, *see* Oxford, University of
Lincolnshire, 458
Lincoln's Inn, *see* Inns of Court
Lisbon, 438–439
London, 46, 126–27, 160, 173, 333, 359, 367, 383–84, 387, 392, 394, 405, 407, 410, 419, 437, 445, 448–51, 453, 457, 468–69, 472, 475, 477–78, 480–82, 504, 508–12, 517–18, 537–40,

543, 545, 551, 554–55, 560–61, 567, 569, 572, 574, 585, 589, 592–94, 596–97, 602, 610–11, 613, 617, 621–22, 625, 628, 634, 641, 643, 651–53, 685. *See also* London, see of; Tower of London; **Index 1**: Conceptual tools, DONNE, **Biography**, and London; DONNE, **Writings**, and London
London, see of, 369, 377, 473, 556, 558, 567–68, 572–74, 583, 602, 605, 611–12, 629, 638
Long Marston, Yorkshire, 498
Loseley, 38, 358–59, 379, 385, 457, 472, 477, 480
Louvain, 386–88, 391–92, 409, 413, 419
Low Countries, 376, 407, 435–40, 442, 462.
 See also Belgium; Netherlands
Ludgate prison, 451
Lutzen, 634

Madrid, 550, 592–93, 595, 598, 620, 622–23
Mannheim, 620
Marshalsea prison, 475
Mermaid Tavern, 24, 160, 173, 243, 451, 577
Merton College, *see* Oxford, University of
Middle Temple, *see* Inns of Court
Middlesex, County of, 29, 355
Milan, 593
Mitcham, 164, 359, 367, 512, 671, 674–75
Mitre Tavern, 173, 243, 392, 577
Monzón, 626
Mousehole, 442

Naples, 422   Neoplatonism ?
Netherlands, 93, 412–13, 418, 537, 597, 601, 618, 622–23. *See also* Low Countries
 Dutch Republic, 594
 Holland, 618
 United Provinces, Republic of the, 542, 618
Newark Priory, 478
Newbattle Abbey, 685
Newcastle, 409, 480
Newgate prison, 423, 451
Newmarket, 535, 557–58, 561, 568–70, 575
Norfolk, 374, 376
Normandy, 413, 440
Norwich, see of, 611, 639, 645

Ouse Bridge, 746
Oxford, see of, 398, 570, 572
Oxford, University of, 160, 263, 387, 390–91, 396–98, 401–04, 409, 411–14, 419–21, 425, 499, 568, 571, 586, 665. *See also* **Index 1**: DONNE, **Biography**, at Oxford; academic degrees
 All Souls College, 390–91, 409
 Bodleian Library, 47, 62, 74, 76, 499
 Christ Church College, 76–77, 419

 Hart Hall, 381, 402, 411
 Lincoln College, 588
 Merton College, 391, 404
 Oxford University Press, 2, 11, 21, 47, 50, 52, 55, 70, 78–79, 175, 348
 Queen's College, 49
 St. John's College, 83
 Wadham College, 586
 Worcester College, 77

Palace Academy, 421
Palatinate, 28, 368, 505, 541, 544, 581–84, 607, 618–23, 634.
Pale, The, 446
Paris, 358, 377, 412, 414, 486, 489, 500, 503, 510, 514, 520, 542, 593, 624, 639, 706, 752
Paul's Cross, 327, 386, 451, 469, 560–61, 605–06, 609, 617, 621, 640, 667, 680–81, 697
Peniche, 439
Penzance, 442
Peterborough, see of, 391
Peterhouse, *see* Cambridge, University of
Petworth House, 520
Pillars of Hercules, 113–15, 428–29
Plymouth, 429–431, 445
Portugal, 437–40
Prague, 406, 619
Puerta da Santa Maria, 429
Pyrford, *see* **Index 1**: Conceptual tools, DONNE, **Biography**, residence at Pyrford

Queen Elizabeth's Summer House, 478
Queen's Bench, *see* **Index 1**: Conceptual tools, Law courts
Queen's College, *see* Oxford, University of

Rhé, Isle of, 628, 633
Rheims, 411, 413
Rhine, River, 619–20
Rochester, see of, 568
Rolls Office, 449–50, 453, 455
Rome, 123, 125–26, 130, 135, 148, 210, 263, 377, 391, 409, 411–12, 422, 485 493, 500, 677. *See also* **Index 1**: Conceptual tools, Catholicism, Roman
Rome, see of, 486, 493
Romney Marsh, 392–93
Rouen, 440–41
Royston, 557–58

Saftingen, 416
St Andrew's Church, Holborn, 555
St Clement Danes, 451
St David's, see of, 572, 574–75, 602

St Dunstan's-in-the-West 451, 608. *See also* **Index 1**: Conceptual tools, DONNE, **Biography**, vicar at St. Dunstan's
St. Edmund's Church, Salisbury, 588
St Gregory, church of, 641
St John's College, see Oxford, University of
St Mary of Bethlehem Hospital, 647
St Mary's Hospital, 560
St Omer, 398, 411
St Paul's Cathedral, 6, 71, 240, 262, 327, 332–33, 379, 387, 450–51, 491, 499, 520, 554–56, 558, 564–65, 569, 574–75, 605, 607–10, 640–642, 652, 654–56, 670, 700, 736, 741–42. *See also* **Index 1**: Conceptual tools, DONNE, **Biography**, as Dean of St. Paul's
St Paul's Cathedral Library, 83, 92
Salisbury, see of, 574–75, 602
Savoy, 472–74, 541, 593, 597–98, 618
Scotland, 546, 560, 590–91, 594, 626, 681
Sevenoaks, rectory of, *see* **Index 1**: Conceptual tools, DONNE, **Biography**, rector of Sevenoaks
s'Hertogenbosch, 416, 418–19
Shrewsbury, 482
Smithfield, 31
Sorbonne, The, 162, 165, 169, 500, 503, 510
Soviet Union, 716
Spa, 537
Spain, 5, 126, 142–43, 166, 172, 213, 295, 376–77, 407, 412, 424–26, 428, 435–40, 442, 444–46, 465, 469, 482–83, 497, 502, 509, 541, 550, 552, 568, 572–73, 590–96, 598–99, 618, 620–23, 629, 631, 633, 665, 681, 698. *See also* **Index 1**: Conceptual tools, DONNE, **Biography**, and Spain; **Writings**, and Spain
Spital, *see* St Mary's Hospital
Star Chamber, Court of, see **Index 1**: Law courts
Steeken, 416–18
Stratford, 381
Suffolk, County of, 275, 285, 376
Surrey, County of 183, 194, 209, 359, 379, 385, 472, 475, 477–78, 508
Surrey History Centre, 38
Sussex, County of, 379, 520
Sweden, 596, 631, 634, 639

Taunton, 544, 549
Thames, River, 229

Thavies Inn, *see* Inns of Chancery
Theobalds, 480
Tower of London, 39, 175, 304, 377, 386, 410, 413, 519–20, 544–46, 551–52, 607, 746
Trinity Chapel, Lincoln's Inn, 585–58
Tuscany, 541, 618
Twickenham Park, 359
Tyburn, 146, 386, 516
Tynemouth, 412

Ulster, 446
United Provinces, Republic of the. *See* Netherlands
Uphall Manor, 458

Valladolid, 509
Venice, 169, 211, 259, 261, 397, 489, 497, 504, 509, 514–17, 520–22, 529, 531–32, 539, 547, 573, 591, 593, 597–98, 721
Vienna, 406, 596
Vigo, 438
Villa Franca, 483
Virginia, 298, 606
Virginia Company, 529, 606, 610

Wadham College, *see* Oxford, University of
West Looe, Cornwall, 497
Westminster, 344, 387, 478, 515, 519, 564, 602, 607, 617, 620, 636
Wey, River, 478
White Mountain, (Battle of), 227, 584, 619–20
Whitehall, 87, 342, 405, 554, 557, 560–61, 564, 634, 636, 638, 640, 642, 650, 702, 729–30
Wight, Isle of, 358
Winchester, 481
Winchester, see of, 499, 568, 572, 575, 639
Wisbech Castle, 377
Wittenberg, 493, 666
Worcester, see of, 571
Worcester College, *see* Oxford, University of
Worms, 565
Wrest Park, 610

York, 122, 490, 745
York, see of, 508, 520–21, 555, 639
York House, 15, 449, 468, 471–72, 478, 568
Yorkshire, 498

Index 4: Individual works discussed

Air, 90, 198, 705
AltVic, 20
Amic, 506–07, 517
Anniv, 203, 676, 686, 711
Annun, 52, 237, 240
Antiq, 109, 114
Appar, 106, 205

Bait, 15, 24, 103, 709
BedfCab, 290
BedfDead, 216
BedfReas, 25
BedfRef, 27, 681–82
BedfShe, 290–91
Biathanatos, 12–14, 25, 27, 29, 35–36, 41, 68, 74–75, 100, 153–57, 160, 204, 246, 259, 357, 730, 732–33, 752
Blos, 205
BoulNar, 30, 293–94
BoulRec, 292
Break, 30, 32, 45, 52, 198, 684

Cales, 109, 431
Calm, 31, 35, 103, 207, 213, 425, 432–33, 684
Canon, 24, 185, 191–95, 197, 204, 223, 229, 307, 346, 390, 683, 738–39
Carey, 18, 62–63, 199, 214–15, 456
CB, 577
Christ, 239, 241, 504, 733
Citizen, 21, 52
Commun, 202, 676, 679
ConfL, 202
Corona, 44, 52, 100, 163–64, 219–21, 223–25, 227–28, 232, 236, 238, 709, 734
Cor1, 223–24
   Cor2, 223
   Cor3, 223
   Cor4, 223
   Cor5, 223
Coryat, 173, 518
Courtiers Library, 75–76, 152, 165–68, 469, 512–13, 732, 735, 746
Cross, 236–37, 707
Curse, 52, 457

Damp, 30
Devotions, 12–14, 71–72, 77, 207, 308–17, 347, 350, 529, 602, 607–08, 613, 616, 631, 651–53, 691, 730, 735–36, 752
Disinher, 110–12

Eclog, 28, 62, 102, 103, 304–05, 307, 532–34, 548, 718, 722, 724, 726, 739–40
Ecst, 102, 163, 347, 683, 686–87, 705, 711
ED, 210, 220
EG, 210, 454
ElAnag, 143–44, 148
ElAut, 21, 24, 54, 136, 138
ElBed, 21, 23, 37, 45, 50, 54, 138, 143, 146–48, 303, 684
ElBrac, 18, 22–23, 38, 45, 58, 61, 137–41, 143, 146–48, 743, 746–48, 750, 755
ElChange, 137, 147–48, 676
ElComp, 44, 49–50, 140, 143–44, 146–48, 679
ElExpost, 21, 32, 52, 137–38
ElFatal, 137–38, 147–48, 705
ElJeal, 137, 140, 142, 144, 148, 460, 613, 743
ElNat, 144, 148, 746
ElPart, 21, 45, 52, 58–59, 61, 136–37, 460
ElPerf, 140, 143–44, 460–61, 676, 745–46
ElPict, 45, 137, 147–48
ElProg, 45, 52, 86, 136–38, 142–44, 148, 189, 684
ElServe, 148, 470, 676
ElVar, 21, 44, 52, 676
ElWar, 20, 46, 142, 146, 148, 218, 434
EpEliz, 28, 301–05, 307
EpLin, 103, 49, 299–301, 307, 613, 680
Essayes, 12–14, 76–78, 102, 151, 228, 264–72, 319, 535, 666
EtAD, 18, 228, 287
EtED, 275, 285
Expir, 30

Fare, 18, 53
Father, 24, 30, 38, 49–51, 237, 240–41, 607, 656, 676, 734
Fever, 686–87
FirAn, 14, 28, 53, 160, 273–77, 279–83, 290, 518, 678, 680, 706, 719

Flea, 24, 106, 112, 191, 205, 706, 739
Fun, 205, 705
FunEl, 14, 273–77, 280, 290, 518

GHerb, 655
Goodf, 237–38, 241, 530, 565, 654–55, 674, 677, 680, 734
GoodM, 52, 198, 203, 205, 683, 686

Ham, 57–58, 197, 287, 297, 705–06, 738
Har, 17, 27, 30, 287, 296, 733
Henry, 14, 44, 48, 278, 294–96, 301, 518, 721
Hero, 113
HG, 212, 243
HSBatter, 64, 218, 226–27, 347
HSBlack, 64, 222, 225, 226–27, 675
HSDeath, 64, 222
HSDue, 64, 222, 224–27, 233, 675
HSLittle, 52, 64, 226
HSMade, 64, 225–26, 675
HSMin, 64, 222, 227
HSPart, 64, 222, 226–27
HSRound, 64, 222, 226–27
HSScene, 23, 51, 64, 222, 226–27
HSShe, 18–19, 50, 55, 60, 64, 227–29, 231–32, 287, 649
HSShow, 60, 64, 227–28, 230–31, 675, 677
HSSighs, 45, 54, 222, 226
HSSouls, 51, 226, 649
HSSpit, 64, 222, 227
HSVex, 60, 64, 231, 676, 740–41
HSWhat, 55, 64, 224, 227, 231–32, 239
HSWhy, 64, 227
HSWilt, 64, 227
HuntMan, 682
HWHiber, 211
HWKiss, 211, 454, 528, 613, 667, 728
HWNews, 211, 454, 467–68, 613
HWVenice, 211

Ignatius, 12–13, 68–69, 76–77, 158, 168–73, 246, 257, 367, 496, 500, 503–04, 507, 518, 520–21, 590–91, 645
ILRoll, 210
Image, 52
Ind, 15, 32, 185, 188, 202, 679

Julia, 21, 52

Lam, 235, 620
Lect, 203
Letters, see **Index 1: Conceptual tools**, DONNE: **Writings**, Genres: Prose Letters
Liar, 20, 46

Libro, 16, 217, 727
Licent, 114
Lit, 235–36, 240, 262, 318, 527–28, 644, 655, 680, 734
LovAlch, 679, 687
LovGrow, 15, 635

Macaron, 20, 173–74
Mark, 276–77, 291–92
Martial, 24, 118, 120–21
Marriage Letters, see **Index 1: Conceptual tools**, DONNE: **Writings**, Genres: Prose Letters
Mess, 724
Metem, 2, 35–36, 41, 44, 52, 84, 99, 103, 106, 120, 158, 161–64, 171, 181, 203, 497, 505, 518, 613, 678–80, 684, 686, 688, 734
MHPaper, 190, 199–200, 215, 729

Noct, 198–99, 228, 738

Para, 203
Paradoxes, see **Index 1: Conceptual tools**, DONNE: **Writings**, Genres: Paradoxes
Phrine, 109
Prim, 205
Problems, see **Index 1: Conceptual tools**, DONNE: **Writings**, Genres: Problems
Pseudo-Martyr, 3, 12–13, 29, 66–72, 77, 100, 152, 160, 173, 246, 249–63, 321, 356, 367, 377, 380, 408, 410, 466, 492–94, 496, 498–500, 503–04, 507, 518, 520–22, 533, 555, 558, 591, 612, 645, 665–67, 669, 671, 697, 702, 718, 727, 744, 746, 750, 753–55
Pyr, 113, 741

Ralph, 118–21
Relic, 23, 192–93, 197, 200, 205, 646, 648
Res, 197, 238
RWSlumb, 432
RWThird, 181, 210

Sal, 215
Sappho, 21, 52, 138, 203, 683, 688, 739
Sat1, 127, 130–32, 306, 466, 739
Sat2, 26–27, 114, 127–29, 132
Sat3, 22–23, 100, 102, 127–28, 132, 142, 157, 229–31, 257, 378, 649, 675, 730, 737
Sat4, 49, 127, 129–30, 132, 168, 171, 306, 366, 318, 430, 452–54, 528, 555, 743–44, 746, 748, 751
Sat5, 114, 125, 132, 229, 448–49, 750
SecAn, 14, 28, 33, 53, 277, 279–83, 290, 518, 729
SelfL, 21, 44, 52
Sermons, see **Index 1: Conceptual tools**, DONNE: **Writings**, Genres: Sermons

SGo, 15, 30, 162, 680, 705, 742
Sheaf, 105, 107, 109, 117, 366, 414–20, 433, 512–13, 732, 735
Ship, 108, 426, 428, 606
Sickness, 218, 239–40, 607, 656–57
Sidney, 235–36, 239, 241, 603, 707
Sorrow, 25, 390
SSweet, 684, 737
Storm, 30, 35, 103, 190, 213, 425, 428, 430–31, 433, 577, 712
SunRis, 103, 190–91, 195, 307, 613, 709

Tilman, 28, 733–34
TMC, see **Index 1: Conceptual tools**, DONNE: **Writings**, Genres: Prose Letters
Token, 21, 52

Triple, 185, 212
TWHail, 210
TWPreg, 210–11
Twick, 15, 200–01

Under, 204, 686

ValBook, 42, 95, 192, 197, 199, 204
ValMourn, 86, 185, 189–91, 196–99, 205, 346, 476, 647–48, 676, 704, 713–14
ValName, 86, 185
ValWeep, 15, 218

Will, 52, 647
Wing, 109, 112–15, 428–29
WomCon, 197, 202–03, 676, 736, 739.

Lightning Source UK Ltd.
Milton Keynes UK
UKOW05f0008180116

266522UK00004B/4/P